P9-AQG-807

the AMERICANA ANNUAL

1992

AN ENCYCLOPEDIA OF THE EVENTS OF 1991

YEARBOOK OF THE ENCYCLOPEDIA AMERICANA

This annual has been prepared as a yearbook for general encyclopedias. It is also published as *Encyclopedia Year Book*.

Library of Congress Catalog Card Number: 23-10041
ISBN: 0-7172-0223-2
ISSN: 0196-0180

Printed and manufactured in the United States of America

Contents

Feature Articles of the Year

The Alphabetical Section

Entries on the continents, major nations of the world, U.S. states, Canadian provinces, and chief cities will be found under their own alphabetical headings.

© Sipa

Sonia Gandhi mourns her assassinated husband.

© Mario Villafuerte/Picture Group

Workers protest proposed U.S.-Mexico trade pact.

© Focus on Sports

Roger Clemens pitches to another Cy Young Award.

© Michael Rondou/"San Jose Mercury News"/Sipa

A Review of the Year 1991

When the final chapter on the 20th century is written, 1991 well may be judged with 1917 and 1945 as one of the most significant years of the 100-year period. As 1991 opened, attention was focused on whether Saddam Hussein would withdraw Iraq's forces from occupied Kuwait. The Iraqi president did not, and a U.S.-led coalition overwhelmed Iraq militarily during some six weeks of hostilities *(photo below)*. As the year evolved, Israel and its Arab neighbors gathered at the negotiating table in Madrid and Washington; another Gandhi was assassinated in India; nations of Africa took democratic steps; Croatia and Slovenia declared their independence and civil war broke out in Yugoslavia; the Philippines wrestled with the effects of an erupting volcano as well as the future of U.S. military bases on its soil; Javier Pérez de Cuéllar ended his term as secretary-general of the United Nations in the glow of the release of most of the hostages in the Middle East; Europe was looking to greater unity as it continued to witness its greatest change since 1945 and the end of World War II; the political scene in China remained constant; significant peace talks were held regarding El Salvador and Cambodia; a democratically elected president was overthrown in Haiti; and the divided Korean peninsula was seeing initiatives of rapprochement.

© Steve Liss/"Time" Magazine

However, it was developments in the USSR that set 1991 apart and gave the year its historic note. Although an August coup by Soviet hard-liners against Mikhail Gorbachev and his *glasnost* and *perestroika* failed *(photo left)*, the Nobel Prize-winning leader gave up the presidency on Christmas Day. In fact, the Union of Soviet Socialist Republics, the Communist state that resulted from the 1917 Bolshevik Revolution, was breaking up and was being replaced by a Commonwealth of Independent States with free-market economies.

Meanwhile in the United States, the state of euphoria that existed following the success of the Gulf war turned to concern about a lingering economic recession. Many states faced fiscal crises. President Bush sought a new trade agreement with Mexico. The term sexual harassment came to the forefront as Clarence Thomas was confirmed to the Supreme Court. Similarly, the issue of date rape was examined in the televised trial and acquittal of William Kennedy Smith.

Miss Saigon was Broadway's big musical and readers rushed to find out what happened to Scarlett in the *Gone With The Wind* sequel. Several sports veterans attempted comebacks. Magic Johnson tested positive for the HIV virus, gave up pro basketball, and spoke out about AIDS—a disease whose effects became even more tragic.

THE EDITORS

JANUARY

1 A 7% federal tax on goods and services goes into effect in Canada.

3 The first session of the 102d U.S. Congress convenes.

4 The United Nations Security Council votes unanimously to condemn Israel's treatment of the Palestinians in the occupied territories.

6 In Guatemala, Jorge Serrano Elias, an engineer and educator, is chosen president in a runoff election.

7 In Haiti loyalist army forces crush an attempted coup led by Roger Lafontant, the former head of the Tontons Macoutes (the private militia of the deposed Duvalier dictatorship).

9 Six and one-half hours of talks between U.S. Secretary of State James Baker and Iraq's Foreign Minister Tariq Aziz conclude in Geneva, Switzerland, without agreement concerning Iraqi withdrawal from occupied Kuwait.

13 In a crackdown on pro-independence forces in the Baltic republic of Lithuania, Soviet army troops kill 15 protesters in the republic's capital of Vilnius.

Boris N. Yeltsin, president of the Russian Federation, and representatives of the Baltic republics of Estonia, Latvia, and Lithuania sign a mutual-security agreement.

14 Two leaders of the Palestine Liberation Organization (PLO), Salah Khalaf (Abu Iyad) and Hayel Abdel-Hamid (Abu al-Hol), are assassinated in Tunis, Tunisia.

15 In the USSR the Supreme Soviet confirms Aleksandr A. Bessmertnykh as foreign minister, succeeding Eduard A. Shevardnadze, who resigned in December. On January 14 the legislature had confirmed Finance Minister Valentin Pavlov as premier, succeeding Nikolai I. Ryzhkov, who gave up the post for reasons of health.

16 Following the expiration of the United Nations Security Council deadline for Iraq to withdraw from Kuwait, an international force led by the United States begins air and missile attacks against Iraq. On January 12 the U.S. Congress had voted to give President Bush the authority to use military force to drive Iraq from Kuwait.

U.S. Secretary of State James A. Baker III and Iraq's Foreign Minister Tariq Aziz, below left, *met in Geneva, Switzerland, for six and one-half hours on January 9 in a last-minute effort to avert war in the Persian Gulf. After the talks failed to produce an agreement regarding Iraq's withdrawal from occupied Kuwait, fighting between Iraq and a U.S.-led multinational force began on January 16. Newspaper headlines in rural Illinois,* top page 9, *and around the world announced the war's outbreak.*

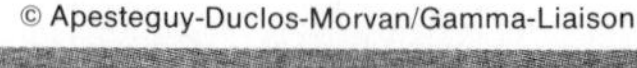
© Apesteguy-Duclos-Morvan/Gamma-Liaison

© Steve Liss/"Time" Magazine

18 Eastern Airlines halts its flights and announces that it will liquidate its assets.

25 President Bush names Rep. Edward Madigan (R-IL) to succeed Clayton Yeutter as secretary of agriculture. Yeutter had resigned the post to become chairman of the Republican National Committee.

27 The New York Giants defeat the Buffalo Bills, 20–19, in professional football's Super Bowl XXV.

28 Meeting in Washington, Secretary of State Baker and Soviet Foreign Minister Bessmertnykh announce the postponement of a summit meeting between Presidents George Bush and Mikhail Gorbachev, planned for February 11–13 in Moscow.

29 In South Africa, Nelson Mandela, deputy president of the African National Congress, and Mangosuthu Gatsha Buthelezi, president of the Inkatha Freedom Party, meet in Durban in an effort to end the violence between their two groups.

Pierre Joxe succeeds Jean-Pierre Chevènement as France's defense minister. Chevènement resigned the post in protest against his government's involvement in the Persian Gulf war.

President Bush delivers the annual State of the Union address, and Sen. George J. Mitchell (D-ME) presents the Democratic Party's response.

FEBRUARY

1 A major earthquake kills up to 400 persons in Afghanistan and at least 300 in Pakistan.

4 President Bush sends to Congress his budget for fiscal year 1992. Spending would total $1.446 trillion and revenue is estimated at $1.165 trillion, leaving a deficit of $281 billion.

7 In London three mortar shells are fired at 10 Downing Street, the British prime minister's official residence. The Provisional Irish Republican Army later takes responsibility for the attack, during which two policemen and a government worker suffered minor injuries.

During the early weeks of 1991, parts of California, below, were experiencing the state's worst drought since 1977. On February 15, Gov. Pete Wilson announced a series of proposals to fight the shortage, including a nonbinding 50% reduction in water usage, the establishment of a water bank, and the creation of a $100 million fund for forest-fire fighting, wildlife protection, and other conservation measures.

© Michael Schumann/Saba

© Les Stone/Sygma

On February 7, Jean-Bertrand Aristide (center) was inaugurated as Haiti's first democratically elected president. An elderly peasant woman presented the presidential sash to the 37-year-old ordained Roman Catholic priest.

Jean-Bertrand Aristide, the winner of Haiti's presidential election in December 1990, takes the oath of office.

9 In an unofficial "public-opinion poll" (nonbinding plebiscite) on independence, Lithuanians overwhelmingly support secession from the Soviet Union.

15 At the conclusion of a summit in Visegard, Hungary, the leaders of Czechoslovakia, Hungary, and Poland sign the so-called Visegard agreement, by which they plan to cooperate in transforming their nations to free-market economies.

22 In Albania, President Ramiz Alia names a new government, headed by economist Fatos Nano, in an effort to halt pro-democracy unrest.

23 Thailand's government, led by Chatichai Choonhavan, is overthrown in a military coup.

25 In Budapest, Hungary, the foreign and defense ministers of the six Warsaw Pact nations sign an agreement to disband the alliance's military structure by March 31, 1991.

27 President Bush announces that allied forces have liberated Kuwait and will suspend military action against Iraq.

In Bangladesh, Khaleda Zia, the widow of Gen. Ziaur Rahman, the nation's leader from November 1975 until his assassination on May 30, 1981, wins sufficient electoral support to become the nation's next prime minister.

The U.S. Senate Ethics Committee ends deliberations in the so-called Keating Five case, the investigation of five senators accused of exerting improper influence on behalf of Charles H. Keating, Jr., owner of the failed Lincoln Savings and Loan Association in California. The committee finds "substantial credible evidence" of misconduct by Sen. Alan Cranston (D-CA), "an appearance of impropriety" by Sen. Dennis DeConcini (D-AZ) and Sen. Donald W. Riegle, Jr. (D-MI), and the exercising of "poor judgment" by Sen. John Glenn (D-OH) and Sen. John McCain (R-AZ).

MARCH

2 The United Nations Security Council adopts Resolution 686, establishing the terms for a formal end to hostilities in the Persian Gulf.

3 In nonbinding plebiscites, significant portions of the voters in the Baltic republics of Estonia and Latvia cast ballots in support of independence from the USSR.

5 Soviet President Gorbachev assures visiting British Prime Minister John Major that the USSR supports the UN Security Council's actions for peace in the Persian Gulf.

9 In Belgrade, Yugoslavia, two persons are killed in clashes between anticommunist protesters and security forces.

12 In his first visit to Israel as U.S. secretary of state, James A. Baker III confers with Prime Minister Yitzhak Shamir and ten Palestinian leaders from the West Bank and Gaza.

14 In Los Angeles four white police officers are indicted by a grand jury in connection with the beating of a black motorist.

21 The British government announces that it is suspending the widely unpopular local tax known as the poll tax.

22 The United Nations Security Council ends its embargo on food shipments to Iraq and eases its sanctions on other humanitarian items.

24 In Benin's first free presidential elections in some 30 years, Prime Minister Nicephore Soglo defeats Brig. Gen. Mathieu Kérékou, the incumbent president who came to power in a 1972 coup.

25 In the midst of a political crisis in Yugoslavia, leaders on the federal and republic levels hold conciliatory talks in Belgrade. Borisav Jović, who resigned from the federal collective presidency on March 15, agreed to return to the executive body on March 20.

At the annual Academy Awards ceremony, *Dances with Wolves* wins seven Oscars, including the prize as best picture.

Addressing a joint session of the U.S. Congress and a national television audience on March 6, President George Bush was interrupted by frequent applause as he spoke of his goals for the United States and for peace in the Middle East now that the war in the Persian Gulf was over.

© Brad Markel/Gamma-Liaison

© Trippett/Sipa

Bob Martinez, above, *who was defeated in his bid for reelection as governor of Florida in November 1990, was sworn in as director of the U.S. Office of National Drug Control Policy in the White House Rose Garden March 28.*

26 By a five-to-four vote, the U.S. Supreme Court rules that the use of a coerced confession in a criminal case does not void a conviction automatically.

In the West African nation of Mali, the government of President Moussa Traoré is overthrown in a coup.

The presidents of Argentina, Brazil, Paraguay, and Uruguay sign an agreement creating the Southern Cone Common Market, a four-nation free-trade zone, by Jan. 1, 1995.

28 Former Florida Gov. Bob Martinez takes the oath of office as director of the Office of National Drug Control Policy.

APRIL

1 Choreographer Martha Graham, 96, dies in New York City.

Duke University defeats the University of Kansas, 72–65, to win the National Collegiate Athletic Association Division I basketball tournament.

2 In the USSR retail prices increase and goods remain scarce as state controls over the economy are relaxed.

Chicago Mayor Richard M. Daley (D) is elected to a full term.

William Vander Zalm resigns as premier of British Columbia. He is succeeded by Deputy Premier Rita Johnson, who becomes the first woman premier of a Canadian province.

4 President Bush and Japan's Prime Minister Toshiki Kaifu discuss world trade and funding for the Persian Gulf war in Newport Beach, CA.

Sen. John Heinz (R-PA) and six other persons are killed as the senator's chartered plane and a helicopter crash in midair over a Philadelphia suburb.

9 The United Nations Office of the High Commissioner for Refugees estimates that 750,000 Iraqi Kurds had crossed Iraq into Iran, while some 280,000 had arrived in Turkey, and some 300,000 were along the Iraq-Turkey border. The Kurds were escaping the Iraqi army. On April 5 the United Nations Security Council passed a resolution condemning Iraq's repression of the Kurds and other Iraqi dissidents.

11 The U.S. space shuttle *Atlantis*, with a five-member crew aboard, completes a six-day mission during which the Gamma Ray Observatory, a 17-ton astronomy satellite, was deployed into orbit.

The Gamma Ray Observatory (GRO), below, *was released into orbit from the grasp of the Remote Manipulator System of the "Atlantis" space shuttle on April 7. Earlier two astronauts had performed an emergency space walk to extend the high-gain antenna of the astronomy satellite.*

NASA

15 In Albania the opposition Democratic Party boycotts the opening of the newly elected People's Assembly to protest the slayings of four party members by security forces in the city of Shkoder on April 2. The ruling Albanian Workers' (Communist) Party had gained a two-thirds parliamentary majority as a result of runoff elections on April 7.

16 In a speech to a joint session of the U.S. Congress, Nicaragua's President Violeta Barrios de Chamorro asks for increased U.S. economic aid to her country.

17 In Italy, Christian Democrat Giulio Andreotti forms a new coalition government. His previous cabinet had fallen on March 29.

18 President Bush signs legislation ordering striking freight-railroad workers to return to work, and unveils "America 2000," his plan to improve the quality of U.S. education.

19 Soviet President Gorbachev and Japan's Prime Minister Kaifu end three days of talks in Tokyo. The leaders failed to agree on the future of the Kurile Islands, which had been seized from Japan by the USSR at the end of World War II.

20 President Gorbachev is the first Soviet head of state to visit South Korea. He and South Korea's President Roh Tae Woo agree on a series of diplomatic and economic accords.

21 Canada's Prime Minister Brian Mulroney reshuffles his cabinet. Former Prime Minister Joseph Clark becomes minister for constitutional affairs; Barbara McDougall succeeds Clark as minister of external affairs.

23 President Gorbachev and leaders of nine of the USSR's 15 constituent republics, including Russian President Boris Yeltsin, sign an agreement to cooperate in trying to solve the nation's economic and political difficulties.

25 Following general elections in Finland on March 17, Esko Aho of the Center Party forms a new four-party government.

30 A powerful cyclone kills an estimated 125,000 persons and leaves millions homeless in Bangladesh.

The U.S. Federal Reserve Board votes to cut its basic interest rate for loans to member banks to 5.5% from 6%.

Taiwan's President Lee Teng-hui declares an end to 43 years of emergency rule.

© Tomas Muscionico/Contact from Woodfin Camp & Associates

Residents of Bangladesh's Sandwip Island, above, *in the Bay of Bengal were devastated by the heavy loss of life and extensive property damage that resulted from the April 30 cyclone.*

On May 15, Edith Cresson, below, *a 57-year-old Socialist and former cabinet minister, became the first woman to be named prime minister of France.*

© Chamussy/Sipa

MAY

6 President Bush returns to the White House after being hospitalized since May 4 for an irregular heart rhythm.

The space shuttle *Discovery*, with a seven-member crew aboard, completes a military mission which had begun on April 28.

14 Winnie Mandela, the wife of South Africa's African National Congress leader Nelson Mandela, is sentenced to six years in prison after being convicted of four counts of kidnapping and acting as accessory to assault in a case involving four black youths at her Soweto home in 1988. Mrs. Mandela was acquitted of four more-serious charges of direct assault.

15 France's Prime Minister Michel Rocard resigns; President François Mitterrand names Socialist Edith Cresson as Rocard's successor.

16 During a visit by Chinese Communist leader Jiang Zemin to Moscow, China and the USSR sign an agreement to resolve part of their border dispute.

© Demulder/Sipa

Life in Ethiopia began to return to normal in late May after rebel troops, above, overwhelmed government forces, causing the resignation of President Mengistu Haile-Mariam; took control of the capital; and promised a new democratic government.

Following parliamentary elections and the assassination of Congress(I) party leader Rajiv Gandhi on May 21, P.V. Narasimha Rao, below, *a member of the Congress(I) party and a former cabinet minister, assumed the prime ministership of India on June 21.*

© Robert Nickelsberg/"Time" Magazine

Queen Elizabeth II becomes the first British monarch to address the U.S. Congress.

18 The Nepali Congress Party is declared officially the winner of Nepal's first multiparty elections since 1959.

20 The Supreme Soviet enacts legislation easing restrictions on travel and emigration by Soviet citizens.

In an address to the Israeli Knesset, Poland's President Lech Walesa asks Israel's forgiveness for the suffering caused by Polish anti-Semitism.

German Chancellor Helmut Kohl confers with President Bush at the White House.

21 India's former Prime Minister Rajiv Gandhi, the 46-year-old Congress(I) party leader, is assassinated at an election-campaign stop some 25 mi (40 km) southwest of Madras.

In Ethiopia, Lt. Col. Mengistu Haile-Mariam resigns as president and flees, as rebel forces advance against government troops. Lt. Gen. Tesfaye Gebre-Kidan, the nation's vice-president, is named acting president.

22 Lebanon's President Elias Hrawi and Syria's President Hafiz al-Assad sign a treaty of friendship and cooperation.

South Korea's Premier Ro Jai Bong resigns as the nation faces nearly one month of demonstrations against the killing of a student protester by riot police.

23 President Bush names Gen. Colin Powell to a second two-year term as chairman of the Joint Chiefs of Staff.

25 The Pittsburgh Penguins win their first National Hockey League Stanley Cup by defeating the Minnesota North Stars, four games to two.

26 An Austrian charter jet explodes in midair and crashes over Thailand, killing all 213 passengers and ten crew members.

Rick Mears wins the Indianapolis 500 auto race.

28 The defense ministers of the member nations of the North Atlantic Treaty Organization (NATO) approve a military restructuring of the alliance.

29 Pope John Paul II names 22 new cardinals, including two Americans—Archbishop Anthony J. Bevilacqua of Philadelphia and Roger M. Mahony of Los Angeles.

31 Angola's President José Eduardo dos Santos and Jonas Savimbi, leader of the rebel National Union for the Total Independence of Angola (UNITA), sign an agreement to end Angola's 16-year-old civil war.

JUNE

4 President Bush names Robert S. Strauss, a former chairman of the Democratic National Committee, ambassador to the USSR.

5 Albania's President Ramiz Alia appoints Ylli Bufi to head an interim government. The cabinet of Prime Minister Fatos Nano had resigned on June 4 in the midst of labor unrest and urban opposition to Communist rule.

Following 12 days of unrest in Algiers, Algeria, President Chadli Benjedid declares a state of emergency, postpones parliamentary elections planned for late June, and dismisses Premier Mouloud Hamrouche and his cabinet.

The Organization of African Unity concludes its annual summit in Abuja, Nigeria.

© Klaus Reisinger/Black Star

Boris N. Yeltsin enjoyed Russian customs, above, *while campaigning for the newly created position of executive president of the Russian Republic. On June 12 the 60-year-old political independent was elected to the post with some 60% of the vote, becoming Russia's first leader to be chosen directly by the people.*

9 Pope John Paul II completes a nine-day visit to his native Poland.

10 Mount Pinatubo volcano, located about 65 mi (90 km) northwest of Manila, the Philippines, erupts, forcing the evacuation of Americans from nearby Clark Air Force Base. On June 4, Mount Unzen, a Japanese volcano that had been dormant for two centuries, had erupted, killing at least 38 persons.

12 Boris N. Yeltsin is elected by popular vote to the newly created position of executive president of the USSR's Russian Republic.

President Bush and El Salvador's President Alfredo Cristiani meet for two hours at the White House.

The Chicago Bulls win their first National Basketball Association championship by defeating the Los Angeles Lakers, four games to one.

17 Leaders of Germany and Poland sign a treaty of friendship and cooperation.

20 After the Congress(I) Party wins a plurality in India's general elections May 20-June 15, President Ramaswamy Venkataraman names the party's president, P.V. Narasimha Rao, as prime minister.

U.S. House Majority Whip William H. Gray 3d (D-PA) declares that he will resign from the U.S. House of Representatives to become president of the United Negro College Fund.

21 The seventh annual International Conference on AIDS concludes in Florence, Italy.

22 Thousands of Albanians cheer visiting U.S. Secretary of State James A. Baker 3d.

25 The U.S. National Commission on Children issues a 519-page report, recommending a national health-insurance plan to provide coverage for children and pregnant women.

27 Vietnam's Communist Party announces the election of Do Muoi, 74, as its new leader.

JULY

AP/Wide World

Jeffrey L. Dahmer, 31, was arrested in Milwaukee, WI, on July 22 after police discovered human heads and other body parts in his apartment. A July 24 affidavit said that he had confessed to killing at least 11 people. Police said later that they believed he had killed at least 17.

1 President Bush names Clarence Thomas, a 43-year-old judge of the U.S. Court of Appeals for the District of Columbia Circuit, to the U.S. Supreme Court. He would succeed Associate Justice Thurgood Marshall, who announced his retirement on June 27. Both Marshall and Thomas are black.

4 In honor of Colombia's new constitution that is to take effect on July 5, President César Gaviria Trujillo removes the state of siege that was imposed in 1984.

5 During its first national conference to be held within South Africa in 32 years, the African National Congress, the nation's largest antiapartheid movement, elects Nelson Mandela as president.

7 Germany's Michael Stich wins the men's singles tennis title at Wimbledon. Steffi Graf, also of Germany, took the women's singles crown on July 6.

8 The Yugoslav government and the rebel republic of Slovenia agree to a three-month truce and discussions on a new federal structure.

10 President Bush lifts the U.S. economic sanctions imposed against South Africa by the Comprehensive Antiapartheid Act of 1986. On July 9 the International Olympic Committee had removed its ban against South Africa's participation in the Olympic Games.

President Bush announces that he is appointing Alan Greenspan to a second term as chairman of the U.S. Federal Reserve Board.

11 The Democratic Party caucus of the U.S. House of Representatives elects Rep. David E. Bonior (MI) to succeed Rep. William Gray 3d as House majority whip.

15 U.S. Secretary of Commerce Robert A. Mosbacher announces that the 1990 U.S. census would not be adjusted statistically to account for those who may have been missed in the count.

17 At the conclusion of their annual conference, the leaders of the Group of Seven major industrial democracies confer with Soviet President Gorbachev in London. The Western leaders offer the USSR a plan of technical assistance.

18 Twenty-three heads of state from South and Central America, the Caribbean, Spain, and Portugal gather at Guadalajara, Mexico, for the first Ibero-American Summit Conference.

21 President Bush concludes a three-day visit to Turkey. He was in Greece July 18–19.

30 In a report to the UN Security Council, UN weapons inspectors confirm that Iraq tried to conceal its nuclear-weapons program by destroying or burying equipment related to nuclear research.

31 In Moscow, President Gorbachev and President Bush sign the Strategic Arms Reduction Treaty.

AUGUST

1 Israel's Prime Minister Yitzhak Shamir reveals that Israel would participate in U.S.- and USSR-sponsored peace talks on the Middle East, provided that its conditions on the composition of the Palestinian delegation at such a conference were met.

2 Responding to a mysterious photo released to the press on July 15, President Bush pledges that the U.S. government would "run down every single lead" regarding the possibility of Vietnam War-era U.S. servicemen being held captive in Southeast Asia.

10 Japan's Premier Toshiki Kaifu arrives in Beijing for talks with Chinese leaders.

11 Edward A. Tracy, an American who had been held hostage in Lebanon since October 1986, is released and Jérôme Leyraud, a French relief-organization administrator who was seized by the previously unknown Organization for the Defense of Prisoners' Rights on Aug. 8, 1991, also is freed. British journalist John McCarthy, who had been a hostage since April 1986, had been released in eastern Lebanon on August 8.

13 Clark M. Clifford and Robert Altman resign as chairman and president, respectively, of First American Bankshares Inc., the largest bank holding corporation in Washington, DC. The two men have been under investigation for allowing the Bank of Credit and Commerce International (BCCI) to gain a secret and illegal controlling interest in First American.

17 President Bush signs legislation to provide additional benefits to the long-term unemployed but refuses to declare a fiscal emergency, necessary to release the required funds.

22 Soviet President Gorbachev returns to Moscow after being detained for three days by Soviet hard-liners and security forces in the Soviet Crimea in an unsuccessful coup d'état.

© Filip Horvat/Saba

© Chesnot/Sipa

Thousands of Russians gathered in Moscow's Red Square, left, on August 22 to celebrate the collapse of an attempted coup by Soviet hard-liners against President Gorbachev. Boris Yeltsin, placard above, *the president of the Russian Republic, who led the resistance against the failed uprising, addressed the crowd.*

27 The premiers of nine of Canada's ten provinces conclude their annual meeting in Whistler, B.C.

28 In New York City a subway train derails at high speed and crashes into a station support column, killing five passengers and injuring more than 200.

29 In the wake of the failed coup attempt, the Supreme Soviet votes to curtail the activities of the Communist Party. President Gorbachev had resigned as head of the party on August 24.

30 At the World Track and Field Championships in Tokyo, Mike Powell leaps 29′4.5″ (8.95 m), surpassing Bob Beamon's long-jump record of 29′2.5″ (8.9 m) set at the 1968 Olympics.

SEPTEMBER

3 A fire in a chicken-processing plant in Hamlet, NC, claims the lives of 25 workers.

4 Representatives of the United States and Kuwait initial a ten-year security pact that allows the U.S. armed forces to stockpile weapons and conduct military exercises in Kuwait.

5 Britain's Prime Minister John Major concludes an international tour during which he met with President Bush in Kennebunkport, ME; became the first Western leader to visit Moscow since the abortive coup; and was the first Western leader to visit China since the 1989 crackdown against the prodemocracy movement.

The trial of former Panamanian strongman Manuel Antonio Noriega, on drug-trafficking and money-laundering charges, gets under way in U.S. District Court in Miami.

6 The State Council, the new Soviet provisional executive body, formally recognizes the independence of the Baltic republics of Estonia, Latvia, and Lithuania.

In Beijing in early September, Britain's Prime Minister John Major (left), *his Foreign Minister Douglas Hurd, and China's Foreign Minister Qian Qichen shared a toast. While the British leaders were in China, the two nations signed an agreement regarding the construction of a new international airport for Hong Kong.*

AP/Wide World

8 In a referendum, Macedonia joins Croatia and Slovenia in declaring its independence from Yugoslavia.

Stefan Edberg of Sweden wins the men's singles tennis title at the U.S. Open. Czechoslovakia's Monica Seles had captured the women's crown on September 7.

11 Israel releases 51 Palestinian and Lebanese prisoners after receiving confirmation that two Israeli soldiers, captured in South Lebanon in 1986, had died.

13 The United States and the Soviet Union agree to end their military aid to government and rebel forces in Afghanistan.

14 In South Africa, President F. W. de Klerk, African National Congress President Nelson Mandela, and Inkatha Freedom Party President Mangosuthu Gatsha Buthelezi sign a plan to end factional violence in the black townships.

16 All charges against Oliver North in the Iran-contra case are dropped.

The Philippine Senate rejects a treaty that would have extended the U.S. lease on the Subic Base Naval Station. President Corazon Aquino vows to bring the decision to a national referendum.

17 North Korea, South Korea, the three newly independent Baltic states, Micronesia, and the Marshall Islands are admitted as members of the United Nations as the 46th session of the General Assembly opens in New York.

18 A nine-day strike by federal government workers in Canada ends.

22 The Huntington Library in San Marino, CA, agrees to make its set of photographs of the Dead Sea Scrolls available to the public.

23 President Bush calls upon the UN General Assembly to repeal its 1975 resolution equating Zionism with racism.

24 Theodor Seuss Geisel, the children's book author and illustrator known as Dr. Seuss, dies in La Jolla, CA.

25 Representatives of El Salvador's government and the nation's five main rebel groups sign a pact on El Salvador's political and economic future.

27 In a televised address, President Bush outlines a planned unilateral reduction of about 2,400 U.S. nuclear weapons.

30 Jean-Bertrand Aristide, Haiti's freely elected president, is overthrown in a coup.

OCTOBER

3 In Sweden, Moderate Party leader Carl Bildt is sworn in as head of a four-party center-right coalition government, succeeding a coalition headed by Ingvar Carlsson, whose Social Democratic Labor Party was defeated in September 15 elections.

4 In Madrid, Spain, representatives of 24 nations sign an agreement extending the provisions of the 1959 Antarctic Treaty. The new agreement prohibits all mining activity and oil exploration in Antarctica for 50 years.

5 Soviet President Gorbachev unveils his own plan for nuclear cuts in response to President Bush's proposal of September 27.

6 In Portugal the Social Democratic Party of Premier Aníbal Cavaco Silva retains its parliamentary majority in national elections.

15 By a 52–48 vote the U.S. Senate confirms the nomination of Clarence Thomas as a justice of the U.S. Supreme Court. The vote followed three days of televised hearings into charges of sexual

Photos, © Brad Markel/Gamma-Liaison

The United States watched attentively as U.S. Supreme Court nominee Clarence Thomas (top right) *defended himself against charges of sexual harassment before the Senate Judiciary Committee. His former colleague and current law professor Anita Hill* (above) *brought the charges. Thomas was confirmed to the court by a 52-48 vote on October 15.*

harassment brought against Thomas by Anita F. Hill, a law professor and former Thomas aide.

16 A gunman identified as George Jo Hennard, 35, goes on a shooting rampage in a Killeen, TX, cafeteria, killing 24 persons, including himself.

Leaders of the Commonwealth gather in Harare, Zimbabwe, for the opening of their biennial Commonwealth meeting.

18 President Gorbachev and the presidents of eight of the 12 Soviet constituent republics sign an economic union treaty.

21 Jesse Turner, a U.S. university professor who had been held hostage in Lebanon since January 1987, is released.

Roy Romanow, a member of Canada's New Democratic Party, is elected premier of Saskatchewan. Michael Harcourt, also a member of the New Democratic Party, had been elected premier of British Columbia on October 17.

22 The European Community (EC) and the European Free Trade Association (EFTA) agree in principle to form a 19-nation free-trade area.

23 In Paris the four factions warring for control of Cambodia sign a comprehensive peace agreement, under which the United Nations would administer a transition to democracy.

27 In Poland's first fully free parliamentary elections, no party emerges with anything near a ruling majority.

The Minnesota Twins win baseball's World Series, defeating the Atlanta Braves, four games to three.

29 The United States Treasury Department announces a federal budget deficit of $268.7 billion for fiscal 1991.

30 In Madrid, Spain, representatives of Egypt, Israel, Jordan, Lebanon, Syria, and the Palestinians of the Israeli-occupied territories attend the opening session of the Middle East peace talks. Presidents Bush and Gorbachev open the discussions.

31 A furious Atlantic storm batters coastal areas of the Northeast and mid-Atlantic states of the United States, causing extensive damage.

NOVEMBER

2 Civil-rights leader Jesse Jackson announces that he will not seek the 1992 Democratic presidential nomination.

4 The Middle East peace conference in Madrid, Spain, adjourns without any substantive progress but with a general agreement to hold future bilateral talks between Israeli and Arab delegates.

5 Off-year elections are held throughout the United States. In Pennsylvania, Harris Wofford (D) defeats former Attorney General Richard Thornburgh (R) to fill the unexpired term of the late Sen. John Heinz (R). Voters in the state of Washington defeat a measure that would have set limits on the number of terms that the state's U.S. congressional delegation could serve. Kirk Fordice (R) and Brereton C. Jones (D) are elected governors of Mississippi and Kentucky, respectively.

By a vote of 64-31, the U.S. Senate confirms the nomination of Robert M. Gates as director of the Central Intelligence Agency (CIA).

China and Vietnam reestablish diplomatic relations, which had been broken after Vietnam invaded Cambodia in 1979.

The body of media baron Robert Maxwell is found floating several miles from his yacht in the Atlantic Ocean off the Canary Islands.

6 In Japan, Kiichi Miyazawa, who was chosen leader of the ruling Liberal Democratic Party on October 27, succeeds Toshiki Kaifu as premier of Japan.

7 Floods resulting from tropical storm *Thelma* have killed at least 3,400 people in the Philippines.

Basketball star Earvin (Magic) Johnson announces that he has tested positive for the HIV virus that causes AIDS and retires immediately as a player with the Los Angeles Lakers.

8 A summit meeting of the North Atlantic Treaty Organization (NATO) draws to a close in Rome as the post-Cold War role of the alliance continues to change.

9 For the first time scientists produce a significant amount of energy from controlled nuclear fusion. The achievement, which occurred at the Joint European Torus laboratory in Oxfordshire, England, is considered a major step in harnessing for human use the type of thermonuclear fire that lights the Sun.

14 The United States indicts two Libyan intelligence officers for the bombing of Pan Am Flight 103 over Lockerbie, Scotland, in December 1988, which resulted in 270 deaths.

After nearly 13 years in exile, Prince Norodom Sihanouk returns to Phnom Penh.

During a seven-day trip to the United States, Argentina's President Carlos Saúl Menem addresses a joint session of the U.S. Congress.

15 A U.S. appeals court panel reverses the Iran-contra convictions of John Poindexter. The former national security adviser had been convicted in 1990 of five felony charges in the case.

In Japan, Kiichi Miyazawa, 72-year-old former cabinet minister, was elected president of the ruling Liberal Democratic Party on October 27. A special session of the Diet (parliament) formally appointed him premier, and he named a 20-member cabinet on November 6.

© Najlah Feanny/Saba

Reuters/Bettmann

In a gubernatorial race that drew considerable attention in Louisiana as well as throughout the United States, former Louisiana Gov. Edwin Edwards (D), top, *defeated state Rep. David Duke,* below, *in a November 16 runoff by a 61%-39% margin. Duke, a former leader of the Ku Klux Klan, later announced his candidacy for the U.S. presidency.*

16 In a runoff gubernatorial election in Louisiana, former Gov. Edwin Edwards defeats former Ku Klux Klan leader David Duke.

18 Church of England envoy Terry Waite and U.S. professor Thomas Sutherland are released after years of captivity as hostages in Lebanon.

23 Russian President Boris Yeltsin concludes a three-day visit to Germany.

25 Egypt's President Hosni Mubarak confers with Syria's President Hafiz al-Assad in Syria.

26 William P. Barr takes the oath of office as U.S. attorney general.

The United States agrees to pay Iran $278 million in compensation for U.S.-Iranian arms agreements canceled following Iran's 1979 Islamic revolution.

27 The first session of the 102d U.S. Congress adjourns.

Khieu Samphan, a high-ranking official of Cambodia's Khmer Rouge faction, is attacked by a mob as he tries to reenter Cambodia.

29 A sudden dust storm causes a series of chain-reaction auto accidents on Interstate Highway 5 near Coalinga, CA, causing the death of 17 persons.

DECEMBER

1 The U.S. space shuttle *Atlantis* concludes a weeklong military mission.

France captures the Davis Cup tennis title.

4 Pan American World Airways ceases operations.

Charles H. Keating, Jr., former chairman of the Lincoln Savings & Loan Association, is convicted in Los Angeles of 17 counts of securities fraud.

5 U.S. Transportation Secretary Samuel K. Skinner is named to succeed John H. Sununu as White House chief of staff. Sununu's resignation from the post had been announced on December 3.

7 President Bush attends ceremonies in Hawaii commemorating the 50th anniversary of the Japanese attack on Pearl Harbor.

8 Russia's President Boris Yeltsin and the leaders of the Ukraine and Byelorussia sign an agreement establishing the Commonwealth of Independent States to replace the USSR.

10 Conservative columnist Patrick Buchanan announces that he will seek the 1992 Republican presidential nomination.

The U.S. Supreme Court declares unconstitutional a New York state law—known as the Son of Sam law—that limits the ability of convicted criminals to profit from selling stories of their crimes.

11 The European Community (EC) takes steps toward an "ever closer union" at a summit meeting in Maastricht, the Netherlands.

William Kennedy Smith, the nephew of Sen. Edward M. Kennedy (D-MA), is acquitted of sexual battery (rape) charges in Palm Beach, FL.

13 The premiers of North and South Korea sign a pact entitled "Agreement on Reconciliation, Nonaggression, Exchange, and Cooperation."

16 The United Nations General Assembly rescinds its 1975 resolution equating Zionism with racism.

AP/Wide World

Associated Press correspondent *Terry Anderson*, center—*the last U.S. hostage in Lebanon—who was released from captivity on December 4, enjoys a joyful reunion with fellow hostages Joseph J. Cicippio, left, and Alann Steen at the U.S. Air Force Base in Wiesbaden, Germany. Cicippio and Steen, who were employed by the American University in Beirut before their capture, had been released on December 2.*

Canada announces that it has reached an agreement with Inuit leaders on a massive land-claim settlement. The pact would lead to the establishment of a new territory, Nunavut.

Trinidad and Tobago's People's National Movement Party, led by Patrick Manning, defeats the ruling National Alliance for Reconstruction in national elections.

18 General Motors announces the closing of 21 assembly plants and the elimination of 70,000 positions.

Peace talks between Israel and its Arab neighbors adjourn in Washington.

19 Australia's former Treasurer Paul Keating is elected to succeed Bob Hawke as leader of the ruling Labor Party and, therefore, prime minister.

20 New York Gov. Mario Cuomo announces that he will not seek the Democratic presidential nomination in 1992.

The Federal Reserve System cuts the discount rate to 3.5%, the lowest level since 1964.

21 The ruling Nationalist Party is victorious in elections in Taiwan.

25 Mikhail S. Gorbachev gives up the presidency of the USSR.

26 President Bush names Barbara H. Franklin as secretary of commerce, succeeding Robert A. Mosbacher. The latter is resigning to direct the president's 1992 reelection campaign.

In Algeria the Islamic Salvation Front, a fundamentalist Muslim movement, wins 44% of the seats in the first round of parliamentary elections.

27 The Philippines tells the United States that it must withdraw from Subic Bay naval base by the end of 1992.

31 North and South Korea announce that they have agreed to ban nuclear weapons from the Korean peninsula.

AP/Wide World

THE SECOND SOVIET REVOLUTION

By Robert Sharlet

© Filip Horvat/Saba

The 20th century has witnessed the rise and fall of Soviet communism. Revolutions are defining moments in a nation's history and the people of the Soviet Union have experienced two in little more than seven decades. The Bolshevik Revolution of 1917 had ushered in the era of communism as a ruling ideology which came to include one-party dictatorship, a planned economy, social collectivism, and an expansionist foreign policy. The Moscow coup of 1991 brought this era to an end, fully opening the way to the second Soviet revolution, a systemic change complete with a new set of code words—democracy, the market, individualism, and national independence. By August 1991 the Soviet Union was in decline politically, economically, socially, and internationally.

© Wojtek Laski/Sipa

During the First Soviet Revolution in November 1917, Vladimir Lenin, top page 24, *led the movement that brought the Bolsheviks to control and established the Communist system. During the Second Soviet Revolution in August 1991, Boris Yeltsin,* above right, *president of the Russian Republic, was a vocal force against a hard-line coup that sought to remove Mikhail Gorbachev,* above left, *as Soviet president. As the 1991 takeover attempt failed, the statues of such Communist stalwarts as Feliks Dzerzhinsky,* page 24, *the founder of the KGB—the Soviet political police, were toppled.*

Six years of Mikhail Gorbachev's *perestroika*—his ambitious program for reforming the Soviet system launched in the mid-1980s—had inspired many positive changes, but at the same time it had unleashed great social forces over which Gorbachev progressively lost control. As a result, social unrest and ethnic rebellion were rife, economic life was in disarray, the external empire in Eastern Europe was gone, and the Communist Party and its allied social-control mechanisms were in a severely weakened state. In this context, the coup and its quick collapse finished off the Soviet system, and by year's end the USSR had exited the stage of history.

Background to the Coup. The coup as a conservative backlash against the consequences of *perestroika* could be seen coming from the late summer of 1990. Gorbachev and his political rival Boris Yeltsin, presidents of the USSR and Russian parliaments respectively, had agreed to go forward with a radical 500-day plan for converting the Soviet Union to a market economy when, abruptly, Gorbachev reneged on the agreement. He had experienced pressure from his conservative constituencies—the party, the KGB or secret police, and the military-industrial complex—all of which feared the adverse impact of privatization and marketization on their interests. From that point on, signs of conservative concern and backstage maneuvering were apparent.

The coup was not the product of a single, well-planned, long-gestating conspiracy. It was more the result of a conservative mind-set that tolerated only tinkering with the status quo and therefore recoiled at and actively resisted Gorbachev's reform policies and their consequences. By 1990, from the conservative point of view, Gorbachev had lost effective control over his policies on public information (*glasnost*) and political participation (''democratization''), the projected radical economic reforms were considered contrary to the interests of the party-state, while Gorbachev's foreign policy was

About the Author. Robert Sharlet, professor of political science at Union College in Schenectady, NY, specializes in Soviet and East European affairs. Dr. Sharlet was in the Soviet Union immediately following the August 1991 coup, for a personal assessment of the situation. During the year he also completed his fourth book, *Soviet Constitutional Crisis,* which is to be published by M. E. Sharpe in 1992. Dr. Sharlet was graduated from Brandeis and Indiana universities and was an exchange fellow at Moscow University Law School. He has appeared as a guest expert on various television programs and is consulted regularly by leading newspapers and magazines.

regarded as a threat to the Soviet Union's status as a superpower.

The conservative leaders gathered their anti-*perestroika* forces slowly, opposing the program behind the scenes and operating through surrogates while occasionally attacking at the flanks over the course of a year, until they finally decided on an open, frontal assault on power late in the summer of 1991. Their precoup opposition was expressed in three patterns: (1) public and sub-rosa criticism of Gorbachev's principal reform advisers, (2) small-scale military and police attacks on the periphery of the reform movement, and (3) parliamentary and media broadsides calling for strong measures against the systemic crisis created by *perestroika.*

Historians eventually may conclude that harbingers of the coup first appeared in Tbilisi, Georgia, in 1989 when Soviet troops put down a peaceful demonstration with unwarranted force, causing death and injury to a number of people; or in Baku, Azerbaijan, at the beginning of 1990 when the military, in the process of restoring order after serious violence, used excessive firepower, killing and wounding hundreds of civilians. In fact, the immediate coup season began in September 1990 with the mysterious nocturnal movement of units of the elite Pskov parachute division into the environs of Moscow. Nothing ensued, but to quiet fearful rumors flying about, the military put out the story that the troops, in full battle dress, had arrived to help with the potato harvest.

During the fall of 1990 conservatives openly and behind the scenes conducted a vilification campaign against leading reformers, including Alexander Yakovlev, considered the architect of *perestroika;* Foreign Minister Eduard Shevardnadze; and the national police minister, Vadim Bakatin. By early December parliamentary conservatives had engineered Bakatin's removal and his replacement by the hard-line former KGB and party official, Boris Pugo. The conservative faction next set their sights on Shevardnadze, whom they scape-

As the August 1991 coup began, the hard-liners dispatched thousands of military units, including hundreds of tanks, to key positions in Moscow. Later, as the coup began to fail, Muscovites gleefully mingled with the dispersing forces.

A CHRONOLOGY OF A COUP THAT FAILED

Coup Leaders: KGB's Vladimir Kryuchkov

Premier Valentin Pavlov

Photos, AP/Wide World

August 19. The Soviet news agency Tass announces that Soviet Vice-President Gennadi I. Yanayev and seven other members of a State Committee for the State of Emergency in the USSR have taken over the government. Soviet President Mikhail Gorbachev, who is at his summer home in the Crimea with his family, is said to be ill. A state of emergency is declared. Leaders of the emergency committee suspend all civil rights, establish curfews, and ban opposition political activity. Military units take up positions at key points in Moscow. . . . Thousands of civilians rush to the Russian Republic parliament building and are addressed by Russian Republic President Boris N. Yeltsin. Standing on the top of an army tank, he declares the coup unconstitutional and the coup leaders traitors.

August 20. President Yeltsin, backed by the heads of other republics, asks security forces to join the resistance and calls for a general strike. Yeltsin is supported by tens of thousands of people who gather in large cities around the USSR to build barricades and defy the new government and armed forces. . . . Some troops called into Moscow exhibit divided loyalty. . . . Valentin S. Pavlov resigns as prime minister of the USSR and as a member of the emergency committee. . . . The foreign ministers of the European Community condemn the coup and freeze all but humanitarian aid to the USSR.

August 21. In the midst of domestic and international pressure, the coup collapses. In their first telephone conversation since the attempted overthrow, President Gorbachev assures U.S. President Bush that "constitutional authorities" have regained power in the USSR. Gorbachev is released from house arrest in the Crimea late in the day. . . . The Presidium of the Supreme Soviet voids all decrees of the emergency committee.

August 22. President Gorbachev returns to Moscow and declares he is again in full control of the country. He hails Boris Yeltsin and the Soviet people. . . . Thousands of Muscovites, celebrating the coup's failure, cover the headquarters of the secret police (the KGB) in Red Square with graffiti and topple the statue of KGB founder Feliks Dzerzhinsky. . . . Boris K. Pugo, a member of the emergency committee, commits suicide, and the arrest of other coup members begins.

August 23. President Yeltsin rejects President Gorbachev's appointments of the interim heads of the military and KGB; Gorbachev then names Air Force Gen. Yevgeny I. Shaposhnikov, who had refused to support the coup, and Vadim V. Bakatin, who is considered a reformist, as defense minister and KGB chief, respectively. . . . The Soviet president also dismisses Foreign Minister Aleksandr A. Bessmertnykh, who claimed to be ill during the uprising. . . . Yeltsin unilaterally suspends publication of the Communist Party daily *Pravda* and five other newspapers. . . . Gorbachev, who generally is blamed for having brought the coup leaders to power, is heckled when he addresses the Russian Republic's parliament.

August 24. President Gorbachev resigns as Communist Party leader. All party property is placed under the management of the Soviet parliament and all political activity in public institutions and elsewhere is banned or curbed. . . . As many as 100,000 people gather in Moscow for the seven-hour funeral of three men killed during the coup. . . . Ivan Silayev, prime minister of the Russian Republic and a Yeltsin aide, is appointed by Gorbachev to oversee the national economy.

August 26. President Gorbachev appeals to the republics to stick together.

August 28. Thirteen former officials, including the seven surviving members of the emergency committee, are charged with treason for their actual or alleged involvement in the coup. . . . President Gorbachev appoints Boris Pankin, currently the Soviet ambassador to Czechoslovakia, foreign minister.

August 29. The USSR legislature, the Supreme Soviet, votes to suspend all activities of the Communist Party.

August 30. KGB chief Bakatin announces plans to reorganize and depoliticize the KGB.

September 2. The United States grants diplomatic recognition to the Baltic states—Estonia, Latvia, and Lithuania. Several other nations had done so previously.

September 3. Communist Party apparatchiks and government officials on all levels continue to be fired. A few are arrested.

September 5. The Congress of People's Deputies, the overall Soviet parliament, approves a plan whereby an interim political structure would direct the country pending the writing of a new constitution and the drafting of a new union treaty to redefine the relationship between the central government and the republics.

September 6. The Soviet Union's new State Council recognizes the independence of the three Baltic republics.

Coup Leaders:

Interior Minister Boris Pugo

Vice-President Gennadi Yanayev

Defense Minister Dimitri Yazov

goated for the recent loss of Communist East Europe and reunification of Germany. The foreign minister, fed up with the constant criticism and furious that his friend Gorbachev did not defend him, abruptly announced his resignation in late December. Ominously, he warned that a dictatorship was coming.

Possibly emboldened by their successes, the conservative opposition turned to action in the first weeks of January 1991. In a nearly instant manifestation of Shevardnadze's dire warning, special KGB and military units attacked two communications facilities in independence-minded Lithuania, killing a number of people and wounding many others. In effect, this was an attempted coup against the outspoken nationalist government of the Lithuanian republic which was called off quickly due to domestic and international protest. Seven months later, several of the senior Soviet officials involved in planning the Lithuanian action appeared in the ranks of the plotters of the Moscow coup.

The Lithuanian assault was the beginning of a period of low-level acts of violence, semi-open as well as clandestine, directed at the maverick nationalists in the Baltic region, especially Lithuania and Latvia, running up through the end of July. It was then, during the 1991 Moscow summit between President Gorbachev and U.S. President George Bush, that six Lithuanian customs officers were found brutally murdered execution-style by means of military weapons. All the circumstances of the crime pointed to the special services of the USSR who then were commanded by Minister Pugo and KGB chief Vladimir Kryuchkov.

Finally, in the lead-up to the August coup, conservatives in the Soviet and Russian parliaments, in the upper echelons of the party, and in the media carried on a vigorous verbal and print effort to raise public alarm over the web of crises generated by Gorbachev's reforms. The conservatives' critique included the rampant crime problem, declining public morality, the faltering economy, a disintegrating state, the demoralized military, and the Soviet Union's diminished prestige abroad. Leading the criticism of Gorbachev in the union parliament was People's Deputy Viktor Alksnis, an air-force colonel and the articulate coleader of the conservative bloc called "Union." Gorbachev had other critics in the disgruntled party leadership, frustrated at watching their power dissipate under *perestroika*.

Among the media critical of Gorbachev and his program were the main party paper *Pravda,* the conservative daily *Soviet Russia,* and a new far-right weekly called *The Day*. As if in a single voice from their common mind-set, the conservatives in these various venues pounded away at *perestroika* as reform run riot, urging Gorbachev to use his presidential powers of emergency rule to restore order and discipline and restabilize the economy. In late July, just weeks before the coup, as the patience of the conservatives was running out, a group of generals, politicians, and writers—three of whom would go on to lead the seizure of power—issued an "Address to the People," a clarion call to action:

© Michael Rondou/"San Jose Mercury News"/Sipa

© Filip Horvat/Saba

Moscow street scenes, August 1991: A Russian woman, left, expresses her views on the uprising to a group of soldiers, and a Soviet flag with the hammer and sickle removed is displayed defiantly. The lack of full military support, especially among junior officers who sided with Yeltsin, contributed to the coup's failure.

> *An enormous, unprecedented misfortune has befallen us. Our homeland and country, a great state that was given into our care by history, nature, and our glorious ancestors, is perishing, breaking up, and being plunged into darkness and nonexistence. . . . Let us unite to stop the chain reaction of the ruinous disintegration of the state, the economy, and the individual. . . .*

The Coup That Failed. The coup was not a surprise to everyone, although no one foresaw its exact timing. President Bush, on the strength of intelligence reports, a few months earlier had warned Gorbachev, who assured him everything was under control. On the very eve of the seizure, Gorbachev's ally Yakovlev publicly predicted a coup by hard-line elements, but the president, vacationing at his summer house in the Crimea, was not listening. It was there on Sunday afternoon, August 18, that a delegation of conspirators arrived unannounced and presented Gorbachev with an ultimatum either to join them or to resign the presidency. Rejecting their proposals out of hand, President Gorbachev found himself and his family incommunicado and under virtual house arrest. Returning to Moscow, the plotters met with their waiting comrades and formed the State Committee for the State of the Emergency with Vice-President Gennadi Yanayev as its head. In the early hours of Monday morning, the conspirators publicly set the coup in motion under cover of a constitutional transfer of power to Yanayev as acting president, based on their false report of Gorbachev being ill and incapacitated.

The Emergency Committee's initial public documents made clear its conservative lineage from the opposition of the past year. In this spirit, the committee's opening proclamation even echoed the July "Address":

> *Fellow countrymen! Citizens of the Soviet Union! In a dark and critical hour, we address you! A mortal danger hangs over our great homeland! The policy of reform initiated by M.S. Gorbachev . . . has . . . come to a dead end.*

Several hours later, a comprehensive decree on the emergency was issued, effectively suspending *perestroika*. The provisions of the decree were aimed directly at the policies of *glasnost* and democratization and were intended to bring an abrupt end to the "war of laws" between competing jurisdictions as well as a decisive halt to the so-called "parade of sovereignties" by would-be secessionist republics.

Predictably, troops were deployed in Moscow; radio and television were brought under control; proreform papers were shut down; strikes and demonstrations were banned; and arrest orders were issued. Almost immediately, however, things went awry in the capital. Yeltsin, who in June became executive president of the Russian Republic, was not arrested and became the cynosure of public resistance to the coup. An independent radio station managed clandestinely to resume broadcasting, while Soviet TV personnel quietly passed vital satellite equipment to CNN, which inexplicably was allowed to cover the coup live. Pro-Yeltsin papers pooled their resources and turned out underground bulletins. Sizable crowds of Muscovites gathered at the Russian parliament building—Yeltsin's headquarters—and, crucially, some troops and police crossed over and came to Yeltsin's defense. Faced with growing resistance at home and abroad, the refusal of several important military commanders to comply with the Emergency Committee's orders, and more troop defections, the conspirators lost their nerve and by Wednesday, August 21, the coup had collapsed with only minimal casualties.

"The country is emerging from a crisis. The forces which organized it [the coup] have been condemned by history. The people have made their decision and they clearly have no intention of going back again."

Boris Yeltsin
Aug. 22, 1991

Why did the plotters strike when they did? The coup was directed against *perestroika* as personified by its author, Gorbachev, and its champion, Yeltsin. In the previous month, both presidents had taken decisions which, once implemented, irreversibly would have undermined the sources of the conservatives' power—the monolithic party, the centralized state, and a unified military and police establishment. Thus, the coup makers were reacting against Yeltsin's July decree removing party organizations from all Russian enterprises, Gorbachev's new plan to eviscerate the party's Marxist-Leninist identity, and both presidents' intention of signing on Tuesday, August 20, an historic new Treaty of Union which constitutionally would have shifted substantial powers from the center to the republics.

Why, then, with such strong motivation and the enormous coercive forces of the state at their disposal, did the leaders of the coup fail? Three reasons seem apparent: (1) the absence of detailed preparations, (2) the failure of political resolve, and (3) irreversible changes in Soviet society brought about by *perestroika*. After his arrest, Marshal Dimitri Yazov, the former minister of defense, confirmed that there had been little advance planning; the plotters first had come together as a

© Sichov/Sipa

group at an informal meeting on Saturday afternoon, August 17. Secondly, while Kryuchkov was the prime mover of the coup, Yanayev—a weak and ineffectual politician—served as its constitutional front man. Therefore, without a political strongman, the group's cohesion cracked under pressure of the resistance; Yazov quit, Pavlov checked into a hospital, while Yanayev drank himself into a stupor. Finally, the hastily undertaken coup counted on military discipline and social acquiescence to achieve its objective of stopping the country's descent into chaos. The military, however, mirrored the changes which had taken place in society, including the reform-conservative split, with many junior officers and servicemen siding with Yeltsin against the coup. Similarly, while the vast majority of the population, beset with scarcities and disillusioned with politics, remained on the sidelines, the activist public did turn out in sufficient numbers in Moscow, St. Petersburg, and several other cities to help Yeltsin prevail over the poorly organized, irresolute conspirators.

© Filip Horvat/Saba

Expressions of grief were vivid on August 24 as some 100,000 people jammed Moscow streets to honor the three men killed during the coup. Presidents Gorbachev and Yeltsin both addressed the crowd.

Aftermath. President Gorbachev was freed and returned to Moscow to resume his rivalry with President Yeltsin, but now from a position of considerable weakness. Gorbachev had come back to a different country from the one he had left to go on vacation. The authority of the center and its institutions, including the once hegemonic Communist Party, had collapsed along with the coup. Yeltsin, hero of the resistance, took the lead in forging the second Soviet revolution. Accruing to himself and the Russian government extensive new powers at the expense of Gorbachev and the discredited union government whose most-senior officials had usurped power, Yeltsin and Russia set the pace for the other republics. In the wake of the coup, the three Baltic republics regained their

© Keren/REA/Saba

Foreign Minister Aleksandr Bessmertnykh, who for the most part was absent from the scene during the coup and claimed illness when he reappeared in Moscow late on August 21, was removed from his post by President Gorbachev on August 23.

independence and world recognition, while ten of the remaining 12 union republics had declared—newly or previously—their independence of the Soviet Union. Gorbachev's efforts to reconstitute the state in one form or another—as a loose confederation or a minimal political and economic union—all proved futile in face of the republics' irrepressible nationalism and irresistible determination to seek their own paths to the future. By year's end, Gorbachev had become a superfluous president of a vanishing country as the presidents of Russia, Ukraine, and Belarus (Byelorussia) created a new Commonwealth of Independent States open to other republics as well, with its center in Minsk, far from Moscow.

The effect of the coup's aftermath on the populace was much more mixed and less decisive. Although only a small minority actually had opposed the coup, the vast majority were buoyed up initially by the outcome. For many, hope, which had flagged as the Soviet Union drifted rudderless earlier in the year, was revived temporarily. In the interest of averting total chaos, Yeltsin and Gorbachev had managed, although at arm's length, to work together in the weeks following the coup to fashion with other leaders a set of interim institutions for guiding the country through a "transitional period" to a radically different USSR. These institutions included new executive and legislative bodies and a coordinating committee for the union economy, but none of them took root in the changing landscape of the second Soviet revolution.

In this atmosphere of decolonialization and self-determination, what remained of the national economy fell into unworkable pieces and the citizen-consumer sank back into despair. As a woman in St. Petersburg observed, freedom of speech is important, but freedom to purchase is necessary as well, and the former without the latter is not of much use in the daily struggle for existence. As citizens of the former Soviet Union pondered the second Soviet revolution at 1991's end, the liberation of the nations of the Soviet internal empire was under way, with political freedom racing ahead and economic necessity lagging far behind.

Future Outlook. Gorbachev's *perestroika* began as an ambitious attempt to reform communism in the Soviet Union and in its client states in East Europe. In the end, the reforms proved fatal to the system built by Lenin and Stalin, bringing about the collapse of communism, first in Eastern Europe in 1989 and finally, two years later in 1991, in the Soviet Union itself, costing Gorbachev himself his presidency. As such, *perestroika* became the Trojan horse of the Bolshevik Revolution, subverting its creation, the Communist system, and clearing the way for the second Soviet revolution. Unlike its predecessor, though, the new revolution which will carry the nations of the former USSR into the 21st century is likely to take diverse and plural forms, some hopeful and promising and others foreboding and regressive, in the quest for human freedom and self-realization.

See also Alphabetical Section, USSR article.

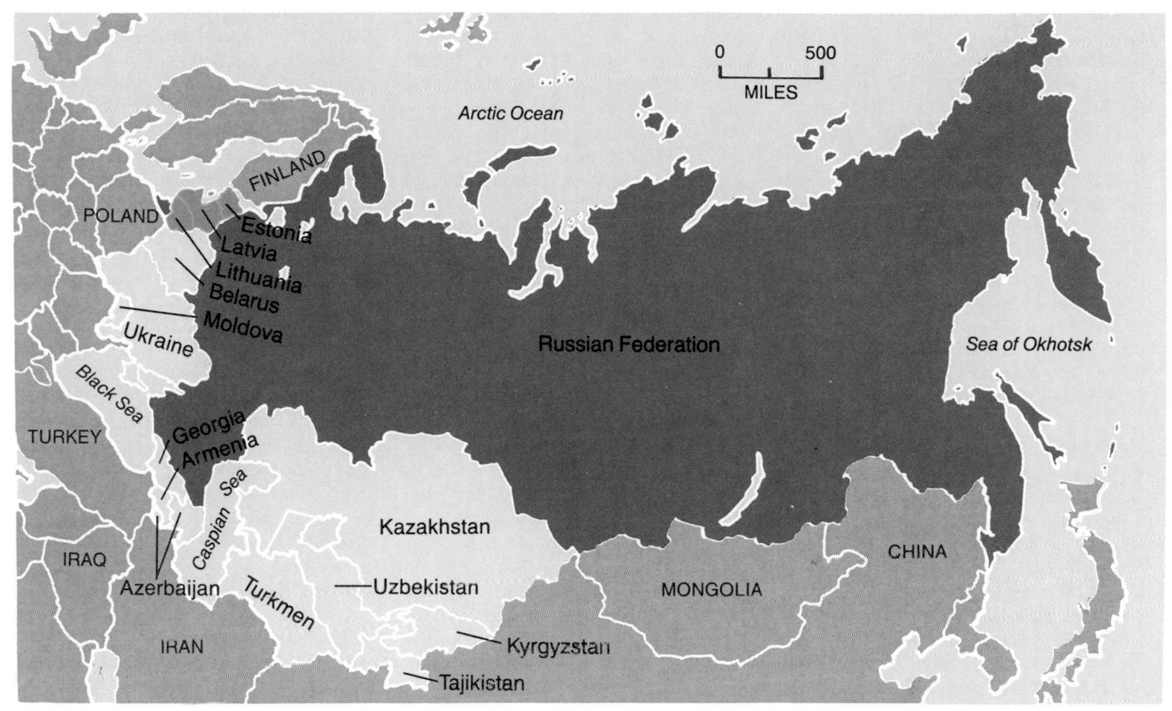

The Former Republics of the USSR

Armenia. The Armenian people have lived in the region between the Black Sea and the Caspian Sea since ancient times. The Kingdom of Armenia, which lasted from around 190 B.C. to around 1070 A.D., included not only the present Republic of Armenia, but also part of Azerbaijan and a large slice of what is now eastern Turkey. The country later was divided between Persia and the Ottoman Empire. Persian Armenia, annexed by Russia in 1828, became an independent republic after the breakup of the Russian Empire in 1918. It was incorporated into the USSR in 1922, and became the Armenian Soviet Socialist Republic in 1936. Since 1988, Armenia has been involved in an armed conflict with neighboring Azerbaijan over the status of Nagorno-Karabakh, a territory in Azerbaijan inhabited mostly by ethnic Armenians. In August 1990 the Armenian parliament voted to declare its independence of the USSR, and changed the country's name to the Republic of Armenia; with the dissolution of the USSR in December 1991, the international community recognized Armenian independence.

The Armenians were the first nation to adopt Christianity (300 A.D.) officially. Their church, the Armenian or Gregorian Church, is an independent body. Armenia is mountainous, but vineyards, fruit, and tobacco are cultivated in the valleys. It has a chemical industry, and its mineral products include copper and zinc. **Area:** 11,500 sq mi (29 800 km²); **Population:** 3,580,000 (1991 est.); **Capital:** Yerevan.

Azerbaijan. Situated on the western shore of the Caspian Sea, Azerbaijan Republic originally was part of the pre-Christian Persian Empire. It was annexed by Russia between 1813 and 1828, and became a union republic of the USSR in 1936. It includes the Nakhichevan Autonomous Republic (which is an enclave within Armenia) and the territory of Nagorno-Karabakh, a largely ethnic Armenian enclave that recently triggered fighting between Azerbaijan and Armenia. Azerbaijan declared its independence after the failed Moscow coup of August 1991. As in some other republics, Azerbaijan's President Ayaz Mutalibov is a former Communist official. Its most important products are petroleum and natural gas. The Azeri (Azerbaijani) people, who make up 83% of the population, are mostly Muslim, speak a Turkic language, and have close ties to their fellow Azeris in Iran. **Area:** 33,400 sq mi (86 400 km²); **Population:** 7,145,600 (1990 est.); **Capital:** Baku.

Belarus (Byelorussia). Belarus, or White Russia, was part of Poland until the late 1700s, when it was annexed by Russia. The republic, established in 1919, was enlarged by territory taken from Poland in 1939. With Russia and Ukraine, it was one of the three Slavic republics that formed the nucleus of the new Commonwealth of Independent States which replaced the USSR in December 1991. The Belarus city of Minsk was designated as the Commonwealth's center. The Belarus people, who comprise 78% of the population, are related closely to the Russians in language and culture. The republic's industrial products include cement, steel, and TV sets. **Area:** 80,151 sq mi (207 590 km²); **Population:** 10,259,000 (1990 est.); **Capital:** Minsk.

Estonia. The northernmost of the three Baltic countries, Estonia was ruled by the German Teutonic Knights, Poland, Denmark, and Sweden before being conquered by Russia in 1721. Like its Baltic neighbors, Estonia was independent from 1918 to 1940, when it was annexed forcibly by the USSR. A renewed drive for nationhood in the early 1990s was opposed by the large (30%) ethnic Russian population that had settled in the country during the period of Soviet rule. Many of them boycotted the independence referendum of March 3, 1991, in which 77% of the participants voted "yes." Estonia finally seceded from the USSR on Aug. 20, 1991, and its independence was recognized by the Soviet government on September 6. Estonia was admitted to the United Nations on September 17 and rejoined the Olympic movement the following day.

The Estonians, who comprise about 62% of the population, are mostly Lutheran and are related closely to the people of nearby Finland. Agriculture is important to the economy, and animal fodder is a major product. Manufactured items include textiles and wood products, especially paper. Oil shale is mined in the northeast for use as a fuel. **Area:** 17,400 sq mi (45 065 km^2); **Population:** 1,600,000 (1990 est.); **Capital:** Tallinn.

Georgia. Located on the eastern shore of the Black Sea, Georgia was annexed by Russia in 1801 and became a union republic of the USSR in 1936. In April 1991, Georgia declared its independence; after that it was troubled by ethnic strife and political quarrels. The authoritarian style of Zviad Gamsakhurdia, a non-Communist who was elected president in May 1991, aroused opposition. In September 1991 the president's political opponents, accusing him of trying to establish a dictatorship, took up arms against him, unleashing a full-scale civil war and driving the president from the capital. Georgia did not join the post-Soviet Commonwealth.

The Georgians, a proud mountain people who constitute 69% of the population, have been Christians since the 4th century A.D., and have their own Orthodox Church. Notable Georgians have included Joseph Stalin and Eduard Shevardnadze, who served as Soviet foreign minister under Mikhail Gorbachev. Other peoples in the republic include the Abkhaz and Adzhars (both Caucasian peoples, like the Georgians) and the Iranian-speaking South Ossetians. The South Ossetians, who wish to secede from Georgia, have been in rebellion against the Georgian government since 1990. Wine, tea, and fruit are important Georgian agricultural products, and manganese is a major mineral resource. **Area:** 27,000 sq mi (70 000 km^2); **Population:** 5,449,000 (1989); **Capital:** Tbilisi.

Kazakhstan. The Central Asian nation of Kazakhstan, the second-largest (next to Russia) of the former Soviet republics in area, was traditionally the domain of the Kazakhs, nomadic horsemen who were subdued by the Russians in the 19th century. A union republic of the USSR since 1936, it declared its independence in December 1991. Kazakhstan's President Nursultan Nazarbayev achieved prominence in the early 1990s as a spokesperson for the Central Asian republics and a strong proponent of a free-market economy; he and other Central Asian leaders were quick to support the new Commonwealth that took shape after the demise of the USSR, insisting on equal status with the European members. Kazakhstan's adherence was especially important because it possessed part of the former Soviet nuclear arsenal, which the international community wanted to keep under unified control.

The Kazakhs, a Muslim people who speak a Turkic language, comprise 36% of the population; Russians constitute 40%. Kazakhstan is a major grain-producing region; oil and gas, coal mining, and electric power are major industries. **Area:** 1,049,155 sq mi (2 717 300 km^2); **Population:** 16,690,300 (1990 est.); **Capital:** Alma-Ata.

Kyrgyzstan (Kirghizia). Kyrgyzstan, a mountainous country on the western border of China, was formerly part of the Khanate of Kokand, annexed by Russia in 1876. A union republic of the USSR since 1936, it declared its independence on Aug. 31, 1991. The Kyrgyz people, who are Muslim and speak a Turkic language, form 52% of the population. Tension between them and the Uzbek minority (13%) provoked bloody riots in 1990. Kyrgyzstan's mineral resources include coal, petroleum, natural gas, and uranium. **Area:** 76,640 sq mi (198 500 km^2); **Population:** 4,372,000 (1990 est.); **Capital:** Bishkek (Frunze).

Latvia. Latvia, one of the Baltic nations, was part of medieval Livonia, ruled by the Teutonic Knights; later divided between Sweden and Poland, it was absorbed into the Russian Empire in 1721. Latvia was independent from 1918 to 1940, when it was annexed forcibly by the USSR. Violent confrontations occurred between Soviet troops and Latvian nationalists as the USSR moved to halt Latvia's independence drive in January 1991. Following the failed Moscow coup of August 1991, Latvia did secede from the USSR; the Soviets recognized its independence on September 6. Latvia joined the UN and returned to the Olympic movement in September.

The Latvians, or Letts, who constitute 52% of the population, are mostly Lutheran and speak a Baltic language related to Lithuanian. Russians, who comprise 34%, were divided on the independence issue. Latvia's products include transportation and electrical equipment, and chemicals. **Area:** 24,600 sq mi (63 700 km^2); **Population:** 2,700,000 (1990 est.); **Capital:** Riga.

Lithuania. Lithuania is the southernmost and most populous of the three Baltic nations. A small country today, in medieval times it ranked as a grand duchy and was one of the great powers of Eastern Europe. In 1386 it was united with Poland; the resulting kingdom of Poland-Lithuania included most of what is now Belarus and Ukraine. Annexed by Russia in 1795, Lithuania regained its independence in 1918, but was subjected to Soviet rule along with Estonia and Latvia in 1940. In the late 1980s, Mikhail Gorbachev's *glasnost* policy encouraged a revival of Lithuanian nationalism, represented by the Sajudis Party. Lithuania was the first of the Soviet republics to declare its independence (March 11, 1990) and elected Vytautas Landsbergis, a music professor and political activist, president. The Soviet government declared the declaration illegal and imposed economic sanctions on Lithuania in an attempt to stifle the independence movement. In June the Lithuanians agreed to suspend the independence declaration and try to negotiate a compromise settlement. No compromise was reached, however, and meanwhile the drive for nationhood spread to other Soviet republics. A Soviet military crackdown early in 1991 failed to resolve the crisis, and the USSR finally was forced to recognize the independence of Lithuania and the other Baltic countries in September 1991.

The Lithuanian people are traditionally Roman Catholic and speak a Baltic language related to Latvian; they comprise 80% of the population. Agriculture, especially dairy farming, is a mainstay of the economy. Hydroelectric power, shipbuilding, and the manufacture of textiles and construction materials are major industries. **Area:** 25,174 sq mi (65 200 km^2); **Population:** 3,700,000 (1990 est.); **Capital:** Vilnius.

Moldova (Moldavia). The Moldovan Republic is the eastern part of the historic region of Moldova, the rest of which lies in neighboring Romania. Annexed by Russia in 1812, it belonged to Romania from 1918 to 1940, when it was incorporated into the USSR. The Moldovans, a Romanian-speaking people, form about 64% of the population; Russians and Ukrainians, who comprise about 27%, are concentrated in the easternmost portion of the republic, along the Dniester River. When the Moldovan Popular Front, a Moldovan nationalist group, won control of the government in 1990, they made Romanian the republic's official language and began talking about a possible reunion with Romania. These moves were resisted by the Russians and Ukrainians, who tried to establish a separate republic in the Trans-Dniester region, and by the Gagauzi, a Turkic people in the south. Ethnic tensions increased when the Moldovan government declared itself independent of the USSR in August 1991. In December 1991, however, Moldova joined with ten of the other former Soviet republics to form the Commonwealth of Independent States. **Area:** 13,000 sq mi (33 700 km²); **Population:** 4,341,000 (1989); **Capital:** Kishinev.

Russia. The Russian Federation, formerly the Russian Soviet Federated Socialist Republic, extends from the Baltic Sea across the Russian heartland and the vast reaches of Siberia to the Pacific Ocean. It was the largest and most powerful of the union republics of the USSR; now, as a separate nation, it is by far the largest country in the world in terms of area, and the sixth-largest in population. The majority (83%) of its inhabitants are ethnic Russians, but it also includes more than 38 other national groups, many of them living in the 16 autonomous republics, five autonomous regions, and ten national areas within the Russian Federation. As the principal industrial and agricultural producer of the USSR, Russia for decades has been one of the world's major economic powers. Today its economy is in crisis as it tries to make the difficult transition from state socialism to a free-market system.

In 1991 the government of the Russian Federation, led by Boris Yeltsin, persistently challenged the supremacy of the Soviet regime under Mikhail Gorbachev, and eventually drove it out of existence. Early in the year, Yeltsin denounced the Soviet military crackdown in Lithuania and demanded that Gorbachev resign; later, however, he made a pact with Gorbachev to work for a new union with greater autonomy for the republics. In April the Russian parliament reorganized the government of the Federation, establishing a popularly elected presidency. When the first presidential election was held in June, Yeltsin was the victor. In August, when Communist hard-liners staged a coup to oust Gorbachev, Yeltsin led the successful opposition to the plotters, and the headquarters of the anti-coup resistance was the Russian parliament building in Moscow. After that, Yeltsin's power increased, and when the USSR was dissolved in December, the Russian Federation took over most of its functions, at the same time taking the initiative in forming a new Commonwealth with the other republics. Within the Federation, the Russians had difficulty containing separatist movements among the Tatars, Chechens, and other national groups. As 1991 ended, Russia was preparing to take the seat formerly held by the USSR on the UN Security Council. **Area:** 6,592,812 sq mi (17 075 303 km²); **Population:** 147,386,000 (1989); **Capital:** Moscow.

Tajikistan (Tadzhikistan). One of the Central Asian republics, Tajikistan borders on Afghanistan and China. Formerly part of the Emirate of Bukhara, it was organized as an autonomous republic of the USSR in 1924 and became a union republic in 1929. The Muslim Tajiks, who comprise 59% of the population (23% are Uzbeks), speak an Iranian language and have close ties to their fellow Tajiks in Afghanistan and Uzbekistan. Tajikistan is an important cotton-growing region. Former Tajik Communist Party chief Rakhman Nabiyev took power in September 1991 and was elected president of the republic in November, receiving 58% of the popular vote. The Islamic Revival Party is also a powerful force in the new nation. **Area:** 55,251 sq mi (143 095 km²); **Population:** 5,112,000 (1989); **Capital:** Dushanbe.

Turkmenistan (Turkmenia). Established as a republic of the USSR in 1924, Turkmenistan is north of Iran on the eastern side of the Caspian Sea. Its main physical feature is the Kara Kum desert. The Turkmen people, who make up 68% of the population, are Muslim and speak a Turkic language. Turkmenistan is a major producer of petroleum, natural gas, and cotton. Known as the most conservative of the former Soviet republics, it declared its independence in October 1991, but remained dominated by the Turkmen Communist Party. **Area:** 188,455 sq mi (488 096 km); **Population:** 3,621,700 (1990 est.); **Capital:** Ashkhabad.

Ukraine. Ukraine, along with its fellow Slavic nations Russia and Belarus, took the initiative in forming the Commonwealth of Independent States in December 1991. As the second-most-populous of the former Soviet republics and a major industrial and agricultural center, its adherence was considered vital to the Commonwealth's success. In addition, a large number of Soviet nuclear warheads were located on Ukrainian territory. The Ukrainian people, who form about 75% of the population of Ukraine (about 21% are ethnic Russians), are related closely to the Russians in language and culture, but have a strong sense of their own identity. Ukraine belonged to Poland from the 1300s to the 1600s, and some areas (Galicia and Carpatho-Ukraine) did not join the Soviet Union until 1945. Religiously, the Ukrainians are mostly Orthodox, with a minority of Eastern Rite Catholics.

Considerable resentment against the Soviet authorities existed in Ukraine because of their handling of the disastrous Chernobyl nuclear accident (1986). In 1990 a rash of strikes and student protests forced the republic's Communist government to adopt a more independent stance toward the USSR. At the same time, Rukh, a Ukrainian nationalist party founded in 1989 and with strength in the western section of the republic, began to advocate full independence for Ukraine. The nationalist movement gained support in the spring and summer of 1991 with Leonid Kravchuk, president of the Ukrainian parliament, replacing Rukh leaders as its most influential advocate. Ukraine declared its independence after the failed Moscow coup of August 1991, a move ratified by the voters in a referendum held on December 1. On the same day, Kravchuk was elected president of Ukraine. After the formation of the Commonwealth on December 8, Kravchuk agreed to surrender control of Ukraine's nuclear weapons to the new central authority and to negotiate a compromise with Russia on control of the former Soviet Black Sea fleet. The status of the Crimea, which has been part of Ukraine only since 1954, remained unsettled.

Ukraine has rich deposits of coal and iron and is a major producer of grain and steel. **Area:** 233,089 sq mi (603 698 km²); **Population:** 51,704,000 (1989); **Capital:** Kiev.

Uzbekistan. Uzbekistan is the most populous of the new Central Asian nations and the third-most-populous of the former Soviet republics. Its cities, including Samarkand and Tashkent, were major centers of Islamic civilization in the Middle Ages. More recently it was dominated by the Muslim states of Bukhara and Khiva, which came under Russian control in the 1800s. A union republic of the USSR since 1925, Uzbekistan declared its independence on Aug. 31, 1991. Like its neighbors, Tajikistan and Turkmenistan, Uzbekistan is a cotton-growing region. Diversion of water from Uzbekistan's rivers to irrigate the cotton fields have caused the Aral Sea, fed by these rivers, to lose 60% of its water. The government, dominated by President Islam Karimov, has resisted democratization. Karimov's Uzbek nationalism has alienated the country's ethnic Russians, who form 8% of the population. The Uzbeks, a Muslim Turkic people, make up about 69% of the total. **Area:** 172,740 sq mi (447,400 km²); **Population:** 19,906,000 (1989); **Capital:** Tashkent.

Compiled by JOHN R. ROBINSON
Reviewed by ROBERT SHARLET

© Halstead/Gamma-Liaison

THE MIDDLE EAST

THE INTERTWINING OF WAR AND DIPLOMACY

By Arthur Campbell Turner

For the Middle East, 1991 saw war and peace talks. The year opened with a U.S.-led coalition successfully battling Iraq to force it to leave Kuwait, which it had occupied in August 1990. By the end of October 1991, representatives of Israel, Egypt, Jordan, Lebanon, Syria, and the Palestinians of the Israeli-occupied territories were gathered at the Spanish Royal Palace in Madrid, above, *for the first round of U.S.- and Soviet-sponsored peace talks.*

No recent year has seen changes in the Middle East as great as those that occurred in 1991. The extraordinary events of the year provided a magnificent illustration of the dictum of Karl von Clausewitz (1780–1831), the Prussian theorist of war, that policy and war are a continuum—that war is a continuation of policy "with an admixture of other means."

The year opened with Iraq under pressure from the international community to withdraw from Kuwait, which it had invaded on Aug. 2, 1990, conquered, and incorporated in its own territory. Sanctions had been authorized by the United Nations (UN) Security Council to create economic coercion on Iraq to withdraw, and a deadline, after which force would be used, was set at Jan. 15, 1991. Then a short and successful war gave way to pressure and diplomacy. As far as Iraq was concerned, unsuccessful war yielded to prolonged, and in some degree successful, attempts to evade the stringent terms imposed by the UN in the cease-fire resolutions. Observance of these rulings, so far as it was achieved, was attained only because of the always-present threat of the resumption of war. So war and policy were interwoven.

The focus of attention, however, shifted from Iraq to another issue—the strenuous drive by the United States to make progress toward the resolution of Arab-Israeli hostility by the convoking of an international conference in which Israel and its neighbors would negotiate face to face. This object in fact was achieved, at least in the sense that the conference was brought into being; but such a diplomatic triumph was made possible because of the recent and impressive demonstration of military muscle by the United States. Successful diplomacy was part of the payoff of a successful war.

The Stakes and Achievements. The stakes were obvious and high in the Gulf war. Kuwait was a major oil producer, and its successful conquest well might have encouraged Iraq to push on to conquer Kuwait's and Iraq's neighbor, that greatest of all oil-exporting states, Saudi Arabia. It was this manifest threat that induced Saudi Arabia in the first days of August 1990 to agree, however reluctantly, to the deployment of foreign troops on its territory.

Despite the highly satisfactory outcome of a war fought and won with the overwhelming support of U.S. public opinion, some degree of disappointment surfaced in the spring and summer months after the war. Kuwait had been liberated, indeed, but Saddam Hussein remained in power in Iraq, and thus certainly the triumph was not unalloyed. Yet perhaps the best way to assess the achievements of the year, which were striking, was to contrast the situation of December 1991 with that in December 1990. As 1990 drew to an end the international community as represented in the United Nations had agreed to condemn Iraq's aggression and to vote sanctions against the aggressor. The lineup in favor of such action included the majority of Arab states. (Jordan, Yemen, and

About the Author. A longtime observer of the Middle East scene, Arthur Campbell Turner is professor of political science at the University of California, Riverside. A graduate of the University of Glasgow, Oxford, and the University of California, Berkeley, he was one of the founders of the Riverside campus. He also has taught at such institutions as Berkeley, the University of Toronto, Claremont Graduate School, and UCLA. Professor Turner is author of *The Unique Partnership: Britain and the United States* (1971) and coauthor of *Tension Areas in World Affairs* (1964) and *Power and Ideology in the Middle East* (1988). He is a former member and chairman of the Editorial Committee of the University of California Press.

Kuwaiti citizens inspect the emir's palace, which was looted and damaged heavily during the Iraqi occupation.

© Abbas/Magnum Photos

Libya were the exceptions.) However, the coalition seemed fragile; the concurrence of the Soviet Union was welcome but uncertain to stay the course. It had taken immense diplomatic efforts by the United States at the end of November to secure the Security Council's authorization of the use of force against Iraq. The possibility of war soon after January 15 was a very disquieting one. Many saw the prospects as dire. One heard a great deal about Saddam Hussein's "battle-hardened army, one million strong." It was only after the war that commentators could say casually: "The outcome was hardly in doubt."

The U.S. armed forces, certain to be outnumbered greatly, were an unknown quantity. The troops already there under the rubric of "Desert Shield" had not enjoyed summer and fall in the Arabian desert. There was considerable doubt how sophisticated weaponry would operate in conditions of heat and omnipresent sand. Heavy casualties were feared. It also was difficult to prognosticate political developments. How staunch would the Arab partners in the coalition be, especially if Iraq attacked Israel, and Israeli retaliation brought Israel into the war?

Groundless Fears. Surprisingly and quite unpredictably, these apprehensions were proven to be largely groundless. The coalition forces held together and functioned very well

(Continued on page 43.)

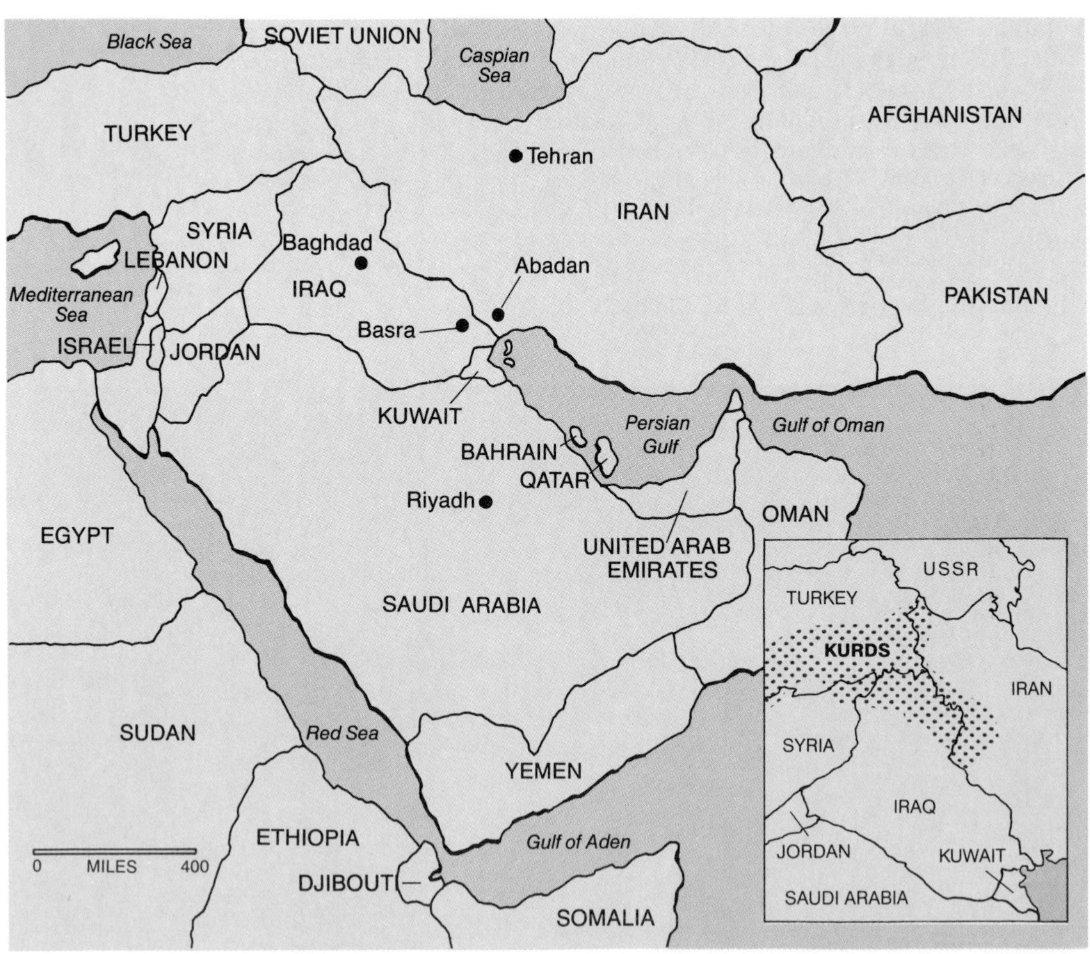

Saddam Hussein became president of Iraq in July 1979. His August 1990 invasion of Kuwait led to the world's first post-Cold War hostilities.

© Sygma

On Sept. 27, 1990, the exiled emir of Kuwait told the UN of the "horrors" his nation was enduring "inside and outside its occupied homeland."

© N. Tully/Sygma

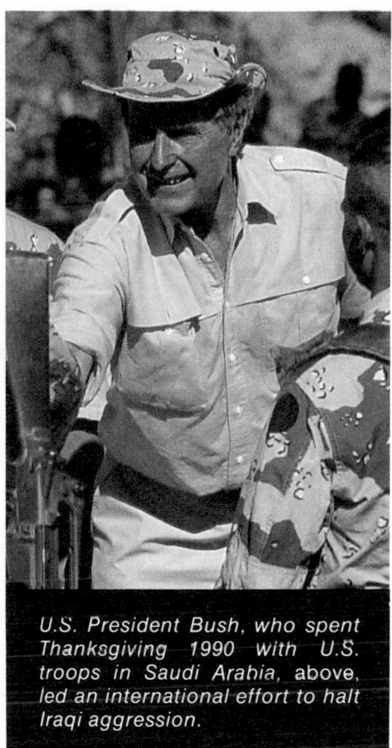
U.S. President Bush, who spent Thanksgiving 1990 with U.S. troops in Saudi Arabia, above, led an international effort to halt Iraqi aggression.

© J.L. Atlan/Sygma

The Gulf War - A Chronology

Early in 1991 the United States, joined by forces from more than 20 countries from five continents and with the full support of the United Nations, engaged in a major war to liberate Kuwait, a Persian Gulf state of some 1.4 million people, from Iraqi occupation. Following less than two months of hostilities, U.S. President George Bush told a joint session of the U.S. Congress that the allied coalition had "lifted the yoke of aggression and tyranny from a small country." A chronological summary of the highlights of the conflict follows.

1990

August 2. Iraqi forces invade and occupy the oil-rich desert sheikdom of Kuwait. . . . The United Nations Security Council condemns the invasion and demands Iraq's immediate withdrawal from Kuwait.
August 6. The UN Security Council votes to impose a trade embargo against Iraq and occupied Kuwait. . . . U.S. President George Bush orders the deployment of U.S. military forces to the Persian Gulf.
August 10. At an emergency meeting, the Arab League votes to send troops to Saudi Arabia and other Persian Gulf states to protect them from Iraqi aggression.
August 16. President Bush confers with Jordan's King Hussein and Saudi Arabia's Foreign Minister Saud al-Faisal Al Saud.
August 18. The UN Security Council unanimously demands the release of all foreign nationals from Iraq and Kuwait.
August 22. President Bush orders the mobilization of a part of the U.S. military reserve to augment the U.S. military presence in the Persian Gulf, now known as Operation Desert Shield.
August 25. The UN Security Council authorizes a U.S.-led naval armada in and around the Persian Gulf to use force to prevent violations of economic sanctions imposed by the United Nations against Iraq.
August 28. An Iraqi presidential decree declares Kuwait as Iraq's 19th province.
September 1. Two days of talks between UN Secretary-General Javier Pérez de Cuéllar and Iraq's Foreign Minister Tariq Aziz end inconclusively.
September 9. After conferring in Helsinki, Finland, President Bush and Soviet President Mikhail Gorbachev "call upon the government of Iraq to withdraw unconditionally from Kuwait, to allow the restoration of Kuwait's legitimate government, and to free all hostages now held in Iraq and Kuwait."
September 11. In a televised address to Congress, President Bush states that "vital issues of principle are at stake" in the crisis.
September 14. ,Great Britain declares that it is sending 8,000 troops and 120 Challenger tanks to Saudi Arabia.
September 25. The UN Security Council votes to extend its land and sea blockade of Iraq to include an embargo on air traffic.
October 2. The U.S. Senate passes a resolution supporting President Bush's actions in the Persian Gulf. The U.S. House had supported a similar motion on October 1. Members of both bodies emphasize that the resolutions do not authorize the use of force.
October 29. The UN Security Council passes a resolution making Iraq liable for damages, injuries, and losses in-

© Bob McNeely/Sipa

The troika of U.S. Gulf policy included (l-r) Secretary of Defense Dick Cheney, Joint Chiefs of Staff Chairman Colin Powell, and Gen. Norman Schwarzkopf.

© J. Langevin/Sygma

curred as a result of its invasion and occupation of Kuwait.

November 8. President Bush orders an increase in the number of U.S. forces deployed in the Persian Gulf. The president states that the additional troops are required to ensure that the multinational force opposing Iraq "has an adequate offensive military option."

November 23. After spending the Thanksgiving holiday with U.S. troops in Operation Desert Shield and conferring with Egypt's President Hosni Mubarak in Cairo, President Bush meets with Syria's President Hafiz al-Assad in Geneva.

November 27. The U.S. Senate Armed Services Committee opens hearings on U.S. policy in the Persian Gulf.

November 29. By a 12-2 vote, with one abstention, the UN Security Council approves Resolution 678, authorizing the use of "all means necessary" if Iraq does not withdraw from Kuwait by Jan. 15, 1991.

November 30. "To go the extra mile for peace," President Bush announces he is ready to send Secretary of State James Baker to Baghdad, Iraq, and to meet with the Iraqi foreign minister in Washington.

December 1. Iraq's ruling Revolutionary Command Council announces that it will continue to link a solution of the Persian Gulf crisis to Israel's occupation of Palestinian territory.

December 6. Iraq's President Saddam Hussein declares that all of the foreigners held hostage in Iraq and Kuwait will be freed soon.

December 8–13. Most of the more than 2,000 Western hostages held in Iraq and Kuwait for some four months are flown to freedom.

1991

January 9. U.S. Secretary of State Baker and Iraq's Foreign Minister Aziz fail to reach any agreement that would curtail a possible war during six and one-half hours of talks in Geneva.

January 12. Both houses of the U.S. Congress authorize the president to use military power to force Iraq to withdraw from Kuwait.

January 13. During two and one-half hours of talks in Baghdad, UN Secre-

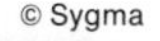

© Sygma

© M. Milner/Sygma

tary-General Javier Pérez de Cuéllar fails to convince Saddam Hussein to withdraw from Kuwait.

January 14. Iraq's National Assembly votes to support President Saddam Hussein, giving him the authority to fight a "holy war" to defend Kuwait's occupation.

January 15. By a 534–57 vote, Britain's House of Commons approves the use of force against Iraq.

January 16. Under the code name Operation Desert Storm, U.S.-led multinational military action begins against Iraq and Kuwait in an effort to liberate Kuwait.

January 17. Iraq launches the first long-range missile (Scud) attack against Israel.

January 19. The United States sends Patriot antimissile missiles to Israel. . . . Antiwar protests are held in Washington and San Francisco.

January 20. Iraqi television broadcasts the first of a series of interviews with reported allied prisoners of war.

January 22. Kuwaiti oil facilities are set on fire by Iraq. . . . Three persons are killed in Tel Aviv, Israel, by a Scud missile attack.

January 23. A large oil spill, reportedly released on purpose by Iraq from occupied Kuwaiti offshore facilities, begins to foul the waters of the Persian Gulf. . . . Iraq prohibits the sale of gasoline to consumers.

January 30. Eleven Marines become the first U.S. soldiers killed in ground

© L. van der Stockt/Gamma-Liaison

The Gulf War — A Profile

Nations Contributing Troops, Warships, or Planes to Allied Cause

Afghanistan *(mujahidin)*†	Denmark	Morocco†	Saudi Arabia†
Argentina	Egypt†	Netherlands	Senegal†
Australia	France†	New Zealand†	South Korea†
Bahrain*†	Germany	Niger†	Spain
Bangladesh†	Great Britain†	Norway	Syria†
Belgium	Greece	Oman*†	Turkey†
Canada†	Hungary†	Pakistan†	United Arab Emirates*†
China	Italy	Poland†	United States†
Czechoslovakia	Kuwait*†	Qatar*†	

*Member Gulf Cooperation Council † had ground combat forces in Saudi Arabia

Allied Contributions	**Commitments**	**Cash**	**In-kind**	**Total**
Saudi Arabia	$16.839	$9.036	$3.693	$12.729
Kuwait	$16.006	$11.775	$.032	$11.807
United Arab Emirates	$4.087	$3.870	$.217	$4.007
Japan	$10.072	$0.377	$.567	$9.944
Germany	$6.572	$5.772	$.782	$6.554
Korea	$.355	$.150	$.070	$.220
Others	$.021	$.004	$.017	$.021
Total in billions; As of mid-1991	$53.952	$39.984	$5.378	$45.362

	United States	**Iraq**
Troop Strength	540,000	1,000,000*
Casualties	376	c 100,000

*Total regular army and reserves plus 850,000-member militia

© Christopher Morris/Black Star

© J. Langevin/Sygma

Less than 17 hours after the expiration of the UN Security Council deadline for Iraq's evacuation from Kuwait, U.S. planes launched massive air attacks against Iraq, including its capital, Baghdad, page 40, bottom left. *In response to the allied attacks, Iraq fired Scud missiles against Saudi Arabia and Israel. Although U.S. Patriot missiles intercepted many Scuds, a section of the Israeli city of Tel Aviv was damaged in the war's early days,* page 40, bottom right. *Some 94,000 U.S. Marines, including the task force operating in Saudi Arabia,* page 41, center, *were part of Operation Desert Storm. Members of the Saudi force, totaling some 45,000 troops, participated in the battle for the liberation of Kuwait in late February,* right. *Nearly half of the 1,300 oil wells in Kuwait, including one in Ahmadi,* top, *were burning out of control as the latter battle got under way.*

© Boccon-Gibod/Sipa

Large numbers of Iraqis surrendered as the U.S.-led coalition liberated Kuwait in a four-day offensive. Residents of Kuwait City, below, *warmly greeted the allied forces.*

© P. Durand/Sygma

fighting during the war. (It later is revealed that seven of the Marines were killed by a missile from a U.S. aircraft.)

January 31. Allied forces retake the Saudi town of Khafji, which reportedly was captured by the Iraqis on January 30.

February 9. U.S. Secretary of Defense Richard B. Cheney and Joint Chiefs of Staff Chairman Colin L. Powell confer with military commanders in Saudi Arabia.

February 12. The allies launch what is called their largest combined air, sea, and land-based shelling of the war.

February 13. Some 100 to 200 Iraqi civilians reportedly are killed as U.S. bombs are dropped on a reinforced concrete building in a residential area of Baghdad. Iraqi officials claim that the building was a civilian air-raid shelter; U.S. authorities say that it was a military command-and-control center.

February 15. Iraq's Revolutionary Command Council announces that it is willing to discuss its withdrawal from Kuwait provided that various conditions are met. President Bush rejects the offer as a "cruel hoax."

February 18. Soviet President Gorbachev presents visiting Iraqi Foreign Minister Aziz with a plan for Iraq's withdrawal from Kuwait. . . . Two U.S. warships, operating off Kuwait, are struck by Iraqi mines.

February 22. The USSR declares that Iraq has accepted an eight-point peace plan. In behalf of the allied coalition, President Bush rejects the Soviet initiative and gives Iraq until noon on February 23 to observe UN resolutions.

February 23. After Iraq ignores the allied deadline for evacuating from Kuwait, a "large-scale ground operation" by the coalition against Iraq begins.

February 25. At least 28 U.S. servicemen are killed as an Iraqi Scud missile demolishes a barracks in Dhahran, Saudi Arabia.

February 27. President Bush declares that "Kuwait is liberated" and that Iraq's army is defeated. . . . Iraq agrees to comply with all 12 relevant resolutions of the UN Security Council.

March 2. The UN Security Council approves Resolution 686, establishing the terms of a formal end to hostilities.

March 3. U.S. Gen. H. Norman Schwarzkopf reports that Iraqi military leaders have accepted allied terms for formally ending the Persian Gulf war. The announcement follows a two-hour meeting between the U.S. commander and Iraqi military leaders.

March 4. Crown Prince and Premier Sheik Saad al-Abdallah Al Sabah returns to Kuwait from exile.

March 5. Iraq releases what it claims as the last remaining allied prisoners of war.

March 6. President Bush informs the U.S. Congress that "the war is over." . . . Saddam Hussein names Ali Hassan Majid, the supervisor of the first three months of the occupation of Kuwait, interior minister.

April 7. Iraqi radio announces that President Saddam Hussein had written a letter to UN Secretary-General Pérez de Cuéllar in which Iraq formally accepts the terms of UN Security Council Resolution 687, setting up a permanent cease-fire in the Persian Gulf and bringing a gradual end to international sanctions against Iraq.

May 6–7. A 1,400-member United Nations peacekeeping force takes control of a demilitarized zone along the Iraq-Kuwait border.

© John Ficara/Woodfin Camp & Associates

Days after being released by Iraq, 21 former prisoners of war were received at Andrews Air Force Base, MD, March 10.

under the extremely able command of U.S. Gen. Norman Schwarzkopf (*see* BIOGRAPHY). This was true not only of the European contingents, in which Britain contributed the largest element, but of the Arab and other participants in what became a very large-scale international effort. The high-technology weapons of the United States functioned superbly (*see* SIDEBAR/MILITARY AFFAIRS). That so much of Iraq's army and air power survived was because they were withheld from combat. Iraq did attack Israel with Scud missiles, but the antimissile Patriot missiles rushed to Israel were largely effective, and Israel was persuaded not to make any retaliatory moves. Coalition casualties were light. The Iraqi army proved rather ineffective in combat—as indeed it had also against the Kurds, before 1975, and in the Iraqi-Iranian war (1980–88).

Soviet Influence Withers. During the balance of 1991 the general international political situation changed greatly with the disintegration of the Soviet Union. In December 1990 the USSR still was of some weight. In the last days of the air war against Iraq, and just before the land assault to free Kuwait began, the Soviet Union was touting actively the possibility of a compromise solution. But as the year passed, the former giant empire became so embroiled in internal conflicts and dissolution that it became more and more an international nullity. This had far reaching effects on the Middle East. The rug was pulled out from under some foreign policies. The great game of playing off the United States and the Soviet Union against each other, indulged in by so many states for so long, was possible no more. The effect on Syria particularly was striking. The wily Syrian President Hafiz al-Assad, who had begun in 1990 to adjust his policies, donned the mantle of respectability, sent a small contingent to the war, and courted U.S. approval.

A Change of Mood. There was something new in 1991 in the general mood, the climate of opinion, in the Middle East. Intangible factors sometimes can be quite real. Some policies seemed to be becoming more reasonable; some favorable developments occurred—whether due to the constant pressure of U.S. policy or, more likely, because of it in conjunction with other factors. Such factors included fatigue, the passage of time, and the failure to achieve results of totally intransigent policies. The Arab-Israeli peace conference did convene; but it was not the only welcome event. By December all U.S. hostages held in the Middle East had been released, some after years of captivity, and were home again. At one time there had been 17 U.S. hostages in Lebanon. Only three Europeans (two Germans and one Italian who was presumed dead) remained unaccounted for in Lebanon as 1991 ended. A price had been paid, however. For example, Israel had released 91 Arab prisoners; at least one terrorist had been freed by France; the United States had released $278 million to Iran, whose intermediary role had been essential. It, however, had been shown that hostage-taking was not an effective means in bringing about major changes in the policies of states.

Again, U.S. diplomacy was successful in securing, on December 16, the rescinding by the UN General Assembly of the anti-Zionist resolution of 1975. The vote was 111 to 25 in favor of rescinding. Among the cosponsors of the rescinding resolution advanced by the United States was the USSR, which had voted for the original 1975 motion. It also may be noted that even Iraq's 1991 actions were not wholly obstructive. In August, Iraq returned to Kuwait $700 million in gold bullion that had been looted during the Iraqi occupation.

Conciliation and Changing Roles. When the coalition went to war to rescue Kuwait, it was supposed widely that Iraq would unleash anti-Western terrorist activity on a worldwide basis. Accordingly, the travel industry was hurt particularly. Such terrorism did not happen: There were no major terrorist activities of Middle East origin in 1991. This was not the only incorrect prophecy. Just after the war, it was said that the fires in the oil fields set by Iraq might take three to five years to extinguish fully; they were all extinguished by November.

Again, the Palestine Liberation Organization (PLO), led by Yasir Arafat, backed the wrong horse when Iraq invaded Kuwait, and only lamely and partially reneged on support of Iraq later. However, the PLO was not, as seemed likely, permanently ruined as a political force, though its influence certainly was lessened. It was still of some importance that the Palestine National Council, meeting in Algiers September 23–28, did endorse in general terms the idea of Palestinian participation in a peace conference. The approval, however, was hesitant and conditional, and the conditions laid down were ignored by the United States. The major permanent result of PLO support of Iraq was the damage done to individual Palestinians. Scores of thousands of them worked in Kuwait and other Gulf states before the invasion. Almost all of them were excluded permanently from Kuwait after the restoration, even if they had lived there for a long time; and they became more or less *personae non gratae* in all the Gulf emirates.

Jordan, likewise, had sided with Iraq, but was back in the good graces of the West by midyear, though Saudi Arabia still was wary. There was some, if hardly total, readiness to forgive and forget. The Arab League meeting of March 30—attended by all members, including Iraq—was brief but showed some eagerness to paper over the dissension. By May even Libya and Egypt were drawing closer together.

The climactic events since the summer of 1990 evoked some significant changes of role in Middle East states. Syria's successful quest for legitimacy has been noted. Saudi Arabia, much given to hanging back and long reluctant to accept any prominent part in regional politics, shed some of its hesitations and adopted more positive stances. The Saudi ambassador in Washington, Prince Bandar bin Sultan, U.S. Secretary of State James Baker's chief link with King Fahd in Riyadh, was important here. Egypt sent troops to support the coalition but, much beset by internal difficulties, played a less prominent role thereafter than might have been expected and than it had done previously.

Unfinished Business. Successful as the Gulf war was, it left behind much that might be called unfinished business. Most obvious was the internal situation of Iraq. At the onset of the war, the United States in a somewhat ambiguous way encouraged actions within Iraq that might overthrow the government of Saddam Hussein. In March two regional rebellions occurred, that of the Shiites in the southern half of Iraq, and that of the Kurds in the north. That of the Shiites received no serious help from outside sources and was suppressed before the end of March. The Iraqi government proceeded with equal vigor against the Kurds (*see* page 48), but coalition forces established a Kurdish security zone and conducted a relief organization. Sporadic clashes between government forces and Kurds in fact continued throughout the summer and fall. So also did negotiations in Baghdad about a possible grant of Kurdish regional autonomy. These negotiations had not reached any conclusion by year's end.

President Bush's Middle East Agenda. The Gulf war was scarcely over when in a March 6 address to a joint session of the U.S. Congress, President Bush outlined his goals for the Middle East. These were four in number—a new security structure for the Gulf; a reduction in the amount of arms in the region; new opportunities for peace and stability in the Middle East; and the fostering of economic development for the sake of peace. In the speech the president also noted that Hussein and those around him were accountable for their war actions. Two points here should be noted. None of these velleities had been stated by the UN Security Council to be aims of the war, and only the last one had any bearing on the Kurdish and Shiite uprisings.

The new security structure for the Gulf at first envisaged was for the Gulf Cooperation Council states (Saudi Arabia, Kuwait, Bahrain, Qatar, Oman, and the United Arab Emirates), which are wealthy but small in population, to use Egyptian and Syrian troops as their first means of defense. This "six plus two" group met at intervals throughout the rest of

© Matias Nieto/Saba

The Palestinian delegation arrives in Madrid for the opening of the peace conference. Israel had insisted that no Arabs with overt ties to the Palestine Liberation Organization (PLO), no Arabs from East Jerusalem, and no Arabs from outside the occupied territories be allowed to attend the Madrid conference. Dr. Haidar Abdel-Shafi, a physician from the Gaza Strip, led the Palestinian delegation.

the year, but no agreement emerged. A much more likely pattern for Gulf security was seen in the U.S.-Kuwait defense pact signed on September 4. Arms reduction proved equally difficult to achieve, and indeed the potential spread of atomic weapons to Middle East states, beginning with Iraq and Iran, was one of the most ominous postwar developments. In the aftermath of the war, Middle East nations bought arms at an increased rate, and the United States was one of the chief suppliers. In addition, little occurred to increase Middle East prosperity except a natural upswing when hostilities ceased.

Arab-Israeli Conference. Secretary of State Baker expended enormous energy and persuasion in his numerous trips to the Middle East, which eventually produced the conference that opened in Madrid on October 30. That it ever did so was a triumph for him and for the United States. Key stages on that road were Saudi Arabian participation, secured in May; Syrian agreement to go, obtained in July; and the significant hardening of U.S. policy toward Israel shown, in September, by the insistence on delay in considering the $10 billion in U.S. housing-loan guarantees desired by Israel, the funds being needed to house the large influx of Russian Jews already arriving. Israel was successful, however, in insisting that Palestinian representation should take only the form of a joint Jordanian-Palestinian delegation and that no Palestinian directly associated with the PLO should be a member.

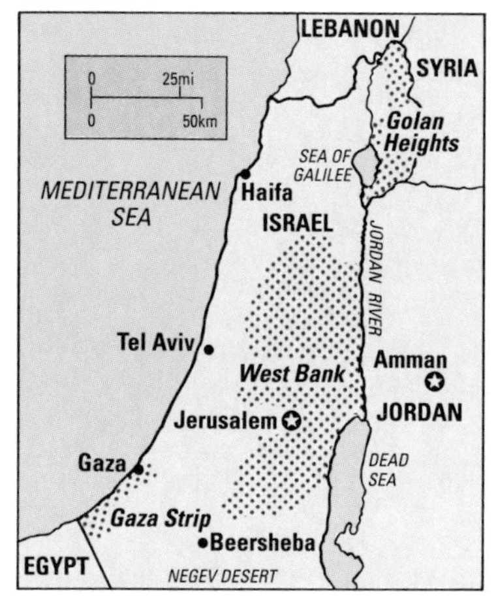

The main questions were territorial. In the Arab-Israeli war of 1967, forced on Israel by the ill-advised attempt of Egypt to blockade the Israeli port of Elath, Israel won control of five pieces of territory: the Sinai peninsula and the Gaza strip on the Mediterranean—both of these taken from Egypt; East Jerusalem and the "West Bank" (Judea and Samaria), taken from Jordan; and the Golan Heights, taken from Syria. The Sinai was returned to Egypt by the Camp David accords (1978) and subsequent peace treaty (1979). East Jerusalem and the Golan Heights have been incorporated formally in Israel,

Although Iraq was overwhelmed quickly in the 1991 war, its longtime dictatorial leader, Saddam Hussein, remained in power throughout the year.

Photos, © Ricki Rosen/Saba

The personal diplomacy of U.S. Secretary of State Baker (above left) *convinced the various parties, including Israel's Prime Minister Shamir* (right), *to attend the Madrid conference. Israelis* (left) *feared that territorial concessions would be granted at the talks.*

Gaza and the West Bank have not. The relevant UN resolutions call for the return of territories taken in 1967; since the resolutions speak of "territories" and not "the territories," Israel claims to have fulfilled this condition by returning the Sinai, a claim the Arabs deny. The oft-repeated slogan that the obvious solution is "land for peace" à la Camp David fails completely to appreciate the basic Israeli security problem. Without the West Bank, Israel is in two pieces connected by a narrow waist, a configuration hardly defensible.

One of the most visible aspects of the problems is the large Arab population of the West Bank, where, despite extensive settlements, Israelis are outnumbered greatly. It was important for Israel that the Palestinian cause was represented not by the PLO, living in exile, but by actual residents of the area, with whom some possibility of compromise existed. The plan for the conference between Israel and its neighbors called for three phases. In the first, opened by President Bush and Soviet President Mikhail Gorbachev on October 30, speeches were made in plenary session. In the second phase, meeting in Washington and delayed by Israel, face-to-face negotiations were supposed to take place between Israel and each surrounding state. The third phase, yet to come at year's end, is perhaps the most interesting and promising. It would involve general discussions on topics of broad interest, such as water resources and arms control. Within 1991 the two opening phases at least had begun, though much bedeviled by procedural preliminaries. The remainder of the proposed program might take many months or years. But the fact that such meetings were taking place at all was, at the very least, a great and promising breakthrough.

Photos, © Bruno Barbey/Magnum

During 1991 international attention was focused on the Kurds, a mountain people of some 13 million who live in substandard conditions, mainly in Iran, Iraq, and Turkey.

THE KURDS

✦

A Distinct and Ancient Mountain People

In the weeks following the end of the 1991 Gulf war international attention was focused on the Kurds, a mountain people whose homeland lies where the western ends of the Zagros and Elburz mountain chains come together and where the nations of Iran, Iraq, and Turkey are contiguous. The great majority of Kurds are to be found in those three countries, with small numbers in Syria and the Soviet Union.

One cannot say exactly how many Kurds there are in each state or overall. What is clear is that the largest group of Kurds is in Turkey. The number of Turkish Kurds has been estimated at between 3 million and 10 million; somewhere between 6 and 8 million is reasonably accurate. In Iran there are between 3 and 4 million, and nearly as many in Iraq. The total number of Kurds is about 13 million.

In Iraq and in Turkey the Kurds are easily the largest minority group—second in size in Iraq only to the Arabs, and in Turkey to the Turks. In Turkey the Kurds amount to perhaps 12% or more of the population, but the Kurdish area of Turkey, in the southeast, is between one quarter and one fifth of Turkey's total area. In Iraq the Kurdish population is between 15% and 20% of the total, and the Kurdish area is nearly one quarter of the whole. However, Kurds in Iran—perhaps 8% of the population—are only one of the many minority groups who together nearly equal the Persian population, the core people of the nation.

The harshest treatment of Kurds historically has been in Turkey, where there was a sustained attempt to blot out their language and deny their claim to be a distinct people. In Iran (Persia) they were treated about the same as other minorities. Only in Iraq, over the seven decades of its existence, have the Kurds been accepted as a separate people and entitled to some degree of special treatment. Agreements to that effect have been made often but they seldom, if ever, have been implemented to the Kurds' satisfaction.

"Kurdistan." The Kurds' homeland has been known as Kurdistan for 1,000 years, but despite the use of this name there never has been a single, independent Kurdish state. The Kurds' destiny has been extraordinary and melancholy. The most eminent Kurds known to history have pursued their careers outside their homeland. Yet the Kurds constitute a distinct and ancient people; and a people numerous enough so that, if they ever were united into a sovereign state, that state's population would be larger than those of at least half the member states of the United Nations. Moreover, it would be a state with its own, and only one, language—Kurdish—an Indo-European language related to Persian. Kurdish has its own grammar and vocabulary and is spoken in two principal versions, northern and southern. There is a written language dating back to the tenth century, but the level of literacy is low throughout Kurdistan. Teaching in Kurdish has been permitted only in Iraq.

Religion and Character. The Kurds were converted to Islam during the 7th century, and nearly all Kurds are Sunni Muslims, i.e., they belong to the mainstream of Islam. This sets them apart in Iran, with its preponderance of Shiism (though there are some Kurdish Shiites in Iran), but aligns them in religion with the majority in Turkey, and in Iraq with the Sunni Arabs who consistently have ruled Iraq.

The Kurds have a distinct style of dress and a strong historical consciousness of their identity and their way of life. They were traditionally a nomadic people, though that began to change in the 19th century. Great loyalty was given to local chiefs, and in the remoter parts of Kurdistan the tribe is still the all-important social group. The settled Kurds are farmers growing a variety of crops. Some live in towns. For example, the Iraqi town of Mosul is mostly Kurdish in population, and the area between Mosul and Kirkuk is half-Arab and half-Kurd. It is also one of Iraq's two great oil-producing areas, and control of it has been a bone of contention. However, many Kurds have been resettled forcibly in the south by recent Iraqi governments.

The Kurds possess extreme personal bravery, pride, and quarrelsomeness and, as a corollary, an inability to cooperate to gain common objectives. They are not liked by their neighbors. Antipathy between Arab and Kurd and between Turk and Kurd has been a potent and continuing factor.

History. Kurds always have shown a resistance to any external rule, but they were very slow to develop anything that could properly be called national feeling or a national move-

In early April some 1 million Kurds fled Iraq and established refugee camps in Iran and Turkey. The Kurds, who had staged an unsuccessful uprising against Iraq's President Saddam Hussein in March, feared reprisal. After receiving international aid (photo inset), *the Kurds began to return to their homes or "safety zones" some weeks later.*

© Patrick Robert/Sygma

© Kevin McKiernan/Sipa

ment. They hardly have done so even now. That they are an ancient people is not open to doubt. They may be the same people as the wild *Karduchoi* of the Zagros Mountains whom Xenophon (5th-4th centuries B.C.) describes in the *Anabasis*, but Kurdish tradition maintains that they are the descendants of the Medes.

In the medieval period local rulers in Kurdistan established some degree of local power. The Persian Empire and Ottoman Turkey contested the Tigris-Euphrates area (site of today's Iraq), but a 1639 treaty set the frontier between the two empires more or less as it remained until the 20th century, with about three quarters of Kurdistan in the Ottoman dominions. Neither Turkey nor Persia made any serious attempt to impose their rule in detail on the Kurds until the middle of the 19th century. Semiautonomous local chieftains ruled their tribes without much interference. Then more vigorous attempts in both empires to enforce central authority led to rebellions.

At the end of World War I, both oppressors of the Kurds were in disarray. The Ottoman Empire had suffered defeat and was disintegrating. The Persian Empire was going through the last incompetent years of the Kajar dynasty, to be replaced in 1925 by the more vigorous Pahlavi dynasty. The first peace treaty imposed on Turkey, the Treaty of Sèvres (1920), envisaged in Articles 62–64 "a scheme of local autonomy" possibly leading to independence for Turkey's Kurds. The revival of national Turkey under Mustafa Kemal Atatürk made the Treaty of Sèvres unenforceable. It was replaced by the Treaty of Lausanne (1923), which made no mention of Kurdistan.

For the Kurds, World War I meant that they now were held down not by two decrepit empires but by three vigorous states—Turkey, Persia, and the newly created Iraq. There were three major Kurdish rebellions in Turkey, in 1925, 1930–31, and 1937. There also were some minor revolts in Iranian Kurdistan. In Iraq, Kurds could be elected to parliament and serve in government at all levels, including the cabinet. The Iraqi Kurds thus became more politically experienced than their ethnic brethren.

The Soviet Union exercised control in northern Iran during World War II (as the British did in the south), and in the chaotic period at the end of the war (1945–46), a Soviet puppet state, the Mahabad Republic, emerged in northern Iran, giving a brief reality to Kurdish dreams of independence. When Soviet power was withdrawn from northern Iran, the Mahabad Republic collapsed.

The greatest Kurdish leader of recent times was Mustafa Barzani (1904–79). The Barzanis are tribal leaders from Barzan in the remotest northeast area of Iraq. Mustafa was a guerrilla fighter of genius with a fairly sophisticated knowledge of politics. He emerged in the 1930s as a leader of insurgency. He was a general in the Mahabad Republic and its military mainstay. In 1961, Barzani became the leader of the Iraqi Kurds in a civil war against Baghdad which lasted, with some intermissions, for 14 years. It was made possible by the steadily increasing help supplied to the Kurds by the shah of Iran.

Disaster hit the Kurds when the shah and Saddam Hussein of Iraq struck a bargain in 1975, as part of which the shah withdrew his support of the Kurds. The rebellion collapsed, and Barzani died in Washington in 1979. However, in 1970 the Iraqi government had issued a decree in which it offered a very substantial degree of autonomy to Iraqi Kurds. This offer, never formally withdrawn or fully implemented, has been the basis of subsequent negotiations.

During the Iran-Iraq war of 1980–88, both nations gave aid to the other's rebels, a traditional ploy in which Iran was more successful. Kurds cooperated with Iranian troops and caused the diversion of a large part of the Iraqi army to hold down the north in 1987. Toward the end of the war, Iraq, not surprisingly, turned savagely on its Kurdish rebels. In August 1988 some 70,000 Iraqi Kurds fled over the border into Turkey. With the end of the 1991 Gulf war the Kurds were again—temporarily—an object of international solicitude. There was at first an internationally protected zone in northern Iraq, but then the joint forces were withdrawn, with vague promises of intervention if called for. Also Turkey, which had given support to Iraqi Kurds, briefly conducted bombings of its own Kurds, some of whom have been engaged in a smoldering rebellion.

Through the spring and early summer of 1991—following an abortive uprising of Iraqi Kurds—prolonged negotiations about autonomy went on between Masoud Barzani, son of Mustafa Barzani, and the Baghdad government. The Baghdad government held the high cards. But some degree of autonomy within Iraq always has been the most that the Iraqi Kurds have attempted to achieve. Even such a modest aspiration is, presumably, quite beyond the grasp of the Kurds of Iran and Turkey.

In the early 1990s the leadership of the Kurds was taking the form of a cooperation between Masoud Barzani, a traditionalist leader of the Kurdish Democratic Party—the largest group in the Kurdistan Front—and Jalal Talabani, the leader of the Patriotic Union of Kurdistan. Talabani, who emerged in the 1960s as an opponent of the elder Barzani and has lived in Syria and Turkey, has views more leftist than those of either Barzani. The cooperation is thus likely to be fragile; but, in some fashion or another, the flame of Kurdish nationalism will survive.

ARTHUR CAMPBELL TURNER

© D. Ludwig/Sipa

Family members circle the funeral pyre of Rajiv Gandhi, who was assassinated while campaigning to return as India's prime minister on May 21, 1991.

INDIA

After the Nehru-Gandhi Dynasty

A New Chapter?

By Norman D. Palmer

By mid-1991, India was facing the most serious crisis in the nearly 45 years of its existence as an independent nation; and it was doing so without the continued leadership of the Nehru-Gandhi "dynasty." Since independence on Aug. 15, 1947, this dynasty—Jawaharlal Nehru, his daughter Indira Gandhi, and her son Rajiv Gandhi—had been in power for all but about six years and was a major political force even in opposition (between March 1977 and January 1980, and December 1989 and June 1991). Just as the dynasty seemed about to return to power in the nation's tenth general elections in May 1991, its last prominent leader, Rajiv, was assassinated by a female suicide bomber in a small town in the southern state of Tamil Nadu.

The crisis confronting India is a multifaceted one, with major political, economic, social, and religious dimensions. It is a crisis within the usually ruling Congress Party of the Nehru-Gandhi dynasty and within the political system; but more significantly, it is a crisis that threatens to undermine the social fabric and the territorial integrity of the country. The tragedy of the Nehru-Gandhi dynasty is a reflection of the

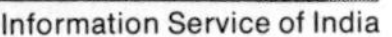

Information Service of India

© Maous/Gamma-Liaison

© Bartholomew/Gamma-Liaison

The Nehru-Gandhi dynasty—(l-r) Jawaharlal Nehru (1889-1964), his daughter Indira Gandhi (1917–84), and her son Rajiv Gandhi (1944–91)—led India's government for all but about six years from independence on Aug. 15, 1947.

deeper tragedy that is hampering India's continuing struggle for survival and viability. Thus far, India has not been able to mobilize its great human and natural resources in a way that would enable it to overcome this ominous larger tragedy.

The Assassination. In an article in *The New York Times Magazine* of May 19, 1991, on the eve of India's tenth and perhaps most "defining" national election, Barbara Crossette, the chief of the *Times*' New Delhi bureau, wrote: "With this election, India begins the torturous task of redefining itself, laying the foundation of a post-Nehruvian, post-Cold-War future. The major question is whether that future will be forged through religious confrontation, caste war, and civil strife or through the ballot box and Parliament. As India begins its odyssey, the world can neither look away nor assume that the eternal, otherworldly 'India of the Imagination' . . . can survive endless assaults on its down-to-earth institutions."

Two days after that article was published, Barbara Crossette, together with another foreign journalist, had the last interview Rajiv Gandhi ever gave, as they were riding with him toward the town of Sriperumbudur where he was scheduled to address a large election rally; and the *Times* correspondent was not far from him when the bomb explosion ended his life shortly after he had plunged into the waiting crowd.

A few days later, as the nation—and the world—mourned, Gandhi's remains were cremated on the very spot on the banks of the Jumuna River in Delhi where the body of his mother, Indira, also the victim of assassination, had been cremated in early November 1984, and near the site of the cremation of modern India's greatest son, Mahatma Gandhi (no relation to Indira and Rajiv) in early February 1948. "In a haze of sandalwood smoke," wrote a staff correspondent of *Newsweek* in the magazine's June 3, 1991, issue, "the dynasty that ruled India for most of its 44 years of independence came to an end on a funeral pyre in Delhi. . . . for the first time since independence in 1947, Indians could no longer expect leadership from their country's first family."

About the Author. Norman D. Palmer is a professor emeritus of political science and South Asian studies at the University of Pennsylvania, where he taught for many years. A frequent visitor to India, he is a former Fulbright professor at the University of Delhi and a visiting professor at Bombay University. Professor Palmer has written/cowritten numerous books, including *Leadership and Political Institutions in India* (1959), *The Indian Political System* (1971), and *The United States and India: The Dimensions of Influence* (1984). He has been a consultant to the U.S. State Department and a life member of the Indian Political Science Association.

The Dynasty's End?. Unless Rajiv Gandhi's son Rahul or his daughter Priyanka, now both college students—at Harvard and a Catholic college in New Delhi, respectively—enter political life and rise to national leadership at some time, it is quite possible that the Nehru-Gandhi era came to an end with the assassination of Rajiv. But it should be remembered that on previous occasions the same prediction had been made.

Toward the end of Jawaharlal Nehru's long reign as India's first prime minister (1947–64)—and, as many Indians insisted and as he recognized, he also was more than prime minister—speculation was rife regarding his possible successor. There were many gloomy predictions that India would be leaderless after his death. In fact, the transition proved to be a smooth one, without any threat to political stability. After the less spectacular but still effective service of Lal Bahadur Shastri ended with his sudden death in Tashkent, USSR, in January 1966, Nehru's daughter Indira was chosen as prime minister by the Congress bosses—presumably because they assumed she would be amenable to their wishes—and the dynasty resumed.

© Sipa

Sonia Gandhi, Rajiv Gandhi's 44-year-old, Italian-born widow, turned down a bid to succeed her late husband as leader of the Congress(I) Party.

Again the question of the end of the dynasty arose when Indira was defeated soundly at the polls in the general election of March 1977; but less than three years later she was back in power. She remained in the top post until her assassination in October 1984. Her first chosen successor, her younger son Sanjay, died in a plane crash in June 1980; but her elder son Rajiv, who had been drafted, against his wishes and inclinations, to take Sanjay's place, was nominated immediately to succeed his mother after her death. In the eighth general elections in December 1984 he won a larger percentage of votes—including, no doubt, many sympathy votes—than either his grandfather or mother ever had obtained.

When Rajiv, after losing much of the popularity that he enjoyed in his first months in office, was defeated by a National Front coalition in the election of November 1989, again predictions of the end of the dynasty were voiced strongly. Yet after nearly 19 months of ineffective rule by two weak coalitions, one dominated behind the scenes by Rajiv Gandhi, the other having a representation of hardly more than one tenth of the members of the Indian Parliament, Gandhi seemed almost certain to return to power, with some help from allies, in the elections of May 1991. Has an assassin's bomb finally ended the dynasty that opposition politicians could interrupt only for relatively brief and ineffective intervals over a period of nearly 45 years?

The Dynasty's Peaks and Valleys. Like the history of India since independence, there are many peaks of grandeur and some valleys of gloom in the Nehru-Gandhi story. Most of the peaks came in the Nehru years, although there were some when his daughter was in power, notably her success in defeating the bosses of the Congress Party and gaining control of the major branch of the party in 1969 and her triumphal return to the prime ministership in January 1980. There were a few more peaks after Rajiv became her reluctant successor,

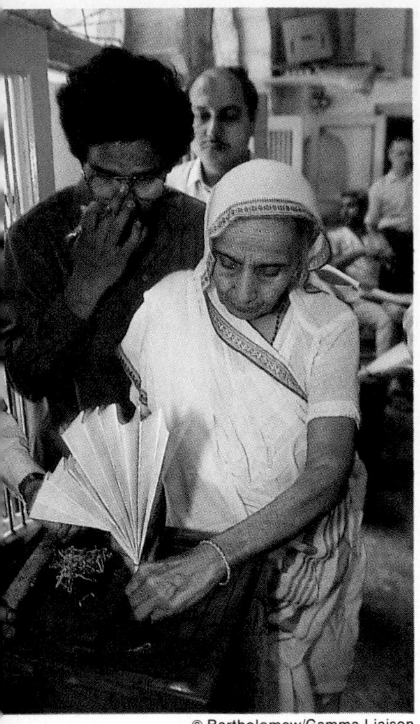

© Bartholomew/Gamma-Liaison

© Robert Nickelsberg/Gamma-Liaison

After being criticized as an aloof campaigner, Rajiv Gandhi, right, *the leader of the opposition since late 1989, sought to become more accessible during his 1991 campaign appearances. The first round of the balloting,* above, *was on May 20. The second and third rounds were postponed until June 12 and June 15 following the assassination.*

especially in the first one and one-half years of his administration. There also were many lows, especially during the last years of Nehru's life, when his health was failing and when problems at home and abroad were multiplying; during the grim years of the national emergency imposed by Indira (June 1975 to March 1977) and during her years out of office (1977–80); and during the last years of Rajiv's tenure after he had lost the image of "Mr. Clean" and after his electoral defeat in November 1989.

Undoubtedly there is some basis for the recurring charges that all three of the Nehru-Gandhi clan ruled or tried to rule more like emperors or empresses than like democratic leaders, and that they had a common addiction to autocratic practices and closed-circle rule. It is no serious reflection on Indira and Rajiv to point out that they were lesser mortals than Jawaharlal, one of the greatest political leaders of modern times. A more serious charge would be that they were more willing to flout the conventions of democracy than was Jawaharlal, who strictly observed most of these conventions, however much he may have used them to cloak some of his autocratic actions. Mahatma Gandhi proved to be wise in designating Nehru as his political heir and prescient in assuring his countrymen that India would be safe in Jawaharlal's hands. The same observation could not be made with equal assurance about either Indira or Rajiv. But on the whole they served India well, at great cost to themselves, ending in ultimate tragedy for both.

As time went on, however, the dynasty deteriorated and became out of touch with the vast changes that were under way in the country and with the cascading problems as well as the new challenges that India faced. It was a great dynasty in many ways, but perhaps it had outlived its usefulness.

Without the Dynasty. Rajiv Gandhi's sudden removal from the Indian scene, at a time when all political fortunes seemed to be on the rise again, was obviously a great shock to most Indians. As a well-known Indian political scientist wrote, "the assassination . . . has not only removed a charming figure from India's political arena but also has raised complex and sensitive questions about the future of its political structure and territorial integrity." But while India may be described correctly as "adrift" after this unexpected tragedy, its basic institutions, even under continued weak and compromise leadership, were hardly "in shambles," as some analysts, Indian and foreign, have characterized them.

In fact, one could argue that in the long run the apparent end of the dynasty might have some salutary effects. "You have overemphasized India's dependence on a single family for political stability," wrote an Indian citizen to *Time* Magazine in June 1991. "At the grass-roots level, we Indians are independent, self-reliant, and strong enough to absorb national tragedy. Ironically, the death of Rajiv Gandhi may herald a new and powerful India." An informed foreign observer, Emily MacFarquhar, discussing "Passage from Regal India" in *U.S. News & World Report* shortly after Rajiv's assassination, observed: "His [Rajiv's] removal could have a galvanizing effect on India's body politic, simply by eliminating the centralizing force of dynastic succession. Without a Gandhi in command, power will start flowing from Delhi, where it has been held far too closely for far too long."

In the aftermath of Rajiv's assassination a veteran Indian journalist, Pran Chopra, wrote: "Far from weakening democratic traditions, the end of the Nehru-Gandhi dynasty, while happening under tragic circumstances and at a fragile period in India's polity, will likely strengthen democratic institutions." And he added: "It does not change the nature of Indian politics; it does not change the Congress Party."

Today's Political Parties. India needs a strong political system that will provide fair, enlightened, democratic leadership in a period of mounting crisis on many levels. Instead the outlook is for an indefinite period of coalition politics, with the Congress as the dominant but still minority party. This is clearly evident in any analysis of the present and probable future state of the political parties.

Since 1969 the Indian National Congress, founded in 1885 and one of the largest and oldest parties in the world, has been weakened by splits and, since 1972 when Mrs. Gandhi suspended internal elections in the party, by the absence of organizational democracy. Rajiv Gandhi's successor as president of the Congress(I) Party and as prime minister, P.V. Narasimha Rao, is a respected party veteran who was associated closely with Gandhi. He was chosen prime minister largely as a result of the support of pro-Gandhi loyalists; but he was a compromise candidate, in ill health and with little

"And this [the Rajiv Gandhi assassination] is a terrible tragedy. It tests the souls of India, and it tries the hearts of all of us. But I fear not for India's democracy."

President George Bush
May 24, 1991

India's Prime Ministers

Jawaharlal Nehru, Congress Party, Aug. 15, 1947, to May 27, 1964
Lal Bahadur Shastri, Congress Party, June 9, 1964, to Jan. 11, 1966
Indira Gandhi, Congress Party, Jan. 24, 1966, to March 24, 1977
Morarji Desai, Janata Party, March 24, 1977, to July 28, 1979
Charan Singh, Janata-Secular Party, July 28, 1979, to Jan. 14, 1980
Indira Gandhi, Congress(I) Party, Jan. 14, 1980, to Oct. 31, 1984
Rajiv Gandhi, Congress(I) Party, Oct. 31, 1984, to Dec. 1, 1989
V. P. Singh, Janata Dal Party, Dec. 2, 1989, to Nov. 10, 1990
Chandra Shekhar, Janata Dal Party faction, Nov. 10, 1990, to June 21, 1991
P. V. Narasimha Rao, Congress(I) Party, June 21, 1991

N.B. Gulzarilal Nanda served briefly as acting prime minister in 1964 and 1966.

© Rakesh Sahai/Black Star

A large crowd attends a campaign rally for the Bharatiya Janata Party (BJP). Although the Congress(I) Party was returned to power with a plurality in the 1991 elections, the Hindu-fundamentalist BJP scored the biggest election gains, finishing in second place overall.

political base of his own. Apparently he was selected, not elected, to conduct a holding operation until the Congress Party could increase its minority representation and allied support in the Lok Sabha and chart a new course to strengthen its position throughout the country.

With one outstanding exception, no political parties emerged from the national election in May-June 1991 with significant strength on the national level. The Socialist Janata Party (SJP), led by Chandra Shekhar, was reduced to an even smaller rump group than it was when it headed a minority government from November 1990 to June 1991. The Janata Dal, the leading party in the National Front government that was in office with Congress sufferance for nearly a year after the 1989 elections and is led by V.P. Singh, lost 74 of its previous 129 seats in the Lok Sabha and was reverted to its former limited and hesitant cooperation with the Congress.

The one party that improved its position significantly in the 1991 elections, proportionately but not absolutely more than the Congress, was the Bharatiya Janata Party (BJP), a nationalist party that espouses Hindu fundamentalist ideals. This party, with nonsecular, pro-Hindu, and potentially divisive goals, was led by two of the ablest political leaders in India, L.K. Advani and Atal Behari Vajpayee. It became the major opposition party in the Lok Sabha, and it routed the Congress and the SJP in Uttar Pradesh, India's most populous state.

Future Prospects. The malaise that India is experiencing is far more than a political crisis. The deeper tragedy is to be found in the deepening divisions in Indian society; the worsening cult of violence; the mounting economic problems; the widespread corruption that is becoming endemic in politics and society; the persistence of separatist movements—particularly in Punjab, Jammu and Kashmir, and Assam; and the general anomie in the internal scene. Some analysts have spoken of "the tragic dismemberment and retribalization of India" and have questioned whether it can survive as a united nation or become a viable society. In his last months, Rajiv Gandhi frequently voiced gloomy warnings. A tremendous frustration, he pointed out again and again, was building up in the country. In one of his last interviews he said that the main issue facing India was "survival, survival as a nation."

All of these and many other problems seemed to worsen, or at least to become more conspicuous, in the first five months of 1991. India's influence and credibility abroad and its basic internal viability seemed to be declining simultaneously. Externally the Persian Gulf crisis added greatly to its near-desperate economic conditions. Internally the weakness of the Chandra Shekhar government, which took over in November 1990, complicated the problem of governing.

It was hoped that the 1991 elections—which, it was thought, would restore Gandhi and the Congress to power—would enable the country to begin to cope effectively with its enormous problems. The Congress(I) did return at the head of the minority government after the elections, but its only strong and nationally popular leader had been struck down.

© Eric Bazin/Gamma-Liaison

© Richard Vogel/Gamma-Liaison

© Robert Nickelsberg/Gamma-Liaison

As India began to look to the post-Nehru-Gandhi era, tensions between its Hindus, above left, *who currently number more than 600 million, and its Muslims,* bottom page 56, *who total some 100 million, continued to persist. Like its predecessors, the new government, led by P.V. Narasimha Rao, also faced increased separatist violence in several states, including the Punjab. In June 1984, Indian troops had stormed the holiest of Sikh shrines, the Golden Temple complex,* above, *in Amritsar, the Punjab, in an effort to oust Sikh extremists. The action led to prolonged unrest.*

The apparent and perhaps the final end of the Nehru-Gandhi dynasty was indeed a major break in India's political leadership; but while it obviously meant new directions for the country, it did not necessarily mean, as Pran Chopra sagely observed, a change in the basic nature of Indian politics, and certainly not in the basic nature of Indian society.

The present Indian picture, moreover, is not wholly a gloomy one. The country has tremendous human and natural resources. It is not just another failing developing country, but the giant among those countries and potentially one of the major nations of the world. It has more of "the poorest of the poor" than any other country, but it also has a large developed sector, encompassing perhaps 10% of its population; the world's largest pool of scientific and technological manpower (a fact that is pointed out often by Indians); and a growing middle class, estimated at 100 million to 300 million. In 1991, India was experiencing an economic crisis, but, except for successive years of drought, it has become self-sufficient in food production (admittedly at a low level of consumption), and its annual growth rate is impressive, about 5%.

India, in short, for all its problems, has advantages that few of the other developing countries enjoy. It must "get its act together" before it can hope to cope effectively with its present difficulties and claim its rightful place in the modern comity of nations.

See also INDIA in the Alphabetical Section.

© Ira Wyman/Sygma

For the spouses, other family members, and health-care workers who must minister to the 4 million persons in the United States who suffer from Alzheimer's disease, special understanding and patience are prerequisites. Support groups, such as the one above, offer advice and comfort for caregivers.

ALZHEIMER'S DISEASE

By Edward F. Truschke

About the Author. Edward F. Truschke is president and chief executive officer of the Chicago-based Alzheimer's Association. A founding member of the Business Leadership Task Force, a collaborative effort by San Francisco-based businesses to seek new solutions to community needs, he is a member of the Board of the National Health Council.

Alzheimer's disease (AD) is a progressive, degenerative disease that results in impaired memory, thinking, and behavior and, finally, death. Approximately 4 million Americans suffer from Alzheimer's disease. It is the most common form of dementia-causing illness and claims an estimated 100,000 lives annually, making it the fourth-leading cause of death in adults in the United States after heart disease, cancer, and stroke.

Description and Diagnosis. The disease, first described by Alois Alzheimer, a German neuropathologist, in 1907, knows no social or economic boundaries and affects men and women almost equally. Approximately 10% of people over age 65 are affected by Alzheimer's disease. This percentage rises to 47.2% in those age 85 or older. Alzheimer's disease can occur in middle age as well, with the youngest documented case being that of a 28-year-old individual.

Symptoms of AD include a gradual memory loss, decline in ability to perform routine tasks, impairment of judgment, disorientation, personality change, difficulty in learning, and loss of language skills. Although there is variation in the rate of change from person to person, the disease eventually renders its victims totally incapable of caring for themselves.

There is no single clinical test to identify AD. Before a diagnosis of the disease can be made, other conditions must be excluded. These include potentially reversible conditions such as depression, adverse drug reaction, metabolic changes, nutritional deficiencies, head injuries, and stroke. Each person with possible AD symptoms should have a thorough evaluation. The evaluation should include a complete medical history, a thorough physical examination, neurological and mental-status assessments, and diagnostic tests—including blood studies, urinalysis, electrocardiogram, and chest X rays. Other studies often recommended include psychiatric assessment, neuropsychological testing, and, occasionally, examination of the cerebrospinal fluid by spinal tap. While the latter evaluation may provide a clinical diagnosis, confirmation of AD requires examination of brain tissue, which usually is performed at autopsy.

A family physician, geriatrician, or internist can begin the diagnostic process. Any of those doctors then may consult with or refer the patient to a physician in a specialized Alzheimer diagnostic center. Because of the seriousness of AD, a second opinion is appropriate if there is any doubt about the diagnosis. In some patients it is difficult to tell from a single testing whether there has been any decline of memory and other skills or abilities. Retesting then is recommended to provide comparisons that will show if there has been such a decline. Retesting also is recommended in cases where the patient is experiencing symptoms that are not defined clearly.

Alzheimer's disease is distinguished from other forms of dementia by characteristic changes in the brain that are visible only upon microscopic examination. At autopsy, the brains of

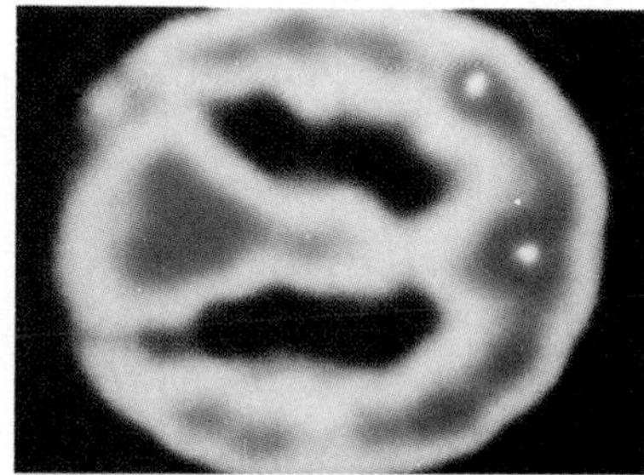

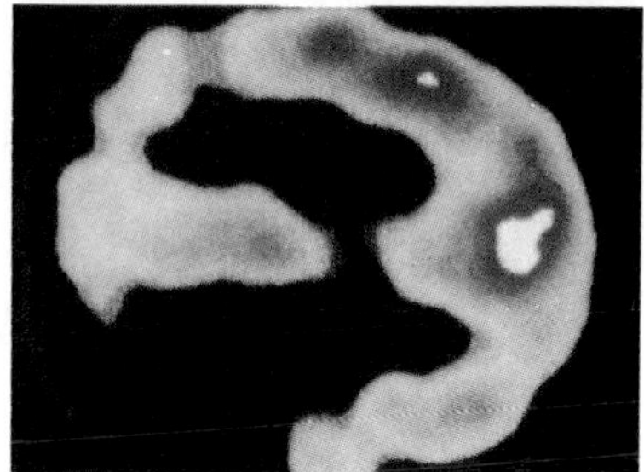

Photos, © NIH/Science Source/Photo Researchers

The PET scan (positron emission tomography) of the brain of a healthy person, top, is compared with the PET scan of the brain of a person suffering from Alzheimer's disease, lower. The shrinkage of the brain of the Alzheimer's patient is accompanied by degenerative changes

© SIU/Photo Researchers

Under the watchful eye of an Alzheimer's specialist, a volunteer undergoes extensive testing at a research laboratory. Scientists continue to search for the cause of the disease.

© Ira Wyman/Sygma

Institutions specializing in the treatment of Alzheimer's disease help patients cope with memory loss, a prime trait of the infirmity.

those afflicted with AD show the presence of characteristic tangles and fibers (neurofibrillary tangles) and clusters of degenerative nerve endings (neuritic plaques) in areas of the brain that are important for memory and intellectual functions. Another AD characteristic is the reduced production of certain brain chemicals, especially acetylcholine and somatostatin. These chemicals are necessary for normal communication between nerve cells.

Cause and Treatment. The search for the cause of Alzheimer's disease has led scientists to pursue several avenues of investigation, including genetics, toxins, infectious agents, and the body's metabolic process. For one form of the disease, called Familial or Early Onset Alzheimer's disease, there is strong evidence that a defect exists in a single gene on Chromosome 21. However, for most AD patients the genetic involvement is less clear. Although there does seem to be a genetic predisposition for the disease, other factors influence whether or not an individual develops Alzheimer's disease. Scientists continue to explore the importance of such things as a slow virus, environmental toxins, and other physical conditions that may interact with the genetic defect.

© Lynn Johnson/Black Star

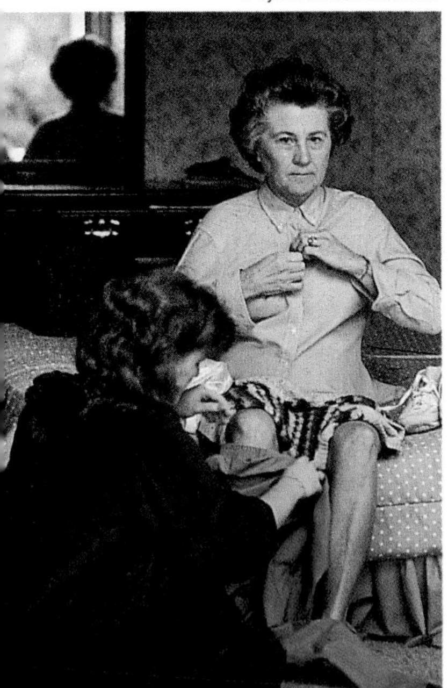

By mid-1991 there was no treatment or cure available to stop or reverse the mental deterioration of Alzheimer's disease. However, new research findings were giving reason for hope. Several drugs used to relieve the symptoms of memory loss were in clinical trials. Other medications were available to assist in managing some of the most troubling symptoms of AD. Under a doctor's supervision, medication can be used to control depression, behavioral disturbance, and sleeplessness. Physical exercise and social activity are important, as are proper nutrition and health maintenance. A calm and well-structured environment may help the afflicted person to maintain as much comfort and dignity as possible.

Prevention of the disease will not be possible until a cause is known. However, scientific advances are bringing us closer to answers that can lead to treatments/strategies for prevention. Meanwhile, focus on improved care and support for the caregiver are helping to ease the burden of Alzheimer's disease.

Care. Caring for a person with Alzheimer's disease or a related disorder is never easy. It is important for the caregiver to remember that he or she is not alone and that there are many people—family, friends, health-care professionals, and others—who can help look after the AD patient. There are also programs and services that can improve the quality of life for both the person with the disease and the caregiver. Alzheimer caregivers need help in giving the care—and in caring for themselves as well. Not everyone will need the same services to the same degree. Timely access to relief services will help guarantee proper treatment of both the Alzheimer patient and caregiver.

People with Alzheimer's disease are in a unique situation. They may need services similar to those required by the frail elderly or the handicapped, but such services may not be appropriate for persons with AD because of their mental impairment. AD patients need help that is designed for *their* needs and abilities, which vary widely over time and from person to person. They require patience and compassion from people who have the training and experience to work effectively with them. Support services and educational information are available through local and state organizations such as the agencies on aging, and various private, nonprofit organizations such as the Alzheimer's Association.

The 1991 report "Time Out" by the Alzheimer's Association demonstrates how family caregivers are strained under intense pressure from the unrelenting emotional, physical, and financial demands of providing round-the-clock care for a severely disabled person. The increasing age and failing health of both caregivers and care recipients and changing family structures often result in inadequate support for primary caregivers. The report cites how Alzheimer caregivers experience reduced feelings of stress, frustration, depression, and sleeplessness if provided with respite. Three out of four of those caregivers who receive assistance in administering to their patients reported improved physical and mental health and 76% said they can manage themselves and their loved ones better.

Responding to the plight of Alzheimer patients and their caregivers, the U.S. Congress, with the support of many private organizations, including the Alzheimer's Association, has enacted legislation for Alzheimer research and support services. Each year the Alzheimer's Association publishes its "National Program to Conquer Alzheimer's Disease." The program's purpose is to help government decision-makers frame policies and programs needed to help alleviate the tremendous toll Alzheimer's disease and related disorders exact on society.

© Ira Wyman/Sygma

Persons suffering from Alzheimer's disease must be assisted with such tasks as getting dressed, bottom page 60, *and be reminded frequently to lock the front door, turn off the stove, and unplug the coffee maker.*

Editor's Note. The Alzheimer's Association is a national voluntary organization dedicated to finding the cause and cure of as well as the proper treatment for Alzheimer's disease and related disorders. Founded in 1980, the association works through a network of 211 chapters with more than 1,600 support groups and 35,000 volunteers nationwide. Through its nationwide network, the association provides support groups, help lines, respite services, information and referral data, and caregiving training. The association offers free information through its toll-free Information and Referral Services Line (800–272–3900).

© David Muench

The National Park Service at 75

By Jenny Tesar

The 75th anniversary of the founding of the U.S. National Park Service was marked in 1991, focusing attention on the 357 sites that the service administers. The Grand Teton National Park, above, in Wyoming was established in February 1929 and includes a winter feeding ground for the American elk herd.

In Florida a panther moves silently through the saw-grass marshes of the Everglades. In Alaska, Dall sheep graze near huge glaciers on the slopes of Denali (Mount McKinley), the highest mountain in North America. In Maine seabirds search for food along the rocky shores of Acadia. In Hawaii rare silverswords grow on Haleakala, the world's largest dormant volcano.

As our world becomes more congested, such places of scenic beauty and environmental uniqueness become ever more precious. In the United States many such places are under the protection of the National Park Service (NPS), which celebrated its 75th anniversary in 1991. The Everglades, Denali, Acadia, and Haleakala are national parks, protected by law and entered by visitors only under conditions that preserve the areas' special features. The other 46 national parks include such treasures as Yellowstone, gracing the states of Wyoming, Montana, and Utah; Yosemite, embracing a dramatic California mountain region; the Grand Canyon, enhancing Arizona's landscape; Zion, covering a beautiful part of southwestern Utah; and Mount Rainier, adding excitement to the state of Washington.

In addition to 50 national parks, the NPS, which is a part of the Department of the Interior, protects 307 other units of scenic, cultural, and historic importance. These include scenic trails, such as the Appalachian Trail that extends from Maine to Georgia; scenic parkways, such as Blue Ridge National Parkway in North Carolina and Virginia; seashores, lakeshores, and recreation areas, such as Cape Hatteras National Seashore in North Carolina, Pictured Rocks National Lakeshore in Michigan, and Glen Canyon National Recreation Area in Utah and Arizona; and historic places, such as Martin Luther King, Jr. National Historic Site in Atlanta, GA, and Gettysburg National Military Park in Pennsylvania.

The NPS also has an inventory of some 26 million objects of archaeological, cultural, and historic value, most of them accumulated through digs and donations. These artifacts range from 6,000-year-old Indian sandals to the surrender cannons from Revolutionary War battles and the derringer believed used by John Wilkes Booth to assassinate Abraham Lincoln. They include the 1899 Kenwood sewing machine used by the Wright brothers to make wing covers for their gliders, plus hundreds of valuable papers and books displayed in the library of the house bought by John Adams in 1787, two years before he became the first U.S. vice-president.

Unfortunately, celebration of the many treasures and notable achievements of the NPS is tempered by growing threats to the resources under the bureau's protection. Overcrowding, encroaching development, and air pollution are harming sites throughout the nation. Insufficient budgets and inadequate staffing compound the problems. Unless this trend is reversed, many people fear that priceless pieces of the nation's heritage will be lost forever.

About the Author. A free-lance writer who specializes in the fields of science, medicine, and technology, Jenny Tesar spent much of 1990–91 completing a series of books on environmental issues for young readers. The volumes discuss such timely topics as global warming, the waste crisis, shrinking forests, endangered habitats, the threatened oceans, and food and water problems. A computer enthusiast and former science teacher, Ms. Tesar enjoys traveling, including visiting the national parks.

Stephen Mather, below extreme right, *the first director of the National Park Service (1917–29), and Albert B. Fall, the secretary of the interior (1921–23), inspected Glacier Point, Yosemite National Park, in August 1921. The Gallatin Gateway Arch*, below left, *at the Gardiner north entrance of Yellowstone, the world's first national park, opened on Aug. 1, 1926.*

© F.P. Farquar/National Park Service/HFC

© Culver Pictures, Inc.

© Tom Bean/Aperture Photo Bank & Alaska Photo

Alaska's 3.2-million-acre (1.3-million-ha) Glacier Bay National Park and Preserve, featuring McBride Glacier, above, *was a national monument before becoming a national park and preserve on Dec. 2, 1980. A park ranger,* below, *assists a foreign tourist. Overwork, poor pay, and inadequate housing are among the problems facing the park rangers of the 1990s.*

© Annerino/Gamma-Liaison

Establishing a Mission. The idea of creating large national parks to preserve natural features and ecosystems, including plants and animals, developed primarily in the United States during the second half of the 19th century. U.S. wilderness was disappearing rapidly as populations moved westward and people exploited minerals, forests, and other natural resources with little regard to the environment or to future generations. A growing conservationist movement stressed that certain lands were too important to be divided up for private gain, and instead should be set aside for permanent public use.

The world's first national park was established by the Yellowstone National Park Act of 1872. This act protected a portion of the upper Yellowstone River region and set the pattern for preserving other undisturbed areas, such as Yosemite, General Grant (now part of Kings Canyon), and Sequoia national parks, which were established in California in 1890. Then, in 1906, Congress passed the Antiquities Act, which gave the president authority to preserve scenic, historic, and scientific treasures by declaring them national monuments.

As the number of protected sites grew, overseeing them became increasingly complex. Many people began to advise that a single managing body be formed. In response, the National Park Service was created by an act of Congress which President Woodrow Wilson signed on Aug. 25, 1916. The act established the mission of the NPS: "to conserve the scenery and the natural and historic objects and the wildlife therein and to provide for the enjoyment of the same in such manner and by such means as will leave them unimpaired for the enjoyment of future generations."

When the NPS was founded, it was responsible for 36 parks and monuments, covering 5 million acres (2 million ha). Approximately 350,000 people visited the sites annually. Over time, the NPS acquired more and more sites. In 1933 responsibility for national military parks and monuments passed from the War Department to the NPS. National monuments previously managed by the Forest Service also came under NPS control. In addition, the types of protected sites expanded. For instance, the first national seashore was created in 1937. In 1980, NPS acreage more than doubled when new parks were created in Alaska, including the huge Wrangell-St. Elias National Park and Preserve, which covers 13.2 million acres (5.1 million ha)—more than five times the area that comprises Yellowstone National Park.

By mid-1991 the National Park System encompassed 358 different areas that covered more than 80 million acres (31.1 million ha); some 260 million people were visiting these sites annually. To maintain the parks and meet the needs of visitors, the NPS had a 1991 operational budget of $876 million.

Facing Growing Challenges. "The natural resources of the parks are under increased stress," notes NPS Director James M. Ridenour; "the present and future 'health' of the system depends, to a great extent, on the level of public support we can achieve."

In one sense, there is too much public support. National parks and monuments never have been as crowded as they are today. Yet the number of visitors is expected to double within 15 years. As a result of the influx, campsites quickly fill, urban-like gridlock develops on roads, and the natural ecosystems suffer. Each year the period of heavy use begins earlier and earlier in the most popular parks and extends later and later. This means that a park's resources have less opportunity to recover before the next onslaught of visitors. It also means increasing conflicts between tourists and wild animals. In Yellowstone, for example, grizzly bears visit Yellowstone Lake each spring to feed on spawning trout. In years past few

© Matthew Naythons/Gamma-Liaison

© G. Gropp/Sipa

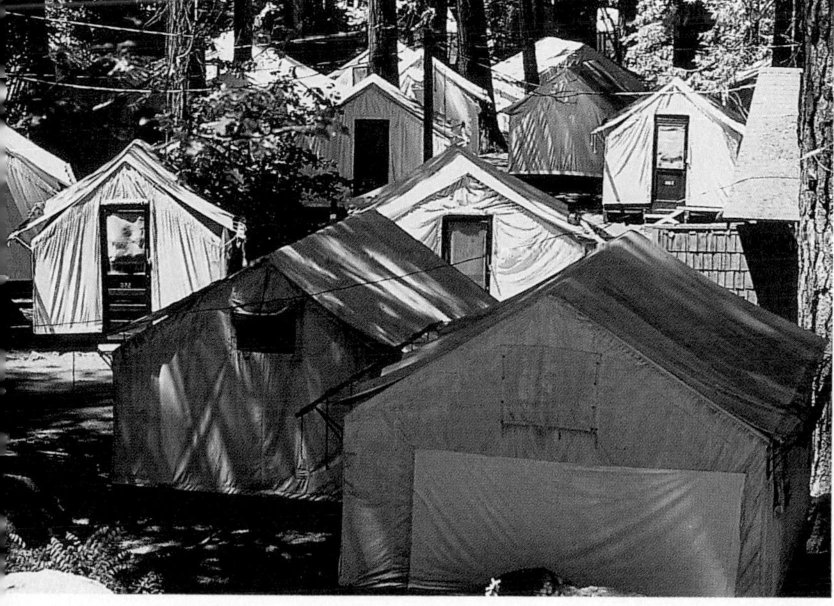

To help cope with the increasingly overcrowded conditions at many of the national parks, including Yosemite in California, above and left, all campers are required to make reservations.

© Rich Mahan/Stock South

Efforts have begun to preserve Florida's Everglades National Park, above, *the largest remaining subtropical wilderness in the coterminous United States. Insufficient water supply and phosphorus pollution from pesticides are among the Everglades' problems. The Lincoln Boyhood National Memorial,* below left, *in Lincoln City, IN, commemorates the 16th U.S. president. The Montezuma Castle National Monument,* right, *in Camp Verde, AZ, is a well-preserved cliff dwelling.*

people were around to disturb the bears. Today, Yellowstone campgrounds and hotels are filled with springtime visitors, creating a potential for dangerous encounters. Park rangers move grizzlies to less-visited areas, but the more a bear is moved, the greater the likelihood that it becomes a fatality.

Environmental threats also come from outside the parks. Tons of pesticides and other agricultural wastes pollute the waters of the Everglades in Florida. Air pollution from coal-burning power plants obscures views and kills fish and forests at Shenandoah National Park in Virginia. Erosion caused by logging activities on neighboring hills fills streams in Olympic and Mount Rainier national parks in Washington with silt.

As a result of such threats, many parks have recorded significant declines in their wildlife populations. In the Everglades, for example, the population of wading birds has declined 90% since the 1930s, only two Florida panthers are known to reside where hundreds once roamed, and expanses of saw grasses have been replaced by cattails, which remove oxygen from the wetlands and suffocate the tiny organisms at the bottom of the food chain.

In contrast, some animals have thrived in the parks. At the beginning of the century, about 50 bison inhabited Yellowstone. Today, there are more than 3,000 bison. The animals increasingly wander outside the park in search of food, leading

© Jeff Gnass/The Stock Market

© Dale E. Boyer/Photo Researchers

© Rocky Weldon/Leo deWys

New Mexico's White Sands National Monument contains the world's largest gypsum dune field, covering some 230 sq mi (596 km²). The white dunes rise as high as 60 ft (10 m).

to clashes between park managers and cattle ranchers who use public lands around the park.

Despite the ever-greater demands made on the parks, many of them have seen their budgets decline in real dollars or in purchasing power during the past decade. As a result, park managers have had to postpone maintenance, reduce staffing and park hours, and eliminate programs for visitors. Valued employees, frustrated by low pay, substandard housing, and limited opportunities for career advancement, have resigned. Few facilities are immune. At Wrangell-St. Elias poaching of Dall sheep and other wildlife is rampant. At the Jefferson Memorial in the national capital the marble is crumbling. At the San Francisco Maritime National Historical Park the last surviving wooden-hull steam schooner has deteriorated to the extent that it never can be refloated.

Commented U.S. Rep. Chester G. Atkins (D-MA): "At some point, we ought to be honest with the American public and say, we are not going to protect these things that we call jewels in our system. And we are going to let them go because we are not prepared to pay the money for it, rather than pretending that we are going to protect them and letting them gradually deteriorate."

Meanwhile, Congress continues to add new sites to the NPS but fails to provide adequate funds for their upkeep. Critics charge that some of the additions are of dubious national significance and not worthy of NPS recognition. Perhaps no addition has received more criticism than Steamtown in Scranton, PA, a collection of old locomotives and rolling stock in the former Delaware, Lackawanna, and Western railroad yards. Steamtown may be attractive to tourists and economically beneficial for local businesses, but to many historians and other experts, it degrades the image of the NPS. John White, former curator for transportation at the Smithson-

At Arizona's Grand Canyon, photos right, *air quality varies in accordance with atmospheric conditions. The nearby Navajo Generating Station, completed in 1976, has accounted for 70% of the park's smog on the worst winter days. In August 1991 the owners of the power plant agreed to measures to control air pollution and curb haze at the park by the end of the 1990s.*

Photos , © Air Resource Specialists, Inc.

ian Institution, has called it "a third-rate collection in a place to which it had no relevance." Yet between its designation as a national historic site in 1986 and 1990, Steamtown received $43.6 million in federal funds. In 1991 it received $13 million —while the 8.6-million-acre (3.5-million-ha) Gates of the Arctic National Park and Preserve in Alaska received only $847,000.

Looking Toward the Future. The NPS is using various tactics in an effort to safeguard the future of its treasures. It has limited the number of campers in many parks and requires would-be campers to reserve space in campsites prior to entering the parks. Trail bikes and rafts are restricted in some places. At Yosemite there is a quota system to control auto traffic inside the valley. At South Dakota's Mount Rushmore only the first 2,000 people were admitted to the early-morning celebration of the monument's 50th anniversary in July 1991.

The NPS also is becoming active in the fight for stricter antipollution standards. It has pushed for a 90% reduction in sulfur-dioxide releases from Navajo Generating Station, a massive power plant north of the Grand Canyon that dumps

© Robert Frerck

up to 265 tons of sulfur dioxide (a precursor of acid rain) into the air each day, in contravention of Clean Air Act amendments passed in 1977. And it has opposed construction of new power plants in Virginia, fearing that pollutants from the plants could spell disaster for Shenandoah National Park.

Maine's Acadia National Park unites the coastal area of Mount Desert Island, the picturesque Schoodic Peninsula on the mainland, and the cliffs of Isle au Haut. One of the smaller U.S. national parks, it is visited by some 2.5 million tourists annually.

The NPS also is a leading proponent of a system that would link national, state, and local parks together with other public and private areas of open land. Such a system would include "greenways" and other paths to connect forests, meadows, riversides, and even city parks. The concept would give people throughout the United States greater access to nature and would make it easier for wildlife to move from one suitable habitat to another.

Efforts to preserve significant sites are not limited to the United States. Although the national-park concept originated in the United States, it has been adopted by more than 100 nations. The NPS has helped Poland, Saudi Arabia, India, Australia, Thailand, and other nations to establish and maintain parks. It works with Canada to manage the Waterton-Glacier International Peace Park that straddles the U.S.-Canadian border. And in 1991 a joint effort was under way with the Soviet Union to develop an international park bridging Alaska and Siberia.

As it moves toward the 21st century, says Ridenour, "the National Park Service . . . will continue to be a catalyst for parks everywhere—local, state, national, and international."

© Win McNamee/Duomo

THE SUPER BOWL AT 25

By Paul Attner

It began as just another championship game. Fans thought so little of the first meeting between the champions of the National Football League (NFL) and the American Football League (AFL) that there were some 30,000 empty seats in the Los Angeles Coliseum. That was in 1967; 25 years later, tickets for what now is known as the Super Bowl sell for $150, and customers of scalpers are willing to pay hundreds more. And there no longer are empty seats for the most popular, most hyped, most anticipated game in American sports.

© Paul J. Sutton/Duomo

During its 25-year history, pro football's Super Bowl has become the premier sports event in the United States. For today's Super Bowl, the stadium is filled to capacity, fan hysteria is widespread, and television coverage is extensive—before, during, and after the contest.

© Focus on Sports

Sports' Social Event. For the 25th-anniversary game between the New York Giants and Buffalo Bills on Jan. 27, 1991, more than 73,000 fans filled the stadium in Tampa, FL. The sun-coast region of Florida realized more than $140 million in revenues generated by the game and events associated with it. Three out of every four Americans—more than 150 million—watched the contest on television; another 1 billion viewed it worldwide, either live or on delayed tape. There never has been an accurate count of how many parties are held on Super Sunday or how little work is done for the four hours tied up by the game. But a survey of professional caterers estimates that $750 million is spent nationwide on game-day parties. As a social event, the Super Bowl is Number 1.

Time magazine has called the Super Bowl "The Great American Time Out." Clergyman Norman Vincent Peale has said, "If Jesus were alive today, He would be at the Super

About the Author. Paul Attner is one of the foremost authorities on professional football's Super Bowl. As a senior writer for *The Sporting News*, Mr. Attner covers not only football but the other major sports, including basketball, baseball, golf, and tennis, as well. The author of three books, he has been the recipient of numerous writing awards from the Pro Football Writers Association and similar organizations.

AP/Wide World

The 1991 Super Bowl (official logo above) *was one of the most exciting championships as the outcome remained in doubt until the final seconds.*

Bowl.'' Even the most lukewarm sports fan watches the game, because it is the ''in'' thing to do. Of the top ten most-watched television programs of all time, nine are Super Bowls, including Number 1 (Super Bowl XX between Chicago and New England in 1986). The only outsider to crack television's most-watched list is the last show in the series *M*A*S*H*. But the television penetration extends even further. All of the last 20 Super Bowls are among the top 25 shows of all time. Advertisers are willing to pay a staggering $850,000 for a 30-second commercial; the audience strength generated by the game is that alluring.

During the two weeks normally set aside as a buildup to the game, the nation's sports pages are dominated by stories on the Super Bowl. More than 3,000 media members from around the world cover the game. The Super Bowl Party, which is held the Friday before the game, began as a small event for the media. It has grown so large that the NFL now rents an entire convention center to house it; one party was held on the *Queen Mary*. The halftime show has become an extravaganza of its own, each with an individual theme and usually featuring a big-name entertainment star. Nothing about the Super Bowl is small, but the irony is that the games themselves often have turned out to be lopsided and dull.

The Super Bowl halftime show has become a Hollywood spectacular for the fans at the game as well as the large television audience. Each show features its own stars and theme. The show at Super Bowl XXI, below, *ended with Frank Sinatra's rendition of "New York, New York," honoring the game's eventual winner —the New York Giants.*

Popularity. Still, the Super Bowl's popularity remains unchallenged. Although it is the climactic event of the most popular sport in the United States, NFL officials continue to be awed by its growth and place in the nation's fabric. Only 25 years ago, for that first game between the soon-to-be-merged pro leagues, just 62,000 attended the matchup between Green Bay of the NFL and Kansas City of the AFL. Two networks (CBS and NBC) televised the game simultaneously; tickets were scaled at $12, $10, and $6 and commercials sold for no more than $85,000 a minute. Green Bay, which was coached

© Focus on Sports

© David Madison/Duomo

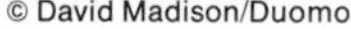

© Brent Jones

Super Bowl Madness: *On Jan. 23, 1989, some 300,000 persons lined San Francisco's Market Street as members of the victorious 49ers, including quarterback Joe Montana and his family, above left, paraded in decorated cable cars. Even the famous Art Institute of Chicago lions wore helmets after the Bears' win in Super Bowl XX.*

by Vince Lombardi, won, 35–10. The Super Bowl trophy now is named for Lombardi, who is a member of the Pro Football Hall of Fame.

It was not until the third championship game, in 1969, that the event became what then-commissioner Pete Rozelle describes as "a permanent part of the American sports and entertainment consciousness." In that contest the AFL representatives, the New York Jets, upset the heavily favored NFL champs, the Baltimore Colts, 16–7 in Miami. But what made it especially memorable was the outlandish prediction of Jets quarterback Joe Namath, who had "guaranteed" a victory during a speech a few days before kickoff. The merger between the leagues was a season away, but the Jets had proven the AFL was the equal of the older, more established organization. And the title game never would be the same either.

The Jets' victory coincided with the renaming of the game. For two years it had been called the AFL-NFL World Championship Game. But Kansas City owner Lamar Hunt urged a change. His daughter had been playing with a popular children's toy called a Super Ball, which bounced dramatically higher than a regular ball. Hunt knew a good thing when he saw it—Super Ball, Super Bowl—and suggested to Rozelle that the game officially become the Super Bowl. At the time, it seemed arrogant on the NFL's part, but it became a marketing move cast in genius.

Now, cities bid furiously for rights to host the game, as much for the prestige as for its acknowledged economic impact. Nothing seems to reduce its importance—not players, strikes, ongoing wars, or lopsided matchups. Now, only the World Cup attracts greater international sports interest than the Super Bowl, even in countries whose citizens do not have the foggiest idea of what offsides or flea-flicker means. All the interest and hype are derived from a humble beginning when even the United States did not know what to do with this Super of all games.

National Football League Commissioner Paul Tagliabue presents the Vince Lombardi Trophy to the Super Bowl winner.

© Duomo

A TIME TO REMEMBER

© Focus on Sports

Super Bowl I: The Green Bay Packers' Bart Starr

Super Bowl I. Memorial Coliseum, Los Angeles, Jan. 15, 1967: Green Bay Packers 35, Kansas City Chiefs 10. Bart Starr completes 16 of 23 passes and is voted the game's most valuable player (MVP) as the Packers of the National Football League (NFL) take the first Super Bowl. Attendance: 61,946.

Super Bowl II. Orange Bowl, Miami, Jan. 14, 1968: Green Bay Packers 33, Oakland Raiders 14. Vince Lombardi concludes his coaching career at Green Bay by directing the Packers to a second consecutive Super Bowl win. Bart Starr again is MVP. Attendance: 75,546.

Super Bowl III. Orange Bowl, Miami, Jan. 12, 1969: New York Jets 16, Baltimore Colts 7. In a major upset, New York quarterback Joe Namath completes 17 of 28 passes for 206 yards as the Jets win the first Super Bowl for the American Football League (AFL). MVP Namath had "guaranteed" the Jets win. Attendance: 75,377.

Super Bowl III: The New York Jets' Joe Namath

© Walter Iooss, Jr./"Sports Illustrated"

Super Bowl IV. Tulane Stadium, New Orleans, Jan. 11, 1970: Kansas City Chiefs 23, Minnesota Vikings 7. The AFL takes a second consecutive Super Bowl as Kansas City stretches a 16–0 halftime lead into a 23–7 victory. Chiefs quarterback Len Dawson is MVP. Attendance: 80,562.

Super Bowl V. Orange Bowl, Miami, Jan. 17, 1971: Baltimore Colts 16, Dallas Cowboys 13. In the first Super Bowl following the merger of the AFL and the NFL, the Colts' Jim O'Brien kicks a game-winning field goal with seconds remaining. Dallas linebacker Chuck Howley is the first nonquarterback to be named MVP of a Super Bowl game. Attendance: 79,204.

Super Bowl VI. Tulane Stadium, New Orleans, Jan. 16, 1972: Dallas Cowboys 24, Miami Dolphins 3. Cowboys quarterback Roger Staubach is the game's MVP as Dallas completely dominates Miami, offensively and defensively. Attendance: 81,023.

Super Bowl VII. Memorial Coliseum, Los Angeles, Jan. 14, 1973: Miami Dolphins 14, Washington Redskins 7. The Miami Dolphins complete the season without a loss by shutting down the NFL rushing leader Larry Brown. Miami safety Jake Scott intercepts two passes and is named MVP. Attendance: 90,182.

Super Bowl VIII. Rice Stadium, Houston, Jan. 13, 1974: Miami Dolphins 24, Minnesota Vikings 7. Miami scores touchdowns on its first two possessions and goes on to an easy win. Larry Csonka of the Dolphins rushes for a Super Bowl record of 145 yards and MVP honors. Attendance: 71,882.

Super Bowl IX. Tulane Stadium, New Orleans, Jan. 12, 1975: Pittsburgh Steelers 16, Minnesota Vikings 6. Pittsburgh's defense limits Minnesota to 119 total yards as the Steelers crush Minnesota, 16-6. Steelers fullback Franco Harris rushes for a record 158 yards on 34 carries and is named MVP. Attendance: 80,997.

Super Bowl X. Orange Bowl, Miami, Jan. 18, 1976: Pittsburgh Steelers 21, Dallas Cowboys 17. In a battle between quarterbacks Terry Bradshaw of Pittsburgh and Roger Staubach of Dallas, the Steelers gain the upper hand for their second consecutive Super Bowl victory. Wide receiver Lynn Swann makes four receptions for 161 yards and MVP honors. Attendance: 80,187.

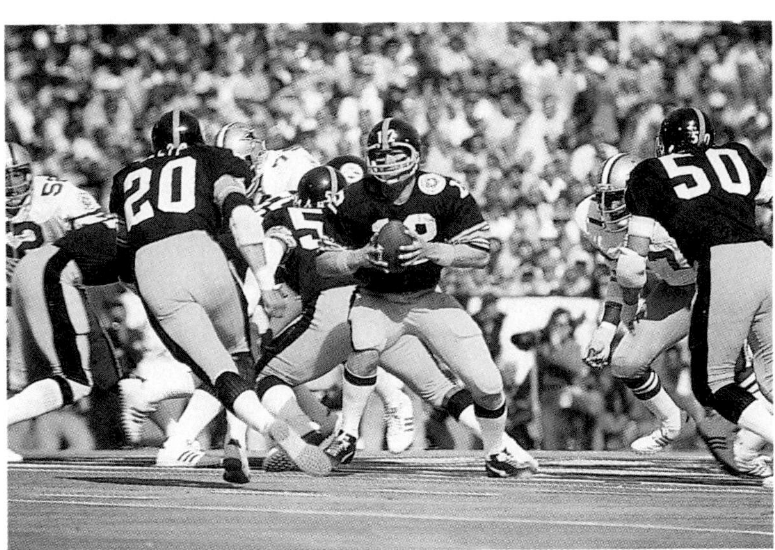

© Focus on Sports

Super Bowl X: The Pittsburgh Steelers' Terry Bradshaw

Super Bowl XI. Rose Bowl, Pasadena, Jan. 9, 1977: Oakland Raiders 32, Minnesota Vikings 14. Minnesota suffers its fourth Super Bowl loss in as many appearances as Oakland scores 16 points in the second quarter and coasts to a 32-16 win. MVP Fred Biletnikoff of the Raiders catches four passes for 79 yards. Attendance: 100,421.

Super Bowl XII. Louisiana Superdome, New Orleans, Jan. 15, 1978: Dallas Cowboys 27, Denver Broncos 10. Dallas linemen Randy White and Harvey Martin are the first cowinners of the Super Bowl MVP award as the Cowboys dominate defensively. During the first half alone, Dallas converts two interceptions into a touchdown and a field goal. Attendance: 75,583.

Super Bowl XIII. Orange Bowl, Miami, Jan. 21, 1979: Pittsburgh Steelers 35, Dallas Cowboys 31. The Steelers become the first team to win three Super Bowls as quarterback Terry Bradshaw throws for four touchdowns and the MVP award. Dallas scores two late fourth-quarter touchdowns but still comes up short. Attendance: 79,484.

Super Bowl XIV. Rose Bowl, Pasadena, Jan. 20, 1980: Pittsburgh Steelers 31, Los Angeles Rams 19. Pittsburgh and Terry Bradshaw win the Super Bowl and the MVP trophy, respectively, for a second consecutive time. Two long, fourth-quarter touchdown passes by Bradshaw are the Steelers' margin of victory. Attendance: 103,985.

Super Bowl XV. Louisiana Superdome, New Orleans, Jan. 25, 1981: Oakland Raiders 27, Philadelphia Eagles 10. For the first time a play-off wild-card team captures the Super Bowl as Oakland takes control of the contest early. Raiders quarterback Jim Plunkett, the MVP, completes 13 of 21 passes for 261 yards and three touchdowns. Attendance: 76,135.

Super Bowl XVI. Silverdome, Pontiac, MI, Jan. 24, 1982: San Francisco 49ers 26, Cincinnati Bengals 21. With San Francisco's defense making some key plays, the 49ers jump to a 20–0 halftime lead and hold on for a 26–21 win. Bengals quarterback Ken Anderson completes a record 25 passes but his opposing counterpart, Joe Montana, is named MVP. Attendance: 81,270.

Super Bowl XVII. Rose Bowl, Pasadena, Jan. 30, 1983: Washington Redskins 27, Miami Dolphins 17. Washington's unheralded defense holds Miami to 34 yards in the second half and their offense scores two fourth-quarter touchdowns for the Redskins' first Super Bowl win. Redskins fullback John Riggins rushes for a Super Bowl-record 166 yards and is the MVP. Attendance: 103,667.

Super Bowl XVIII. Tampa Stadium, Tampa, Jan. 22, 1984: Los Angeles Raiders 38, Washington Redskins 9. MVP Marcus Allen rushes for a new record of 191 yards on 20 carries, scores two touchdowns, and leads the Raiders to a lopsided victory. The Raiders' offense, defense, and special team all score touchdowns. Attendance: 72,920.

Super Bowl XIX. Stanford Stadium, Stanford, CA, Jan. 20, 1985: San Francisco 49ers 38, Miami Dolphins 16. With 49ers quarterback Joe Montana

© Globe Photos

Super Bowl XIX:
The San Francisco 49ers' Joe Montana

completing 24 of 35 passes for a record 331 yards and rushing for 59 yards in five carries to capture the MVP honors, San Francisco dominates the Dolphins. Attendance: 84,059.

Super Bowl XX. Louisiana Superdome, New Orleans, Jan. 26, 1986: Chicago Bears 46, New England Patriots 10. After New England scores first with a 36 yard field goal, Chicago, led by quarterback Jim McMahon, responds with 44 unanswered points for an easy win. New England commits six turnovers as Chicago's defensive end Richard Dent is the MVP. Attendance: 73,818.

Super Bowl XXI. Rose Bowl, Pasadena, Jan. 25, 1987: New York Giants 39, Denver Broncos 20. After trailing 10–9 at halftime, quarterback Phil Simms directs the Giants to a 30-point second half. Simms, who tosses three touchdown passes, is the unanimous choice for MVP. Attendance: 101,063.

Super Bowl XXII. Jack Murphy Stadium, San Diego, Jan. 31, 1988: Washington Redskins 42, Denver Broncos 10. Denver opens the game with ten quick points, but the Redskins score 35 points in the second quarter and go on to a 42-10 victory. Washington quarterback Doug Williams passes for a record 340 yards and is the MVP. Attendance: 73,302.

Super Bowl XXIII. Joe Robbie Stadium, Miami, Jan. 22, 1989: San Francisco 49ers 20, Cincinnati Bengals 16. In one of the more exciting Super Bowls, 49ers quarterback Joe Montana throws a game-winning touchdown pass to John Taylor with 34 seconds left in the contest. San Francisco's wide receiver Jerry Rice, who has 11 receptions for a Super Bowl record of 215 yards, is voted MVP. Attendance: 75,179.

Super Bowl XXIV. Louisiana Superdome, New Orleans, Jan. 28, 1990: San Francisco 49ers 55, Denver Broncos 10. With Joe Montana throwing for a record five touchdowns and becoming the first to win a third Super Bowl MVP award, the 49ers play near-perfect football for their fourth Super Bowl crown. Attendance: 72,919.

Super Bowl XXV. Tampa Stadium, Tampa, Jan. 27, 1991: New York Giants 20, Buffalo Bills 19. In a superior Super Bowl, the Giants, directed

© Duomo

***Super Bowl XXV:** The Buffalo Bills miss a field-goal attempt to assure the Giants' win.*

by substitute quarterback Jeff Hostetler, capture their second championship in five years as Buffalo's Scott Norwood misses a field goal in the final seconds. New York's running back Otis Anderson rushes for 102 yards and scores a touchdown for MVP honors. Attendance: 73,813.

Super Bowl XXVI. *See* SPORTS—*Football.*

© North Wind Picture Archives

The Admiral of the Ocean Sea

© The Bettmann Archive

By Richard C. Schroeder

World attention centers on Christopher Columbus—the Admiral of the Ocean Sea—as 1992 marks the 500th anniversary of his famous transatlantic voyage. The navigator is an Italian Renaissance gentleman in Sebastiano del Piombo's 1519 portrait, above right. F.E. Wright's late 19th-century engraving shows Columbus' ships, the "Santa Maria," the "Niña," and the "Pinta," as restored from models in a museum in Madrid, Spain.

Throughout the course of 1992 and beyond, the attention of scholars and laymen around the world would be focused on the life and times of Christopher Columbus and the astonishing transatlantic voyage he made 500 years ago.

Quincentennial commemorative commissions have been set up on both sides of the Atlantic in at least 32 countries. In the United States, 39 states and more than 100 cities have established such groups. Billions of dollars have been committed by governments, businesses, museums, universities, and the media to commemorative events—ranging from parades and fireworks to exhibitions, symposia, construction of monuments, books, television programs, commemorative coins and stamps, sailing races, and guided tours. One of the most colorful of these celebrations was likely to be the voyage of copies of Columbus' three ships, the *Niña*, the *Pinta*, and the

Santa Maria. Following as closely as possible Columbus' route, they would sail from Spain to the Bahamas by way of the Canary Islands and thence visit several U.S. and Caribbean ports. Worldwide, 12 full-scale replicas of the original ships, including one commissioned by the government of Japan, have been planned.

Seville would be the host of a Columbian world's fair with exhibits from more than 100 nations at a cost of $4 billion to $5 billion. Barcelona would be the principal site of the 1992 Summer Olympic Games, dedicated to Columbus. Genoa, the birthplace of the Admiral of the Ocean Sea, was planning an international conference of Columbus specialists, an exposition of Columbiana collected worldwide, and the display of its own version of the *Santa Maria*. The Dominican Republic, site of the first permanent colony established by Columbus, was building a 390-ft (119-m) lighthouse at a cost of $10 million that would be the largest Columbian monument in the world.

Negative Views. The quincentennial celebrations would have to compete with a burgeoning number of counterdemonstrations, especially in Latin America and the United States. "The 1991 Columbus quincentennial is already causing friction between groups that see it as a celebration of Western civilization and those that view it as a commemorative of native cultures victimized by European imperialism," Karen J. Winkler wrote in the March 15, 1991, issue of the *Chronicle of Higher Education*. The latter point of view sees Columbus' "discovery" of the New World as the spark that ignited centuries of pillage and exploitation bringing about the slaughter of millions of Native Americans and the destruction of their environment. In the summer of 1990 about 300 Native Americans from throughout the Western Hemisphere met in Quito, Ecuador, for the "First Continental Meeting of Indigenous Peoples—500 Years of Resistance," and voted to send a 500-member delegation to Spain in 1992 to demand reparations for the Spanish conquest.

The Native American protesters have been joined by numerous environmental and religious groups. The largely Protestant National Council of Churches issued a statement condemning the discovery as an "invasion" and resolved that "a celebration is not an appropriate observation of this anniversary." Instead, the council declared, the quincentennial should be a time for penitence rather than jubilation. The Roman Catholic Church, on the other hand, planned to celebrate 1992 for 500 years of Christianity in the Western Hemisphere. Writing in the Jesuit weekly *America*, James Muldoon, a professor of history at Rutgers University, said the resolution

The earliest known chart of the New World was drawn by Juan de la Cosa, circa 1500. He was the navigator of the Niña on Columbus' second voyage.

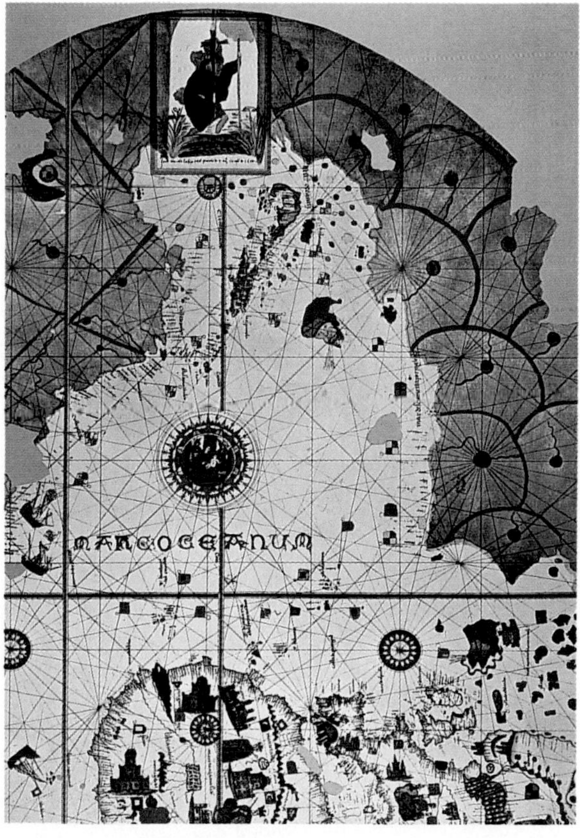

of the National Council of Churches amounted to a "condemnation of the entire history of the modern world."

A prominent environmentalist and founder of the New York Green Party, Kirkpatrick Sale, joined the fray in 1990 with the publication of a book, *The Conquest of Paradise: Christopher Columbus and the Columbian Legacy*. In it, Sale portrayed Columbus' behavior during his four journeys to the New World as a model for later conquistadores who plundered the Native Americans and committed genocide and ecocide against the natives and their environment.

Background. Columbus was born in Genoa between 1450 and 1452. As with many other details of Columbus' life and exploits, the time of his birth and, for some, even the place, are in dispute. His Italian name was Cristoforo Colombo, Hispanicized later to Cristóbal Colón.

© North Wind Picture Archives

Columbus' coat of arms features the emblems of Castile and León, drawings of scattered islands, and some anchors.

Columbus was of lower-middle-class origin. His father was a master clothier who pursued a sideline as a wine merchant. As a youth the future Admiral of the Ocean Sea almost certainly worked with his father, and his first seagoing experiences—possibly as early as 1471—were coastal trips to purchase wool and wine for his father's businesses. The sea apparently attracted him more than did wine and wool. He began making longer voyages out of Genoa, probably as a deckhand or common seaman. During one of these voyages, his ship was attacked and sunk by privateers off the southern coast of Portugal in the year 1476. Reaching shore—a distance of 6 mi (14 km)—he landed at the port of Lagos, from where he made his way to Lisbon. There he lived, on and off, for the next nine years.

During his time in Lisbon, Columbus expanded his seafaring experience, signing on for voyages as far away as the Gulf of Guinea, off the west coast of Africa, to England, and possibly to Iceland in the North Atlantic. In Lisbon he learned to read and write in Portuguese and Castilian and absorbed a fair amount of Latin. (The Genoese dialect of his day was a language of common speech that never was written.) While in Portugal he married Felipa Perestrello e Moniz, a member of a distinguished family with ties to Madeira, where Diego, his only legitimate son, was born. (Diego would become admiral of the Indies in 1509 and govern Hispaniola until his recall in 1523.) Dona Felipa died in Portugal; Columbus later lived in Spain with Beatriz Enríquez de Harana but from all evidence never married her. From that union came a second son, Ferdinand, who was to become one of his father's principal biographers.

In Lisbon, Columbus began to formulate what he called "The Enterprise of the Indies," a plan for a voyage west into the unexplored Ocean Sea. Some scholars say that Columbus intended to search for the mythical islands, such as Antilla, reputed to lie in the Atlantic. Others insist that Columbus already had a vision of a New World. Samuel Eliot Morison in his 1942 biography, *Admiral of the Ocean Sea: A Life of Christopher Columbus*, says that his goal was to "reach 'the Indies,' that is, Asia, by sailing westward." All Columbianists

About the Author. As a specialist in Latin American affairs and consultant to the Organization of American States (OAS), Richard C. Schroeder has taken a keen interest in the quincentenary of Christopher Columbus' discovery of America. A syndicated writer, editor, and editorial consultant, Mr. Schroeder has been a columnist for Latin America Service and *Américas* magazine, chief of the Washington Bureau of *Visión* magazine, and editor of *OAS/CECON Trade News* and the *Latin America Index*. Coauthor of the book *Dateline Latin America* (1971), he has served as coordinator of the Alliance for Progress Information Program.

agree, however, that Columbus and many others in that period believed the Earth was round, and one could arrive in the East by sailing west. It was a rather widely held view at the time. Pythagoras declared the Earth round in the sixth century B.C. Aristotle reported rumors of lands to the west of Europe. Moreover, Marco Polo returned to Europe in 1295 after an overland trip to Asia, with vivid tales of the wealth and splendor of India, China, and Japan. Columbus then was not alone in rejecting the flat-Earth theory.

© Culver Pictures Inc.

Isabella I (1451–1504), queen of Castile, drawing above by unknown artist, *and her husband Ferdinand, the king of Aragon, were the principal patrons of Columbus in his "Enterprise of the Indies," a plan for a voyage west into the unexplored Ocean Sea.*

The Voyage. Columbus sought support for his scheme in Portugal and England to no avail. Finally, after eight frustrating years of importuning, he obtained it in Spain, where King Ferdinand and Queen Isabella provided him with ships and crew at an estimated cost of $14,000. The price of building an empire never again would be so low. The bulk of the money came from the treasury of Aragon and was not, as myth promulgated in the 17th century maintained, raised by Queen Isabella pawning her jewels.

The fleet, assembled at the port of Palos in the Andalusian region of southern Spain, consisted of three ships. Two, the *Niña* and the *Pinta*, were caravels with a capacity of approximately 60 tons each and of a type used in coastal trading. The

© The Granger Collection

Columbus departed from Palos, Spain, on his first voyage on Aug. 3, 1492. In the 1893 U.S. lithograph, left, *he bids farewell to Isabella and Ferdinand.*

© The Granger Collection

The navigator and his party landed on an islet in the Bahamas, Oct. 12, 1492. Holding the royal standard of Castile, 19th-century lithograph above, *Columbus reportedly "asked all those with him to give faith and witness how he took possession of this island for their sovereigns, the king and queen, with all due ceremony."*

third, the *Santa Maria*, was a somewhat larger vessel called a *nao*, with a capacity of about 100 tons. The caravels were captained by the brothers Martín Alonso Pinzón and Vicente Yáñez Pinzón. Columbus commanded the expedition from the flagship, the *Santa Maria*. The crew complement of the fleet was 90, most of whom were experienced seamen and only four of whom, besides Columbus, were not Spaniards. The crew was not composed, as another myth would have it, of criminals promised pardons for sailing with Columbus.

Most of what we know about the first voyage is gleaned from Columbus' shipboard log. The fleet sailed from Palos half an hour before dawn on Aug. 3, 1492. A stop was made in the Canary Islands for refitting the sails of the *Niña* and for wood and fuel. The ships weighed anchor on September 6, cleared the Canaries on the ninth, and heading due west with a fortuitous following trade wind, made landfall on an islet in the Bahamas 33 days later on October 12.

The voyage had been uneventful. Reports that his crew threatened mutiny are discounted by most scholars. The Lucayo Indians who inhabited the area called the site of the landfall Guanahani; Columbus named it San Salvador (Holy Savior), and took possession of it in the name of King Ferdinand and Queen Isabella of Spain. The actual location of the islet is much in dispute, with more than a dozen different sites proposed.

Columbus was enchanted by the people he found on San Salvador and at other points he touched on his first voyage. He found them docile and generous to a fault. "I believe they would easily be made Christians,'' he noted in his log. Later he would change his mind as resentment among the Indians against Spanish brutality mounted. The Indians would be considered ugly, treacherous, and lazy, particularly when they were unable to supply much of the gold the Spaniards so ardently desired.

On this first voyage, Columbus sailed to numerous islands, including Cuba and Hispaniola. Off the latter, his flagship, the *Santa Maria*, was wrecked on Christmas Day. Salvaging the timbers, his men built a fortress, the first Spanish structure in the New World, forming the center of a settlement on the north coast of what is now Haiti. Columbus named the settlement Navidad (Christmas). When he set sail for Spain, he left behind 40 of his crew in Navidad with instructions to build houses and hunt for gold mines. On his return to the site in November 1493, he found the settlement destroyed and its inhabitants slaughtered.

With his two remaining ships, Columbus left Hispaniola on Jan. 16, 1493, arriving in the Azores on February 11. Bad weather between the Azores and the Iberian peninsula forced him to make a temporary landing in Portugal. As a result, in an ironic twist, Columbus' first report on his epic voyage was made not to the king and queen of Spain, but to their intense rival, King John (Dom João) of Portugal.

Columbus made three more voyages to the New World from 1493 to 1504. And although he added many new lands to his discoveries—Jamaica, Puerto Rico, the islands of the Lesser Antilles, and the mainland of South and Central America—his star never shone as brightly as it did after his first trip. Its luster became so dim, in fact, that on the third voyage he was relieved as governor of the Indies because of growing turmoil and corruption in the new colony of Hispaniola. He returned to Spain in irons. Many of the titles and privileges that were stripped from Columbus in that sad affair were restored eventually. He died, not penniless as many have claimed, yet in relative obscurity at Valladolid, Spain, on May 20, 1506, while still seeking new favors and old benefits from King Ferdinand. (Queen Isabella, his principal benefactor, had died in 1504.)

The Admiral of the Ocean Sea was fascinated initially by the people he found at the sites where he landed during his first voyage. As the engraving, below, illustrates, the natives were glad to trade items with Columbus and his crew.

Columbus' Impact. The role of Columbus in the conquest and colonization of the New World he had opened to Europe was minimal. Other men and forces shaped the bitter course of empire in the Western Hemisphere. Yet, despite the controversies that surrounded him, it cannot be gainsaid that Columbus' exploits triggered events that transformed the course of Western and world history. Whatever his goal, he sailed the uncharted Atlantic Ocean to a *terra incognita*, a vast land unknown to most of the inhabitants of Europe and the other continents in 1492. There is ample evidence from Columbus' own writings that he thought his goal, and India as well, were close to his landfall in the Bahamas.

By the end of his fourth voyage, however, Columbus well may have come to perceive, however dimly, that what he found was not the Orient he had set out to reach, but a wholly new world that lay between the western shores of Europe and Japan, China, and India. Sale declares unequivocally that "There is no doubt about this extremely important fact: Admiral Colón claimed to have found a new continent, surmised its dimension, calculated its rough geographic position, and asserted as much, more than once, to his royal patrons."

In contrast to Sale, however, Morison concludes that Columbus never altered "his conviction that he had discovered a western route to Asia. In his cosmographical ideas, Columbus remained stubbornly and obstinately, to the end of his life, absolutely and completely wrong."

It generally is accepted that Columbus was not the first European to reach the shores of the New World. In the 10th and 11th centuries, Norsemen explored the coast of North America from Labrador as far south as present-day New England and may have established a few rudimentary settlements. Fishermen from England also are known to have worked off the coast of Newfoundland decades before Columbus' first voyage, and may have put ashore there on several occasions. Columbus

The colored woodcut, above, *is from an illustrated edition of the navigator's writings. Columbus maintained a 20-page journal of his first voyage, reporting steady winds and a calm sea.*

© The Granger Collection

With a group of captured natives, Columbus returned to Spain in the spring of 1493, where he was received warmly by Ferdinand and Isabella, 1892 U.S. lithograph, above. *Columbus was directed by the king and queen to prepare immediately for a second voyage.*

himself may have had word of the existence of islands or even *terra firma* in the western sea. But the earlier European incursions were short-lived and little-noticed in Europe. In the wake of Columbus' expeditions, on the other hand, the Spanish, quickly followed by other European nations, began a movement of widespread conquest and settlement of the New World.

In this sense, it was Columbus who "brought Europe to the New World, with all the consequences that resulted," as Wilbur E. Garrett has observed in the *National Geographic*. His discovery or invasion, whichever it was, marked one of the great discontinuities in history, the end of an age in Europe and the encounter between two worlds that had coexisted for millennia without being aware of each other.

Robert H. Fuson, a professor of geography at the University of South Florida, wrote in the 1985 book *In the Wake of Columbus: Islands and Controversy* that, "From the standpoint of sheer significance, the first voyage of Christopher Columbus has very few historico-geographical parallels. It was one of those rare events that altered the course of history, immediately and directly. It finalized the destruction of the Middle Ages and it provided geographers with that complete planetary laboratory they had so long envisioned." Or as the historian Edward Channing put it succinctly in 1905, "No man has done more to change the course of human history than Christopher Columbus."

Latin America Then and Now

The debate about the good and the bad of the legacy of Christopher Columbus did not begin with the quincentennial observance. The question has troubled the consciences of men and women on both sides of the Atlantic from the earliest days. The maltreatment of the indigenous populations, the stratification of societies into very rich and very poor, the exploitation of the land and the ecosphere, militarism, and state-dominated economies have been the heritage of European colonialism in the New World, particularly in Latin America. Only now, as the end of the 20th century approaches, does Latin America appear to be throwing off the dark yoke of the conquest and the stultifying institutions that grew up during more than 300 years of colonial rule.

The Native Peoples. The greatest shame of the colonial period in Latin America was the devastation of the indigenous peoples of the region, those whom Columbus mistakenly named "Indians." The effect of European contact with the indigenous population was catastrophic. The Indians were slaughtered in battle with the invaders. They died of privation in slavery. Most of all they fell victim to their exposure to epidemic diseases, principally smallpox and measles, against which they had no immunity. In the first half century of European occupation of the New World, it has been estimated, the Indian population fell to 5% of its preconquest level.

The state of the European attitude toward the native peoples of the New World was foretold by Columbus in the journal of his first voyage, which he addressed to the sovereigns of Spain. "Your Highnesses may believe," Columbus wrote, "that this island and all the others are as much yours as Castile, that here is nothing wanting save a settlement, and to command them to do what you will. For I with these people aboard, who are not many, could overrun all these islands without opposition; for already I have seen but three of these mariners go ashore where there was a multitude of these Indians, and all fled without their seeking to do them ill. They bear no arms, and are all unprotected and so very cowardly that a thousand would not face three; so they are fit to be ordered about and made to work, to sow and do aught else that may be needed, and you may build towns and teach them to go clothed and to adopt our customs."

Such a state of mind gave rise to the *leyenda negra*, the black legend of Spanish (and to some extent, Portuguese) cruelty, rapaciousness, and bigotry, that even today colors the way the conquest and the colonial period are viewed. At the time, voices were raised against the view that the Indians were chattel to be used and abused at the will and for the enrichment of their European conquerors. Among the most prominent was that of Bartolomé de las Casas, a Dominican friar and bishop of Chiapas, Mexico. Las Casas urged the abolition of the *encomienda* system of forced Indian labor. He proposed, instead, the importation of black slaves from Africa, a suggestion he later regretted, deciding that all slavery was unjust.

There are demurrers to the *leyenda negra*. The late historian Hubert Herring argued that "Spain did not topple the Indian peoples from an Elysian state of perfection to one of abysmal misery. . . . Spain did not bring hunger and poverty to Indian America; life was meager and hunger was general before the conquerors came. . . . Spain did not introduce cruelty and war; exploitation was an old story to the Indians. . . . Spain did not destroy ancient systems of noble moral standards; the Indians were masters of gluttony, drunkenness, sexual excesses, and refined torture. . . . It is possible that the Indians of Mexico and Peru had more to eat under Spanish rule, more protection against each other and against their masters, more security of life and happiness than they had under Indian nobles and priests."

The Economies. Be that as it may, it cannot be denied that the conquerors came to the New World primarily to extract its riches and only incidentally, if at all, to improve the lot of

Library of Congress

The "Apostle of the Indies," Bartolomé de las Casas (1474–1566), one of the first Spanish missionaries in Latin America, advocated improved treatment of the Indians in the New World. His work "History of the Indies" is a major reference source for the early period of colonization.

© Jerry Frank/DPI

A market in Pisac, Peru, above, and a Nicaraguan farmer harvesting coffee are examples of Latin America's commodity-based economy. Some Latin nations now are encouraging more free-market, less state-controlled economies.

© Steve Northrup/Black Star

its inhabitants. The Latin economies throughout the colonial period and even after independence were commodity-based, oriented by European mercantilism. Latin America was assigned the role of producing the primary products needed by the industrialized countries, from gold to grain and from meat to petroleum. Under such a system the region was consigned to a marginal economic status, dependent first on Europe and later on the United States for markets for raw materials and for the supply of manufactured goods. The Latin American countries prospered or suffered with the rise and fall of world commodity markets.

Latin America, for example, came out of World War II with a huge foreign-exchange surplus, the result of supplying vast amounts of industrial raw materials to the Allies, but its economy was skewed seriously. Aside from their dependence on external markets and sources of finance, the Latin American economies had become precariously specialized. A few commodities accounted for most of the foreign trade in the majority of Latin American nations well into the 1980s. Petroleum represented 89% of Venezuela's foreign-exchange earnings. In Guatemala it was coffee and bananas (95%); in Cuba, sugar and tobacco (79%); in Bolivia, tin (71%); and in Chile, copper and nitrates (66%).

So long as the colonial-mercantile pattern prevailed, the Latin American economies languished. In the 1980s, the region moved into the most serious foreign-debt crisis and the most severe depression in its history. In the 1990s, the debt crisis lingers on, although somewhat abated. But for the first time, the Latin countries have embarked on a series of structural reforms that could break the bonds of the past. Countries such as Mexico, Brazil, Argentina, and Venezuela have begun intensive efforts to make a transition from rigidly controlled, state-dominated economies to free-market structures. State-owned companies are being privatized at a remarkable rate, huge unwieldy bureaucracies are being pared down, fiscal discipline is being imposed on central governments, export sectors are being diversified, and foreign investment is being sought actively.

The United States is lending its support to the modernization process. President George Bush has proposed the Enterprise for the Americas Initiative, which envisions the creation of a hemisphere-wide free-trade area where all tariff and nontariff barriers among the countries of North and South America will be eliminated. The Enterprise Initiative also proposes debt relief, incentives for foreign investment, and programs to protect the environment. At the same time, economic-integration movements are gathering strength in the hemisphere, with common markets developing in the Southern Cone (Argentina, Brazil, Paraguay, Chile, and Uruguay), Central America, and the Caribbean.

Optimism should be restrained prudently; many times in the past efforts to revitalize the Latin economies have been tried and faltered. But if the present efforts succeed, future historians may mark the 1990s as the time when Latin America finally emerged from the 500-year trauma of the discovery and conquest.

RICHARD C. SCHROEDER

© Scala/Art Resource

Alexander the Great (356–323 B.C.), at left in the above mosaic, *conquered and explored the known world of his day.*

The Constant Search

From prehistoric times through the present, the history of mankind has been one of discovery and exploration. From Alexander the Great to today's astronauts and cosmonauts, humans always have felt the need to investigate their surroundings and venture into the unknown. The 500th anniversary of Christopher Columbus' famous discovery during the height of the era of the "unrolling of the map" offers an appropriate time to review a chronology of major discoveries and explorations—undertakings that changed the course of human history.

334–323 B.C. Alexander the Great, the king of Macedonia, advanced into Asia as far as northern India, spreading Greek influence and increasing Greek geographic knowledge. Although Alexander's primary motive was military conquest, he also possessed a great geographic curiosity, and took on trips with him land surveyors, botanists, and scribes.

circa 795 A.D. A group of Irish monks discovered Iceland and established a retreat there. They apparently had traveled between 300 and 500 mi (477 and 795 km) in wicker-frame, hide-covered boats. Vikings from Scandinavia reached Iceland in about 870 and ousted the monks.

984. Eric the Red, fleeing Iceland after being convicted of several crimes, sailed northwest to an "unknown land" he had heard of—thus discovering Greenland. He later returned to the area with his family, friends, and other settlers to colonize its west coast. The colonists were dependent for their survival on supply ships from Norway, and the colony later died out when ships ceased to come because of the Black Death and other problems being encountered in Europe.

1001. Leif Ericson (the son of Eric the Red) sailed west from Greenland in search of new lands and wood, since Greenland had no trees. He reached and explored Labrador and Newfoundland. He and his crew sailed further south and settled for a few years in an area they named Vinland. Vinland well may have been on the North American mainland, but Ericson's discoveries never were followed up on.

1271–95. Marco Polo, a Venetian, together with his father and uncle began a journey to China and the court of Kublai Khan at Kaifeng. After reaching Beijing in 1275, Polo traveled in the service of Khan for 17 years, visiting central Asia, northern China, India, and southeastern Asia. The expedition returned to Venice in 1295.

1418–60. Prince Henry of Portugal (Henry the Navigator) sponsored explorations down the west coast of Africa. Interested in geography and anxious to further the importance of his country, he wished to find a route to India which would not be under Arab control. The beginning of this exploration of the African coast generally is agreed to have ushered in the Great Age of Exploration. Before proceeding, Henry's sailors had to overcome superstitions about "boiling seas" and sea monsters. Eventually, Henry's men discovered the Madeira islands and introduced sugar and wine production there. In 1455 his sailors Alvise da Cadamosto and Antonio Noli discovered the Cape Verde islands. By the time of the prince's death in 1460, his explorers had reached Guinea, past the bulge of the west African coast.

1487–88. Bartholomeu Dias, a Portuguese navigator, became the first European to round the southern tip of Africa; he reached the east African coast, opening the long-sought sea passage to India. Ironically, Dias later was killed during a storm off the southern tip, which he originally had named Cape of Storms.

1492–93. Christopher Columbus sailed across the Atlantic and discovered the Bahamas, Hispaniola, and Cuba on his first trip, claiming them for Spain. In a second voyage in 1493, he claimed Puerto Rico and Jamaica, and on later voyages he explored the South and Central American coasts.

(*See* accompanying article.)

1497–99. Vasco da Gama of Portugal sailed around Africa—establishing a path used by sailing ships ever since—and reached India, opening a sea trading and exploration route.

1497. Exploring for the English king Henry VII, Italian-born John Cabot sailed to northern North America and claimed the area for England. This marked England's entry into large-scale exploration and discovery in the New World.

Ferdinand Magellan (c.1480–1521) led the first circumnavigation of the globe. The "Victoria," the only one of his five ships to complete the voyage, is in full sail in the above 1590 map of the Pacific Ocean by Flemish geographer Abraham Ortelius.

1499–1502. Amerigo Vespucci, an Italian navigator, claimed to have been the first to discover the New World and to have made four voyages there. He is credited with at least two voyages (1499–1500 and 1501–02), during which he explored the mainland coast of South America. Despite doubts as to the veracity of his claims, his name later was given to both the newly discovered continents.

Hernán Cortés conquered Mexico and the Aztec empire in the early 16th century. The Mexican painting (below) *illustrates the Spanish conquistador negotiating with a Tlaxcaltec Indian chief; the Indian maid Marina is the translator.*

1500. Heading down the African coast on da Gama's sea route to India, Portuguese explorer Pedro Álvares Cabral was blown off course and reached the coast of South America, claiming Brazil—and a good portion of the continent—for Portugal.

1513. Vasco Núñez de Balboa, a Spanish conquistador who had gone to America to gain a fortune, crossed the Isthmus of Panama in search of gold. Instead, he found and claimed the "Great South Sea" (the Pacific Ocean) for Spain. With this discovery, it became apparent that Columbus was much mistaken in assuming America was, in fact, Asia. . . . Searching for gold and glory, Spanish explorer Juan Ponce de León discovered Florida.

1519–21. Hernán Cortés, a ruthless and brilliant conquistador from Spain, conquered Mexico and its Aztec empire, opening much of North America to Spain.

1519–22. Ferdinand Magellan, a Portuguese aristocrat sailing for King Charles I of Spain (Holy Roman Emperor Charles V), set sail ostensibly to find a western trading route to the Indies. He also believed that he could find a passage from the Atlantic to the Pacific oceans. After landing at Brazil, Magellan continued south and found what now is called the Strait of Magellan. He and his crew set off across the Pacific, reaching Guam and the Philippines, where Magellan was killed by natives. However, his voyage became the first to circumnavigate the globe when one of his sailors, Juan Sebastián del Cano, brought the lone remaining ship, the *Victoria*, back to Spain by traveling west around Africa.

1524. Giovanni da Verrazano, a Florentine sailor and surveyor serving France's King Francis I, explored the North American coast from Cape Fear, NC, to Nova Scotia, searching for the "Northwest Passage" to the Pacific Ocean. He and his crew were welcomed and entertained by Indians when they entered New York Bay during the voyage.

1531–35. Francisco Pizarro, a Spaniard, came to South America, entrusted by Spain with the task of conquering the as yet unknown land of Peru. He and his conquistadores defeated the mighty Incan empire with small losses to their own men. In 1535 the Spanish established the city of Lima in Peru.

Photos, © The Granger Collection

Francis Drake was the first Englishman to sail around the world. Following the three-year voyage (1577–80) during which he looted Spanish property, Drake was knighted by Queen Elizabeth I aboard his "Golden Hind" (above 19th-century engraving).

1534–35. Jacques Cartier of France, leading an expedition to search for the elusive Northwest Passage, traversed the St. Lawrence River; he reached areas which later were to become Quebec and Montreal, and laid the foundation for the French colonies in North America.

1541–43. Hernando de Soto, a Spanish navigator, set out from Florida, reaching the Mississippi River and exploring the Ozark Mountains in a fruitless search for gold and other riches like those described by Pizarro. After his death near the mouth of the Mississippi in 1542, his party continued the search, finally reaching the Gulf of Mexico in 1543. This was the first widespread exploration by Europeans of what now is the southern United States.

1568. Álvaro de Mendaña de Neyra of Portugal sailed west from Peru into the southern Pacific in search of islands rumored to contain great stores of gold. He discovered the Solomon islands some 200 mi (318 km) east of New Guinea, so naming them in the belief that they were the site of the fabled Solomon's mines. Later efforts to rediscover the islands were unsuccessful; even Mendaña himself could not locate them on a later voyage.

1577–80. Englishman Sir Francis Drake, during his circumnavigation of the globe, found that there was open sea south of Tierra del Fuego (the southern tip of South America) and went on to discover San Francisco Bay while searching for the Northwest Passage. He and his party also engaged in looting of Spanish ships and property, since England and Spain were engaged at the time in a "cold war." He returned to England, crossing the Pacific and Indian oceans and sailing up Africa's west coast.

1603–08. During several trips to the New World, Samuel de Champlain, a French explorer and colonizer, helped settle parts of the territory of New France. He helped found Port Royal in Acadia, and in 1608 established the colony of Quebec. He also mapped the entire east coast of North America south to Martha's Vineyard.

1606. Spanish explorer Pedro Fernandes de Queirós discovered the New Hebrides islands northeast of Australia and southeast of the Solomon islands. He was seeking "Terra Australis Incognita," or the great unknown land to the south. This mythical continent, said to be a vast area of land extending from the southern polar regions up toward the equator, had been sought since Ptolemy, a 2d-century geographer, first had hypothesized its existence.

1609–11. Searching for the Northeast Passage to Asia for the Dutch, Englishman Henry Hudson explored the Hudson River, traveling up to what is now Albany, NY. This gave the Dutch their

Sailing for the Dutch and searching for a northern passage to Asia, English navigator Henry Hudson discovered the New York river that bears his name in 1609. His ship, the "Half Moon," is anchored in the background of the 19th-century engraving (below).

© The British Library

James Cook explored the Pacific Ocean during three voyages (1768–79). In 1778 he discovered the Hawaiian islands. The following year the British captain (standing foreground in the above 1785 drawing) *was killed there during a native uprising.*

claim to the Hudson region in present-day New York. During a 1610 voyage for the English, he sailed through Hudson Bay in northern Canada. However, his men mutinied while in the Bay and in June 1611 killed Hudson and his son, still a child, by setting them adrift.

1616. Dutch explorers Willem Schouten and Jakob Le Maire searched for an alternate route to the Pacific other than the Strait of Magellan. They rounded the southern tip of the South American continent, proving that Tierra del Fuego was not attached to the hypothetical southern continent as well as providing a new route to the western ocean.

1642. Abel Tasman, a Dutch explorer, discovered the island of Tasmania, which he called Van Diemen's Land (after the governor-general of the Dutch East Indies). In his search for the mysterious southern continent, he discovered many islands and circumnavigated Australia without realizing it, proving it to be an island.

1673–74. French explorer and fur trader Louis Jolliet and Jacques Marquette, a French Jesuit missionary, entered the Fox River in Wisconsin, found a portage to the Wisconsin River, and followed the river for more than 100 mi (161 km) to its junction with the Mississippi River. The expedition followed the Mississippi as far as the Arkansas River.

1682. Sieur de la Salle (born René Robert Cavelier), a French explorer who built several forts in Canada, sailed down the Mississippi River to the Gulf of Mexico and claimed its entire drainage area for France, calling the area Louisiana.

© The Granger Collection

1741. Vitus Bering, a Danish captain in the Russian Navy, discovered the Bering Strait between Asia (Siberia) and North America (Alaska), reaching the coast of America with great difficulty. His ship ran aground on Bering Island, where Bering and many of his crew succumbed to scurvy.

1768–79. Captain James Cook of England surveyed the coasts of New Zealand and in April 1770 reached the previously unexplored eastern coastline of Australia, calling the area New South Wales. In a second voyage, he circumnavigated the globe in as southerly a latitude as possible, thus disproving once and for all the existence of the mythical great southern continent. In 1778, Cook discovered the Hawaiian islands, but was killed there by natives in 1779.

1804–06. Meriwether Lewis and William Clark, two U.S. army officers, reached the Pacific Ocean by way of the Missouri River, the Rocky Mountains, and the Columbia River, and returned safely. The two split up on the return journey, reuniting at St. Louis, MO.

The Sieur de la Salle, a French explorer and fur trader, was the first European to sail the Mississippi River to its mouth. The 1698 engraving (left) *depicts his landing on the Gulf of Mexico coast (now Matagorda Bay) in 1685.*

© North Wind Picture Archives

Scottish physician and missionary David Livingstone and Welsh-born U.S. journalist Henry Morton Stanley explored Africa in the 19th century. In 1871, Stanley found the missing Livingstone in a village near Lake Tanganyika (above 1872 engraving).

They thus covered more ground and collected even more information. Their journey showed the possibility of a route across the mountains, thus opening up the West for exploration and settlement. It also disproved the theory that North America could be crossed by an all-water route.

1871–90. Welsh explorer Sir Henry Morton Stanley reached Zanzibar, east Africa, in January 1871 and subsequently found Scottish explorer David Livingstone, who had not been heard from for more than two years. Stanley later explored equatorial Africa and descended the Congo River to the Atlantic Ocean.

U.S. naval officer Richard E. Byrd (1888–1957), below, *was the first man to fly over the North and South poles, May 1926 and November 1929, respectively.*

© U.S. Navy Department

1872–76. The H.M.S. *Challenger*, a steam corvette, conducted the first circumnavigation of the world's oceans primarily for scientific purposes.

1878–79. Swedish scientist and explorer Baron Nils A.E. Nordenskjöld discovered the long-sought Northeast Passage to Asia, sailing along the northern coast of Asia and through the Bering Strait.

1903–11. A Norwegian, Roald Amundsen, became the first to traverse the Northwest Passage. In 1911 he was the first to reach the South Pole, traveling by dogsled.

1909. After extensive training and several unsuccessful attempts, Robert E. Peary, a U.S. naval officer, apparently reached the North Pole, traveling by dogsled. He formed a team made up of many Eskimos. The white men on the team adopted the survival techniques of the Eskimos.

1926. Richard E. Byrd of the United States made the first air crossing of the North Pole. He made the first flight over the South Pole in 1929.

1953. Sir Edward Hillary, a New Zealander, and Tensing Norkay, a veteran Sherpa guide, were the first to reach the summit of Mount Everest, the world's tallest peak, in the Himalayas.

Oct. 4, 1957. The USSR launched the first earth satellite, *Sputnik 1*. The satellite was only 23 inches (58.4 cm) in diameter, and weighed 184.3 lbs (83.6 kg). This launch marked the beginning of the Space Age and set into motion the "space race" between the Soviet Union and the United States.

April 12, 1961. Yuri A. Gagarin of the Soviet Union became the first human being in orbit in the spaceship *Vostok 1*.

July 20, 1969. The spacecraft *Apollo 11* of the United States landed on the Moon. Astronauts Neil A. Armstrong and Edwin E. Aldrin, Jr., became the first humans to walk on the Moon's surface.

June 13, 1983. After a flight of 2.8 billion mi (4.5 billion km), the unmanned U.S. spacecraft *Pioneer 10* crossed the orbit of the planet Neptune and became the first manmade object to leave the solar system. The spacecraft had been launched March 2, 1972, and had flown by Jupiter in December 1973.

NASA

In "one small step for a man, one giant leap for mankind," Neil A. Armstrong was the first man to set foot on the lunar surface, July 20, 1969. Moments later, Edwin E. Aldrin, Jr., descended the ladder of the "Eagle" (above) *to become the second man on the Moon.*

Compiled by
MEGHAN O'REILLY LEBLANC
Staff Editor

People, Places, and Things

The following five pages recount the stories behind a selection of people, places, and things that may not have made the front-page headlines in 1991 but drew attention and created interest.

On July 3, 1991, President George Bush traveled to the Black Hills of South Dakota to mark the 50th anniversary of the Mount Rushmore National Memorial, right. *Earlier, on May 9, Vice-President Dan Quayle participated in ceremonies at the John F. Kennedy Space Center in Florida dedicating "Space Mirror,"* below, *a 42.5-ft (12.86-m)-high and 50-ft (15-m)-wide mirror-finished black granite memorial, to honor the U.S. astronauts who have died in the line of duty. The monument is mounted on a steel framework which turns to track the Sun. The names of the fallen astronauts are cut through the granite.*

© "Florida Today" from Gamma-Liaison

© Roemer/Argus Leader from Sipa

Courtesy, Ronald Reagan Presidential Library

© Joffet/Sipa

The Ronald Reagan Presidential Library, top, *designed by Stubbins Associates of Boston and containing the papers of the 40th U.S. chief executive, opened in Simi Valley, CA, in November 1991. A crowd of 4,200 invited guests, including five presidents and six first ladies—Lady Bird Johnson* (left), *President and Mrs. George Bush, President and Mrs. Reagan, President and Mrs. Jimmy Carter, President and Mrs. Gerald Ford, and President and Mrs. Richard Nixon* (right)*—attended the November 4 dedication. Actor Charlton Heston* (podium) *was among the ceremony's speakers. The occasion marked the first gathering ever of five White House occupants.*

© Louise Gubb/JB Pictures

In August off the coast of South Africa the Greek cruise liner "Oceanus" sank. Although all of the ship's 571 passengers were rescued, her captain was criticized severely for leaving the liner by rescue helicopter, while 160 passengers remained on board. A South African entertainer who looked after the remaining passengers was considered the incident's hero. Meanwhile Chicago baseball fans had to travel across the street from Comiskey Park to the new Comiskey Park to watch their White Sox play. Featuring traditional bleacher seats and a playing field of grass, the new Comiskey represents a "return to the intimacy and character of the old ball park."

© David Walberg/"Time" Magazine

© Thomas Kristich/"Time" Magazine

Several popular products celebrated anniversaries in 1991. For example, Cheerios cereal turned 50; the Fig Newton cookie and the American Express Travelers Cheque reached 100; and the Tube Council of North America rejoiced over the 150th birthday of the tube. Adults and children alike were enjoying the latest summer pastime—the Velcro paddle and ball, right. *Alexandra Ripley,* below, *became a celebrity as "Scarlett," her long-awaited sequel to "Gone With the Wind," reached the bookstores and sold out quickly.*

© Luc Novovitch/Gamma-Liaison

© Markus Boesch/Allsport

Professional beach volleyball, first organized in California in 1976, was boasting a 24-city U.S. tour and would become an exhibition sport at the 1992 Olympics. The television show "American Gladiators" also was in the midst of a nationwide tour and was enjoying cult status among its followers. The program features bodybuilders and former football players employed by Samuel Goldwin Television of Los Angeles.

© Rob Brown

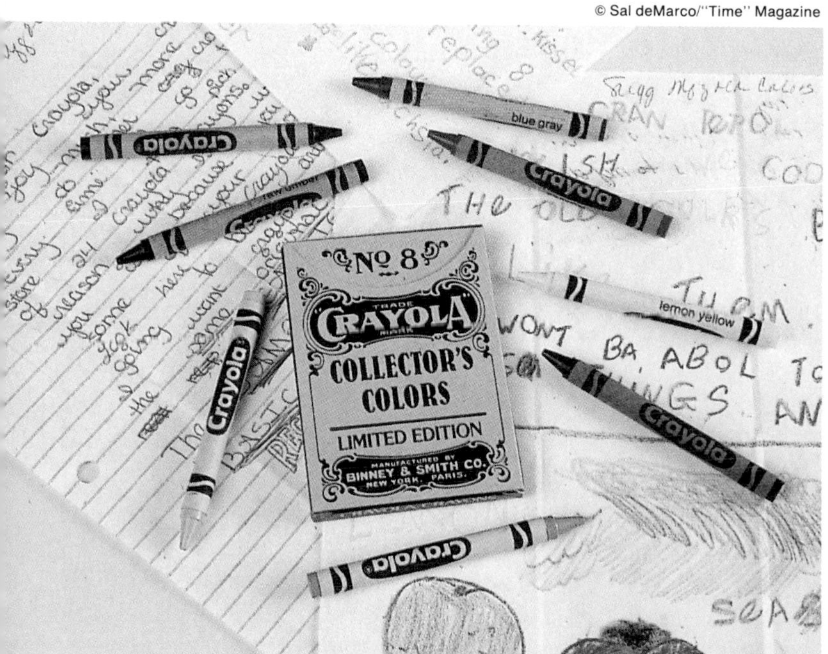

© Sal deMarco/"Time" Magazine

For years the basic colors of the eight Crayolas were the same. In 1990 the crayons' manufacturer introduced flashy new shades. However, customer complaints forced the company to return to the former eight colors late in 1991. The president of CRAYON (the Committee to Reestablish All Your Old Norms) called the action "a great moral victory."

The Alphabetical Section

© Haviv/Saba

© Filip Horvat/Saba

While most of Eastern Europe spent 1991 continuing to adapt to new political and economic systems, Yugoslavia—a federation of six republics—was fighting a civil war caused by political manipulation of nationalistic passions. The republics of Slovenia and Croatia, where demands for separation were strong *(page 96)*, declared their independence in late June. Hostilities between the increasingly Serbian-dominated Yugoslav army *(left)* and forces in Croatia *(above)* broke out shortly thereafter. Despite numerous efforts at a cease-fire, heavy fighting between the two sides continued for much of the remainder of the year. (*See also* YUGOSLAVIA.)

ACCIDENTS AND DISASTERS

AVIATION

Feb. 1—Thirty-four persons are killed when a jet collides with a commuter plane while landing at Los Angeles International Airport.

Feb. 5—A Greek military transport plane goes down during stormy weather in the eastern mountains of Greece; all 66 aboard are feared dead.

Feb. 20—A chartered Chilean airliner carrying tourists to Antarctica crashes near the southern tip of Chile, killing 19 persons.

March 3—A passenger jet en route from Denver to Colorado Springs nose-dives into a park in Colorado Springs, killing all 25 aboard.

March 5—Forty-three persons are killed when a Venezuelan airliner strays off course and crashes near the Andean town of La Puerta, Venezuela.

March 21—Two U.S. Navy planes collide during a training mission off the coast of southern California, killing all 27 aboard.

March 21—Ninety-two Senegalese soldiers and six Saudi crewmen are killed when their military transport plane crashes while landing at a Saudi air base. Smoke from Kuwait's burning oil wells was said to block visibility.

March 25—An Indian air force transport plane crashes near Bangalore, India, killing 28 persons.

April 5—A commuter plane crashes while approaching the Brunswick, GA, airport, killing all 23 on board, including former Sen. John Tower (R-TX).

May 26—An Austrian charter airliner explodes in midair and crashes over rural Thailand, killing all 223 on board.

July 11—A charter jet carrying Nigerian Muslims home after a trip to Saudi Arabia crashes while attempting to make an emergency landing at Jidda, Saudi Arabia; all 261 on board are killed.

Aug. 16—Sixty-nine persons are killed when a jet catches on fire and crashes into a remote jungle area of eastern India.

Sept. 11—A commuter plane crashes in Houston, TX, killing all 14 aboard.

Oct. 5—A military transport plane crashes shortly after take-off at Jakarta, Indonesia, killing all 132 aboard.

FIRES AND EXPLOSIONS

March 4—Nine elderly persons are killed when fire sweeps through a retirement home in Colorado Springs.

June 29—A gas explosion and fire in a coal mine in the Ukrainian city of Donetsk kills 30 miners.

Sept. 3—Fire sweeps through a chicken-processing plant in Hamlet, NC, killing 25 persons.

Oct. 20–21—At least 24 are left dead when fire sweeps through residential areas of Oakland and Berkeley, CA.

LAND AND SEA TRANSPORTATION

Jan. 12—A large cargo ship carrying a crew of 33 and a Spanish fishing trawler with 22 crewmen sink in stormy seas off the coast of Newfoundland. All the crew members are presumed dead.

March 1—More than 150 Somali refugees drown while fleeing their country on a small, overcrowded boat when the craft runs aground several miles from the shore of Kenya.

March 14—A 40-ton steel girder falls from a monorail under construction in Hiroshima, Japan, crushing 11 vehicles below and killing 14 persons.

April 10—At least 140 are feared dead after a car ferry rams an anchored oil tanker off the northwest coast of Italy during foggy conditions.

May 14—An overcrowded tourist train crashes into a local commuter train in western Japan, killing 42 persons.

June 8—In the second-worst rail disaster in Pakistani history, at least 100 persons are killed and more than 200 injured when a crowded passenger train collides with a stationary freight train near Sukkur, Pakistan.

June 26—More than 120 are killed when two ships collide in the Straits of Malacca, Malaysia.

July 31—Seven persons are killed when part of a passenger train derails near Camden, SC, sideswiping a parked freight train.

July 31—A bus carrying some 60 Girl Scouts skids off a winding mountain road in Palm Springs, CA, killing seven passengers.

Aug. 3—An overcrowded bus flips over southeast of Harare, Zimbabwe, killing 87 persons, 80 of them schoolchildren.

Aug. 15—Twelve persons are believed dead after a barge carrying oil workers in the South China Sea capsizes and sinks 65 mi (104.6 km) off the coast of Hong Kong.

Aug. 28—In the worst New York City subway disaster since 1928, five are killed when a subway train derails and crashes into a steel support column.

Oct. 17—Sixteen persons are killed when an overnight passenger train en route from Nice to Paris, France, collides with a freight train about 30 mi (50 km) southeast of Paris.

Nov. 19—A freight train derails and crashes into a line of cars and trucks in Tehuacán, Mexico, killing up to 60 persons.

Nov. 21—A sailboat carrying Haitian refugees bound for Miami capsizes off the coast of Cuba in stormy seas; 135 are feared dead.

Dec. 15—A ferry is swept up by high waves in stormy weather in the Red Sea and thrown against a reef. As many as 471 persons are feared dead.

STORMS, FLOODS, AND EARTHQUAKES

Jan. 6—At least 28 persons are presumed dead after gales sweep across Ireland and Great Britain over a period of several days.

Feb. 1—A major earthquake strikes a mountainous area of Pakistan and Afghanistan, leaving up to 700 dead.

Feb. 26—A mud slide caused by recent torrential rains wipes out several villages in the northeastern mountains of Papua New Guinea, leaving at least 200 persons dead.

March 10—More than 500 persons are left dead after floodwaters pour down from Mulanje Mountain in Malawi.

April 4–5—Three earthquakes strike Peru, killing 38 persons.

April 22—A powerful earthquake hits Costa Rica and Panama, killing a total of 75 persons.

April 27—At least 28 persons are killed when tornadoes slash through Kansas.

April 29—A powerful earthquake and several severe aftershocks shake Soviet Georgia, leaving more than 100 persons dead and demolishing entire villages.

April 30—More than 125,000 persons are left dead when a strong cyclone strikes coastal areas of Bangladesh.

June 18—Intense storms in northern Chile cause heavy rains, snow, and mud slides; 116 are left dead.

July 4—A strong earthquake strikes several southeastern Indonesian islands, killing at least 22.

July 20—Severe floods hit southeast China, leaving at least 1,700 dead.

July 30—A river swollen from heavy rains overflows into a village in western India, killing as many as 500 persons.

July 31—After two days of flooding caused by two months of torrential rain, more than 100 are feared dead in northeastern Romania. The rain followed seven years of drought.

Aug. 24—At least 24 persons are feared dead after a typhoon strikes the southern tip of the Korean peninsula.

Oct. 20—An earthquake rocks the foothills of the Himalayas in India, near the Nepal border; at least 360 are feared dead.

Nov. 5—At least 3,500 persons are killed when typhoon-caused flash floods sweep through villages in the central Philippines.

MISCELLANEOUS

Jan. 13—Fighting erupts during a soccer match at Orkney, South Africa, killing 40 persons.

Feb. 13—Worshipers surge into an overcrowded church in Chalma, Mexico, during Ash Wednesday services; at least 41 are trampled to death or suffocate.

June 4—At least 38 persons die when the volcanic eruption of Mount Unzen in southwestern Japan destroys an entire village.

July 14 (reported)—Up to 435 persons are killed by the continuing eruption of Mount Pinatubo in the Philippines; the eruption of the volcano began June 9.

Dec. 28—Nine youths are killed in a stampede when thousands try to enter an overcrowded gymnasium at City College in New York City to view a benefit basketball game featuring well-known rap stars.

ADVERTISING

The recession that began plaguing the U.S. advertising, marketing, and media industries in 1990 continued with a vengeance in 1991. The downturn in advertising spending led to sweeping layoffs at ad agencies and the media nationwide and forced several publications to close. Among the publications closing in 1991 was the nation's first daily sports newspaper, *The National*, which folded after 16 months of publication. Family Media, publisher of six magazines, was another fatality of the soft advertising market.

Speculation among industry executives on when business might improve was generally pessimistic. Most agreed that the recession would last at least until the second quarter of 1992, and perhaps longer.

Controversies. New U.S. Food and Drug Administration (FDA) Commissioner David Kessler began cracking down on food-label violations with the seizure of some Citrus Hill Fresh Choice orange juice for "false and misleading" use of the word "fresh" in its name—the juice is made from concentrate. The FDA also served notice it would institute action against fraudulent claims of health benefits.

Italian clothing marketer Benetton's controversial print campaign—featuring photos of a priest and a nun kissing, a placenta-covered newborn baby with umbilical cord, and an angelic Caucasian girl paired with a black boy whose hair was cropped to resemble devil's horns—was rejected by many U.S. and foreign magazines, but garnered extensive publicity.

In other news, Coca-Cola Co. reacted to criticism that lackluster advertising had caused it to lose momentum, if not market share, to rival Pepsi-Cola Co. Critics maintained that Pepsi's advertising featuring singer Ray Charles was more creative. In the fall, Coke began hearing presentations from ad agencies other than McCann-Erickson, which had held the account for more than 40 years. Coke also surprised the industry by hiring Hollywood superagent Michael Ovitz and his Creative Artists Agency to help develop marketing strategies, the first time a major marketer had turned to a talent agency for marketing assistance. Some saw the Coke move as the beginning of a trend.

Account Shifts. A handful of prominent advertising accounts changed hands in 1991. The most notable shift occurred when Miller Brewing Co. moved its $85 million account for Miller Lite beer from Backer Spielvogel Bates, New York, to Leo Burnett, Chicago. In other major changes, the $50 million Subaru account moved from Levine, Huntley, Vick & Beaver, New York to Wieden & Kennedy in Portland, OR; Isuzu switched its estimated $70 million business from Della Femina McNamee in New York to Goodby, Berlin & Silverstein of San Francisco; and American Express was said to be reviewing a $60 million account held by its longtime agency Ogilvy & Mather.

Ad Volume. The McCann-Erickson agency, which had predicted U.S. ad spending would increase 4.6% in 1991 to $136 billion, revised the forecast to between 3% and 4% and $132 billion. Publishers Information Bureau reported magazine ad pages were down 5% for the first half of 1991, compared with the same period in 1990. The Newspaper Advertising Bureau said total ad spending in U.S. newspapers fell 7% during the first six months of 1991, and the Television Bureau of Advertising reported ad spending on network television had dropped 7.1% during that time. The three major TV networks, ABC, CBS, and NBC, along with Fox Broadcasting, reported $3.5 billion in sales for the 1991–92 network-TV upfront market, a 19% decline from 1990's record $4.3 billion.

Creative. The Clio awards, the most prestigious in the ad industry, suffered a potentially fatal black eye in 1991. The annual print-and-radio-awards ceremony erupted into chaos when lists of award winners proved incomplete, confusing the presenters and prompting finalists to rush the stage for the Clio statuettes. The scheduled TV-awards ceremony was canceled and the disorganization, coupled with rumors that Clio organizers were heavily in debt, led to speculation the awards could not survive. Bill Evans, president of Clio Inc., the independent, for-profit organization that runs the awards show, was said to be negotiating for its sale.

At the International Advertising Film Festival in Cannes, France, Perrier's ad—created by Ogilvy & Mather, Paris—showing a woman and a lion climbing opposite sides of a mountain to confront over a bottle of Perrier, won Grand Prix as best TV commercial of the year. Designer Calvin Klein broke new ground with a jeans campaign that consisted of a 116-page, free-standing "outsert" that looked like a magazine and was attached in a polybag to selected copies of *Vanity Fair*'s October issue.

Acquisitions. Two important acquisitions took place in the media business in 1991. One was British media baron Robert Maxwell's purchase of the ailing *New York Daily News*, which had suffered from a prolonged strike. Another was the sale of eight magazines owned by Rupert Murdoch—including *Seventeen, Premier,* and *New York*—to a new player on the magazine scene, K-III Holdings.

There were few acquisitions of ad agencies in 1991 and most involved foreign companies. French agency BDDP switched from minority to majority control of U.S. agency Wells Rich Greene. And French agency Eurocom merged with French shop Roux, Seguela, Cayzac & Goudard to form the largest agency in Europe.

JOHN WOLFE, *"Advertising Age"*

AFGHANISTAN

As the second anniversary of the last Soviet occupation troops to leave Afghanistan came and went on Feb. 15, 1991, the regime they left behind remained in power, thanks partly to a massive arms-supply program. On Jan. 1, 1992, however, Soviet military support to President Najib (also known as Najibullah) and his ruling Homeland Party (HP) was to cease. And just 150 years after an Afghan victory over another superpower (Great Britain), disunited but implacable resistance forces hoped to remove Najib and his followers from power.

Internal Political Developments. The apparent lack of legitimacy of the Najib government remained its biggest problem. The disunited resistance controlled 80% to 85% of the country as 1991 ended, including 200 district capitals and six provincial capitals. Najib's four-year-old calls for "national reconciliation" and for the return of nearly 5 million refugees from Pakistan and Iran largely went unheeded. The resistance groups, though badly fragmented, were unanimous in refusing to deal with a regime seen as a purely Soviet creation.

Najib continued efforts to shed the puppet image. He switched the country's national day from April 27—the anniversary of the 1978 Communist coup (formerly dignified as the "Great Saur Revolution")—to the traditional independence holiday of Jeshyn (August 19), which celebrated the 1919 liberation from British rule. He later decreed that the terms "PDPA" (People's Democratic Party of Afghanistan—former name of the HP), "primary party organization," and even "Saur Revolution" be dropped from all government and legal documents. Eight Communist-associated medals and awards were abolished. The blessings of a multiparty democratic system, an independent judiciary, and a free press were hailed in regime propaganda, which now forswore socialism. In September, Foreign Minister Abdul Wakil, who had helped found the Marxist-Leninist PDPA in 1965, declared that there was "no place for communism in Afghanistan."

These cosmetic changes in no way affected the HP's determination to remain in power, however. Repeated government demands for peace were offset by ongoing efforts to glorify the army. In the preceding three years the role of the HP had been deemphasized, but April saw its return to public prominence.

In June former Afghan leader Babrak Karmal returned from his four-year exile in the Soviet Union, as did the disgraced economic expert and former Prime Minister Soltan Ali Keshtmand. The homecomings were apparently a Soviet initiative, and they evoked no enthusiasm from Najib and his followers, who denied their political significance and placed armed guards outside Karmal's door. The Soviets may have hoped that the returnees would help shore up and unify the party, but if so the hope was in vain. Both men immediately sank from view, and in July resignations from the party reportedly climbed.

Military Developments. The most significant military development was the resistance's March victory at Khost, a fortified town near the Pakistani border. Defended by 10,000 to 12,000 troops led by 25 generals, and supported by the Afghan air force, tanks, and heavy artillery, the town fell after a lightning attack by coordinated resistance forces under field commander Jalaluddin Haqqani. Najib later hinted—and the Soviets stated outright—that treachery by some of the regime's 25 generals, all of whom were taken prisoner along with 600 members of the elite Republican Guards, was responsible for the defeat.

In late summer and early autumn, a resistance offensive against Gardez, another garrison town, failed. In this instance, good weather favored the Afghan air force, which decisively turned back the resistance thrusts.

Although the resistance had a growing capability for large-scale attacks against fortified targets, most field commanders (including the renowned Ahmed Shah Massoud) believed in a strategy of minimizing casualties by picking off smaller, lightly defended posts and isolating the larger cities. There was no effort to starve out the townspeople, most of whom did not sympathize with the government, but shipments of munitions were interdicted where possible. In the fall there were reports of quiet truces between resistance and government forces in some areas, possibly indicating that both expected the regime soon would fail.

Economic Developments. The Afghan economy continued to spiral downward in 1991, despite official boasts of progress. In June the gross domestic product for the preceding Islamic year ending in March was estimated at 115 billion afghanis ($2.27 billion), and the gross national product at 160.8 billion afghanis ($3.18 billion). Increases totaling 1.6 billion afghanis ($31.6 million) were registered in industry, trade, communications, and construction,

AFGHANISTAN • Information Highlights

Official Name: Republic of Afghanistan.
Location: Central Asia.
Area: 250,000 sq mi (647 500 km^2).
Population: (mid-1991 est.): 16,600,000.
Chief Cities (1984 est.): Kabul, the capital, 1,179,000; Kandahar, 203,000; Herat, 160,000.
Government: Najibullah, general secretary, People's Democratic Party (appointed May 1986) and president; Fazil Haq Khaliqyar, prime minister (named April 1990). *Legislature*—bicameral National Assembly.
Monetary Unit: Afghani (50.6 afghanis equal U.S.$1, June 1991).
Gross Domestic Product (1989 est. U.S.$): $3,000,000,000.
Foreign Trade (1990 U.S.$): *Imports,* $884,000,000; *exports,* $235,000,000.

but there was a net loss of 5 billion afghanis ($99 million) in agriculture. The above figures are derived from the unrealistic official exchange rate of 50.6 afghanis to the U.S. dollar. The real value of the afghani, according to official sources, fell from 525 to the dollar in 1990 to 1,000 to the dollar in 1991. Foreign trade totaled $1.025 billion, but only $230 million were exports.

In March, Najib referred to the "appalling situation" concerning food and fuel in the capital, and in June to the "critical economic situation." The only apparent bright spots in the economy during the year were the reported resumption of natural-gas production and a first-ever claim of oil production.

Media coverage of the economy promoted private enterprise, especially in the transportation field. "State monopoly in most cases . . . will be eliminated," stated Prime Minister Fazl Haq Khaliqyar. He singled out consumer goods as deserving private-sector attention.

Outside Powers' Involvement. In January the Soviet Union budget for 1991 showed that Afghanistan would receive 280 million rubles ($165 million), 70% of all Soviet foreign aid. The unstated military aid, however, came to about $300 million per month and included such weapons as Scud missiles. The United States, which had budgeted about $200 million in military aid to the resistance in 1991, unilaterally stopped all arms deliveries on October 15.

The Soviets continued efforts to consolidate economic links by arranging for direct trade agreements between Afghanistan and various Soviet communities, especially in the Central Asian republics. They also continued a decade-long policy of hosting Afghan children in summer camps, but Soviet influence in Afghan schools declined as Marxist-Leninist writings began to be discarded.

In May both the resistance and the regime endorsed four out of five points of a vague United Nations plan covering the Afghan rights to sovereignty, territorial integrity, independence and nonalignment, an Islamic government, and self-determination. The plan also called for an end to arms deliveries. On September 13, Soviet and U.S. negotiators finally were able to agree on this point: The supply halt was scheduled for Jan. 1, 1992.

In November, Moscow yielded to resistance demands for recognition of an interim Islamic government, an Afghan right to cancel agreements reached since 1978, withdrawal of all Soviet military personnel, immediate reduction of military supplies, reparations, and official condemnation of the invasion. In return, the resistance promised to free Soviet prisoners of war and hold internationally supervised elections within two years. In effect, the Soviets were abandoning Najib.

ANTHONY ARNOLD
Hoover Institution, Stanford

AFRICA

Many longtime observers of sub-Saharan Africa may look back on 1991 as one of the most hopeful years for the African continent since many of its individual countries gained their independence in the 1960s.

A veritable wave of political liberalization swept the region, with one government after another legalizing opposition political parties, freeing the press, and setting dates for national elections. The year also brought hope for a resolution of some of Africa's bloody conflicts, including those in Angola, Mozambique, Liberia, Ethiopia, and Somalia. But events in the region during 1991 were not entirely positive. Violence continued in South Africa, where the major political groups moved haltingly toward negotiations on the country's future. Some conflicts, like the one in Sudan, remained unresolved, with untold numbers of people displaced and starving. Political change threatened to provoke conflict and starvation in Zaire. And economic conditions throughout most of the region remained depressed.

Democratic Reform. The biggest news of 1991 involved political change. Prolonged economic decline combined with the dramatic overthrow of communism in Eastern Europe and the USSR over the previous several years fed the deep discontent felt by many Africans toward their governments and a willingness on their part to take to the streets and demand democratic reform. Political changes in Africa itself demonstrated to many Africans that their

In Benin in March 1991, Nicephore Soglo defeated incumbent President Mathieu Kérékou in the nation's first free presidential elections in 30 years. He took office April 4.
© Susan Katz Miller

© R. Bouget/Sygma

Protesters jammed the main square of Antananarivo, Madagascar's capital, as opposition parties campaigned for the resignation of President Didier Ratsiraka. Some 50 persons were killed as troops fired on the demonstrators in August.

governments were vulnerable to pressures for more open political systems.

In January the first freely elected prime minister in Cape Verde assumed office. In March a new president was elected freely in Benin. In the Congo a national conference convened, declared itself "sovereign," rewrote the Congolese constitution to expand and protect human and political rights, set dates for a constitutional referendum and local and national elections, and installed an interim prime minister. The months of debate were televised live and watched avidly both in the Congo and across the river in Kinshasa, Zaire. National conferences were held in Togo, Niger, and Mali, and were demanded by the opposition throughout much of Francophone Africa. The governments of Sierra Leone, Tanzania, and Ghana permitted debates about constitutional change, while in Zambia, October presidential elections ended the 27-year rule of President Kenneth Kaunda. Only in a handful of countries—including Kenya and Malawi—did governments continue to resist demands for political liberalization.

South Africa. Political change also occurred in South Africa, where the government of President F. W. de Klerk repealed the Land Acts, the Group Areas Act, the Black Communities Act, and the Population Registration Act, all key foundations of apartheid. In response to these and other initiatives by the de Klerk government, the United States and the Europeans lifted most of the economic sanctions imposed on South Africa. However, continuing violence between the African National Congress (ANC)—the country's leading black political party)—and Inkatha—a Zulu-based group—and revelations that the South African government had been financing Inkatha slowed progress toward negotiations on a new constitution. A peace accord signed by the government and the two factions in September failed to halt the violence. However, talks on a new constitution got under way in December.

Civil Wars. Several of Africa's chronic and bloody conflicts appeared to have ended in 1991. The three-decade-old civil war in Ethiopia was resolved, at least temporarily, with the flight in May of Ethiopian President Mengistu Haile-Mariam and the military victory of the Ethiopian People's Revolutionary Democratic Front, which established a new government in Addis Ababa. The Front, led by Meles Zenawi, a guerrilla leader from the province of Tigre, expressed its commitment to establishing democracy in Ethiopia and to holding the country's first free elections in 1993. President Zenawi and the new provisional government set up in Eritrea by the Eritrean People's Liberation Front also agreed that in two years, a referendum would be held in Eritrea on the issue of independence.

The second of Africa's long civil wars to be resolved was that in Angola, which had lasted for more than 25 years. The government in Luanda and representatives of UNITA, the insurgency movement led by Jonas Savimbi, signed a peace pact on May 31. In October a cease-fire took effect between the two sides and Savimbi returned to Luanda to begin campaigning for elections scheduled for 1992.

It looked like a halt in the fighting also was holding in Liberia where Charles Taylor had led his National Patriotic Front of Liberia against the government of the late President Samuel Doe. An intervention force organized by the Economic Community of West African States had attempted to end the conflict, which had resulted in the deaths of many Liberians, the displacement of nearly one third of the country's population, and spillover violence into neighboring Sierra Leone. By the end of the year, after peace talks among parties to the conflict had been held in Ivory Coast, the fighting appeared to have died down and an interim government led by Amos Sawyer was installed in Monrovia. However, it remained unclear whether a permanent cease-fire and a schedule for elections would be agreed on and observed.

Violence again erupted in Somalia. As 1991 began, clan-based armies opposed to the government of Mohammed Siad Barre forced the president and his supporters to flee from Mogadishu, the country's capital. A new government, drawn in part from southern clans, took over. The northern-based Isaak clan and its political arm, the Somali National Movement, then declared itself independent. It was unclear whether the northerners would be able to realize that goal. Their declaration challenged the long-held African belief that state boundaries should remain unchanged once independence had been achieved. As 1991 ended, continued violence between clan-based factions in the capital left Somalia's future in doubt.

The conflict between the Arab and Islamic northern Sudan and the peoples of the south (Nilotic or Bantu clans made up largely of Christians or believers in traditional religions) continued with no promise of resolution. A drought in the country and interruption of food supplies threatened millions with starvation or severe malnutrition.

Conflicts also broke out in Rwanda as Rwandan refugees invaded from neighboring Uganda; a low-level conflict in the Casamance region of Senegal continued with groups there demanding greater autonomy. Several bloody outbreaks of violence between Muslims and Christians in Nigeria, resulting in a number of deaths, added a worrisome note to Nigerian politics as that country proceeded toward presidential elections scheduled for 1992.

Zaire Crisis. Perhaps the most disturbing political situation in Africa developed in Zaire. The autocratic and corrupt regime of President Mobutu Sese Seko, in office since 1965, continued to cling to power in the face of growing opposition and demands from newly formed political parties for a national conference. Mobutu recognized that if he agreed to such a conference, it likely would follow the path of the ones in Benin and the Congo, with participants

© Allx/Gamma-Liaison

Following four days of strikes and protests in Mali in March 1991, President Moussa Traoré was overthrown in a coup led by Lt. Col. Amadou Toumani Toure (left). Dissident troops reportedly opposed to Toure's plan to transform Mali into a multiparty democracy tried unsuccessfully to depose Toure himself in July.

declaring themselves sovereign, stripping him of his presidential powers, and setting dates for elections. They also would be likely to air publicly the allegations of widespread corruption in his government. Mobutu first resisted demands for a conference; then he agreed to hold one but objected to its being "sovereign"; then he reportedly created a number of bogus political parties and civic associations from which conference participants (loyal to him) would be drawn.

At each stage in this process, opposition forces called rallies, demonstrations, and strikes to show their growing strength among the people. With inflation running at 1000% per year (resulting from the uncontrolled expansion of the money supply by the government) and an apparent political stalemate, rioting and looting by unpaid army troops broke out in the capital, provoking the dispatch of French and Belgian troops to evacuate their nationals. The year ended with continuing maneuvers by Mobutu to retain power, periodic outbreaks of violence, growing economic and political chaos, and the threat of starvation facing many of the residents of Kinshasa and other cities unable to afford the accelerating cost and the drop in the availability of food as the economy spiraled downward.

Economy. The economic situation in most of sub-Saharan Africa showed little overall improvement during 1991. Much of the region had suffered from sustained economic decline since the beginning of the 1980s, with stagnant or falling incomes, decreasing agricultural and industrial production, and heavy debt burdens. As the 1980s ended, roughly 37 of the 48 independent nations of Africa south of the Sahara had adopted economic-reform programs supported by the International Monetary Fund, the World Bank, or both. Some countries had experienced an increase in economic growth but for most, the prospects for coming years included the continuing implementation of often-painful economic reforms and at best a slow improvement in economic conditions.

These gloomy economic prospects did not deter the enthusiasm of African heads of state to commit themselves once again to continental economic integration. At the Organization of African Unity meeting in Nigeria in June, African heads of state signed a treaty creating an African common market by the year 2020. Foreign observers, along with many Africans, wondered whether this treaty would lead to any more action by African governments in promoting economic integration than in the past, or whether existing integration schemes —the Economic Community of West African States, the Preferential Trade Area of East and Southern Africa, or the Economic Community of Central African States—would prove more effective in realizing their goals than they had been.

Finally, in September a special United Nations meeting to review economic progress in Africa was convened. That progress remained disappointing, as did the level of aid and debt relief. But perhaps reflecting the apparently declining worldwide interest in Africa and the dramatic changes elsewhere in the world, the discussions in the UN barely were reported in the Western press.

Elephant "Management." The African elephant, the world's largest land mammal, long has been a favorite with animal lovers the world over. Concern over the wholesale slaughter of elephants for their ivory—the total number declined from 1.3 million in 1979 to 650,000 by the end of the 1980s—led to an international ban on the ivory trade in 1989. This had resulted in a dramatic decline in elephant poaching in countries such as Kenya, where the problem was especially serious. The price of ivory had dropped from $14 per pound to less than $2.

In some countries, however, the elephant population has been growing, and large herds, no longer permitted to roam freely but confined to national parks, were causing widespread damage to forestland. South Africa, Botswana, and Zimbabwe have elephant-management programs which permit designated numbers of the animals to be killed each year in an effort to control the population. In Botswana the tusks, hides, and meat taken from the destroyed elephants are sold and the proceeds are shared with the local inhabitants, so that the people can benefit from the revenues generated by the wildlife-management program. Some environmentalists oppose these practices and claim that the governments exaggerate the size of the elephant herds. African park officials argue that if the excess elephants were not destroyed humanely they would die of starvation.

In June 1991, Botswana, Zimbabwe, Malawi, Namibia, and Zambia joined forces to establish the Southern African Center for Ivory Marketing (SACIM). They plan to apply for an exemption from the international ivory-trading ban and to resume exporting ivory to Japan, Taiwan, and other East Asian countries where there is a great demand for it. The trade would be carried on under strict controls to prevent any black-market activities. Kenya and other countries with endangered elephant populations oppose any relaxation of the ban, fearing that it would lead to a resumption of poaching. But the SACIM governments maintain that they need the revenue from the sale of ivory to support their wildlife-conservation programs. The Convention on International Trade in Endangered Species (CITES) was to make a decision on the SACIM proposal when it meets in Kyoto, Japan, in March 1992.

See also articles on individual countries.

CAROL LANCASTER, *African Studies Program Georgetown University*

AGRICULTURE

World grain production suffered from unfavorable weather in 1991 in the United States, the USSR, and South America. Smaller crops tightened supplies and raised food costs in developing and former centrally planned countries. U.S. crops in some areas were hurt by excessive rain, late plantings, killing frosts, and drought. These problems cut world grain production below 1990, while oilseed production increased slightly, about 2%.

The United States

Grain Supplies Tighten. With population growth, the 5% drop in world grain production reduced per capita production by 7%. Smaller crops reduced grain inventories as a percent of annual use to the lowest level in 17 years and strengthened demand for U.S. grain.

Inventories were slightly below accepted minimum standards for world food security. While global food supplies were not threatened seriously, small stocks make it more difficult to mobilize supplies quickly to meet emergency food needs of some areas. Also, the low stocks provide little reserve to offset possible future weather problems. Grain is used to produce bread, cereal, dairy foods, eggs, and meat. Other uses include gasoline additives to reduce air pollution, starch, corn oil, and high fructose corn sweeteners used in soft drinks and processed foods. Oilseeds provide protein and vegetable oil for human consumption and are needed for efficient dairy and meat production.

Large U.S. Farms Become Larger. In the United States, large farms grew in size and number, especially in the pork, poultry, beef feeding, and dairy industries. Larger operations reflect specialized management skills required in today's agriculture. Skills needed for successful livestock and poultry production include financial management; purchasing; marketing; engineering; strategic and detail planning; understanding of government regulations; and management of personnel, nutrition, and animal health.

With these management challenges, many U.S. farmers now specialize in a single product, in contrast to the diversified farming of the past. Specialization is especially evident in cattle feeding, where expansion continued in 1991 in large feedlots in central and western Nebraska and Kansas and northeastern Colorado. Shifts of beef production to these areas are due to low rainfall and population density, which minimize environmental pollution concerns stemming from odors, animal wastes, and feedlot runoff. Expanded beef production brought new meat-packing plants, feed mills, and other industries supplying inputs for animal agriculture. These industries provide employment in a region where other job opportunities are limited.

In the dairy industry, large farms are concentrated more on the West Coast and in Texas than in other areas. Nearly 47% of California's dairy farms in 1991 had more than 100 cows each. Approximately one fourth of the dairy farms in Texas and Washington now had more than 100 cows, compared with only 7% in Wisconsin. Wisconsin is the nation's top dairy state and produces nearly one fourth of the U.S. milk supply. However, it lost market share to the South and West due to rapid growth in larger dairy farms. U.S. farms with more than 500 dairy cows account for about 12% of the nation's dairy farms but produce about half of the nation's milk.

Growth in Fruit and Vegetable Production. U.S. consumers have become increasingly

Cantaloupes are harvested in Imperial Valley, CA. Growers acknowledged that high melon yields depressed prices in 1991.

health conscious, strengthening the demand for fruits and vegetables in 1991 and providing a ready market for large summer and fall production. Weather was favorable for summer crops after a freeze in California and damage to Florida's winter crops.

The U.S. fruit and vegetable industry experienced strong growth in exports through the first two thirds of the year. Canada was an important market, especially for lettuce. In 1991, Canadian tariffs on U.S. vegetable imports were 30% lower than in January 1989 when the U.S.-Canadian Free-Trade Agreement took effect. That agreement lowers the cost of most imported vegetables and has stimulated demand. U.S. vegetable-seed exports through mid-1991 were 21% above a year earlier.

Cotton and California Water Problems. Springtime brought fears that the nation's cotton crop would be hurt by a severe California drought and reduced irrigation water supplies. However, preliminary estimates indicated that 1991 U.S. cotton production was 14% above the previous year and the largest since 1937. Production in Arizona, California, and New Mexico dropped nearly one tenth below 1990 because of water shortages, but was more than offset by increases of 14% in the mid-South and 70% in the Southeast, where weather was exceptionally favorable.

California's drought brought conflict between urban groups and agriculture over extensive use of water to irrigate cotton, fruit, vegetables, and other crops. Under pressure from urban groups, its farmers planted less land and sharply reduced water utilization. The state's harvested area of cotton in 1991 was 11% below a year earlier, along with declines of 18% for rice, 31% for wheat, 20% for barley, 19% for corn, and 6% for potatoes. When rains returned, concern over agricultural water use diminished. But the issue of urban versus agricultural use will continue in future years as industrial and residential water needs expand.

Conservation and Animal-Welfare Concerns. U.S. agricultural legislation enacted in late 1990 brought increased priority to conservation of natural resources. The legislation encourages preservation of existing wetlands and reclamation of some former wetlands now used for farming. Its intent is to provide wildlife habitat and to control agricultural pollution of water supplies. Penalties for failing to meet soil-conservation requirements were strengthened slightly. The legislation also created an Agricultural Resources Conservation Program (ARCP) authorizing continued long-term contracts to remove highly erodible land and wetlands from agricultural production.

In Europe restrictions on poultry producers were tightened to enhance animal welfare. European Community (EC) regulations for egg farms now specify the minimum cage size and other dimensions, as well as feeding and watering equipment standards that must be met to improve welfare of laying flocks. Caging simplifies feeding, watering, and egg collecting; keeps eggs cleaner; reduces cannibalism among chickens; and aids in disease control. It also lets individual workers care for more birds while reducing costs. The new standards, which will become more stringent in 1995, will increase egg costs. Similar concerns were beginning to develop in the United States. In response, the California Cattlemen's Association in 1991 developed a code of ethics that includes standards for livestock health care, safety, and humane treatment. In North Dakota livestock organizations jointly developed animal husbandry standards for farm animals, pets, zoo animals, and competitive exhibitions.

International

Europe. In Eastern Europe farmers, government officials, bankers, and other agricultural interests struggled to create an economy where market-determined prices guide production and marketing decisions. The shift to privatization has been slow and difficult. Despite problems, East European grain production in 1991 rose an estimated 4% from a year earlier. For the first time in seven years, the area fully met its domestic grain needs and exported modest quantities to neighboring countries. Eastern Europe's production of broilers, eggs, and beef declined slightly, while its pork production increased.

Meanwhile, in Western Europe the EC continued to struggle with manure-disposal problems from its intensive animal agriculture. Agricultural wastes are responsible for high levels of nitrates in lakes, streams, and underground-water supplies in some areas and have been linked to acid rain. Farms in Belgium and the Netherlands are estimated to produce 23 million tons more manure each year than can be disposed of as crop fertilizer under current practices. Pollution-control methods being studied include limiting field applications of manure to certain times of the year, incorporating livestock wastes immediately into the soil upon application, converting some pollution-prone lands to forests, prohibiting increased size of livestock farms, and modifying rations to reduce ammonia levels in manure.

Soviet Union. USSR production of meat, grain, oilseeds, and other farm products declined in 1991 because of unfavorable weather and coordination problems as it shifted away from a government-managed agriculture. Soviet grain production fell 20% to 25% below 1990.

Future Soviet agricultural production and trade will depend heavily on changes begun in 1991 and not yet completed. Production and distribution will be affected by the governmental structure that replaces communism, its will-

© Bruno Barbey/Magnum

Workers at a collective farm in Moldavia, USSR, take a lunch break during corn-harvesting time. With the USSR undergoing political change, it was a difficult year for Soviet agriculture. Grain production was down 20% to 25%.

ingness to encourage Western investment, and the amount of financial assistance provided by Western governments. On October 18 eight Soviet republics signed an agreement to establish a free-market community. One challenge of the new union will be to manage the transportation and distribution system so that equipment as well as imported goods are distributed equitably among republics.

Because of monetary problems that reached a peak in 1991, Soviet agricultural imports in 1992–93 are likely to be maintained largely by Western financial assistance. The USSR's deteriorating financial position reflected lower production of petroleum, natural gas, and coal, and a decline in its gold inventory. Exports of these products formerly paid for massive food imports. Over several years, USSR agricultural production should rise as it completes the changes begun in 1991. A market-directed agriculture will encourage new investment and increased efficiency as its farmers respond to profit incentives.

China. Weather and crop production in the world's most populous nation varied considerably from area to area. While many provinces reported record or near-record wheat and corn crops, severe floods in central China held the nation's wheat output below a year earlier. As a result, wheat imports remained sizable. China's corn crop was large enough to allow modest exports to neighboring countries. Its imports of U.S. cattle hides and cotton increased to support growth in textile and leather industries, which provide large exports to Western nations.

India. Agricultural production was favorable in India in 1991. This country is the world's second-most-populous nation and sometimes is a large importer of food. However, good weather and near-record grain and oilseed production allowed it to export from its 1991 crops. Agriculture is a major part of the Indian economy, accounting for one third of its gross national product and one fifth of its export earnings. Important exports include tea, coffee, spices, protein meal, and cashews. A healthy agricultural sector was beneficial to the nation's economy.

Africa. Chronic food problems continued in parts of Africa. However, sections of north Africa enjoyed the best harvest in years, with plentiful rains benefiting wheat, barley, and other crops and greatly reducing import needs. At the other end of the continent, South Africa, once a major corn exporter, experienced drought which kept its corn crop one third below the recent peak in 1988–89.

Latin America. Low grain prices, large external debts, and reduced government financial assistance to farmers led to a sharp decline in harvested soybean area in Brazil in 1991, after decades of expansion. These same conditions slowed land clearing in the Amazon rain forest.

Mexico in 1991 outlined goals to bring its agricultural and food production to self-sufficiency in the next few years. Mexican officials also began background studies for a proposed U.S.-Mexican Free-Trade Agreement similar to the U.S.-Canadian agreement (*see* SPECIAL REPORT/MEXICO). A free-trade agreement could benefit some agricultural sectors of both nations.

See also BIOGRAPHY—*Madigan, Edward R.*; FOOD.)

ROBERT WISNER, *Iowa State University*

ALABAMA

Financial problems and the activities of the legislature and Gov. Guy Hunt (R) dominated Alabama news in 1991.

Legislative Sessions. The state legislature, which was lopsidedly Democratic in both houses, was disinclined to concentrate on issues of interest to the governor in its 1991 regular session. Early on, members focused most of their attention on the question of their own pay. The first plan, approved on April 25, called for a 25% increase. However, by executive amendment, Governor Hunt cut this to 19.5% and the lawmakers agreed to the reduction on May 7. Alabama legislators now would earn $30,660 a year, up from $25,650.

Education Problems. Governor Hunt had identified education reform as the Number 1 item on his agenda when he opened the legislature's annual meeting on April 16. He called for tax reform to help finance needed improvements, but did not give strong backing to any of the recommendations made by recent study groups. The legislature did pass a largely symbolic Alabama Education Improvement Act on July 21. However, revenues needed to implement its ambitious provisions (approximately $500 million more per year) were lacking. The legislature approved the state education budget on July 29, in the closing hours of the session. It appropriated $2.65 billion in state aid to school programs at all levels.

On August 8 the governor attempted unsuccessfully to use a line-item veto to cut $25 million from the education programs voted by the legislature. The governor vetoed the entire $805 million general-fund appropriation bill, forcing the legislature to go into special session on September 9 to fund noneducational activities of state government. Action came quickly; the legislature passed an $815 million general-fund budget on September 13.

On September 18 a Montgomery county circuit judge, and then on October 2 the state supreme court, ruled that the governor's efforts to employ the line-item veto after the legislature had gone out of session was unconstitutional. However, on the very first day of the fiscal year, October 1, Governor Hunt stated that revenue deficiencies combined with the state's balanced-budget requirements demanded a 6% across-the-board reduction in all state educational appropriations. This would mean $120 million more in cuts than contained in the line-item vetoes, which had succumbed to judicial challenges. On October 10, in the face of continuing financial pessimism, the state school board urged the 129 local school systems to delay the school year by one month in 1992.

The Governor's Travels. The year 1991, Governor Hunt's fifth one in office, was his most controversial. On September 20 the Alabama Ethics Commission recommended to Attorney General Jimmy Evans, a Democrat, that the governor be prosecuted because there was "probable cause" that Hunt, a Primitive Baptist minister, had broken state law by using state planes 18 times to travel to churches in and out of state in which he had preached and had received some $10,000 in offerings. While Hunt did give the state a check for a smaller amount of money, on September 26 he filed suit in federal court to claim that the legislature could not limit the executive, as it had sought to do in the 1973 ethics act. At year's end no action had been taken on the alleged violations of the ethics law. October polls showed that only 31% of those surveyed rated the governor's performance good or excellent.

ALABAMA • Information Highlights

Area: 51,705 sq mi (133 915 km²).
Population (1990 census): 4,040,587.
Chief Cities (1990 census): Montgomery, the capital, 187,106; Birmingham, 265,968; Mobile, 196,278; Huntsville, 159,789.
Government (1991): *Chief officers*—governor, Guy Hunt (R); lt. gov. Jim Folsom, Jr. (D). *Legislature*—Senate, 35 members; House of Representatives, 105 members.
State Finances (fiscal year 1990): *Revenue*, $9,041,000,000; *expenditure*, $8,108,000,000.
Personal Income (1990): $60,776,000,000; per capita, $15,021.
Labor Force (June 1991): *Civilian labor force*, 1,899,800; *unemployed*, 149,000 (7.8% of total force).
Education: *Enrollment* (fall 1989)—public elementary schools, 525,730; public secondary, 197,613; colleges and universities, 208,562. *Public school expenditures* (1989), $2,188,020,000.

Talladega Prison Uprising. On August 21, 121 Cuban inmates at the Talladega Federal Correctional Institute took ten hostages to protest plans to send some of them back to Cuba. The incident lasted nine days, ending on August 30 when Federal Bureau of Investigation (FBI) SWAT teams stormed the facility and rescued the hostages. No lives were lost.

WILLIAM H. STEWART
The University of Alabama

ALASKA

The year 1991 proved to be tumultuous for Alaska in terms of politics, economics, and social matters.

Government Affairs. Independent Gov. Walter Hickel, who first was elected to that office in 1966 on the Republican ticket but resigned to become the U.S. secretary of the interior (1969–70), began his second term in January 1991. His first year in office was marked by conflict and controversy over his administration's approaches to almost all program and policy areas. The governor emphasized the need for several large projects, including the proposed water pipeline from

Alaska to California, the construction of a second trans-Alaska pipeline running the length of the state to enable the export of Prudhoe Bay natural gas, the extension of the Alaska Railroad from interior Alaska to the Northwest coast/Bering Sea region, the construction and upgrading of roads to isolated regions and communities, and development of space-age technology to beam power from urban to rural areas in the state.

At the same time, he called for cuts in the state operating budget of up to 5% per year for the next four years, based upon executive-branch estimates of projected revenues available over that period of time. Gubernatorial vetoes resulted in the deletion of several million dollars from the fiscal year 1992 budget, with funding for local governments and the university system particularly hard hit.

Management of hunting on all federal land in Alaska (60% of the state) remained in the hands of federal agencies, given the inability of two task forces appointed by the governor to reach agreement on a plan which would provide for a rural "subsistence" priority in cases where resources were scarce, as is required by the Alaska National Interest Lands Conservation Act (ANILCA) of 1981. In a related issue, Governor Hickel issued Administrative Order No. 125, stating that "Alaska is one country, one people," thereby revoking an order by the previous administration that had recognized Alaska Native villages as tribal governments in some cases.

Recall Movement. A movement to recall Governor Hickel and Lt. Gov. Jack Coghill was initiated by elements of the Alaska Independence Party (AIP). Backers of the recall movement ranged from active AIP members to members of the general public and well-organized interest groups. Coming in the midst of the recall movement were conflict-of-interest charges brought against Hickel relating to stock that he held in a company that would benefit from the natural-gas pipeline promoted by the governor. Hickel, accused of seven violations of the state's ethics law, reached a December settlement, agreeing to give up his stock.

© Mark Kelley/NYT Pictures

In 1991, Walter J. Hickel, 72, returned for a second stint as governor of Alaska, this time as an Independent. Economic and development issues were his prime concerns.

Another controversy was the drive by the state to open the Arctic National Wildlife Refuge for oil development. Concerns ranged from those focused on the amount of revenues available to the state to those of conservationists about maintaining the integrity of the refuge. In addition, two attempts by the governor's office to settle the state's federal-court suit over the 1989 Prince William Sound *Exxon Valdez* oil spill prior to the date of trial caused problems for Hickel. A settlement was approved in early October. Included in the terms were that the Exxon Corporation pay $1.025 billion in fines and restitution payments through 2001 and that native Alaskans and other private litigants be guaranteed the right to bring separate suits.

Economy. Alaska's economy, like that of most other areas in the United States, cooled off considerably during 1991. Unemployment figures were once again on the rise, partially due to the completion in August of cleanup work on the *Exxon Valdez* oil spill by the industry and the Coast Guard. Extremely low prices paid by processors for salmon made the commercial-fishing season in most areas an official disaster, further exacerbated by strikes by some fishermen. Sport fishing and the related tourist industry in the South Central and Kenai Peninsula regions were affected adversely by the Alaska Board of Fisheries' closures of rivers during major spring and summer fish-spawning runs. Finally, the timber industry in southeast Alaska remained depressed as a consequence of both market conditions and environmental concerns.

CARL E. SHEPRO, *University of Alaska*

ALASKA • Information Highlights

Area: 591,004 sq mi (1 530 700 km²).
Population (1990 census): 550,043.
Chief Cities (1990 census): Juneau, the capital, 26,751; Anchorage, 226,338; Fairbanks, 30,843; Sitka, 8,588.
Government (1991): *Chief Officers*—governor, Walter J. Hickel (I); lt. gov., John B. Coghill (I). *Legislature*—Senate, 20 members; House of Representatives, 40 members.
State Finances (fiscal year 1990): *Revenue,* $5,500,000,000; *expenditure,* $4,688,000,000.
Personal Income (1990): $11,956,000,000; per capita, $21,688.
Labor Force (June 1991): *Civilian labor force,* 264,600; *unemployed,* 20,600 (7.8% of total force).
Education: *Enrollment* (fall 1989)—public elementary schools, 81,698; public secondary, 27,582; colleges and universities, 28,627. *Public school expenditures* (1989), $739,020,000.

ALBANIA

During 1991 the Albanian government under President Ramiz Alia continued its efforts to cope with the demand for change unleashed by the collapse of the Communist system in Eastern Europe; meanwhile, thousands of Albanians registered their discontent with the economic situation by fleeing the country, and relations with Yugoslavia worsened.

Emigration. As the regime began to liberalize and open up the country to outside influence, increasing numbers of citizens clamored to leave Albania. In January more than 11,000 Albanians, many of them ethnic Greeks, left southern Albania to seek refuge in Greece. About 7,000 were sent back across the border by Greek officials. Beginning in March huge numbers of people commandeered boats in the ports of Durres and Vlora to take them across the Strait of Otranto to Italy, where more than 20,000 were given asylum. A second exodus by sea occurred in August, but this time the refugees were turned back by Italian authorities.

Political Developments. The refugee crisis and growing public protests by students and workers reflected and intensified power struggles within the ruling Albanian Workers' (Communist) Party between reformist and Stalinist factions. Alia's reformist wing gained the upper hand in the early part of the year, and the People's Assembly agreed to hold the country's first multiparty parliamentary elections since World War II. The elections were scheduled for March 31, and newly emerging non-Communist political parties were allowed to participate. In the polling, the Communists ran strongly in the rural areas, winning 68% of the vote and 169 of the seats in the 250-seat legislature. The Democratic Party—the main opposition group, led by cardiology professor Sali Berisha—did well in the cities but came in second with 30% of the vote and 75 seats in the legislature. Ramiz Alia, running in a Tiranë constituency, lost his seat, but was reelected by parliament to the presidency in April.

The Communists won a majority because they held a clear advantage in terms of funds, infrastructure, and access to the mass media, in comparison to the immature democratic parties. There were also charges of voter intimidation in the countryside and other election irregularities. Four people were shot dead by the police during demonstrations protesting the election results. Sustained public pressure and a general strike among industrial workers forced the government to resign in June and agree to a power-sharing arrangement with the Democrats.

The new coalition that took office on June 12 included 12 Communists—among them Ylli

Albania's first multiparty parliamentary elections since World War II were held March 31, 1991. The Communists did well in the rural areas, such as the one below, *and the Democratic Party, the main opposition, ran strong in the cities.*

© Chris Niedenthal/"Time" Magazine

Bufi, the new prime minister—and seven ministers from the Democratic Party. This coalition government made some headway in calming political discontent, and began to accelerate the reform program. Various branches of government were restructured, and the authorities began to depoliticize the judiciary, police, army, and diplomatic corps. Amid disclosures of widespread corruption by the previous regime, investigations were begun against several high-ranking officials. One of these was Nexhmije Hoxha, widow of Enver Hoxha, the Communist dictator who ruled Albania from 1944 until his death in 1985. Mrs. Hoxha is an ardent Stalinist and leader of a hard-line Communist Party faction. The party renamed itself the Socialist Party and began the process of internal democratization. Political pluralism continued to develop, and 15 new parties were registered by the fall of 1991 in preparation for new general elections scheduled for the spring of 1992.

The Economy. Despite Albania's political progress, the economic situation remained chaotic. The country's dilapidated infrastructure was crumbling, food output slumped in the collective farms, and industrial production fell due to shortages of raw materials and disarray in management. Spontaneous and poorly planned land-reform programs exacerbated the chaos and confusion in the agricultural sector. The flight of refugees to Italy during the summer was triggered largely by deteriorating economic conditions and severe food shortages. This crisis prompted several Western countries to begin furnishing much-needed humanitarian aid to the Albanian people. Albania urgently needed to import food during the 1991–92 winter to help feed its population, the poorest in Europe.

The People's Assembly had yet to enact a comprehensive privatization program, while guarantees of employment and high wages to forestall further worker unrest seriously depleted the state budget. The passage of a viable market-reform program remained hamstrung by continuing tensions in both the government and parliament between reform socialists and liberal democrats, as well by fears of renewed social turmoil.

ALBANIA • Information Highlights

Official Name: People's Socialist Republic of Albania.
Location: Southern Europe, Balkan peninsula.
Area: 11,100 sq mi (28 750 km^2).
Population (mid-1991 est.): 3,300,000.
Chief City (mid-1987): Tiranë, the capital, 225,700.
Government: *Head of state,* Ramiz Alia, president (took office November 1982). *Head of government,* Ylli Bufi, prime minister (took office June 12, 1991). *Legislature* (unicameral)—People's Assembly, 250 members.
Gross National Product (1989 est. U.S.$): $3,800,000,000.

Foreign Affairs. The Albanian government moved swiftly to reestablish diplomatic ties with all Western countries, including the United States. The latter effort was capped by the visit of Secretary of State James Baker to Tiranë in June. Albania also joined the Conference on Security and Cooperation in Europe (CSCE), obtained International Monetary Fund (IMF) status, and hosted a conference of Balkan leaders in Tiranë. But continuing legal impediments and the absence of a stable business climate discouraged foreign investment.

Albania's most pressing foreign-policy problem was a dispute with the neighboring country of Yugoslavia, which was torn apart by civil war in 1991. Relations with the Serbian-dominated Yugoslav government suffered a major setback because of Serbia's conflicts with the 2 million ethnic Albanians that form the majority of the population in its province of Kosovo.

In September, while Serbia was engaged in a major armed conflict with Croatia, Kosovo's leaders held a referendum on the question of turning their province into an independent republic. The result was an overwhelming victory for the pro-independence forces. The Albanian government became more outspoken on the Kosovo issue, and in October the Albanian parliament formally recognized the independence of Kosovo. This moved Serbia to charge Tiranë with interfering in Yugoslavia's internal affairs. As the war in Yugoslavia intensified, fears grew that the fighting might spread to Kosovo. If this were to happen, it would be difficult for Albania to avoid involvement, since its political leaders probably would feel bound to offer aid and protection to their fellow Albanians across the border.

JANUSZ BUGAJSKI
Associate Director of East European Studies
Center for Strategic and International Studies

ALBERTA

Alberta remained economically and politically stable in 1991. Although behind opposition parties in popularity polls, Progressive Conservative Premier Don Getty had until 1993 to hold a provincial election.

Budget. Provincial Treasurer Dick Johnston unveiled a C$12.6 billion budget of widespread tax increases and user fees, but promised it would be balanced, with a surplus of C$33.4 million. The budget slashed 600 government jobs and eliminated a variety of subsidies and grants. Critics attacked the government for planning to transfer C$225 million in lottery revenues to general revenues in order to balance the budget, since lottery revenues were earmarked to fund culture, amateur sports, and hospitals. In September there were reports that the government already had overspent the budget by C$22 million and planned to sell off C$200 million in assets in order to battle rising costs. The accumulated provincial deficit was estimated at C$11 billion.

Oil Industry. Although the oil industry, given a temporary boost by the Persian Gulf war, continued to suffer severe profit declines and sharp staff cuts in 1991, the federal government won praise for announcing the relocation of the National Energy Board to Calgary from Ottawa. The board is the federal regulatory body for oil and gas development.

The federal government started to privatize its Calgary-based national oil company, Petro-Canada, by selling off 19.5% of the 16-year-old company. This long had been a demand of the Alberta oil industry, which had opposed the creation of Petro-Canada as unnecessary. The initial public offering brought in C$540 million. However, within weeks investors learned that in the first six months of 1991 prior to the share offering the company had lost C$149 million, and had considerable long- and short-term debt. Some analysts suggested Petro-Canada, which cost C$6 billion to create, now might have assets worth only C$3 billion. Others believed the company was viable and a good long-term investment.

Controversial Laws. Regulations were passed to allow cocktail lounges and bars to serve liquor on Sundays without the provision that customers also order a meal, and to permit wine stores in resort communities to open on Sundays. The laws received heavy criticism from temperance and church groups.

The sale of domestically raised game-farm elk for human consumption was legalized. The move was opposed by animal-rights activists, and became more controversial when it was discovered there was bovine tuberculosis in many herds. Some experts believed perhaps half of Alberta's 4,200 domestically raised elk might have to be culled to halt the disease's spread.

ALBERTA • Information Highlights

Area: 255,286 sq mi (661 190 km²).
Population (September 1991): 2,525,200.
Chief Cities (1986 census): Edmonton, the capital, 573,982; Calgary, 636,104; Lethbridge, 58,841.
Government (1991): *Chief Officers*—lt. gov., Gordon Towers; premier, Don Getty (Progressive Conservative). *Legislature*—Legislative Assembly, 79 members.
Provincial Finances (1991–92 fiscal year budget): *Revenues,* $12,633,000,000; *expenditures,* $12,600,000,000.
Personal Income (average weekly earnings, July 1991): $546.47.
Labor Force (September 1991, seasonally adjusted): *Employed* workers, 15 years of age and over, 1,250,000; *Unemployed,* 8.0%.
Education (1991–92): *Enrollment*—elementary and secondary schools, 523,900 pupils; postsecondary—universities, 49,600; community colleges, 28,000.
(All monetary figures are in Canadian dollars.)

Political Scandal. The Progressive Conservative government came under attack in August when it was revealed that the chairman of the province's electoral boundaries commission had resigned in June after the province refused to give him more funds to continue his work of redrawing constituencies' sizes. Although Judge Charles J. Virtue had given his resignation to Premier Getty, Getty kept the move secret until it leaked out. Critics charged Getty was trying to stifle attempts toward a fair boundaries revision plan, and that the government wanted fewer seats in urban high-density ridings where it was generally unpopular and more seats in low-density rural ridings.

Prominent Deaths. One of Alberta's most prominent entrepreneurs, Dr. Charles Allard, 71, died in August. Allard began professional life as a surgeon, then built up a huge real-estate and communications empire. Canada's first elected senator, Stan Waters, died in October. The Calgary businessman entered politics when Alberta made a revolutionary move of holding an election to fill a vacant Alberta seat in the federal institution.

PAUL JACKSON, *"The Calgary Sun"*

ALGERIA

The prospect of Algeria's first multiparty national legislative elections strained the nation's political institutions to the limit. In June 1991, President Chadli Benjedid declared a state of siege under which the army proceeded to arrest the most prominent leaders of the Islamic Salvation Front (FIS). In the first round of voting in December, however, the FIS—advocating an Islamic republic—won the most legislative seats.

Politics. Having pledged in July 1990 to hold elections for the National People's Assembly (APN) early in 1991, the president subsequently adjusted the timetable by fixing the June date, which allowed his own party, the National Liberation Front (FLN), more time to prepare its electoral strategy. Prime Minister Mouloud Hamrouche chose the classic tactic of gerrymandering. A new electoral bill submitted to the parliament increased the number of seats from 295 to 542, creating a disproportionate number of districts in the sparsely populated southern regions, the only part of the country in which the FLN had prevailed in the local elections of June 1990. As the assembly, elected under the single-party system in 1987, was controlled completely by the FLN, the law passed easily.

The FIS vehemently denounced this maneuver. Late in May it called a general strike and Islamist militants occupied parts of Algiers, insisting that the law be abrogated and that early presidential elections be scheduled as well. Violence flared when the government

© Hocine Zaourar/Sipa

The Algerian government responded to demonstrations by the fundamentalist Islamic Salvation Front, left, *by declaring a state of emergency and imposing a curfew in June 1991.*

took measures to clear the streets. Declaring martial law on June 5, Benjedid ordered the military to restore order. Before carrying out the order, Minister of Defense Gen. Khaled Nezzar insisted that Hamrouche be dismissed and that presidential elections be promised. On June 7, Sid Ahmed Ghozali, who was foreign minister in the Hamrouche government, was named prime minister. He pledged to organize "free and clean" elections sometime in 1991.

Despite Ghozali's pledge, the climate of agitation persisted. As further clashes occurred, Islamist firebrand Ali Belhadj urged his followers to stock weapons for the defense of Islamic values. On the night of June 30 the army surrounded FIS headquarters and arrested party leaders Belhadj and Abassi Madani; some 750 other party activists were taken into custody elsewhere. Martial law was lifted at the end of September, but the military continued to hold Madani and Belhadj on charges of inciting rebellion.

ALGERIA • Information Highlights

Official Name: Democratic and Popular Republic of Algeria.
Location: North Africa.
Area: 919,591 sq mi (2 381 740 km²).
Population (mid-1991 est.): 26,000,000.
Chief Cities (1987 census): Algiers, the capital, 1,507,241; Oran, 628,558; Constantine, 440,842.
Government: *Head of state,* Chadli Benjedid, president (took office Feb. 1979). *Head of government,* Sid Ahmed Ghozali, prime minister (appointed June 7, 1991).
Monetary Unit: Dinar (18.385 dinars equal U.S.$1, June 1991).
Gross Domestic Product (1988 est. U.S.$): $54,100,000,000.
Foreign Trade (1988 U.S.$): *Imports,* $7,396,000,000; *exports,* $8,164,000,000.

Prime Minister Ghozali undertook to revise the election law, and after much debate the APN defined 430 constituencies. As the election campaign resumed, Ghozali named Maj. Gen. Larbi Belkheir as minister of the interior. The elections, held in December, were not decisive; thus a second round of voting (scheduled for January 16) was required. Leading after the first round was the FIS with 189 seats. The Socialists, in second place, gained 20 seats, and the ruling FLN had 16 seats.

Diplomacy and Economy. Facing a public opinion that was heavily pro Iraq during the Persian Gulf crisis, Benjedid sought to negotiate an Iraqi withdrawal from Kuwait virtually up to the commencement of hostilities. After the war, Algeria returned its focus to the unresolved Palestinian issue, serving as the site for a critical session of the Palestine National Council in September.

Saharan affairs commanded attention as tensions between Mali's government and its Tuareg population caused refugee problems in southern Algeria, and the ever-delicate Western Saharan dispute moved into a new phase with the arrival of the first members of a United Nations monitoring group there.

Regionally, the Union of the Arab Maghreb located its parliament in Algiers while the secretariat was lodged in Morocco under a Tunisian secretary-general. Debt remained a strain on the economy, prompting Ghozali to propose that Algeria sell certain oil rights to foreign companies—a heretical proposition in a country that was a leader in nationalizing its oil industry two decades earlier. Financial pressures also caused the government to devalue the dinar by 22% on September 30.

ROBERT MORTIMER, *Haverford College*

ANTHROPOLOGY

In 1991, anthropologists debated whether Neanderthals once lived alongside modern humans in the Middle East; new fossils shed light on the earliest known members of the human evolutionary family; and a fossil jaw yielded clues to the only known ancient ape in southern Africa. The mummified remains of a 4,600-year-old man were found in the Tyrolean Alps.

Middle Eastern Neanderthals. Researchers presented starkly opposing views on the prehistoric presence of Neanderthals in the Middle East. Some held to the more accepted notion that Neanderthals and anatomically modern humans inhabited neighboring Israeli caves from around 100,000 to 40,000 years ago. But others argued that fossils unearthed in the caves represent a single population of early or formative modern humans.

Anthropologists generally agree that Neanderthals lived in Europe from about 130,000 to 35,000 years ago. "Classic" European Neanderthals had thick, heavy bones, sloping foreheads, bulging brows, and projecting jaws holding peg-like front teeth. During the past 50 years, skeletal remains uncovered in several Israeli caves usually have been assumed to represent Neanderthals at some of the sites and modern humans at others.

The Israeli fossils indeed represent two species, Neanderthals and modern humans, reported Yoel Rak of Tel Aviv University. Middle Eastern Neanderthals had skulls much like those of European Neanderthals, he contended, and a Neanderthal pelvis found in Israel displays a markedly different shape than those of modern humans excavated at nearby sites.

But Baruch Arensburg, also of Tel Aviv University, responded that the entire Israeli fossil collection fits into one big, anatomically diverse population of early modern humans. And Milford H. Wolpoff of the University of Michigan suggested that the fossils show the racial differences of a single species of "archaic" humans.

***Afarensis* Fossils.** Scientists announced the discovery of fossils at an Ethiopian site that expand the anatomical diversity of the earliest known species in the human evolutionary family. "Lucy," a partial skeleton found at the same site in 1974, is the best-known member of the more than 3-million-year-old species, known as *Australopithecus afarensis* by anthropologists.

A team led by Donald C. Johanson, William H. Kimbel, and Robert C. Walter of the Institute of Human Origins in Berkeley, CA, found 18 pieces of fossilized bone from 15 *A. afarensis* individuals. Most of the specimens are tooth and jaw fragments that closely resemble previous finds, but three fossils shed new light on the anatomy of Lucy's species. An upper jaw contained much shallower roots for the front teeth than previously observed in *A. afarensis*; a lower jaw with some teeth still in place displayed primitive features similar to those of extinct apes that lived in Africa more than 8 million years ago; and an upper right arm bone preserved two large grooves that anchored powerful shoulder muscles used for hoisting the body with the arms.

Although the new arm fossil indicates that Lucy and her kin spent some of their time in the trees, other skeletal evidence shows they were on the way to a full-time upright stance, Johanson said.

Ancient Ape. A team of fossil hunters working in Namibia discovered part of a jaw that may have belonged to one of the last common ancestors of modern African apes and the human evolutionary family. The find, assigned a preliminary age of 10 million to 15 million years, represents the first ancient ape-like creature found in southern Africa, according to expedition director Glenn C. Conroy of Washington University in St. Louis.

On Sept. 19, 1991, German mountain climbers sighted the frozen corpse of a 4,600-year-old man in the Tyrolean Alps. Dating from the Neolithic Period, it is the oldest naturally preserved corpse ever found.

The new fossil, a lower right jaw, contains several cheek teeth and largely intact roots for a canine and other teeth at the front of the mouth. As with early species in the human evolutionary family, the ancient ape apparently had a vertically aligned face without protruding jaws, small front teeth, and a relatively short canine tooth, Conroy asserted. But the wisdom teeth at the back of the mouth probably erupted soon after the other cheek teeth, a pattern seen in living apes.

Conroy and his coworkers hope to date the Namibian fossil more accurately and, using comparisons with ancient ape fossils from eastern Africa, place it within a genus (a group of related species) and species.

BRUCE BOWER, *"Science News"*

ARCHAEOLOGY

The discovery of extensive catacombs built by Mogollon Indians in Arizona some 800 years ago, the excavation of more than 300 additional terra-cotta statues of ancient warriors in China, and the finding that wine existed much earlier than previously believed were among 1991 highlights in archaeology.

Eastern Hemisphere

Terra-cotta Army. Chinese archaeologists reported the excavation of more than 300 terra-cotta statues of ancient warriors—with at least 10,000 statues still buried—near the tomb of an emperor who died in 144 B.C.. In 1974 a trove of 7,000 life-sized terra-cotta warriors turned up in the same region.

The new army, discovered during construction of a highway to the site of the 1974 find, lies within 24 vaults that cover an area the size of about 12 soccer fields. The statues portray naked men with no arms who stand about 20 inches (51 cm) high. Their clothes apparently disintegrated over time, and the arms may have been fashioned of wood that also disintegrated. Each statue has a carefully sculpted face with a distinctive expression. Weapons of copper and iron, arrowheads, spears, swords, coins, and other artifacts surround the terra-cotta soldiers.

Stone-Age Greeks. Boston University archaeologists searching an ancient lake bed in Greece uncovered a flint hand-ax assigned a preliminary age of between 200,000 and 400,000 years old. The 9-inch (23-cm)-long artifact, which features two sharp edges converging to a point at one end, resembles similar implements found at western European and African sites spanning the period from 1.6 million to 200,000 years ago. A species of "archaic" modern humans may have fashioned the Greek hand-ax, according to Curtis Runnels, who first noticed the specimen in the lake bed. The same species first may have settled Europe, he says. However, many archaeologists suspect an earlier human ancestor, *Homo erectus*, gained first entry to Europe.

Early Wine Makers. Chemical evidence from ancient jars indicated that wine existed about 5,500 years ago, several hundred years earlier than scientists previously thought. Analysis of reddish stains on jars excavated at an Iranian site yielded the same chemical composition as a stain in an Egyptian vessel known to have contained wine. Tartaric acid, a chemical abundant only in grapes, appears in both the Egyptian and Iranian jars.

The Iranian finds include 7- and 14-gallon (26.5-liter and 53-liter) containers with long, narrow necks and a body shape that suggests they once stored liquids while resting on their sides, just as wine is stored today.

Ancient Harbor. Underwater exploration at the ancient port city of Caesaria in Israel indicated that early engineers ingeniously enlisted help from the sea in building the first modern harbor 2,000 years ago. Large stone and concrete blocks were laid out in checkerboard fashion during construction of two massive walls used to protect the harbor from incoming waves. Natural sea action quickly filled in the adjacent spaces between blocks with sand, which workers then capped with rubble, concrete, and paving stones to form continuous sea walls. The 100-acre (40-ha) harbor was the world's first port constructed in the open sea without the aid of natural bays, islands, or peninsulas. Construction on the harbor began in 20 B.C. and lasted nearly ten years.

Heroic Monument. A research team reported the unexpected discovery in Greece of a long-lost inscribed monument described in a 1st-century A.D. document written by the Greek historian Plutarch. The monument, found atop a hill near Plutarch's hometown of Chaironeia, clearly establishes the location of a battle between the Roman army occupying Greece and invaders from the Black Sea area in 86 B.C. Classical scholars had proposed several hills around Chaironeia as possible battle sites based on Plutarch's writings.

The 3-ft (.9-m)-high, 1-ft (.3-m)-wide marble monument lay amid a pile of rubble. It contains the names of two Chaironeia townsmen who helped the Romans thwart the invaders and the word *aristis*, which means "heroes" in Greek.

Early Cyprus Settlers. A collapsed rock shelter on Cyprus yielded evidence that people inhabited the site at least 10,000 years ago, about two millennia earlier than any other documented human occupation on the Mediterranean island. Stone artifacts made by humans turned up among the bones of extinct animals, including dwarf elephants and pygmy hippopotamuses, suggesting that early colonizers may have helped wipe out the creatures through hunting. Stone artifacts uncovered at the rock shelter include chisels and thumbnail-sized scrapers. Excavators also found beads fashioned from stone and shells. Radiocarbon dates for sediments containing these artifacts cluster around 10,000 years of age.

Western Hemisphere

Maya Tomb. An archaeological team working beneath the ruins of a pyramid in Dos Pilas, the capital of an ancient Maya city-state in what is now Guatemala, found the tomb and remains of an 8th-century A.D king. The tomb contained the skeleton of an adult male, as well as a jade headdress, conch and pearl, obsidian blades probably used in bloodletting rituals and ceramics inscribed with hieroglyphics.

Although reasons for the demise of classic Maya civilization by 900 A.D. remain unclear, archaeologists who found the tomb said its discovery, combined with the presence of large fortifications at Dos Pilas, suggests that the buried ruler participated in devastating wars between Maya states that hastened the collapse of royal power and urban centers.

Maya Water Control. The construction of extensive reservoirs apparently spurred the growth of classic-period urban centers in the Maya lowlands between 250 A.D. and 900 A.D., two archaeologists reported. The scientists reconstructed the reservoir system of the ancient Maya city of Tikal using previously published maps of the site. To provide water during annual four-month droughts, Tikal's residents constructed at least ten central reservoirs fed by clay-lined drainage ditches. Smaller reservoirs stored water for individual households. Reliable water storage attracted as many as 80,000 people to Tikal and influenced the emergence of powerful kings at most lowland Maya cities, the archaeologists argued.

Early Cotton Farmers. Excavations at one of the earliest major settlements in the New World indicated that it was geared solely toward cotton production, rather than the grain cultivation practiced by early civilizations in Europe and Asia. Inhabitants of the coastal Peruvian site, founded around 3,800 years ago and covering more than 125 acres (50 ha), did not cultivate grain for food. Instead, they apparently traded cotton products for food from inland communities and also gathered "fast foods" such as anchovies, mussels, clams, and wild plants. Although huge stone structures dot the Peruvian center, investigators found no evidence of a central ruler or political bureaucracy.

Indian Tombs. Archaeologists announced the discovery of extensive catacombs—underground cemeteries with galleries for tombs—built by the Mogollon Indians around 800 years ago in what is now eastern Arizona. The catacombs run beneath a large pueblo and ceremonial room built on a terrace cut into a massive

© David McIntyre/NYT Pictures

Archaeologist Christopher Adams inspects the pre-Columbian burial caverns of the Mogollon Indians in Arizona. The find was expected to shed light on a vanished people.

cliff. The Mogollons apparently constructed vaulted chambers as large as 20 ft (6 m) high and 100 ft (30 m) long that hold the tombs within a natural underground network of tunnels. The find may shed light on the enigmatic culture of the Mogollons, who disappeared suddenly in 1400 A.D.

Slum Remains. The foundations of at least four structures from the "Five Points" slum, a center of crime, poverty, and violence in New York City for much of the 19th century, turned up during an archaeological excavation in lower Manhattan. The foundations outline the basements of former slum buildings where residents lived packed together in squalid apartments. A brick fireplace remains in one wall, along with an iron crane used to hang cooking pots over the open flames. Five drainpipes jut out of another section where occupants probably dumped their liquid wastes. Most of the Five Points area was razed at the beginning of the 20th century to make way for government buildings and a city park.

Salvadoran Village. Ongoing excavations of a village in El Salvador buried by volcanic ash 1,400 years ago yielded the remains of carefully cultivated household gardens and a community sauna. The gardens include the remains of a type of cassava, corn, flowers, and cacti that provided fiber to make rope and twine. A 10-sq-ft (.9-m^2), earthen-domed building, with a central kiln surrounded by a rectangular adobe bench, probably served as a sauna, and resembles community saunas still used by Maya people living in the same region. The ancient villagers had cultural links to both the Maya and Lenca societies, but their architecture reflects a greater Maya influence, according to excavators.

BRUCE BOWER, *"Science News"*

ARCHITECTURE

The 1991 Honor Awards from the American Institute of Architects (AIA) demonstrated the wide variety of design directions that characterized current practice. "Our choices reflect the particular spirit of our time, its range and its quality," said jury chairman Robert Venturi, who himself won the prestigious Pritzker Architectural Prize for a quarter century of influence on the profession—mostly through a highly individualistic design idiom of his own. (*See also* BIOGRAPHY.)

The New Eclecticism. AIA honor-award choices ranged from the caricature of a turn-of-the-century office building complete with a massive cornice made from a overhanging roof and a forest of projecting stick-like supports (360 Newbury Street, Boston, designed by Frank O. Gehry & Associates) to a revival of pure Classicism (Rice Building, Art Institute of Chicago, by Hammond Beeby and Babka) to the crisp lines of Modernism (Meyerson Symphony Center, Dallas, by Pei Cobb Freed & Partners—the architects of the massive Neoclassical Federal Triangle Project in Washington, DC, which after many delays finally was moving ahead). Two award recipients (Stanley Tigerman's Fukuoka Mixed Use Apartment Building and Eisenman Architects'—with K Architects and Associates—Koizumi Sangyo Building, both in Japan) might have been labeled Deconstructivist, a style in which the parts appear to be disjointed and exploding outward, although this style had been labeled stillborn by its many critics when it first appeared.

Other projects receiving the AIA award evidenced more popular vernacular styles, such as a shingle-style house which fit right in with its turn-of-the-century neighbors in East Hampton, NY, by Cooper Robertson & Partners; and several West-Indies-style houses in Seaside, FL, by Scott Merrill Architect. Charleston Cottages in Charleston, SC, by Chris Schmitt & Associates, Inc., followed local custom by turning their gable ends to the street; front doors lead onto side porches. Robert A. M. Stern Associates' Courtyard Houses at Wood Duck Island in Vero Beach, FL, with red-tile roofs and stucco walls, followed another local tradition, the Spanish Revival. Recognizing the many directions that architectural design was taking, Paul Sachner, the executive editor of *Architectural Record*—which celebrated its 100th anniversary in 1991—stated: "Our goal is a deliberately eclectic magazine."

Regional Styles. As revealed by the AIA awards, the search for regional styles often meant relying on local tradition. Among the more conspicuous examples of regional styles was the Church of the Nativity outside San Diego, designed by Charles Moore of Moore Ruble Yudell together with The Austin Hansen Group. (Moore was the recipient of the AIA's 1991 Gold Medal.) The church resembles a Spanish colonial mission around a traditional courtyard. Less obviously derivative but fitting in with a surrounding 1930s neo-Gothic campus

U.S. architect Robert Venturi was awarded the 1991 Pritzker Architectural Prize for expanding and redefining "the limits of the art of architecture in this century." Venturi's works include the Gordon Wu Hall, Butler College, at Princeton University, right.

were the vertical lines of the 15-story, limestone-clad Northwestern University medical-research tower by Perkins & Will, Architects in Chicago.

An architect with one of the longest careers of searching for regional styles in the United States is Antoine Predock. Active primarily in the Southwest, producing muscular buildings reminiscent of the adobe tradition, he was commissioned in 1991 to design two buildings for different University of California campuses.

Perhaps the example of historic influences on design of the most dubious merit was an announced 70,000-sq-ft (6 500-m^2) "golf-park" clubhouse on Maui, HI, to be synthesized from designs for three unbuilt houses, including that of Marilyn Monroe and Arthur Miller, by Frank Lloyd Wright.

Americans Abroad. The demand for U.S. architectural services overseas was evidenced by the announcement or completion of several massive new projects. Work continued on the $148 million aquarium and shopping center in Osaka, Japan, designed by Cambridge Seven Associates of Boston in a style that might be called modified Modernism. Although the building follows its rectilinear unadorned predecessors of the 1960s and 1970s, it is enlivened by brightly colored Cubist elements. Gunnar Birkets and Associates unveiled plans for four major projects: a U.S. Embassy in Caracas, Venezuela; an 865,700-sq-ft (80 423-m^2) mixed-use building in Florence, Italy; a complex including a high-rise for the University of Turin, Italy; and the national library in Riga, Latvia.

U.S. architects, beset by depressed construction volume at home, were heartened by the enormity of rebuilding plans for Kuwait following heavy damage in the Persian Gulf war. Cost estimates ran as high as $100 billion, and the lion's share of design and construction commissions was expected to go to U.S. firms. The rebuilding of Kuwait City was compared to rebuilding a city the size of Phoenix, AZ. Taiwan announced an even more ambitious $300 billion development plan, although it was far less certain that U.S. architects would be favored.

Landmarks and Restoration. Challenges to local landmark preservation laws (which had seemed a past issue after a suit to overturn the designation of Grand Central Station in New York City was defeated by the U.S. Supreme Court) became front-page news again after Washington's Supreme Court overturned the designation of Covenant Church in Seattle. The court ruled that a local landmark ordinance could not be applied to a church building. The U.S. Supreme Court instructed Washington's high court to reconsider the ruling. Indeed, churches recently had posed the most visible threat, beginning with New York City's St. Bartholomew's suit, started several years earlier. The Supreme Court refused the case, in which St. Bartholomew's had challenged the city's landmark preservation law, without comment. The case against the church was based on the contention that designation infringed on 1st Amendment rights to free pursuit of religion.

But churches were not alone. The Pennsylvania Supreme Court removed designation of a theater in 1991 after the owners claimed they were being deprived of their property rights. A more constructive solution to the churches' problems was found by the landmarked St. Jean Baptiste in New York City, which managed to sell its unused air rights to the developer of a new adjacent building.

New restoration projects included a $149 million program for the Texas state capitol, which included a 600,000-sq-ft (55 740-m^2) extension underground to avoid visual competition with the original 1886 structure. Project architects were 3D/I for the extension and Ford, Powell, and Carson for the restoration. Notter Finegold + Alexander completed the restoration of the 1905 Berkeley Building in Boston, a daring combination for the time of large plate-glass windows and elaborate terracotta, which had, like many older commercial buildings, been defaced badly in later years. One of the largest rebirths was that of a 1.9-million-sq-ft (176 510-m^2) 1930s warehouse in Jersey City, NJ, which was remodeled as part of the first phase of Harborside Financial Center by architects Beyer Blinder Belle. Another reuse of an industrial building was an aging aircraft hangar which became USAir's terminal at Washington National Airport through redesign by Giuliani Associates.

Growing Social Concern. Changing demographics within the profession promised heightened activism. Some 30% of students in architectural schools were women and 20%, minorities. These groups had been missing conspicuously in the field, but, even so, architects had been very vocal on a wide range of topics ranging from preserving historic structures, to raising government and private-sector monies for housing the poor and homeless, to boycotting timber from South American forests—which were being depleted at an alarming rate. Now even louder voices could be expected as new groups with deeper social concerns graduated and entered practice.

New Legal Protections. As a result of the U.S. entry into the Berne Copyright Convention with its stringent provisions long in place in Europe, architects finally got federal protection of their designs. Previously, only the unauthorized use or copying of plans had been prevented by copyright law, but copying a building had not. Still, lawyers admitted that it might be difficult to establish when similarities cross the line into copying.

CHARLES K. HOYT, *Architectural Record*

ARGENTINA

During 1991 cabinet changes by President Carlos Saúl Menem moved Argentina in the direction of reform and stability. Progress was made in deregulation and economic recovery, and inflation was brought under control. In foreign policy, Argentina moved closer to the United States.

Government and Politics. President Menem reshuffled his cabinet in January. Guido di Tella took over the foreign ministry and Antonio Ermán González was shifted to defense. Domingo Cavallo picked up the economy portfolio. A Harvard-trained economist, Cavallo was not a member of Menem's Peronist (Justicialist) Party.

Gubernatorial and congressional midterm elections were held on August 17, September 8, and October 27. The Peronists retained the governorships they previously held and gained additional seats in the Chamber of Deputies, where they had been the largest party. The government forces campaigned on having brought about economic stability, while the opposition stressed the social and labor conflicts that accompanied privatization programs.

Voters tended to focus on lower rates of inflation (1.3% in August) rather than the scandals and corruption that reached the highest levels of the Menem administration. The president only reluctantly gave up a red Ferrari that he had received from an Italian businessman. His adviser and brother-in-law Emir Yoma was investigated and dismissed in January on bribery charges, following a complaint by U.S. Ambassador Terence Todman. Menem was sued for divorce in March by Zulema Yoma. On July 24 his sister-in-law and press secretary, Amira Yoma, was indicted along with her former husband, Ibrahim al-Ibrahim, a customs official, for involvement in a drug-money-laundering operation. Interior Minister Julio Mera Figueroa resigned in August amid charges of influence peddling.

In December 1990, Menem pardoned and released from prison the military leaders who had been in positions of authority during the brutal "dirty war," between 1976 and 1983. The next day 50,000 protesters from political parties and human-rights groups demonstrated against this move. Menem cited "national reconciliation" as the reason for the pardons. Others attributed his action to army loyalty weeks earlier during an attempted coup. Among those freed were former junta leaders Jorge Videla and Roberto Viola, as well as ranking naval, air-force, and police officers. Upon his release, Videla launched a campaign for his reintegration into the armed forces and vindication of the military for stamping out "subversion" during the period of army rule. His sympathizers wanted the armed forces' "oversight" role of civilian regimes restored.

On September 2 a federal appeals court upheld a January ruling by the highest military tribunal in the cases of 13 military personnel implicated in a December 1990 mutiny by the nationalist Painted Face faction that cost 21 lives. The leader of the mutiny, former Col. Mohammed Alí Seineldín, was given life imprisonment. Fourteen other officers were given sentences of two to 20 years. All were stripped of their military rank. Twenty-six other rebels were court-martialed on August 15 and received sentences of from 30 days to nine years. As the threat from the army's right wing diminished, the government proceeded with permanent reductions in the military budget.

Economy. Economy Minister Cavallo's recovery program stabilized the austral by linking it to the dollar at a ratio of 10,000 to 1. The printing of paper money not backed by dollar or gold reserves was prohibited. Tax collections and payments from the sale of public enterprises increased revenues. Additional government-owned companies were offered for sale. Most government controls over business were eliminated, and barriers were removed in order to stimulate trade. Cavallo claimed that, even though his "modernization" program resulted in the severance of thousands of public-sector employees, foreign investment increased, creating 150,000 new jobs. The economy was expected to grow by 5% in 1991. On July 29 the International Monetary Fund (IMF) announced its approval of a $1.04 billion standby credit for Argentina, in support of its economic program through 1992. One fourth of the IMF loan was set aside for use in future commercial-bank debt-reduction talks. That debt amounted to $33 billion. Cavallo promised a debt-reduction plan by mid-1992. As of December 1991 unpaid interest amounted to $9 billion, on which Argentina had been making token $60 million monthly interest payments.

Privatization. Four major oil- and gas-producing areas were opened on January 1 to 50% private-sector joint ventures with YPF, the na-

ARGENTINA • Information Highlights

Official Name: Argentine Republic.
Location: Southern South America.
Area: 1,068,297 sq mi (2 766 890 km²).
Population (mid-1991 est.): 32,700,000.
Chief Cities (mid-1985 est., incl. suburbs): Buenos Aires, the capital, 10,728,000; Cordoba, 1,055,000; Rosario, 1,016,000.
Government: *Head of state and government,* Carlos Saúl Menem, president (took office July 8, 1989). *Legislature*—Senate and Chamber of Deputies.
Monetary Unit: Austral (9,918.8 australs equal U.S.$1, financial rate, Dec. 3, 1991).
Gross National Product (1989 est. U.S.$): $72,000,000,000.
Economic Indexes: *Consumer Prices* (1990, 1988 = 100), all items, 79,530.5; food, 62,807.6. *Industrial Production* (1989, 1980 = 100), 79.
Foreign Trade (1989 U.S.$): *Imports,* $4,204,000,000; *exports,* $9,579,000,000.

tional oil monopoly, in a sweeping deregulation of that industry. Bid winners, announced in April and May, included Argentine, U.S., Spanish, and French firms. The combined payment for acquiring half ownership amounted to $600 million. Despite criticism, the privatizing program moved ahead in May with calls for bids on 67 additional areas that either had been left undeveloped or were producing very little crude. In August the economy ministry authorized purchasers of the four initial oil- and gas-producing areas to increase their participation to 80%-90%, from which Argentina expected another $400 million. President Menem announced on October 20 that about one third of the national territory would be opened to oil exploration by foreign companies, with 40% of the area located offshore. His decision to allow foreign interests into exploratory activity was attacked as contravening national sovereignty.

Foreign Relations. President Menem arrived in the United States on November 13 for a week of activities that included calling on U.S. President George Bush at the White House; Menem was the first Peronist president to have been so honored. He addressed a joint session of Congress, in which he called for democracy in Cuba. An investment protection treaty was signed and debt-reduction talks were held at the international lending agencies. Bush had visited Argentina in December 1990.

Pursuant to a request by President Bush in March, Menem ordered his delegate to the UN human-rights commission to vote for a special probe by the UN of Cuba's alleged rights violations. In April, Menem decided to accept an offer of U.S. assistance in combating arms-smuggling, drug-trafficking, and money-laundering operations. The plan did not include placing U.S. military personnel on Argentine soil; that idea was opposed by two thirds of the Argentine public in an August poll. As a member of MERCOSUR—the Southern Cone common market created in March by Argentina, Brazil, Paraguay, and Uruguay—Argentina signed a free-trade and investment agreement in Washington on June 20. During a visit to Buenos Aires by U.S. Vice-President Dan Quayle in August, Argentine representatives signed agreements with the United States that loosened longstanding Argentine protectionist policies on satellite technology, tourism, and mining development. At the same time they expressed to Quayle their objections to U.S. wheat subsidies.

As a result of improved relations with Great Britain, an investment-protection treaty was signed on Dec. 11, 1990, encouraging British investment in Argentina. About 360 Argentines were allowed to visit grave sites of loved ones in the Falklands on March 18. A total of 750 Argentines had died in the British reconquest of the disputed islands in 1982. Military restrictions in the South Atlantic were eased.

A state visit to Buenos Aires by Chilean President Patricio Aylwin in August provided a backdrop for an agreement to resolve remaining border disputes peacefully. During the stay 22 disputed areas were delineated and the final case would be turned over to a panel of Latin American judges for arbitration.

LARRY PIPPIN
University of the Pacific

ARIZONA

After a fringe candidate denied the election of a governor in Arizona in the November 1990 election, the state finally chose a chief executive in February 1991. J. Fife Symington III, a Republican businessman, easily defeated Terry Goddard, a Democratic former mayor of Phoenix, in a gubernatorial runoff mandated by a constitutional requirement that more than 50% of the vote was necessary to win. Neither candidate had received such a margin in 1990.

Morris K. Udall (D), who had represented Arizona's 2d District in the U.S. House of Representatives since 1961, resigned for reasons of health in May. Democrat Ed Pastor was elected to the seat in a special election in September, becoming the state's first Hispanic to serve in the U.S. Congress.

Scandal. Early 1991 saw the unfolding of the greatest political-corruption scandal in the state's history. Early in 1990 the Phoenix police had begun a probe of illegal gambling in the city. They structured a "sting" in which an operative posed as a Las Vegas mobster wanting to legalize casino gambling. In all, 23 people—including seven legislators, one former legislator, one justice of the peace, and several lobbyists—were charged with various crimes. Six of the seven legislators resigned and the seventh was expelled by a unanimous vote. Most of the accused pleaded guilty and some were sentenced to prison terms, one as long as five

ARIZONA • Information Highlights

Area: 114,000 sq mi (295 260 km²).
Population (1990 census): 3,665,228.
Chief Cities (1990 census): Phoenix, the capital, 983,403; Tucson, 405,390; Mesa, 288,091; Glendale, 148,134; Tempe, 141,865.
Government (1991): *Chief Officers*—governor, J. Fife Symington (R); secretary of state, Richard Mahoney (D). *Legislature*—Senate, 30 members; House of Representatives, 60 members.
State Finances (fiscal year 1990): *Revenue,* $8,598,000,000; *expenditure,* $8,265,000,000.
Personal Income (1990): $58,946,000,000; per capita, $16,012.
Labor Force (June 1991): *Civilian labor force,* 1,728,900; *unemployed,* 92,800 (5.4% of total force).
Education: *Enrollment* (fall 1989)—public elementary schools, 451,311; public secondary, 156,304; colleges and universities, 252,614. *Public school expenditures* (1989), $2,143,148,000.

© Miguel Luis Fairbanks/Peter Menzel

In southern Arizona in the fall, four men and four women prepared to seal themselves in Biosphere 2, a giant glass and steel greenhouse. During a two-year period the eight Biosphere residents planned to assess the ecology of closed systems.

years. As part of the political fallout from the affair the chief of the Phoenix police resigned.

Although staggered by the scandal, the legislature managed to close a budget gap of more than $100 million without a tax increase. This was accomplished in large part by reducing mandated increases in education funding.

Governor Symington came under a cloud in September when *The Washington Post* published a memo leaked from the Resolution Trust Corporation which alleged that the governor was on the board of a failed thrift that had loaned nearly $26 million to one of his development projects. Several of his projects were in financial trouble due to the collapse of the commercial real-estate market in Arizona.

Biosphere and Central Arizona Project. In southern Arizona, September saw the "closing" of Biosphere 2. (Earth is considered to be Biosphere 1.) This $150 million project is essentially a giant terrarium in which eight people are sealed inside a 3-acre (1.2-ha) glass enclosure with nearly 4,000 animals, plants, and insects. The Biosphere includes five "wilderness ecosystems"—desert, marsh, rain forest, savanna, and a 25-ft (2.3-m)-deep ocean. The complex is powered by a five-megawatt generator. The eight people planned to stay inside the Biosphere for two years to assess the ecology of closed systems. Critics questioned the value of the project and considered it pseudoscience.

Also in southern Arizona, water from the Colorado River arrived in Tucson via the $3.6 billion Central Arizona Project. This was the Bureau of Reclamation's largest single authorized project, and it lifts the water of Lake Havasu 2,900 ft (269 m) and carries it across 335 mi (539 km) of desert to provide 60% of Arizona's renewable water supply. The project was authorized in 1968.

Peter MacDonald. On the Navajo reservation, former tribal chairman Peter MacDonald was indicted in federal court on charges of assault, kidnapping, burglary, and conspiracy to overthrow the tribal government. These charges stem from a riot in 1989 in which two died. The tribal court convicted MacDonald of 41 counts of bribery in 1990.

PETER GOUDINOFF
University of Arizona

ARKANSAS

The demise of a major newspaper and activities of the legislature dominated news in Arkansas during 1991.

Newspapers. The oldest newspaper west of the Mississippi River, the *Arkansas Gazette,* was closed by its parent company, the Gannett Co., Inc., just one month short of its 171st birthday. Assets were sold to the *Gazette*'s bitter rival, the *Arkansas Democrat,* thus ending a 12-year "newspaper war" that cost both papers millions of dollars in advertising revenue.

Legislature. The General Assembly passed more than 1,200 pieces of legislation, notably increases and broadening of the sales tax, gasoline and diesel-fuel tax, and tobacco tax. Also passed was a mandatory seat-belt law and approval for the distribution of contraceptives in school-based health clinics as long as no state money was involved. A bill suspending the driver's license of students dropping out of school before age 18; an amendment to the state Freedom of Information Law, which opens state records on incentives and discounts to private businesses; and legislation reorganizing the state's vocational-technical education system also were enacted.

Legislators rejected a new civil-rights bill that would have provided damages for individuals subjected to harassment, vandalism, or violence due to race, religion, or ethnic background. Also defeated was a bill to legalize sexual relations of homosexuals and lesbians.

Politics and Population. Five-term Gov. Bill Clinton resigned his position as chairperson of the Democratic Leadership Council to run for the U.S. presidency.

Final data released by the U.S. Census Bureau showed a population increase of only 2.8% in the 1980s, compared with a growth of almost 19% in the 1970s. Four of the state's ten largest cities lost population. Reflecting the new data, the state board of apportionment, despite protest from some members of the black community, approved new legislative districts. A three-member panel of federal judges was reviewing the plan.

University of Arkansas. Bad news hit the University of Arkansas when the Pine Bluff campus reported a $3 million deficit in its operating budget and its chief operating officer resigned. The Fayetteville campus was rocked with charges of sexual misconduct by several members of its athletic programs, the felony conviction of a member of that institution's department of athletics for theft of several thousand dollars from the school's athletic fund, and a dispute with the U.S. Postal Service over more than $500,000 in research contracts. And in Little Rock, pro-life advocates picketed and then filed a lawsuit against the medical sciences campus in an effort to stop the institution from performing abortions and genetic-screening research.

ARKANSAS • Information Highlights

Area: 53,187 sq mi (137 754 km²).
Population (1990 census): 2,350,725.
Chief Cities (1990 census): Little Rock, the capital, 175,795; Fort Smith, 72,798; North Little Rock, 61,741; Pine Bluff, 57,140.
Government (1991): *Chief Officers*—governor, Bill Clinton (D); lt. gov., Jim Guy Tucker (D). *General Assembly*—Senate, 35 members; House of Representatives, 100 members.
State Finances (fiscal year 1990): *Revenue,* $4,511,000,000; *expenditure,* $4,223,000,000.
Personal Income (1990): $33,389,000,000; per capita, $14,188.
Labor Force (June 1991): *Civilian labor force,* 1,137,600; *unemployed,* 86,700 (7.6% of total force).
Education: *Enrollment* (fall 1989)—public elementary schools, 311,060; public secondary, 123,900; colleges and universities, 88,572. *Public school expenditures* (1989), $1,319,370,000.

Other News. A proposed $111.8 million tax package ("Little Rock 2000") to finance city operations and a broad range of capital projects was defeated by Little Rock voters in a special election held in October. . . . Hazardous-waste disposal continued to be a matter of dispute between environmentalists and private-business interests, with the incineration of medical waste at issue. . . . The U.S. Congress approved the closing of Eaker Air Force Base in Blytheville and Fort Chaffee Army Post near Fort Smith.

C. FRED WILLIAMS
University of Arkansas at Little Rock

ARMS CONTROL AND DISARMAMENT

Since the nuclear era began in 1945, no year has been as important for the disarmament of nuclear weapons as 1991. The emphasis on nuclear disarmament began with the United Nations victory in the Persian Gulf war and concluded with important actions taken by the world's two major nuclear-weapons powers, the United States and the Soviet Union. Both nations also moved ahead with a treaty to reduce conventional forces in Europe. The Conventional Forces Europe Treaty, ratified by the U.S. Senate late in 1991, was somewhat redundant due to the dismemberment of the Warsaw Pact and unilateral reduction in North Atlantic Treaty Organization (NATO) forces.

The Strategic Arms Reduction Treaty (START). On July 30–31 in Moscow, U.S. President George Bush and Soviet President Mikhail Gorbachev signed the first agreement ever to reduce substantially the number of strategic nuclear weapons in the U.S. and Soviet arsenals. The U.S. government described the purpose and character of the treaty in these terms: "The principal U.S. objective in strategic arms control is to increase stability in the U.S.-Soviet nuclear relationship at significantly lower levels of nuclear weapons. . . . Furthermore, limits in START are designed specifically to constrain the most destabilizing weapons of the Soviet arsenal—heavy Intercontinental Range Ballistic Missiles (ICBMs)—while encouraging greater reliance on slower, stabilizing delivery systems.

The complex agreement contained numerical restrictions on nuclear weapons and their delivery systems, of which the following are the most important: A ceiling of 1,600 was placed on the number of Strategic Nuclear Delivery Vehicles (SNDVs) that each nation may possess. The figure pertains to ICBMs, Submarine Launched Ballistic Missiles (SLBMs), and heavy bombers. Further, the two signatory nations each may deploy no more than a total of 6,000 nuclear weapons in the form of warheads on missiles, or as gravity bombs and air-launched cruise missiles, both of which are carried aboard bombers. Achieving these levels of deployment would approximate a 33% overall reduction in strategic nuclear forces.

Verification of compliance with the START requirements would be based upon six procedures: (1) Each nation may use satellites to monitor the other's compliance; (2) the telemetry regarding the flight tests of missiles is to be shared; (3) prior to the treaty entering into effect, both sides will exchange data on numbers, locations, and technical characteristics of all weapons accountable under the agreement; (4) seven times per year either side may request the other to display in the open road-mobile launchers, rail-mobile launchers, and heavy bombers; (5) each side will establish continuous monitoring at the perimeter and portals of the other side's mobile ICBM assembly facilities—for the USSR this provision means the United States has the right to maintain monitoring capabilities at Votkinsk, the final assembly plant for the SS-25 ICBM, and at Pavlograd, which is the final assembly plant for the SS-24 ICBM; for the United States this provision means that Soviet inspectors may be based at the Thiokol Strategic Operations plant, Promontory, UT; and (6) 12 types of on-site inspections may be made by either side of the other's strategic nuclear-weapons establishment.

Both sides have seven years to complete the reductions required by the treaty. The duration of the agreement is 15 years, unless it is decided to supersede it with another agreement. If both sides agree, the treaty then may be extended in five-year increments.

As the year ended the U.S. Senate prepared to debate the merits of the treaty prior to giving or withholding its consent as required by the Constitution. While observers expected that the treaty would be approved, some wondered what type of government would be operating in 1992 to enforce the START provisions.

Unilateral U.S. Initiatives. Noting the reduction in the threat by the Soviet Union, President Bush announced on September 27 that the United States would commence the largest unilateral cuts in nuclear weapons ever made. The subjects of his remarks were short-range nuclear weapons such as artillery shells for 155-mm and 203-mm guns and short-range missile warheads. Such weapons for years had been deployed in Western Europe to offset the numerical advantage in soldiers and tanks that the Soviet-backed Warsaw Pact held over NATO forces of the West. Further, the president announced that all tactical nuclear weapons would be removed from U.S. surface ships and attack submarines, and from land-based naval aircraft. He urged the Soviets to join in the reduction of tactical nuclear weapons. Several weeks later, Washington announced that U.S. tactical nuclear weapons in South Korea also would be removed. Thereafter, North and South Korea signed a nonaggression pact, and international pressure mounted on North Korea to open its nuclear facilities to UN inspection.

In the same speech the president made other unilateral pronouncements. These included taking all of the strategic bomber force off alert status, and removing the ICBMs scheduled for deactivation under START from an alert condition. Bush also announced that he was canceling the development of the mobile ICBM known as the Peacekeeper, or MX, and terminating further development of the mobile version of the Midgetman single-warhead ICBM. Also canceled was the program to build a replacement for the nuclear short-range attack missiles carried aboard strategic bombers.

With an eye on the potential proliferation of nuclear weapons and associated missile-delivery systems, Bush suggested the 1972 Anti-Ballistic Missile Treaty with the Soviet Union be renegotiated to permit each nation to deploy nonnuclear antiballistic missiles around its territory. The ABM Treaty currently permitted only one such installation.

The disintegration of the Soviet Union created a new nuclear-weapons proliferation problem. With the dismantlement of a large portion of the former Soviet military-industrial complex, concerns developed in the West that those skilled in the manufacture of nuclear weapons and missiles would seek greener pastures provided by nations seeking a quick route to nuclear-weapons acquisition.

Responding to the collapse of the Soviet Union, U.S. Secretary of Energy James D. Watkins announced in December that plans were being formulated to cut back the nation's production of fissionable materials used in nuclear weapons. Instead of producing upward of 6,000 warheads per year, the secretary said that by 1996 the nuclear industry would be engaged principally in maintaining the declining nuclear-weapons stockpile and in cleaning up the pollution left by 45 years of nuclear production.

Toughened Nuclear-Weapons Inspection. As a result of the United Nations victory in the Gulf war, the International Atomic Energy Agency (IAEA) was instructed by the United Nations Security Council to search Iraq for hidden facilities not destroyed by the allied bombing, as well as for biological and chemical plants. During 1991 such inspections were carried out despite obstruction by the Iraqi government, including the detention of 44 IAEA inspectors in Baghdad. Later in the year the IAEA charged Iraq with cheating on its obligation to refrain from producing nuclear weapons as prescribed by the Nuclear Non-Proliferation Treaty, which it had signed in 1969.

ROBERT M. LAWRENCE
Colorado State University

ART

Museum art exhibitions in 1991 mainly took the form of retrospectives. However, a number of exhibitions were group shows which offered new concepts in art history. It was a great year for museum acquisitions despite the dismal economic scene in the United States.

Exhibitions. There were a number of fine shows in 1991, but it would be difficult to say which was the most important or most discussed. One long-overdue show was the Georges Seurat retrospective marking the centenary of the artist's death in a diphtheria epidemic at age 31. The show, organized jointly with the Musée d'Orsay with 185 paintings and drawings, opened at the Metropolitan Museum of Art in New York in September after having been at the Grand Palais in Paris from April to August. Since other notable Post-Impressionists—Cézanne, Gauguin, and Van Gogh—have had recent retrospectives, the Seurat exhibition was a show whose time had come.

A ground-breaking exhibit that challenged long-held views about the place of Impressionism in modern art premiered at the IBM Gallery of Science and Art in New York in August. The show, entitled "The Rise of Landscape Painting in France: Corot to Monet," went on to the Dallas Museum of Art in November and would travel to the High Museum of Art in Atlanta in 1992. Two other exhibits showcasing the works of the popular Impressionist Monet were "Monet to Matisse: French Art in Southern California," which opened in June at the Los Angeles County Museum; and "Claude Monet: Impressionist Masterpieces from the Museum of Fine Arts, Boston," which showed only at the Baltimore Museum of Art in the fall.

Another interesting retrospective was an exhibition of the works of the Russian constructivist and one of the most accomplished artists of the Russian avant-garde, Liubov Popova (1889–1924). The show premiered at the Museum of Modern Art (MoMA) in New York in February with 50 paintings and 60 works on paper, as well as theater and textile design. The exhibit traveled to the Los Angeles County Museum in June, and then to the Ludwig Museum in Cologne, Germany, and on to Madrid, Spain.

Shows of contemporary artists included "Jenny Holzer: The Venice Installation" at the Albright-Knox Art Gallery, Buffalo, NY, which opened in July. Holzer was the winner of the Golden Lion Award for best pavilion at the 11th Venice Biennale in 1990. Lynda Benglis' works were on view with a retrospective of 50 pieces dating from 1969 to 1989. The show opened at the High Museum in Atlanta in January.

Biennials and triennials included the Whitney Museum of American Art's always-controversial "Biennial" survey of current trends in American art, which opened in April, and the 1991 Carnegie International "Triennial" survey of contemporary art from around the world, which offered U.S. viewers a chance to see international avant-garde or cutting-edge art. The latter show opened at the Carnegie Museum in Pittsburgh in October.

Retrospectives of 19th-and 20th-century U.S. artists represented one of the most popular themes of museum shows in 1991. Among these was the first major retrospective of the 19th-century African-American artist, Henry Ossawa Tanner, with 120 paintings and other works. The exhibition opened at the Philadel-

The Metropolitan Museum of Art

To mark the centenary of the death of Neo-Impressionist Georges Seurat (1859–91), New York's Metropolitan Museum of Art and the Réunion des musées nationaux/Musée d'Orsay in Paris jointly organized an exhibit of 185 of his paintings and drawings. "The Roadstead at Grandcamp" (1885), right, *was on view only at the Metropolitan.*

phia Museum of Art in January and moved to the Detroit Institute of Arts in May, traveling to the High Museum, Atlanta, in September, and on to the De Young Memorial Museum, San Francisco, in December. Another African-American artist, Romare Bearden, had his first major retrospective since his death in 1988 with an exhibit of 144 works which opened at the Studio Museum in Harlem in April and moved to the Museum of Contemporary Art in Chicago in September. The show would travel to museums around the country.

An exhibition entitled "Albert Bierstadt: Art and Enterprise" was a major retrospective of the 19th-century American landscape painter. The show, which included 74 oil paintings—both small oil sketches and monumental western panoramas—premiered at the Brooklyn Museum in February. It moved to the Fine Arts Museum of San Francisco in June, and then to the National Gallery of Art in Washington, DC, in November.

The first retrospective of the 20th-century American cubist, Stuart Davis, in more than 20 years included 175 paintings, watercolors, gouaches, and drawings. Organized by Lowery Sims, the show opened at the Metropolitan Museum in November. It would travel to the San Francisco Museum of Modern Art in 1992. Also opening in November, at the Whitney Museum of American Art only, was a display of the works of the 20th-century U.S. sculptor Alexander Calder. And a much-talked-about exhibition of the abstractionist painter Ad Reinhardt, who died in August 1967, opened at MoMA in mid-1991 and then traveled to the Los Angeles Museum of Contemporary Art in October.

Exhibitions of Old Master works included two superb drawing shows. One, entitled "Guercino, Master Draftsman," celebrated the 400th anniversary of the birth of the Emilian Baroque master, Giovanni Francesco Barbiero, called Guercino. More than 800 drawings were culled from the Royal Library at Windsor Castle. The show premiered in Fort Worth, TX, at the Kimbell Art Museum in December. It would travel to other museums in 1992. The second show, "The Drawings of Anthony Van Dyck," commemorated the 350th anniversary of the Baroque Flemish painter's death with 100 drawings. That show appeared at Washington's National Gallery from January until mid-February, and moved to New York's Pierpont Morgan Library until April, ending at the Kimbell Art Museum in Fort Worth, TX, from June through August.

Exhibitions of non-European art included "The Triumph of Japanese Style," which explored the 16th-century beginnings of modern Japan through a survey of art from the late Muromachi (1392–1573) and Momoyama (1573–1615) periods. This show appeared only at the Cleveland Museum of Art in the fall.

The Metropolitan Museum of Art

An exhibit of the works Walter Annenberg gave to New York's Metropolitan Museum of Art, including van Gogh's "La Berceuse," above, *ran from June 4 to Oct. 13, 1991.*

Museums. Major acquisitions were the principal museum news in 1991. Perhaps the most-discussed museum acquisition was that announced by former ambassador and publishing magnate Walter Annenberg on the eve of his 83d birthday in March. Annenberg stated that his coveted collection of more than 50 Impressionist and Post-Impressionist works would go to New York's Metropolitan Museum of Art after his death. The Metropolitan Museum won out over the Philadelphia Museum, the Los Angeles County Museum of Art, and the National Gallery in Washington.

Indeed, that billion-dollar bequest almost overshadowed the National Gallery's 50th-birthday celebration. In the spring, works were put on view showcasing the more than 320 Old Master through Modern works given to the museum by 150 donors. The National Gallery also received $7.5 million from the Andrew Mellon Foundation in 1991 to endow three new senior positions—two posts and one visiting scholar.

Another anniversary celebration of note was the Cleveland Museum's 75th-anniversary exhibition. The majority of 70 works in the show were purchased by the museum because it believes the best way to collect is with purchases by curators. The Cleveland Museum has one of the country's largest acquisition endowments, which generates more than $6 million annually.

In two other large-scale bequests, the San Francisco Museum of Modern Art received Matisse's 1905 Fauve masterpiece, "Femme

Winslow Homer's "Dad's Coming" (1873) was among the gifts promised by Mr. and Mrs. Paul Mellon to the National Gallery of Art in Washington, DC, in honor of its 50th anniversary. The work was shown at a special anniversary exhibit in 1991.

National Gallery of Art

au Chapeau," plus 30 other artworks from the estate of Elise Stern Haas; included are works by Picasso, Arp, Brancusi, Derain, Gris, Moore, O'Keeffe, and Rivera. And William S. Paley bequeathed 84 Modernist works to MoMA in New York. In return for the gift, MoMA promised to organize a total of 20 loan exhibitions of Paley's collection. Paley's foundation would not transfer the bequest formally until the loan exhibitions have been completed.

The Fort Lauderdale Museum received more than 200 works by William Glackens and his circle through a bequest from Ira Glackens, the artist's son, who died in November 1990. The gift included 61 oils, 54 drawings, and 18 etchings.

The John and Mable Ringling Museum of Art in Sarasota, FL, featuring large tapestry paintings by Rubens, reopened in January 1991 following a decade-long restoration.

The John and Mable Ringling Museum of Art

Major new museum openings in 1991 included the $55 million Seattle Museum, a five-story Post-Modern structure which opened in November. It was designed by Venturi, Rauch and Scott Brown of Philadelphia. New York's Pierpont Morgan Library reopened in October after receiving a thorough cleaning, renovation, and $30 million expansion which added about 50,000 sq ft (4 645 m^2) to the library. Another reopening took place at the John and Mable Ringling Museum of Art in Sarasota, FL, after an extensive $20 million restoration funded largely by the state of Florida.

The Detroit Institute of Arts launched Phase I of a 35-year master plan which calls for extensive modernization of the existing building. There also will be a new eastern addition designed by Michael Graves to be used for new galleries, a shop, a restaurant, and a shipping department. This $75 million project will be overseen by A. Alfred Taubman, the real-estate developer and head of Sotheby's, Inc.

The Dia Foundation of New York, originally founded by Texas oil heir Philippe de Menil, officially changed its name to Dia Center for the Arts.

Changes in museum personnel included the retirement of John Szarkowski, director of photography at New York's Museum of Modern Art. Deborah Gribbon was named associate director and chief curator at the J. Paul Getty Museum in Malibu, CA, where she had been associate director for curatorial affairs. Three new museum appointments were Katharine C. Lee as director of the Virginia Museum of Fine Arts, Richmond, VA; Thomas K. Seligman, as the new director of the Stanford University Museum of Art; and Ned Rifkin, who accepted the position of director of Atlanta's High Museum of Art.

The Art Market

Auction prices for works of art during 1991, with few exceptions, continued to spiral downward. In August the top auction houses, Christie's and Sotheby's, reported declines of 50% or more. Anxiously-awaited November sales of Impressionist, modern, and contemporary artworks proved that the market remained weak. Sales continued to fall sharply below their presale estimate, while 20% to 50% of works simply did not sell. However, great works of art with reasonable estimates did very well.

Reasons for the price decline included the U.S. recession, the Persian Gulf war, and finally, the retreat of the Japanese from the market due to art-related scandals. With the withdrawal of the Japanese and the speculators of the 1980s, the major buyers in the art market during 1991 were private European and U.S. collectors, both new and experienced. The most serious decline in sales was for Impressionist, modern, and contemporary art.

The highest-priced painting for the year was Degas' "Racehorses," which went for $9.98 million at Christie's London June 24 sale. It was followed by Fernand Léger's "Les Maisons Sous les Arbres," which sold for $9.9 million at Christie's New York spring sale. Another Léger—"Petit Déjeuner" from the Burton and Emily Tremaine collection, which sold for $7.7 million at Christie's November 5–6 sale in New York—was the star painting of the fall season. Other top prices in the same sale included Robert Delaunay's "Premier Disque" of 1912 for $5.17 million and Juan Gris' Cubist painting "Poires et Raisins sur une Table." Delaunay's tondo was important historically because it was considered to be the first abstract picture painted in France. A 1940 painting by Matisse, "The Persian Robe," brought $4.5 million at Sotheby's.

Prices for Surrealist works continued to rise. Miró's "Danseuse Espagnelle" fetched $5.94 million at Sotheby's spring sale, while Giorgio de Chirico's "Delights of the Poet" brought $2.42 million at Sotheby's in the fall. At Christie's May 8 auction, Belgian surrealist René Magritte's "Les Barricades Mystérieuses" was sold for $2.2 million.

Aristide Maillol's "Monument to Paul Cézanne," which sold for $2.2 million at Sotheby's in November, fetched the top price for a modern sculpture.

The top price for a contemporary work went to Robert Rauschenberg's "Rebus" for $7.26 million at Sotheby's New York on April 30. In November at Sotheby's, Jasper Johns' "Jubilee" sold for $4.95 million, while at Christie's November sale, Johns' "Device Circle" fetched $4.4 million and Willem de Kooning's "Woman" sold for $3.41 million. An example of how prices had fallen came with the sale of Andy Warhol's 1963 silk screen "Red Jackie" for $352,000 at Sotheby's November 13 sale. The same work sold for $825,000 in 1989.

Sales of artworks of artists of more recent vintage included Brice Marden's "Nico Painting," for $374,000; Robert Ryman's "Director," for $330,000; and Frank Stella's "Joatinga I," for $220,000. All were sold at Sotheby's in November and were from the collection of Charles Saatchi, the advertising magnate. At Sotheby's April 30 auction, records were set with works by 11 artists, including Julian Schnabel's "Ethnic Type #4" for $242,000 and Cy Twombly's untitled abstraction from 1959 for $2.2 million.

Old Master paintings were the least disturbed by speculation and the most underpriced. At Sotheby's New York May 30 auction, Goya's "A Maja and Celestina," a 2-inch (5-cm)-square miniature ivory, brought $550,000.

The market for 19th-century European painting, except for the Goya, did not fare well in 1991. The top price for a painting was at Sotheby's May 22 auction for Joaquín Sorolla y Bastida's "Salida Del Bano," which brought $2.64 million. At the same sale, Giovanni Boldini's "The Portrait of Pedro and Luis Subercaseax" brought $396,000, and Franz van Stuck's "Sphinx" brought $242,000.

Like the 19th-century European painting market, the 19th-century U.S. art market was not memorable except for works of quality. Good American Impressionist painting proved to be the easiest work to sell, though no longer a hot market. Top prices were gotten for Maurice Prendergast's "Gloucester," which sold for $1.32 million at Sotheby's spring sale, and J.H. Twachtman's "Winter Landscape," which sold for $517,000 at Christie's. American Western art also did well in 1991.

The antiquities market was healthy and thriving. More liquid than contemporary art, antiquities are fueled by divorce, death, and debt. At Sotheby's June 18 sale, a Greek marble grave stele brought $176,000.

The Latin American market continued to rise due to the influence of museum exhibitions and buyers from Mexico and Venezuela, whose economies accelerated in 1991. The sale of Diego Rivera's "Vendedora de Flores" for $2.97 million at Christie's November 19–20 sale established a record not only for Rivera but also for any Latin American work of art. The sale of Frida Kahlo's "Self Portrait With Loose Hair" for $1.65 million at Christie's spring sale established a record for her. At Sotheby's November 18 sale the top lot was José María Velasco's "Valle de Mexico," which brought $2.42 million, with records set for 19 artists, including Rufino Tamayo and Fernando Botero.

MARGARET BROWN HALSEY
New York City Technical College of the City University of New York

ASIA

Asia's importance to the United States continued in 1991. Between 1985 and 1989 two-way transpacific trade grew by 60%. In 1990 such trade reached $303 billion, outstripping U.S. trade with Western Europe by $113 billion. The effects of the Cold War's demise also were causing changes in Asian military affairs. During 1991 the United States was in the middle of a program to reduce its 135,000 Asia-based personnel by 12%, though security commitments to Japan, South Korea, the Philippines, Thailand, and Australia remained.

While movements toward reconciliation were occurring, long-standing Asian conflicts —South Korea versus North Korea, mainland China versus Taiwan, the northern territories claim by Japan against the USSR, and rival claims in the South China Sea by China, Taiwan, Vietnam, Malaysia, and the Philippines—continued. None of these, however, portended imminent hostilities in 1991.

Economic Groups. Efforts at promoting economic regionalism focused on two groups—one consensual, the other controversial. The former is the Asia-Pacific Economic Cooperation Council (APEC), which provides for regular consultations among the market economies of the western Pacific plus the United States and Canada. In 1991 a breakthrough occurred with the admission of China, Taiwan, and Hong Kong as members. China, which agreed to the admission of the latter two, is the only Communist member of APEC, an organization dedicated to promoting economic growth.

More controversial was the East Asian Economic Caucus (EAEC), proposed by Malaysia's Prime Minister Mahathir bin Mohamad; EAEC would include the six members of the Association of Southeast Asian Nations (ASEAN)—Brunei, Indonesia, Malaysia, Philippines, Singapore, Thailand—plus China, Hong Kong, Taiwan, South Korea, and Japan. The United States would not be included. Mahathir's proposal was a reaction to the failure of the December 1990 Uruguay Round of the General Agreement on Tariffs and Trade (GATT), which failed to lower trade barriers for Asian products into the European Community (EC). Mahathir's original vision for EAEC would be a Japan-led Asian trade group to compete within a world of three trade blocs—Europe, North America, and Asia. Responses to the EAEC proposal were unenthusiastic. The United States opposed any regional trading bloc. Thailand and Indonesia privately expressed reservations at any group that could obstruct their access to the U.S. market. Most important, Japan would resist any Asian organization that might cut Tokyo's trade.

Foreign Policy/Security Issues. Japan displayed a more active foreign-policy profile in 1991. Its $13 billion total contribution to defray the costs of the U.S.-led coalition against Iraq made Tokyo one of the largest financial contributors to the war effort. Prime Minister Toshiki Kaifu's subsequent dispatch of Japanese minesweepers to help clear the Persian Gulf constituted Japan's first military mission away from the home islands since World War II. Significantly, most Asian states welcomed the Japanese deployment. Only China warned that Japan should not be encouraged to undertake any new military role.

An era ended in Southeast Asia in September when the Philippine Senate refused to ratify a treaty extending the U.S. naval facility at Subic Bay to the end of the century. (The United States opted to leave Clark Air Field in the Philippines after Mount Pinatubo's eruption rendered it unusable.) President Corazon Aquino and the Senate split over the issue, and subsequent negotiations failed to resolve the impasse, resulting in a decision that the United States withdraw from Subic Bay by the end of 1992. The U.S. Navy did not plan to replace the facilities with a single alternative.

Korea as a Site of Regional Instability. The Republic of Korea (ROK—South Korea) has become an important economic partner for both the USSR and China, while the Democratic People's Republic of Korea (DPRK—the North) is seen as an economic albatross by its old allies. Pyongyang's need for food, oil, and the hard currency to buy them led it to a political compromise whereby the North and South both joined the United Nations in September. Previously, the DPRK had opposed separate memberships as ratifying the split peninsula. Pyongyang also pressed Japan for diplomatic recognition and war reparations for the 35 years of Japan's Korean occupation. Reparations would substitute for the loss of Soviet subsidies, as the USSR had curtailed financial aid to its Asian allies.

Possible North Korean nuclear-weapons development at Yongbyon caused concern. Intelligence estimates put the DPRK only three to four years away from possessing nuclear warheads which could be dropped on the South. Pyongyang stated a willingness to permit International Atomic Energy Agency inspection of its facilities only if the ROK agreed to abrogate the U.S. defense guarantee.

Endgame in Indochina? The year 1991 witnessed significant progress toward a political settlement of the 13-year Cambodian civil war. Collaboration among the five permanent members of the UN Security Council, the ASEAN states, and the four Cambodian factions led to an agreement that created an interim Supreme National Council that would rule Cambodia under United Nations auspices until general elections were held for a new government, possibly in 1993. (*See* CAMBODIA.)

SHELDON W. SIMON
Arizona State University

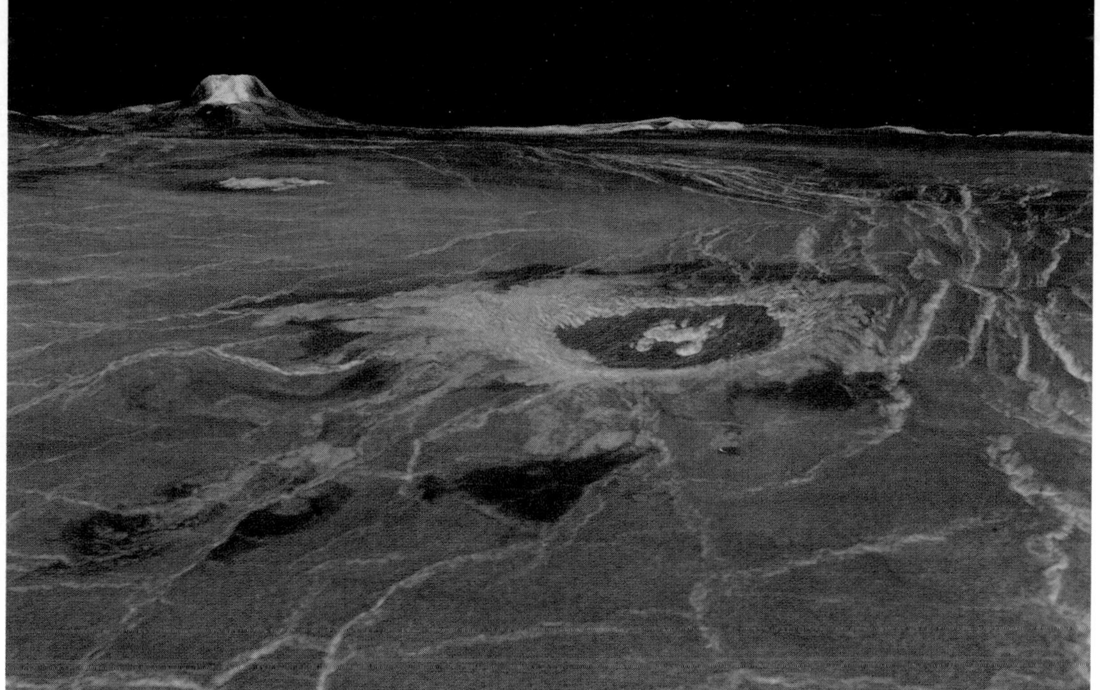

© JPL

The 1991 radar image of the planet Venus, taken from the Magellan spacecraft, showed evidence of a 3-mi (4.8-km) - high volcano and a large crater. According to the project's chief scientist, Venus "is dominated by volcanism on a global scale."

ASTRONOMY

The launching of several space-based observatories in 1991 gave astronomers simultaneous access to more of the electromagnetic spectrum than ever before. Also, "Star Wars" optical technology became available to ground-based scientists, promising them much sharper views of the heavens. Geologists identified the scar from a meteorite that struck Earth 65 million years ago and was the likely cause of the dinosaurs' extinction. Consequences of the Big Bang theory of the creation of the universe continued to perplex theoreticians. And planetologists made surprising discoveries about two of Earth's neighbors in the solar system.

Mercury, the closest planet to the Sun, is the last place in the solar system one would think to go for ice. At Mercury's equator the midday surface temperature reaches 825 Kelvin (1,134°F). But at the planet's poles there is only grazing sunlight, and the floors of deep craters remain permanently dark and frigid. Mercury's north pole is where strong radar reflections were detected in 1991—similar to ones from Mars' ice-rich polar cap—and they have been interpreted as probably marking an ice layer several hundred kilometers wide.

Venus Alive. On August 30 scientists at NASA's Jet Propulsion Laboratory (JPL) announced that the spacecraft Magellan had discovered a giant landslide on Venus. This crustal movement, the first seen on a planet other than Earth, reportedly involved some 9 km^3 of debris. Yet by late September the JPL planetologists admitted they may have misinterpreted Magellan's images. The truth would not be known until about April 1992, when the spacecraft would have another opportunity to view the area.

Incontrovertible was Magellan's discovery on Venus of the largest channel known in the solar system. It is 4,200 mi (6 800 km) long, slightly longer than the Nile River, but less than 1 mi (1.6 km) wide. Scientists had not discovered yet how such a groove could be carved and were wondering how the eroding material could have remained liquid under Venus' extremely high temperature and atmospheric pressure.

Killer Crater Identified? What began as a bizarre idea in 1980—that the impact of a celestial body 65 million years ago was responsible for the extinction of the dinosaurs—has become gospel. Debate now has shifted from "Did it occur?" to "Where did it happen?" Perhaps the denouement took place in 1991 when several lines of evidence indicated that a small asteroid, 6 mi (10 km) across, blasted a crater 112 mi (180 km) in diameter at the northern tip of the Yucatán peninsula. This cataclysm is imagined to have spawned a chain reaction: So much dust was thrown into Earth's atmosphere that sunlight was suppressed, plant life died, and the herbivorous dinosaurs perished.

The Astro Mission. In January the first results became available from the Astro observatory, which reached space in December 1990 aboard space shuttle *Columbia*. Astro's main mission was to observe the universe in ultraviolet light (largely absorbed by Earth's atmosphere) emitted by very hot objects. One of Astro's discoveries was the probable presence of graphite in interstellar space.

Gamma-Ray Enigma. Bursts of gamma rays appear suddenly in the sky, last for 0.01 to 1,000 seconds, and then disappear. Although they have been recognized since 1973, their source has yet to be matched with any physical object; thus they remain thorns in the sides of astronomers who study the universe at the highest energies known. (Gamma rays have energies millions to billions of times greater than visible light.)

Starquakes or explosions on neutron stars (gravitationally collapsed suns of enormous density) had been proposed as the most likely source of gamma-ray bursts. This idea seemed secure in May when French and Soviet scientists reported that these bursters are concentrated along the plane of the galaxy. Since this is where the most stars are, it is the place where most neutron stars (and bursters) should also be.

But by September a much more comprehensive survey from the Arthur Holly Compton Gamma Ray Observatory showed 117 bursts *uniformly* distributed over the sky. Thus, only five months after its launch, this second "Great Observatory" threw high-energy astronomy into turmoil. Only two possibilities remained as sources of these energetic outbursts: an unknown phenomenon within the solar system or something truly bizarre in extragalactic space. If the latter, scientists might be looking at the signature of an unrecognized physical process or a new inhabitant of the cosmos.

The Billion-Dollar Question. The Hubble Space Telescope (HST)—the first "Great Observatory"—despite its flawed optics, continued to return unique results, though not the revelations touted before launch in April 1990. Unfortunately, the telescope had experienced a growing number of debilitating and potentially terminal illnesses. Two of its six pointing gyroscopes had been lost and a third was hinting failure. Three were needed, and only one backup remained. Also, the winglike solar arrays that power HST flap, causing the telescope to jiggle and sometimes lose its target. In 1991 it was realized that the flapping could buckle the arrays' support booms, collapse them, and lead to a catastrophic loss of electricity. Finally, in late summer observations were halted with HST's high-resolution spectrograph because of malfunctions.

The billion-dollar HST clearly was not a healthy craft, and it continued to weaken. Yet the refurbishment space-shuttle mission scheduled for 1993 had been delayed until 1994. So many things now were wrong with HST that it was unlikely a single flight could fix them all. Ironically, the installation of optics to correct HST's infamous blurry vision might be the first repair to be cut.

© Larry Reider/Sipa

Vendors in Mexico sold special glasses as a total eclipse of the Sun, visible across parts of Central and South America as well as Hawaii, occurred July 11, 1991.

No Trouble for the Big Bang. In January newspapers carried stories describing the death of the Big Bang theory of the universe's formation. In fact, reporters had misinterpreted a debate about how galaxies congregate into structures tens of millions of light-years long. Although astronomers were under increasing pressure to explain how these gigantic "walls" and "bubbles" developed after the Big Bang, their problem had not cast doubt on the Big Bang itself.

Eclipse '91. Except for the 1986 appearance of Halley's Comet, no celestial event received more media attention nor was awaited more anxiously than the July 11, 1991, total eclipse of the Sun. It became a celestial celebrity for three reasons: It was the longest such eclipse visible to anyone now alive; the spectacle could be seen from Hawaii's Big Island, where many of the world's most sophisticated astronomical telescopes are situated; and the eclipse track passed over Mexico City, the largest metropolis in the world. Fortunately, clear skies prevailed along most of the track, and the spectacle was seen by tens of millions of people, unquestionably more than any previous total solar eclipse.

But most important were images obtained by observatories on Hawaii. They revealed the Sun's atmosphere (corona) with unprecedented clarity. Motions were seen to take place in the coronal plasma (a sea of free electrons and protons) within only ten seconds, which should help astronomers understand how the Sun's atmosphere is heated. And for the first time the full extent of the corona was imaged in infrared light, permitting studies of warm dust in the innermost solar system and perhaps giving insight about its origin.

LEIF J. ROBINSON, *"Sky & Telescope"*

AUSTRALIA

A recession rated the most severe in decades swept the Australian economy in the ninth year of Robert J. Hawke's Australian Labor Party (ALP) government and resulted in Hawke's overthrow. The effects of persisting balance-of-payments deficits were compounded by a sharp rural decline and a severe business downturn, with 11% of the work force jobless. By mid-1991 inflation had fallen and interest rates were down from previously onerous levels, but declining business profitability and the massive debt overhang inhibited recovery. The setback was most severe in the states of Victoria and Western Australia, both suffering from the collapses of large-scale speculative enterprises.

A general level of personal prosperity defied the broader trend, and household spending held up relatively well except on new cars and some other large-ticket items.

By year's end, growing dissatisfaction with Hawke's performance led to the ALP caucus move that gave the prime ministership to Paul J. Keating, a former treasurer.

In the international arena, strong support for U.S. initiatives continued; in particular, Australia lent support to the U.S-led coalition in the Persian Gulf war.

The Economy. With manufacturing slack and rural industries squeezed by high costs and low returns, the business downturn was seen in virtually every sector. Outlays on plant and equipment continued to decline as corporate cash flows were squeezed. Also, farm spending was minimal, and reports told of a spate of bankruptcies. One of the few sectors able to boost activity was tourism.

Increasingly, concern was expressed that the problems were deep-seated in the Australian economy and resulted from decades of cost escalation. Business leaders pointed to the fact that in the changing world economy Australian living standards would hinge upon economic expansion in a highly competitive environment; a need to raise workplace efficiency also was underscored. Tax changes to increase incentives to save were advocated. Financial experts deplored the strength of the Australian dollar, which remained at levels harmful to export potential and supportive of imports at the expense of local industry.

Wage reforms, which also were advocated, proved more difficult than hoped, with the wage accord between the government and the Australian Council of Trade Unions (ACTU) a central issue. In April the Industrial Relations Commission handed down a decision described as "a stinging rebuff" for ACTU and the government. The commission's refusal to endorse a formula for continuing escalation of wages and benefits became a turning point.

A clear reorientation of longer-term policy was outlined by Prime Minister Hawke in a March parliamentary statement on industry, the most far-reaching proposal of which was a phasing out within a decade of the basic commitment to a protective-tariff structure. The statement also pledged adoption of microeconomic reforms to achieve more-productive work practices. Some commentators shared Hawke's view that the statement set a positive new agenda, while others found that the proposals provided "too little too late."

A ten-year review of federalism was on the agenda of a constitutional conference that met in Sydney in April with the aim of creating a new economic union out of the current profusion of federal, state, and local governments.

In other economic news, the government sold off 30% of the Commonwealth Bank (established in 1911) in the nation's biggest-ever share issue. Plans to privatize the nationally owned airlines (Qantas and Australian) were thwarted by the profit downturn. The rural sec-

AP/Wide World

In one of his first acts as Australia's new Labor Party leader and prime minister, Paul Keating (right), 47-year-old former government treasurer and union clerk, greeted U.S. President George Bush and Mrs. Bush upon their arrival in Sydney for a four-day, year's-end state visit.

tor struggled under heightened difficulty at a time of excessive costs and bedrock prices for wool and an indifferent market for grains. Adding to the setback, a widespread drought blighted the principal inland pastoral and farming areas of Queensland and New South Wales and caused a reduction in wheat exports.

Japanese investment in Australia remained strong in spite of lessened attention to real estate (generally the principal interest of the Japanese investors). In 1991, Japanese investors tended to support local subsidiaries of Japanese carmaking firms and other manufacturing enterprises as well as mining operations linked with Japanese markets.

Politics. Nationwide opinion polls showed support for the ALP at less than 35%, with the Liberal-National Party coalition enjoying a 12% to 15% lead. Minor parties (including the Democrats and the Greens) held varying levels of support from state to state. The ALP was weakest in Western Australia and Victoria, where long shadows were cast by ALP governments' financial excesses of the 1980s.

Restiveness within the ALP's federal caucus was apparent throughout the year. In June, after a failed attempt to oust Hawke, deputy ALP leader and Treasurer Paul Keating, a right-winger, was demoted, with Brian Howe, the left's nominee, becoming Hawke's deputy. Declining popularity weakened Hawke's caucus backing, leading to the year-end move by Keating supporters that overthrew Hawke.

Liberal Party leader John Hewson announced a major tax-reform plan as a key element of the opposition's electoral platform; the plan involved a broadly based "goods and services" consumption levy to be balanced by lowered income tax as a means of encouraging savings.

The Budget. Federal accounts ended the fiscal year in June with A$1.9 billion in surplus; however, the 1991–92 budget presented by Treasurer John Kerin in August brought the first deficit since 1986–87 with a projected shortfall of A$4.7 billion (outlays A$101.5 billion, or 25.7% of gross domestic product (GDP), and revenues A$96.7 billion, or 24.5% of GDP).

Major initiatives included changes in medicare aimed at limiting the growth of health expenditure, increased assistance to families, and increased spending aimed at achieving "better" cities. A superannuation (pension) guarantee levy foreshadowed the establishment of a compulsory 5% of wages contribution by employers beginning in 1992. Employers were critical, declaring that retirement income was a community issue and employers should not be forced to carry the burden. Other criticism centered around the budget's failure to encourage business investment or private-sector savings.

Immigration Policy. In spite of widespread political reluctance to provoke debate on immigration policy, questions were raised about continuing high levels of immigration. In particular, adverse effects on the current-account deficit and on unemployment, as well as infrastructure and environmental problems, brought suggestions that the 110,000 annual intake of immigrants should be halved.

Other. An innovative means of fleece removal was demonstrated publicly for the first time at Sydney's Royal Easter Show. The process, known as biological wool harvesting and developed after 13 years of nationally funded research, offered the prospect of fleece removal through use of a hormone; six weeks after injection, it would become possible to peel the fleece from the sheep.

R. M. YOUNGER
Author, "Australia and the Australians"

AUSTRALIA • Information Highlights

Official Name: Commonwealth of Australia.
Location: Southwestern Pacific Ocean.
Area: 2,967,896 sq mi (7 686 850 km²).
Population (mid-1991 est.): 17,500,000.
Chief Cities (June 30, 1987, metro. areas): Canberra, the capital, 285,800; Sydney, 3,430,600; Melbourne, 2,931,900; Brisbane, 1,171,300.
Government: *Head of state,* Elizabeth II, queen; represented by Bill Hayden, governor-general (took office February 1989). *Head of government,* Paul Keating, prime minister (took office Dec. 19, 1991). *Legislature*—Parliament: Senate and House of Representatives.
Monetary Unit: Australian dollar (1.2646 A$ equal U.S.$1, Nov. 26, 1991).
Gross National Product (1989 est. U.S.$): $240,800,000,000.
Economic Indexes (1990): *Consumer Prices* (1980 = 100), all items, 218.0; food, 204.2. *Industrial Production* (1988, 1980 = 100), 129.
Foreign Trade (1990 U.S.$): *Imports,* $38,847,000,000; *exports,* $39,659,000,000.

AUSTRIA

The year 1991 was one of stability and prosperity in Austria. There were countless concerts and other celebrations commemorating the bicentennial of Mozart's death (*see* MUSIC—*Classical*).

Government. Austria started the year with a new government, for it was not until Dec. 17, 1990, after the parliamentary elections on October 7, that a new cabinet of 20 members—including three women—was sworn in. It was again a coalition with Socialist Franz Vranitzky as chancellor and Joseph Riegler of the People's Party as vice-chancellor. Alois Mock continued as minister of foreign affairs. In presenting his program, Vranitzky emphasized European integration and preservation of the environment as two major challenges.

At the Socialist Party conference on June 14–15, the party officially changed its name to Social Democratic Party of Austria. Vranitzky, with 98.5% of the vote, again was elected chairman. On June 21, Jörg Haider of the right-wing Freedom Party was removed as governor of Carinthia for praising Nazi employment policies. Past relations to the Nazis remained a touchy issue in Austria. In a major address to parliament on July 8, Vranitzky offered a formal apology for Austria's role in the Holocaust. The address was well received by Jewish organizations both at home and abroad. So too was President Kurt Waldheim's announcement on June 21 that he would not seek reelection in 1992. Earlier that month he made an official visit to Iran where he was received with honors. Hopes that he might help Western hostages did not materialize.

Foreign Affairs. Having been chosen in November 1990, Austria began a two-year term as a nonpermanent member of the United Nations Security Council in January. Peter Hohenfellner, Austria's permanent representative to the UN, took on the new responsibilities. In March he assumed the presidency of the council for a month. Austria regularly voted with the permanent members of the council during the Persian Gulf crisis. At the close of the conflict, Austrian Major General Gunther Greindl was put in command of the UN peacekeeping mission in Kuwait. Moved by humanitarian considerations, on January 29 the cabinet approved granting some 135 million schillings (about $13 million) to alleviate war-related hardships in various states, notably Jordan.

On March 18 the Conference on Security and Cooperation in Europe (CSCE) opened the International Conflict Resolution Center in Vienna. In a meeting in Bologna, Italy, the Pentagonale (Austria, Czechoslovakia, Hungary, Italy, Yugoslavia) foreign ministers issued a statement in support of Yugoslavia remaining a federal republic founded on democratic reform. The civil conflict in Yugoslavia, however, accelerated and Austria called the first meeting of the International Conflict Resolution Center on July 1. Austria charged that its air space had been violated by Yugoslavia and refuted claims by Yugoslavia that Austria secretly was arming Slovenia's militia. Yugoslavia also requested that Austria withdraw additional armed forces it had stationed along the Slovenian border. The meeting was well attended by CSCE states and brought a call for a cease-fire in Yugoslavia. On August 26, Chancellor Vranitzky announced that Austria would grant diplomatic recognition to Slovenia and Croatia only if other European states did so.

Austria remained opposed to nuclear power and was concerned about the safety of nuclear plants in neighboring Czechoslovakia. Agreement was reached to establish a joint commission to study the issue.

Economy. Although the growth rate of the gross domestic product (GDP) was estimated to be about 3.3% for 1991—compared with 4.6% for 1990—the economy was booming. The decline was related to the Persian Gulf crisis. On the other hand, unification of Germany and the opening of trade with Eastern Europe had had a very favorable effect. During the first half of 1991, Austria held the presidency of the European Free Trade Association (EFTA). Approximately 75% of Austria's merchandise exports go to EFTA countries and to the members of the European Community (EC). Germany is by far Austria's leading trade partner and the Austrian schilling is pegged to the German mark.

Serious negotiations regarding Austria's 1989 application for membership in the EC are not expected to begin until 1993. With current political changes in Eastern Europe, the whole question of EC membership remained in flux. The active privatization program begun in 1987 was continuing. Up until late 1991 no more than 49% of any company had been sold to private interests. Inflation was expected to rise from about 3.3% to 4% in 1991 and unemployment to 5.5%.

Other Events. On May 26 an Austrian charter jet belonging to Laudi Air crashed shortly after takeoff from Bangkok en route to Vienna, with the loss of all 223 aboard. On September 19, German climbers on the receding Similaun glacier in the Tyrolean Alps found the body of a man and some artifacts that dated from the Neolithic Period (*c.* 2600 B.C.). The find, discovered in Italian territory, was being investigated by the University of Innsbruck. (*See also* ANTHROPOLOGY.)

Although Austria has a very liberal policy toward refugees and exiles it refused to grant asylum to Markus Wolf, former East German spy official. He had fled to the Soviet Union and from there to Austria, where on September 21 he elected to be turned over to Bavarian border guards.

ERNST C. HELMREICH
Professor of History Emeritus
Bowdoin College

AUSTRIA • Information Highlights

Official Name: Republic of Austria.
Location: Central Europe.
Area: 32,375 sq mi (83 850 km²).
Population (mid-1991 est.): 7,700,000.
Chief Cities (1981 census): Vienna, the capital, 1,531,346; Graz, 243,166; Linz, 199,910; Salzburg, 139,426; Innsbruck, 117,287.
Government: *Head of state,* Kurt Waldheim, president (took office July 1986). *Head of government,* Franz Vranitzky, chancellor (took office June 16, 1986). *Legislature*—Federal Assembly: Federal Council and National Council.
Monetary Unit: Schilling (12.00 schillings equal U.S. $1, Oct. 23, 1991).
Gross Domestic Product (1989 est. U.S.$): $103,200,000,000.
Economic Indexes (1990): *Consumer Prices* (1980 = 100), all items, 141.3; food, 132.7. *Industrial Production* (1980 = 100), 133.
Foreign Trade (1990 U.S.$): *Imports,* $50,017,000,000; *exports,* $41,881,000,000.

AUTOMOBILES

The U.S. new-car and light-truck market endured a second year of deeply recessed sales in 1991, seemingly unaffected by the quick end of the Persian Gulf war and the lowest interest rates in nearly 20 years. With arrival of the 1992-model year, a massive campaign to regenerate consumer demand was mounted by the domestic Big Three and foreign-owned automakers.

Not only were U.S. dealerships offering a host of all-new and redesigned nameplates, but sales incentives which had failed to halt volume declines in the 1991-model season were carried over and expanded upon rollout of 1992-model vehicles. Competition was intensified by spread of the sales slowdown to Japanese brands, both those assembled in the growing number of "transplant" U.S. facilities and units exported from Japan. The industry's woes, which brought the Big Three net financial losses close to an estimated $4 billion in 1991, also touched off a shakeout of market entrants as the French Peugeot and British Sterling bowed out of the U.S. market in August.

Sales. During the first eight months of 1991, U.S. retail sales of new cars and light trucks (including utility vehicles and minivans) plunged 13.2% from the comparable 1991 period to 8,393,143 units. The Big Three's decline amounted to 15.1%, with General Motors experiencing a drop of 14.1%; Ford Motor Co., 17.3%; and Chrysler Corp., 13.9%. Although Japanese makes sustained a 5.7% falloff in the January-August period, the share of U.S. sales taken by the nine Japanese producers rose to 24.9% from comparable 1991 levels. This gain reflected increased demand for Japanese cars assembled in U.S. plants, such as the Toyota Camry and Honda Accord, the latter of which was the top-selling car or truck in 1990 and remained so in the first eight months of 1991.

The domestic Big Three's market share fell from 71.8% in 1990 to 70.2% a year later, while that of European producers dropped from 3.3% to 2.9%. Growing sales of Japanese luxury cars, combined with a new U.S. tax of 10% on new cars priced above $30,000, dealt a severe blow to volume of higher-priced European lines.

In an effort to stir up reluctant consumers, many of whom admitted to "price-sticker shock" after being out of the market since the mid-1980s or earlier, manufacturers turned to a wide array of aggressive promotions. Leasing of new vehicles, often with rates subsidized by the producers' finance subsidiaries, was pursued as a new-vehicle acquisition mechanism requiring no substantial equity down payment. Dealers also were boosting sales of so-called "program cars," consisting of 1991 or 1992 new vehicles repurchased from daily rental fleets and then auctioned or directly shipped to retail outlets at suggested prices sharply below those of "unused" new cars and trucks.

Other Trends. The intense competition to overcome the auto industry's recession was benefiting consumers in other ways. Basic warranties were expanded by many automakers to up to three years or 36,000 mi (58 000 km), compared with as little as one year and 12,000 mi (19 300 km) on 1990 and 1991 models. Oldsmobile and Volkswagen offered to refund purchase prices or replace without charge cars whose owners were dissatisfied after a month of use.

As the 1992-model year debuted, with some introductions as early as the spring of 1991, automakers were concerned by tighter credit requirements imposed by financial institutions on replacement vehicles sought by owners who had little difficulty qualifying for loans or leases of up to five or six years in the mid-1980s. This reduced auto loans outstanding in the 1990–91 model year by a record $15 billion, but analysts were cautiously optimistic that new-vehicle

Chrysler's Dodge Viper, right, *was the only all-new U.S. car nameplate to be introduced for the 1992-model year. The sports coupe resembles the roadsters of the 1960s.*

The Electric Car

By the turn of the century, electric-powered cars will be produced for sale by all of the world's automakers engaged in the U.S. market.

That became certain in 1991 when the California Air Resources Board, which administers pollution regulations in the most populous state, mandated that 2% of every automaker's California sales by 1998 must produce "zero emissions." This decree, which elevates the minimum ratio of no-emissions vehicles to 10% of California sales by 2003, translates into electric-vehicle production worldwide since no other feasible power source is guaranteed at this stage to meet the standard.

Farthest ahead among U.S. automakers in electric-car development is General Motors, which announced that a futuristically designed, battery-powered coupe called the Impact is being targeted for mid-decade production at GM's Lansing (MI) Craft Centre. The Impact uses a battery pack consisting of 32 ten-volt sealed lead-acid batteries. The pack weighs 870 lb (395 kg), amounting to 40% of the car's total vehicle weight, and has a driving range of 120 mi (193 km) before it needs recharging.

The low cruising range and lengthy recharging cycle—from two hours on a 240-volt supply source to eight hours on 110 volts—admittedly pose problems for electric-car marketing. But Japan's Nissan Motor Co. said it had built an electric car with a nickel-cadmium battery which can be recharged in 15 minutes. However, the Nissan car has only a 100-mi (160-km) range and accelerates at a slower speed than the Impact.

With a $7 million grant from the city of Los Angeles, an Anglo-Swedish company, Clean Air Transport, unveiled a family-sized electric sedan which was ticketed for 1993 production. The car features a 216-volt lead-acid battery and will be assembled in England. It has a range of only 60 mi (96 km) and will be priced at about $25,000.

Other electric-car developments were announced by Germany's BMW, which displayed the "El" prototype at the Frankfurt motor show; Japan's Mitsubishi Motors, which said it would develop a commuter-vehicle-production program with Tokyo Electric Power Co.; and Italy's Fiat Auto, whose Panda Elettra minicar entered production with an automatic eight-hour battery recharger as standard equipment.

Underscoring the need to perfect a longer-use battery system for electric cars, the United States Advanced Battery Consortium, a power-development venture, was formed by GM, Ford, and Chrysler. It is working with the U.S. Department of Energy, the electric utility industry, and the Electric Power Research Institute.

MAYNARD M. GORDON

The U.S. overdependence on oil and the environmental problems caused by today's cars have led auto manufacturers and experts to take a new look at the electric car. In response, General Motors is developing the two-seat electric Impact, prototype at right.

loan windows would open further after September's prime-rate cutback by the Federal Reserve Board.

The United Auto Workers (UAW), having concluded peacefully a round of three-year contracts with the Big Three in late 1991, enjoyed mild successes in organizing Japanese-owned "transplant" parts plants, but made no appreciable gains in recruiting members at transplant assembly plants in Ohio (Honda), Kentucky (Toyota), Indiana (Isuzu-Subaru), or Tennessee (Nissan).

The industry's best-known chief executive officer, Chrysler chairman and former Ford president Lee A. Iacocca, announced he would retire on Dec. 31, 1992, at the age of 68.

The New Models. All-new car nameplates were introduced for U.S. 1992-model buyers by six Japanese manufacturers, Korea's Hyundai, and only one domestic automaker—Chrysler

Corp. The Chrysler arrival was a limited-production sports coupe, the Dodge Viper, priced at upward of $50,000. The Big Three were concentrating on the truck side of the business insofar as newborn hardware was concerned. Chrysler prepared to enter production in January 1992 of its Grand Cherokee replacement for the popular all-wheel-drive Jeep Cherokee at a new Detroit assembly plant.

Ford, whose Explorer utility vehicle outsold Chrysler's Cherokee in 1991 for the first time, planned to open a joint-venture minivan plant with Japan's Nissan in the summer of 1992 at Avon Lake, OH. GM's Chevrolet division, leading Ford in 1991 in all new-car segments, rolled out redesigned full-size truck and van models as its main "new for '92" products.

GM and Ford divisions did greet the heightened competition from overseas-based automakers with a broad array of redesigned new cars. Modernized aerodynamic exteriors were introduced for 1992 on the Buick LeSabre and Skylark; Cadillac Eldorado and Seville; Ford Taurus and Mercury Sable; Oldsmobile Achieva (replacing the Cutlass Calais) and 88; and Pontiac Bonneville and Grand Am. Buick dropped the Reatta two-seater coupe, blaming poor sales. Chrysler disclosed that its long-awaited new midsize sedans, scheduled for 1993-model introduction, would be called the Chrysler Concorde, Dodge Intrepid, and Eagle Vision. GM's new car division, Saturn, sold 41,739 cars through August, below its 75,000 first-year goal.

WORLD MOTOR VEHICLE DATA, 1990

Country	Passenger Car Production	Truck and Bus Production	Motor Vehicle Registrations
Argentina	81,107	18,532	5,600,000
Australia	360,912	23,183	9,489,500
Austria	14,741	5,265	3,159,177
Belgium	311,803	73,460	4,118,826
Brazil	663,084	251,587	13,000,000
Canada	1,045,498	850,608	16,269,686
China	24,202	406,840	5,274,663
Czechoslovakia	188,000	54,000	3,382,140
France	3,294,815	474,178	27,758,000
Germany, East	152,537	34,353	4,368,700
Germany, West	4,660,657	315,895	32,066,513
Hungary	–	8,525	2,055,384
India	176,609	187,572	3,971,154
Italy	1,874,672	246,178	26,382,000
Japan	9,947,972	3,538,824	55,093,128
Korea, South	986,751	334,879	2,658,598
Mexico	598,093	222,465	9,014,583
The Netherlands	121,300	29,832	5,928,000
Poland	295,000	70,000	5,910,500
Spain	1,679,301	374,049	13,736,980
Sweden	335,853	74,415	3,887,473
USSR	1,200,000	840,000	22,075,000
United Kingdom	1,295,611	270,133	25,672,545
United States	6,077,449	3,702,787	187,260,547*
Yugoslavia	289,362	29,754	4,121,400
Total	35,675,329	12,437,314	556,931,486**

* U.S. total does not include Puerto Rico, which has 1,508,048 vehicles. ** World total includes 424,365,795 cars and 132,565,691 trucks and buses. Other countries with more than one million vehicle registrations include: Bulgaria, 1,397,971; Colombia, 1,300,000; Denmark, 1,900,024; Finland, 2,183,625; Greece, 2,358,265; Indonesia, 2,099,000; Malaysia, 1,775,000; New Zealand, 1,865,000; Nigeria, 1,379,000; Norway, 1,933,085; Portugal, 1,908,000; Saudi Arabia, 4,300,000; South Africa, 4,416,500; Switzerland, 3,177,993; Taiwan, 2,130,000; Thailand, 2,239,466; Turkey, 2,101,458; and Venezuela, 2,000,000. Source: Motor Vehicle Manufacturers Association of the United States, Inc.

© Toyota Public Relations

Toyota's Paseo sports coupe is offered with a five-speed manual overdrive or a four-speed automatic transmission.

From Japanese automakers and Hyundai came a welter of new entries in all segments of the market. Korea's Number 1 automaker unveiled the Elantra, positioned as a compact between its subcompact Excel and midsize Sonata. Japan's leading manufacturer of vehicles, Toyota, introduced the Paseo sports coupe in the subcompact class, added the SC 400 sports coupe to its highly acclaimed Lexus luxury lineup, and restyled the Camry midsize car built at Georgetown, KY.

Honda's six-year-old luxury network, Acura, added the Vigor sedan in a range between the midsize Legend and compact Integra. Mazda followed up on the appeal of its two-year-old hit, the Miata two-seat sportster, with the MX-3 roadster in the subcompact segment. A pricier V-6 coupe called the Subaru SVX replaced the Subaru GT.

Redesigned 1992 offerings from Japan included Honda's Civic subcompact and Prelude sports coupe and Mazda's 929 midsize sedan, the latter accompanying a Mazda announcement that it would join Toyota Lexus, Nissan Infiniti, and Honda Acura in à separate luxury-car channel, starting in 1994 under the name "Amati."

Three German imports checked in with freshened 1992-model editions—Audi with the 100, BMW with the 325 in entry-level segments, and Mercedes-Benz in the upper range with the S-Class sedan. Volkswagen unwrapped restyled 1993-model Golf and Vanagon vehicles and signified its intention to remain a U.S. player by opening a new VW of America headquarters building in Auburn Heights, MI.

Technical advancements featured the debut by Honda of the 1992-model Civic VX, boasting a "lean-burn" engine with average fuel-economy ratings of up to 55 miles per gallon on the highway. Antilock brakes and front-seat airbags were spreading fast throughout all price segments in stepped-up safety programs. Volkswagen reintroduced a diesel engine on its Jetta Compact.

MAYNARD M. GORDON
Detroit Bureau Chief, "Auto Age" Magazine

BANGLADESH

A return to competitive democracy potentially threatened by the worst cyclonic devastation since 1970 dominated events in Bangladesh in 1991.

Politics. With the ouster and arrest of former President H. M. Ershad in December 1990, parliamentary elections were held on Feb. 27, 1991. A multiparty council of advisers developed a "code of electoral conduct" to be observed during the campaign and election. Tight security was maintained by the army assisting the police. Most observers concurred the elections were free and fair. Turnout was high: Some 70% of the electorate voted.

Major contesting political parties were the Bangladesh Nationalist Party (BNP), the Awami League (AL), former President Ershad's Jaitya Party (JP), the Jamaat-e-Islami (JI)—an Islamic fundamentalist party, and a coalition of leftist groups—the Ganatantrik Oikya Jote (GOJ). The field, however, included more than 70 parties and 427 independent candidates for a total of more than 2,700 candidates vying for 300 seats.

Final results showed the BNP with the largest number of seats (140 with 31% of the popular vote), AL with 95 (28% of the vote), the JP garnering 35 seats (12% of the vote), and JI winning 17 seats with 6% of the vote. Thirty seats reserved for women were filled by an indirect election, adding 28 to BNP's total (for 168 seats) and two to JI's (19). BNP, whose popular support came from rural and urban middle classes, poor people, and women, had a bare 50.9% majority but also the parliamentary support of the JI. Acting President Shahabuddin Ahmed asked BNP leader Khaleda Zia to form the government, which was sworn in on March 20 with Zia as prime minister.

The AL was stunned. Its leader Sheikh Hasina Wajed called the election rigged. She accused the BNP of having close ties with the military. But infighting among the AL's factions spelled potential instability to many voters who cast their votes elsewhere. The JP's 35 seats indicated dissatisfaction with its performance under President Ershad, but also problems of campaigning while many of its leaders were under arrest. The formation in 1990 of the fundamentalist Zaker Party (ZP) and its declared intention to name Islam as the state religion had raised expectations of considerable support. However, the ZP won no seats and the JI's scant 17 indicated the greater importance of secular issues.

Aside from critical economic problems exacerbated by the cyclone of April 30, major issues faced by Zia's government were its inexperience, instability, and whether or not to return to a strong parliamentary system, which she had opposed. In a September 15 referendum, voters indicated overwhelming (84%) support for a Westminster parliamentary form of government.

A Devastating Cyclone. On April 30, Bangladesh was hit by a devastating cyclone and heavy rains. The estimated death toll was more than 125,000, with an indeterminate number of later deaths from dehydration and disease. Approximately $250 million was provided in humanitarian assistance by several countries. A U.S. naval task force was diverted on its way home from the Persian Gulf to aid relief efforts. An official estimate of $1.4 billion needed for reconstruction was only half the sum named by some observers. Agriculture, transportation, power, and vital export industries such as textiles were affected badly, as was the main port at Chittagong. A previously anticipated 6% growth rate was shelved with no further predictions possible, even though the government's plan for fiscal 1992 projected a growth rate of more than 5%.

Apart from the human tragedy, the devastation and recurring cycle of storms and floods underscored the need for basic structural and

Khaleda Zia—the widow of Gen. Ziaur Rahman, the leader of Bangladesh (1976–81)—was sworn in as the nation's prime minister on March 20, 1991. She had led the Bangladesh Nationalist Party in February elections.

BANGLADESH • Information Highlights

Official Name: People's Republic of Bangladesh.
Location: South Asia.
Area: 55,598 sq mi (144 000 km²).
Population (mid-1991 est.): 116,600,000.
Chief City (1981 census): Dhaka, the capital, 3,430,312.
Government: *Head of state,* Shahabuddin Ahmed, acting president (assumed power Dec. 5, 1990). *Head of government,* Khaleda Zia, prime minister (sworn in March 20, 1991). *Legislature*—Parliament.
Monetary Unit: Taka (36.49 taka equal U.S.$1, July 1991).
Economic Index (1989): *Consumer Prices* (Dhaka, 1980 = 100), all items, 255.9; food, 247.6.
Foreign Trade (1990 U.S.$): *Imports,* $3,143,000,000; *exports,* $1,512,000,000.

economic reforms in Bangladesh. Poverty is endemic and overpopulation forces the poorest to eke out their livelihoods on the low islands of the disaster-prone delta. Family planning may not be as critical as land reform, generation of nonagricultural employment, massive investments in education, and human-resource development.

Additionally, although much had been done to provide warning and protection in the event of storms, much more was needed. Estimates included $350 million for shelters and $4 billion for flood-control measures. A long-range strategy would include cooperation between the countries of the subcontinent and China on reforestation of the Himalayan range and water management to prevent flooding of lowlands.

Foreign Relations. Relations between Bangladesh and aid donors dominated foreign relations. Since 86% of development costs came from foreign aid, there was considerable pressure by donors to liberalize and privatize the economy, cut domestic subsidies and consumption, and raise productivity.

Additionally, there was a growth in the almost uncontrollable smuggling of goods and girls for prostitution between Bangladesh and India. Strains also appeared with Myanmar over refugees from the latter, further draining Bangladesh's scarce resources.

ARUNA NAYYAR MICHIE
Kansas State University

BANKING AND FINANCE

In 1991, U.S. banks and savings associations faced their most tumultuous period since the Great Depression as the first nationwide recession in almost a decade aggravated an already weak condition. Congress had to move three times during the year to pump tens of billions of taxpayer dollars into insurance programs that protect depositors. And in a cause-and-effect relationship that made matters worse, the tightening of bank credit was viewed as a cause of the recession, while the continued economic slide further hurt banks by lowering demand for commercial and consumer loans and causing a wave of corporate and personal bankruptcies.

Downturns. Federal regulators continued their aggressive cleanup of the nation's saving associations, and by December the number of savings associations seized by the two-year-old Resolution Trust Corporation (RTC) had grown to a total of 674. Of the total, 583 either were sold or closed. Another 200 to 300 institutions were expected to be taken over by the government.

Real-estate markets sank further in the Northeast, the South, and California, and many banks and savings associations found themselves holding near-record numbers of delinquent loans for commercial and residential real estate.

Lower interest rates for bank accounts and certificates of deposit (CDs) encouraged many bank customers to seek greater returns in higher-yielding mutual funds and other investments. By midyear, deposits at commercial and savings banks had shrunk by $31 billion, while investments into stock and bond mutual funds had grown by $93 billion during the first ten months of the year. By December, one-year CDs were averaging a yield of about 5%, their lowest interest level in years, and other kinds of accounts also posted low yields. The banks' lower interest rates resulted from the Federal Reserve Board's attempts to stimulate the economy by pushing down rates.

In the year's most important personnel shift, L. William Seidman retired in October after his terms expired as chairman of both the Federal Deposit Insurance Corporation (FDIC) and the RTC.

Thrifts. As the savings and loan industry continued to shrink there was finally some good news: for the first time in four years, those savings and loans outside of government control posted a profit, earning $1.1 billion for the first nine months of 1991. The results were due largely to continuing federal efforts to seize and close the most ailing institutions. By the end of 1991 there were about 2,200 such institutions, nearly half those existing in 1980.

Congress twice provided new money for the RTC, giving $30 billion in March and $25 billion in November. Administration officials estimated that another $55 billion would be needed to complete the job, bringing the total to more than $200 billion, excluding the interest charges that taxpayers would be paying for decades.

The inventory of seized assets from failed institutions being held by the government grew dramatically. By October the RTC held $147 billion in assets, including $26 billion in delinquent loans and $19 billion in real estate. As a sign of the agency's enormous growth, Congress in November extended until September 1993 the time for the agency to seize failed in-

© Don Wright/"The Palm Beach Post"

Many U.S. banks continued to face serious problems. A total of 124 failed during 1991.

stitutions. It, however, could be years before the RTC finally sells all of its assets.

With Seidman's departure, the Treasury Department named Albert V. Casey the new RTC chief executive officer. Casey, a former American Airlines chairman, would face confirmation proceedings in 1992. In the fall the administration split the FDIC from the RTC and in November, Congress moved to streamline further the bailout set up in 1989. Legislation adopted by Congress merged the two boards overseeing the FDIC and RTC into a seven-person panel to be chaired by the secretary of the treasury and include Casey, the Federal Reserve chairman, the FDIC chairman, the director of the Office of Thrift Supervision, and two persons from outside of government.

The structural changes did little to reduce the enormous costs. The rescue effort made the trust corporation the world's largest consumer of legal services, spending $700 million for more than 1,675 law firms.

Banks. The year began badly when one of the nation's largest banks, the Bank of New England—the third-largest in the region and 33d-largest in the nation—was declared insolvent at an ultimate cost to the bank-insurance fund approaching $2.5 billion. It was the third-costliest failure in U.S. banking history. Just a few days earlier, New England depositors were jolted by the collapse of the private insurance corporation that protected depositors at 45 Rhode Island credit unions and banks.

The side-by-side events led regulators to avert a regional panic by declaring the Bank of New England "too big to fail," and thus to protect all of its depositors, even those above the $100,000 coverage limit. The bank and two other affiliates, Connecticut Bank and Trust Company and Maine National Bank, were sold in April to a partnership consisting of the Fleet/Norstar Financial Group Inc. and Kohlberg, Kravis, Roberts & Company, the big corporate-buyout firm.

In July deposit insurance rose to 23 cents per $100 in deposits, an increase of 92% over 1990, and some government officials said it would rise again in 1992 by as much as 30%. But it was not enough. By year's end the insurance fund that protects almost $2 trillion in deposits was considered insolvent by government auditors and had to be bailed out by Congress, which provided "taxpayer loans" to be repaid over 15 years by the banks.

The industry responded to the turbulent times by a wave of bank mergers aimed primarily at reducing costs. In November federal regulators approved two of the largest mergers in history. Chemical and Manufacturers Hanover merged to produce the nation's third-largest bank, and the NCNB Corporation and the C&S/Soveran Corporation merged to make the nation's fourth-largest bank, which was renamed NationsBank. Pending was a merger of BankAmerica and Security Pacific to create the second-largest banking company after Citicorp.

Regulation. President Bush named William Taylor, a veteran regulator at the Federal Reserve, to succeed Seidman at the FDIC. Taylor, who took office in October, pledged to consider new ways for the government to resolve ailing banks. In November, Robert L. Clarke was denied reappointment to a second five-year term as the comptroller of the currency by the Senate Banking Committee. Clarke had been attacked by Democrats, who said that his lax policies contributed to the banking crisis in Texas and New England and that his tough response to those problems helped create a "credit crunch."

With banks in many regions shying away from making new loans, federal banking and savings regulators moved several times to ease that logjam by recommending relaxations of the standards used by banks to put values on

Banking Reform

Hopes were high at the beginning of 1991 that the woes of the banking industry finally would provide a vehicle for sweeping away more than 60 years of laws that sharply had restricted banks. But under repeated attack from Wall Street, the insurance industry, small banks, and some lawmakers who viewed the recommendations as dangerous new deregulation, the U.S. Congress in November rejected every major proposal of the Bush administration. In its place, the House and Senate passed legislation that provided a badly needed infusion of tens of billions of dollars in taxpayer loans to the nearly insolvent fund that insures bank deposits.

The Bush Proposal. The Bush administration's proposal was born out of the 1989 savings and loan bailout law, which required the Treasury Department to conduct a comprehensive study of the nation's banking system. With great fanfare, Treasury Secretary Nicholas F. Brady unveiled the long-awaited recommendations in February.

The plan had five key elements. Broader new access to the securities and insurance industries would permit banks to diversify their businesses and become more profitable. Costs would be reduced by easing restrictions that had made it expensive to open new branches and take over banks in other states. Industrial enterprises, such as General Motors, would be permitted to own banks in an attempt to attract new capital to the industry. Four agencies that regulate banks and savings associations would be merged into two. And modest limits would be imposed on the coverage of deposit insurance in an attempt to reduce the government's exposure to greater losses.

From the outset, the plan was challenged as repeating the mistakes of the savings and loan debacle by deregulating the banks and permitting them to speculate in the insurance and securities businesses. It ultimately was doomed by a confluence of factors. Estimates to bail out the banks through heavy taxpayer loans rose steadily during the year. At the same time there was mounting criticism of the savings and loan rescue, which by some estimates could cost taxpayers $500 billion over 40 years. And President Bush did not push strongly for a banking overhaul, leaving the lobbying to Secretary Brady.

Action. The measure ultimately approved increases the amount that could be borrowed by bank regulators from taxpayers from $5 billion to $30 billion. It also provides for an unspecified amount of tens of billions of dollars in borrowing from working capital that is supposed to be repaid through the sale of assets from failed banks. The legislation, adopted on the last day Congress was in session in 1991, also tightened bank regulations, giving officials greater authority to seize weak but solvent institutions.

Bush administration officials and some lawmakers vowed to renew their efforts to overhaul the banking system in 1992. But the prospects for comprehensive change were not good. The political climate was set by the administration's failure to get any major changes enacted in 1991. Adding to the difficulty was the fact that any substantive changes in the banking system would require that kind of bipartisan support that typically is absent during an election year.

STEPHEN LABATON

their loans. The moves were intended to ease the tightening of credit, although some critics said that they would come back to haunt the industry and the government, likening them to the decisions in the 1980s to relax standards for saving institutions and refraining from closing weak institutions.

The credit crunch was the least of problems for minorities seeking bank loans. In a comprehensive report on mortgage lending nationwide, the Federal Reserve Board found that blacks continued to suffer from severe discrimination by banks. The Fed concluded that even among the same income group, whites were nearly twice as likely as blacks to be approved for loans.

Federal Reserve. In July, President Bush appointed Alan Greenspan to a second term as chairman of the Federal Reserve Board. By the end of the year the Senate had not confirmed the appointment, although Greenspan was not expected to encounter any serious opposition.

Since Congress and the Bush administration had decided in 1990 to limit federal spending as part of a budget agreement, the role of the Federal Reserve grew enormously as the only federal institution capable of stimulating the economy. Through its control over interest rates and monetary policy the Fed moved repeatedly to bolster the economy and increase lending and spending. Between December 1990 and the end of 1991, the Federal Reserve moved six times to cut the discount rate—the fee that the Fed charges banks—from 7% to 3.5%, the lowest rate since 1964. In December the Fed also moved to cut the federal funds rate—the overnight interest rate among banks—for the 15th time since the recession began, to 4%, its lowest rate since 1963.

STEPHEN LABATON, *"The New York Times"*

BELGIUM

A relatively stable year in terms of economic and political life in Belgium was punctuated by concern over events in the Persian Gulf and Zaire and by ethnic disturbances in Brussels. Protest votes in the November 24 elections demonstrated, however, that Prime Minister Wilfried Martens' program of devolution no longer controlled the political situation.

Foreign Affairs. Belgium acceded to a nonpermanent seat on the United Nations Security Council on Jan. 1, 1991, in the midst of final diplomatic efforts to force Iraq to relinquish its seizure of Kuwait and avert war. Belgian jets were among the North Atlantic Treaty Organization (NATO) fighters sent to Turkey at the beginning of the year to bolster that nation's defenses against Iraq. Belgium supported a French initiative for an Iraqi withdrawal from Kuwait in return for the promise of a peace conference on Middle East problems "at an appropriate moment." When this and other peace efforts failed, Belgian planes participated in the Gulf war, but the country sent no ground troops.

After the war, Belgian troops helped to establish medical services in northern Iran for Kurdish refugees. Belgian soldiers also took part in an international peace force stationed at Silopi, Turkey, intended to protect refugee Kurds along the Turkish border. Belgium was chosen by the United Nations Security Council to head the governing council of the UN Compensation Fund, which was to oversee reparations for Iraq's invasion of Kuwait. (*See also* FEATURE SECTION, page 36.)

Belgium joined the other European Community (EC) nations in recognizing the independence of Estonia, Latvia, and Lithuania on August 27. It supported EC efforts to arrange a truce in Yugoslavia but cautioned against deeper involvement in the region.

In September unrest and rioting by underpaid soldiers in Zaire led Belgium to fly approximately 500 troops to Zaire to protect Belgian nationals. A number of families were evacuated. The French government also sent troops and joined the Belgians in negotiations that resulted in an announcement by the dictatorial president of Zaire, Mobuto Sese Seko, that he would relinquish some of his powers and make other reforms.

Domestic Events. On May 10 a minor incident—a police check of the license plate of a moped driven by a 17-year-old—led to three days of street riots in south Brussels. Young Moroccans—living in cramped housing and often lacking education, recreation, and job opportunities—focused their animosity on the police. Immigrant families told of being treated roughly and with disrespect; they asserted they were singled out for frequent checks of identity cards and drug possession.

No persons were injured seriously, though cars and buildings were firebombed. Television coverage of the event—which actually involved only a few blocks in the run-down commune of Forest—sparked discussion of the situation of immigrant families in Belgium. About 9% of the country's 9.9 million population and one quarter of that of Brussels is foreign. While European immigrants are assimilated, other groups are not. The some 135,000 Moroccans and 80,000 Turks remain social outsiders.

The government's first efforts were to restore order by adding to police forces. Later, 40,000 immigrants were granted citizenship and the process simplified for persons born in Belgium to foreign parents. Proposed long-term solutions included an education and urban-development program for immigrants, specially trained social workers, and the addition of Moroccans to police forces.

The surprising election results weakened the governing parties. The nationalist and anti-immigrant Flemish bloc fared well. In Wallonia the Greens gained at the expense of the Socialists. With his coalition lacking a majority in Parliament, Martens continued in a caretaker position while efforts to form new combinations foundered.

Other. By the end of 1994 the number of Belgian units assigned to NATO will be cut for financial reasons. . . . Curbs were announced on the export of chemical agents useful in production of chemical weapons. . . . The complex tax code was reformed in the hope of reducing tax evasion and bolstering civic responsibility. . . . Parliament approved a constitutional change allowing women to accede to the throne. . . . A new and larger building for the European Commission in Brussels was planned.

J. E. HELMREICH, *Allegheny College*

BELGIUM • Information Highlights

Official Name: Kingdom of Belgium.
Location: Northwestern Europe.
Area: 11,780 sq mi (30 510 km²).
Population (mid-1991 est.): 9,900,000.
Chief Cities (Dec. 31, 1988): Brussels, the capital (incl. suburbs), 970,501; Antwerp (including suburbs), 473,082; Ghent, 230,822; Charleroi, 208,021; Liège, 199,020; Bruges, 117,653.
Government: *Head of state,* Baudouin I, king (acceded 1951). *Head of government,* Wilfried Martens, prime minister (formed new government Oct. 1985). *Legislature*—Parliament: Senate and Chamber of Representatives.
Monetary Unit: Franc (34.92 francs equal U.S.$1, commercial rate, Oct. 23, 1991).
Gross Domestic Product (1989 est. U.S.$): $136,000,000,000.
Economic Indexes (1990): *Consumer Prices,* all items (1980 = 100), 150.7; food (1988 = 100), 103.2. *Industrial Production* (1980 = 100), 123.
Foreign Trade (1990 with Luxembourg, U.S.$): *Imports,* $120,067,000,000; *exports,* $118,295,000,000.

BIOCHEMISTRY

For biochemistry the period 1990–91 was highlighted by major breakthroughs involving Alzheimer's disease (AD), colon cancer, and cystic fibrosis.

Alzheimer's Disease (AD). AD is characterized by a gradual loss of memory and reasoning and eventually by severe disorientation. Biologists have known for some time that the brains of AD patients are studded with abnormal plaques and forming the central core of these plaques is a small protein—ß-amyloid. The paradox had been whether ß-amyloid actually caused the nerve-cell degeneration of AD or was merely the result of that degeneration.

Three major studies have pinpointed ß-amyloid as the cause of AD. In one such study, John Hardy of St. Mary's Hospital in London and his colleagues discovered a single mutation in a gene that can cause AD. And what is interesting is that the gene encodes the amyloid protein. Apparently the defective ß-amyloid protein accumulates and causes the progressive neurological illness. This discovery also is important from the therapeutic point of view in that drugs might be developed to prevent the accumulation and removal of amyloid protein.

A second study conducted by Neil W. Kowall of Massachusetts General Hospital unambiguously established a direct link between ß-amyloid and neuron destruction in live animals. In this study of 69 rats, pure ß-amyloid was injected directly into two areas of the rat brain —the hippocampus and cortex—that are affected severely in AD. The protein showed toxicity generally similar to that in AD. Interestingly, in a subsequent study, the scientists discovered that another brain protein—substance P (a naturally occurring neurotransmitter)—injected directly into the brain with the ß-amyloid, within a day or so, reduced the extent of toxicity and prevented neuron damage by amyloid. This discovery raised the possibility of effective treatment for AD.

In a third study, Barbara Cordell of California Biotechnology, Inc., and her associates underscored the importance of ß-amyloid by discovering that mice genetically engineered to overproduce amyloid precursor protein (from which ß-amyloid is derived) developed plaques similar to those found in the disease. (*See* FEATURE ARTICLE/ALZHEIMER'S DISEASE, page 58.)

Colon Cancer. Biochemists identified a key gene that may be linked to an early stage of colon cancer. Over the previous few years, research had indicated that many types of cancer, including colon cancer, arise from a series of gene mutations in cells. Some genes—called oncogenes—cause abnormal cell growth, while others—called suppressor genes—normally prevent the abnormal growth. It is when a suppressor gene mutates that it no longer can function normally and a natural check of abnormal growth is removed. Two research groups, working independently, identified the gene underlying familial adenomatous polyposis (FAP), which affects about 1 in 5,000 people in the United States and carries a very high risk of developing colon cancer. The researchers named the gene APC (for adenomatous polyposis coli). The FAP patients who have inherited a defective copy of this gene develop polyps in the colon early in life which, if not removed surgically, progress into cancer.

Both groups concentrated their studies on a small segment—designated q21—of chromosome 5 which is missing in many colon-cancer patients and was suspected to contain one or more suppressor genes. One group headed by Kenneth Kinzler and Bert Vogelstein at Johns Hopkins identified the APC gene by comparing the genes in the q21 segment that were active in normal colon cells but were damaged in patients with FAP and in patients with colon cancer, but not FAP. The other group located the APC gene by searching for common mutations in the q21 segment of chromosome 5 of several unrelated FAP patients.

It is believed that APC is a suppressor gene and that a mutation in this gene is one of the early changes that occur in colon cancer. Studies were under way to determine if the insertion of a normal APC gene into a cancerous colon cell would suppress the cancerous growth. The discovery of the APC gene was expected to lead to improved screening for colon cancer and to help in identifying individuals who may be susceptible to inherited colon cancer. Although it remained unknown how the APC gene prevented colon cancer, the biochemical basis of the inhibition of cell growth by another suppressor gene—retinoblastoma—was becoming clear.

Cystic Fibrosis. In late 1989 the gene for cystic fibrosis was identified. A year later biochemists succeeded in correcting the defect in cells taken from cystic-fibrosis patients. Cystic fibrosis affects about 30,000 children and young adults in the United States. Their cell membranes are defective and the cells are unable to expel charged particles called chloride ions. In effect, the chloride channels are clogged and water is pulled into the cell, resulting in the buildup of thick, dry mucus in the lungs that is characteristic of the disease.

Using virus as a vehicle, two groups of biochemists succeeded in inserting the normal gene into cells taken from cystic-fibrosis patients. Once integrated into the chromosome it started to produce the normal protein which then stimulated the chloride channel to open. Several difficulties remained, including how to deliver the gene into the airways of a cystic-fibrosis patient successfully.

PREM P. BATRA
Wright State University

BIOGRAPHY

A selection of profiles of persons prominent in the news during 1991 appears on pages 143–57. The affiliation of the contributor is listed on pages 591–94; biographies that do not include a contributor's name were prepared by the staff. Included are profiles of:

ALEXANDER, Andrew Lamar, Jr.

Lamar Alexander, a former two-term governor of Tennessee who had gained a reputation as one of the first state chief executives to champion school reform, took office as U.S. secretary of education on March 22, 1991. The president of the University of Tennessee system had been named to the cabinet post by President Bush on Dec. 17, 1990, and the appointment was approved by voice vote without dissent by the U.S. Senate. During Alexander's confirmation hearings, Sen. Edward Kennedy (D-MA), the chairman of the Senate Labor and Human Resources Committee, stated that Alexander "has the background and record to push us on the right path of progress toward our goals in education."

During his first weeks in office, Secretary Alexander was instrumental in formulating President Bush's education-reform program. The plan was unveiled in mid-April.

Background. Andrew Lamar Alexander, Jr., was born on July 3, 1940, in the small east Tennessee town of Maryville. He attended high school in Maryville, where he was a superior student, won awards in piano and debating, and earned varsity letters in basketball and tennis. He then earned a bachelor's degree from Vanderbilt University on a scholarship and obtained a law degree from New York University Law School. After serving as a legislative assistant to Sen. Howard Baker (R-TN) and in the congressional relations office of the Nixon White House, he returned to Tennessee and ran unsuccessfully for governor in 1974. Four years later he was elected governor; he won reelection in 1982.

Despite a Democratic-controlled legislature, the Republican governor oversaw enactment of Tennessee's Comprehensive Education Reform Act of 1984. Governor Alexander had traveled personally across the state lobbying in behalf of the measure after it suffered an earlier defeat. The act imposed stiffer standards for students and teachers alike. It also provided for an annual bonus for teachers based on performance reviews, a provision that was opposed by the teachers themselves. A one-cent increase in the state sales tax was approved to fund the act. Alexander, whose parents were teachers, also used his position as chairman of the National Governors' Association (1985-86) to encourage other states to examine and, if necessary, improve their education programs.

Alexander left the governorship in January 1987 and spent six months with his family traveling throughout Australia, during which time he reflected on his years in public service. The trip was the subject of his book *Six Months Off: An American Family's Australian Adventure*, published by William Morrow & Company in 1988. In January 1988 he became president of the University of Tennessee system.

Lamar Alexander and his wife Leslee (known to her friends as Honey) are the parents of four children. The former governor plays the trombone.

© Piko-Media/Sipa

Peter Arnett

ARNETT, Peter

As the only accredited Western newsman in Baghdad for most of the six-week Gulf war of 1991, Cable News Network (CNN) correspondent Peter Arnett dominated the world airwaves as few ever had done before, earning him acclaim as well as charges of collaborating with the enemy.

Transferred to Baghdad just four days before hostilities began in January, Arnett and his team aimed a TV camera out of the window of their ninth-floor room at the Al-Rashid Hotel and, with the only secured open telephone link with the outside world, gave a nonstop, 17-hour eyewitness account of the allied bombing of the Iraqi capital. Pulitzer Prize-winner Arnett, who was reporting his 17th war in 29 years, then took a calculated risk and refused evacuation out of the country, becoming the sole correspondent to report on the beleaguered and hostile Iraqi government and population.

While Arnett, whose coverage included a 90-minute interview with Iraq's President Saddam Hussein, openly admitted that his reporting was censored heavily, the more than 700 correspondents working the allied side of the war complained bitterly as the U.S. military kept them on a tight rein, permitting only selective, guided news-pool coverage of the fighting. (*See* SPECIAL REPORT/PUBLISHING.)

Background. Peter Arnett was born on Nov. 30, 1934, in Riverton, a small whaling village on the southernmost point of New Zealand, to Eric, a local builder, and his wife Jane. A tough, scrappy boy, Arnett chose to become a newspaperman rather than finish college. After a number of local newspaper jobs he drifted first to Australia and then to Southeast Asia, where his reporting of opium operations, revolutions, and corrupt governments kept him in constant trouble with gangsters, warlords, and government officials.

Arnett arrived in Vietnam in 1962 as a correspondent for The Associated Press (AP). His no-holds-barred reporting this time earned him the enmity of both South and North Vietnamese governments as well as U.S. military and civilian authorities. None other than President Lyndon B. Johnson himself angrily condemned his eyewitness accounts of the war, calling him a Communist and trying to get him fired. Arnett's reporting of the Vietnam War won him a Pulitzer Prize in 1966. Refusing evacuation as Saigon was falling in April 1975, he remained to report the arrival of the conquering Vietcong troops and their occupation of the city.

In 1981, Arnett joined the newly formed CNN. He first spent an uncomfortable six months covering the White House, but then returned to covering international news as a TV correspondent. An unlikely TV reporter with his balding head, crooked nose, and hesitant on-camera delivery in a flat New Zealand accent, Arnett was sent to cover wars in El Salvador, Afghanistan, and Africa. He was in Jerusalem reporting on the Palestine *intifada* when he was rushed to Baghdad to augment the CNN crew there.

Following the end of the Gulf war, Arnett, now an international celebrity, received various honors and awards as well as a seven-figure advance for a book, which he began writing in his Jerusalem apartment.

Separated from his wife Nina, a Vietnamese, with whom he has a son, 26, and a daughter, 23, Arnett became engaged in 1991 to Kimberly Moore, a reporter he met in Washington, who is the same age as his daughter. He became a U.S. citizen in 1985.

Aung San Suu Kyi

© Jeffrey Aaronson/Sipa

Aung San Suu Kyi

On Oct. 14, 1991, the Nobel Peace Prize was awarded to Myanmar's Aung San Suu Kyi for "her nonviolent struggle for democracy and human rights"; she was cited as "one of the most extraordinary examples of civil courage in Asia in recent decades." The 46-year-old opposition leader had been under house arrest and held incommunicado by the military junta in Yangon, Myanmar (formerly Rangoon, Burma) since 1989.

The government claimed Aung San Suu Kyi was free to leave Myanmar, provided she never returned. She maintained that she never would leave until the government freed all political prisoners, turned power over to those elected in the May 1990 election, and permitted her to explain her decision over radio and television.

Background. Aung San Suu Kyi was born in Rangoon, Burma, on June 19, 1945. Her father, Aung San—called by some the "father of modern Burma"—was the leader of the Anti-Fascist People's Freedom League. He was assassinated in 1947—shortly before Burma became independent. Her mother, Daw Khin Kyi, also active in politics, raised her daughter in Burma, India, and England. Aung San Suu Kyi was graduated from Oxford University and married Michael Aris, a British professor, in 1972. The couple had two sons and lived in Japan, Bhutan, and England.

Aung San Suu Kyi led an apparently apolitical life until 1988. Early that year, her mother's terminal illness brought her back to Myanmar, where she felt compelled to enter politics. The collapsing economy, U Ne Win's resignation as head of Burma, and the resultant political limbo emboldened groups seeking economic reform and political freedom.

Aung San Suu Kyi became the daring and charismatic leader of the National League for Democracy (NLD), the largest opposition group. She defied bans on public speaking, faced down armed soldiers, and provided an almost mythic focus for the fragmented democratic opposition. The junta was reluctant to move against the popular leader, but she was arrested after a fiery antigovernment speech on Martyr's Day, July 20, 1989—a date commemorating her father's assassination.

Ignoring May 1990 election results giving 80% of the parliamentary seats to the NLD, the junta launched a public-relations effort against Aung San Suu Kyi designed to appeal to the country's xenophobia. She was reviled for marrying a foreigner and having mixed-race children, and was accused of being a pawn of the U.S. Central Intelligence Agency.

No contact between Aung San Suu Kyi and her family had occurred for about two years. The government claimed she was in good health, but there was no independent confirmation that she even was alive. Late in 1991 there were unconfirmed reports that she was critically ill.

Aung San Suu Kyi also was a recent recipient of the European Parliament's Sakharov Prize for human rights. It was accepted in her behalf by her younger son Kim.

LINDA K. RICHTER

BARR, William Pelham

When U.S. President George Bush selected William P. Barr as his nominee for attorney general in October 1991, he chose a conservative government lawyer who had gained popularity with Justice Department employees through his reputation for accessibility. Unlike the president's two most recent nominees to major federal posts—Judge Clarence Thomas to the Supreme Court and Robert M. Gates to the Central Intelligence Agency (CIA)—Barr sailed through the Senate confirmation hearings with relative ease, winning approval by voice vote. He was sworn into office on November 26, three months after Richard Thornburgh resigned the post to mount an unsuccessful run for a U.S. Senate seat from Pennsylvania.

Barr had served as deputy attorney general under Thornburgh since the spring of 1990. In that position he helped Thornburgh carry out investigations of the savings and loan industry and the scandal involving the Bank of Credit and Commerce International (BCCI). Thornburgh had been criticized for moving those investigations along much too slowly. During his confirmation hearings, Barr defended the department's performance but also made it clear that he would be responsive to lawmakers. That promise of responsiveness and his candid answers to politically hot questions, including his stated opposition to *Roe v. Wade,* the 1973 Supreme Court decision that legalized abortion, earned him the praise of even liberal senators.

Barr is one of a group of young, conservative officials who rose quickly during the Reagan administration. He has strong White House ties.

Background. Born in New York City on May 23, 1950, William Pelham Barr received his undergraduate degree from Columbia University in 1971 and his master's degree in 1973. He served as a staff officer of the CIA (1973–77), while getting his law degree from George Washington University (1977). He then was an associate in the Washington law firm of Shaw, Pittman, Potts & Trowbridge (1978–82), leaving to become deputy assistant director of the domestic policy staff at the White House (1982–83), and then rejoining the law firm as a partner. He joined the Justice Department in 1989 as an assistant attorney general.

He and his wife Christine have three daughters.

BUTHELEZI, Mangosuthu Gatsha

Mangosuthu Gatsha Buthelezi, reviver and head of the South African cultural and political organization Inkatha KwaZulu, has been a prominent and controversial black political leader in South Africa since the 1970s. Although willing to work with the prevailing white political system to bring about change, he often strongly has opposed the actions of the government. The rival African National Congress (ANC) remains highly critical of Buthelezi's willingness to work within the political system but recognizes that he cannot be discounted as an important participant in any negotiations on the constitutional future of South Africa.

Although the ANC and Inkatha once were aligned closely, they have been at odds for a decade. Since the mid-1980s violence between the ANC and its allies and Inkatha has intensified. The conflict has resulted in the loss of thousands of lives, and the violence has spread from Natal province to other regions of the nation, especially near Johannesburg.

In January 1991 a long-awaited meeting took place between Nelson Mandela, then deputy president of the ANC, and Buthelezi. This was the first meeting between the two men in more than 30 years, and it ended with an accord to set aside differences and to fight apartheid. There were high expectations that this meeting might help ease the violence; however, it only intensified.

In July 1991 serious allegations were made that the government secretly had given nearly $100,000 to Inkatha for it to organize rallies and even larger sums to support the Inkatha-backed trade union. Buthelezi denied all knowledge of these transactions, insisting they had been carried out by Inkatha subordinates.

Background. Mangosuthu Gatsha Buthelezi was born Aug. 27, 1928, in Mahlabatini, Zululand. His mother was Princess Constance Magogo Zulu, daughter of King Dinuzulu. Her husband was Chief Mathole Buthelezi, whose family were prime ministers to the Zulu kings. Buthelezi began high school at Adams College in the Cape province in 1944. While continuing his studies at Fort Hare University, he joined the Youth League of the ANC. In 1950 he was expelled from Fort Hare for protesting a visit from the governor-general of South Africa. He later completed his degree at the University of Natal.

© Martin Simon/Saba

Mangosuthu Gatsha Buthelezi

In 1953, Buthelezi became a hereditary Zulu chief; however, because the government was suspicious about his motivations, he was not confirmed in office until 1957. From 1959 until the death of King Cyprian in 1968, he was prime minister of the Zulu nation. After Cyprian's death, he was elbowed out of Zulu political activities until June 1970, when he was elected chief executive officer of the KwaZulu Territorial Authority, one of the "homelands" created by the South African government. In 1976 he became chief minister of KwaZulu, although he never was willing to endorse the limited "independence" which other homeland leaders accepted from South Africa.

In July 1975, Buthelezi formed Inkatha KwaZulu (Zulu National Cultural Liberation Movement), named after a movement formed in the 1920s by King Solomon to foster a sense of Zulu nationalism. The 1975 movement sought to rally followers around a sense of Zulu consciousness. Over the years Buthelezi and Inkatha have been concerned with such issues as a single Natal province/KwaZulu legislative assembly, a constitution for that region (reforms which were opposed by the South African government), and the issue of sanctions against South Africa. As the United States and European nations imposed economic sanctions in the 1980s, Buthelezi was adamant in his opposition. He insisted that overseas investment should continue. In contrast to the ANC, he also strongly favors a free-enterprise economic system for South Africa.

Buthelezi married Irene Audrey Thandekile Mzila, a nurse, in 1952. The couple have seven children.

PATRICK O'MEARA

CAREY, George Leonard

The Rev. George L. Carey stirred controversy two months before he was installed as the 103d archbishop of Canterbury when *Reader's Digest* published an interview in which he said, "The idea that only a male can represent Christ at the altar is a most serious heresy." In response to a storm of protest, he substituted the term "theological error" for "heresy," but refused to back down on his approval of women priests although only eight of the 29 autonomous churches in the worldwide Anglican communion have them. The archbishop's Church of England does not.

When his election as Anglican primate was announced in July 1990, Carey said, "Today the church seems light-years away from ordinary people, people like the ones I grew up with. I want to reassure them that the Church of England is for them." In keeping with this, Carey's enthronement in April 1991 as the successor of Archbishop Robert Runcie departed from tradition by featuring guitars, a synthesizer, and modern gospel music.

An evangelical who is sympathetic to the charismatic movement, Carey illustrated his willingness to take bold stands when he told his critics, "If you want a wishy-washy archbishop who is just a flag blowing in the wind, then it's not me."

Background. George Leonard Carey was born Nov. 13, 1935, within the sound of Bow Bells in London's East End. He left school at age 15 and worked as an office boy with the London Electricity Board. Carey says he did not "encounter living Christianity" until he was 17, when he went to the local Anglican church, "found the worship appallingly boring but the fellowship and preaching riveting." There, he told the *Church Times*, "I found Christ, or should I say, he found me."

Carey entered the Royal Air Force in 1954, and after serving as a wireless operator in Egypt and Iraq, he decided to seek ordination. He became a priest of the Church of England in 1962 after earning a bachelor of divinity degree at King's College in London. The Reverend Carey later received a doctorate in divinity from London University.

He served as curate of Saint Mary's Church in Islington, lectured in theology at Oakhill Theological College, and was chaplain at Saint John's College in Nottingham. He was vicar of Saint Nicholas' Church in Durham from 1975 to 1982, when he was appointed principal of Trinity College in Bristol. He served there until his appointment as bishop of Bath and Wells in 1987.

Carey is the author of several books, including *The Meeting of the Waters* (1985), about relationships between evangelical Protestants and Roman Catholics, and *The Message of the Bible* (1988). His hobbies include jogging and soccer.

Carey and his wife, the former Eileen Harmsworth Hood, have two sons and two daughters.

DARRELL J. TURNER

CLEMENS, William Roger

As the 1991 baseball season began, Roger Clemens, the pitching ace of the Boston Red Sox, had won two Cy Young Awards (given annually to the best pitcher in each league), narrowly missed two others, and added a most valuable player (MVP) trophy. He also had led the American League (AL) in victories, earned run average (ERA), and complete games twice each and in shutouts three times. In general the 6′4″ (1.9-m), 220-lb (100-kg) right-hander was one of baseball's best players. After signing a four-year, $21.5 million contract extension in February that tied him to the Boston Red Sox through 1995, with a club option for 1996, he also was the game's highest-paid player. At the same time the star right-hander periodically antagonized the fans, front office, his teammates, and the media with his conduct.

In fact, early in the 1991 season he underwent a five-game suspension as the result of an incident in the 1990 American League (AL) play-offs. In the second inning of the fourth game on October 10, Clemens exploded after umpire Terry Cooney called ball four on a pitch to Oakland's Willie Randolph. Boston's star pitcher was ejected immediately from the game. After reading Cooney's report and watching videotapes of the incident, AL president Dr. Bobby Brown slapped Clemens with the suspension and a $10,000 fine.

In another incident, Clemens had spent 12 hours in jail in mid-January 1991 after he and his brother Gary scuffled with Houston police at Bayou Mama's Swamp Bar. Though the felony charge was reduced to a misdemeanor in April, a trial was pending.

© Focus on Sports

Roger Clemens

Clemens, known as Roger the Rocket more for his fastball than his temper, enjoyed another fine season in 1991. He finished the year with an 18-10 record and led the league in ERA (2.62), strikeouts (241), shutouts (four), and innings pitched (271). For his efforts, he was awarded a third Cy Young Award.

Background. Roger Clemens was born in Dayton, OH, on Aug. 4, 1962. The last of five children born to Bill Clemens and the former Bess Wright, Roger was less than four months old when his parents separated. His mother later married Woody Booher and moved to Vandalia, TX. Clemens was graduated from Spring Woods High School in Houston in 1980. A pitcher-first baseman in high school and American Legion ball, he won all-state honors and helped his American Legion team win the 1979 state championships. Clemens also starred in football and basketball.

He turned pro after posting a 25–7 record at the University of Texas. The two-time All-American was Boston's first choice in the June 1983 free-agent draft. After appearing in only 18 minor-league games, Clemens reached the majors—revealing a style strikingly similar to that of Nolan Ryan, his childhood hero. Though disabled by a right-forearm injury in 1984 and shoulder problems in both 1985 and 1990, Clemens has been a consistent star since turning pro. In 1986, his best season, the right-hander became the only man ever to win MVP honors in both the All-Star Game and the regular season, as well as the Cy Young Award. He opened the year with a 14–0 record en route to a 24–4 season. On April 29 of that year, he struck out 20 Seattle Mariners in a 3–1 victory. In 1987 he became the fourth pitcher to win the Cy Young trophy in successive seasons.

Clemens and his wife, the former Debbie Godfrey, are the parents of two sons, Koby and Kory.

DAN SCHLOSSBERG

CLIFFORD, Clark McAdams

On Aug. 13, 1991, 84-year-old Clark Clifford, one of Washington's most prominent lawyers and statesmen and friend and adviser to many leading Democrats, resigned as chairman of First American Bankshares Inc., the largest bank-holding corporation in the nation's capital. At the same time, Robert Altman, a 44-year-old Clifford protégé, gave up his post as First American Corporation's president. The two men, also partners in

AP/Wide World

Clark Clifford

the law firm of Clifford & Warnke, had been under investigation for allowing the Bank of Credit and Commerce International (BCCI), a loosely regulated institution owned by Arabs and operated by Pakistanis, to acquire a secret and illegal controlling interest in the bank.

Both Clifford and Altman, who as lawyers had represented BCCI and reportedly had bought stock in First American with loans from BCCI and had repaid the loans after selling the stock for profit, denied any wrongdoing. Testifying before the U.S. House of Representatives Banking Committee, Clifford said that he had been duped by BCCI and that he had not known that it owned a controlling interest in First American. The former presidential adviser admitted that his judgment in the case was "questionable" and that he "should have learned" in some way of BCCI's involvement in his bank but that he did not. He also pointed out that he had been a "practicing lawyer for 63 years" and there never before "been a cloud placed against" his name.

Although no revelations against Clifford or Altman emerged during the House hearings, many members of Congress questioned Clifford's account. They wondered how such an experienced and sophisticated member of the capital's establishment could have been so duped. Meanwhile federal investigations of the BCCI case continued. (*See also* SPECIAL REPORT/INTERNATIONAL TRADE AND FINANCE.)

A public figure since 1945 and an adviser to every Democratic president since World War II, Clifford also made the news in 1991 with the publishing of his memoirs, *Counsel to the President*, written with Richard Holbrooke. The work includes a firsthand account of his dramatic rise to power under President Truman and presents Clifford's view of his role in formulating Vietnam-war policy as a presidential adviser and secretary of defense (March 1968-January 1969) in the Johnson administration. The biography was a best-seller.

Background. Clark McAdams Clifford was born in Fort Scott, KS, on Christmas day, 1906, one of two children of railroad official Frank Andrew Clifford and his wife Georgia (McAdams) Clifford, an author of children's books and the teacher of a college writing course. Shortly after his birth the family moved to St. Louis, where he attended grammar and high schools and Washington University, where he earned a law degree in 1928. That year he ranked second among the 350 people who took the St. Louis bar examination.

Clifford practiced law in St. Louis until he joined the Navy as an officer in 1944. He served stateside in the logistics command before being transferred to Washington, DC, where he became assistant to President Truman's naval aide. As special counsel to President Truman (1946–50), he helped set up the U.S. intelligence system, was a principal architect of post-World War II defense and foreign policy, and was a guiding force in Truman's upset election victory in 1948. He took up law practice in Washington, DC, in 1950. In that capacity, he served as an adviser to President-elect and later President John F. Kennedy, and assumed special diplomatic missions for President Jimmy Carter.

Clark Clifford has been married to the former Margery Pepperell Kimball since 1931. They have three daughters. In January 1969, President Lyndon Johnson awarded him the Presidential Medal of Freedom.

COSTNER, Kevin

The triumph of Kevin Costner at Hollywood's Oscar ceremony on March 25, 1991, was particularly sweet. Already a charismatic star sometimes described as a new Gary Cooper, Costner had followed his urge to produce and direct as well as act in his obsessively ambitious film *Dances with Wolves.* Many had scoffed at the very idea of a first-time director attempting a film that itself was problematical.

The common view was that Westerns had seen their day, and that a three-hour movie about the relationship between an idealistic Civil War soldier and Sioux Indians —speaking Lakota translated into subtitles—was doomed. But Orion Pictures Corporation agreed to finance partly and to distribute Costner's film, made by Tig, his own production company.

His tenacity vindicated, Costner not only won an Oscar for best director, but *Dances with Wolves* was chosen best picture, in addition to earning five more Oscars, including one to Michael Blake for the screenplay adapted from his novel. Costner already had received the prestigious Best Director Award of the Director's Guild of America. There was also victory at the box office: By mid-1991 the gross for the United States and Canada topped $177 million.

Costner fared less favorably with critics for his unexciting title performance in the 1991 Warner Brothers summer release *Robin Hood: Prince of Thieves.* Nevertheless, the film was instantly popular with audiences,

Kevin Costner

© J. Markowitz/Sipa

and in less than a month grossed some $100 million. Next Costner was cast as controversial New Orleans attorney Jim Garrison in Oliver Stone's Kennedy assassination drama *JFK*. Following that performance, he was to produce and star in *The Bodyguard*.

A major new force in Hollywood, Costner has earned a reputation for choosing films carefully, setting high standards, and approaching his work with thorough professionalism. He is also extremely versatile. He has played a gunslinger in *Silverado* (1985), lawman Eliot Ness in *The Untouchables* (1987), a Navy officer in *No Way Out* (1987), a has-been baseball player in *Bull Durham* (1988), and a man with a dream in *Field of Dreams* (1989). He projects an on-screen presence as a handsome, easygoing, and likable star, and readily establishes rapport with admiring audiences.

Background. Kevin Costner, the younger of two brothers, was born in Los Angeles on Jan. 18, 1955, to Bill and Sharon Costner. He traces his ethnic heritage to a mix of Irish, German, and, on his father's side, Cherokee Indian. Growing up with a talent for sports, Costner considered becoming a baseball player, but instead opted for a bachelor's degree in marketing from the University of California. All along, acting also had fascinated him, and it took but a few experiences in community theater to alter his course.

He moved to Hollywood, studied his craft, and began to win minor film parts. A break came with the 1983 film *Testament*, in which he played a nuclear-war survivor. Oddly, he made further headway with *The Big Chill* (1983), even though all his scenes were cut. There was much publicity about his ill fortune, and the film's director, Lawrence Kasdan, compensated by casting him in *Silverado*. Costner then was truly on his way.

Costner has been married to the former Cindy Silva, whom he met at college, since 1978. They have three children.

WILLIAM WOLF

CRESSON, Edith

With his popularity in steep decline after the euphoria of the 1991 Persian Gulf war, French President François Mitterrand decided to shake things up. On May 15 he replaced his competent and consensual, but unarresting, prime minister, Michel Rocard, with the combative and outspoken Edith Cresson, a former government minister and one of Mitterrand's most faithful soldiers. In an advanced Western country where women are underrepresented widely in government, Mitterrand assured himself some additional words in history books by naming France's first woman prime minister.

Mitterrand said he named Cresson to give the country a "new impetus" in preparing France for the European Community's single market in 1992. Cresson, known for her lambasting of Japanese commercial tactics and her calls for more activist industrial policies, seemed to many well suited for the task. It also was assumed that she was named to prepare the Socialists for legislative elections, scheduled for 1993. Initial public response was positive, with polls showing more than two thirds of the French approving her appointment.

But in little more than a month—after her first speech before the National Assembly fell flat, after reports of dissatisfaction with Cresson among her own ministers, and after a number of unpopular measures—including a jump in social-security taxes—Cresson's approval rating had plunged to less than one third of the electorate, a record low for a French premier. Cresson, who, a decade earlier as the country's first woman agriculture minister, had described her presence as "traumatizing" for many male farmers, laid her troubles at the feet of French sexism. But the blame was equally Mitterrand's, for having named an unabashedly partisan and divisive personality to Matignon (the prime minister's palace) at a time when France's great left-right ideological divide had blurred and most voters were identifying with a welfare-state government of the center.

Cresson's popularity rose slightly in July, ironically after a speech on illegal aliens with a "send 'em home" theme that sounded more right-wing than socialist. She then proceeded to find kind words for Japanese investment in France, indicating an evolution toward a more pragmatic, centrist political stance.

Background. Edith Campion was born on Jan. 27, 1934, in the well-off Paris suburb of Boulogne-Billancourt. She attended some of the country's best schools, earning a doctorate in demography. Cresson's first taste of national politics came when she joined a Mitterrand-run political group in 1965. She followed Mitterrand as he took the leadership of the Socialist Party in 1971, joining the party leadership herself in 1975. Cresson was elected to the European Parliament in 1979, then to the National Assembly in 1981 in the Mitterrand Socialist sweep. She was agriculture minister (1981–83), minister of foreign trade and tourism (1983–84), and minister of industrial redevelopment and foreign trade (1984–86). In 1988 a reelected Mitterrand appointed her minister of European Affairs, a post she kept until October 1990. Her frequent calls for a super ministry to "wage economic war" having gone unheeded, she resigned.

The prime minister, who married Jacques Cresson, an executive with Peugeot, in 1959, has two daughters.

HOWARD LAFRANCHI

GATES, Robert Michael

Robert M. Gates had wanted to be a doctor or teacher, only interviewing with the Central Intelligence Agency (CIA) on a lark in 1965, but on Nov. 12, 1991, he became the 15th director of the agency. It was his second try for the post, having been nominated by President Reagan in 1987 but forced to withdraw amid questions regarding his knowledge of the Iran-contra affair. Since the beginning of that scandal, the 48-year-old Gates had said he learned that profits from arms sales to Iran were being diverted to the Nicaraguan contras only shortly before the scandal broke. In 1991 a majority of U.S. senators believed him.

Critics, however, contended that as deputy director of the CIA under William Casey in 1986, Gates was in a position to know more. During Senate confirmation hearings, testimony was presented indicating that he had been told about the diversion several months earlier

Robert Gates

© Diana Walker/Gamma-Liaison

but dismissed it as hearsay. Gates blunted much of the criticism during his first day of testimony by admitting that he should have acted more aggressively when he first heard of the diversion and by stating that he would lay his job on the line should he learn of such wrongdoing in the future.

Also at issue were questions about whether Gates deliberately skewed intelligence reports to present a position consistent with Casey's beliefs and his own pessimistic view of the Soviet Union. A lifelong bureaucrat who has served in the White House and CIA, Gates is a specialist in Soviet affairs and has been a hard-liner, skeptical of Soviet reform and Mikhail Gorbachev's chances for economic overhaul.

Confirmed by a Senate vote of 64–31 and sworn in on November 12, Gates took control of the CIA during a time of flux. Concern over a confrontation with the Soviet Union no longer was the overriding reason for intelligence gathering, but of new concern were coming budget cuts and recent CIA shortcomings, including its failure to detect early on Iraq's planned invasion of Kuwait. Agency changes already under way included more emphasis on recruiting Third World agents; targeting drug trafficking, terrorism, and nuclear proliferation; and a greater emphasis on human intelligence rather than electronic surveillance.

Gates won the support of many senators with his relative candor and promises to maintain a strong relationship of "trust and confidence" with Congress. He comes from the analytical arm of the CIA and is not known to operate with a cloak-and-dagger style of management.

Background. Robert Michael Gates was born Sept. 25, 1943, in Wichita, KS. He received an undergraduate degree from the College of William and Mary, a master's degree in history from Indiana University, and a doctorate in Soviet studies from Georgetown University. He joined the CIA in 1965 as a junior analyst and won praise for his cogent analysis and crisp writing. His big break came in 1974 when he was assigned to work at the White House on the National Security Council, under Air Force Gen. Brent Scowcroft. He was appointed deputy CIA director in 1986 under Casey and then nominated for the directorship in 1987 when Casey was diagnosed with a brain tumor. In 1989 he again moved to the White House as deputy national security adviser, again under Scowcroft.

He and his wife, Becky, have two children.

HARALD V

King Harald V ascended the throne of Norway upon the death of his father, King Olav V, on Jan. 17, 1991. A formal swearing-in ceremony followed on January 22. Harald became the third king of Norway since the separate monarchy was reestablished following the dissolution of the union with Sweden in 1905. His reign as the constitutional monarch started auspiciously when he and his wife, Queen Sonja, traveled through a large part of Norway in June and received the blessings of the Norwegian church at the historic Cathedral of Nidaros in Trondheim on June 23.

Background. Born at Skaugum (the crown prince and princess' royal residence) in Asker, Norway, on Feb. 21, 1937, Prince Harald was the first Norwegian prince born in Norway in 566 years. His mother was Crown Princess Märtha (1901–54). At the time of the German invasion in April 1940, Märtha, with Harald and her two daughters, Princess Ragnhild and Princess Astrid, fled first into Sweden and then to the United States. The family lived near Washington, DC, while Harald's father, Crown Prince Olav—in England with his father King Haakon—assumed command of the Norwegian forces taking part in the struggle against the Nazis. Princess Märtha and the children returned to Norway in June 1945.

Prince Harald attended a local primary school and high school and passed preliminary examinations at the University of Oslo in 1955. His military service included

© Holmvarig/Sipa

King Harald V of Norway

studies at the Norwegian Cavalry Officers' Candidate School and the Military Academy, from which he was graduated in 1959. This service was followed by studies at Oxford University, with majors in political science, history, and economics.

The crown prince served as regent for the first time in 1960 when his father—who had become king in 1957—fell ill; he made his first official journey to the United States in 1969 at the time of the 50th anniversary of The American-Scandinavian Foundation. In following years he shared with his father numerous official duties both in Norway and abroad, helping to promote Norwegian business interests.

In 1968 the crown prince married a commoner, the present Queen Sonja. She shares in numerous official duties at home as well as in wide-ranging travel abroad. The couple have two children, Princess Märtha Louise (born Sept. 22, 1971) and Crown Prince Haakon Magnus (born July 20, 1973). Like his father, King Harald loves sports and has been outstanding in international sailing competitions, representing Norway in several Summer Olympics. He also won the Gold Cup Races in 1968, the world championship in the half-ton class in 1982, and the world championship in 1987.

ERIK J. FRIIS

KRZYZEWSKI, Mike

He may have the most difficult name in college basketball to pronounce, so call him "Coach K" and be happy. But Mike Krzyzewski (it is pronounced Sha-shef-ski), the hard-working Polish lad from Chicago, has made the Duke University basketball program easy to remember. The Blue Devils are a prototype sports program, the best in college basketball. Not only is the program successful, but it also graduates the vast majority of its players. There are no admission "exceptions" at Duke for athletes. To gain entrance and stay eligible, the athletes have to have good grades in high school and they have to continue to study in college. Coach K's players, who do not live in athletic dorms, have competed successfully in the classroom.

Coach K also has shown you can win consistently with scholar-athletes. His Duke team captured the 1991 National Collegiate Athletic Association (NCAA) basketball title, but only after pulling off one of the great upsets in college-basketball history, beating undefeated and highly favored University of Nevada-Las Vegas in the semifinals. The Blue Devils had been in the Final Four five of the last six years, a stunning accomplishment. For Krzyzewski the championship was the climax of years of hard work.

Background. Born on Feb. 13, 1947, Mike Krzyzewski was a star athlete in high school. He wanted to attend the U.S. Military Academy but his parents were opposed. But he prevailed, and he wound up playing basketball under coach Bob Knight, who later turned Indiana University into a preeminent program. Krzyzewski was a hard-nosed, intense college player, traits he later brought to coaching. After fulfilling his military obligation, he eventually became an assistant under Knight at Indiana.

When the head coaching job at Army became available, Krzyzewski was hired. After five years, he took over the job at Duke in 1981. His first team made it to the National Invitation Tournament but his next two won only a combined 21 games. Since then, his Blue Devils have won no less than 24 games in every season. Besides his college duties, he also coached the U.S. entry in the 1987 World University Games and in the amateur world championships in 1990.

Coach K has become involved in the community around Durham, NC, where Duke is located. He is chairman of the Duke Children's Miracle network and has campaigned against alcohol, drugs, and drunk driving.

Krzyzewski is married to the former Carol Marsh. They have three children (Debbie, Lindy, and Jamie).

PAUL ATTNER

LEE, Spike

Film director Spike Lee not only is an inspiration to a new generation of African-Americans with a passion for making movies, but also is a role model for young would-be directors who begin their careers by making low-budget, independent films. His success in breaking into the mainstream and contributing importantly to U.S. cinema holds out the promise to others that they too can fulfill their aspirations.

Lee's special priority, reflected in his films, has been to portray the lives of his own people and culture boldly and freely, thus striving to help redress a long-festering shortcoming. In the 1970s director Melvin Van Peebles broke new ground by proving that films about African-American life could make money, but before long the new opportunities resulted in a spate of exploitative action films. Lee's assault on the movie power structure could have more staying power. Some 19 films by black filmmakers were due to be released by the end of 1991, and most were concerned with vital issues of racial equality and survival.

With a volatile, often original style that expresses strong emotions without fear of controversy, Lee films his world as he sees it. Audiences, whatever their composition, have not been accustomed to movies made with such a candid perspective. Not unexpectedly, he has been attacked, by those who disagreed with his portrayal of black characters in *Jungle Fever* (1991), those who feared—mistakenly as it turned out—that his Universal release *Do the Right Thing* (1989) would lead to race violence, and by skeptical militants who demand that his vision of Malcolm X, the subject of his $25 million Warner Bros. film, conform to their own.

Lee, who also acts in his films and is known for his frenetic Nike television commercials, has a strong public persona and reaps publicity by striking back at his critics. He also has been waging an ongoing battle for greater opportunities for blacks to work in Hollywood.

Background. Spike Lee was born on March 20, 1957, in Atlanta, GA. His name at birth was Shelton Jackson Lee. His father, Bill Lee, is a musician and composer whose work the director has used in his films. His mother, Jacqueline Shelton Lee, who died in 1977, was an art and literature teacher. The family (Lee has three brothers and a sister) moved to Chicago and then to Brooklyn, NY.

Spike Lee

Lee earned a bachelor of arts degree at Morehouse College (1979), where his experiences ultimately were reflected in his Columbia release, the musical film *School Daze* (1988). He received a master's degree in filmmaking at New York University in 1982, where he met and worked with his cinematographer-to-be Ernest Dickerson. They collaborated on Lee's thesis film *Joe's Bed-Stuy Barbershop: We Cut Heads* (1982), which won a student Academy Award, was showcased by The Film Society of Lincoln Center and the Museum of Modern Art in New York, and drew public attention to Lee's evident talent. *She's Gotta Have It* (1986), his independent film about a free-spirited young black woman, was a critical and financial success and paved the way for his studio-backed films.

Lee works through his own Brooklyn-based production company, Forty Acres and a Mule Filmworks.

WILLIAM WOLF

MADIGAN, Edward R.

On Jan. 25, 1991, President Bush named U.S. Rep. Edward Madigan as the next U.S. secretary of agriculture. Following unanimous confirmation by the U.S. Senate on March 7, the Illinois Republican publicly took the oath of office to the Cabinet post on March 12. He succeeded Clayton Yeutter, who became chairman of the Republican National Committee.

Although Madigan is from one of the most important corn-soybean areas in the United States, he has no direct experience as a farmer himself. He, however, had served on the Agriculture Committee for 16 of his 18 years as a member of the House and had been the committee's ranking Republican for eight years. At the swearing-in ceremony the president noted that Madigan "played a leading role in the writing of both of the past two farm bills. And that's a major reason that we've been able to build more free-market flexibility into our federal farm policy."

© Trippett/Sipa

Edward Madigan

The new agriculture secretary would face the continuing problems of increasing farm efficiency and productivity in a time of advancing technology, and maintaining favorable farm prices.

Background. Edward R. Madigan was born in Lincoln, IL, on Jan. 13, 1936, and was graduated from Lincoln College in 1955. Prior to entering politics in the mid-1960s, he ran his father's car-rental and taxi-company business. He was a member of the Illinois House of Representatives (1967–72) and was elected to the first of ten terms in the U.S. House in November 1972. During his tenure in the House, Madigan not only served on the Agriculture Committee but also on the House Energy and Commerce Committee, was chairman of the House Republican Research Committee, and was House Republican chief deputy whip.

Secretary Madigan is married to the former Evelyn M. George. They are the parents of three daughters. He has been awarded various honorary degrees and in 1974 was given Lincoln College's Outstanding Alumni Award.

MADONNA

Since she burst onto the music scene almost ten years ago, pop star Madonna has become one of the world's most well-known and controversial celebrities. When she first appeared in 1983, wearing underwear as outerwear and proclaiming herself a "Boy Toy," virtually no one took her seriously. However, as her image constantly changed and her music evolved, Madonna became recognized as having a talent for provoking controversy and for making one think. She is considered a master of the relatively new form of the music video and is credited with influencing greatly the development of this genre. More than video or music, however, her medium is herself. In her 1991 documentary film, *Truth or Dare*, she went further than any star in memory in revealing her private and public selves to the world at large. With Madonna, however, there is always the question of whether one is seeing the "real" Madonna or another carefully crafted image.

Background. Madonna Louise Veronica Ciccone was born Aug. 16, 1958, in Bay City, MI, to Sylvio ("Tony")—a first-generation Italian-American—and Madonna Ciccone. Her mother died when Madonna was only 5, and she never was able to accept her father's remarriage. The third child and oldest girl in a family of six children, Madonna helped raise her younger siblings. The family was strictly Catholic, and Madonna attended parochial schools, becoming rebellious early on.

After an early graduation from high school, Madonna attended the University of Michigan on a dance scholarship. After two years, in 1978, she dropped out and headed to New York City to make a career in dance. She joined the third company of the Alvin Ailey Dance Theater, but soon left. After a brief stint in France as a dancer and backup singer, she returned to New York and began to compose songs, forming several short-lived bands.

Madonna's climb to fame began late in 1982, when a disc jockey heard a demo recording she had made and secured a contract for her with Sire Records. Madonna's self-titled first album, released in July 1983, was not an immediate hit, but the single "Borderline" reached the Number 1 spot on the charts in spring 1984. She appeared briefly in the film *Vision Quest* (1984), singing "Crazy for You."

Madonna's second album, *Like a Virgin* (1984), helped along by the newly popular music video, led to her domination of the record charts throughout 1985. She presented a more serious musical image in 1986's *True Blue*, addressing the topic of teen pregnancy in "Papa Don't Preach," and in *Like a Prayer* (1989). In the title single and video, Madonna used the familiar symbols of her Catholic childhood to stir controversy once again. The title video pictured the singer apparently seducing a saint. A late 1990 video single, "Justify My Love," was banned from MTV because of its sexual content, and her 1990 Blond Ambition tour received heavy criticism because of its sexual content and suggestions of sadomasochism. In 1990 a greatest-hits package entitled *The Immaculate Collection* was released.

Madonna also has tried acting, first in the 1985 movie *Desperately Seeking Susan*, for which she received good reviews. After appearances in several mediocre films, she was praised for her role in *Dick Tracy* (1990). She also demonstrated talent in the Broadway play *Speed-the-Plow* (1988).

Divorced from the actor Sean Penn since 1989, Madonna is a strong supporter of AIDS-awareness campaigns and is active in many such groups.

Madonna

© V. Vlamos/REA/Saba

© David Valdez/The White House

Lynn Martin

MARTIN, Judith Lynn Morley

Lynn Martin, who gave up a safe seat in the U.S. House of Representatives to run unsuccessfully for the U.S. Senate against the incumbent Democrat Paul Simon in November 1990, took office as the 21st U.S. secretary of labor on Feb. 22, 1991. The former congresswoman had been named to the cabinet post by President Bush on Dec. 14, 1990, and the appointment was approved unanimously by the U.S. Senate on February 7.

Although a Bush loyalist, Martin supported the 1989 bill increasing the minimum wage and 1990 civil-rights and parental-leave legislation. The three measures were vetoed by the president, although he and Congress reached a compromise on the minimum-wage increase. During her confirmation hearings, Martin noted that the president did not "want yes women and yes men" and that she planned to give Bush her "best advice."

In late April the new labor secretary unveiled a voluntary plan to encourage small businesses to establish pension programs for their employees. A feature of the proposal would permit employees who change jobs to divert their pensions to an individual retirement account and to penalize those who did not.

Background. Judith Lynn Morley was born on Dec. 26, 1939, in Evanston, IL. After receiving a bachelor of arts degree from the University of Illinois in 1960, she taught in public and parochial schools during much of the 1960s. A member of the Winnebago County Board (1972–76), she served in the Illinois House of Representatives (1977–79) and in the state Senate (1979–81). As a state senator she cosponsored with Richard M. Daley, Jr., legislation to improve the state's nursing homes. On Nov. 4, 1980, the Illinois Republican was elected to the first of five terms in the U.S. House from the 16th District. The House seat was vacated by John Anderson (R), who ran for the presidency as an independent that year.

As a member of the House, she served on the budget and rules committees and was vice-chair of the House Republican Conference (1984) and the Committee on Rules (1984–88). Representative Martin also served as national cochair of the 1988 Bush-Quayle presidential campaign and was named Republican Woman of the Year in 1989. In 1988 she lost in a bid to win the chairmanship of the Republican Conference.

In January 1987 the future labor secretary married Harry D. Leinenweber, a federal judge in Illinois. She is the mother of two daughters from a previous marriage to John Martin, which ended in divorce.

MIYAZAWA, Kiichi

Kiichi Miyazawa, 72, like many Japanese politicians the son of a member of the (lower) House of Representatives, devoted almost half a century to preparing to become prime minister. On Oct. 11, 1991, the largest faction of the Liberal Democratic Party (LDP), controlled by former Prime Minister Noboru Takeshita, supported Miyazawa as president of the ruling party. (It earlier had withdrawn backing of Prime Minister Toshiki Kaifu.) Accordingly, on November 6 the Diet (parliament) elected Miyazawa to be Japan's 20th postwar prime minister.

An "internationalist" like one of his predecessors, Yasuhiro Nakasone, Miyazawa is even more fluent in English than is Nakasone. He was regarded with favor by Americans for being among the first to urge Japan to shift from export-driven growth to enhancement of domestic demand. However, he also has been known to recall the U.S. occupation (1945–52), when as a junior finance-ministry aide he had to take orders from the staff of Gen. Douglas MacArthur. Later, he occasionally grew restive under what he regarded as dictation from the United States.

It was expected that Miyazawa would bring more self-confidence to the prime ministership than recently had been seen. He seemed eager for Japan to participate in helping solve international financial problems, but was strongly critical of what he considered to be a recent U.S. trend toward blaming Japan for a worsening economy.

Miyazawa's success marked a remarkable political comeback, since he had been forced to resign as finance minister amid the turmoil of the Recruit influence-peddling scandal of less than three years earlier.

Background. Kiichi Miyazawa was born in Hiroshima prefecture on Oct. 8, 1919, and was graduated from Tokyo Imperial University (department of law) in 1941. He entered the finance ministry and in 1949 became private secretary to Finance Minister Hayato Ikeda. In 1953 Miyazawa resigned to run in an election for the (upper) House of Councillors, where he served two terms.

Since 1967, Miyazawa has been a member of the lower house, and has occupied a variety of posts in LDP-led governments. Three times he served as director-general of the Economic Planning Agency: in 1962–64 (under Prime Minister Ikeda, when Miyazawa was identified with the "doubling national income plan"); in 1966–68; and again in 1977–78. He was minister of international trade and industry (MITI) in 1970–71. He served as foreign minister (1974–76 under Prime Minister Takeo Miki), and has been minister of finance twice (1986–87 under Nakasone and 1987–88 in the Takeshita cabinet). He also served as chief cabinet secretary (1980–82) and as deputy prime minister (1987–88).

Miyazawa has headed the executive council of the LDP (1984–86), and since September 1986 has chaired the third-largest faction of the ruling party.

Miyazawa married his wife, Yoko, in 1943. The couple has a son, Hiro, and a daughter, Keiko. The new prime minister enjoys watching *Noh* drama, reading history, and playing golf.

ARDATH W. BURKS

ÖZAL, Turgut

During the Persian Gulf conflict of 1990–91 Turkey's President Turgut Özal added to his already controversial domestic political reputation by joining the anti-Iraq coalition firmly, closing the pipelines through which Iraq exported much of its oil (at a considerable financial loss to Turkey), and allowing the stationing of U.S. warplanes in his country. The actions were taken in part to show continued solidarity with the West and to boost implicitly Turkey's bid to join the European Community, but they generated domestic dissent from the many who did not want to risk military involvement.

President Özal is accustomed to controversy, however, having taken Turkey onto a road of an economy

© Haviv/Saba

Turgut Özal

increasingly open to the world. Most observers think that his economic program promises vigorous growth in the long run but has serious short-term domestic costs, including high inflation and unemployment. His devotion to Islam (he ran for parliament in the 1970s on the ticket of a religion-oriented political party) is also the source of a great deal of domestic debate between those who consider it a proper pillar of Turkish society and those who are alarmed at the increasing public role religious forces have played in recent years.

Background. Turgut Özal was born in 1927 in the eastern city of Malatya, the son of two teachers. He received his education in electrical engineering from Istanbul Technical University. After further training in the United States he held positions in several government agencies and was appointed to an important position in the State Planning Organization (SPO) in 1967. During the 1970s he spent two years at the World Bank in Washington, DC, and also worked in private industry. Rejoining the SPO as undersecretary in 1979, he is credited with devising a reform program designed to replace its state-dominated and inward orientation with increased liberal capitalism, privatization, and export-oriented integration with the world economy.

In 1983, when the armed forces returned Turkey to multiparty politics after its suspension (in 1980) and restructuring, Özal's personality, modern campaign tactics, and the electorate's desire to show defiance of the wishes of the generals for a different party won him and his Motherland Party a solid electoral victory and an absolute majority in the Grand National Assembly. As prime minister and as a skilled and flamboyant politician he dominated Turkish politics, but in 1987 his party was returned to power only through peculiarities of the electoral system. The setback was attributed mainly to the unpopular short-run social and economic costs of Özal's economic program, though his reputation also was tarnished by resentment at his giving important political offices to members of his family. His wife Semra, a strong supporter of women's rights, was chosen leader of the Istanbul branch of the Motherland Party in April 1991. In November 1989 he moved to the supposedly less partisan office of president, but he continued to head the Motherland Party and to direct Turkish foreign and domestic politics.

Özal and his wife are the parents of three children. Health problems have required that Özal receive specialized treatment in the United States on several occasions.

WALTER F. WEIKER

SCHWARZKOPF, H. Norman

Emerging from relative obscurity in late 1990 and early 1991, U.S. Army Gen. H. Norman Schwarzkopf, in a skillfully executed campaign highlighted by minimal allied casualties, forced occupying Iraqi troops out of Kuwait and severely damaged a menacing Iraqi military machine that had been growing relentlessly for more than a decade.

The four-star general dominated the entire operation from its inception. In a few short months he molded 690,000 disparate troops from various nations into a trained, cohesive fighting force ready to do battle on difficult desert terrain. Bringing to bear an impressive military skill, the highly decorated Vietnam veteran first destroyed the enemy's military infrastructure with six weeks of relentless air bombing. Then, after feigning an amphibious attack on the Kuwaiti coast, Schwarzkopf's forces made an end run around the other flank, cutting the Iraqi army off from its command and supplies and forcing surrender within 100 hours.

To Americans still recalling the bitter feelings of the Vietnam war and smarting from the beating their industrial sector was taking from Japanese and other foreign competitors, General Schwarzkopf appeared as a genuine, much-needed hero. To the international community of nations, Schwarzkopf's convincing win in the Persian Gulf proved without a doubt that the United States was still the world's major superpower.

Background. Born Aug. 22, 1934, in Trenton, NJ, to a retired army brigadier general—then head of the New Jersey state police—also named H. Norman, and his wife Ruth, Schwarzkopf knew from a very young age that he would make the army his career. After attending several military academies he spent a year in Iran, where his father was on assignment, before going on to private schools in Germany and Switzerland. He was graduated in the top 10% of the West Point class of 1956, was a member of its wrestling and football teams, and both sang in and conducted the cadet choir.

After undergoing infantry and airborne training, Schwarzkopf chose the infantry as his branch of service and was stationed in various stateside and overseas posts before his two tours of duty in Vietnam—the first as an adviser to the South Vietnamese Army, and the second as commander of a U.S. Infantry battalion. Schwarzkopf, known as a frontline officer, culminated his Vietnam service in a heroic effort that, at the risk of

H. Norman Schwarzkopf

© David Turnley/"Detroit Free Press"/Black Star

his life, helped rescue soldiers who had strayed into a mine field.

Schwarzkopf left Vietnam with three Silver Stars, three Bronze Stars, two Purple Hearts, and a Distinguished Service Medal, plus disillusionment concerning the competence of the U.S. general staff and bitterness about political interference in the conduct of the war and the lack of support by the people at home. These memories guided his conduct during the Gulf war.

The general also served as deputy commander of the 1983 Grenada invasion and was commander in chief of the U.S. Central Command since 1988.

In 1991 the general received an honorary knighthood from Queen Elizabeth and a contract of more than $5 million for his memoirs, in addition to other honors and acclaim. He retired from the army in August 1991. The 6′3″ (1.9-m), 240-lb (109-kg) general is married to the former Brenda Holsinger. They have two daughters and a son. Schwarzkopf is a folksy family man and avid outdoorsman who is fond of steak and ice cream.

SELES, Monica

Monica Seles came to the attention of tennis fans worldwide in 1990 by upsetting top seeds at major tennis tournaments—Martina Navratilova at the Italian Open and Steffi Graf at the German and French opens. With this last feat, Seles became, at age 16, the youngest woman ever to win the French Open, and the youngest since 1887 to win a Grand Slam title. Even more notable was the fact that it was Graf she defeated in the finals—a player considered virtually invincible until recently.

In 1991, Seles continued her meteoric rise to the top of women's tennis. She had a promising start to the year, winning the Australian and French opens and displacing Graf in March as the world's top-ranked woman player. Matters took a confusing turn when Seles dropped out of Wimbledon with almost no advance notice; she resurfaced two weeks later, explaining shin splints as the problem. Then it was back to business as usual, with Seles defeating Navratilova to take the U.S. Open and regain the Number 1 ranking Graf had recovered briefly. Seles concluded her stellar season by winning the Virginia Slims Championship in November. She became only the second woman in professional tennis (Graf was the other) to attain the final of every tournament she had entered. Fans were left wondering, however, if Seles would have become the first player since Graf in 1988 to win a Grand Slam, had she participated in Wimbledon.

Although controversial off the court, Seles is a consummate professional on the court, a powerful and aggressive player with great stamina. A left-hander who hits both forehands and backhands two-handed, Seles is expected by many to become known as one of the greatest woman players of all time.

Background. Monica Seles was born Dec. 2, 1973, in Novi Sad, Yugoslavia. Her father, Karolj, is a cartoonist, and her mother Esther, a computer programmer. Seles first took up tennis seriously at age 9. She was the European junior champion by age 10, and in 1985 was named Yugoslavian Sportswoman of the Year—the youngest recipient ever of this award. Seles was spotted by U.S. tennis coach Nick Bollettieri while playing a tournament in Florida. He offered her a full scholarship at his tennis academy, and the Seles family moved to Bradenton, FL, in 1986.

Seles' parents gave up their jobs to help support their daughter's career. In 1990, however, the Seles family broke bitterly with Bollettieri, claiming that Karolj really had been his daughter's coach all along, and that Bollettieri had spent too much time coaching other students.

The 5′9″ (1.75-m), 120-lb (54-kg) Seles is an excellent student. She spends time with her parents and her brother, Zoltan, in her spare time, and cites pop icon Madonna as her idol. Seles aims to bring a sense of glamour, as well as tennis ability, to the game.

See also SPORTS—*Tennis*.

SHULA, Donald Francis

Professional football coach Don Shula recorded the 300th win of an illustrious 29-year career when his Miami Dolphins defeated the Green Bay Packers, 16–13, on Sept. 22, 1991. The Dolphins went on to win six more games in 1991, extending Shula's victory total to 306—19 short of the record held by the late Chicago Bears coach George Halas. Consequently his career record as 1991 ended was 306 wins, 145 losses, and six ties—a percentage of .676, one of the best in the game's history. Although Shula has said that, "of course," he would like to surpass Halas' victory mark, his son Mike, a coaches' assistant with the Dolphins, claims that what his father really wants is another Super Bowl victory. He has won two of the six championships in which he has coached.

Bill Walsh, the former coach of the San Francisco 49ers, had said that "what makes Don the best" is his "ability to win with different teams in different eras. He's done it with passers like Unitas and Marino. He's done it with runners like Csonka, Jim Kick, and Mercury Morris. He's even done it with a rollout quarterback like Woodley, who really wasn't much of a passer." Shula himself has said: "You try to get the most out of the talent" of your players—"make 'em work and let 'em play."

Background. Donald Francis Shula was born Jan. 4, 1930, in Grand River, OH. Shula was a four-letter man in high school and played football at John Carroll University. A ninth-round draft pick by the Cleveland Browns in 1951, Shula began his professional career as a reserve defensive back on the taxi squad. After two seasons he was traded to the Baltimore Colts where, in addition to a starting position as right cornerback, he assisted the defensive coach (1953-56). He then played for one season with the Washington Redskins.

After working as assistant coach at the universities of Virginia and Kentucky, Shula joined the Detroit Lions in 1960 as defensive coordinator. In 1963 he succeeded Weeb Ewbank as head coach of the Baltimore Colts, compiling a 71-23-4 record over seven seasons. After the 1969 season, Shula signed a long-term contract with Miami. In 1972 he became the only coach to guide a team through an undefeated season.

In 1958, Shula married Dorothy Alice Bartish. They had two sons and three daughters. His older son, David, an assistant with his father (1982–88), was named head coach of the Cincinnati Bengals in December 1991, becoming at 32 the youngest coach in modern NFL history. The Don Shula Foundation was established in memory of his wife, who died of breast cancer in February 1991.

Norodom Sihanouk

SIHANOUK, Norodom

In November 1991, Cambodia's former king, Prince Norodom Sihanouk, returned home after more than a decade of exile to become his country's new president. A descendant of the centuries-old Khmer dynasty, the charismatic 69-year-old prince still commanded the loyalty of many Cambodians, especially those of the older generation, who remembered him as a colorful young man who liked to play the saxophone in a jazz band. In 1982, Sihanouk joined forces with the Communist Khmer Rouge and a smaller faction, the Khmer National Liberation Front, to form a government-in-exile in opposition to the Vietnamese-backed regime that controlled Cambodia.

In 1990 he and his colleagues opened negotiations with the Phnom Penh government in Paris under the sponsorship of the United Nations. An agreement signed in October 1991 established a Supreme National Council representing all factions and headed by Sihanouk, which was to administer the country in cooperation with UN authorities until free elections could be held. Once back in Cambodia, however, the prince assumed the presidency in an attempt to forestall a takeover by his erstwhile Khmer Rouge allies and restore peace.

Background. Born Oct. 31, 1922, Sihanouk succeeded his grandfather, King Monivong, on the Cambodian throne in 1941, when the country was part of French Indochina. Encouraged by the Japanese, who occupied Cambodia during World War II, he proclaimed Cambodia's independence in March 1945, but was forced to accept the return of French rule later the same year. In 1947 he established a constitutional monarchy, and in subsequent years struggled to contain a rebellion by the Khmer Issarak nationalist movement while working to achieve independence for Cambodia, under his leadership. France agreed to independence in 1953.

In 1955, Sihanouk abdicated in favor of his father, Norodom Suramarit, in order to free himself to take on a more direct political role. For the next 15 years Cambodia was a virtual one-party state dominated by Sihanouk and his Sangkum Reastr Niyum (People's Socialist Community); he ruled first as prime minister and, after his father's death in 1960, as chief of state. In foreign affairs he pursued a policy of neutrality, maintaining friendly relations with Communist China and North Vietnam and distancing himself from the anti-Communist West. In March 1970 his government was overthrown by a civilian-military coup led by the pro-Western Gen. Lon Nol, a move that was followed by the extension of the Vietnam war into Cambodia. Sihanouk fled to Beijing, where he remained until Lon Nol was ousted by the Khmer Rouge in 1975. After serving once more as head of state in 1975–76, he was placed under house arrest by the Communists, and went into exile again in 1979.

THOMAS, Clarence

U.S. President George Bush's choice in July 1991 of Clarence Thomas to replace retiring Supreme Court Justice Thurgood Marshall ultimately touched off a convulsive political battle unlike any in recent memory. It was not intended to be that way, and it did not start out explosively. Bush denied that he was filling an affirmative-action quota in selecting the black conservative judge to replace the only black ever to sit on the high court, indicating instead that Thomas was the best qualified candidate for the job.

Women's-rights activists and civil-rights groups disagreed. They pointed to remarks that Thomas had made seeming to suggest an opposition to abortion and to his stern criticism of affirmative action.

At the subsequent Senate confirmation hearings, Thomas refused to discuss his views on abortion and whether he would vote to overturn the court's 1973 ruling in *Roe v. Wade* that legalized abortion nationwide. He said he had no fixed views on the matter and never even had discussed it with friends. He also backed away

© Markel/Gamma-Liaison

Clarence Thomas

from controversial stands he had taken on some issues and endorsed a constitutional right to privacy. The Democrat-controlled Senate Judiciary Committee split, 7-7, on the nomination and sent it to the full Senate in late September.

That, however, was all a mild prelude to the real battle. On October 6, practically on the eve of the Senate's confirmation vote, it was revealed that a black law-school professor, Anita Hill, alleged that she had been the victim of sexual harassment by Thomas when she had worked for him in two different federal agencies during the 1980s. The ensuing avalanche of publicity and concern caused the Senate to postpone the vote and to conduct three days of televised hearings on the matter. During the hearings, Hill said that Thomas repeatedly had asked her out on dates and had refused to take no for an answer. She said that he described in explicit detail the sexual high jinks he had seen in pornographic movies. Thomas, in turn, unequivocally denied that there was any truth to the allegations, calling the Senate process a "high-tech lynching" of an "uppity" black man by unscrupulous liberals. Witnesses and Republican senators attacked Hill's credibility—and questioned her sanity. On October 15 when it was all over, Thomas had won confirmation by the narrow margin of 52–48. He took the oath of office as the 106th justice of the Supreme Court at a White House ceremony on October 18 and privately at the court on October 23.

Background. Thomas' life story—from his birth on June 23, 1948, in the segregated rural South of Pin Point, GA, to the doorstep of the Supreme Court—was the foundation of the White House campaign to win confirmation. A sharecropper's grandson who escaped from poverty to graduate from Holy Cross College and Yale Law School, Thomas became a federal appeals-court judge in 1990 after serving from 1982 to 1990 as chairman of the Equal Employment Opportunity Commission (EEOC). He earlier had served as the Education Department's civil-rights chief (1981–82) and as an assistant attorney general in Missouri (1974–77). He also had been a legislative aide (1979-81) to Sen. John Danforth (R-MO), his staunchest backer throughout the confirmation fight and someone who played a key role in helping Thomas finally win a high-court seat.

After his first marriage ended in divorce, Thomas was a single parent, raising his son, Jamal, during much of his tenure at the EEOC. His second wife, Virginia, who is white, is a deputy assistant secretary at the U.S. Department of Labor.

JIM RUBIN

© N. Tully/Sygma

Tommy Tune

TUNE, Thomas James

In 1990 the dancer, choreographer, and director Tommy Tune was honored as best choreographer and best director of a musical for his work in *Grand Hotel.* In 1991 he was presented Tonys in the same two categories for *The Will Rogers Follies.* It was the first time in the history of the theater awards that a single person had captured two Tonys in consecutive years. However, as Jack Kroll noted in reviewing *The Will Rogers Follies* for *Newsweek,* "with the tragic deaths of Gower Champion, Bob Fosse, and Michael Bennett, Tune is pretty much alone as Broadway's major choreographer."

In all, Tune has captured nine Tony Awards during his career, and not just for choreography and direction but for acting as well. He was named best supporting actor in a musical for *Seesaw* (1974) and best actor in a musical for *My One and Only* (1983). Of his success on both sides of the footlights, Tune has commented that performing "is like running away and joining the circus," but directing brings "adult" challenges. "A balance of the two makes a man happy."

Background. Thomas James Tune was born on Feb. 28, 1939, in Wichita Falls, TX, and developed a love of dance early. As his father trained Tennessee walking horses, the boy mimicked their gaits. He went to dance class at age 5. But a dream of ballet stardom died when Tune sprang to 6′6″ (1.98 m) by his early teens.

After graduating from the University of Texas in 1962 and studying theater at the University of Houston, he went to New York City, immediately landing a chorus role. Parts in regional theater, summer stock, and touring companies followed. He also appeared in such films as *Hello Dolly!* (1969) and *The Boy Friend* (1971) and on television's *The Dean Martin Show.*

In 1973 director Michael Bennett summoned Tune to Detroit to join a wounded version of *Seesaw*, the musical version of *Two for a Seesaw.* When the show opened on Broadway, Tune, who was cast as a homosexual choreographer who is the heroine's best friend, was given much of the credit for its critical success. During the next few years, he took odd jobs in television and directing/choreographing summer stock. In 1977 he was awarded an Obie award for his direction of the off-Broadway musical review *The Club.*

The Best Little Whorehouse in Texas, which opened off-Broadway before beginning a long Broadway run in 1978, marked Tune's return to the Great White Way and earned him a share of a Drama Desk award as best director. Choreographing *A Day in Hollywood/A Night in the Ukraine* (1980) and directing *Nine* (1982) followed and led to Tonys. He not only took accolades for his acting in *My One and Only* (1983) but also shared a Tony for its choreography.

Tommy Tune's overall success, especially with *Grand Hotel* and *The Will Rogers Follies,* led *Vanity Fair* to claim that when Tune shines "the Broadway musical is more than an antiquated pop form."

TYLER, Anne

After seeing her novel *The Accidental Tourist* (1985) made into a popular motion picture and winning a Pulitzer Prize for *Breathing Lessons* (1988), Anne Tyler delighted her many readers with her 12th novel, *Saint Maybe,* in 1991. The novel began appearing in bookstores in late summer and was a best-seller by September.

In *Saint Maybe,* Tyler once again turns to a family as the center of her plot. This time it is the Bedloes of Baltimore, who believed that "every part of their lives was absolutely wonderful." The main character is Ian, the youngest of the three Bedloe children, who feels responsible for the death of his older brother and gives up college to help care for his late brother's baby daughter and two stepchildren. The story covers a period of nearly 25 years.

As one critic noted, in *Saint Maybe,* Tyler "explores the myriad ways in which dreams get deferred and hopes revised, infusing the prosaic details of domestic

Anne Tyler

© Diana Walker/Gamma-Liaison

life with honor, humor, and deep affection," and raises "ordinariness to an art form."

Background. Anne Tyler was born in Minneapolis, MN, on Oct. 25, 1941, to Lloyd Parry and Phyllis Mahon Tyler. She spent her early years in various Quaker communities in the Midwest and South before living in North Carolina. She enrolled in Russian studies at Duke University at the age of 16. While at Duke, she came under the influence of the novelist Reynolds Price, who tried to foster a literary career for her. After doing postgraduate work in Russian at Columbia University, Tyler married Taghi Modarressi, a psychiatrist from Iran, in 1963.

Although Tyler's first two novels, *If Morning Ever Comes* and *The Tin Can Tree,* were published in 1964 and 1965, it was not until after the Modarressis moved to Baltimore in 1967 that she took up writing in earnest. *A Slipping-Down Life,* which Tyler reportedly considers one of her most bizarre works, and *The Clock Winder* were published in 1970 and 1972. It was with her next novel, *Celestial Navigation* (1974), the story of a disoriented artist who fears leaving his Baltimore block, that Tyler gained much critical acclaim and recognition as an important literary figure.

Searching for Caleb (1976) and *Earthly Possessions* (1977) were followed by *Morgan's Passing* (1980), the tale of Morgan Gower, a 42-year-old hardware store manager who takes on other roles. It was nominated for a National Book Critics Circle Award in hardcover and an American Book Award in paperback. According to novelist John Updike, in her ninth novel, *Dinner at the Homesick Restaurant* (1982), Tyler achieved "a new level of power and gives us a lucid and delightful yet complex and somber improvisation of her favorite theme, family life."

The appropriately titled *The Accidental Tourist* recounts the life of the well-organized travel writer Macon Leary—the tragic death of his son, his separation from his wife, and his attraction toward the carefree dog trainer Muriel Pritchett. The plot of Tyler's award-winning *Breathing Lessons* centers on one day in the life of Maggie and Ira Moran, who have been married for 28 years, as they drive to the funeral of a friend.

Anne Tyler, who also has written for *The New Yorker* and other magazines, is a member of P.E.N. and the American Academy and Institute of Arts and Letters. Of her endeavors, she has said: "I want to live other lives. I've never quite believed that one chance is all I get. Writing is my way of taking chances."

The Modarressis continue to live in Baltimore, the setting of many of her novels. They are the parents of two daughters.

VENTURI, Robert Charles

In April 1991, U.S. architect Robert Venturi was announced as the year's winner of the prestigious Pritzker Architectural Prize in recognition of a quarter century's influence on the profession. Although he has remained outside the mainstream of established architectural thought, he greatly has influenced that thought throughout his career, but not always in direct ways. Venturi has been the recipient of numerous awards, including the Brunner Memorial Prize in Architecture, awarded in 1973.

The year 1991 saw the completion of Venturi's most visible building to date, the Sainsbury Wing of the National Gallery in London. His idiosyncratic neoclassic design—combining columns, moldings, and other formal elements in unexpected ways—replaced a much-criticized, starkly modern design by a British firm. The building's plastic three-dimensional emphasis breaks with Venturi's usual design vocabulary of two-dimensional facades (or "billboards," as he calls them). These facades usually are decorated with flat designs and given profiles that recall popularly familiar associations.

Believed by some to be the first and one of the most influential in starting Post-Modernism, which depends heavily on the near-literal interpretation of historic styles, Venturi has been quoted as saying: "The modern movement was almost all right." Indeed he does not think of himself as a Post-Modernist, setting himself apart by a wholehearted acceptance of the industrial age. He applies builders-standard parts to what he calls "the decorated box," producing far different results from the stripped-down buildings that the Modernists thought to be the logical outcome of industrialism.

Courtesy, Jensen and Walker, Inc.

Robert Venturi

Background. Robert Charles Venturi was born June 25, 1925, in Philadelphia, PA. He was the only child of Robert Charles, a wholesale fruit merchant, and Vanna Venturi. Aspiring since childhood to become an architect, he attended Princeton University, becoming a member of Phi Beta Kappa and receiving a bachelor of arts degree summa cum laude in 1947. Venturi received a master of fine arts degree from Princeton in 1950 and attended the American Academy in Rome under a Rome Prize Fellowship awarded in 1954 and 1956.

After returning to Philadelphia, Venturi began by working in the firm of Louis I. Kahn. By 1958 he had organized his first firm, Venturi, Cope & Lippincott. In 1966 he published *Complexity and Contradiction in Architecture,* described by critic and then Yale professor Vincent Scully as the most important book on the subject since Le Corbusier's 1923 *Vers une Architecture,* thought to be the greatest influence on the establishment of Modernism. Venturi's book argued that symbolism, popular appeal, and decoration were important. "Less is a bore," said Venturi in answer to a famous quotation of Mies van der Rohe: "Less is more." His subsequent books include *Learning from Las Vegas* (1972), which argued for more popular appeal and the "billboard" approach to design. It was written with then associate Steven Izenour and wife Denise Scott Brown—an architect, author, and educator—who has collaborated on many of Venturi's books. She is a member of the firm Venturi, Scott Brown and Associates, and is credited with a strong influence on his design.

Venturi and his wife have been married since 1967; they have one son, born in 1971.

CHARLES KING HOYT

BIOTECHNOLOGY

The year 1991 brought encouraging advances in the development of an efficient blood substitute and an environmentally safe bacterial insecticide, the use of coral in reconstructive bone surgery, and the use of a nasal spray in gene therapy. Understanding of the biological activity of dioxin also increased.

Human Hemoglobin from Yeasts. Advances in modern medicine have produced a need for blood that far has surpassed its availability. The simplest solution would be to produce human hemoglobin that would function outside a red blood cell as well as it does within it. Two problems exist. First, outside the red blood cells, hemoglobin tends to break up into its component parts which are filtered out of the bloodstream by the person's kidneys. Second, the remaining intact hemoglobin binds so tightly to oxygen that the oxygen is not released to the tissues in adequate amounts.

Dr. G. Stetler and his colleagues at the biotechnology firm Somatogen, Inc. in Boulder, CO, announced that they have succeeded in altering human-hemoglobin genes so that the above problems are avoided. They also have transferred these altered genes to yeast cells which produced the desired human-hemoglobin molecules in large amounts. This genetically engineered human hemoglobin must be tested in people. If effective, this blood substitute will save countless lives.

Bacterial Insecticide. In the battle against crop-destroying insects, one approach has been to spray plants with bacteria to which the gene for the Bt protein—an endotoxin which kills insects that swallow the bacteria while feeding on a plant—has been transferred. An objection of the Environmental Protection Agency (EPA) to bacterial insecticides is that the gene-altered bacteria will reproduce and spread from their point of application in a field, with unknown consequences to the natural ecosystem.

Mycogen Corp., an agricultural-biotechnology company in San Diego, kills the bacteria before selling them to the farmers. Under these conditions, the bacterial pesticides present no danger to the environment, although they are as effective against insects as when they were alive. This new approach to the preparation of genetically engineered bacterial insecticides received EPA approval.

Coral for Bone Repair. When the repair of severe bone fractures requires a connecting segment to bridge the gap between broken sections, surgeons usually insert pieces of bone which they have removed from other parts of the patient's body. Dr. P. Spiegel at the University of South Florida Medical Center in Tampa and others elsewhere have been experimenting successfully with the use of coral—the hard (calcium carbonate) porous skeleton of certain marine animals (sea anemones)—for bone repair. Because of the porous nature of coral, when it is inserted between sections of broken bone, blood vessels and cells (osteocytes) from the adjacent bone sections move into the spaces of the coral, resulting in a solid seal between them. Of great importance is the fact that coral does not elicit an immune response from the patient's body, as can occur when bone from another individual is used. The biotechnology company Interpore International of Irvine, CA, now prepares blocks of coral for use in reconstructive bone surgery.

Adenovirus and Genetic Emphysema. Two million Americans suffer from emphysema, a disease which involves the progressive destruction of an individual's lung tissue. About 40,000 of them suffer because of the lack of a gene-produced protein alpha-1 antitrypsin, which limits the activity of neutrophil elastase, an enzyme that normally destroys only worn-out lung cells. In the absence of alpha-1 antitrypsin, neutrophil elastase also destroys healthy lung cells.

Dr. R. G. Crystal and his associates at the National Heart, Lung and Blood Institute transferred copies of the human alpha-1 antitrypsin gene to the adenovirus which infects lung cells, causing various respiratory diseases ranging from the common cold to pneumonia. Prior to the gene transfer, however, the adenovirus was modified so that it was incapable of reproducing and causing disease. The scientists then squirted solutions containing the genetically engineered virus into the lung passages of rats. After one week, the experimenters detected human alpha-1 antitrypsin in the rats' lung secretions, indicating the adenovirus had entered the rats' lung cells and the human gene was functioning normally. If this nasal-spray adenovirus procedure can be used successfully with humans, it opens tremendous possibilities for the cure of genetic emphysema and other lung-involving genetic diseases (such as cystic fibrosis).

Dioxin's Biological Activity. Dioxin (TCDD) is an industrial waste product which contaminates the environment. Laboratory studies with animals have shown that dioxin is lethal at high doses and—depending on the species and dosage—can cause cancer, birth defects, liver damage, and depression of the immune system. Dr. O. Hankinson of the University of California at Los Angeles has reported that after entering a cell, TCDD moves into the nucleus, where it binds to a particular chromosomal site close to the gene that specifies the enzyme cytochrome P-450 protein. This induces the P-450 gene to become active, leading to the synthesis of excessive amounts of the cytochrome enzyme. When present in very large amounts, this enzyme makes a number of toxic compounds in the cell even more potent, resulting in one or more dioxin-caused diseases.

LOUIS LEVINE, *City College of New York*

BOLIVIA

Bolivia continued to make progress on several economic fronts in 1991, but poverty, the unequal distribution of income, and the scarcity of foreign investment presented the central government with formidable challenges.
The government had to deal with public-health problems, principally scattered outbreaks of cholera (*see* SIDEBAR/LATIN AMERICA) and yellow fever. It also came under criticism for its handling of antidrug-trafficking programs supported by the United States.

Economy. In recent years, Bolivia has kept rampant inflation in check. The rise in prices, which reached 24,000% in 1985, was held to 18% in 1990, one of the lowest inflation indices in Latin America. Nevertheless, a World Bank mission found in 1991 that the gross national product (GNP) per capita had been stagnant since 1986, consumption per capita had fallen steadily, and private investment had declined by 6%, despite various private-sector incentives.

The bank's mission found that a large portion of the country's economic activity still was dominated by government enterprises. In Bolivia, the mission said, there were 157 state-owned companies with 30,395 employees, representing 66% of public expenditures. In April 1990 the government had announced an ambitious plan to sell two thirds of the state enterprises, but, the mission said, the privatization plan still had to be executed.

In April, Exxon, the U.S. oil company, announced that it would invest at least $40 million in oil exploration on the Bolivian altiplano. In August, President Jaime Paz Zamora and Uruguay's President Luis Alberto Lacalle said they had agreed to work toward an international accord to govern shipping on the Paraguay-Panama waterway system that extends from southeast Bolivia to Buenos Aires, Argentina.

Integration. The two presidents also said they would explore ways for Bolivia to join the newly formed MERCOSUR, a common-market movement involving Argentina, Brazil, Paraguay, and Uruguay in South America's Southern Cone. Bolivia is a member of the Andean Group, which includes Colombia, Ecuador, Peru, and Venezuela. Membership in the Andean Group was an impediment to Bolivia's entry into the MERCOSUR. For its part, the Andean Group announced in 1991 that it would seek to create its own common market by 1995. Late in 1991 legislation was pending in the U.S. Congress to provide preferential tariff treatment for certain Andean exports to the United States.

Drugs. One of the most difficult political problems for the Bolivian government has been the question of how to deal with international drug trafficking. Bolivia exports an estimated 30 to 55 tons (27 200 to 50 000 kg) of cocaine per year, most of it bound for the United States. The government was under heavy pressure from the United States to participate in coca-eradication programs and other antidrug efforts and came under fire at home for seeming to bow to U.S. demands.

The February appointment of retired Army Col. Faustino Rico Toro as head of Bolivia's antinarcotics forces set off a crisis in relations with the United States. Rico Toro had been an intelligence chief in the dictatorship of Gen. Luis García Meza during 1980–81 and was charged by U.S. officials with corruption, human-rights violations, and links to cocaine traffickers. Rico Toro resigned his post on March 4, barely a week after his appointment. Bolivia's Minister of the Interior Guillermo Capobianco Rivera also resigned following accusations in U.S. newspapers that he had accepted payments from drug traffickers.

In April, President Paz Zamora provoked waves of angry demonstrations when he announced his decision to allow the Bolivian army to participate in the war on drugs. The Union of Bolivian Workers called a nationwide one-day strike to protest the decision.

Tempers were inflamed further in May, when Bob Martinez, the director of the U.S. Office of National Drug Control Policy, visited Bolivia to press the government to sign a treaty permitting the extradition of Bolivians charged with drug crimes in the United States. Paz Zamora declined to sign the treaty, which had been under study for two years.

U.S. efforts were set back still more in July, when Paz Zamora pledged to block extradition of Bolivian drug traffickers who turned themselves in to the government within four months. Bolivian officials also said the offer included possible reduction of sentences for persons convicted of drug crimes, if they cooperated with the government in identifying other traffickers.

RICHARD C. SCHROEDER, *Consultant to the Organization of American States*

BOLIVIA • Information Highlights

Official Name: Republic of Bolivia.
Location: West-central South America.
Area: 424,162 sq mi (1 098 580 km²).
Population (mid-1991 est.): 7,500,000.
Chief Cities (mid-1988 est.): Sucre, the legal capital, 95,635; La Paz, the actual capital, 1,049,800; Santa Cruz de la Sierra, 615,122; Cochabamba, 377,259.
Government: *Head of state and government,* Jaime Paz Zamora, president (took office Aug. 5, 1989). *Legislature*—Congress: Senate and Chamber of Deputies.
Monetary Unit: Boliviano (3.590 bolivianos equal U.S.$1, June 1991).
Gross National Product (1988 U.S.$): $4,600,000,000.
Economic Index (1990): *Consumer Prices* (La Paz, 1983 = 100), all items, 1,104,426; food, 998,735.
Foreign Trade (1990 U.S.$): *Imports,* $715,000,000; *exports,* $900,000,000.

BRAZIL

Amid economic stagnation, spiraling inflation, charges of wrongdoing, and military grousing, President Fernando Collor de Mello's government launched a long-delayed drive to privatize key sectors of Brazil's economy in 1991. Congress declined to act on his proposal to amend the nationalistic constitution.

Politics. Collor, who took office in March 1990 as a popular champion of growth and reform, saw his public-approval rating plummet during the year. Contributing to these negative sentiments were irregularities and political favoritism allegedly practiced by Collor's wife, Roseane, before she resigned as president of the Legiao Brasileira de Assistencia (LBA). No sooner had the government come to grips with the LBA scandal then it was discovered that the office of the presidency, even as it demanded austerity in other agencies, had purchased 26 new cars.

In an attempt to give some direction to his administration, Collor renewed his privatization efforts later in the year. In late October the government sold Usiminas, the country's largest steel mill. The auction occurred amid massive security after a bomb was hurled at the Rio de Janeiro stock exchange on the eve of the transaction. Riot-squad police used tear gas on demonstrators who protested the sale.

Such demonstrations emboldened demagogic politicians to protest the Usiminas sale, as well as a proposal, pending in the National Congress at year's end, to allow private firms to sign risk contracts for oil exploration. The nationalistic 1988 constitution reserved such prospecting to Petrobrás, the state oil firm.

The most strident critic was Rio de Janeiro Gov. Leonel Brizola. A disciple of Petrobrás founder Getúlio Vargas, the populist Brizola, 69, sought to craft a nonpartisan front opposed to "divesting the country of its national patrimony." In addition to foes of Collor, Brizola solicited support from Vice-President Itamar Franco, an opponent of the Usiminas sale, and elements of the military. Even as the opposition to Collor mounted, Delfim Neto, Roberto Campos, and other members of the Bloc of Modern Economists applauded Collor's initiatives to modernize the nation's hugely statist economy.

Advocates of a plebiscite on converting Brazil's government to a parliamentary regime sought to advance the vote, scheduled for 1993. Collor thwarted this drive for an early plebiscite because the Workers' Party (PT) and other Collor opponents hoped to use the election to abbreviate his four-year presidential term.

In May, Zélia Cardoso de Mello, the "super minister" of economics and one of the architects of Collor's economic shock program, resigned. She had become the center of attention in October 1990 when her affair with Justice Minister Bernardo Cabral, a married man, became public. Cardoso de Mello was replaced by Marcílio Marques Moreira, the fifth economics minister in six years.

Economy. While other Latin American nations moved ahead with economic change, Brazil found itself caught in a vexing cycle of

Miners search for gold in the Brazilian Pantanal. Such mining as well as soy farming and inexpensive development for tourism are threatening the area, the world's largest wetland. About 80% of the Pantanal is in Brazil, with the balance in Bolivia and Paraguay.

recession, government deficits, stagnation, and inflation. Upon taking office, Collor had tried to strike a "death blow" against inflation. He froze billions of dollars worth of individual savings accounts and took other steps to restrict the money supply. In addition, he promised to cut the number of state employees, while privatizing white-elephant state firms. He also advocated new social programs to uplift the masses whose standard of living fell 3% in 1991 compared with 1990.

Collor claimed that his bold stabilization plan would have succeeded except for the Persian Gulf war. This conflict drove up energy prices and impeded anti-inflation schemes in Brazil and other oil-importing countries.

More of an obstacle to Collor's attempted changes, however, was the 1988 constitution that guaranteed job security to government workers, making it extremely difficult to slash the bloated public payroll. The constitution also placed a ceiling on interest rates, mandated public spending in several areas, and restricted foreign investment, particularly in exploiting Brazil's oil and mineral wealth.

To gain control over the economy and spur growth, Collor presented a reform package to Congress. These measures included: 1) allowing only the federal government, not states and municipalities, to issue public debt bonds; 2) applying the same rules to inefficient, overstaffed state companies that affect private firms—for example, permitting them to go bankrupt; 3) allowing greater participation by foreign investors in national corporations; 4) lifting the banking secrecy rules; 5) implementing "fiscal adjustments" to boost federal revenues; and 6) returning public employees to a social-security system separate from private-sector workers.

The chief executive, however, failed to win support for his initiatives. Any constitutional amendment must twice pass Congress by a 60% vote, and legislative leaders declined to act in 1991.

BRAZIL • Information Highlights

Official Name: Federative Republic of Brazil.
Location: Eastern South America.
Area: 3,286,473 sq mi (8 511 965 km^2).
Population (mid-1991 est.): 153,300,000.
Chief Cities (mid-1989 est.): Brasília, the capital, 1,803,478; São Paulo, 10,997,472, Rio de Janeiro, 6,011,181; Belo Horizonte, 2,339,039.
Government: *Head of state and government,* Fernando Collor de Mello, president (took office March 15, 1990). *Legislature*—National Congress: Senate and Chamber of Deputies.
Monetary Unit: Cruzeiro (866.21 cruzeiros equal U.S.$1, Dec. 11, 1991).
Gross Domestic Product (1989 est. U.S.$): $377,000,000,000.
Economic Indexes (1990): *Consumer Prices* (Sao Paulo, 1988 = 100), all items, 39,039.3; food, 38,110.2. *Industrial Production* (1980 = 100), 100.
Foreign Trade (1990 U.S.$): *Imports,* $20,501,000,000; *exports,* $31,408,000,000.

The stalemate further eroded public confidence and threatened to wipe out Collor's successes against inflation. Prices—which fell during the spring—began to rise in the summer, with the inflation rate exceeding 260% for the year.

Also discouraging were setbacks in foreign trade, long the motor of Brazilian growth. Even though the trade surplus ($8.7 billion) for the first eight months was 1.9% higher than in 1990, the October surplus was $426 million, the smallest monthly surplus of the first ten months of 1991. Thus foreign-exchange holdings fell to a disturbing low level of $6.3 billion. While Brazilians imported more foodstuffs through August, lower export levels were caused by poorer sales of orange juice, coffee, soya, and other agricultural commodities. Crucial to sagging exports was the U.S. recession. Between January and August the United States purchased 19.1% of Brazilian sales abroad, down from 25% during the first half of 1990.

Earlier, in late March, Brazil, Argentina, Paraguay, and Uruguay had signed an accord establishing the Southern Cone Common Market (SCCM), to be effective by Jan. 1, 1995. The organization, modeled after the European Community, would be headed by a president. This office was to be rotated among the member nations every six months.

Foreign Affairs. The Persian Gulf war caused a decline in Brazil's weapons-industry exports as Arab nations, once among Brazil's biggest arms customers, turned to the United States and Western European nations as the "natural suppliers" of weaponry during the conflict. In addition, Brazil incurred Washington's wrath for leaking sensitive military-research information to Iraq and other Third World states, a move that resulted in increased U.S. pressure on the Collor regime to tighten controls over the dissemination of such data. Brazil responded by adopting and implementing principles of the Missile Technology Control Regime, a 1987 pact restricting the circulation of sensitive military technology.

The presidents of Argentina and Brazil jointly denounced the proliferation of nuclear weapons, insisting that developments in nuclear technology in their nations was intended exclusively for civilian purposes. On September 5, Brazil joined Argentina and Chile in signing a joint resolution that condemned the production and use of chemical weapons.

From June 17 to 20, Collor was in Washington, where he met with U.S. President George Bush to discuss Brazil's emerging role in the world economy and his country's foreign debt. During a September address to the United Nations, Brazil's chief executive castigated the United States for failing to fulfill its "inescapable obligation" to help protect the environment. In mid-1992 Brazil was to host the first Earth Summit on global ecological concerns. In planning the agenda for the conference, Washington reportedly had resisted including a discussion of mandatory limits on carbon-dioxide emissions.

In October, Pope John Paul II traveled to Brazil for the first time in 11 years. He visited ten state capitals as part of a ten-day whirlwind tour during which he castigated public and private morals in the country.

GEORGE W. GRAYSON
College of William & Mary

BRITISH COLUMBIA

In 1991, British Columbia more than lived up to its reputation for political turbulence. The provincial economy had an encouraging year.

Government and Politics. The controversy surrounding Social Credit Premier William Vander Zalm's activities in connection with the September 1990 sale of his Fantasy Gardens theme park led the premier to initiate an investigation by Conflict-of-Interest Commissioner Edward Hughes. On March 29, Vander Zalm announced his intention to step down; he resigned on April 2 following the release of the Hughes report, which found there had been a conflict of interest in the C$16 million sale.

After Vander Zalm's resignation, the Social Credit caucus of Legislative Assembly members chose Rita Johnston as interim leader; Johnston thus became Canada's first woman premier. In a cabinet shuffle April 15, Premier Johnston brought three new ministers into a smaller, 19-member cabinet. Former Finance Minister Melville Couvelier, who early in March had become the 11th minister to resign from the cabinet since the 1986 election, was reappointed, but a month later was asked to resign. At the subsequent party leadership convention July 18–20, Johnston narrowly defeated Grace McCarthy, 941 votes to 881, on the second ballot in a contest among five leadership candidates, including Couvelier.

In the long-awaited provincial general election held October 17, the Social Credit government not only was defeated but was relegated to third-party status with 24% of the popular vote, giving it seven seats in the enlarged 75-seat House. The Liberal Party led by Gordon Wilson had not held a seat since 1979, but this time captured 17 to become the official opposition with 33% of the vote. New Democratic Party leader Mike Harcourt became the province's 29th premier. His party secured 51 seats with 41% of the vote. This new political mood was demonstrated further in the overwhelming support given to two government-sponsored referendum questions to permit voter recall of members of the legislature and to allow voters to initiate their own referendum questions.

Budget. The provincial budget estimated general-fund revenue for 1991–92 at C$16.15 billion after dissolution of the Budget Stabilization Fund, and expenditures at C$16.545 billion. The deficit was reported at C$395 million, but total gross borrowing requirements amounted to C$1.982 billion. New revenue measures included increases in some taxes and in Medicare premiums. A commitment was made to balance the budget over a five-year business cycle. The legislature adjourned in July without authorizing the full budget.

Concern over the federal government's offloading of its deficit grew further after the province lost a court challenge to the federal capping of Canada Assistance Plan transfer payments for social-assistance programs.

Economy. As the unemployment rate fell below 10%, British Columbia's economy seemed largely to have escaped the recession which had plagued eastern Canada. However, the forestry and mining resource sectors were faced with lower metal and lumber prices toward year's end. Low newsprint demand prompted mill closures and layoffs.

Other News. Antilogging protests by environmentalists continued during the summer. . . . Research and development received a boost from the federal government's confirmation of its one-third share, C$236 million, of the University of British Columbia's KAON project in subatomic-particle physics research.

NORMAN J. RUFF, *University of Victoria*

BRITISH COLUMBIA • Information Highlights

Area: 365,946 sq mi (947 800 km²).
Population (September 1991): 3,218,900.
Chief Cities (1986 census): Victoria, the capital, 66,303; Vancouver, 431,147; Prince George, 67,621; Kamloops, 61,773; Kelowna, 61,213.
Government (1991): *Chief Officers*—lt. gov., David C. Lam; premier, Michael Harcourt (New Democratic Party). *Legislature*—Legislative Assembly, 75 members.
Provincial Finances (1991–92 fiscal year budget): *Revenues,* $16,150,000,000; *expenditures,* $16,545,000,000.
Personal Income (average weekly earnings, July 1991): $546.89.
Labor Force (September 1991, seasonally adjusted): *Employed* workers, 15 years of age and over, 1,502,000; *Unemployed,* 9.7%.
Education (1991–92): *Enrollment*—elementary and secondary schools, 593,200 pupils; postsecondary—universities, 43,550; community colleges, 27,500.
(All monetary figures are in Canadian dollars.)

BULGARIA

Bulgaria began 1991 under a new transitional government with politically independent judge Dimitar Popov as prime minister. Of 17 cabinet positions in the Popov government only eight went to the Bulgarian Socialist Party (BSP) (formerly the Bulgarian Communist Party—BCP). The remaining nine positions had been distributed among the opposition.

Political Affairs. The new government's efforts were concentrated on the passage of a new constitution, stabilized labor relations, and economic reform. February saw the passage of the Land Reform Law, returning appropriated land to original owners or their heirs. In June a unified tax administration, using the United States as a model, was initiated. After an August strike by 21,000 miners (nearly one third of Bulgaria's miners) demanding wage increases, the Federation of Miners forced the government to double their salaries.

Debate in the Grand National Assembly over restoration of the monarchy proved to be short-lived with the revocation, eight days after approval, of a planned July 6 referendum to decide the issue. Former Czar Simeon II was issued a Bulgarian passport on June 12, but would not disclose if he would visit.

Former Communists faced increasing unpopularity in 1991. By the beginning of the year membership in the BSP had plummeted from more than 1 million to an estimated 250,000. In late April the BSP and other former Communist organizations were ordered to compensate for funds illegally expropriated from the government between 1949 and 1990. On October 1 the Bulgarian Supreme Court froze most BSP assets. The first of the trials of former party members and government officials for corruption began on February 13. The trial of former head of state Todor Zhivkov began February 25, but was discontinued in June due to his health.

On July 9 the Grand National Assembly passed the third reading of the new constitution and on July 14, 307 of the 400 delegates signed the new constitution into law, while 80 members of the Union of Democratic Forces (UDF) and the Turkish Movement for Rights and Freedoms (MRF) abstained.

Elections were held on October 13, and only three parties—UDF, BSP, and MRF—passed the minimum threshold of 4% of the vote necessary to receive seats in parliament, the final distribution being UDF, 110; BSP, 106; and MRF, 24. The UDF nominated its chairman, Filip Dimitrov, as prime minister and sought the support of the ethnic Turkish MRF, though without a coalition, fearing that appointment of an ethnic Turk to a cabinet position might cause an eruption of nationalist furor. Presidential elections were set for Jan. 13, 1992. Under the new constitution the president would serve a five-year term and would be limited to two terms.

Domestic and Social Affairs. Resistance to the reversal of the "Bulgarization" campaign against the ethnic Turkish minority continued in 1991, especially over the planned introduction of Turkish-language instruction in elementary schools. In March the Grand National Assembly decided to introduce optional Turkish-language courses, but on October 1, in a dramatic reversal, it passed a law prohibiting the teaching of any minority languages.

BULGARIA • Information Highlights

Official Name: People's Republic of Bulgaria.
Location: Southeastern Europe.
Area: 42,823 sq mi (110 910 km²).
Population (mid-1991 est.): 9,000,000.
Chief Cities (Dec. 31, 1988 est.): Sofia, the capital, 1,136,875; Plovdiv, 364,162; Varna, 306,300.
Government: *Head of state,* Zhelyu Zhelev, president (took office August 1990). *Head of government,* Filip Dimitrov, premier (took office October 1991). *Legislature*—Grand National Assembly.
Monetary Unit: Lev (18.3 leva equal U.S.$1, July 1991).
Gross National Product (1989 est. U.S.$): $51,200,-000,000.
Economic Index (1989): *Industrial Production* (1980 = 100), 139.
Foreign Trade (1990 U.S.$): *Imports,* $13,089,-000,000; *exports,* $13,428,000,000.

Economic Affairs. Food prices rose to five to seven times 1990 levels; the prime interest rate rose from 15% to 45%; and economists predicted an inflation rate of 288% in 1991. By September unemployment was estimated at 320,000 (nearly 8% of the total work force).

Throughout 1991, Bulgaria sought to alleviate its debt problems. The Paris Club rescheduled Bulgaria's $2 billion debt over the next ten years. In March the International Monetary Fund granted a loan of $503 million, with $109 million for energy needs. A new currency-convertibility regime, limited to established financial institutions and national banks, was introduced to realign the official rate with the black market. In June, Bulgaria's first commodity exchange opened for trade once a week. In August the World Bank granted Bulgaria $250 million to finance structural changes in the economy.

Bulgaria's energy crisis became critical in January, disrupting industry and transportation. On January 1 gasoline sales to nonessential private and state vehicles were discontinued due to low reserves, aggravated by the Soviet failure on oil deliveries, the Persian Gulf war, and frequent breakdowns of the Kozlodui nuclear-power plant. The situation deteriorated to the point that the country possessed no energy reserves and many households had electricity for only a few hours each day.

Diplomatic Affairs. In 1991, Bulgaria concluded a 20-year friendship treaty with Greece. It also improved relations with the United States. In April the two nations signed agreements on trade, economic cooperation, and tourism, moving Bulgaria closer to most-favored-nation status. In June, Vice-President Dan Quayle became the highest-ranking U.S. official ever to visit Bulgaria. President Zhelyu Zhelev reciprocated by traveling to Washington in mid-September.

VLADIMIR TISMANEANU
University of Maryland

BURMA. *See* MYANMAR.

BUSINESS AND CORPORATE AFFAIRS

It was a year of stress, disappointments, and change for businesses in the United States throughout 1991—a year in which companies large and small were compelled to face long-delayed decisions. Downsizing and restructuring—marked by mass layoffs, plant closings, write-offs, and refinancings—were frequent. Shareholders became more restive and active, and critical of high management salaries. Small businesses complained about a credit crunch, and retailers strained to induce insecure consumers to spend.

Troubled Areas. Many industries or segments of them, including banking, insurance, airlines, automobiles, real estate, retailing, housing construction, and the media, were in serious condition. Crimped advertising budgets affected the media in particular. Business profits overall were depressed; third-quarter earnings of the 30 Dow Jones industrials fell 30% from a year earlier. Dividends were slashed. In just the first half of the year, 244 cuts and omissions were recorded, the highest six-month total of unfavorable dividend actions since the first half of 1982.

Losses and write-offs reached immense levels. Citicorp lost $885 million in just the third quarter, and the company said it would eliminate its dividend. Ford, General Motors, and Chrysler already had cut their dividends in anticipation of further losses; their total deficit was $1.7 billion in the third quarter alone. International Business Machines (IBM), still highly profitable despite lower earnings, said in March that it would charge off $2.3 billion and reduce its work force by 14,000. In November it announced another restructuring and charge to earnings, this one involving 20,000 more workers and an additional $3 billion. The latter was to pay for termination expenses and a "fundamental redefinition" of its business. Small businesses suffered badly, many claiming banks cut existing lines of credit. Lenders said that they had sufficient problems of their own and could not risk more.

Financial disasters were common. Dun & Bradstreet said third-quarter business failures jumped 51.5% to 50,641 from 33,425 in the same period of 1990, with total liabilities soaring to $56.5 billion from $37.1 billion.

Banking. The most spectacular failures were in banking. On New Year's Day, Rhode Island shut down 45 banks and credit unions to prevent a run on deposits after their private insurer collapsed. At the time, 1,000 of 12,400 U.S. commercial banks were ranked troubled by the federal government, and the Federal Deposit Insurance Corporation (FDIC) said it expected 180 banks with assets of $70 billion to fail during the year. Within days the Bank of New England, burdened by nonperforming real-estate loans, collapsed in spite of its $22 billion in assets. And by midyear, in the largest bailout ever of a savings bank, the FDIC seized New York state's Goldome Bank. In March, Congress agreed to spend $30 billion in taxpayers' money to pay off insured depositors at failed savings and loans. The amount was insufficient, however, and the Bush administration requested an additional $80 billion in June, a sum that was reduced to $25 billion by Congress. (*See also* BANKING AND FINANCE.)

Insurers. Public confidence was eroded further by the poor condition of many insurers, their asset base weakened by declines in the value of real estate and junk bonds. After weeks of rumors that company assets were insufficient to guarantee 245,000 policyholders, the state of California seized Executive Life Insurance, a company with $46.11 billion of life insurance and annuities on its books. Executive, founded in the early 1980s, was a relative newcomer to the insurance industry. But some of the biggest names in the industry—old-line firms such as John Hancock, New England Mutual, and Travelers—were among those whose finances were downgraded by Moody's. The realization that such pillars of finance had quivered was unnerving to an already apprehensive public. (*See also* INSURANCE.)

Scandals. Concern became dismay with public knowledge of two almost unbelievable financial scandals that suggested intrigue at the very heart of the government's financing system. In the first case, evidence became public that the Pakistani-managed, Abu Dhabi-owned Bank of Credit and Commerce International (BCCI) was infiltrated by thieves, implicated in spying and drug trafficking, and involved in financing weapons merchants. It also controlled First American Bankshares, the largest commercial bank in the Washington, DC, area, which was headed by former presidential adviser Clark Clifford as chairman. Clifford claimed he was unaware of the institution's control by BCCI. (*See also* SPECIAL REPORT/INTERNATIONAL TRADE AND FINANCE.)

Atop this scandal came the discovery that the most powerful dealer in U.S. government securities, the esteemed and highly profitable Salomon Brothers firm, had attempted to control the market and to some degree had done so. Moreover, the firm's top management had learned of the activity and failed to report it to regulators. Senior officers, led by Chairman John Gutfreund, were replaced by a team headed by Warren Buffett, owner of $700 million of Salomon's preferred stock and widely regarded as a savvy investor and upright businessman.

Working It Out. Buffett had much company in dealing with challenges. Unable to pay his bills, Donald Trump saw many of his assets divided among creditors. Carl Icahn, an otherwise successful investor, had to sell his investment in USX in order to calm his TWA bondholders. Robert Dilenschneider, seemingly at the peak of a much-praised public-relations career as chief executive officer of Hill & Knowlton, lost his job. William Farley's ownership of the $1.6 billion West Point-Pepperell company collapsed in a bankruptcy deal to 5% from 95%. Owen Bieber, United Auto Workers president, lost his seat on the Chrysler board when membership was cut to 13 from 18. Media magnate Rupert Murdoch remained oppressed by huge debts. The sons of Robert Maxwell, the media giant, were confronted by a unique problem—the unraveling of their father's publishing empire after his sudden and mysterious death on November 5.

New Managers. Financial tensions and marketplace changes forced boards to seek new managers. Lawrence Bossidy replaced a suddenly retired Edward L. Hennessy, Jr., as chairman of Allied Signal. Michael Walsh replaced a similarly reluctant James L. Ketelsen at Tenneco. Stanley Gault took over the reins at Goodyear from Tom Barrett, who had been named to the job only two years earlier. Michael Miles replaced Hamish Maxwell as chairman of Philip Morris. Many new chairmen had in common a desire to cut costs that had soared in the 1980s, and some also were intent on reorganizing their companies.

It was a chairman who retained his job, however, who announced the most startling reorganization. IBM's John F. Akers said late in the year that the company would reorganize into a "family" of loosely affiliated companies and that parts of IBM even might be spun off. Earlier, IBM and Apple Computer, one of its chief competitors, announced they would share their advanced technology and deep secrets, while remaining competitors in marketing. Similar alliances were made by otherwise competing companies.

See also STOCKS AND BONDS.

JOHN CUNNIFF, *The Associated Press*

CALIFORNIA

Major news events in California in 1991 centered on the state Supreme Court's decision to uphold term restrictions of the legislature, tax increases and an economy budget, redistricting, and drought.

Term Limits. The state Supreme Court upheld a 1990 initiative that limited members of the state Assembly to three two-year terms and senators (along with statewide officers) to two four-year terms. Proponents of the initiative argued that legislators made lifetime careers out of elective office, altering the rules to make successful challenge to an incumbent almost impossible.

Taxes and the Budget. Although the new Republican Gov. Pete Wilson had hoped to avoid any tax increase, he found a budget shortfall that eventually reached a record $14.3 billion. He and Democratic legislative leaders with difficulty worked out a compromise resulting in $7.7 billion in higher taxes. The personal-income tax was increased, and the sales tax was raised by 1.25% and broadened in scope. Other taxes also were increased. Republican Assembly leader Ross Johnson voted against the tax compromise, resulting in his removal from the leadership by the party caucus.

© Terrence McCarthy/NYT Pictures

San Francisco's Mayor-elect Frank Jordan (second from left) *introduces his sons* (l-r) *Jim, Thomas, and Frank, Jr., to the press. The former police chief defeated Mayor Art Agnos by a 52%-48% margin in a nonpartisan December 1991 runoff.*

After four months of hard bargaining, a $55.7 billion budget was enacted. It provided for $5.1 billion in service cuts and $2 billion in savings created by bookkeeping changes. Welfare provisions were cut by 4.4%, but population increases and inflation added 4.6% to the dollar increase. The governor vetoed items totaling $191 million.

Other Political News. Governor Wilson also sought to deal with longtime problems in expensive and controversial workers' compensation. He tried to tie reforms to the budget but achieved little except to anger legislators. He vetoed two controversial bills, one outlawing job discrimination against homosexuals and the other prohibiting sexual harassment in the workplace.

State Sen. John F. Seymour was appointed to the governor's vacated U.S. senate seat; he would face election in 1992. . . . Former Democratic Gov. Jerry Brown announced he was a candidate for the U.S. presidency.

Redistricting. Legislators adopted plans to redistrict for both the state legislature and the federal congressional delegation, but the governor vetoed both. The task of drawing the lines then went to the state Supreme Court, which, as in 1970, was to appoint a panel to carry out the task.

Drought. This was the fifth year of a major drought, but the legislature failed to enact water legislation, though it nearly adopted a plan to simplify the sale of water to cities by farmers and to move toward a free market in water. (Most water is controlled, not by individuals, but by public water districts.) This proposal was to be reconsidered in 1992. Farm-city conflict over water has been severe, with the most water used by farmers. Santa Barbara water districts voted by more than 2–1 to pay the cost of connection to the State Water Project, a move long at issue. Some local government officials also asked Congress for research funds to make desalinization economically feasible.

Education. The public schools received a 1.5% increase per student and faced another year of strict economy.

State university budgets called for 20% to 40% fee increases for students, with no salary increases for faculty or staff, not even for promotions. The University of California (UC) Regents raised fees by $650, the highest single increase in its history. UC moved to raise admissions standards to curtail enrollment.

Barry Munitz, former head of the University of Houston, was named chancellor of the 20-campus California State University.

Disasters. A tanker car was derailed in July and spilled thousands of gallons of pesticide into the Sacramento River, killing or injuring wildlife over a 45-mi (70-km) area to Lake Shasta, where it was contained.

A bus carrying Girl Scouts skidded off a mountain road near Palm Springs on July 31, killing seven.

A brush fire on October 20 spread through the Oakland and Berkeley hills, killing at least 24 people, destroying more than 3,000 homes and apartment units, and injuring dozens.

See also Los Angeles.

Charles R. Adrian
University of California, Riverside

CALIFORNIA • Information Highlights

Area: 158,706 sq mi (411 049 km²).
Population (1990 census): 29,760,021.
Chief Cities (1990 census): Sacramento, the capital, 369,365; Los Angeles, 3,485,398; San Diego, 1,110,549; San Jose, 782,248; San Francisco, 723,959; Long Beach, 429,433; Oakland, 372,242.
Government (1991): *Chief Officers*—governor, Pete Wilson (R); lt. gov., Leo T. McCarthy (D). *Legislature*—Senate, 40 members; Assembly, 80 members.
State Finances (fiscal year 1990): *Revenue,* $88,704,000,000; *expenditure,* $78,867,000,000.
Personal Income (1990): $619,381,000,000; per capita, $20,677.
Labor Force (June 1991): *Civilian labor force,* 14,823,700; *unemployed,* 1,190,900 (8.0% of total force).
Education: *Enrollment* (fall 1989)—public elementary schools, 3,470,574; public secondary, 1,301,404; colleges and universities, 1,744,879. *Public school expenditures* (1989), $19,370,242,000.

CAMBODIA

On Oct. 24, 1991, a treaty aimed at ending 21 years of civil war in Cambodia was signed in Paris. Representatives of four Cambodian factions and 18 foreign nations took part in the ceremony. The treaty was a remarkable experiment, because it placed Cambodia under United Nations rule for a period of 18 months. During this time, the UN would seek to arrange a cease-fire and then organize and run free elections for a constitutional assembly, which would draft a new constitution for Cambodia.

During this transitional period, the highest Cambodian authority would be a Supreme National Council, composed of six members of the existing government in Phnom Penh and two representatives from each of the three insurgent factions that have been fighting for years to overthrow the government.

Politics. Prince Norodom Sihanouk (*see* Biography), who turned 70 a week after the Paris treaty was signed, would chair the Supreme National Council. He was supposed to have the power to make decisions if the other council members could not agree. His main strengths were his close ties with foreign leaders and the fact that he had been the dominant personality in Cambodian public life for 50 years. In that time, he became an expert diplomat and politician, and many people gave him credit for the Paris peace treaty.

© Reuters/Bettmann

Accompanied by Cambodia's Premier Hun Sen, Prince Norodom Sihanouk (left) *returned to Phnom Penh after more than a decade in exile on Nov. 14, 1991. Six days later the Vietnamese-backed regime named Sihanouk president of Cambodia.*

But Prince Sihanouk had serious health problems, and no one doubted that taming the murderous rivalry between Cambodian factions would take all his strength and skill. For older Cambodians, he carried an aura of legitimacy, because French colonial rulers placed him on the throne in 1941. Fourteen years later, after the French were expelled, he abdicated in favor of his father and won the first of many national elections.

In 1970, Sihanouk was ousted by a right-wing coup, which plunged the country into civil war. For a time, he served as titular head of the brutal Khmer Rouge regime, which killed more than 1 million Cambodians, including several of Sihanouk's own relatives. In 1982 he became head of a government in exile composed of the three insurgent factions. So he was used to working with these factions, and he seemed to have a cordial relationship with Hun Sen, who headed the Phnom Penh regime. But the problems of bringing peace to Cambodia were enormous, and even the presence of a UN force of 10,000 or more civilian and military officials did not guarantee success. Their first task would be to arrange a cease-fire between Cambodian forces that might total as many as 100,000 (no one had complete data on their strength or armament). They were spread over a country half again as large as Louisiana which includes dense forest and jungle. An advance UN mission, headed by Brig. Gen. Jean-Michel Loridon of France, began arriving in October.

Removing the last Vietnamese troops from Cambodia would be the next task. Then, the UN forces would have to begin clearing the country of thousands of land mines, which had been placed on roads and along the borders. Roads and bridges throughout the country would have to be rebuilt so the UN personnel could move about.

Economy. Approximately 350,000 Cambodian refugees were housed in camps in Thailand at the time the Paris treaty was signed. The Khmer Rouge faction had begun returning some to areas of Cambodia under their control. According to press reports they did this in order to gain popular support in the coming struggle for control of the country. Prince Sihanouk claimed they had promised him they would leave the repatriation to the UN, which has worked out a plan to bring the refugees home and provide them with the means to support themselves without being beholden to any of the factions.

The repatriation of the refugees may cost about $100 million, and the entire UN mission was expected to cost about $1 billion. Even though this was far less costly than waging a war, no one knew for certain that the UN member states would be willing to foot the bill.

Cambodia is rich in good farmland and has timber, precious stones, and other resources, but war had reduced it to poverty. In the 1960s it was an exporter of rice, but now one half million Cambodians have too little to eat. It remained to be seen whether 18 months of UN rule would be enough to turn the country around.

PETER A. POOLE
Author, "Eight Presidents and Indochina"

CAMBODIA • Information Highlights

Official Name: Cambodia.
Location: Southeast Asia.
Area: 69,900 sq mi (181 040 km²).
Population (mid-1991 est.): 7,100,000.
Chief City (1989 est.): Phnom Penh, the capital, 800,000.
Government: *Head of state and government:* Prince Norodom Sihanouk, president (named Nov. 20, 1991).

CANADA

For Canadians 1991 was a grouchy, uncomfortable year. An economic recession combined with changes from the Canada-U.S. Free Trade Agreement left one worker in ten unemployed. A new federal sales tax added to the cost of living. The renewed search for constitutional accommodation scratched the national self-image of compromise. Politicians, notably federal Prime Minister Brian Mulroney, plumbed new depths of unpopularity.

The Constitutional Crisis. The Meech Lake accord of 1987 had tried to give Canada's French-speaking province, Quebec, special constitutional status as a "distinct society," but met a last-minute defeat in June 1990. In Quebec the Meech debacle produced bitter disillusionment on the part of Premier Robert Bourassa and fellow federalists and soaring popular support for full sovereignty. In Ottawa a government that had been confident that the prime minister's notable deal-making skills would prevail had to start fresh.

Bourassa acted first. A 37-member commission, headed by prominent business leaders Michel Bélanger and Jean Campeau, with a membership carefully balanced between federalists and separatists, was ordered to consult Quebeckers and report early in 1991. Bourassa's Liberal party met in March and endorsed a constitutional report from a committee headed by Montreal lawyer Jean Allaire that demanded transfer to Quebec of 22 federal powers—11 of which were already under provincial control—from external affairs to regulatory agencies. The Bélanger-Campeau Commission reported a few weeks later. The commission declared that it was up to Canada to come up with constitutional proposals and that Quebeckers would decide their future in a referendum held no later than October 1992.

Ottawa's first post-Meech initiative was a "Citizens' Forum on Canada's Future," set up to meet the complaint that constitutions should not be settled by "11 white middle-class men in a closed room." Headed by Keith Spicer, chair of the federal broadcasting regulatory agency, forum members spent an estimated C$24 million and a contentious six months listening to people with axes to grind about immigration and language. Critics noted that the forum made few forays into Quebec and swelled its 700,000 response rate by conscripting schoolchildren. Its report, issued on Canada Day, July 1, claimed support for a strong Canada, opposition to special status for Quebec, opposition to multicultural programs, and general disillusionment with politicians. Several provinces launched their own constitutional inquiries, with similar results. Newfoundland Premier Clyde Wells, a major figure in killing the Meech Lake accord, demanded a constituent assembly; Ontario's New Democratic Party Premier Bob Rae agreed.

Preston Manning, leader of a burgeoning Reform Party, called for a "New Canada" that Quebec could join only if it accepted equality with the other provinces. His party, Manning explained, would not be running candidates in Quebec. Opponents claimed that Manning's policy would lead to the breakup of Canada as surely as Jacques Parizeau's Parti Québécois. For their part, 80% of Canadians, both French- and English-speaking, insisted that they preferred Canada to stay together, but agreement stopped there.

To reconcile such divergence and to manage the next and perhaps final round of Canada's constitutional negotiations, Mulroney turned to the man he had humiliated and undermined as party leader, Joe Clark. One of the few ministers to grow in public esteem during the Conservative years, Clark reluctantly left external affairs for the weary round of internal diplomacy. Months of preparation, speculation, and intense consultation ended on September 24 with Clark's presentation of a 28-point constitutional proposal.

Joe Clark (left), *who stepped aside as Canada's foreign minister to become minister for constitutional affairs in April 1991, shakes hands with Prime Minister Brian Mulroney after a proposal for constitutional reforms was presented to the House of Commons on September 24.*

In the government-proposal package called *Shaping Canada's Future Together,* constitutional connoisseurs could recognize a host of old ideas, from a so-called Canada Clause defining the country's presumed goals, to a favorite of the real-estate industry—entrenching "property rights" in the Charter of Rights and Freedoms. Other proposals included aboriginal self-government within ten years and an elected Senate with considerable powers to replace the appointed upper house. Whether provinces would have equal representation was left for future debate. While some federal powers—immigration, culture, and skills training—would be passed to the provinces, the biggest innovation was the proposal for a federal-provincial Council of the Federation to flatten interprovincial trade barriers into an "Economic Union." Decisions on fiscal and trade policy would carry if Ottawa and seven provinces with 50% of the population agreed. The same majority would be needed before Ottawa could launch spending programs in areas of provincial jurisdiction.

Response to the constitutional package was predictable. Manitoba Cree lawyer Ovide Mercredi, newly elected leader of the Assembly of First Nations, cried betrayal, insisting that natives never had lost the right to self-government and that ten years was an intolerable delay. In Quebec nationalists dismissed the Ottawa proposals as a waste of time; others condemned the Economic Union proposals for, once again, subjecting Quebec to rule by outsiders. Sensing a make-or-break for confederation, most English-Canadian leaders, including Premier Wells, were cautious. A federal parliamentary committee, cochaired by Manitoba Member of Parliament (MP) Dorothy Dobbie and Quebec Sen. Claude Castonguay, set out to consult the grass roots. In November the committee lapsed into partisan wrangling. Castonguay withdrew and Dobbie continued only after the Liberals backed down. The government itself retreated from a national referendum at the insistence of its Quebec MPs. By late 1991, Canadians had no clear idea about constitutional substance or procedure. Many questioned the issue's importance.

Party Politics. As Spicer's forum had noted, it was tough to save Canada if no one trusted the people in charge. In Quebec, the base for Mulroney's 1984 and 1988 victories, federal economic mismanagement fed the separatist cause. The proindependence Bloc Québécois, formed in 1990 by former Mulroney confidant Lucien Bouchard as the Meech Lake accord collapsed, led other federal parties in Quebec opinion polls much of 1991. During a Conservative convention in August, Tory MP Pierrette Venne announced that she had become the Bloc's ninth member in Parliament.

Preston Manning's Reform Party, already out polling Conservative supporters in the West, won the permission of its members in a May referendum to extend its organization to Ontario and the Atlantic region.

Tories took some comfort from their rivals' apparent troubles. Jean Chrétien, the Trudeau stalwart who swept up the Liberal leadership in June 1990, seemed almost invisible through most of 1991 except when he shifted stands—against and then for the Persian Gulf war in January, and against and then for a national referendum on the constitution. When federal New Democrats met in Halifax in June, they

THE CANADIAN MINISTRY

M. Brian Mulroney, prime minister
Harvie Andre, minister of state and leader of the government in the House of Commons
Perrin Beatty, minister of communications
Pierre Blais, minister of consumer and corporate affairs and minister of state for agriculture
Benoit Bouchard, minister of national health and welfare
Pauline Browes, minister of state for the environment
Pierre H. Cadieux, minister of state for fitness and amateur sport, minister of state for youth, and deputy leader for the government in the House of Commons
Kim Campbell, minister of justice and attorney general of Canada
Jean Charest, minister for the environment
Joe Clark, president of Queen's Privy Council for Canada and minister responsible for constitutional affairs
Mary Collins, associate minister of national defense and minister responsible for the status of women
Jean Corbeil, minister of transport
John C. Crosbie, minister of fisheries and oceans and minister for the Atlantic Canada Opportunities Agency
Marcel Danis, minister of labor
Robert R. DeCotret, secretary of state of Canada
Paul Dick, minister of supply and services
Jake Epp, minister of energy, mines, and resources
Tom Hockin, minister of state for small businesses and tourism
Otto J. Jelinek, minister of national revenue
Monique Landry, minister for external relations and minister of state for Indian affairs and northern development
Doug Lewis, solicitor general of Canada
Gilles Loiselle, president of the Treasury Board and minister of state for finance
Elmer M. MacKay, minister of public works
Shirley Martin, minister of state for transport
Marcel Masse, minister of national defense
Charles J. Mayer, minister of Western economic diversification and minister of state for grains and oilseeds
Donald F. Mazankowski, deputy prime minister and minister of finance
John McDermid, minister of state for finance and privatization
Barbara J. McDougall, secretary of state for external affairs
William H. McKnight, minister of agriculture
Gerald S. Merrithew, minister of veterans affairs
Lowell Murray, leader of the government in the Senate
Frank Oberle, minister of forestry
Thomas E. Siddon, minister of Indian affairs and northern development
Bernard Valcourt, minister of employment and immigration
Monique Vézina, minister of state for employment and immigration, and minister of state for seniors
Gerald Weiner, minister of multiculturalism and citizenship
Michael H. Wilson, minister of industry, science, and technology and minister for international trade
William Winegard, minister for science

© Canapress

Michael Harcourt, a Vancouver lawyer, was proud to display "The Vancouver Sun" announcing the victory of his New Democratic Party in British Columbia elections.

had dropped from first place in the polls. The media blamed Audrey McLaughlin's lackluster leadership; her caucus insisted that her opposition to the Gulf war and refusal to be "one of the boys" were strengths.

In May the prime minister met a new session of Parliament with a shuffled cabinet and few promises. Among major changes, Barbara McDougall replaced Joe Clark at external affairs; the West's strongest minister, Don Mazankowski, took on finance. After producing seven difficult budgets, Michael Wilson moved from finance to international trade, with a special mandate to improve Canada's competitiveness. Despite cutting C$580 million from postsecondary education since 1989, the government consciously echoed U.S. President George Bush by declaring its commitment to a "learning culture."

By the time Mulroney met his colleagues in a late-summer retreat at Kelowna, polls showed Tory support at 12%. Tough repression of a round of public-service strikes in September restored a bit of popularity. Ministers even could take comfort when the courts dismissed charges by former Tory businessman Glen Kealey that 13 Tories and even top Royal Canadian Mounted Police (RCMP) officers had shared in or covered up a multimillion-dollar contract kickback scheme; only former Public Works Minister Roch LaSalle had to face trial.

Provincial-election results from British Columbia and Saskatchewan, in which new Democrats swept out sympathetic Social Credit and Conservative regimes, reflected both local issues and resentment of Ottawa. A C$800 million federal handout to wheat farmers just before the Saskatchewan election was contrasted with the C$2 billion the Conservatives had made available for a similar contest in 1986.

Joe Clark and Ovide Mercredi, chief of the Assembly of First Nations, discuss a plan under which native leaders would be allowed to conduct hearings on constitutional reform.

© Canapress

Economics. Some of the political dissatisfaction came from Canadians facing the new goods and services tax (GST), a federal 7% levy on just about everything but food, rent, and financial services. Quebec integrated the GST with its existing sales taxes; Ontario collected it separately. Albertans, who never had had a sales tax, had another reason to blame Ottawa. One result, encouraged by a surge in the exchange rate for the Canadian dollar, was a cross-border spending spree, shifting more than 1 billion shopping dollars to U.S. stores from Ontario alone. The chief barrier to cross-border shoppers, once customs officials were told to speed up queues of returning bargain hunters, was blockades by angry truckers, facing ruin from untaxed U.S. competitors. Government officials promised to look into their plight.

The GST replaced the former hidden manufacturers' sales tax and, the government insisted, would be "revenue neutral." In fact, the new tax produced bigger revenues than expected. And they were needed as the recession that had begun in 1990 deepened in most of Canada. Despite the additional revenues, Ottawa's deficit was back at C$30.5 billion and devouring 27% of federal spending.

In February, Finance Minister Michael Wilson's last budget cut 6,000 more government jobs; slashed spending on culture, retraining, and environmental cleanup; froze transfer payments to the provinces; and continued the

© Joe Traver/Gamma-Liaison

For several days in September, members of Canada's Public Service Alliance were on the picket lines, protesting the government's wage-freeze plan. In early October, Parliament enacted a "back-to-work" bill, imposing heavy fines on striking civil servants.

freeze on Ottawa's share of welfare costs in Ontario, Alberta, and British Columbia.

The government's wage policy made a mockery of federal laws on public-service bargaining and a conciliation report that recommended 6% raises for the lowest-paid. It also drove the 150,000 members of the usually weak and divided Public Service Alliance into uncharacteristic militancy. After two walkouts in September, there were angry scuffles when Parliament forced alliance members back to work on the government's terms. However, many Canadians accepted the union claim that MPs and senior officials hurriedly had given themselves fat increases in advance of the restraint program.

There was also little help for two sets of victims of world economics—Atlantic fishery workers, whose ravaged industry could not provide even ten weeks' work, and wheat growers, whose bumper harvest was made worthless by the U.S.-European Community trade war.

Legal Matters. Kim Campbell, the first woman to be the federal minister of justice, faced two agonizing issues during the year—abortion and gun control. Personally pro-choice on abortion, Campbell had devised a compromise—which ultimately failed—that in some instances would have recriminalized abortion. Gun control, an issue since the 1989 slaughter of 14 women engineering students in Montreal, had 79% national support, but the minority could count on support from rural Conservative MPs.

Various court decisions also created problems. A Quebec appeal court struck down federal legislation controlling tobacco advertising as a breach of Charter guarantees of free speech. Canada's Supreme Court ruled 7–2 that a 1983 law sparing alleged rape victims from being questioned about their sexual past prevented a fair trial; feminists protested, and Campbell promised a new law. The issue of fair trials affected David Milgaard, whose 1969 conviction for a murder in Saskatoon, Sask., looked increasingly questionable, and Lawrencia Bembenek, a U.S. prison escapee who insisted, with some forensic support, that her Milwaukee murder trial was a frame-up.

Racial incidents also occurred. Montreal police in July shot a black man though he bore no resemblance to the robbery suspect they were seeking. A riot between white and black youths followed. In Halifax, N.S., blacks attacked downtown bars that had refused to admit them. In Winnipeg, Man., the police chief resigned after an inquiry into justice for natives claimed that his force had demonstrated racist attitudes. A former police commissioner and successful candidate for Toronto's mayoralty, June Rowlands, was criticized for stating that blacks provided a disproportionate share of the city's crime.

CANADA • Information Highlights

Official Name: Canada.
Location: Northern North America.
Area: 3,851,792 sq mi (9 976 140 km^2).
Population (mid-1991 est.): 26,800,000.
Chief Cities (1986 census): Ottawa, the capital, 819,263; Toronto, 3,427,168; Montreal, 2,921,357.
Government: *Head of state,* Elizabeth II, queen; represented by Ramon Hnatyshyn, governor-general (took office January 1990). *Head of government,* M. Brian Mulroney, prime minister (took office Sept. 17, 1984). *Legislature*—Parliament: Senate and House of Commons.
Monetary Unit: Canadian dollar (1.1313 dollars equal U.S.$1, Nov. 13, 1991).
Gross Domestic Product (1989 est. U.S.$): $513,600,000,000.
Economic Index: *Consumer Prices* (1990, 1980 = 100), all items, 178.1; food, 163.2.
Foreign Trade (1990 U.S.$): *Imports,* $116,461,000,000; *exports,* $126,995,000,000.

Native Peoples. Economic hard times were not new for most native peoples, and assaults by environmentalists on hunting and trapping further undermined their traditional industries. However, the public sympathy, revealed when Manitoba Cree Elijah Harper dealt the fatal blow to the Meech Lake accord in 1990, gave natives added political leverage. On June 12, 500 chiefs of the Assembly of First Nations gave the leadership of 600,000 status Indians to Ovide Mercredi. While huge land claims and jockeying for a renewed influence in constitutional negotiations were Mercredi's priority, the year's biggest native issue was the struggle between Inuit and Cree in northern Quebec against the Bourassa government's C$12.7 billion, 3,168-megawatt Great Whale River hydro project. By aligning with environmentalists and targeting the project's U.S. customers, the Crees succeeded by the end of 1991 in delaying and perhaps derailing the venture.

External Affairs and Defense. Faced with so much unpleasantness at home, Canadian ministers found comfort in foreign travel. With Liberals equivocating and the NDP opposed, Canada went along with U.S. leadership in the Gulf war. Thanks to limited roles, professionalism, and good luck, Canada's three warships, 26 CF-18 aircraft, and 2,400 men and women returned without a single loss. At home an Edmonton imam called for holy war against the United Nations (UN), and Arab-Canadians complained of encountering prejudice and being interviewed by security officials. A minor related scandal broke in April when Mohammed al-Mashat, a defecting Iraqi diplomat, slipped into Canada. The opposition blamed the government, which fingered civil servants, one of them a nephew of the Liberal leader.

Though Canadians complained more about their contribution to the Gulf war than most U.S. allies, Mulroney could feel that he had added to his fund of goodwill in the White House. President Bush's annual visit in March produced signatures on a long-awaited accord on acid-rain emissions. Free trade with Mexico was not mentioned.

Canada had little influence on events in Eastern Europe. After urging financial assistance, Mulroney dutifully approved the Group of Seven Nations' (G-7) cool response to USSR President Mikhail Gorbachev in August. After the Moscow coup failed, Ottawa was quick to recognize the Baltic republics. In October, Mulroney gave a stirring speech to Stanford graduates on the need to send tangible aid to the emerging fragments of the USSR, but Ottawa signed no checks. Still it was a suitable campaign speech for a politician who was nominated by Britain and the United States as a potential successor to the UN Secretary-General Perez de Cuellar. After giving voters long enough to realize that their unpopular prime minister had stature abroad, Mulroney indicated that he would not leave.

The meltdown of the Cold War brought renewed thoughts of a peace dividend, but realism intervened. Canada's forces were already tiny and most of the C$13 billion defense budget subsidized industries and otherwise impoverished regions. In September, Defense Minister Marcel Masse announced that Cana-

On October 25, Britain's Prince Charles and his wife Princess Diana were welcomed to Toronto's City Hall, below. Sudbury, Kingston, and Ottawa were other stops on the seven-day royal tour, which was intended to promote social causes.

© "Maclean's"/Saba

© Reuters/Bettmann

Theo Fleury and goalie Bill Ranford, who was named most valuable player, celebrate Team Canada's victory in the Canada Cup. It was Canada's fourth win in five Canada Cups.

da's two bases in Germany would close by 1995 and all but 1,100 Canadians would come home. Regular Canadian Forces strength would fall by 8,000, and certain bases in Canada might close.

Life and Times. Canadians looking for distraction could follow the endless hockey season to Pittsburgh's final victory in June. The national junior team narrowly won its second consecutive world championship. The team's star, Eric Lindros, added to Quebec's grievances by refusing National Hockey League (NHL) orders to play for the Quebec Nordiques. The Canadian Football League got costly but welcome glamour when the U.S. owner of the Toronto Argonauts signed a top National Football League (NFL) draft pick, Raghib "Rocket" Ismail, for C$30.1 million. Canada's own top footballer, Nick Mazzoli, signed with Seattle for a mere $100,000. Toronto's Blue Jays baseball team reached the American League play-offs. Their Skydome stadium broke attendance records for the league—and went still deeper into debt. Sprinter Ben Johnson returned to competition after a two-year ban for steroid use at the 1988 Seoul Olympics.

DESMOND MORTON
Erindale College, University of Toronto

The Economy

During 1991 the Canadian economy continued to suffer through the effects of a yearlong recession. There were some signs of sluggish recovery, however.

The first half of the year saw the new goods and services tax fuel inflation and erode real personal disposable income. The value of retail trade for the period fell 2.8%, causing sales to dwindle for all retailers and in every province except British Columbia, where business was essentially flat. July's dismal tally of C$934 million in sales showed that consumers still either were postponing purchases of clothing, appliances, and furniture or were taking their shopping dollars south to the United States.

Similarly, the housing sector was squeezed tightly by the recessionary twist. The first-quarter construction starts on houses, apartments, and condominiums were the weakest in any quarter since 1957. Falling mortgage rates during the second quarter stimulated new construction. This caused the seasonally adjusted level of housing construction, including apartments and condominiums, to rise by 58% to 152,000. But this impetus was eliminated partially by the repeat of the sector's dismal performance when August starts, compared with July, slipped 13%. Spurred by the falling mortgage rates, however, home sales posted their sixth consecutive monthly gain in August.

The manufacturing sector recorded a similar impact from the recessionary punch. The value of manufacturing shipments for the first half of the year, as compared with the same period a year earlier, was down 7%. Lower exports due to the high value of the U.S. dollar and sagging domestic demand slashed the after-tax, second-quarter earnings of 154 major firms. Corporations reacted by laying off workers, causing the seasonally adjusted jobless rate for August to hit 10.6%, a six-year high. Employment fell by 20,000 to 12,338,000 with most of the job losses packed into the trade and construction sectors, down 37,000 and 9,000, respectively. Job losses hit men more than women because of the higher proportion of men employed in the hard-hit goods-producing sector.

Some signs of economic upturn were recorded during the second quarter, however, when the use of manufacturing capacity rose by 1.7% and the merchandise-trade surplus shot up C$417 million, following three quarters of consecutive declines. Wholesale trade, which had experienced strong growth in the spring, advanced 1% in July. Manufacturing output grew 1.1% in July, putting it 5.1% above the March 1991 low point. Most of the growth was contributed by producers of food, primary and fabricated metal products, and wood products.

Propelled by a resurgence in manufacturing and construction, the economy grew for the fourth consecutive month in July when real gross domestic product rose by a seasonally adjusted rate of .2%. The growth rate was well below the 1.2% surge in April, however, indicating that the downturn was not over.

R.P. SETH
Mount Saint Vincent University

The Arts

The government-owned Canadian Broadcasting Corporation (CBC)—because it employs many actors, writers, and the like—is the bellwether of Canadian artists. The year 1991, however, brought these artists little comfort, as an anticipated year's shortfall for the CBC of C$108 million forced the layoff of 1,100 staff members and the closing or cutting back of 11 CBC television stations. A coalition, called 100 Days of Action and comprising representatives of concerned groups, launched a national campaign attempting to persuade federal politicians to give the CBC emergency funding. The government complied, providing the CBC with a once-only C$50 million—C$10 million of it being a repayable loan.

Ballet lovers rejoiced that the federal government gave C$88 million toward Toronto's proposed Ballet Opera House. In Montreal the Monument National, the city's most important historic theater, was undergoing restoration for its reopening at its centenary in 1993. The C$16 million cost was to be shared equally by the federal and Quebec governments.

Visual Arts. At the National Gallery of Art in Ottawa, two exhibits claimed wide attention. The first was the master work "Jupiter and Europa" by the 17th-century Italian artist Guido Reni; the work was acquired by the National Gallery for C$3.46 million, the highest figure ever paid by the gallery for any acquisition.

The second exhibit claiming national attention was "Vanitas: Flesh Dress for an Albino Anorexic." By Montreal artist Jana Sterbeck, it consisted of 50 flank steaks sewed together and hung on a hanger like a shift dress. Also displayed by a live model, it symbolized, among other things, that earthly things, including human bodies, decay and perish. An Ottawa alderman and others opposing the display claimed it was criminal to waste $300 worth of food when so many are hungry, while gallery officials indicated that they had no authority to use acquisition funds to feed the hungry. Art experts pointed out that portraying decay, especially in flowers and fruit, was an artistic convention dating back to medieval times. Amid the controversy the work dripped blood on the gallery floor before drying as it matured.

Also at the National Gallery was "Masterful Studies: Three Centuries of French Drawing." Among the 113 exhibits were works by Seurat, Delacroix, and Degas.

Other exhibits included that at the McMichael Gallery in Kleinberg, Ont., which showed "North by West: The Arctic and Rocky Mountain Paintings of Lawren Harris," featuring Harris' impressive and towering "Mount Lefroy." Among its 60th-birthday celebrations the Vancouver Art Gallery showed "60 years 60 Artists," including Emily Carr's painting, "The Red Cedar."

At the Montreal Museum of Fine Arts a big and brilliant show, "The 1920s: Age of the Metropolis," displayed some 700 items—mainly paintings, drawings, and etchings but including photos, cars, and an airplane—in a splendid remembrance of that decade.

Performing Arts. Theater highlights included the Stratford [Ont.] Festival, which opened with Shakespeare's *Hamlet,* directed by David William and with Colm Feore as Hamlet and Patricia Collins as Gertrude. A surprise hit was the difficult Shakespeare drama, *Timon of Athens,* performed at Stratford for the first time since 1962. Director Michael Langham daringly set the play in the 1920s, and Brian Bedford played the role of Timon. Another highly praised offering was the world premiere of a new English translation of Michel Tremblay's *Les Belles Soeurs,* directed by Marti Maraden. The play, about the repercussions of a working-class Montreal woman winning one million dollars' worth of trading stamps, featured 15 fine actresses, including Kate Reid, Goldie Semple, Michelle Fisk, and

Tamara de Lempicka's "Portrait of the Duchesse de la Salle," an oil on canvas, was shown at "The 1920s: Age of the Metropolis" exhibit at the Montreal Museum of Fine Arts.

© Michael Cooper

During the bicentennial of Mozart's death, the Canadian Opera Company presented his "Cosi fan tutte" at Toronto's Elgin Theatre in June. Federico Davia (left), *Louise Winter, Richard Croft, and Joanne Kolomyjec* (right) *sang the leading roles.*

Susan Wright. Rodgers and Hammerstein's musical *Carousel,* directed and choreographed by Brian Macdonald, earned praise for the dancing.

The Shaw Festival at Niagara-on-the-Lake presented *Henry IV,* a play by Luigi Pirandello about a madman who thinks he is an 11th-century Italian emperor, Henry IV. Directed by Paul Lampert, it starred David Schurmann, Jennifer Phipps, and Roger Rowland. Glynis Leyshon directed one of George Bernard Shaw's less frequently performed plays, *Press Cuttings*. Shaw wrote it for the Women's Suffrage Society as a satire on the antifeminism of British Field Marshal Horatio Herbert Kitchener and various other politicians. A production of Henrik Ibsen's *Hedda Gabler,* adapted and directed by Judith Thompson, took the unusual but effective step of having Hedda shoot herself on stage rather than off.

The Canadian Opera Company's new production of *Die Fledermaus,* directed by Brian Dickie, with a new translation by John Mortimer, starred Gwynnar Geyer as Rosalinda and John Janssen as Eisenstein. In Vancouver a new production of *The Barber of Seville,* directed by Christopher Newton and designed by Cameron Porteous, had Figaro as a magician who allowed the characters to travel through time. It starred J. Patrick Rafferty as Figaro and Kathryn Cowdrick as Rosina. The same opera company also had a production of Richard Strauss' *Electra,* starring Johanna Meier.

A highlight of the ballet year was the National Ballet of Canada's presentation of the world premiere of William Forsythe's *The Second Detail.*

Film. Under the direction of festival president Serge Losique, Montreal's 12-day World Film Festival presented a fine series of films in the late summer. In addition, the festival celebrated its 15th anniversary with special tributes to two actors, Anthony Hopkins and Sidney Poitier, and several directors. Two of these directors entered their films at the festival: Jeri Menzel's *The Beggar's Opera* and Alan Tanner's *l'Homme qui a perdu son ombre*.

Toronto's 16th annual Festival of Festivals film event under executive director Helga Stevenson began in September, increasing its box-office receipts by more than 10% over 1990. Atom Egoyan's *The Adjuster* won the C$25,000 award for the best Canadian feature film. The award money was given by Egoyan to John Pozer, whose *The Grocer's Wife* had won honorable mention. Among a number of gay films was Derek Jarman's adaptation of Christopher Marlow's 1592 play, *Edward II*. Critics voted Gus Van Sant, Jr.'s *My Own Private Idaho* the top cinematic achievement.

DAVID SAVAGE
Free-Lance Writer, Vancouver, B.C.

CARIBBEAN

The countries of the Caribbean showed cohesion on several fronts during 1991. They unanimously condemned the September 30 coup that ousted the elected president of Haiti, a Caribbean country, and joined with the Organization of American States (OAS) in applying economic and trade sanctions against the interim government that replaced President Jean-Bertrand Aristide. The foreign ministers of Jamaica and Trinidad and Tobago were members of the OAS delegation that went to Port-au-Prince in October to press for Aristide's reinstatement. (*See* HAITI.)

Economic integration in the Caribbean region also made progress in 1991, although at a slower pace than regional leaders had predicted. The 13-member Caribbean Community (CARICOM) missed a January 1 deadline for implementing a common external tariff (CET) in trade with countries outside the region, a first step in creating a Caribbean common market programmed to take effect by the beginning of 1994.

However, in July, Caribbean government leaders, at a summit meeting in St. Kitts, approved a plan drafted by a West Indies Commission on ways to implement several critical integration targets, including the unrestricted movement of skilled workers throughout the region, accelerated adoption of a common currency, and steps toward the establishment of a single market. In addition, by the end of the year ten CARICOM countries had instituted or were in the process of adopting the CET. Two countries, St. Lucia and Antigua and Barbuda, said it would be several months before they could take action on the CET. The Bahamas did not sign the original tariff agreement.

International Initiatives. Although integration within the region was proceeding more slowly than planned, Caribbean leaders were establishing stronger ties with other Western Hemisphere countries during the year.

In July, Venezuela offered unilaterally to eliminate its tariffs on the exports of the CARICOM countries. Under the Venezuelan initiative, tariffs will be reduced gradually over a five-year period, until there is duty-free entry for imports from the Caribbean. After the initial five years, negotiations will begin on reciprocal tariff concessions by the Caribbean countries on Venezuelan products.

Three months later, Venezuela submitted a formal application for membership in the Caribbean Community. The application was scheduled to be considered at a Caribbean summit meeting in January 1992. If approved, Venezuela would become the first Latin American member of the community, which has been made up solely of former British colonies in the region. (Montserrat, a member of the community, remains a British colony.) The Dominican Republic and Haiti also applied for CARICOM membership. Their requests were pending at the end of the year.

In another significant outreach step, CARICOM in July signed a framework trade agreement with the United States under the U.S. Enterprise for the Americas Initiative, which envisions the eventual creation of a Western Hemisphere free-trade area. The framework agreement provides for the establishment of a bilateral council to promote two-way trade and investment and to explore further trade-liberalizing arrangements.

In November, CARICOM foreign ministers met with their counterparts from Central American countries in San Pedro Sula, Honduras, to begin talks on a future integration pact with the six member countries of the Central American Common Market.

CBI Expansion. In October the United States announced that it would provide new or expanded duty-free treatment under the U.S. Caribbean Basin Initiative (CBI) to 94 product categories from beneficiary countries. The enhanced benefits would affect some $47 million in 1991 exports, the U.S. announcement said. The changes took effect on October 2.

A month earlier, the U.S. Customs Service had ruled that the upper portions of shoes and sneakers could be imported into the United States duty-free from CBI beneficiary countries if they were made of U.S. components. A previous customs ruling permitted duty-free imports of completed shoes from CBI countries. Similar imports from other shoe-exporting countries were subject to duty. It was believed that the two rulings would spur increased investment in shoe-manufacturing operations in the Caribbean.

Not all the trade news was positive for the Caribbean during the year, however. In October the United States said that it would make substantial cuts in its tariff-rate quota for sugar imports during the 1991–92 import year. According to analysts, the tariff-rate quota reductions would cut Caribbean duty-free sugar exports to the United States by nearly one third from 1991 levels. The country most severely affected by the reductions was the Dominican Republic, which saw its duty-free limit slashed from 358,010 metric tons in 1990–91 to 232,555 metric tons in 1991–92.

Politics. In January, Belize and Guyana were admitted as the 34th and 35th member countries of the OAS. The two countries had held observer status in the inter-American body, but were barred from full membership because of territorial disputes with other OAS members. An OAS charter change, initiated in 1985, opened the way for their eventual acceptance. With their entry, the OAS came to include all the independent countries in the Western Hemisphere. Of the 35 OAS members, 12 are also members of CARICOM and

© Tony Savino/Sipa (inset); © Steve Starr/Saba

The military was much in evidence in Haiti after President Jean Bertrand Aristide was ousted in a coup, led by Brig. Gen. Raoul Cedras (top right). *Supreme Court Justice Joseph Nerette* (top left) *then took office as interim president.*

two more—the Dominican Republic and Haiti —are located in the Caribbean (Suriname, often considered a Caribbean nation although it is in South America, is an OAS member.)

In a second significant international political development, Guatemala took steps to relinquish its long-standing territorial claims on the neighboring country of Belize. In a statement issued in August, Guatemalan President Jorge Serrano said: "The government of Guatemala . . . recognizes the right of the Belizean people to self-determination." Representatives of the two countries and Britain had been meeting in Miami to find a peaceful settlement to the dispute, which dates back to colonial days when Belize was the British colony of British Honduras. A final resolution of the dispute must be ratified in a referendum in Guatemala. Britain said that until that occurred, British troops would remain stationed in Belize.

Suriname and Other Elections. Along with Haiti, Suriname was an exception to the general pattern of democratic progress seen throughout the Caribbean in 1991. On Christmas Eve 1990, Suriname's elected government was dismissed in a swift and bloodless coup by the army. A provisional president was installed, but real power resided in the hands of army commander Désiré Bouterse. Suriname returned, tentatively, to the democratic fold in September, however. District councils and the national assembly elected a former government minister, Ronald Venetiaan, to a five-year term as president. Venetiaan headed a four-party coalition that held 30 of the 51 seats in the National Assembly. The new president said he would seek constitutional changes to restrict military influence.

In Barbados the governing Democratic Labor Party, led by Prime Minister Lloyd Erskine Sandiford, was reelected to another five-year term in January. In Guyana the government was approaching its term limit, but elections were postponed pending the completion of a new voter-registration list.

AIDS. A report released during the year by the Pan American Health Organization (PAHO) indicated that the Caribbean had one of the highest incidences of AIDS cases in the world. In all of Africa, there were 6 million reported cases of AIDS, while the Caribbean, with a fraction of Africa's population, reported nearly 1 million cases. The highest rates of infection in Africa were just more than 30 per 100,000 people. In the Bahamas, Bermuda, and French Guiana, however, the rates exceeded 60 per 100,000. According to the U.S. Agency for International Development (AID), the disease began to appear in the Caribbean in the early 1980s and has spread rapidly through all population sectors, including an increasing number of children.

RICHARD C. SCHROEDER, *Consultant to the Organization of American States*

CENTRAL AMERICA

As Central Americans pondered the problems they would face in the 1990s, they also looked back at the vast waste of the 1980s. A number of democratic elections had been held, but they almost always were supervised by outsiders. Furthermore, it would be risky to claim that an election or two might guarantee a nation's fragile democracy. Chronologically the period coincided with U.S. President Ronald Reagan's war on communism, and Central America frequently was buffeted about by opposing superpowers. Outrageous inflation, civil wars (some of which still continued), huge foreign debts, and disjointed commerce resulted in unparalleled economic decline and very little progress. Together it totaled a lost decade.

In spite of unprecedented U.S. aid to Central America during the 1980s, regional per capita income fell nearly 20%. Trade within Central America in 1991 approximated one half that of 1980. The physical and psychological damage of civil wars in El Salvador, Guatemala, and Nicaragua would require many years of repair. Increased financial assistance from Washington was virtually out of the question. In 1990 and 1991 total U.S. aid to Central America was reduced by about 40% because Central America was no longer "the last defense against communism." U.S. anger over the narcotics trade also helped reduce Central America's share of its largess. Demand for U.S. aid from other parts of the world was unprecedented. Central America got some help, but not enough.

Central American leaders went back to an old idea in 1991, the Central American common market of the 1960s. Mexico played the lead in hosting bilateral and multilateral trade discussions among the Central Americans and, at times, even with Spain and Portugal. Mexico and Venezuela proposed arrangements to provide lower oil prices to Central America, and President George Bush urged the creation of some kind of North American trading bloc.

These ideas were complex and faced many entrenched groups who opposed outside interference, but no better suggestions were forthcoming. A few trade barriers within the region were lowered and many international investors thought they saw some opportunities as the small nations sought to change old habits and to seek less-traditional exports. The danger lay in continued reliance upon the United States as the major market, seemingly the goal of most of the world. But as political tensions subsided, it was hoped that regional commerce could revive and help stimulate investment as well.

Belize

Boundary Disputes Settled. In the 17th century, Great Britain established the lumber-cutting colony of British Honduras in the midst of Spanish Central America. When the Spanish colonies became independent in the 1820s, Mexico and Guatemala each contended that British Honduras belonged to it. Throughout much of the 19th century both the status and the boundaries of British Honduras remained in dispute. In 1981, Great Britain granted the colony independence under the name Belize. Mexico dropped its claims, but Guatemala became more aggressive. British troops remained behind to discourage any Guatemalan adventurism. In time national status became less a matter of doubt. In January 1991, Belize was accepted as the 34th member of the Organization of American States (OAS). In August, Guatemala's government announced that it recognized the "right of the people of Belize to self-determination" and declared its intention to live in peace and harmony with Belize. The following month, Guatemala opened diplomatic relations with Belize for the first time. It would seem that the matter of Belizean sover-

Although Belize, the former British Honduras, is one of Latin America's more remote nations, its advantages as a tourist center were beginning to catch on in 1991. Fishing, especially for tarpon, is a prime activity for the visitor.

An earthquake, measuring 7.4 on the Richter scale, struck Costa Rica on April 22, 1991, killing 47 persons. Parts of Panama also felt the tremors.

eignty finally was settled, although Guatemala had not agreed that the present boundaries were correct. Probably because of that caveat, small detachments of British troops remained in Belize.

The Environment. Peaceful, if not entirely viable economically, Belize continued to develop its tourist program by promoting its clear coastal waters and the Mayan ruins of the interior. The citizenry take much pride in their devotion to the environment. Most of Belize's great rain forest appeared to have been saved from the world's lumber demands, and a popular new zoo was used to impress the public with the need for saving the wildlife of that forest. A 1991 postage stamp bore the photograph of a tapir. The zoo's resources were strained badly, but supported by the public as the most visible means of demonstrating concern for their small land.

Costa Rica

Earthquakes. As so often happens in the tropics, modest economic gains twice were compromised by natural disasters in Costa Rica. The nation had suffered from an earthquake in December 1990, killing one, injuring 229, and leaving some 14,000 homeless. The quake of April 22, 1991, brought far worse havoc to the land. (It also was felt in Panama.) The April quake, measuring 7.4 on the Richter scale, was the worst since 1910. The estimated number of deaths totaled 47. More than 100 persons were injured. The quake flattened much of the Caribbean town of Limón, including two hotels, and wiped out many beaches. The region is the poorest in Costa Rica, and the disaster particularly hurt workers whose jobs were threatened when great banana farms, the nation's only oil refinery, and most roads were made temporarily useless. More than 80% of the nation's trade passes through the port of Limón, so all of Costa Rica's economy was affected by the quake.

The Economy. Although Costa Rica's economy remained the most stable in Central America, in 1991 it still lacked vigor. During the 1980s growth was a negative 5%. Inflation was still high, and the administration of President Rafael Angel Calderón Fournier was forced to cut government jobs and boost some taxes. Costa Rica has been one of only three Latin American states to benefit so far from the plan of U.S. Secretary of the Treasury Nicholas Brady to renegotiate foreign debts (known as the Brady Plan). The reduction in interest payments was expected to spur business. Costa Rica also led Central America in diversification programs, with newer, nontraditional exports including vegetables, cut flowers, and ornamental plants. However, coffee, bananas, textiles, and sugar still provided most of its export income.

Landmark Environmental Lawsuits. In 1979 the U.S. Environmental Protection Agency (EPA) banned the use of dibromochloropropane (DBCP), a strong pesticide. A few years later a number of Costa Rican workers, mostly men who worked on banana farms, claimed that Shell Oil, Dow Chemical, and Occidental Petroleum still sold the chemical in Costa Rica as late as 1984. Contending that DBCP caused cancer and sterility among them, the workers attempted to sue in U.S. courts. The companies replied that they had discontinued the use of the chemical in Costa Rica about the time of the EPA ruling. Florida and California courts refused to accept the cases, but in 1990 the Texas Supreme Court ruled that the Costa Ricans could sue in Texas courts provided they could prove the companies had a "sizable Texas presence." No decisions had been rendered by late 1991.

El Salvador

Peace Talks. In 1991 the civil war in El Salvador entered its 11th year. Over a span of 18 months peace talks were held in Caracas, New York, and Mexico City. United Nations (UN) mediators used all their prestige and position to pressure the government and the rebels of the Farabundo Martí National Liberation Front (FMLN), but there still was no peace. In part the issues dividing the parties were constitutional questions and could not be remedied quickly. The most difficult matters concerned the land-reform program, restructuring the military and the police, negotiating a cease-fire, and amending the constitution to implement some of these reforms. Under considerable pressure from the UN, the parties came up with a number of agreements about constitutional issues in April and May. But between May and August no progress was achieved, and in some ways the brutal war continued.

The United States, the USSR, and Cuba played declining support roles, substantially reducing the arms flow into El Salvador. In September the two sides agreed in principle to integrate rebels into a new national police force, and the government promised to protect the right of rebel families to retain occupied lands. But there was no cease-fire and no significant reform of the military, although the government promised to make some unspecified changes later. Finally in November, five rebel commanders announced that they were enforcing an immediate unilateral cease-fire, to remain in effect until a peace treaty was signed. President Alfredo Cristiani acknowledged the action as most helpful, but did not reciprocate. The army dismissed the announcement as a trick and deployed troops into rebel strongholds the next day. In the early hours of Jan. 1, 1992, a peace agreement between the government and the rebels was reached at the United Nations. Although several points remained to be resolved, a cease-fire was to go into effect on Feb. 1, 1992.

Election. In March an election was held for a new National Assembly as well as many local offices. The first election in 11 years that saw formal rebel participation resulted in the Republican National Alliance (ARENA) losing its majority in the National Assembly. ARENA, however, did win a plurality—39 of 84 seats—and continued to rule through a coalition of conservative parties. The Christian Democrats captured 26 seats, the ARENA-allied National Conciliation Party won nine, representatives of the guerrillas took eight, and a Communist party and a spinoff of the Christian Democrats each gained one. ARENA won most of the mayoral races. The outgoing legislature approved the constitutional reforms resulting from the peace talks, but by year's end these

In a controversial trial in El Salvador in the fall of 1991, two army officers were convicted and seven other soldiers were cleared of the murders of six Jesuit priests and two women in mid-November 1989.

changes had yet to be approved by the new National Assembly as the constitution required.

Controversial Trial. The trial of nine military men for the 1989 murder of eight persons, including six Jesuit priests, finally began in September amid charges of cover-up. Jurists were threatened; witnesses disappeared. Confessions were recanted, and a judge even warned he would pass sentence, then flee the country. Once the evidence was presented the jury acted quickly, if strangely. It convicted a colonel and a lieutenant and cleared seven other soldiers, including four who once had confessed to complicity in the killings. Along with many Salvadoreans, a U.S. congressional investigative team made up of 20 House Democrats disputed the decision and in November concluded that the shootings had been the plot of senior army officers led by Gen. René Emilio Ponce—the chief of staff—and the current minister of defense. The House report was tied closely to the negative attitude of Democratic House members toward giving more military aid to El Salvador, most of which was delayed in 1991 because of the nation's human-rights record.

The worst fraud in the country's history was reported in July when a judge ordered the arrest of 21 prominent business people for looting millions of dollars from a government-owned bank. The investigators, trained by Americans, spent two years researching huge loans made with little concern for security. By late 1991 no one had been arrested; many of the 21 already had fled the country.

Economic Difficulties. The slackening of the civil war's intensity in 1991 aided the faltering economy. Production of coffee and other agricultural products grew almost 10%, although the overall economic growth was only about 3% and still was far behind the 1978 level. Inflation remained high, around 24%. Probably the least welcome economic statistic was the estimate that the nation's chief source of foreign exchange was the thousands of Salvadoreans in exile. It was estimated that nearly one fifth of the nation lived in Canada or the United States, and many of these supported their families back home with portions of their salaries.

Guatemala

A New President. As expected Jorge Serrano Elías won the January runoff for the presidency. Serrano, a member of the Solidarity Action Movement and a close ally of former President Efraín Ríos Montt, decisively defeated Jorge Carpio Nicolle of the National Center Union. Serrano, an educator and engineer, is a conservative and, like Ríos Montt, an evangelical Christian.

Within a few months the new president settled a long-standing irritant when he extended diplomatic recognition to neighboring Belize.

AP/Wide World

In a runoff election on Jan. 6, 1991, Jorge Serrano Elías, an engineer and educator, was chosen president of Guatemala. He is a member of the Solidarity Action Movement.

Facing a stagnant economy with a growth rate of less than 3% and inflation of nearly 75%, Serrano blamed his predecessor for a "bankrupt" nation. The foreign debt was a persistent problem, and tax revenues had shrunk. Serrano's counteractions included a 10% cut in the national budget, new taxes and collection procedures, and the laying off of some 3,000 government workers. Talks with labor-union leaders were ongoing to help reduce the worst effects of these actions. As elsewhere in Central America, Guatemala was attempting, with some success, to move away from traditional exports. Fruits, flowers, and vegetables were of increasing importance in its export trade.

U.S. Relations. Relations between Guatemala and the United States were strained seriously throughout much of 1991 because of human rights; the two governments simply did not view the matter in the same fashion. In December 1990 the U.S. State Department formally deplored the number of violent noncombat deaths in Guatemala, finding the record much worse than that of El Salvador. The consequence was the loss of U.S. military aid. The Guatemalan government's own ombudsman reported 599 extrajudicial killings and 140 disappearances in 1990, and 321 claims of similar killings in the first six months of 1991. On taking office, President Serrano revealed his sensitivity about the issue, denying responsibility for the actions of previous administrations and claiming his nation's dignity and sovereignty were hurt by Washington's threats. But he did little toward prosecuting anyone in the rape of a U.S. nun or the murder of a U.S. rancher. Late in the summer both houses of the U.S. Congress passed legislation that tied resumption of aid to Guatemalan progress in human rights and other reforms—including taxes, freedom of the press, control of the military, and peace negotiations with the rebels.

Washington received support from the OAS in August when it warned Guatemala to protect the lives of foreign judges investigating various killings. In October, President Serrano saw President Bush in Washington to discuss some of these criticisms.

Peace talks between the rebels and the Guatemalan government continued on and off throughout the year with small result. Earthquakes of 5.8 and 4.0 intensities struck the nation in September, killing perhaps 20 people and creating landslides that destroyed homes and blocked portions of the Pan American Highway. Many Colombian drug traffickers appeared to have increased the importance of Guatemala as an entrepôt, shifting cargoes from Miami to remote Guatemalan towns because their more-central locations made refueling more practical. Archaeologists continued their Mayan findings, discovering the tomb of an 8th-century ruler of great significance in 1991. The importance of the ruler reopened major questions about the fate of the Mayan empire.

Honduras

Abuses by the Military. The Honduran record for the protection of human rights was somewhat better than that of its neighbors, Guatemala and El Salvador, in 1991. In June, Amnesty International (AI) announced that it had received no reports of "disappearances" or killings by the army since the presidential inauguration of Rafael Leonardo Callejas in January 1990. However, AI did find that torture and illegal detention were "rife" in Honduras. In July a 17-year-old student had gone to a military base to request the release from service of her boyfriend, who had been recruited forcibly. Soon thereafter she was found dead, her body horribly mutilated. Two officers were arrested, but the repeated issue of judicial jurisdiction arose. Civil courts insisted upon the right to prosecute the officers, but as usual the military claimed full control over its personnel. At the question's heart was the matter of who ran Honduras, the military or civilian administrations. In a similar instance a colonel killed five peasants over a land dispute, and his case was prosecuted by military court. The continued interference of the military in domestic affairs greatly concerned many Hondurans.

In turn, the army worried about losing its long-standing prestige. U.S. military aid, which for a decade had been so vast as to make the armed forces almost independent of the government, was cut 50% in 1990. Washington's use of Honduras as a base and staging area in the Nicaraguan civil war had made the military the major political force in the land. Its 1991 strength of about 17,000 made it a highly privileged group.

Economy. The economy improved little in 1991. Like so many other heavily indebted nations, Honduras had been forced by international lending agencies to attempt the adoption of a number of austere financial measures. The nation suffered badly from a lack of credit in 1990 for its failure to achieve certain of these goals. In 1991, however, President Callejas inaugurated many of these reforms. His administration increased some taxes, reduced government spending, cut thousands of workers from the government payroll, and increased utility rates. The lending agencies approved these actions, meaning the probable resumption of foreign aid, but the measures critically damaged the finances of most of the nation, where three fourths of the people live below the poverty level.

Nicaragua

Nicaragua moved ahead in 1991, but very slowly and only in a few areas. Merely being able to retain her office and accomplish a few matters must be looked upon as a major achievement for new President Violeta Barrios de Chamorro.

President Chamorro. With a variety of tactics, President Chamorro generally controlled the legislature enough to get her way. She worked closely with moderate elements of the opposition parties in order to reduce the size and influence of the military and reestablish an

CENTRAL AMERICA • Information Highlights

Nation	Population (in Millions)	Area (sq mi)	Area (km²)	Capital	Head of State and Government
Belize	0.2	8,865	22 960	Belmopan	Minita Gordon, governor-general George Price, prime minister
Costa Rica	3.1	19,730	51 100	San José	Rafael Angel Calderón Fournier, president
El Salvador	5.4	8,124	21 040	San Salvador	Alfredo Cristiani, president
Guatemala	9.5	42,042	108 890	Guatemala City	Jorge Serrano Elías, president
Honduras	5.3	43,278	112 090	Tegucigalpa	Rafael Leonardo Callejas, president
Nicaragua	3.9	49,998	129 494	Managua	Violeta Barrios de Chamorro, president
Panama	2.5	30,193	78 200	Panama City	Guillermo Endara, president

open economy. Even these changes had their opponents. Sandinistas were divided by her approach; many worked freely with her, but others saw the steps as a measure to destroy the Sandinistas as a party. The rest of the world, and especially the international banks, applauded the freeing of business, but the changes meant huge adjustments to many Nicaraguans who were familiar only with the waste, cumbersome bureaucracy, and strong governmental controls of the recent Marxist rulers.

The most explosive issue Chamorro faced concerned the ownership of vast amounts of land, a question which had turned into a national debate. The lame-duck Sandinista legislature had passed two measures just before Chamorro took office. The laws confirmed titles to the holdings of thousands of people who obtained property during the Sandinista regime. The new owners included the very poor as well as a few rich families, but all supported the Sandinistas. Some members of the new Chamorro government wanted to cancel all such titles; others favored the president's plan to pay the former owners and not to dispossess anyone using the land properly. (Former President Daniel Ortega was one of those enjoying a confiscated mansion.) President Chamorro established a commission to deal with the conflicting claims; so far about 300 families out of 6,000 affected had had their land returned by the commission. Alfredo César Aguirre, a close adviser to the president, split with her on the tenure question, insisting that all the land be returned to the pre-Sandinistas. The property at issue was worth tens of millions of dollars.

Many old Sandinistas and former contras still fought the civil war—in a fashion. No significant battle took place, but small skirmishes increased in number throughout the year as each side claimed persecution. The Sandinistas convened a party convention in July, voting by secret ballot for a party assembly to replace the old directors who fought the war. The leadership looked much like that of old, if less militant. No program or platform was announced. Meanwhile former contras, apparently getting funds from exiles in Miami, made random attacks on remote farms—perhaps over land titles, perhaps to get former Sandinistas out of the security forces. Workers' complaints were agitated by Daniel Ortega, who encouraged unions to strike and take over the factories in the midst of the crucial sugar harvest. Several were shut down through these actions. Ortega insisted he was not attempting to overthrow the government.

AP/Wide World

U.S. Vice-President Dan Quayle (top left) *and House Speaker Tom Foley applaud as Violeta Barrios de Chamorro prepares to address the U.S. Congress on April 16, 1991. The Nicaraguan president told a joint session that Nicaragua needs "steadfast financial assistance from the United States throughout this entire decade to reconstruct" its economy.*

During this first year of post-Sandinista rule some progress was made in reforming the military, much of this because Humberto Ortega—former Sandinista and brother of Daniel—remained head of the security forces and worked closely with President Chamorro. The military draft was eliminated; Cuban military advisers were sent home; forces were reduced from 80,000 to 20,000; and the military budget was cut more than 50%. Most of the 1,700 secret police were disbanded as fast as the economy could absorb their demobilization.

The Economy. The Nicaraguan economy remained Central America's sickest and ranked only above Haiti's in the hemisphere. Productivity and exports were both well below 1980 levels. Inflation and the debt almost baffled comprehension. Unemployment averaged about 40% for the year. Strong reform measures were introduced, including devaluation of the currency and reductions in price supports of basic foods. In April, President Chamorro visited Washington seeking financial relief for her destitute state. Her severe economic measures were welcomed by various lenders, and Nicaragua received promises of international help to cover the arrears in interest due on its $11 billion foreign debt. The United States, Germany, and Japan made contributions, and the United States wrote off some debt dating back to the 1960s.

Panama

Striving Toward Economic Recovery. By the end of 1991, Panama appeared to be reaching the starting line in the race to economic recovery. The U.S. embargo and the war that resulted in the capture of former dictator Manuel Noriega had brought about negative growth during 1989–90. The immediate consequence was the disruption of the famed international banking system, the massive withdrawal of foreign bank deposits, and great unemployment. As occurred elsewhere in Central America, the republic introduced a number of fiscal reforms. These were harsh in many ways, but helped to restore the confidence of the international financial community in Panama's will to bring needed change. Panamanian banks began opening their records to aid investigations into money laundering and drug activities, and President Guillermo Endara promised to privatize certain government operations and reduce some tariffs. However, his administration did nothing to cope with the problems of hunger, lack of housing, and poor education.

Panama Canal. To no small extent the nation's future economic position would depend upon the performance of the Panama Canal and adjacent U.S. bases. Panama had but eight years to assume full responsibility for the canal's operation, and certain signs were disappointing. Those ports and the railway already under total Panama management were being run poorly. Some shippers were considering alternative routes and methods in the event Panama did badly with the canal. The Persian Gulf war proved beneficial, with the canal enjoying a record year in tonnage and tolls. But the government assumed those conditions would not be repeated. U.S. and Japanese trade had predominated in recent years, but their growth virtually had stopped. The biggest increase in world shipping now was found within the Asian theater and was of little value to the canal.

President Endara established a commission to make recommendations to him by April 1992 about the future of the canal and the development of some 360,000 acres (145 750 ha) of land that also will be transferred from U.S. jurisdiction at the end of the century. In July plans were approved to widen an 8-mi (12.9-km) section of Gaillard Cut to make possible two-way transit of the largest ships through those narrows. Estimated cost was $200 million. While many Panamanians were embittered by the U.S. invasion of 1989, polls showed that nearly two thirds of the population wanted U.S. troops to remain after 1999 when the canal treaty is completely operational and ten Southern Command bases are closed. The bases provide 6,000 civilian jobs and pour about $250 million into the Panamanian economy each year. This is in addition to the spending power of about 10,000 U.S. troops. Some Panamanian officials would like to reopen the treaty terms, but that was unlikely.

The coalition government put together by President Endara in 1989 appeared to be falling apart in 1991. Various differences over economic policies and the role of former followers of Manuel Noriega caused Endara to remove five members of his cabinet, all of who were Christian Democrats, the leading opposition party. Polls showed Endara's popularity to be less than 15%, as much of the public blamed him for trying to accommodate international banks and ignoring domestic problems.

Manuel Noriega. After nearly two years of imprisonment and months of closed-door hearings, Manuel Noriega finally went to trial in Miami on drug-trafficking charges. He had been indicted in 1988 by Florida grand juries, then was captured during the U.S. invasion of Panama in December 1989. Since then he had been in prison awaiting trial. The prosecution wanted to limit the trial to drug matters, and had witnesses testifying to huge bribes Noriega received for cooperating with Colombian drug lords. The defense was emphasizing Noriega's connections with past U.S. administrations as a paid agent of the Central Intelligence Agency and Drug Enforcement Agency for three decades. Testimony from scores of witnesses portended a long trial.

THOMAS L. KARNES
Arizona State University

CHEMISTRY

Events in chemistry in 1991 included the discovery of potentially useful properties of hollow carbon molecules called "buckyballs," the synthesis of new compounds with exotic geometries, and the introduction of polymers with novel properties.

Buckyballs. If a compound were to be named "molecule of the year," for 1991 it would have to be the buckyball. In 1985 chemists at Rice University startled the scientific world with an announcement that they had discovered a new form of elemental carbon consisting of symmetric, hollow cages of carbon atoms bonded like chicken wire. The most prominent form was C_{60}, with 60 carbons joined like the seams of a soccer ball. Since the arrangement reminded the Rice workers of the geodesic domes of architect R. Buckminster Fuller, they called the new form buckminsterfullerene. In time the entire class of compounds came to be called fullerenes or, less formally, buckyballs.

Because these compounds could be prepared only in minute quantities they remained curiosities until 1990, when workers in Germany and Arizona reported a simple method for making them in large amounts. This sparked an explosion of activity, and in 1991 hardly a week passed without report of a discovery involving fullerenes or their derivatives.

Until 1991 the symmetric, hollow shape attributed to C_{60} was only speculative. The problem was that the C_{60} molecules' spherical shapes allowed them to orient freely in a crystal; thus the exact ordering needed for an X-ray-diffraction picture, the traditional means for determining molecular structure, was missing. In the spring of 1991 chemists at the University of California solved this problem by attaching osmium adducts chemically to the C_{60} molecule. With these new "tails" holding the molecules in their places the X-ray crystal structure was obtained and the hollow, symmetric shape confirmed. At about the same time chemists at IBM's Almaden Research Center in California reported that they had measured the bond lengths in C_{60} using NMR spectroscopy, again confirming the soccer-ball shape.

Among the most interesting properties of the fullerenes are their electrical properties. In 1991 it was found that when potassium was added to C_{60} to yield K_3C_{60} the material became an electrical conductor, and at the very low temperature of just 19 kelvins (19 K) above absolute zero, it was a superconductor, i.e., it allowed an electric current to flow without resistance. Later studies showed that doping with rubidium raised the superconductivity temperature to 30 K, and thallium and rubidium raised it to about 45 K. Other work showed that several fullerenes possess magnetic and optical properties.

Synthesis. Synthetic chemists continued to create fascinating new compounds, among them a "bow-tie" compound produced by chemists at Rice University. Formally called spiropentadiene, the compound contains five carbon and four hydrogen atoms—one carbon at the center, and two carbons connected by double bonds lying perpendicular to one another on either side. Long of theoretical interest, this compound had frustrated earlier attempts at synthesis because its highly strained structure makes it very unstable. After producing the compound in the gas phase, the Rice workers trapped it at low temperatures using liquid nitrogen.

Cyclobutadiene, C_4H_4, another chemical of great theoretical interest, has been called "the Mona Lisa of organic compounds." This enigmatic compound is highly reactive, and normally can be obtained only at very low temperatures or with large protecting groups bonded to it. In 1991, UCLA chemists synthesized cyclobutadiene by means of a photochemical reaction carried out inside the cavity of a hemicarcerand, a clam-like compound that restricts the entrance and exit of other species. Inside a hemicarcerand the newly formed C_4H_4 was protected from attack and remained stable even at ordinary temperatures.

Polymers. Polymers are giant molecules that make up modern plastics and synthetic fibers such as nylon and polyester. It long has been recognized that a durable magnetic polymer might have a number of commercial applications, e.g., in magnetic-storage devices for computers. Such materials might be individually tailored for specific purposes, unlike common iron-containing magnets. The trouble has been that these materials tend to work only at very low temperatures, often near absolute zero. In 1991 workers at Ohio State University and DuPont's Central Research Department in Wilmington, DE, reported that they had created a vanadium-containing organic polymer that remains magnetic at room temperature and above. They first noticed this material's promise when it was found sticking to a magnetic stirring bar in their reaction container. Despite its potential, the polymer has the disadvantage that it must be kept in an inert atmosphere or it loses its magnetism.

The amine-quinone polymer that adheres so strongly to metals that it displaces water and oils also was attracting attention. Developed by a Philadelphia chemist, the material holds promise as an anticorrosion coating. Since more than $200 billion is spent annually to overcome corrosion in the United States, there would be a big market for such a material. Both synthesis and application of the material are claimed to be relatively simple.

PAUL G. SEYBOLD, *Wright State University*

© Ralf-Finn Hestoff/Saba

Richard M. Daley, his wife, mother, and children celebrate his election to a full term as mayor of Chicago. Daley, who had been elected to fill the unexpired term of the late Harold Washington in 1989, won with more than 70% of the vote.

CHICAGO

Mayor Richard M. Daley established his own political power in an April 1991 mayoral election by garnering 73% of the vote in a three-way race. His impressive victory struck a blow to efforts by some black political leaders to revive the political coalition that twice elected Harold Washington mayor. Third-party candidate R. Eugene Pincham, a former judge who had hoped the 1 million blacks in Chicago would unite behind him, received 22% of the vote. Four percent of the vote went to the Republican candidate and 1% to a candidate from the Socialist Workers Party.

Daley, son of the legendary five-term Mayor Richard J. Daley, first was elected in 1989 to fill the unexpired term of the late Mayor Washington. Experts predicted that with this victory and control of the Chicago City Council, Daley would become a more aggressive mayor. But as he embarked on his first full term, he was haunted by many of the same problems that faced previous mayors. Crime again soared in 1991, the city's tax base continued to erode, and financial woes and poor student performance plagued Chicago's school system.

Crime. Daley promised to put 600 more policemen on Chicago streets in response to a record number of homicides. It was expected that more than 900 people would be killed in 1991 in this city of 3 million people. Much of the killing was believed to have been caused by drug use and turf wars between drug dealers, brought on by the infiltration of crack cocaine.

Critics of the plan included John Dineen, president of the Fraternal Order of Police, who said more policemen was not the answer, that there was no longer a respect for law and order. Meanwhile efforts also were under way to sweep crime-ridden housing projects of the gangs that were filling vacant apartments and terrorizing residents. Several projects were renovated in the hopes of again making them a good place for working families to live.

Schools. In the Chicago schools, huge spending cuts were made by Schools Superintendent Ted Kimbrough to eliminate an estimated $315 million shortfall in funds that Kimbrough predicted could reach as high as $500 million in fiscal 1993. He urged state legislators to raise taxes to fund schools.

New Structures. White Sox fans got a new stadium in 1991 with the opening of a new Comiskey Park (*see* PEOPLE, PLACES, AND THINGS) and book lovers got a new library with the opening of the $144 million Harold Washington Library Center, the largest public library anywhere with 2 million volumes.

ROBERT ENSTAD, *"Chicago Tribune"*

CHILE

Chile began 1991 by rekindling bitter memories of the repression suffered under the 17-year dictatorship of Gen. Augusto Pinochet. At the same time, though, the country, now under a freely elected government headed by a civilian, Patricio Aylwin, was being welcomed back into the community of democratic nations.

Human Rights. In March the Aylwin government released a long-awaited report on human-rights violations committed during the Pinochet regime. Formally titled "The National Truth and Reconciliation Report," the 1,700-page document described 2,279 "victims of political violence"—of which 815 represented "executions and torture deaths," 957 persons "arrested by agents of the state and disappeared," and 101 "alleged escape attempts" during the 1973–90 military rule. The result of a ten-month investigation by an eight-member panel headed by Raul Rettig, an 81-year-old jurist, the report was compiled from more than 4,000 interviews. The public reaction in Chile to the report was to blame the atrocities almost equally on the army and the judiciary for its failure to bring human-rights violators to justice.

Public officials, however, refrained from attacking Pinochet, who was still chief of the Chilean armed forces, or the army as an institution, and few advocated that the military leaders be tried on human-rights charges. In any case, military officers responsible for atrocities committed during the dictatorship were protected from prosecution by an amnesty law dictated by Pinochet in 1976.

Scattered incidents of violence erupted when the report was published, but in general the nation remained calm. It was apparent, though, that the army was unrepentant for the massive abuses it had committed. As a result, tension smoldered throughout the year between the civilian government and the military. Pinochet, reacting to the discovery of mass graves of leftists killed following the military coup of 1973, and told that the remains of two persons were found in the same coffin, commented, "but how economical." Minister of Government Enrique Correa said that the government was "deeply shocked" by Pinochet's "cruel statements."

International. Despite such incidents, in 1991, Chile regained much of the international respect it had lost under the Pinochet regime. An agreement signed with Argentina in August ended more than a century of border disputes between the two countries, which in 1978 almost had led to war.

In February the United States reinstated Chile as a beneficiary of the U.S. Generalized System of Preferences (GSP). The redesignation made Chile eligible for duty-free entry to the U.S. market for certain exports. GSP privileges had been withdrawn from Chile in 1988 for its violations of workers' rights. During the year the United States also signed a framework trade agreement with Chile which eventually could lead to free trade between the two countries under President George Bush's Enterprise for the Americas Initiative.

In June, Chilean Finance Minister Alejandro Foxley said his country was interested in association with MERCOSUR, the common market recently initiated by Argentina, Brazil, Paraguay, and Uruguay. Foxley added that his government also was negotiating liberalized trade arrangements with Mexico and Venezuela. And on September 22, President Aylwin and Mexican President Carlos Salinas de Gortari did sign a free-trade pact which projected the bilateral reduction of import tariffs beginning in 1992, and the elimination of all customs duties by 1994. The Chile-Mexico agreement was the first such bilateral pact signed by two Latin American countries. Aylwin said he expected that when the agreement came into effect it would more than triple Chilean-Mexican trade, which reached $150 million in 1990, to $500 million per year.

Economy. During the year foreign investors showed increasing interest in opportunities in the country. By September some $1.6 billion in new investment had been approved, 11% more than the $1.47 billion record set in 1990, according to Economy Minister Carlos Ominani. "The figures show that Chile is still the leader in the amount of foreign investment on the continent," Ominani said in announcing $604 million in new Finnish, Spanish, Brazilian, and U.S. investment in mining, energy, construction, and financial services.

G. Edward Tillman, president of the Chilean-American Chamber of Commerce, commented that he expected the Chilean economy to grow at a rate of 4% to 6% in 1991, and he predicted that inflation would go no higher than 20% during the year.

Storms. Intense storms in northern Chile on June 18 left 116 people dead and produced unusually heavy snowfalls in the Atacama Desert. Rain swept away 600 homes and damaged another 6,000 in the city of Antofagasta. Streets in the city were buried in mud up to 3 ft (.9 m) deep. Roads into the city were blocked, telephone communications were cut off, and port facilities were closed for several days.

RICHARD C. SCHROEDER
Consultant to the Organization of American States

CHILE • Information Highlights

Official Name: Republic of Chile.
Location: Southwestern coast of South America.
Area: 292,259 sq mi (756 950 km^2).
Population (mid-1991 est.): 13,400,000.
Chief Cities (June 15, 1990): Santiago, the capital, 4,385,481; Concepción, 306,464.
Government: *Head of state and government,* Patricio Aylwin, president (took office March 1990). *Legislature*—National Congress: Senate and Chamber of Deputies.
Monetary Unit: Peso (349.65 pesos equal U.S.$1, official rate, Nov. 8, 1991).
Gross Domestic Product (1989 U.S.$): $25,300,-000,000.
Economic Index (Santiago, 1990): *Consumer Prices* (1980 = 100), all items, 635.5; food, 612.5.
Foreign Trade (1990 U.S.$): *Imports,* $7,272,000,000; *exports,* $8,580,000,000.

© Chine Nouvelle/Sipa

Parts of eastern China, including a residential area of the city of Wuxi (above) *suffered from severe flooding that began in May 1991. The disaster took some 1,700 lives, left millions homeless, and cost numerous farmers their livelihood.*

CHINA, PEOPLE'S REPUBLIC OF

The state of suspended animation that marked the political scene in China in 1990 prolonged itself throughout 1991. The tug of war between those elder statesmen cautiously inclined toward continued economic reform and those elder statesmen firmly committed to a renewal of central planning continued through the year. Indeed, it was unlikely to be resolved even by a projected change of leadership at the 14th congress of the Chinese Communist Party scheduled for early 1992. As a result of this continuing stalemate, most of the change in China that occurred during the year could be traced to external sources.

The Collapse of Soviet Communism. The most important of these external sources was the failed coup in the Soviet Union, the subsequent collapse of the Soviet Communist Party, and, ultimately, of the Soviet Union itself. Initial reports of the coup came as music to the ears of the elderly conservatives. They took the news of its collapse two days later as indicative of the need to exercise care in selecting a successor generation in order to avoid entrusting the future of Chinese communism to an unreliable figure like Mikhail Gorbachev who would squander its heritage. In the months following the coup attempt, the collapse of Soviet communism exerted an important influence over both domestic and international policy in China.

Preserving the Socialist Base. In domestic terms, the response to the failure of socialism abroad has been to redouble efforts to prop up the socialist base in China. Overall, the Chinese economy did very well in 1991, achieving a growth rate in excess of 7% and an inflation rate of less than 5%. On the other hand, its health could be attributed more to the private and collective sectors than to the state-owned sector.

Growth rates in the private and collective sectors in 1991 were 45% and 25%, respectively. Meanwhile the state sector grew at a rate of only 11%. With this differential growth rate, China would reach the point in mid-1992 at which production in the state sector would account for less than half of the total gross national product for the first time since 1949.

A slow rate of growth was only one of the problems encountered by China's 10,000-odd state-owned enterprises. Just less than half of them lost money during 1991. The backlog of unsold stock produced by state-owned factories totaled more than $42 billion by year's end. Their ability to turn a profit was hampered severely by the fact that most of these enterprises were responsible for the livelihood of a very large group of people, only a fraction of whom were engaged in production. The majority were retired or were providing a wide range of services for the remainder of the staff. Moreover, state enterprises were operating in a new environment where some but not all of their costs and some but not all of their prices were controlled by state plan. The remainder were determined by a fluctuating market over which they had no control.

While a new bankruptcy law was passed in 1989, the central government has discouraged its application to state-sector factories. Two reasons appeared to lie behind this potentially problematic decision. The first was an ideologically determined commitment to hold together what remains of the socialist system in China in the face of the collapse of socialist systems in what was the Soviet bloc. The second was an overriding fear of political instability. Closing factories means dismissing workers, and unemployed workers well may take to the streets to express their dissatisfaction with those responsible for putting them out of work.

Instead of allowing unprofitable firms to go out of business, the government provided them with more than $10 billion in loans and covered losses totaling an additional $15 billion in 1991. The cost of these subsidies exceeded government expenditures for the military and for education combined, and contributed significantly to the more than $10 billion deficit in the national budget for the year.

Realizing that these subsidies could not be maintained over the long term, government planners cast about for another cure for the ills of the state sector. Technological upgrading was one of the straws at which they grasped, but few observers had faith in the efficacy of this very costly remedy. The real solution would appear to be to close down the hopelessly inefficient factories and to sell off the rest to individuals or collectives prepared to cope with the vagaries of the expanding market economy. Such a radical approach as this, however, must await the advent of a new and bolder set of leaders less governed by nostalgia for a socialist past than are China's gerontocrats.

China's Place in the New World Order. In recent years, China's perception of its place in the international order was determined primarily by the great power rivalry that existed between the Soviet Union and the United States. With the Persian Gulf war and the collapse of the Soviet Union this framework of what the Chinese called "great power hegemony" suddenly disappeared.

In its place was a new and tentative world order in which the United States occupied a position of primacy that soon would be challenged by a newly united Europe and a rapidly developing Japan. Under these circumstances, China has had to abandon its position as a balancing force situated equidistant between the two great powers. Lest it find itself hopelessly sidelined in the new world order, China attempted, over the course of 1990–91, to carve out a role for itself as a regional power in East Asia, as a leader among developing nations, and, less overtly, as a patron of the remaining members of what used to be the socialist camp.

Toward these ends, China's leaders engaged in a flurry of diplomatic activity during 1991. Premier Li Peng visited the Middle East in July and India in December. President Yang Shangkun visited Pakistan and Iran in November. Diplomatic ties with Vietnam were restored in November after a 12-year rupture that began with a border clash in 1979. Visits also were exchanged with North Korea. Li Peng visited Pyongyang in June and North Korea's Kim Il Sung was greeted with great fanfare in Beijing in October.

Attempting to mark an end to the isolation imposed on China following the suppression of the democracy movement in Beijing in 1989, highly publicized visits to Beijing were arranged for Japan's Prime Minister Toshiki Kaifu in August, Britain's Prime Minister John Major in October, and U.S. Secretary of State James Baker in November.

Baker arrived in Beijing with a full agenda of issues to take up with his Chinese hosts. The year had been marked by a steady deterioration of relations between the United States and China. The U.S. Congress manifested its displeasure with China by raising a number of issues in conjunction with its attempt to withdraw most-favored-nation (MFN) status from China or at least to impose conditions on its subsequent renewal. The issues included both new, trade-related problems and lingering questions of human rights.

Trade related issues were exacerbated by the fact that, while two-way trade between China and the United States grew to more than $20 billion in 1991, by its reckoning the United

Becoming the first major U.S. official to visit Beijing since China's 1989 prodemocracy crackdown, Secretary of State James Baker conferred with Foreign Minister Qian Qichen (right) *and other government leaders in November 1991.*

AP/Wide World

States experienced a deficit in that trade of some $13 billion. The Chinese government denied the existence of the problem, excluding from its calculations those goods transshipped through Hong Kong to the United States and thus claiming a deficit of its own amounting to more than $1 billion.

Seeking to redress what it takes to be an imbalance in trade, the U.S. government made formal complaint to the Chinese government about its restrictions on the free flow of goods into China. Under investigation by the U.S. side were direct quotas and bans on certain imports, complex import-licensing requirements, detailed technical specifications that served to bar most imports, and the failure to publish rules and regulations governing imports.

The U.S. side also complained of loopholes in the Chinese copyright law that permitted the copying of patented products and copyrighted software. Losses by U.S. firms that could be attributed to these loopholes were estimated to run as high as $400 million per year. Finally, violations of a U.S. law prohibiting the importation of goods produced by prison labor were given wide publicity in the United States beginning in the spring of 1991, and culminating in a cover story in *Newsweek* magazine that also was run as a segment on the television news program *Sixty Minutes*.

Most-favored-nation status for nonmarket economies must be renewed annually by Congress. Since 1989, Congress had taken that occasion to express its dissatisfaction with the repressive policies of China's conservative leaders and with what many take to be President Bush's excessively accommodating attitude toward them. In addition to the specific trade-related problems just cited, Congress continued to manifest its dissatisfaction with China's human-rights record in general and specifically with the government's treatment of those arrested at the time of the suppression of the prodemocracy demonstrations in Beijing in 1989.

CHINA • Information Highlights

Official Name: People's Republic of China.
Location: Central-eastern Asia.
Area: 3,705,390 sq mi (9 596 960 km^2).
Population (mid-1991 est.): 1,151,300,000.
Chief Cities (Dec. 31, 1988 est.): Beijing (Peking), the capital, 6,800,000; Shanghai, 7,330,000; Tianjin, 5,620,000.
Government: *General Secretary of the Chinese Communist Party,* Jiang Zemin (chosen June 1989); *Head of government:* Li Peng, premier (took office Nov. 1987); *Head of state:* Yang Shangkun, president (took office March 1988). *Legislature* (unicameral)—National People's Congress.
Monetary Unit: Yuan (5.363 yuan equal U.S.$1, official rate, August 1991).
Gross National Product (1989 est. U.S.$): $413,000,-000,000.
Foreign Trade (1990 U.S.$): *Imports,* $53,369,-000,000; *exports,* $62,089,000,000.

In July the House of Representatives voted 313 to 112 in support of a bill extending MFN status to China for another year, but imposing conditions on its renewal in 1992. A similar measure was passed by the Senate with a 55-to-44 vote. Neither body was able to muster sufficient votes to override President Bush's veto, though the president did feel obliged to take several steps designed to placate congressional critics of his policy toward China. Among these steps were his advocacy of membership in the General Agreement on Tariffs and Trade (GATT) for the authorities on Taiwan, as well as a formal investigation of China's trade practices that led to the imposition in late November of high tariffs on certain Chinese imports.

Secretary Baker left Beijing after his November visit saying that "the gulf" between the two sides was "too wide to bridge." For their part, the Chinese described their problematic relations with the United States to a visiting American journalist as falling into three categories: On certain international issues there is broad agreement; on trade issues there is hard bargaining; and on ideological principles (including those governing human rights), there is flat-out disagreement. At year's end it was clear that both sides must prepare to live with this state of affairs for the foreseeable future.

The Arms Merchant. One issue on which Baker claimed to have made progress during his talks with the Chinese was also the subject of conversation during Major's and Kaifu's visits to Beijing. As a means of augmenting its only slowly expanding budget, the Chinese army for several years has been engaged in an active program of arms sales. The principal customers for this arms trade have been countries in the Middle East, Southwest Asia, and, most recently, China's isolated and regressive neighbor, Myanmar (formerly Burma). Much of this trade has been conducted apparently without the knowledge of and often in direct contradiction to the policies of China's foreign ministry.

Since Iraq was among the recipients of Chinese arms, the question was given substantial publicity during and after the Gulf war. China's response to this publicity was to assert its sovereign right to engage in such sales and to point out that many of those nations calling attention to the problem, the United States most prominent among them, engaged in arms sales far in excess of those undertaken by the Chinese.

Ultimately, however, international pressure appeared to have some effect. During the Japanese prime minister's visit to Beijing in August the Chinese announced that they had decided to sign the Nuclear Nonproliferation Treaty and were considering becoming a party to the Missile Technology Control Regime. In

© Chine Nouvelle/Gamma-Liaison

To cultivate relations with the remaining Communist states, North Korea's President Kim Il Sung spent nearly two weeks in China in October 1991.

October tentative agreement was reached among the governments of the United States, France, Britain, the Soviet Union, and China on limiting the sale of conventional weapons. Following Baker's visit the Chinese agreed to consider an arrangement whereby pending weapons sales to Syria and Iran would be canceled in exchange for a U.S. agreement to sell certain military-related technology to China and to treat China in future as an equal player in arms-sales-limitation agreements.

While these steps were encouraging, their effectiveness would be limited by the degree to which control over arms sales was wrested from the exclusive purview of those who benefit most directly from them, namely the army and a handful of companies closely controlled by China's elderly conservatives and their family members.

Will the Center Hold?. Support for the nostalgic policies of China's aging autocrats was by no means universal or even widespread in China. Indeed the patriotic and ideologically correct rhetoric surrounding the celebration of the 70th anniversary of the founding of the Chinese Communist Party on July 1 rang hollow for many. Most observers agreed that the party's legitimacy had hit an all-time low in recent months.

Disaffection from the conservative line was running especially strong among those who benefited most from the reformist policies in effect prior to June 1989. The coastal communities of Shanghai, Fujian, and Guangzhou all have developed economies that are heavily dependent on outside investment and trade. None of them have anything to gain from the center's ill-starred efforts to revive central planning and the state sector it controls. The tendency among these communities is to ignore conservative central directives or, at best, to pay them lip service in principle while violating them in practice. Concrete evidence of this tendency came at the end of 1990 when provincial and municipal leaders were called into conference in Beijing and told to increase the proportion of their revenues that they transmitted to the central government. Contrary to past practice, they did not accede meekly to the central government's plan; instead, they rejected it out of hand and walked out of the meeting.

Under circumstances such as this there was little that the center could do to assert its control short of calling in the military, as was done in Beijing in 1989. Not only would such a solution be counterproductive, but it well might not work a second time. The central authorities used a carrot-and-stick approach to maintain control of the army in 1991. The military budget was increased each year and strenuous efforts were exerted to ensure that loyal officers were promoted and potentially disloyal officers were transferred or punished.

Despite these efforts it was highly questionable whether the military would agree to be used to enforce central directives over an openly resisting local populace. To become embroiled in civil disputes interferes with building the professional capability the military seeks. Moreover, the military would be reluctant to cut itself off willingly from international contacts that could provide it the technical equipment and expertise it requires to bring about its effective modernization. The appropriateness of these latter goals only was reinforced in the eyes of the Chinese military by the respective performances of the U.S. and Iraqi forces in the Gulf war.

And so China moved forward at a lumbering pace, loosening a bit at the seams, keeping a wary eye on the outside world, and waiting for a new era to begin.

JOHN BRYAN STARR
Yale-China Association

CITIES AND URBAN AFFAIRS

Developments in 1991 foreshadowed the issues that would face U.S. cities throughout the 1990s. For more than a decade cities had been experiencing a new wave of immigration. The political consequences of this continuing population movement will reverberate for years to come. Minority representation had become as contentious as partisan wrangling in the apportionment battles that followed the 1990 census. The census itself revealed that though older cities did better in the 1980s than in previous decades, they continued to lose ground to the suburbs and to the Sunbelt. As a result of a national recession, many cities ended 1991 with serious fiscal problems.

Apportionment and Population Change. Once again the United States had become a nation of immigrants. About 6.3 million immigrants were granted permanent residence during the 1980s, but the total number of legal and illegal immigrants was much higher, probably 8 million to 9 million, a number that approached the previous peak of 8.8 million immigrants in the first decade of the century. And the impact was far-reaching. Leading immigrant ports were transformed. About half of Miami's population was foreign-born, compared with more than 30% of Los Angeles' population. About 4 million Hispanics lived in the Los Angeles area, and more than 2 million in the New York area. The Miami, Chicago, San Francisco, Houston, and San Antonio metropolitan areas also had more than 500,000 Hispanics each. Four cities—Los Angeles, San Francisco, New York, and Honolulu—accounted for nearly 20% of the nation's Asian population. In the Los Angeles and San Antonio metropolitan areas, non-Hispanic whites now were outnumbered by minority groups. By the year 2000 this probably would be the case for more ports of entry.

One effect of the new immigration was a heightened awareness of minority representation in the political system. Minority representation was at the forefront of the political infighting over the reapportionment that would take place in 1992. In 1991 there were 37 blacks and Hispanics in Congress. As a result of redistricting there could be 20 more minority representatives in Congress after 1992. In Texas the Democrats were trying to create one black-majority district (in Dallas) and two Hispanic-majority seats (in Houston and San Antonio). In Illinois the Democratic speaker of the state House of Representatives promised to create a Hispanic-majority district in Chicago, which would result in several incumbents losing seats.

In some cases redistricting created tensions between blacks and Hispanics. In California, Hispanics outnumbered blacks by three to one, and Asians accounted for almost 10% of the state's population. For Hispanics and Asian-Americans, questions about their immigrant status loomed large as public-policy issues, as did issues of bilingualism in the schools. In national as well as local politics, the biracial politics of the past was being replaced by multiethnic and multicultural politics. City politics, as a result, will become more complex.

The increasing complexity of urban politics was coming at a time when cities were losing political leverage in state and national politics. In the 1980s older cities in the Frostbelt rebounded somewhat from the huge population losses of the previous decade, and several metropolitan areas that had declined in the 1970s actually grew in the 1980s. However, the fastest-growing cities were suburban. As of the 1990 census, 48% of Americans lived in suburbs. The number of states with suburban majorities increased from three in 1980 to 14 in 1990. The influence of cities in state legislatures, in Congress, and in presidential politics had eroded to the point that central cities, on their own, exerted very little political influence outside their borders. In the 1988 election, for example, George Bush could have carried almost all of the northern industrial states without a single vote from the big cities. Redistricting in 1992 would weaken the political voice of cities still further. (*See also* SPECIAL REPORT/UNITED STATES, page 548.)

Urban Policy. As a result of the long-term restructuring of political influence in the federal system, cities could not expect to find a sympathetic ear in statehouses or in Washington. The Community Development Block Grant (CDBG) program, which had been the cornerstone of many cities' revitalization efforts, would be cut from $3.2 billion in 1991 to $2.92 billion in 1992. Congress once again failed to support the Bush administration's enterprise-zones proposal, which would have cost about $1 billion in lost federal taxes over a four-year period. The Department of Housing and Urban Development's main new initiative was its Homeownership Opportunities for People Everywhere (HOPE) plan to sell public-housing units to tenants. The program, which potentially would involve 2 million housing units, was moving slowly. The cost of refurbishing and financing was estimated at $50,000 to $60,000 per unit. There was considerable opposition to the idea.

In 1991 the Bush administration offered to give $15 billion in block grants over to the states. Urban leaders expressed opposition to the idea of giving the states the authority to distribute CDBG as well as funds for mass transit and other services; in general, they believed that the states have not been responsive to cities. And as the recession of 1991 hit state budgets particularly hard, it was unlikely that they would be more responsive to the cities in the future.

Fiscal Stress. The recession of 1991 hit city budgets even harder than the recessions of 1973–75 and 1982–83. According to a report issued by the National League of Cities, more than 70% of cities said they were less able to meet their needs in 1991 than in 1990, and more than 60% reported that expenditures were expected to exceed revenues. Eighty-five percent of cities had raised taxes in 1990, and almost 10% actually had reduced service levels. Among the nation's largest cities, 41% reported that service levels had been reduced. After eliminating street cleaning and recreational programs, and cutting money for its libraries and services for the elderly, Bridgeport, CT, filed a bankruptcy petition, which later was denied. If the recession continued, other cities also would be forced to make harsh budget cuts, and some also might teeter on the edge of financial insolvency. (*See also* SPECIAL REPORT/UNITED STATES, page 550.)

DENNIS R. JUDD
University of Missouri-St. Louis

COINS AND COIN COLLECTING

U.S. Mint

The 1991 Mount Rushmore Silver Dollar Coin

As the slumping U.S. economy faltered in 1991, numismatics as an investment vehicle suffered a dramatic downturn. The hobby's three major grading and encapsulation services —Professional Coin Grading Service (PCGS), Numismatic Guaranty Corporation (NGC), and ANACS—all reported substantially reduced submissions. Bereft of investor dollars, coin prices fell sharply, and many dealers were left with large, overpriced inventories.

The collector—long the backbone of traditional dealer sales—began to emerge as the hobby's salvation, and sight-unseen sales of coins declined. As the market bottomed out, new complaints from investors and collectors regarding overvalued coins began to surface. The Federal Trade Commission advised dealers that government regulation of numismatic sales was a real possibility.

Numismatic education once again assumed paramount importance for the dealer and collector alike. Ancient and foreign coins, historical gold issues, medals, and type sets began to fetch substantial prices, while inflated values for common investor coins, such as the Morgan silver dollar, mostly were a thing of the past.

Commemoratives. Amid much fanfare, in February the U.S. Mint released the first in a series of three commemorative issues scheduled for 1991. Commemorative coins honoring the golden anniversary of the Mount Rushmore Memorial were unveiled at a ceremony held February 15 at Ford's Theater in Washington, DC. The coins—a gold $5, a silver dollar, and a copper-nickel-clad half-dollar—were the product of designs from six different artists whose entries were selected from a competitive field of well-known medalists and Mint engravers.

The Mount Rushmore coins, as well as the year's other two commemoratives—honoring the Korean War and the United Service Organizations (USO), respectively—sold well throughout 1991. Initial sales of the Mount Rushmore commemorative topped 1 million pieces before the advance-sale discount cutoff on March 28. By May 17, sales of Korean War commemorative silver dollars approached the half-million mark. And USO commemorative dollars, unveiled at a huge Desert Storm victory parade June 8, were promoted extensively in connection with U.S. military accomplishments in the Persian Gulf.

After their unveiling, the designs for all three commemorative issues were criticized roundly. The U.S. Commission of Fine Arts, the official counselor to the Treasury Department, termed the submissions "mediocre." In response, the Mint announced an open design competition for the 1992 Olympic commemoratives—the first open competition since 1973.

Other. The viability of a $1 coin again was debated, but outgoing U.S. Mint Director Donna Pope stated that the public has shown no interest in such a coin. The Susan B. Anthony $1 coin, issued for only three years (1979–81), never achieved general usage. Pope noted that the Mint pays the Denver Federal Reserve Bank $35,000 per year to store 122 million Susan B. Anthony dollars.

A 1927-D Saint-Gaudens "double eagle" ($20 gold piece), one of only 12 specimens thought to exist, sold for $475,000 in a spring 1991 auction conducted by Stack's of New York City. During the summer, a New England 1652 sixpence, one of only eight known, was authenticated by the American Numismatic Association Authentication Bureau. A woman had found the coin in a Long Island, NY, potato field with the aid of a metal detector.

The American Numismatic Association celebrated its centennial with a gala convention in Chicago. A highlight of the convention was a display of U.S. proof gold coins valued at $10 million.

NAWANA MOS BRITENRIKER
American Numismatic Association

COLOMBIA

The year 1991 well may have marked a turning point in Colombia's continuing efforts to bring drug-related violence under control. President César Gaviria's dynamic and decisive approach to the problem appeared to have brought about a substantial diminution in violence and also in the political influence of at least the Medellín drug cartel. As a sign that violence was abating, President Gaviria on July 4 lifted a national state of siege that had been in effect since 1984. A new constitution, drafted by a special constituent assembly, was proclaimed on July 5. In his proclamation, Gaviria stated that the new constitution "does not mark the end of a reform process; it is, rather, the beginning of a new chapter in our history." Millions of Colombians hoped he was correct.

Drug Trade. Amid international criticism of the president's new policy of leniency toward drug traffickers who surrendered to the government, Gaviria announced on June 19 the surrender of Pablo Escobar Gaviria (no relation), reputedly the leader of the violence-prone Medellín cartel. Escobar's surrender included an agreement by the government not to seek his extradition to the United States, a policy which later was incorporated into the new constitution. While the surrender of Escobar and other cartel members did not mean the end of drug trafficking, it appeared to diminish substantially the amount of drug-related violence in the country. Kidnapping and assassinations of political figures went almost to zero, and several journalists who had been kidnapped in 1990 were released unharmed. The president also was able to sign peace agreements with all but two of the country's left-wing guerrilla organizations.

Efforts to break up the Medellín cartel, however, may have had the unintended effect of spreading the drug trade elsewhere. During 1989–90 drug traffickers in the southern Colombian city of Cali quietly had increased their share of the world cocaine market to an estimated 50%.

Politics. One result of the new constitution was the election of a new congress on October 27. In the election the old-line Liberal Party was the big winner, maintaining an absolute majority in both the Senate and the Chamber of Deputies. The big (and expected) loser was the Democratic Action M-19 (AD M-19), which garnered only 8% of the vote, down from 26% in the Constituent Assembly elections of December 1990. Both the AD M-19 and the Conservative splinter group under Andres Pastrana gained nine seats in the Senate.

In the nation's first popular election of governors, the Liberals gained more than half of these posts as well. The election results were further evidence of Gaviria's continuing popularity and resulted in at least a temporary halt in the meteoric rise of AD M-19 leader Antoni Navarro Wolff.

COLOMBIA • Information Highlights

Official Name: Republic of Colombia.
Location: Northwest South America.
Area: 439,734 sq mi (1 138 910 km²).
Population (mid-1991 est.): 33,600,000.
Chief City (Oct. 15, 1985): Bogotá, the capital, 3,982,941.
Government: *Head of state and government,* César Gaviria Trujillo, president (took office Aug. 1990). *Legislature*—Parliament: Senate and Chamber of Deputies.
Monetary Unit: Peso (600.00 pesos equal U.S.$1, Nov. 18, 1991).
Gross Domestic Product (1988 U.S.$): $35,400,-000,000.
Economic Index (Bogotá, 1990): *Consumer Prices* (1988 = 100), all items, 150.1; food, 145.5.
Foreign Trade (1990 U.S.$): *Imports,* $5,590,000,000; *exports,* $6,745,000,000.

Economics. The Colombian economy continued to perform well in 1991, at least in comparison with other Latin American countries. Unemployment continued at close to 10% for the second year in a row. Inflation for the year was at an estimated 27.1%, which was approximately the same as the 1990 level. The nation's gross domestic product (GDP) increased by slightly more than 3% for the year.

ECOPETROL, the nationalized Colombian oil company, announced several new oil finds during the year. The big economic news, however, was Gaviria's announcement in October of a three-year program of economic and social development labeled "Revolución Pacífica" (Peaceful Revolution). The plan is a three-year effort to pull at least 4 million Colombians out of poverty, eliminate illiteracy in urban areas, extend educational services to at least 95% of the rural population, and greatly increase the provision of basic sanitation throughout the nation. According to the president, the plan would concentrate on improving both the physical and social infrastructure of the country.

ERNEST A. DUFF
Randolph-Macon Woman's College

COLORADO

Colorado began 1991 on a high note as the University of Colorado Buffaloes defeated Notre Dame, 10–9, in the Orange Bowl. The victory won for the university the coveted—though hypothetical—national championship in The Associated Press college-football rankings. Sports fans got another boost in the summer when the National League announced that Denver and Miami would receive expansion baseball franchises in 1993.

Economy. The end of the Cold War brought some negative "peace dividends" to Colorado's economy as major defense contractors,

© Bruce McAllister

City Auditor Wellington Webb (D), 50-year-old former regional director of the U.S. Department of Health, Education, and Welfare in the Carter administration, became the first black to be elected mayor of Denver in a June 18, 1991, runoff election. He took office on July 1.

including Martin Marietta, announced layoffs. The worst blow was the decision to close Lowry Air Force Technical Training Center in Denver.

To offset those losses, Gov. Roy Romer convened a special session of the legislature in August to offer United Airlines $148 million in state subsidies to locate a new 6,500-job maintenance facility in Denver. United declined but gave Colorado a consolation prize, choosing Denver for its new reservations center, which would bring in 2,000 jobs.

Colorado Springs, also hurt by defense cutbacks, diversified its economy during 1991. Apple Computer announced that it would open an assembly plant in nearby Fountain, and MCI Communications also expected to bring 1,400 jobs to the area by 1995.

September Special Legislative Session. Many Colorado elementary and secondary public schools faced a severe budget crunch in 1991 because a school-finance law passed in 1988 caused a drop in local property-tax collections without replacing the lost property taxes with state aid. Governor Romer, a Democrat, called a second special session of the legislature in September to increase state school aid. But Republicans, who controlled both legislative chambers, refused to increase taxes. Facing an overall shortfall, Romer cut $80 million from the state budget.

The Colorado Supreme Court, which earlier had approved a 1985 death-penalty law, struck down a revised 1988 version of the law in 1991. During the September special session, legislators readopted and the governor signed the court-approved 1985 version.

Transportation. Transportation made news as the Regional Transportation District won approval to build a 3.1-mi (5-km) light-rail demonstration project in Denver and pushed ahead on a federally aided project to add a lane reserved exclusively for buses and carpools on Interstate 25 north of Denver. The E-470 toll road, which eventually would span the eastern half of the Denver metropolitan area, opened its first link, from Interstate 25 to South Parker Road.

Denver Politics. In a nonpartisan election runoff in June, Denver elected its first black mayor when former City Auditor Wellington Webb defeated Denver District Attorney Norm Early, who is also black. Denver voters in May rejected a citizen-initiated effort to repeal a homosexual-rights law passed by the City Council.

Other News. Operations remained suspended throughout 1991 at the Rocky Flats plant north of Denver that produces plutonium triggers for nuclear weapons; a federal safety audit reported ongoing safety problems. . . . On March 3 a United Airlines jet crashed in Colorado Springs, killing 25. . . . Casino gambling began in October in three old mining towns—Central City, Black Hawk, and Cripple Creek. . . . Denver unveiled its new $28 million Temple Buell theater, with a 2,830-person capacity.

BOB EWEGEN, *"The Denver Post"*

COLORADO • Information Highlights

Area: 104,091 sq mi (269 596 km²).
Population (1990 census): 3,294,394.
Chief Cities (1990 census): Denver, the capital, 467,610; Colorado Springs, 281,140; Aurora, 222,103; Lakewood, 126,481.
Government (1991): *Chief Officers*—governor, Roy Romer (D); lt. gov., C. Michael Callihan (D). *General Assembly*—Senate, 35 members; House of Representatives, 65 members.
State Finances (fiscal year 1990): *Revenue,* $7,527,000,000; *expenditure,* $6,510,000,000.
Personal Income (1990): $62,378,000,000; per capita, $18,890.
Labor Force (June 1991): *Civilian labor force,* 1,799,800; *unemployed,* 84,200 (4.7% of total force).
Education: *Enrollment* (fall 1989)—public elementary schools, 407,525; public secondary, 155,230; colleges and universities, 201,114. *Public school expenditures* (1989), $2,266,667,000.

COMMUNICATION TECHNOLOGY

The year 1991 was marked by heightened interest and activity in personal communication systems (PCSs), in which the user carries a small pocket-size telephone capable of operation anywhere—in or out of buildings—and connectable by wireless means to existing local and long-distance telephone networks. The concept is an extension of cellular vehicular mobile radio without restriction as to area or the number of users who can be served.

Data traffic continued to increase and was becoming a substantial portion of all telecommunications, growing three times as fast as voice messages. It was expected that within a few years almost half of all traffic would consist of data, graphics, and video signals.

Computer processing and telecommunications continue to be synergistic and inseparable in the information age. Making a strong move in the direction of "open" computer communications, six large computer companies formed a consortium to ensure that ongoing hardware and software developments will allow information to be sent freely worldwide between different types of computers. It was estimated that the necessary programming and equipment modifications would be completed by 1993.

Transmission and Switching Technology. Field tests of a new high-speed, broad-band digital fiber-optic system were conducted by Philips N.V. in Spain (in preparation for the 1992 Summer Olympics) and in Australia. The system, operating at a pulse rate of 2.5 gigabits (2,500 megabits) per second can send simultaneously more than 30,000 digital speech channels on a pair of optical fibers.

A new ultra-long-distance light-wave transmission system was demonstrated by AT&T Bell Laboratories. It is capable of spanning the Atlantic or Pacific Ocean with no electronic amplifiers in the entire length. A world-record transmission rate of 5 gigabits per second was achieved over a distance of some 5,600 mi (9 000 km). The experiment utilized a circulating loop of optical fiber with optical amplification provided by spliced-in segments of glass fiber containing the rare-earth element erbium. The photonic amplifiers obviate the need for conversion to electronic signals for amplification and then reversing the procedure in reconversion to light pulses.

The need for business and personal communications free from the limits set by a telephone cord and wiring between stations has intensified interest in the development of personal-communication networks. By using low-power transmitters to cover small space cells (microcells) a few hundred feet in size and by reusing the same radio frequencies, the microcell system can accommodate up to 100,000 customers per square mile, a number 100 times as great as the capacity of typical present-day mobile-vehicular systems. Since the available radio spectrum no longer can support a significant increase in communications capacity, the advantages of PCS are of importance to all segments of the industry.

Such companies as Northern Electric, AT&T, and Philips N.V. are incorporating computer chips, display screens, and data-handling circuitry into the plain old telephone. The chips will provide capabilities to permit such interactive services as paying bills, shopping, banking, selective dialing, and screening of incoming calls. A viewing screen, about 4 inches by 6 inches (10 cm by 15 cm) in size, lists the options available with the touch of a finger.

The use of satellites for direct broadcasting to homes equipped with dish antennas has been ventured but without noteworthy commercial success. In 1991 additional plans were announced for the dissemination of pay-to-view television movies, sporting events, and other programs. With higher-power satellites combined with digital-transmission technology, it now appears possible to achieve nationwide coverage offering superior quality and yet requiring only a 1- or 2-foot (.3- or .6-m) dish at the receiving location.

In the competition for high-definition television acceptance, tests of four digital TV systems were conducted in 1991. Digital systems carry picture and audio information in the form of coded on-off pulses which are more immune to noise and electrical interference than the present analog-modulation system. Picture quality is improved and the signal can be processed for the desired height and width.

Microelectronics and Microprocessors. In 1991 records were surpassed in speed and capacity of microprocessors, memory devices, analog-digital converters, and other solid-state components. Two companies announced semiconductor chips utilizing 64-bit architecture capable of executing 100 million instructions per second (MIPS). This was twice the data-processing capacity of the previously available 32-bit microprocessors.

IBM developed a transistor with a switching time of 33 picoseconds (billionths of a second). Typical transistors of current design require about 100 picoseconds. AT&T Bell Laboratories scientists generated the world's shortest and fastest light pulses with a new type of semiconductor laser producing 350 billion light pulses per second, each one shorter than a trillionth of a second. In comparison, the fastest commercial light-wave system in service was operating at a pulse rate of about 2.5 billion pulses per second. The use of shorter pulses in a communication system increases its capacity for handling traffic, thus reducing the cost per channel.

M. D. FAGEN
Formerly, AT&T Bell Laboratories

COMPUTERS

Fierce competition within the computer industry increased during 1991, shrinking profit margins, threatening the future of some firms, and leading to unexpected alliances. Particularly hard hit were makers of mainframe computers, who watched sales decline while sales of smaller machines continued their rapid growth. For instance, Unisys Corporation announced it would lay off 10,000 of its 70,000 employees. IBM announced its first quarterly loss ever.

In what some industry analysts called "the deal of the decade," archrivals IBM and Apple agreed to share technology and jointly to develop advanced hardware and software. IBM also agreed to work with the German electronics firm Siemens to build a factory to produce 16-megabit D-RAMs—advanced memory chips. Early in 1991, IBM became the first company in the world to achieve volume production of these chips. The Advanced Computing Environment consortium was formed to try to set standards for workstations; the more than 20 member firms included both hardware and software firms.

Ever-smaller PCs. The hottest-selling personal computers (PCs) were those small enough to be easily portable; analysts predicted that by 1995 they would comprise 50% of all computer sales. Many of the latest laptop and notebook-sized computers matched the power and features of desktop models, and their prices continued to fall, narrowing the price advantage enjoyed by desktops.

The next important rival of desktops was expected to be palm-sized computers weighing less than 1 lb (.45 kg). Hewlett-Packard began selling a portable IBM-compatible computer that weighs only 11 oz (.3 kg). The machine has a built-in spreadsheet program, text editor, and communications link, and is powered by two AA batteries that last up to two months with average use. Its main disadvantage: keys so small that typing is awkward and slow.

Several companies introduced notebook-sized computers designed to be controlled with an electronic stylus rather than a keyboard. The stylus is used like a pen to write, draw, and make program choices directly on the computer's liquid-crystal screen. This eliminates the need to know how to type as well as the difficulties presented by trying to use lilliputian keyboards. Among the most powerful new stylus models was NCR's System 3125, weighing less than 4 lbs (1.82 kg). It can decipher upper- and lowercase block-printed letters with great accuracy, but cannot recognize cursive writing.

Supercomputers. Efforts to create the world's fastest computer are driven by the desire to tackle complex problems requiring vast amounts of computer time. The goal, expected to be reached within a few years, was to create a teraflop computer—one capable of handling 1 trillion mathematical calculations per second. In 1991, Intel Corporation demonstrated its Touchstone Delta supercomputer, which can run 8.6 billion calculations per second, and Thinking Machines introduced a new model capable of performing 9.03 billion calculations per second. Both machines are examples of what are called massively parallel systems: They have thousands of microprocessors connected in parallel. A computational problem is divided into parts, with portions assigned simultaneously to various processors, which calculate subtotals and return them to a central processor for combining.

Supercomputer manufacturers were facing competition not only from one another but also from manufacturers of smaller machines. New workstation models were able to solve problems in only twice the time of a supercomputer, but were selling for less than 10% of the cost of a supercomputer. At Yale University, scientists created an inexpensive supercomputer by linking together 40 workstations scattered throughout the school's computer-science department. The scientists were able to produce a complex color image from a mathematical formula in seven minutes. It took ten times as long to complete the task on a $15 million Cray 2 supercomputer—and four hours to compute the image on a single workstation.

Privacy and Piracy. In today's "age of information," businesses depend on masses of data about individuals: their health, life-styles, financial status, and so on. Individuals who wish to safeguard the privacy of such information find that it is difficult, if not impossible, to determine what information about them is on file and how it is being used. Efforts to create oversight mechanisms in the United States so far have been thwarted. In Europe, however, many nations have enacted laws to restrict the flow of personal information, and the European Community was considering the adoption of the European Privacy Directive. Proposals for the directive, scheduled to become law in 1993, include requiring companies using personal data to tell the subjects of that use; notifying credit-card holders before selling their names to mail-order firms; and prohibiting the transfer of data to another country unless that country offers adequate protection of records.

Piracy—the illegal copying of software—continues to cost the U.S. software industry more than $2 billion in lost revenues each year. According to the Software Publishers Association (SPA), most of the loss is due to business corporations that are unwilling to purchase software legitimately. However, theft of educational and entertainment software also is believed to be a significant problem. Intensified legal efforts to combat unauthorized copying have resulted in record monetary settlements.

JENNY TESAR, *Free-lance Science Writer*

Ever-Broadening Applications

Computers, already part of so many aspects of modern life, continue to be put to new uses. Home sewers now can buy a sewing machine with 481 stitch designs in its computer memory —and the ability to turn a freehand sketch into a stitch. Dairy farmers can use computers to monitor milk production and temperature, and soon may be installing milking robots.

The Food Business and Speaking Machines. When people stop at a fast-food restaurant these days they may face a computer rather than a human at the order counter. Customers place their orders on a computerized touch screen. If an order consists of a hamburger and pie but nothing to drink, the screen illuminates a printed message asking, "Would you like a refreshing soda?" The completed orders appear on similar screens in the kitchen area. The system saves time, improves accuracy, and may result in larger orders.

Computers also are improving their ability to speak. The Kurzweil Personal Reader uses a hand-held scanner to read print electronically, then reads the copy aloud—in any of nine distinct voices. The machine dramatically has transformed the lives of blind people who previously had relied on other people to read them letters, books, office papers, and other documents. And Bell Canada has installed a system that reads the location of broken phone equipment to its repair people and then tells them how to fix the equipment.

Geographical Use. Large databases give cartographers the ability to create highly accurate maps based on photographs from satellites and airplanes. The cartographers then can merge the geographic data used to make the maps with almost any other kind of data: rainfall patterns, income distribution, the location of dinosaur fossils, disease prevalence, and so on. A city map that combines data on elevation, soil, and water tables can help city planners find the best site for new housing. An area map with information on geological formations can aid petroleum engineers in locating likely spots for drilling. And a map of Alaska with data on caribou herds can assist scientists to determine the impact of an oil pipeline on caribou migrations.

On the Road. Automakers are testing electronic navigation systems to help drivers find their way. To use such a system, a driver first indicates the car's starting location and destination to the computer, which plots the car's location on a map stored in its memory and then displays the map on a small screen built into the dashboard. A dotted line drawn on the map shows the driver the recommended route of travel. The computer continually monitors the car's movements and adjusts its location on the map. Automakers hope someday to expand these systems to include up-to-the-minute data on traffic conditions. However, this would require the installation of road sensors to measure traffic speed; cables to carry data from the sensors to a central computer, which would monitor conditions throughout the area; and radio equipment that would broadcast information on traffic conditions to the cars' navigation systems.

Technology developed by the U.S. armed forces for top-secret communications has been adapted to help trace stolen cars. In a system offered in southern California by International Teletrac Systems, a radio transceiver hidden inside a car is inactive unless someone tries to start the car by short-circuiting the ignition system or by forcing the ignition with a dummy key. The radio unit then sends a signal that is picked up by Teletrac's receiving antennas, which relay the information to a central computer. As the car moves, the radio signal is picked up by different antennas, allowing the computer to track the car. This information is relayed to the police, who follow the car using computerized road maps.

A mobile communications system from Qualcomm allows dispatchers in a trucking company to keep in constant touch with truckers on the road. The system also automatically indicates the location of each truck on electronic maps used by the dispatchers. Each truck has a computer terminal that the driver uses to send and receive messages. The terminal is connected to an antenna mounted on the roof, which transmits messages to a satellite, which in turn relays the messages to a central computer at Qualcomm. The messages then are transmitted to the trucking-company headquarters, where a computer routes them to the proper dispatcher. A dispatcher can send a message to the driver using the same system.

The Nissan Motor Corporation has introduced a computerized suspension system that adjusts each of a car's four shock absorbers independently. Sensors mounted near the wheels and around the car monitor the car's height off the road, bounce, and side-to-side motion. The data are fed into a computer connected to a controller that pumps hydraulic fluid into or out of each shock absorber.

JENNY TESAR

SPECIAL REPORT/COMPUTERS

Virtual Reality

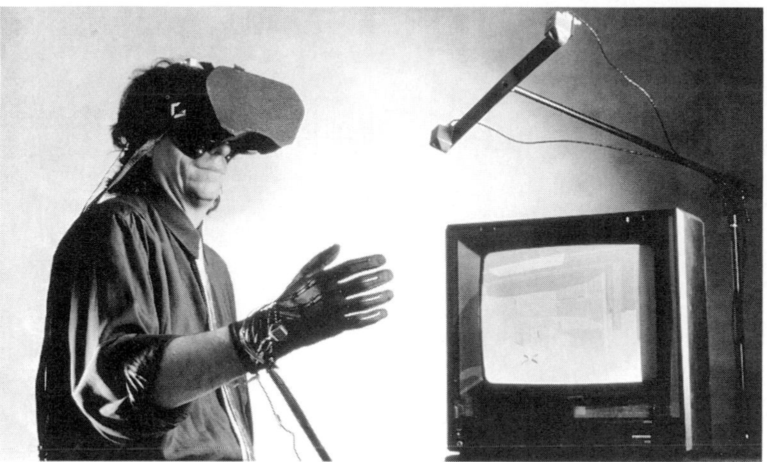

© Autodesk, Inc.

Walk through a house before it is built . . . perform a heart-transplant operation . . . play tennis with someone far away . . . be the Mad Hatter in a production of *Alice in Wonderland*! How? A developing area of computer technology promises to let you experience such activities while sitting in an easy chair.

Called virtual reality, artificial reality, or cyberspace, this technology creates the illusion that you are moving through an artificial universe that seems as "real" as the real world. Your body may be in a chair in your home, but as far as your senses are concerned, you are exploring a coral reef off Australia, moving through a nuclear reactor, or trying to land a spaceship on Mars. You might even become a hummingbird hovering over a flower or a dinosaur sloshing through a Mesozoic swamp. The illusion of reality is so complete that your body experiences seasickness as you sail over rough seas, aching muscles as you try to push together two molecules, or dizziness as you whirl around the dance floor.

With standard computer simulations, users simply look at representations on a computer screen and use joysticks or computer keyboards to change their view. With virtual reality, however, users feel as if they are actually inside a three-dimensional simulation, and a natural turn of the head lets the person "see" what is to the left or right.

How It Works. Virtual reality combines full-color computer simulations with equipment that senses the movements of the person who uses, or "enters," the simulations. The standard equipment consists of two pieces of attire. One is a headset that contains two miniature liquid-crystal-display screens, one in front of each eye. The screens feed the computer imagery to the eyes and hence to the brain. The second piece of attire is a skintight glove. Both the headset and the glove contain electromagnetic sensors that track the wearer's movements, and both are linked by fiber-optic cables to the computer (photo *above*).

As the person looks at the screens in the headset, his or her hand is visible as a computerized hand. Movements of the hand act as commands. To pick up an object, one makes a fist. To fly in a certain direction, one merely points a finger.

Instead of a glove, some virtual reality systems allow a user to wear a special bodysuit. This gives an even greater sense of immersion in an artificial world, as the user becomes a full body on the screen. Some systems allow two people to share an artificial environment.

Practical Applications. Even in its infancy, virtual reality is finding practical applications. Architects are using it to let clients tour a building before it exists. The clients can move walls, add doors, change light fixtures, and make other alterations. These changes are fed into the computer, which automatically adjusts electrical systems and other building components. When everyone is satisfied, the computer prints out blueprints, supply requirements, and a construction schedule.

In the coming years, medical simulators will let medical students practice surgical techniques on virtual patients. Military flight simulators will allow pilots to fly over virtual enemy land in a virtual jet, to rehearse bombing attacks. And families will take virtual vacations to virtual resorts.

JENNY TESAR

CONNECTICUT

Connecticut wage earners began paying a state income tax on Oct. 1, 1991. The state legislature narrowly approved a 4.5% tax on wages on August 22, ending a 53-day impasse over a state budget for the fiscal year that began July 1. In adopting the income tax, the legislature lowered the state sales tax from 8% to 6%, but extended the sales tax to 22 items that previously were untaxed.

Connecticut had been one of ten states without an income tax. One had been adopted by the 1971 legislature but was repealed before it became effective. Antitax rallies across the state called for repeal of the levy and at an October 5 rally at the State Capitol that attracted 40,000 persons, Independent Gov. Lowell P. Weicker, Jr., was hanged in effigy. A special legislative session in December failed to repeal or alter the tax.

Economy. The newly enacted income tax came at a time when Connecticut's economy was reeling under economic stress. Twenty banks failed in 1991, most of them brought down because large loans made to real-estate developers in the 1980s were in default. Bridgeport, the state's largest city, filed for bankruptcy, and major employers, largely dependent on defense contracts, were forced into widespread layoffs as the Pentagon announced cutbacks in military-weapons programs. United Technologies Corporation, the state's largest private employer with 49,000 workers on its Connecticut payroll, announced a $1 billion cutback in its operations budget by 1993, a move that would include a 25% reduction in its Hartford headquarters staff.

In other economic news, Sage-Allen & Company moved its headquarters to Syracuse, NY, in May, ending the retailer's 102-year-long presence in downtown Hartford; the company merged with Addis & Dey, a Syracuse retailing chain. The *Manchester Herald,* a 109-year-old afternoon daily newspaper in Manchester, ceased publication in June. The *Middletown Press,* an afternoon daily in Middletown, announced its purchase in August by the Eagle Publishing Company, which owns papers in Massachusetts, Vermont, and Connecticut.

CONNECTICUT • Information Highlights

Area: 5,018 sq mi (12 997 km²).
Population (1990 census): 3,287,116.
Chief Cities (1990 census): Hartford, the capital, 139,739; Bridgeport, 141,686; New Haven, 130,474; Waterbury, 108,961.
Government (1991): *Chief Officers*—governor, Lowell P. Weicker, Jr. (I); lt. gov., Eunice Groark (I). *General Assembly*—Senate, 36 members; House of Representatives, 151 members.
State Finances (fiscal year 1990): *Revenue,* $9,591,000,000; *expenditure,* $9,886,000,000.
Personal Income (1990): $83,842,000,000; per capita, $25,484.
Labor Force (June 1991): *Civilian labor force,* 1,815,000; *unemployed,* 113,000 (6.2% of total force).
Education: *Enrollment* (fall 1989)—public elementary schools, 338,378; public secondary, 123,182; colleges and universities, 169,438. *Public school expenditures* (1989), $2,984,542,000.

Legislation. Other action by the 1991 state legislature included the decriminalization of adultery. The legislature also enacted a gay-rights law, prohibiting discrimination based on sexual orientation in employment, housing, extension of credit, the awarding of state contracts or benefits, and in places of public accommodation. The same legislative session declared the footprints of the dinosaur Eurbrontes the official state fossil. The dinosaur footprints are the latest to join the state's official list that includes the mountain laurel as the state flower, the American robin as the state bird, and the praying mantis as the state insect.

Other News. A mystery that had tugged at Connecticut's heartstrings for 47 years was solved in 1991. Little Miss 1565, an unidentified victim of the July 6, 1944, circus fire in Hartford in which 168 persons perished, was identified. She was 8-year-old Eleanor Emily Cook, who had gone to the circus with her mother and

© Bob East III/"The News Times," Danbury

Following prolonged legislative debate, Lowell P. Weicker, Jr., who was elected governor of Connecticut on an Independent ticket in 1990, signed the 1991–92 budget on August 22. The budget included a 4.5% income tax, which became the subject of widespread public outcry.

two brothers. One of her brothers died from burns and her mother, Mildred Cook, was hospitalized for six months because of the burns that she suffered. Little Miss 1565—her morgue number—became a symbol of the circus holocaust as she was remembered on every anniversary of the fire. Although there was evidence that Little Miss 1565 might be Eleanor Cook, her mother never would confront the evidence. Early in 1991 she finally accepted the fact that Little Miss 1565 was her daughter. Eleanor Cook's body was transferred from a cemetery near Hartford to the Cook family plot in a cemetery in Southampton, MA.

A major fire in a New Britain house in February caused the deaths of ten persons. The fire was caused by an electric heater.

Names in the News. Bob Steele, 80, ended a 55-year-long stint as host of Hartford radio station WTIC-AM's morning show on September 30. Archbishop John F. Whealon, 70, head of the Roman Catholic Hartford archdiocese for 22 years, died August 3 of cardiac arrest. Bishop Daniel A. Cronin, 64, of Fall River, MA, was named as his successor. Waterbury Mayor Joseph J. Santopietro, 32, was charged in a federal indictment with several counts of graft. In November he was defeated in his bid for a fourth two-year term.

ROBERT F. MURPHY, "*The Hartford Courant*"

CONSUMER AFFAIRS

"Consumers hesitate to spend, impeding economic recovery." This headline in *The Wall Street Journal* pointed out how consumers felt about their financial well-being in 1991. Although some experts believed that the recession had bottomed out, there was not the optimism that was needed to persuade consumers to rush into the market and spend. Two significant reasons for the consumers' hesitancy were job insecurity and indebtedness. Household indebtedness averaged $15,554 for each person.

Credit Problems. As most interest rates were declining during the year, credit-card-interest rates held firm. Banks were trying all kinds of promotional gimmicks to encourage more and more persons to get credit cards, but they were not reducing interest rates. A U.S. congressional proposal to cap credit-card interest rates failed. Another serious problem was that credit-reporting companies were filling consumers' files with errors and illegally selling sensitive data to "junk-mailers." Attorneys general in six states launched a legal assault against one of the largest credit bureaus.

The U.S. Federal Trade Commission (FTC) reported that consumer complaints about credit files rose 50% during the year. Such grievances were the number one subject of FTC complaints. Legislation was introduced in Congress to reform the credit-reporting system. The credit-reporting industry, in hopes of forestalling action by Congress, launched a campaign to improve its public image.

U.S. Government Action. Ann Windham Wallace took over as director of the U.S. Office of Consumer Affairs within the Department of Health and Human Services. There was an unannounced but subtle change in the title for the position. Wallace's predecessor, Bonnie Guiton, held the titles of director and special adviser to the president; Wallace was given just the title of director. However, President Bush also named her chairperson of the Federal Consumer Affairs Council, a composite of consumer representatives from various federal agencies that reviews consumer policy.

What well may turn out to be a most significant government action benefiting consumers is the strong stand being taken by the new Food and Drug Administration (FDA) Commissioner David Kessler. A *New York Times* article pointed out that he "has been making waves, seizing mislabeled products, and using his office as a bully pulpit to inform the food industry that the laissez faire policies of the last decade are no longer in the political fashion." The FDA's staff was increased and its regulatory division was working on a far-reaching assortment of rules to carry out the 1990 Nutritional Labeling and Education Act. The rules would transform most of the food labels in the supermarket by making the nutrition and ingredient labels less confusing and more useful.

The Consumer Product Safety Commission remained a listless watchdog in the eyes of many top agency officials and safety advocates. It has the responsibility of regulating the safety of all consumer products other than cars, boats, drugs, alcoholic beverages, tobacco products, and food. The problem seems to stem from weak leadership and a decline in staffing in the 1980s from about 1,000 to 500 employees. Budget considerations led to the decline.

Just prior to adjourning, Congress sent to the president legislation protecting consumers from unsolicited telephone calls and "junk faxes." Legislation protecting phone customers from unscrupulous marketing ploys and invasion of privacy awaited action in 1992.

Life-insurance Jitters. Public confidence, already shaken by the collapse of many savings and loan associations and the weakened position of a number of commercial banks, was shaken anew by the bankruptcy of some large insurance companies and the revelation that other big insurance companies took shelter in the arms of regulatory authorities. An added concern was what appeared to be a too-easy rating procedure used by insurance-rating firms in judging the financial strength of life-insurance companies. (*See* INSURANCE, LIABILITY.)

STEWART M. LEE, *Geneva College*

CRIME

Though most of the world's attention in early 1991 was focused on activities in the Persian Gulf, problems associated with crime in the United States also occupied much of the U.S. scene throughout the year. Twenty-four Americans died in air operations against Iraq during the Gulf war, while in the same time period 52 Americans died as the result of homicide in Dallas, TX.

Much of the criminal activity in the United States continued to be associated with the use of and trafficking in illicit drugs (*see* DRUGS AND ALCOHOL). On the international level, the Florida trial of former Panamanian dictator Manuel Noriega began in September for his alleged involvement in narcotics smuggling and racketeering. In October agents of the U.S. Drug Enforcement Administration (DEA) arrested Dandeny Muñoz Mosquera in New York City. Muñoz Mosquera was believed to be the most trusted hit man of the Medellín drug cartel in Colombia and was thought to have killed 40 Colombian police officers. The purpose of the alleged hit man's presence in New York was unknown but it was expected that he would be extradited to Colombia to face trial on charges of murder and robbery.

The fact that drugs were a major influence on overall crime in the United States was reflected in a Bureau of Justice Statistics' study of jail inmates, which found that in about one of every three cases, convicted robbers and burglars had committed their crimes to obtain drug money. At least four of every ten convicted inmates in local jails said they had used drugs during the month before committing their crimes. Another study found that 80% of prison inmates had a history of drug abuse.

In the area of federal law-enforcement leadership, William P. Barr succeeded Dick Thornburgh as attorney general and former Florida Gov. Bob Martinez took over as director of the Office of National Drug Control Policy.

Famous Crimes of 1991. Some of the crimes that made headlines in 1991 were both bizarre and alarming. The grisly deeds of one of the most unusual serial killers in history were discovered during the summer. Jeffrey L. Dahmer, a quiet and unassuming resident of Milwaukee, WI, confessed to having dismembered and mutilated 11 men. Police discovered severed heads and other body parts in Dahmer's apartment, including that of a 14-year-old Laotian immigrant named Konerak Sinthasomphone.

Sinthasomphone's death was especially controversial and painful to the community in that he had escaped Dahmer's apartment in May and was seen running naked and bleeding in the street. When police were called, Dahmer explained the incident as a homosexual "lover's quarrel" and the police returned the boy to Dahmer, who reportedly murdered him after the officers departed. Dahmer, a convicted child molester, was believed to have killed 17 men, mostly black homosexuals.

Another possible serial killer surfaced in 1991. When police arrested and questioned Donald Leroy Evans about the rape and murder of a 10-year-old girl in Mississippi, the Texas drifter claimed to have killed more than 60 people in at least 21 states. The year also saw the trial on another charge of the man suspected of killing five University of Florida college students in 1990. Danny Rolling, a 36-year-old convict from Shreveport, LA, was connected to the Gainesville, FL, killings through DNA "fingerprints" obtained from blood samples. He was convicted of a September 1990 supermarket robbery and sentenced to life in prison for the offense in September 1991. Evidence relating to the Gainesville murders was submitted to a grand jury in November. The jury indicted him on five counts of murder, three of rape, and three of armed burglary. The year also marked the conviction of Walter Leroy Moody, Jr., for the mail-bombing deaths of a federal judge and a civil-rights attorney in 1989. Moody was convicted of all 71 federal charges stemming from the slayings.

One of the most tragic cases of 1991 occurred in October in a shopping mall in Killeen, TX. George J. Hennard, Jr., drove his pickup truck through the window of a cafeteria in the mall, got out of the vehicle, and started shooting customers and employees at random. Hennard killed 22 and wounded 23 more, making the incident the deadliest mass shooting in U.S. history. Hennard was wounded by police and committed suicide.

In Exeter, NH, Pamela Smart, a 23-year-old high-school aide, reportedly seduced a 15-year-old student and then convinced him and his friends to kill her husband. Smart was found guilty and sentenced to life imprisonment. William Flynn, Smart's student lover, and his two friends pleaded guilty to lesser charges in exchange for their testimony, and received sentences of 18 to 28 years.

A Houston, TX, trial that received much attention was that of Wanda Webb Holloway, convicted in September of plotting to solicit the murder of the mother of her daughter's rival for a cheerleader slot at their junior high school. In November, Holloway was granted a new trial on the basis of new evidence and the fact that one of the original jurors should have been disqualified because he was on probation for a drug offense.

Famous names also made crime headlines during 1991. Paul Reubens, better known as Pee-wee Herman, was arrested in July for allegedly masturbating in an adult movie theater in Sarasota, FL. As Pee-wee, Reubens was a successful star in both movies and in television programs made for children. In November he

Rape

Largely because of the women's movement, media attention, and a greater willingness on the part of victims to speak out, public awareness of the nature, severity, and extent of the crime of rape—sexual penetration without permission—has risen significantly. Recent statistics indicate that rape is committed mostly by young men and that in the United States it is committed once every five minutes. There also has been increased awareness of the concept of acquaintance or date rape—encounters where the perpetrator and the victim are acquainted—and of marital rape.

Several professions—including the law and other areas of public policy—have responded to the more intense focus, prompting changes in practice and theory relating to rape. Likewise, state and federal legislators have proposed ever-more-progressive measures in efforts to demythologize the crime.

Privacy Rights. An issue particularly associated with the crime of rape is the victim's right to privacy. Traditionally, the media voluntarily refrained from naming victims of rape, but during 1990 the *Des Moines Register* sparked debate by publishing the name of the woman victim in a series of articles on her abduction and rape and on her experience testifying at the resulting trial. The woman permitted the newspaper to use her name in the hope that more thorough coverage of rape as a crime would act as a preventive measure.

The pros and cons of public identification of the victim have been aired in recent years. Those favoring disclosure assert that treating rape victims differently from other crime victims further stigmatizes them and is unfair to the accused, who is innocent until proven otherwise. Others fear that revealing names further traumatizes victims, slows their recovery, and discourages other rape victims from reporting the crime. Legislation proposed at state and federal levels in 1990–91 would allow rape victims to choose whether their names are publicized.

Legislative Action. With regard to legislative action, two more states made marital rape a crime in 1990, leaving only one state that retained the "marital exemption," whereby the rape of one's spouse is not considered a crime. A number of states still regarded marital rape as a crime only under certain circumstances, such as when the couple is separated legally.

In 1990 the federal Crime Awareness and Campus Security Act was passed, requiring institutions of higher education that receive federal financial aid to develop policies and procedures for addressing rape on campus. All such institutions were required to publish and distribute annual statistics on all rape cases reported to campus-security authorities or to local police agencies. The federal Campus Sexual Assault Victims' Bill of Rights that was proposed in 1990 assured that victims would have the right to have any rapes investigated and adjudicated by local criminal and civil authorities and that they would be so informed by campus officials.

In 1991 the Violence Against Women Act was introduced in Congress, but by year's end no final action had been taken. Among its provisions were strengthened penalties for those convicted of rape and the establishment of a National Commission on Violent Crimes Against Women. The bill also treated sexual assault as a "hate" crime and a violation of women's civil rights. It provided grants to programs aimed at combating violent crimes against women (including rape) and providing training for law-enforcement personnel, prosecutors, judges, and court personnel in state courts to assure equal justice for women in the legal system. In addition the bill would fund education and prevention programs that strengthened victim-service efforts. One provision of the bill would require that 15% of granted funds to education and prevention programs target junior and senior high-school students.

BETH STAFFORD-VAUGHAN

entered a plea of no contest and received a small fine and some community-service work. Another person with a well-known name was arrested in Florida for rape. William Kennedy Smith, the 30-year-old nephew of Massachusetts Sen. Edward Kennedy, was charged with raping a woman at the Kennedy compound in Palm Beach during Easter weekend. The case caused extreme political and personal embarrassment for Senator Kennedy. Smith was acquitted of the crime in December at the conclusion of a highly publicized and controversial trial.

The shooting death in Detroit of a soldier made news in 1991. Army Specialist Anthony Riggs was gunned down outside his wife's grandmother's residence shortly after returning from the Persian Gulf war. The incident was publicized initially as an example of random "drive-by violence" in U.S. cities. Further investigation, however, led police to believe that Riggs had been shot by his brother-in-law, Michael Cato, in alleged collusion with Riggs' wife, in order to collect his life insurance. Riggs' wife, Toni Cato Riggs, later was cleared of all charges by a judge who found that there was not enough evidence to base a case against her. Cato was convicted of first-degree murder in December.

Crime Rates. The Federal Bureau of Investigation (FBI) released its compilation of crime statistics for 1990 in August. The data verified the comments of Sen. Joseph Biden (D-DE), chairman of the Senate Judiciary Committee, that 1990 was "the bloodiest year in United States history." The murder toll reached an all-time high of 23,440, the largest one-year increase in ten years. Washington, DC, again had the distinction of being the nation's "murder capital" with a murder rate eight times the national average. (Washington also had that distinction in 1991.) Washington was followed by New Orleans, Atlanta, Detroit, and St. Louis in the murder rankings. Preliminary figures indicated that 1991 crime rates probably would exceed those of 1990. Reported crime overall increased 2% for the first half of 1991, according to FBI figures. Robberies were up 9%, the number of murders increased 5%, forcible rape was up by 4%, and aggravated assault by 2%. The six-month figures also showed a 1% increase in burglaries, larcenies, and motor-vehicle thefts.

The Death Penalty. Since 1976, when the U.S. Supreme Court reinstated the death penalty, the issue surrounding the execution of convicted murderers has been one of the most controversial topics in U.S. criminal justice. By the beginning of 1991, 143 individuals had been executed since 1976 and 2,356 persons were under a death sentence in U.S. prisons.

Among the 1991 court decisions affecting the death penalty were the Supreme Court limitation of death-row inmates' ability to appeal to the federal courts. The decisions were expected to increase the rate of executions in the United States, which never has exceeded 25 per year since 1976. Also, the Supreme Court allowed prosecutors to justify the imposition of the death penalty based on the suffering, loss to society, or extent of harm caused to others by the death of the murder victim. In California a federal judge upheld a ban on television cameras at executions, thereby prohibiting public viewing of the procedure. The ruling came in response to a lawsuit filed by a San Francisco television station that wanted to record the first execution in California in 25 years.

Gun Control. As in years past, the controversy over gun control was a continuing key issue in federal, state, and local debates on crime. In 1991 the focus of the debate concerned the ban of assault weapons and the attempt to prohibit individuals with histories of criminal activity or mental illness from purchasing handguns. In regard to assault weapons, various versions of the crime bills introduced in Congress attempted to ban the sale of assault-style semiautomatic weapons. Though the Senate version of the crime bill approved the ban, the House version rejected this provision as part of its crime legislation.

The House approach to attempting to screen prospective gun owners was embodied in two versions. The so-called Brady bill—named for former White House Press Secretary James S. Brady, crippled in an assassination attempt against President Ronald Reagan—proposed a seven-day waiting period for individuals seeking to purchase a handgun, thereby allowing law-enforcement authorities to check the background of the buyer. The Brady bill received unexpected support when former President Reagan, a lifetime member of the National Rifle Association (NRA)—a principal opponent of gun control—endorsed it. The other approach to gun control, represented by the "Staggers bill"—named after its sponsor, Rep. Harley O. Staggers, Jr. (D-WV)—attempted to screen gun buyers through the use of an "instant check," where gun retailers could call a state-maintained file which would contain the names of individuals ineligible to purchase firearms. Though this form of gun legislation was supported by the NRA and the Justice Department, opponents of the Staggers bill argued that the lack of adequate criminal-history files and financial resources made the instant-check provision of the bill unfeasible. Though Congress failed to enact a crime bill during 1991, the Brady-bill version of gun-control legislation was included in the last-minute passage by the House of the crime bill conference committee report. The passage of this committee report virtually ensured that the Brady bill again would face congressional action during 1992.

White-Collar Crime. The year's most controversial case regarding white-collar crime concerned the Bank of Credit and Commerce International (BCCI). The alleged bank fraud and other illegal activities conducted by BCCI were believed to have involved some 70 countries and about $5 billion in lost or stolen assets. BCCI was purported to have been involved in pervasive money-laundering operations for Colombian drug barons, terrorist organizations, and world leaders such as Panama's former strongman Manuel Noriega and Iraq's President Saddam Hussein. The investigation of BCCI was complicated further by the alleged use of the bank by U.S. and foreign intelligence agencies to fund covert operations. In November the U.S. Justice Department handed down a criminal indictment of BCCI and three businessmen associated with the bank. On December 19 the Justice Department and New York City prosecutors announced that BCCI had agreed to plead guilty to federal and state criminal charges and would forfeit $550 million, resolving all U.S. charges against BCCI. (*See* SPECIAL REPORT/INTERNATIONAL TRADE AND FINANCE.)

JACK ENTER, *Free-lance Writer*

Police Misconduct

On March 3, 1991, a bystander videotaped a group of Los Angeles police officers beating Rodney King, a black. The videotape created a national sensation when it was broadcast on television news and provoked a political crisis over the issue of police misconduct.

The King beating raised a number of questions about the police, including: How prevalent is police misconduct? Are black citizens the primary victims? Was the King incident an "aberration," as Los Angeles police chief Daryl Gates argued? Is the Los Angeles police department worse than other big-city departments? What can be done about police misconduct?

Definition and Prevalence. Police misconduct takes many forms. It includes unjustified use of deadly force, excessive use of physical force, verbal abuse (especially racial epithets), discriminatory arrest practices, and police corruption. The commonly used term "police brutality" refers to excessive use of physical force. The key question is how much physical force is "excessive"? The law allows police officers to use enough force to accomplish their lawful goals. When a person under arrest resists physically, officers may use enough force to effect the arrest. Anything more than that is excessive. Most observers thought the Rodney King beating involved excessive force because the officers continued to beat him even though he was lying on the ground and apparently not resisting.

Measuring the extent of police misconduct is extremely difficult. Police departments do not keep records on this problem. The only available statistics are the number of formal complaints filed by citizens. These records, however, are difficult to interpret. Many victims of police misconduct do not file complaints, while some of the filed complaints are not valid.

Sociologists have attempted to measure the prevalence of police misconduct through direct observation of police officers on the job. The most thorough study, by Professor Albert Reiss, now of Yale University, in the 1960s found that officers acted improperly in three out of every 1,000 encounters with citizens. Statistically, then, the rate of misconduct is not very high. Reiss was quick to point out, however, that incidents accumulate over time and can create the perception of systematic police brutality.

Are the Police Racist?. The perception of systematic police brutality is particularly strong in urban black communities. Police misconduct is a major issue for local black leaders. The sociological data present a very mixed picture. Reiss and others find only a slight pattern of racial discrimination. The victims of excessive use of force are generally lower-class males of all races. Additionally, black and Hispanic police officers are just as likely to use excessive force as are white officers. Black Americans are more often the victims of police misconduct because blacks are disproportionately poor, and because big-city police departments assign more officers to low-income neighborhoods. This means the police have more contact with poor black males than with any other group.

Was the Rodney King Incident an Aberration?. Civil-rights groups in Los Angeles argued that the Rodney King beating was typical of a broad pattern of brutality and racism within the Los Angeles police department. Many national experts agreed. They were shocked by the fact that so many officers participated in the beating, that a sergeant participated, and that the officers talked about it casually over the police radio afterward. An independent commission created to examine the Los Angeles police, chaired by former U.S. Deputy Secretary of State Warren Christopher, also found a pattern of brutality and racism.

Remedies. Many remedies have been proposed for police misconduct. Since the U.S. urban riots of the 1960s, police departments have hired more black and Hispanic police officers. Nationally, about 12% of all officers are black. Departments also have raised their educational standards. About 65% of all police officers now have some college education. Nearly all police departments have created a formal process for investigating citizen complaints. Yet, the problem of police misconduct persists.

Civil-rights leaders long have charged that police departments do not discipline officers guilty of misconduct. To remedy this problem, they have called for civilian review of the police. Civilian review is a procedure designed to provide a more independent investigation of complaints by involving persons who are not sworn police officers in the process. The concept of civilian review has spread rapidly in recent years. Thirty of the 50 largest U.S. cities have some form of civilian review.

Police misconduct is a serious problem with a long history. Experts generally are agreed that there is no easy solution to it.

SAMUEL WALKER

CUBA

The collapse of communism in the Soviet Union plunged Cuba in 1991 into its deepest economic and political crisis since 1959, when Fidel Castro seized power. As the Soviets drastically reduced subsidized trade with Cuba, the country was affected severely by shortfalls in the deliveries of such vital Russian products as petroleum, grains, lumber, chemicals, steel, and spare parts. In October, Havana cut the workday and, thus, salaries by 30% in many sectors. The future of the country's three largest, multibillion-dollar projects—a nickel plant and two nuclear power stations—whose completions were dependent on Soviet assistance, was uncertain.

The Domestic Scene. President Castro, repeatedly warning that the worst was yet to come, said adoption of "zero option"—restrictions in every aspect of the country's life—might be necessary. Stark austerity was being felt by the population, often left without such basic products as medicines, clothes, or soap and with food rations steadily diminishing. To save resources the traditional Havana carnival was canceled, as was the election for the National Assembly, Cuba's parliament, which was rescheduled for late 1992. Cubans were fleeing the country in record numbers, using makeshift boats and even inner tubes to reach the United States.

While industrial production dropped significantly, Cuba still managed a better-than-average sugar harvest of 7.63 million metric tons, enabling it to fulfill its export commitments. Sugar is the mainstay of the country's exports and generates 20% of its gross national product (GNP). To save fuel, for the first time in decades, oxen replaced tractors and were used in many areas to haul sugarcane to the mills.

Severe austerity and general grumbling notwithstanding, there were no signs in 1991 of widespread popular opposition to the Castro rule. The small and constantly harassed internal dissident movement was divided and disorganized. President Castro, who turned 65 in August and was completing his 32d year in power, appeared to have the loyalty of the military, the security apparatus, and the vast governmental bureaucracy, most of whose members would be uncertain of their jobs and their safety in case of an internal upheaval. Castro repeatedly rejected any notion of change, either political or economic.

While minor changes were made by the October congress of the ruling Communist Party of Cuba, the top leadership—President Castro and his deputy, brother Gen. Raúl Castro—remained entrenched. The principal tenet of the Castro regime continued to be its faith in Marxism-Leninism. "Whatever happens in the Soviet Union," editorialized *Granma,* the official Cuban newspaper, "we will not move away from the path we have chosen. We will continue with our independent, Cuban socialist line." Among the few cosmetic changes adopted by the congress were opening the party doors to religious believers who accepted Marxist principles, and recommending that the National Assembly be chosen by direct elections, even though the candidates still would be selected by the government. A few younger Communist leaders emerged at the congress, which increased the Party's Central Committee to 225 members and its Politburo to 25, an increase of more than one third in their memberships.

Foreign Affairs. Although Cuba hosted the XI Pan American Games (*see* SPORTS—*Pan American Games*), its overall international role diminished to almost zero in 1991. In May, ending 16 years of military support for Angola's embattled leftist government, the last Cuban soldiers departed that country. Since 1975 more than 500,000 Cuban soldiers had served in Africa. In 1978 the Cubans helped repel a Somalian invasion of Ethiopia's Ogaden province.

In September the Soviet Union announced it would withdraw its military contingent of 11,000 stationed in Cuba since 1962. According to the U.S. State Department, the contingent included a combat brigade of more than 3,000 to provide security for a large electronic intelligence installation in Lourdes, southeast of Havana, where another 3,000 Russians worked; and roughly 3,500 military advisers to the Cuban armed forces. Sales of Soviet arms to Cuba also would be phased out, Moscow said. Cuba reacted angrily to Moscow's unilateral move. It said that a Soviet troop pullout should be linked to the withdrawal of U.S. forces from the U.S. Guantánamo naval base. That was rejected by the Bush administration which, if anything, hardened its policy toward Havana and tried to tighten the 30-year-old U.S. economic embargo against Cuba.

More damaging for Havana was a statement by Soviet President Mikhail Gorbachev that, ending years of generous grants, a new Soviet-Cuban economic relationship would be based strictly on free trade, eliminating the $2-billion-per-year subsidy that Moscow had been giving

CUBA • Information Highlights

Official Name: Republic of Cuba.
Location: Caribbean.
Area: 42,803 sq mi (110 860 km^2).
Population (mid-1991 est.): 10,700,000.
Chief Cities (Dec. 31, 1989 est.): Havana, the capital, 2,096,054; Santiago de Cuba, 405,354; Camagüey, 283,008; Holguín, 228,053.
Government: *Head of state and government,* Fidel Castro Ruz, president (took office under a new constitution, December 1976). *Legislature* (unicameral)—National Assembly of People's Power.
Foreign Trade (1988 U.S.$): *Imports,* $7,579,000,000; *exports,* $5,518,000,000.

Cuba by bartering oil for sugar and other products on terms that greatly overvalued the sugar.

Trying to find other markets, Cuba offered economic incentives to foreign capital. In 1991 about 200 foreign companies, many from Western Europe, operated 50–50 joint ventures—mostly in the tourist industry, which had been growing at a rate of 10% annually since 1989. A French consortium signed a six-year contract in 1991 to explore Cuba's north coast for oil.

The Castro government succeeded in improving relations with Latin America in 1991. Chile and Colombia reestablished diplomatic ties with Havana, leaving only El Salvador, Honduras, and Guatemala without representation in Cuba. In October, Castro met in Mexico with Presidents Carlos Salinas de Gortari of Mexico, César Gaviria of Colombia, and Carlos Andrés Pérez of Venezuela. After the meeting, the three presidents urged Havana and Washington to normalize ties, with President Pérez noting that while the Cold War was over in Europe, it was still on in the Americas. He urged Washington to end the Cuban embargo, arguing that this could lead to peaceful change in Havana, an argument that apparently fell on deaf ears in Washington.

GEORGE VOLSKY
University of Miami

CYPRUS

Cyprus, an island republic, remained divided in two in 1991, as it has been since 1974 when a Turkish invasion supporting the minority Turkish Cypriots took over about 37% of the country's northern territories. Since 1983 these territories had been proclaimed unilaterally as the Turkish Republic of Northern Cyprus, and a Turkish Cypriot, Rauf Denktas, was president there. The rest of Cyprus was under the government of the Greek Cypriot George Vassiliou, who as president of the Republic of Cyprus steadfastly refused to acknowledge the validity of the state headed by Denktas, which was recognized only by Turkey. Vassiliou and his internationally recognized government continuously condemned not only the Turkish occupation, which included armed forces estimated at 35,000, but also the fact that the Turkish government had brought into the occupied territory some 80,000 Turkish settlers to replace the 200,000 Greek Cypriots driven from their homes by the 1974 invasion. The UN retained a peacekeeping force (UNFICYP) of 2,100 on the island.

Reconciliation Efforts. Although attempts to reconcile the majority Greek Cypriots with the minority Turkish Cypriots had been unsuccessful, UN Secretary-General Javier Pérez de Cuéllar continued to seek a solution in 1991. The key to a solution involved the assent of Greece and Turkey, as well as agreement among the Greek Cypriots and the Turkish Cypriots. Hopes were raised in July when U.S. President George Bush visited both Athens, Greece, and Ankara, Turkey, making clear his wish to help find an equitable solution through the UN.

In August, President Bush announced that Prime Minister Constantine Mitsotakis of Greece and President Turgut Özal of Turkey would attend a UN-sponsored meeting in the United States about Cyprus in September if sufficient progress toward finding a common ground had been reached by then. However, a meeting of Mitsotakis and Turkish Prime Minister Mesut Yilmaz in Paris on September 11 showed that the two countries were far apart, and the September UN-sponsored meeting was not held. In early October the UN secretary-general reported to the Security Council that last-minute demands by Rauf Denktas had placed obstacles in the way of an understanding.

Under these circumstances the Security Council on October 11 unanimously adopted Resolution 716, stating that the Republic of Cyprus should remain an independent, sovereign state with the two communities being politically equal. Meanwhile, elections in Turkey on October 20 in which Özal's party finished second slowed down the negotiating process, and an impasse developed.

Elections. Parliamentary elections, the first since 1985, were held for the House of Representatives in the nonoccupied parts of Cyprus on May 19, 1991. The two parties which won the largest number of the 56 seats in the House were the conservative Democratic Rally, which received 35.8% of the votes—giving it 20 seats—and the Communist AKEL, which garnered 30.6% of the votes and 18 seats. Both of these parties supported President Vassiliou, an independent, in his efforts to seek discussions with the Turkish Cypriots under UN aegis. The Democratic Party of former President Spyros Kyprianou won only 19.5% of the votes and 11 seats. His platform was in oppo-

CYPRUS • Information Highlights

Official Name: Republic of Cyprus.
Location: Eastern Mediterranean.
Area: 3,571 sq mi (9 250 km^2).
Population (mid-1991 est.): 700,000.
Chief Cities (1982 census): Nicosia, the capital, 48,221; Limassol, 74,782.
Government: *Head of state and government,* George Vassiliou, president (took office Feb. 1988). *Legislature*—House of Representatives.
Monetary Unit: Pound (0.480 pound equals U.S.$1, August 1991).
Gross Domestic Product (1988 est. U.S.$): $4,200,000,000.
Economic Index (1990): *Consumer Prices* (1980 = 100), all items, 160.9; food, 172.2.
Foreign Trade (1990 U.S.$): *Imports,* $2,558,000,000; *exports,* $956,000,000.

© Georges Merillon/Gamma-Liaison

Czechoslovakia's President Václav Havel (right) *hosted a conference on "European confederation," an idea proposed by France's President François Mitterrand* (left) *as 1989 ended, in Prague, June 12–14, 1991. More than 150 persons attended.*

sition to direct negotiations with Turkish Cypriots. The Socialist Party, EDEK, which also criticized Vassiliou's negotiating plans, took 10.9% of the votes and seven seats.

The Economy. The Persian Gulf war and its aftermath greatly impaired unoccupied Cyprus' tourist industry and affected importing and exporting as well. In addition, agricultural production was affected by a widespread drought. But as the year progressed, the usually strong economy in the south showed definite signs of recovery. In the northern occupied territories the drought was also a problem as was the fact that Asil Nadir, a Turkish Cypriot who had vast holdings in the north, was undergoing charges in Great Britain for theft and other irregularities.

GEORGE J. MARCOPOULOS, *Tufts University*

CZECHOSLOVAKIA

Two issues dominated the political and economic scene in the post-Communist Czechoslovakia of 1991: The ever more bitter controversy about the future of Czech-Slovak relations, a controversy that poses a serious threat to the very survival of Czechoslovakia as a unified country; and the continuing disagreement about restructuring Czechoslovakia's economy.

The Czech-Slovak Dissension. While in 1990 the Czech-Slovak argument turned mainly around the distribution of powers between the federal government and those of the two constituent republics, in 1991 voices began to be heard in Slovakia advocating a much looser confederative arrangement, and the Slovak premier even spoke of eventual Slovak independence. Advocates of Slovak separatism began to organize demonstrations protesting against what they called "Czech colonialism," and clamoring for Slovakia's independence. To counter the separatists' campaign, Slovak supporters of a unified Czechoslovakia began to collect signatures on a petition pleading for Czech-Slovak unity. A heated argument developed about the Slovak demand that the drafting of the new Czechoslovak constitution be preceded by the conclusion of a treaty between the "sovereign Czech Republic" and the "sovereign Slovak Republic." The demand was rejected by President Václav Havel and the federal government. Instead, they proposed that the basic constitutional principles of Czech-Slovak relations be stipulated in a joint Czech-Slovak declaration as an intrastate document.

Thus the preservation of a united Czechoslovak federation faced a major challenge. To resolve the problem President Havel and the federal government intended as 1991 came to an end to conduct a referendum asking Czech and Slovak voters whether they wanted a united country or would prefer independence. Should more than 50% of the eligible voters in either of the two republics vote to live in separate countries, Czechoslovakia would cease to exist. Public-opinion polls indicated that the majority of Slovaks were for a united Czechoslovakia.

The Government and Political Parties. In spite of the threat of Slovak separatism, work continued in 1991 on the new federal constitution. Its proposals provided for a popularly elected Federal Assembly and a smaller Federal Council with equal representation for Czechs and Slovaks. The federal president would be elected by both the Assembly and the Council.

Substantial changes occurred in 1991 in the alignment of political forces. The two civic groupings that spearheaded the "velvet revolution" of 1989, the Czech Civic Forum and the Slovak Public Against Violence, split along liberal-conservative lines. A multiple process of fragmentation and realignment occurred also in a number of political parties, most of all the former Communist Party.

Responding to the often-repeated wishes of the people, the Federal Assembly in October approved a law that bars higher functionaries of the former Communist Party from holding high or middle positions in the government and other public institutions for five years. Exempt from the measure were those who held such functions in the "Prague spring," the period from Jan. 16, 1968, to May 1, 1969.

The Economy. The government's efforts to replace the stagnating command economy inherited from the Communist regime with a privatized free-market system gathered momentum in 1991. In the first step, dubbed "small privatization," more than 15,000 smaller publicly operated enterprises—such as restaurants, hotels, and retail stores were put on the auction block to be sold to the highest bidders. By August, 7,058 of them were sold for a sum equivalent to $190 million. However, as many as 8,723 enterprises remained unsold and had to be offered again at a lesser price in a second round of auctions. In the second step, called "big privatization," some 4,127 larger state enterprises—such as factories and assembly plants—with an estimated value of $7 billion, began to be converted into joint-stock companies. Some of them were to be sold to private entrepreneurs for cash, but most were to be offered to individual investors. Every permanent-resident Czechoslovak citizen over 18 years of age was entitled to buy a book of coupons which would be used to purchase shares of enterprises included in the privatization.

To encourage entrepreneurial zeal, 85% of prices were decontrolled, but ceilings were retained on food, some services, and a few other staple items. Rents were being allowed to rise by as much as 180%, and in October consumers began to pay 70% more for electricity. Government subsidies of the Communist era were being reduced gradually.

The Pain of Transition. As the country moved closer to its goal of a free-market economy it encountered more problems and difficulties. A great many enterprises were burdened with heavy debts and so were the majority of state and cooperative farms. It was feared that many of them would not make it in free-market conditions. The situation was complicated by growing export difficulties, as orders for Czechoslovak products from the Soviet Union and the East European countries fell sharply and substitute markets in the West were hard to find. The agricultural sector was in deep trouble as farmers had to pay much more for fertilizers, feeds, and tools and could not compensate by getting high enough prices for what they produced. Thus they were stuck with huge surpluses of grain and meat. Entrepreneurs encountered problems with financing as banks practiced tight-credit policies and charged interest as high as 17%.

This economic malaise was borne out by official figures on the performance of Czechoslovakia's economy. In the first half of 1991 industrial production fell by 16.8% (and by as much as 32.3% since June 1990); construction decreased by 26.3%; labor productivity fell by 9.3% in industry and by as much as 24.8% in construction; between December 1990 and June 1991 consumer prices rose by 49.2% and the cost of living by about 45%. As of June 1991 only 3.8% of the work force was reported to be unemployed, thus indicating that the Communist legacy of excessive overemployment had yet to be dealt with. Nor was the economic scenario likely to improve soon. A government report in 1991 saw the gross national product achieving its 1989 level again only by the mid-1990s.

International Relations. On October 7 a Czechoslovak-German treaty of Good Neighborliness and Cooperation was signed ceremoniously in Prague in the presence of the heads of both countries. The treaty's preamble proclaims the inviolability of Czechoslovak-German borders and affirms German recognition of the uninterrupted existence of Czechoslovakia since 1918. Czechoslovakia was admitted to membership in the Council of Europe and was granted a $450 million loan by the World Bank.

EDWARD TABORSKY
University of Texas, Austin

CZECHOSLOVAKIA • Information Highlights

Official Name: Czech and Slovak Federative Republic.
Location: East-central Europe.
Area: 49,371 sq mi (127 870 km^2).
Population (mid-1991 est.): 15,700,000.
Chief Cities (Dec. 31, 1989 est.): Prague, the capital, 1,214,885; Bratislava, 440,629; Brno, 390,986.
Government: *Head of state,* Václav Havel, president (elected June 1990). *Head of government,* Marian Calfa, premier (took office Dec. 10, 1989). *Legislature*—Federal Assembly.
Gross National Product (1989 est. U.S.$): $123,200,000,000.
Economic Indexes (1990): *Consumer Prices* (1980 = 100), all items, 124.0; food, 126.8. *Industrial Production* (1980 = 100), 120.
Foreign Trade (1990 U.S.$): *Imports,* $13,106,000,000; *exports,* $11,882,000,000.

A 1991 ballet highlight was the New York City Ballet's performance of "Sleeping Beauty," a $2.8 million version of the 19th-century classic staged by Peter Martins. Starring in the acclaimed production were Ben Huys and Darci Kistler (above).

DANCE

For dance lovers 1991 was marked especially by the deaths of major personalities, including Martha Graham and Margot Fonteyn (*see* OBITUARIES). It was a year in which ballet companies, folk groups, and modern-dance troupes from abroad were highly visible in the United States, thanks to the many festivals that sponsored them. U.S. companies also remained active and innovative despite severe financial problems.

Ballet. The New York City Ballet's artistic director, Peter Martins, staged an acclaimed version of *The Sleeping Beauty*. Although he retained the set pieces of Marius Petipa's original choreography of 1890, Martins gave the $2.8 million production a contemporary look by speeding up the tempo and compressing some of the action with rechoreographed passages.

The City Ballet presented several new works. Robert La Fosse turned to Carl Maria von Weber, Franz Liszt, and Tchaikovsky for three contrasting sections in his *Waltz Trilogy*. Martins choreographed two ballets: Michael Torke's strongly rhythmic score propelled five couples along in *Ash;* Bach's music accompanied taut, yanking duets and a display of the academic idiom in *A Musical Offering*.

The Joffrey Ballet celebrated its 35th anniversary at Lincoln Center in New York with three premieres. These were Charles Moulton's *Panoramagram,* Christopher d'Amboise's *Runaway Train,* and Edward Stierle's *Empyrean Dances*. A week earlier, Stierle had presented his first ballet, *Lacrymosa*. His two works passionately expressed an acceptance of death and signaled a major new choreographic talent. But Stierle, already a brilliant dancer, died shortly afterward (March 8) of AIDS at the age of 23. The Joffrey's dancers finished the season with public sympathy and another premiere, Alonzo King's *Lila*.

American Ballet Theatre (ABT) in a cost-conscious season presented no new works. There were three partially successful revised productions: *Coppélia,* staged by Enrique Martinez, *Don Quixote* by Vladimir Vasiliev, and Act III of *Raymonda* by Fernando Bujones. The troupe danced Jiri Kylian's 1978 ballet, *Sinfonietta,* for the first time.

An ABT gala honored Cynthia Gregory, who was leaving the company she had joined in 1965 but said she would continue to dance elsewhere. Ballet Theatre presented Carla Fracci from Italy and Sylvie Guillem, formerly with the Paris Opera and now with the Britain's Royal Ballet, as guest artists.

The San Francisco Ballet presented its first season in New York since Helgi Tomasson became its artistic director in 1985. The former New York City Ballet star had raised visibly the company's level of classical dancing. For Elizabeth Loscavio, the San Francisco troupe's rising young ballerina, Tomasson choreographed an elegant neoclassic Mozart ballet, *Haffner Symphony*. There were two other Tomasson premieres, the frolicsome *Meistens Mozart* and the austere Bach ballet, *Aurora Polaris*. Val Caniparoli offered a more sweeping style in *Connotations,* set to Benjamin Britten's *Violin Concerto*.

Two scores by Alberto Ginastera were used for premieres by Dance Theatre of Harlem: Glen Tetley choreographed *Dialogues* and Billy Wilson created *Ginastera*. Premieres by Eliot Feld for Feld Ballets/NY included *Common Ground* to Bach, *Savage Glance* to Shostakovich, and *Fauna* to Debussy.

Modern Dance. Martha Graham, who died on April 1 at the age of 96, was honored as the foremost pioneer of U.S. modern dance in a free performance by her company on June 3 in New York. The troupe's season in October included part of an unfinished work that Graham had begun choreographing for Spain's Columbian Quincentenary Exposition in Seville. Graham's images in this 14-minute segment, *The Eyes of the Goddess,* were richly baroque and alluded to a journey to the unknown. Marisol designed the set, including a symbolic death cart. During the same season, Mikhail Baryshnikov gave a dramatic performance in the title role of Graham's *El Penitente*. On Graham's death, Ron Protas and Linda Hodes became the company's codirectors.

The year's most popular premiere was *Company B,* which Paul Taylor choreographed to recordings by the Andrews Sisters. Taylor created the piece for the Houston Ballet and transferred it to his own company. Enthusiastic audiences included President George Bush, who saw the Houston Ballet premiere at the Kennedy Center in Washington. Taylor's appeal was on two levels. The innocence and patriotism of the United States in the 1940s were implied in the songs and undercut by images of war and complex personal relationships in the dancing. Taylor also choreographed *Fact and Fancy* to reggae music for his own company.

Merce Cunningham used a computer to create *Trackers*. His other premiere was called *Neighbors*. Judith Jamison, artistic director of the Alvin Ailey American Dance Theater, used a commissioned score by Nona Hendryx for *Rift,* which was concerned with an outsider's relation to a group. Erick Hawkins' *Intensities of Space and Wind* and Trisha Brown's *Foray Forêt* were other notable new pieces.

Unusual experimental pieces came from Garth Fagan in *Griot,* with an evocative jazz score by Wynton Marsalis, and from Jawole Willa Jo Zollar, whose Urban Bush Women company presented *Praise House*. The work imaginatively probed the inner world of Minnie Evans, a black folk painter. Eiko and Koma were less successful in their evocation of the Southwest in *Land*.

Non-U.S. Companies. Britain's Royal Ballet, visibly in a decline during its last U.S. visit in 1983, returned renewed under its current director, Anthony Dowell. The 22-year-old Darcey Bussell created a sensation with the bold power of her dancing. Kenneth MacMillan cast her perfectly in his *Prince of the Pagodas* and *Winter Dreams,* his distillation of Chekhov's *Three Sisters*.

Irek Mukhamedov and Sylvie Guillem, who had a greater impact dancing with the Royal Ballet than with Ballet Theatre, gave outstanding dramatic performances in MacMillan's *Manon*. Other novelties were *'Still Life' at the Penguin Cafe,* David Bintley's charming ecological fable, and Dowell's well-received staging of *Swan Lake*. The decor by Yolanda Sonnabend was in Art Nouveau style.

The Matsuyama Ballet from Tokyo was led by the ballerina Yoko Morishita. The Kirov Ballet from St. Petersburg essayed three Western ballets on its tour: Antony Tudor's *Jardin aux Lilas* and George Balanchine's *Apollo* and *Tchaikovsky Pas de Deux*. Igor Zelensky stood out among the young soloists.

The Moiseyev Dance Company from Moscow included the U.S. premiere of Moiseyev's *Greek Suite* and *Tsam,* a richer work inspired by Mongolian theater.

Experimental choreographers also traveled to the United States. Anne Teresa de Keersmaeker, the leader of the Belgian avant-garde, offered a complex essay on context and meaning in *Stella*. Wim Vandekeybus, a younger Belgian, played with physical risk in *Always the Same Lies*. Pina Bausch's brand of German dance theater found inventive expression in *Bandoneón* and *Palermo, Palermo,* which opens with a huge wall falling down.

Festivals. The Festival of Indonesia continued a season begun in 1990. The New York International Festival of the Arts sponsored groups from Asia and European experimental choreographers like Angolin Preljocaj and Philippe Genty from France, and Philippe Saire from Switzerland. The New York festival introduced 95 Russian folk performers under the title *Gulyane*.

The American Dance Festival in Durham, NC, sent teachers to train China's first modern-dance troupe and presented the U.S. debut of the troupe, the Guangdong Modern Dance Company.

People. Anna Sokolow received the Samuel H. Scripps-American Dance Festival Award; the Nicholas Brothers—tap dancers Harold and Fayard Nicholas—received Kennedy Center Honors.

Among others who died in 1991 were Ruth Page, the dancer and choreographer whose Chicago-based ballet company in the 1930s was one of the country's first; and Roman Jasinski, the Polish-born ballet star who cofounded Tulsa Ballet Theatre.

ANNA KISSELGOFF
"The New York Times"

DELAWARE

Reapportionment, recession, and budget cutting dominated public concerns in Delaware in 1991. While considered by many analysts to be relatively well-off compared to neighboring states, Delaware saw its economic growth level off as unemployment rose, construction slowed, and the automobile and chemical industries furloughed workers and shut down plants for multiweek periods. The state government cut its budget, raised some business taxes, and initiated an early-retirement program.

Legislative Session. The first session of the 136th General Assembly was low-key with relatively few bills passed. The specter of legislative reapportionment, declining revenues, and unhealed battle wounds from the 1990 election brought a somber mood which lasted throughout the regular session. Finally in a special legislative session held in August, a reapportionment bill was passed. The new plan shifted political strength to suburban and downstate areas, while increasing the potential for minority representation.

Early in the regular session, the General Assembly passed major legislation proposed by Gov. Michael N. Castle that created an early-retirement option for state employees, including public-school teachers. When the retirement option was taken by more employees than originally predicted, it caused great hardships for some agencies and schools.

The only other major legislation to be enacted set up a farmland-protection program. Delaware, one of the most rural states on the east coast, nonetheless has much prime agricultural land in the path of urban or recreational development. Under the plan farmers can place their lands in special districts that protect its agricultural use for a minimum of ten years.

Economy. The Du Pont Company, Delaware's largest employer, announced a $1 billion cost-reduction program. While many details of the program remained to be announced, it was expected to have a significant impact on the Delaware work force and economy. Layoffs and retirements at Du Pont and other local industries would increase unemployment, which at year's end stood at close to the U.S. average rate of 6.8%. As recently as June 1990, Delaware's unemployment rate was just 3.5%.

While economic stagnation became a reality in 1991, the impact of a major increase in employment and population during the 1980s continued to foster controversy and new demands to slow development. Greater traffic volume was one of the most visible and least appreciated results of the economic boom. It was within this context that three major new shopping malls were proposed for development along the already heavily congested U.S. Route 202 corridor in northern Delaware. While furiously opposed by civic groups in their immediate environs, all three malls were approved by the New Castle County Council. The approvals were labeled by an irate Governor Castle as "Mall Mania," as he and other state leaders called for major reforms in the land planning and regulation process.

As 1991 came to a close, memories of the troublesome Persian Gulf war began to fade. Delaware played a major role in the war through its National Guard, reserves, and Dover Air Force Base. During the early weeks of summer, Delawareans took time to celebrate the contributions and sacrifices of the servicemen and servicewomen through parades, air shows, and memorial services.

JEROME R. LEWIS, *University of Delaware*

DELAWARE • Information Highlights

Area: 2,045 sq mi (5 295 km²).
Population (1990 census): 666,168.
Chief Cities (1990 census): Dover, the capital, 27,630; Wilmington, 71,529; Newark, 25,098; Milford, 6,040.
Government (1991): *Chief Officers*—governor, Michael N. Castle (R); lt. gov., Dale E. Wolf (R). *General Assembly*—Senate, 21 members; House of Representatives, 41 members.
State Finances (fiscal year 1990): *Revenue,* $2,316,000,000; *expenditure,* $2,128,000,000.
Personal Income (1990): $13,397,000,000; per capita, $20,022.
Labor Force (June 1991): *Civilian labor force,* 368,500; *unemployed,* 24,100 (6.5% of total force).
Education: *Enrollment* (fall 1989)—public elementary schools, 70,699; public secondary, 27,109; colleges and universities, 40,562. *Public school expenditures* (1989), $479,327,000.

DENMARK

The political balance was changed in Denmark in 1991 following a hastily called election at the end of 1990.

Politics. The fifth general election in nine years was held on Dec. 12, 1990, in response to pressure from opposition parties, who were unhappy with government finance and tax policies. The Social Democrats scored a significant advance, gaining 14 seats and becoming with a total of 69 seats the largest party in the legislative assembly. The ruling three-party coalition did not fare well—the Conservatives lost five of their 35 seats; the Liberals gained seven seats for a total of 29; and the Radicals saw their representation reduced from ten to seven. The Center Democrats and the Christian People's Party retained nine and four seats, respectively; the Socialist Party ended up with 15 seats (a loss of nine); the Progress Party lost four seats, dropping to 12.

Although commanding only 59 seats in the 179-member Folketing (parliament), a coalition of Conservatives and Liberals was empowered

Queen Margrethe II of Denmark met with U.S. President George Bush in Washington during a state visit to the United States in February. The queen's itinerary included a tour of colonial Williamsburg in Virginia.

AP/Wide World

to lead Denmark. Prime Minister Poul Schlüter and Foreign Minister Uffe Ellemann-Jensen continued in office, but they now were dependent on the various parties to the right of the Social Democrats.

Much of the summer's political calm was disrupted by the so-called "Tamil case," in which former cabinet member Erik Ninn-Hansen was accused of unjustifiably having prevented several Sri Lankan political refugees from joining relatives. The controversy continued at year's end.

Foreign Affairs. Denmark was in full agreement with UN Security Council resolutions condemning the invasion of Kuwait by Iraq. The Danes sent a naval corvette to the Gulf and dispatched a medical team to the war zone. Fifty observers also joined nine church workers in the Gulf.

Denmark supported the attempts of the three Baltic states of Latvia, Lithuania, and Estonia to achieve full sovereignty. In February, Denmark joined the other Nordic countries in signing an agreement of cooperation with the Baltic states, confirming recognition of their independence and offering to extend economic and technical cooperation.

As a member of the European Community (EC), Denmark favored admitting the former Communist nations of Eastern Europe into the EC. The Danes, however, together with the British and other EC members, opposed transforming the community into a federal state.

Queen Margrethe II and Prince Henrik in mid-February made an official visit to the United States.

Economic Affairs. The economic situation was on the whole encouraging. Inflation was kept within bounds and the trade balance showed a surplus during the summer. Unemployment remained a factor to be reckoned with. In March representatives of labor and industry signed a biennial agreement that was characterized by moderation on the part of both factions.

An agreement on linking Denmark and Sweden by a bridge across the Sound was signed on March 23, but plans did not call for the $2.5 billion span to be completed until 1999. In the meantime, work on the tunnel under the Great Belt to link the main islands of Sjaelland and Fyn was proceeding slowly and was expected to be completed sometime in 1994.

Cultural Affairs. The restored home of author Karen Blixen at Rungstedlund opened as a museum on May 15. Restoration expenses came from the revenue received from two motion pictures based on her works *Out of Africa* and *Babette's Feast*.

ERIK J. FRIIS
"The Scandinavian-American Bulletin"

DENMARK • Information Highlights

Official Name: Kingdom of Denmark.
Location: Northwest Europe.
Area: 16,629 sq mi (43 070 km²).
Population (mid-1991 est.): 5,100,000.
Chief Cities (Jan. 1, 1990 est.): Copenhagen, the capital, 1,337,114 (incl. suburbs); Århus, 261,437; Odense, 176,133.
Government: *Head of state,* Margrethe II, queen (acceded Jan. 1972). *Head of government,* Poul Schlüter, prime minister (took office Sept. 1982). *Legislature* (unicameral)—Folketing.
Monetary Unit: Krone (6.3615 kroner equal U.S.$1, Nov. 13, 1991).
Gross Domestic Product (1989 est. U.S.$): $73,700,000,000.
Economic Indexes (1990): *Consumer Prices* (1980 = 100), all items, 177.4; food, 165.0. *Industrial Production* (1980 = 100), 131.
Foreign Trade (1990 U.S.$): *Imports,* $31,766,000,000; *exports,* $35,112,000,000.

DRUGS AND ALCOHOL

There was mixed news in 1991 about the national fight against the importation, sale, and use of illegal drugs. Two years after President George Bush called the drug problem "the gravest domestic threat facing our nation" and significantly expanded federal antidrug efforts, government studies indicated that marijuana and cocaine use were down, but that heroin was making a comeback and drug-related violent crime remained a national problem. "I think we are winning a lot of individual battles, but there are a number of areas of great concern," said Bob Martinez, the former Florida governor who became director of the Office of National Drug Control Policy on March 28.

President Bush and other federal officials stressed the successes of the administration's "war" against drugs. "The clear message of available data is that drug use is on the way down. Since I've come into office, we've seen an important and encouraging shift in drug-use trends," the president said in a January 31 speech, during which he proposed an expanded $11.7 billion federal antidrug program.

Law-enforcement agencies throughout the country confiscated unprecedented amounts of illegal drugs in 1991. In May, for example, federal agents and New York City police found 1,237 lbs (561 kg) of cocaine worth more than $300 million inside a van driven, police said, by an employee of the Cali, Colombia, cocaine cartel. The seizure was the sixth-largest made in the city. During June, July, and August federal drug agents in Boston seized nearly 5 tons (4 500 kg) of cocaine worth some $1 billion. U.S. Customs Service agents raided a container ship in Oakland, CA, on June 21 and confiscated some 1,080 lbs (490 kg) of heroin—the largest heroin seizure ever made in the United States. The heroin, which was shipped from Thailand through Taiwan, was estimated to be worth as much as $1.5 billion.

National surveys buttressed the administration's claim of a steady decline in general drug use. The annual survey by the University of Michigan's Institute for Social Research released January 24, for example, found that some 48% of the high-school seniors interviewed reported using an illegal drug at least once in their lives. That compared to a high of 66% in 1982. A report issued by the Drug Control Policy Office in June estimated that Americans spent some $40.4 billion in 1990 on illegal drugs, compared with $51.6 billion in 1988 and $49.8 billion in 1989.

Critics of the government's drug policy pointed out that drug use declined only among the affluent and middle class. The critics contended that drug use—especially of heroin and crack (the relatively inexpensive and highly addictive smokable form of cocaine)—was an intractable and dangerous problem among Americans at the bottom rung of society. Critics pointed to the continuing flourishing of drug trafficking in Latin America as well as to record numbers of drug-related violent crimes.

Law-enforcement and health officials in Chicago, Detroit, Los Angeles, New York, Pittsburgh, Washington, DC, and other cities continued to cope with the devastating social costs of what they called an ongoing crack "epidemic." In Chicago, where street gangs took over the crack trade, murder rates were at an all-time high. Chicago police estimated that 40% of the city's homicides in 1991 were related to drugs, primarily crack, or gangs.

Health officials estimated that during 1991 some 375,000 children were exposed to drugs in the womb. Many of those newborns were addicted at birth to crack. "All you have to do is move through the cities to see that the statistics are not telling the whole story," said Davene M. White of Howard University Hospital in Washington, DC, where some 30% of the babies born in 1990 were exposed to drugs in the womb.

Another concern in 1991 was a resurgence of heroin smuggling and use. Evidence strongly indicated that increasing amounts of heroin, the highly addictive narcotic, were coming into the United States from Asia and South America. The heroin imported was significantly purer and less expensive than it had been in recent years. This led to street prices as low as $3 per dose and to widespread popularity of purer blends that could be snorted or smoked.

Alcohol. The multibillion-dollar fight against drugs did not include a substance that many health officials consider to be the United States' most abused drug—alcohol. "Since the beginning of the war on drugs, there has been so much focus on illicit drugs that there's been a tendency to forget that the drug that most profoundly affects people's lives is alcohol," said Christine Lubinski of the National Council on Alcoholism and Drug Dependence.

A survey released in September by the National Center for Health Statistics estimated that there were some 10.5 million alcoholics in the United States and that 76 million American adults—43% of the adult population—have either grown up with an alcoholic in the family, married an alcoholic, or had a close alcoholic relative. A series of reports issued in 1991 indicated widespread use of alcohol among young persons. In June, for example, a Department of Health and Human Services survey estimated that some 10.6 million junior and senior high-school students were weekly alcohol users, despite the fact that the legal drinking age is 21 in all 50 states. Many colleges put into effect tighter alcohol-consumption regulations. But the use of alcohol among the nation's 12 million college students remained exceptionally high.

MARC LEEPSON, *Free-lance Writer*

ECUADOR

Ecuador proved to be as difficult to govern in 1991 as it was in 1990. Pulled in diverse directions by foreign creditors, workers, Indians, and the military, President Rodrigo Borja steered a cautious course that satisfied few and failed to solve any of the country's daunting problems but at least averted disaster.

At the onset of the U.S.-led coalition's war against Iraq in early 1991, oil prices fell slightly below even the prudent budget estimate of $17 per barrel, creating a $90 million shortfall in government revenues in the first half of the year. Without the anticipated infusion of petroleum earnings, economic growth was estimated to be a positive but sluggish 2% for the year, little better than the 1.5% figure for 1990.

Politics. Party politics was typically turbulent in 1991. In February, Borja's coalition fell apart as the Democratic Popular Movement (MPD), the Broad Leftist Front (FADI), and the Socialists joined the opposition in censuring two cabinet ministers for economic policies that had sparked riots and a general strike. By July six members of the cabinet had been forced to resign in little more than a year, and the congress decided to initiate impeachment proceedings against Vice-President Luis Parodi for alleged corrupt dealings during Borja's absence. Fears of a constitutional crisis grew as Parodi refused to appear before congress and the congress debated taking away some of the president's appointment powers.

Economy. Finding himself unable to satisfy both popular-sector groups and the international financial community, and too isolated to propose any bold initiative, Borja resorted to half measures to deal with the country's economic problems. Unlike most other Latin American countries, Ecuador continued to pay only 30% of the debt service due on its $11.7 billion foreign debt. Official creditors, the World Bank, and the Inter-American Development Bank held up loans to Ecuador until a new agreement could be signed with the International Monetary Fund (IMF), but the last IMF agreement expired in February and there was little progress on talks for a new one.

Important progress was made toward economic integration as Ecuador agreed to join Peru, Bolivia, Colombia, and Venezuela in an Andean Pact free-trade area by 1992 and a common market by 1995. Even in this milestone, however, Ecuador insisted on lowering its trade barriers more slowly than the other members. The most dramatic economic development was the liberalization of foreign-investment rules in May. Foreign investment now would be permitted in all sectors of the economy except defense, radio, television, and print media, and the regulation limiting profit remittances to 40% of the total investment was eliminated.

ECUADOR • Information Highlights

Official Name: Republic of Ecuador.
Location: Northwest South America.
Area: 109,483 sq mi (283 560 km²).
Population (mid-1991 est.): 10,800,000.
Chief Cities (mid-1990 est.): Quito, the capital, 1,281,849; Guayaquil, 1,764,170; Cuenca, 227,212.
Government: *Head of state and government,* Rodrigo Borja Cevallos, president (took office August 1988). *Legislature* (unicameral)—Chamber of Representatives.
Monetary Unit: Sucre (1,035.51 sucres equal U.S.$1, floating rate, Oct. 21, 1991).
Gross Domestic Product (1989 U.S.$): $9,800,000,000.
Economic Index (1990): *Consumer Prices* (1981 = 100), all items, 1,906.3; food, 2,696.5.
Foreign Trade (1990 U.S.$): *Imports,* $1,862,000,000; *exports,* $2,722,000,000.

In domestic economic policy, the Borja administration cut government spending twice, but not enough to close an estimated $300 million fiscal deficit, which was far too large to blame on unexpectedly low oil prices. Continued deficit spending made it unlikely that the inflation rate would fall below 1990's 49.5%.

Indian Groups and Guerrilla Warfare. Indian groups, potentially representing one third of the population, continued to challenge the government's authority. In May their confederation, CONAIE, occupied the legislature in Quito for two days, threatening to set up a government of its own if its demands for land, investment, amnesty, and respect were not met. The group also called for a more effective response to the cholera epidemic, which claimed hundreds of lives (*see* SIDEBAR/LATIN AMERICA). The Indians' demands alarmed the military, which demanded that the president "neutralize" groups that sought an independent Indian state. The confrontation ended with a Catholic Church-mediated resumption of negotiations between the Indian groups and the government.

There was mixed progress on the guerrilla front as *¡Alfaro Vive Carajo!* laid down its arms in February under the terms of a peace accord. In September, however, members of a dissident wing of the rebel group occupied parts of the British embassy in Quito, demanding the release of their jailed leader.

The Future. One probable reason for the growing political weakness of President Borja was the fact that he was starting to be treated as a lame duck. Presidential and congressional elections were scheduled for June 1992, so presidential candidates began surfacing to challenge Borja's leadership during 1991. Burdened by responsibility for political deterioration and disappointing economic performance, Borja's Democratic Left Party (ID) was not expected to make a strong showing.

MICHAEL COPPEDGE
Johns Hopkins University

© Robert Maass

With 77% of all college students attending state schools, cuts in the states' education budgets, mandated by fiscal difficulties, were a nationwide problem. Above, *students from the City University of New York demonstrated their concern.*

EDUCATION

If the 1980s were characterized as the decade of education reports in the United States, then 1991, the first full year of policy-making and debate of national education goals, was the year of the report card. The National Education Goals Panel released the first of what were to be annual reports on progress on the national goals. It painted a "sobering" picture of how students, teachers, and schools stacked up to the standards set by the panel and adopted by the nation's governors and the White House in 1989.

Questionable Progress. By broadening the high-school completion rate to include 19- and 20-year-olds, the panel claimed progress on the goal of high-school completion—now only 7% under the goal of a 90% completion rate. The other positive news in the first goals report concerned a decrease in drug abuse by teenagers and a slight improvement in mathematics and science achievement, compared with early in the 1980s.

The rest of the goals panel's report to the U.S. public described a baseline that was discouragingly low. For example, only one of every five students demonstrated competency in mathematics; the goal is to be first in science and math achievement by the year 2000. Another goal is for all children to be ready for school, but the panel learned that only 40% of three-to-five-year-olds from low- and moderate-income families were enrolled in preschool programs (75% of children from families with incomes above $75,000 attend preschools).

A very telling aspect of the first report of the goals panel was how much policymakers do not know about children and youth. The report has big gaps. For example, on the goal of school readiness, the panel could give itself only a grade of incomplete because there is no real way available yet to measure if a child is ready for school—and much controversy over what measurements to use. The report gives individual state reports, but they are full of blanks, either because the data were not collected or because they were not comparable across states. The National Education Goals Panel lamented this lack of reliable information and said the reports would become more complete as better systems for collecting data were developed.

Nevertheless, 1991 would be remembered by many policymakers as the year when they were inundated with data. Certainly by the end of the year the public had a much clearer idea of the status of U.S. children and youth than ever before. For example, the National Assessment of Educational Progress (NAEP) issued its first state-by-state comparison of student achievement—limited in the trial year to eighth-grade math. As might be expected, states with fewer students in large-city schools, with fewer students receiving free lunches, and smaller percentages of black and Hispanic students were the higher-performing states (North Dakota, Montana, Iowa, Nebraska, Minnesota, and Wisconsin).

The NAEP governing board also adopted a controversial standard that spells out what students should be able to do at certain levels—basic, proficient, and advanced. Its analysis of the 1990 math assessment, covering fourth and 12th grades as well as the state comparisons for eighth grade, said that less than 20% of the students in all of the grades reached the proficient level. Only 2.6% of high-school seniors achieved at the advanced level. The poor performance was not limited to groups that usually do not do well in math—minorities and females. "Even in the most successful demographic groups," said the NAEP governing board, "the majority of the students do not meet the performance standards set for the proficient level and only a small fraction of the students reach the advanced level." The use of proficiency levels, however, was questioned seriously by evaluators hired—then fired—by the NAEP, and the National Educational Goals Panel did not use the governing board's definitions, noting that its process had not been validated yet.

NAEP also reported that students were achieving at about the same levels in 1990 as they were 20 years earlier, gaining back the ground lost in the ensuing two decades in science, math, reading, and writing. In fact, students significantly had increased their abilities to solve complex problems in math and science. However, Secretary of Education Lamar Alexander (*see* BIOGRAPHY) noted that the standard of 20 years ago was not good enough for today's internationally competitive world.

U.S. Public and Private Schools

	1991–92	1990–91
Enrollment		
Kindergarten through Grade 8	34,313,000	33,765,000
High school	12,529,000	12,427,000
Higher education	14,105,000	13,558,000
Total	60,947,000	59,750,000
Number of Teachers		
Elementary and secondary	2,826,000	2,785,000
Higher	762,000	762,000
Total	2,588,000	3,547,000
Graduates		
Public and private high school	2,446,000	2,522,000
Bachelor's degrees	1,081,000	1,024,000
First professional degrees	75,000	67,000
Master's degrees	338,000	322,000
Doctor's degrees	39,000	36,000
Expenditures		
Public elementary-secondary school	$229,400,000,000	$212,900,000,000
Private elementary-secondary	19,200,000,000	18,100,000,000
Public higher	106,500,000,000	98,200,000,000
Private higher	58,700,000,000	54,300,000,000
Total	$413,800,000,000	$383,500,000,000

Status of Children. Other data reported during the year confirmed a growing disparity between the poor and the rich, with more than 20% of U.S. children now living in poverty. The Center for the Study of Social Policy did its own ranking of states on eight indicators of child well-being and found little to praise. It reported increases in the percentage of children living in poverty, the violent death rate among teenagers, the percentage of adolescents giving birth out of wedlock, and the juvenile incarceration rate. It also noted some improvement in the graduation rate. Other positive trends occurred in reducing percentages of low-weight births, infant mortality, and child deaths. Similar statistics were cited by the congressionally chartered National Commission on Children, a bipartisan group which spent two years investigating the status of children. (*See also* FAMILY.)

Another significant contribution to knowledge about U.S. youth was produced by the Children's Defense Fund (CDF), ordinarily known for its work with young children. It amassed data on adolescents and young adults, showing just how much things had changed from a few decades ago. For example, birth rates among unmarried teenagers and young women were higher than they ever had been—and teenagers with the poorest basic academic skills were most likely to have babies. On every possible indicator, including quality of teachers, availability of technologies, and access to college-preparatory courses, schools enrolling a large percentage of minority students compared unfavorably with other schools, said CDF.

The public also found out in 1991 what various groups thought about the preparation of young people for jobs or for college. The opinions split down the middle, with employers and higher-education officials not pleased, but recent high-school graduates and their parents quite satisfied with the education system. On 15 indicators—including skills, attitudes, and capacity to learn—only 30% of employers responded positively. However, the average of positive responses by students was 70% and by their parents, 65%. The Louis Harris poll, conducted for the National Education Goals Panel and the Committee for Economic Development, concluded that "the current crop of students and their parents are deluding themselves." Nonetheless, all of the groups, including 87% of recent high-school graduates, were overwhelmingly in favor of higher achievement standards.

In many ways, studies and initiatives on school-to-work transitions combined a number of issues that dominated in 1991, including curriculum and national assessment. More than 400 educators, youth-training experts, and researchers had come together at the end of 1990 to launch a national campaign for youth ap-

Home Schooling

Growing numbers of U.S. parents are teaching their school-aged children at home, instead of sending them to public or private schools. In the 1990–91 school year, an estimated 249,000 to 359,000 children did their kindergarten to grade-12 schoolwork at home.

Out of necessity, schooling at home was common in early America. However, the growth of public schools and compulsory-education laws almost eliminated it by the middle of the 20th century. A few religious groups—Seventh Day Adventists, Mormons, the Amish, and others—continued to consider it an option, but by the 1970s only about 20,000 children were in home schools. Then the contemporary home-schooling movement flowered. An estimate for fall of 1983 suggests that at least 50,000 children were being schooled at home. If present trends continue, the number will exceed 500,000 by the mid-1990s. This would be about 1% of the total school-aged population; or about 10% of the privately schooled population.

Parents' reasons for home schooling vary. Some want to spend more time with young children. Some believe they have a religious duty to school their children at home. Others feel that their child is not reaching his or her full potential in a regular classroom, or needs a unique program of instruction.

Legislation and Objections. At the outset of the modern home-school movement, many states did not allow the practice and home-schooling families operated underground. Today all states either make home schooling an option in the state's compulsory-education law or interpret the law to allow a school to meet in a home. States also have liberalized requirements for the home teacher. For example, parents do not need a teacher certificate, except in Michigan. Even there, a lower-court decision has restricted the scope of the requirement.

Some states test home-school students. While some families ignore the requirement, the tested group scores above average. This does not mean that home schooling produces above-average results. Some (less than half) of those tested are below average. Some of those who score above average could do so wherever they attended school.

The practice has been controversial. Those school officials who frown on the practice have prosecuted parents under state compulsory-education laws. Parents have fought back with lawsuits demanding a right to home school. Some courts have stricken compulsory-education laws because they are too vague. Some have stricken state regulations if they go beyond the terms of state law. Other courts have allowed prosecution of parents if they find that the home school does not meet state requirements. Thus far, legislatures always have responded favorably to home schoolers seeking more lenient compulsory-education laws. To be sure, legislative change takes time, but after several years of lobbying, home schoolers generally win favorable changes in state law.

In mid-1990 the national Parent-Teachers Association (PTA) had a resolution opposing the practice and the National Education Association (NEA) had a resolution calling for more rigorous regulation of it. Other groups, including the American Civil Liberties Union (ACLU), maintain that parents have a constitutional right to home school. Even though most Americans do not approve of home schooling, a majority responding to a Gallup poll believes that parents have a right to do it.

PATRICIA M. LINES

Editor's Note. Patricia M. Lines, holder of the Haynes Chair in the Department of Education at Catholic University of America in Washington, DC, is the author of *Estimating the Home School Population* for the U.S. Department of Education. The statistical estimates included in this report are hers.

prenticeships. The U.S. Department of Labor increased its investment in apprenticeship programs, and the General Accounting Office (the investigative arm of Congress) recommended that cooperative education be restructured along the lines of apprenticeship systems in Europe, with students receiving skills certificates that would be valid nationwide. In addition, foundations gave their support to the development of a performance-assessment system, recommended by the National Center on Education and the Economy, which all 16-year-olds would be required to pass. (A bill in Congress also supported the idea.)

However, the major school-to-work transition event was the release of the report of the National Commission on Achieving Necessary Skills (SCANS), sponsored by the U.S. Department of Labor. The report, "What Work Requires of Schools," outlined three foundations—basic skills, thinking skills, and personal qualities—necessary to be effective in five competencies—resources (allocating time, money, materials), interpersonal skills, information (acquiring and using data), understanding social and organizational systems, and using technology. These were drawn up by business people, educators, and researchers.

The commission anticipated its recommendations would become part of President Bush's America 2000 initiative; Oregon stepped out in front by approving a plan for an "exit" proficiency examination for high-school students that would certify them for work or postsecondary education.

Federal Action. To give the public something far-reaching and mold-breaking to think about in education, President Bush announced his America 2000 plan, with a cornerstone being a model school in each congressional district, plus another two schools in each state. These schools would be selected, funded, and evaluated through a development corporation supported by up to $200 million raised from the private sector. The president's plan also called for a national assessment system, an expansion of school-choice plans to include private schools, and support for alternate certification of educators. However, despite these preparations, the House and Senate each drafted their own bills for elementary and secondary school reforms instead of acting on the president's proposed package.

With no control over the private-sector approach in the president's plan, Congress chose to go categorical in 1991. By the fall there were dozens of pieces of proposed legislation dealing with a children's trust fund, teacher recruitment and training, youth training, merit schools, technology, and research. Congress went head-on with the governors and the White House over the development of national standards and assessment. A National Education Goals Panel subgroup on standards and assessment was reconfigured to help soothe the bad feelings that had developed because Congress had been left out of the national goals process. The new congressionally established National Council on Education Standards and Testing, which includes members of Congress, was charged to study the feasibility and impact of national standards and testing. However, without the congressional delegation present, the council voted in August to go ahead with the setting of standards and development of a national assessment system. At its September meeting, key members of Congress politely but firmly asked that the decision be rescinded until the required studies were completed.

It became obvious in public debates of the two groups—the goals panel and the standards/assessment council—that there was strong sentiment for the setting of curriculum standards and for a national testing system. On the latter issue, the proposal receiving the most attention was one presented by a task force headed by Lauren Resnick of the University of Pittsburgh, calling for voluntary participation in regionally developed tests that would be calibrated to a national one. NAEP would not be discarded but would be a parallel system providing needed trend data. This was the plan initially adopted by the council but temporarily, at least, halted by congressional opposition. Funding for a national assessment system would depend upon Congress' support.

Curriculum. Former Tennessee Gov. Lamar Alexander took over the secretary of education post in March, succeeding Lauro F. Cavazos. As a former chairman of the National Governors' Association, Alexander had started that organization on the road to investment in education reform and was well-respected among his former colleagues. However, Alexander's strong defense of the Bush administration's plan to expand choice to private schools did not sit well with influential members of Congress. Secretary Alexander also was criticized on Capitol Hill for threatening to withhold funds from a regional accrediting agency because of its use of multicultural indicators in staffing and curriculum to evaluate schools and colleges.

In the curriculum area, multiculturalism came to the forefront during 1991 in several ways. The release of a report on reshaping the social-studies curriculum in New York state to reflect "multi-perspectives" brought a rash of media attention to multicultural issues throughout the country—and to the growing number of ethnic/language minorities in the schools. (It was up to 31% in New York, more than half in California.) The report gave more attention to non-Western cultures. Christopher Columbus, for example, would be portrayed as a voyager to an already settled land, not the discoverer of America.

What the media coverage portrayed, however, was a movement already under way, especially in urban school districts, to provide cultural-awareness training to teachers and integrate multicultural perspectives into the curriculum. However, most headlines began to center on one particular form of multiculturalism—ethnic separatism—reflected in efforts for separate schools for black males. Appalled at the high failure rate of black males, Milwaukee school officials approved separate schools for this population in order to provide an Afrocentric curriculum and better support for black males. Detroit soon followed with a similar plan, but both school districts modified their plans to avoid legal problems, agreeing to admit girls as well as boys.

In another curriculum area, the Carnegie Commission on Science, Technology, and Government concluded that only the federal government and presidential leadership could gain the attention of the public and educators and provide sustained support for mathematics and science reform. The commission wanted a separate agency—a Joint Office for Math and Science Improvement—run by the U.S. Department of Education and the National Science Foundation. But perhaps the most unifying curriculum development of the year

University Research

© Matthew McVay/Saba

The practice by which U.S. colleges and universities engaged in federally funded research recoup overhead expenses by overbilling the U.S. government came under fire in 1991. The issue came to light when a federal auditor revealed that Stanford University was recouping expenses for such unrelated costs as depreciation on a 72-ft (22-m) yacht and flowers and other items for the home of the university's president. The incident unleashed a U.S. congressional investigation not only into the charges against Stanford but into the entire system of underwriting university-based research. Other universities whose expenses were questioned included the University of Michigan, Massachusetts Institute of Technology (MIT), Harvard Medical School, and Johns Hopkins University.

For Stanford and other major universities, research grants are big business. In 1991 alone, Stanford received nearly $300 million in such funds. Under rules started after World War II, when the federal government became the prime sponsor of university research, the government agreed to pay a portion of the overhead costs of such work. Such costs involve administration, libraries, utilities, and building maintenance; are in addition to the researchers' salaries and equipment costs; and are based on a rate negotiated by the school and the government. For example, Stanford's rate was 74%—later dropped to 55.5%; in other words, it would receive $1.74 ($1.55) for every $1 in research funds granted.

Although Stanford University agreed to pay back more than $2 million to the U.S. government and, together with other schools, was overhauling its accounting practices, the scandal was cited as a main reason why Donald Kennedy (*above*) submitted his resignation as the university's president. U.S. Rep. John D. Dingell, chairman of the subcommittee investigating the affair, called it "a story of excess and arrogance, compounded by lax governmental oversight."

was the creation of the Alliance for Curriculum Reform, representing more than 30 national curriculum organizations. The alliance said it was not seeking a national curriculum but a voice in the development of national curriculum standards in various disciplines.

Funding and Leadership. Considering the fiscal problems of the states, it was logical that most of the debate, policy-making, and innovation in school reform took place at the national level during 1991. The final results of the various state legislative sessions were not as drastic as had been expected. Still, teacher-salary increases were the smallest in many years, more than half of the states made cutbacks or held steady on school spending, and some school districts declared bankruptcy. The grand experiment in Chelsea, MA, for example, where Boston University had made a ten-year commitment to improving the school system, was jeopardized by the city's bankruptcy. Richmond, CA, which had relied upon a districtwide—and expensive—school choice plan to improve academic achievement and integration, had to be rescued by the state. New Jersey state school officials took over a second urban school system because of continued student failure.

As great as the financial problems of urban school systems were their leadership crises. This was reflected by the more than two dozen vacancies among urban superintendencies during the year. Apparently, there were several root causes, including a dwindling number of experienced minority administrators prepared for top jobs and simmering conflicts between urban superintendents and their school boards. In fact, the leadership capabilities of school boards were being questioned generally. In Boston, city political leaders eliminated problems with a fractious school board by changing it to an appointed board. New studies by the Institute for Educational Leadership and the Twentieth Century Fund focused on the weaknesses in the current school-governance structure and how to improve school-board effectiveness. Their recommendations were due in 1992.

Anne C. Lewis
Education Policy Writer

EGYPT

The Persian Gulf war overshadowed both domestic and foreign events in Egypt during 1991 (*see* FEATURE SECTION, page 36). The economic crisis precipitated by the war was relieved somewhat as a result of increased foreign aid provided in compensation for Egypt's role in the conflict. Domestic unrest continued, but without undermining government stability or President Hosni Mubarak's dominant position in the country's internal and foreign affairs.

Economic Rescue. Egypt's already precarious economy was worsened severely by the Persian Gulf crisis, first by severing relations with Iraq during 1990, then by the war itself in early 1991. The number of Egyptians who lost their jobs in Iraq and Kuwait and returned home to face unemployment was estimated at between 500,000 and 700,000. As a result the country lost more than $2 billion in foreign-currency remittances these workers had been sending home annually. The tourist economy, another mainstay of scarce foreign currency, collapsed. Although ancient monuments and historical sites closed during the war were reopened in March, regional instability continued to keep visitors away. Officials estimated that some $2 billion was lost during the 1991 tourist season. Suez Canal revenues, another principal hard-currency earner, also declined early in 1991 because of the war. Revenues from oil exports diminished because of increased consumption by a growing population. When the war ended President Mubarak calculated overall losses at some $20 billion.

In appreciation for its assistance during the war the United States and several other creditor nations agreed to wipe out nearly half of Egypt's $50 billion foreign debt, which had made it the world's fourth major debtor among developing nations. At a meeting during May of the so-called Paris Club, negotiators from 17 creditor nations hammered out a package of write-offs and reschedulings to be stretched out until 1994. Of the $20 billion owed to the seven major creditors, 15% would be written off immediately. Another 15% reduction was linked to a tough economic-reform program devised by the International Monetary Fund (IMF). A final 20% cut would be implemented in 1994, contingent on progress toward realization of the IMF-inspired economic-liberalization program. The United States previously had written off some $7 billion in military debts owed by Egypt as a reward for support in the anti-Iraq coalition. The Gulf states also had forgiven another $7 billion as their share of the reward. If the debt-reduction program was implemented as planned, Egypt's total remaining debt would be reduced to $20.2 billion, much of it long-term at low interest rates.

In addition to its war costs, Egypt would have to pay a severe economic price for the debt-reduction package. According to the agreement, Egypt would be required to impose a 10% sales tax on its citizens, increase domestic energy prices, and raise customs duties on imported items. Interest and currency-exchange rates would continue to be decontrolled; government subsidies on basic food items such as bread and meat would be reduced greatly, leading to substantial price increases. Plans also were introduced to privatize state-owned industries accounting for 70% of industrial production.

Among many Egyptians there was apprehension that these IMF terms could lead to unrest and mass protests against sharp price increases in basic household items long kept inexpensive by government subsidies. The price of kerosene for cooking stoves increased by 50% during May; utility costs also rose between 30% and 50%. Saudi Arabia and Kuwait promised to help relieve the situation by employing large numbers of Egyptians to compensate for those who lost their jobs during the war. The number of Egyptians employed in Saudi Arabia increased to more than 300,000. Kuwait promised large contracts to Egypt to help reconstruct war damage.

Other Domestic Matters. Although groups ranging from Muslim fundamentalists to small leftist factions opposed Egypt's role in the Persian Gulf war, the government prevented protests from escalating into major incidents. Riot police broke up an antiwar demonstration by pro-Saddam Hussein leftists early in February. Cairo University was closed briefly at the end of that month when an estimated 2,000 students held an antiwar demonstration. In May the People's Assembly extended for three years emergency legislation adopted in 1981 after President Anwar Sadat's assassination.

Far more serious than protests against the war were continued outbreaks of ethnic violence in various parts of the country. Clashes between police and Islamic militants, and attacks by the militants on Coptic Christian

EGYPT • Information Highlights

Official Name: Arab Republic of Egypt.
Location: Northeastern Africa.
Area: 386,660 sq mi (1 001 450 km²).
Population (mid-1991 est.): 54,500,000.
Capital: Cairo.
Government: *Head of state,* Mohammed Hosni Mubarak, president (took office Oct. 1981). *Head of government,* Atef Sedki, prime minister (took office November 1986). *Legislature* (unicameral)—People's Assembly.
Monetary Unit: Pound (3.3305 pounds equal U.S.$1, free-market rate, Dec. 3, 1991).
Gross Domestic Product (1989 est. U.S.$): $38,300,000,000.
Economic Index (1990): *Consumer Prices* (1980 = 100), all items, 477.3; food, 548.3.
Foreign Trade (1990 U.S.$): *Imports,* $9,202,000,000; *exports,* $2,234,000,000.

churches and other property occurred periodically throughout Egypt. One of the most severe incidents was in the Imbaba section of Cairo where two churches, homes, and shops were burned in a flare-up between Muslims and Christians leading to the arrest of several hundred rioters.

A cabinet reshuffle in May gave Egypt a new foreign minister, Amr Moussa, who replaced Ismat Abd al-Magid. Al-Magid was elected secretary-general of the Arab League, whose headquarters had been moved back to Cairo from Tunis in 1990. The new defense minister was Gen. Muhammed Hussein Tantawi, a veteran of five wars who had been chief liaison officer with U.S. forces in the Gulf war.

Diplomacy. As the Gulf war approached, Egypt increased the number of its troops in the combat zone to more than 38,000, the largest Arab contingent. Egyptian casualties were light —19 killed and 74 wounded during hostilities.

After the war Egypt joined seven other Arab countries in the Damascus Agreement, providing for a multilateral Arab force to maintain future Gulf security. In August, President Mubarak withdrew all Egyptian forces from the Gulf region because of his disappointment in the economic assistance he was to receive from his Gulf allies. The reason for the withdrawal was given as Mubarak's opposition to participation of non-Arab (Turkish and Iranian) forces in regional security arrangements.

Relations with Libya improved greatly as President Mubarak ordered removal of all border barriers between the two countries. Cross-border traffic surged and trade between Egypt and Libya increased to an all-time high.

Egypt participated in the Madrid Middle East peace conference in October as an observer and played an active role as intermediary in making arrangements for the conference.

DON PERETZ
State University of New York, Binghamton

ENERGY

Historically, it always has taken a major crisis to force Americans to reassess their energy-consumption habits, and 1991 proved no exception. The year began with a major U.S. military offensive in the Persian Gulf to drive Iraqi forces out of Kuwait, a key Middle Eastern oil producer and U.S. ally that the Iraqis had occupied since August 1990. That occupation had caused a panic in world oil markets, sending the price of crude from $13 per barrel before the invasion to more than $40 by Jan. 1, 1991. Gasoline prices in the United States, by far the world's largest oil consumer, followed suit, rising about 30 cents per gallon as the crisis mounted.

In the United States the gyrations in oil prices sparked the familiar calls for a national energy policy that had accompanied oil crises since the 1970s. Early in 1991, President George Bush announced a new energy strategy aimed at reducing U.S. dependence on foreign oil, and a bill endorsing many of the administration's recommendations began to wend its way through Congress. But the initial enthusiasm for energy policy soon cooled as the feared disruption in world oil supplies never materialized. By March 1991, with Operation Desert Storm—the U.S.-led allied campaign in the Gulf—nearing completion, world oil prices had fallen to about $17 per barrel, only $4 more than before the Gulf crisis began. By the year's end, oil supplies were stable and prices were holding steady at $20-$22 per barrel. A national energy policy had taken a backseat and Congress adjourned in late November without acting on the issue.

Fossil Fuels. Once calm was restored to the world oil market, Americans resumed their old energy-consumption habits. Despite efforts to reduce oil consumption, including conservation measures and fuel-switching for electric utilities, industry, and homes, the United States continued to grow increasingly dependent on foreign oil in 1991, according to a congressional study released in October by the Office Of Technology Assessment.

As it had been for decades, oil was the leading source of energy in the United States in 1991, accounting for 41% of U.S. energy consumption and two thirds of the fuel used for transportation. As a fossil fuel—the end product of a geological process requiring millennia to complete—oil is a finite resource that was being consumed faster than new reserves could be discovered. With domestic oil production falling since 1970's peak of more than 9 million barrels per day to less than 7 million barrels per day in 1991, the United States has grown increasingly dependent on foreign sources. Imported oil now was accounting for 40% of the oil consumed in the United States.

Coal and Natural Gas. The other main fossil fuels, natural gas and coal, each accounted for about one quarter of U.S. energy supplies in 1991. In contrast to the situation with oil, with gas and coal the United States could rely on domestic sources of both to run its plants and generate electricity. Natural gas has become more widely used for home and business heating since the energy crises of the 1970s made it a cheaper and more reliable source of energy than oil. Thanks to recent technological advances, natural gas also has emerged as a feasible alternative for powering automobiles.

As the United States' most abundant energy source, coal held out the promise of energy independence. But coal also is the dirtiest fossil fuel and its use produces severe environmental damage, including air pollution and acid rain. Research continued to enhance the efficiency of scrubbers—special filtering devices installed inside smokestacks of coal-fired plants. But they still were of limited effectiveness.

Environmental Impact. Joining the call for reducing America's growing dependence on foreign oil were scientists who cited the potentially devastating environmental impact of burning fossil fuels. Oil and coal, in particular, were blamed for a progressive rise in the Earth's surface temperature over the past four decades. Many believe that the global warming trend occurs because the carbon dioxide and other gases released during fossil-fuel combustion trap the Sun's radiant energy inside the atmosphere, acting much the same as the glass ceiling and walls of a greenhouse. In December scientists at the Worldwatch Institute, an environmental research organization in Washington, DC, reported that global emissions of carbon dioxide actually fell slightly in 1991. But they attributed the dip in greenhouse-gas emissions to the collapse of industrial production in the Soviet Union and Eastern Europe.

The Bush administration remained skeptical about global warming and called for further scientific research into the phenomenon. Consistent with this stance, the United States was the only leading energy-consuming nation that remained opposed to setting timetables for limiting national carbon-dioxide emissions. Limits on greenhouse-gas emissions were the object of international negotiations throughout 1991 and the subject of a treaty scheduled to be signed in June 1992 at the Earth Summit in Rio de Janeiro. Because the United States was the biggest emitter of greenhouse gases, the Bush administration's position placed that treaty in jeopardy. (*See also* ENVIRONMENT.)

Alternative Energy Sources. The link between fossil-fuel consumption and environmental degradation lent new weight to calls for the substitution of renewable-energy sources for traditional fuels. Unlike fossil fuels, renewable sources cannot be depleted easily and are widely available. They exploit the energy contained in such natural forces as wind, moving water, and the Sun's rays. More-recent renewable-energy technologies also permit the production of ethanol, a clean-burning fuel, out of the fermentation of agricultural waste. Renewable-energy sources, especially solar power, were promoted as a matter of federal energy policy during the oil crises of the 1970s. When the world oil market became glutted and oil prices fell during the 1980s, however, the Reagan administration eliminated most of the development incentives.

By 1991 renewable sources provided less than 10% of U.S. energy sources, most of which was generated by hydroelectric dams. There is little room for expansion of hydroelectricity in the United States because the most suitable rivers already are dammed. The biggest obstacle to widespread use of other alternative energy sources continued to be cost; oil,

© Matthew L. Wald/NYT Pictures

The Yankee Rowe nuclear plant in Rowe, MA, began closing in October 1991 after the Nuclear Regulatory Commission said it had "reduced confidence" in the plant's safety.

coal, and gas still were cheaper to use than most renewable sources. But as research and applications expanded in 1991, the cost of using renewable sources continued to fall. And because the price of oil was projected to rise over the long run as world supplies dwindled, the U.S. Department of Energy predicted that renewable-energy sources may satisfy almost one third of U.S. energy needs by 2030.

Nuclear Power. As an energy source that normally emits virtually no greenhouse gases or other pollutants and is practically immune to international supply disruptions, nuclear energy offered solutions to many of the problems debated in 1991 and, in fact, nuclear power from the existing 111 operating plants in the United States provided 19% of the electricity in the nation in 1991. But the U.S. nuclear-power industry continued to flounder amid lasting concern about the safety of nuclear reactors following the 1979 accident at Three Mile Island outside Harrisburg, PA, the catastrophic explosion of the Soviet reactor at Chernobyl in 1986, and the disposal of the radioactive waste the plants generate.

Despite the fact that no new nuclear reactors had been ordered since 1978, the nuclear-power industry looked forward to renewed growth in the 1990s as concern builds over the nation's growing reliance on foreign oil supplies. The federal government supported the development of new and safer light-water reactors that were expected to be approved by the Nuclear Regulatory Commission as soon as 1992.

National Energy Policy. The need for a comprehensive national energy policy topped the federal legislative agenda. Early in the year, while U.S. troops still were engaged in the Gulf war, the Bush administration presented its strategy for reducing the country's dependence on foreign sources of oil. Many of the administration's recommendations found their way into a massive energy bill sponsored by Sen. J. Bennett Johnston (D-LA). The National Energy Strategy bill addressed many areas of energy policy, including regulation of the electric-utilities industry, gas-pipeline construction, and licensing procedures for nuclear-power plants. The bill also required greater use of cars powered by methane and other alternative fuels and called for more federal energy research.

To the dismay of environmentalists and other administration critics, however, both the Bush and the Johnston proposals relied heavily on expanding domestic oil production and less on promoting conservation and the development of alternative energy sources to wean the country of its dependence on foreign oil. Critics were incensed particularly over the bill's provision to promote exploratory drilling for oil in Alaska's Arctic National Wildlife Refuge, which oil analysts think harbors the biggest remaining untapped oil reserve in the United States. Citing the 1989 *Exxon Valdez* oil spill, environmentalists countered that the pristine wilderness area should not be exposed to the danger of a similar catastrophe just to provide a temporary boost to the country's dwindling oil supplies. The debate ended in deadlock with a November filibuster effort succeeding in blocking Senate action for the year.

The main alternative to the energy-strategy bill was an initiative to cut oil consumption by raising gasoline-mileage standards for new cars. Initially introduced in 1975 in the wake of the first major oil crisis, Corporate Average Fuel Economy (CAFE) standards had forced automakers to make smaller, lighter, and more energy-efficient cars. The standards had been relaxed, however, by the Reagan administration. The 1991 bill, introduced by Democratic Sen. Richard H. Bryan of Nevada, would require automakers to raise CAFE standards 40%, from 27.5 miles per gallon to 38 miles per gallon by 2001, a step supporters said would save 2 million barrels of oil per day. Automakers claimed the tougher standards would pose an intolerable financial burden for the industry at a time when it already was weakened by foreign competition. This energy bill also failed to gain final action before Congress adjourned.

State Initiatives. Even as national energy policy stalled in Congress, U.S. consumers faced requirements from other sources to change their energy habits. California, which suffered some of the worst smog conditions in the country, took the lead in introducing strict new rules on auto emissions and fuel requirements. The state required oil refiners to begin selling gasoline that produces 30% to 40% less smog than current blends no later than 1996. California also announced that automakers would be required in 1994 to begin selling cars that produce much less pollution. By 2003, one car in ten sold in California must be free of harmful emissions, that is, powered by electricity or hydrogen fuel cells.

California served as a model for other smog-ridden states. The District of Columbia and nine Eastern states from Virginia to Maine announced that they jointly would adopt California's tough auto-emission standards. Together with Illinois and Texas, which also expressed interest in adopting California's standards, those states accounted for almost half the cars sold in the United States. With so many consumers living under the strict rules, automakers were faced with the need to develop cars powered by electricity or hydrogen before the end of the decade.

There were signs that the state initiatives already were affecting production decisions by U.S. automakers. In November, General Motors Corp. announced plans to introduce in 1992 Chevrolet Luminas that run on either methanol or gasoline—the first "variable-fuel" cars ever to be sold to the public in the United States. Ford Motor Co. followed suit with a plan to sell vans and Taurus sedans that also run on either ethane or gasoline. (*See* SIDEBAR/AUTOMOBILES.)

The absence of a national energy policy did not prevent the nation's electric utilities from promoting one of the most innovative conservation ideas of recent years. Forced by the 1990 Clean Air Act to reduce their emissions of sulfur dioxide, a greenhouse gas produced by burning coal, electric utilities in many states took steps to meet the bulk of the growing demand for electrical power through conservation efforts rather than simply by burning more fuel. In many parts of the country, utilities encouraged conservation by subsidizing the purchase of new energy-saving light bulbs and efficient electrical motors.

MARY H. COOPER
"CQ [Congressional Quarterly] Researcher"

ENGINEERING, CIVIL

Advances in materials and technology continued in civil engineering in 1991; major repair projects advanced or were completed.

Restorations and Repairs. In 1991 the Portland, OR, district of the U.S. Army Corps of Engineers wrapped up a major portion of the $1 billion cleanup and restoration of the area damaged when Mount St. Helens erupted in 1980, killing 60 people and wreaking havoc throughout the Northwest, particularly up and down the Columbia River. The Corps built two permanent structures to ensure the safety of the area. Because the eruption had enlarged Oregon's Spirit Lake dangerously, a permanent outfall tunnel was installed to hold it to a safe level. Engineers can adjust the flow of the intake structure to lower the lake level even further if the volcano should erupt again. But releasing water from Spirit Lake would move sediment throughout the Columbia River and its tributaries. The eruption already had caused the river to silt up, halting river traffic. So the Corps designed a sediment-retention structure to keep the river flowing freely. For their efforts, the American Society of Civil Engineers awarded the agency the Outstanding Civil Engineering Achievement Award for 1991.

The Corps would remain busy well into the 1990s, as the agency was beginning work on the Santa Ana River Mainstream Project in southern California. When completed at the turn of the century, the $1.45 billion project will eliminate one of the worst flood threats in the United States. The Corps will oversee construction of a new dam in the Santa Ana River Canyon, raise the Prado Dam near Corona, CA, by 28 ft (8.53 m) and add 2,000 acres (810 ha) of reservoir, restore more than 20 mi (32 km) of the concrete floodwall along the Santa Ana River, and upgrade more than 23 mi (37 km) of the river's existing channel.

Also in southern California, the 50-year-old Coachella Canal was found to be leaking 115,000 acre-feet (141.45 billion l) of water annually. Without draining the canal, engineers relined it with 60-ft x 200-ft (18.3-m x 61-m) geosynthetic sheets. This relining, under the direction of the U.S. Bureau of Reclamation, was the first such use of a geosynthetic in North America.

Materials and Technology. Geosynthetics, or geotextiles, increasingly appear in civil-engineering works due to their durability and cost effectiveness. More than 800 million sq yds (668 901 890 m^2) have been used in recent years for landfill liners, highway construction landscaping and reinforcement projects, and flood control, according to the North American Geosynthetics Society. Dr. Robert Koerner, director of the Geosynthetics Research Institute at Drexel University, predicted the materials eventually would become competitive with steel and concrete in civil-engineering applications. Geosynthetics are made up primarily of melted and extruded polyester, nylon, polypropylene, and high-density polyethylene.

A discovery about another civil-engineering material, asphalt, may eliminate potholes and ruts from highways. Researchers at the National Research Council's Strategic Highway Research Program in Washington, DC, have discovered the key chemical components, called amphoterics, that control asphalt's tendency to crack. Researchers were developing new tests to help refiners and manufacturers modify asphalt cement for better performance.

Concrete and steel continued to dominate public works. To protect these materials, engineers were installing cathodic systems. Cathodic protection works electrochemically by driving low-voltage current to steel, preventing chloride ions from reacting with steel reinforcing bars. This technology has been used on ship hulls, underground pipelines, and buried tanks, but is fairly new to bridge construction and rehabilitation projects.

The Brooklyn Battery Tunnel in New York would become the first tunnel in North America to have cathodic protection for its steel deck reinforcement. Engineers began installing the $15.2 million system in 1991. An inspection showed that the concrete in the tunnel had become saturated with chlorides from cars carrying de-icing salts. The corrosion had spread across the bottom of the roadway, damaging the reinforcing steel.

Repair efforts also were under way on the Washington, DC, Bi-County Water Tunnel. More than 6 mi (9.6 km) of steel will line the concrete tunnel as part of a $70 million fix enabling the tunnel to carry treated drinking water from the Potomac River to Maryland's Montgomery County. In 1987 a pressure test in the tunnel led to a structural failure.

Engineers would install the 96-inch (244-cm) internal-diameter liner with concrete backfill between the liner and the original tunnel. They would spray the full interior of the liner with .5 inch (3.2 cm) of cement mortar to prevent corrosion and would install a cathodic system to protect the tunnel from stray electrical currents.

In addition to concrete, steel, and asphalt, marble too falls prey to materials deterioration. In 1991 engineers installed sensitive instrumentation systems to document and analyze the movements of the Jefferson and Lincoln memorials in Washington, DC. Small sensors were placed across minute cracks to track slight movements of the monuments' structural materials. Information gleaned from the sensors would help determine whether the cracks are the result of characteristics of the particular stone, or due to influences from other parts of the structure or the surrounding land.

TERESA AUSTIN, *Free-lance Writer*

© J. Langevin/Sygma

The 1991 Persian Gulf war had a devastating effect on the environment as various actions by Iraqi troops led to the largest oil spill in history. The Iraqis also set fire to more than 600 Kuwaiti oil wells, causing extensive air pollution.

ENVIRONMENT

The war in the Persian Gulf inflicted 1991's most visible environmental scars. However, new research suggested that industrial and residential pollution pose more pervasive threats and health hazards.

War Wounds. Most Arab and Western industrial nations challenged Iraqi President Saddam Hussein's annexation of oil-rich Kuwait. While the United States and its allies waged war to free Kuwait, Hussein's armies unleashed a series of what since have been described as terrorist attacks on the environment.

The first of those attacks took place at the Kuwaiti port of Mina al-Ahmadi around January 20. Iraqi troops not only discharged several million barrels of crude oil there from five berthed supertankers but also opened an underwater pipeline carrying oil from onshore storage tanks to a tanker-loading terminal about 10 mi (16 km) offshore. Oil from these maneuvers caused the largest spill in history, as well as a slick that blackened beaches, killed more than 20,000 birds, and contaminated many fragile fish-spawning regions.

According to an October 25 Environmental Protection Agency (EPA) report to Congress, the initial spill totaled about 6 million to 8 million barrels of oil—up to 30 times as much oil as the 1989 *Exxon Valdez* accident had unleashed. The sabotage of several other facilities in Kuwait added hundreds to thousands of barrels more oil into the Gulf daily through April.

Moreover, oil experts note, because "light" Kuwaiti oil contains more volatile organic hydrocarbons than does the heavier Alaskan crude spilled by the *Exxon Valdez,* the Kuwaiti oil is more toxic. In all, only about 1.4 million barrels of that oil was recovered. Ecologists suspected it might take five years or more to assess the extent to which the remaining oil harmed the Gulf's fisheries, which had been among the most productive on Earth.

Before the United States and its allies drove Hussein's army out of Kuwait, Iraqi troops also set fire to more than 600 oil wells, posing a monumental environmental threat. The tons of black soot spewed into the atmosphere risked initiating a "nuclear winter"-style global cooling. However, by midsummer researchers from the United States and Europe were reporting that most of the sunlight-blocking soot particles were not remaining aloft high in Earth's atmosphere—where they could circle the globe and remain aloft for several years—but instead returned rather quickly to Earth in an acid rain. Though the fires polluted the air about Kuwait City with choking concentrations of soot, the October EPA report said that "there was no documented increase in the proportion of visits to hospital emergency rooms for acute upper- and lower-respiratory infections or asthma."

Stratospheric Ozone. On March 7 revisions to the Montreal Protocol went into effect. This international treaty limits the amount of stratospheric-ozone-depleting pollutants—chiefly chlorofluorocarbons (CFCs)—that nations may produce. By the year 2000, industrial nations must end production of CFCs, halons, and carbon tetrachloride completely. Developing nations have an additional ten years to phase out these chemicals.

The new limits had been prompted by a June 1990 report that stratospheric ozone—which shields plants and animals on Earth's surface from sunlight's biologically damaging ultraviolet radiation—had begun thinning even over the United States. Indeed, on April 4, 1991, EPA announced that new data suggested that the atmosphere above the United States was losing 6% to 8% of its ozone every ten years—double the previously suggested rate.

An annual thinning of ozone over the Antarctic also worsened in 1991. This seasonal ozone hole began a week earlier than normal—the second week in September. At its maximum in mid-October, the stratosphere contained just 54% of the ozone that had been typical for that time of year—a record low.

Global Warming. The United Nations worked to draft a climate treaty for signing in June 1992. But after a February 1991 meeting in Virginia and a September meeting in Nairobi, Kenya, the negotiators had resolved few of their divisive conflicts on how best to limit a global warming. The United States split from other industrial nations in its refusal to accept firm limits on when and how much it ultimately must cut carbon dioxide emissions. Developing countries also wanted far more financial help in paying for pollution-controlling technologies than the industrial nations were willing to offer.

Meanwhile, British scientists reported in January that, globally, 1990 had been the hottest year in more than 100 years—and a "likely" early sign that a greenhouse warming was under way. However, it may take several years to see a return to this warming trend, atmospheric scientists noted in June, because of the millions of tons of sulfur dioxide and other gases emitted by the eruption of the Philippine volcano Mount Pinatubo (*see* SIDEBAR/GEOLOGY). Pollutants released into the atmosphere by major volcanic eruptions often lead to a slight, several-year-long global cooling.

Air Pollution. More than 74 million Americans breathed air that violated at least one federal air-quality standard, EPA announced in a November 20 report on urban air-quality trends. For instance, it noted that 63 million people live in counties exceeding the smog-ozone limit, nearly 22 million are exposed periodically to carbon-monoxide levels above the federal standard, and almost 19 million inhaled levels of airborne particles exceeding the particulates limit. However, the report showed that most communities made substantial progress in reducing atmospheric levels of the most pervasive pollutants "without hindering this country's economic growth," noted EPA Administrator William K. Reilly.

Acid Rain. Several new developments should help further improve air quality. On March 13, for instance, the United States and Canada signed a new air-quality treaty. Thirteen years in the making, the new accord requires the United States to reduce sulfur-dioxide emissions by the year 2000 to a level 10 million tons below its releases in 1980, and to establish a permanent national cap on these releases of 14.6 million tons annually by 2010. Total annual air releases of nitrogen oxides also would drop 2 million tons from 1980 levels by the year 2000. Canada agreed to make comparable reductions.

Automotive Limits. In May, EPA issued new emission controls for cars and trucks—the first major tailpipe-emissions reduction since 1981. Over a three-year period, manufacturers must begin reducing existing hydrocarbon emissions another 31% and nitrogen oxides another 60%.

On August 16 a landmark agreement was announced between EPA, gasoline makers, states, and the environmental community. It outlined how EPA would implement new rules for cleaner-burning gasolines as required under the Clean Air Act—such as characteristics that will be required of the new fuels, where they must be used, and when. In general the new gasoline must be sold in the nine smoggiest cities—regions accounting for 25% of all gas sales. However, any other community voluntarily may require the sale of this gasoline—a quick fix for reducing seemingly intractable smog-ozone problems. Ordinarily, EPA announces proposed rules, solicits public comments on them, issues a final rule—and then postpones final enactment of the change pending near-certain litigation by companies hardest hit under the new rules. But in the cleaner-gasoline decision, all affected parties helped draft the rules—with the understanding that none later would sue to delay their implementation.

Air Pollutants. In another example of EPA's new strategy of prompting rapid, cost-effective change, its administrator sent letters to leaders of the nation's 600 largest industrial polluters. He asked these companies to agree voluntarily to cut their emissions of the 17 air pollutants that EPA had identified as posing the biggest toxic risks to health—at least 33% by the end of 1992, and to just 50% or less of 1988 levels within another three years.

EPA's traditional rule-making procedures typically take years. But by pointing out the cost savings that can occur by preventing pollution, the agency by July had won pledges from 200 companies to work toward achieving the voluntary limits that Reilly proposed.

Particulates. In mid-September, EPA announced plans to reduce the levels of particulates that it would allow diesel buses and trucks to emit. In explaining the move, Reilly noted that: "We have received more complaints about the huge, black billows of smoke from buses than any other issue relating to vehicles." Beginning with the 1993-model year, bus manufacturers must reduce their vehicles' emissions by 60%. The next year's emissions must drop another 50%-90% from uncontrolled levels. The new rules would phase in controls on buses in many large cities and on heavy-duty diesel-fueled trucks.

EPA epidemiologist Joel Schwartz reported data also indicating that particulates may be much more toxic than had been thought. By correlating air pollutants, daily weather, and mortality in five U.S. cities, he found that rates of nonaccidental deaths tend to increase and decrease in near lockstep with outdoor particulate levels. No other pollutant or weather characteristic showed a similar trend.

The magnitude of the effect was the same for each city—nearly a 6% increase in deaths from disease for every 100 micrograms of total particulates measured in the air. Moreover, this correlation was seen at even low-dust levels—in one city at just 23% of the federal limit. The finding suggests that up to 60,000 U.S. residents may die each year from levels of particulates at or below the current EPA standard, Schwartz concluded at a Society for Occupational and Environmental Health conference in March.

Drinking Water. EPA issued new federal limits for 38 drinking-water contaminants in January. They included 17 pesticides, ten volatile organic chemicals, polychlorinated biphenyls (PCBs), eight inorganic materials, and two water-cleaning chemicals. One third of these substances represent "probable" carcinogens.

© George Goodwin/Monkmeyer

In 1991 the U.S. Environmental Protection Agency issued new guidelines for 38 drinking-water contaminants. Lead joints remaining in old plumbing systems were a concern.

In May the environmental agency also lowered its drinking-water standard for lead, a toxic heavy metal, from 50 parts per billion (ppb) to just 5 ppb. Most lead in drinking water leaches out of lead pipes and pipe solder. EPA recommends that municipal water suppliers treat water having high lead levels with alkaline chemicals to reduce its corrosivity—and, hence, ability to leach lead. In announcing the new rule, EPA's Reilly said that "approximately 600,000 children will have their blood-lead content brought below our level of concern because of these standards."

But even that may not protect all children from lead's toxic effects. Data from the National Health and Nutrition Examination Survey of Mexican-American children showed that lead levels as low as 10 micrograms per deciliter (μg/dl) of blood stunted their height. Because a host of studies have shown adverse effects of low levels of lead in children, the Department of Health and Human Services announced on October 7 that it was revising the level of lead considered toxic in children to 10 μg/dl.

Endangered Species. In August 1986 the U.S. Fish and Wildlife Service (FWS) announced it would capture the world's last remaining black-footed ferrets. These 18 animals became the basis of an experimental breeding colony in Wyoming, which was aimed at saving the species from extinction. In early September 1991 wildlife officials began releasing 49 juveniles at Shirley Basin, WY—the first black-footed ferrets reintroduced into the wild.

The ten- to 14-week-old animals were let go into a village of prairie dogs. The ferrets not only eat prairie dogs but also live in abandoned prairie-dog burrows. Roughly 260 black-footed ferrets remained in captivity. And if all went well, FWS expected to release another 100 young animals in 1992.

Seven North American zoos established a similar species-survival program for Puerto Rico's crested toad in 1991. There are two genetically distinct populations of the species, separated by mountains. At most, an estimated 25 exist north of the mountains, and probably no more than 3,000 south of the geological divide. Some 700 tadpoles from a breeding pair at the Cincinnati Zoo—representing the northern crested toads—were distributed to other zoos for raising. Late in the year wildlife biologists expected to fly 600 of these thumbnail-sized toadlets home for reintroduction into the wilds. Their destination was to be a cattle trough the size of a small swimming pool—the only known breeding site for this northern population.

JANET RALOFF
Environment/Policy Editor, "Science News"

ETHIOPIA

Ethiopia's 17-year-old Marxist government led by Mengistu Haile-Mariam was toppled in 1991, replaced by a leadership once also steeped in Marxist ideology but now proclaiming itself pro-Western and supported by the United States. The 31-year struggle for Eritrean independence also came close to fruition. And all Ethiopian Jews were flown out of the country to Israel, most during the final days of Mengistu's regime.

Civil War Ends. President Mengistu Haile-Mariam, who headed a government that for almost two decades was viewed as one of the most revolutionary Marxist regimes in Africa, fled to Zimbabwe on May 21 after 14 years in power.

The beginning of the end was seen in February as the regions of Gondar and Gojjam were captured by the Tigre People's Liberation Front (TPLF). In May the TPLF occupied Wollo region, seizing Ethiopia's Third Army Division and isolating Addis Ababa from the northern sector of the country. As this was taking place the Eritrean People's Liberation Front (EPLF), which had fought for secession for 31 years, moved into Asmara, Eritrea's capital, and attacked and captured the port of Assab, the only port left through which Ethiopia could import goods. Ethiopia's northern army disintegrated as some troops fled to Djibouti, most were captured, and tens of thousands died. By the third week in May the Ethiopian military was in total disarray, the government was on the verge of collapse, and the TPLF was poised to invade the capital.

During most of the crisis in the Persian Gulf, Ethiopia consistently had voted in the UN to support U.S. efforts against Iraq, in some part to curry U.S. favor. In April, Mengistu also tried to appeal to the United States by shifting his cabinet, selecting more liberal pro-Western figures. Tesfaye Dinka became prime minister and Tesfaye Gebre-Kidan was made vice-president. Washington, however, which had opposed Mengistu's government from the beginning, was not appeased. Left with neither power, authority, nor political leverage, Mengistu deserted the country.

Tesfaye Gebre-Kidan became acting president in a scene reminiscent of the final days before the fall of Saigon. He begged the U.S. embassy to exert its good offices to obtain a cease-fire so that his government could retain power. He also sent Prime Minister Tesfaye Dinka to London to attend previously scheduled peace talks that had been arranged by U.S. Assistant Secretary of State for African Affairs Herman J. Cohen, to negotiate a cease-fire. But the United States refused to support a cease-fire; indeed it approved of the TPLF's plan to move into Addis Ababa immediately. On May 28, without much fighting, the capital was captured. Tesfaye Gebre-Kidan fled to the Italian embassy, where he remained, and Prime Minister Dinka received asylum in Washington. Seventeen years of communism in Ethiopia had ended.

© Gamma-Liaison

A group of Ethiopian Jews arrive in Israel. In the mission called "Operation Solomon," some 14,000 Jews were transported from Addis Ababa to Tel Aviv in late May 1991.

Meles Zenawi. The 36-year-old head of the Ethiopian People's Revolutionary Democratic Front (EPRDF)—a coalition of political groups dominated by the TPLF—led the new government upon his return to Ethiopia from London. Born in Adowa, Tigre, of peasant origin, Meles Zenawi attended high school in Addis Ababa and entered Addis Ababa University in 1973. Although he studied medicine he moved rapidly into politics after the 1974 revolution. In the mid-1970s he set up the Marxist-Leninist League of Tigre, which eventually became the core of the TPLF, to combat the Mengistu government from the left. The withdrawal of the Soviet Union from Ethiopia in 1990–91 and the terror of the Mengistu regime, along with the need to appease the United States as the sole remaining superpower, apparently turned Meles into a liberal democrat proclaiming the values of human rights and individual freedoms.

Beginnings. As the EPRDF organized itself to hold power, anti-U.S. demonstrations by segments of the largely Amhara population of

ETHIOPIA • Information Highlights

Official Name: People's Democratic Republic of Ethiopia.
Location: Eastern Africa.
Area: 471,776 sq mi (1 221 900 km^2).
Population (mid-1991 est.): 53,200,000.
Chief Cities (1984 census): Addis Ababa, the capital, 1,412,577; Asmara, 275,385; Dire Dawa, 98,104.
Government: *Head of state,* Meles Zenawi, transitional president (took office 1991). *Legislature*—Council of Representatives (transitional; established 1991).
Monetary Unit: Birr (2.07 birr equal U.S.$1, May 1991).
Gross Domestic Product (1989 est. U.S. $): $6,600,000,000.
Economic Index (Addis Ababa, 1990): *Consumer Prices* (1980 = 100), all items, 153.9; food, 149.5.
Foreign Trade (1988 U.S.$): *Imports,* $1,075,000,000; *exports,* $448,000,000.

Addis Ababa erupted in June. Blaming the United States for supporting the largely Tigrean leadership, riots broke out at the central market and some 40 people were shot and killed. Remnants of the defeated Ethiopian army attacked a munitions depot in Addis Ababa where more than 100 died.

Transitional Government. A conference attended by 24 political groups, with U.S. Assistant Secretary of State Cohen as an observer, established a national charter creating a transitional government. Made up of an 87-member council of representatives, the new government represented 27 ethnic and political groups. The council was given responsibility to draw up a constitution to be presented to a new National Assembly that would be elected by 1993. The charter guaranteed individual human rights; freedoms of expression, association, and assembly; and proclaimed that the overthrow of Mengistu provided "the peoples of Ethiopia with the opportunity to restructure the state democratically."

Of the 87 seats the EPRDF received 32, the Oromo Liberation Front (OLF) 12, and the Afar Liberation Front (ALF) three, with the remaining groups receiving one or two seats each; six seats remained vacant. Meles Zenawi was chosen transitional president and he appointed Tamrat Layne, an Amhara of the Ethiopian People's Democratic Movement (EPDM), as prime minister. Tamrat's appointment was met with opposition by the Oromos who, as the nation's largest ethnic group, demanded the position.

Eritrea. The EPLF, which had battled Ethiopian governments for three decades, attended the July 5 conference only as observers. Viewing Eritrea as virtually a sovereign state, the EPLF felt it was negotiating with Ethiopia as an equal. It achieved major political concessions from the conference as the national charter recognized an Eritrean provisional government, and further stated that in 1993 an Eritrean referendum held under United Nations auspices would be conducted so that Eritreans could decide whether or not they want independence. The United States, in a major policy shift, supported Eritrea's right of secession, something it consistently had opposed in the past.

The 46-year-old secretary-general of the EPLF, Isaias Afewerki, was selected by his organization to head Eritrea's provisional government. To prevent Ethiopia from being landlocked, Eritrea's port of Assab was made "a free port to Ethiopia." Until the referendum, high-level Eritrean and Ethiopian delegations were to be established in Asmara and Addis Ababa to facilitate cooperation. In essence, from 1991 to 1993, Eritrea was granted equal sovereignty with Ethiopia without independence.

Famine. With Oxfam America proclaiming in June that 7 million Ethiopians were at risk of famine, the EPRDF and the EPLF moved to organize famine relief. Eritrea, however, intermittently diverted food for Ethiopia coming through its ports to feed its own people, doing so to emphasize its status as a coequal with Ethiopia and not under its control. In addition, with roads having been destroyed, continuing drought, and almost no internal transportation facilities available, relief efforts were constrained even though the United States and Western Europe were shipping food supplies into the country. Under the new government, too, drought, famine, and malnutrition seemed to be permanent fixtures.

Airlift of Ethiopian Jews. In a massive and complicated effort Israel airlifted 14,500 Ethiopian Jews from Addis Ababa to Israel during a 36-hour period beginning May 25. With the Marxist state crumbling, Israel was frightened that the Jews would be caught in a vice between the rebels and the government. It paid a $35 million bribe to Mengistu-government officials to approve the airlift and successfully urged President George Bush to call for a 24-hour cease-fire during which time it removed the Jews. By late in the year the 2,600 Jews remaining in the country also were flown to Israel.

Endgame. Ethiopia's Marxist leadership had tried to construct a social and political revolution. Using the theories of Lenin and Stalin it had engaged the country in massive political upheaval in an attempt to resocialize the population toward Communist values. The revolution with its attendant terror failed and Mengistu, who originally was seen by many as a revolutionary hero, must be given much of the blame for the failure. His ideals turned into tyranny, his leadership into dictatorship. Corrupted by power he destroyed the very revolution he led. His ignominious departure symbolized the failure of his rule and the failure of communism in Ethiopia.

PETER SCHWAB
State University of New York at Purchase

ETHNIC GROUPS

The year 1991 raged with arguments about the roots and nature of the United States. The results of the 1990 census reaffirmed American diversity, while planning for the quincentenary of Christopher Columbus' discovery of America set off a debate about multiculturalism and the "ownership" of America's past (*see* FEATURE SECTION, page 76).

Multiculturalism. The issue of multiculturalism was effecting a major overhaul of U.S. historical writing and school curriculum. In California and New York state, attempts at a multicultural curriculum ignited charges of ethnic favoritism, falsifying the past, and using history for political propaganda. Adding to the controversy were efforts of universities to achieve ethnically diverse student populations through preferential admissions and required courses. Racial-ethnic tensions especially worsened in the University of California system, which favored black, Mexican-American, and American Indian applicants for admission in order to comply with the state's legislative directive to have the university reflect populations of high-school graduates. Asian Americans complained of the decline in the number of Asian students.

First Amendment rights and academic freedoms came under the spotlight in the cases of two City University of New York professors—one who opined that blacks were less intelligent than whites and another who maintained that Jews underwrote the slave trade and later conspired to denigrate blacks in movies. The university rebuked the professors but upheld academic freedom.

Reports of racial and ethnic violence were up in many areas—from black-Latino gang wars over turf in Los Angeles; to the Crown Heights section of Brooklyn, NY, where black-Jewish tensions exploded; to Dubuque, IA, where attempts to recruit a black population led to violence directed at the newly located black families. The beating of a black motorist, Rodney King, by Los Angeles policemen in March was videotaped and set off a debate on police brutality (*see* SPECIAL REPORT/CRIME).

The 1990 census told the tale of U.S. multiculturalism. It showed that the nation's racial makeup had changed more profoundly during the 1980s than at any other time in the 20th century. According to the census, one in every four Americans claimed African, Asian, Hispanic, or American Indian ancestry in 1990, as compared with one in five in 1980. The Census Bureau reported that the number of Asian Americans doubled and the Hispanic population grew by more than 50%. And more people listed themselves as American Indians.

The census also showed that the black population remained stable or declined in the metropolitan North and Midwest but rose in the Sunbelt and Pacific Northwest. Much of this was attributed to a search for jobs. A bureau survey admitted that it might have missed as many as 6 million Americans, including about 2 million blacks. A decision not to change the count angered some officials. Redistricting was an important issue following the 1990 census as minority groups invoked the Voting Rights Act and court decisions to challenge plans in numerous states and cities that gerrymandered minorities out of seats or did not afford them maximum representation.

Legislation, Court Ruling, and Studies. After a year of debate, President Bush signed a compromised civil-rights bill in November. The act expanded the rights of alleged job-discrimination victims to sue and collect damages, extended protection of the 1964 Civil Rights Act to U.S. companies operating overseas, and reversed or modified eight 1989 U.S. Supreme

Indian-like chants and a chopping arm motion known as the "tomahawk chop" were common cheers at Atlanta's Fulton County Stadium as the Braves went to the 1991 World Series. Various Native Americans not only protested the practices of the Atlanta fans but also the use of Indian terms for sports teams.

Court rulings that made it difficult for victims of job bias to win lawsuits against their employers. The bill also prohibits "race-norming"—the adjustment of employment tests to score individuals differently because of race.

In January the U.S. Supreme Court, in a 1972 case involving an Oklahoma City busing program, ruled that school systems that had "complied in good faith" with desegregation orders and eliminated the "vestiges of past discrimination . . . to the extent practicable" need not continue indefinitely such judicially mandated orders as busing. Meanwhile, figures on enrollment in historically black colleges showed that the number of blacks applying for admission increased dramatically in 1991. School districts across the United States reported that the percentage of blacks finishing high school had risen steadily. The U.S. Health and Human Services Department reported that blacks and American Indians bore the "disparate burden of poor health in this country." Asians were the healthiest group overall. Mexican-Americans, Puerto Ricans, and blacks had the least health-care coverage.

Blacks. On the political scene, U.S. Rep. William Gray (D-PA), who as House majority whip was the highest-ranking U.S. black official, resigned to accept the presidency of the United Negro College Fund. Jesse Jackson declined to join the field for the 1992 Democratic presidential nomination after Virginia Gov. L. Douglas Wilder, a black, stepped in. Race figured prominently in Louisiana where former Ku Klux Klansman David Duke rode to a runoff in the governor's contest by opposing hiring quotas and affirmative action and urging cutbacks in welfare. He lost the election, however—in part due to a heavy turnout by black voters. Kirk Fordice was elected Mississippi's first Republican governor since Reconstruction, on a call for repeal of the Voting Rights Act and the end to racial quotas under affirmative action. W. Wilson Goode retired after two terms as Philadelphia's first black mayor, but three major cities elected their first black mayors. Kansas City, MO, chose Emanuel Cleaver; Denver elected Wellington Webb; and Memphis chose Willie Herenton.

When U.S. Supreme Court Justice Thurgood Marshall resigned, President George Bush nominated another black man—U.S. Appeals Court Judge Clarence Thomas (*see* BIOGRAPHY)—to succeed him. Thomas' confirmation hearings were marked by charges that Thomas had sexually harassed Anita Hill, a former colleague, and by concerns about Thomas' support for civil rights. Thomas nevertheless was confirmed and joined the high bench in October.

Even as more blacks entered the middle class, the gap between the pay of blacks and whites widened and other blacks fell deeper into the "underclass" of poor and unemployed. Black leaders worried that blacks would suffer from military cutbacks as military service had been a route for blacks to achieve a better education, income, and career advancement.

The opening of the National Civil Rights Museum in Memphis, on the site where Martin Luther King, Jr., was shot in 1968, brought visitors but also criticism about "cheapening" King's memory with showmanship.

Hispanic Americans. The political power of Hispanics began to be recognized in 1991 as Gloria Molina was elected to the Los Angeles County Board of Supervisors and several big-city mayors appointed Hispanics to visible positions. Yet legislators proved reluctant in Illinois, Pennsylvania, and elsewhere to create Hispanic-majority congressional or legislative districts. Although Hispanic Americans' buying power increased by 70% between 1982 and 1990, they were twice as likely as anyone else to be poor. Only half of all Hispanic Americans had completed high school.

Native Americans. A major issue facing Indians in 1991 was the federal government's definition of tribal status. A dispute over the way to obtain such recognition—and the benefits that go with it—arose in July after the U.S. Select Committee on Indian Affairs granted federal recognition to the Mowa band of Choctaws over the objections of the Poarch band of Creeks, who wanted Congress to abide by the Bureau of Indian Affairs (BIA) standards. Federal legislation was introduced establishing an independent commission to oversee tribal recognition. Indian groups, meanwhile, continued efforts to reduce the authority of the BIA, which various Indian leaders charged with corruption and waste.

Indian preservationists won a major victory in March when the Smithsonian Institution announced an extensive repatriation policy for Indian relics and human remains. At the same time, the U.S. Forest Service approved exploratory oil and gas drilling on land sacred to the Blackfeet in Montana. The most controversial development was in Washington state where the Quinault Indian Nation embarked on a three-year experiment in self-government. Six other tribes joined the experiment. In April the Supreme Court cleared the way for the Mashantucket Pequot Indian tribe to open a casino in Connecticut that would be the largest in the nation run by an Indian tribe.

Asian Americans. Asian Americans remained the fastest-growing U.S. minority. Although Asian Americans had a median family income higher than that of whites, great disparities in wealth and culture divided them. In an educational switch, Asian Americans increasingly were abandoning the emphasis on sciences, engineering, and mathematics in favor of the humanities and social sciences.

RANDALL M. MILLER
Saint Joseph's University, Philadelphia

EUROPE

In 1991, Europe grappled with the problems arising from the collapse of Communist power in Eastern Europe. While disarmament negotiations made fast progress, Western plans for economic aid to Eastern Europe and the Soviet Union remained hesitant. The European Community (EC) continued to thrive economically, but negotiations for creation of an Economic and Monetary Union (EMU) and of a political union caused continual bickering among its 12 disparate members. Although the EC remained committed to achievement of full economic union by December 1992, many members questioned whether more effort should not be made to come to terms with the new political and economic realities in Eastern Europe and with the urgent problem of admitting to membership present applicants from Western Europe and future applicants from Eastern Europe.

Europe and the Soviet Union. The breakup of the Soviet Union and the collapse of the Communist Party had major consequences for the whole of Europe. The USSR desperately needed massive aid from the West. By August, at the time of the attempted coup by hard-liners, inflation was 100%, food supplies for the winter dangerously low, and production dropping. The estimated gross national product for 1991 was likely to be at least 18% less than in 1990, and perhaps as much as 25% less. Germany took the lead, pledging $33 billion in aid. The EC promised $1 billion in credits for food and technical assistance in 1991. But most European countries followed the United States in holding back large-scale assistance other than food supplies and advice until they were certain that the Communist command economy had been replaced by a genuine market economy. When Soviet President Mikhail Gorbachev made a dramatic appearance in July at the London meeting of the so-called G-7 countries (Canada, France, Germany, Italy, Japan, United Kingdom, and the United States) plus the EC, he was promised special associate status for the Soviet Union in the International Monetary Fund, and more technical aid. The failure of the West to offer more economic aid probably encouraged the coup planners to move.

Militarily, the weakening of the Soviet Union had positive results in encouraging disarmament. On Nov. 19–21, 1990, the heads of state or government of the 34 members of the Conference on Security and Cooperation in Europe (CSCE) met and signed an ambitious agreement on conventional forces in Europe. The forces were to be limited in size and armaments. CSCE also was given permanent institutions: a Conflict Prevention Center in Prague; a center in Warsaw to monitor elections; and a ministerial council. The Warsaw Pact, which had linked the East European countries in an anti-Western alliance since 1955, was disbanded officially in March. The last Soviet troops left Czechoslovakia and Hungary in June. Those remaining in Poland were the subject of current negotiations, while those in eastern Germany would be gone by the end of 1994. In July, at a summit meeting in Moscow, President George Bush and Gorbachev signed the Strategic Arms Reduction Treaty (START), in which they agreed to sharp reductions in the number of their nuclear warheads.

Finally, in September, Bush announced that he was withdrawing tactical nuclear weapons unilaterally and was ready to join the Soviet Union in banning land-based missiles with multiple warheads. Gorbachev replied with even further-reaching promises of nuclear disarmament, including reductions of strategic warheads to below the limits of the START treaty.

© Chip Hires/Gamma-Liaison

In mid-July 1991, British Prime Minister John Major (front row, center) *was host of the annual summit of the leaders of the Group of Seven (G-7) major industrial democracies and the European Community (EC). At the close of the meeting's regular session, the leaders met with Soviet President Mikhail Gorbachev at London's Lancaster House and offered the USSR a technical-assistance package.*

The North Atlantic Treaty Organization (NATO) made plans to reduce its own role. On May 28 its defense ministers agreed that U.S. military forces in Europe should be halved. Central Europe was to be defended by seven defense corps; and a Rapid Reaction Corps was to be organized for action outside Europe. Some protection even was offered to former Communist countries of Eastern Europe. The French, however, pressed for the strengthening of the nine-member Western European Union, which they proposed to make the defense arm of the EC, and in October joined Germany in planning the creation of a Franco-German brigade of 35,000 to 40,000 soldiers that could become the nucleus of a European army.

Hope and Fear in Eastern Europe. After free elections, beginning in East Germany in March 1990 and culminating in Albania in March 1991, the non-Communist governments (Czechoslovakia, East Germany, Hungary, Poland) or reforming governments of former Communists (Albania, Bulgaria, Romania) abandoned the economic links imposed on them by the Soviet Union. After January 1991, trade among them was conducted in hard currency. As a result, COMECON, the one integrative organization in Eastern Europe that had attempted ineffectually to coordinate economic planning and trade since 1949, ceased to exist. Following the lead of Poland and Hungary, the East European countries tried to shift their trade to the West, from where they hoped to gain investment capital for privatization of nationalized industries and opening of new ventures. Much hope was placed on the European Bank for Reconstruction and Development, which was inaugurated in London on April 15, 1991, and endowed—largely by the United States and Western Europe—with $12 billion to provide credit for private enterprises in Eastern Europe and the Soviet Union. A separate G-24 fund administered by EC would act as a clearinghouse for direct Western aid to East European trade and development. The three East European countries making the most rapid progress toward a creation of market economies (Czechoslovakia, Hungary, Poland) even declared their intentions of becoming full members of EC eventually, but they ran into stubborn opposition, especially from France. Large increases in Eastern Europe's exports of farm products and textiles would have compelled EC to increase purchases of its own farmers' surpluses and bloat the cost of the Common Agricultural Policy beyond the expected total of $43 billion for 1991. Moreover, EC warned the East European countries that they would have to make far greater economic changes before their memberships could be considered. This suspicion seemed justified by the difficulties Eastern European countries were undergoing. Inflation was expected to range from 36% in Hungary to 200% in Bulgaria, and a drop in industrial output from 4.5% in Czechoslovakia to 20% in Romania.

A Dynamic European Community. EC remained the powerhouse of the continent, increasing the attractiveness of membership to countries such as Austria, which had applied in 1989; Sweden, which applied in July; and Finland and Norway, which were considering application. After two years of bitter discussions, EC and the seven-member European Free Trade Association (Austria, Finland, Iceland, Liechtenstein, Norway, Sweden, and Switzerland), agreed in October to form a European Economic Area (EEA) which would be the world's largest trading bloc.

Meanwhile, within EC disagreements in the parallel talks on EMU and political union provoked tension. In 1989 it was proposed that EMU be created in three stages. In the first, which began on July 1, 1990, monetary policies were to be coordinated. In the second, a central EC bank was to be created and currencies aligned. In the third, EC would use a common currency. In March 1991, Germany attempted to delay establishment of a central bank, scheduled for 1994, and to impose stringent conditions for "convergence" of members' economies during the second stage. In October, however, it agreed that in the second stage, starting in 1994, a European Monetary Institute would coordinate monetary policies and that the Institute and the European Commission would report in 1996 whether the economies of a minimum of seven or eight members had "converged" sufficiently for them to create a currency union.

The failure of EC members to formulate a common policy in the Persian Gulf war emphasized the Community's need for common political institutions. A draft treaty presented by Luxembourg in June proposed that foreign, economic, and security policy should be administered separately, although by common institutions. The Dutch, however, who presided over EC from July, offered a federalist draft which would have strengthened the European Commission, Parliament, and Court, only to have the foreign ministers revert to the Luxembourg proposal in September. Meanwhile, the failure of EC's attempts to broker a cease-fire in the Yugoslav civil war illustrated the futility of attempting to implement an EC foreign policy without giving it military backing. At Maastricht, the Netherlands, in December, the European Council made major progress toward unification by agreeing to create a central bank and, by 1999 at the latest, to adopt the ecu as its common currency. The members also decided to adopt common foreign and security policies and to strengthen the Western European Union, the military organization, which nine EC members already had joined.

F. ROY WILLIS
University of California, Davis

FAMILY

Family leave, health care, economic and education conditions, as well as the effects of divorce and child abuse, continued to be issues of focus for the U.S. family in 1991.

Changes and Trends. The percentage of so-called traditional families—a married couple and one or more children under age 18—continued the decline begun in the 1970s, according to the U.S. Census Bureau. Only 26% of the nation's 93.3 million households met the definition of traditional in 1990 as compared with 31% in 1980 and 40% in 1970. Growth came in the number of single parents (up 41% from 1980) and unmarried couples living together (up 80%).

The number of men and women living alone also grew, from 18.3 million in 1980 to 23 million in 1990. And economic factors were cited as one reason for 32% of single men and 20% of single women ages 25–34 living with their parents in 1990.

Of the 9.7 million single-parent households, 8.4 million were headed by women. The number of babies born to single women also grew, according to the most recent figures. In 1988, 26% of newborns were born to single women, up from 18% in 1980.

Marriage. For those who did marry, marriage came later. The median age for a first marriage in 1990 was 26.1 years for men and 23.9 years for women, up from 24.7 and 22 years, respectively, in 1980.

The divorce rate in the United States continued to surpass that of other industrialized nations, with 1.2 million Americans divorcing in 1990. Debate on how this affects children intensified on the heels of the 1989 publication of a comprehensive study by Judith S. Wallerstein and Sandra Blakeslee, *Second Chances: Men, Women and Children a Decade After Divorce*.

Economics. Poverty continued to be a worry, especially for children. The Census Bureau found that the likelihood of a child living in poverty increased almost twofold when parents were separated or divorced. There was a 36% poverty rate among children whose parents had been single for four months. Lack of jobs, however, was not necessarily the reason for the poverty. According to a report by the Children's Defense Fund, 63% of families living below the federal poverty line—$12,675 in annual income for a family of four—had at least one wage-earning member. Additionally, almost one half of these families did not receive welfare and 55% lived in rural or suburban areas.

National Commission on Children. The National Commission on Children, headed by U.S. Sen. John D. Rockefeller IV (D-WV), issued its report in June 1991. The 34-member panel's chief recommendation was the adoption of a $1,000 federal-tax credit for every child under age 18. This tax credit would replace the current $2,150 per-child tax exemption and would be paid to low-income families even if they owed no taxes. The panel also urged more vigorous collection of child-support payments and recommended that welfare be reoriented as short-term relief.

Regarding education, the commission urged making Head Start programs available to every eligible three- and four-year-old and 30% of five-year-olds and allowing parents to enroll children in schools outside their geographic area. Also recommended were changes in federal funding policies so that there would be a greater incentive to keep troubled families together and a streamlining of the adoption process. On health care, the group was divided but the majority recommended developing a universal system of insurance coverage for pregnant women and children through age 18 and expanding existing health-care programs for low-income and medically underserved populations.

Family Leave. Although the U.S. Senate and House both passed national family-leave bills in October and November, respectively, they failed to meet in conference to develop a joint bill before Congress adjourned in late November. The legislation, which was expected to come up again in 1992, would require many employers to grant up to 12 weeks of leave for workers to care for a newborn, a newly adopted child, or a sick relative. President Bush had threatened to veto such a bill, saying that the matter should be answered by private industry and not by the federal government.

The idea of family leave seemed to be getting the attention of more employers as such businesses as Lotus Development and Eastman Kodak allowed men paternity leaves. The number taking such offers was small, but there were increasing signs that more men were willing to accept slower career advancement in exchange for time with their families.

Child Abuse and Foster Care. The number of reported cases of child abuse in the United States in 1990 climbed yet again, rising 4% from the previous year. More than 2.5 million cases of abuse were reported and more than 1,200 children died from abuse-related incidents. An independent study also showed that children who are abused or severely neglected have lower IQs and an increased risk of depression, suicide, and drug problems.

The foster-care system received attention as Congress and the Bush administration debated how best to spend limited funds, particularly as the caseloads of troubled children rise. At the heart of the debate was the current funding method which seemed to encourage taking children from their families rather than working to solve the family's problems.

KRISTI VAUGHAN

Today's Military Family

The deployment of U.S. forces to the Persian Gulf and the call-up of reserve personnel in support of the deployment in 1990–91 brought into public awareness changes that have taken place in military families during the past 20 years. Unlike the bachelor Army of old, today's armed forces are composed primarily of people with families. Reservists, on whom the military is increasingly dependent, tend to be older and are more likely to have family responsibilities than are active-duty personnel.

Societal Changes. General changes in family patterns and gender roles affect the military. Civilian wives of military men are increasingly likely to be in the labor force. The number of uniformed women has increased dramatically since the end of conscription in 1973. The services in 1991 included more than 370,000 women, constituting 11% of active-duty personnel and 13% of ready reserves. Though military women are less likely than their male peers to have spouses or children, most of those who are married have husbands in the military. (It is only since the 1970s that pregnant women and mothers of minor children have been allowed to remain in service.) Most single parents are men, but a larger proportion of military women than men are single parents.

Parents in many occupations experience pressures from balancing work requirements with children's needs. But conflicts may be felt more keenly in the armed forces due to the demands of the military life-style that become especially apparent during crises.

Concern for Children. More than 33,300 women were deployed to the Persian Gulf; they constituted about 6% of the U.S. force. Special concerns were raised about the well-being of children when deployment involved two military parents, a single custodial parent, or the mother of an infant (regardless of the presence of the father). Such concerns prompted various reactions, including the introduction in Congress of bills to prevent such deployments.

Extant military policies require dual-service couples and single parents to file a dependent-care plan specifying who will care for their children during a deployment. Children of servicemembers with civilian spouses are assumed to be cared for. Local commanders may postpone or cancel deployment of servicemembers for various reasons, including dependent-care plans that fail. Research on previous operations shows no difference in ability to deploy for single parents or dual-service couples as compared to other servicemembers. During the Gulf crisis difficulties were encountered due to ambiguous regulations (such as how to arrange a guardian's transportation to pick up a child).

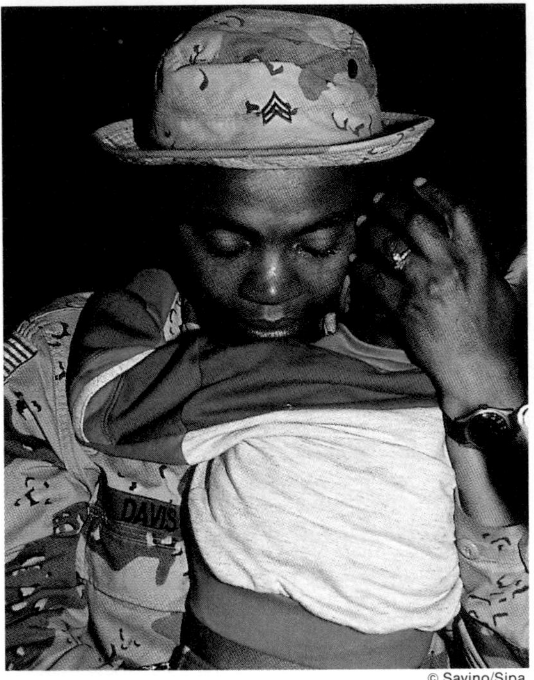

There is very little systematic research on the long-term effects on children when they are separated temporarily from one or both parents due to work demands. From the accumulated research on military families and the experience of the Gulf operations, a number of conclusions can be drawn. While most spouses and children do adjust successfully, family separations and reunions are stressful for most families. Lack of preparation can compound problems, as can unavailability of means of communication. Some families, especially of reservists, experience financial difficulties. Various kinds of support provided by friends and relatives, including child care and financial help, are crucial for most families. Many families also are aided by programs the armed services offer, including support programs, financial help, and information about eligibility for benefits.

Debate about military-family policies will continue. Awareness of the special concerns of military families may spark public attention to broader work and family issues.

MADY WECHSLER SEGAL

© Daniel Simon/Gamma-Liaison

Plaid was a major attraction in the fall collections in American and European fashion centers. The Ungaro collection, above, *from Paris featured multicolored plaids in dressy ensembles that included matching hats.*

FASHION

Fashion moved in many directions in 1991, some extreme, some conservative, but all in an attempt to attract a reluctant customer.

Due to the recession, designers encountered resistance to escalating prices. Some designers, such as Ralph Lauren, announced price reductions; others began less-expensive lines like Anne Klein's "A Line" or Emanuel Ungaro's "Emanuel." Giorgio Armani, impressed by the success of The Gap stores, launched a collection of men's and women's jeans and casual wear—most of which would retail for less than $100—called A/X Armani. Calvin Klein, whose stripped-down minimalist looks were better sellers in less-expensive copies, launched a $1 million advertising campaign to promote his potentially more profitable jeans line. Others, like Carolyne Roehm, simply closed up shop.

Trends in Apparel. Hemlines went up and down like a yo-yo. The predominant length still hovered at or just above the knee, and when skirts were shown mid-calf or lower, designers often gave them thigh-high slits or used transparent fabrics such as chiffon or voile. Also shown were hemlines that curved from high in front to low in back or dipped asymmetrically, jagged handkerchief hems, or long overskirts of fabric strips with minis.

Designers found inspiration in rap-music street style. Motorcycle jackets and bomber looks in sleek black leather were part of every collection. At Chanel, Karl Lagerfeld quilted his leather cycling jackets, teamed them with taffeta or chiffon skirts, and piled on the pearls. Versace used beaded motifs on his jackets and paired them with pleated silk miniskirts. Donna Karan opted for authenticity in her multizippered versions of the biker jacket, while Louis Dell'Olio gave his biker jacket tunic styling. "Biker" boots were part of the look, as were fishnet tights and rap-inspired accessories.

Sweaters were roomy and comfortable, textured in mohairs, chenilles, shetlands, and cashmere. There were thick bulky patterns and bold floral or ethnic designs with a hand-knit look. Most were tunic length to work over stretch tights and boots or with the popular cigarette jeans and stirrup pants.

Fashions for evening took their cue from lingerie. Lace and tulle confections were sexy and seductive offerings for after-five. Bob Mackie did teddy looks in black lace over nude spandex, while Valentino's lace-trimmed satin slip dress was inspired by movie-star lingerie. Lacroix, St. Laurent, and Versace presented corselette looks with stays and horsehair cancan skirts, as well as see-through chiffon, bra tops, bodice lacing, and high slits. Karl Lagerfeld came up with the essential accessory—a Chanel garter purse.

It was cloak-and-dagger time on fashion runways with the popularity of the trench coat. It was shown short in jazz-hot colors at Genny

© Barthelemy/Sipa

Important trends of the fashion year were zippers, prominently displayed as an accessory in all types of fashions ranging from biker jackets to scuba-style designs; colorful stockings, many in popular plaids; and high boots, shown in soft glove leathers, suede, and satin.

© Cavalli/Sipa

and Armani; in a long circle-skirted version by Isaac Mizrahi; and in a long and slim version, done in black velvet by Ralph Lauren. Donna Karan opted for black leather with zippers or, for her DKNY line, a short yellow rubberized version. Michael Kors used gilded leather to give his short trench Hollywood glamour. Short swing coats in bright colors or color-blocked combinations were also popular—many had front-zipper "scuba" closures—and the duffel coat was a strong look in high-voltage brights.

The Gulf war produced a flurry of patriotism early in 1991. Ralph Lauren led the pack with military looks and his popular flag sweater; Tom and Linda Platt's jersey chemise bore a peace symbol on the back, and Steven Stolman tied a yellow ribbon around a navy shift. Camouflage-print "fatigues" were strong and in accessories there were flag pins, military medals, and caps, and stars and stripes appeared on shoes, scarves, and bags. Americana was celebrated in Christian Francis Roth's skirts with Amish quilt patterns and in Isaac Mizrahi's "Totem Pole" gown and shearling coat with lavish American Indian-inspired bead trim.

Color and Fabric Trends. Fashion went mad for plaid in 1991, from authentic tartans to "designer clan" creations in unusual colorations and combinations. Plaids were used for outerwear, lingerie, and everything in between. Oscar de la Renta flooded the runway with sophisticated urban plaids for day and evening, often embellishing them with beading, embroidery, sequins, fringe, and other trimmings. Ungaro's ruched and draped plaid taffeta ballgowns were a favorite of the ladies on the charity-ball circuit, and Ralph Lauren gave his "Polo" plaid military airs in brass-buttoned, tailored, and fitted suits and dresses.

Checks were another prominent pattern. Houndstooth, in all sizes, was used at every price level in apparel and accessories. For the ultimate statement, Jean-Paul Gaultier did a full-body catsuit in houndstooth with matching checked boots, face-covering hood, bag, gloves, and umbrella. Gingham checks took on a 1960s mood in Bardot-inspired sundresses and girlish swimwear and sportswear items.

Denim, especially cotton/spandex blends, was hot not only for classic jeans, rancher jackets, and the newer overall looks but in suits, trench coats, and evening dresses as well as swimwear and accessory items. Karl Lagerfeld paired it with more-elegant fabrics, teaming short blue denim skirts with classic Chanel wool bouclé tweed jackets or bell-shaped denim evening skirts over gold bodysuits. Donna Karan's DKNY resort collection topped short blue denim flounced or pleated skirts with navy crepe jackets. While blue was still the favored color, brights and white were becoming increasingly popular.

Footwear. The year 1991 was definitely a boot year. Besides the heavy, solid bikers, there were sturdy hiking-boot styles and the popular cut-down Western boot. Refined ankle boots took to high heels in brightly colored suedes, patent, and polished leathers with metallic trims. Soft glove leathers and lush suede and satin were used for higher boots done on all heel heights. These went from under-the-knee to thigh-high versions designed for short skirts or tunic-length mini dresses and colorful tights. The most extreme was Anne Klein's all-in-one stretch velvet boot tight worn over a matching bodysuit.

Shoes were down to earth; the ballet slipper was still popular in a variety of leather and fabric versions. Classic designer looks such as the Chanel toe-capped sling and the Gucci loafer were equally strong and were copied widely. The fashion shoe of 1991, though, was the mule. On every heel height, in every material, plain or ornamented, it was shown with everything from the most casual sportswear to elegant evening gowns.

The zipper, in addition to its use in biker jackets, was the major element in the "scuba" styling that was an important look. It also decorated pockets and sleeves, and Bill Blass spiraled a gold zipper around a navy jersey dress. In accessories it showed up on hoods, gloves, shoes, and boots. Functional, too, it transformed Jean-Paul Gaultier's flared skater's coat into a waist-length jacket with a slip of its waist-circling zipper. And in Anne Klein's suede knee-thigh boot with multicolored zippered sections, it gave the wearer the option to vary the height or change the color mix.

Menswear. Menswear reflected many of the same trends as women's fashion. Plaids ran the gamut from refined and subdued glens for business dressing through classic tartans for casual looks. St. Laurent and Versace designed plaid suits in wild color mixes for the truly self-assured male.

Biker looks in zippered black leather were big in menswear, as were bomber jackets in distressed leathers. The macho trend extended to chinos and camouflage print shirts, fatigues, army caps, and the ever-popular trench coat.

Denim in jeans, jackets, and shirts was strong, and great outdoor classics like the duffel coat, hiking jacket, and safari look were most popular.

By and large, menswear had loosened up both in fit and conviction. Corporate dress codes had been relaxed and men were encouraged to adopt a more casual and individual approach to clothes—one that stressed comfort and informality and had a sportier attitude. The result was a colorful, pattern-mixed blend of tailored and casual components that had a thoroughly modern, youthful look.

ANN M. ELKINS
"Good Housekeeping"

© Cavalli/Sipa

Also making a fashion statement were bold colors and color combinations. Gold was popular for evening wear, while the pink and green ensemble, below, denoted trends that included the ankle boot, plaid stockings, and checks.

AP/Wide World

FINLAND

A major election and economic news highlighted 1991 events in Finland. In July the unemployment rate set a new record of 9.7%.

Political Affairs. General elections for Finland's parliament (Eduskunta) took place on March 17, 1991, and had the unexpected result of the Center Party (formerly the Agrarians) taking 24.85% of the vote and gaining 15 new seats. With 55 seats in all in the new legislature, it became the biggest and most important party in the country. The former top vote-getter, the Social Democratic Party, lost eight seats and had to settle for second place with 48 seats, while the National Coalition Party (Conservatives) ended up with 40 seats. Among the other represented parties the Left Association finished with 19 seats; the Swedish People's Party took 11 seats; the Greens had ten seats; and the Christian League, the Rural Party, and the Liberal People's Party captured eight seats, seven seats, and one seat, respectively. The Åland Islands have one representative.

After a six-week delay, a four-party coalition consisting of the Center Party, the National Coalition Party, the Swedish People's Party, and the Christian League formed a new cabinet. Esko Aho, the leader of the Center Party, became the new prime minister, replacing Harri Holkeri. Paavo Väyrynen, also of the Center Party, took over the department of foreign affairs, and the post of minister of defense was retained by Elisabeth Rehn of the Swedish People's Party, who was a holdover from the previous cabinet.

On June 26 the parliament passed a new law on presidential elections. In the future the president of Finland would be elected by a direct vote, and the presidential term would be limited to two terms of four years each.

Economic Affairs. The so-called European Economic Area (EEA), which was planned to bring together the nations of the European Community (EC) and the European Free Trade Association (EFTA), attracted mixed attention in Finland. On October 22, Finland, a member of EFTA, agreed at a meeting in Luxembourg to go along with the other six EFTA nations in creating a new common market, the EEA, in conjunction with the EC. Earlier, in June, the government had decided to follow the example of other European nations and link its currency, the Finnmark, to the European Currency Unit (ecu) and benefit from the exchange regulations maintained by the EC.

A three-week strike by employees within the bus and trucking companies as well as in the harbors took place through the better part of June. The strike ended in late June through the efforts of a national arbitrator.

Foreign Affairs. President Mauno Koivisto and Mrs. Koivisto met with U.S. President George Bush and Mrs. Bush in Washington on May 6–8. The Finnish president invited the Bushes to Helsinki in early 1992 to attend a meeting of the Conference on Security and Cooperation in Europe (CSCE).

Disagreement between Finland and Denmark about the projected bridge-tunnel link between the Danish islands of Fyn and Sjaelland wound up before the International Court of Justice when Finland took the case there. The Finns claimed that the mere 65-ft (19.8-m) height of the bridge above the water's surface would prevent the passage of Finnish oil rigs between the Baltic and the North seas. The plea was turned down on July 23, however.

On August 25, Finland extended full recognition of the independence of the three Baltic nations—Estonia, Latvia, and Lithuania. It also entered into trade agreements with them.

ERIK J. FRIIS
"The Scandinavian-American Bulletin"

FINLAND • Information Highlights

Official Name: Republic of Finland.
Location: Northern Europe.
Area: 130,127 sq mi (337 030 km^2).
Population (mid-1991 est.): 5,000,000.
Chief Cities (Dec. 31, 1989 est.): Helsinki, the capital, 490,629; Tampere, 171,561.
Government: *Head of state,* Mauno Koivisto, president (took office Jan. 27, 1982). *Head of government,* Esko Aho, prime minister (took office April 1991). *Legislature* (unicameral)—Eduskunta.
Monetary Unit: Markka (4.258 markkaa equal U.S.$1, Dec. 9, 1991).
Gross Domestic Product: (1989 est. U.S.$): $74,400,000,000.
Economic Indexes (1990): *Consumer Prices* (1980 = 100), all items, 191.8; food, 183.1. *Industrial Production* (1980 = 100), 130.
Foreign Trade (1990 U.S.$): *Imports,* $27,110,000,000; *exports,* $26,743,000,000.

FLORIDA

Florida continued to reel from the effects of a lingering economic recession in 1991. A projected shortfall of $622 million in tax revenues forced Gov. Lawton Chiles and his cabinet to call a special session of the state legislature for December to institute sweeping cuts in funding for education, social-service programs, and other areas. Exacerbating the problem was the continued frenetic growth of Florida and the absence of a sufficient tax base for funding necessary state services. The 1990 census indicated that nine of the 12 fastest-growing U.S. cities were in Florida.

Politics. Under the leadership of Governor Chiles, Florida passed a stringent campaign-financing law, placing a ceiling of $500 on contributions to candidates for state office and creating a public fund to help finance campaigns for governor and cabinet-level posts.

Chiles took his crusade for governmental reform and spending cuts to many areas of the state. He often was met with strong protests, especially from students and educators.

Florida's U.S. senators were divided over the controversial nomination of Judge Clarence Thomas to the U.S. Supreme Court. While Republican Sen. Connie Mack supported Thomas, Democratic Sen. Bob Graham opposed him. Graham also opposed the nomination of U.S. District Judge Kenneth L. Ryskamp of Miami to the Eleventh Circuit Court of Appeals. The Senate rejected the Ryskamp nomination amid charges that he had shown insensitivity toward minorities.

The Economy. Florida experienced one of its roughest economic years in recent times in 1991. At one time the state's premier banking system, Southeast Bank lost hundreds of millions of dollars in 1991 before it was taken over by North Carolina-based First Union. After tottering on the brink of extinction for several years, Florida's Eastern Airlines went out of business. Ailing Pan Am declared bankruptcy; later the carrier became a virtual appendage of Delta Airlines. Real-estate and construction slumps, along with growing woes among large retail firms, brought additional economic problems.

On a positive note, a record orange harvest led to a rise in sales in this important industry. Miami also gained a major-league baseball franchise, which is expected to inject a few hundred million dollars annually into the economy after it begins play in 1993.

The Environment. An extremely wet rainy season pushed the water levels in the drought-stricken Everglades to their highest point in recent years. Florida and federal authorities instituted a $700 million project to return a portion of the Everglades to nature, thereby reversing a century of harmful human interference. The project included continuing work on restoring the original contours of the Kissimmee River north of Lake Okeechobee, filling in and redesigning miles of deep-water canals, building thousands of acres of experimental marshes to cleanse water of agricultural pollutants, and adding more than 100,000 acres (40 469 ha) to Everglades National Park.

Governor Chiles also called for a wide coastal buffer zone around the state. Oil and gas drilling would be prohibited within the zone.

© Pool/Saba

Attention centered on the Palm Beach county courthouse as William Kennedy Smith, above, *the nephew of Sen. Edward Kennedy, was acquitted of rape in December 1991.*

Crime. William Kennedy Smith, the nephew of Sen. Edward M. Kennedy (D-MA), was acquitted of the rape of a woman at the family compound in Palm Beach.

Law authorities charged Aileen Carol Wuornas, a lesbian, with the murder of seven males found dead on highways in north and central Florida. And Floridians were shocked by the revelation that a Broward county sheriff's deputy and his wife allegedly ran a prostitution service out of their home. It was believed that their list of clients included several prominent members of the community.

Other. Former Florida Gov. LeRoy Collins died at age 82. Collins had served as Florida's chief executive from 1955–61; his moderation and enlightened leadership during the racial crisis of that era caused him to be considered one of the state's greatest governors.

Kimberly Bergalis, a young woman who contracted AIDS from an infected dentist and who argued before the U.S. Congress for testing of all health-care workers, died at her Fort Pierce home in December.

Two thousand rafters fleeing Cuba entered Florida during the year. Haitian refugees in Miami rioted in the aftermath of a military coup d'état that deposed the democratically elected president of Haiti, Jean-Bertrand Aristide. (*See* REFUGEES AND IMMIGRATION.)

PAUL S. GEORGE
Miami-Dade Community College

FLORIDA • Information Highlights

Area: 58,664 sq mi (151 939 km²).
Population (1990 census): 12,937,926.
Chief Cities (1990 census): Tallahassee, the capital, 124,773; Jacksonville, 672,971; Miami, 358,548; Tampa, 280,015; St. Petersburg, 238,629.
Government (1991): *Chief Officers*—governor, Lawton Chiles (D); lt. gov., Buddy MacKay (D). *Legislature*—Senate, 40 members; House of Representatives, 120 members.
State Finances (fiscal year 1990): *Revenue,* $23,868,000,000; *expenditure,* $21,723,000,000.
Personal Income (1990): $241,713,000,000; per capita, $18,530.
Labor Force (June 1991): *Civilian labor force,* 6,454,900; *unemployed,* 506,900 (7.9% of total force).
Education: *Enrollment* (fall 1989)—public elementary schools, 1,303,439; public secondary, 468,910; colleges and universities, 573,712. *Public school expenditures* (1989), $7,245,515,000.

FOOD

Food-industry developments in 1991 included new, healthier beef products, efforts to revise the number and amount of chemicals used in U.S. food production, and a U.S. government campaign to improve food labeling (*see* CONSUMER AFFAIRS). A tightening of global food supplies and dramatic changes in the Soviet Union that brought temporary food shortages also occurred.

New Beef Products. U.S. poultry consumption per person exceeded both beef and pork for the second straight year due to consumer health consciousness, a desire for more variety in diets, and a wide range of poultry products offered by processors. In an effort to regain its former position as the preferred meat, the beef sector introduced several new low-fat, low-cholesterol products. McDonald's McLean Deluxe sandwich was a success for the company. The McLean Deluxe contains a 91% fat-free patty with carrageenan, a seaweed-based product that helps maintain moisture and flavor.

Quaker Oats introduced "lean maker," a product utilizing oat bran and designed to help maintain desirable flavor, texture, and juiciness in low-fat ground beef. A Minneapolis-St. Paul-based firm specializing in food products for institutional trade introduced "smart meat," a product also low in fat and cholesterol but processed to simulate traditional fat in highly finished beef.

Other low-fat beef products include 96% fat-free ground beef to be marketed by Momford of Colorado, along with similar products by Excell and IBP, both large beef-processing firms. The new products are more expensive per pound than traditional ground beef. However, they have less weight loss during cooking. The U.S. beef industry has established a goal of reducing fat in its products by 20% by 1995.

Global Chemical Standards. Some U.S. officials proposed adopting the international chemical safety standard for food. The international standard is from Codex, an affiliate of the United Nations Food and Agricultural Organization (FAO). An international standard would simplify U.S. exporting and importing of food products. However, public-health, consumer, and environmental organizations expressed serious concern about the move since it could shift control of pesticide standards from the national to the international level.

A study by the U.S. General Accounting Office (GAO) reported that adopting the international standard would increase maximum allowable U.S. pesticide limits for 11 chemicals or 27% of those listed as probable human carcinogens. The change would reduce allowable U.S. limits for 55% of the suspected carcinogens and would leave the standards approximately unchanged for the remainder. The study found maximum U.S. limits were below those of the international standards for about one third of all food-related chemicals.

U.S. and international standards also specify allowable average daily consumer intake of chemical compounds. U.S. standards, according to GAO, specify lower average daily intake levels than Codex for two thirds of the food chemicals it studied. For nearly one fifth of the chemicals, the U.S. limits were found to be at least ten times lower than the international standards. In light of the food-safety concerns of U.S. consumers, the issue was unlikely to be resolved soon.

In other food-safety developments, EPA banned the use of the pesticide parathion on 81 out of 90 U.S. crops. A total ban on the use of parathion also was being considered.

The International Scene. Weather problems in parts of the United States, China, the USSR, Brazil, and Argentina reduced world food supplies modestly in 1991. World grain stocks dropped slightly below accepted minimum standards for food security. No major food crises developed although localized food shortages occurred in parts of Africa, Iraq, and the USSR. Lower grain stocks increased the world's vulnerability to the effects of adverse weather.

Dramatic political changes and unfavorable weather reduced the Soviet grain crop by 20% to 25%. Decentralized control of the economy brought shortages of inputs in the food and agricultural sector and problems in storing, processing, and distributing food. Political turmoil and inflation led to a hoarding psychology where farms held back food supplies, while consumers rushed to buy available products. The result was adequate food supplies in rural areas but shortages in larger cities. To deal with these problems, the Soviets looked to the United States, Japan, and the European Community for financial aid to help cover the cost of food imports.

Mexico developed plans to expand food production so as to reduce food imports substantially by the turn of the century. China announced plans to raise wheat prices sharply to encourage more production and reduce imports. Research in food-related sciences continued in many parts of the world in order to keep global food production in step with the nearly 2% annual population growth.

Other Developments. A study by the American Dietetic Association showed three fourths of U.S. consumers are not as careful about their diets as they should be. Researchers in animal nutrition, genetics, and breeding continued to work toward the development of more healthful food products. Efforts to introduce greater variety and lower-fat products into U.S. school-lunch programs were initiated.

See also AGRICULTURE.

ROBERT WISNER, *Iowa State University*

FOREIGN AID

The first U.S. foreign-aid authorization bill since 1985 fell victim to domestic politics in late October 1991 as the opening salvos of the 1992 presidential-election campaign were launched. Charging that President George Bush was paying too much attention to problems overseas while ignoring the plight of the jobless, homeless, and uninsured at home, congressional Democrats and Republicans joined forces to scuttle a measure that would have authorized about $25 billion in foreign aid for fiscal 1992 and 1993 to be administered bilaterally and through the International Monetary Fund and other international organizations.

Political Motives. Opposition to foreign aid had been building long before the bill's defeat. The United States today spends about $15 billion annually on economic, humanitarian, and military assistance to foreign nations. That comes to less than 0.3% of the country's gross national product (GNP), or economic output, and is far less in relation to wealth than that spent by many other industrial nations. The highest U.S. rate of spending for international aid ever was 3.2% of GNP, registered in 1949.

In the past, Democrats usually could be counted on to support foreign-aid initiatives. This time, however, many Democrats joined with conservative Republicans in calling for a shift of attention to the domestic scene. Just how sensitive the 1992–93 foreign-aid measure was to domestic political concerns became clear as the bill made its way through Congress. Initially opponents of the measure focused on two abortion-related provisions. One would have overturned a seven-year-old U.S. policy barring funding for international organizations that promote abortion as a method of family planning. The other provision authorized $20 million for the United Nations Population Fund. The Reagan administration suspended U.S. contributions to this agency in 1985 because it provided aid to China and other countries that are accused of promoting forced abortions. Bush had threatened to veto the foreign-aid bill over both these provisions.

By late October congressional support for the foreign-aid bill had crumbled, as abortion opponents were joined by those who criticized Bush's alleged insensitivity to the plight of the economically oppressed. With an eye on 1992 elections, lawmakers on both sides of the aisle abandoned the foreign-aid bill. On October 30 the House overwhelmingly rejected the conference report the Senate had approved three weeks before.

Existing Programs. Congress separately appropriated funds for existing foreign-aid programs at their fiscal 1991 levels through March 31, 1992. The Senate had agreed to a White House request to postpone action on a foreign-aid appropriations bill for all of fiscal 1992, ending Sept. 30, 1992. Bush had asked for the delay as part of an agreement to put off consideration of an Israeli request for $10 billion in loan guarantees. Israel is the largest recipient of U.S. aid, receiving more than $3 billion per year.

The U.S. pullback from overseas assistance came at a particularly hard time for much of the Third World. The United Nations reported that about 10% of the world's population suffered from chronic hunger in 1991. In sub-Saharan Africa alone some 30 million people were threatened by famine.

Soviet Union. Ironically, one of the few countries to receive increased foreign aid was the Soviet Union, the United States' chief adversary in the 45-year Cold War. After severe economic and political upheaval left the USSR's economy in shambles and with an uncertain political future, Soviet President Mikhail S. Gorbachev asked Western donors for a massive infusion of economic assistance. Reflecting ambivalence in Washington over the advisability of helping the Soviets construct a free-market economy, Congress authorized no economic assistance for either the Soviet central government or the 12 remaining republics.

Congress, however, did authorize Bush to grant $15 million to the Baltic states of Estonia, Latvia, and Lithuania, which gained their independence from the Soviet Union in 1991. Bush also announced on November 20 that the United States would provide the Soviet Union with $1.5 billion in grain credits and food shipments to help avert a food emergency over the winter, bringing to $4 billion the total 1991 U.S. food aid to the Soviet Union.

Then, hours before adjourning for the year on November 27, Congress approved an additional $100 million to help the Soviet people get enough food and medicine to survive the winter and gave the president the authority to use up to $400 million in defense spending to help the Soviets quickly destroy their 27,000 nuclear weapons. Supporters said that failure to dismantle the weapons posed a significant threat to the U.S. national interest. About 5,000 nuclear warheads were thought by Western intelligence agencies to be deployed in non-Russian republics.

Earlier, Democratic Sen. Sam Nunn of Georgia and Democratic Rep. Les Aspin of Wisconsin, chairmen of the two armed services committees, had proposed diverting $1 billion of the defense budget to help the Soviets, arguing that the end of the Cold War was yielding a "peace dividend" in the form of savings on weapons that no longer were needed to protect against Soviet aggression. Congress rejected the plan under pressure to divert all available defense and foreign-aid funds to domestic needs.

MARY H. COOPER
"CQ [Congressional Quarterly] Researcher"

© Chamussy/Sipa

French President François Mitterrand (right) *and German Chancellor Helmut Kohl held frequent discussions during 1991. The political and economic future of Europe—with attention to the European Community—was high on their agendas.*

FRANCE

France in 1991 marked the ten-year anniversary of the election of Socialist François Mitterrand to the presidency on May 10, 1981. With characteristic restraint for such events, the French people observed the milestone from a middle ground between the dark judgments of political figures on Mitterrand's right—former Prime Minister and Gaullist Paris Mayor Jacques Chirac announced that after ten years the France of Mitterrand was a "sinking ship"—and the president's near-deification by Socialist Party admirers and collaborators. Throughout the year the country's media rumbled with the recurring theme of "ten years is enough!" But by the end of 1991, and despite an unshakable malaise among the French resulting from disruptive public-sector strikes, stubbornly high unemployment, worries over immigration, and the stunning unpopularity of Edith Cresson, the country's first woman prime minister, Mitterrand appeared secure in his mandate set to end in May 1995. This was true if only because intraparty squabbles among Mitterrand's potential successors on both the left and the right put the president somewhat above the fray—a position he cultivated. Nevertheless, on November 10, Mitterrand announced in a television interview his intention to organize a national referendum to decide, among other institutional changes, whether to reduce the presidential term from seven to five years—a constitutional change he had favored since before his election. The 75-year-old Mitterrand did not say whether a "yes" vote in a referendum he suggested be held in late 1992 would cause him to cut his second seven-year term to five, and thus to leave office in 1993.

For France the decade of Mitterrand's presidency was not simply a date to be noted, however. It marked the country's evolution from an economic maverick, where the role of the state remained central and in many cases determinant, to a solid student of free-market capitalism along the lines of other Western European economies—and this under a Socialist president. It also marked the convergence of France's frequently traveled separate road in international affairs with the main thoroughfares of Western policy. Thus France in 1991 gave up its claim to an original Arab policy to stand beside the United States and the coalition it assembled in the Persian Gulf conflict, just as it had altered or abandoned other independent policies in recent years.

International Affairs. The Gulf conflict dominated the first quarter of 1991. In a press conference January 9, President Mitterrand stated that armed conflict would become completely "legitimate" as of January 16, the day after the expiration of the United Nations (UN) ultimatum for Iraq to leave Kuwait. Until that date, however, he said France would attempt all diplomatic means to avoid a war. In that context, Mitterrand dispatched Michel Vauzelle, president of the National Assembly's Commission on Foreign Affairs, to Iraq for a long meeting with President Saddam Hussein. France also made one last-ditch peace proposal to the UN Security Council on January 14, but failed to win the support of the United States or Great Britain.

When U.S. and British jets began bombing Baghdad and other Iraqi positions on January

17, France took part. At first Defense Minister Jean-Pierre Chevènement, an opponent of the war, insisted that French planes would attack only Iraqi positions inside Kuwait. But on January 20, Mitterrand contradicted that line, saying Iraq's "military-industrial potential" would have to be destroyed if Iraq were to be forced out of Kuwait. On January 24, French planes bombed their first targets inside Iraq, and on January 29, Chevènement resigned. When the allied land assault began on February 24, France participated there as well. In all, the country provided 10,000 of the allies' 690,000 military personnel, two of whom were killed and at least 25 of whom were injured. All French participants were from the country's professional corps and not from among young men fulfilling their obligatory one-year military service, in keeping with a commitment Mitterrand made to the French people.

While France's participation in the Gulf war was neither large nor decisive, it allowed Mitterrand to declare "with pride that France fulfilled its role and its rank." With the leaders of a united Germany next door maneuvering for a greater international role, France was especially keen to emphasize its "rank" among the world's major powers as a permanent member of the UN Security Council. Yet while France's participation made for a period of unusually close Franco-U.S. relations, it also complicated France's place in the Arab world, particularly across the Mediterranean Sea in North Africa. With pro-Iraq sentiment particularly high in Tunisia, Algeria, and Morocco, Mitterrand was burned in effigy and anti-French slogans were shouted in several North African cities, while diplomatic relations between France and Algeria remained frosty months after the conflict.

One of Mitterrand's central points in arguing for participation in the Gulf war was the necessity to guarantee France "a place at the negotiating table" when the issue of peace in the Middle East was taken up. Yet when some eight months after the war's end the Middle East peace conference opened in Madrid on October 30, France's only presence was through the participation of the European Community (EC), represented by Dutch Foreign Minister Hans van den Broek.

When the Yugoslav republics of Slovenia and Croatia declared their independence and disassociation from the federal Yugoslavia on June 25, Mitterrand immediately recognized the dangerous situation facing Europe. But unlike Germany, France opposed quick recognition of the breakaway republics, fearing a development of German influence over parts of unstable Eastern Europe, and the effect such recognition could have on other European independence movements. France considered it a major diplomatic victory when Germany agreed in August not to proceed to any recognition on its own.

French Middle East diplomacy suffered a blow on August 8 with the assassination of former Iranian Prime Minister Shahpur Bakhtiar, in his home near Paris and while under heavy police security. Since the Persian Gulf war struck down Iraq as the keystone to French strategy for building its influence in the Middle East, France had begun realigning its diplomatic efforts toward Iran. Mitterrand had scheduled a state visit to Iran for November, but an investigation revealing probable official Iranian involvement in Bakhtiar's death rendered the trip politically impossible. Nevertheless, in October, France settled a dispute with Iran over assets frozen after the 1979 Islamic revolution by agreeing to turn over nearly $1.3 billion to Iran.

On August 19, Mitterrand stunned the French by appearing to respond mildly to the coup against Soviet President Mikhail Gorbachev the day before. The French president was criticized for reading, during a television appearance, excerpts from a letter from the Soviet Union's self-proclaimed new leaders. Although Mitterrand said he meant the letter-reading to be a reassuring gesture, surveys showed the French considered Mitterrand's actions to reflect an acquiescence toward the coup. Mitterrand's position was damaged further when Boris Yeltsin came out of the ill-fated coup an international hero, since earlier in the year Mitterrand had snubbed Yeltsin during an official visit to France.

France and Germany announced on October 16 plans to create a Franco-German army corps. Mitterrand and German Chancellor Helmut Kohl described the corps as the possible "embryo" of a future European defense body. The proposal was received cautiously by Britain, which supported development of a European defense capability, but under North Atlantic Treaty Organization (NATO)—and not strictly European—control. Still, Mitterrand interpreted as a positive development for

FRANCE • Information Highlights

Official Name: French Republic.
Location: Western Europe.
Area: 211,208 sq mi (547 030 km²).
Population (mid-1991 est.): 56,700,000.
Chief City (1987 est.): Paris, the capital, 2,078,900.
Government: *Head of state,* François Mitterrand, president (took office May 1981). *Chief minister,* Edith Cresson, prime minister (took office May 15, 1991). *Legislature*—Parliament: Senate and National Assembly.
Monetary Unit: Franc (5.4555 francs equal U.S. $1, Nov. 25, 1991).
Gross Domestic Product (1989 est. U.S.$): $819,600,-000,000.
Economic Indexes (1990): *Consumer Prices* (1980 = 100), all items, 180.7; food, 180.9. *Industrial Production* (1980 = 100), 113.
Foreign Trade (1990 U.S.$): *Imports,* $233,163,-000,000; *exports,* $209,996,000,000.

Europe the statement by U.S. President George Bush at the NATO summit in Rome, November 7, supporting some European defense development.

Meeting in Maastricht, the Netherlands, in December, Mitterrand and the leaders of the other 11 EC member nations agreed on a pact forging greater political and economic ties. Important measures agreed upon at the meeting included the establishment of common foreign and defense policies as well as a single currency and regional central bank by no later than 1999. Relating to a future common defense policy, all community leaders agreed to build up a nine-nation military pact known as the Western European Union into the community's informal defense structure, while at the same time retaining ties to NATO.

Domestic Affairs. The issue of immigration rose from one of secondary importance to center stage during 1991. National agencies and independent sources estimated legal immigration to France at about 100,000 people per year, a lower figure than during the 1970s and much of the 1980s, years of generally high economic growth. But rising unemployment, mounting vandalism and delinquency in the cities, cultural conflicts, and sporadic high-profile violent incidents pitting the police against immigrant youths or French-born youths of immigrant descent combined to keep immigration at the heart of political debate.

On March 26 a young Algerian man was killed by a guard at a suburban Paris shopping center, touching off three nights of violence in several immigrant neighborhoods. In May two nights of violence in another Paris suburb resulted in numerous arrests, including that of an 18-year-old man of Moroccan descent who died while in custody. Then in June a policewoman and a young Algerian were killed after a confrontation and chase. The government allocated emergency resources to provide summer activities for ghetto youths, and the summer passed quietly.

Despite the calm in the streets, France's political leaders watched as opinion polls showed the far-right, anti-immigration National Front (FN) gaining strength. One poll released in October, confirming the findings of other surveys earlier in the year, showed that 32% of the French agreed with the ideas espoused by the FN—a gain of 14 percentage points in one year. In response, mainstream political leaders escalated their anti-immigration rhetoric. Jacques Chirac, leader of the Gaullist RPR party, declared in June that France suffered from an "overdose of foreigners," and that the French were tiring of the "odor" of immigration. Those statements caused Prime Minister Edith Cresson to denounce Chirac as sounding "more like Jean-Marie Le Pen," the FN leader, "than Le Pen himself." Less than a month later, however, Cresson caused her own

The issue of immigration occupied center stage in France during 1991. Turmoil and various violent incidents involving immigrants sparked demonstrations and political advantage for the anti-immigration National Front Party.

© Malanca/Sipa

furor by evoking the possibility of "charters" to ferry illegal immigrants back to their countries of origin. She was followed, in September, by former President Valéry Giscard d'Estaing, who wrote in a prominent weekly of an "invasion" of foreigners that required, among other solutions, a change in French laws to make attaining French nationality more difficult.

In a less emotional vein—and with an eye on falling birthrates and tens of thousands of unfilled job offers despite record-high unemployment—Gaullist Senator and former Interior Minister Charles Pasqua declared in July that "to pretend that France has no need of immigrants is nonsense." He proposed an immigration system with quotas, akin to those of the United States, Canada, or Australia, based on nationality and profession, but his plan failed to receive backing from other politicians.

The immigration debate and the rising popularity of the FN did, on the other hand, cause continuing discussions among the French right and center-right political parties over whether to strike an electoral accord with the far right. France would hold regional elections in spring 1992, an important precursor to national parliamentary elections in spring 1993. Surveys over the year showed the traditional conservative parties surpassing the ruling Socialists and their minor-party allies, but not by enough to govern without third-party participation. Le Pen, eager to join the political mainstream, declared himself ready for an electoral accord, but the issue continued to convulse the traditional right.

On May 15, Mitterrand replaced Michel Rocard, his prime minister of almost exactly three years, with Edith Cresson (*see* BIOGRAPHY), a former minister of such high-profile portfolios as agriculture, industry, and European affairs, and a longtime Mitterrand follower and confidante. In announcing the change, Mitterrand said he wanted to give the government a "new impetus" to guide France energetically to "objective 1993," when the EC's single market is set to become reality. Most political observers, however, assumed that the French president had another 1993 objective in mind: the parliamentary elections. If so, his gamble provided little initial payoff, since both his own public rating and that of his new prime minister sagged.

A growing impatience among French public employees over the government's tightfisted policies resulted in a proliferation of strikes during the fall. Public transport was disrupted over pay and retirement demands in October. On November 17 more than 250,000 representatives of the medical profession jammed Paris boulevards to protest government plans for reining in ballooning social-security outlays. Already on September 29, nearly 200,000 farmers had marched in Paris to demand higher subsidies and programs to safeguard French rural life. But at that time sporadic acts of violence by farmers around the country met with swift condemnation from Mitterrand and a warning that "there is no alternative" to Finance Minister Pierre Bérégovoy's tight-budget, low-inflation, strong-franc policies. There was no indication as 1992 neared that the mounting social discontent was swaying the government in its fiscal determination.

In October, France was shaken by revelations that more than 400,000 people had been contaminated over the last decade by transfusions involving infected blood. In the overwhelming majority of cases the contamination involved one of several strains of hepatitis, but in the case of an estimated 3,500 individuals—mostly hemophiliacs—contamination was with the virus that causes AIDS. The ensuing controversy enveloped past ministers and other past and current government officials accused of either knowing of the dangers, or of rebuffing warnings about them. Three doctors, former high-ranking health officials, were charged in the affair. By the end of the month the government announced an accord with insurance companies for covering the victims' indemnification, and in early November the government unveiled a complete overhaul of the country's system of transfusion regulation.

The Economy. France in 1991 sustained itself as a model of low-inflation, strong-currency, and moderate unit-labor-cost economics that was all the more impressive because just eight years earlier the country, in Mitterrand's more truly Socialist economic phase, still was following a growth-through-spending regime that produced high inflation and destabilizing budget deficits. But in 1991 inflation fell to a 2.5% annual rate, the lowest of the large industrialized nations and at least a full point below next-door neighbor Germany. The bad news was that this was caused partly by high unemployment, which hovered just below the 10% rate and which threatened to cross the psychologically devastating threshold of 3 million unemployed individuals by year's end. France's dogged pursuit of a strong currency was motivated in large part by a desire for binding agreements on European Monetary Union, which came in December at the EC meeting in Maastricht.

While leaving macroeconomic matters in Finance Minister Bérégovoy's hands, Prime Minister Cresson, soon after her arrival in office, announced a series of measures designed primarily to boost employment. By June these involved increasing apprenticeships and training for unskilled laborers, and reducing the costs to small and medium industries of new hires. Cresson noted that the percentage of workers in France who are unskilled far exceeds the German level.

HOWARD LAFRANCHI
"The Christian Science Monitor"

GARDENING AND HORTICULTURE

In 1991 the third annual "Organic Index," a nationwide Harris poll conducted for *Organic Gardening* magazine, indicated that more than 60% of U.S. backyard fruit and vegetable gardeners used organic methods and did not use pesticides, herbicides, or synthetic chemical fertilizers in their gardens. This was a 15% increase in just two years.

Award Winners. The All-America Selections (AAS) judging committee announced four AAS Bedding Plant and Flower Awards for 1992. The winners were determined from test results from 33 flower trial gardens across North America. The AAS Bedding Plant Award was presented to Dianthus F_1 "Ideal Violet," the first dianthus ever to receive the award. Both greenhouse and outdoor field trials proved this bedding plant to be of superior quality. "Ideal Violet"—with large, single, deep violet to almost purple blooms with small white eyes—flowered early on compact plants. It is adaptable to container culture or for use as a spring bedding plant. Although it is considered an annual, it may overwinter in areas without extremely cold temperatures. This cultivar was developed by Elidia Flower Seeds Co., Avoine, France.

The three AAS Flower Awards were presented to Salvia coccinea "Lady in Red," Verbena "Peaches & Cream," and Canna "Tropical Rose." "Lady in Red" is an improved dark red, dwarf salvia on a compact plant, reaching 12 to 15 inches (30–38 cm) in height. This plant may attract hummingbirds and butterflies to the garden. Verbena "Peaches & Cream" received the award because of its new flower color, a pastel blend of apricot and salmon. "Peaches & Cream" produces flowers throughout the summer on a plant that spreads to 10 to 12 inches (25–30 cm) and attains a height of 8 to 10 inches (20–25 cm). Both Salvia "Lady in Red" and Verbena "Peaches & Cream" were developed by K. Sahin in Alphen Aan der Rijn, the Netherlands. Canna "Tropical Rose" can be flowered in gallon containers or grown to a height of 2.5 ft (.76 m) in a full sun garden. This new seed canna was bred by American Takii Inc.

There were five Fleuroselect, Wassenaar, Netherlands Gold Medal winners for 1992. Three more floral selections were awarded in addition to a gold medal to Salvia "Lady in Red" and Verbena "Peaches & Cream." The three additional Fleuroselect Gold Medal Award winners were Impatiens wallerana "Mega Orange" for its exceptional weather tolerance and vigorous growth; Callistephus chinensis "Starlight Rose," an aster with wilt-resistance exhibiting 3-inch (7.6-cm) rose-color double blossoms; and Tagetes patula "Safari Tangerine," an early 12-inch (30-cm)-high French marigold with 2-inch (5-cm) tangerine-orange blossoms.

© Griffith Greenhouses Inc.

The genetically created Citrosa Mosquito Fighter releases a lemony smell that is pleasant to humans but a natural repellent for mosquitoes, blackflies, and most biting insects.

The All-America Rose Selections Awards (AARS) were presented to three outstanding rose introductions for 1992. Hybrid tea rose "Brigadoon" is a lightly fragrant, coral-pink blossom staged on an upright plant growing to a height of 6 ft (1.8 m). "Brigadoon" was developed by William A. Warriner, a renowned rose hybridizer. Miniature rose "Pride 'n' Joy," also developed by Warriner, exhibits fiery orange flowers with yellow reverse measuring 1.5 inches (3.8 cm) across. This compact plant reaches a mature height of 3 ft (.9 m), making it ideal for containers or small space gardens. "All that Jazz" is a coral and salmon flower shrub rose recommended for landscape planting because of its vigorous, highly disease-resistant growth. It was introduced by DeVor Nurseries, Inc., Watsonville, CA.

New Plant Introduction. Citrosa, Pelargonium citrosum Van Leenii "The Mosquito Fighter," which was developed by Dirk Van Leeni, a Dutch horticulturist, is a new genetically engineered plant that emits citronella oil, a natural mosquito repellent. This new plant was produced by a process known as protoplast fusion—the combining of the chromosomes from the grass of China and a geranium from South Africa. The grass of China provides the citrosa with the ability to produce citronella and citral, and the African geranium provides the fleshy leaves that release the fragrance.

RALPH L. SNODSMITH

GENETICS

The year 1991 brought the discovery of a mechanism for correcting DNA deficiencies, a mutation that increases the life span of an organism, a case of interspecies transfer of a courtship song, and a report on the progress of the first gene-therapy trials.

mRNA Editing. It has been known for some time that the messenger RNA (mRNA) for the energy-related mitochondrial protein cytochrome oxidase of the human-skin-ulcer-causing protozoan parasite *Leishmania tarentolae* contains 39 nucleotides which are not encoded in the mitochondrial gene for this protein. Without these 39 nucleotides, located at various sites in the mRNA, a nonfunctional protein would be produced by the protozoan and the parasite would die. It is clear that between the time the mRNA is formed (transcription) and the time it is used in the synthesis of cytochrome oxidase (translation), it has to be "edited" so as to add the missing 39 nucleotides in their proper places.

Through the extensive work of Dr. L. Simpson and his colleagues at the University of California in Los Angeles, this situation finally has been explained. These geneticists found that in addition to producing the deficient mRNA for cytochrome oxidase, the mitochondrial DNA also produces a short segment of RNA called *guide RNA* (gRNA), which contains the missing nucleotides. The gRNA attaches to the deficient mRNA and, with the help of RNA-cutting and RNA-splicing enzymes, directs the insertion of the needed nucleotides in their proper places. Examples of mRNA editing, involving both nuclear and mitochondrial genes, have been discovered in plants, animals, and other microorganisms.

Life-Span Mutation. Single-gene mutations, chromosomal deletions, etc., generally reduce life expectancy. An exception to the life-span-reducing effect of mutations has been found in the nematode (round worm) *Caenorhabditis elegans*. This organism has a normal life expectancy of 19 days and a maximum life span of 37 days. Dr. T. E. Johnson of the University of Colorado at Boulder reported on studies of a recessive mutation, named *age*-1. This mutation, when homozygous, increases the organism's life expectancy by 65% and its maximum life span by 110%. It further was reported that the lengthening of these animals' life spans was the result of a general slowing down of the age-specific mortality rate which characterizes aging and senescence. This discovery will stimulate the search for comparable gene mutations in humans and other organisms.

Interspecies Transfer of a Courtship Song. Part of a *Drosophila* male's courtship behavior involves the production of a "song" which is generated by the extension and vibration of one or the other of his wings. The duration of the song is species-specific: *D. melanogaster* produces a song that lasts 50–65 seconds, whereas the closely related species *D. simulans* generates a shorter 30-to-40-second song. The females of a particular species respond only to their own species-specific song.

Dr. J. C. Hall and his colleagues at Brandeis University in Waltham, MA, have been studying the songs of the above species and have found that, in both species, a section of the flies' X chromosomes—labeled *period* (*per*)—controls song production. In *D. melanogaster*, various mutations of this gene have been found, including one which is caused by the loss (deletion) of this section of the X chromosome. Males with this mutation, called per^{01}, produce songs that have no fixed duration.

Using modern molecular techniques, a wild-type (nonmutant) *per* section of *D. simulans* was transferred to *D. melanogaster* flies which were per^{01} mutants. The genetically altered *D. melanogaster* males produced a courtship song with the characteristics of *D. simulans'* song.

Gene-Therapy Trials. The first gene-therapy trial conducted under the auspices of the U.S. National Institutes of Health (NIH) began on Sept. 14, 1990, and involved a 4-year-old child suffering from a form of Severe Combined Immunodeficiency (SCID) caused by a lack of production of the enzyme adenosine deaminase (ADA) by the patient's lymphocytes.

Through genetic engineering, one can transfer normally functioning ADA genes from lymphocytes of a healthy person to lymphocytes of a person suffering from SCID. Thereafter, repeated divisions of the patient's gene-altered cells result in a huge population of lymphocytes, all capable of producing ADA.

About 1 billion gene-altered lymphocytes were transfused into the child by Drs. W. F. Anderson and R. M. Blaese of the National Heart, Lung and Blood Institute of the NIH. There have been monthly infusions of the genetically engineered blood cells and the patient was reported as showing improved immune function. Since that time another child was treated similarly for SCID but no progress report had been issued by the fall of 1991.

DNA Fingerprinting. Congress was considering a bill entitled the DNA Proficiency Testing Act of 1991. This bill would set standards for DNA-fingerprinting laboratories and mandate proficiency testing of these laboratories every six months. The bill was designed to eliminate any confusion over the admissibility of DNA-fingerprinting evidence which has, since 1987, been used increasingly to establish the guilt or innocence of individuals accused of violent crimes where bloodstains or semen of the criminal are available but where there are no reliable eyewitnesses as to whether the accused is the perpetrator of the crime.

LOUIS LEVINE, *City College of New York*

GEOLOGY

In 1991 deadly earthquakes and volcanic eruptions shook the globe, while geologists discovered important information about ancient animals and the inner Earth.

Volcanoes. The Pacific "Ring of Fire" lived up to its name in 1991. During mid-May shallow earthquakes began shaking the Japanese volcano Unzen, signaling an imminent eruption. The Japanese government evacuated thousands of people from the area during late May. But at least 38 perished on June 4 when part of Unzen's summit collapsed, unleashing a large stream of lava, ash, and hot gas that raced down the mountain at reported speeds of up to 62.5 mph (100 km/h). Many of the casualties were journalists and scientists who had ventured into a "forbidden" zone. Unzen last erupted in 1972, when some 15,000 people died after an avalanche created a tsunami wave.

Two weeks after Unzen's June eruption, the Philippine volcano Pinatubo unleashed a blast that killed hundreds and threatens to alter the global climate (*see* sidebar).

On August 12, Hudson volcano in southern Chile erupted, sending ash and gas 10 to 11.25 mi (16 to 18 km) into the atmosphere. Ash fell as far away as the Falkland Islands, 625 mi (1 006 km) to the southeast. The plume of gas from Hudson caught wind currents in the atmosphere and circled the globe in just one week's time. Hudson last erupted in 1971.

Scientists studying an ancient eruption in Siberia have linked this geological event to the most severe biological crisis known, a time when an estimated 96% of ocean species died out along with many of the dominant land animals. This mass extinction at the end of the Permian period set the stage for the world of the dinosaurs, and researchers long have wondered what caused such extraordinary die-offs. Scientists now think eruptions may be the answer, after finding evidence that a huge volcanic deposit in Siberia formed at roughly the same time as the extinctions occurred 248 million years ago. This eruption, one of the world's largest, may have sparked the extinctions by upsetting Earth's climate.

Earthquakes. A devastating earthquake shook the Hindu Kush region of northern Afghanistan on February 1, killing an estimated 400 people there and at least 300 in nearby Pakistan. The magnitude 6.8 quake occurred in a mountainous area that forms the western edge of the Himalaya range. Scientists believe the seismic activity in Hindu Kush results from stress in the Earth, caused by a tectonic collision between the Indian subcontinent and the Asian landmass. This same collision created the Himalaya mountains.

Northern Peru suffered a magnitude 6.7 earthquake on April 5 that killed 38 persons and left some 750 injured. The seismic waves were felt throughout the northern part of the country and in nearby Ecuador.

A strong earthquake hit the eastern coast of Costa Rica on April 22, killing 47 persons in that country and 28 in neighboring Panama. Geologists think the magnitude 7.4 quake may have been generated by a tectonic-plate collision involving the Pacific seafloor, which slides under Central America in a jerky motion, generating earthquakes when it moves.

A magnitude 7.3 shock on April 29 killed more than 100 people in Soviet Georgia. The earthquake occurred in the Caucasus, a region where two of Earth's plates collide. The disaster left some 75,000 persons homeless.

Fossils. Paleontologists in China discovered the fossilized remains of a bird that reveals an important stage in the evolution of flight. Dating back 135 million years, this sparrow-sized specimen is the earliest known example of a bird with wing structure similar to modern birds. The unnamed species is 10 to 15 million years younger than the oldest known bird, *Archaeopteryx,* and has several adaptations to flight that the older bird lacks.

Scientists studying the fossilized bones of the longest known dinosaur report finding proteins that apparently have remained intact through 150 million years. These proteins were isolated from the bones of seismosaurus, the unofficial name for an animal being excavated in central New Mexico. Seismosaurus has an estimated length of 160 ft (49 m), making it the largest animal ever to walk on Earth. If future studies confirm that these proteins really belong to the seismosaurus, scientists could use such molecules to help study the relationships between various dinosaurs.

A discovery of ancient centipedes and spiderlike arachnids is forcing a revision of theories about the origin of land animals, a critical step in the history of life. Investigators uncovered these fossils in England and date them to 414 million years ago. Before this discovery, scientists considered 398-million-year-old fossils as the earliest land animals. The find suggests that the first land creatures climbed out of the ocean very soon after plants began to take root on the continents.

An extraordinary discovery in China is helping scientists understand the history of life right after a biological explosion that filled the seas with the first examples of modern animal phyla. This global event 570 million years ago shaped the development of all future animal evolution. The Chinese site, located in Yunnan province and discovered in 1984, dates to 530 million years ago. In 1991, Chinese and Swedish researchers described a newfound fossil from the Yunnan site that helps make sense of a strange animal called *Hallucigenia* found at other sites. Although this animal has evaded explanation, it resembles the new Chinese fossil, which scientists believe fits in a phylum

The Eruption of Mount Pinatubo

After resting quietly for more than 600 years, the Philippine volcano Mount Pinatubo came to life in 1991 in a violent eruption that killed hundreds of people and would cool the Earth's climate for several years.

The volcano, located on Luzon Island, first gave signs of reawakening in early April when a small explosion ejected steam and ash into the air. In early June several stronger blasts and earthquakes spurred Philippine authorities to evacuate people living near the volcano. The U.S. Air Force evacuated Clark Air Force Base, situated about 9 mi (15 km) east of Pinatubo. The largest explosions occurred on June 15 when the volcano blew its top, sending plumes of steam and hot gas rising some 16 mi (26 km) into the atmosphere. Pyroclastic flows—streams of superheated ash, gas, and rocks—raced down the sides of the volcano, wiping out structures in their path.

The volcano erupted at the same time as a typhoon brought heavy rains to that part of Luzon Island. Water-soaked ash caused roofs to collapse, contributing to the death toll from the eruption. The number of victims continued to climb months after the blast as storms during the rainy season set off destructive mudflows and disease claimed people in evacuation shelters. The death toll had exceeded 500 people by the end of September.

© Reuters/Bettmann

Effects. One of the largest eruptions of the 20th century, the explosion from Mount Pinatubo will affect people around the globe by cooling the climate and thinning the protective ozone shield. The eruption will spur such changes because it ejected millions of tons of superheated sulfur-dioxide gas straight up into Earth's stratosphere. The sulfur-dioxide gas reacts with water in the atmosphere to form tiny droplets of sulfuric acid that slowly would spread around the globe during late 1991 and into 1992.

Sulfuric-acid droplets cool the climate by reflecting sunlight back toward space, slightly dimming the amount of light hitting the Earth's surface. Scientists expect the haze of volcanic-acid droplets could lower global average temperatures by 0.5°C before the droplets fall out of the sky in two or three years. If it occurs as expected, the cooling temporarily will reverse the recent warming trend of global temperatures.The warming has sparked concern because climate experts long have predicted that greenhouse-gas pollution eventually will raise global temperatures. Indeed some scientists say the greenhouse warming has begun.

The sulfuric-acid droplets from Pinatubo also may cause a temporary thinning of the world's protective ozone screen. Atmospheric chemists believe the droplets alter the chemistry of the stratosphere, making chlorine pollution more destructive to ozone than it would be normally. The stratospheric ozone layer absorbs ultraviolet radiation dangerous to plants and animals. Such radiation can cause skin cancer as well as other diseases in humans.

RICHARD MONASTERSKY

called Onychophora. The enigmatic *Hallucigenia,* therefore, may be of the same phylum.

Plate Tectonics and Inner Earth. The lonely continent of Antarctica once may have been connected to North America, according to a startling theory raised by two geologists. Similar rocks found on both continents suggest the two joined together more than 1.6 billion years ago and then remained side by side for at least 1 billion years. Between about 800 million to 600 million years ago they may have formed part of a giant supercontinent consisting of most of the world's continents. Geologists long have believed such a supercontinent existed. The splitting apart of this giant landmass may have changed the atmosphere profoundly, spurring development of the first large, multicellular creatures.

An important discovery on the floor of the Pacific Ocean has helped oceanographers understand the process of seafloor spreading, which creates the ocean floor that covers about two thirds of Earth's surface. Investigators examining sonar images of the seafloor made in 1989 spotted a lava flow that did not show on a sonar map made in 1981. Normally, geologists have no way of dating deep-sea eruptions. The scientists who discovered the recent lava flow believe it occurred when two of Earth's plates pulled apart by several meters, leaving a crack that was filled with molten rock rising from under the seafloor.

European scientists have discovered evidence that the rules of plate tectonics have not changed appreciably in the last 2 billion years. Using sound waves to probe the interior of the Earth, they have found evidence near Finland of an ancient crash between two plates. This collision zone, which dates back 1.9 billion years, resembles more recently formed collision regions, suggesting a close similarity between the plate tectonics of the ancient Earth and that of the modern world.

RICHARD MONASTERSKY, *"Science News"*

GEORGIA

As the Georgia sports dome—under construction in Atlanta—rose higher each month, Georgians focused their attention on business and sports during 1991.

Economics. Reeling from the collapse of Eastern Airlines, the Georgia economy welcomed the news that such companies as Saab Cars USA, United Parcel Service, and Holiday Inn chose to locate their headquarters in Atlanta. The economy also was given a boost in April when Lockheed Corporation in Marietta, GA, landed a lucrative Pentagon contract, called the biggest single defense project of the 1990s. The contract would mean 2,000 new jobs and would solidify Lockheed's position as the top U.S. defense contractor.

GEORGIA • Information Highlights

Area: 58,910 sq mi (152 576 km²).
Population (1990 census): 6,478,216.
Chief Cities (1990 census): Atlanta, the capital, 394,017; Columbus, 179,278; Savannah, 137,560.
Government (1991): *Chief Officers*—governor, Zell Miller (D); lt. gov., Pierre Howard (D). *General Assembly*—Senate, 56 members; House of Representatives, 180 members.
State Finances (fiscal year 1990): *Revenue,* $13,108,000,000; *expenditure,* $12,213,000,000.
Personal Income (1990): $110,886,000,000; per capita, $17,049.
Labor Force (June 1991): *Civilian labor force,* 3,174,900; *unemployed,* 203,800 (6.4% of total force).
Education: *Enrollment* (fall 1989)—public elementary schools, 828,426; public secondary, 298,109; colleges and universities, 239,208. *Public school expenditures* (1989), $4,006,069,000.

Although Georgia's exports in telecommunications equipment, chemicals, and poultry rose, the state government faced a financial crisis that required cuts in public services, hiring freezes, and layoffs. This governmental slump, along with declines in the housing market and increased bankruptcy petitions, reflected the national recession.

Sports. Georgians, still incredulous that Atlanta would host the 1996 Summer Olympics, hardly dared to think that the state at last also might have a championship team. But the Atlanta Braves baseball team surprised everyone by coming from last place to first in the National League and bringing the World Series to the city. Although the Braves lost the series, more than 500,000 people lined Peachtree Street for a post-series parade.

In the meantime, preparations for the Olympic Games continued. The Georgia sports dome neared completion, sites were selected for the equestrian and tennis competitions, and construction was about to begin on the Olympic village. Atlanta also was an official contender for the 1993 World Indoor track and field championships and the 1994 World Cup soccer games.

Politics. Zell Miller became Georgia's 79th governor in January, and within ten weeks of his inauguration, the General Assembly passed all major items on Miller's agenda. These included a constitutional amendment to allow a statewide lottery, boot-camp-style prisons for nonviolent criminals, a bill lowering the standard level of legal intoxication, and a $7.9 billion budget that included tax credits for the working poor. Miller's early success was tempered later, when he announced budget cuts in education and state services and initiated a furlough program for state employees. Amid public outcry and demonstrations by state workers, Miller defended his furlough policy, later rescinded by a court ruling.

Other News. The April crash of a Southeastern Airlines plane traveling from Atlanta to Brunswick took the lives of some prominent figures, including former U.S. Sen. John Tower (R-TX), astronaut Manley L. "Sonny" Carter, Jr., and the president-elect of the American College of Physicians, Nicholas Davies. . . . Native Georgian Clarence Thomas became a U.S. Supreme Court justice in October. . . . Former U.S. Rep. Pat Swindall was denied a retrial for his 1988 perjury charge. . . . Georgia native Walter Leroy Moody, Jr., was convicted in June in the 1989 mail bombings that killed a judge and a civil-rights attorney. . . . Wayne Williams, convicted of murder in the famous Atlanta child-murders case of the early 1980s, was again in the news as well-known attorneys William Kunstler and Allan Dershowitz petitioned to reopen the case.

KAY BECK
Georgia State University

© Contrast Press/Photoreporters

In November 1991, German Chancellor Helmut Kohl, right, *and Russian Republic President Boris Yeltsin signed a declaration providing for "peaceful, comprehensive, and close cooperation" between Germany and the Russian Republic.*

GERMANY

With the euphoria of the 1990 unification past, Germans in 1991 began the complex process of putting their country back together again. Initial hopes that the 40-year (1949–89) division could be overcome quickly were dashed. The reconstruction of the former German Democratic Republic (GDR) or East Germany would take longer and cost much more than was estimated in the heady days of 1990. But more importantly, Germans—East and West—began to realize just how different they had become during the four decades and how difficult genuine social unification would be. The Berlin Wall was down, but a wall still existed in the minds of many Germans.

Politics. After profiting from unification euphoria in 1990, the ruling Christian Democrat Union (CDU) Party, led by Chancellor Helmut Kohl, suffered from unification's downside in 1991. Reneging on his "no new taxes" pledge during the 1990 campaign, Kohl in February announced increases in gasoline taxes, social-security contributions, and a 7.5% surtax on incomes. In making the announcement he cited the unexpectedly high costs of unification and Germany's multibillion-dollar contribution to the Persian Gulf war. Voter backlash against the tax rise in the West was largely responsible for the poor performance of the CDU at several state elections throughout the year. As 1991 ended the CDU governed in only two of the ten "old" states in the West.

In the East the CDU was hurt by the declining economy and a widespread belief that Kohl, following the election, had lost interest in the unique problems of the former East Germany. The CDU in the East also was damaged by its revealed association with Communists, specifically the hated secret police, or Stasi. In September the last prime minister of East Germany, Lothar De Maizière, resigned as deputy chairman of the CDU and withdrew from politics after being accused of collaborating with the Stasi. Throughout the East several CDU members of state parliaments also resigned because of past Stasi connections.

The major opposition party, the Social Democrats (SPD), were the major beneficiaries of the CDU's problems. The party regained control of Germany's upper house of Parliament where it now could veto some of the government's legislative program. The party, however, did not propose any viable alterna-

In state elections in Rhineland-Palatinate on April 21, the Christian Democratic Union, led by the state's Premier Carl-Ludwig Wagner, left, *suffered a surprisingly big defeat.*

© dpa/Photoreporters

© Contrast Press/Photoreporters

A sign showing higher gas prices was changed at night. The increase was a result of new taxes, which went into effect on July 1 and were to fund the cost of German unification.

tive to the government's policies. Its new leader and probable chancellor candidate at the next election, Björn Engholm, was relatively unknown and untested in national politics.

The Free Democrats (FDP), who have been the coalition partners of the CDU since 1982, were spared the wrath of the electorate over the tax increases. Their titular leader, Foreign Minister Hans-Dietrich Genscher, remained the most popular politician in the country. There were increasing signs in 1991 that the FDP considered the Kohl government a sinking ship and was considering a change of partners. In April it formed a coalition in one of Germany's 16 states with the SPD, its third such alignment at state level in two years.

GERMANY • Information Highlights

Official Name: Federal Republic of Germany.
Location: North-central Europe.
Area: 137,931 sq mi (357 241 km²).
Population (mid-1991 est.): 79,500,000.
Chief Cities (Dec. 31, 1989 est.): Berlin, the capital, (1990 est.), 3,400,000; Hamburg, 1,626,220; Munich, 1,206,683, Leipzig, 530,010; Dresden, 501,417.
Government: *Head of state,* Richard von Weizsäcker, president (took office July 1, 1984). *Head of government,* Helmut Kohl, chancellor (took office Oct. 1982). *Legislature*—Parliament: Bundesrat and Bundestag.
Monetary Unit: Deutsche mark (1.6120 D. marks equal U.S.$1, Dec. 4, 1991).
Economic Indexes (1990): *Consumer Prices* (1980 = 100), all items, 129.5; food, 123.5. *Industrial Production* (1980 = 100), 123.
Foreign Trade (1990 U.S.$): *Imports,* $349,417,-000,000; *exports,* $406,483,000,000.

The Greens, Germany's environmentalist party, which failed to gain enough seats in the 1990 election to return to the national Parliament, were able in 1991 to regroup. Throughout the year they made impressive gains in state elections. While not in the national Parliament, they now were in a record three state governments.

German political leaders in 1991 had to deal with three issues that had not been resolved in the 1990 unification treaties—abortion, the millions of Stasi files, and whether the government and Parliament should remain in Bonn or move to Berlin.

In East Germany under the Communists, abortion on demand was permitted during the first trimester of pregnancy. In the West a woman had to prove that a "social" (poverty, mental illness) or medical emergency existed before an abortion could be performed in the first trimester. The certification of such an emergency had to be obtained from a family-planning service approved by the government. The abortion also had to be carried out by a different physician from the one who certified the emergency. The 1990 unification treaty called for the Parliament to resolve the differences in these two laws by the end of 1992. In the meantime, each part of the country would retain its law and women from the West who traveled to the former East Germany could avail themselves of the East German law without penalty. Public opinion favored the more liberal East German law. Christian Democrats from the East probably would join with Social Democrats and Free Democrats from throughout the country to make the old East German law, or a revised version of it, valid for the entire country. This controversial topic was dividing the ruling CDU and could threaten the stability of the Kohl government.

The Stasi Files. East Germans wanted the 6 million files collected by the former Communist secret police to be the special responsibility of the five new eastern states. They also supported public access to the documents so that citizens could find out whether they had been spied upon and, above all, by whom. West Germans, less affected by the files than East Germans, wanted them transferred to the Federal Archives in the West where public access would be limited. As in the case of abortion, the issue was postponed by assigning it to the all-German Parliament. Until then the documents remained in Berlin under the supervision of a special commissioner responsible to the Parliament.

In November a new law was passed that attempted to resolve the problem. The documents would remain in Berlin and citizens would be allowed to examine their files and identify those individuals who had spied on them. The access of the media, however, would be restricted to the publication of the names of the spies and informants. The files of Stasi "victims" could not be publicized. Some publishers and journalists criticized this latter provision as an infringement on press freedom. They also charged that it was intended to prevent the media from publicizing the information the Stasi had gathered on leading West German politicians. The legislation would be tested in the courts.

Bonn or Berlin as Capital. In June, following an emotional 11-hour debate, the Bundestag (lower house of Parliament), by a narrow margin, voted to return the seat of government to Berlin. In the vote the deputies were not bound by party discipline, but only by their individual consciences. Support for both cities cut across party lines. President Richard von Weizsäcker and Chancellor Kohl supported Berlin, while Finance Minister Theodor Waigel wanted the government to remain in Bonn. The decision for Berlin was one of the most important in the Parliament's history. It affirmed West Germany's commitment to integrate the former East Germany into the larger Federal Republic as soon as possible. The move to Berlin, however, would take at least five to eight years and some government agencies and institutions would remain in Bonn.

Even before the decision to move the capital from Bonn, Berlin's economy was booming. Industrial production in the city increased by 13.5% in the first four months of 1991, double the West German average. More than 100,000 new jobs were created in 1991, and the city gained more than 75,000 new residents. By the year 2000, Berlin will have 5 million residents. Since 1989 real-estate prices in the city had more than doubled.

The Economy. In 1991 unified Germany's economy was characterized by rapid growth and near-boom conditions in the West, and rapid deterioration in the East as hundreds of formerly state-run enterprises unable to compete in the free market were forced to close. Real economic growth in the West, fueled by consumer demand in the East, increased by about 4% in 1991. Unemployment, at 5.5%, dropped to its lowest level since 1981. In the East, however, by the end of the year more than 25% of the old GDR's work force was unemployed or on government-subsidized part-time work. The region's gross national product dropped by almost 20% in 1991 following a 13% drop in 1990. Because the 1990 currency union increased the money supply by about 20% without a corresponding increase in productivity, inflation at around 4% became a problem in 1991. The 1991 tax increases also contributed to the rise in prices.

Unification now was hitting the average West German in the wallet. Aid to the East from the West in 1991 averaged almost $4,900 for every man, woman, and child in the region. Government borrowing financed some of this aid, but the unification-related tax and price increases added about $75 to the monthly budget of a typical West German family of four.

Economic development in the East also was hindered by disputes over property ownership. Almost 1.3 million claims were made on property confiscated either by the Nazis after 1933 or the Communists after 1945. Many East Ger-

Mercedes Benz automobiles are manufactured in East Germany. Following unification in late 1990, East Germans continued to adapt to the free-market system of the West during 1991. The unemployment rate in the East was registered at some 25%.

© Novosti/Sipa Press

Soviet troops based in Germany prepare to depart for home. Two treaties on the withdrawal of Soviet troops and on transitional matters related to the withdrawal were approved in principle by the Supreme Soviet of the USSR on April 2.

mans, however, acquired these homes, shops, and farms under laws and regulations issued by the Communist regime, which was a sovereign state until 1990. The courts now had to decide whether the rights of East Germans, who in many cases had lived on the properties for decades, took precedence over the rights of former residents or their heirs who fled or were deported from the country.

In spite of these problems, by the end of the year the massive infusions of Western capital into the East were beginning to show results. The construction industry, small business, and the service sector were expanding even as the overall employment picture continued to worsen. In spite of all the difficulties of modernizing the economy, studies showed that the average East German in 1991 enjoyed a substantially higher standard of living than before unification.

The Environment. Throughout the year the full extent of the East's environmental problems became apparent. The former East Germany was seen as an environmental disaster area and the cleanup was considered to be a harder task than the rebuilding of its economy. Water, ground, and air pollution were among the highest in Europe. Since unification the closing down of some of the worst polluters, largely for economic reasons, produced some marginal improvement in air and water quality, but the monumental task of restoring this area would last well into the 21st century.

Only 3% of the region's rivers and streams were ecologically intact and only 1% of its lakes were free from pollution. Almost 80% of the area's water resources were either biologically dead or heavily polluted. The remainder were poisoned only "moderately." The most important waterway in the East, the Elbe River, which flows from Czechoslovakia through Germany before emptying into the North Sea, was the most polluted river in Europe. Most industrial waste was discharged, untreated, into the Elbe or its tributaries.

Minorities. Germany in 1991 became the target country for almost 240,000 foreigners seeking political asylum, three times the number of any other European country. Article 16 of the German constitution contains one of the most liberal asylum laws in the world. The framers of the constitution in 1949, many of whom were political refugees themselves during the Third Reich, wanted the country's borders to remain open for any refugee from political oppression. People seeking asylum in 1991, however, were seen as fleeing for economic rather than political reasons. All applicants were entitled to due process under German law. While most applications for political asylum were rejected in 1991, the legal process could last for months and even years. In the interim the applicants remained beneficiaries of Germany's generous welfare state.

The growing number of asylum seekers, the poor economic situation in the East—especially among young people—and a general shortage of affordable housing throughout the country were important factors in the growing resentment toward foreigners in 1991. In September outbreaks of violence against foreigners erupted throughout the country. Beginning in the former East Germany, gangs of skinheads and young neo-Nazis attacked hostels and apartment buildings housing the foreigners, most of whom were seeking political asylum. The gangs threw rocks and bottles at the foreigners and in some cases were cheered on by local residents. The decision by local officials in the East German town of Hoyerswerda to evacuate their foreigners spurred similar attacks in other areas, including West Germany. In some cases firebombs were thrown and shots were fired. Some foreigners were assaulted on the street. In October alone authorities registered more than 900 attacks on foreign residents, the most extensive violence against foreigners in Germany since the Third Reich.

The incidents sparked demonstrations by many Germans against the violence. In early November more than 100,000 Germans in 30 cities turned out to express their support for the foreign residents. All major political leaders condemned the violence, but Chancellor Kohl was criticized by many for not participating in the demonstration and for not speaking out more forcefully. Kohl and the CDU wanted a constitutional amendment restricting the right to asylum. The Social Democrats opposed this and proposed a speedier evaluation process or a quota system similar to that used in the other European countries and the United States. All major political parties agreed, however, that the traditional asylum policy had not worked and must be changed.

Terrorism. In April, Detlev Rohwedder, the head of the agency charged with transforming the former East Germany into a market economy, was shot and killed at his home in West Germany. The Red Army Faction (RAF), Germany's most radical terrorist group, claimed responsibility. In February the RAF raked a U.S. embassy building in Bonn with 250 rifle shots, but no one was injured. The terrorists apparently hoped to disrupt the unification process and gain support among East Germans angered over the loss of their jobs. The agency which Rohwedder led, the Trusteeship Authority, has the task of closing the formerly state-run enterprises in the East that could not compete in the market economy and privatizing those that could become competitive.

Foreign Policy. Germany in 1991 continued to be the strongest supporter of the Soviet Union in Western Europe. Soviet President Mikhail Gorbachev was invited to the June economic summit in London at the insistence of Chancellor Kohl, who also urged unsuccessfully that the seven major Western nations offer a generous aid package to the Soviet leader. The abortive August coup against Gorbachev was a shock to the Kohl government. No foreign country had benefited more from *perestroika* than Germany. Since 1989 the Federal Republic had granted more than $30 billion in grants and loans to the Soviet Union, by far the largest amount of any country.

Fearful that a breakup of the Soviet Union would unleash a flood of refugees into Germany, the Kohl government also initiated direct contacts with several Soviet republics. In November, President Boris Yeltsin of the Russian Republic, during an official visit to Germany, signed an agreement calling for cooperation in arms control, scientific research, and the protection of minorities. The Kohl government appealed to President Yeltsin to extradite the former East German Communist boss, Erich Honecker. In March, Honecker fled to the Soviet Union from a Soviet military hospital near Berlin. He was under indictment for issuing a shoot-to-kill order that resulted in the deaths of more than 200 East Germans since the construction of the Berlin Wall.

Germany went to great lengths in 1991 to assure its West European neighbors and allies that unification had not made the country turn inward and become more "German" and less "European." In October it announced plans for stepped-up military cooperation with France and invited other European nations to join in what could become a unified European defense force. Germany also took the lead within the European Community (EC) on the planned monetary union, which would replace the separate national central banks and currencies with a single bank and currency by the end of the century. The Kohl government, however, wanted the currency-union treaty linked to moves toward more political union.

Germany, while supporting the various EC efforts to end the civil war in Yugoslavia, was also the strongest advocate of recognizing the independence of the republics of Slovenia and Croatia, the major belligerents.

Like Japan, Germany sent no combat troops to the Middle East during the Persian Gulf war. However, it did contribute almost $10 billion to the allied effort, including almost $800 million in military and economic aid to Israel. Chancellor Kohl said he would like to amend the German constitution to allow the deployment of combat forces outside North Atlantic Treaty Organization (NATO) territory. But such an amendment also would require the support of the Social Democrats, who wanted German military participation limited to United Nations "blue helmet" or peacekeeping operations. Unified Germany in 1991 had yet to define its international role in the post-Cold War world.

DAVID P. CONRADT, *University of Florida*

GREAT BRITAIN

For the first time in more than a decade, Britain was led in 1991 by someone other than Margaret Thatcher; despite the change at No. 10 Downing Street, the nation remained uncertain if the Thatcher revolution had ended or merely entered another phase. The Iron Lady had been replaced by the Gray Man, as the media referred to Prime Minister John Major, but to the concern of some Conservatives, Thatcher continued to cast a long shadow. In June she spoke out in the United States and in the House of Commons against closer European union; that same month, the conservative *Sunday Telegraph* newspaper reported that she had told friends that Major, her chosen successor, "stands for nothing—he is nothing. He is gray. He has no ideas. I have been totally deceived." Thatcher disclaimed the newspaper account, but the impression remained that all was not well between the woman who lent her name to the Thatcher revolution and the man who inherited it.

Domestic Politics. At least one legacy of Thatcherism was relegated to history in 1991: the hugely unpopular flat-rate community charge or "poll tax." In April, Major announced that the per-capita tax for local services, which had sparked rioting and protest on its introduction to England and Wales in 1990, would be replaced by a new "council tax" based on property values.

As the poll tax was earmarked for abolition, privatization, another pillar of Thatcherism, remained in place. Major restated his determination to sell off British Rail and British Coal, but political tempers were exercised most by the government's plans for the National Health Service. The government, having decreed that National Health hospitals could become "self-governing trusts" responsible for their own budgets, saw two such trust hospitals forced to shed hundreds of jobs in April—shortly after the trust program began. While the government insisted that the purpose of self-governing trusts was to increase management efficiency, the Labour Party warned that they were a step toward privatization, an accusation vehemently denied by Conservatives. Despite Major's personal assurances that the service was not being readied for sale in the free market but simply being reformed, there was widespread concern that the Conservatives would privatize the health service if they won a fourth term in government; according to *The Economist* magazine, the health service's future came second only to the economy among voter concerns.

Though Major won acclaim for his performance on the world stage in 1991, and earned consistently high personal approval ratings, speculation that he would call an early general election was squelched in May, when the Conservatives took a beating in a number of local elections, losing 850 local council seats while Labour gained more than 450 and the Liberal Democrats more than 500. In July, Major unveiled his plans for a "Citizen's Charter" calling for improvements in public services. That same month, his government issued proposals to curtail the armed services and defense spending.

Election fever waxed again in the autumn, as the political parties held their annual conferences. After seeing the approval ratings of its party chairman Neil Kinnock dip, the Labour Party and Kinnock rebounded by holding a slick, made-for-television conference in Brighton. It was a more subdued Conservative Party that met a week later in Blackpool; the Tories saved their enthusiasm for Thatcher, giving her a five-minute standing ovation when she appeared on the platform beside Major. At the end of October, as the question of Britain's future in the European Community once again

Great Britain's Prime Minister John Major visited with members of the Royal Air Force in Kuwait early in 1991. Britain strongly supported the allied coalition during the Persian Gulf war.

dominated British political debate, *The Sunday Times* of London reported that a poll conducted by Market & Opinion Research International (MORI) gave the Labour Party a six-point lead over the Conservatives. With eight months to go before a general election had to be called by law, the year ended with all of the political parties gearing up for a long campaign.

Economy. As elsewhere in the world, recession hit hard in Britain in 1991; among the worst-affected regions was previously booming southeast England. In the same week in February that Britain made its first reduction in interest rates since joining the European Monetary System, Thatcher's former adviser Sir Alan Walters and five other economists wrote to *The Times* to warn that a major depression might be in the offing unless the government devalued the pound. In April, Dun & Bradstreet reported that nearly 8,000 businesses folded in England and Wales in the year's first quarter—the highest failure rate in any quarter since 1980. In May, Major told the Confederation of British Industry that "on any sensible measure," the government was beating inflation. The price, however, was high unemployment and the intransigent recession, and homeowners and business owners alike were suffering. The uneasy state of the economy, no doubt, added to Major's reluctance to call a general election. In October, Chancellor of the Exchequer Norman Lamont was reported as saying that "business optimism is at its highest level since 1988, after the biggest quarterly rise—adjusted for seasonal factors—for 17 years." Given the political pain inflicted by the recession, Lamont's cheer could be understood, but his notion of "seasonally adjusted optimism" drew scorn from opponents and media commentators. According to the Department of Employment, seasonally adjusted unemployment in September registered its smallest rise for nearly a year, but unemployment still had reached a whopping 2.45 million. Figures in November showed unemployment at 8.7%, compared with 5.9% the previous November.

Northern Ireland. In a harbinger of the escalating violence that was to follow, the Irish Republican Army (IRA) launched an audacious attack on No. 10 Downing Street on February 7, firing three mortar bombs at the prime minister's official residence as Major and his Cabinet sat inside discussing the Persian Gulf war. Three people were injured, but Major and his ministers were unharmed. Less than two weeks later, the IRA targeted two of London's busiest rail stations: At Victoria a bomb stashed in a trash can exploded during the early-morning rush hour, killing one man and injuring 38; at Paddington a bomb had gone off several hours before, causing structural damage but claiming no casualties.

In March, six men, originally from Northern Ireland, were freed by a British Court of Appeal after serving more than 16 years for the 1974 IRA bombings of two Birmingham pubs in which 21 people died. The confessions and forensic evidence employed to convict the "Birmingham Six," who had maintained their innocence from the beginning, finally had been deemed unreliable. There was a clamor for the resignation of Lord Chief Justice Geoffrey Lane, who had denied the men's earlier appeal in 1988. In June an appeals court overturned the convictions of the "Maguire Seven," who spent years in prison for supposedly making bombs for the IRA; the forensic evidence used to convict them in 1976 also was discredited. And in September the case of Judith Ward, imprisoned in 1974 for an IRA bombing of a military bus, was referred to an appeals court; the forensic evidence used to convict her also was called into question. All of this fired widespread debate about the British justice system. The government announced in March that it would establish a royal commission to study the system, and in October, Foreign Secretary Douglas Hurd, formerly the home secretary, told an inquiry that home secretaries should surrender the power to refer for appeal possible miscarriages of justice to an authority independent of the government.

AP/Wide World

On February 7 three mortar bombs exploded at No. 10 Downing Street as the prime minister met with his cabinet. The Irish Republican Army took responsibility for the attack.

Against this canvas, Northern Irish Secretary Peter Brooke and other would-be architects of peace in Northern Ireland struggled to get political talks on the future of the province off the ground. In June roundtable talks began with most of the province's major political leaders, but by July the discussions had collapsed, as the participants were no closer to agreeing on a form of regional government for Northern Ireland. Unionists balked at proposals that hinted at participation by the Republic of Ireland; the 1985 Anglo-Irish Agreement that gave Dublin a consultative role had been abhorred by Unionists since its inception. The failure of the talks triggered yet another wave of tit-for-tat killings by loyalist and nationalist paramilitaries that continued through the end of the year. In one of the worst incidents, the IRA bombed the military wing of a Belfast hospital in November, killing two British soldiers and injuring ten others, including a 5-year-old patient. In December business at stores around Britain was disrupted by incendiary devices planted by the IRA.

Foreign Affairs. Britons greeted the advent of 1991 with some trepidation, largely because of the looming conflict in the Persian Gulf. On January 3, Britain gave Iraqi diplomats 24 hours to leave Britain; hundreds more would be deported or imprisoned over the ensuing months. When war was declared in mid-January, Britain had some 35,000 troops in the Gulf, the second-largest Western force after the United States. Major lent fervent support to U.S. President George Bush, as did the British people and most Parliamentarians, save for several left-wing Labourites. Toward the end of January, Britons reacted with horror to televised pictures of two British pilots who had been taken prisoner by Iraq; Major called Iraqi President Saddam Hussein's treatment of prisoners of war "amoral." As the war drew to a close, Major visited British troops in the Gulf. Despite Germany's reluctance to support the Gulf war, Major also visited Chancellor Helmut Kohl in Bonn seeking to mend Anglo-German relations, which had been poor during the Thatcher years.

In April, Major won agreement from Bush and the European Community for his proposal to send troops into northern Iraq to protect Kurdish refugees forced to flee from Iraqi forces. That month, Roger Cooper, a Briton held by Iran for more than five years on espionage charges, was released and returned home. Optimism that all of the Western hostages held in the Middle East soon would be released heightened in August, when British television journalist John McCarthy was freed after spending more than five years as a hostage in Lebanon. His release was followed by the freeing in September of former Royal Air Force pilot Jackie Mann, who had been held hostage in Beirut for more than two years, and by the mid-November release of Terry Waite, an official of the Church of England.

In July, Major hosted a London summit of the Group of Seven. A joint communique issued by the group included calls for a "revitalized United Nations," the maintenance of sanctions against Iraq, the launch of a peace process in the Middle East, and support for market reforms in Eastern Europe. Soviet President Mikhail Gorbachev addressed the summit, seeking economic aid.

In September, Major visited the Netherlands, where he reportedly told the Dutch prime minister that he opposed sending a European Community military force to Yugoslavia. A month later, Major was reported to have been infuriated by a European Commission order telling Britain to halt work on seven important building projects; Britain, said the commission, had failed to comply adequately with a directive requiring environmental-impact studies for such projects.

Issues regarding Europe continued to plague Major into November. Former Conservative Party chair Norman Tebbit rekindled the often-rancorous Conservative debate over Europe when he warned Major on national television not to sign a treaty on economic and political union at the European Community's December summit in Maastricht. Nevertheless, Britain joined the other EC members in agreeing on a draft treaty that took the bloc on a closer road to political and economic unity, including common foreign and defense policies and a single currency by the year 2000. A last-minute formula was accepted whereby Britain

Terry Waite, an envoy of the Church of England, returned to Britain on November 18 after being released from captivity in Lebanon. He had been held hostage since January 1987.

© Reuters/Bettmann

The Royalty Issue

© Nils Jorgensen/Rex USA Ltd.

During her visit to the United States in May 1991, Queen Elizabeth II was received enthusiastically nearly everywhere she went. It must have been a relief, for trouble and dissent had been brewing at home. In Britain, loyalty to "queen and country" remained strong, but it was no longer an unquestioning loyalty and indeed it was a matter of some contention that it ever had been.

During the 1991 Persian Gulf war, the right-of-center *Sunday Times* newspaper lambasted some members of the royal family for not doing enough for the war effort; this was no small slight, for the queen is officially head of the armed services. Some of the family members, railed the newspaper, paraded "a mixture of upper-class decadence and insensitivity which disgusts the public and demeans the monarchy."

The Tax Issue. In February a poll conducted by Numbers Market Research for the *Independent* found that 79% of those polled believed that the queen should pay tax. In June author Phillip Hall revealed the contents of his new book, which asserted that contrary to the widely held belief that the monarch never has paid taxes, both Queen Victoria and Edward VII paid income tax; total exemption, he said, was not secured until the reign of George VI, the current queen's father. Hall's assertions fueled an already raging debate about the queen's untaxed private annual income, which one modest estimate put at about £20 million (about $34 million) per year. (The total private wealth of the Windsors, on which no income tax is paid, had been estimated at $10.73 billion by *Fortune* magazine.)

Noting that the Japanese emperor and the Swedish monarch paid tax, Liberal Democratic Parliamentarian Simon Hughes pressed for a bill that would abolish the queen's tax-free status. Speaking on television, Lord St. John of Fawsley, former Conservative leader of the House of Commons and a devoted royalist, admitted that the queen's tax-exempt status was "not totally accepted in the modern world" and "may be modified at some time in the future."

The Overview. Just as troubling, perhaps, were the results of a Gallup poll conducted for the *Daily Telegraph* newspaper in July that found that 22% of those questioned said that Britain did not need a royal family; of that percentage, 36% was under the age of 25. The same poll showed that 51% of those questioned believed the royal family did not provide "a good example of family life"; in other words, the royals were failing in one of their prime duties. The poll reflected not just fears about family relations among the many peripheral royals, but concerns about the relationship between the heir to the throne and his wife. The couple, the prince and princess of Wales, marked their tenth wedding anniversary on July 29, amid unconfirmed but persistent reports that their marriage was in trouble. Prince Charles would lose his claim to the throne if there were a divorce, a circumstance the crown might not withstand.

Some expressed their belief that the demise of the crown would be no bad thing, arguing that Prime Minister John Major's professed aim of creating a "classless society" never would be achieved until the crown was retired to history. Republicans proposed that the monarch be divested of all constitutional powers; at present, the sovereign is head of the Church of England and head of state of 13 Commonwealth countries. These, however, remained minority views. Britons may want the queen to be taxed, but a relative few wish for the crown to lose its status altogether.

SUZANNE CASSIDY

could decide which measures it would adopt. Under the accord, Britain would be able to "opt out" of the monetary union.

On another long-debated issue, the British and Vietnamese governments signed an agreement in October allowing for the repatriation of Vietnamese economic refugees in Hong Kong.

The Royal Family. The royal who probably had the best year was a long-gone one: Henry VIII, whose 500th birthday was celebrated throughout England (*see* SPECIAL REPORT, page 261). In February, Queen Elizabeth II, the head of the armed services, made her first-ever wartime broadcast, congratulating her troops for their efforts and expressing hopes for a quick and victorious end to the war. In April a former royal police officer told the British press that all was not well in the marriage of the prince and princess of Wales; he claimed that the prince preferred gardening to his wife. That month, Prince Charles reentered the debate on educational standards in Britain, denouncing educators who ignored William Shakespeare. In June the prince was lambasted by the British tabloid press for spending what some regarded to be insufficient time with his son, Prince William, when William was hospitalized after being hit in the head with a golf club by a fellow student at his prestigious private school; by contrast, Princess Diana was said to have been reluctant to leave William's bedside. In August the royal couple celebrated their tenth wedding anniversary with an Italian cruise; sons William and Prince Harry were also aboard. In September the Duchess of York visited New York City, where she was honored at a reception hosted by New York Mayor David Dinkins. The following month, Prince Charles and Princess Diana visited Canada with their sons. Britons were outraged to learn that an Ottawa hospital had called in former patients to fill empty beds on the day the Princess visited.

GREAT BRITAIN • Information Highlights

Official Name: United Kingdom of Great Britain and Northern Ireland.
Location: Island, western Europe.
Area: 94,525 sq mi (244 820 km²).
Population (mid-1991 est.): 57,500,000.
Chief Cities (mid-1989 est.): London, the capital, 6,756,400; Birmingham, 992,500; Leeds, 711,700; Glasgow, 695,600; Sheffield, 526,600.
Government: *Head of state,* Elizabeth II, queen (acceded Feb. 1952). *Head of government,* John Major, prime minister and First Lord of the Treasury (took office November 1990). *Legislature*—Parliament: House of Lords and House of Commons.
Monetary Unit: Pound (0.5566 pound equals U.S.$1, Nov. 20, 1991).
Gross Domestic Product (1989 est. U.S.$): $818,000,-000,000.
Economic Indexes (1990): *Consumer Prices* (1980 = 100), all items, 188.6; food, 165.2. *Industrial Production* (1980 = 100), 118.
Foreign Trade (1990 U.S.$): *Imports,* $224,938,-000,000; *exports,* $185,976,000,000.

Other News. The drama of the Bank of Credit and Commerce International (BCCI), shut down in July because of revelations of extensive fraud, dominated Britain's financial news in 1991. The scandal left British politicians and bank officials reeling because the bank had had its headquarters in Britain and had been supervised by the Bank of England. London depositors, many of them Asian business people with huge sums to lose, demanded to know why the Bank of England had waited so long before taking action. A parliamentary committee was established to investigate the scandal, but the committee's findings were not expected until 1992. (*See also* SPECIAL REPORT/INTERNATIONAL TRADE AND FINANCE.)

In April, London Zoo officials threatened that they would have to displace or destroy thousands of animals unless the government came up with the cash the zoo needed to go on; the government refused and the 163-year-old institution was forced to consider radical reorganization or closure.

In May the leader of the House of Commons, John MacGregor, overruled the House of Lords and cleared the way for war-crimes trials of suspected Nazis residing in Britain. Also that month, the government introduced proposals for controlling dangerous dogs such as American pit bull terriers, which had been responsible for horrific attacks on British children and adults.

In the summer two men claimed that they had been responsible for Britain's "crop circles," the unexplained patterns that mysteriously had appeared on cornfields throughout Britain; crop-circle researchers denied that the patterns were the work of hoaxers.

In September riots by youths in Oxford, Cardiff, and Newcastle, and looting by youths in Birmingham led to a national debate on the reasons for the unrest; while Archbishop of Canterbury George Carey blamed urban deprivation and unemployment, government ministers charged the youths with criminality and moral laxity. In October the death of an adolescent girl in Liverpool, killed by a car driven by "joyriding" youths, threw into sharp relief the need for solutions to the crisis.

That same month saw a shakeup of Britain's independent television network as broadcasting franchises were awarded to new companies and taken away from existing ones. . . . Also, the House of Lords ruled that husbands could be convicted for raping their wives; women's rights campaigners told the British press that the decision ended "250 years of legal sexual slavery." . . . And Charter 88, a movement for constitutional reform, held a "constitutional convention" in Manchester in November, calling for a written constitution and electoral reform.

SUZANNE CASSIDY
Free-lance Journalist, London

The Arts

In 1991 the British arts world looked east, holding a six-month Japan Festival that included Kabuki versions of *Hamlet* and *Jesus Christ Superstar,* a national tour by the Tokyo Symphony Orchestra, a Visions of Japan exhibition at the Victoria and Albert Museum, and Japanese film at the National Film Theatre.

Theater. The year opened uneasily for British theaters, as the economic recession cramped spending at home and the Persian Gulf war kept American visitors away in droves.

With new artistic director Adrian Noble at the helm, the Royal Shakespeare Company returned to its two theaters at London's Barbican Center in March after a four-month hiatus forced by cash shortages. In June the Royal National Theatre told the Arts Council, the quasi-governmental body that helps fund the arts, that it might have to cut its season if it did not receive an extra £1 million (about $1.6 million) per year.

Sadly, too, 1991 saw the loss of Dame Peggy Ashcroft (*see also* OBITUARIES).

Despite its woes, London's West End produced a score of fine shows in 1991. Members of the Olivier family, including Sir Laurence's widow, Joan Plowright, starred in *Time and the Conways,* while sisters Vanessa and Lynn Redgrave, along with niece Jemma, took on *The Three Sisters.* Other notable plays included *Five Guys Named Moe,* a Clarke Peters musical about American jazz great Louis Jordan, and Dublin's Abbey Theatre's production of *Hedda Gabler,* directed by Deborah Warner and starring Fiona Shaw. Less successful was a revival of Thornton Wilder's *Our Town,* with Alan Alda. The autumn saw the eagerly awaited premieres of Arthur Miller's *The Ride Down Mount Morgan,* Alan Ayckbourn's *The Revengers' Comedies,* David Hare's *Murmuring Judges,* and Alan Bennett's *The Madness of George III.* Also in 1991, the Royal Shakespeare opened its new $3 million theater in Stratford-upon-Avon.

Music. Financial trouble plagued the nation's opera companies, too. In April staff members at the Royal Opera House, among them music director Bernard Haitink, petitioned to discontinue job cuts. In October a pay dispute between management and the orchestra closed the Royal Opera House for two weeks, delaying the start of the ballet season and the opening of the opera production *Les Huguenots.* The dispute ended when the orchestra agreed to management's original pay offer. At the cash-strapped English National Opera, general director Peter Jonas announced that he would be leaving in 1993; Dennis Marks, head of music programs for British Broadcasting Corporation (BBC) television, was chosen as Jonas' successor. Also in April, Andre Previn resigned as principal conductor of the Royal Philharmonic Orchestra, moving to the London Symphony Orchestra as conductor laureate; and the Birmingham Symphony Orchestra, led by Simon Rattle, moved into the concert hall built for it by the city of Birmingham. In May controversy at the Royal Opera involved the world premiere of Sir Harrison Birtwistle's new opera, *Gawain;* in one scene, French baritone François Le Roux appeared naked.

In June former Beatle Paul McCartney went classical, staging his *Liverpool Oratorio,* and in July, Luciano Pavarotti marked the 30th year of his career with an outdoor concert at London's Hyde Park; despite a downpour, some 125,000 people, including the Prince and Princess of Wales and Prime Minister John Major,

A highlight of the British theater year was the appearance together in Anton Chekhov's Three Sisters *of certain members of the famed Redgrave theatrical clan. Performing in the turn-of-the-century Russian drama were the sisters Vanessa and* Lynn *(center) and their niece Jemma Redgrave.*

© Annely Juda Fine Art, London and Gallery Lelong, Paris

The fall Tate Gallery exhibit of works by Sir Anthony Caro drew attention to that 20th-century sculptor. One of the major sculptures in the exhibit, Night Movements *(1987–90), above, consists of four freestanding steel units.*

turned out. In September, Prince Charles organized a concert featuring Jessye Norman, Placido Domingo, and Phil Collins to raise cash to restore the spire of Salisbury Cathedral. At the Royal Opera, Haitink conducted the complete cycle of Wagner's *Ring*. Also in 1991, the English Chamber Orchestra held Mozart 200, a series of 21 concerts marking the 200th anniversary of the composer's death.

Visual Arts. The National Gallery commanded much attention in 1991, first with the reopening of its three Impressionist galleries—which had been closed for two years for a restoration—and then in July with the long-awaited opening of the new Sainsbury Wing, a $60 million extension created to house the National Gallery's paintings from 1260 to 1510. The wing was designed by the U.S. firm of Venturi, Scott Brown and Associates; they took over after the Prince of Wales made his first foray into the realm of criticism, calling the original design "a monstrous carbuncle on the face of a much-loved and elegant friend."

In August the Prince rocked architectural circles once again when he resigned as president of the patrons of the Museums of Scotland over the design for a new building to house historical and archaeological artifacts.

Major exhibitions of the year included a Max Ernst retrospective and a massive John Constable survey, both at the Tate Gallery; a Pop Art show at the Royal Academy of Arts; an exhibition of Queen Elizabeth II's paintings at the National Gallery's Sainsbury Wing; and an exhibition of the works of Toulouse-Lautrec at the Hayward Gallery.

Dance. In February, British balletomanes mourned the death of Dame Margot Fonteyn, prima ballerina assoluta, who died at age 71 in Panama. At Covent Garden the Royal Ballet performed works ranging from Kenneth MacMillan's *Winter Dreams* to David Bintley's *Cyrano*. In May the Birmingham Royal Ballet returned to its old London home, Sadler's Wells, for a brief stint, performing among other ballets David Bintley's *Hobson's Choice*. At the Coliseum the English National Ballet's repertoire included *The Taming of the Shrew* and *Onegin*, both choreographed by John Cranko.

Film and Television. Sadness visited British film circles when Sir David Lean died at age 83 in April. The maker of such films as *Lawrence of Arabia* and *Doctor Zhivago* was honored in a memorial service at St. Paul's Cathedral attended by Peter O'Toole, Omar Sharif, Sir John Mills, and Sir Alec Guinness.

Notable films in 1991 included Peter Greenaway's *Prospero's Books,* starring Sir John Gielgud; Derek Jarman's *Edward II;* and Hanif Kureishi's *London Kills Me*.

On television, Britons watched *GBH,* Alan Bleasdale's blistering drama series on militant Laborites and right-wing conspirators, starring Michael Palin and Robert Lindsay, and *Bringing it All Back Home*, a BBC series about the odyssey of Irish music to and back from England and the United States.

SUZANNE CASSIDY

GREECE

During 1991, Greece struggled internally with political and economic problems which were exacerbated by such external issues such as the Cyprus issue, the Persian Gulf war, and the instability of Greece's northern neighbors —Yugoslavia and Albania.

Mitsotakis' Government. Prime Minister Constantine Mitsotakis' New Democracy Party retained a slim one-vote parliamentary majority during the year. His chief critic and longtime antagonist was Andreas Papandreou of the Panhellenic Socialist Union (PASOK). The first political casualty of the year was Education Minister Vassilis Kontoyannopoulos, who was forced to resign after riots precipitated by antagonism against the government's proposals for education reform. The prime minister faced opposition even within the New Democracy Party. In one spectacular incident, Industry, Energy, and Technology Minister Stavros Dimas submitted his resignation to Prime Minister Mitsotakis while both were on an official visit to the Soviet Union. Dimas suddenly tendered his resignation, following an exchange of words with Marika Mitsotakis, the prime minister's wife. The incident created an uproar over her role in politics.

Equally, questions were raised over the fact that Mitsotakis' daughter Dora Bakoyiannis was a member of the cabinet. In August, Mitsotakis made changes in his ministry, and Bakoyiannis was not included in the new list, which reduced the number of members to 36 from 42. Further turmoil occurred in October when Miltiadis Evert, hitherto minister to the prime minister's office, and second-most-important government official, lost his position following a controversy involving the ministry of foreign affairs.

The Economy. The Mitsotakis government also faced grave problems in trying to impose an austerity program to help the moribund Greek economy. Plagued by high inflation and the need to borrow heavily to meet expenses, Mitsotakis' every attempt seemed to provoke opposition leading to strikes and much public discontent. In addition, the Gulf war and its residual effects cut down on Greek tourism and the turbulence in Yugoslavia interfered with the overland transportation of Greek goods.

Embezzlement Trial. In March former Prime Minister Papandreou went on trial before a 13-member tribunal on charges relating to purported wrongdoing concerning the Bank of Crete. Along with Papandreou three others—Deputy Prime Minister Agamemnon Koutsogiorgas and former Ministers Dimitris Tsovolas and George Petsos—also were charged. Calling the trial political, Papandreou refused to appear or even to be represented by counsel. Also absent as the trial opened was the chief accuser George Koskotas, the former Bank of Crete chairman, who had fled to the United States in 1988 and was fighting extradition from a U.S. jail. In April, Koutsogiorgas suffered a stroke and died a few days later, but the trial continued. Koskotas finally was extradited from the United States and he made some sensational charges. After being delayed by a general strike of Greek lawyers, the trial dragged on.

Foreign Affairs. The liberalization of Albanian exodus regulations resulted in thousands of Albanian refugees, many of them Greek Orthodox, flooding into Greece and placing a strain on the country's ability to provide for them. With Yugoslavia in ferment, the Greek government had to consider the possibility that the Yugoslav federal republic of Macedonia might achieve independence. Under this scenario, Macedonia also might make claims to Greek territory disputed in prior eras. Greece, however, continued to emphasize that it had no territorial claims on Yugoslavia. Greece's relations with Turkey remained strained over air and sea rights in the Aegean Sea and most particularly over Turkey's continued occupation of part of Cyprus.

In July the Turkish chargé d'affaires and two Turkish embassy personnel were injured in a car-bomb explosion in Athens. In October, Cetin Gorgu, Turkey's assistant press attaché in Athens, was assassinated. The Greek government strongly condemned both acts. Meanwhile, responsibility for the assassination was claimed by November 17, a clandestine organization that had carried out a number of terrorist actions. The same group was suspected in the bombing death of U.S. Sgt. Ronald Steward in an Athens suburb in March 1991.

U.S. President Bush visited Athens in July, just before going on to Turkey. The president, who was pleased with Greece's support during the Persian Gulf war, called for a UN-mediated settlement in Cyprus. The two leaders met again in Washington.

Other News. In May the 50th anniversary of the Battle of Crete was commemorated. The

GREECE • Information Highlights

Official Name: Hellenic Republic.
Location: Southeastern Europe.
Area: 50,942 sq mi (131 940 km^2).
Population (mid-1991 est.): 10,100,000.
Chief Cities (1981 census): Athens, the capital, 885,737; Salonika, 406,413; Piraeus, 196,389.
Government: *Head of state,* Constantine Karamanlis, president (took office May 1990). *Head of government,* Constantine Mitsotakis, prime minister (took office April 1990). *Legislature*—Parliament.
Monetary Unit: Drachma (180.55 drachmas equal U.S.$1, Dec. 16, 1991).
Gross Domestic Product (1989 est. U.S.$): $56,300,000,000.
Economic Indexes (1990): *Consumer Prices* (1980 = 100), all items, 569.7; food, 566.9. *Industrial Production* (1980 = 100), 110.
Foreign Trade (1990 U.S.$): *Imports,* $19,777,000,000; *exports,* $8,019,000,000.

World War II battle pitted Greece and its allies —Great Britain, Australia, and New Zealand —against Nazi Germany. In a spirit of reconciliation, Chancellor Helmut Kohl of Germany attended the anniversary ceremonies.

In October, Prime Minister Mitsotakis traveled to Istanbul for the funeral of the Ecumenical Patriarch Dimitrios I, the ranking prelate of the worldwide Orthodox Church. The prime minister also attended the installation of the new ecumenical patriarch.

GEORGE J. MARCOPOULOS, *Tufts University*

HAITI

HAITI • Information Highlights

Official Name: Republic of Haiti.
Location: Caribbean.
Area: 10,714 sq mi (27 750 km²).
Population: (mid-1991 est.): 6,300,000.
Chief City (1987 est.): Port-au-Prince, the capital, 797,000 (incl. suburbs).
Government: *Interim president,* Joseph Nerette (took office after coup, October 1991). *Legislature*—suspended.
Monetary Unit: Gourde (5.0 gourdes equal U.S.$1, buying rate, July 1991).
Gross Domestic Product (1988 est. U.S.$): $2,400,-000,000.
Economic Index (1990): *Consumer Prices* (1980 = 100), all items, 191.1; food, 177.3.
Foreign Trade (1988 U.S.$): *Imports,* $344,000,000; *exports,* $200,000,000.

Anarchy and chaos reigned in Haiti during the latter part of 1991 when a military coup deposed the nation's first freely elected president after only eight months in office.

A New President. The year began auspiciously with the inauguration on February 7 of Jean-Bertrand Aristide, a populist Roman Catholic priest who had been swept into presidential office in December with some 67% of the vote.

Aristide immediately launched a series of far-reaching reforms. He took steps to redistribute land, combat illiteracy, and improve health. He also moved to control the army and shrink a swollen bureaucracy.

The new president also began to repair Haiti's poor relations with the international community, particularly the United States. U.S. aid, which had been cut off since 1987, resumed and was programmed to reach $85 million in 1991, with a larger amount planned for 1992. Other countries, along with international lending institutions, also restarted interrupted assistance programs.

The Coup. Aristide's reforms alienated Haiti's minuscule upper class and its traditional ally, the army. Finally, when Aristide began to create a 300-man militia outside the normal army chain of command, resentment grew into revolt. On the night of September 29 mutinies against the Aristide regime broke out. Within hours troops occupied the National Palace and seized Aristide. Although the rebellion at first appeared leaderless, Brig. Gen. Raoul Cedras, named army commander by Aristide in July, soon emerged as the head of a three-man junta that took control of the government. Aristide was deported to Venezuela.

International reaction to the coup came swiftly. The Organization of American States (OAS) condemned the overthrow and called for Aristide's return. The United States and other OAS members imposed a trade embargo which quickly caused food and fuel shortages and the closure of more than 100 assembly plants.

The Haitian legislature, nonetheless, named an interim president and prime minister. Army officers warned that Aristide would be killed if he should return to Haiti. An OAS delegation, sent to Port-au-Prince, arranged a meeting between Aristide and Haitian legislators in Cartagena, Colombia, but the lawmakers balked at restoring Aristide.

As the diplomatic maneuvering continued, violence mounted. According to the Inter-American Commission on Human Rights more than 1,500 Haitians were killed during the first two months following the coup.

Refugees. Thousands of Haitians tried to flee. Most of them crowded into unseaworthy wooden boats and headed for the United States. Many were picked up by the U.S. Coast Guard and some were returned to Haiti under terms of a 1981 refugee-return agreement.

A U.S. federal court in November ordered the repatriation to cease. The Bush administration appealed the order, but while the case was moving through the courts the Coast Guard landed more than 6,000 refugees at the U.S. naval base in Guantánamo, Cuba, where an emergency tent city was built to house the Haitians until order could be restored in their homeland. The problem in Haiti in 1991 was, as a leading U.S. newspaper observed, "not a malign government, but anarchy."

See also CARIBBEAN.

RICHARD C. SCHROEDER, *Consultant Organization of American States*

HAWAII

Hawaii's tourist-oriented economy sputtered during the first half of 1991 but got back on track by midyear, leading economists to predict a 2% growth over 1990.

The Economy. Visitor arrivals, the main barometer of the state's fiscal health, dropped precipitously after war broke out in the Persian Gulf and recession hit the continental United States. In the first five months of the year, visitor arrivals were down 9.1% from the same period a year earlier. However, by August there was an all-time monthly high of 706,420 visitors.

Other key economic components such as construction and credit demand were well ahead of 1990, although agriculture, once an economic mainstay, hit new lows and new highs. Pineapple production, facing competition from Asian markets, continued its decline with the phasing out of Dole's Lanai island plantation and the closing of its landmark cannery in Honolulu. On the brighter side, coffee production was the highest since 1972.

Government Issues. State-tax revenues were up 11.6% from 1990 and there was a surplus in the state treasury of about $350 million. Gov. John Waihee III (D) urged using the surplus to meet the critical housing shortage.

Politicians were criticized strongly for authorizing $64 million for asbestos removal and alterations to the state capitol, which cost only $23 million when built in 1969. During the four years of renovation, the legislature and the executive offices would operate from a nearby state office building.

Japanese Nationals. Hawaii's future prosperity depends in great part on Japanese nationals, who not only make up the bulk of travelers from Asia but also are heavy investors in the islands' tourism industry. They spent an estimated $2.86 billion for real estate in 1990, most of it for hotels and condominiums. They now owned an estimated 65% of all statewide hostelries.

The infusion of Japanese capital has not been without its critics. Honolulu Mayor Frank Fasi tried unsuccessfully to get the city council to agree to a $100 million levy for each golf course built by the Japanese. The levy would have been a condition for obtaining zoning permits. In defending his proposal, the mayor said the money could be used to build low-income housing, which, according to the U.S. Census Bureau, is at a premium in Hawaii. The bureau's 1990 figures showed that Hawaii had the highest average cost of single-family homes in the nation at $245,300. Average monthly rentals were $599.

© Galente/Gamma-Liaison

On Dec. 7, 1991, President Bush led the nation in ceremonies marking the 50th anniversary of Japan's attack on Pearl Harbor that led to the U.S. entry into World War II.

The Bishop Estate. Hawaii's largest private landowner, the Bishop Estate, which has been criticized for impeding home ownership and fueling the housing crunch, said it would fight any government attempt to force it to sell its leasehold properties. However, the estate offered to convert certain lands from leasehold to fee simple status, giving those holding leases an opportunity to purchase the land under their homes for costs up to $750,000. Outraged leaseholders asked their state representatives to introduce a cap on leasehold-conversion costs. No action could be taken until the legislature met in mid-January 1992.

Pearl Harbor. The 50th anniversary of the Japanese attack on Pearl Harbor was commemorated with four days of ceremonies in December. More than 40,000 people, many of them relatives of those 2,403 people killed in the attack, attended.

CHARLES H. TURNER
Free-lance Writer, Honolulu

HAWAII • Information Highlights

Area: 6,471 sq mi (16 759 km²).
Population (1990 census): 1,108,229.
Chief Cities (1990 census): Honolulu, the capital, 365,272; Hilo, 37,808; Kailua, 36,818; Kaneohe, 35,448.
Government (1991): *Chief Officers*—governor, John D. Waihee III (D); lt. gov., Benjamin J. Cayetano (D). *Legislature*—Senate, 25 members; House of Representatives, 51 members.
State Finances (fiscal year 1990): *Revenue,* $4,326,000,000; *expenditure,* $3,832,000,000.
Personal Income (1990): $22,663,000,000; per capita, $20,356.
Labor Force (June 1991): *Civilian labor force,* 565,700; *unemployed,* 17,800 (3.1% of total force).
Education: *Enrollment* (fall 1989)—public elementary schools, 121,660; public secondary, 47,833; colleges and universities, 54,188. *Public school expenditures* (1989), $643,319,000.

© Ron McMillan/Gamma-Liaison

In November, Hong Kong authorities began forcing Vietnam refugees to return to Vietnam under an agreement between Britain and Vietnam that would lead to the repatriation of many of the 63,000 boat people in Hong Kong.

HONG KONG

The year 1991 in Hong Kong was noted for the first direct election to the Legislative Council and the enactment of a Bill of Rights on June 8. The Hong Kong government contributed $29.5 million to Great Britain for the Persian-Gulf-war effort. The Tate's Cairn Tunnel, linking Siu Lik Yuen in Sha Tin and Diamond Hill in Kowloon, was opened in June, and the Hong Kong University of Science and Technology opened in October.

Chinese Intervention. Initially, China, which is scheduled to take control of the colony in 1997, wanted to suspend the $16.3 billion project to build a new airport and expand the shipping port. China feared the project would exhaust the reserve funds for the post-1997 government. After much discussion, the Hong Kong government reached an agreement with China to implement the project. China, in turn, was granted the right to participate in major franchises that would extend beyond 1997.

Three-tier Elections. The district board election for 274 seats, which was a litmus test to determine the prevailing philosophy of Hong Kong's political groups, was held on March 3. Seventy-seven candidates, supported by four liberal political groups, and 62 candidates, supported by two pro-Beijing groups, were elected. The elections for 27 councillors for the Urban and Regional Council were held on May 6. The liberal groups won 14 seats, the pro-Beijing groups won five seats, and the remaining seats went to independents.

The first direct election for 18 Legislative Council seats was held on September 15. Independent candidates took three seats and pro-democracy liberal candidates won the remainder: 12 from the United Democrats, two from Meeting Point, and one from the Association for Democracy and People's Livelihood.

Economy. Capital continued to leave Hong Kong. By 1990, 61 companies based in Hong Kong (10.83% of the territory's total market capitalization) had moved their headquarters elsewhere. Local businessmen also were considering moving overseas. In 1991 the Hong Kong and Shanghai Bank (HSB), the territory's biggest financial institution, set up a British nonresident HSB Corporated Holdings. This new company, owning about 30% of the HSB's overall assets, will continue after 1997.

After the Hong Kong government liquidated the local franchise of the Bank of Credit and Commerce International (BCCI) on July 8, four local banks—the International Bank of Asia, Dao Heng Bank, Citibank, and Standard Chartered Bank—experienced a bank run within a month as panicked depositors withdrew their savings.

China remained the leading source of foreign investment in Hong Kong, accounting for more than $10 billion in 1990. Japan and the United States were next, with $8 billion and $6 billion, respectively.

British Citizenship and Migration. Response to a British plan offering citizenship to a limited number of Hong Kong residents opposed to the Chinese takeover fell below expectations. Only 65,623 applications were received for the 43,500 passports offered, far lower than the anticipated 300,000.

In January 1991 the first group of 29 Vietnamese boat people returned to South Vietnam under the voluntary repatriation program. Some 63,000 Vietnamese refugees remained in Hong Kong. Hong Kong authorities in November reinstated a program of forced repatriation, backed by Great Britain. Fifty-nine refugees were returned to Vietnam against their will on November 9.

David Chuenyan Lai
University of Victoria, British Columbia

HOUSING

U.S. housing-market activity for 1991 was at the lowest level since World War II. The multifamily sector was depressed all year, and the single-family market posted only a modest recovery from a cyclical trough it hit in January when the Persian Gulf war erupted.

Foundations for a stronger single-family-housing recovery were built during 1991. A sizable amount of pent-up demand had accumulated following several years of below-trend home sales. Furthermore, housing affordability improved as mortgage interest rates fell to the lowest levels in 15 years and home prices receded in the weakest regions of the country. On the supply side of the single-family market, inventories of unsold new homes dwindled to their lowest levels since the 1982 recession, paving the way for an upswing in production.

Market fundamentals in the multifamily sector, on the other hand, were quite weak throughout 1991. Apartment vacancies remained high and provisions of the Tax Reform Act of 1986 continued to weigh heavily on investment incentives for building more rental units. The condominium market also remained depressed, particularly in the Northeast region where heavy production of earlier years overhung a market in which demand had fallen back as the economy weakened.

Thus 1991 ended with the single-family-housing market poised for expansion and the multifamily market still in the process of healing. On the policy front, the Federal Reserve Board (Fed) was easing monetary policy aggressively in an attempt to bolster housing and economic activity, and Congress and the Bush administration were working on fiscal-stimulus packages to further those objectives.

Bottoming Out. The U.S. housing market hit bottom in 1991 following several years of contraction. Total housing starts were about 1 million units for the year, down 45% from the recent peak in 1986 and the lowest since 1945.

The 1986–91 down slide in housing activity was concentrated in the multifamily sector, where both rental and condominium markets collapsed. Indeed, multifamily starts amounted to only 175,000 units in 1991, about one fourth of the peak production levels of the mid-1980s. Multifamily activity appeared to hit bottom around mid-1991, but little improvement was recorded during the second half of the year.

Single-family-housing activity had been good throughout the entire 1983–89 period, with starts of new units above 1 million in each of those years. However, single-family activity weakened considerably during 1990 and plunged to a seasonally adjusted annual rate of 650,000 units in January 1991. This low point coincided with the outbreak of war in the Persian Gulf and an associated collapse of consumer confidence in the United States.

Quick victory in the Persian Gulf war generated a rebound in both consumer confidence and housing-market activity. Single-family starts exceeded 800,000 by April and sales activity also bounced back. But consumer confidence weakened badly in subsequent months as the economic recession proved to be more persistent than expected. As a result, the housing-market upswing stalled in the second half of the year and single-family starts were about 830,000 for all of 1991—down 7% from 1990.

Affordability. The affordability of single-family housing improved dramatically in 1991, at least for those households that maintained their jobs and income levels. House prices receded in many metropolitan areas, particularly in previously overheated markets in the Northeast and California. Even more important, mortgage interest rates fell to the lowest levels in 15 years as the Fed eased monetary policy several times in an environment of weak economic activity and decreasing inflation.

By the end of the year, fixed-rate mortgages were down to about 8.25% and adjustable-rate mortgages were widely available for about 6%. Rate declines during the year prompted a surge of mortgage-refinancing activity as well as reductions in the cost of outstanding adjustable-rate loans—factors that bolstered the discretionary income of existing homeowners. The rate declines also helped to buoy home-sales activity in the face of flagging national employment and income and the associated erosion of consumer confidence.

In the rental market, high vacancy rates and recession-induced weakness in demand for apartment space led to stabilization of median rent levels in 1991, and declines in rental rates occurred in some local markets. Even a sharply reduced rate of completions of new apartment units failed to lower rental vacancy rates in the face of weakening demand.

Although declines in house prices and interest rates, along with softness in apartment rents, improved housing affordability for many people in the United States during 1991, affordability remained a serious issue for prospective first-time home buyers as well as lower-income renters. Indeed, a study conducted by the Joint Center for Housing Studies of Harvard University, entitled "The State of the Nation's Housing: 1991," concluded that the economic recession did not provide a cure for these persistent affordability problems. The Harvard study drew a number of conclusions that pose serious challenges for housing policy in the United States:

- Young families still found it very difficult to achieve first-time homeownership in 1991, and these difficulties would increase as economic recovery proceeds and house prices and interest rates move up again.
- Despite a general oversupply of rental space, the supply of apartments available to

low-income renters continued to dwindle in 1991 as demolitions and conversions to luxury units exceeded new production of low-cost units.

• Rising rents of rental units at the low end of the market, along with stagnant income at the low end of the income distribution, combined to worsen the housing-affordability problem for U.S. low-income renters, thus contributing to a growing problem of homelessness in the United States.

National Policy. Substantial easing of general monetary policy by the Federal Reserve was quite important to the interest-sensitive housing sector during 1991. The U.S. central bank cut its key discount rate by three percentage points during the year to 3.5%, the lowest level since 1964. Aggressive Federal Reserve action toward the end of the year helped push yields on both fixed-rate and adjustable-rate mortgages to historic lows.

But there were few key changes in national housing policy, per se, during 1991, despite glaring housing-affordability problems for first-time buyers and low-income renters. Passage of the Cranston-Gonzalez National Affordable Housing Act (NAHA) at the end of 1990 had set the stage for an increase in federal funding of direct subsidies for new construction of low-income rental housing and an expanded role for state and local governments in allocating such federal-housing assistance. For these purposes, NAHA authorized the creation of a new matching-grant program for states and local governments, called HOME, that would allow federal funds to be used for rehabilitation and new construction of low-income housing. However, no funds were appropriated for the HOME program in 1991 and only modest funding was appropriated for 1992. Within the total, grants for housing construction would be limited mostly to rehabilitation of existing housing and only 15% of the money would be reserved for new construction.

Passage and funding of the HOME program sent a strong signal that Congress intended to allow states and localities greater flexibility in the use of federal housing dollars. Congress had started down that path when it authorized the Community Development Block Grant program in 1974, and HOME channeled additional federal housing dollars through state and local governments.

The NAHA also created the National Homeownership Trust, a program designed to provide special mortgage assistance to first-time home buyers, addressing both interest rates and down payments. However, no funds were appropriated for this program in 1991 and funding was unlikely in 1992.

Two long-standing tax programs designed to provide at least partial solutions to affordability problems for first-time buyers and low-income renters were in grave danger of expiring in 1991. The mortgage-revenue-bond program, which channels low-rate mortgage money to moderate-income first-time buyers, and the low-income-housing tax credit, which provides some incentives for development of low-income rental housing, were extended on only a temporary basis by Congress and the administration. The longer-term future of both programs was in serious doubt as 1991 ended.

The persistent economic recession intensified discussion of certain housing support policies as possible components of an emergency economic-stimulus program to be proposed by the president early in 1992. Tax credits for moderate-income, first-time home buyers were being given serious consideration. Support also was gathering behind a proposal to permit usage of savings in individual retirement accounts and other types of pension accounts for down payments on homes—without the usual penalties and tax consequences associated with early withdrawals.

On the rental-housing front, the White House and Congress were considering restoration of limited tax incentives for investors in rental projects. The Tax Reform Act of 1986 had stripped away most of these incentives, leading to the collapse of rental-housing production as well as to sharp declines in the market values of existing apartment buildings, contributing to financial strains in both the banking and thrift industries.

International. Housing-market activity declined in most industrialized countries during 1991 as the economic recession took on international dimensions. The index of construction activity for the "major 7"—the United States, Canada, Japan, France, Britain, Germany, and Australia—declined by 4% in 1991, following increases of 3% and 1%, respectively, in 1989 and 1990. The index for the 12 countries in the European Community fell by 3% in 1991, following increases of 5% and 4% in 1989 and 1990. For the 24 countries that are members of the Organization for Economic Cooperation and Development (OECD), the index of construction activity fell by 4%, following increases of 3% in 1989 and 1% in 1990.

Housing-market activity increased in only a few OECD countries in 1991, and declined abruptly in others. The strongest performance was in Spain, where housing starts vastly exceeded the 1990 pace. Preparation for the 1992 Olympic Games in Barcelona was responsible for Spain's surge. Housing starts fell sharply in Japan during 1991, but the level of activity remained above that of the United States for the fifth consecutive year. In fact, Japan maintained its position as the world's top housing producer, at least in terms of the number of new units.

See also UNITED STATES—*The Economy*.

KENT W. COLTON and DAVID F. SEIDERS
National Association of Home Builders

HUMAN RIGHTS

In a 90-page encyclical letter dated May 1, 1991, to mark the 100th anniversary of an encyclical on labor by Pope Leo XIII, Pope John Paul II made ten separate references to human rights. The term did not appear at all in the 1891 encyclical *Rerum Novarum* ("Of New Things"). Human rights has resonated in international vocabulary—and in international debate—only in recent years, and never more so than in 1991.

State Department Report. One index of the trend was the annual U.S. State Department report on human rights published in February, which at 1,707 pages was the longest ever. Summarizing the survey, which covered 168 countries and territories, Richard Schifter, assistant secretary of state for human rights and humanitarian affairs, said: "Respect for the rights of the individual by governments is on the rise." He cited progress toward democracy not only in Eastern Europe but in Africa, Asia, and Latin America; in such diverse countries as Benin, Cape Verde, Chile, Mongolia, Nepal, Nicaragua, and São Tomé and Príncipe.

Although "the overall trend is distinctly positive," Schifter said, widespread violations continued in both Communist and non-Communist countries. The State Department report was particularly harsh in its judgments of some Asian countries: North Korea ("one of the most severely repressive regimes in the world"), Iraq (an "abysmal record"), Myanmar, formerly Burma ("severe and brutal repression"), and China ("far short of internationally recognized norms"). Nor were Saudi Arabia and Syria, two key U.S. allies in the anti-Iraq coalition, spared from criticism for their human-rights violations, including discrimination against women.

China. During the course of 1991, no country came under stronger and more sustained reproaches than China. Not only the State Department but influential private organizations—Asia Watch and Freedom House in New York City, Amnesty International in London, and the International Confederation of Free Trade Unions in Brussels, among others—issued lengthy reports assailing China for a variety of offenses, including forced labor of political prisoners to produce goods for export. Although Chinese officials repeatedly denied the existence of prison labor to make goods for export, Asia Watch produced evidence from official Chinese documents, and a CBS *60 Minutes* telecast showed proof of prison-labor exports to the United States. As a result, the human-rights case against Beijing echoed more loudly in Congress as both houses debated President George Bush's decision to renew China's most-favored-nation trade privileges.

But the Chinese government vociferously and systematically rejected foreign pressure. The standard response of Chinese officials to outside criticism, such as the State Department human-rights report, was to denounce it as an unacceptable interference in "internal affairs." As communism collapsed in the Soviet Union and Eastern Europe, the Beijing regime repeatedly reaffirmed its commitment to Marxism-Leninism and rededicated itself to a special view of human rights: not the Western concept, based on the individual, but the Marxist-Leninist concept, emphasizing collective rights, especially the right of national sovereignty and the "right of the oppressed nations and oppressed peoples to stay alive." Chinese Communist Party leader Jiang Zemin explained to a visiting dignitary that in China, a poor country, the government must concentrate on the basic right of its people to be fed, clothed, and housed.

At a National Endowment for Democracy conference in Washington, DC, Chinese exile Fang Lizhi, an astrophysicist, asked why Communist China's repeated efforts to achieve modernization and a better life for its people achieved so little success. "Obviously, it is not because the Chinese are not good at working or doing business," he said. "The economic success of overseas Chinese around the world belies such a conclusion." He blamed the country's failures on its "authoritarian political system" and on how the regime "has trampled upon the most basic dignity, rights, and freedoms of its own citizens."

Action Elsewhere. In June the 12-nation European Community (EC) announced its intention to place human-rights conditions into foreign-trade and aid agreements with Third World countries. The issue came to a head at meetings with the six-nation Association of Southeast Asian Nations (ASEAN), when the EC asked ASEAN to join the United States and the EC in applying sanctions against the military regime in Myanmar until it allows a duly elected civilian government to take office. The ASEAN countries, several of which have a big stake in trade with Myanmar, refused and accused Europeans of a wrongful application of Western values and norms.

Indications in 1991 were that international concern for human rights would continue to grow. The United Nations began preparations for a World Conference on Human Rights in Berlin in 1993. At congressional hearings in Washington, John T. Kamm, a Hong Kong-based U.S. businessman, predicted that the global economy and human-rights-motivated business people would bring dramatic changes in a country such as China. Kamm later announced that he was resigning his well-paying executive position to become a human-rights activist among business people in East Asia.

See also BIOGRAPHY—*Aung San Suu Kyi*; individual country articles.

ROBERT A. SENSER, *Free-lance Writer*

HUNGARY

In 1991, a year after the reestablishment of democracy in Hungary, the country was experiencing severe economic dislocation, and the public seemed largely indifferent to the political rivalries in its new government.

Politics. The governing coalition was composed of the Hungarian Democratic Forum (HDF), the Christian Democratic People's Party (CDPP), and the Independent Smallholders' Party (ISP); it was led by Jozsef Antall of the HDF. Opposition parties in the National Assembly included the Alliance of Free Democrats (AFD), the Alliance of Young Democrats (AYD), and the former Communist Party —now called the Hungarian Socialist Party (HSP). The government's popularity in the opinion polls hovered around the 35% mark, but its majority in parliament, where strict party-line voting was the rule, virtually guaranteed passage of its pet projects.

One example was the law on restitution, passed in April, which provided that persons whose property had been confiscated by the Communist regime might be compensated with state-owned property privatized by the government. In May the legislature passed a coalition-sponsored local government law which freed the central government of some of its former responsibilities, and at the same time increased its control over local authorities. The so-called Zetenyi-Takacs law, passed in October, was aimed at facilitating prosecution of offenses committed by former Communist officials by extending the statute of limitations for such offenses. Over the objections of the Budapest city government, parliament also voted to hold a world's fair in Budapest in 1996. In all these cases, coalition politics won the day.

The power of the ruling coalition was limited by two institutions: the presidency and the Constitutional Court. President Arpád Goncz, whose authority was bolstered by his great popularity with the public (his approval rating in the opinion polls was 85%), refused to approve the Zetenyi-Takacs law and government appointments to the directorship of the Hungarian radio and television network, and asked the Constitutional Court for a ruling on the constitutionality of his refusal to sign the government decrees. The court, the majority of whose members were appointed by Prime Minister Antall, frequently sided with the government, but despite this it clearly did exercise a moderating influence over the coalition.

A potential setback for the government came from within the coalition itself when Jozsef Torgyan, president of the ISP, threatened to limit his party's support in an effort to extract concessions from the prime minister. Antall was able to weather this challenge. A majority of the ISP deputies in the National Assembly sided with him rather than Torgyan.

Among the opposition parties the AFD had become largely ineffective. Having concluded a pact with the HDF in 1990, it could not perform its proper role as the leading opposition party. The AFD's abstention on the Zetenyi-Takacs law puzzled its liberal supporters. Moreover, following the resignation of AFD president Janos Kis, the party became involved in a bitter quarrel over the choice of a successor that nearly tore it apart. The election of Peter Tolgyessy as president seemed to signal a return to opposition activities.

The most popular opposition party in parliament was the AYD, the Young Democrats, also known by the acronym FIDESZ, whose distinguishing feature was that applicants for membership must be under 35. Strong advocates of economic reform and a free market system, the Young Democrats were uninterested in the controversies of the past that preoccupied older parties. They won close to 5% of the vote in the parliamentary elections of 1990, but their popularity has grown.

Most of the other parties—the front-running HDF included—tended to be groups without any clear program, held together by the least common denominator.

Economy. Meanwhile, the economy was doing badly. Industries that had produced goods for export to the other Communist countries of Eastern Europe had to close their doors after the dissolution of the Council for Mutual Economic Assistance (COMECON, the East European trading bloc). Because its products were not of sufficiently high quality to compete with Western competitors on the open market, the state-owned Hungarian industrial sector largely collapsed. Unemployment rose from 86,000 in January to 330,000 by year's end and was expected to reach 600,000 in 1992. It was estimated that about 2 million family members would be affected by this rise.

The privatization of the economy, meanwhile, moved at a snail's pace. The government spent more time trying to reassert control

HUNGARY • Information Highlights

Official Name: Republic of Hungary.
Location: East-central Europe.
Area: 35,919 sq mi (93 030 km^2).
Population (mid-1991 est.): 10,400,000.
Chief Cities (Jan. 1, 1990): Budapest, the capital, 2,016,132; Debrecen, 212,247; Miskolc, 196,449.
Government: *Head of state,* Arpád Goncz, president (elected August 1990). *Head of government,* Jozsef Antall, prime minister (took office May 1990). *Legislature* (unicameral)—National Assembly.
Monetary Unit: Forint (76.270 forints equal U.S.$1, August 1991).
Gross National Product (1989 est. U.S.$): $64,600,-000,000.
Economic Indexes (1990): *Consumer Prices* (1980 = 100), all items, 277.1; food, 278.5. *Industrial Production* (1980 = 100), 102.
Foreign Trade (1990 U.S.$): *Imports,* $8,764,000,000; *exports,* $9,707,000,000.

over the privatized industries than in speeding the country's much-needed economic transformation. While Western investment in joint ventures rose, Hungarian investment in industrial growth declined rapidly. The antibusiness sentiment that clearly persisted in the bureaucracy directly conflicted with official rhetoric about the benefits of a free market. The dismissal of Gyorgy Suranyi as president of the Hungarian National Bank in November 1991 further reinforced the impression that the government prized political loyalty over and above economic-development needs.

Foreign Affairs. In 1991 the Warsaw Pact was dissolved, the last Soviet troops left Hungary, and the country became an associate member of the European Community (EC) on November 22. Foreign visitors included Pope John Paul II, Britain's Queen Elizabeth II, and U.S Vice-President Dan Quayle. The bloody conflict in neighboring Yugoslavia (Croatia) placed Hungary on the edge of a war zone. More than 30,000 Croatians fled across the border into Hungary, where they were housed in refugee camps. Relations with Czechoslovakia remained troubled by Hungary's opposition to the planned construction of a Czechoslovak hydroelectric dam along the Hungarian-Czechoslovak border with that country.

Problems. At the end of 1991, Hungary was a troubled country. Crime and homelessness were rampant, social supports were dwindling, and public frustration was growing. Hungarians seemed in need of a clear direction—a road toward stability and social peace that would not impoverish the vast majority in the name of creating a market economy.

IVAN VOLGYES
University of Nebraska, Lincoln

ICELAND

Following April 1991 elections, Iceland's center-left four-party coalition led by Prime Minister Steingrímur Hermannsson was replaced by a center-right alliance of the conservative Independence Party (IP) and the Social Democrats (SDP). Taking over as prime minister was David Oddsson, leader of the IP and former mayor of Reykjavík. SDP leader Jón Baldvin Hannibalsson remained foreign minister.

Firmly supporting the independence struggles of the Baltic states—Lithuania, Latvia, and Estonia—Iceland in August became the first country to recognize and establish diplomatic relations with the three republics.

Trade and the Economy. In a dramatic all-night marathon meeting in Luxembourg in October, Iceland and six other countries of the European Free Trade Association (EFTA) signed an agreement with leaders of the European Community (EC) to create a European Economic Area (EEA). Beginning in 1993, Iceland would have duty-free access to markets for exports of fish and industrial products.

ICELAND • Information Highlights

Official Name: Republic of Iceland.
Location: North Atlantic Ocean.
Area: 39,768 sq mi (103 000 km^2).
Population (Dec. 1, 1991 est.): 259,581.
Chief City (Dec. 1, 1991 est.): Reykjavík, the capital, 99,653.
Government: *Head of state,* Vigdís Finnbogadóttir, president (took office Aug. 1980). *Head of government,* David Oddsson, prime minister (took office April 1991). *Legislature*—Althing: Upper House and Lower House.
Monetary Unit: Króna (61.39 krónur equal U.S.$1, selling rate, July 1991).
Gross Domestic Product (1989 est. U.S.$): $4,000,-000,000.
Foreign Trade (1990 U.S.$): *Imports,* $1,677,000,000; *exports,* $1,590,000,000.

Exports of fish and marine products account for an average 70% of Iceland's annual exports. Even with the present system of duties, ranging from 2% on exports of lobster and salmon to 18% on salt cod exceeding a predetermined quota, there had been a rapid increase in European trade in recent years. More than two thirds of the country's exports were heading to the continent. Per capita fish consumption in European countries had been increasing steadily and demand for the prime catch of the North Atlantic waters had resulted in price increases of up to 40% annually.

Forecasts by marine scientists, however, warned that the biomass of major demersal species such as cod and haddock has been depleted seriously. Catch quotas thus were cut by an average of 20%. The reduced catches for the 1991–92 quota year were expected to set off the most serious economic downturn since 1951. Iceland's inflation had been averaging 8%-12% on an annual basis. However, new wage agreements providing for negligible increases were expected to reduce the inflation rate in 1992.

Industry. Negotiations with Atlantal—an aluminum consortium consisting of Alumax of the United States, Granges of Sweden, and Hoogovens of the Netherlands—on the construction of a new 200-ton smelter in southwest Iceland failed in November. Although the parties reported agreement on most major questions, the decisive question of the price of hydroelectricity was unresolved. Metal prices, however, had been dropping steadily on world markets and construction, which was scheduled to begin in 1991, was postponed. As a result, the Icelandic government was faced with an extensive surplus of hydropower. As a possible alternative to building up a power-intensive industry in Iceland, the National Power Authority was considering exporting power by way of submarine cable to the power-hungry industries of Great Britain, including Scotland.

KENEVA KUNZ, *University of Iceland*

IDAHO

Just as Idaho had been late to follow the United States out of economic lethargy in the early 1980s, the state's economy remained healthy through much of the 1991 recession. But in August, Gov. Cecil Andrus (D) hedged official optimism with a 1.3% holdback in state spending. Petitioners also earned a place on the 1992 ballot for an initiative restricting local property taxes to 1% of market value.

Andrus waged a yearlong battle to prevent the federal Department of Energy from storing nuclear waste from outside the state at the Idaho National Engineering Laboratory near Idaho Falls. He successfully blocked shipments at the border in February, and in November a federal-court ruling blocked any further shipments into the state until the Department of Energy complied with state environmental laws. The ruling was appealed.

Natural Resources. As the year ended the stage was set for conflict over a proposal to draw down reservoirs behind Snake and Columbia river dams in an attempt to rescue endangered Idaho salmon runs. Andrus and other Northwest governors endorsed the plan to help flush juvenile fish downstream to the Pacific Ocean, as the National Marine Fisheries Service recommended protection for three runs. But shippers, farmers, and utility operators warned the drawdown would sap local economies, while driving power costs higher.

The amount of timber cut from national forests in Idaho continued to decline as local Forest Service officials warned they could not meet federal targets. Mediated negotiations to end the state's wilderness stalemate reported little progress. In August, John Mumma, who supervised forests in Idaho, Montana, and the Dakotas, retired upon being reassigned to Washington, DC. Mumma blamed political pressure from such figures as Sen. Larry Craig (R-ID) for his ouster. Craig denied the charge.

IDAHO • Information Highlights

Area: 83,564 sq mi (216 432 km²).
Population (1990 census): 1,006,749.
Chief Cities (1990 census): Boise, the capital, 125,738; Pocatello, 46,080; Idaho Falls, 43,929.
Government (1991): *Chief Officers*—governor, Cecil Andrus (D); lt. gov., C. L. Otter (R). *Legislature*—Senate, 42 members; House of Representatives, 84 members.
State Finances (fiscal year 1990): *Revenue,* $2,417,000,000; *expenditure,* $2,047,000,000.
Personal Income (1990): $15,423,000,000; per capita, $15,249.
Labor Force (June 1991): *Civilian labor force,* 520,400; *unemployed,* 31,100 (6.0% of total force).
Education: *Enrollment* (fall 1990)—public elementary schools, 156,602; public secondary, 58,330; colleges and universities, 48,969. *Public school expenditures* (1989), $571,159,000.

Politics. Sen. Steve Symms (R) announced in August he would not seek reelection in 1992. Symms, who first was elected to the House in 1972 and moved to the Senate after unseating Frank Church in 1980, faced declining popularity at home after divorcing his wife, Frances, and announcing his engagement to a congressional aide. Boise Mayor Dirk Kempthorne faced opposition from stockbroker Milt Erhart and probably from state Sen. John Hansen of Idaho Falls for the Republican nomination for Symms' seat, and 2d District U.S. Rep. Richard Stallings appeared a shoo-in for the Democratic nomination.

In March, Idaho's legislators repealed the last vestige of a 1978 property-tax limitation, which held growth in local tax revenues to 5% per year. (Idaho has no state property tax.) The Idaho Property Owners Association, which was behind the move to get the 1% initiative on the ballot, predicted that the initiative, if passed in 1992, would lead the state legislature to assume total financial responsibility for public schools and medical care of the poor.

Despite a failed petition from the League of Women Voters and a request from Governor

Jesse Turner, a 44-year-old native of Cedar Rapids who had been held hostage in the Middle East since Jan. 24, 1987, was welcomed home at the Idaho statehouse in Boise following his release from captivity on Oct. 21, 1991. His wife and daughter (left) *participated in the celebrations.*

Andrus to establish a citizens' reapportionment commission, a legislative committee met through the summer and fall in an attempt to do the job itself. By November prospects appeared uncertain.

JIM FISHER
"Lewiston Morning Tribune"

ILLINOIS

A new style of leadership and some belt-tightening was ushered in in Illinois when Republican Gov. Jim Edgar took office in January 1991.

Budget and Taxes. Less flamboyant than his Republican predecessor, James R. Thompson, who had held the post for 14 years, Edgar inherited a financial mess in Springfield. And with a General Assembly controlled by Democrats eager to play partisan politics, compromise was needed to bring state spending in line with state revenues. In the end, Edgar succeeded in trimming $1.5 billion in spending for a stripped-down budget of $26 billion. He also convinced legislators to extend the state's income-tax surcharge, the only tax hike he supported in his successful 1990 campaign. "We're now in a position where we've put the state on the soundest fiscal footing you can be," Governor Edgar said of the budget compromises.

By far the most sticky part of the tax plan was the permanent 10% increase in the state income tax, the first permanent increase in the tax since it was imposed in 1969. The tax prompted one state senator, Democrat Patrick Welch, to remark, "This reminds me of a dead carp along the Illinois River at moonlight. It shines and stinks at the same time."

The budget package included a $1 billion public-works project to more than double the size of Chicago's McCormick Place exhibition and convention center, an unpopular cause with downstate legislators. Funding would be through a mix of convention-related taxes in Chicago and Cook county.

In a move aimed at placating property owners, local governments in the collar counties around Chicago were forced to curtail spending as Illinois legislators passed a property-tax cap for Kane, DuPage, Will, McHenry, and Lake counties. The legislation limited annual property-tax hikes to 5% or the rate of inflation, whichever is higher, for hundreds of local school, library, and park districts and municipalities. This effort at tax relief was not successful initially, however, as scores of local governments went on a spending spree before the tax cap took effect. Taxing districts in the five counties approved more than $1 billion in bonds in the nine months preceding October 1, the effective date of the tax cap. That was 60% more than in the same period in 1990.

Many local leaders conceded that they approved the 11th-hour bonding because of the tax cap. They feared voters would not approve the spending if it went to referendum, as required by the new law when the tax increase exceeds 5%.

Politics. In his first year in office, Governor Edgar stayed close to home. He abandoned the costly foreign-trade missions undertaken by his predecessor and closed many of the trade offices the Thompson administration had opened in foreign countries.

In politics, Republicans won a lottery that allowed them to reapportion the state's legislative and congressional districts. They promptly moved to draw up districts that, if past voting trends held up, would give them more seats in the General Assembly in the 1990s. At least 24 Democratic lawmakers were threatened by the Republican map. Republicans estimated that the reapportionment would allow them to pick up at least four state Senate seats and four House seats in the 1992 election. Among Democrats threatened were state Sen. John Daley of Chicago, the brother of the Chicago mayor. The new Senate seats could give the GOP control of that body for the first time since 1975. Democrats were expected to remain in control of the House, which they had held since 1981.

Census. The 1990 census showed a 3% population loss in Cook county, which includes Chicago, during the 1980s. Chicago's population dropped 7.4% to 2,783,726, the first time it had been below 3 million in 70 years. The only significant population growth in Illinois was in the suburban counties, and that was marginal. The five suburban counties and the suburbs in Cook county, which gained 70,000 people, grew by 9% to nearly 4.5 million people. DuPage county west of Chicago gained the most people, adding 122,831, or 19%, for a total population of 781,666.

See also CHICAGO.

ROBERT ENSTAD
"Chicago Tribune"

ILLINOIS • Information Highlights

Area: 56,345 sq mi (145 934 km²).
Population (1990 census): 11,430,602.
Chief Cities (1990 census): Springfield, the capital, 105,227; Chicago, 2,783,726; Rockford, 139,426.
Government (1991): *Chief Officers*—governor, Jim Edgar (R); lt. gov., Bob Kustra (R). *General Assembly*—Senate, 59 members; House of Representatives, 118 members.
State Finances (fiscal year 1990): *Revenue*, $24,313,000,000; *expenditure*, $22,072,000,000.
Personal Income (1990): $233,661,000,000; per capita, $20,419.
Labor Force (June 1991): *Civilian labor force*, 6,116,900; *unemployed*, 443,700 (7.3% of total force).
Education: *Enrollment* (fall 1989)—public elementary schools, 1,280,021; public secondary, 517,334; colleges and universities, 709,937. *Public school expenditures* (1989), $7,655,153,000.

INDIA

India lost its best-known political leader when Rajiv Gandhi was assassinated on May 21, 1991 (*see* FEATURE ARTICLE, page 51). The political situation became somewhat more stable after the tenth general election in May-June, which resulted in the installation of a Congress(I) government headed by P. V. Narasimha Rao. The economy showed some improvement after the new government inaugurated a series of reforms, designed to move India toward greater economic liberalization. The year also was marked by recurrent violence, especially in Assam, Jammu and Kashmir, and Punjab.

Politics. Prime Minister Chandra Shekhar, who took office in November 1990, began the year in a precarious position. His Janata Dal (Socialist) party held only 54 seats in the 545-seat Lok Sabha (the lower house of the Indian Parliament). He was able to remain in nominal control only because the Congress(I) Party, with 194 seats, chose to support him.

As the economic and social situation deteriorated, the central government became increasingly ineffective and virtually impotent; on March 6, Shekhar, apparently frustrated by his difficulties with Congress(I) leader Rajiv Gandhi, suddenly resigned. After deliberating for a week, President Ramaswamy Venkataraman decided to dissolve the Lok Sabha and call for new national elections. In the meantime he asked Shekhar to remain as head of a caretaker government.

The elections were scheduled in all of the 25 states except Jammu and Kashmir—where the troubled situation seemed to rule out a fair and peaceful poll—on May 20, 23, and 26. Later the election in Assam was set for June 6 and 8 and in Punjab for June 22. Elections also were scheduled for the Assemblies in six states. The campaign was a three-way contest among the Congress(I), the Janata Dal-National Front, and the Hindu-oriented Bharatiya Janata Party (BJP). About 55% of the approximately 500 million eligible voters would turn out in "the world's largest democratic elections." A comeback for the Congress(I) was anticipated widely.

The first round of voting on May 20 was held with relatively little violence, and it seemed that the country was on its way to finding a stronger and more stable government through the electoral process. Then, on the following day, the nation was shocked when Rajiv Gandhi was killed by a bomb as he arrived at an election meeting in the small Tamil Nadu town of Sriperumbudur. The crime was linked to a Tamil nationalist group from Sri Lanka. The sudden loss of Gandhi, India's former prime minister and head of its most respected political family, on the eve of his expected return to power, opened the way to a dramatic shift in the country's political direction.

As a consequence of the assassination, the elections scheduled for May 23 and 26 were postponed until June 12 and 15. In Assam they were held on June 6 and 8, as scheduled, but those in Punjab, scheduled for June 22, were postponed first until September 25 and later until February 1992. The Congress(I) won 225 Lok Sabha seats, with majorities in ten major states. The BJP became the major opposition

P.V. Narasimha Rao, below center, *who became India's ninth prime minister in June 1991, meets with members of Parliament. Rao's position as Congress(I) Party leader and prime minister was strengthened as a result of November by-elections.*

© Bob Nickelsberg/Gamma-Liaison

party with 119 seats, mainly in Uttar Pradesh and Gujarat. The Janata Dal captured 55 seats, including a majority in Bihar.

On the state level, the Congress(I) formed governments in Assam, Haryana, and Kerala (at the head of a United Democratic Front). The BJP took control in Uttar Pradesh; in Tamil Nadu a local party, the All-India Anna Dravid Munnetra Kazhagam (AIADMK) was the victor; and in West Bengal the Left Front government headed by Jyoti Basu of the Community Party (Marxist) retained control.

Although the Congress(I) was short of a majority, it was able to assume power in New Delhi by forming coalitions with some minor parties and independents. A veteran congressman, 70-year-old former foreign minister P. V. Narasimha Rao, who had succeeded Gandhi as leader of the Congress(I), was sworn in on June 21 as India's ninth prime minister.

In spite of his weak political base, lack of real national stature, ill health, and old age, Rao proved to be an active and far-seeing leader. In his Council of Ministers he included such prominent leaders as Sharad Pawar (defense), Manmohan Singh (finance), S. B. Chavan (home affairs), Madhav Rao Scindia (civil aviation and tourism), and Arjun Singh (human resource development). Rao himself retained 11 portfolios.

On July 15 the new government was given an overwhelming vote of confidence in the Lok Sabha, in spite of the negative votes of members of the BJP and the abstention of the Janata Dal and its National Front allies. In his first major speech in Parliament after becoming prime minister, Rao said his government would seek a consensual approach to the problems facing the country. In these efforts he had more difficulty with dissidents in his own party (mostly Gandhi loyalists who tried unsuccessfully to persuade Gandhi's widow, Sonia, to become actively involved in politics) than he did with opposition parties or influential groups in the private sector. By-elections were held on November 16 in 14 Lok Sabha and 56 State Assembly constituencies in 13 states. Prime Minister Rao and Defense Minister Sharad Pawar, who did not contest the elections in May and June, both were returned with overwhelming majorities. The Congress(I) won the majority of Lok Sabha seats but only about one fourth of the State Assembly seats, with no victories at all in the 29 State Assembly contests in Uttar Pradesh and Bihar—India's most populous states. It remained a minority party in the Lok Sabha. Nevertheless, the by-elections strengthened Rao's position in the party and in the country.

The Economy. Early in 1991, India was approaching financial bankruptcy. For the first time it was faced with the prospect of a default in interest payments on its foreign debt, which had risen to more than $70 billion, the third-highest in the developing world. Only a last-minute credit of $1.8 billion from the International Monetary Fund (IMF) averted this unwelcome step. India's international creditworthiness plunged to an all-time low. Its trade deficit reached a record high—$5.5 billion in 1990–91, with the likelihood of about $6.5 billion in 1991–92. Foreign-exchange reserves declined to alarmingly low levels. Foreign investment, always disappointingly low, declined still further. Prices of basic commodities rose to record highs, worsening the already poor conditions of millions of Indians. By the fall the rate of inflation exceeded 15%. The economic crisis was aggravated by the uncertain political situation and the mounting violence in the country.

India was one of the countries most adversely affected by the impact of the Persian Gulf war early in the year, which caused a rise in oil prices, a loss of major export markets and of remittances from Indian nationals working in Iraq and Kuwait, and extra financial and other burdens involved in bringing thousands of Indians back from the Gulf and in assisting them after their return.

In June the new Congress(I) government embarked on a series of sweeping economic reforms in the direction of economic liberalization. These were designed to reverse the economic decline, to open up the economy, to stimulate industrial growth, to attract a much larger flow of direct foreign investment and trade, and to enable India to rejoin the world economy. In July the rupee was devalued by about 20%, bringing the currency more into line with its real value and making Indian exports, which had been lagging, more competitive in international markets. On the downside, the devaluation also led to higher prices for imports and for domestic goods and services.

The new directions in economic policy were spelled out in an important industrial-policy statement, presented to the Parliament on July

INDIA • Information Highlights

Official Name: Republic of India.
Location: South Asia.
Area: 1,269,340 sq mi (3 287 590 km²).
Population (1991 census): 844,000,000.
Chief Cities (1981 census): New Delhi, the capital, 273,036; Bombay, 8,243,405; Calcutta, 3,305,006.
Government: *Head of state,* Ramaswamy Venkataraman, president (took office July 25, 1987). *Head of government,* P. V. Narasimha Rao, prime minister (sworn in June 21, 1991). *Legislature*—Parliament: Rajya Sabha (Council of States) and Lok Sabha (House of the People).
Monetary Unit: Rupee (25.907 rupees equal U.S.$1, official rate, Nov. 19, 1991).
Gross National Product (1989 est. U.S.$): $333,000,-000,000.
Economic Indexes (1990): *Consumer Prices* (1980 = 100), all items, 235.1; food, 234.3. *Industrial Production* (1980 = 100), 209.
Foreign Trade (1990 U.S.$): *Imports,* $23,396,-000,000; *exports,* $17,787,000,000.

24, announcing major changes in the oppressive licensing system, in policies regarding foreign investment, and in public-sector policy. These changes, and many others, were incorporated in a budget presented to Parliament on the same day by Finance Minister Manmohan Singh. The budget proposed to reduce the deficit to $3.09 billion (compared with $4.3 billion in the revised budget estimates of the previous fiscal year). Food and fertilizer subsidies were cut, defense expenditures were reduced slightly in real terms, many incentives in the export sector were eliminated, and corporate taxes and petroleum prices were increased by 5% and 20%, respectively.

The budget and the new industrial policy were hailed by *The Times of India* as "a historic change, an attempt to attain the old Nehruvian goals of growth and social justice by using very different means." Most opposition parties opposed the new directions in economic policy, mainly on the grounds that they would make India more dependent on capitalist powers and therefore would decrease India's self-reliance and independence.

The new policies were welcomed by aid-giving countries and international organizations. During the latter half of the year, India received an additional credit of $2.2 billion from the IMF, $500 million from the World Bank as a "structural adjustment" loan, and nearly $1 billion from the Asian Development Bank. In September the Aid India Consortium pledged a record $6.7 billion during fiscal year 1991–92, ending on March 31, 1992.

By late 1991 the economy showed some encouraging signs. Food-grain production reached a record level of more than 171 million tons, and the overall growth rate for the year was around 5%.

Census. India's fifth census since independence, conducted in 1991, indicated that the country's population as of March 1 was nearly 844 million. For the first time the number of literates slightly outnumbered the illiterates. About 30% of the population still lived below the subsistence level, and some 50% were poor "by any standard."

Foreign Policy. India's stand during the Gulf war was criticized widely at home and abroad as being too ambivalent, too standoffish, and occasionally too sympathetic with Iraq's President Saddam Hussein. However, as a member of the United Nations Security Council (on January 1 it became a member of the council for the sixth time) it generally supported actions designed to force Hussein to get out of Kuwait and avert war.

Prime Minister Rao made several trips abroad, including a visit to Germany and brief appearances at the nonaligned summit in Accra, Ghana, in September and at the Commonwealth summit in Harare, Zimbabwe, in October. On September 26 he addressed the General Assembly of the United Nations, where he and his foreign minister advocated a greater democratization of the world body.

India's relations with Pakistan continued to be strained, in spite of high-level official and unofficial contacts, and many professions by the leaders of the two countries of a desire to resolve the issues that divided them. India made repeated charges that Pakistan was giving military aid and training to anti-Indian militants in Jammu and Kashmir and, to a lesser extent; in Punjab, and continued to express concern over Pakistan's alleged nuclear buildup. Pakistan often voiced its frustrations over India's continued unyielding stand on the Kashmir question.

In the early months of the year relations with Sri Lanka seemed to be improving, but they again deteriorated after Rajiv Gandhi's assassination, in which the Liberation Tigers of Tamil Eelam were alleged to have been involved.

For many years, India's ties with the Soviet Union had been close, particularly in the areas of military assistance and rupee trade, both of which were affected adversely by the dramatic changes in the Soviet Union and its constituent republics. Because of the USSR's weakened position and shifts in foreign policy its role in India inevitably declined, forcing the Indians to turn elsewhere—mainly to the capitalist West—for enhanced political, economic, and military support. Nevertheless, in February, Rajiv Gandhi visited Moscow, and on August 8 the two countries announced an extension of the Indo-Soviet Treaty of Peace, Friendship, and Cooperation for a further period of 20 years.

India's relations with the United States broadened and deepened during the year, especially after Rao became prime minister. India's ambassador to the United States, Abid Hussain, was particularly assiduous and effective in fostering improved relations. In January, U.S. President George Bush expressed gratitude to Prime Minister Chandra Shekhar for allowing the refueling of U.S. Air Force aircraft in transit from the Philippines to the Persian Gulf; and when the Indian government, under strong pressure from Rajiv Gandhi, all major opposition parties, and influential private groups, withdrew the permission, Bush's reaction was relatively mild. Military cooperation between India and the United States increased markedly during the year, especially after the exchange of visits by top-level military leaders. The main unresolved issues were in the fields of business and trade. U.S. business people continued to complain about the many "unnecessary impediments" that India placed on trade and investment, which remained low in spite of the fact that the United States had become India's leading trade partner.

NORMAN D. PALMER, *Professor Emeritus*
University of Pennsylvania

© Nielsen/Purdue University

Severe drought following increased spring rains affected Indiana's agricultural crop in 1991. Corn production, left, *was down some 24% from 1990 because of the weather conditions.*

INDIANA

As in many other states, government and politics in Indiana were preoccupied in 1991 with budgetary problems created in large part by the nationwide recession. These economic difficulties soon became intertwined with political wrangling over the redrawing of the boundaries of the state's congressional and other election districts. The political discord of Democratic Gov. Evan Bayh and the Democratically controlled House versus the Republican-controlled Senate resulted in governmental deadlock. The regular session of the legislature ended without a budget or redistricting agreement. Bayh called a special session, but it, too, ended in deadlock. The political stalemate in Indianapolis caused concern throughout the state as a plethora of activities dependent upon state funding was delayed. Finally, during a second special session a combination budget-redistricting bill was passed.

INDIANA • Information Highlights

Area: 36,185 sq mi (93 720 km²).
Population (1990 census): 5,544,159.
Chief Cities (1990 census): Indianapolis, the capital, 741,952, Fort Wayne, 173,072; Evansville, 126,272.
Government (1991): *Chief Officers*—governor, Evan Bayh (D); lt. gov., Frank L. O'Bannon (D). *General Assembly*—Senate, 50 members; House of Representatives, 100 members.
State Finances (fiscal year 1990): *Revenue,* $11,456,000,000; *expenditure,* $10,414,000,000.
Personal Income (1990): $93,805,000,000; per capita, $16,890.
Labor Force (June 1991): *Civilian labor force,* 2,864,900; *unemployed,* 170,400 (5.9% of total force).
Education: *Enrollment* (fall 1989)—public elementary schools, 671,036; public secondary, 283,129; colleges and universities, 275,821. *Public school expenditures* (1989), $3,779,468,000.

U.S. Census. The 1990 census revealed that the resident population of Indiana increased by 0.98% during the 1980s, far behind the national average of 9.8%. More than half (49 of 92) of the state's counties lost population, while 16 of its 30 largest cities and seven of its ten largest also lost population. Of the few cities that showed substantial growth, most were Indianapolis suburbs or major college towns, such as West Lafayette and Bloomington. Evansville became the state's third-largest city despite a small population loss. Gary, which had been third, experienced a dramatic loss caused by the flight of about half of its minority white population.

The average age of Indiana's inhabitants increased significantly from 29.2 years in 1980 to 33 years, the same as the national average, in 1990. For one of the few times in its history, the mean age of Indiana's population was not well below the national average. The reason for the age increase was the departure of a large number of younger people, who left in search of employment.

Economy. The economic problems caused by the recession were exacerbated in Indiana by the effects of the weather on the state's farm production. Unusually heavy spring rains led to disease and rotting problems that caused the state's wheat crop to plummet 22% from the 1990 level. As had happened in 1983, a severe summer drought followed the excessive precipitation of the spring. Drought caused a 23% drop in hay production from 1990, while, as of October 1, agricultural experts at Purdue University estimated that Indiana's important corn crop would be down 24% from 1990. Production of soybeans, another major Hoosier crop, was projected to be near 1990 levels, and some minor commodities, such as apples, showed increased production.

Hoosier wage workers—including factory workers, government employees, and construction workers—experienced an increase in average salary in 1990, but it was substantially less than those in the same occupations in the surrounding states of Ohio, Michigan, and Illinois. One interesting but temporary boost to the Hoosier economy came from the filming of *A League of Their Own* in the Evansville area. The movie, which was directed by Penny Marshall and starred Tom Hanks, Geena Davis, and Madonna, pumped about $10 million into the local economy and used thousands of southwest Indiana residents as film extras.

THOMAS E. RODGERS
University of Southern Indiana

INDONESIA

In 1991, Indonesia continued to maintain a strong economy and a stable political system under the unchallenged 24-year-rule of President Suharto.

Domestic Politics. The political scene was dominated by maneuverings leading to the June 1992 parliamentary elections and 1993 indirect presidential election. Speculation that 70-year-old President Suharto would step down was replaced by signs pointing to the probability that he would stand for a sixth five-year term. Suharto strengthened his hold on the army, his partner in power, with judicious appointments. He improved his credentials within the Muslim constituency by making the Haj, the obligatory pilgrimage to Mecca. Attention then turned to who would be the vice-presidential candidate and possible successor to Suharto in 1998.

The apparent intention to maintain the political status quo led to a curtailment of the cautious process of political liberalization as internal security officials again began to act against speech and behavior that could be interpreted as "destabilizing." One possible destabilizing issue was the popular perception of a growing income gap in the country and a resulting resurgence of antagonism toward the prosperous ethnic Chinese minority. Related to this was the highly sensitive subject of the business activities and associates of the Suharto family. Smoldering ethnic discontent still plagued the security situation in Aceh, Sumatra's resource-rich and strongly Islamic northern province. Although the Free Aceh Independence Movement's rebellion was crushed, antigovernment sentiments persisted.

Economy. Indonesia's economy continued to perform well. The 1990 real growth rate was 7.4%, the same as in 1989. Sticking firmly to its tight money policy, the government allowed interest rates to run as high as 30%. This left the small indigenous Indonesian entrepreneur at a disadvantage, since Chinese businessmen had greater access to foreign funds than did their Indonesian counterparts. The government indicated that it would not loosen its grip on money supply until the inflation rate (9.5% annually) was brought down to 7%.

Continued confidence in Indonesia's medium- to long-term prospects was reflected in the accelerating pace of direct foreign investment. It amounted to $8.7 billion in 1990, an 80% boost over 1989, and in the first six months of 1991 was already $6.5 billion. The flow of investment was overloading the overburdened infrastructure. Bureaucratic procedures and the need for well-connected deal brokers made the process of contracting for infrastructure development frustratingly slow.

Foreign Affairs. The year brought two long-desired successes to Indonesian foreign policy under the stewardship of Foreign Minister Ali Alatas. First, in September, Indonesia finally won the coveted chairmanship of the nonaligned nations movement. This meant that President Suharto would host the 1992 nonaligned summit. At that time the movement, originally founded to find a path between the East and West superpower blocs, would face the challenge of redefining itself in a post-Cold War world. Previous Indonesian overtures for leadership had been turned down because of the lingering criticism of Indonesia's 1975 seizure of East Timor. Also, the more politically radical nonaligned nations have been critical of the Suharto government's domestic anticommunism.

The second success was the October signing in Paris of a peace agreement between the warring parties in Cambodia. Indonesia and France had cochaired the long diplomatic process that finally had brought the antagonists to the negotiating table. Foreign Minister Alatas then staked out Indonesia's next venture into peacemaking with initiatives to defuse the simmering South China Sea conflict over the Spratly Islands.

DONALD E. WEATHERBEE
University of South Carolina

INDONESIA • Information Highlights

Official Name: Republic of Indonesia.
Location: Southeast Asia.
Area: 741,097 sq mi (1 919 440 km²).
Population (mid-1991 est.): 181,400,000.
Chief Cities (Dec. 31, 1983 est.): Jakarta, the capital, 7,347,800; Surabaya, 2,223,600; Medan, 1,805,500; Bandung, 1,566,700.
Government: *Head of state and government,* Suharto, president (took office for fifth five-year term March 1988). *Legislature* (unicameral)—House of Representatives.
Monetary Unit: Rupiah (1,977.03 rupiahs equal U.S.$1, Nov. 7, 1991).
Gross National Product (1989 est. U.S.$): $80,000,000,000.
Economic Index (1990): *Consumer Prices* (1980 = 100), all items, 112.5; food, 109.5.
Foreign Trade (1990 U.S.$): *Imports,* $21,837,000,000; *exports,* $25,675,000,000.

INDUSTRIAL PRODUCTION

Industrial countries were in the grip of recession in 1991. In the countries emerging from what was the sphere of influence of the Soviet Union, industrial production was in a free-fall by year's end 1991.

U.S. industrial production dropped 1.8% in 1991, the first annual decline since a severe recession in 1982 dragged output down by 4.4%. For 1990, the year the 1991 recession started, the Federal Reserve Board's index of industrial production showed a 1.0% gain. Production declines were pronounced especially in industries that supply manufacturers of motor vehicles and the construction industry. Thus, the amount of raw steel produced in 1991 dropped 13% from the 89.7 million tons poured in 1990. Paint production dropped 6.5%. Cement output declined 11%. Hardware, tools, fasteners, lumber, and furniture registered production declines in excess of 6%.

Transportation and Energy Industries. The motor-vehicle industry itself has become complex and intertwined. For instance, General Motors (GM) uses the Chevrolet network to market the GEO nameplate cars. GEO products include a 50% GM and 50% Toyota venture in California. Subcompact and sport-utility vehicles are made in Canada in a 50-50 joint venture between GM and Suzuki. Mazda builds Ford-plated cars in Japan for the Japanese market and in Michigan for the U.S. market. As the tabulation below shows, foreign producers account for more than one fifth of the automobiles actually produced in the United States.

Autos Produced in Plants Located in the United States

Manufacturer	*Output in 1990*
Chrysler	726,466
Ford	1,377,351
GM	2,653,391
Honda	435,438
Mazda	184,368
Mitsubishi	148,379
Nissan	95,844
Subaru	32,377
Toyota	415,416
Total	6,069,030

Automobile sales in the U.S. market dropped 13% in 1991 to 8.3 million. The Big Three (GM, Ford, and Chrysler) accounted for 74% of domestic production. Back in 1980 their share was 97%. Considering import versus domestically sourced car sales, the Big Three's share in 1991 shrunk to 65%. The industry was saddled with excessive capacity. For instance, GM has a capacity to build 5.5 million cars and trucks annually in North America, nearly 30% more than it can sell. Facing that bleak fact of life, the company decided to shut 21 factories and to lay off 74,000 employees in the United States and Canada by 1995. The U.S. market absorbed 12.5 million cars and trucks in 1991, 23% fewer than in 1986, the year sales peaked.

The aerospace industry began facing a serious challenge. Historically half the business came from military orders. While the 1991 Persian Gulf conflict caused a short-term increase in the demand for certain aerospace products, notably the Patriot missile, the long-term outlook was for a decline in defense spending among developed countries. Also, U.S. leadership in aerospace technology was being challenged by the Japanese and the Europeans.

Civilian air transport still was dominated by U.S. manufacturers. Boeing and McDonnell Douglas exported more than 50% of their combined output of commercial aircraft in 1991. U.S. shipments of large transports totaled 583 units in 1991, up from 521 in 1990. The dollar volume was up 18%, to $26 billion. Military-aircraft shipments came to 1,005, a 13% decline from 1990. An indication of growing international competition was the fact that the Airbus Industrie took 35% of worldwide orders in 1991, and Fokker Aircraft of the Netherlands took an additional 7%.

The good news on the energy front was the speed with which the oil fires were put out in Kuwait after the Gulf war. Oil shipments from

U.S. Industrial Production

	Percent Change 1989 to 1990	Index (1987=100) 1991 level*	Percent* Change 1990 to 1991
Total Production	0.9	107.2	−1.8
Mining	2.1	101.6	−0.9
Utilities	0.9	109.0	0.9
Manufacturing	0.9	107.5	−2.1
Consumer Goods	0.6	107.4	0.0
Business Equipment	3.3	122.0	−0.8
Defense and Space Equipment	−0.2	91.1	−6.3
Durable Goods Manufacturing	0.6	107.5	−3.6
Lumber and products	−1.9	94.7	−6.4
Furniture and fixtures	0.6	99.1	−6.4
Clay, glass, and stone products	−2.1	96.2	−9.1
Primary metals	−0.9	99.8	−7.8
Fabricated metal products	−1.3	100.5	−5.1
Nonelectrical machinery	3.9	124.0	−1.9
Electrical machinery	1.7	111.4	−0.8
Transportation equipment	−1.5	99.4	−5.7
Nondurable Goods Manufacturing	1.3	107.5	−0.2
Foods	2.0	108.2	0.6
Tobacco products	−0.9	98.7	0.0
Textile mill products	−1.1	100.6	−0.1
Apparel products	−5.3	96.2	−2.6
Paper and paper products	2.1	104.9	−0.5
Printing and publishing	3.1	111.4	−0.5
Chemicals and products	1.6	110.3	0.1
Petroleum and products	2.1	108.2	−0.1
Rubber and plastic products	1.2	109.9	−0.3
Leather and products	−3.7	90.3	−9.6

* Preliminary Estimate
Source: Board of Governors of the Federal Reserve System

Value of New Construction Put in Place in the United States
(Billions of 1987 dollars)

	1990	1991*	Percent Change
Total new construction	402.8	380.4	−6
Private construction	304.1	280.3	−8
Residential buildings	164.9	153.0	−7
Nonresidential buildings	139.2	127.2	−9
Industrial	21.5	20.4	−5
Office	25.9	22.0	−15
Hotels and motels	8.7	7.0	−20
Other commercial	30.8	24.6	−20
Religious	3.1	3.1	0
Educational	3.8	3.8	0
Hospital and institutional	8.5	8.9	5
Miscellaneous buildings	4.1	4.0	−3
Railroads	2.5	2.1	−15
Electric utilities	11.3	11.6	3
Gas utilities	4.7	4.8	3
Petroleum pipelines	0.4	0.4	0
Farm structures	2.4	2.4	0
Miscellaneous structures[1]	3.0	3.0	0
Telecommunications	8.5	8.9	5
Public construction	98.7	100.1	1
Housing and redevelopment	3.5	3.4	−2
Federal industrial	1.3	1.4	10
Educational	18.5	21.1	14
Hospital	2.4	2.3	−5
Other public buildings[2]	15.8	16.8	2
Highways and streets	28.2	27.4	−3
Military facilities	2.5	2.0	−20
Conservation and development	4.2	4.6	10
Sewer systems	9.3	8.8	−5
Water supply facilities	4.6	5.1	10
Miscellaneous public[3]	8.6	8.0	−2

[1] Includes amusement and recreational buildings, bus and airline terminals, animal hospitals, and shelters, etc. [2] Includes general administrative buildings, prisons, police and fire stations, courthouses, civic centers, passenger terminals, postal facilities. [3] Includes open amusement and recreational facilities, power generating facilities, transit systems, airfields, open parking facilities, etc.
Source: Bureau of the Census * Preliminary Estimate

Kuwait reached 300,000 barrels per day by year's end. The bad news was the sharp decline in what used to be the Soviet oil industry. The official estimate put production at 10 million barrels per day, some 12% less than in 1990, but that may be too optimistic in view of supply shortfalls that crippled transport within the country and played havoc with the economies of the countries that historically depended on Soviet oil. Worldwide oil demand at year's end 1991 was about 68 million barrels per day, barely balanced by output capacity.

U.S. crude petroleum production averaged less than 7 million barrels per day, just below the level of 1990. Natural-gas production totaled 17.4 trillion cubic ft (4.9 billion m^3), up 1.5% from 1990. Coal production reached 1 billion short tons, down 2% from 1990. While there are 2,700 coal mines in the United States, nearly two thirds of the domestic production comes from 211 large mines. New technologies used in coal mining require large capital inputs that only large firms can muster.

Other Trends. Investment in new plant and equipment amounted to $530 billion in 1991, a 0.5% decline. That was the first drop since investment fell 2.4% in 1986. Manufacturing industries as a group curtailed investment by 4.3%. Durable-goods producers reduced investment by 6.7% and nondurable-goods manufacturers registered a 2.5% decline. The only industries to increase outlays for new plant and equipment were food and beverages—8.3%, chemicals—2.9%, and petroleum—7%. Sharpest reductions were in paper—28%, stone-clay-glass—14.3%, blast furnaces and steel works—12.3%, motor vehicles—10.5%, aircraft—9.5%, nonelectrical machinery—9.8%, textiles—9.8%, and fabricated metals—8.3%.

Nonmanufacturing industries increased investment by 1.7%. While railroads cut spending by 8.7%, airlines raised outlays by 10.9%. Public utilities showed a 1.8% decline.

New construction in the United States dropped to $389 billion, down 6% from 1990. Housing starts plummeted 16% from the 1.2 million in 1990. With starts at just about the 1 million level, construction in 1991 had the worst performance since 1982. The industry's misfortunes were exacerbated by the collapse of hundreds of financial institutions. High vacancy rates and weak building prices made new construction unprofitable in many areas. Especially large drops came in nonresidential construction. Office and hotel construction boomed in the first half of the 1980s. Compared to the peak year of 1985, office construction in 1991 was off by 24%. Construction contributed 7.3% to gross national product (GNP) in 1991, lower than the cyclical low of 7.7% in 1982. The post-World War II peak was in 1966, when construction accounted for 11.9% of GNP.

In contrast to new construction, remodeling and repair work made 1991 a record year. New construction accounted for less than 60% of the construction industry's work in 1991.

Employment in goods-producing industries declined in 1991 for the second year in a row. Of all nonagricultural jobs, goods-producing industries account for 22%. All industry groups registered job drops, with the sharpest declines in construction and transportation equipment.

New products introduced in 1991 included "microportable" telephones that weigh about 10 oz (311 grams) and retail from $800 to

Industrial Production: International Overview
1985=100

	1985	1986	1987	1988	1989	1990	1991*
Industrial Countries	100	101	104	110	114	116	115
Australia	100	105	101	105	111	111	108
Austria	100	101	102	106	113	121	123
Belgium	100	101	103	109	114	119	114
Canada	100	99	106	112	112	108	104
Denmark	100	108	104	106	108	108	109
Finland	100	101	106	110	113	114	109
France	100	101	103	107	111	112	110
Germany	100	102	102	106	111	117	121
Ireland	100	103	114	126	142	148	148
Italy	100	104	108	114	118	118	116
Japan	100	100	103	113	120	125	127
Luxembourg	100	103	103	115	125	125	122
Netherlands	100	100	101	101	106	109	111
Norway	100	103	111	117	136	141	147
Spain	100	102	107	111	117	116	114
Sweden	100	100	103	104	108	105	99
Switzerland	100	104	104	111	117	120	121
United Kingdom	100	102	106	110	110	109	105
United States	100	101	105	110	113	114	112

*Preliminary Estimate
Source: International Monetary Fund

Employees on Nonagricultural Payrolls
(in thousands)

	1990	1991*	Percent Change
Good-producing industries	24,960	23,850	−4.4
Mining	710	700	−1.7
Construction	5,140	4,710	−8.4
Manufacturing	19,110	18,440	−3.5
Durable goods	11,120	10,570	−5.0
Lumber and wood products	741	697	−5.9
Furniture and fixtures	510	482	−5.6
Stone, clay, and glass products	557	522	−6.2
Primary metal industries	756	721	−4.5
Fabricated metal products	1,423	1,360	−4.5
Machinery, except electrical	2,095	1,996	−4.7
Electrical and electronic equip.	1,673	1,591	−4.9
Transportation equipment	1,980	1,859	−6.1
Instruments and related products	1,004	971	−3.4
Miscellaneous mfg. industries	377	367	−2.7
Nondurable goods	8,000	7,870	−1.5
Food and kindred products	1,668	1,675	0.4
Tobacco manufacturers	49	48	−1.2
Textile mill products	691	667	−3.5
Apparel and other textile goods	1,043	1,023	−2.0
Paper and allied products	699	692	−1.1
Printing and publishing	1,574	1,537	−2.3
Chemicals and allied products	1,093	1,091	−0.2
Petroleum and coal products	158	160	0.8
Rubber and misc. plastics products	889	859	−3.3
Leather and leather products	132	121	−8.6

* Preliminary Estimate
Source: Bureau of Labor Statistics

$1,200. Small enough to fit in a pocket, the microportables are aimed at consumers who cannot go anywhere without their beepers. Miniaturization continued in computers as well: An 11.6-oz (361-gram) powerful palmtop was introduced by Hewlett-Packard.

The World Scene. Among industrial countries, there were none that could show production gains over the year as 1991 ended. Still, year-to-year comparison showed advances by Norway, Germany, Japan, and Austria. While the economic slowdown in the West was relatively mild, the situation in what was the USSR was disastrous. The post-Communist countries of East Europe Hungary, Poland, and Czechoslovakia, not to mention Yugoslavia—were estimated to have recorded industrial production losses ranging upward from 15% as their raw-material and fuel supplies were interrupted, and the Soviet market was in effect lost as the USSR disintegrated. Of the post-Communist countries, Hungary made the most successful effort to reorient its trade to the West. Even so, the loss of the Soviet market led to sharp production drops.

AGO AMBRE
U.S. Department of Commerce

INSURANCE, LIABILITY

The liability-insurance crisis in the United States that peaked in the mid-1980s continued to abate in 1991. With evidence that juries were being less generous in awards to victims of malpractice and consumers injured by faulty products, liability insurers lowered the premiums they charged to many of their policyholders.

But while the crisis in insurance availability and affordability waned, it continued to have an impact on policy-making, and tort reform gained momentum on the federal level.

Federal Tort Reform. Consumer groups and trial lawyers long had blocked efforts to limit damage awards, saying it unfairly would penalize the victims of defective merchandise and remove an important incentive for manufacturers to ensure product safety. But with the United States mired in recession and businesses falling behind their foreign competitors, business claims that the tort system was driving up business costs through higher liability premiums and discouraging research into product innovation found a more sympathetic audience in Congress.

The Product Liability Fairness Act, introduced in 1991 and expected to be acted on in 1992, would set limits on each party's liability in cases involving more than one defendant, encourage out-of-court settlements, and establish standards on damage awards. Similar reforms were contained in legislation aimed at lowering medical-malpractice premiums by placing a cap on punitive damages and lawyers' fees in malpractice cases. The Bush administration endorsed these and other reforms of the medical-malpractice system as a way to curb spiraling U.S. health-care costs.

Supreme Court Ruling. While Congress appeared to be more hospitable toward tort reform, the advocates of the movement were disappointed when the Supreme Court ruled in March that there was no constitutional basis for limiting the size of punitive-damage awards. The case in question, *Pacific Mutual Life Insurance v. Haslip,* involved an Alabama resident who had been awarded $200,000 in compensatory damages and $840,000 in punitive damages stemming from a health-insurance scam. Business groups representing insurance companies, physicians, and manufacturers supported the insurance company's appeal for caps on damage awards. The Supreme Court's ruling, however, did not affect state laws limiting these awards.

Another setback for liability insurers and their allies occurred in November, when District of Columbia residents approved a referendum initiative holding the manufacturers of assault weapons liable for injuries or deaths caused by the guns.

MARY H. COOPER
"CQ [Congressional Quarterly] Researcher"

INTERIOR DESIGN

The "greening" of the 1990s came to interior design in 1991. Additionally, in the throes of the recession, consumers astutely demanded fashion-forward looks at sensible prices. Manufacturers responded by offering larger pattern scale or dimensions to give a sense of value.

No longer willing to change interior decor on a whim, consumers sought authenticity of design and lasting quality in their purchases. Major multiple-category museum-reproduction programs were launched from the Henry Ford Museum, Mar-a-Lago, and the Newport Preservation Society. Colonial Williamsburg revamped its lauded furniture line through a new association with Baker Furniture.

Design Inspirations. Throughout the home-furnishings industry, new products expressed both the beauty of and human responsibility to the environment. Gone were the stiff floral chintzes of recent memory. Vibrant blooms growing out of roots or bulbs and tropical birds prevailed. Animals, birds, and sun and moon motifs all flourished.

Active caring for the environment took the form of "green" products such as furniture that eschewed endangered tropical hardwoods. Consumers wanted natural, nonpolluting fiber fabrics and filling in upholstery.

Influenced by the Persian Gulf war, Americans experienced renewed patriotism. Accordingly, the April International Home Furnishings Market in High Point, NC, launched Pennsylvania House's American Sampler collection and Broyhill's American Frontier collection.

An emerging style trend was the use of motifs from ethnic or ancient cultures. Textiles embellished with geometric mystical symbols of the early cultures of Central America, accessories and lamps which seemed to be made from Aegean sculptural fragments, and accent furniture vibrant with African tribal motifs were part of this trend.

European country themes continued strong, with the Bombay Company in late 1990 introducing its new Alex & Ivy Stores format offering casual French provincial/country styles.

High-fashion apparel's strongest influence on home furnishings in 1991 appeared in the proliferation of plaid motifs. The Ralph Lauren Home Collection for fall 1991 delivered the most coordinated expression of this undoubtedly short-lived trend.

Technological Breakthroughs. The year 1991 saw the introduction of "video catalogs" to aid in special-order upholstery sales. The consumer now could view a selected frame and various fabric options.

DuPont's Micromattique, a silk-look microdenier polyester fiber, was announced as the first improvement on silk since its discovery 4,500 years ago. Monsanto followed with its own version.

Trends in Color, Textiles, and Finishes. Greens dominated 1991, appearing in a full range of shades. The yellow family warmed many of the premier furniture showrooms at the April market in High Point. Blues appeared in sapphire, denim, and aquamarine. Browns and purples also were favored.

Velvets returned as part of the desire for surface interest. "Dry looks" included linens, bark cloth, duck, tapestries, nubby and slubby weaves, and chenilles. Patterns were bigger and bolder.

Light finishes revealing the grain of the wood continued in favor. Brighter, painted finishes were offered as part of the overall drive to move products fashion-forward and away from the commodity business of brown, homogenized furniture. To that end, more light washed finishes on cherry and mahogany wood were to be expected in 1992.

CARLA BREER HOWARD, *"Traditional Home"*

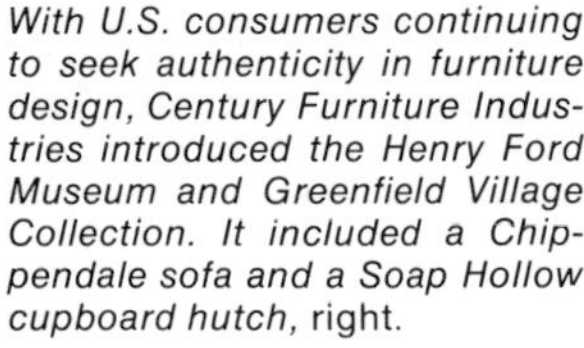

With U.S. consumers continuing to seek authenticity in furniture design, Century Furniture Industries introduced the Henry Ford Museum and Greenfield Village Collection. It included a Chippendale sofa and a Soap Hollow cupboard hutch, right.

© Century Furniture

INTERNATIONAL TRADE AND FINANCE

One of the biggest surprises of 1991 was an unsuccessful three-day coup by Communist Party, military, and KGB hard-liners against Mikhail Gorbachev. The Soviet president was reinstated August 21. German, Austrian, and other continental European equity and bond markets were hard hit briefly by the events in the USSR, while the more distant markets in the United States, Great Britain, Canada, and Australia seemed relatively insulated.

Another surprise was the pause in the U.S. economy in the fourth quarter after a mild recovery from recession in the summer.

A third shock was a dramatic drop in the U.S. stock market on November 15. Investors had been nervous in October, a month that has been prone to huge stock price declines. So it was somewhat unexpected when the Dow Jones industrial average took its largest one-day plunge in more than two years, falling nearly 4%. It closed at 2,943.20, off 120.31. The largest-ever drop in the Dow had been in October 1987 when it fell 508 points. The 1991 dive was blamed on the weak economy in general, an abrupt downturn in biotechnology stocks seen by some investors as overpriced, reports of real-estate problems plaguing several leading insurance companies, and a move by the U.S. Senate to put a cap on interest rates on consumer credit cards. A late December rally caused the Dow to close at 3,168.83—up 20.32% for the year, however.

Soviet Union. The failure of the Gang of Eight's coup was important in that it made unlikely the preservation of a unified Soviet Union (*see* FEATURE ARTICLE, page 24). The old Soviet power structure—the Communist Party, the KGB, the military—had lost its ability to hold the empire together. As the year progressed, the disintegration of the union moved forward, with power shifting to the republics, especially the Russian Republic. The secession of the Baltic states appeared assured and the Ukraine voted December 1 for independence. Moldavia, Georgia, Azerbaijan, and other republics also showed signs of seeking independence. Nonetheless, on October 18, eight of the Soviet Union's 12 remaining republics signed an economic pact linking them together. The Ukraine and Moldavia signed November 6, leaving Georgia and Azerbaijan as holdouts. On December 8, Russia, Ukraine, and Byelorussia (Belarus) declared that the USSR had ceased to exist and proclaimed a Commonwealth of Independent States.

The failure of the coup also opened the way for more radical economic reforms. On October 28, Boris N. Yeltsin, president of the Russian Republic and the decisive leader in blocking the coup, told the Congress of the People's Deputies that he intended to lift price controls in the Russian Republic by year's end, to accelerate sharply the privatization of agriculture and light industry, to stop financing central ministries and all foreign aid, and to bolster the ruble. As many as half of all small and medium enterprises could be privatized within three months, he said. The denationalizing of large enterprises would begin immediately. Spending on the bureaucracies and military would be cut sharply. Yeltsin said he hoped economic recovery would begin by the fall of 1992, but some Soviet experts doubted that it would come so soon. They were reckoning on a 17% fall in Soviet output in 1991 alone. With no other feasible choice, the legislature approved Yeltsin's drastic reforms, aimed at reviving the economy out of the ashes of communism, on November 1.

The weakening of the Soviet Union meant the West could continue with plans for considerable disarmament, an important economic change for the world. On November 1, U.S. House and Senate negotiators approved a $291 billion military budget for the 1992 fiscal year.

AP/Wide World

In November 1991 the World Bank agreed to devote $30 million to assist the Soviet Union restructure its food, banking, and social-security systems during its transition to a free-market system. Lewis T. Preston (extreme left), former chairman of J.P. Morgan & Co., who began a five-year term as the bank's president on September 1, and Soviet President Gorbachev signed the agreement at the Kremlin.

The BCCI Scandal

Most fraud victims get taken for perhaps several thousand dollars. Abu Dhabi's Sheikh Zayid bin Sultan al-Nuhayan, the ruler of the United Arab Emirates, lost billions as a result of management fraud at the Bank of Credit and Commerce International (BCCI). He and his tiny oil-rich Persian Gulf sheikhdom own 77% of the shares of the bank, which was depleted of much of its resources by the mistakes and crooked operations of its management. New York District Attorney Robert M. Morgenthau termed the BCCI scandal "the largest bank fraud in history."

On November 15 the U.S. Justice Department indicted Agha Hasan Abedi, the bank's principal founder and president; Swaleh Naqvi, the bank's acting president; and Ghaith Pharoan, a major shareholder. They were charged with fraud and racketeering. Similar charges, including money laundering, had been filed against BCCI and its principals by state officials in Florida and New York.

At year's end the liquidators of the bank, Touche Ross & Company in London, reportedly were negotiating with Abu Dhabi to make commitments of up to $2 billion in cash and another $3 billion by assuming various liabilities of the bank. That would give BCCI's more than 1 million depositors in some 70 countries between 30 and 40 cents on the dollar to cover their losses. In return, creditors would be asked to waive all further claims.

BCCI was shut down in a coordinated swoop on July 5, 1991. The bank's assets were seized by the countries and locales with its largest operations—Great Britain, Luxembourg, the Cayman Islands, the United States, France, Spain, and Switzerland. Financial regulators in more than 60 other countries were asked to cooperate.

The affair echoed around the world. One of the bank's techniques had been to court prominent individuals by appointing them to boards, making donations to their charities (for example, the museum and conference center of former U.S. President Jimmy Carter), or simply by making bribes. The bank even touched the White House when a former senior aide took a $600,000 contract to represent the former head of Saudi Arabian intelligence who was under investigation in the case. Edward M. Rogers, Jr., withdrew from the contract in late October.

A Pakistani banker, Aga Hasan Abedi, and some compatriots launched the bank in 1972 with a grubstake of $2.5 million and dreams of creating a world-class, Muslim-owned bank competing with the big Western financial institutions and serving developing countries. Bank of America had a 25% interest until 1980. The bank always was desperate for funds.

The *Financial Times of London* reported in November that BCCI engaged in four major frauds, each of several hundred million dollars. In addition to acquiring the U.S. banks illegally

That represented a modest 2% decline after inflation from the previous year's military budget. This followed the path that Defense Secretary Dick Cheney had announced in 1990, calling for a cut in Pentagon spending by about 20% over five years.

Aid. Meanwhile, the West was opening its wallet to help the Soviet Union—something unthinkable only a year or two earlier. Most of the money was to help feed the Soviets after a 30% drop in the grain harvest to 165 million tons, according to official figures. The United States was providing $2.5 billion in credits for food imports; the European Community (EC) was granting the same amount for food and medical supplies; Japan gave $2.5 billion for food and other aid; and Saudi Arabia was allocating $2.5 billion for food, clothing, medicine, and loans. The United States, Europe, Japan, and the World Bank provided technical aid.

At the October joint meeting of the International Monetary Fund (IMF) and the World Bank in Bangkok, Thailand, Soviet economist Grigory A. Yavlinsky pleaded unsuccessfully with the Group of Seven industrial democracies (the United States, Canada, Britain, France, Germany, Japan, and Italy) for a deeper financial commitment.

The United States called for debt relief for the Soviet Union. (An independent news agency, Interfax, on November 11 put the Soviet foreign debt at $81 billion, considerably higher than previously estimated.) The U.S. suggestion annoyed the Europeans, who were owed most of that money. Some bankers in the West expressed concern that the Soviet Union would default on some of its debts, with its supply of foreign currency expected to run out by year's end. There was an agreement October 29 by the 12 Soviet republics to shoulder responsibility jointly for the debt, but there also was talk two weeks later by Andrew Zverev, the deputy finance minister of the Russian Republic, of Russia taking on the entire debt itself in return for other concessions from the other republics. Russia owns 90% of Soviet oil and 75% of natural gas, both of which earn hard currency.

and secretly, it covered up some $633 million of losses on trading in government securities, attempted to prop up its largest borrower—the Gulf shipping group of Pakistan—by lending more than $725 million at a massive loss, and acquired 56% of its own shares at a cost of more than $500 million. The cost of manipulating these secret losses added another $2 billion in losses, the paper said.

BCCI had convinced Zayid and several businessmen in the Middle East early in the game to pose as owners of the bank's Luxembourg holding company, providing an illusion of financial stability. By April 1990, that mistake already was proving costly for Zayid. He and his government provided $400 million in additional capital, increasing their ownership from about 30% to 77%. Without Zayid's knowing it, oil revenues deposited in the bank also were being siphoned off to cover losses.

At its peak, BCCI reported $20 billion in assets. Losses were hidden through fictitious loans and other transactions within an extremely complex corporate structure of shell companies, offshore banks, branches, and subsidiaries, which let BCCI operate virtually unregulated. At least 20 central banks, many in Africa, were expected to take sizable losses.

BCCI gained attention in 1988 when a U.S. sting operation led to the indictment of the bank and ten executives in Florida on charges of laundering drug money. Under a plea bargain, the bank pled guilty and was fined $15 million. Five of its executives were sent to jail.

In the United States, BCCI secretly and illegally owned three banks. The largest was First

© G. Merillon/Gamma-Liaison

American Bankshares Inc. in Washington, DC. Its chairman, Clark M. Clifford (*see* BIOGRAPHY), denied knowing anything about BCCI ownership in testimony to Congress. He and his law partner and president of First American, Robert A. Altman, had resigned their First American positions August 13 after describing as "legal and proper" a deal in which they used a 100% loan from BCCI to buy stock in First American. This stock was sold two years later at a combined profit of $9.8 million.

On December 19 the U.S. Justice Department and New York City prosecutors announced that BCCI had agreed to plead guilty to federal and state charges of racketeering and fraud and would forfeit $550 million. Attorney General William Barr noted that the action "resolves all U.S. charges against BCCI as an institution."

DAVID R. FRANCIS

The difficulty of finding Western funds was demonstrated in mid-November when both Republican and Democratic lawmakers shelved a plan to tap the U.S. military budget for $1 billion to transport and distribute surplus food and medicine, private relief supplies, and other humanitarian aid to the Soviet people. It also would have allowed the Defense Department to help the USSR demilitarize in defense-related enterprises with technical aid, investment incentives, and the expansion of military exchange programs and advice on retraining military personnel. However, U.S. domestic politics killed this proposal. Just prior to adjourning, Congress approved legislation giving the president the power to use up to $400 million in defense funds to help the former USSR dismantle its nuclear arsenal. The president also would be able to allocate up to $100 million from the defense budget to transport humanitarian aid to the Soviet people.

The Overseas Private Investment Corporation in Washington did agree November 11 to provide partial insurance against expropriation, political violence, and currency-convertibility problems for an investment fund that planned to purchase $250 million worth of minority stakes in the commercial affiliates of Soviet military companies.

Stock Markets. The November plunge took back some of the gains in the U.S. stock market. Many such losses were recouped in the December rally. Through October, Japanese stocks were up 5.76% in terms of the yen, French stocks were up 22.32% in the domestic currency, British stocks were up 19.71%, German stocks rose 13.15%, Canadian stocks were up 7.95%, Swiss stocks increased 5.8%, and Italian stocks were down 1%.

Industrial Production. In the United States industrial production was flat in October, the third straight month of virtual stagnation after some recovery in the summer from the recession that began in July 1990. The Commerce Department's revised estimate of the third-quarter gross national product had the output of goods and services rising at a 2.0% annual rate. That was slow compared to most economic recoveries. The slack economy worried officials in both the Federal Reserve System and the White House. The Fed did lower interest rates gradually. By December 6 the federal funds rate which commercial banks charge each other on overnight loans stood at 5%, down from 8% a year earlier; the prime rate banks charge their better customers stood at 7.5%, down from 10% a year earlier. As the 1991 session ended, Congress was considering several measures to cut taxes, with final action put off until 1992. Congress and the Bush administration agreed on an extension of unemployment benefits.

Elsewhere, Canada and Great Britain were emerging from recessions. An October survey of some 48 international economists by Globescope found that in their consensus view, national output would be down 0.2% in the United States in 1991, down 0.7 % in Canada, and down 1.5% in Great Britain. It would be up 3.8% in Japan, up 2.9% in Germany, plus 1.5% in France, and up 1.4% in Italy. The IMF figured both world output and world trade volume were up only 1% in 1991. The Organization for Economic Cooperation and Development in Paris, the club of 24 industrial democracies, offered similar figures.

Trade. In the trade area, the EC and the seven-nation European Free Trade Association (EFTA) agreed October 22 on the creation of a 19-nation free-trade zone. This would result in a market of 380 million consumers if the European Economic Area treaty is ratified by all 19 national parliaments as well as the European Parliament. The goal was to have that completed by 1993. Eventually it was expected the EFTA nations would become full members of the EC. EFTA's members are Norway, Iceland, Finland, Sweden, Switzerland, Austria, and Liechtenstein. (The latter joined in May 1991.) EFTA's total population is 32.5 million. At the time of the treaty signing, Switzerland, Sweden, and Austria were about to apply or already had applied for EC membership. Finland said it would take a stance on EC membership early in 1992.

Negotiations also were under way with the post-Communist democracies of Eastern Europe about "affiliate" EC membership. On November 21, Poland, Hungary, and Czechoslovakia signed association agreements with the EC that would give them a ten-year transition to full free trade. Talks on similar agreements also had started with Bulgaria, Romania, and Albania. Yugoslavia was deep in the midst of a bloody civil war as Slovenia and Croatia sought independence.

Another trading bloc was being negotiated across the Atlantic. Formal talks toward formation of a North American Free Trade Area (NAFTA) began in June. Mexican President Carlos Salinas de Gortari and U.S. President Bush had signed a joint statement approving the idea of a comprehensive agreement between the United States and Mexico a year earlier. In September 1990, Canada indicated it wanted to join the negotiations. The intent was to create a market with 360 million consumers and a total output of $6 trillion. The deal could begin as soon as 1993. (*See also* SPECIAL REPORT/MEXICO.)

As the year neared an end, the five-year-long negotiations for another round of trade-barrier reductions under the auspices of the General Agreement on Tariffs and Trade (GATT) took a favorable turn. The talks by 108 nations had stalled in December 1990 in a dispute over high EC agricultural subsidies that have harmed the exports of such nations as the United States, Canada, Australia, and Argentina. Bush met with EC President and Dutch Prime Minister Ruud Lubbers and EC Commission President Jacques Delors in the Hague, the Netherlands, on November 9 in an effort to break the roadblock. Subsequent negotiations brought the parties closer together, with renewed hopes that the Uruguay Round might conclude successfully in the early months of 1992. One reason was that the EC's spending on farm subsidies—some $41 billion in 1991—had become so expensive that some reform was essential. Change was resisted by many of the EC's 10 million farmers. Success was expected to reduce the danger of the world breaking into three competing trade blocs—those of NAFTA, Europe, and some sort of grouping around Japan.

Other Highlights. At the Economic Summit in London on July 17, the Group of Seven industrial democracies agreed to grant the Soviet Union a sort of permanent-observer status. . . . Presidents Gorbachev and Bush agreed on a strategic arms treaty, the first to mandate reductions by the superpowers.

The United States pushed through an initiative calling for a 50% reduction in the debts of Poland and Egypt. . . . The developing-country debt issue faded as several Latin American debtor nations got their economic houses in better order and the reserves of commercial banks for their debts offered better protection to their solvency. . . . Holders of so-called Brady bonds—international bonds issued by Mexico, Venezuela, the Philippines, Costa Rica, and Uruguay—showed a 66% rate of return over 17 months. . . . The U.S. merchandise-trade deficit averaged $64 billion at an annual rate in the first eight months of 1991—down sharply from the all-year 1990 merchandise-trade deficit of $108 billion. The broader current account, which includes tourism, shipping, and capital flows, was expected to be in deficit by only $4 billion to $5 billion in 1991. One reason was massive cash contributions from coalition partners in the Persian Gulf war.

DAVID FRANCIS
"The Christian Science Monitor"

© Richard Sobol/Sipa

Iowa's Sen. Tom Harkin announced his candidacy for the 1992 Democratic presidential nomination in September, emphasizing traditional Democratic Party values—from better education and health care to improved roads and energy systems. A lawyer and former Navy jet pilot, Harkin had served five terms in the U.S. House of Representatives and was in his second term as a U.S. senator from the state.

IOWA

Monetary matters grabbed attention in Iowa in 1991 as the legislature coped with a budgetary shortfall from 1990–91 and passed the largest budget in state history for 1991–92.

Financial Matters. A financial crisis resulted when state-tax revenues for fiscal 1991 did not meet projections. Consequently appropriations were reduced by 3.5% and Republican Gov. Terry Branstad vetoed all pay increases for state employees for the fiscal year, including pay raises approved by collective-bargaining arbitrators. The union representing state employees sued the governor and other executive officers, asserting that state law had been violated. In anticipation of a ruling against his veto, the governor instructed each department to reduce personnel. More than 1,800 state employees were laid off.

For the 1992 fiscal year the Democratic-controlled General Assembly passed Branstad's record-breaking $3.3 billion budget. To support it, the legislature approved a $.05 increase in the state cigarette tax—bringing it to $.35 per pack; increased fees for fishing and hunting licenses; and a doubling of the cost of a marriage license from $15 to $30.

The July unemployment rate was 4.3%, well below the national average of 6.8%.

Legislature. In other legislative action, Iowa became the first state in the nation to make citizens under age 18 guilty of a misdemeanor for smoking a cigarette. The parimutuel tracks were allowed to take bets on live television races at any time; the age to gamble on riverboat casinos was lowered to 18; home-schooling rules were eased; smoke detectors were required in all new houses; and the Sunday sale of liquors was expanded. Additionally, a law was passed allowing Iowa cities and counties to reorganize into consolidated metropolitan corporations. Six new environmental laws provided for increases in solid-waste tonnage fees, doubling of fines for the emission of pollutants, and higher fees for cleanup of leaking underground gas tanks. The legislature gave second-round approval to a state constitutional amendment that would assure equal rights to women. Residents would vote on it in 1992.

Politics. Democrat Tom Harkin, a former five-term U.S. representative now in his second term as a U.S. senator, announced plans to run for president of the United States. A congressional redistricting plan mandated by Iowa's population decline placed Democratic Congressman David Nagel and freshman Re-

IOWA • Information Highlights

Area: 56,275 sq mi (145 753 km²).
Population (1990 census): 2,776,755.
Chief Cities (1990 census): Des Moines, the capital, 193,187; Cedar Rapids, 108,751.
Government (1991): *Chief Officers*—governor, Terry E. Branstad (R); lt. gov., Joy C. Corning (R). *General Assembly*—Senate, 50 members; House of Representatives, 100 members.
State Finances (fiscal year 1990): *Revenue,* $6,728,000,000; *expenditure,* $6,317,000,000.
Personal Income (1990): $47,870,000,000; per capita, $17,218.
Labor Force (June 1991): *Civilian labor force,* 1,513,400; *unemployed,* 67,600 (4.5% of total force).
Education: *Enrollment* (fall 1989)—public elementary schools, 338,422; public secondary, 140,064; colleges and universities, 169,901. *Public school expenditures* (1989), $1,925,623,000.

publican Congressman Jim Nussel in the same district.

Weather and Agriculture. The biggest spring rainfall in 99 years was followed by a drought in July and August. Corn and soybean yields were the largest of any state but lower than in 1990. Corn yield in Iowa was 1.3 billion bushels or 112 bushels per acre, while soybeans totaled 330 million bushels or 38 bushels per acre.

Other. A Chinese graduate student at the University of Iowa, apparently distraught over his failure to receive an academic honor, killed five people and wounded another before killing himself on November 1. . . . Riverboat gambling, which was seen as a financial boost to local communities, began April 1 on the Mississippi River. Revenue for the first five months was above projections. No riverboats were launched on the Missouri River, however.

RUSSELL M. ROSS, *University of Iowa*

IRAN

In the major developments of 1991, Iran stood somewhat on the sidelines. Though it recently fought an eight-year war with Iraq, it did not join the international coalition that made war on Iraq and forced it to relinquish Kuwait. In the fall, Iran opposed strongly the convening of a peace conference on the Middle East. In domestic affairs, while there was slow progress toward a more moderate line, a certain hesitancy and indecision prevailed. The shadow of the late Ayatollah Khomeini still lay on the land two years after his death, and President Ali Akbar Hashemi Rafsanjani was obliged to avoid stirring up opposition from those who revered Khomeini's memory.

Domestic Affairs. Rafsanjani was elected president overwhelmingly in July 1989, one month after Khomeini's death. Since then he has had control over the central levers of power and has moved to augment his authority. The election in October 1990 of a new Assembly of Experts—the body that elects the supreme religious leader—was a step in this direction since the new assembly was strongly supportive of Seyyed Ali Khamenei, Rafsanjani's ally and Khomeini's successor as spiritual leader.

On the other hand, the 270-seat *Majlis,* Iran's parliament, in 1991 had a hard-line majority, led by Ali Akbar Mohtashemi, a defeated candidate for the post Khamenei holds, and a bitter enemy of the two leaders and of anything moderate or pro-Western. In May the *Majlis* reelected Speaker Ayatollah Mehdi Karrubi, a vocal opponent of closer relations with the United States. In addition to the opposition in the *Majlis,* there continued to be large numbers of bureaucrats and officials who were able to frustrate any reforms that they opposed.

Economic Progress. The ideological hostility of many still in power to anything smacking of a market economy and the enormous losses from the war with Iraq (1980–88) hampered Iran's economic advance in 1991. A UN team estimated Iran's total war-related losses at $916 billion. Yet the government's moves in the direction of a freer economy undoubtedly stimulated a vigor in productivity. Within 1990–91, light industrial output trebled; wheat production almost doubled; and gross overall production rose more than 10%. The Tehran stock exchange reopened and was flourishing. There was a general shift from the military economy called for by the war with Iraq to a peacetime economic basis. The process was being directed by new Rafsanjani appointees. They were practical men rather than ideologues; some were U.S.-educated.

Iranian oil sales abroad rose about one third in 1991 over 1990. A number of foreign countries already were involved in investment or joint ventures in Iran, notably France, Germany, Italy, Japan, and Great Britain. The great exception to this trend was the United States, which severely restricted its trade with Iran. However, there were three U.S. contributions to Iran's economic health. One was the permission given by the U.S. Treasury on June 11 for a U.S. oil company to buy up to 2.5 million barrels of Iranian crude, worth about $35 million to $40 million. No Iranian oil had been imported since 1987. Second, the United States neither opposed nor supported Iran's application to the World Bank for a massive loan to be used to repair damage from the great earthquake in northwest Iran in June 1990; and the World Bank on March 16 extended to Iran a $250 million, 15-year loan. In addition, in late November, Iran and the United States reached agreement on compensation of $278 million to Tehran for undelivered Iranian-owned, U.S.-made military equipment dating from before the Islamic revolution.

Popular Discontent. The transition to a market economy was roughest on the poorest. Benefits were visible for the middle and upper strata of society, but the elimination of food subsidies and price controls led to severe price increases that made life hard for the poor. The problem also had political importance since elections for a new *Majlis* were scheduled for early 1992, and the president's opponents would exploit the discontent. Graffiti hostile to him became common, and there were six mysterious, presumably arsonist-set, fires in the summer in Tehran's Grand Bazaar, citadel of the new market economy. On the other hand, some aspects of discontent might be regarded as pro-change. Such was the riot, leading to 300 arrests, in Isfahan on July 26. The protesters were objecting to attempts to enforce the late Ayatollah's dress code for women—a dress code now quite largely ignored.

Persian Gulf War. Iran's attitude to the Gulf war was determined by two directly contrary pulls. On the one hand it was gratifying to see Iraq, the great and recent enemy, heavily and rapidly defeated. On the other hand, it was detestable that the United States along with other Western states suddenly had a great military presence in the Gulf. Even the participation of Egypt and Syria in the allied coalition was viewed askance. In its approach to the war, Iran strove for a peaceful solution, while condemning Iraqi occupation of Kuwait and opposing any foreign, especially Western, military activity in the Gulf.

Iran maintained a respectable neutrality throughout the war. It observed the sanctions (some inevitable smuggling excepted). It never took any formal stand against the UN resolutions authorizing the war. On January 17, Rafsanjani condemned both Iraq and the United States. This stance did not have unanimous support. Mohtashemi declared on January 20 that Iran had a religious duty to ally with Iraq; and in the course of January there were anti-U.S. demonstrations, but of limited size, in Tehran and three other cities.

Between January 26 and 29 just more than 100 Iraqi warplanes were flown across the border into sanctuary in Iran. This produced a brief flurry of fear of Iraqi-Iranian cooperation, which proved groundless. Iran said the planes would be confiscated, and they never were returned. Most of the planes were MiG 29s. Since Iran had purchased a number of such planes from the Soviet Union in 1991, spare parts were assured and the former Iraqi planes would be sustainable as part of Iran's air force.

Diplomatic Relations Restored. Iran devoted much effort in 1991 to maintaining or restoring good relations with neighboring states. On January 14 normal diplomatic relations with Jordan, severed at the start of the Iraqi-Iranian war—in which Jordan like all Arab states except Syria had supported Iraq—were restored. Embassies reopened in March. On March 12 it was announced that Egypt and Iran would set up interests sections—a low level of representation—in each other's capital. This was "as a first step toward the restoration of full diplomatic relations."

Normal relations with Saudi Arabia recommenced March 26—three years after the breach occasioned by the 1987 clashes between Iranian pilgrims and Saudi security forces. Agreements were made about numbers of Iranian pilgrims to be permitted annually to visit Mecca on *hajj* (pilgrimage). Mohtashemi was bitterly critical of this rapprochement. Rafsanjani visited Syria, April 27–29, in his first trip as president outside Iran. While there he underlined Iran's commitment to Iraq's territorial integrity. In Lebanon he conferred with leaders of Iranian-supported factions. In Turkey, April 29-May 2, Rafsanjani and Turkish leaders concurred that no Kurdish state should be carved out of northern Iraq; agreements were made about the sale of Iranian oil and gas to Turkey.

Strengthening of foreign ties also occurred outside the region. A high-level European Community delegation was in Tehran in April for trade discussions, and the foreign ministers of France and Germany both visited Iran in May. Austria's President Kurt Waldheim visited Iran June 9–11, the first European head of state to do so since the shah's overthrow.

Iran in Opposition. In the fall, Iran was much opposed to the long course of diplomacy which led to the convening of an Arab-Israeli peace conference in Madrid on October 30 (*see* FEATURE SECTION, page 36). For Iran, Israel is an enemy even worse than the United States. Iran's retort was the holding in Tehran from October 19 to 22 of an "International Conference for the Support of the Muslim Palestinian People's Revolution," also dubbed the anticonference conference. More than 400 delegates, Islamic extremists from more than 40 countries, attended.

Iran did make some conciliatory gestures. On April 1, Robert Cooper—a British businessman who had been arrested in 1985 accused of spying, and held without trial ever since—was released. Iran no doubt played a major role in achieving the release from Lebanon of the remaining U.S. and British hostages. But there were many items on the other side of the ledger. On April 18 in Paris, Abdul Rahman Broumand, a member of the opposition National Iranian Resistance Movement, was stabbed and killed. More striking, on August 6, also in Paris, Shahpur Bakhtiar, who held office briefly in 1979 as the last prime minister of the shah (whom he long had opposed), was murdered. Rafsanjani was accused widely of responsibility for these murders. And as 1991 drew to an end there were reports that Iran, with Chinese help, was well on the way toward the development of nuclear weapons.

ARTHUR CAMPBELL TURNER
University of California, Riverside

IRAN • Information Highlights

Official Name: Islamic Republic of Iran.
Location: Southwest Asia.
Area: 636,293 sq mi (1 648 000 km^2).
Population (mid-1991 est.): 58,600,000.
Chief City (1986 census): Tehran, the capital, 6,042,584.
Government: *Head of state and government,* Ali Akbar Hashemi Rafsanjani, president (took office August 1989). *Legislature* (unicameral)—Islamic Consultative Assembly (*Majlis*).
Monetary Unit: Rial (69.173 rials equal U.S.$1, July 1991).
Gross National Product (1989 U.S.$): $97,600,-000,000.
Foreign Trade (1988 U.S.$): *Imports,* $12,000,-000,000; *exports,* $12,300,000,000.

IRAQ

Saddam Hussein, the ruler of Iraq for more than a decade, continued to demonstrate two notable characteristics in 1991. One was poor judgment in matters of international politics that has led to major blunders. To cite examples, in 1980 he embarked quite needlessly on an unprovoked aggressive war against Iran, which lasted eight years, caused enormous losses, and gained nothing. In 1990 he invaded Kuwait and occupied it, evoking a consensus of opposition to his aggression not merely in the West but also from the majority of Arab states. This led to a war in 1991 in which Iraq was ousted from Kuwait and suffered great destruction and total defeat.

Hussein's second characteristic has been an amazing ability to survive such blunders and to remain in power, with his dictatorial grasp of the reins of government not impaired and indeed sometimes enhanced, and with his prestige at home and among the Arab masses—as distinct from Arab rulers—diminished hardly at all. In 1991 he survived defeat in war by an international coalition as well as two simultaneous and serious rebellions, and emerged with his power, more than half of his army, and his state's territory intact. As 1991 ended, reasons for his resilience only could be suggested. The most obvious one was Hussein's tight control of government. His closest advisers and cabinet ministers had been long-standing associates whom he believed he could trust completely and who in many cases were related to him. He also had been completely ruthless and with good cause feared.

There was more to it than merely terror, however. The Baath Party regime that has ruled Iraq since the latter 1960s has been in many respects beneficial. Iraq's level of literacy is high by Middle East standards. The large oil revenues probably have been used more wisely for broad economic development, including agriculture, than in any other oil-producing country of the region. Although Saddam Hussein and almost all his entourage are Sunni, an effort has been made to conciliate the Shiite southern area by building hospitals and other public works there.

In addition to these factors, no visible candidate had emerged by late 1991 who might replace Hussein as the ruler of Iraq. All rivals had been eliminated. The multifarious dissident groups in exile, who held two conferences in Beirut in 1991, lacked plausibility. Most Iraqi people appeared to believe that Hussein's disappearance would produce not an improvement but an unpredictable worsening of their situation. This belief has been reinforced by ideological considerations that have made the Iraqi dictator something of a folk hero to the Islamic masses not only in Iraq but throughout the region. It was no small thing to have defied the United States and the whole West and, though defeated, to have survived. There was a class-struggle dimension, too—the oil-rich rulers of Saudi Arabia and the smaller Gulf states, on whose behalf the West intervened, were not much beloved by the poor Arabs of the more populous states to the north and west.

Sanctions, War, and Defeat. The central and most important event of the year was the culmination of the crisis that had begun on Aug. 2, 1991, with the Iraqi invasion and occupation of Kuwait. The United Nations (UN) deadline for Iraq to leave Kuwait, Jan. 15, 1991, passed without any Iraqi withdrawal and the next day hostilities against Iraq began with punishing air bombardments, which continued for five and one half weeks. The second phase of the war began on February 23 when coalition forces launched large-scale ground operations. This phase was completed in four days. On February 27, Iraq agreed to comply with all 12 of the UN resolutions passed in 1990, and on March 3, Iraq's military leaders accepted terms for the ending of the Gulf war.

The UN passed resolutions in April that defined Iraq's dealings with the international community. The 34 points of Resolution 687, passed on April 3, ordered Iraq to submit information concerning chemical and biological weapons stocks by April 17, to permit on-site inspection of weapons of mass destruction by a UN-International Atomic Energy Agency (IAEA) team, and to destroy all nonconventional weapons and ballistic missiles with a range above 93 mi (150 km) by July 2. Iraq also was required to renounce international terrorism. The resolution envisaged the creation of a UN fund to pay war reparations financed by a percentage of Iraq's oil earnings. (The latter was not realized in 1991.) The embargo on food exports to Iraq was removed, but other sanctions were retained with exceptions for humanitarian purposes. The provisions were subject to bimonthly review. On April 9, Resolution 689 approved the establishment of a demilitarized zone between Iraq and Kuwait, 6 mi (10 km) deep on the Iraq side and 3 mi (5 km) wide on the Kuwaiti side. The resolutions were combined with a formal cease-fire.

IRAQ • Information Highlights

Official Name: Republic of Iraq.
Location: Southwest Asia.
Area: 167,923 sq mi (434 920 km^2).
Population (mid-1991 est.): 17,100,000.
Chief City (1987 census): Baghdad, the capital, 3,844,608.
Government: *Head of state and government,* Saddam Hussein, president (took office July 1979).
Monetary Unit: Dinar (0.311 dinar equals U.S.$1, selling rate, August 1991).
Gross National Product (1989 est. U.S.$): $35,000,000,000.
Foreign Trade (1988 est. U.S.$): *Imports,* $10,200,000,000; *exports,* $12,500,000,000.

Nuclear and Chemical Weapons. The enforcement of the various conditions imposed on Iraq proved much more difficult and contentious than the resolutions suggested. The Iraqi government engaged in a tireless game of evasion, concealment, and deceit in an effort to protect as much of its military might as possible. And in a very short while the victorious allies no longer had any means, short of a renewal of the war, to enforce their wishes. By midsummer no U.S. or other foreign troops remained on Iraqi soil, apart from a small peacekeeping force on the Kuwait border. Vague late July threats by the United States to launch air strikes against Iraq if it did not reveal the complete extent of its nuclear program ran into opposition from the Soviet Union and two Arab allies of the United States, Egypt and Syria.

Jaafar Dhia Jaafar, deputy chairman of Iraq's Atomic Energy Commission, asserted to the IAEA experts on July 18 that Iraq had disclosed all of its nuclear equipment that could be used to make weapons, and the inspection team to a large extent agreed with him. However, many experts were skeptical and emphasized Iraq's repeated attempts to conceal its nuclear activities, which indeed eventually proved to be much more advanced than had been thought. It emerged that without the war, Iraq would have been able to produce nuclear weapons, as well as chemical weapons in quantity, by the mid 1990s.

The high-water mark of Iraqi intransigence was reached in two incidents in September when the UN weapons team was blockaded for several days in parking lots in Baghdad by Iraqi troops. The inspectors had found records of the Iraqi Atomic Energy Commission proving conclusively that Iraq had plans to manufacture nuclear weapons. In the second incident the inspectors were able to keep in touch with the outside world by satellite telephone—an embarrassment to Iraq—and refused the demand to hand over documents they had discovered. The incident ended with the inspectors keeping the documents but providing Iraqi officials with an inventory of them.

Iraq's repeated violations of the cease-fire agreements evoked many exasperated comments from U.S. President George Bush. On September 8, Iraq said that it would not allow UN inspectors to fly their own helicopters. Iraq yielded on this point when President Bush said that inspecting helicopters would be escorted by U.S. air force planes if necessary.

Internal Conditions. There could be no doubt that the war did great damage to Iraq, that the conflict and its aftermath caused loss of life—military casualties were estimated at 100,000—and that the standard of living—surprisingly little affected in the 1980–88 war with Iran—declined during 1991. There, however, was much difference of opinion and a paucity of information about the precise extent of damage and loss. The Iraqi government embarked immediately after the cease-fire on a vigorous program of restoration and rebuilding. By March 8, about one week after the end of the war, all of Baghdad again had electricity at night, though full repair of the capital's generating equipment might take up to a year. The oil ministry announced on March 6 that it was beginning to restore pipelines and buildings. Work was begun on rebuilding telecommunications facilities and repair of roads and bridges also began. All primary and secondary schools in areas of Iraq not in rebellion reopened on March 23.

© Francoisc Demulder/Sipa

Immediately after the cease-fire, Iraq began to restore and rebuild that which was damaged during the 1991 Persian Gulf war. The repair of bridges and roads was a priority.

It, of course, is an unfortunate aspect of sanctions, as of war, that they have the worst impact on those least in a position to affect policy decisions. Pollution of drinking water caused grave health problems in all major cities, and there were epidemic diseases in the south to an extent not known since the Iraqi government seldom permitted foreign observers to go there. In the war unintended deaths of civilians as a result of bombing did occur, but on a very small scale as compared with World War II. A mid-November report by Middle East Watch claimed an "upper limit" of 2,500 to 3,000 civilians dead from the bombing.

Humanitarian efforts to bring food and medical supplies to Iraq in quantity were initiated by UN and various national agencies. Iraq, however, adamantly refused to accept the help offered in Security Council Resolution 706 of June 7, which would have permitted Iraq to export $1.6 billion worth of oil over a six-month period to pay for the import of food, medicine, and other necessities. Iraq balked at the conditions that called for some of the money to be used for reparations to Kuwait and other states that had losses in the war. However, another humanitarian program, without strings, providing relief in distressed areas, was accepted reluctantly by Saddam Hussein.

A U.S. Senate Foreign Relations Committee study, released on November 27, concluded unequivocally that Iraq was exporting massive amounts of goods in violation of sanctions and was using the earnings to buy luxuries as well as food and medicine, and that a high percentage of the funds was going to maintain the morale of the army. The land trade across Iraq's borders resumed openly, though the oil blockade was apparently still effective. The Iraqi harvest of 1991 was a good one; the difficulties concerned distribution. In early December visitors to Baghdad reported that the food situation had improved and that prices had stabilized, though at a level higher than in 1990. The only really bad conditions were in the south.

Rebellions. In the immediate aftermath of the war, Saddam Hussein was obliged to deal with two simultaneous large-scale rebellions, one in the Kurdish area in the north and the other in the Shiite region of south Iraq. The Kurdish problem had international dimensions and continued unresolved throughout the year. The Shiite uprising, however, was dealt with by a combination of political and military steps by the end of March. On March 6 pay bonuses were announced for all soldiers and an amnesty declared for deserters and draft dodgers. The same day, Hussein appointed Ali Hassan Majid, the hard-line local government minister, as interior minister, with orders to suppress the uprising, which he did with ruthless efficiency. Majid, a cousin of Hussein, had used poison gas against the Kurds in 1988 and had been the brutal governor of Kuwait after the conquest of August 1990. Some reports said that 30,000 people died in the southern rebellion. For the remainder of the year the southern area remained sealed off from the rest of Iraq.

Ministerial Changes. During the year, Saddam Hussein carried out several reshuffles among his closest advisers. A new Council of Ministers was appointed on March 23. The longtime foreign minister, Tariq Aziz, able, but no relative and never a member of the inner circle, was replaced by Ahmad Husayn Khudayir al-Samarrai; Aziz remained a deputy premier. Sadoun Hammadi, a deputy premier, became prime minister, a post previously held by Saddam Hussein himself. But Hammadi proved too outspoken and was replaced on September 14 by Mohammad Hamza al-Zubaidi. In a speech on March 16, Hussein promised major reforms in a "new phase," and held out the vision of a "democratic society based on constitution, law, institutions, and pluralism." Observers were skeptical.

On November 6, Majid was named defense minister and replaced as interior minister by Wathban Ibrahim Hassan. The latter had been governor of the most important Salah al Din province just north of the capital—the family stronghold—as well as head of military intelligence. Hassan is the oldest of Saddam Hussein's three half brothers. One of the other two was heading the secret police and the third was Iraq's chief agent in Europe, based in Geneva.

See also FEATURE SECTION/MIDDLE EAST, page 36.

ARTHUR CAMPBELL TURNER
University of California, Riverside

IRELAND

Rumors and accusations of corruption in the highest circles of Ireland's government and business broke into the public domain in September 1991 with the news that several prominent financiers, who were friends of Prime Minister Charles J. Haughey, had made huge profits through means that smacked of insider trading. Against a background of alleged fraud at a giant beef-exporting company owned by Lawrence Goodman and amid charges of windfall profits from the privatization of the Irish Sugar Company, tne press reported another alleged scandal involving the purchase of an old factory in Ballsbridge for company headquarters of the semi-state entity Telecom Eireann.

The Ballsbridge property had been owned by United Property Holdings (UPH), whose principal shareholder, Dermot Desmond, had founded one of Ireland's biggest stockbroking firms, National City Brokers (NCB). Desmond, who was a good friend of both Prime Minister Haughey and Telecom Chairman Michael Smurfit, sold the site to Telecom in January 1990 for 9.4 million Irish pounds (about $16.7 million) after having paid 4 million Irish pounds (about $6.2 million) for it in 1989. It later was revealed that Smurfit held a 10% stake in UPH through another company. Telecom also had leased a large office building from UPH without the knowledge of its own board of directors. The press also reported that NCB had furnished confidential information to the prime minister's son, a leading shareholder in Celtic Helicopters, on a rival company.

The strong impression of collusion between members of the political and business elite gave rise to calls for Haughey's resignation. According to an opinion poll in the *Irish Times* on October 14, 63% of those surveyed believed that the prime minister should step down, while the satisfaction rating for Haughey's government had fallen to a mere 29%—its lowest level in five years. Criticism came not just from the opposing Fine Gael and Labour parties but also from backbench members of his own Fianna Fail Party in the Dail. Uneasy about their alliance with the government, the Progressive Democrats called for an official inquiry. The prime minister denied any wrongdoing and told his followers at an October 2 meeting that he would be vindicated. In the meantime the scandal moved Desmond to resign as chairman of Aer Rianta, the Irish airports authority, and to give up temporarily his directorship of NCB. Smurfit also stepped down as head of Telecom Eireann.

After a heated debate in the Dail over allegations of corruption, Haughey survived an October 18 vote of confidence in the Dail by a margin of 84 to 81. The price of the Progressive Democrats' support was acceptance of their demand for reductions in the tax rate and government borrowing.

All these discontents came to a head early in November, when Haughey faced a vote of no confidence within his own parliamentary party. On November 7 he fired his chief rival in the cabinet, Albert Reynolds, minister of finance, who refused to support him at the upcoming meeting. Although Haughey won an endorsement by a margin of 55 to 22 votes on November 9, three junior ministers voted against him. All three were sacked shortly thereafter. To prevent further erosion of power, the prime minister embarked on a major reshuffle of his cabinet, naming Bertie Ahern as finance minister, Vincent Brady as minister of defense, and Noel Davern as minister for education. Acrimony and suspicion continued to swirl around the Fianna Fail party, however.

Foreign Policy. Although the Irish government tried to remain neutral during the Persian Gulf war, U.S. planes bound for the Gulf were allowed to land and refuel at Shannon Airport. On June 28–29 Irish ministers met with the leaders of the other 11 members of the European Community (EC) in Luxembourg to discuss closer economic and political union.

Britain's Secretary of State for Northern Ireland Peter Brooke launched a new round of talks involving all the constitutional parties in the six counties on April 30. He had hoped that any agreement arising out of these discussions would be placed before the voters in both the Irish Republic and Northern Ireland. After several weeks of wrangling, however, the delegates could not agree even on a site for future meetings and further talks were canceled.

Economy. An official unemployment rate of 17.1% gave Ireland the dubious distinction of having the highest such rate in the EC. Beset by symptoms of recession, the government tried to stimulate the economy with modest adjustments. The budget, introduced by Minister for Finance Reynolds on January 30, called for a 1% reduction in the income-tax rate and a 4% increase in welfare benefits. While taxes on cars and tobacco were raised, the government reduced the higher (but not the lower) value-added tax (VAT) rate from 23% to 21%, which brought it closer to the VAT in other EC countries. The combination of rising prices and more layoffs increased antigovernment feelings among trade-union members, who had agreed not to ask for more than 4% increases.

Social Issues, the Presidency, and Other News. Haughey sought to fend off his critics with assurances that he would try to liberalize the laws concerning birth control and divorce. Some political observers construed this shift in Fianna Fail policy as a sign of Haughey's anxiety about the growing popularity of President Mary Robinson since her election in November 1990. Determined to breathe new life into the largely ceremonial office of the presidency, Robinson toured every county in Ireland during her first ten months in office.

On January 2 the body of Provisional IRA member Patrick Sheehy was found in the town of Nenagh, County Tipperary, with a bullet wound in the head. The victim of an apparent suicide, Sheehy had been high on the British government's "most wanted" list for his alleged involvement in bombings in England.

L. Perry Curtis, Jr., *Brown University*

IRELAND • Information Highlights

Official Name: Republic of Ireland.
Location: Island in the eastern North Atlantic Ocean.
Area: 27,135 sq mi (70 280 km²).
Population (mid-1991 est.): 3,500,000.
Chief Cities (1986 census): Dublin, the capital, 920,956 (incl. suburbs); Cork, 173,694; Limerick, 76,557.
Government: *Head of state,* Mary Robinson, president (took office Dec. 3, 1990). *Head of government,* Charles Haughey, prime minister (took office March 1987). *Legislature*—Parliament: House of Representatives (Dail Eireann) and Senate (Seanad Eireann).
Monetary Unit: Pound (0.6120 pound equals U.S.$1, Nov. 12, 1991).
Gross Domestic Product (1989 est. U.S.$): $31,400,000,000.
Economic Indexes (1990): *Consumer Prices* (1980 = 100), all items, 209.8; food, 461.7. *Industrial Production* (1980 = 100), 184.
Foreign Trade (1990 U.S.$): *Imports,* $20,716,000,000; *exports,* $23,778,000,000.

© P. Kern/Sygma

New settlements continued to be developed in the Israeli-occupied territories of Gaza and the West Bank (above). *Damage caused by Iraqi Scud missiles and increased immigration from the USSR further complicated Israel's housing crisis.*

ISRAEL

In 1991 the Persian Gulf war and the Middle East peace conference dominated events in Israel although problems from previous years continued to be critical. Such problems included massive Jewish immigration from the Soviet Union, an influx of several thousand Ethiopian Jews, and the Palestinian Arab uprising or *intifada*.

The Persian Gulf War. The most immediate impact on Israel of the Persian Gulf war was Iraq's Scud-missile attacks on Tel Aviv and Haifa. Although casualties were few, hundreds of dwellings were destroyed, adding to an already critical housing shortage. The war cost Israel an estimated $3 billion, but an Israeli official was quoted as saying that most damage was temporary and that the war did not "hurt the economy very much."

One of the first emergency measures taken by the government was to stop Arab labor from the occupied territories, Gaza and the West Bank—more than 100,000 workers—from entering Israel. This undermined plans to construct some 100,000 new units by the end of the year, adding to the continuing problem of finding quarters for hundreds of thousands of new immigrants, most of them from the USSR.

Agriculture, also heavily dependent on Arab labor, was slowed. Hundreds of millions of dollars were lost in the fruit-and-flower-export business. A number of high-tech companies reported loss of sales because of the uncertainties of war and failure of foreign suppliers to renew orders.

The impact of emergency measures in the occupied territories was far more severe than in Israel proper. In addition to closing borders and the bridges to Jordan, the longest curfew during the 24 years of occupation was imposed on Gaza and the West Bank. The total economy of the territories nearly was halted; farmers were unable to water, harvest, or market their crops; and most Palestinian business ceased. Economists calculated that the territories were working at only 25% of capacity by the time the curfew was lifted in March. The United Nations (UN) appealed for funds to feed the Palestinians and the European Community (EC) prepared an $8 million food-aid package.

By spring some Palestinians were permitted to return to their jobs in Israel, but the number of permits was reduced greatly. Paradoxically, within Israel itself unemployment climbed steadily to more than 10% with projections that it probably would peak at 14% by 1994. In Israel's parliament, the Knesset, questions were raised about the incongruity of paying large amounts of unemployment insurance when agriculture and the construction industry were begging for workers. Some employers even requested government permission to import labor from Turkey, Portugal, or Yugoslavia.

Economic pressures in 1991 were relieved somewhat by increased aid from the United States. Israel was compensated for its "restraint" in the face of the Iraqi missile attacks with substantial additions to the $3.2 billion it considered due in annual U.S. assistance. The additions included $650 million for the destruction and "pain and suffering" resulting from the Iraqi attacks, a special military grant of $700 million, $400 million in housing guarantees, and several smaller items. These additions were assured before the squabble between the Bush administration and Prime Minister Shamir over Israel's demand for another $10 billion in housing-loan guarantees to cover construction of homes for new immigrants during the next five years.

The Palestinians. Outbreaks of zealous Palestinian support for Iraq's President Saddam Hussein greatly deepened the suspicions and hostility between Israeli Jews on the one hand, and Israeli Arabs and Palestinian inhabitants of the territories on the other. Unlike the 1982 war in Lebanon or the army's campaign against the *intifada,* which were criticized widely, the Gulf war galvanized Israeli public opinion behind the government. But by March, after the war ended, this national unity began to unravel. The prime minister was attacked sharply from the right and the left. Three right-wing parties —Tehiya, Tzomet, and Moledet—opposed Prime Minister Yitzhak Shamir's 1989 plan, the basis for Israeli policy for a peace settlement. These three nationalist groups adamantly objected to proposals for elections by Palestinians in the territories and to granting them autonomy under Israeli control.

In July the judicial inquiry into the October 1990 Al Aksa mosque incident in Jerusalem was completed. Judge Ezra Kama concluded that the police, not the Palestinians, initially provoked the violence in which at least 17 Arabs were killed. His findings contradicted a government-appointed commission that had exonerated the police. The judge observed that neither Israelis nor Palestinians were blameless and that both were responsible for turning what began with a "trivial incident" into a "tragedy." However, Judge Kama concluded, no charges should be brought against any of the police officers since it was impossible to determine which officers were guilty.

Politics. The Labor opposition and the six parties to its left were highly critical of the prime minister for appointing former Gen. Rehavam Zeevi to his cabinet as minister without portfolio. Zeevi is leader of Moledet, a party that called for the expulsion of all Arabs from the West Bank and Gaza. Former Prime Minister Shimon Peres, leader of the Labor Alignment, launched an attack on Shamir in October for placing Israel on a "collision course" with the United States by "insulting" President George Bush in the controversy over immigrant-housing-loan guarantees.

The Peace Conferences. Although both Israel and the United States had insisted that there was no linkage between the confrontation with Iraq and the Arab-Israel conflict, the war was a catalyst that led to convening a Middle East peace conference in Madrid during October. It required eight trips to Israel and the surrounding countries by U.S. Secretary of State James Baker to complete arrangements for the conference. Among the conditions that the Shamir government imposed for its participation were: No Arab inhabitants of Jerusalem could be represented; none with any Palestine Liberation Organization (PLO) connections might participate; and Palestinians would be represented only by residents of Gaza or the West Bank and only as part of a Jordanian delegation. The Israeli leader also opposed UN sponsorship or participation in the conference and agreed to Soviet cosponsorship on the condition that the Soviet Union reestablish full diplomatic relations with Israel. While agreeing to a brief formal opening session attended by all parties concerned, Prime Minister Shamir insisted that the following meetings be bilateral, face-to-face discussions between Israeli representatives and those of Syria, Lebanon, and Jordan/Palestine.

Most of these conditions were accepted. In October, after a visit by Soviet Foreign Minister Boris D. Pankin, diplomatic relations were renewed with Moscow for the first time since the 1967 Arab-Israeli war. At the opening sessions in Madrid, Israel was represented by Prime Minister Shamir, and although many of the exchanges in the opening sessions were acrimonious, the conference was seen as historic because it was the first in which the two sides engaged in public, direct negotiations. Major differences between Israeli and Arab representatives focused on convening the second phase of the conference, involving bilateral negotiations. Israel insisted the next round of meetings occur in Israel and the surrounding countries, while Arab representatives demanded a European site. When the conference adjourned at the end of October these procedural disputes had yet to be resolved. The meetings commenced again during December in Washington, where procedural wrangling again dominated the first sessions.

(*See also* FEATURE SECTION/MIDDLE EAST, page 36.)

DON PERETZ
State University of New York, Binghamton

ISRAEL • Information Highlights

Official Name: State of Israel.
Location: Southwest Asia.
Area: 8,019 sq mi (20 770 km²).
Population (mid-1991 est.): 4,900,000.
Chief Cities (1989 est.): Jerusalem, the capital, 493,500 (including East Jerusalem); Tel Aviv-Jaffa, 317,800; Haifa, 222,600.
Government: *Head of state,* Chaim Herzog, president (took office May 1983). *Head of government,* Yitzhak Shamir, prime minister (took office October 1986). *Legislature* (unicameral)—Knesset.
Monetary Unit: Shekel (2.275 shekels equal U.S.$1, Dec. 16, 1991).
Gross National Product (1989 U.S.$): $38,000,-000,000.
Economic Indexes (1990): *Consumer Prices* (1980 = 100), all items, 65,417.6; food, 60,230.7. *Industrial Production* (1989, 1980 = 100), 124.
Foreign Trade (1990 U.S.$): *Imports,* $15,104,-000,000; *exports,* $11,576,000,000.

© Bari Press/Sipa Press

Thousands of Albanians, seeking a better economic lot, fled by ship to Italy in 1991, posing a crisis for the Italian government. Although some of the refugees were able to remain in Italy, many were forced to return to their homeland.

ITALY

Fear that Italy might slip to second-class status in the more tightly integrated Europe of 1992 led to new calls for reform of Italy's constitution and economic practices in 1991.

Another Coalition Government. The year began with Italy administered by a fragile five-party *(pentapartito)* government headed since July 1989 by Giulio Andreotti, a right-wing Christian Democrat. His coalition also consisted of Socialists, Social Democrats, Republicans, and Liberals. The government supported the United Nations (UN) in the Persian Gulf war, and Italy contributed naval and air-force units to this effort. But as soon as the war ended it reverted to wrangling over domestic policies.

On March 29, Premier Andreotti resigned. His action was triggered by the ambitions of Bettino Craxi, leader of the Socialist Party and a key partner in Andreotti's cabinet. Craxi argued that Italy must have a new government capable of dealing with such thorny issues as runaway budget deficits and soaring crime rates. He also called for changes in the constitution that would strengthen greatly the powers of the now largely figurehead president of the republic, and would modify the voting system of proportional representation to reduce the clout of minor parties. The Republican, Social Democratic, Liberal, and other small parties viewed such changes as a threat.

On April 11, Andreotti announced that he had organized a new government composed of the same five parties as before. This was the seventh government the 72-year-old premier had headed, and Italy's 50th since World War II.

Four days after Andreotti's announcement, Giorgio La Malfa's Republican Party, angered by its failure to obtain more than three low-level ministries, decided not to join the new coalition after all. Rather than allow his shaky new government to collapse, Andreotti chose to get along with just four parties: his own Christian Democrats, the Socialists, Social Democrats, and Liberals.

Controversy Over Political Reform. On June 9, Italy held a referendum designed to simplify the country's voting procedures. It was instigated by a Sardinian Christian Democrat, Mario Segni, whose immediate aim was to reduce opportunities for electoral fraud—a common practice in Mafia-dominated sections of the south. But Segni also wanted to give Italians a chance to signal their desire for far-reaching political reform. The response surprised even the referendum's most enthusiastic champions. Not only did 95.5% of those who voted back the referendum, but 62.5% of the electorate went to the polls, comfortably over the 50% turnout needed for the vote to stand.

Clearly, the voters had sent a resounding message to Rome. But Premier Andreotti shrugged off the results because his coalition partners were divided deeply over the vote. Andreotti was especially anxious not to alienate his main ally, Socialist Party leader Craxi, who was the most vocal critic of this particular referendum but who nevertheless had his own agenda for constitutional reform.

Craxi had proposed a referendum that would institute a directly elected, powerful president of the republic, an office to which he himself aspired. Such a referendum, however, presupposed rewriting the constitution of 1948, because referenda, at present, only can abrogate existing laws; they cannot introduce new ones. To get his way, Craxi would need a two-thirds parliamentary majority to amend the constitution. This would not be easy as most of the other parties had their own schemes for a "Second Republic."

Confusion was compounded when President Francesco Cossiga, a Christian Democrat, made statements on national television that went far beyond the ceremonial role Italian heads of state generally have played. The increasingly outspoken president, whose seven-year term would end in July 1992, asserted his right to dissolve parliament "even against its will" and to call a general election prior to the spring of 1992, when it normally would occur. This assertion caused such a furor that he had to back down.

In other pronouncements, Cossiga asked Premier Andreotti to initiate at once the process for constitutional revision. He recommended that the next parliament complete the revision within two years. The president also advocated reform of the system of proportional representation and called for differentiating the powers of the two houses of parliament. In addition, he urged expansion of regional autonomies—a burning issue in Piedmont, Lombardy, and Venetia, where new political "leagues" had emerged, demanding that the affluent north no longer subsidize the backward south. Cossiga went on to declare that the budgetary process must be improved drastically if Italy was to be ready for tighter integration of the European Community (EC) in 1992.

On still another occasion, President Cossiga angered many leftists when he defended those politicians who had taken part in the "Gladio" guerrilla network that was organized secretly with the help of the North Atlantic Treaty Organization (NATO) in 1956 to forestall possible subversion by the Warsaw Pact.

Former Communists. Ever since 1947 the Italian Communist Party (PCI) had been excluded from government coalitions, even though it had been the second-largest vote-getter at every election since World War II, trailing only the center-right Christian Democrats. After the PCI adopted a Eurocommunist stance independent of the Kremlin in 1976, it polled 34.4% of the national vote. But in the 1980s the party steadily lost strength. It garnered only 26.6% of the national vote in 1987 and just 19.4% in regional elections in 1990.

In the wake of the collapse of Communist regimes in Eastern Europe, the PCI decided in February 1991 to rename itself the Democratic Party of the Left. A small minority refused to go along and formed a separate Communist Refoundation. Both groups opposed Italy's participation in the Persian Gulf war. In August, when Communist hard-liners in Moscow tried to overthrow President Mikhail Gorbachev, Italy's Democratic Party of the Left denounced the coup; the Communist Refoundation supported it.

In November the Democratic Party of the Left voted to begin impeachment proceedings against President Cossiga over accusations that he had exceeded his constitutional role by asserting that former Italian Communists had maintained contacts with East European security guards.

The Mafia. In 1991 the national government continued its long offensive against the Mafia in Sicily. But there was little evidence that it was having any effect. Indeed, many mafiosi kingpins had managed, through technicalities, to gain early release from long prison terms. And in Calabria and Naples, similar crime syndicates tightened their grips.

The Economy. Whereas in the booming 1980's Italy's economy was among the fastest-growing in the industrialized world, in 1991 this was no longer true and Italy seemed in danger of slipping to second-class status in the renovated EC of 1992. Observers noted that Italy's national debt, equal to $1.1 trillion, exceeded the country's gross national product (GNP). And where state spending had accounted for only 30% of Italy's GNP in 1970, by 1991 it had risen to 52%. Many were shocked when, in the summer, Moody's Investors Service downgraded Italy's triple-A credit rating to AA1.

Italy's huge public sector of the economy (more than one fifth of the total) remained especially inefficient. Political patronage in the public sector was rampant, and salaries there were 15% higher than in the private sector. Italy's archaic banking system also needed rapid modernization if it were to compete with northern European banks.

Although Italy belongs to the elite G-7 group of industrialized nations, a 1991 Swiss study revealed that Italy had slipped to 17th place in productivity in the world. For every dollar that a worker took home, Italian companies had to pay out another $1.05 in social security, taxes, and health benefits, whereas in France and Germany the comparable figure was about 85 cents; in the United States and Britain, 50 cents; and in Japan, 30 cents. One out of every three Italians was drawing a pension, and some more than one. On the brighter side, Italy cut its annual inflation rate to about 6% in 1991, and its GNP rose a modest 1.4%.

Albanian Refugees. When the economy of Albania's Communist state collapsed in 1991, thousands of desperate Albanians dreamed of emigrating to Italy, which they imagined to be a veritable El Dorado. Thus in March more than 20,000 of them (mostly young men) commandeered ships and small boats and landed illegally in Brindisi. Local officials could not cope with the crisis, and the central government did not do much better. In the end many were granted temporary sanctuary. Some were shunted off to other countries.

In August a second wave of some 18,000 "boat people" overwhelmed port authorities in Bari. Losing its patience, the Italian government took the position that this new horde of Albanians had no valid claim to political asylum. And since Italy itself was suffering from 10% unemployment (about 20% in the south), it could not tolerate the influx of unskilled, poorly educated workers from the former Communist world. (There were perhaps 1 million immigrants in Italy from outside the EC, with fewer than two thirds of these registered as legal residents.)

The government ordered police and army units to herd the half-naked Albanian refugees into Bari's soccer stadium in preparation for sending them home. Sanitary conditions were abysmal. Despite the intense heat, almost no water or food were provided to the unruly internees. Appalled by the shocking spectacle, many Italians wondered if this was a portent of things to come as the economies of Eastern Europe continued their downward spirals. High Italian officials hurried to Albania to extend $135 million of immediate aid in an effort to forestall new attempts at illegal immigration.

Foreign Affairs. Italy's Foreign Minister Gianni De Michelis sought to launch a new regional grouping (the Hexagonale), composed of Italy, Austria, Czechoslovakia, Poland, Hungary, and Yugoslavia. It was designed to serve as a vehicle for Italian influence as well as a barrier to German expansion into post-Communist Central Europe. Yugoslavia was supposed to coordinate the regional transport plans for the Hexagonale. But this scheme collapsed in the summer when Yugoslavia broke apart in civil war. Italy was alarmed greatly that Yugoslavia's ethnic conflict could unleash a new flood of refugees and also encourage regional separatism in parts of northern Italy. De Michelis, therefore, called for a cease-fire.

Italy, along with Germany, was one of the most vocal advocates of massive economic aid by the West to the Soviet Union. In a September speech to the UN, Foreign Minister De Michelis proposed sweeping changes in the UN structure, including an increase in both the permanent and nonpermanent members of the Security Council.

In November, Italy hosted a summit meeting in Rome of the 16 heads of state of NATO. The conference debated the kind of role NATO should play in the post-Cold War era. A related question concerned whether the EC should organize a military force of its own, perhaps through the nine-member Western European Union (WEU). Italy strongly supported the Anglo-American position that NATO, with a continuing strong U.S. presence, should remain the primary authority for the defense of Western Europe. "Europe wants a transatlantic partnership, including the military role," De Michelis declared.

In December, on the eve of the EC's "new look," Italy joined the 11 other EC members for an important summit conference held in Maastricht, the Netherlands. The agenda included further discussion of such urgent issues as new military-security arrangements, monetary coordination, possible enlargement of the EC, and procedures for decision-making.

In May, Columbia University announced creation of a $17.5 million Italian Academy for Advanced Studies in America, to be financed entirely by the Italian government.

Obituaries. Mario Scelba, a founder of the Christian Democratic Party, minister of the interior (1947–53), and premier (1954–55), died in Rome at the age of 90. Randolfo Pacciardi, an antifascist exile who commanded the Garibaldi Battalion in the Spanish Civil War and was minister of defense in several of Italy's postwar governments, died in Rome at age 91.

CHARLES F. DELZELL, *Vanderbilt University*

ITALY • Information Highlights

Official Name: Italian Republic.
Location: Southern Europe.
Area: 116,305 sq mi (301 230 km²).
Population (mid-1991 est.): 57,700,000.
Chief Cities (Dec. 31, 1989): Rome, the capital, 2,803,931; Milan, 1,449,403; Naples, 1,204,147.
Government: *Head of state,* Francesco Cossiga, president (took office July 1985). *Head of government,* Giulio Andreotti, prime minister (sworn in July 10, 1989). *Legislature*—Parliament: Senate and Chamber of Deputies.
Monetary Unit: Lira (1,231.0 lire equal U.S.$1, Nov. 15, 1991).
Gross Domestic Product (1989 est. U.S.$): $803,300,000,000.
Economic Indexes (1990): *Consumer Prices* (1980 = 100), all items, 250.8; food, 232.6. *Industrial Production* (1980 = 100), 114.
Foreign Trade (1990 U.S.$): *Imports,* $180,105,000,000; *exports,* $168,680,000,000.

JAPAN

In Japan, 1991 was marked by a damaging financial scandal involving the nation's top brokerage houses, a visit by Soviet President Mikhail Gorbachev, a major volcanic eruption, and the fall of Prime Minister Toshiki Kaifu's government.

Domestic Affairs

Despite the evidence of Japan's achievement of world economic power, its diplomatic stance remained uncertain. This and a succession of embarrassing incidents at home eroded support for Premier Kaifu among the leaders of Japan's ruling Liberal Democratic Party (LDP).

Party Politics. Kaifu was already in difficulties when the year began. In the 1990 general election for the lower house, the LDP had won a slim victory, but with margin enough to control committees. In December 1990, in a struggle to survive, the prime minister had reshuffled his cabinet. He retained Finance Minister Ryutaro Hashimoto, a rival for party leadership; he reappointed Foreign Minister Taro Nakayama; and he kept Ichiro Ozawa, another promising candidate for president, as secretary-general.

As of January 1, the 512 seats in the lower house of the Diet were distributed as follows: LDP—281, Social Democratic Party of Japan (SDPJ)—140, Komeito—46, Japan Communist Party (JCP)—16, Democratic Socialist Party (DSP)—14, independents and small parties—11, vacancies—4. The LDP, with 113 in the 252-seat (upper) House of Councillors, lacked a majority. Combined opposition parties—the SDPJ, Komeito, JCP, DSP, and Rengo (a labor federation)—controlled 139 seats (with one vacancy).

Nevertheless, because the lower house takes precedence in fiscal proceedings (as it does in electing a prime minister), on April 11 the Kaifu government was able to pass a budget for fiscal year 1991. It provided expenditures of 70.2 trillion yen ($521 billion), a 6.2% increase over the previous year. Foreign aid (especially to Eastern Europe and the Persian Gulf states) rose 8%; defense expenditures actually declined by 2 billion yen ($14.8 million).

Moreover, by the end of the session (May 8), most of the bills submitted by the Kaifu government were passed by the Diet. After the conclusion of the Persian Gulf conflict, there was little opposition to sending Japanese minesweepers to the area. It was argued that they were on a peacekeeping mission and thus raised no constitutional issue on defense. Finally, the SDPJ, the major opposition force, was showing signs of pragmatism after its dismal showing in the April local elections.

One clue lay in the change of the party's translated name to the Social Democratic Party of Japan. The Japanese title for Japan Socialist Party (*Shakaito*) remained the same. On June 21, one day after the Socialists adopted a moderate and less ideological platform, their leader Takako Doi, the first woman to head a major Japanese party, resigned and was succeeded by Makoto Tanabe.

The first incident that presaged Kaifu's downfall came on April 7, when local elections were held throughout the country. In Tokyo the 80-year-old incumbent governor, Shinichi Suzuki, was reelected despite withdrawal of LDP support. The party secretary-general, Ichiro Ozawa, had backed Suzuki's opponent and, after the election, resigned to take responsibility for the defeat.

Then, on August 5, a 61-day extraordinary Diet session began to focus on yet another financial scandal, which was an additional blow to the Kaifu government. Japan's "Big Four" among securities firms (Nomura, Daiwa, Nikko, and Yamaichi), as well as smaller brokerage houses, revealed that they had paid

© Koichi Sakamoto/Sipa Press

Kiichi Miyazawa, extreme left, 72-year-old former cabinet minister, took office as Japan's 20th post-World War II prime minister in November 1991.

clients more than $1 billion in compensation for stock losses over two years. Kaifu termed the affair "most deplorable" and proposed a revision of the securities and exchange law.

On July 10 the finance ministry had announced a four-day suspension of the largest firms' activities with corporate clients. Several local governments and cities delayed business with the big four. Finance Minister Hashimoto took a 10% pay cut over three months to assume responsibility for the scandal. On October 14 he officially announced his resignation from the finance ministry.

Although no hearings were held nor judicial actions instituted, Chairman Tabuchi Setsuya of Nomura and President Takuya Iwasaki of Nikko resigned from their posts. On August 20 the finance ministry introduced a bill in the lower house that would ban covering of losses, and on August 29 Setsuya and Iwasaki appeared before an ad hoc Diet committee, using the occasion to apologize to the public. Nevertheless, the brokerage houses continued to oppose an independent investigatory agency.

The immediate reason for Kaifu's fall arose, strangely enough, out of the issue that originally had brought him to power. Having taken office after the so-called Recruit influence-buying scandal of 1989, he had promised to enact electoral reforms and to control "money politics." Most LDP faction members (as well as the opposition parties), however, opposed his plans for reform. The election of the LDP president was scheduled for Oct. 27, 1991. As the day approached, Kaifu, preoccupied with preparing the electoral reform on which he had staked his future, abstained from campaigning for reelection. On October 4 the party's leading faction withdrew its support for his presidency, which forced him to step down as premier.

On October 27 the LDP chose as its leader former Finance Minister Kiichi Miyazawa (*see* BIOGRAPHY), who became the new prime minister on November 6. Miyazawa's associates included a number of politicians formerly excluded from power because of their implication in the Recruit scandal, and his cabinet choices reflected the continuing influence of former Premiers Yasuhiro Nakasone and Noboru Takeshita.

Economy. Just as the stock scandal broke, the Bank of Japan lowered the discount rate for the first time in four years, to 5.5%. The bank had raised the rate five times since the historic low of 1989 (2.5%) to the high of August 1990 (6%). The bank's governor, Yasushi Mieno, had justified the tight-money policy as a campaign against speculative assets.

On the heels of the scandal, the Tokyo Stock Exchange (TSE) directly punctured the "bubble economy." The Nikkei stock average plunged from the historic high of 39,000 (end of 1989) to about 23,000 (August 1991), with daily volume dramatically declining and current prices of major issues at one half or one third in value. The "Big Four" investment houses suffered the most (down an average 11.2%).

The Japanese economy continued its remarkable expansion during the year. In fact, May marked the 57th consecutive month of growth. In the fiscal year ending March 1991, according to the Economic Planning Agency (EPA), the gross national product (GNP) grew 5.7% in real terms. This rate was, however, a slight decline from a recent high of 6.2% (1988). The EPA estimated that in February the annualized GNP at constant price totaled 421 trillion yen ($3.2 trillion at the current rate of exchange, compared with $2.8 trillion in 1990 and $1.35 trillion in 1985).

Japan's labor force was in full employment, with an unemployment rate of only 2% in May. The inflation rate was relatively modest: The consumer price index stood at 110.7 in May, compared with 107.1 in May 1990 and 100 in the base year 1985.

During 1991 a task force of 121 Japanese academic experts and businessmen was chosen to serve under the Economic Council, an advisory body to the prime minister. Called the Committee for the Year 2010, the task force was assigned to project the nation's economic growth. The committee noted that Japan's share of global GNP had expanded to 13% (second to that of the United States). The nation's official development assistance (ODA) topped those of all the industrial democracies. The committee predicted that real economic growth would slow from an average 3%-4% (1990s) to 2%-3% (2000–2010). The proportion of Japanese 65 years old or more would rise from 12% (1991) to 17% (2000) and to 21% (2010). Energy conservation based on UN guidelines to offset global warming would reduce real economic growth to 1.5%.

Imperial Family. Emperor Akihito proclaimed his eldest son Naruhito (honorific title, Crown Prince Hiro) heir to the throne at a tra-

JAPAN • Information Highlights

Official Name: Japan.
Location: East Asia.
Area: 145,882 sq mi (377 835 km²).
Population (mid-1991 est.): 123,800,000.
Chief Cities (March 31, 1988 est.): Tokyo, the capital, 8,155,781; Yokohama, 3,121,601; Osaka, 2,543,520; Nagoya, 2,099,564.
Government: *Head of state,* Akihito, emperor (acceded Jan. 9, 1989). *Head of government,* Kiichi Miyazawa, prime minister (took office Nov. 6, 1991). *Legislature*—Diet: House of Councillors and House of Representatives.
Monetary Unit: Yen (130.30 yen equal U.S.$1, Nov. 11, 1991).
Gross National Product (1989 est. U.S.$): $2,670,000,000,000.
Economic Indexes (1990): *Consumer Prices* (1980 = 100), all items, 122.5; food, 121.6. *Industrial Production* (1980 = 100), 149.
Foreign Trade (1990 U.S.$): *Imports,* $234,800,000,000; *exports,* $286,949,000,000.

ditional ceremony in the Imperial Palace, Tokyo, on February 23, which was the prince's 31st birthday. Prime Minister Kaifu, government officials, and some 300 foreign representatives witnessed the ritual. Born in 1960, Naruhito had celebrated his coming of age in 1980. After graduating from the Japan Academy in 1983, he went to Merton College, Oxford, where he studied European history for two years.

Emperor Akihito and Empress Michiko, arriving in Bangkok, Thailand, on September 26, embarked on the first tour of the region by a reigning emperor since Japan's military intervention there during World War II. At an opening banquet, the emperor assured the Thais that Japan is determined never to repeat "the horrors of that most unfortunate war." He did, however, stop short of apologizing for the nation's militaristic past. After four days in Thailand, the imperial couple flew to Malaysia and Indonesia, both of which also had been invaded by Japan during the war.

Volcanic Eruption. In June, Mount Unzen, a volcano on the southern Japanese island of Kyushu, erupted for the first time since 1792, killing 38 people. In the 1792 eruption, some 15,000 had died; this time the area had been evacuated in advance.

© Miladinovic/Sipa Press

Emperor Akihito (center) *visited several Southeast Asian nations in the fall of 1991. The emperor was welcomed to Bangkok by Thailand's King Bhumibol Adulyadej* (left).

Foreign Affairs

Both during and after the Persian Gulf war of 1991, Japan was charged by foreign governments and press with giving insufficient support to the allied coalition. In the wake of the conflict, former Finance Minister Miyazawa called on the government to play a leading role in postwar reconstruction, recommending the creation of a Middle East fund that would match the Marshall Plan.

The Middle East. On April 10, Tokyo decided to extend emergency aid to Iran and to Turkey, including the dispatch of medics. The Diet approved an additional $9 billion to aid the multinational effort in Kuwait (bringing Japan's total contribution to $13 billion), and on April 27 a flotilla of six ships left Yokosuka for Dubai, with orders to help U.S. forces with mine-clearing operations in the Gulf. This was Japan's first military excursion abroad since World War II. Nonetheless, many Japanese feared the delay in extending help had cost the nation a permanent seat on the Security Council of the UN.

U.S. Relations. Although U.S. spokespersons, including Ambassador Michael Armacost, expressed frustration with Japan's Gulf policy, on other issues the two allies often agreed. Washington was pleased to see that Japan's current-account surplus had declined dramatically from a peak of $94 billion (1987) to $35.7 billion in 1990. The surplus, however, showed an increase again in 1991. In addition, the Japanese finance ministry announced that in 1990 investors sold $16.1 billion more in U.S. securities than they bought. (They were net buyers of $26.5 billion in 1989.) Declining interest rates in the United States contributed to the drop. Ironically, Tokyo was implementing a request made by Washington in the so-called "Strategic Impediments Initiative" (SII): The Japanese were investing less and spending more on social overhead. This created a risk to the United States, in that a lower savings rate meant fewer investments available to offset the U.S. budget deficit.

SII negotiations resumed in Tokyo on January 17 (pursuant to a joint agreement of June 1990). Topics included investment patterns, the persistence of cartels (*keiretsu*) in Japan's economy, and land policy. U.S. Deputy Trade Representative Linn Williams warned that the outcome of the Tokyo talks would be important to U.S.-Japanese trade relations.

A two-day meeting followed, concentrating on Japan's construction market. Later, on May 31, after U.S. Trade Representative Carla Hill had exerted extreme pressure, Tokyo agreed to help U.S. firms in their bids on 17 large-scale projects. Their main target was the new Kansai International Airport in Osaka, to be opened late in 1994. The scale of the terminal had been reduced in April but still boasted a $10.6 billion budget.

Another trade problem involved the desire of U.S. rice growers for access to the Japanese market, which conflicted with Japan's traditional protection of its agricultural sector. In March, U.S. Secretary of Agriculture Edward Madigan filed a protest with Secretary of State

Japan's role in the 1991 Persian Gulf war was debated nationally and internationally. In April, Japan sent six naval vessels to the Gulf to search for mines laid by Iraq. It was the first foreign mission by Japanese military personnel since World War II.

© Kaku Kurita/Gamma-Liaison

James Baker as he met with Foreign Minister Nakayama in Washington. The issue was an alleged threat to arrest a U.S. rice-industry group for displaying products in Tokyo.

On April 5, in a two-hour meeting with President George Bush in Newport Beach, CA, Prime Minister Kaifu agreed to seek a "successful conclusion" to the rice problem. Visiting Tokyo on May 20, Vice-President Dan Quayle reiterated Washington's call for Tokyo to open the rice market, which was linked to the ongoing GATT negotiations.

Meanwhile, a consensus was building among Japanese business leaders, politicians, and even bureaucrats to liberalize rice trade. President Gaishi Hiraiwa of Keidanren (Japan's most powerful corporate federation) urged the Kaifu government toward a solution, after talks with the union of agricultural cooperatives (Zenchu). Takeshi Nagano, the newly elected head of Nikkeiren (an employers' association), also called for a decision. In a May 24th television interview, Takeo Nishioka, chairman of the LDP policy council, became the first party leader to advocate opening the market after taking sufficient measures to protect domestic growers of rice.

On June 9, however, Minister of Agriculture Motoji Kondo reversed the stand of a subordinate and stated that Japan was not ready for a decision to liberalize the rice market. He reflected the traditional feeling that the country should not become dependent on imports for its basic food supply, and that "not a single grain of rice" should cross Japan's borders.

On other issues Tokyo attempted to synchronize policy with that of Washington. After the April minisummit meeting in California, Prime Minister Kaifu visited President Bush again in Kennebunkport, ME, July 11–12, just prior to the London conference of G-7 industrial-democracy leaders. The two announced that they would not offer the USSR massive economic assistance at the forthcoming summit. Bush accepted Kaifu's invitation to visit Japan in November, but the visit later was postponed by the president for domestic political reasons.

Soviet Relations. In a press conference held in Tokyo on July 8, Prime Minister Kaifu had defined conditions for an offer of financial aid to the Soviet Union. Moscow would have to display a concerted shift of resources from the military to the civilian sector. And Tokyo would not extend financial help until a long-standing territorial dispute between the nations was settled. Tokyo had normalized relations with Moscow in 1956, but a peace treaty between the World War II foes remained stalled over the question of some southern Kuril Islands, claimed by Japan but occupied by the Soviets since 1945.

Soviet President Gorbachev made a long-expected visit to Tokyo in April. The unstable situation in the USSR, however, made Gorbachev hesitant to agree to the transfer of the southern Kurils. He, in turn, was disappointed in Japan's denial of large-scale aid. Later, Kaifu did pledge technical assistance to help the USSR convert weapons to nonmilitary uses and build transport systems, and to support special status for the USSR in the International Monetary Fund and in the International Bank for Reconstruction and Development.

During the attempt by hard-line Communists to overthrow Gorbachev in August, Kaifu was noncommittal. After the failure of the coup, however, he welcomed the "resumption of constitutional order" in Moscow, and gave special recognition to the role played by Russian President Boris Yeltsin in defeating the plotters. In October, Japanese trading companies agreed to a five-year $1.4 billion plan to develop Siberian lumber resources. This was the first joint venture between Japan and Yeltsin's Russian Republic, which has jurisdiction over Siberia.

Asia. On August 10, Prime Minister Kaifu received a warm welcome in Beijing, including a 21-gun salute in Tiananmen Square. His five-day visit was the first to China by a leader of a major democracy since the Chinese government suppressed the prodemocracy movement in 1989.

Before his departure, Kaifu announced Japan's plan to continue the fiscal 1991 portion of a $5.96 billion loan package to China that would run through 1995. Chinese Premier Li Peng for his part agreed in principle to sign the Nuclear Nonproliferation Treaty of 1968. The leaders agreed to schedule events in 1992 to commemorate the 20th anniversary of the normalization of diplomatic relations.

In a two-day visit to Seoul, South Korea, in January, Prime Minister Kaifu tried to prepare the South Koreans for Tokyo's possible establishment of diplomatic relations with the Communist government of North Korea. South Korean President Roh Tae Woo expressed concern that a hasty Japanese tie with North Korea would undermine progress in unification of the two regimes on the peninsula.

On April 25 in Tokyo, Foreign Minister Nakayama was reported to have told his South Korean counterpart, Lee Sang Ok, that Japan would support South Korea's bid for separate UN membership. (Both South and North Korea were accepted as members of the UN in the fall.)

Negotiations between Japanese and North Korean representatives in Beijing, however, continued to be snagged on various issues. Japan insisted that North Korea must comply with international nuclear-inspection accords. The North Koreans refused, insisting that the United States first must remove its nuclear arsenal from South Korea.

In May, Prime Minister Kaifu visited four of five of the ASEAN member states (Brunei, Malaysia, the Philippines, Singapore, and Thailand).

ARDATH W. BURKS, *Rutgers University*

JORDAN

In the year of the Persian Gulf war, policy for Jordan became a delicate exercise in tightrope walking. Nor were things much better on the domestic front. The flood of refugees from Kuwait and Iraq had passed but enormous financial problems remained. But the monarchy, in refusing to line up with the coalition against Iraq, garnered increased popularity at home; while later in the year, Jordan regained Western approval by helping enthusiastically to facilitate a Middle East peace conference.

Cabinet Reshuffle. In January, Foreign Affairs Minister Marwan al-Qasem was replaced by a leading Palestinian figure, Taher al-Masri, who had been chairman of the foreign-affairs committee of the Jordanian House of Representatives. Whereas Qasem supposedly had been lukewarm in approval of King Hussein's neutral policy in the Gulf crisis, Masri—though in general, liberal and pro-Western—had voiced strong support for neutrality. At the same time the king appointed five new ministers belonging to the Muslim Brotherhood, recognizing the strength of that right-wing movement. The Brotherhood held 22 of the 80 seats in the lower house of Parliament and was the largest bloc there. Brotherhood members were assigned to the portfolios of education, health, justice, religious affairs, and social development.

National Charter. A significant step in Jordanian political reform was consummated on June 9, when the king and representatives of all main groups ratified the National Charter, which had been formulated by a royal commission over a two-year period. The charter's reforms aimed at mollifying the disparate elements that make up Jordanian society. In the past, leftist and pan-Arab groups had opposed the British-created monarchy and refused to accept the country's basic institutions—though this attitude had been changing gradually for more than a decade. The charter established Islamic law (*sharia*) as the basic source of legislation and Arab Islamic civilization as the basis of national identity. It also legalized political parties, which hitherto were banned. (The Muslim Brotherhood was registered as a charitable organization.) In his address at the formal inauguration of the charter, King Hussein called pluralism "the only guarantee against all forms of dictatorship and despotism, particularly despotism by one party." No one party, he said, can claim a monopoly on the truth.

New Government. King Hussein was hospitalized briefly in Amman, June 11–13, for treatment of an irregular heartbeat, but very soon thereafter, on June 19, he issued a decree appointing a new prime minister and cabinet. Foreign Minister Taher al-Masri replaced Mudar Badran as prime minister; the new cabinet included a number of Palestinians but no members of the Muslim Brotherhood. Masri

JORDAN • Information Highlights

Official Name: Hashemite Kingdom of Jordan.
Location: Southwest Asia.
Area: 35,475 sq mi (91 880 km²).
Population (mid-1991 est.): 3,400,000.
Chief Cities (Dec. 1986): Amman, the capital, 972,000; Zarqa, 392,220; Irbid, 271,000.
Government: *Head of state,* Hussein I, king (acceded Aug. 1952). *Head of government,* Sherif Zeid bin Shaker, prime minister (took office November 1991). *Legislature*—Parliament: House of Representatives and Senate.
Monetary Unit: Dinar (.68970 dinar equals U.S.$1, Nov. 25, 1991).
Gross National Product (1989 U.S.$): $5,200,000,000.
Economic Index (1990): *Consumer Prices* (1980 = 100), all items, 202.1; food, 185.7.
Foreign Trade (1990 U.S.$): *Imports,* $2,603,000,000; *exports,* $922,000,000.

himself is a native of the West Bank and was expected to be better able to seek a compromise solution of the Palestinian problem than Badran and his Brotherhood supporters. Analysts viewed his appointment as signaling Hussein's commitment to flexibility and compromise both at home and abroad.

On July 7 the king canceled most of the martial-law provisions concerning press restrictions, arbitrary arrest, and other matters, that had been in force since 1967.

Despite the National Charter, Jordan's internal difficulties did not disappear. Masri hardly had had time to embark on any serious program of changes before encountering difficulties about the proposed Middle East peace conference with Israel. On October 3 he dismissed from the cabinet five ministers all more or less opposed to Arab-Israeli negotiations; their replacements were less intransigent. On October 7 some 50 members of Parliament's lower house signed a petition criticizing Masri's policies—internal and external—and calling for his resignation. As Parliament was in recess, no adverse vote of confidence was possible. The king bypassed Parliament by seeking support from a Jordanian National Congress on October 10 (the same body that had endorsed the charter in June), and used his constitutional prerogative to postpone the opening of Parliament for 60 days. Masri, however, resigned as prime minister in mid-November and was replaced by Sherif Zeid bin Shaker, a trusted court official, who had been prime minister for six months in 1989.

Financial Matters. The somewhat complex story of Jordan's finances perhaps may be summarized by saying that, while enormous burdens were imposed on the country by circumstances in 1990 and 1991, assistance was forthcoming or was promised from a variety of sources sufficient to ensure that the situation, though serious, did not become desperate. On February 24 the then-premier, Mudar Badran, announced that the confrontation in the Gulf so far had cost Jordan $8 billion—twice the country's annual economic output. Major U.S. aid—except for medical and humanitarian assistance—was withheld throughout the spring because of Jordan's refusal to join the coalition against Iraq, but was resumed in the fall. Aid from Germany, Japan, the United Nations, and the European Community was given without interruption, and the king's impassioned speech to the European Parliament at Strasbourg on September 12, in which he painted a grim picture of his country's plight, produced promises of substantial increases.

Foreign Relations. Jordan's Middle East policies in 1991, though indeed inconsistent, were not hard to understand given the country's geographical position between Iraq and Israel. No one, at the beginning of the year, knew how a coalition war with Iraq over Kuwait might go, and it seemed possible that Jordan itself might become a battleground between Iraqi and Israeli forces. So King Hussein in early January continued the desperate efforts at mediation in which he had been engaged since August. He opposed a war against Iraq, while at the same time condemning the Iraqi conquest of Kuwait. Jordan continued to recognize the legitimacy of the Kuwaiti government-in-exile, and the Kuwaiti embassy in Amman remained open throughout the 1990–91 crisis. Jordan claimed to be observing all UN-mandated sanctions against Iraq.

In a televised speech on February 6 the king strongly attacked U.S. policy, reflecting Jordanian outrage at U.S. bombing attacks against Jordanian trucks on the road to Baghdad. After the victory of the allied coalition, however, a different tone prevailed. In another television speech on March 1, Hussein stressed that he wished to repair Jordan's strained links with the West and with the Arab members of the anti-Iraqi coalition. The former, at least, proved fairly easy to do. U.S. Secretary of State James Baker, who had cold-shouldered Jordan on his first postwar Middle East trip, visited Amman on April 20 and on a number of later occasions.

In the latter half of the year, Jordan, more directly concerned than any other Arab state with the Palestinian question—it ruled the West Bank from 1948 to 1967, and more than half of its population is Palestinian—played the major role in the furtherance of the peace process and in the preparations for the peace conference that convened at Madrid at the end of October. Jordanian cooperation alone made possible the creation of the joint Jordanian-Palestinian delegation which went to Madrid. Jordan also later accepted immediately the U.S. invitation to attend resumed peace talks in Washington in December.

See also MIDDLE EAST/FEATURE SECTION, page 36.

ARTHUR CAMPBELL TURNER
University of California, Riverside

KANSAS

A number of controversies marked 1991 in Kansas—including the governor's veto of major tax legislation, the loss of millions of dollars for the Kansas Public Employees Retirement System, and anti-abortion protests in Wichita.

Legislation. Joan Finney, a Democrat, was inaugurated as the first woman governor of Kansas in January and soon found herself at odds with legislators from both parties. Property-tax relief was a major issue, following dramatic increases in property taxes caused by reappraisal and a classification implemented in 1990. Finney proposed the elimination of nu-

© Al Schaben/Sygma

Members of the antiabortion group Operation Rescue demonstrated at abortion clinics in Wichita, KS, during the summer, leading a U.S. district judge to issue a temporary restraining order preventing protesters from blocking the entrance to the clinics. More than 1,900 arrests were made between mid-July and the first week of August.

merous sales-tax exemptions, while the legislature, in a record-setting 102-day session, passed a tax package based on increases in the sales tax and income-tax rates. Much of the increase was to provide funding for schools. Governor Finney vetoed the bill, which then led to mill-levy increases for most Kansas school districts and, therefore, additional property-tax increases. Efforts to override the veto failed.

The legislature passed laws to strengthen the state's ethics commission, to make it more difficult for insurance companies to refuse coverage to small groups, and to allow limited interstate banking. A major issue during the session was an investigation of the Kansas Public Employees Retirement System (KPERS), which reported losses of more than $230 million from the $4.4 billion state-pension fund. Alleged mismanagement and poor decision-making by several investment companies, primarily in real-estate investment, were viewed as the reason for the loss. By late fall, KPERS' special counsel had filed several civil lawsuits aimed at recovering funds.

Agriculture. Kansas agricultural production declined as the result of a summer and fall drought. The 1991 Kansas wheat crop totaled 356.4 million bushels, down 24% from the 1990 record high. The average yield per acre was 33 bushels, with 10.8 million acres harvested. Estimated crop totals for fall crops of sorghum grain and soybeans were approximately 8% lower than in 1990. For the second year in a row, corn production exceeded sorghum production, and the 1991 crop was the largest since 1906.

During fiscal year 1990, Kansas ranked sixth in the nation as an exporter of agricultural products, though cash value of $2.2 billion was more than 20% lower than in 1989. Kansas remained first in the sale of wheat and wheat products and accounted for 13% of the total of U.S. wheat exports. Income from livestock remained one of the leading cash producers in the Kansas agricultural economy.

Other. Two medical clinics in Wichita were the target of a radical out-of-state antiabortion group. Leaders of the protest and hundreds of others were arrested for contempt after they violated a court order aimed at keeping the clinics open. Rallies by pro-choice and pro-life supporters were held and tensions remained high for weeks. Efforts to pass more restrictive abortion legislation failed.

On April 26 a destructive tornado hit Andover, a suburb of Wichita, killing 28 people and damaging more than 500 homes. . . . Following his failed bid for reelection in 1990, former Kansas Gov. Mike Hayden was named assistant secretary of the interior for fish and wildlife and parks.

PATRICIA A. MICHAELIS
Kansas State Historical Society

KANSAS • Information Highlights

Area: 82,277 sq mi (213 098 km^2).
Population (1990 census): 2,477,574.
Chief Cities (1990 census): Topeka, the capital, 119,883; Wichita, 304,011; Kansas City, 149,767.
Government (1991): *Chief Officers*—governor, Joan Finney (D); lt. gov., James L. Francisco (D). *Legislature*—Senate, 40 members; House of Representatives, 125 members.
State Finances (fiscal year 1990): *Revenue,* $5,136,000,000; *expenditure,* $4,705,000,000.
Personal Income (1990): $45,050,000,000; per capita, $18,162.
Labor Force (June 1991): *Civilian labor force,* 1,332,100; *unemployed,* 61,200 (4.6% of total force).
Education: *Enrollment* (fall 1989)—public elementary schools, 313,588; public secondary, 117,276; colleges and universities, 158,497. *Public school expenditures* (1989), $1,712,260,000.

KENTUCKY

Electoral politics—especially a gubernatorial contest—dominated events in Kentucky in 1991. Other important developments included two special legislative sessions, state revenue shortfalls, the loss of one congressional seat, and the first-year benefits of historic education reform. Economic changes included the expansion of the state's Toyota auto operations, the sale of IBM's Lexington facility, and the bankruptcy of the thoroughbred stables, Calumet Farms.

Gubernatorial Election. Lt. Gov. Brereton Jones, who earlier had won the Democratic primary, was elected governor after the costliest race in state history, defeating seven-term Republican U.S. Rep. Larry Hopkins by a nearly two-to-one margin. Jones, a 52-year-old thoroughbred horse farmer, spent more than $4 million on the primary campaign alone. More than $19 million (a new record) was spent in the quest for the governorship overall. The front-runner from start to finish, Jones had faced personal negative campaigning from his primary opponents—Martha Wilkinson, the incumbent governor's wife, who withdrew 18 days before the contest; Scotty Baesler, the three-term mayor of Lexington; and Dr. Floyd Poore, a former state transportation secretary and fund-raiser for Governors Martha Layne Collins and Wallace Wilkinson. Gatewood Galbraith, a maverick pro-marijuana attorney, also ran.

Although the election had been expected to be the GOP's best chance to win the state's highest office in 24 years, Jones outspent Hopkins two to one. Having focused his campaign on Jones' finances, Hopkins was hurt badly when it was revealed that he had 32 overdrafts in the U.S. House bank. Hopkins carried only 13 of 120 counties, losing every county in his 6th District. Only 44% of registered voters voted—the next-to-lowest turnout in a Kentucky gubernatorial election in the 20th century. All other statewide Democratic candidates also were victorious.

Legislature. During a special session in January the legislature strengthened the state's laws against drunken driving, made restrictive changes in the control of landfills and waste disposal, approved economic incentives in the state for Delta Airlines and Scott Paper, and altered Medicaid financing.

Because of stagnant population growth, Kentucky lost one of its seven U.S. House seats following the 1990 census. Heated interparty and intraparty battles preceded the reapportionment accomplished by a second special session in December 1991.

State Finances. A revenue shortfall of at least $155 million resulted from such factors as the national recession, the allocation of a $1.3 billion tax increase to elementary and secondary education in 1990, the commitment of one-time windfalls from the lottery, and the sluggish state economy. Cuts in spending for higher education, construction projects, and some state agencies probably would cover the shortfall.

School Reform. The Kentucky Education Reform Act of 1990, which resulted in innovative changes in the governance, curriculum, and financing of Kentucky's public schools, was hailed nationally for its initial successes. The state Department of Education was reorganized and there now was an appointed commissioner of education. Locally, the power of the school boards was reduced through the formation of local school councils and repeated attacks on nepotism in hiring. Most local school systems saw increased funding.

Zachary Taylor. The body of Zachary Taylor, which is buried in Lexington, was exhumed amid a report that the late president might have been poisoned. Tests revealed no signs of arsenic, however.

PENNY MILLER
University of Kentucky

KENTUCKY • Information Highlights

Area: 40,410 sq mi (104 660 km²).
Population (1990 census): 3,685,296.
Chief Cities (1990 census): Frankfort, the capital, 25,968; Louisville, 269,063; Lexington-Fayette, 225,366.
Government (1991): *Chief Officers*—governor, Wallace Wilkinson (D); lt. gov., Brereton Jones (D). *General Assembly*—Senate, 38 members; House of Representatives, 100 members.
State Finances (fiscal year 1990): *Revenue*, $8,593,000,000; *expenditure*, $7,772,000,000.
Personal Income (1990): $55,351,000,000; per capita, $15,001.
Labor Force (June 1991): *Civilian labor force*, 1,823,400; *unemployed*, 132,100 (7.2% of total force).
Education: *Enrollment* (fall 1989)—public elementary schools, 451,858; public secondary, 178,830; colleges and universities, 166,014. *Public school expenditures* (1989), $1,918,741,000.

KENYA

In December 1990, Kenya's ruling Kenya African National Union (KANU) met in special session to discuss a package of political reforms. The reforms—including reinstituting secret ballots and returning an element of independence to the judiciary—were opposed at the conference, but, following a plea by President Daniel arap Moi, were adopted. The changes fell far short of permitting opposition to KANU and failed to reduce criticism of Moi's human-rights record of 1991. It was only following the dramatic events of the year that Moi proposed to amend Kenya's constitution to permit a legal opposition.

Growing Opposition. In February 1991 veteran politician and former Vice-President

© Daily Nation for NYT Pictures

Kenya's President Daniel arap Moi, who assumed power in 1978, came under increasing criticism during 1991 relating to official corruption, human-rights abuses, and one-party rule. Facing financial consequences from international donors, he moved toward reform late in the year.

Oginga Odinga announced that in direct violation of Kenya's constitution he was forming an opposition party, the National Democratic Party (NDP). While the government refused to permit its registration, an announcement of the party's formation, its manifesto, and criticism of the "tribal biases" in Moi's administration appeared in the *Nairobi Law Monthly*. Its editor, Gitobu Imanyara, was detained without bail and charged with sedition—a move condemned by the U.S. ambassador.

Moi attempted to appease his critics, including Kenya's legal profession, by appointing Amos Wako, a prominent human-rights lawyer, as attorney general. After Wako's appointment, Imanyara and others were released, but these moves were overshadowed by the final report on the February 1990 death of Kenya's Foreign Minister Robert Ouko. Prepared by Britain's Scotland Yard at President Moi's request, the report implicated Kenya's police force and pointed to a high-level conspiracy. In the public inquiry that followed, Energy Minister Nicholas Biwott, one of Moi's closest political allies, was identified as one of two "prime suspects." In late November, one week after dismissing Biwott from the cabinet, Moi ordered his arrest and abruptly shut down the inquiry, turning over responsibility to the police instead. These developments undermined Moi's support among Ouko's ethnic group, the Luo. And Biwott was released.

International Affairs. Following a freeze which the U.S. Congress placed upon $15 million in aid to Kenya in 1990, Kenya became increasingly sensitive to its human-rights image in the United States. Kenya's embassy in Washington began to provide human-rights organizations with regular information.

Kenya's cooperation in evacuating U.S. officials from Somalia and Sudan, and its willingness to accept guerrillas opposed to Libya's Qaddafi who were stationed in Chad, led the Bush administration to award it $5 million in military aid in early February. The move drew harsh criticism from the U.S. Congress when, two weeks later, Kenya detained Imanyara. At the time, Kenya was the largest recipient of U.S. aid in Africa. International aid remained critical to Kenya's ability to balance its budget and meet its international payments. In November, Kenya's major donors met in Paris and refused to commit specific amounts for the coming year, agreeing to make new assistance contingent upon reforms. In a further effort to appease donors, in mid-December, Moi announced that he was proposing to amend Kenya's constitution to permit legal opposition parties. By year's end, however, further international financial assistance had been held up.

Kenya came under harsh criticism for strengthening its official ties to South Africa. In June, Kenya hosted South Africa's President F. W. de Klerk on a state visit. Subsequently, Kenya reestablished sports ties with South Africa and opened a commercial mission there. Moi also came under fire when, after an attempt to negotiate a settlement in Mozambique, it was disclosed that Kenya secretly had been supporting the rebel Mozambique National Resistance (MNR).

WILLIAM CYRUS REED
The American University in Cairo

KENYA • Information Highlights

Official Name: Republic of Kenya.
Location: East Coast of Africa.
Area: 224,961 sq mi (582 650 km²).
Population (mid-1991 est.): 25,200,000.
Chief Cities (1989 est.): Nairobi, the capital, 1,286,200; Mombasa (1985 est.), 442,369.
Government: *Head of state and government,* Daniel T. arap Moi, president (took office Oct. 1978). *Legislature* (unicameral)—National Assembly, 188 elected members, 12 appointed by the president.
Monetary Unit: Kenya shilling (28.605 shillings equal U.S.$1, July 1991).
Gross Domestic Product (1989 est. U.S.$): $8,500,000,000.
Economic Index (1989): *Consumer Prices,* (Nairobi, 1980 = 100), all items, 289.5; food, 236.8.
Foreign Trade (1990 U.S.$): *Imports,* $2,227,000,000; *exports,* $1,054,000,000.

KOREA

The year 1991's most conspicuous development was the entry of both Koreas into the United Nations. The most dangerous one appeared to be North Korea's continuing progress toward developing a nuclear-weapons capability at a time when the United States had decided to withdraw all its nuclear weapons from South Korea.

Republic of Korea (South Korea)

Politics and Government. The ruling establishment, institutionalized in President Roh Tae Woo's Democratic Liberal Party, managed to enhance its position in 1991 at the expense of both the parliamentary and the radical opposition.

In late March elections were held for 3,562 low-level local posts that previously had been filled by appointment. Although political parties were not allowed to nominate candidates, 49.8% of the winners were affiliated with the Democratic Liberal Party. The remaining winners were divided between independents and the leading opposition party, Kim Dae Jung's Party for Peace and Democracy. Disappointed at this poor showing, Kim dissolved his party in April and created a new one, the New Democratic Union, by merging with other opposition groups. He evidently saw this move as part of his preparation for the presidential election scheduled for 1992. In elections for provincial and municipal councils held in June, the Democratic Liberal Party won only 40% of the popular vote, but it took 65% of the seats. Kim Dae Jung's new party won 19% of the seats.

In September, Kim reorganized and expanded his party, now known as the Democratic Party, by amalgamating with a smaller party with that name. One concern troubling the opposition was the possibility of President Roh using the Democratic Liberal Party's two-thirds majority in the National Assembly to amend the constitution to create a parliamentary system of government. Roh, who was ineligible for reelection as president, could serve indefinitely as premier. In late May, however, Roh announced that, in view of widespread popular opposition, he was abandoning any idea of instituting a parliamentary system.

The militant opposition to the South Korean establishment long had been led by radical students, whose season for antigovernment demonstrations normally was the spring. Accordingly, May and June saw the biggest and most violent demonstrations since the last months of former President Chun Doo Hwan's tenure in mid-1987. In addition to general objections to the regime, the demonstrators were protesting some human-rights violations attributed to the police. The demonstrations occurred in cities across the country, in addition to the capital of Seoul. In an unusual development, some protesters committed suicide, with at least nine of them dying by self-immolation. These excesses had much to do with the fact that, in contrast to 1987, the militants failed to win broad public support. For its part, the government took some relatively ineffective measures to calm the demonstrators, including the dismissal of Minister of the Interior Ahn Eung Mo; the release of 258 political prisoners; and some minor amendments to the National Security Law, one of the main objects of the militants' wrath. Minister of Education Yoon Hyoung Up resigned because of the demonstrations. Premier Ro Ja Bong also was forced to resign but was replaced by Chung Won Shik, another conservative.

On balance, it appeared that the ruling party and the government not only had ridden out the crisis but had improved their political position

© Sisa Journal/Sipa Press

In the spring in South Korea, nearly a month of demonstrations against the killing of a student protester by riot police led to the resignation of the premier. Offering "apologies to the people," Premier Ro Ja Bong resigned May 22, 1991.

at least a little. This was possible because the opposition had discredited itself somewhat—the moderate wing by its ineffectiveness and the radical wing by its excesses. The country continued, however, to be troubled by labor unrest, although its level had been reduced by substantial wage increases.

Economy. South Korea, after a long period of impressive growth, continued in 1991 the difficult transition from an export-led economy to a market economy. But it was a market economy overshadowed by a fear of Japanese domination. South Korea's growth rate had slowed in 1989 but quickened to 9% in 1990. The gross national product (GNP) was $179.5 billion in 1990; per capita income was $5,569, an 11.5% jump from 1989. There was some concern, however, that growth was being fueled more by an increase in consumption than by improving export performance. Rising labor costs and lagging technological innovation had acted as significant constraints to exports.

In 1991 the declining growth rate for exports and higher import rates, linked to increased consumption, hurt South Korea's foreign-trade situation. The oil-price increases that followed the Iraqi invasion of Kuwait in August 1990 also impacted the trade balance. Foreign trade in 1990 totaled $128.3 billion—exports stood at $63.2 billion (up 3% from 1989) and imports were at $65.1 billion (up 14.6% from 1989). This deficit widened in early 1991. The government's response included the continuation of policies protecting agriculture from foreign competition; the diversification of export markets away from the United States and toward Asia and the Soviet Union; and an austerity campaign against imported "luxury" goods. Trade with China continued to grow rapidly, with the balance in China's favor. Trade with the Soviet Union was at a considerably lower level than with China, but in January, Seoul extended a $3 billion credit to the Soviet Union—in effect, a quid pro quo for diplomatic recognition the previous September.

Exports to the United States fell to $19.4 billion in 1990 (down 6.2% from 1989), while imports rose to $16.9 billion (up 6.5%). The trade surplus with the United States decreased from $4.7 billion in 1989 to $2.4 billion in 1990. U.S. investment in South Korea in 1990 approximated $2 billion, and like other foreign firms operating in South Korea, U.S. companies found much to complain of. Among the problems were complicated customs regulations and procedures, restrictions on both Korean and foreign banks interested in extending credit to U.S. firms involved in South Korea, inadequate access to distribution channels for imported goods, high taxes on consumer goods, the official austerity campaign against imported "luxuries," and harassment of U.S. firms in retaliation for U.S.-government pressures for South Korea to open its markets.

Foreign Affairs. Even more than economic issues, security considerations dominated South Korea's relations with its sole ally, the United States. Many Koreans long had demanded a restructuring of the Combined Forces Command, under which a U.S. general had commanded all South Korean as all as U.S. troops in the peninsula. The Koreans wanted to play a leading rather than a supporting role. The United States was open to change and in March, over North Korean protests, a South Korean general was appointed to head the United Nations mission at the continuing talks at Panmunjom. In June it was announced that another South Korean general would head the combined ground forces, with Gen. Robert W. RisCassi still in overall command.

In view of North Korea's evident decision to acquire nuclear weapons, a unilateral U.S. decision to remove all nuclear warheads—whether based on land or sea, or deliverable by aircraft—aroused considerable concern in South Korea, especially on the part of the military, even though other U.S. nuclear weapons were to remain in nearby places such as Guam. Similarly, there were reservations in Seoul about the withdrawal of 7,000 of the 43,000 U.S. troops from South Korea scheduled for 1991–92. In light of North Korea's nuclear threat, U.S. Secretary of Defense Dick Cheney halted the U.S. withdrawal in November.

It was mainly in order to accommodate its U.S. ally that South Korea made its contribution to the Gulf war effort—by dispatching a military medical team and a military transport group equipped with five C-130s.

For the past several years, Seoul had been establishing friendly, including diplomatic, relations with the USSR. Both sides were interested in promoting trade and South Korean investment in Siberia, and Seoul wanted to make North Korea more flexible by increasing its isolation from its Soviet and Chinese allies. President Roh and Soviet President Mikhail

SOUTH KOREA • Information Highlights

Official Name: Republic of Korea.
Location: Northeastern Asia.
Area: 38,023 sq mi (98 480 km²).
Population (mid-1991 est.): 43,200,000.
Chief City (1985 census): Seoul, the capital, 9,639,110.
Government: *Head of state,* Roh Tae Woo, president (formally inaugurated February 1988). *Head of government,* Chung Won Shik, prime minister (took office 1991). *Legislature*—National Assembly.
Monetary Unit: Won (726.1 won equal U.S.$1, July 1991).
Gross National Product (1990 U.S.$): $179,500,-000,000.
Economic Indexes (1990): *Consumer Prices* (1980 = 100), all items, 183.6; food, 190.8. *Industrial Production* (1980 = 100), 300.
Foreign Trade (1990 U.S.$): *Imports,* $65,100,-000,000; *exports,* $63,200,000,000.

© J. Markowitz/Sygma

South Korea's President Roh Tae Woo (at dais) *and U.S. President George Bush held their fourth summit meeting at the White House in July 1991. Security and economic issues dominated the agenda, but no major agreements were announced.*

Gorbachev met April 19–20 on the island of Cheju Do. The Soviet side promised to support South Korea's admission to the UN, and both agreed that North Korea ought to submit to inspection of its nuclear facilities by the International Atomic Energy Agency (IAEA).

In addition to the rapid growth of Sino-Korean trade, Beijing promoted better relations with Seoul by promising to reject Pyongyang's demand that it block South Korea's entry into the United Nations, and it gave the impression that it was preparing to grant diplomatic recognition to South Korea.

South Korea's relations with Japan retained a strongly ambivalent quality: deep resentment of four decades of colonial rule, combined with important economic ties and considerable popular admiration for some aspects of Japanese culture, such as films. In January a long-standing grievance was removed by an agreement under which Tokyo promised to stop fingerprinting members of the large Korean community (almost 1 million) in Japan.

In July, South Korea became the seventh "dialogue partner" of the Association of Southeast Asian Nations (ASEAN)—after the United States, Japan, Australia, New Zealand, Canada, and the European Community.

Seoul's main international achievement of the year was its admission to the UN in September. North Korea was admitted at the same time, after dropping its previous demand for a joint (North-South) seat and agreeing to separate memberships. On September 24, President Roh, in an address to the General Assembly, hailed the entry of the two Koreas as a major step toward Korean unification.

South Korea had belonged to the Asia-Pacific Economic Cooperation (APEC) forum since its creation in 1989. In November, Seoul hosted APEC's third ministerial meeting and arranged for the introduction of China, Taiwan, and Hong Kong into the organization.

Democratic People's Republic of Korea (North Korea)

Domestic Affairs. In 1991, North Korea remained what it had been since its founding in 1948: a self-isolated, militarized, totalitarian state with no visible political dissent.

It appeared that the self-styled Great Leader Kim Il Sung was ill, and daily affairs reportedly were directed by his heir apparent, his son, the so-called Dear Leader Kim Jong Il. Clearly a political transition could not be far off, and few expected that the younger Kim would prove more than a temporary successor to his father. The recent collapse of Communist states in Eastern Europe and the unsuccessful hard-line coup against President Gorbachev in August had heightened North Korea's sense of isolation. The Soviet Union reduced aid and demanded hard currency in trade. This forced North Korea closer to China than before.

Burdened by a uniquely rigid form of socialism and by heavy military expenditures, the North Korean economy was in very poor condition. The GNP dropped by an estimated 3.7% in 1990. Informed Soviet estimates put North Korean per capita income at only $300-$500 per year. There were few signs of any desire to liberalize the economy. There were shortages of basic necessities, including food.

Foreign Affairs. North Korea's external relations continued to be strained by the widespread belief that North Korea was working to acquire nuclear weapons. One complex of installations for this purpose had been identified near Yongbyon, about 40 mi (64 km) north of Pyongyang, and at least one more was thought to exist at Pakchon, not far from Yongbyon. The neighbor most seriously concerned was South Korea, but even the Soviet Union, which had provided most of the aid that had made the North Korean nuclear-weapons program possible, now joined in deploring the program and urging Pyongyang to open it to inspection by the IAEA. For its part, Pyongyang was withholding agreement to inspection of its nuclear facilities until the United States withdrew its nuclear weapons from South Korea and guaranteed in writing not to use nuclear weapons against North Korea. The U.S. decision in the fall to do the first of these things was greeted with approval in Pyongyang, which insisted that the withdrawal must be completed and verified before inspection of the North Korean nuclear facilities could begin.

On November 8, President Roh stated that after the withdrawal of U.S. nuclear weapons, no further nuclear weapons would be permitted on South Korean soil. Other South Korean sources made clear at that time that Seoul was opposed to the use of force against North Korea's nuclear facilities. The moves were designed to encourage Pyongyang to agree to inspection or even dismantlement of its nuclear installations, and Tokyo was making a similar outcome a condition for any granting of diplomatic recognition or aid to North Korea.

Pyongyang's belief that the United States was a threat to North Korean security evidently was reinforced by the impressive U.S. military performance in the Gulf war. This sense of enhanced respect for the United States probably had something to do with Pyongyang's unprecedented return in June of the remains of 11 U.S. soldiers killed in the Korean War and its promise to cooperate in a search for 9,000 other personnel of the United Nations forces missing in action during the war.

Pyongyang's relations with its Soviet ally were soured badly by Moscow's diplomatic recognition of Seoul and its cutback of economic support for North Korea. Pyongyang's relations with its other ally, China, were somewhat better. During a visit to Beijing in October, Kim Il Sung reportedly was told to reform his economy along Chinese lines and to stop acquiring nuclear weapons.

In late January, North Korea began talks with Japan on normalization, including the establishment of diplomatic relations. The Japanese side offered an apology for the period of colonial rule but was confronted with a demand for compensation not only for the colonial period but also for the division of the peninsula since 1945, for which Pyongyang claimed to hold Japan partly responsible.

North Korea continued to foster its reputation as an international troublemaker and indeed as a "terrorist state," by selling improved Scud missiles to Syria, Libya, and, reportedly, Iraq after the Gulf war.

The Two Koreas

Continuing Confrontation. As for some years, North Korea's powerful 1-million-man army mostly was deployed in essentially offensive formations not far from the so-called Demilitarized Zone separating the North and South. Against this backdrop, the apparent North Korean quest for nuclear weapons was especially troubling, and there were threats by some South Korean military sources to knock out the facilities. As always, Pyongyang claimed to be upset by the annual (in February) Team Spirit exercises, involving South Korean and U.S. troops.

Political Contacts. In the spring athletic exchanges began between the two sides, and a joint women's table tennis team took the world championship away from the defending Chinese team. In July trade began on a limited scale; South Korean rice was exchanged for North Korean coal.

In his address to the UN General Assembly on September 24, President Roh laid down three principles for unification. First, the two Koreas should renounce the use of force against each other and replace the 1953 armistice with a peace treaty. Second, they should undertake confidence-building measures, such as arms-control agreements and the abandonment of its nuclear-weapons program by the North. Third, they should expand contact in the areas of trade, travel, and communication.

On December 13, North and South Korea signed an Agreement on Reconciliation, Nonaggression, Exchange, and Cooperation. By the treaty the two countries said they formally would end the Korean War. On December 31 they announced an agreement banning nuclear weapons from the Korean peninsula, but did not settle on a method of inspections.

HAROLD C. HINTON
The George Washington University

NORTH KOREA • Information Highlights

Official Name: Democratic People's Republic of Korea.
Location: Northeastern Asia.
Area: 46,540 sq mi (120 540 km²).
Population (mid-1991 est.): 21,800,000.
Chief Cities (1986 est.): Pyongyang, the capital, 2,000,000; Hamhung, 670,000.
Government: *Head of state,* Kim Il Sung, president (nominally since Dec. 1972; actually in power since May 1948). *Head of government,* Yon Hyong Muk, premier (appointed Dec. 1988). *Legislature* (unicameral)—Supreme People's Assembly. The Korea Workers' (Communist) Party: General Secretary, Kim Il Sung.
Gross National Product (1989 U.S.$): $28,000,000,000.

KUWAIT

The Aug. 2, 1990, Iraqi invasion of Kuwait and its liberation in February 1991 profoundly affected that small but rich Persian Gulf state. Political, social, and economic reconstruction took place at a slow but steady pace.

Invasion and Liberation. Hundreds of thousands of Kuwaitis fled Iraq's harsh rule as local resistance was crushed. After the United Nations strongly condemned the conquest and annexation, a coalition of countries acting with United Nations approval, and led by the United States, Saudi Arabia, and the Kuwaiti government in exile, unsuccessfully sought by diplomatic means to compel Iraq to withdraw from Kuwait. The use of force began with air attacks on Iraq and occupied Kuwait on Jan. 17, 1991. Just before the ground war officially began on February 24, Iraqis set afire 640 of Kuwait's oil wells and damaged another 132 of the total 940 wells, thereby creating an unprecedented disaster for the local ecological system (*see* ENVIRONMENT). The coalition's ground forces completed the liberation of Kuwait on February 27.

Military and Political Consequences of the War. While the fighting stopped, the chaos brought about by the war did not end easily. Emir Jabir al-Ahmad al-Sabah declared a state of martial law and appointed Crown Prince Saad al-Abdallah al-Sabah as military governor. Homes, shops, municipal services, and oil fields had been damaged extensively, first by the Iraqis and then in the subsequent fighting. Angered by this, many Kuwaitis took the law into their own hands as they killed and harassed persons accused of collaboration with the Iraqi occupiers. Feelings also were bitter because more than 5,000 Kuwaitis were forced to go to Iraq during the war and they were repatriated very slowly.

Kuwait's borders with Iraq returned to the prewar situation, but with a demilitarized zone 6 mi (9.6 km) into Iraq and 3 mi (4.8 km) into Kuwait patrolled by the UN Iraq-Kuwait Observer Mission. Although Iraq rescinded its annexation of Kuwait on March 5, since Iraq's President Saddam Hussein remained in power, Kuwait's safety from future attacks seemed precarious. Kuwait turned first to Egypt and Syria for military guarantees, but ultimately decided in September to make a security agreement with the United States that called for prepositioning military equipment, conducting joint military exercises, and allowing U.S. vessels to use Kuwaiti ports. However, there would be no permanent stationing of U.S. forces in Kuwait. As the United States sought support for an end to the Arab-Israeli dispute, ultimately leading to the Madrid peace conference, Kuwait joined Saudi Arabia on May 11 in pledging publicly its participation in the U.S. initiative.

Emir Jabir returned to Kuwait on March 14. Political reform was slow, and many Kuwaitis wanted a more-democratic political system. In response to this and other criticism the cabinet resigned on March 18; demonstrators demanded early parliamentary elections. The emir appointed a new cabinet on April 20, ended martial law on June 26, and on July 9 reopened the national council that had been elected in June 1990. Parliamentary elections and a full restoration of the 1962 constitution were set for October 1992. U.S. Secretary of State James Baker, during a visit to Kuwait on April 22, strongly urged the emir to take additional steps toward political democracy and the preservation of human rights for all residents of Kuwait. In June many army officers threatened to resign unless the leaders responsible for Kuwait's weak resistance to the Iraqi invasion were removed from office.

Social Consequences of the War. While hundreds of thousands of Kuwaiti citizens began in May to return to their devastated country, Kuwait did not permit noncitizen longtime residents to come back. Resentment was especially strong toward the Palestinian community, since the Palestine Liberation Organization (PLO) had seemed to favor Iraq and some Palestinians living in Kuwait had collaborated with the Iraqi-occupation authorities. Many Palestinians were arrested and tried arbitrarily; some were tortured and killed. Tens of thousands of Palestinians had left during the

The Emir of Kuwait, Jabir al-Ahmad al-Sabah, extended his hands as he returned to Kuwait in March after months in Saudi Arabia during the Iraqi occupation of his homeland.

© Reuters/Bettmann

A cause for celebration in Kuwait in November was the extinction of the final oil-well fire, one of many that had been set by the Iraqis during the Persian Gulf war. The first oil-well fire was capped in April and during the ensuing months oil crews worked diligently to contain the environmental threat.

© Gustavo Ferrari/Sipa Press

Iraqi occupation; later, more were encouraged or forced to leave Kuwait as the Kuwaitis sought to establish themselves as a majority of the population in their own country. The *bidoons,* Kuwaiti residents who were not full citizens of the country, often were treated harshly. Although they had composed most of the army before the Iraqi invasion, they were not welcomed back after the liberation; this plus the general chaos of the country helped explain much of the lawlessness prevalent from March to May.

The Economy and Oil. Kuwait pledged as much as $22 billion to the coalition countries during the war, but it also had to spend vast amounts to support Kuwaitis living abroad, encourage the resistance, and maintain the exiled government in Taif, Saudi Arabia. After liberation the finances of the Kuwaiti government depended upon income from the $100 billion of investments abroad, since most of Kuwait's economy, physical infrastructure, and oil industry were damaged severely or destroyed.

With help from the U.S. Corps of Engineers and international businesses the Kuwaitis began to restore power lines, generating facilities, water distribution, public hospitals, sanitation services, telephone service, roads, the international airport, and a host of other facilities. On March 12 the chief port was reopened and food supplies could enter the country more easily. On March 24 the government reopened banks and issued new currency. By May and June most services were functioning, although in many cases not yet at full capacity. Particularly dangerous were the mine fields and unexploded ordnance in the desert regions.

Smoke from the burning oil wells and crude oil spewing from the ground created a dire environmental threat and also deprived Kuwait of income from petroleum exports. The first oil well fire was extinguished by U.S. crews on April 7, and the last fires were put out on November 6. Oil-tanker exports began in July, and production reached about 500,000 barrels per day by November. That was less than 25% of the prewar production level. Kuwait still faced the challenge of rebuilding refineries, oil-gathering centers, booster stations, and port facilities destroyed by the Iraqis.

See also FEATURE SECTION/MIDDLE EAST, page 36.

WILLIAM OCHSENWALD
Virginia Polytechnic Institute and State University

KUWAIT • Information Highlights

Official Name: State of Kuwait.
Location: Southwest Asia.
Area: 6,000 sq mi (17 820 km²).
Population (mid-1991 est.) 1,400,000.
Chief Cities (1985 census): Kuwait, the capital, 44,335; Salmiya, 153,369; Hawalli, 145,126.
Government: *Head of state,* Jabir al-Ahmad al-Sabah, emir (acceded Dec. 1977). *Head of government,* Saad al-Abdallah al-Sabah, prime minister (appointed Feb. 1978). *Legislature*—National Council.
Monetary Unit: Dinar (0.292 dinar equal U.S. $1, July 1991).
Gross Domestic Product (1988 U.S.$): $20,500,-000,000.
Economic Index (1989): *Consumer Prices* (1980 = 100), all items, 132.6; food, 115.0.

© Rodney Curtis

With the unemployment rate jumping from 6.1% in January to 7.1% in December, jobs were scarce in the United States in 1991. In New Hampshire (above), *where the June jobless rate was 7.3%, some 1,200 applicants applied for 100 openings.*

LABOR

Employment in the United States was down in 1991, unemployment was up, and part-time workers were replacing full-time employees in many companies. The only bright spots in the U.S. economy were the sharp decline in the Consumer Price Index (CPI) and an increase in productivity over the previous year. On the international scene many other countries also were suffering from high unemployment.

United States

Employment, Wages, and Prices. Employment in the United States in the third quarter of 1991 was 116,764,000, a sharp drop of 1.15 million from the previous year. By comparison, 1990 employment was 572,000 higher than in 1989. Unemployment stood at 8,477,000 in the third quarter of 1991, a whopping increase of 1.6 million over 1990. The unemployment rate of 6.8% of the labor force compared with 5.5% in 1990 and 5.3% in 1989. Long-term unemployment—those unemployed for 27 weeks or longer—increased by almost 500,000 to a total of 1,148,000 in September 1991.

The unemployment rate rose sharply for workers in all age groups, for women as well as for men, and for blacks and Hispanics as well as for whites. The unemployment rate for adult men (20 years and over) was 6.5%, for adult women 5.5%, and 19.2% for teenagers. Unemployment of blacks at 12.1% was double that of whites and higher than unemployment among Hispanic workers, which stood at 10.2% for the third quarter.

Real wages rose for the first time in several years due to the sharp decline in consumer prices. The CPI for urban wage earners and clerical workers rose at a seasonally adjusted rate of only 2.7% for the 12 months ending in November 1991. This compared most favorably with annual rates of 6.1% in 1990, 4.6% in 1989, and 4.4% in 1988. The small increase in 1991 reflected falling prices of petroleum-based energy products, which affected prices of motor fuels, household heating oil, and airline fares. Reduced costs of materials and labor also contributed to the low inflation rate during the first half of 1991.

Average weekly earnings in private industry rose by 3.0% between November 1990 and November 1991. Though this was a smaller increase than for 1990, real earnings were higher because of the small increase in consumer prices. However, real compensation in 1991 was still lower than in 1982.

Productivity and Gross Domestic Product. The U.S. Bureau of Labor Statistics reported that productivity, exclusive of farming, increased at the rate of 2.4% during the third quarter of 1991. This was the first gain in a year and the fastest pace since the summer of 1988. Unit-labor costs fell in manufacturing, while in services, where costs had been rising at the rate of 6%, the increase slowed to 2% during the third quarter.

Productivity almost always revives during the early stages of a recovery as employers hold off recalling laid-off employees and hiring new workers. The rise in productivity reflected the fact that nonfarm business output rose at the rate of 3% while hours worked rose only .6%.

In 1991 the U.S. government began using gross domestic product (GDP) to measure the economy rather than gross national product (GNP). GDP counts only economic activity within the borders of the United States, excluding production of U.S. companies in other countries, which was included in GNP. The GDP grew at a disappointing annual rate of 1.8% during the third quarter of 1991. It previously had been estimated that the growth rate would be approximately 2.5%. The 1.8% increase followed a 1.4% increase in the second quarter of 1991 and declines of 3.9% and 2.5% during the preceding two quarters. The outlook for GDP growth in the fourth quarter was not good, according to economists.

Legislation. After two years of negotiations between U.S. congressional leaders of both the Democratic and Republican parties and the administration, President George Bush signed a civil rights bill on November 21. The law significantly enhances the rights of plaintiffs in employment-discrimination cases. It reverses a series of 1989 Supreme Court decisions that were unfavorable to plaintiffs and, for the first time, expands remedies under Title VII of the 1964 Civil Rights Act to include jury trials and compensatory and punitive damages for intentional discrimination. The new law allows plaintiffs to collect up to $300,000 in punitive damages if they prove they were denied intentionally a job or promotion on the basis of race or sex. This is the first time plaintiffs would be allowed to collect punitive damages for sex discrimination.

On November 15, President Bush signed a temporary extension of unemployment benefits for unemployed workers who had exhausted their regular 26 weeks of benefits under existing law. The president previously had vetoed two similar bills because of their funding arrangements as well as the manner in which eligibility for benefits was to be determined. About 3 million of the nation's 8.47 million unemployed were expected to receive benefits under the new law. Nine states and Puerto Rico were expected to qualify for 20 weeks of extended benefits and 41 states for 13 weeks of benefits. The formula for determining the duration of benefits depends on a state's insured unemployment rate and benefit exhaustion rate. The benefits extension was expected to cost about $5.3 billion.

Employment at Will. The United States is the only major industrialized nation that does not have a federal statutory prohibition against unjust dismissal. Only one state, Montana, has a law requiring that employees may be discharged only for just cause. In all other states, employees who are not protected by grievance procedures in collective-bargaining agreements or by civil service are considered to be employed at will and subject to dismissal without a showing of cause by employers.

During the past two decades, courts in almost all states have recognized exceptions to the employment-at-will doctrine. This has resulted in a proliferation of court suits seeking redress for alleged wrongful termination under the public policy or implied contract exception recognized in many states. Court judgments, many for large monetary damages, have eroded the employment-at-will doctrine to some extent. However, such suits have benefited middle- and upper-level employees much more than lower-paid workers who have not had the financial resources to go to court and whose cases are not attractive to attorneys because the potential damages are relatively small.

Bills have been introduced in a number of states to deal with wrongful termination but, except in Montana, none have been enacted into law. These legislative proposals, as well as adverse decisions involving substantial judgments against employers in some cases, led the National Conference of Commissioners on Uniform State Laws to attempt to draft a Uniform Employment Termination Act for consideration by state legislatures as a means of limiting employer liability, reducing costly litigation, and extending protection to all employ-

U.S. Employment and Unemployment (Armed Forces excluded)

	1990**	1991*
Labor Force	124,787,000	125,242,000
Participation Rate	66.4%	65.9%
Employed	117,914,000	116,764,000
Unemployed	6,874,000	8,477,000
Unemployment rate	5.5%	6.8%
Adult men	4.9%	6.5%
Adult women	4.8%	5.5%
Teenagers	15.5%	19.2%
White	4.7%	6.1%
Black	11.3%	12.1%
Hispanic	8.0%	10.2%

*N.B.** Third-quarter average; ** annual average. Source: U.S. Bureau of Labor Statistics. The participation rate is the number of persons in the labor market, whether employed or unemployed, as a percentage of the civilian noninstitutional population.

ees. The committee drafting the model legislation was composed of representatives from employers and unions as well as plaintiff and management lawyers. After two years of deliberation the committee agreed on a model law on wrongful termination.

The proposed law would cover an employee who works for the same employer for an average of at least 20 hours per week for 26 weeks. An employer would be able to discharge an employee for good cause, which is defined as a reasonable basis for termination taking account of the employee's duties and responsibilities, conduct, job performance, and employment record. Good cause also would include the good-faith exercise of business judgment by an employer in setting its economic goals and determining methods of achieving those goals.

A complaining employee would have to prove that the termination was without good cause or that the employer violated a severance-pay agreement. The employer would have the ultimate burden of proving that the termination was for good cause.

Possible remedies may include reinstatement or, if reinstatement is not ordered, the arbitrator may award severance pay not exceeding 36 months. The award would be subject to limited court review.

AFL-CIO. Eighty-nine unions representing 14 million workers belonged to the American Federation of Labor-Congress of Industrial Organizations (AFL-CIO) at the close of 1991. This represented an increase of 377,000 since the organization's 1989 biennial convention and approximately 140,000 less than the record high membership in 1975.

The International Brotherhood of Teamsters, the largest AFL-CIO affiliate, reported a membership of 1.4 million. It was followed by the American Federation of State, County and Municipal Employees with 1.2 million members, the United Food and Commercial Workers with 997,000 members, and the Service Employees International Union with 881,000 members.

The shift away from manufacturing to a more service-oriented economy in the United States was reflected in the declining membership in such unions as the United Auto Workers with 840,000 members and the United Steelworkers with 459,000 members, both of which were among the largest unions prior to the 1980s.

The nation's largest union, the National Education Association, which has approximately 2 million members, is not included in the above figures.

The convention reelected President Lane Kirkland and Secretary-Treasurer Thomas Donahue. Three new vice-presidents were elected to the 33-member AFL-CIO executive council, including the first Hispanic member, Jack Otero, international vice-president of the Transportation Communications International Union.

In keeping with the organization's strong disagreement with the policies of the Bush administration, Secretary of Labor Lynn Martin was not invited to address the convention. It was addressed by Lithuanian President Vytautas Landsbergis, who appealed to the AFL-CIO to help establish independent trade unions in his country to replace the state-controlled unions that existed before Lithuania declared independence from the Soviet Union.

The convention adopted a resolution opposing a new trade agreement with Mexico which, it argued, would result in reduced employment in the United States. It favored reducing car imports from Japan, which have resulted in unemployment among U.S. autoworkers. Top priority for future legislation was given to a bill prohibiting employers from hiring permanent replacements for workers on strike for economic reasons. The Bush administration opposed such legislation and the president promised a veto if such a bill were to be passed by Congress.

International

Unemployment Trends. The United States was not alone in experiencing rising unemployment in 1991. The U.S. rate of 6.8% was lower than the rate of unemployment in Canada (10.3%), Australia (9.8%), France (9.6%), and Great Britain (8.7%). Every one of those countries had a much higher rate of unemployment during the first half of 1991 than in 1990.

On the other hand and perhaps more significant, the U.S. unemployment rate was much higher than that of its major economic competitors. Japan's unemployment rate was 2.1%, the same as in 1990, and the western part of Germany reduced its rate of unemployment to 5.5%, the lowest level since 1981. (Unemployment in former East Germany stood at approximately 25%, however.) Sweden, which consistently has experienced relatively low unemployment, showed a sharp increase from 1.5% in 1990 to 2.5% in the second quarter of 1991. While this was a cause of concern in Sweden, it was well below the U.S. unemployment rate during any period since World War II.

OECD. The Economic Policy Committee (EPC) of the Organization for Economic Cooperation and Development (OECD)—the Paris-based group of 24 major industrial nations that fosters economic growth—said that, as of November 1991, weak private-sector confidence was holding back economic recovery. To rectify this situation, Bernard Molitor, EPC vice-chairman and director-general of the German economics ministry, recommended continuing budget-deficit-reduction policies, reform of financial systems, and other structural adjustments.

Business confidence was weak, according to Molitor, because the positive aftereffect of the Persian Gulf war was overestimated and because of the psychological impact of the U.S. recession. He predicted that unemployment in OECD countries would continue to rise and would peak in 1992, leaving "an unacceptably high level of structural" joblessness.

The OECD revised downward its projection of U.S. economic growth to 2.2% for 1992. This was down from the 3.1% 1992 growth rate for the United States that the OECD had predicted previously. For the entire OECD area the prediction was for an average growth rate of 2.2% in 1992, down from the previous prediction of 2.9%. Except for Great Britain, Molitor believed that most countries that were in recession were starting to pull out of it.

Japan. At a time when legislation to permit U.S. workers to take unpaid leave for child care was being considered—but not enacted—in the U.S. Congress, a child-care-leave bill was passed in Japan, to become effective April 1, 1992, in the private sector. Employees, both men and women, would be allowed to take leaves of absence until a child is 1 year old. The new law expands an existing labor-standards law allowing women leaves of six weeks before and eight weeks after childbirth. Japan's management originally opposed child-care legislation. However, rapid economic growth and a tight labor market were important factors leading to a change in employer attitudes. The increasing voice of women in Japanese politics also was significant. A similar bill for public employees was being proposed, also to take effect in 1992.

A survey by Rengosoken, a Japanese research institute, reported in October on various attitudes of the Japanese toward work and leisure as compared to workers in four other countries. According to the report, Japanese workers feel they do not have "affluence" and "comfort" in their lives because of their long work hours in comparison with workers in the United States, Britain, France, and Germany. Average work-related hours—including time on the job, commuting, and break periods—were 12 hours daily in Japan, 10 hours and 22 minutes in the United States, 9 hours and 24 minutes in France, and 9 hours and 11 minutes in Britain. The report also pointed out that Japanese workers are "company people" and give top priority to work. They daily spend one hour more on the job than do their counterparts in France and Germany. Japanese workers also spend more time "hanging around" the workplace before and after work than do workers in France and Germany. The survey also found a difference in the average amount of time spent for leisure and socializing during the workday—2 hours and 28 minutes in Japan; 3 hours and 20 minutes in France; and 4 hours and 15 minutes in Germany.

AP/Wide World

In December 1991, Ronald Carey, 55, head of a local union of United Parcel Service drivers in Queens, NY, was elected president of the International Brotherhood of Teamsters.

Belgium. A royal decree abolished the requirement for unemployed people to sign on (register) every day, a long-standing feature of Belgian unemployment insurance. That requirement was intended to ensure that the unemployed were not working while collecting unemployment insurance. Trade unions long had opposed the procedure, but employers had opposed its abolition on the ground that the unlimited duration of Belgian unemployment benefits was subject to abuse. Under the new rule those registered as unemployed would have to sign on twice a month.

Denmark. The Danish Employers' Confederation (DA) reported that average weekly pay rose by 2.2% in 1990, the lowest annual rise since the 1950s. In 1989 the increase was 2.7%. Average hourly pay rose by 3.7% in 1990. The lower weekly figure was due to cuts in working hours. Inflation for 1990 was 2.6%.

Finland. The severity of the economic recession in Finland hindered the conclusion of a new central agreement between Finnish employers and unions. After a decade during which Finland enjoyed one of the fastest growth rates in the Western world, the economy had deteriorated sharply. The Ministry of Trade and Industry estimated that the GNP for 1991 would fall by 6%, while unemployment was expected to rise to 8.5% in 1992 as compared with only 3.4% in 1990.

As a result of the economic crisis employers asked unions for a 10% pay cut and the abolition of the holiday bonus, which is equivalent to two weeks' wages. They also asked for a 50-hour increase in annual working time and a 10% reduction in supplementary labor costs in the form of pensions and sickness and unemployment benefits. Another demand was for the end of centralized wage bargaining.

JACK STIEBER
Michigan State University

LAOS

Laos improved relations with China, the United States, and Vietnam during 1991. Laos' Communist leaders wanted to follow their neighbors' example by opening their economy to market forces, while keeping tight controls.

Politics. The fifth congress of the Lao People's Revolutionary Party, held March 27–29, emphasized economic reform and one-party rule, which the new constitution—promulgated in August—underscored. There was little change in political direction. Prince Souphanouvong, who had stepped down as president for health reasons and was replaced by a temporary/acting president in 1986, resigned as a Politburo member, along with other elder members. Kaysone Phomvihan became the new president and was reelected as party chairman. Khamtai Siphandon replaced him as head of government.

Economics. With Soviet aid declining, Kaysone visited China and Vietnam in the fall to seek closer ties. However, Laos' rugged terrain limits the amount of trade that can be carried on with these two countries, despite efforts to upgrade the Laotian road system.

Laotian trade with Thailand is aided by the Mekong River, which forms their common border for hundreds of miles. Construction of an Australian-financed bridge across the Mekong was begun and is scheduled to be completed by 1994. Laos' main export to Thailand is electricity from its huge hydroelectric dams.

Foreign Relations. Relations between the ethnically similar Lao and Thai people remained strained, however, because of Thailand's size and wealth. In September, Laos announced a ban on timber exports. Thai consumer goods flooded Lao towns along the Mekong, and Thai television programs dominated in Vientiane.

Relations between Laos and the United States continued to improve steadily. Americans found it easier to travel to Laos. A number of Lao officials received grants to visit the United States and study its system of democratic government. U.S. counternarcotics officials visited Laos.

PETER A. POOLE
Author, "Eight Presidents and Indochina"

LAOS • Information Highlights

Official Name: Lao People's Democratic Republic.
Location: Southeast Asia.
Area: 91,430 sq mi (236 800 km^2).
Population (mid-1991 est.): 4,100,000.
Chief City (1985 census): Vientiane, the capital, 377,409.
Government: *Head of state:* Kaysone Phomvihan, president and party chairman; *Head of government,* Khamtai Siphandon. *Legislature* (unicameral)—national Congress of People's Representatives.

LATIN AMERICA

Latin America showed signs of emerging from its decade-long recession in 1991. Progress was uneven, with some countries performing better than others, but on the whole, the region seemed ready to put the dismal record of the debt-ridden 1980s behind it.

Democracy. Politically, democratic systems continued to show strength throughout the region. The exception was Haiti, where a military-led coup ousted popularly elected President Jean-Bertrand Aristide in September.

Elsewhere, the governing Peronist party in Argentina scored impressive victories in gubernatorial and congressional elections in September. The Institutional Revolutionary Party (PRI) holding power in Mexico overwhelmed its opposition in midterm elections in August. The PRI victory was marred, however, by charges of vote fraud and the subsequent removal of two PRI state governors who had been declared elected.

In Suriname a new civilian president was inaugurated for a five-year term, replacing an interim government controlled by the military. A tentative peace agreement was reached in negotiations at the headquarters of the United Nations between the government of El Salvador and rebel guerrilla forces. The government of Guatemala recognized the independence of neighboring Belize, ending a territorial dispute dating back to colonial times. The government's action was subject to ratification by a national referendum.

Economy. The most salient feature of the year in Latin America was the degree to which the economies of the region began to display new dynamism.

In a midyear assessment released in September, the United Nations Economic Commission for Latin America and the Caribbean (ECLAC) predicted that "at the end of 1991, there will have been an increase in the number of countries experiencing growth or recovery to past levels of activity. Thus, regional output will show a slight rise (over 2%), which will cause per capita GDP [gross domestic product] to register its first increase in four years."

The ECLAC concluded that "the gloomy atmosphere of stagnation, recession, and inflation presented in recent years by most of the countries of Latin America shows signs of beginning to clear up, although some contradictory trends still persist." The ECLAC attributed the turnaround to structural reforms under way in many countries of the region.

The World Bank concurred with that analysis in its annual report, also issued in September. The bank referred to "profound political and economic changes that are taking place within many countries [which] could lay the foundation for future growth." The reforms are radically different from those adopted in recent decades, the bank declared. "The movement has been away from a broad role for government, highly protected industrial development, extensive regulation of the private sector, public ownership of productive assets, and large budgetary deficits."

The new policy, the bank said, "emphasizes smaller and more efficient governments, privatizations of government enterprises, more open foreign-trading regimes, deregulation of financial and commodity markets, and reductions in public sector expenditure imbalances."

Enterprise Plan. President George Bush's proposal for the creation of a hemisphere-wide free-trade area gained momentum in 1991. The United States signed framework trade agreements with a number of Latin American and Caribbean countries. The agreements provide for continuing negotiations on the liberalization of trade arrangements in the hemisphere. Included among the agreements were two signed with subregional economic integration groups —the 13-member Caribbean Community (CARICOM) and the four-member Southern Cone Common Market (MERCOSUR). The number of Latin countries signing such agreements reached 26 in 1991. In addition, the United States signed a debt-reduction plan with Chile, the first such accord reached under the Enterprise for the Americas Initiative.

Also during the year the five countries of the Andean Pact announced plans for the creation of a free-trade zone by the end of 1991 and a common market in 1995. The Andean countries said they too would seek to negotiate a framework agreement with the United States.

Social Development. Despite the encouraging macroeconomic performance of the hemispheres in 1991, poverty remains endemic throughout the region. The debt crisis of the 1980s left a legacy of social deterioration that experts said will persist through the 1990s.

Unemployment remains high and real income levels are some 25% lower than they were in 1980. The dilemma is compounded by high population growth rates and severely limited social services in such areas as education and health. The incidence of disease is rising, including AIDS and cholera (*see* sidebar).

Natural disasters also afflicted the region in 1991—strong earthquakes in Panama, Peru, and Costa Rica and torrential rains in Chile. Trafficking in illicit drugs remained a major problem. In Colombia, for example, where millions of opium poppies have been destroyed in recent years, authorities found the first heroin laboratory in more than 30 years. Latin America, in short, made significant progress in 1991, but by the end of the year it was evident that enormous tasks lay ahead.

See also FEATURE SECTION/CHRISTOPHER COLUMBUS, page 76.

RICHARD C. SCHROEDER, *Consultant Organization of American States*

The Cholera Epidemic

In January 1991 a cholera epidemic broke out in Peru. It was the first major outbreak of cholera in the Western Hemisphere in the 20th century. By the end of August, Peru had reported 246,246 cases, 2,416 of them fatal. Meanwhile, the disease also had moved into other Latin American countries, particularly Ecuador (34,123 reported cases), Colombia (5,466), and Mexico (696).

Cholera is caused by a bacterium, *Vibrio cholerae.* To catch the disease, people must swallow the bacteria. The bacteria multiply in the victims' bodies and are excreted in their fecal wastes, which then may contaminate drinking water and food supplies in places with poor sanitation. For instance, millions of Peruvians obtain their water from rivers that are used to carry untreated human wastes to the sea. The vegetables they eat are grown on fields irrigated with water from these rivers. Much of their seafood is taken from contaminated waters and eaten raw.

In August, following 15 cases of cholera among tourists returning from South America, U.S. health officials cautioned travelers to protect themselves against the disease. Four of the tourists contracted the disease in Ecuador; the other 11 became ill after eating improperly prepared crabmeat.

Many people who swallow *Vibrio* bacteria do not become ill, though they become carriers who spread the disease through their excrement. Other infected people experience high fever, severe vomiting, and diarrhea. They can recover if quickly treated with antibiotics and intravenous solutions. Left untreated, however, the victims may become dehydrated rapidly, dying from loss of body fluids within hours of the onset of symptoms.

To combat cholera's spread, officials in Peru and other Latin American nations mounted widespread educational campaigns, explaining that people can safeguard against infection by washing their hands and food, by boiling drinking water and foods, and by buying safe water. Authorities also allocated increased funds to improve water supply and sewage systems, although their depleted national treasuries do not contain sufficient funds to tackle this need. The Pan American Health Organization estimated it would cost Peru alone $320 million per year for ten years to build adequate water and sewage systems.

Many health experts believe that cholera will remain a serious problem in Latin America through the 1990s. The World Health Organization estimated in May that cholera would infect up to 6 million people in South America over the next few years.

JENNY TESAR

LAW

For the second year in a row the hectic conclusion of a U.S. Supreme Court term was marked by the retirement of a liberal member. Hours after the court handed down its final rulings of the 1990–91 term, Justice Thurgood Marshall announced that failing health and his advanced age—he was about to celebrate his 83d birthday—compelled him to step down. The moment was historic and overshadowed the climax of a term in which conservatives further solidified their control of the high court. The retirement of Justice Marshall, the court's only black member and a towering civil-rights figure for nearly four decades, came one year after Justice William J. Brennan departed and was replaced by David H. Souter. Justices Brennan and Marshall, close friends, had been steadfast liberal allies since Marshall joined the court in 1967.

President Bush wasted little time in picking a conservative black judge, Clarence Thomas (*see* BIOGRAPHY), to replace Justice Marshall. Thomas was opposed by many leading civil rights and women's rights groups. He appeared headed for Senate confirmation after a contentious round of hearings before the Senate Judiciary Committee. But on the eve of the final vote, charges that he had sexually harassed a woman who worked for him a decade earlier threatened the nomination and he barely was confirmed by the Senate, 52–48.

There was controversy on other legal fronts as well. Vice-President Dan Quayle blasted lawyers at the annual convention of the American Bar Association (ABA). Calling for major changes in the nation's legal system—including limits on punitive-damage awards in lawsuits—he blamed lawyers for the United States' falling economic competitiveness. ABA President John J. Curtin, Jr., told the vice-president to his face that the charges were unfair.

As for the Supreme Court, led by Chief Justice William H. Rehnquist, conservatives prevailed on most key issues—most notably in cases affecting the rights of those accused or convicted of crimes. Often the division on the court in such cases was 6–3 with Justices Marshall, John Paul Stevens, and Harry A. Blackmun comprising the dwindling liberal wing.

In the lower courts, the nephew of Sen. Edward M. Kennedy was acquitted of rape charges in Florida in one of the most publicized cases of the year. Other matters making news included the resentencing of evangelist Jim Bakker; conviction of a Cuban refugee in the death of 87 people killed in a New York City social-club fire; and a ruling that allowed a Virginia military academy to continue to exclude women.

Issues involving the Persian Gulf war and the definition of the term "state" as the USSR broke up and Yugoslavia was in the midst of civil war dominated international-law circles.

United States

Supreme Court. Criminal defendants fared poorly before the high court in the 1990–91 term, one in which the work load again was scaled back. The justices handed down signed decisions in 112 cases, the fewest since 1970. Several key features emerged in criminal cases. Justice Souter voted against defendants in all

After lengthy confirmation hearings, Clarence Thomas (left) *became the 106th justice of the U.S. Supreme Court in October 1991. The other justices are* (l-r): *David H. Souter, Antonin Scalia, Sandra Day O'Connor, Chief Justice William H. Rehnquist, John Paul Stevens, Harry A. Blackmun, Byron R. White, and Anthony M. Kennedy.* AP/Wide World

but a handful of the cases in which he participated, essentially matching the voting record of Chief Justice Rehnquist. The court displayed a readiness to overturn liberal precedents. And often the division in the most significant cases was 6–3, supplanting the 5–4 splits that had prevailed in past years.

Four times the court explicitly scrapped precedents that had favored criminal defendants. The justices, in effect, tossed aside a precedent in a fifth case—without acknowledging that was their express purpose.

The court called a virtual halt to repeated death-penalty appeals, ruling that federal judges must dismiss such petitions except in rare circumstances (*McCleskey v. Zant*). The court also said that state-prison inmates who were barred from raising some federal claims in state courts because of procedural flaws generally may not raise them in federal court (*Coleman v. Thompson*). The ruling means that a defense lawyer's error can cost the right of federal appeal. The ruling overturned a 1963 decision (*Fay v. Noia*) that said state prisoners were entitled to seek federal-court help unless they deliberately circumvented state courts.

The use of a coerced confession does not automatically mean a conviction must be overturned, the court said. The justices said the conviction may stand if it rests on other evidence properly introduced at the trial (*Arizona v. Fulminante*). The decision threw out a key part of a 1967 precedent (*Chapman v. California*). Two other recent precedents that had banned so-called victim-impact testimony during sentencing in capital cases went by the wayside on the final day of the court term. The court said prosecutors seeking death sentences may show the impact of a murder on the victim's family and may reveal evidence about the victim's character (*Payne v. Tennessee*). Discarded were precedents established in 1987 (*Booth v. Maryland*) and in 1989 (*South Carolina v. Gathers*)

The court said inmates suing over inhumane prison conditions must prove that authorities acted with deliberate indifference and were not prevented from improving matters because of lack of money (*Wilson v. Seiter*). Police without a warrant or even suspicious of a crime may board buses and ask passengers to consent to being searched for drugs, the court ruled (*Florida v. Bostick*). The court said states may impose life in prison without parole for people convicted of possessing at least 1.5 lbs (.68 kg) of cocaine. The court rejected arguments that such harsh sentences violate the Constitution's ban against cruel and unusual punishment (*Harmelin v. Michigan*).

Evidence thrown away by people fleeing from police may be used as evidence against them even if the police lacked any reason to suspect the commission of a crime when they gave chase, the court ruled (*California v. Hodari D.*). The court also made it easier for police to search closed containers found in cars when they lack a search warrant, ruling the search is lawful as long as authorities have probable cause to believe there is hidden contraband (*California v. Acevedo*). In a 1979 ruling (*Arkansas v. Sanders*), the court had barred such warrantless searches.

The justices did not address the issue of abortion directly. But in one of the key cases of the term, the court upheld federal regulations adopted during the Reagan administration that bar family-planning clinics from receiving federal aid if they discuss abortion with their patients (*Rust v. Sullivan*). The decision prompted intense anger among women's rights groups and free-speech advocates and ignited an effort in Congress to override the ruling. In another case involving freedom of expression, the court said states may ban nude dancing in adults-only establishments (*Barnes v. Glen Theatre*).

Two disputes over freedom of the press captured widespread attention. The court ruled that news organizations may be sued for revealing the identities of sources who were promised confidentiality (*Cohen v. Cowles Media Co.*). The justices also said fabricated quotations attributed to a public figure may be libelous, but only if the quotes changed the meaning of what the speaker actually said (*Masson v. The New Yorker*). The case involved two highly publicized magazine articles about a prominent psychologist who accused the author of making up quotations.

The court broke important new ground in the areas of civil rights and women's rights. The justices ruled that under the Civil Rights Act of 1964 women of childbearing age may not be barred from hazardous jobs because the work may pose a danger to fetuses (*United Automobile Workers v. Johnson Controls Inc.*). The court said the same law does not protect U.S. workers in foreign countries who claim that U.S. companies overseas are discriminating against them (*Equal Employment Opportunity Commission v. Arabian American Oil Co*). The court allowed public-school officials to end court-ordered racial desegregation plans after achieving integration even if it results in a return to single-race schools (*Board of Education v. Dowell*).

Also, the court said potential jurors may not be excluded from noncriminal trials because of their race (*Edmonson v. Leesville Concrete Co.*). The court said that defendants in criminal trials have grounds to stop prosecutors from excluding jurors based on race—even if the defendant is white and the jurors in question are black (*Powers v. Ohio*). The court said that neither federal law nor the Constitution are violated when states impose mandatory retirement ages for appointed state judges (*Gregory v. Ashcroft*).

© Robert Trippett/Sipa

Citing advancing age and poor health, Thurgood Marshall announced his resignation from the U.S. Supreme Court—to which he was appointed by President Johnson in 1967—in June 1991. The first black to serve on the high court, he was considered one of its most liberal members. Earlier he had been the chief counsel to the civil-rights movement, a judge of the U.S. Court of Appeals, and U.S. solicitor general. He was born July 2, 1908, in Baltimore, MD, and was graduated from Howard University Law School.

In two cases from the South, the court ruled that elected judges are covered by federal voting-rights law aimed at helping minorities (*Chisom v. Roemer* and *Houston Lawyers v. Attorney General of Texas*).

The most important business case decided during the term was a major defeat for corporations. The court said punitive damages awarded in personal-injury lawsuits against businesses generally do not violate constitutionally protected due-process rights even when the awards are many times greater than the actual losses suffered (*Pacific Mutual Life Insurance Co. v. Haslip*).

The court also held that the alphabetical listing of names and addresses in the white pages of a phone directory may be copied without violating federal copyright law (*Feist Publications v. Rural Telephone Service*). The decision could have a big impact on the computerized information industry.

Local Law. William Kennedy Smith, nephew of Sen. Edward Kennedy (D-MA), was acquitted of rape in Palm Beach, FL, in December. The much-publicized, televised trial, during which the accuser testified—with her face blocked out for the TV audience, brought into the open such issues as the role of live television coverage in the courtroom and the right of the accuser in such a case to remain anonymous. The fact that the trial judge had ruled against introducing testimony involving the past sexual history of the accuser or the accused also became a subject of discussion.

In Charlotte, NC, television evangelist Jim Bakker had his prison sentence reduced to 18 years. Bakker had been sentenced to 45 years in prison after he was convicted for conspiracy and fraud in 1989, but the term was overturned by an appeals court. He will be eligible for parole in 1995.

A federal judge in Roanoke, VA, ruled that Virginia Military Institute (VMI) may continue to exclude women. U.S. District Judge Jackson Kiser said the academy "truly marches to the beat of a different drummer" and that all-male VMI, a public college, increases educational diversity in Virginia even though there is no equivalent school for women. The Justice Department said it would appeal the ruling.

A jury in New York City convicted Julio Gonzales, a 37-year-old Cuban refugee, of causing one of the worst mass murders in the nation's history, a fire that killed 87 people in the Happy Land social club in the Bronx. Gonzales was convicted of murder, arson, and assault for setting the blaze after arguing with his former girlfriend about being thrown out of the club. Gonzales was sentenced to 25 years to life in prison.

The 9th U.S. Circuit Court of Appeals in San Francisco reinstated a lesbian's lawsuit over her discharge from the Army Reserve. The appeals court said social prejudice against homosexuals does not justify excluding them from the military. The appeals court relied in part on a 1984 Supreme Court ruling that said social disapproval of an interracial marriage cannot justify denial of child custody to such a couple. The appeals court decision was a victory for the Rev. Dusty Pruitt, who remained an officer in the Army Reserve after leaving active service to become a Methodist minister. The ruling did not overturn the U.S. military policy against homosexuals, but said the Pentagon must justify the policy in individual cases by proving it is rational.

A federal judge in Virginia overturned the suspension of a fraternity at state-run George Mason University that had staged an "ugly woman" contest in which a white man dressed in women's clothing and blackface. U.S. District Judge Claude M. Hilton said that even racist and obnoxious student performances are protected by constitutional free-speech guarantees. The university said the performance was disruptive and wanted to suspend the fraternity for two years.

In Houston, TX, in September, Wanda Holloway was convicted and sentenced to 15 years in prison for trying to hire a hit man to kill the mother of her daughter's rival for the junior-high-school cheerleader squad. The jury found that Holloway wanted Verna Heath killed in hopes that Heath's daughter would be too upset to compete in cheerleader tryouts against Holloway's daughter. In November, however, Holloway was granted a new trial on the basis of new evidence and the fact that one of the jurors should have been disqualified because he was on probation on a drug offense.

JIM RUBIN, *The Associated Press*

International Law

The year 1991 posed difficult problems for international law. The very definition of states, the principal subjects of international law, was put in question by the dissolution, or attempted dissolution, of such states as the Soviet Union, Yugoslavia, and possibly Ethiopia. The success of the Baltic republics in gaining formal independence stood in stark contrast with the struggle for statehood of the Yugoslav republics of Slovenia and Croatia. The international community refused early recognition to Croatia, apparently trying to maintain Yugoslavia's territorial integrity.

Sovereignty. Another basic tenet of international law, the doctrine of sovereignty, also was placed under heavy pressure. The right of governments to exercise untrammeled authority within their territories was challenged by the international community in the case of Liberia, where the armed intervention of a regional integration organization to end a fratricidal struggle within the country was endorsed by the United Nations Security Council early in 1991. When a military coup took place in Haiti later in the year, the United Nations refused recognition to the military junta and supported the previous government, which could base its legitimacy on democratic elections in December 1990.

However, the UN continued to exercise restraint in a number of other cases. In deference to the principle of territorial sovereignty, the Security Council was initially reluctant to intervene on behalf of Kurds, Shias, and other minorities within Iraq who were faced with annihilation at the conclusion of the Persian Gulf war. When the Security Council finally imposed an obligation upon Iraq to accept the activities of international humanitarian-aid agencies on its territory, military forces of the international coalition intervened in northern Iraq and created safe havens for displaced Kurds. But attempts to secure the position of Kurds and other minorities within Iraq through an international autonomy agreement were unsuccessful. (*See* FEATURE ARTICLE/THE KURDS, page 48.)

Persian Gulf Conflict. Other aspects of the Gulf crisis continued to dominate the 1991 international legal agenda, and a number of difficult legal questions remained to be resolved. Most issues arising from the Persian Gulf war were covered by the stringent UN cease-fire terms which Iraq had been invited to accept prior to a formal termination of hostilities. They related to the deployment of an observation force on the Iraq-Kuwait boundary, the demarcation of that boundary, the acceptance by Iraq of supervised arms limitations, the maintenance of economic sanctions, and the payment of compensation for damage suffered as a result of the conflict.

Difficulties were encountered when Iraq resisted the highly intrusive inspections of its nuclear and other armaments-production facilities. The Baghdad government also appeared to lay the groundwork for revindicating its territorial claims against Kuwait at a later stage, despite the work of the boundary-demarcation commission.

The United Nations set up another commission, provisionally located in Geneva, to deal with the avalanche of financial claims against Iraq. Draft guidelines for the processing of claims were adopted by the UN Security Council, preference being given to comparatively small claims. Iraq was obliged to pay some 30% of its oil revenue into the compensation fund for disbursement by the claims commission. However, Iraq failed to generate sufficient revenue for a commencement of any settlement.

Other Developments. Before the Gulf conflict, the UN General Assembly had requested that the UN International Law Commission should concentrate its work on offenses against the peace and security of mankind. But the failure of the international community even to attempt to try those responsible for aggression against Kuwait gave an air of unreality to the proceedings. Even if results were achieved in the future, it was doubtful that they would be acceptable to the member states of the UN.

The commission also dealt with the question of liability for injurious consequences of harmful acts not prohibited by international law. The commission was under pressure to reach at least a preliminary conclusion for submission to the 1992 environmental conference in Rio de Janeiro. But the commission members remained split on this important area of law which has been on its agenda for years.

The commission did manage to adopt a draft text on state immunity at second reading and also approved rules governing nonnavigable international watercourses at first reading.

Work at the International Court of Justice proceeded comparatively swiftly. A record number of 12 cases were being adjudicated. The last case to be submitted concerned a bridge across the Baltic sea-lane of the Great Belt. The bridge is to connect Copenhagen with the Danish mainland. Finland has objected to this project as it would restrict the right of passage through the Belt—a right on which Finland claims to be economically dependent. An application by Finland for interim protection was rejected by the court.

The United States was contesting jurisdiction of the court in an action brought by Iran in connection with the downing of an Iranian airliner by the U.S. warship *Vincennes* during the Iran-Iraq war. Iran alleged that the compensation offered by the United States to relatives of the victims of that event was outrageously low and demanded higher payment.

MARC WELLER, *University of Cambridge*

LEBANON

For the first time in more than a decade, most of Lebanon experienced a year without violence and dislocation. Apart from the south of the country, which remained outside the control of the national government, Lebanon enjoyed both stability and security. However, the price for this new tranquility was the autonomy of the government and the country from foreign control. However, the new peacefulness suffered a blow in late December as a powerful car bomb exploded, killing 20 persons in Beirut. It was the most powerful attack since the peace process began in Lebanon.

Stability. The Greater Beirut security plan, undertaken in late 1990, was extended under the new "national unity" government to much of the country. With two exceptions, all militias agreed to disarm. Some turned their heavy weapons over to the army, others to Syria. Many small arms were retained in hiding, and some groups, such as the Lebanese Forces (the largest Christian militia), shipped major weapons into secure hiding places. Most of the major militias retained an organizational cadre on which to reconstitute themselves if necessary.

The two militias that refused to disarm were the Palestinians—really a complex of different groups, and Hezbollah—the movement of fundamentalist Shia. Both claimed their status as resistance groups against Israel should exclude them from disarming. However, the armed Palestinian movement in southern Lebanon was primarily under the control of Yasir Arafat's al-Fatah, a movement opposed by Syria, which essentially controlled the Lebanese government. Consequently, the Lebanese army moved against the Palestinians in July and in a series of battles effectively defeated them. The Palestinians then agreed to disarm and submit to Lebanese authority.

By contrast, Hezbollah remained closely linked to elements in Iran, and the Iranian government continued to use its influence in Damascus to secure an exception for Hezbollah as an indigenous Lebanese resistance to the Israeli occupation of the south. However, Iran announced in October that it planned to withdraw gradually the approximately 1,500 Iranian Revolutionary Guards deployed in Lebanon since 1982.

By midyear government authority nominally extended to all of Lebanon north of the Israeli "security zone" in the south—more than 90% of the country—in part as a result of the deployment of the army along national highways. Actual government control varied and depended upon the degree to which Syria permitted the government to operate autonomously. In spite of these limitations, the entire area nominally under government control experienced a resurgence of internal travel and visits by Lebanese who had been limited to their own areas of habitation. Even regions such as Baalbek, which remained under de facto domination of Hezbollah and Iranian revolutionary guards for most of the year, were opened. By midyear numerous foreign airlines and embassies that had discontinued operation in Lebanon were returning.

Economy. Contrary to some predictions, the Lebanese economy did not rebound. Only a fraction of the promised foreign aid materialized, and government revenues continued to be but a fraction of expenditures. Although the pound remained relatively stable at about 900 to the U.S. dollar, there was little internal or external investment. The economy was burdened with public lack of confidence, mismanagement, and rampant corruption.

© Beaudenon/Sipa

In Beirut, Lebanon, members of Hezbollah, a fundamentalist Muslim faction, protest the U.S.-sponsored Middle East peace talks. At the conference that opened in Madrid, Spain, in late October, the Lebanese delegation followed Syria's lead on virtually all issues.

Syrian Control. Political progress in Lebanon had occurred under the facade of the Taif agreements reached by a majority of the members of parliament in late 1989. These accords laid out a general program of political reforms and a menu for bilateral relations with Syria. Many who signed the agreements, however, had seen them as only a blueprint that would be elaborated as the national political process was renewed. Instead the government of "national unity" that was named at the end of 1990, and composed almost entirely of pro-Syrian elements, moved ahead with a Syrian-backed agenda. This included appointing new members of parliament to fill seats created by its enlargement and negotiating agreements with Syria. The newly appointed members of parliament were virtually all pro-Syrian, as were key appointments in such areas as security, intelligence, and the armed forces. The army was reorganized, purportedly to create units that integrated Christian and Muslim soldiers. However, the "mixing" was done on a highly selective basis, leaving some battalions (particularly Druze and Shia) essentially untouched. The effect was to dilute further any resistance to Syrian control.

On May 22 the Lebanese government signed a Treaty of Brotherhood, Cooperation, and Coordination with Syria, transferring significant decision-making power to mixed Lebanese-Syrian committees under the two nations' presidents. In September, Syria asserted even greater control when Lebanon ratified a bilateral "security agreement" that authorized Syrian training and "exchange" throughout the internal security establishment. It also provided for action against persons, including journalists, who harm or offend Syria.

International Relations. With its decreasing autonomy, Lebanon was even less able to mount an independent foreign policy than it had been in the past. The new Lebanese government quickly asserted its determination to extend the area of its control into the south.

By disarming the Palestinian resistance the government sought to demonstrate its ability to maintain security in southern Lebanon, which would obviate the need for continued Israeli maintenance of its "security zone" there. However, Israel looked at the army as an extension of a Syrian-controlled Lebanese government, and this was far from an acceptable security force on its northern border. Therefore, when the Lebanese government asserted it soon would take over Jazzine, essentially an enclave under the control of the Israeli-supported South Lebanon Army (SLA), Israeli officials objected. Intermittent attacks against the SLA and Israeli units in the security zone generated Israeli retaliatory raids.

The major Lebanese event involved developments in the Western hostage saga. Both Syria and Iran had been working to improve

LEBANON • Information Highlights

Official Name: Republic of Lebanon.
Location: Southwest Asia.
Area: 4,015 sq mi (10 400 km^2).
Population (mid-1991 est.): 3,400,000.
Chief Cities (1982 est.): Beirut, the capital, 509,000; Tripoli, 198,000.
Government: *President,* Elias Hrawi (took office November 1989); *prime minister,* Umar Karami (took office December 1990). *Legislature* (unicameral)—National Assembly.
Monetary Unit: Lebanese pound (880 pounds equal U.S.$1, Dec. 4, 1991).
Foreign Trade (1987 U.S.$): *Imports,* $1,500,000,000; *exports,* $1,000,000,000.

their relations with the United States, and Washington appeared intent on reciprocating. The problem of the Western hostages held in Lebanon constituted the single greatest obstacle to such improvement. Thus, Damascus and Tehran, using a number of intermediaries, and with renewed UN activity, initiated a new effort to break the impasse. The general outline of an arrangement involving Lebanese and Palestinians held in Israel as well as Westerners held in Lebanon emerged, but implementing the process proved difficult, in part because of factional divisions among the groups holding the Western hostages. Further complicating things was the demand of some groups that the Hamadeh brothers, held on terrorist charges in Germany, be included in any exchange.

Nevertheless, a series of highly publicized releases of Western hostages brought the crisis to a near end. Those released included Britons John McCarthy in August, Jack Mann in September, and Terry Waite in November; and Americans Edward Tracy in August, Jesse Turner in October, Thomas Sutherland in November, and Joseph J. Cicippio, Alann Steen, and Terry Anderson in December. Following the latter's release, only two Germans remained in captivity; a missing Italian was reported to be dead. As 1991 ended, the bodies of Lt. Col. William R. Higgins and William Buckley—two U.S. hostages who had been slain by their captors—also were released.

Another drama involved the status of mutinous Gen. Michel Aoun. Aoun, named prime minister by then-outgoing President Amin Gemayel in 1988, had refused to recognize Lebanon's president and to leave the presidential palace he occupied. Aoun was ousted in a general offensive by Syrian and Lebanese armed forces in October 1990, but fled to the French embassy. France was willing to grant Aoun asylum, but the Lebanese government insisted he face criminal charges. The standoff continued until August 29, when Aoun was spirited out of Lebanon following a grant of amnesty. He was admitted to France but was prohibited from taking part in Lebanese politics.

RONALD D. MCLAURIN
Abbott Associates Inc.

LIBRARIES

In 1991 two extraordinary events occurred in the world of librarianship in the United States. The Second White House Conference on Library and Information Services was held, and librarians staged a "rally on wheels" from Atlanta to Washington to call the nation's attention to the funding crisis facing libraries.

The White House Conference. The second White House Conference on Library and Information Services (WHCLIS) was held July 9-13 in Washington, DC. The conference, authorized by a law signed by President Ronald Reagan in 1988, brought 700 delegates and some 1,300 alternates, observers, and others together to make recommendations for the future of U.S. library and information services.

The delegates represented library and information professionals, library supporters (including trustees and members of Friends of Libraries groups), government officials, and the general public. These representatives passed 94 recommendations dealing with access to information, government information, literacy, intellectual freedom, and library services to a diverse population.

The delegates' top five priorities were recommendations calling for: a national Omnibus Children and Youth Literacy Through Libraries Act; the National Research and Education Network (an electronic information highway) to be available in all libraries; a national investment in library services; the development of model marketing programs for libraries; and amendments to the 1991 National Literacy Act.

President Bush received the final report from the WHCLIS in November and would report to Congress on the conference's recommendations early in 1992. U.S. national, state, and regional library associations were developing plans for implementing these recommendations.

The Librarians Rally. The American Library Association (ALA) staged a "Rally on Wheels" from Atlanta to Washington in mid-1991.

The rally was held to call the nation's attention to libraries' fight for survival. While Americans ask their librarians more than 200 million reference questions each year and while there are more public libraries than there are McDonald's restaurants, federal funding for libraries in the last 25 years had totaled less than the cost of one aircraft carrier. Libraries currently were costing taxpayers an average of only $15.10 per capita annually.

And while library use had risen dramatically over the last decade, libraries faced successive years of budget cuts that now literally were threatening their ability to keep their doors open. Libraries from Brooklyn, NY, to Portland, OR, had closed branches either entirely or on certain days each week.

Key library leaders and library supporters led the rally's kickoff in Atlanta on June 29. The kickoff, attended by some 4,000 librarians, began a yearlong "Rally for America's Libraries." Other media events were held in Atlanta, and on July 4 a caravan of library leaders and supporters began a five-day trek to Washington, DC, for the WHCLIS.

Along the road, rallies were held in various communities. Speaking for libraries at a rally in Greenville, SC, Jesse Jackson said, "Our dream today is not just to save libraries, it's to save the country." At the rally's end in Washington, DC, a library compact signed by some 500,000 library supporters was displayed.

Associations. The ALA held its 110th annual conference June 29–July 4 in Atlanta. Presided over by Richard M. Dougherty, the conference had a theme of "Kids Who Read Succeed." Patricia Glass Schuman was inaugurated as the ALA's new president at the end of the conference and Marilyn L. Miller was welcomed as president-elect.

The ALA passed a preservation policy entitled "Permanence and Durability of Information Products." This policy speaks to the permanence of information media, their intelligibility and readability over time, the threat to information posed by technical obsolescence, the long-term retention of information resident in commercial databases, and the security of library and commercial databases. ALA passed this policy to provide a framework in which to address the very serious threats to the nation's heritage posed not only by books which are rotting on shelves, but also by the fragility of information stored in electronic formats.

The Canadian Library Association (CLA) held its 46th annual conference in Montreal, Que., June 1–5 with the theme "Libraries—Threads in the Fabric of the Information Society." President Ernie Ingles presided and First Vice-President/President-Elect Marnie Swanson welcomed the CLA's new executive director, Karen Adams.

CHARLES HARMON
American Library Association

Library Awards for 1991

Beta Phi Mu Award for distinguished service to education or librarianship: Edward G. Holley, professor, School of Information and Library Science, University of North Carolina, Chapel Hill

Randolph J. Caldecott Medal for the most distinguished picture book for children: David Macaulay, *Black and White*

Melvil Dewey Award for recent creative professional achievement of a high order: Lucia J. Rather, Library of Congress

Grolier Award for unique contributions to the stimulation and guidance of reading by children and young people: Dorothy M. Broderick, *Voice of Youth Advocates*

Joseph W. Lippincott Award for distinguished service to the profession of librarianship: Peggy Sullivan, Northern Illinois University

John Newbery Medal for the most distinguished contribution to literature for children: Jerry Spinelli, *Maniac Magee*

LIBYA

Libya's opposition to both Iraq's invasion of Kuwait and the presence of massive international forces in the Middle East led it to pursue diplomacy seeking a peaceful solution to the Persian Gulf crisis. As a result, Libyan relations with Egypt and most European states improved in the course of the year. The country's dealings with the United States and Great Britain became even cooler, however.

Gulf Diplomacy. In an effort to avert the outbreak of war in the Gulf, Libyan leader Muammar el-Qaddafi hosted a summit attended by the presidents of Egypt, Syria, and Sudan on January 3. Although this meeting produced no peace strategy, Libya continued to advocate a diplomatic rather than a military approach to the regional crisis. On January 15—the United Nations (UN) deadline for an Iraqi withdrawal from Kuwait—Libya joined France, Algeria, and Yemen in an unsuccessful call for Iraqi forces to leave Kuwait in exchange for a commitment that the U.S.-led coalition would not attack and that international attention would be focused on resolving the Arab-Israeli dispute over Palestine. After the bombing of Iraq began, Libya and its partners in the Arab Maghreb Union (AMU)—Tunisia, Algeria, Morocco, and Mauritania—requested that the UN Security Council demand a cease-fire. The motion again was unsuccessful.

Throughout the war, President Qaddafi honored a pledge to support the decisions of his Egyptian counterpart, Hosni Mubarak. The Libyan government, which had from the outset regarded the Iraqi invasion as a blow to the cause of Arab unity, issued few public pronouncements during the war. Libyan demonstrations protesting the large number of Iraqi civilian casualties occurred in mid-February.

Support for Egypt stemmed partly from Libya's desire to build on bilateral accords, signed late in 1990 and envisioning significant cooperation in future development projects. Following the war the two countries strengthened their economic linkages. The elimination of customs and tariff barriers during the summer permitted the free movement of goods and persons across the Libyan-Egyptian border. Increased Egyptian exports to Libya eased shortages of consumer goods there, while substantial infusions of Libyan capital benefited Egyptian industries. The August completion of the first phase of Libya's Great Man Made River project, which would tap extensive underground water reserves to bring previously arid land under cultivation, was accompanied by the announcement of plans to settle as many as 500,000 Egyptian peasants to help underpopulated Libya work the newly arable land.

Other members of the Arab Maghreb Union expressed concern that Libya's improved relations with Egypt came at their expense. In addition to a shift of Libyan investments from AMU countries to Egypt, they cited as evidence the shelving of Libyan plans to permit the immigration of a large number of Moroccan laborers. A project to establish a railway between Libya and Tunisia was abandoned in favor of a line linking Libya and Egypt.

U.S. Relations. A U.S. trade blockade against Libya, in effect since 1986, had been especially harmful by preventing the acquisition of spare parts and maintenance services needed by the Libyan oil industry. Although Libya profited from the increase in oil prices that accompanied the Gulf crisis, the boycott prevented it from pushing its production to full capacity. Egypt's attempt to facilitate a Libyan-U.S. rapprochement made little headway.

The United States insisted that Libya was continuing to manufacture illegal chemical weapons and was supporting insurgents in Liberia, Ghana, Senegal, and other sub-Saharan African countries. In turn, it was the exposure of secret U.S. efforts to undermine the Libyan government that angered Qaddafi.

In the spring the United Kingdom rebuffed Libyan overtures for a resumption of diplomatic relations, broken since the murder of a British policewoman at the Libyan embassy in London in 1984. Refusing a Libyan contribution to a police benevolent fund, the British government insisted on the extradition of the individual responsible for the shooting and firm evidence that Libya had severed its links with the Irish Republican Army.

In mid-November the United States and Scotland indicted two Libyan intelligence agents for their alleged role in the 1988 bombing of Pan American flight 103 over Scotland that killed 270 persons. The U.S. government came just short of blaming Qaddafi for the bombing. The indictments further damaged relations between Libya and the United States and Britain and threatened the improving relations with other European nations.

KENNETH J. PERKINS
University of South Carolina

LIBYA • Information Highlights

Official Name: Socialist People's Libyan Arab Jamahiriya ("state of the masses").
Location: North Africa.
Area: 679,359 sq mi (1 759 540 km^2).
Population (mid-1991 est.): 4,400,000.
Chief Cities (1984 census): Tripoli, the capital, 990,697; Benghazi, 435,886.
Government: *Head of state,* Muammar el-Qaddafi (took office 1969). *Legislature*—General People's Congress (met initially Nov. 1976).
Monetary Unit: Dinar (0.288 dinar equals U.S. $1, July 1991).
Gross National Product (1988 est. U.S.$): $20,000,-000,000.
Foreign Trade (1988 est. U.S.$): *Imports,* $5,879,-000,000; *exports,* $6,683,000,000.

LITERATURE

Overview

Political action and artistic accomplishment, potent companions in the contemporary literary world, again were spotlighted in 1991 with the news that Nadine Gordimer had won the Nobel Prize in literature. Over the course of her long writing career, this white South African woman, a political activist and longtime foe of apartheid, saw several of her novels banned in her homeland. While certain apartheid restrictions recently have been lifted in South Africa, Gordimer remains a controversial figure there for her novels exploring the conflicts and contradictions of a racist society and her political commitment to the African National Congress. Upon hearing of her prestigious award, she indicated that the news was her second great thrill of recent years—her first being Nelson Mandela's release from prison in 1990. The Swedish Academy, conferring the literary prize on a woman for the first time in 25 years and only the seventh time in its history, referred to her as, through her writing, "of very great benefit to humanity." Soon after the announcement of the award, *Jump and Other Stories*, Gordimer's latest offering, was published.

© Marilyn K. Yee/NYT Pictures

South African writer Nadine Gordimer, 67, whose body of work speaks to the consequences of apartheid, was awarded the Nobel Prize in literature in 1991.

Political and/or religious issues also were at the heart of the continuing consequences originating from the late Ayatollah Khomeini's 1989 pronouncement of death upon Salman Rushdie, the author of *The Satanic Verses* (first published in Britain in 1988). In 1991 the Japanese translator of the novel was stabbed fatally; the Italian translator had been stabbed only days before, but survived the attack. The Indian-born British author accused by Khomeini of blasphemy against the Islamic faith remained under a threat of death even though Khomeini died in 1989.

Literary Controversy. The conflict between a biographer's need for information about a subject and a doctor's duty to provide confidentiality surrounded the 1991 publication of *Anne Sexton: A Biography*. In what was the first known time that a biography of a major American figure relied on material from psychiatric sessions, the biographer Diane Wood Middlebrook was given access to medical records and tapes of therapy sessions between the poet, who committed suicide in 1974, and Dr. Martin Orne. Although Orne, who treated Sexton between 1956 and 1964, acted with the permission of Sexton's older daughter and literary executor, an uproar ensued in literary and psychiatric circles. Many in the field of psychiatry felt that the doctor had committed a breach of medical ethics. Others took a more positive view, suggesting that Sexton, a so-called confessional poet who herself drew heavily on very personal autobiographical material, would have approved.

"Scarlett." Creating a sensation of another sort was *Scarlett*, the long-awaited sequel to *Gone with the Wind*, Margaret Mitchell's 1936 epic romance of the Old South. Written by Alexandra Ripley, who was chosen to write the book after a nationwide contest, *Scarlett* soared quickly to the top of the best-seller list despite a considerable drubbing by many critics. One million copies of the book were in stores within about a week, and personnel at Warner Books, which paid $4.94 million for the rights to the sequel, estimated that 500,000 were sold during the same period. The sequel, which sold ten times as many copies as the number two best-seller, also provided brisk sales for *Gone with the Wind*.

U.S. Poet Laureate. Joseph Brodsky, an emigrant from the Soviet Union and the winner of the 1987 Nobel Prize in literature, was appointed in May 1991 to be the fifth poet laureate of the United States, effective in September. The poet, who came to the United States in 1972 after being deprived of his Soviet citizenship and forced into exile, was appointed to the post by James H. Billington, librarian of Congress. Brodsky, who is now a U.S. citizen, has taught at several prestigious American universities and colleges. He has been at Mount Holyoke College in Massachusetts since 1981.

SAUNDRA FRANCE

American Literature

Although it is said that nobody reads anymore, books attracted significant media attention in 1991. The most spectacular if not the most literary event was the publication of Alexandra Ripley's *Scarlett: The Sequel to Margaret Mitchell's "Gone With The Wind."* In addition to large book sales, it was purchased by television for $8 million.

The Novel. After the success of his first novel *The Naked and the Dead* (1948), Norman Mailer predicted that he would write a novel that would be great in concept and scale. Although he did memorable reportage, as in *Armies of the Night* (1968), and produced several novels, most recently *Ancient Evenings* (1983), Mailer's later fiction was not as acclaimed as his first novel. *Harlot's Ghost,* a more-than-1,300-page account of a U.S. secret agent's life and an imaginary history of the Central Intelligence Agency, was proclaimed in 1991 as his major work. With fine writing and powerful insights into the American psyche and the twists and turns of U.S. policies, the book, nevertheless, probably would remain more admired for its ambition than its achievement.

Harold Brodkey was another writer at the center of a long-awaited event, the publication of his novel *The Runaway Soul.* Since the publication of his first story collection, *First Love and Other Sorrows* (1958), those who admire his densely evocative prose have anticipated a major novel. *The Runaway Soul,* a coming-of-age story focusing on a young man from the Midwest, proved to be deeply internalized and full of endless digressions.

Don DeLillo's *Mao II* proved once more that he is a prescient observer of society. He seemed to be writing about such artists as Mailer, Brodkey, or J. D. Salinger as he centered on a reclusive, worshipped writer who has not produced a book in so long that its absence promises to have greater impact than its presence.

The acceptance of the "graphic novel"—a narrative told in words and pictures in the manner of the traditional comic book—as a serious literary form was signaled by the *New York Times Book Review*'s front-page review of Art Spiegelman's *Maus: A Survivor's Tale II: And Here My Troubles Began.* With the humans often represented by mice, cats, and other animals, it shows the Spiegelman family in the United States, the parents haunted by their World War II experience in Nazi concentration camps. Their story began in *Maus: A Survivor's Tale* (1986).

American literature inevitably was becoming more international in scope, but the themes

Among the notable novels of 1991 were "A Dangerous Woman," the second novel of Mary McGarry Morris, about an emotionally disturbed young woman struggling against her circumstances, and "Harlot's Ghost" (above), a long-awaited major work by Norman Mailer.

Jane Smiley (right), *in her provocative novel "A Thousand Acres," evokes comparisons to the classic tragedy of King Lear. Set in Iowa, the book revolves around the perils of family and property as a father divides his land among his daughters, leaving the youngest without a share.*

© Stephen Mortensen

were not so much about delineating customs as about the psychological effects of cultural conflict. Louis Begley's *Wartime Lies* tells of a Polish Jewish boy and his older sister trying to survive the Nazi occupation during World War II. Mark Helprin's *A Soldier of the Great War* recounts World War I, but not, as might be expected, the U.S. experience. Helprin focuses on a philosophical Italian who fought the Austro-Hungarians in northern Italy.

America's cultural diversity also was expressed vigorously. Amy Tan's great success with her story of the conflict of generations in Chinese families, *The Joy Luck Club* (1989), was followed in 1991 by *The Kitchen God's Wife,* in which a mother reveals the secrets of her life in China to her daughter. Gish Jen's *Typical American* tells of a Chinese couple learning, for better or worse, American values. Frank Chin's *Donald Duk* describes a young boy from San Francisco, embarrassed by his Chinese heritage, who in his dreams finds himself working on the Central Pacific railroad in 1869. Yvonne Sapia's *Valentino's Hair* focuses on a Puerto Rican barber in New York whose life was changed forever by a fleeting, dramatic contact with Rudolph Valentino. Paule Marshall's *Daughters* travels back and forth between a Caribbean island and the United States to delineate two women's struggles for meaningful social and political action. John Sayles' *Los Gusanos* recreates the Cuban community in Miami, wrestling with its past and future.

Male characters have been said to dominate serious U.S. fiction; that clearly was no longer true. Whitney Otto's *How to Make an American Quilt,* one of the most successful first novels of the year, takes the metaphor of a traditional American craft to show the interrelated lives of a California women's quilting circle. Alice Adams' *Caroline's Daughters* shows how a mother and her three grown daughters have fashioned very different lives. Even more striking, male novelists were turning to women as protagonists. Ron Hansen's *Mariette in Ecstasy* tells of a woman's intense and problematic search for God. Bret Lott's *Jewel* is about a mother's unfailing devotion to her retarded daughter. Norman Rush's *Mating* is presented from the point of view of a woman student in Africa finding love with a male anthropologist who runs a utopian community for women.

Although realism was the dominant mode in American literature, the philosophical novel still lived. Robert Pirsig in *Lila: An Inquiry into Morals* continued the quest for truths begun in his *Zen and the Art of Motorcycle Maintenance* (1974). Richard Powers' *The Gold Bug Variations* weaves a romantic plot and brilliant imagery into a dense matrix of scientific ideas. John Barth's *The Last Voyage of Somebody the Sailor* is a complex disquisition on the nature of fiction and the irreality of realism. Evan S. Connell's *The Alchymist's Journal* explores the boundaries between science and magic.

Short Stories. Short-story writers explored the same themes that captured U.S. novelists: America's problematic relationship to the rest of the world, its own diverse population, its stormy domestic landscape, and the ironies of trying to understand the world through fiction. Maria Thomas' *African Visas* shows Americans confronting Africa and often achieving unexpected or painful insights into themselves. Sandra Cisneros' *Woman Hollering Creek and Other Stories* depicts the lives of Mexican-American women who are trapped by race, language, and gender. Michael Chabon's *A Model World* has a series of stories about a boy watching his family disintegrate, and Rick DeMarinis' *The Voice of America* delves into the issue of fidelity. Padgett Powell's *Typical* wrestles with the impossibility of storytelling.

Poetry. Dana Gioia's essay, "Can Poetry Matter?," published in *Atlantic Monthly,* attacked the state of American poetry on the

AMERICAN LITERATURE: MAJOR WORKS | 1991

NOVELS

Adams, Alice, *Caroline's Daughters*
Banks, Russell, *The Sweet Hereafter*
Barth, John, *The Last Voyage of Somebody the Sailor*
Begley, Louis, *Wartime Lies*
Brodkey, Harold, *The Runaway Soul*
Brown, Larry, *Joe*
Bruccoli, Matthew J., ed., *Zelda Fitzgerald: The Collected Writings*
Busch, Frederick, *Closing Arguments*
Canin, Ethan, *Blue River*
Chin, Frank, *Donald Duk*
Connell, Evan S., *The Alchymist's Journal*
Coover, Robert, *Pinocchio in Venice*
DeLillo, Don, *Mao II*
Dexter, Pete, *Brotherly Love*
Dworkin, Andrea, *Mercy*
Edgerton, Clyde, *Killer Diller*
Elkin, Stanley, *The MacGuffin*
Gaitskill, Mary, *Two Girls, Fat and Thin*
Godwin, Gail, *Father Melancholy's Daughter*
Hansen, Ron, *Mariette in Ecstasy*
Helprin, Mark, *A Soldier of the Great War*
Hiaasen, Carl, *Native Tongue*
Humphreys, Josephine, *The Fireman's Fair*
Jen, Gish, *Typical American*
Johnson, Denis, *Resuscitation of a Hanged Man*
Keillor, Garrison, *WLT: A Radio Romance*
Lee, Gus, *China Boy*
Leonard, Elmore, *Maximum Bob*
Lish, Gordon, *My Romance*
Lott, Bret, *Jewel*
Mailer, Norman, *Harlot's Ghost*
Markus, Julia, *A Change of Luck*
Marshall, Paule, *Daughters*
Morris, Mary McGarry, *A Dangerous Woman*
Oates, Joyce Carol, *The Rise of Life on Earth*
Otto, Whitney, *How to Make an American Quilt*
Pirsig, Robert, *Lila: An Inquiry into Morals*
Porter, Connie, *All Bright Court*
Portis, Charles, *Gringos*
Powers, Richard, *The Gold Bug Variations*
Quindlen, Anna, *Object Lessons*
Ripley, Alexandra, *Scarlett: The Sequel to Margaret Mitchell's "Gone With The Wind"*
Rush, Norman, *Mating*
Sapia, Yvonne, *Valentino's Hair*
Sayles, John, *Los Gusanos*
See, Carolyn, *Making History*
Shawn, Wallace, *The Fever*
Singer, Isaac Bashevis, *Scum*
Smiley, Jane, *A Thousand Acres*
Spiegelman, Art, *Maus: A Survivor's Tale II: And Here My Troubles Began*
Tan, Amy, *The Kitchen God's Wife*
Tyler, Anne, *Saint Maybe*
Wilcox, James, *Polite Sex*

SHORT STORIES

Abbott, Lee K., *Living After Midnight*
Abel, Robert, *Ghost Traps*
Alvarez, Julia, *How the Garcia Girls Lost Their Accents*
Beattie, Ann, *What Was Mine: Stories*
Chabon, Michael, *A Model World: And Other Stories*
Chappell, Fred, *More Shapes Than One*
Cisneros, Sandra, *Woman Hollering Creek: And Other Stories*
DeMarinis, Rick, *The Voice of America*
Dufresne, John, *The Way That Water Enters Stone*
Gurganus, Allan, *White People*
Louie, David Wong, *Pangs of Love: Stories*
Oates, Joyce Carol, *Heat: And Other Stories*
Powell, Padgett, *Typical*
Price, Reynolds, *The Foreseeable Future*
Smith, Charlie, *Crystal River*
Thomas, Maria, *African Visas*
Wiggins, Marianne, *Bet They'll Miss Us When We're Gone*

POETRY

Ackerman, Diane, *Jaguar of Sweet Laughter*
Ashbery, John, *Flow Chart*
Balaban, John, *Words For My Daughter*
Codrescu, Andrei, *Belligerence*
Creeley, Robert, *Selected Poems*
Dunn, Stephen, *Landscape at the End of the Century: Poems*
Goldbarth, Albert, *Heaven and Earth, a Cosmology: Poems by Albert Goldbarth*
Grossman, Albert, *The Ether Dome*
Levine, Philip, *What Work Is*
Macdonald, Cynthia, *Living Wills: New and Selected Poems*
McGrath, Thomas, *Death Song*, edited by Sam Hamill
Miller, Vassar, *If I Had Wheels or Love: Collected Poems of Vassar Miller*
Moss, Thylias, *Rainbow Remnants in Rock Bottom Ghetto Sky: Poems*
Terranova, Elaine, *The Cult of the Right Hand*
Walker, Alice, *Her Blue Body Everything We Know: Earthling Poems 1965–1990 Complete*

CULTURE AND CRITICISM

Ackerman, Diane, *The Moon by Whale Light and Other Adventures Among Bats, Penguins, Crocodilians, and Whales*
Dershowitz, Alan, *Chutzpah*
Dubus, Andre, *Broken Vessels*
Faludi, Susan, *Backlash: The Undeclared War Against American Women*
Fiedler, Leslie, *Fiedler on the Roof: Essays on Literature and Jewish Identity*
Fox-Genovese, Elizabeth, *Feminism Without Illusions: A Critique of Individualism*
Garreau, Joel, *Edge City: Life on the New Frontier*
Goldman, Ari L., *The Search for God at Harvard*
Gordon, Mary, *Good Boys and Dead Girls: And Other Essays*
Gould, Stephen Jay, *Bully for Brontosaurus*
Grumbach, Doris, *Coming Into the End Zone*
Heat-Moon, William Least, *Prairyerth (A Deep Map)*
Kozol, Jonathan, *Savage Inequalities: Children in America's Schools*
Lasch, Christopher, *The True and Only Heaven: Progress and Its Critics*
Lehman, David, *Signs of the Times: Deconstruction and the Fall of Paul de Man*
Lesser, Wendy, *His Other Half: Men Looking at Women Through Art*
Lewis, Michael, *The Money Culture*
Matthiessen, Peter, *African Silences*
Morris, David B., *The Culture of Pain*
Percy, Walker, *Signposts in a Strange Land*
Stewart, James B., *Den of Thieves*

HISTORY AND BIOGRAPHY

Baker, Liva, *The Justice From Beacon Hill: The Life and Times of Oliver Wendell Holmes*
Boyd, Brian, *Vladimir Nabokov: The American Years*
Campbell, James, *Talking at the Gates: A Life of James Baldwin*
Cherkovski, Neeli, *Hank: The Life of Charles Bukowski*
Clayton, Bruce, *W. J. Cash*
Cott, Jonathan, *Wandering Ghost: The Odyssey of Lafcadio Hearn*
Dallek, Robert, *Lone Star Rising: Lyndon Johnson and His Times, 1908–1960*
Eisler, Benita, *O'Keeffe and Stieglitz: An American Romance*
Ferguson, Robert, *Henry Miller*
Gentry, Curt, *J. Edgar Hoover: The Man and His Secrets*
Gottlieb, Robert, ed., *The Journals of John Cheever*
Graham, Martha, *Blood Memory*
Hamalian, Linda, *The Source Behind the San Francisco Renaissance: A Life of Kenneth Rexroth*
Ione, Carole, *Pride of Family: Four Generations of American Women of Color*
Johnson, Haynes, *Sleepwalking Through History: America in the Reagan Years*
Kreyling, Michael, *Author and Agent: Eudora Welty and Diarmuid Russell*
Lax, Eric, *Woody Allen*
Lewis, Anthony, *Make No Law: The Sullivan Case and the First Amendment*
Lewis, R. W. B., *The Jameses: A Family Narrative*
McFeely, William, *Frederick Douglass*
McPherson, James M., *Abraham Lincoln and the Second American Revolution*
Middlebrook, Diane Wood, *Anne Sexton*
Miller, Ruth, *Saul Bellow: A Biography of the Imagination*
Niven, Penelope, *Carl Sandburg: A Biography*
Pyron, Darden Asbury, *Southern Daughter: The Life of Margaret Mitchell*
Remini, Robert V., *Henry Clay: Statesman for the Union*
Roth, Philip, *Patrimony*
Schama, Simon, *Dead Certainties (Unwarranted Speculations)*
Toland, John, *In Mortal Combat: Korea, 1950–1953*
Watson, Steven, *Strange Bedfellows: The First American Avant-Garde*

grounds that there were too many poets, poetry journals, poetry presses, and poetry readings, which was blamed largely on English departments in colleges and universities. It was a curious argument since the widespread activity that might be seen as a sign of health was interpreted as a symptom of sickness. Although U.S. poetry today is almost entirely a noncommercial art form, it continues to thrive.

Enormous diversity in style and subject could be found in such volumes as John Ashbery's intellectually demanding *Flow Chart,* Robert Creeley's minimalist *Selected Poems,* Philip Levine's humane *What Work Is,* and Alice Walker's mystical *Her Blue Body Everything We Know: Earthling Poems 1965-1990 Complete.*

Works by younger writers, such as Thylias Moss' *Rainbow Remnants in Rock Bottom Ghetto Sky: Poems,* showed poetry successfully expressing intense political concern. Diane Ackerman, already one of the finest U.S. writers of nonfiction (*A Natural History of the Senses,* 1990, and *The Moon by Whale Light,* 1991), had her important poetry collection, *Jaguar of Sweet Laughter,* published during the year.

Culture and Criticism. The woes of Wall Street inspired a number of books. James B. Stewart's *Den of Thieves* and Michael Lewis' *The Money Culture* stood out, not only for recounting the rise and fall of Michael Milken and his ilk, but for illuminating how these financial debacles and misadventures reflected the state of our society.

The second generation of feminism examined its progress and setbacks. Susan Faludi's *Backlash: The Undeclared War Against American Women* argues that advertising, mass media, journalism, and politics—threatened by women's progress—have combined to urge women to return to their traditional subservient roles. Elizabeth Fox-Genovese's thoughtful *Feminism Without Illusions* looks at feminism itself, urging a more complex view of the nature of individual and community responsibility. Wendy Lesser's *His Other Half* shows how male artists find their female selves through their painting of women.

The real subject of a book is sometimes the personality of the writer. Doris Grumbach's *Coming Into the End Zone* is a meditation on old age in which she examines her own life. Philip Roth's *Patrimony* explores his relationship to his father. Alan Dershowitz' *Chutzpah* uses himself as the chief point of reference to discuss the position of Jews in America. William Least Heat-Moon's *Prairyerth (A Deep Map)* celebrates life in a single county in Kansas, but raises speculation on the writer's own absorption in this project. No matter what Leslie Fiedler's subjects are in *Fiedler on the Roof: Essays on Literature and Jewish Identity,* the central force is his iconoclastic personality.

Literary criticism was rocked profoundly during the 1970s and 1980s by a group of critics known as deconstructionists. Their radical skepticism about values, knowledge, and language created fierce controversy. David Lehman's *Signs of the Times: Deconstruction and the Fall of Paul de Man* traces the history of the movement and of a leading exponent in America who concealed his Nazi past.

Jonathan Kozol's *Savage Inequalities: Children in America's Schools* argues persuasively that some U.S. school systems had been neglected so massively that it amounted to a virtual abandonment of the historic commitment to public education.

History and Biography. Darden Asbury Pyron's *Southern Daughter: The Life of Margaret Mitchell* not only was well coordinated with the renewed interest in the author of *Gone With the Wind,* but also is a deeply researched, thoughtful book with many insights into Mitchell and Southern intellectual and bohemian life in the 1930s. Brian Boyd's *Vladimir Nabokov: The American Years* is a brilliant and insightful biography of one of the great writers of the 20th century, continuing the work Boyd began in *Vladimir Nabokov: The Russian Years* (1990). James Campbell's *Talking at the Gates: A Life of James Baldwin* shows a deep understanding of an important and complex literary figure. R. W. B. Lewis' *The Jameses: A Family Narrative* perceptively explores one of the most significant intellectual families of our culture.

Diane Wood Middlebrook's *Anne Sexton* precipitated a controversy over Middlebrook's use of intimate revelations supplied by the poet's psychiatrist for the candid biography. Robert Gottlieb's posthumous edition of *The Journals of John Cheever* also generated discussion on the appropriateness of publishing these private ruminations on Cheever's alcoholism, infidelity, and homosexuality.

JEROME STERN, *Florida State University*

Children's Literature

The children's-book field continued to mean big business for publishers in 1991. Established publishing houses expanded their lines and instituted new imprints, and small presses appeared on the scene in ever-increasing numbers. Prevalent in 1991 were nonfiction series books covering every topic imaginable, with a particular emphasis on the environment.

The year 1991 was also one in which many well-known names in children's literature passed away. Most notable was Theodor Geisel, Dr. Seuss (*see* OBITUARIES); among others were award-winning illustrator Margot Tomes, historical novelist Patricia Beatty, and Newbery Medal winner Meindert DeJong.

The year's Newbery Medal was awarded to Jerry Spinelli for his *Maniac Magee*. The Caldecott Medal went to David Macaulay's *Black and White,* an innovative picture book.

Christopher Columbus Books. With the quincentenary of Christopher Columbus' arrival in the Americas looming large, books about the explorer flooded in. One of the most notable was Peter Sis' *Follow the Dream: The Story of Christopher Columbus,* a picture book briefly describing the life of Columbus and illuminating it with Renaissance-style paintings, engravings, and maps. Several fiction books purported to describe life on the voyage as seen through the eyes of young boys. Two have the same title, *I Sailed With Columbus;* one was by Susan D. Martin, the other by Miriam Schlein. Another similarly themed book is Pam Conrad's *I, Pedro*.

Picture Books. The explosion in children's publishing was most evident in the picture-book field, where new authors and illustrators vied for attention with more established writers and artists. Among the best books by favorite authors and illustrators were Cynthia Rylant and Barry Moser's moving collaboration, *Appalachia,* Eric Carle's colorful collage, *Dragons, Dragons, and other Creatures,* and Molly Bang's simple ode to the beach, *Yellow Ball.* Among emerging talents establishing themselves during 1991 were illustrator Caroline Binch with her book about an imaginative black girl, *Amazing Grace,* and Jonathan Allen drawing his hilarious *Mucky Moose*.

Several of the year's best picture books were stories from or about Africa: *When Africa Was Home,* a young boy's wistful look back at the time he spent in Africa; Rachel Isadora's *At the Crossroads,* the moving story of South African children waiting for their fathers, who have been gone for months working in the mines; Tololwa M. Mollel's *The Orphan Boy,* a Masai story; and a tale of the Nkundo of Zaire, *Traveling to Tondo* by Verna Aardema.

Middle-Grade Books. Middle-grade fiction had a rather undistinguished year. The high spots were provided by established authors. Lois Lowry offered another book in her popular Anastasia series, *Anastasia at This Address,* while Zilpha Keatley Snyder turned to fantasy in *Song of the Gargoyle*.

Nonfiction played a predominant role, especially in the area of biography. *The Last Princess,* written by Fay Stanley and illustrated by her daughter, Diane, told the story of Princess Ka'iulani of Hawaii. Jean Fritz looked at the life of the 26th U.S. president in *Bully for You, Teddy Roosevelt!*

Junior High and Young Adult. The young-adult genre, though never very profitable for publishers, won praise as always for its wide-ranging subject matter and high-quality writing. Paul Fleischman's *The Borning Room,* a sophisticated historical novel, and Lloyd Alexander's Chinese fantasy, *The Remarkable*

Photograph by Carol Palmer.
Book jacket by Jerry Spinelli.
Reprinted by permission of Little, Brown and Co.

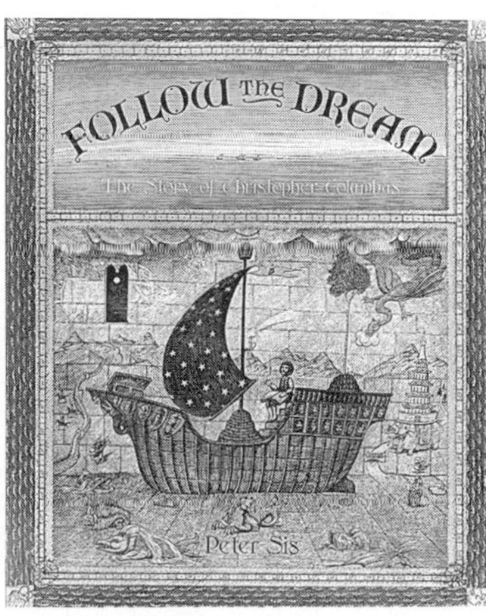

SELECTED BOOKS FOR CHILDREN

Picture Books
Bunting, Eve. *Fly Away Home*
Cole, Brock. *Alpha and the Dirty Baby*
Dorros, Arthur. *Abuela*
Ehlert, Lois. *Red Leaf, Yellow Leaf*
Fisher, Leonard Everett. *Cyclops*
Fleming, Denise. *In the Tall, Tall Grass*
Lear, Edward and Brett, Jan. *The Owl and the Pussycat*
McDonald, Megan. *The Potato Man*
McLerran, Alice. *Roxaboxen*
Wood, Audrey and Don. *Piggies*
Yorinks, Arthur. *Christmas in July*

The Middle Grades
Anno, Mitsumasa. *Anno's Math Games III*
Burleigh, Robert. *Flight*
Conrad, Pam. *Prairie Visions*
Fenner, Carol. *Randall's Wall*
Fox, Paula. *Monkey Island*
Giblin, James Cross. *The Truth about Unicorns*
Hahn, Mary Downing. *Step on the Cracks*
Hurwitz, Johanna. *"E" is for Elisa*
Kesey, Ken. *The Sea Lion*
Leverich, Kathleen. *Best Enemies Again*
Lynn, Joseph. *A Wave in her Pocket: Stories from Trinidad*
MacLachlan, Patricia. *Journey*
Marshall, James. *Rats on the Roof: And Other Stories*
Martin, James. *Chameleons: Dragons in the Trees*
Prelutsky, Jack. *For Laughing Out Loud: Poems to Tickle your Funnybones*
Shreve, Susan. *The Gift of the Girl Who Couldn't Hear*
Soto, Gary. *Taking Sides*

Junior High
Avi. *Nothing but the Truth: A Documentary Novel*
Beatty, Patricia. *Jayhawker*
Blumberg, Rhoda. *The Remarkable Voyages of Captain Cook*
Cleary, Beverly. *Strider*
Dana, Barbara. *Young Joan*
Ferguson, Kitty. *Stephen Hawking*
Kerr, M.E. *Fell Down*
Orlev, Uri. *The Man from the Other Side*
Paterson, Katherine. *Lyddie*
Peck, Richard. *Unfinished Portrait of Jessica*

Journey of Prince Jen, were among the well-crafted novels that invited readers into another world. *Lizard,* by newcomer Dennis Covington, tells the story of a bright, deformed boy who escapes a home for mentally handicapped boys to start a life in theater. A raucous read was *Agnes the Sheep* by William Taylor.

ILENE COOPER
Editor, Children's Books, "The Booklist"

Canadian Literature: English

Increased taxes, the recession, and countrywide postal and civil-service strikes harassed Canadian publishers in 1991. However, some books of exceptional merit appeared.

Nonfiction. Much discussion was caused by *Deconfederation: Canada Without Quebec,* by David Bercuson and Barry Cooper. The book claims that the problems caused by Quebec wanting special status can end only in that province leaving Canada and becoming a new country. Other 1991 books about Canada's relations with Quebec are *Confederation in Crisis,* edited by Robert Young; *Debating Canada's Future: Views From the Left,* edited by Simon Rosenblum and Peter Findlay; and *Toolkits and Building Blocks: Constructing a New Canada,* edited by Richard Simeon and Mary Janigan.

Former publisher Mel Hurtig of Alberta claimed much attention with *The Betrayal of Canada,* stating that the free-trade agreement with the United States was a disaster for Canada. Hurtig criticizes Prime Minister Brian Mulroney's key part in promoting the pact.

Of interest was *Mulroney: The Politics of Ambition,* by John Sawatsky, about the early years of Canada's Conservative prime minister. Lengthily researched, it claims Mulroney was a womanizer and heavy drinker until he married his wife Mila. Another politically themed book was *"I'll Be With You In a Minute, Mr. Ambassador": The Education of a Canadian Diplomat in Washington* by Allan Gotlieb, for years Canadian ambassador to the United States.

Works dealing with both recent and past history were numerous. Included was Peter C. Newman's *Merchant Princes,* the third volume of his history of the Hudson's Bay Company. *Fatal Cruise: The Trial of Robert Frisbee,* by William Deverell, details the sensational trial of Frisbee for murdering his rich employer.

Among biographies and memoirs, several were notable. Poet Dorothy Livesay, 81 years old, with 25 books of poetry and prose behind her, contributed *Journey with My Selves: A Memoir, 1909–1963. To Canada with Love and*

Canadian writer and former "Maclean's" magazine editor Peter Newman finished his "Merchant Princes," the third volume of his history of the Hudson's Bay Company, in 1991.
© Brian Willer

Some Misgivings, edited by Vaughn Palmer, collects Bruce Hutchison's best writing. Hutchison, 90, is considered the dean of Canadian journalists. In *Webster: An Autobiography,* celebrated TV and radio reporter Jack Webster speaks frankly about the tragedy in his life. Rosemary Sullivan's *By Heart: Elizabeth Smart, a Life* tells how the daughter of a rich Ottawa family rebelled by going to England and marrying Herge Barker, an English poet. And David Macfarlane's *The Danger Tree: Memory, War and the Search for a Family's Past* is a Newfoundland family memoir.

Susan Goldenberg's *Global Pursuits* examines the global strategies of 100 big and small businesses in Canada. And Margaret Visser offered *The Rituals of Dinner: The Origin, Evolution, Eccentricities and Meaning of Table Manners.*

Poetry. Patrick Lane's *Mortal Remains* is about the father-son relationship. *Keep the Candle Burning Bright* presents the last poems by the late Bronwen Wallace. Dorothy Roberts' seventh volume, *In The Flight of Stars,* is about age and mortality.

Sudden Miracles, by Eight Women Poets was edited by Rhea Tregobov and includes works by Ann Michaels, Roo Borson, and Bronwen Wallace. Don McKay's seventh work was *Night Field,* and Margaret Avison offered *Selected Poems.* In *The Words The Voice The Text: The Life of a Writer,* Anne Szumigalski illustrates the processes that created her previous books of poetry.

Fiction. In the celebrated Robertson Davies' tenth novel, *Murther & Walking Spirits,* the main character is killed by his wife's lover on the first page. The rest of the book shows how, as a spirit, this main character seeks both vengeance and understanding.

Daniel Richler's *Kicking Tomorrow* is about troubled teens in Montreal's wealthy Westmount. Ottawa writer Clive Doucet's *The Gospel According to Mary Magdalene* has two present-day Canadian women visiting Provence, France, where the original Mary Magdalene is said to have lived for many years and is buried.

Short stories were numerous. *Wilderness Tips,* Margaret Atwood's 26th book, gave additional reason why she is published in 25 countries. Douglas Oliver's *A Guide to Animal Behaviour* presents a gallery of eccentric characters. *Hockey Night in Canada and Other Stories,* by Diane Schoemperlan, is 14 stories of urban life. *The Bridge River Anthology: Stories from Saskatoon,* edited by Susan Gingell, is a collection of stories by past or present teachers in the University of Saskatchewan's English department. *Canadian Short Stories,* the annual selection by Robert Weaver, includes tales by Alice Munro and Margaret Atwood.

DAVID SAVAGE, *Free-lance Writer*

English Literature

British fiction in 1991 tended toward the historical and the biographical. Although some novelists wrote experimental fiction—for example, Martin Amis with *Time's Arrow,* others published what debatably has been termed genre fiction—John Le Carré, for instance, who followed the acclaimed *The Russia House* (1989) with *The Secret Pilgrim,* in which his incomparable George Smiley appears again.

Because of the romance and realities of the past, from isles to empire, the historical in Britain has remained for writers a rich and varied lode to mine. Thus India of almost any period and focus seems ever to fascinate, as in Ian Buruma's *Playing the Game,* in which the narrator seeks to research the life of K. S. Ranjitsinhji (Ranji), the great Indian cricketer of the 1890s. In yet another reminder of the British Raj, David Dabydeen wrote in his compelling first novel, *The Intended,* of a Hindu boy from Guyana transported at the age of 10 to the grim realities of south London.

In a social-realistic vein were Thomas Healy's short novel *It Might Have Been Jerusalem,* which grimly depicts a Glasgow of the 1950s in which its characters all fatefully suffer; and Michael Curtain's *The Plastic Tomato Cutter,* a novel ambitiously narrated in voices of alternative generations that depicts social change in an Irish town. A collection of stories—*The Burn,* and one of plays—*Haride and Baird and Other Plays,* by the talented Scottish writer James Kelman also were well-received.

Not necessarily more comforting was A. N. Wilson's third volume of his Lampitt saga, *Daughters of Albion,* which continues his serial treatment of English social life. Lawrence Norfolk offered a tangled and clever historical novel, *Lembriere's Dictionary,* set in 1788, and admirers of Isabel Colegate's novels of keen observation were treated to *The Summer of the Royal Visit,* another chronicle of the Edwardian years. Joan Aiken intriguingly blended the historical and fictional in her novel *The Haunting of the Lamb House.* The house was once the abode of Henry James who, with Edith Wharton, William James, and Hugh Walpole, figures prominently in the novel. Pat Barker's fifth novel, *Regeneration,* follows an individual poet's reactions to the Great War (World War I) and includes insights into the works of Robert Graves, Siegfried Sassoon, and Wilfred Owen.

Not forgotten among all these ventures was the old and respected talent of story telling. Angela Carter's *Wise Children,* her first novel in seven years, added luster to her reputation as a highly regarded writer of fiction. And a collection of Audrey Lilian Barker's short stories written over a 40-year period entitled *Any Excuse for a Party: Collected Stories* was published during the year.

© Douglas Brother

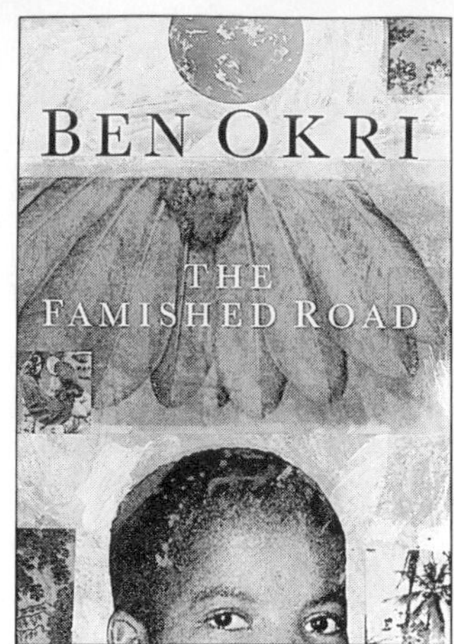

Nigerian writer Ben Okri, who now lives in London, was awarded the British Booker Prize in 1991 for "The Famished Road." The prize carried a cash award of $34,350.

Booker Prize nominees in 1991 were William Trevor for "Reading Turgenev" from *Two Lives;* Martin Amis for *Time's Arrow;* Roddy Doyle for *The Van;* Rohinton Mistry for *Such a Long Journey;* Timothy Mo for *The Redundancy of Courage;* and the Booker Prize winner, Nigerian writer Ben Okri for *The Famished Road*.

Nonfiction. The year saw the publication of a rich assortment of nonfiction. Related to the intense interest in the Middle East flamed by the Persian Gulf war were Daniel Yergin's *The Prize: The Epic Quest for Oil, Money and Power,* which provided a sweeping historical analysis of the oil industry; and Albert Hourani's *A History of the Arab Peoples*. In a lengthy (more than 1,000 pages) and detailed account, Correlli Barnett's *Engage the Enemy More Closely: The Royal Navy in the Second World War* offers vivid reading in a strong narrative with keen analysis that is supported by maps and photographs. Also on the subject of the British in World War II was Angus Calder's examination of the civilian war experience, *The Myth of the Blitz*.

In the field of letters, volume three of *The Letters of Alfred Lord Tennyson, 1871-1892,* edited by Cecil Y. Lang and Edgar F. Shannon, Jr., was published despite that poet's expressed distaste for such things. Also, the *Memoirs* of Kingsley Amis, consisting of essays and sketches, made for a good read. Leading in the crowded field of biographies in 1991 was Michael Holroyd's *Bernard Shaw, Volume Three: The Lure of Fantasy, 1918–1950,* which appeared to the delight of Shaw enthusiasts. Volume one of Nicholas Boyle's detailed and unified biographical study, *Goethe: The Poet and the Age,* subtitled *The Poetry of Desire (1749-1790),* did much to bring that genius into needed perspective in the English-speaking world. Also of interest was *Darwin,* a lengthy biography by Adrian Desmond and James Moore.

Finally, *The Making of "The Golden Bough": The Origins and Growth of an Argument,* by Robert Frazer, celebrated the centenary of the publication of Sir James Frazer's great work. And J. F. Took's study *Dante: Lyric Poet and Philosopher, An Introduction to the Minor Works* offers a fuller appreciation of the great Italian poet.

Poetry. That poetry continued to be published in such variety suggested that the insights, encapsulated realities, or simply the sheer delight in the poet's gifts continued to have appeal. Christopher Logue, who worked at renditions of Homer's *Iliad* for some 30 years although he knew no Greek, saw his *Kings* published in 1991. The volume proved an energetic and bold departure in translation, reminiscent of the kind done by Robert Lowell in his *Imitations* (1961). Quite a different treatment of the Greek poet was Derek Walcott's *Omeros* (1990), which aimed more at being a modern epic. Set in Walcott's native Caribbean, the work was lively with echoes of Homer, whose name in Greek provides the title.

The Scottish poets D. M. Black and Norman MacCraig both had volumes published during the year. Black's *Collected Poems, 1964–1987* contains long narrative poems as well as lyrical works, while the 80-year-old MacCraig provided a major publishing event with his thick volume *Collected Poems*. Also of interest was *Seeing Things* by the Irish poet Seamus Heaney.

Other notable works of poetry that appeared during the year included Oliver Reynold's *The Oslo Tram;* Steve Griffiths' *Uncontrollable Fields;* and, after a lengthy silence, Michael Longley's *Gorse Fires*.

DONALD L. JENNERMANN
Indiana State University

World Literature*

In a year that saw startling change in the Soviet Union and continued democratization in the formerly socialist nations of Central Europe, it is surprising that the literature of the region did not register these changes, given the new freedom suddenly available in the arts. Part of the explanation lay in the fact that many prominent writers now were participating in the new governments in one capacity or another. For many of them, literature was not an indulgence they now could afford.

Eastern Europe. What notable new works did emerge in 1991 from the region came largely from the émigré community and from well-established authors. Aleksandr Solzhenitsyn's vision of a post-Communist Soviet Union in the book-length essay *Rebuilding Russia* correctly predicted the release of the non-Slavic republics from the union. Longtime survivor Yevgeny Yevtushenko picked the perfect moment to release his collected poems of 40 years in several editions worldwide, including English. Vladimir Kunin's 1987 best-seller *Intergirl,* depicting a deeply stratified society in a supposedly classless one, where even prostitutes have a strict hierarchy, made its debut in English. The recently emigrated Zinovy Zinik's exuberant novel *The Lord and the Gamekeeper* tracks several oddballs from a miserable Moscow flat to the posh estate of an eccentric Englishman. Nina Berberova's novella collection *The Tattered Cloak,* by contrast, derives from the Russian-expatriate Paris of the 1930s and 1940s. The late Sergei Dovlatov's last novel, *A Foreign Woman,* casts an entertaining light on an émigré yuppie's attempts to adapt to life in a Russian neighborhood in New York. And the multitalented Vassily Aksyonov weighed in with a collection of his plays, most of them satires with elements of the grotesque and the absurd.

From Poland came at least two important works: The novelist and unofficial jester-in-chief of Polish letters, Tadeusz Konwicki, published a provocative diary cum meditation called *New World Avenue and Vicinity,* in which he ruminates on the political and moral issues of the 1980s; and, perhaps more significant, the novel *Who Was David Weiser?* by Pawel Huelle is a tale about the disappearance of a gawky Jewish youth in late-1950s Danzig. From abroad came the familiar voices of Nobel laureate Czesław Miłosz, in the informal autobiographical work *Beginning with My Street,* and of Adam Zagajewski with a new verse collection in translation titled *Canvas.*

The two best-known Czech émigré writers, Milan Kundera and Josef Škvorecký, brought out new works in 1991. Kundera's *Immortality* is a complex but very readable novel of ideas that moves between a slightly rarefied present-day Paris and the late-18th-century Germany of Goethe and Bettina von Arnim. Škvorecký's 1972 novel *The Miracle Game,* making its debut in English, presents a satiric look at Czech life during the 1950s and 1960s and at the crushing of the Prague Spring (the 1968 campaign toward freedom).

The outstanding Albanian novelist Ismail Kadare brought out both the first French edition of his short 1963 novel *The Monster,* a modern-day reenactment of the Rape of Helen, and *The Early Spring,* an essay explaining his 1990 emigration to Paris. Yugoslavia's Milorad Pavic weighed in with another elegantly playful crossword puzzle of a novel, *Landscape Painted with Tea.*

German. The German-speaking countries enjoyed a good literary year in 1991. Martin Walser's *Defense of Childhood* offers the story of a former wunderkind's pure, obsessive love for his mother. Gabriele Wohmann brought out a new collection of her finely crafted short stories under the provocative title *He Sat in the Bus That Ran Over His Wife.* Günter Herburger's *Thuja* closed out a trilogy on the subject of reconciliation with the German past. Gerhard Köpf's novelette *There Is No Borges* recounts the case of a philologist who has retreated into the world of books. Friederike Mayröcker's novel *Still Life* presents a Beckettian exercise about an enclosed domestic world that is anything but the tranquil one promised by the title. The multitalented Hans Magnus Enzensberger brought out his first verse collection in more than a decade, and the late, great Austrian writer Thomas Bernhard's verse of nearly 40 years appeared in a collected edition, revealing his consistent excellence in that genre.

French. French literature also enjoyed a decent year in 1991. The academician Hervé Bazin's *School of Fathers* transmutes autobiography into fiction in an account of a youthful rebel of 1968 whose life is changed by fatherhood. Roger Knobelspiess' *Chicken Thief* is even more successful in its recasting of the author's checkered early life into a droll, ultimately disturbing picaresque narrative. The eminent poets Jean Cayrol and Yves Bonnefoy brought out new collections of verse titled *Viva Voce* and *The Snow's Beginning and End,* respectively. And Françoise Sagan's *False Fugitives* tells the story of a country outing gone madly awry for four French thirtysomething yuppies.

Other European Languages. Spain's Manuel Vázquez Montalbán was honored with his country's National Prize in Fiction for the novel *Galíndez,* about the ethics of distinct generations embedded in a story of the 1956 kidnapping and assassination of a Basque politician. The Argentine writer Luisa Valenzuela created in *Black Novel with Argentines* a tantalizing text that turns on itself and cannibalizes all the clues necessary to solve the murder mystery at the center of what little plot there is. *An Explanation of the Birds* by Portugal's António Lobo Antunes charts the tragicomic disintegration of a young leftist radical in revolt against his bourgeois family during the political chaos that followed the fall of the Salazar regime. And Greece's Nobel laureate, the poet Odysseus Elytis, presents in *Private Way* two prose meditations on poetry and painting, a relationship which has had a seminal effect on his own exquisite work in both fields.

Middle East. From Turkey came several fine new works: Orhan Pamuk's *White Castle,* the tale of a young 17th-century Italian scholar captured by Turkish pirates who later rises to a position of influence at court; and Nedim Gürsel's short-story collection *The Last Tram,* which explores multiple facets of émigré life. Güneli Gün uses the language of her adopted home, the United States, in *On the Road to Baghdad,* a "picaresque novel of magical adventures begged, borrowed, and stolen from *The 1001 Nights.*"

Egypt's Nobel winner Naguib Mahfouz saw two more of his earlier novels brought out in English translation: *The Search,* a powerful psychological portrait of a young criminal; and *Palace of Desire,* the second installment in his monumental *Cairo Trilogy*. Sonia Rami's *Antiquity Street* charts the changes of post-Nasser Egyptian life from the vantage point of an articulate, willful young woman. Israel's Amos Oz toys with the spy-thriller genre in *To Know a Woman,* a highly ironic account of a former Mossad agent's uneasy settling into the mundane domesticity of retirement in the Tel Aviv suburbs. And David Grossman saw his precocious first novel, *The Smile of the Lamb,* issued in numerous translations, including English.

Asia. A bounty of quality writing and translations emerged from Asia in 1991. From mainland China came at least six noteworthy new works, foremost among them the novel *Turbulence* by Jia Pingwa. Set in a village on the Zhou River, the story follows the lives of two peasants, star-crossed lovers, through the post-Mao years. *Getting Used to Dying* by Zhang Xianliang presents the autobiographical account of a Chinese novelist just released from a forced-labor camp and now famous enough to be allowed to travel abroad. *Hunger Trilogy* by Wang Ruowang takes up a similar theme, recounting three episodes of hardship in the writer-narrator's life—incarceration by the Kuomintang in the 1930s, flight from Japanese invaders during the 1940s, and imprisonment as a reactionary during the 1966-76 Cultural Revolution. Two short-story collections by women writers—*Old Floating Cloud* by Can Xue and *As Long as Nothing Happens, Nothing Will* by Zhang Jie—employ, respectively, an experimental, surrealist style and biting yet compassionate humor in their depictions of Chinese life in the 1980s.

In Japan, *The Hard-Boiled Wonderland and the End of the World* by Haruki Murakami tells a tale of technological espionage and brainwave tampering that conveys a distinct fear and loathing of the microchip age. Kobo Abe saw some of his earliest short fiction at last presented to an international audience in the collection *Beyond the Curve*. The noted novelist Morio Kita weighed in with *Ghosts,* a Proustian exercise in memory and the interplay of past and present.

From India came several ambitious novels. *The Salt of Life* is the third installment in Chaman Nahal's *Gandhi Quartet*. *Cyrus Cyrus* by Adam Zameenzad is about a lowborn genius and visionary forced by fate into the role of outcast both in this world and in the afterlife. *The Redundancy of Courage* by Timothy Mo is the story of a Third-World war that wreaks devastation on the small Indian Ocean island nation to which it is confined. Shashi Tharoor's *The Great Indian Novel* constitutes at once a parody and a 20th-century retelling of the *Mahabharata*. Lastly, perhaps the finest living prose writer in Hindi, Nirmal Verma, saw more of his short fiction presented to a worldwide audience in English translation as *The Crows of Deliverance*.

From elsewhere in Asia came *Not Out of Hate* by the Burmese writer Ma Ma Lay, who uses the story of a young girl's struggle against a suffocating love to provide insights into the late colonial period; and *Tiger!* by the Indonesian writer Mochtar Lubis, which tells the story of villagers on a jungle trip that turns into a nightmare of fear, deception, and betrayal through the appearance of a marauding, godlike tiger.

Africa. Though not as strong as in previous years, African writing in 1991 did bring forth several fine new works. Nadine Gordimer of South Africa, who was awarded the 1991 Nobel Prize in literature, published two new collections of short stories, *Jump* and *Crimes of Conscience*. *Emergency Continued* by Richard Rive updates the story told in the late author's 1988 novel *Emergency,* about the tense relations between the older and younger generations in South Africa's black community. *The Famished Road* by Ben Okri of Nigeria presents a study of brutality and injustice in a poverty-bound village, and of political strife where ancestral spirits coexist alongside contemporary African personalities. From Algeria came *The Vigils* by Tahar Djaout, a portrait of modern-day Algerian society. Lastly, the superb Moroccan novelist Tahar Ben Jelloun's latest effort, *Downcast Eyes,* tells of a young Berber shepherdess in a poetic coming-of-age story spanning two civilizations, the Berber village and worldly, metropolitan Paris.

WILLIAM RIGGAN
"World Literature Today"

*Titles translated

AP/Wide World

Los Angeles Police Commissioner Daryl F. Gates (foreground) came under fire following the videotaped beating of a black motorist by several Los Angeles police officers. In July, Gates announced that he would retire in April 1992, provided that a successor had been found by then. He later seemed to be coy about retiring, stating that the city might have to "drag me out and try to fire me."

LOS ANGELES

Crises in the police department and in water supply were the chief factors in Los Angeles' news for 1991. In late October a strike by nurses and their coworkers halted services at Los Angeles county hospitals.

Police Matters. On the evening of March 3, 1991, Rodney King, a black motorist, was stopped by Los Angeles police on a minor traffic matter. A resident made a videotape of him being beaten severely by several police officers and sold it to a local television station. Four of the officers involved were indicted on felony charges and the case was converted into a trial of the department and of Daryl F. Gates, 64, police chief since 1978.

The four charged pleaded not guilty. An appeals court granted a change of venue to a place to be selected outside the county and removed the trial judge as being biased against the defendants. The judge appealed.

A commission to investigate the department, under Warren Christopher, issued a report charging "racism" and frequent brutality. It urged adoption of a "community-based" approach to replace "confrontational" practice but did not show that these police behaved differently from those in other large cities.

Blacks and Latinos led in a call for Gates' resignation, which he resisted. The report did not blame Chief Gates directly for shortcomings, but did recommend that he retire in 1992 and the method of selecting the chief, now under civil service, be changed. (*See* SPECIAL REPORT/CRIME.)

Sheriff Sherman Block appointed a group of "community leaders" to advise him on implementing Christopher's recommended reforms. Since 1990, 30 deputies had been suspended, with felony indictments against 18. Four shootings were most controversial and seven former deputies were imprisoned for theft of $893,000 during narcotics raids.

Water. The area entered its fifth year of a major drought. The most serious water shortage in 60 years was regarded in a survey as second only to crime as an area problem. The giant Water Project of the 1950s, drawing from the Sierra Nevada, could not cope.

In February, Mayor Tom Bradley called for a 15% cutback in use with severe penalties for violations, but the council refused to make this mandatory. Then, incredibly, in March all parts of the state were rocked by heavy rainstorms. The summer was the coolest in many decades. And people had changed water-use habits. By August, with some purchase of water, all reserves had been replaced. But officials still worried for the future.

Elections. In February, Gloria Molina became the first Latino elected to the county board of supervisors in the 20th century and the first woman ever. In April two young blacks replaced two veteran black council members and a second Latino was elected to that body. Four union endorsees were elected to the financially strapped school board as it began a year-round schedule. The overall city voting turnout was a light 18%. A proposal to update community-college buildings was defeated narrowly.

Malibu. After a long struggle, affluent Malibu became Los Angeles county's 87th city. Residents had opposed county control of growth and the construction of a sewer system.

Fire. A county fire investigator said a private security guard admitted he started the $25 million Universal Studios fire of November 1990 that destroyed 20% of the exterior sets on the historic lot.

CHARLES R. ADRIAN
University of California, Riverside

LOUISIANA

With the eyes of the nation and the world on Louisiana, the state's voters overwhelmingly elected former Democratic Gov. Edwin Edwards to his fourth term, handing a crushing defeat to former Ku Klux Klan leader and Nazi sympathizer David Duke.

Roemer Administration. Incumbent Gov. Charles "Buddy" Roemer, an early favorite for reelection, did not make the runoff in the state's open primary, which requires candidates of all parties to run together. In the first primary, Edwards led the field with 33.6% of the vote, Duke was second with 31.6%, and Roemer was third with 26.6%.

The Harvard-educated Roemer, who switched from the Democratic to the Republican Party earlier in 1991, had what was considered a mixed record as the state's chief executive. He sponsored some tougher environmental laws and a teacher-evaluation bill. And there was no hint of scandal during his administration. But his efforts at fiscal and tax reform accomplished little because of a reluctant legislature, many of whose most powerful members he had alienated. The state's economy continued to limp along in the wake of the oil-field bust.

Election. Many Louisianans expressed horror at the choice facing them in the runoff. Duke had worn the swastika on his arm when he was young, had celebrated Hitler's birthday as late as the mid-1980s, and had denied that the Holocaust—the murdering of 6 million Jews—had taken place. Edwards, meanwhile, had been indicted twice (though never convicted) on federal racketeering charges and was known for his cronyism, his gambling, and his womanizing.

Early polls showed Edwards, who had served three previous terms, in the lead. But Duke, who had run well statewide in the primary—even running strong in the Cajun country, Edwards' traditional home base—was a force to contend with. Duke had attracted not only the hard-core racist vote, but protest votes from others who were tired of taxes, dangerous crime, and governmental interference in their lives. His stand against affirmative action and for welfare reform also appealed to moderate conservatives.

The key to victory was to attract most of the 409,000 Roemer voters, who tended to be white, middle-class professionals. Edwards promised to reform his ways, to protect the environment, and to appoint only the best people to state office. He succeeded in forming an extraordinary coalition of business people, educators, environmentalists, and Republicans, all normally foes of the populist Edwards. Even the head of the state National Guard came out for him. In the end, Edwards captured 61.4% of the vote, including 96% of the vote of blacks. He even won Duke's home Jefferson parish with 59%. After the election, Edwards said he wanted to bring Louisiana together. Duke, meanwhile, announced that he would seek the 1992 Republican presidential nomination.

Melina Schwegmann became the first woman to be elected lieutenant governor.

Other News. A law that would prohibit all abortions, except to save the life of the mother or in certain cases of rape or incest, in the state was passed by Louisiana legislators in June but struck down by a federal district court judge in August. Although Roemer vetoed the law, the legislature overrode the veto.

The U.S. Supreme Court on June 20 ruled that the federal Voting Rights Act applied to judicial elections as well as to representative elections. Questions about the issue arose from cases in Louisiana and Texas.

U.S. Labor Secretary Lynn Martin announced a record $10 million fine levied against Angus Chemical Co. to settle a government investigation of worker-safety violations after a May 1 blast at its Sterling plant. That explosion killed eight people and injured 120. The fine came on top of a $5.8 million settlement in August of charges of worker-safety violations brought at a Citgo Petroleum Company plant near Lake Charles. A March 3 refinery blast there killed six workers and injured six others.

JOSEPH W. DARBY III
"The Times Picayune," New Orleans

LOUISIANA • Information Highlights

Area: 47,752 sq mi (123 677 km^2).
Population (1990 census): 4,219,973.
Chief Cities (1990 census): Baton Rouge, the capital, 219,531; New Orleans, 496,938; Shreveport, 198,525.
Government (1991): *Chief Officers*—governor, Charles E. Roemer (R); lt. gov., Paul Hardy (R). *Legislature*—Senate, 39 members; House of Representatives, 105 members.
State Finances (fiscal year 1990): *Revenue,* $10,096,000,000; *expenditure,* $9,420,000,000.
Personal Income (1990): $61,237,000,000; per capita, $14,542.
Labor Force (June 1991): *Civilian labor force,* 1,961,900; *unemployed,* 145,800 (7.4% of total force).
Education: *Enrollment* (fall 1989)—public elementary schools, 581,702; public secondary, 201,323; colleges and universities, 179,927. *Public school expenditures* (1989), $2,468,307,000.

MAINE

Unable to avoid the Northeast's economic woes, Maine citizens and their government spent much of 1991 trying to cope with budget deficits and rising unemployment. The struggle reached its peak on July 1, when Republican Gov. John R. McKernan refused to sign a budget sent to his office by a state legislature controlled by Democrats.

© Gary Guisinger/NYT Pictures

With the state of Maine shut down due to the lack of a budget in mid-July 1991, some 100 state workers formed "Union City"—an encampment of tents in Capitol Park across from the capitol in Augusta. The protest was intended to encourage passage of a new budget.

Without a budget, state government shut down, idling some 10,000 state workers and ending all but emergency state services for 16 days. The impasse was broken on July 16 when a compromise budget was approved in the House and Senate and signed by the governor. Negotiating a resolution to disagreements over a workers' compensation measure, which had emerged as the battleground on which the budget war was waged, the new $3.2 billion budget also imposed $300 million in new taxes while cutting some $500 million from government services and subsidies.

Economy. The budget standoff, which left the state's 47 parks and beaches unstaffed at the height of the tourist season, cost Maine much-needed revenues. With unemployment climbing from 5% in 1990 to 7.8% in 1991, any additional losses in revenue weakened an already shaky economy. "The number of jobs lost in Maine since 1990 has continued to accelerate during 1991," said Steven Adams, state economist at the Maine State Planning Office. "I believe, however," he said in October, "that we have reached the low point of our decline. The state economy will continue to remain stagnant for awhile. Then, at the start of 1992, we can anticipate a weak recovery."

Further signals of the economic slowdown showed up across the state. Classified advertising, long considered a reliable economic indicator, declined at all newspapers, with one of Maine's largest dailies reporting an overall 24% drop. Real-estate sales lagged throughout the state, and especially in the greater Portland region, where office space constructed during the 1980s was, for the most part, vacant and likely to stay that way, at least until real-estate prices came down.

Weather. Adding to the year's general malaise, a summer-long drought withered much of the year's cash crops. During the driest summer in 25 years, a relentless sun and sparse rains took their greatest toll in northern and central Maine. In Aroostook County, where potatoes are Maine's largest crop, growers said the June-July drought cost them tens of millions of dollars in lost yields.

The rains came, however, on August 19 when Hurricane Bob's eye brushed the Maine coast near Portland, bringing gusts up to 60 mph (97 km/h) and dumping 8 inches (20.3 cm) of rain on coastal communities. Three persons died in storm-related accidents and power was not restored in some areas for several days. Many roads and bridges were washed out. Property owners reported scores of felled trees and millions of dollars in damage.

A coastal storm in late October caused heavy damage to the summer home of President George Bush on Walker's Point in Kennebunkport. During the president's August vacation in Kennebunkport, several demonstrations by pro- and anti-abortion groups, the unemployed, and those who believe that the administration should play a greater role in the fight against AIDS disrupted business.

Transportation Referendum. In a referendum held November 5, voters defeated by a

MAINE • Information Highlights

Area: 33,265 sq mi (86 156 km²).
Population (1990 census): 1,227,928.
Chief Cities (1990 census): Augusta, the capital, 21,325; Portland, 64,358; Lewiston, 39,757; Bangor, 33,181.
Government (1991): *Chief Officers*—governor, John R. McKernan, Jr. (R); secretary of state, G. William Diamond (D). *Legislature*—Senate, 33 members; House of Representatives, 151 members.
State Finances (fiscal year 1990): *Revenue,* $3,246,000,000; *expenditure,* $3,044,000,000.
Personal Income (1990): $21,146,000,000; per capita, $17,175.
Labor Force (June 1991): *Civilian labor force,* 656,500; *unemployed,* 50,000 (7.6% of total force).
Education: *Enrollment* (fall 1989)—public elementary schools, 152,267; public secondary, 61,508; colleges and universities, 58,230. *Public school expenditures* (1989), $921,931,000.

59%–41% margin a proposed $100 million bond issue to finance the widening of the Maine Turnpike from York to South Portland. The subject had generated much controversy in the state.

JOHN N. COLE, *"Maine Times"*

MALAYSIA

In 1991, Malaysia's multiethnic character (59% Malay and other indigenes, 32% Chinese, 9% Indian) continued to define the national agenda, although the positive effects of moderation and economic success could be seen. A proposal for establishing a Chinese Cultural Center put forward early in the year by the Malaysian Chinese Association, a member of Malaysia's multiparty National Front governing coalition, posed a touchy question for the country's Malay prime minister, Mahathir bin Mohamad. Though unresolved, the matter subsided.

The Dakwah movement, which had attracted many Malay Muslims seeking a return to a more traditional way of life, appeared to be leveling off. And Parti Islam (PAS), which represents the fundamentalist side of the country's Islamic community, gave evidence of moderating its position in anticipation of the next general elections. More important was the government's June 27 announcement of the New Development Plan (NDP), signaling a departure from the use of racial quotas (to benefit Malays) as a basis for national development. The NDP acknowledged that many of the goals of the previous New Economic Policy, such as greater participation in the economy by Malays, had been achieved. Together with Vision 2020, it provided a blueprint for turning Malaysia into an advanced industrial nation by 2020.

Politics. The Malaysian federal government in Kuala Lumpur faced yet another challenge to stability in the East Malaysia state of Sabah. The chief minister of Sabah, Joseph Pairin Kitingan, was arrested on three counts of corruption. His ruling political party, Parti Bersatu Sabah, had switched from Prime Minister Mahathir's National Front coalition to the opposition. The situation in Sabah remained tense throughout the year. In West Malaysia the opposition party Semangat 46 won two important August by-elections in Kelantan state, where an opposition coalition of Semangat 46 and PAS now controlled the government.

Economy. The Malaysian economy experienced another good year. Gross domestic product (GDP) grew by 9%. Inflation was held to 4.5%, a relatively low rate for the region. The country's rapid industrialization led to a trade deficit of $3.2 billion for the year. National debt declined to about $15 billion, and foreign investment totaled approximately $3 billion. Under a new investment policy, Malaysia would give priority to capital-intensive, high-technology projects, using skilled workers.

MALAYSIA • Information Highlights

Official Name: Malaysia.
Location: Southeast Asia.
Area: 127,317 sq mi (329 750 km²).
Population (mid-1991 est.): 18,300,000.
Chief City (1980 census): Kuala Lumpur, the capital, 919,610.
Government: *Head of state,* Sultan Azlan Shah, king (elected March 1989). *Head of government,* Mahathir bin Mohamad, prime minister (took office July 1981). *Legislature*—Parliament: Dewan Negara (Senate) and Dewan Ra'ayat (House of Representatives).
Monetary Unit: Ringgit (Malaysian dollar) (2.787 ringgits equal U.S.$1, July 1991).
Economic Indexes (1990): *Consumer Prices* (1990 = 100), all items, 100.0; food, 100.0. *Industrial Production* (1980 = 100), 231.
Foreign Trade (1990 U.S.$): *Imports,* $29,261,000,000; *exports,* $29,418,000,000.

Foreign Relations. During 1991, Malaysia came under considerable criticism internationally for the continuing destruction of forests in the East Malaysia state of Sarawak. The government continued to push for the creation of the East Asian Economic Caucus (EAEC), a loose consultative forum seeking ways to liberalize trade. In October, Malaysia offered the United States access to its naval base at Lumut —for maintenance and repair purposes only— when it withdraws from the Philippines. Relations with the United States nevertheless were strained over the U.S. decision to end Malaysia's general system of preferences (GSP) privileges for exports to the United States. In mid-December it was announced that Malaysia and Singapore would use each other's airspace for military training.

PATRICK M. MAYERCHAK
Virginia Military Institute

MANITOBA

In 1991, Manitobans were concerned with criticisms of the Winnipeg city police and recommendations by provincial politicians for new proposals regarding the status of Quebec.

Police Matters. In March 1988 a police officer shot aboriginal leader J. J. Harper during a scuffle. This had led to an inquiry on aboriginal justice by a two-judge commission, which issued its report in August 1991. The report had especially harsh words for the Winnipeg city police administration; it condemned the handling of the Harper shooting and recommended that an aboriginal system of justice be established, using as a model the tribal judicial systems of the United States. Some of the recommendations aroused opposition, and by late 1991 none of them had been implemented.

In September, Justice Ted Hughes produced another report condemning the Winnipeg city police, this time for their handling of a sexual-harassment case. A well-known Winnipeg defense lawyer, Harvey Pollock, had been accused of harassing a client. However, at his trial, the client denied there had been any harassment, and said that the police had told her to make up the charges. Pollock, the Harper family's lawyer, had been critical of the role of the police during the aboriginal-justice inquiry, and Hughes said his support for aboriginal clients against the police had been the motive for the manufactured charges against him. Hughes recommended that the police chief be suspended, but before the city could act on the recommendation, Chief Herbert Stephen announced his intention to retire in February 1992.

Post-Meech Lake Proposals. In 1990, Manitoba politicians had been instrumental in defeating the Meech Lake accord, and an all-party commission was established to come up with new proposals which could be set before a federal-provincial constitutional conference. This commission reported in late October 1991 after extensive deliberations. It suggested that Quebec be recognized as a "unique" society; a major innovation was that Manitoba proposed an immediate guarantee of aboriginal self-government, a topic ignored in the original Meech Lake formula. Manitoba also sought increased federal Senate representation for smaller provinces.

Budget and Economy. The 1991 provincial budget, which increased spending slightly, also increased taxes on cigarettes and motor fuels. Almost 1,000 government jobs were eliminated, some services were cut, and C$12 million in grants for nonprofit groups was eliminated. Despite depressed international grain prices, net farm income rose by 16.4%, to C$470 million. Much of the increase was due to payments from the federal government. Further payments were expected to bring net farm income up another 5%. Other sectors of the Manitoba economy showed modest gains, and the province's real gross domestic product was up by 0.7%, compared with the nationwide average of 0.9%.

Nurses' Strike. All but about 1,000 of the 10,500 members of the Manitoba Nurses Union walked off their jobs January 1 in a salary dispute. The pay scale of Manitoba's nurses ranked eighth out of the ten provinces. The strike was resolved February 1 with a two-year contract granting registered nurses a 14% pay raise over two years, and licensed practical nurses, an 11% increase.

MICHAEL KINNEAR
University of Manitoba

MANITOBA • Information Highlights

Area: 250,946 sq mi (649 950 km²).
Population (September 1991): 1,097,000.
Chief Cities (1986 census): Winnipeg, the capital, 594,551; Brandon, 38,708; Thompson, 14,701.
Government (1991): *Chief Officers*—lt. gov., George Johnson; premier, Gary Filmon (Progressive Conservative). *Legislature*—Legislative Assembly, 57 members.
Provincial Finances (1991–92 fiscal year budget): *Revenues,* $4,976,000,000; *expenditures,* $5,300,000,000.
Personal Income (average weekly earnings, July 1991): $484.72.
Labor Force (September 1991, seasonally adjusted): *Employed* workers, 15 years of age and over, 495,000; *Unemployed,* 9.3%.
Education (1991–92): *Enrollment*—elementary and secondary schools, 220,200 pupils; postsecondary—universities, 20,000; community colleges, 3,950.
(All monetary figures are in Canadian dollars.)

MARYLAND

Major news in Maryland in 1991 included a fiscal crisis, the behavior of the governor, and a controversy over congressional redistricting.

Budget. The dominant issue in Maryland in 1991 was a fiscal crisis which saw more than $1 billion slashed from the state budget. The legislature refused to raise taxes despite shrinking state revenues and large increases in the demand for welfare and Medicaid programs. The result: In mid-October the legislature and Gov. William Donald Schaefer agreed on a budget-cutting plan. It necessitated layoffs of 1,600 state workers; $180 million less in state aid for the counties and Baltimore; major cuts in state funding for drug and alcohol treatment for the indigent; reduced funding to the University of Maryland; and welfare payments rolled back to 1989 levels.

Meanwhile, fiscal experts were predicting that the state would have to cut another $150 million from the 1992 budget before the budget year ends on June 30. Even antitax legislators were predicting in October that the legislature would enact a major tax increase in 1992. Despite the budget problems the state retained its AAA bond rating.

Politics. Maryland's legislature enacted far-reaching measures on abortion and the environment in 1991. On abortion, the legislature passed a law protecting the right of women to get abortions in the early stages of pregnancy. After that, abortions would be permitted if the health of the mother was in jeopardy or if the baby would be deformed severely. Females under the age of 18 would need parental consent for abortions unless a doctor decided that was not in the girl's best interest. On the subject of the environment, the general assembly enacted a law requiring builders to plant trees to replace those cleared during real-estate development.

In February, Governor Schaefer commuted the prison sentences of eight women convicted of killing or assaulting men who had abused them; he said he believed they had acted in self-defense and were no threat to society.

AP/Wide World

Maryland Gov. William D. Schaefer conducts a half-hour call-in radio show from the statehouse in Annapolis.

The thorny issue of congressional redistricting reared its head in September, the result being a deadlock between the state House and Senate over competing plans for congressional reapportionment. Complicating the plans was the creation of a minority district in the Washington, DC, suburbs. Leading Democrats wanted to draw a new district to protect Democratic Rep. Steny Hoyer—the white congressman that had represented that area—because he was the fourth-ranking Democrat in the House of Representatives.

The final meaning of this was that two existing congressmen would have to face each other in the 1992 elections. Senate Democrats were adamant that two Republicans face each other; the Democrat-controlled House wanted a Democrat to face a Republican. The House won, but residents of Anne Arundel county sued to overturn the plan because it split the county into four congressional districts.

MARYLAND • Information Highlights

Area: 10,460 sq mi (27 092 km²).
Population (1990 census): 4,781,468.
Chief Cities (1990 census): Annapolis, the capital, 33,187; Baltimore, 736,014; Rockville, 44,835.
Government (1991): *Chief Officers*—governor, William Donald Schaefer (D); lt. gov., Melvin A. Steinberg (D). *General Assembly*—Senate, 47 members; House of Delegates, 141 members.
State Finances (fiscal year 1990): *Revenue,* $12,195,000,000; *expenditure,* $11,296,000,000.
Personal Income (1990): $104,631,000,000; per capita, $21,789.
Labor Force (June 1991): *Civilian labor force,* 2,555,200; *unemployed,* 152,000 (6.0% of total force).
Education: *Enrollment* (fall 1989)—public elementary schools, 507,007; public secondary, 191,799; colleges and universities, 255,326. *Public school expenditures* (1989), $3,505,018,000.

The Governor. Governor Schaefer, reelected in 1990 with 60% of the vote, became a major issue in state politics after a series of strange antics which began with his comparison of the state's eastern shore to an outhouse. (The governor had lost the shore in the election.) It became a cause célèbre for the residents of the mostly rural peninsula. Schaefer finally apologized, but it was too late.

Later in the year came widespread accounts in the press of Schaefer's penchant for writing nasty, handwritten notes to constituents who criticized him. He allegedly also made an unannounced personal visit to the home of another critic, and had his bodyguards track down a driver who had made a rude gesture toward him. By summer the once-popular governor's approval ratings had plummeted.

DAN CASEY, *"The Annapolis Capital"*

MASSACHUSETTS

Troubled economic conditions continued to dominate the news and shape major public action in Massachusetts in 1991. Some economists believed that the recession was the worst since 1946. The state's unemployment rate remained above 9%, the highest of the 11 large industrial states. A recovery was not predicted until mid-1992 at the earliest.

In November, Boston's Mayor Raymond L. Flynn was reelected to a third term with a record 75% of the vote.

Bank Failures. In January the Bank of New England, one of the region's biggest, was declared insolvent by federal regulators. It was the largest of more than two dozen banks and credit unions that failed during the year, all due to investments in unsuccessful real-estate ventures. Two other large and troubled banks, the Shawmut Bank and the Bank of Boston, discussed a merger that could head off federal seizure for both. A major problem for bank recovery was the large amount of foreclosed real estate that banks were unable to sell in the state's depressed realty market. (*See* BANKING AND FINANCE.)

Budget Crisis. The recession posed a major challenge for the state's new governor, William Weld, the first Republican to hold the office in 15 years. The state's bond rating, which sets the cost of borrowing funds, was reduced by major Wall Street rating firms to one of the lowest in the nation. This put pressure on state officials to make budget reductions. At the same time, revenue projections continued to decline in the first half of the year, adding to the sense of crisis.

Weld proposed large budget cuts and reaffirmed his campaign pledge of no new taxes. He faced opposition by the Democratic-controlled legislature, but in April and May a series of compromises were worked out that led, after

© 1991 Richard Howard/"People Weekly"

Kathy Betts won the gratitude of Massachusetts Gov. William Weld, above. The part-time employee at the state's welfare department discovered that by combining several regulations regarding Medicaid reimbursement, the state could be eligible for additional funds. Accordingly, the federal government agreed to give Massachusetts $489 million.

a 19-hour marathon session, to passage of a $12.8 billion budget. This marked the first time in 30 years that the state spent less money than it had the year before. Reductions in Medicaid, public welfare, and aid to cities and towns led the list of cuts, and social-service advocates warned of major negative effects on the poor and elderly. The consensus among political leaders, however, was that a single major cut was preferable to several smaller reductions over a period of months. The sharply reduced budget was seen as a major victory for Weld, who remained popular despite his advocacy of cuts in state programs.

The state's revenue collections exceeded forecasts during the second half of the year, in some months as much as 10% higher. This prompted some legislators to call for restoration of some budget cuts. The Weld administration's projections remained cautious, however. While tax revenue—which covers about 70% of state spending—was up, nontax revenue—such as federal grants, fees, and the state lottery—remained behind predictions.

MASSACHUSETTS • Information Highlights

Area: 8,284 sq mi (21 456 km²).
Population (1990 census): 6,016,425.
Chief Cities (1990 census): Boston, the capital, 574,283; Worcester, 169,759; Springfield, 156,983.
Government (1991): *Chief Officer*—governor, William Weld (R); lt. gov., Argeo Paul Celluci (R). *Legislature*—Senate, 40 members; House of Representatives, 160 members.
State Finances (fiscal year 1990): *Revenue*, $17,034,000,000; *expenditure*, $18,736,000,000.
Personal Income (1990): $135,861,000,000; per capita, $22,569.
Labor Force (June 1991): *Civilian labor force*, 3,167,200; *unemployed*, 300,300 (9.5% of total force).
Education: *Enrollment* (fall 1989)—public elementary schools, 590,238; public secondary, 235,350; colleges and universities, 426,476. *Public school expenditures* (1989), $4,522,119,000.

Bankrupt City. A highly visible reminder of continuing economic troubles was provided in August when Chelsea, a community of 60,000 located just to the north of Boston, appealed for a takeover by the state when it was unable to cover a $9.5 million deficit. Special legislation was passed quickly, placing the city in receivership, the first municipality in the state to be officially bankrupt since the 1930s. A receiver was appointed to run the government and create a plan to stabilize finances. The city was expected to take two years to recover.

Legislative Proposals. In the latter part of the year, with budget matters under control, Governor Weld announced a number of proposals for changes in state policy. The most controversial of these was for restoration of the death penalty for first-degree murder. There had been no executions in Massachusetts since 1947. Another proposal that sparked debate was a public-education-reform plan setting standards which school systems would have to meet to receive state aid.

Nuclear Plant Closed. Back in August 1960, many Bay State residents were excited by the opening of the first nuclear-powered generating plant. Located in the small town of Rowe, on the Vermont border in western Massachusetts, the plant operated continuously for 31 years. In October 1991 the federal Nuclear Regulatory Commission ordered it shut down, citing concerns that its reactor vessel had become too brittle for safe use.

HARVEY BOULAY, *Rogerson House*

Quality health care, including its cost, became even more of a concern among the U.S. public during 1991. Although no federal legislation was enacted during the year, various plans were considered and further action was expected in 1992.

MEDICINE AND HEALTH

Medical headlines during 1991 were dominated by rising health-care costs; ethical dilemmas, including questions regarding whether health-care workers carrying the AIDS virus should be allowed to perform invasive medical procedures; and the continued growth of such scourges as cancer, AIDS, and malaria. New drugs and technologies improved prospects for many patients, but at the same time doubts about safety were raised concerning products already on the market. Also of concern was cholera, a medical threat in Latin America that broke out in Peru in January (*see* SIDEBAR/LATIN AMERICA). In the area of mental health, the U.S. Congress established the 1990s as the Decade of the Brain, with research initiatives aimed at understanding the brain in relation to mental illness.

Overview

Autoimmune Disorders. In May, Graves' disease was diagnosed in U.S. President George Bush. A form of hyperthyroidism, or overactive thyroid gland, the disease earlier had been diagnosed in his wife, Barbara. The cause of Graves' disease is unknown, but the disorder is not known to be contagious. Some scientists suspect, however, that it may be triggered by a bacterium, virus, or other environmental factor.

Graves' disease patients are treated either with radioactive iodine, which destroys thyroid cells, or by removing surgically all or part of the gland. A complication for such patients can be hypothyroidism, or underactive gland, later in life. The president's doctors put him on radioactive-iodine therapy, but said that if the iodine destroyed too much of his thyroid, he might need to take thyroid pills.

Graves' disease is an autoimmune disorder—a disease in which the immune system, for unknown reasons, forms antibodies that attack the body's own tissues. Other autoimmune disorders include lupus, rheumatoid arthritis, and juvenile-onset diabetes.

Heart Disease. Kelly D. Brownell, a psychologist and weight specialist at Yale University, found that people who repeatedly lose and regain weight ("yo-yo dieters") are at greater risk of developing heart disease and have a higher overall death rate than people whose weight remains relatively stable. Indeed, the risks of such dieting appear to equal or even exceed those of being overweight.

Harvard Medical School physician Patricia Hebert reported that a survey of more than 22,000 U.S. male doctors found that short men are more likely to suffer heart attacks. Men 5′7″ (1.7 m) or shorter had a 60% greater risk of developing a first heart attack than men 6′1″ (1.85 m) or taller. "Over the five-year period of the study, for every added inch of height there was a 3% decrease in the risk of a heart attack," said Hebert.

Women often are excluded from clinical studies, even though the results of such studies usually are applied to both sexes, a practice that does not take into account hormonal and other differences between the sexes. Charges of sexism have increased in recent years, and some steps have been taken to remedy the problem. The National Heart, Lung and Blood Institute announced it would underwrite a study of 45,000 nurses age 50 and older to learn if low doses of aspirin protect women against heart disease. Studies of men have shown conclusively that aspirin can cut the risk of heart attacks, but there was some evidence that taking aspirin increases the risk of strokes from bleeding into the brain. Since women more often tend to develop strokes from bleeding, it was hoped that lower doses will avoid increasing this tendency.

A ten-year study involving more than 48,000 nurses found that women who take estrogen after menopause can cut their risk of heart disease almost in half. Directed by Meier J. Stampfer, a physician at Brigham and Women's Hospital in Boston, the study supported earlier evidence that the benefits of estrogen substantially outweigh the risks. Estrogen taken after menopause also prevents thinning of the bones, or osteoporosis, a common ailment among the elderly. However, it increases the risk of cancer of the uterine lining and breast. The researchers noted that a white woman age 50 to 94 has a 31% chance of dying

Dr. Healy and the NIH

Bernadine P. Healy, a former chairman of the Research Institute at the Cleveland Clinic Foundation in Ohio, was sworn in publicly as director of the U.S. National Institutes of Health (NIH) on June 24, 1991. Her appointment in January 1991 had ended a prolonged search for an NIH director. It was seen as good news for women who may benefit from her call to balance the amount of research money spent on men's and women's diseases. In the past, far less was spent studying women's diseases, and women were used less as test subjects. Healy is the first woman to take the NIH helm.

AP/Wide World

Born on Aug. 2, 1944, Healy, a cardiovascular researcher and past president of the American Heart Association, was graduated from Vassar College in 1965 and received her medical degree from Harvard Medical School in 1970. Prior to joining the Cleveland Clinic Foundation in 1985, she served in various positions at Johns Hopkins School of Medicine and was deputy director of the White House Office of Science and Technology (1984–85). She also served on several federal science advisory committees, including one that recommended approving the use of fetal tissue for research. Both the Reagan and Bush administrations have overruled that recommendation. The new NIH director is married and the mother of two daughters.

Dr. Healy took over the NIH—the principal biomedical-research agency of the U.S. government that includes 13 institutes and employs more than 3,000 scientists—at a time of mounting problems. In 1990 alone, NIH researchers located the cystic-fibrosis gene, developed a drug to reduce paralysis from spinal-cord injuries, and showed that the drug AZT can prolong the life of AIDs patients. Nevertheless, NIH has a difficult time attracting new researchers because its salaries are two to three times less than what a scientist can receive in nongovernmental work. Additionally, political sensitivities have made it hard to do research in certain areas, including contraception, and investigations of scientific misconduct have caused concern.

During her first months in office, Dr. Healy announced a major research effort on the neglected medical problems of women and called for greater funding for research. She also told a reporter that she was not afraid of shaking things up a bit and was not concerned about being popular.

KRISTI VAUGHAN

from heart disease but only a 2.8% and 0.7% chance, respectively, of dying from breast cancer and cancer of the uterine lining.

Following a heart attack a patient is likely to be given a drug to dissolve blood clots in the coronary arteries. An international study by scientists at Britain's Oxford University evaluated the three competing "clot-busters": streptokinase, Eminase, and TPA (tissue plasminogen activator). All were found to be equally effective in saving lives, with streptokinase resulting in significantly fewer strokes from bleeding into the brain. The drugs' costs, however, were far from equal. The oldest drug, streptokinase, preferred by doctors in most countries, cost $200 per treatment. Eminase cost $1,700 per treatment. The newest drug, TPA, favored by U.S. doctors, cost $2,200 to $2,700 per treatment.

Cancer. The number of cancer cases continued to soar. Lung cancer was killing more smokers than heart disease, according to the National Cancer Institute, which estimated that cigarette smoking would cause more than 157,000 cancer deaths in 1991. The lifetime risk of an American developing malignant melanoma—the deadliest type of skin cancer—was now 1 in 105, and was likely to increase to 1 in 75 by the year 2000. According to the National Cancer Institute, the U.S. incidence of breast cancer increased 32% between 1982 and 1987, and was continuing its rapid rise. The American Cancer Society estimated that the average U.S. woman now ran a one-in-nine risk of developing breast cancer during her life.

Scientists were zeroing in on the causes of ever more cancers. During 1991 scientists detected the gene that causes colon cancer (*see also* BIOCHEMISTRY) and linked a common bacterium to stomach cancer. Two different studies found that the spiral-shaped bacterium *Helicobacter pylori* may be responsible for up to 60% of all stomach cancer, which is the second-most-common cancer in the world after lung cancer. *H. pylori* previously had been shown to cause gastritis, an inflammation of the stomach lining that may predispose a person to cancer.

Can diet help prevent cancer? Chemoprevention is a developing area of cancer research, and some epidemiological evidence suggests that certain foods may have a protective effect. For instance, several teams of scientists reported that green tea, a popular drink in parts of the Far East, has potent anticancer properties in tests conducted with mice.

A simple, inexpensive blood test combined with a rectal examination can improve detection of prostate cancer. The new test checks blood levels of a protein called prostate-specific antigen (PSA), which is produced by cells on the surface of the prostate. An enlarged prostate, caused by cancer or other problems, results in higher PSA levels.

One of the most promising new cancer drugs is taxol, made from the bark of rare Pacific yew trees. Studies indicate that taxol is effective in treating ovarian, breast, and lung cancers. Unfortunately, supply is limited. About six 100-year-old Pacific yew trees are needed to produce enough taxol to treat one patient for a year. In the past, the yews were considered weeds by loggers, who usually burned them during clear-cut logging operations. The remaining trees suddenly are valuable, and in March the U.S. Forest Service ordered an end to the burning of downed yews. Several groups of scientists were developing methods for making taxol in the laboratory, which could provide unlimited supplies, but it may be several years before such products are ready to be marketed.

In January researchers at the National Cancer Institute, led by Steven Rosenberg, made the first attempt to treat cancer patients by injecting genetically altered cells. Genes for an immune-system hormone, tumor necrosis factor, which has been shown to be an effective anticancer agent, were inserted into a type of white blood cell that attacks cancerous tissue. Large numbers of these cells were grown in the laboratory and then injected into the patients. The initial two patients had advanced melanoma and were not expected to survive more than a few months. By July, however, they still were alive and had not shown any ill effects from the therapy.

AIDS. Between 1981, when it first was recognized, and late 1991, Acquired Immune Deficiency Syndrome (AIDS), a disease caused by HIV viruses, had claimed the lives of more than 126,000 Americans. Some 200,000 additional people had symptoms of the disease and an estimated 1 million were infected with the viruses. Worldwide, an estimated 10 million adults were infected. The situation was most acute in sub-Saharan Africa. For example, 40% of the adults in some cities in Tanzania were infected; in Rwanda's capital, Kigali, 30% were infected.

Apparently it takes about six months between the time that the HIV virus enters the body and the time that antibodies to the virus become detectable in the person's blood. (Detection of such antibodies is the basis of the standard AIDS test.) Then it takes an average of 10.5 years before the person shows symptoms of AIDS. This long latency period means that the infected person may be unaware of the infection, even as he or she is spreading the virus to other people.

There are four major transmission routes for HIV viruses: sexual contact, the sharing of contaminated needles and syringes by drug abusers, from a mother to her fetus during pregnancy, and infected blood transfusions.

Worldwide, heterosexual transmission was accounting for 75% of all infections. In the

© Markel/Gamma-Liaison

© Bill Nation/Sygma

Kimberly Bergalis, top, who contracted AIDs from her dentist, campaigned for mandatory testing of all health-care workers for the virus that causes AIDs. The 23-year-old Floridian died in December. Basketball's Magic Johnson, above, became a spokesperson against AIDS after being infected with the HIV virus.

United States, most infections had occurred among homosexuals and drug abusers. But the epidemic was increasing fastest among heterosexuals, who accounted for 5.6% of reported cases. The United States was shocked in November when the great basketball player Earvin (''Magic'') Johnson announced that he had been infected by the HIV virus through heterosexual contact and would retire immediately from the Los Angeles Lakers.

Johnson's infection was discovered during a physical exam for a health-insurance policy. He did not have the symptoms of AIDS yet but the early diagnosis was valuable because it allowed early use of azidothymidine (AZT), a drug that appears in at least some cases to slow the onset of symptoms and prolong life.

Until October, AZT was the only drug to combat the HIV virus that had been approved by the U.S. Food and Drug Administration (FDA). Then the FDA approved didanosine (DDI) for treatment of patients with advanced AIDS who cannot tolerate or are not helped by AZT. During 1991 approval also was given to foscarnet, to combat a viral infection called cytomegalovirus retinitis, which often causes blindness in AIDS patients.

Ever since it became known in 1990 that Florida dentist David J. Acer infected five patients with the HIV virus, debate has raged over how to prevent infected health-care professionals from transmitting the virus to their patients. Despite a major investigation by epidemiologists, it was unclear how Acer, who died soon after the disclosure, transmitted the virus; by late 1991 his was the only known case of a health practitioner infecting patients. The Centers for Disease Control issued guidelines recommending that health-care workers who perform invasive surgical procedures be tested for the HIV virus, but dropped the guidelines following strong opposition from the medical community, which asserted that there is no scientific reason for such broad restrictions. However, local health panels may set restrictions on a case-by-case basis.

Malaria. ''Despite heroic efforts to eradicate malaria in the 1950s and 1960s, this disease not only has prevailed but has made a dramatic resurgence within the past two decades,'' reported the Institute of Medicine, an organization affiliated with the National Academy of Sciences. Some 300 million people were believed to be infected worldwide; 1 million to 2 million deaths due to malaria were occurring annually. A major problem was that the malarial parasites had become resistant to chloroquine and other drugs commonly used to treat malaria.

Malaria is a problem primarily in equatorial countries, but even the United States experienced a significant rise in cases. The great majority of the approximately 1,100 Americans who contract malaria each year get the disease while traveling in countries where the parasites are widespread. But some people get the disease when U.S. mosquitoes transfer the parasites from one person to another. Such transmission is most common in California, and is thought to be due to infected migrant farm workers in the state.

Scientists at the U.S. Naval Medical Research Institute reported the successful inoculation of mice against malaria. This was the first time that animals had been immunized fully with a man-made vaccine, created through genetic engineering. It was hoped that a similar approach would lead to a human vaccine. (*See also* MICROBIOLOGY.)

Unsafe Drugs? Two widely used drugs came under attack during 1991 following reports of dangerous side effects. Halcion, the world's top-selling prescription sleeping pill, was banned in Britain after newly disclosed data supported earlier evidence that the drug may cause memory loss, depression, anxiety, and other behavioral problems. In some European nations, where doses up to 1.0 milligrams (mg) once were prescribed, the recommended dose was lowered to 0.25 mg, the same as in the United States.

The pharmaceutical firm F. Hoffmann-La Roche was charged with withholding data on the safety of Versad, a sedative used during minor surgery or before and during general anesthesia. Sold in the United States since 1985, Versad originally was marketed in a concentrated formulation that could lead to life-threatening side effects—a problem that internal documents indicated the company knew about, yet, contrary to FDA regulations, did not report.

Transplants. Survival rates for the most common types of organ transplants continued to improve, due largely to better matches of organs and patients and to the development of anti-rejection drugs. However, the number of people awaiting transplants far exceeds the number of available organs. Approximately 25,000 people who die each year are suitable organ sources, but only one sixth of them actually donate their organs. Blacks donate fewer organs than whites, which has been one factor in the lower rate of successful transplant operations among blacks, since it is difficult to obtain a good donor-recipient match between races. A campaign to improve donor participation among minorities, led by Clive O. Callender, director of Howard University Transplant Center, met with some success.

Surgeons at the University of Pittsburgh reported the first successful transplants of the small intestine. The five patients—two adults and three children—suffered from short-gut syndrome, which meant they were unable to eat and had to receive their nutrition intravenously.

A single donor can provide material for dozens of transplant operations: two kidneys, four heart valves, six ear bones, bone marrow, ligaments, blood vessels, skin, and so on. If the donated organ is infected, the disease may be passed on to the recipient. For instance, three people died of AIDS after receiving organ transplants from a man infected with the AIDS virus. In 1991 the New England Organ Bank reported that hepatitis C, a liver disease, also can be spread through transplants.

Implants. In May a 52-year-old man became the world's first recipient of a fully portable heart pump. Surgeons at Texas Heart Institute in Houston implanted the device below the diaphragm, leaving the patient's heart in place. The pump assisted the left ventricle, the chamber of the heart that pumps blood into the aorta. Two weeks after the operation, the patient died; according to the institute, the heart pump worked well, but the patient's liver and other organs failed. Surgeons also soon may test artificial pancreases in humans.

U.S. surgeons perform more than 140,000 knee-replacement operations annually, as well as thousands of operations to replace hip, shoulder, elbow, and other joints. Improved designs of artificial parts coupled with better fits between an implant and the patient's bones have meant that implants last longer and allow the person to resume normal activities more completely. A computer system developed at Cornell University's Department of Mechanical and Aerospace Engineering allows surgeons to visualize how an implant will fit and move within a particular patient before the operation is performed.

More than 2 million U.S. women had received silicone breast implants, mostly for cosmetic reasons, in the nearly 30 years they had been on the market. The implants had been marketed without proof of safety; not until 1991 were manufacturers required to submit safety data. In September the FDA indicated that the data provided by manufacturers were inadequate, and a moratorium or even a ban of the implants became a possibility. Risks of breast implants include allergic reactions; hardening or lumping of tissue around the implant; and rupturing of the implant with subsequent leakage of silicone, which may increase the risk of autoimmune diseases and cancer. Also, the implants can interfere with mammography, preventing detection of tumors.

Other types of implants also create a significant number of problems. A survey of data collected by the U.S. National Center for Health Statistics indicated that 49% of the people who receive lens implants have problems with the implants, as do 32% of those with artificial joints, 30% with ear vent tubes, and 27% with cardiac pacemakers.

See also FEATURE ARTICLE/ALZHEIMER'S DISEASE, page 58.

JENNY TESAR
Free-lance Science Writer

Health Care

The year 1991 saw much discussion about problems with the U.S. health-care system but very little action.

For the first time all the major players in health care—doctors and other providers, insurance companies, employers, labor unions, and consumers—urged Congress and President George Bush to do something to fix a system that was costing more each year but covering fewer people. While just about everyone agreed on the problem, no consensus emerged about how to fix it. That left politicians the unpalatable choice of doing nothing or doing something bound to infuriate one or more influential interest groups.

Controlling costs was the top priority for employers and labor unions. Indeed, by 1990 the nation's total medical bill had reached $666.2 billion, another double-digit increase from the previous year. Doctors, hospital officials, and other health-care providers seemed most concerned with ensuring that all Americans had access to needed health-care services. More than 34 million Americans—16% of the nonelderly population—lacked health insurance in 1989, according to the latest estimate.

The Bush Administration and Congressional Plans. Although President Bush ordered a study of the health-care problem in both his 1990 and 1991 State of the Union addresses, in 1991 administration officials also were admitting that they did not know what to do. But even they conceded the growing seriousness of the situation. In April the White House's director of the Office of Management and Budget, Richard G. Darman, told a Senate committee that the rate of growth in federal health spending, principally the Medicare program for 34 million elderly and disabled Americans, was "unsustainable."

In the meantime, health was heating up as a political issue for the 1992 presidential election. Three of the leading Democratic candidates—Sens. Tom Harkin of Iowa and Bob Kerrey of Nebraska, and Arkansas Gov. Bill Clinton—made universal health care a lead issue in their campaigns.

But while the lack of consensus prevented comprehensive action from Washington, it did not stop members of Congress from offering their own plans. The most visible was unveiled in June by several senators influential in health-care policy, led by Senate Majority Leader George J. Mitchell (D-ME). It featured a "play-or-pay" system under which employers would have to provide workers and their families with health insurance or pay into a fund from which insurance would be provided. Those without jobs also would get insurance through the new program, to be called AmeriCare.

Several Democrats, however, did not think the plan went far enough. A competing bill introduced in the House in March would institute a "single-payer" system similar to the one in Canada, in which the federal government would replace health-insurance companies. Backers of the proposal said it would save enough money in administrative costs alone to pay for coverage of all uninsured Americans.

Republicans paid more attention to health care in 1991 as well, but most of their plans were far less sweeping, and several GOP members of Congress limited themselves to pushing the Bush administration to come forward with a plan.

JULIE ROVNER, *"Congressional Quarterly"*

Medical Ethics

The dominant theme in bioethics for 1991 was a battle for control over death and dying, a battle fought in hospitals, courtrooms, and at the ballot box. A second important theme for the year was at the other edge of life—having children.

To End a Life. The United States has become accustomed to discussion over whether a terminally ill patient should be allowed to die: the family pleading for an end, doctors and hospital or nursing home insisting the person be kept alive. Helga Wanglie and her husband turned the tables. Wanglie, 86 years old, had been in a persistent vegetative state since May 1990. Her husband insisted that she would have wanted to be kept alive, even if she never regained consciousness. Her doctors believed it was futile to continue her life-prolonging treatment and asked a court to allow them to remove life-support. In July, Wanglie's husband won the legal battle; but his wife died three days later.

The Wanglie case proposed a major revision of the principle that patients and families should make decisions about life-prolonging treatment. Should physicians have the authority to deny certain interventions on the grounds that they are futile, even though patients or families want them?

In March 1991, Timothy E. Quill, a physician practicing in Rochester, NY, published in a prestigious medical journal his account of how he helped a patient commit suicide. Diane, the name he gave the patient, had had a difficult life but was doing well when she was found to have a severe form of leukemia. The three-step treatment for her disease, successful in 25% of cases, was extremely painful and debilitating. Diane refused the treatment, preferring to live her remaining months out of the hospital. She asked for barbiturates to help her sleep and wanted enough to take her own life if and when she chose. Quill complied. She died, presumably of a drug overdose, nearly four months later. Timothy Quill's story of Diane starkly posed the question of whether a compassionate, thoughtful physician should assist, even indirectly, in a patient's suicide.

Quill's story differed from the June 1990 case in which Dr. Jack Kevorkian hooked up Janet Adkins to a suicide machine he invented. Quill had known his patient well for years, had long discussions with her about her prognosis, and acted with deliberation. Kevorkian had known Adkins a few days. In October 1991, Kevorkian also assisted in the suicides of two women whom he did not know well.

© Brookins/"Richmond Times-Dispatch"

Dr. Jack Kevorkian, a Michigan doctor who connected an Alzheimer's patient to a homemade suicide machine and watched her die in 1990, assisted in two more suicides in 1991. His actions were the cause of extensive debate.

In November 1991 voters in Washington state defeated Initiative 119, which would have permitted "physician aid in dying." If the initiative had been approved, physicians would have been permitted to assist in suicide as well as to perform active euthanasia for terminally ill people. For several years the Netherlands has tolerated physicians performing euthanasia by not prosecuting them if they observe certain safeguards. But the Netherlands has not made euthanasia itself legal.

Wanglie, Quill, and Kevorkian were 1991's major names in the struggle for control over death and dying. Increasingly, the timing and manner of death are not consequences of disease but, instead, conscious decisions made by patients, families, and physicians—even, on occasion, by judges. More than 80% of older Americans die in institutions, such as hospitals and nursing homes. It is believed that 70% of such deaths—that is, 50-60% of all deaths among the elderly—result from decisions to forgo life-prolonging measures.

In 1990 the U.S. Congress passed the Patient Self-Determination Act, which took effect on Dec. 1, 1991. This law requires health-care organizations paid by Medicare and Medicaid to inform patients about the availability of instruments—living wills and durable powers of attorney for health care—for enabling their desires about treatment or nontreatment to be recognized. The law also requires these organizations to educate their staffs and surrounding communities about decision-making for dying patients. The new law would be monitored by the medical and legal professions.

To Start a New Life. A case in California highlighted the other end of life. Mary and Abe Ayala's 19-year-old daughter Anissa developed leukemia. Her best chance for successful treatment was a bone-marrow transplant from a compatible donor. Her parents' marrows were not suitable, but there was a chance that a sibling's would be. Her father's vasectomy was reversed, and her parents conceived a child.

The Ayalas were criticized, sometimes harshly, for their actions. They were accused of creating a child solely for its usefulness to another child. The Ayalas said that they wanted this child for several reasons: to love for its own sake; to have another child to raise in the event Anissa died; and in the hope that the child would be a compatible marrow donor for its older sister.

The Ayala case helped to open a discussion of the reasons why people conceive, bear, and raise children, and the ethical implications of those reasons. As human reproduction becomes more a matter of conscious choice, there may be increasing discussion about the ethics of having children, just as control over dying forces us to confront the ethics of prolonging life and assisting death.

THOMAS H. MURRAY
Center for Biomedical Ethics
Case Western University

Mental Health

Major 1991 advances in research on mental illnesses contributed to the growing body of knowledge of the biological and behavioral underpinnings of depression, schizophrenia, addictions, and other disorders that disable millions of people.

Depression. In a study supported by the National Institute of Mental Health (NIMH), scientists found that a more aggressive approach to treatment can prevent or delay new bouts of recurrent unipolar depression, a disorder characterized in part by repeated severe episodes of fatigue, sadness, and hopelessness. All the patients in the study first received the antidepressant imipramine in doses sufficient to bring about a remission of depressive symptoms and stabilize their condition. Of those patients who continued receiving imipramine in the same dosage, 80% remained well for the study's three years.

These findings accentuate the importance of maintaining patients on therapeutic doses of antidepressant medication long beyond the acute phase of their illness. The study also revealed that monthly sessions of psychotherapy designed to treat depressive illness helped delay the recurrence of depression.

Panic Disorder. More than 3 million Americans have panic disorder—a potentially disabling condition involving repeated and unexpected attacks of intense fear. Expert panelists participating in a 1991 consensus-development conference sponsored by the NIMH and the National Institutes of Health (NIH) determined that effective treatments for panic disorder include several medications and a relatively new form of psychotherapy called cognitive-behavioral therapy. Treatment should be chosen according to the patient's individual needs and preferences, the panelists recommended, and any treatment that has not shown positive results after six to eight weeks should be reevaluated. The NIMH, with private voluntary health organizations, undertook a nationwide campaign to acquaint the public and health-care professionals with panic disorder.

Hyperactivity. Hyperactivity—or attention deficit hyperactivity disorder (ADHD)—afflicts up to 4% of youngsters under the age of 13. Children with ADHD are impulsive and easily distracted, have difficulty sitting still, and are at greater risk for juvenile delinquency. In the first PET scan study of its kind, NIMH researchers studying adults with histories of childhood ADHD have discovered abnormally low activity in those areas of the brain involved in movement and attention span. Investigators now can focus on determining what goes wrong to produce this abnormality and work toward better therapies.

Severe Mental Illnesses. In 1991 the NIMH and its National Advisory Mental Health Council published a plan of research aimed at improving services for the millions who suffer from chronic disabling mental illnesses. The plan, "Caring for People with Severe Mental Disorders," considers how research can contribute to improving the standard of care for individuals with these conditions and to finding ways to deliver that care widely.

Substance Abuse. A new NIMH study demonstrated a higher-than-expected overlap, or comorbidity, of mental illness with drug or alcohol abuse. The findings indicate that 30% of U.S. adults who have had a mental disorder also have had a diagnosable alcohol or drug-abuse disorder. Nearly half of those with schizophrenia, for example, and more than half of those with manic-depressive illness have had a history of substance abuse. Conversely, more than half of adults diagnosed with drug-abuse disorders also have had one or more mental disorders, as have 37% of adults who have been alcohol abusers. The high failure rate of substance-abuse treatment programs may be due in part to co-occurring mental disorders.

Mother-Infant Interactions. Studying newborn rats, NIMH-supported scientists showed that early separation from the mother leads to increased levels of stress hormones in the infant. This finding has significant implications for the newborn's developing nervous system, since elevated stress-hormone levels may impair nerve-cell functions critical to memory and learning.

Other researchers have demonstrated in animals and humans that in the first day of life human babies learn to recognize their mother's odor and to locate and maintain contact with her breast. Since this type of learning relies on normal functioning of the brain's temporal lobe and limbic system, the findings can be used to assess cognitive function in newborn human infants. With early detection, it might be possible one day to treat nervous-system defects in newborns while the brain is at its most flexible.

Decade of the Brain. With Congress establishing the 1990s as the Decade of the Brain, researchers are pursuing a number of initiatives to increase understanding of the brain and its role in mental illnesses. One area attracting particular research interest is AIDS. Investigators in four NIMH-supported AIDS research centers are studying the causes of central-nervous-system disease in AIDS, including the molecular and cellular mechanisms involved in AIDS dementia complex. This brain disorder deprives some AIDS patients of memory and reasoning ability. An intensified effort also is under way to study nervous-system development in infants and children infected with the AIDS virus (HIV) and to develop animal models to study how HIV infection impairs the function of the central nervous system.

ALAN I. LESHNER, *Acting Director*
National Institute of Mental Health

METEOROLOGY

Natural and man-made changes to the atmosphere commanded international attention for much of 1991, even while a vigorous debate continued on the broader question of long-term effects.

Oil Fires. Although brief, the 1991 war in the Middle East resulted in near-total devastation of Kuwait's oil fields. An international team of scientists assembled by the World Meteorological Organization rushed to the area to evaluate the damage being caused by smoke billowing from well fires. At their height the fires were estimated to be burning 3 million barrels of oil and 1.4 billion cu ft (40 million m^3) of natural gas per day. Although the scientists concluded that the effects were primarily regional, contamination by black, oily residue was identified as far away as the Himalaya Mountains in Kashmir. (*See also* ENVIRONMENT.)

Volcanic Eruption. Mount Pinatubo, located on the island of Luzon in the Philippines, became extremely active during the summer. The explosions of June 15–16 sent a plume of ash and smoke 100,000 ft (30 480 m) into the atmosphere. This height (some 50,000 ft—15 240 m —into the stratosphere) experiences very little "weather," so it was expected to take as long as three to four years for the pollutants to be removed. Aerosols (tiny particles condensed from the volcanic gases) efficiently reflect incoming sunlight, so their net effect is to cool the Earth. Parts of Japan were reported to be receiving up to 15% less sunlight in late summer. The Mount Pinatubo eruption injected about twice the aerosols into the stratosphere as did the last significant eruption, El Chichón (Mexico) in 1982, so it was estimated that the global average temperature would be lower by as much as .9°F (.5°C) for the next few years. Such declines do not occur uniformly worldwide, and the effects are mixed in with other major forcings, such as El Niño. The blankets of fresh volcanic ash from Mount Pinatubo caused numerous mud slides whenever heavy rain occurred. (*See also* SIDEBAR/GEOLOGY.)

Ozone Depletion. Once again a hole in the stratospheric ozone was observed over Antarctica in the Southern Hemisphere spring. Satellite-based measurements reached their lowest single-day values in the 13 years of monitoring.

The continuing occurrence of the ozone hole spurred action on several fronts. First, China ratified the 1990 Montreal Protocol on stratospheric-ozone depletion. This brought a large developing nation into the group (now numbering 70) committed to phasing out the ozone-layer-destroying family of chlorofluorocarbons (CFCs) by the end of the century. Second, the Environmental Protection Agency (EPA) proposed rules implementing the Montreal Protocol in the United States. Third, the search for CFC substitutes moved into high gear. And fourth, scientists mounted a study of the 1991 ozone hole, focusing on the appearance of stratospheric ice-crystal clouds.

Global Warming. The scientific debate over the "greenhouse effect" became more heated during 1991. In part the debate reflected the normal course of science in which all theories are reassessed critically. The other factor was the demand in the political process for definitive statements from scientists. It is clear that increases in radioactive trace gases tend to force the atmosphere toward warmer temperatures. The key issue is whether every important interdependency that helps determine surface temperature has been included in the calculations.

Observing Systems. Surface-based observing systems continued to be upgraded in the United States as all three systems now under development were put to operational use.

The WSR-88D (developed as NEXRAD—next-generation radar) replaces antiquated weather radars with modern technology, including Doppler capabilities. Three units were operating in late 1991, with seven more in progress. The Automated Surface Observing System (ASOS) eliminates the need for most routine visual observations of the weather at airports. Three ASOS units were operating, with 51 more in progress. Because ASOS units are less expensive than human observers, some 200 to 500 more airports will have ASOS by 1996 than were reporting the weather in 1991. The Wind Profiler uses a vertically pointing Doppler radar to report the wind continuously at various levels of the atmosphere. A "demonstration network" of 29 Wind Profiler units in the plains states was operating as the year ended.

Satellites. In May the NOAA-D polar-orbiting meteorological satellite was launched successfully (becoming NOAA-12 upon achieving orbit). This TIROS-N class satellite joined three similar satellites already in orbit.

In October the National Aeronautics and Space Administration (NASA) successfully launched the Upper Atmosphere Research Satellite. Among its capabilities it was expected to measure winds at heights between 6 mi (10 km) and 186 mi (300 km), where observations were very sparse.

Throughout the year problems continued to plague GOES-NEXT, the next-generation Geostationary Operational Environmental Satellites. With the project already well behind schedule and over budget, new technical difficulties raised questions about continuing it. During the fall it was decided to continue development, even while a contingency plan was made in case the current GOES satellite fails before the first new model is launched (scheduled for late 1992). Under the plan, Meteosat-3 would be borrowed from Eumetsat—the 16-nation group that operates Europe's weather-sat-

© Brent Ward/Sipa

A combination of high winds, warm temperatures, low humidity, and dry conditions caused by five years of drought led to a sweeping wildfire in the Oakland and Berkeley region of California, Oct. 20–21, 1991. At least 24 persons were killed and some 1,800 homes and 900 apartment units were destroyed by the fires. It was one of the costliest disasters in California's history.

ellite system—and repositioned to view the United States and adjacent waters.

Finally, NASA announced in late summer that the design for the Earth Observing System (EOS) would be shifted from two large satellites to a number of smaller satellites. EOS is a major, long-term effort to monitor the environment slated to start late in the 1990s.

Weather Highlights. The year was characterized by extremes in precipitation in the United States. California suffered a fifth year of drought. As the summer progressed, drought conditions in the northern plains eased, while the corn belt and mid-Atlantic states dried out. The Gulf states received copious rainfall the entire year. Shreveport, LA, received a year's worth of rain by May 9, then surpassed its all-time record by mid-October. The most notable single event was a slow-moving cluster of thunderstorms over south Florida in mid-October. North Miami Beach received 11 inches (279 mm), while Hollywood got 15 inches (381 mm).

Temperatures in many parts of the country were average or above average during the first eight months of the year. A widespread heat wave in early August helped guarantee that the summer was above average from the corn belt through the mid-Atlantic states (as well as being dry). The pattern later shifted to cool in the West and warm in the East.

Tornado activity was similar to that in 1989 and 1990, with higher-than-normal occurrence (1,147 versus 803) and lower-than-normal deaths (36 versus 82). A late-April event spawned 70 tornadoes from Texas to Nebraska, including the Andover, KS, storm, which caused more than half the year's fatalities.

The Atlantic Ocean tropical-storm season produced a relatively small number of storms, but managed to wreak havoc twice on the mid-Atlantic and Northeast coasts. There were seven named storms and three hurricanes. In mid-August, Hurricane Bob went onshore at Narragansett, RI, causing massive damage to buildings, power lines, and boats from Rhode Island across Cape Cod in Massachusetts. Then in late October the remnants of Hurricane Grace teamed up with a developing northeaster. The storm churned southeast of Cape Cod for two days, resulting in additional devastation, including severe damage to President George Bush's summer house in Kennebunkport, ME.

Notable events outside the United States included the tropical cyclone that hit Bangladesh on April 30. It was estimated to be the fourth-worst storm ever observed in the Bay of Bengal in terms of fatalities. The onset of the summer monsoon was delayed, soaking southern and eastern India, while the other regions baked in premonsoon heat. When the monsoon finally arrived, severe flooding occurred in Indochina. Also, prolonged heavy rains and severe flooding occurred during early July in the Yangtze River in China, leaving 2 million people homeless.

Finally, in November the Climate Analysis Center of the National Weather Service announced that a weak warm episode of El Niño had begun. The apparent start of an El Niño was blamed for the coldest winter in New Zealand in 15 years and for the unusual occurrence of rain in Chile's Atacama Desert.

GEORGE J. HUFFMAN
Universities Space Research Association

MEXICO

Mexico thrived in 1991. Government efforts to stimulate the economy by encouraging private enterprise continued to pay off as the economy performed well for still another year. Less successful, however, were efforts to rid the nation's electoral system of its reputation for fraudulent practices. Negotiations for a North American free-trade agreement began in June (*see* SPECIAL REPORT, page 360).

Politics. The August 18th elections for the national Chamber of Deputies, half of the Senate seats, and six governorships served as a test of the government's willingness to democratize the political system. In addition, fraud-free elections were important to improve the nation's reputation in the United States, with which it was negotiating a free-trade agreement. In 1988, President Carlos Salinas de Gortari of the Institutional Revolutionary Party (PRI) barely squeaked to a victory amid widespread charges of voter fraud. Since then, Salinas had promised a fraud-proof electoral system. New laws created a relatively independent Federal Electoral Institute, tough vote-fraud penalties, and a hard-to-counterfeit voter credential. Fear that PRI was losing control prompted the passage of a provision giving an automatic majority in the Chamber to any political party which received 35% of the national vote; PRI was the only party likely to obtain such a percentage.

The Federal Electoral Institute was so slow in issuing the new voter credentials that perhaps as many as 9 million potential voters never received them. Opposition parties complained. Some demanded the postponement of the elections; others asked that foreign observers be invited to monitor the elections to prevent fraud, a demand the government rejected on the grounds of national sovereignty. Government welfare expenditures rose significantly before the election, particularly in places where PRI faced electoral difficulties.

As expected, PRI steamrolled the opposition with about 61% of the national vote. The National Action Party (PAN) was second with more than 18%. The Democratic Revolutionary Party, whose candidate almost beat Salinas in 1988, saw its vote percentage drop from about 30% to below 10% because of internal dissension. PRI won 320 of the 500 deputy seats, including all 40 in the Federal District, where opposition parties had been strong. It also won back a Senate seat there and claimed victory in all the gubernatorial races. PAN won 100 deputy seats and a Senate seat in North Baja California state. The other parties fared poorly.

Two gubernatorial races provoked so much controversy that the PRI candidates had to abandon the posts they just had won. PAN claimed that its candidate, Vicente Fox, former president of Coca-Cola of Mexico, won the Guanajuato governorship but that it was stolen by PRI. In the face of PAN-led demonstrations, the newly elected PRI governor took the oath of office and then resigned, forcing a new election. To ensure that Fox could not run, the Guanajuato state legislature enacted a law requiring gubernatorial candidates to be natives of the state, which Fox was not. In nearby San Luis Potosí, the new PRI governor also resigned amid charges that the opposition candidate actually had been elected.

Most observers agreed that these elections demonstrated Salinas' determination to achieve economic reform before tackling political reform. To do so, he must have the support of the PRI machinery and a free hand in the Chamber of Deputies. During the 1988-91 term, he had to bargain with PAN to pass some laws. The new PRI majority, added to the votes of some small, tame opposition parties, not only guaranteed passage of ordinary laws but also enactment of new constitutional amendments. Speculation quickly arose that Salinas wanted a constitutional amendment allowing him to run for another six-year term in 1994. More important, however, was the fact that the new

AP/Wide World

With trade and other economic issues on the agenda, Mexico's President Carlos Salinas de Gortari (right) *visited several European capitals during the summer. In Moscow he conferred with Soviet President Mikhail Gorbachev* (left).

majority allowed Salinas to pass any laws necessary to implement the forthcoming free-trade agreement with the United States and Canada.

In his State of the Union address on November 1, President Salinas broached the idea of amending the constitution to eliminate some of its anticlerical provisions. By year's end legislators had approved constitutional changes giving legal recognition to religious institutions for the first time since 1917, subject to approval by state legislatures.

Mexico remained politically stable, but its political system showed signs of trouble. In March, Salinas had to fire his attorney general and launch a probe and reorganization of the federal judicial police because of alleged human-rights violations. In April bugging devices were discovered in the offices of the National Commission on Human Rights.

Economics. The Mexican economy performed well even though it is tied closely to that of the United States, which was in recession. The gross domestic product grew almost 5% between January and June. Exports, led by nonpetroleum products, rose almost 16% compared to the previous year. The stock market boomed, with the index rising 90% in the first eight months of the year. The labor-business solidarity pact helped reduce inflation to about 15%, its lowest level in 13 years. The foreign debt declined. Foreign investors, principally from the United States and Japan, significantly increased their participation in the economy. Automobile and truck manufacturing rose from 550,000 units in 1990 to 650,000 in 1991. The rising domestic economy and the demand for oil led PEMEX, the government oil monopoly, to adopt a $3 billion exploration budget.

Liberalization of the economy was accounting for its consistent improvement. President Salinas continued to sell state-owned corporations to private investors, encourage both domestic and foreign capital investment, and unplug bottlenecks to economic growth. The government sold controlling interest in its largest bank, BANAMEX, to a group of Mexican private investors for more than $3 billion. Returning control of banks to private hands stimulated capital investment more than any other act, for it signaled the government's commitment to private enterprise. Mexican financier Carlos Slim gained control of the former government-owned telephone company through a $1.7 billion investment. Another 20% of the company's stock was sold abroad. In June, Salinas ordered the union-controlled Veracruz Port Service, long noted for corruption and inefficiency, dismantled and replaced by a private-sector firm. This reorganization quickly increased cargo handling at the nation's largest port. Foreign companies were invited to explore and drill for oil, a move reversing more than 50 years of government policy. In November the president also hinted that he would seek to eliminate some collective farming organizations, allowing private individuals—including foreigners—to own more land.

Mexican firms launched a number of cooperative ventures with U.S. firms. Vitro, the $2.76 billion glass manufacturer in Monterrey, signed an agreement with Corning Glass that would put Vitro's products in U.S. stores. Wal-Mart, the U.S. retailing giant, planned to open three stores in Mexico in collaboration with a Mexican retail firm.

Social Welfare. Salinas created a new agency, Solidarity (PRONASOL), to encourage private citizens to invest in efforts to improve health conditions and to build small public-works projects. Funded at more than $3 billion, Solidarity made important gains in improving living conditions among the nation's poor, reaching people who never had benefited from previous programs. The adoption of this approach represented a break with past government policies whereby the central government distributed welfare benefits, often on purely political grounds.

Foreign Affairs. The main foreign-policy goal of the Salinas administration was the successful negotiation of a free-trade agreement with the United States and Canada. Simultaneously, Mexico sought expansion of its economic activity in Central America. In January the presidents of Costa Rica, Guatemala, Honduras, Nicaragua, and El Salvador met with President Salinas in southern Mexico to discuss plans for a free-trade agreement by 1996. Continued trade and investment initiatives also were made in Japan and Europe as the government sought to open new markets and attract more foreign capital.

Mexico supported the Persian Gulf war but limited its participation. Many citizens opposed any such action, but the government joined the coalition in order to improve relations with the United States.

DONALD J. MABRY
Mississippi State University

MEXICO • Information Highlights

Official Name: United Mexican States.
Location: Southern North America.
Area: 761,602 sq mi (1 972 550 km²).
Population (mid-1991 est.): 85,700,000.
Chief Cities (March 1990 census): Mexico City (Federal District), the capital, 8,236,960; Guadalajara, 1,628,617; Nezahualcóyotl, 1,259,543.
Government: *Head of state and government,* Carlos Salinas de Gortari, president (took office Dec. 1988). *Legislature*—National Congress: Senate and Chamber of Deputies.
Monetary Unit: Peso (3,070.01 pesos equal U.S.$1, floating rate, Nov. 12, 1991).
Gross Domestic Product (1989 U.S.$): $187,000,000,000.
Economic Indexes (1990): *Consumer Prices* (1980 = 100), all items, 15,058.3; food, 14,031.9. *Industrial Production* (1980 = 100), 120.
Foreign Trade (1990 U.S.$): *Imports,* $29,993,000,000; *exports,* $26,524,000,000.

The Free-Trade Issue

The U.S. battle over a free-trade agreement with Mexico could have more permanent results than the 1991 Persian Gulf war. At stake is the creation of the world's largest trading bloc—the North American Free Trade Area (NAFTA), comprised of Canada, Mexico, and the United States. If the United States and Mexico sign a free-trade agreement similar to the one signed by Canada and the United States in 1988, the resulting NAFTA would contain 360 million people and produce $6 trillion in goods and services annually (25% more than the European Community). The NAFTA eventually might become a hemispheric free-trade area. Thus, the issue of negotiating a U.S.-Mexican free-trade agreement presents the possibility of a new world economic order.

The key skirmish in 1991 was the congressional vote on extending fast-track authority to the Bush administration. Under fast-track authority, Congress has no role in free-trade negotiations and only can vote yes or no on a final agreement. Democrats were reluctant to give the Republican president another victory, especially so close to the 1992 presidential election. Economic issues largely determined the sides in the battle, however.

Pros and Cons. Because Mexico is poor by U.S. and Canadian standards, its integration into a North American common market means that some will prosper while others will suffer. The U.S. and Canadian economies are similar except in size. Both the Mexican economy and standard of living are high by world standards but puny compared to those of its northern neighbors. Labor unions in the United States and Canada fear that jobs will be lost to cheaper Mexican labor because plants will be moved south of the Rio Grande River. The U.S. National Association of Manufacturers and Business Roundtable, ardent supporters of the free-trade pact, counter that such plant relocations would benefit all three countries. Admitting that some industrial jobs will be lost to Mexico, they argue that these jobs would go to Asia if not to Mexico. By going to Mexico, North American industry can remain competitive. Mexican purchasing power would increase, and new export-related jobs would be created in the United States, for Mexico buys 70% of its imports from the United States.

Unconvinced, the AFL-CIO tried to defeat the bill granting the Bush administration the right to use fast-track authority. Joining labor unions in trying to defeat fast-track authorization were Canadians and Mexicans who feared that their countries would be dominated by the gigantic U.S. economy or who feared that lax Mexican pollution controls further would destroy the environment or, possibly, lead to a relaxation of environmental protection standards. The Bush administration, in alliance with the Mexican and Canadian governments, free-enterprise advocates, southwestern U.S. states, and business groups, promoted the agreement as the best means of ensuring prosperity to all three nations in the long term. The Mexican government argued that its recent ef-

© Mario Villafuerte/Picture Group

As Mexico's President Carlos Salinas de Gortari visited Texas in April 1991, U.S. labor-union members protested against the proposed U.S.-Mexican free-trade agreement. U.S. workers fear the pact would lead to the loss of their jobs.

© Keith Dannemiller/Saba

Lamps are produced for export at a Mexican factory, left. Although the proposed U.S.-Mexican trade pact could undercut some Mexican industries, 71% of Mexicans favor free trade without conditions or restrictions.

forts to create a pro-business climate would be institutionalized by the agreement.

U.S. Congressional Action. The Bush administration and its allies triumphed when the votes were taken in the U.S. House of Representatives on May 23 and in the Senate on May 24. Both branches passed the bill—the House by a 231–192 margin and the Senate by 59–36. Although the bulk of the opponents in both houses were Democrats (170 of the 192 "no" votes in the House; 31 of the 36 "no" votes in the Senate), Democratic leaders such as Sen. Lloyd Bentsen (TX) and Reps. Dan Rostenkowski (IL) and Richard Gephardt (MO) voted for the fast-track extension. Representatives from states with heavy industries and strong unions (principally in the Northeast and Midwest) or with large textile industries (such as North Carolina) tended to vote against the extension, while representatives from southwestern states voted for it. At the last minute, four of the six largest environmental groups announced support for the bill after Bush promised that environmentalists would be appointed to the task force advising the negotiators. Formal talks on the pact began in June.

Effects, Prospects, and Other Agreements. The economies of all three countries will change significantly if agreement is reached, for specialization should make each nation more competitive. Mexican exports of farm products would increase dramatically as U.S. tariffs are dropped, for 60% of Mexican farm exports are taxed by the United States. Agribusiness in Canada and the United States will have to compete against Mexican farm products. U.S. orange-juice producers, for example, are likely to suffer. U.S. exports of corn, soya, and sorghum and exports of Canadian wheat and timber to Mexico would increase, however. Some manufacturing plants in both Canada and the United States would move to Mexico, but Mexican industries also would face more competition. In the short term, the number of illegal immigrants to the United States would increase but eventually it would decline as more jobs open up in Mexico.

In spite of its approval of fast-track authority, the U.S. Congress is likely to try to amend the U.S.-Mexican free-trade agreement when it finally is submitted, probably in 1993. In the summer of 1991, Sen. Donald Riegle (D-MI) began seeking support for a congressional resolution to allow amendment of the final trade agreement in the areas of environmental protection, settlement of disputes, aid to dislocated workers, labor standards, and origin of the content of goods. The United States will want to stipulate a North American content percentage to prevent Mexico from becoming a gigantic assembly plant for Asian and European producers. U.S. businesses will demand that the agreement ensures that Mexican producers not have a competitive advantage by not having to pay the costs associated with labor and environmental regulations. U.S. manufacturers might want to restore tariffs if flooded by foreign goods or if the non-U.S. content became too high.

Discussions about a North American Free Trade Area encouraged similar free-trade initiatives throughout Latin America. Nations there began to liberalize their economies and seek admission into a hemispheric common market. In January, Mexico and the Central American nations agreed to create a free-trade area within six years and Mexico later signed an agreement with Colombia and Venezuela to create a free-trade area by 1994.

DONALD J. MABRY

MICHIGAN

A new Republican governor put his stamp on Michigan politics in 1991. Controversy arose in Detroit over plans to build a new stadium at public expense for Detroit's major-league baseball team and allegations of criminal activity by top police officials.

State Cutbacks. Republican John Engler assumed the governorship on January 1 and, in keeping with his conservative ideology, began a drastic reduction in state services. As the months passed, the governor slashed millions of dollars from the state budget through administrative orders and budget vetoes.

State employment was reduced from 66,080 workers on January 1 to 62,604 by October 12. Reduced support for the arts, including cutbacks in state funding for the Detroit Symphony and Detroit Institute of Arts, brought Engler under sharp criticism, but the most vehement objections were to cutbacks in welfare services—reduced support for families with dependent children and the elimination of general welfare assistance for almost 90,000 "employable" single adults. Republicans insisted the cutbacks were necessary to avoid tax increases and rising budget deficits.

Police Charges. Detroit Police Chief William L. Hart, 67, was indicted in February by a federal grand jury on charges of embezzling $1.3 million from a police fund; filing false tax returns for 1985, 1986, and 1987; and obstructing justice by tampering with a witness who was to testify against him before the grand jury. Hart, who insisted he was innocent, was suspended with pay pending his trial, scheduled for 1992.

Kenneth A. Weiner, 45, a former deputy police chief and business associate of Detroit Mayor Coleman A. Young, was sentenced in May to ten years in prison for masterminding a phony investment scheme and failing to pay taxes. In September, Weiner pleaded guilty to another charge of embezzling $1.3 million from a police fund under an agreement with federal prosecutors that he would serve no more than three additional years in prison.

Tiger Stadium. Proposals to build a new stadium for the American League Detroit Tigers baseball team aroused controversy on several grounds. Critics assailed multimillionaire Tigers owner Tom Monaghan not only for his insistence that public money help finance a new $200 million baseball stadium, but that the stadium include luxury boxes to be rented to businesses for entertainment purposes. Critics argued that the existing Tiger Stadium could be renovated at far less cost. Detroit and Wayne county officials lobbied the state legislature to allow them to assess a county hotel/motel tax to help finance the stadium.

On another front, Tigers president Bo Schembechler and public officials—Wayne County Executive Edward McNamara most prominently—battled publicly over possible sites. McNamara and Detroit's Mayor Young wanted any new publicly financed stadium to be located in downtown Detroit. Schembechler maintained it should be on the west side of downtown, close to the existing stadium—and hinted the franchise would be moved to Florida if the Tigers' demands were not met.

Other News. Detroit automakers posted major losses attributed to a continuing national recession. General Motors Corp. reported losses of $2.98 billion in the first three quarters of 1991. Ford Motor Co. and Chrysler Corp. also reported losses of $1.78 billion and $892 million, respectively . . . A former postal worker, bitter because of his dismissal from his job in 1990, went on a shooting spree in November at the Royal Oak regional postal center, killing four postal workers and himself.

CHARLES W. THEISEN, *"The Detroit News"*

MICHIGAN • Information Highlights

Area: 58,527 sq mi (151 586 km^2).
Population (1990 census): 9,295,297.
Chief Cities (1990 census): Lansing, the capital, 127,321; Detroit, 1,027,974; Grand Rapids, 189,126; Warren, 144,864; Flint, 140,761; Sterling Heights, 117,810.
Government (1991): *Chief Officers*—governor, John Engler (R); lt. gov., Connie Binsfeld (R). *Legislature*—Senate, 38 members; House of Representatives, 110 members.
State Finances (fiscal year 1990): *Revenue*, $23,405,000,000; *expenditure*, $23,098,000,000.
Personal Income (1990): $171,003,000,000; per capita, $18,360.
Labor Force (June 1991): *Civilian labor force*, 4,597,300; *unemployed*, 423,100 (9.2% of total force).
Education: *Enrollment* (fall 1989)—public elementary schools, 1,127,921; public secondary, 448,864; colleges and universities, 560,320. *Public school expenditures* (1989), $7,493,266,000.

MICROBIOLOGY

The year 1991 brought new hope for the development of a malaria vaccine, evidence of the presence of a new rat-transmitted disease in the United States, the discovery of a symbiotic relationship involving a biosynthetic pathway, the detection of an association between the incidence of AIDS and the practice of circumcision, and the use of DNA sequence analysis to track the history of a disease-causing organism.

Malaria Vaccine. Malaria is a protozoan-caused disease that strikes 270 million people worldwide each year, killing more than 2.5 million. Of the various species that cause malaria in humans, *Plasmodium falciparum* is responsible for most of the deaths.

Research has shown that the production of antibodies by a vaccinated individual is induced by the proteins that are present in a parasite's cell surface. In laboratory experiments involving mice and the protozoan *P. yoelii*, which causes malaria in this animal, it was found that there are two cell-surface proteins (CS and SSP2), each of which when used separately as an antigen stimulates antibody production in about 50% of the mice.

Dr. S. L. Hoffman and his colleagues at the Naval Medical Research Institute in Bethesda, MD, have used a combination of both the above surface proteins as a vaccine. None of the immunized mice developed malaria even when injected with more than ten times the number of parasites known to cause the disease. It remains for scientists to isolate the *P. falciparum* cell-surface proteins that are comparable to those used in the mouse vaccine and to develop a malaria vaccine for humans.

A New Danger From Rats. It has been known for some time that rats in some Asian countries harbor a virus called the *Hantaan* virus which when transmitted to human beings causes high fever, internal bleeding, high blood pressure, and kidney failure. If the disease is untreated, death ensues. Transmission of the virus from rats to humans is through airborne droplets exhaled by infected rats and through contact with rat urine and feces.

Dr. J. W. LeDuc of the U.S. Army Medical Research Institute and others studied hospital patients in the Baltimore area who were suffering from high blood pressure and chronic kidney problems. They found that the blood of a number of these patients contained antibodies against the *Hantaan* virus, indicating that these people were infected with the virus and at risk of developing the disease's other symptoms. It further was found that about two thirds of the rats captured in the Baltimore area and tested were infected with the virus.

Symbiosis and a Biosynthetic Pathway. Legumes (peas, beans, etc.) grow well in nitrogen-poor soils because, in their roots, they encase nitrogen-fixing bacteria which convert the nitrogen present in air into nitrate which the plants need. The bacteria in turn receive nutrients from the plants. This type of mutually beneficial relationship between diverse organisms is called symbiosis.

A crucial biosynthetic pathway for both the legume and the bacteria is the one that leads to the formation of the oxygen-carrying compound heme (the same as in human hemoglobin). A precursor molecule in the synthesis of heme is the chemical compound delta-aminolevunilic acid (ALA). Working with the nitrogen-fixing bacterial species *Bradyrhizobium japonicum*, Drs. I. Sangwan and M. R. O'Brian at the State University of New York in Buffalo selected a mutant strain which is incapable of producing ALA, and hence cannot make heme. They injected the mutant bacteria into the roots of soybean (*Glycine max*) seedlings. After becoming incorporated into the root tissues, the mutant bacteria began to make heme; specifically, they took ALA which was produced by the soybean plant and used it to make heme. Thus, a symbiotic relationship can involve parts of a biosynthetic pathway.

AIDS and Circumcision. Surgical removal of the penile foreskin has been practiced by various groups for thousands of years. However, most of the world's males are not circumcised. With the present worldwide increasing frequency of AIDS (1991 World Health Organization estimate of 1.5 million active cases and 10 million carriers of the virus), a number of scientists have investigated whether circumcision protects against the disease. Dr. A. Ronald of the University of Manitoba in Winnipeg and his colleagues at the University of Nairobi in Kenya reported on 140 geographical districts in Africa. In areas where carriers of the AIDS virus make up less than 1% of the population, 97% of the groups practice circumcision, whereas in areas where carriers of the virus constitute more than 10% of the population, only 6% of the groups practice circumcision. This finding may prompt governments to encourage circumcision.

Tracking a Disease-Causing Microbe. In 1975, Lyme disease was described as a distinct clinical entity, occurring in Lyme, CT. The disease is caused by a bacterium (*Borrelia burgdorferi*) which is transmitted to humans through the bite of a tick (*Ixodes dammini*). In order to determine whether the bacteria were present in the area before 1975, Dr. D. H. Persing and his colleagues at Yale University went to various museums of natural history and examined specimens of ticks that were known to have been collected in Connecticut in the 1940s. The tissues of a number of the ticks contained *B. burgdorferi*-specific DNA sequences, indicating that the organisms were present in the area at least one generation before the disease was described.

LOUIS LEVINE, *City College of New York*

MIDDLE EAST

The Middle East commanded major headlines in 1991. By mid-January a U.S.-led coalition was engaged in a major Persian Gulf war to force Iraq to evacuate from Kuwait. In the aftermath of Iraq's defeat, the plight of Iraq's Kurdish minority gained attention. In November the last oil-well fire of the war was capped in Kuwait. . . . Representatives of Israel, its Arab neighbors, and the Palestinians of the occupied territories assembled for peace talks in Madrid in late October and in Washington in December. . . . Terry Anderson, the last of the U.S. hostages held in Lebanon, was released in December; only two Germans and one Italian, who was believed dead, remained in captivity as 1991 ended. (*See also* FEATURE SECTION, page 36.)

MILITARY AFFAIRS

The Persian Gulf war—its weapons, strategies, and logistics—was the year's major military event (*see* FEATURE SECTION, page 36; SIDEBAR, page 366). But other forces at work elsewhere also contributed to making 1991 a year of transition for both the U.S. and Soviet military establishments. As the Soviet Union disintegrated, the United States wrestled with the question of how to trim its massive armed strength to fit into the post-Cold War world.

U.S. Base Closures and Realignments. After months of arguments among members of the U.S. Congress, and pleas by their constituents as to which military bases were the most important to national security, Secretary of Defense Dick Cheney endorsed the evaluations of the Defense Base Closure and Realignment Commission. This body had been appointed to review the initial proposals regarding which military bases no longer were required. On October 1 the recommendations of the base-closure commission became law.

By 1996, 13 Air Force facilities, eight Navy and Marine stations, and four Army bases would be closed. Among the largest and best-known military installations to be terminated would be the Bergstrom and Carswell Air Force bases in Texas, Castle Air Force Base in California, and Lowry Air Force Base in Colorado; Navy stations at San Francisco and Long Beach in California, Philadelphia, PA, and on Puget Sound in Washington; and the Fort Ord, CA, and Fort Benjamin Harrison, IN, Army bases, and Sacramento Army Depot in California. Additionally, 48 other domestic military facilities would be realigned. The cries and complaints heard from the various communities slated to lose nearby military bases, and the payrolls which they generate, suggested that President Dwight D. Eisenhower knew what he was talking about in his January 1961 valedictory address to the U.S. people. In that message, Eisenhower had warned against the military-industrial complex which might use its power and influence to pressure for the continuance of military activities far past the time when they could be justified by any conceivable military threat.

Another example of political pressure to maintain unneeded military units was seen when Congress showed reluctance to accept Secretary Cheney's proposed cuts in national guard and reserve units. Congress was reacting to numerous letters from communities which did not want their local armories closed or reduced in size.

Restructuring of Armed Forces of the Former Soviet Union. As the Soviet Union was replaced by a commonwealth composed of former USSR republics, the largest and most powerful of the successor governments, Russia, assured the West that it would continue with the former government's announced plan to remove all Red Army units and other military forces from the former Communist countries of Eastern Europe. At year's end most of the troops had left except for contingents remaining in Poland and what had been East Germany, now incorporated into the Federal German Republic. The expectation was that these forces all would have departed by 1993. A problem facing the former Soviet republics in their military restructuring was the difficulty former enlisted men and officers were having relocating themselves as civilians in a declining economy that offered little opportunity for men mustered out of service. Some observers in Moscow and Washington fretted over the possibility that a large and disgruntled army, including unemployed former army personnel, would constitute a threat to the fragile democratic structures that were being built on the remains of the former Soviet Union. Adding further complexity to the military situation in the former USSR was the interest shown by some republics in forming their own armies independent of any central authority. Of particular concern was the plan announced by the Ukrainian republic to raise its own army of 450,000 troops.

In the last four months of the year, as the Soviet Union lurched toward oblivion, concern mounted as to what political authority now would control the Kremlin's immense stockpile of nuclear weapons. The situation cleared somewhat just before Christmas when Secretary of State James Baker returned from Moscow to address a North Atlantic Treaty Organization (NATO) meeting. Baker told the allies that he had obtained assurances from the former Soviet republics of Ukraine, Byelorussia (now Belarus), and Kazakhstan—areas in which Soviet ICBMs are based—that they would comply with the Non-Proliferation Treaty and rid themselves of former Soviet nuclear weapons on their soil when they become fully independent. However, at year's end the situation regarding Kazakhstan remained ambiguous. Also in late November, Congress authorized up to $400 million to assist in the dismantlement of many nuclear weapons previously held by the USSR. In the interim the weapons were placed under the control of Air Marshal Yevgeni Shaposhnikov, the former Soviet minister of defense, who now was reporting to Russian President Boris Yeltsin.

Late in December, Secretary Baker issued an interesting statement regarding the nuclear weapons not marked for destruction under START that were transferred from Gorbachev's defunct government to Yeltsin's new Russian government. Baker indicated he believes in the balance of power approach to international relations when he said—"I am not prepared to walk away from the concept of nuclear deterrence that has kept the peace for more than 40 years. I would like to see zero weapons targeted on the United States, but I am not prepared . . . to subscribe to the philosophy of denuclearization."

Another problem was whether the Red Army would acquiesce in the transfer of political power from the old Soviet government to the new Russian government. In mid-December, however, senior Red Army officials stated their support for President Yeltsin.

Strategic Weapons of the Future. The United States had to make hard choices in 1991 about what new weapons would be required in the future, and which programs could be canceled without compromising the national defense. In Congress the Bush administration just managed to retain funding for the B-2 Stealth bomber. Equally difficult was the effort, eventually successful, to retain monies in the budget for continued research on the Strategic Defense Initiative (SDI), a program begun under President Ronald Reagan to build a defense against ballistic-missile attack. In both instances the Republicans struggled to justify the large costs and to define a mission for the B-2 bomber and the SDI following the USSR's collapse.

Supporters of the two weapons systems argued that the Iraq war indicated there were external threats to the United States other than the declining one from the Soviet Union. Also, some urged that the nation "keep its powder dry" until it is certain the USSR would not be restructured in some new, but hostile, fashion.

In November the U.S. Congress and the Bush administration agreed to a $291 billion defense budget for fiscal 1992. A last-minute effort by Sen. Sam Nunn (D-GA) and Rep. Les Aspin (D-WI) to transfer $1 billion from Pentagon funding to aid the Soviet Union failed. The president, however, was authorized to use up to $100 million from the Pentagon budget to transport humanitarian aid to the Soviets.

A Reagan-Era Publication Is Canceled. In another sign of the changing times, 1991 ended with a Department of Defense announcement that it no longer would publish *Soviet Military Power,* which had been a mainstay in the Pentagon's efforts to garner support for increased military spending. Since the early days of the Reagan administration the annual publication had carried dire warnings about Soviet military intentions and artists' depictions of new and frightening Soviet weapons systems. In its place the Pentagon announced a new publication, *Military Forces in Transition*.

The North Atlantic Treaty Organization. With the Soviet-sponsored Warsaw Pact dissolved, the members of NATO began to discuss the kind of military alliance needed in a less-bellicose world. The potential for division between the Western allies was sparked by a suggestion from spokespersons for France and Germany that a new multinational European army be formed around a core of 30,000 French and German troops. The suggestion was received negatively by the British, who were suspicious about a continental force run by the French and Germans.

A complicated subject for NATO was raised in the fall when Czechoslovakia's President Václav Havel visited Washington. Speaking also for Hungary and Poland, the Czech leader told Congress that the East Europeans, now without a security alliance, wanted some kind of institutional association with NATO. What that link with the West would be was under discussion by NATO at the end of the year. The task was complicated further in December when Boris Yeltsin said Russia also was interested in joining NATO.

The Proliferation of Nuclear Weapons. With the Cold War tensions between the United States and the USSR easing, both Moscow and Washington showed increased concern over the nuclear weapons possessed by others. This concern was heightened when late in the year United Nations (UN) inspectors filed their reports regarding the extent to which Iraq had moved toward the development of atomic weapons. Another proliferation problem remained unresolved in 1991 when North Korea again refused to permit UN inspection teams to monitor its nuclear facilities, an obligation it assumed when Pyongyang signed the Nuclear Non-Proliferation Treaty. India and Israel also remained outside the treaty, with the former having demonstrated a nuclear device in 1974, and the latter assumed to have made a number of atomic bombs without actually testing them.

Hard Times for the U.S. Navy. The Navy endured two embarrassing incidents in 1991. In October former Assistant Secretary of the Navy for Research, Development, and Acquisition Melvyn R. Paisley was sentenced to four years in prison and fined $50,000. Paisley was the highest-ranking Pentagon official to be convicted in a scandal which broke in 1988, one of 45 individuals and six corporations who pleaded guilty to charges of illegally using confidential information to assist private contractors in securing Department of Defense contracts. One of the corporations, the Unisys Corporation, pleaded guilty to criminal misconduct in September and agreed to pay some $190 million in fines.

And in October, Adm. Frank B. Kelso 2d, chief of Naval Operations, announced that the 1989 explosion of a gun turret on the battleship *Iowa,* which killed 47 sailors, could not be attributed to Clayton M. Hartwig, a gunner's mate second class. Previously the Navy had claimed that Hartwig had been depressed over a failed homosexual relationship with a shipmate and had committed suicide by igniting bags of explosives in the turret. At year's end, Hartwig's family still planned to sue the Navy.

ROBERT M. LAWRENCE
Colorado State University

The Weaponry of the Gulf War

Raytheon Company

The six-week war that was fought in the Persian Gulf between Iraq and the United States and its allies early in 1991 offered an appropriate opportunity for a fresh look at the world's weapons systems. Some of the high-technology systems were developed during the defense buildup of the Reagan administrations and used for the first time in the Gulf conflict; others had been utilized earlier.

Taking note of allied success in a May 8 address to the U.S. Congress, Gen. H. Norman Schwarzkopf thanked Congress and former administrations for the "finest tanks and aircraft and ships and military equipment in the world." According to the commander of U.S. forces during the war, "that is what gave us the confidence necessary to attack . . . our enemy with the sure knowledge that we would prevail."

The **Patriot** antimissile system, *right,* was the most-celebrated U.S. weapon of the conflict and generally was considered a "spectacular success." After launch, the Patriot, a result of the U.S. Strategic Defense Initiative, regularly destroyed an Iraqi Scud in flight, defending Israel and Saudi Arabia from Iraqi attack. A description of other weapons that made the headlines during the Gulf war follows.

AP/Wide World

The **F-4G Wild Weasel,** above, *a U.S. Air Force fighter bomber, connects with a stratotanker for refueling over the Atlantic Ocean. Loaded with electronic jamming devices and High-Speed Anti-Radiation Missiles (HARMs), it was used in the Gulf to remove mobile Iraqi air defenses.*

The **Scud,** below, *was designed by the USSR to deliver nuclear warheads over a short range and later sold to Baghdad. As the Gulf conflict began, it was estimated that Iraq had between 500 and 800 Scuds, with fixed and mobile launchers. Since the Scud warheads, which were nonnuclear in the 1991 war, are attached to the missile, it offered a larger target for the Patriot's radar. Nonetheless, 28 U.S. soldiers were killed in a Scud attack in Saudi Arabia on February 25; Israeli sites also were hit by Scuds.*

© Kol al Arab/Sipa

© Hans Halberstadt/Arms Communications

© Gilles Rivet/Sipa

U.S. Marine helicopters armed with **TOW** *(Tube-launched, Optically tracked, Wire-guided) antitank missiles,* above left, *were successful in halting Iraqi attackers during the final campaign to liberate Kuwait. The* **F-16,** above right, *a ground-attack fighter with a variety of weapons, was used against Iraqi tanks. It has been in service since the late 1970s.*

© Gamma-Liaison

© Bill Gentile/Sipa

The **Tomahawk** *long-range cruise missile,* above left, *was launched from U.S. ships. A U.S. Navy official noted that its "accuracy was absolutely phenomenal" during the Gulf war. The* **AH-64 Apache,** above right, *a U.S. Army battlefield helicopter with laser guided Hellfire antitank missiles and ground-attack rockets, destroyed Iraqi early-warning radar stations.*

The U.S. **F-117A Stealth,** below left, *a medium-range bomber known for its radar-evading abilities, struck at night against high-priority fixed targets. The rotating radar dome of the* **EC-3 AWACS Sentry,** below right, *the U.S. Airborne Warning and Control System, provided continuous air surveillance for the allies, identifying enemy aircraft and blocking radar.*

Lockheed

Boeing Aerospace & Electronics

MINNESOTA

Baseball's Minnesota Twins, an unprecedented prewinter blizzard, Northwest Airlines, turbulent politics, deep budget cuts, and gambling commanded top attention in Minnesota in 1991.

Baseball and Weather. For the second time in five years, the Twins won the world baseball title, defeating the National League Atlanta Braves in a cliff-hanging seven-game series. The Braves' Indian costumes and "Tomahawk Chop" cheer drew protests from the American Indian Movement and focused national attention on sports symbols regarded as demeaning to ethnic groups.

The World Series hardly had ended when the earliest blizzard ever recorded began on Halloween eve, inundating the state with 6 to 30 inches (15–76 cm) of snow. It closed highways, businesses, and schools; caused power outages; buried unharvested crops; and disrupted activity for four days.

The Economy and Business. Minnesota's economy fared slightly better than the nation's. Unemployment in September was 5.2%, compared with 6.4% nationally. An especially dark spot was the dairy industry. Falling prices forced 500 of the state's 5,336 dairy farms to fold during the year.

For more than six months, state officials negotiated with Northwest Airlines (NWA) over a loan of $740 million for financing two NWA maintenance facilities in northern Minnesota that would create 2,000 jobs. Negotiators weighed the value of jobs against the risk to state funds on a tenuous private venture.

Work proceeded in Bloomington on construction of the $625 million Mall of America, believed to be the nation's largest shopping center with 2.6 million sq ft (241 540 m^2) of retail space. It was scheduled to open in August 1992.

Two leading broadcast stations, WCCO-TV and WCCO-Radio, were sold to CBS in a $200 million deal, but Federal Communications Commission (FCC) approval was challenged by a watchdog group, the Media Access Project, claiming the sale would curb diversity and exceed FCC ownership limits.

Politics. Independent-Republican (I-R) Gov. Arne Carlson had a rough first year in office. His popularity dropped sharply following a series of unpopular vetoes (most of which were invalidated by the state Supreme Court), a succession of quixotic staff changes, and fallout from the 1990 election. In a book, Jon Grunseth, who had been the I-R nominee for governor but withdrew amid allegations of sexual misconduct, accused Carlson of conspiring to force him out. Meanwhile, former Democratic-Farmer Labor Gov. Rudy Perpich, who, after losing to Carlson, assumed a U.S. governmental post in Yugoslavia, spoke of a comeback effort as an independent in 1994.

Legislative Action. The 1991 legislature slashed budgets and raised taxes to meet a $1.2 billion shortfall. These cuts hit the University of Minnesota hard, forcing it to freeze salaries, increase tuition, close its Waseca branch, and restructure.

Gambling. The state's new gambling industry was unsettled by a flurry of competition between the state's lottery, the dozen casinos operated by Indian tribes, charitable gambling, horse racing, and a dog track in adjoining Wisconsin. Meanwhile, an effort was under way to have the state legalize riverboat gambling to match the moves of Iowa, Wisconsin, and Illinois; plans to introduce a lottery using the Nintendo computer-game system were canceled, however.

ARTHUR NAFTALIN
Professor Emeritus, University of Minnesota

MINNESOTA • Information Highlights

Area: 84,402 sq mi (218 601 km^2).
Population (1990 census): 4,375,099.
Chief Cities (1990 census): St. Paul, the capital, 272,235; Minneapolis, 368,383; Duluth, 85,493.
Government (1991): *Chief Officers*—governor, Arne Carlson (I-R); lt. gov., Joanell Dyrstad (I-R). *Legislature*—Senate, 67 members; House of Representatives, 134 members.
State Finances (fiscal year 1990): *Revenue,* $13,162,000,000; *expenditure,* $11,355,000,000.
Personal Income (1990): $82,223,000,000; per capita, $18,731.
Labor Force (June 1991): *Civilian labor force,* 2,498,700; *unemployed,* 118,900 (4.8% of total force).
Education: *Enrollment* (fall 1989)—public elementary schools, 528,507; public secondary, 211,046; colleges and universities, 253,097. *Public school expenditures* (1989), $3,282,296,000.

MISSISSIPPI

In 1991, Mississippians stunned political observers by electing a Republican governor for the first time since Reconstruction. Only days before the November 5 balloting, polls had shown the Democratic incumbent, Ray Mabus—the first governor in the 20th century to be eligible for immediate reelection—seemingly headed for a narrow victory. The legislature, the economy, and widespread flooding were among the other items that made headlines in the state during the year.

Quadrennial Elections. Daniel Kirkwood "Kirk" Fordice, Jr., a 57-year-old construction contractor who never had held an elected political office, capitalized upon rampant anti-incumbency sentiment and lower-than-expected turnout among black voters in the Delta to win 51% of the slightly more than 700,000 votes cast in the November 5 election. Governor Mabus gathered 47% of the vote and Shawn O'Hara, an Independent, 2%. Fordice earlier

AP/Wide World

Mississippi Republican Governor-elect Kirk Fordice, with his wife Pat at his side, holds a news conference following his defeat of the Democratic incumbent Gov. Ray Mabus in the November general election. Fordice is the first Republican since the Reconstruction period to be elected governor of Mississippi.

had defeated state Auditor Pete Johnson, a former Democrat, in the first-ever Republican gubernatorial runoff election.

Republicans also captured the lieutenant governorship for the first time in more than 100 years. Republican state Sen. Eddie Briggs received 49% of the votes, third-term Democratic incumbent Brad Dye 42%, and former Independent state Sen. Henry Kirksey, 9%. While the failure of any candidate to win a majority meant that the Democratically controlled House of Representatives would be required by the constitution to choose the lieutenant governor from among the top two vote getters, Dye announced that he would not pursue his candidacy. Democrats retained control of all remaining statewide offices and continued to dominate both houses of the legislature, but a number of incumbents holding leadership roles were defeated.

The Legislature. The 1991 legislature was so bogged down by budget woes and internal bickering that the session was more noteworthy for what it failed to accomplish than for what it enacted.

Chief among the legislature's failures was the inability to fashion an acceptable and timely redistricting plan for the 1991 legislative elections. In the wake of that failure, a three-judge federal panel allowed the state to elect legislators from districts which were drawn prior to the 1990 population count. Although that ruling was affirmed by the U.S. Supreme Court after the elections had taken place, the governor called a special session of the legislature to redraw congressional districts.

Lawmakers refused to enact a tax increase, opting instead to approve a 1992 budget some $20 million leaner than that for 1991. Higher education, already suffering from inadequate funding, was especially hard hit. Two items that had been debated for nearly a decade finally won approval: landlord-tenant guidelines and mail-in voter registration. Other long-term agenda items, such as a state lottery, failed.

The Economy. Lower-than-expected corporate-income-tax receipts forced Governor Mabus to make painful budget cuts in January, but the cuts were not as deep as anticipated. Throughout the year, Mississippi's Index of Leading Economic Indicators fluctuated, suggesting to many that the recession that had come into view in 1990 had not bottomed out. Double-digit unemployment rates continued in a number of counties, and consumer confidence remained weak.

Flooding and Other News. Long-lasting spring floods, primarily in the Delta and in northeast Mississippi, covered more than 2 million acres (810 000 ha), affected approximately 1,700 homes, and caused losses of nearly $280 million. Despite late planting occasioned by the flooding, the state experienced a record cotton crop in 1991.

In November the U.S. Supreme Court heard arguments in the 16-year-old Ayers case charging that segregation continues in Mississippi's system of higher education. Also in November, Mississippians congratulated Democratic U.S. Rep. Jamie Whitten on 50 years of service in the Congress.

DANA B. BRAMMER
University of Mississippi

MISSISSIPPI • Information Highlights

Area: 47,689 sq mi (123 515 km²).
Population (1990 census): 2,573,216.
Chief Cities (1990 census): Jackson, the capital, 196,637; Biloxi, 46,319; Greenville, 45,226.
Government (1991): *Chief Officers*—governor, Raymond Mabus, Jr. (D); lt. gov., Brad Dye (D). *Legislature*—Senate, 52 members; House of Representatives, 122 members.
State Finances (fiscal year 1990): *Revenue,* $5,344,000,000; *expenditure,* $4,838,000,000.
Personal Income (1990): $33,009,000,000; per capita, $12,823.
Labor Force (June 1991): *Civilian labor force,* 1,224,200; *unemployed,* 128,400 (10.5% of total force).
Education: *Enrollment* (fall 1989)—public elementary schools, 369,513; public secondary, 132,507; colleges and universities, 116,370. *Public school expenditures* (1989), $1,372,290,000.

© William Campbell/"Time" Magazine

"Country Music's Broadway": Some 5 million tourists, mostly from a 300-mi (483-km) radius, flock annually to the southwest Missouri town of Branson to listen to country-music stars. Some 24 theaters are filled on most afternoons and evenings.

MISSOURI

Budget crises, education concerns, layoffs, and murder made for major news in Missouri in 1991. Disappointing state-revenue collections forced cutbacks in state programs, while lackluster sales stalled some businesses and industries. Still, Missouri seemed to weather the recession better than many other states.

Education. The state's educational system toyed with disaster as districts grappled with increasing money woes. Administrators cut programs and fired teachers, while some districts headed toward bankruptcy. In November voters unexpectedly rejected a $385 million tax package to boost funding for lower and higher education. The tax plan, known as Proposition B, called for increasing teachers' salaries and improving educational programs.

Desegregation efforts in St. Louis and Kansas City public schools continued despite complaints they cost too much money. The state spent more than $354 million on the two court-ordered programs in 1991, while cutting about $75 million from other school districts.

Crime. A mid-Missouri farm couple became the only husband and wife in the United States on death row after being convicted of killing five transient farm workers. Separate juries found that Faye and Ray Copeland of Chillicothe lured drifters into a cattle-buying scheme, killed them, and buried their bodies near the Copelands' farm.

In St. Louis violence escalated as the city raced toward a record number of homicides. More violent deaths had been recorded by mid-September than in all of 1990. To help combat the growing use of firearms, a police test program turned out to be overwhelmingly popular. The city and private businesses offered up to $50 for every gun turned in to a city police station. In just the first three days, the department had received more than 2,400 guns. In light of St. Louis' success, Kansas City considered a similar program.

Legislature and the Courts. The Missouri general assembly enacted a law to allow individuals to designate someone else to make health-care decisions if they are incapacitated. The law came after the parents of Nancy Cruzan fought their way to the U.S. Supreme Court in 1990 for permission to remove their brain-damaged daughter's feeding tubes.

MISSOURI • Information Highlights

Area: 69,697 sq mi (180 516 km²).
Population (1990 census): 5,117,073.
Chief Cities (1990 census): Jefferson City, the capital, 35,481; Kansas City, 435,146; St. Louis, 396,685; Springfield, 140,494; Independence, 112,301.
Government (1991): *Chief Officers*—governor, John Ashcroft (R); lt. gov., Mel Carnahan (R). *General Assembly*—Senate, 34 members; House of Representatives, 163 members.
State Finances (fiscal year 1990): *Revenue,* $9,343,000,000; *expenditure,* $8,326,000,000.
Personal Income (1990): $89,572,000,000; per capita, $17,472.
Labor Force (June 1991): *Civilian labor force,* 2,710,200; *unemployed,* 191,400 (7.1% of total force).
Education: *Enrollment* (fall 1989)—public elementary schools, 576,243; public secondary, 231,691; colleges and universities, 278,505. *Public school expenditures* (1989), $3,096,666,000.

In what was labeled the state's next right-to-die battle, the father of accident victim Christine Busalacchi asked the Missouri Supreme Court for permission to take his daughter to Minnesota for further testing. The Missouri Health Department was fighting the move, contending the father only wanted to let his daughter die in a state with less restrictive right-to-die laws. The high court's decision was pending late in 1991.

Economy. The nationwide recession hit Missouri like everywhere else, but the state did not show signs of major damage. Hardest hit was St. Louis, with a wealth of layoffs in the aircraft and automobile industries. Smaller towns across southern Missouri also felt the departure of several shoe and clothing factories. Unemployment increased slightly in the state.

The economic picture looked bright for southwest Missouri as the country-music boom town of Branson continued to attract attention. A slew of big-name entertainers—including Johnny Cash, Andy Williams, and Willie Nelson—announced plans to perform in the town of 3,700. The newcomers joined the likes of Roy Clark, Jim Stafford, and Ray Stevens and regularly helped to fill 24 theaters.

Other Developments. Fire broke out in the Taney county jail in Forsyth, killing four prisoners. . . . Kansas City elected the Rev. Emanuel Cleaver as its first black mayor. . . . John C. Danforth, the state's senior U.S. senator, was the principal supporter of Clarence Thomas in his successful campaign to win confirmation as a Supreme Court justice.

LANE BEAUCHAMP, *"The Kansas City Star"*

MONTANA

Montana got a new lieutenant governor in 1991 and learned it would lose one of its two U.S. congressional seats. A strike by state employees, the biennial session of the state legislature, a deadly prison riot, and hunting issues also made headlines in 1991.

MONTANA • Information Highlights

Area: 147,046 sq mi (380 848 km²).
Population (1990 census): 799,065.
Chief Cities (1990 census): Helena, the capital, 24,569; Billings, 81,151; Great Falls, 55,097.
Government (1991): *Chief Officers*—governor, Stan Stephens (R); lt. gov., Dennis Rehberg (R). *Legislature*—Senate, 50 members; House of Representatives, 100 members.
State Finances (fiscal year 1990): *Revenue,* $2,225,000,000; *expenditure,* $2,007,000,000.
Personal Income (1990): $12,205,000,000; per capita, $15,270.
Labor Force (June 1991): *Civilian labor force,* 410,700; *unemployed,* 26,300 (6.4% of total force).
Education: *Enrollment* (fall 1989)—public elementary schools, 109,791; public secondary, 41,474; colleges and universities, 37,660. *Public school expenditures* (1989), $592,454,000.

Politics. Lt. Gov. Allen Kolstad, a Republican, resigned to accept an appointment as U.S. representative to the federal boundary commission, which oversees the U.S.-Canadian border. Dennis Rehberg, an aide to U.S. Sen. Conrad Burns, replaced Kolstad.

The U.S. Census Bureau confirmed that Montana would lose one of its two congressional seats. The state was 3,420 people short of meriting a second seat and would become the most populous congressional district in the country in 1992. Both Republican Rep. Ron Marlenee of the eastern district and Democratic Rep. Pat Williams of the western district announced that they would run for the single seat in 1992.

Legislature. In 1991 the state legislature easily voted down a proposal to expand gambling through the addition of blackjack to the list of legal games.

Legislators introduced a proposal to raise all state employees' pay by $1 per hour. Gov. Stan Stephens insisted that the budget could not stand the additional cost. Legislators then pared the amount to 60 cents. Governor Stephens vetoed the bill and the next morning 4,200 state employees walked out. The strikers were joined by most other hourly state employees a day later.

National Guard troops were called to staff the state prison, state hospitals, and other state institutions. County sheriffs replaced striking state highway patrolmen. Highways, including Interstate 90, closed when a spring snowstorm crossed the state and snowplow operators joined the strike. Five days into the strike, legislative and administration negotiators agreed to a $1.05-per-hour raise over two years for all state employees.

Prisons. The legislature appropriated money to expand the crowded state penitentiary, which was nearly three times over capacity. After objections from labor unions, the state agreed not to use prison labor for the construction. But inmates rioted before work could begin, guards were taken hostage, and five inmates in protective custody were killed. Armed National Guardsmen stormed the prison to restore order.

The legislature also appropriated funds to replace the women's prison in Warm Springs.

Wildlife. Hunting licenses were issued for buffalo that had wandered out of Yellowstone National Park, after state and federal officials said the bison might be carrying brucellosis, a disease that causes cattle to abort their calves. A state judge overturned a lawsuit by conservationists aimed at stopping the hunt. But the legislature later removed the state's authority to issue bison-hunting licenses. In another attempt to reduce the number of buffalo leaving the park, federal officials ordered park rangers to shoot them before they could wander onto private land. But after one day of shooting a federal judge ordered the National Park Service to halt the program.

Montana officials voluntarily postponed the annual grizzly-bear hunt after conservation groups unsuccessfully sued to stop it.

ROBERT C. GIBSON, *"The Billings Gazette"*

MOROCCO

Morocco in 1991 was focused on a single event of intense emotional and historical significance: the United Nations-administered referendum on the Western Sahara scheduled for January 1992. Moroccans never have accepted that the former Spanish colony, roughly the size of England, could be anything other than part of Morocco. But in an effort to gain international recognition for that conviction, and finally to end the guerrilla war that has pitted Morocco against the proindependence Polisario Front since Spain abandoned the Western Sahara in 1975, Morocco's King Hassan II accepted a plan for a referendum on the territory's future drawn up by UN Secretary-General Javier Pérez de Cuéllar and approved by the Security Council.

Western Sahara. All parties to the Western Sahara conflict have agreed to the need for a referendum since 1981. But international agreement on a procedure for finally settling the territory's status was made possible by evolutionary forces outside Morocco, including the collapse of communism in eastern Europe and an accompanying loss of support for the Marxist Polisario Front. In addition, a desire to forge a Maghreb economic union among five North African states led neighboring Algeria to give up its backing for Polisario.

As one of the first steps toward the referendum, a UN-monitored cease-fire was declared September 6. The cease-fire held precariously despite complaints from Polisario leaders of Moroccan violations. The most controversial aspect of the referendum's preparation was agreement on a final list of Western Sahara residents eligible for the January vote. UN officials began working with a 1974 Spanish census listing about 70,000 people, but the Moroccan government rejected that census, saying it neglected perhaps 50,000 nomadic tribesmen.

Impact of Persian Gulf War. Despite intense public interest in the Sahara issue, Morocco was not untouched by the Persian Gulf crisis. On February 3, Rabat, the capital, was the scene of one of the country's largest demonstrations since independence. Nearly 200,000 marchers, called by the country's opposition parties, assembled to protest the Western-led coalition against Iraq in general, and the king's decision to send 1,200 troops to defend Saudi Arabia in particular. But opposition-party leaders, hoping to reactivate a struggling democratization process frozen by Hassan II in the wake of the Gulf crisis, and unanimous in their support of the efforts to establish full sovereignty over the Western Sahara, rallied to keep the demonstration from taking on any strong antigovernment overtones. Unlike bloody riots in Fez in December 1990, the February demonstrations remained nonviolent.

Human Rights. Morocco's human-rights record, long the focus of several Western governments and human-rights organizations, improved in 1991 after Hassan II established an advisory council on human rights in May 1990. The government action, which included generally improved conditions for prisoners and revisions in judicial procedures, was part of an effort to improve ties to the West, and especially with the United States and France, both of which have drawn attention to the issue in the past. International human-rights organizations acknowledged an evolution in Morocco's treatment of prisoners but estimated at several hundred the number of political prisoners still held.

Economy. Hassan II visited Washington, DC, on September 26 and 27. During the visit, President George Bush praised Morocco for its improved human-rights performance, as well for measures aimed at liberalizing the country's economy. During his weeklong U.S. stay the king also met with business leaders. Despite numerous riches, Morocco remains one of the poorest countries of the Arab world, with per capita income well below $1,000. Yet despite a setback to the country's crucial tourist industry as a result of the Gulf war, the government said it would register a 4% growth rate for 1991. In addition, leaders expressed confidence that settlement of the Western Sahara's status in Morocco's favor would open the territory to substantial development of its rich phosphate and fishing resources.

HOWARD LAFRANCHI
"The Christian Science Monitor"

MOROCCO • Information Highlights

Official Name: Kingdom of Morocco.
Location: Northwest Africa.
Area: 172,413 sq mi (446 550 km²).
Population (mid-1991 est.): 26,200,000.
Chief Cities (mid-1987 est., incl. suburbs): Rabat, the capital, 1,287,000; Casablanca, 2,904,000; Fez, 933,000; Marrakech, 1,425,000.
Government: *Head of state,* Hassan II, king (acceded 1961). *Head of government,* Azzedine Laraki, prime minister (appointed Sept. 30, 1986). *Legislature* (unicameral)—Chamber of Representatives.
Monetary Unit: Dirham (9.327 dirhams equal U.S.$1, June 1991).
Gross Domestic Product (1989 est. U.S.$): $21,900,000,000.
Economic Indexes (1990): *Consumer Prices* (1980 = 100), all items, 201.3; food, 200.3. *Industrial Production* (1980 = 100), 133.
Foreign Trade (1989 U.S.$): *Imports,* $5,492,000,000; *exports,* $3,308,000,000.

MOTION PICTURES

The power of movies to trigger passionate arguments and emotional responses on a national scale is evident only on rare occasions. In the 1960s, for example, *Bonnie and Clyde* engendered controversy about violence, as did *A Clockwork Orange* in the 1970s. Similarly, in 1991, *Thelma and Louise* touched a raw nerve among women harboring pent-up anger about injustices inflicted by men. Susan Sarandon and Geena Davis gave rousing performances as pals whose weekend vacation turns into a feminist spree with the police hunting them as outlaws. Their charisma, a knowing script by Callie Khouri, and astute direction by Ridley Scott combined to create a film that caused many to cheer Thelma and Louise on and others to express outrage. The film took in nearly $44 million at the box office, impressive for its type, and prompted much public discussion. Whatever one felt about the picture, the intense response indicated anew that movies could arouse strong reactions.

A striking development of a different sort was the breakthrough of films by Afro-Americans about Afro-Americans. Spike Lee's (*see* BIOGRAPHY) *Jungle Fever,* concerning interracial and family relationships, was the most high-profile of the group. *New Jack City,* directed by Mario Van Peebles, whose father Melvin Van Peebles started a black film trend in the 1970s, was a more conventional action film involving urban drug warfare. John Singleton, age 23, made an auspicious writer-director debut with *Boyz 'N the Hood,* about the struggle for survival in a Los Angeles neighborhood. Even more remarkable was the debut of 19-year-old Matty Rich with his low-budget *Straight Out of Brooklyn*. Hispanics also had an advocate in Joseph B. Vasquez and his *Hangin' With the Homeboys*.

Performers Turned Directors. The year also marked an impressive directorial debut by Jodie Foster, already regarded as an extraordinarily talented actress. Foster, who won an Oscar previously for her portrayal of the rape victim in *The Accused* (1988), scored a triple coup in 1991. First she captivated audiences with her performance as an FBI agent in the harrowing thriller *The Silence of the Lambs,* a box-office hit directed by Jonathan Demme and featuring a mesmerizing performance by Anthony Hopkins as a psychopathic murderer.

Then along came Foster with *Little Man Tate,* in which she effectively starred as the conflicted mother of a 7-year-old genius desperate for a happy childhood. Directing the film as well, Foster showed herself to be as sensitive to emotional nuance behind the camera as she is on screen. Actor Sean Penn also attempted the transition to director with *The Indian Runner*. While he showed potential, the overall result was not impressive.

AP/Wide World

Actress Jodie Foster made her directing debut in "Little Man Tate," in which she also starred as a working-class mother with a brilliant son, played by Adam Hann-Byrd, right.

Film Theme. Alienation, a theme in both Foster's and Penn's efforts, was a subject at the core of other major films. In David Mamet's *Homicide,* which premiered at the New York Film Festival, Joe Mantegna depicted a cop who during a murder investigation faces coming to terms with his Jewish identity and his repressed feelings as an outsider trying to gain acceptance in the police department.

In *My Own Private Idaho,* Gus Van Sant, Jr., hailed by many critics as a rising director, dealt with two male hustlers of different social and economic backgrounds struggling to overcome their feelings of alienation. Variations on the theme were found in such diverse films as Terry Gilliam's *The Fisher King,* costarring Robin Williams and Jeff Bridges; Garry Marshall's *Frankie & Johnny,* in which Michelle Pfeiffer portrayed a woman fearful of becoming romantically involved, with Al Pacino as another wounded soul; John Sayles' ironically titled *City of Hope,* starring Vincent Spano as a young man adrift; and Joel and Ethan Coen's highly stylized *Barton Fink,* a triple winner at the Cannes Film Festival, expressing the feelings of alienation gripping a young writer in 1940s Hollywood.

Irwin Winkler's *Guilty by Suspicion,* a recollection of the days of Hollywood blacklisting that starred Robert De Niro, explored the emotional effects of being career outcasts. Martha Coolidge's *Rambling Rose* starred Laura Dern as an outsider with a troubled past who causes havoc in the household that employs her as a domestic. Two appealing comedies also dealt with alienation. Ron Underwood's *City Slickers,* starring Billy Crystal, found laughs in mid-life alienation from family and work, and Bill Murray was the ultimate outsider in *What About Bob?,* playing a fearful but overbearing loner who wrecks the life of his psychiatrist (Richard Dreyfuss).

Winners and Losers. As expected, the summer release *Terminator 2: Judgment Day,* a sequel for Arnold Schwarzenegger, proved to be a box-office bonanza, tallying more than $200 million by October. *Robin Hood: Prince of Thieves* scored with about $160 million in a similar period even though Kevin Costner (*see* BIOGRAPHY and PRIZES AND AWARDS) received cool notices on the heels of his 1991 Oscar triumph for directing *Dances with Wolves* (1990). The box-office total for *The Silence of the Lambs* reached more than $130 million, followed by *City Slickers* with more than $120 million. The popular slapstick sequel *Naked Gun 2½: The Smell of Fear* topped $85 million, and *Backdraft,* a fireman saga directed by Ron Howard, weighed in with $76 million. The Disney Company had reason to be delighted when the reissue of *101 Dalmatians* garnered almost $60 million within three months. (Orson Welles' *Citizen Kane* was rereleased with more modest results, celebrating the classic's 50th anniversary.)

The biggest fiasco of the year was *Hudson Hawk,* the action film with Bruce Willis, reported to have cost some $60 million. Other films with potential that failed to catch on included *V.I. Warshawski,* in which Kathleen Turner played a tough-talking private eye; *Scenes from a Mall,* which teamed Woody Allen and Bette Midler; *Dying Young,* which died young itself despite the presence of lauded star Julia Roberts; and Mel Brooks' comedy with heart, *Life Stinks.*

The National Film Registry

The Library of Congress in 1991 named an additional 25 American films to the National Film Registry. The films are listed in accordance with a 1988 law, specifying that none can be altered without a designation to that effect.

The 1991 designated films, classified as "culturally, historically, or esthetically significant," were: *Battle of San Pietro* (1945), *The Blood of Jesus* (1941), *Chinatown* (1974), *City Lights* (1931), *David Holzman's Diary* (1968), *Frankenstein* (1931), *Gertie the Dinosaur* (1914), *Gigi* (1958), *Greed* (1924), *High School* (1968), *I Am a Fugitive from a Chain Gang* (1932), *The Italian* (1915), *King Kong* (1933), *Lawrence of Arabia* (1962), *The Magnificent Ambersons* (1942), *My Darling Clementine* (1946), *Out of the Past* (1947), *A Place in the Sun* (1951), *The Poor Little Rich Girl* (1917), *The Prisoner of Zenda* (1937), *Shadow of a Doubt* (1943), *Sherlock, Jr.* (1924), *Tevya* (1939), *Trouble in Paradise* (1932), and *2001: A Space Odyssey* (1968).

As usual, movie companies released a barrage of major films near the end of the year, such as Robert Benton's engrossing *Billy Bathgate,* based on E.L. Doctorow's novel and starring Dustin Hoffman; Martin Scorsese's remake of *Cape Fear,* with Robert De Niro; *The Prince of Tides,* with Barbra Streisand both directing and acting opposite Nick Nolte; *Other People's Money,* Norman Jewison's movie based on Jerry Sterner's play, with Danny DeVito as a ruthless corporate raider; *Beauty and the Beast,* the charming and sprightly new Disney animated version of the fairy tale; *For the Boys,* a musical drama about U.S.O. performers during wartime, costarring Bette Midler and James Caan and directed by Mark Rydell; Lawrence Kasden's *Grand Canyon,* a drama about the difficulties of living in today's world, with a cast headed by Kevin Kline and Steve Martin; and Steven Spielberg's *Hook,* the *Peter Pan* spin-off bolstered by Dustin Hoffman, Robin Williams, and Julia Roberts.

Other noteworthy films included *Dead Again,* the Hitchcock-like thriller that was a tour de force for the director-star Kenneth Branagh; Alan Parker's *The Commitments,* a realistic portrait of a fictitious musical group in Dublin; Oliver Stone's dramatization of the real-life rock group *The Doors,* enhanced by a praised star performance by Val Kilmer and his controversial *JFK,* starring Kevin Costner; Mike Nichols' *Regarding Henry,* in which Harrison Ford played a high-powered lawyer mentally shattered by a gunman's bullet; William Hurt's tour de force as a surgeon who learns a better bedside manner when he must face his own cancer in *The Doctor;* Barry Levinson's *Bugsy,* starring Warren Beatty as gangster Bugsy Siegel; and in a much lighter vein, *The Addams Family,* starring Anjelica Huston and Raul Julia. Not to be forgotten was *Truth or Dare,* the documentary of a tour by Madonna.

Uphill Struggle. Independent films and foreign-language films are two categories that have the most difficult time competing with studio projects backed by high advertising and promotion budgets. Still, some do break through, as was the case with Henry Jaglom's *Eating,* a fascinating conversational film with actresses talking about the problems women have in meeting society's demand that they keep slim. Hal Hartley's *Trust* further demonstrated the writer-director's talent, evident in 1990's *The Unbelievable Truth.* Richard Linklater commanded attention with *Slacker,* his documentary-style musing that presented actors playing various types of dropouts. Another unusual offering was Juan Jose Campanella's *The Boy Who Cried Bitch.* The documentary that evoked the most interest was Jennie Livingston's *Paris Is Burning.*

Several foreign-language imports also succeeded. *Everybody's Fine,* directed by Giuseppe Tornatore (*Cinema Paradiso,* 1990),

© Sygma

Creating much controversy was the buddy road picture "Thelma and Louise," starring Geena Davis, left, and Susan Sarandon. An unexpected summer hit, the film chronicles the adventures of two friends who set out for a getaway weekend only to find themselves in increasing trouble, first with men and then with the law.

MOTION PICTURES | 1991

THE ADDAMS FAMILY. Director, Barry Sonnenfeld; screenplay by Caroline Thompson and Larry Wilson, based on the characters created by Charles Addams. With Anjelica Huston, Raul Julia, Christopher Lloyd.

ANOTHER YOU. Director, Maurice Phillips; screenplay by Ziggy Steinberg. With Richard Pryor, Gene Wilder.

ANTONIA AND JANE. Director, Beeban Kidron; screenplay by Marcy Kahan. With Imelda Staunton, Saskia Reeves.

AT PLAY IN THE FIELDS OF THE LORD. Director, Hector Babenco; screenplay by Jean-Claude Carrière and Babenco. With Tom Berenger, John Lithgow, Daryl Hannah, Aidan Quinn, Tom Waits, Kathy Bates.

AT THE MAX. Creative consultant and location director, Julien Temple; concept by Michael Cohl. In IMAX. With the Rolling Stones.

BACKDRAFT. Director, Ron Howard; screenplay by Gregory Widen. With Kurt Russell, William Baldwin, Robert De Niro, Donald Sutherland, Jennifer Jason Leigh.

BARTON FINK. Director, Joel Coen; screenplay by Ethan Coen and Joel Coen. With John Turturro, John Goodman.

BEAUTY AND THE BEAST. Directors, Gary Trousdale and Krik Wise; animation screenplay by Linda Woolverton.

BILLY BATHGATE. Director, Robert Benton; screenplay by Tom Stoppard, based on the book by E. L. Doctorow. With Dustin Hoffman, Bruce Willis, Nicole Kidman.

BLACK ROBE. Director, Bruce Beresford; screenplay by Brian Moore. With Lothare Bluteau, August Schellenberg, Aden Young, Sandrine Holt, Tantoo Cardinal.

BOYZ N THE HOOD. Written and directed by John Singleton. With Ice Cube, Cuba Gooding, Jr., Morris Chestnut, Larry Fishburne, Angela Bassett, Nia Long.

BUGSY. Director, Barry Levinson; screenplay by James Toback. With Warren Beatty, Annette Bening.

THE BUTCHER'S WIFE. Director, Terry Hughes; screenplay by Ezra Litwak and Marjorie Schwartz. With Demi Moore.

CAPE FEAR. Director, Martin Scorsese; screenplay by Wesley Strick, based on a screenplay by James R. Webb and the novel *The Executioners* by John MacDonald. With Robert De Niro, Nick Nolte, Jessica Lange.

CITY OF HOPE. Written and directed by John Sayles. With Vincent Spano.

CITY SLICKERS. Director, Ron Underwood; screenplay by Lowell Ganz and Babaloo Mandel. With Billy Crystal, Daniel Stern, Bruno Kirby, Jack Palance, Helen Slater.

THE COMFORT OF STRANGERS. Director, Paul Schrader; screenplay by Harold Pinter, based on the novel by Ian McEwan. With Christopher Walken, Natasha Richardson.

THE COMMITMENTS. Director, Alan Parker; screenplay by Dick Clement, Ian La Frenais, and Roddy Doyle, from the latter's novel. With Robert Arkins, Michael Aherne, Angeline Ball, Maria Doyle, Dave Finnegan.

CONVICTS. Director, Peter Masterson; screenplay by Horton Foote, based on his play. With Robert Duvall, Lukas Haas, James Earl Jones.

CURLY SUE. Written and directed by John Hughes. With James Belushi, Alisan Porter, John Getz.

DADDY NOSTALGIA. Director, Bertrand Tavernier; screenplay by Colo Tavernier O'Hagan. With Dirk Bogarde.

DEAD AGAIN. Director, Kenneth Branagh; screenplay by Scott Frank. With Kenneth Branagh, Emmy Thompson, Robin Williams, Derek Jacobi, Hanna Schygulla.

DEFENDING YOUR LIFE. Written and directed by Albert Brooks. With Albert Brooks, Meryl Streep, Rip Torn.

DOC HOLLYWOOD. Director, Michael Caton-Jones; screenplay by Jeffrey Price, Peter S. Seaman, and Daniel Pyne. With Michael J. Fox, Julie Warner.

THE DOCTOR. Director, Randa Haines; screenplay by Robert Caswell. With William Hurt, Elizabeth Perkins.

THE DOORS. Director, Oliver Stone; screenplay by J. Randal Johnson and Stone. With Val Kilmer, Meg Ryan, Kevin Dillon, Kyle MacLachlan, Billy Idol.

THE DOUBLE LIFE OF VÉRONIQUE. Director, Krzysztof Kieslowski; screenplay by Kieslowski and Krzysztof Piesiewicz. With Irène Jacob, Philippe Volter.

EATING. Written and directed by Henry Jaglom. With Nelly Alard, Frances Bergen, Mary Crosby, Lisa Richards.

EUROPA, EUROPA. Written and directed by Agnieska Holland, based on the autobiography of Solomon Perel. With Solomon Perel, Marco Hofschneider.

FATHER OF THE BRIDE. Director, Charles Shyer; screenplay by Frances Goodrich, Albert Hackett, Nancy Meyers, and Shyer. With Steve Martin, Diane Keaton.

THE FISHER KING. Director, Terry Gilliam; screenplay by Richard LaGravenese. With Jeff Bridges, Robin Williams.

FOR THE BOYS. Director, Mark Rydell; screenplay by Marshall Brickman, Neal Jimenez, Lindy Laub. With Bette Midler, James Caan, George Segal.

FRANKIE AND JOHNNY. Director, Garry Marshall; screenplay by Terrence McNally. With Al Pacino, Michelle Pfeiffer.

FRIED GREEN TOMATOES. Director, John Avnet; screenplay by Fanny Flagg and Avnet, based on a novel by Flagg. With Jessica Tandy, Kathy Bates.

GRAND CANYON. Director, Lawrence Kasden; screenplay by Meg Kasden and Kasden. With Danny Glover, Kevin Kline, Steve Martin, Mary McDonnell.

GUILTY BY SUSPICION. Written and directed by Irwin Winkler. With Robert De Niro, Annette Bening.

HEARTS OF DARKNESS: A FILMMAKER'S APOCALYPSE. Written and directed by Fax Bahr with George Hickenlooper. Documentary footage by Eleanor Coppola.

HIGH HEELS. Written and directed by Pedro Almodóvar. With Victoria Abril.

HOOK. Director, Steven Spielberg; screenplay by Jim V. Hart, Malia Scotch Marmo, and Nick Castle, Jr., from the James Barrie play and story *Peter Pan.* With Robin Williams, Dustin Hoffman, Julia Roberts, Bob Hoskins.

HUDSON HAWK. Director, Michael Lehmann; screenplay by Steven E. de Souza and Daniel Waters. With Bruce Willis, Danny Aiello, Andie MacDowell, James Coburn.

THE INDIAN RUNNER. Written and directed by Sean Penn. With David Morse, Viggo Mortensen, Charles Bronson.

THE INNER CIRCLE. Director, Andrei Konchalovsky; screenplay by Konchalovsky and Anatoli Usov. With Tom Hulce, Lolita Davidovich, Bob Hoskins.

JFK. Director, Oliver Stone; screenplay by Stone and Zachary Sklar from *On the Trail of the Assassins* by Jim Garrison and *Crossfire* by Jim Marrs. With Kevin Costner, Gary Oldman, Tommy Lee Jones, Sissy Spacek.

JUNGLE FEVER. Written and directed by Spike Lee. With Wesley Snipes, Lonette McKee, Spike Lee, Ossie Davis.

KAFKA. Director, Steven Soderbergh; screenplay by Lem Dobbs. With Jeremy Irons, Theresa Russell.

THE LAST BOY SCOUT. Director, Tony Scott; screenplay by Shane Black. With Bruce Willis, Damon Wayans.

L.A. STORY. Director, Mick Jackson; screenplay by Steve Martin. With Steve Martin, Victoria Tennant.

LET HIM HAVE IT. Director, Peter Medak; screenplay by Neal Purvis and Robert Wade. With Christopher Eccelston, Paul Reynolds, Tom Bell, Eileen Atkins.

LIFE IS SWEET. Written and directed by Mike Leigh. With Alison Steadman, Jane Horrocks, Jim Broadbent.

LIFE STINKS. Director, Mel Brooks; screenplay by Brooks, Rudy De Luca, and Steve Haberman. With Mel Brooks, Lesley Ann Warren, Jeffrey Tambor.

LITTLE MAN TATE. Director, Jodie Foster; screenplay by Scott Frank. With Jodie Foster, Dianne Wiest, Adam Hann-Byrd, Harry Connick, Jr.

MADAME BOVARY. Written and directed by Claude Chabrol, based on the novel by Gustave Flaubert. With Isabelle Huppert, Jean-François Balmer.

THE MARRYING MAN. Director, Jerry Rees; screenplay by Neil Simon. With Kim Basinger, Alec Baldwin.

MEETING VENUS. Director, Istvan Szabo; screenplay by Szabo and Michael Hirst. With Glenn Close.

MORTAL THOUGHTS. Director, Alan Rudolph; screenplay by William Reilly and Claude Kerven. With Demi Moore, Glenne Headly, Bruce Willis, Harvey Keitel.

MY GIRL. Director, Howard Zieff; screenplay by Laurice Elehwany. With Macaulay Culkin, Anna Chlumsky.

MY OWN PRIVATE IDAHO. Written and directed by Gus Van Sant, Jr. With River Phoenix, Keanu Reeves.

NAKED GUN 2 1/2: THE SMELL OF FEAR. Director, David Zucker; screenplay by Zucker and Pat Proft. With Leslie Nielsen, Priscilla Presley, George Kennedy.

NAKED LUNCH. Written and directed by David Cronenberg, based on the book by William S. Burroughs. With Peter Weller, Judy Davis, Ian Holm, Roy Scheider.

NEW JACK CITY. Director, Mario Van Peebles; screenplay by Thomas Lee Wright and Barry Michael Cooper. With Wesley Snipes, Mario Van Peebles.

ONLY THE LONELY. Written and directed by Chris Columbus. With John Candy, Maureen O'Hara.

OSCAR. Director, John Landis; screenplay by Michael Barrie and Jim Mulholland, based on the play by Claude Magnier. With Sylvester Stallone, Don Ameche.

OTHER PEOPLE'S MONEY. Director, Norman Jewison; screenplay by Alvin Sargent, based on the play by Jerry Sterner. With Danny DeVito, Gregory Peck.

OVERSEAS. Director, Brigitte Rouan; screenplay by Rouan, Philippe Le Guay, Christian Rullier, Cedric Kahn. With Nicole Garcia, Marianne Basler, Brigitte Rouan.

POINT BREAK. Director, Kathryn Bigelow; screenplay by W. Peter Iliff. With Patrick Swayze, Keanu Reeves, Gary Busey, Lori Petty, John McGinley, James Le Gros.

THE PRINCE OF TIDES. Director, Barbra Streisand; screenplay by Pat Conroy and Becky Johnston, based on the Conroy book. With Barbra Streisand, Nick Nolte.

PROSPERO'S BOOKS. Director, Peter Greenaway; screenplay by Greenaway, adapted from *The Tempest* by William Shakespeare. With John Gielgud.

RAMBLING ROSE. Director, Martha Coolidge; screenplay by Calder Willingham, based on his book. With Laura Dern.

REGARDING HENRY. Director, Mike Nichols; screenplay by Jeffrey Abrams. With Harrison Ford, Annette Bening.

RHAPSODY IN AUGUST. Written and directed by Akira Kurosawa. With Sachiki Murase, Hisashi Igawa.

ROBIN HOOD: PRINCE OF THIEVES. Director, Kevin Reynolds; screenplay by Pen Densham and John Watson. With Kevin Costner, Morgan Freeman, Christian Slater, Alan Rickman, Mary Elizabeth Mastrantonio.

ROSENCRANTZ AND GUILDENSTERN ARE DEAD. Written and directed by Tom Stoppard. With Gary Oldman, Tim Roth, Richard Dreyfuss.

© Gamma-Liaison

Arnold Schwarzenegger starred in "Terminator 2: Judgment Day," the sequel to the 1984 thriller. It was the biggest box-office hit among the summer film releases.

RUSH. Director, Lili Fini Zanuck; screenplay by Peter Dexter, based on the book by Kim Wozencraft. With Jason Patric, Jennifer Jason Leigh.

SCENES FROM A MALL. Director, Paul Mazursky; screenplay by Roger L. Simon and Mazursky. With Bette Midler, Woody Allen, Bill Irwin, Paul Mazursky.

THE SEARCH FOR SIGNS OF INTELLIGENT LIFE IN THE UNIVERSE. Director, John Bailey; screenplay by Jane Wagner. With Lily Tomlin.

SEX, DRUGS, ROCK & ROLL. Director, John McNaughton; screenplay by Eric Bogosian. With Eric Bogosian.

THE SILENCE OF THE LAMBS. Director, Jonathan Demme; screenplay by Ted Tally, adapted from a novel by Thomas Harris. With Jodie Foster, Anthony Hopkins.

SLEEPING WITH THE ENEMY. Director, Joseph Ruben; screenplay by Ronald Bass. With Julia Roberts.

SOAPDISH. Director, Michael Hoffman; screenplay by Robert Harling and Andrew Bergman. With Sally Field.

STAR TREK VI: THE UNDISCOVERED COUNTRY. Director, Nicholas Meyer; screenplay by Meyer and Denny Martin Flinn, based on *Star Trek,* created by Gene Roddenberry. With William Shatner, Leonard Nimoy.

THE SUPER. Director, Rod Daniel; screenplay by Sam Simon. With Joe Pesci, Vincent Gardenia.

SWITCH. Written and directed by Blake Edwards. With Ellen Barkin, Tony Roberts, Perry King.

TED & VENUS. Director, Bud Cort; screenplay by Paul Ciotti and Cort. With Bud Cort, James Brolin, Carol Kane, Woody Harrelson, Gena Rowlands, Rhea Perlman.

TEEN-AGE MUTANT NINJA TURTLES II: THE SECRET OF THE OOZE. Director, Michael Pressman; screenplay by Todd W. Langen, based on characters created by Kevin Eastman and Peter Laird. With Michelan Sisti, Leif Tilden, Kenn Troum, Mark Caso.

TERMINATOR 2: JUDGMENT DAY. Director, James Cameron; screenplay by Cameron and William Wisher. With Arnold Schwarzenegger, Linda Hamilton.

THELMA AND LOUISE. Director, Ridley Scott; screenplay by Callie Khouri. With Susan Sarandon, Geena Davis.

TRUTH OR DARE. (concert documentary film) Director, Alek Keshishian. With Madonna.

UNTIL THE END OF THE WORLD. Director, Wim Wenders; screenplay by Peter Carey and Wenders. With William Hurt, Sam Neill, Max Von Sydow.

V. I. WARSHAWSKI. Director, Jeff Kanew; screenplay by Edward Taylor, David Aaron Cohen, and Nick Thiel. With Kathleen Turner, Jay O. Sanders, Charles Durning.

WHAT ABOUT BOB?. Director, Frank Oz; screenplay by Tim Schulman. With Bill Murray, Richard Dreyfuss.

YEAR OF THE GUN. Director, John Frankenheimer; screenplay by David Ambrose. With Andrew McCarthy.

offered a strong role for Marcello Mastroianni. Another special film from Italy was Pupi Avati's *The Story of Boys and Girls,* a homey look at 1930s family life as an engagement celebration unfolds. From France came *Cross My Heart,* Jacques Fansten's tender story of children hiding the body of a boy's mother to conceal her death and keep him from being sent to an orphanage. Other superior films from France included *Overseas, Uranus, My Father's Glory, My Mother's Castle, La Belle Noiseuse,* and *Madame Bovary*. Polish director Agnieszka Holland's *Europa, Europa,* in French, Polish, and Russian, traced the unusual true-life saga of a Jewish boy in World War II.

Business. Hollywood bristled with envy and concern over the accumulating power exercised by super talent agent Mike Ovitz, president of Creative Artists Agency (CAA). CAA's ever more prestigious client list of stars, directors, and writers has enabled Ovitz to construct major film deals and demand top money for the agency's clients. Movie-company executives complained that higher salaries and percentages, coupled with other production tabs, were driving costs far above what the business could bear. Others pointed critically to the executives' gigantic salaries and bonuses.

The soaring budgets, with $26.8 million considered merely the average by the Motion Picture Association of America, have occurred in the context of changing corporate ownership, a revolving door of chief executives, and uncertain conditions at the box office. Results were disappointing in the summer months and fall business dipped from 1990. Little realistic hope existed, however, for changing the long-term situation. Various strategies were in the planning stages, such as the relatively unusual collaboration by two major studios on a film, as Columbia Pictures, now owned by Sony, and Universal Studios, now owned by the Matsushita Electric Industrial Company, intend with *Houdini*. One solution would be to make movies with less expensive talent, but so long as the public will flock to see an Arnold Schwarzenegger, his financial demands will be met. That is the nature of the flamboyant movie business.

WILLIAM WOLF, *New York University*

MOZAMBIQUE

Long-awaited elections promised by President Joaquím Chissano were scheduled for late 1991. The once-dominant Marxist Mozambique Liberation Party (Frelimo) was now only one of the parties involved. The dissident Mozambique National Resistance Movement (Renamo), despite attending peace talks in Rome, continued murderous attacks in northern and southern Mozambique.

MOZAMBIQUE • Information Highlights

Official Name: Republic of Mozambique.
Location: Southeastern coast of Africa.
Area: 309,494 sq mi (801 590 km²).
Population (mid-1991 est.): 16,100,000.
Chief City (1987 est.): Maputo, the capital, 1,006,765.
Government: *Head of state,* Joaquím A. Chissano, president (took office November 1986). *Head of government,* Mário da Graça Machungo, prime minister (took office July 1986). *Legislature* (unicameral)—People's Assembly.
Gross Domestic Product (1988 U.S.$): $1,600,-000,000.

Civil War. Peace talks between the government and Renamo produced a significant agreement for a cease-fire along the 196-mi (315-km) transport route from Zimbabwe to Beira. Renamo agreed not to attack this corridor or the Limpopo rail line further south, provided the permitted 7,000 Zimbabwean troops were deployed only within a 1.86-mi (3-km) strip on each side of the two routes. These secure areas allowed for truck and rail traffic to Beira and Maputo. They were also magnets for some 500,000 people seeking safety within the zones. Renamo's renewed offensive was aimed at controlling areas in the northern provinces of Manica, Tete, and Sofala before elections. In Zambézia province much of the resettlement work undertaken by Italian experts was halted. In the south, Renamo guerrillas in February cut off all power to Maputo for more than two weeks.

Economic Development. Private and foreign-government aid allowed for the reconstruction of the port of Beira and much of the damaged railway system. The World Bank pledged $1.2 billion in support for the period 1991–93, with $130 million targeted for relief efforts. Free enterprise has allowed for the creation of new businesses, but the stagnation of an inefficient socialist system and the civil war created almost insuperable problems. Water systems in the major cities were collapsing, the road network was in disrepair, and the health and educational infrastructures throughout the country were almost nonexistent.

Unemployment and inflation plagued even those fortunate enough to live beyond Renamo's reach. Cities and towns were crowded with more than 2 million internal refugees. The continuation of the drought meant few crops were harvested. Despite more than 1 million persons fleeing Mozambique, millions were kept alive by relief efforts made difficult and expensive by the war, air delivery being the only way to serve remote districts. In Sofala province alone, 250,000 people depended on airlifts. The increased cost of delivery, "donor fatigue" after four worldwide appeals for aid, and competition for funds with other areas left an estimated 5 million rural people on the edge of starvation.

HARRY A. GAILEY, *San Jose State University*

© Winnie Klotz

New York's Metropolitan Opera Company opened its 108th year in September with a 25th-anniversary celebration of its move to Lincoln Center. The grand finale of the gala evening was an all-star presentation from "Die Fledermaus."

MUSIC

For many of the world's large classical-music institutions, a unifying focus of 1991 was the bicentennial of the death of Wolfgang Amadeus Mozart. While such celebrations usually are reserved for birth rather than death anniversaries, Mozart scholarship had made such strides in the 35 years since Mozart's 200th-birthday commemoration in 1956 that the time seemed right to point the spotlight on the current state of Mozart performance. Other commemorations marking the 1991 music year included the 100th-birthday celebrations of composer Cole Porter; New York City's Carnegie Hall's 100th birthday, celebrated with two gala concerts on May 5; the New York Metropolitan Opera's 25th-anniversary celebration of its move to Lincoln Center; and the 100th anniversary of the Chicago Symphony, marked by, among other events, a cultural exchange with the Leningrad [St. Petersburg] Philharmonic.

While there was much to celebrate, the music world was saddened at the passing of jazz trumpeter and composer Miles Davis in late September. An important jazz presence for four decades, Davis was an important influence on many successive jazz styles.

Classical

The worldwide bicentennial celebration of the death of Mozart provided a new opportunity in 1991 to assess the composer's gifts and contributions, and it seemed that almost everyone—from international opera companies and orchestras to chamber groups and soloists—wanted to participate. Certainly the largest Mozart celebration was that mounted by Lincoln Center in New York, which in January kicked off a 19-month series that would involve performances by all of the institution's constituents, among them both the Metropolitan Opera and New York City Opera, the New York Philharmonic, the Chamber Music Society of Lincoln Center, the New York City Ballet, the Juilliard School, and even Lincoln Center's Film Society. The plan, variously described in the press as educational, encyclopedic, and elephantine, was to play every single work Mozart composed, no matter how obscure or minor. Even a group of canons with scatological texts, scribbled for friends at dinner parties, were given their premieres.

Elsewhere, Mozart's light also shone brightly: Glyndebourne, the intimate opera festival in Lewes, England, devoted its entire season to Mozart, reprising various recent productions and adding two new ones—Trevor Nunn's provocative and not wholly successful shipboard staging of *Così Fan Tutte* and a sleek *La Clemenza di Tito* from Nicholas Hytner, the young theater director who also was enjoying an international success with the musical *Miss Saigon*.

Also notable among new Mozart productions was *The Magic Flute,* by the avant-garde director Robert Wilson, at the Bastille Opera in Paris. (Wilson, best known for his work in contemporary theater and opera—his 1976 collaboration with Philip Glass on *Einstein on the Beach,* for example—also delved into earlier opera in a production of Gluck's *Alceste* at the Chicago Lyric Opera in 1991.) In *Magic Flute* he mixed such high-tech touches as white neon bars with more primitive elements like bright primary colors and shapes, as well as images that evoked Japanese theater. The production impressed critics who believe in the application of contemporary transformations of classic works and drew sharp criticism from those who prefer a more traditional approach. A common criticism was that Wilson seemed not to understand the Masonic imagery that pervades the work.

The Metropolitan Opera was to have put on *The Magic Flute* in a production by the film director Werner Herzog, but as the season drew close, it became clear that Herzog's tantalizing designs were too complex for the house to mount. Instead, the company borrowed a traditional David Hockney production that had originated some years before at the Glyndebourne Festival. And Mozart productions, both new and revived, were centerpieces at Aix-en-Provence (*The Marriage of Figaro* and the rarely heard *The Duty of the First Commandment*), the Holland Festival (*Idomeneo*), and the Washington Opera (*The Magic Flute*), not to mention the Salzburg Festival in Salzburg, Austria, Mozart's birthplace and home for part of his life.

Opera. In addition to the Mozart offerings, other parts of the operatic literature also thrived in different ways. A grandiose production of *Tosca,* mounted at Earl's Court in London, proved in the main extremely effective, although the British press expressed doubts in advance about whether it was appropriate to stage the work almost as a rock 'n' roll extravaganza.

Twentieth-century opera also fared well. Bernd Alois Zimmermann's 1965 *Die Soldaten,* reputedly the most difficult opera ever written, was mounted at the New York City Opera in October. That same month saw the premiere at City Opera of a jazz-dance opera, *The Mother of Three Sons,* by Bill T. Jones and Leroy Jenkins. The Chicago Lyric Opera, meanwhile, revived several U.S. works during the year, among them Dominick Argento's *The Voyage of Edgar Allan Poe* (1976), Samuel Barber's *Antony and Cleopatra* (1966), and Carlisle Floyd's *Susannah* (1955).

The Metropolitan Opera, which generally sticks with the standard repertory, offered Jonathan Miller's fine production of Leos Janacek's *Katya Kabanova* in February and the premiere of John Corigliano's long-delayed *The Ghosts of Versailles* in December. At Covent Garden in London the big premiere of the year was Sir Harrison Birtwistle's *Gawain,* an atonal telling of part of the King Arthur legend. And the German avant-gardist Wolfgang Rihm presented his angular, acidic view of *Oedipus* at the Santa Fe Opera.

At the minimalist or post-modern end of the compositional spectrum, there were two major premieres. Meredith Monk's *Atlas* was offered first at the Houston Grand Opera and later at the American Music Theater Festival in Philadelphia, and John Adams' *The Death of Klinghoffer* was presented first at the Théâtre Royal de la Monnaie in Brussels and then at the Lyon Opera and at the Brooklyn Academy of Music. The latter work, which deals with the 1985 hijacking of the cruise ship *Achille Lauro* by Arab terrorists and the murder of a wheelchair-bound U.S. passenger, Leon Klinghoffer, is the latest of several operas by U.S. composers to deal with recent incidents as opera plots (one of its predecessors was Adams' own *Nixon in China,* 1987).

One operatic tour that captured considerable attention was that of the Bolshoi, the famed Soviet company, which performed at the Metropolitan Opera in New York and at the Wolf Trap festival, outside Washington in Virginia, beginning in late June. The troupe offered three of the Russian works for which it is renowned. Its new staging of Tchaikovsky's *Eugene Onegin* at the Metropolitan Opera was the first Bolshoi production ever to open outside Moscow. The other works performed by the Bolshoi were Rimsky-Korsakov's *Mlada* and Tchaikovsky's version of the Joan of Arc story, *Maid of Orleans.* Responses to the per-

© Jim Caldwell

Participating in the worldwide celebration of Mozart on the bicentennial of his death was the Houston Grand Opera, left, which presented "The Magic Flute," staged by author-illustrator Maurice Sendak. The opera was one of five works by the famed Austrian composer that was presented by the company during a Mozart festival.

AP/Wide World

© Michelle V. Agins/NYT Pictures

Carnegie Hall at 100

A gala celebration of the music year was the occasion of the 100th birthday of New York's Carnegie Hall on May 5. The festivities of the day included two concerts, with music for both performed by the New York Philharmonic *(above, right)*. The concerts' highlights included an appearance by Plácido Domingo *(right)*. Much in evidence, too, was the violinist and Carnegie Hall president Isaac Stern, who saved the hall from demolition in 1960. Over the years classical music has dominated in the hall, but many jazz and popular performers have made memorable appearances.

© Michelle V. Agins/NYT Pictures

formances were mixed, with some critics praising the performances' authority and others coming away somewhat disappointed by the state of the Bolshoi, which, like everything else in the Soviet Union, was coming to grips with difficult economic times.

The economy had its effect on Western musical organizations too: Governments and corporations that had supported the arts in past years had to cut back on funding programs, while at the same time the broader problems in the economy were reflected in falling ticket sales for some ensembles.

Nevertheless, there were also expansions: A new opera house, the Maestranza Theater, opened in Seville, Spain, in May, and the City of Birmingham Symphony Orchestra in England moved into a new concert hall in April. And one old hall—Carnegie Hall in New York—gave itself a lavish centennial celebration. Included were concerts by many of the world's great orchestras, soloists, and chamber groups, a series of new works commissioned by the hall, and a daylong gala on the anniversary itself, May 5.

Orchestras. In the orchestral world, new music directors took over two of the biggest U.S. orchestras. Kurt Masur, who had been scheduled to take over the New York Philharmonic in 1992, decided to step in a year earlier and did so with a gala concert in September. Daniel Barenboim, who took over the Chicago Symphony Orchestra, was somewhat less lucky: On what was to have been his first opening night, the orchestra went on strike for 17 days.

© Robert Maass/Sipa

German conductor Kurt Masur debuted as music director of the New York Philharmonic in September. Earlier he was the chief conductor of the Dresden and Leipzig symphonies.

Both their predecessors ended their tenures with big concerts that were recorded for disc release. Sir Georg Solti ended his Chicago years with concert performances of Verdi's *Otello* that featured Luciano Pavarotti and Kiri Te Kanawa, and Zubin Mehta brought his Philharmonic tenure to a close with Schoenberg's *Gurre-Lieder*.

If 1990 had seen the tentative and, by most accounts, unsuccessful entry into the world of opera composition by a rock star (Stewart Copeland, the drummer of the Police), 1991 saw a number of orchestral and choral crossovers. One that got a good deal of attention was *The Forest,* a sprawling and somewhat spotty work by David Byrne of Talking Heads.

Somewhat better received, although by no means a unanimous success, was the *Liverpool Oratorio* by former Beatles bassist Paul McCartney and film-score composer Carl Davis. The 97-minute work for orchestra, chorus, boys' choir, and soloists was unveiled in Liverpool and had performances in London and New York. It was praised for its attractive melodies and effective, colorful scoring.

Other important orchestral premieres included several works by Alfred Schnittke, the most famous contemporary Soviet composer, including the North American premiere of a Cello Concerto, played by Mstislav Rostropovich with the Boston Symphony, and the world premiere of his Concerto Grosso No. 5, played by the Cleveland Orchestra; the first complete performances of David Del Tredici's *Alice Symphony,* by the Boston Symphony at Tanglewood; John Harbison's Symphony No. 3, given by the Baltimore Symphony Orchestra; and Peter Lieberson's *World's Turning,* given by the San Francisco Symphony Orchestra.

Other News. The winner of the Pulitzer Prize in composition was the Israeli-born, Chicago-based Shulamit Ran, for her *Symphony,* composed for the Philadelphia Orchestra in 1990.

Among the notable musicians who died in 1991 were the pianists Rudolf Serkin, Claudio Arrau, Wilhelm Kempff, and Malcolm Frager. (*See also* OBITUARIES.)

ALLAN KOZINN
"The New York Times"

Popular and Jazz

Nothing holds as much sway in the world of popular music as the weekly album charts in the trade magazine *Billboard.* The industry was in tumult in 1991 when *Billboard* changed the way it tabulated the pop and country charts from a poll of top-ranked albums in individual stores to a computer-generated tally of actual sales, and chart positions shifted like kites on a windy day.

The newly fashioned charts more accurately reflected a highly diversified music market that included fans favoring hard rock, rap, dance music, and any number of other popular genres. Country music greatly benefited from the new chart format, with the third album by Garth Brooks, *Ropin' the Wind,* galloping to Number 1 in the first week of its release.

Numerous other albums also debuted at the top of the reconfigured charts, with hard-rock albums exhibiting particularly strong performances, including a self-titled album by the group Metallica, Van Halen's *For Unlawful Carnal Knowledge,* and Skid Row's *Slave to the Grind.* (Hard-rock hits also tend to drop quickly down the charts after stunning initial sales.) The most astonishing first-week showing, however, came when two simultaneous releases by the rock group Guns N' Roses (*Use Your Illusion I* and *II*) landed in the top two slots.

Other hit albums, including Bonnie Raitt's *Luck of the Draw,* Natalie Cole's *Unforgettable,* and R.E.M.'s *Out of Time,* showed that dance and hard rock were not the only genres that could sell in the millions. This diversity was explained partly by the fact that for the first time, more recordings were being bought by consumers over 30 years of age than by purchasers under the age of 19. That meant that the generation that grew up with rock and roll was also the first to continue buying new music well into adulthood.

Reacting to this broad marketplace, MTV—the powerful cable channel largely devoted to music videos—announced that it soon would split into three different channels, each with a different musical menu.

Grammy Awards. The Grammy Awards, coming in the midst of the Persian Gulf war,

© Michael Grecco/Outline

Singer Natalie Cole recorded the best-selling "Unforgettable" during 1991. The album features songs earlier performed by her famous father, the late Nat King Cole.

reflected the conflict with the choice of "From A Distance" as the song of the year. Written by Julie Gold, the tune had been recorded by a number of artists before Bette Midler's version became a song of solace during the war. Midler opened the Grammy program by performing the tune. As if to lend balance, Bob Dylan, on hand to accept a lifetime achievement award, sang one of his early protest anthems, "Masters of War."

Quincy Jones was the year's big Grammy winner, collecting six awards for his *Back on the Block,* a work that featured a number of jazz, pop, and rap performers. Jones, with the most Grammy nominations of anyone in history, now had a total of 25 awards, second only to the 28 won by Sir Georg Solti.

Mariah Carey won the Grammy for best new artist. Many likened Carey's mixture of ballads and dance tunes to the format followed by Whitney Houston, and ironically, Carey's debut album sold far more copies than Houston's most recent release, *I'm Your Baby Tonight*. One significant difference between the two was that unlike Houston, Carey writes her own material.

Sure to be nominated for a Grammy in 1992 was the biggest adult-oriented hit of the year, Natalie Cole's *Unforgettable*. The album reprises the sumptuous pop hits of her late father, Nat King Cole; the title tune is a "duet" in which Cole sings alongside a recording of her father. *Unforgettable,* thought to be a risky commercial venture, rose to the top of the charts, the first time a parent and child each have had a Number 1 album.

Reissues. The proliferation of extravagant boxed sets chronicling the careers of pop artists underscored the diversity of the pop audience. With huge sales racked up by artists from Led Zeppelin to Eric Clapton, record companies continued to raid their vaults to produce collections that were relatively inexpensive to produce and invariably profitable. Among the year's most notable packages were compilations of the Byrds, Barbra Streisand, Bo Diddley, Fats Domino, and an exhaustive nine-compact-disc set containing virtually all the singles released by a seminal soul-music label of the 1960s, Stax/Volt Records.

The most surprising success, however, was the gold-record status achieved by *Robert Johnson: The Complete Recordings*. Johnson, regarded as one of the very best practitioners of the country blues style developed in the Mississippi Delta, made 41 recordings (including alternate takes) over five days in 1936 and 1937. Johnson was a man of mystery and myth—he was said to have won his musical prowess in a deal with the devil, and died from drinking poisoned whiskey at the age of 27. But tall tales were not what caused Johnson's music to endure; rather, it was the artful tension between his voice and guitar, a stunning combination that illuminated a most singular soul.

The Johnson collection keynoted a flood of blues reissues, including sets devoted to the work of T-Bone Walker—a pioneer of the electric blues guitar—and Howlin' Wolf, a Delta-bred singer who gained fame playing electric blues in Chicago. When releases by many more worthy but lesser known figures were added in, it could be argued that one of the greatest benefits of the compact disc was that the format had encouraged the reissue of classic U.S. music, some of which had been unavailable for decades.

Rock and Dance. Much was made of the fact that in all of 1990, not a single rock album had reached the top of the charts, and many prematurely declared the death of rock at the hands of rap (*see* special report) and dance music. But while dance music remained strong in 1991, with major hits produced by performers like Paula Abdul and C & C Music Factory, rock rebounded with major hits by hard rockers as well as such alternative acts as R.E.M. and Jane's Addiction.

Jane's Addiction, a psychedelically-tinged rock band with a strong collegiate following, went from cult status to million-selling success with the release of *Ritual de lo Habitual*. The group also mounted the most noteworthy tour in a year that proved economically perilous for concert promoters. Dubbed the "Lollapalooza Tour," the all-day extravaganza featured a rainbow coalition of punk, rock, and rap acts, and suggested that the pop audience had much wider tastes than those suggested by the narrow playlists of most radio stations.

Rock and dance music also were being forged into a creative new alliance by a number

SPECIAL REPORT/MUSIC

The Latest Is Rap

© Kenneth Johansson/Outline Press

Rap music, or hip-hop, first emerged in the mid-1970s as an outgrowth of dance music. A "D.J." plays staccato bursts of music—created by playing brief portions of various existing songs, often scraping the needle across the record as a sound effect—while rhyming lyrics are sung or spoken over this music by a "rapper." The style, which has been controversial since it first appeared, has made a quantum leap in popularity during the past few years. Once in favor only among a limited group of listeners—primarily urban blacks—rap was everywhere in 1991.

Rap's move to the mainstream began in the late 1980s. The Beastie Boys, one of the very few white rap groups, first brought rap to the attention of most of the record-buying public with their 1986 hit *Fight for Your Right (to Party).* A black group, Run-D.M.C., had a platinum album the same year. In 1989, Tone-Lōc's *Wild Thing* became one of the best-selling singles of all time on the strength of its beat and partying theme. By 1990, MTV's *Yo! MTV Raps* had become its most popular program, and rap albums regularly were featured on Billboard's Top 40 pop chart.

The lyrics in rap songs often are concerned with urban ills such as gang membership, crime, and drug abuse. Critics charge that the music, with its vulgarity and flagrant use of obscenity, teaches youngsters misogyny and celebrates violence and the gang life. Some groups do seem to glorify violence, especially toward women and authority figures, and are occasionally in trouble with the police themselves. Others, however, take care to emphasize the danger involved in drug abuse and gang membership.

It is notable that the rappers most responsible for bringing the style its current mainstream popularity were those most willing to forgo vulgar language and serious messages in favor of innocuous lyrics and a "party" image. MC Hammer (photo left), Vanilla Ice, and Jazzy Jeff and the Fresh Prince (the latter, whose real name is Will Smith, even starred in his own TV show) are prime examples of the rappers most popular with middle-class Americans. They have in common a tendency toward lighthearted, obscenity-free lyrics, and are not socially threatening. However, harsher "hardcore" rap appeared to be gaining a greater following by 1991. N.W.A., a group known for its pornographic, violent lyrics and themes, gained the Number 1 pop-chart slot in June 1991 with an X-rated album.

One of critics' principal complaints about rap is that it uses recycled music rather than original tunes in most cases. However, this characteristic is one reason rap is so wildly popular with record companies. A rap album can be produced for as little as one-tenth the cost of a typical rock recording, yet can bring in similarly high profits. In some cases, rappers even produce their recordings at home using music software programs, giving them the freedom to create new and unique effects—and also saving even more money.

Rap Is Everywhere. The special language, sound, and even the "look" of rap has become part of the U.S. mainstream over the past few years. Rap artists and music are being used to sell everything from soda to cars. Rap-slang words—such as "chillin'," "def," "dis," "fresh," and "word"—have become part of teenagers' vocabulary; and clothing like that worn by rappers—typically quasimilitary attire, oversized sweatclothes, expensive sneakers, and lots of gold jewelry—is a staple of high-school fashion. Dance and even rock music are influenced, with raps and rap rhythm styles appearing in both genres. It would seem that, whatever the critics' complaints, rap music is a strong influence on both popular culture and on the evolution of popular music. Those who said rap would be as dead as disco by the mid-1980s would appear to be dead wrong.

MEGHAN O'REILLY LEBLANC

© Lee Chum/Outline Press

The rock group R.E.M. brought out "Out of Time" during the year. The top-selling album was the seventh by the Georgia rock band, whose members are noted for their concern for the environment and have experienced growing acceptance by the musical mainstream.

of young bands who mixed nimble rhythms and muscular guitar sounds. Bands successfully exploring this provocative new hybrid included Faith No More, Jesus Jones, Living Colour, Urban Dance Squad, and the Red Hot Chili Peppers.

Country. Garth Brooks was unquestionably *the* country star of 1991, and in terms of record sales, the equal of any pop star. What was truly significant about Brooks, however, was that while most recent country stars looked to giants like Hank Williams and George Jones for inspiration, Brooks was aligned more clearly with a pop-rock singer-songwriter like James Taylor. His records might be shelved in the country section, but Brooks drew much of his audience from older rock fans disenchanted with the hyped-up sound and often-adolescent lyrics of dance music and hard rock.

The success of the Grammy Award-winning Kentucky Headhunters similarly reflected how modern country music was drawing both musical inspiration and fans from the world of rock and roll. The Headhunters had much more to do with the country-inflected Southern rock of the Allman Brothers Band and Lynyrd Skynyrd than with the traditional stars of Nashville.

Jazz. An event occurred in 1991 that was likely to be seen as a watershed event in the history of jazz. New York's Lincoln Center—long a mecca for classical music, opera, and ballet—launched a jazz program that symbolically acknowledged that this quintessentially American art form belongs in the concert hall as well as on the bandstand of nightclubs.

Deaths. Miles Davis, as much as anyone in jazz, bridged the gap between high culture and soulful art, and his death at the age of 65 sent a discernible ripple through U.S. musical culture. Davis was renowned as a titan of the trumpet, and was famous for a melodic sense that was the musical equivalent of poetry. Yet the legacy of his nearly 50 years on the bandstand also rested on his eclecticism.

Davis arrived in New York to study at Juilliard, but got serious playing with bebop saxophonist Charlie Parker. In the 1950s he starred in symphonic suites arranged by the late Gil Evans, and led a quartet that epitomized the "cool school" of jazz with landmark albums like *Kind of Blue*. In the late 1960s he formed an electric band and sparked the creation of jazz-rock fusion. His various bands included many of the giants of modern jazz, including John Coltrane, Herbie Hancock, Chick Corea, and John McLaughlin.

The jazz world also mourned the loss of Stan Getz, who was 64. A richly melodic improviser on the saxophone, Getz sparked the bossa nova craze in the early 1960s when he and guitarist Joao Gilberto scored a major pop hit with "The Girl from Ipanema," which won four Grammy awards.

The pop world lost David Ruffin, a principal singer with the original Temptations, and Steve Marriott, known for his work with two British rock bands, Small Faces and Humble Pie. Rock promoter Bill Graham, an influential force in the music world ever since he began producing concerts at San Francisco's Fillmore Auditorium in the mid-1960s, died in a helicopter crash. Country music lost two veteran stars, Dottie West and Tennessee Ernie Ford.

JOHN MILWARD
Free-lance Writer and Critic

MYANMAR

Three years after the army brutally crushed Myanmar's prodemocracy movement, the country still was being run by a military junta known as the State Law and Order Restoration Committee (SLORC), which generally was considered to be a front for retired strongman Gen. U Ne Win.

Political Repression. In 1991 the SLORC, headed by Saw Maung, enjoyed more control over Myanmar than any government has for three decades. It achieved this power by jailing critics; torture; dissolution of alternative institutions such as schools, newspapers, and political parties; and through an ambitious effort to co-opt the guerrilla groups representing the country's ethnic minorities that have opposed the central government since 1945. It changed the name of Rangoon, the capital, to Yangon, which means "no more enemies." That may be wishful thinking, but the government has not lacked for imagination in controlling its citizens.

The leading opposition party, the National League for Democracy (NLD), which won a massive victory in the elections of May 1990, was dissolved in December 1990. The election results had been ignored by the SLORC. More than 300 of the candidates elected to the National Assembly were imprisoned, and several died under mysterious circumstances. A small band of elected opposition leaders escaped to Thailand, where a provisional government-in-exile was formed. Two of the leaders subsequently were abducted by the regime to Myanmar and no nations accorded diplomatic recognition to the provisional government. Only three of the original 12 members of the NLD's central committee were free in 1991; their most famous leader, Aung San Suu Kyi, still was being held incommunicado under house arrest two years after she rallied tens of thousands to fight for democracy.

Enormous areas of the capital city—where prodemocracy forces were strong—were evacuated, and four new cities—one with a population of more than 300,000—were created. Those thought disloyal to the military junta were being used as human mine detectors for the army, which marched them into guerrilla areas. The guerrillas established a loose alliance to confront the regime but proved susceptible to a combination of economic incentives and the army's firepower.

Medical schools reopened in May, but many other schools remained closed. Students were required to sign pledges not to become politically involved. Members of the civil service were required to answer a lengthy and loaded questionnaire designed to gain their written commitment to support the regime. A major purge of the bureaucracy reportedly was under way.

Political repression spurred emigration. More than 10,000 Burmese were living illegally in Japan, a country attractive to them for its Buddhist culture. One thousand moved to Sydney, Australia, and thousands of others also fled Myanmar.

Economic Conditions. The teak forest of central Myanmar had been cut down completely to garner foreign exchange. Despite a dramatic burning of opium by the military, it was estimated that half of the world's opium was being processed in Myanmar, much of it by ethnic minorities on the Thai and Chinese borders. The military also was said to be involved heavily in drug trafficking.

The government claimed a 27% increase in exports and a 53% increase in private investment. The Asian Development Bank saw such figures as grossly exaggerated but acknowledged a temporary increase in revenues because of the sale of national assets. The regime also had three times the amount of currency in circulation as in 1988, which contributed to an annual inflation rate of more than 70%.

Nations such as Japan, Thailand, and Korea have been eager to take advantage of Myanmar's fire-sale prices for teak, oil concessions, and fishing rights. The junta in turn purchased $1.2 billion worth of weapons from China.

International Censure. A report by the United Nations Human Rights Committee has condemned the government's sustained pattern of torture and abuse of dissidents. The SLORC's image was sullied further in October 1991 when the Nobel Peace Prize was awarded in absentia to opposition leader Aung San Suu Kyi (*see* BIOGRAPHY).

LINDA K. RICHTER, *Kansas State University*

MYANMAR • Information Highlights

Official Name: Union of Myanmar.
Location: Southeast Asia.
Area: 261,969 sq mi (678 500 km²).
Population (mid-1991 est.): 42,100,000.
Chief Cities (1983 census): Yangon (Rangoon), the capital, 2,513,023; Mandalay, 532,949.
Government: *Head of government,* Gen. Saw Maung (took power Sept. 18, 1988). *Legislature* (unicameral)—National Assembly.
Monetary Unit: Kyat (6.516 kyats equal U.S.$1, June 1991).
Gross Domestic Product (1988 est. U.S.$): $11,000,000,000.
Economic Index (1990): *Consumer Prices* (1980 = 100), all items, 292.3; food, 299.9.
Foreign Trade (1990 U.S.$): *Imports,* $261,000,000; *exports,* $325,000,000.

NAMIBIA

The world's newest democracy celebrated its first year of independence in March 1991, but the legacy of generations of white minority rule and privilege was presenting Namibia with a formidable challenge. Notwithstanding the constant tension of enduring inequalities, bitter enemies were coexisting and the multiparty democracy put in place at independence was able to avert major crises in 1991.

Politics. To some extent white fears of nationalization were allayed, and the ruling South West African People's Organization (SWAPO), which held 41 of the 72 legislative seats, managed to govern in the midst of six parliamentary opposition groups. Indeed, SWAPO encouraged debate and a free exchange of ideas, while demanding strict adherence to the new constitution which not only protects freedoms of speech, religion, and movement but prohibits racial discrimination and capital punishment.

Throughout the year, President Sam Nujoma and his government insisted on the application of their policy of national reconciliation, which some blacks were interpreting narrowly as the government's promise to whites that, at least relatively speaking, the status quo would be protected. Thus, while the government began to address emergency food and medical needs of the black majority, whites still controlled the economy and Namibia remained dependent on South Africa. For example, the South African rand remained the national currency of Namibia, the phone systems were integrated, and Afrikaans still was used widely as a language of communication. The expected white exodus to South Africa had not taken place, and many whites were accepting Namibian citizenship. On the other hand, while most whites came to terms with living under a black government, racial prejudice still was in evidence and a minority of well-armed reactionary whites continued to pose a threat.

Economy. The new government not only had to contend with the problem of nearly 18,000 unemployed former guerrillas but with the return of more than 40,000 exiles, which greatly exacerbated the already serious unemployment problem. Namibia's economy would continue to struggle to meet the demands of these groups. Three donor and investor conferences attracted only one new industry, Citroen of France, which intended to manufacture luxury cars for export to the South African market. At independence foreign donors promised $220 million in development aid but only a small portion of this was allocated to the country's more than $1 billion budget. One positive sign was a so-called peace dividend of more than $100 million as a result of the end of the guerrilla war and a reorientation of government spending priorities away from defense.

Walvis Bay. The status of Walvis Bay, Namibia's only deep-water port, continued to be disputed in 1991. South Africa maintained that Walvis Bay remained under its control despite Namibian independence. Namibia, on the other hand, with the United Nations Security Council and world opinion on its side, claimed an inherent right to Walvis Bay. Meetings of government officials from both countries to resolve the issue ended in deadlock. The port is of particular value to Namibians because it would lessen their dependence on South Africa. The related issue of the necessity of passports for those traveling between Namibia and Walvis Bay was resolved temporarily with an agreement to waive the requirement.

PATRICK O'MEARA
and N. BRIAN WINCHESTER
Indiana University

NAMIBIA • Information Highlights

Official Name: Republic of Namibia.
Location: Southwestern coast of Africa.
Area: 318,259 sq mi (824 290 km²).
Population (mid-1991 est.): 1,500,000.
Chief City (December 1988): Windhoek, the capital, 114,500.
Government: *Head of state and head of government,* Sam Nujoma, president (sworn in March 1990). *Legislature*—National Assembly.
Monetary Unit: South African rand (2.7925 rands equal U.S.$1, Nov. 4, 1991).
Gross National Product (1987 U.S.$): $1,540,000,000.

NEBRASKA

Nebraska's economy continued strong during 1991. Employment and personal incomes were up; unemployment rates were below the national average; the state's savings and loan institutions were reporting increased strength; and a study found Omaha in second place in terms of growth rate among the nation's 75 largest metropolitan areas. However, the year had an unfinished quality about it in that several pressing issues remained unresolved as the end of the year approached.

Tax Muddle. What was certainly the state's most confused and pressing issue to remain undecided concerned the tax structure. The state Supreme Court ruled that property-tax exemptions long granted on seed, grain, livestock, agricultural machinery, and business inventories violated the clause in the state constitution requiring uniformity in taxing. Numerous tax proposals followed as the legislature sought some means of keeping local governments solvent without creating new inequities. A proposal for a constitutional amendment failed in the regular session of the legislature and also in a special session. Lawsuits challenged a stopgap measure passed to provide a temporary solution, and by late in 1991 the governor, legislature, tax-study groups, and the courts were blaming one another for the impasse.

Radioactive Waste Disposal. Another issue that remained unresolved was the selection of a disposal site for the Central Interstate Low-level Radioactive Waste Compact, involving five states. The site selected was in Nebraska's Boyd county, but conflict followed almost at

© Ted Kirk/NYT Pictures

Bob Kerrey, 48, greeted supporters in Lincoln after the U.S. senator and former Nebraska governor announced his candidacy for the Democratic presidential nomination.

once as proponents and opponents of the site clashed. Demonstrations and political protests over the selection continued. Things became even more bitter when the executive director of the project was convicted on federal charges of embezzling nearly $800,000 in compact funds.

Death Penalty. A bewildering array of appeals, hearings, and court orders delayed the execution of Harold Lamont Otey, convicted of a brutal rape and murder committed in 1977. The U.S. Supreme Court declined to reverse a stay of execution issued by a lower court a few hours before Otey was scheduled to die in the electric chair. Frustrations created by the long delays and uncertain outcome may have contributed to the results of a statewide poll, which showed more than 80% in favor of the death penalty. The last execution in Nebraska had been in 1959.

Weather. The first half of the year produced exceptionally heavy rainfall in Nebraska, delaying planting and threatening crops. Then in mid-June the rain ceased and drought became a threat. Fortunately there were few summer days hot enough to categorize as "stress days," and that fact, coupled with more acres being brought under irrigation, meant surprisingly good yields, including a bumper crop of corn. An unusually early winter storm—termed "the Halloween blizzard of '91"—dropped heavy snow and record low temperatures on the state.

Newsmakers. Two prominent Nebraskans received national attention in 1991. Omaha investor Warren Buffett was selected as interim chairman of the scandal-plagued firm of Salomon Brothers Inc., and U.S. Sen. Bob Kerrey became a candidate for the 1992 Democratic presidential nomination.

WILLIAM E. CHRISTENSEN
Midland Lutheran College

NEBRASKA • Information Highlights

Area: 77,355 sq mi (200 350 km²).
Population (1990 census): 1,578,385.
Chief Cities (1990 census): Lincoln, the capital, 191,972; Omaha, 335,795.
Government (1991): *Chief Officers*—governor, Ben Nelson (D); lt. gov., Maxine Moul (D). *Legislature* (unicameral)—49 members (nonpartisan).
State Finances (fiscal year 1990): *Revenue*, $3,073,000,000; *expenditure*, $2,885,000,000.
Personal Income (1990): $27,734,000,000; per capita, $17,549.
Labor Force (June 1991): *Civilian labor force*, 874,700; *unemployed*, 20,500 (2.3% of total force).
Education: *Enrollment* (fall 1989)—public elementary schools, 194,227; public secondary, 76,693; colleges and universities, 108,844. *Public school expenditures* (1989), $1,105,009,000.

NEPAL

Nepal held national elections in May 1991, the first under the new democratic constitution. Despite this achievement, the new government faced major economic and political challenges.

Elections. The multiparty elections on May 12 were Nepal's first in 32 years. With a turnout of more than 60% of the country's 11 million voters, the polling produced some notable surprises. The Nepali Congress (NC) won 110 seats, a majority of the 205 contested seats in the lower house of Parliament, but far short of the two-thirds majority they had sought. The Communist Party of Nepal-United Marxist Leninist (CPN-UML) won 69 seats to become the major opposition party in the new assembly.

Interim Prime Minister K. P. Bhattarai (NC), who led Nepal through its democratization process, was defeated narrowly by CPN-UML leader Madan Bhandari. Bhattarai was one of four NC candidates who lost in the five Kathmandu constituencies. Despite the defeat of other NC leaders nationwide, the party did well enough in the rural areas to form a government. The new prime minister, Girja Prasad Koirala, is a veteran NC activist.

Economic Issues. In July the Koirala government submitted a budget designed to alleviate the economic plight of Nepal's rural poor. Roughly two thirds of the funds were for development, 70% of it in rural areas. Foreign assistance would underwrite more than two thirds of the development expenditures.

Like many other countries, Nepal was looking to privatization to improve productivity and stimulate growth. The Nepali rupee was devalued by 21% in July to increase foreign trade. The country continued to seek means to reduce its heavy trading dependency upon its giant neighbor to the south, India.

NEPAL • Information Highlights

Official Name: Kingdom of Nepal.
Location: South Asia.
Area: 54,363 sq mi (140 800 km²).
Population (mid-1991 est.): 19,600,000.
Chief City (1981 census): Kathmandu, the capital, 235,160.
Government: *Head of state,* Birendra Bir Bikram Shah Dev, king (acceded Jan. 31, 1972); *Head of government,* Girja Prasad Koirala, prime minister (took office May 1991). *Legislature*—National Assembly.
Monetary Unit: rupee (35.3 rupees equal U.S.$1, buying rate, June 1991).
Gross Domestic Product (1989 U.S.$): $2,900,-000,000.
Foreign Trade (1990 U.S.$): *Imports,* $687,000,000; *exports,* $208,000,000.

The deforestation problem in Nepal had worsened under the new democratic order. Politicians, tourists, landless squatters, and timber smugglers all contributed to the destruction of an estimated 59,300 acres (24 000 ha) of forest in 1990–91.

Foreign Relations. Nepal's relations with India, which had reached a low point in the late 1980s, improved with Nepal's democratization, especially during Chandra Shekhar's period as Indian prime minister. The Nepali Congress has had long-standing ties with India's Congress Party. However, public sentiment against Indian domination still was strong, and was one of the factors which apparently cut into the NC vote in the May elections.

The democracy movement in Nepal also had some effect on ethnic Nepali elements in neighboring Bhutan. The NC and the Communists both were backing "dissidents of Nepalese origin" in Bhutan, in opposition to the Bhutanese king's new policies imposing Bhutanese and Buddhist cultural values on the predominantly Hindu Nepalese.

WILLIAM L. RICHTER
Kansas State University

NETHERLANDS

The year 1991 was marked by novel problems for the Netherlands relating to the environment and to European Community endeavors.

Environment. The long-term consequences of the "greenhouse effect" in raising the level of the ocean were troubling for the Netherlands, more than half of whose territory is below sea level. Yet the protection afforded by the Delta Works, the system of dikes and dams protecting the coastline of Zeeland and Holland provinces, was beginning to be seen as environmentally damaging and probably inadequate. Important for the supply of fresh water, however, were measures adopted in neighboring countries to reduce the pollution of the Rhine River. Efforts to limit the production and overuse of manure fertilizers met bitter resistance from farmers.

European and Foreign Affairs. Increasing attention was paid to the eventual problems of Dutch cultural and linguistic identity in the politically more unified Europe expected to develop after 1992. In particular emphasis was given to the importance of collaboration with the Dutch-speaking population and government in Flanders, in neighboring Belgium. There was sharp debate over a proposal by the minister of education that English be made a working language in the universities alongside Dutch.

During the second half of 1991 the Netherlands, holding the chairmanship of the European Community, was involved in a series of difficult mediation efforts to negotiate a peace in the civil war in Yugoslavia. In addition, a Dutch proposal for a tight political union within the European Community that would reduce the dominance of the big powers was rejected.

The end of the Cold War reduced domestic tensions over the Netherlands' role in foreign policy. The country sent frigates, a hospital ship, and antirocket weapons to the allied forces in the Persian Gulf war. The once-vigorous peace movement put up little resistance.

Domestic Affairs. The central political problem within the country was the costs of the welfare system, with benefits among the highest in the world, that contributed to mounting government deficits and made the competitive position of the Netherlands more difficult. The cabinet, a coalition of the Christian Democratic and Labor parties led by Premier Rudolf (Ruud) Lubbers, met opposition not only to reductions in government-operating expenditures, but also to its attempt to "uncouple" the level of welfare payments from the minimum wages in industry. The position of the cabinet was shaky following proposed measures to reduce the number of persons on sick leave and workers' disability, and brief wildcat strikes broke out. But Wim Kok, the vice-premier and minister of finance who was the head of the

NETHERLANDS • Information Highlights

Official Name: Kingdom of the Netherlands.
Location: Northwestern Europe.
Area: 14,398 sq mi (37 290 km²).
Population (mid-1991 est.): 15,000,000.
Chief Cities (Jan. 1, 1990 est.): Amsterdam, the capital, 695,162; Rotterdam, 579,179; The Hague, the seat of government, 441,506.
Government: *Head of state,* Beatrix, queen (acceded April 30, 1980). *Head of government,* Ruud Lubbers, prime minister (took office Nov. 1982). *Legislature*—States General: First Chamber and Second Chamber.
Monetary Unit: Guilder (1.8445 guilders equal U.S.$1, Nov. 8, 1991).
Economic Indexes (1990): *Consumer Prices* (1980 = 100), all items, 127.2; food, 119.0. *Industrial Production* (1980 = 100), 116.
Foreign Trade (1990 U.S.$): *Imports,* $126,195,-000,000; *exports,* $131,839,000,000.

Labor Party and the former president of the allied trade-union movement, was able to hold Labor Party support.

Although elections for the provincial states (legislatures) and public-opinion polls showed a sharp decline in Labor Party support, the cabinet avoided crisis because the Christian Democrats let their Labor allies serve as a buffer against discontent. The chief potential beneficiary was the progressive party known as Democrats '66, which was excluded from the 1989 coalition government. Among other political parties, the Conservative Party, which had been the former cabinet partner of the Christian Democrats, remained bitter toward them, and the small leftist parties retained their combined identity as "Green Left" (combining environmentalists and political radicals of a socialist cast). The Communist Party disbanded.

HERBERT H. ROWEN
Rutgers University

NEVADA

A stagnant economy, an acrimonious legislative session, new taxes, drought, water controversies, and a troublesome desert tortoise were in the Nevada limelight during 1991.

The Legislature. The biennial session was dominated by a revenue shortfall of $300 million, necessitating some form of new taxes. Democratic Gov. Robert J. Miller proposed a 1% business payroll tax coupled with increased licensing fees to raise $272 million. After the defeat of the governor's tax proposal, a bipartisan group of legislators initiated a plan to raise $317 million through increasing the sales tax by 0.75% and assessing business-license fees from $100,000 to $400,000 per year, based on the number of employees. The legislators' plan passed after a bitter standoff.

The divisive question of reapportionment prolonged the session when a maverick Democratic state assemblywoman refused to vote for the Democratic-sponsored plan, throwing the assembly into a tie. Ultimately a compromise was reached with terms more favorable to the Republican minority.

In other legislation, a right-to-die law was enacted, allowing terminally ill patients to halt medical care with legal documents or through a living will. A separate family-court system was created to handle child-support and custody cases, divorces involving couples with children, underage marriages, child abuse, and other civil cases involving children.

In education the governor's program for elementary class-size reduction was extended through the third grade, with state funds provided for a maximum student-teacher ratio of 15 to one in the first grade, 16 to one in the second grade, and 19 to one in the third grade.

The Economy. Nevada, in the midst of a recession, saw its unemployment rate fluctuate between 5.9% and 6.4% in the first half of the year. Gaming revenues remained flat, increasing only slightly over those of 1990. A governmental fiscal crisis was precipitated when July and August sales-tax revenues were down 1.28%, while the 1991–92 state budget was built on a projected 7.5% increase. In October the 4% pay raise approved for state employees and public-school teachers was delayed for at least three months. Subsequently, the public employees' union filed suit. Additionally, state agencies and public schools were required to cut their state-allocated budgets by 4%.

Other Issues. Water played an important role in Nevada during the year. The attempts of the city of Las Vegas and Clark county to facilitate additional demands for water to meet their rapid growth by importing water from rural Lincoln County met stiff resistance and were delayed. On another note was the settlement after more than 70 years of litigation of the dispute between the Pyramid Lake Paiute Indians and the upstream users of the Truckee and Carson rivers. Northern Nevada suffered through a fifth year of drought, with Lake Tahoe falling to its lowest level since the 1930s and staying below the rim of its outlet into the Truckee River. Mandatory water-use restrictions were applied in Reno, Sparks, and Carson City for the second straight year. Growth in Clark County, where about 60% of Nevada's inhabitants reside, was slowed by the discovery of the endangered desert tortoise in areas slated for development.

TIMOTHY HALLER
Western Nevada Community College

NEVADA • Information Highlights

Area: 110,561 sq mi (286 352 km²).
Population (1990 census): 1,201,833.
Chief Cities (1990 census): Carson City, the capital, 40,443; Las Vegas, 258,295; Reno, 133,850.
Government (1991): *Chief Officer*—governor, Robert J. Miller (D); lt. gov., Sue Wagner (R). *Legislature*—Senate, 21 members; Assembly, 42 members.
State Finances (fiscal year 1990): *Revenue,* $3,266,000,000; *expenditure,* $2,929,000,000.
Personal Income (1990): $23,298,000,000; per capita, $19,035.
Labor Force (June 1991): *Civilian labor force,* 659,500; *unemployed,* 39,700 (6.0% of total force).
Education: *Enrollment* (fall 1989)—public elementary schools, 137,455; public secondary, 49,379; colleges and universities, 56,471. *Public school expenditures* (1989), $615,161,000.

NEW BRUNSWICK

In 1991 events in New Brunswick, the Liberals made it two majority wins in a row with a resounding September election triumph, while a new political force took over the opposition benches. Premier Frank McKenna put a leash on the power commission, and former Premier Richard Hatfield died.

Liberals Returned. Premier McKenna's Liberal Party roared back into office in a provincial general election September 23, winning 46 of the 58 seats in the legislature for their second straight majority victory. The win was less lopsided than in 1987, however, when the Liberals swept all 58 seats.

The Confederation of Regions (CoR) was a surprise runner-up. Contesting its first provincial election, CoR took eight seats to become the official opposition. The Conservatives won three seats and the left-wing New Democratic Party one.

McKenna, in a victory statement, played down the emergence of CoR, which advocates the repeal of the province's Official Languages Act, the statute that recognizes both English and French as official languages of New Brunswick. He called the Liberal win a victory for bilingualism in the province. Later, on October 8, the premier named seven Francophones to his 18-member postelection cabinet, thus assuring French-speaking New Brunswickers a continuing strong voice in provincial affairs.

Tory Leader Quits. Barbara Baird Filliter suddenly resigned as leader of the New Brunswick Conservative Party April 12. She had assumed the leadership in November 1989, filling a vacuum created by the departure of Richard Hatfield. Subsequently, at a convention in Fredericton June 15, the Tories picked Dennis Cochrane as her successor. Cochrane, a former mayor of Moncton, went on to lead the Tories in the ensuing provincial election and won personal victory in the riding of Petitcodiac.

Bittersweet Budget. Finance Minister Allan Maher unveiled a C$4 billion budget in the legislature April 2 that offered New Brunswick residents good news of a sort: no major across-the-board tax increases and a slim operating surplus of C$1.1 million. The price was a year-long freeze on public-sector salaries—affecting more than 40,000 workers and duly passed into law June 6—combined with the elimination of 225 jobs. High-income earners were hit with an 8% income surtax.

New Brunswick Power Cut. Premier McKenna moved to assert greater control over the trouble-prone New Brunswick Electric Power Commission. At a Fredericton news conference February 7, he admitted that the utility was beset with problems ranging from questionable hiring practices to out-of-control spending. Henceforth all jobs would be open to fair competition. The president was to have greater authority over day-to-day operations, the chairman—a provincial cabinet position—less.

Hatfield Dies. Sen. Richard Hatfield, New Brunswick's colorful, widely beloved Conservative premier from 1970 to 1987, died of cancer in Ottawa on April 26 at the age of 60. His 17-year stint in the premier's office was the longest in New Brunswick's history.

JOHN BEST
"Canada World News"

NEW BRUNSWICK • Information Highlights

Area: 28,355 sq mi (73 440 km²).
Population (September 1991): 727,300.
Chief Cities (1986 census): Fredericton, the capital, 44,352; Saint John, 76,381; Moncton, 55,468.
Government (1991): *Chief Officers*—lt. gov., Gilbert Finn; premier, Frank McKenna (Liberal). *Legislature*—Legislative Assembly, 58 members.
Provincial Finances (1991–92 fiscal year budget): *Revenues,* $4,000,000,000; *expenditures,* $3,998,900,000.
Personal Income (average weekly earnings, July 1991): $493.56.
Labor Force (September 1991, seasonally adjusted): *Employed* workers, 15 years of age and over, 285,000; *Unemployed,* 12.8%.
Education (1991–92): *Enrollment*—elementary and secondary schools, 141,850 pupils; postsecondary—universities, 17,410; community colleges, 2,680.
(All monetary figures are in Canadian dollars.)

NEWFOUNDLAND

The year 1991 was not a good one for Newfoundland in spite of activity at the Hibernia oil-field construction site about 1 hour outside of St. John's. In broad terms the provincial economy was hit by the effects of the general Canadian recession and the slowdown in federal transfer payments.

Politics and Government. In spite of the economic difficulties faced by Newfoundland, in an October by-election to fill the seat made vacant by the resignation of opposition leader Tom Rideout, it was the Liberal candidate who won.

Premier Clyde Wells continued his personal interest in constitution making, but when the federal government tabled its proposals for the nation's future in September, Wells' suggestions for a constitutional convention followed by a referendum were not included. In response, Premier Wells followed the lead of other provincial governments in setting up a joint parliamentary committee to consider Newfoundland's position. Debate on the outcome would be held in the new legislative chambers for the House of Assembly, opened in February.

Hibernia Oil Field. The future had looked bright for Newfoundland when in September 1990 three parties—the governments of Newfoundland and Canada and a consortium of oil companies—signed an agreement to develop Hibernia 200 mi (321.9 km) off Newfoundland. Government spending and loan guarantees allowed contracts to be let which were valued at more than C$1 billion. The promise of new money and jobs in the province seemed to fore-

NEWFOUNDLAND • Information Highlights

Area: 156,649 sq mi (405 720 km²).
Population (September 1991): 574,300.
Chief Cities (1986 census): St. John's, the capital, 96,216; Corner Brook, 22,719.
Government (1991): *Chief Officers*—lt. gov., Frederick William Russell; premier, Clyde Wells (Liberal). *Legislature*—Legislative Assembly, 52 members.
Provincial Finances (1991–92 fiscal year budget): *Revenues*, $3,300,000,000; *expenditures*, $3,500,000,000.
Personal Income (average weekly earnings, July 1991): $510.20.
Labor Force (September 1991, seasonally adjusted): *Employed* workers, 15 years of age and over, 198,000. *Unemployed*, 17.8%.
Education (1991–92): *Enrollment*—elementary and secondary schools, 124,150 pupils; postsecondary—universities, 13,300; community colleges, 3,980.
(All monetary figures are in Canadian dollars.)

tell a better future. Work on the project proceeded in 1991, but otherwise Newfoundland had no good news economically.

Economy and Budget. The province suffered financially during 1991. For local resource companies the recession necessitated a reduction in workers to cut costs, and for the provincial government, C$27 million less in transfer payments meant a "savage" budget which led to large cuts in the numbers of civil servants, a freeze in public salaries in spite of collective agreements, and the elimination of 360 hospital beds. Even changing world conditions affected the province as the U.S. government announced in July it would close its air-force base in Goose Bay, Labrador.

Fishing Industry. Added to the economic difficulties, nature itself seemed to turn against the province during 1991. Icebergs from Greenland brought ice-filled harbors and very cold water all along the Labrador and northeast coasts of the island until late in June. The result was a fish harvest far below that of previous years. This in turn meant almost no employment in fish-processing plants and other related industries. Offshore, vessels from Europe continued to overfish in areas beyond the 200-mi (321.9-km) limit, and there seemed to be nothing the government of Canada could do to stop the depletion of the resource itself. Late in the year the federal minister of fisheries announced spending of C$38 million to provide make-work projects for fishermen and plant workers to enable them to qualify for unemployment-insurance payments.

SUSAN MCCORQUODALE
Memorial University of Newfoundland

NEW HAMPSHIRE

Throughout 1991 nothing captured more attention than the continuing economic malaise affecting virtually everyone in the state of New Hampshire. After the heady 1980s, the severity of this economic downturn seemed even worse. Unemployment in the state during the 1980s consistently had been below the national average. In 1991 it remained persistently above the national level—ranging from a high of 7.2% in January to 6.9% in September. Clearly the economic miracle had ended, and New Hampshire had to cope with the excesses of the 1980s boom. As might be expected, the real-estate market remained terrible, with auction notices regularly filling several pages of daily and Sunday newspapers.

The Legislature. Because of the recession, state government had to wrestle with ways to find adequate revenue to fund necessary programs. After much acrimony during the legislative session, the representatives approved and Gov. Judd Gregg signed a $3.9 billion budget for the biennium that included $110 million in higher taxes. Throughout the session considerable attention was directed to tax reform. For the first time in many years, a sizable number of members of the General Court supported major tax reform, including the implementation of an income tax. Although income-tax legislation did not pass, the issue remained alive because many believe the state has a regressive tax structure. State budget problems continued into the new fiscal year as tax revenues failed to meet expectations. In late October the governor and the legislative fiscal committee agreed on a 3.5% across-the-board reduction in spending.

The Economy. Reinforcing the downward trend, the state's second-largest utility, the New Hampshire Electric Cooperative, filed for bankruptcy. Most of its debt had been incurred from investments in the Seabrook nuclear plant. It owed the Rural Electrification Administration $255 million. As the year was ending, the reorganization process continued.

The banking crisis reached New Hampshire as seven banks were taken over by the Federal Deposit Insurance Corporation (FDIC) and then purchased by two banks—First New Hampshire Bank and the newly formed New

NEW HAMPSHIRE • Information Highlights

Area: 9,279 sq mi (24 032 km²).
Population (1990 census): 1,109,252.
Chief Cities (1990 census): Concord, the capital, 36,006; Manchester, 99,567; Nashua, 79,662.
Government (1991): *Chief Officer*—governor, Judd Gregg (R). *General Court*—Senate, 24 members; House of Representatives, 400 members.
State Finances (fiscal year 1990): *Revenue*, $1,922,000,000; *expenditure*, $1,972,000,000.
Personal Income (1990): $23,147,000,000; per capita, $20,827.
Labor Force (June 1991): *Civilian labor force*, 644,300; *unemployed*, 46,900 (7.3% of total force).
Education: *Enrollment* (fall 1989)—public elementary schools, 124,410; public secondary, 47,286; colleges and universities, 58,600. *Public school expenditures* (1989), $733,230,000.

Dartmouth Bank. This action, the seventh-most-expensive bank rescue to that point, cost the FDIC $966 million.

A more optimistic development was the purchase of the famous Mount Washington Hotel in Bretton Woods by a group of five local businessmen, assuring that this grand 89-year-old hotel would continue in operation. The federal government had taken over the resort facility and offered it at auction in late June.

Other News. One of the most dramatic stories of 1991 centered on the trial of Pamela Smart, the high-school media specialist from Derry, NH, who was charged with conspiring to have her student lover murder her husband. For three weeks in March the televised trial enthralled viewers with lurid details of the affair between student and teacher and the alleged manipulation by Smart of her lover. The jury convicted Smart, and she began serving her sentence in the state women's prison.

Other stories making news included the final closing of Pease Air Force Base at Newington, NH; the moving to new facilities of the Dartmouth-Hitchcock medical center; and the good summer tourist season that helped to improve the economic picture.

WILLIAM L. TAYLOR
Plymouth State College

NEW JERSEY

© Frank C. Dougherty/NYT Pictures

New Jersey Senate President John Lynch, bottom, *and his supporters watch the 1991 election returns. Although he was reelected, many of his fellow Democrats in the legislature were defeated.*

Hard times and political infighting dominated the 1991 scene in New Jersey, with Democratic Gov. Jim Florio the focal point.

The Governor. Florio's main task was to repair the damage done in 1990 when, after campaigning on a pledge of no new taxes, he pushed a $2.8 billion increase through the Democrat-controlled legislature without any apparent explanation of why he changed course. His success in image rebuilding was moderate at best. Public-opinion polls showed that the extreme grass-roots anger had abated, but that Florio's overall approval rating was only about 25%.

Democratic state legislators, positioning themselves for fall elections, tried to disassociate themselves from the governor. Senate President John Lynch, for example, led a move to provide tax relief for middle-class suburbanites. He sought to transfer several hundred million dollars earmarked for urban education to property-tax relief. Nevertheless, in November's legislative elections the Republicans completely overwhelmed the Democrats, gaining control of both houses for the first time in 20 years.

Coping with Hard Times. Hard economic times were evident in unemployment figures and Governor Florio's austerity budget. From 1988 to 1991 unemployment rose from 3.8% to 6.5% of the labor force. Meanwhile, the budget called for a record $14.7 billion in spending, accompanied by $800 million worth of cuts in services, the elimination of 2,250 jobs, and wage freezes for those remaining on the state payroll. More radically, $400 million was raised by selling a 4.4-mi (7-km) section of Interstate

NEW JERSEY • Information Highlights

Area: 7,787 sq mi (20 169 km²).
Population (1990 census): 7,730,188.
Chief Cities (1990 census): Trenton, the capital, 88,675; Newark, 275,221; Jersey City, 228,537; Paterson, 140,891; Elizabeth, 110,002.
Government (1991): *Chief Officers*—governor, James J. Florio (D). *Legislature*—Senate, 40 members; General Assembly, 80 members.
State Finances (fiscal year 1990): *Revenue,* $22,624,000,000; *expenditure,* $21,454,000,000.
Personal Income (1990): $192,893,000,000; per capita, $24,936.
Labor Force (June 1991): *Civilian labor force,* 4,096,300; *unemployed,* 265,300 (6.5% of total force).
Education: *Enrollment* (fall 1989)—public elementary schools, 765,810; public secondary, 310,195; colleges and universities, 314,091. *Public school expenditures* (1989), $7,309,147,000.

95 to the New Jersey Turnpike Authority (NJTA). The NJTA's purchase was funded, in part, by massive toll increases. Despite these measures, state Treasurer Douglas C. Berman said that barring wage reductions and a further reduction in state workers there would be a $768 million deficit. On the brighter side, economists felt that New Jersey was better able to survive recession than many Northeastern states.

Legislative Redistricting. Following the 1990 census, legislative redistricting was a controversial issue that highlighted demographic change and political-party power. The suburbanization of New Jersey continued, leaving the older cities increasingly poor and nonwhite. This was good for Republicans and bad for Democrats as redistricting shifted the state's 40 legislative districts south and west. Vain attempts were made by Attorney General Robert Del Tufo and the New Jersey NAACP to reverse the court-ordered redistricting plan.

Insurance. Failing to overthrow Governor Florio's plan requiring insurance companies to pay for the elimination of the New Jersey Underwriters Association, Allstate announced that it no longer would operate in New Jersey, as costs were too high. The company had the most automobile-insurance business in the state.

Marking a sign of the times, New Jersey regulators seized control of the Mutual Benefit Life Insurance Company, the nation's 18th-largest life insurer, which was in deepening financial trouble due to a heavy investment in troubled real estate.

Storm Damage. A late October Atlantic storm, considered the worst in 20 years, took a severe toll on New Jersey's coastline, causing severe beach erosion. Damage was caused by high tides and gale-force winds.

HERMANN K. PLATT
Saint Peter's College

NEW MEXICO

New Mexico's political face changed slightly in 1991 with redistricting resulting from 1990 Census Bureau figures, which showed that the state's population had grown by 16.3% since 1980, to 1.5 million.

Redistricting. Most of New Mexico's population growth was in the northern 3d District, which had about 520,400 people, while the 1st and 2d Districts each recorded about 497,000. State legislators and Gov. Bruce King approved a plan that gave each district 505,000 people.

Dona Ana county, abutting the Mexico and Texas borders, became the state's second Class A county. Bernalillo county, home to Albuquerque, long had been the state's only Class A county.

NEW MEXICO • Information Highlights

Area: 121,593 sq mi (314 925 km²).
Population (1990 census): 1,515,069.
Chief Cities (1990 census): Santa Fe, the capital, 55,859; Albuquerque, 384,736; Las Cruces, 62,126.
Government (1991): *Chief Officers*—governor, Bruce King (D); lt. gov., Casey Luna (D). *Legislature*—Senate, 42 members; House of Representatives, 70 members.
State Finances (fiscal year 1990): *Revenue,* $4,731,000,000; *expenditure,* $4,172,000,000.
Personal Income (1990): $21,677,000,000; per capita, $14,265.
Labor Force (June 1991): *Civilian labor force,* 723,000; *unemployed,* 61,100 (8.5% of total force).
Education: *Enrollment* (fall 1989)—public elementary schools, 203,157; public secondary, 92,900; colleges and universities, 81,350. *Public school expenditures* (1989), $975,552,000.

Border Matters. State officials hoped to have a new international border crossing with Mexico in Dona Ana county by 1992. The crossing would be the third in the state, and legislators hoped it would be an economic boon after a U.S.-Mexico free-trade agreement is finalized. Poising itself for free trade, the state also created the Border Development Authority, which was to oversee development related to Mexico.

Cholera became an acute issue along the border as the disease made its way up from South America, where it killed thousands (*see* SIDEBAR/LATIN AMERICA). State health officials educated health providers along the Mexican border in an effort to head off the disease, which spreads through water and food contamination. By year's end, no cases had been reported along the border.

The federal government in 1991 began earmarking Community Development Block Grant money to improve border communities called Colonias which have inadequate housing and weak or contaminated water systems.

Also close to the border, 1991 saw more mechanical harvesting of the state's prize crop, chiles. Migrant pickers feared the machine could eliminate the jobs of the estimated 15,000 workers who pick the crop.

Environment. The U.S. Energy Department's Waste Isolation Pilot Plant, which would store radioactive waste from around the nation underground, continued to generate controversy during the year. Located near Carlsbad, the 10,240-acre (4 144-ha) site was to have opened in October 1988, but still had not opened by October 1991. Recent questions dealt with truck routes and how much waste could be shipped to the site during the proposed test phase of six to eight years. After negotiations with the U.S. Department of Energy, New Mexico Sens. Pete Domenici (R) and Jeff Bingaman (D) failed to agree over these questions, and Energy Secretary James Watkins assumed control of the site.

Mescalero Apaches in the state were looking to locate a similar storage plant on their 461,000-acre (186 560-ha) reservation near Ruidoso. In 1991 the tribe received a $100,000 federal grant to study the feasibility of such a plant.

On the wilderness front, environmentalists continued to battle loggers in the Lincoln National Forest for what they saw as a diminishing habitat for the Mexican spotted owl. Congress created a timber task force to address the concerns of environmentalists and the state logging industry.

Reintroduction of the Mexican gray wolf remained on environmentalists' agenda in 1991. The U.S. Fish and Wildlife Service held public hearings in February 1991 in New Mexico over the wolf, which is extinct in the U.S. wilderness. New Mexico's White Sands Missile Range was a proposed site for its release.

KEITH WHELPLEY
"Las Cruces Sun-News"

NEW YORK

The lingering national recession exacted a political and economic toll in New York state in 1991, eroding the popularity of elected officials, prompting widespread cutbacks in tax-funded programs as the state and local governments struggled to avoid tax hikes, and pushing the number of New Yorkers seeking public assistance to the highest level in more than 50 years.

Budget. The severity of the fiscal problems was foreshadowed in 1990, when Democratic Gov. Mario Cuomo, fresh from election to a third term, summoned the state legislature for an unusual December session to implement a series of steps designed to eliminate a budget shortfall that had emerged at the midpoint of the state fiscal year.

After the state's 1990–91 problem had been solved, however, deeper fiscal woes remained. When Cuomo sent his proposed $51 billion budget to the legislature on January 31, he warned that the state faced "the most threatening fiscal situation . . . since the Great Depression." He said that unless spending was cut or more money raised, the state confronted a potential deficit in the fiscal year that began April 1 of $6 billion.

Neither the Democrat-controlled State Assembly nor the Republican-led Senate was eager to embrace the painful combination of cuts and taxes Cuomo proposed. It was not until 18 weeks later—ten weeks after the state's fiscal year had begun—that the governor and legislative leaders agreed on a spending plan. The new budget added $2.1 billion in taxes and fees. It cut spending in nearly every program. Grants to local governments, excluding school aid, were reduced by $2.9 billion, 13% below the level required to maintain current programs. School aid was cut by 5.3% from existing levels and the state operations budget, which covers the cost of running state government, was trimmed by 15%.

The result was felt in all corners. Local governments closed hospitals and emergency rooms, cut the work force in even essential services such as police and fire fighting, and raised property taxes. School budgets were slashed and tens of thousands of people on public payrolls lost their jobs. Tuition was hiked at the State University and City University of New York, home-health-care grants were trimmed, new limits were placed on Medicaid services, mental-health facilities were closed, and new community-residence beds for the mentally ill were deferred.

In part because of the cuts, Cuomo's popularity—once the highest of any contemporary governor—plunged. Editorials around the state excoriated the legislature and the governor, and antitax groups were formed. Voters expressed their ire in November local elections, where many incumbents were defeated.

Yet the problems persisted. Food-stamp use reached an all-time high in the autumn, and by November, Cuomo said he would be forced to summon the legislature again for a special session to deal with a midyear deficit of $500 million to $800 million and another projected revenue shortfall of $3.5 billion in fiscal 1993. Meanwhile, the Hunger Action Network of New York state reported that the demand for services from the roughly 2,000 food pantries in the state was 30% higher than a year earlier. (*See also* SPECIAL REPORT/UNITED STATES.)

At the same time, Governor Cuomo had been considering running for the 1992 Democratic presidential nomination. Finally on December 20, Cuomo announced that he could not seek the nomination while the state was facing such a severe fiscal crisis.

NEW YORK • Information Highlights

Area: 49,108 sq mi (127 190 km²).
Population (1990 census): 17,990,455.
Chief Cities (1990 census): Albany, the capital, 101,082; New York, 7,322,564; Buffalo, 328,123; Rochester, 231,636; Yonkers, 188,082; Syracuse, 163,860.
Government (1991): *Chief Officers*—governor, Mario M. Cuomo (D); lt. gov., Stan Lundine (D). *Legislature*—Senate, 61 members; Assembly, 150 members.
State Finances (fiscal year 1990): *Revenue,* $64,253,000,000; *expenditure,* $59,139,000,000.
Personal Income (1990): $397,602,000,000; per capita, $22,086.
Labor Force (June 1991): *Civilian labor force,* 8,738,500; *unemployed,* 627,400 (7.2% of total force).
Education: *Enrollment* (fall 1989)—public elementary schools, 1,790,143; public secondary, 775,698; colleges and universities, 1,018,130. *Public school expenditures* (1989), $17,127,584,000.

Other. The legislature passed and Governor Cuomo signed into law a bill that made it easier for residents to vote. Voters now could register as few as 25 days before a primary and would not be purged from election rolls unless it had been five to eight years since they last voted.

A devastating Atlantic storm struck coastal areas of New England and the mid-Atlantic states on Halloween. Tides 8 ft (2.4 m) above normal pounded the beaches of Long Island's eastern and southern shores. The storm came little more than two months after Hurricane Bob killed three persons in the state.

The fate of the controversial Shoreham nuclear-power plant was all but sealed in October when the State Court of Appeals upheld a 1989 agreement to close the power station. Built at a cost of $5.5 billion, the plant was never operated because of concerns that Long Island could not be evacuated safely in the event of a nuclear disaster.

REX SMITH
Editor, "The Record," Troy, NY

NEW YORK CITY

New York City, largely spared the ravages of August's Hurricane Bob, instead was buffeted by man-made tragedies and swept by winds of political change during 1991. As officials struggled to bridge deficits widened by the recession, the city's fragile physical and social infrastructures were tested sorely by racial disturbances in Brooklyn, a subway crash that killed five people, and a water-main break that flooded midtown Manhattan.

Crown Heights Violence. Census figures confirmed what demographers had guessed for several years: By 1990 the nation's largest city had fractured into a cosmopolis of minorities in which non-Hispanic whites no longer constituted a majority. Periodically, like tectonic plates beneath the Earth, members of New York's ethnic and racial groups rub each other the wrong way until the friction flares into a violent confrontation. That happened in the Crown Heights section of Brooklyn in August after a car driven by a Hasidic Jew accidentally struck and killed a young black boy. Within hours a group of blacks retaliated by fatally stabbing a Hasidic student. The next days were marked by outbursts of civil unrest as David N. Dinkins, confronting special expectations as the city's first black mayor, aggressively waded into the fray to help restore calm.

City Government. A ten-year legal and political process to make New York's government more representative of the population culminated in elections for an expanded City Council. Under a revised charter approved by voters in 1989, the city's newly invigorated legislative body grew from 35 to 51 members. A voluntary system of public campaign financing and the improved prospects for election from 16 new districts attracted a bumper crop of candidates, if not of voters. When the results were in, the proportion of black and Hispanic council members had increased from 25% to 40%.

When the mayor and council were not coping with spontaneous crises, they grappled with budget gaps, reaching agreement on a $29 billion spending plan by the legal deadline—unlike their counterparts in state government. But it was a plan that satisfied virtually no one. It imposed higher taxes and promised a decline in city services, except for the police force, which Mayor Dinkins was expanding under an ambi-

© Fred R. Conrad/NYT Pictures

A subway derailed at New York City's Union Square Station on Aug. 28, 1991, killing five persons and injuring 171. The motorman later was charged with manslaughter.

tious public-safety program that he persuaded the council and state legislature to approve. The budget cuts were not deep enough, however, to appease the municipal-bond market or independent financial monitors who urged further reductions in the municipal work force.

Dinkins delivered a televised address promising "reform and renaissance," but neither progressed as negotiations stalled with municipal-employee unions and as the state, itself facing a growing deficit, offered little immediate relief. Gov. Mario M. Cuomo did provide moral support, combined with a financial and administrative commitment to spur a number of public-works projects to jump start the sluggish local economy.

Also high on the city's agenda was homelessness. The Dinkins administration unveiled a controversial blueprint to disperse homeless individuals from cavernous shelters to a score of smaller ones, many in middle-class neighborhoods. Meanwhile, bowing to community complaints, the mayor approved the demolition of a homeless encampment in Tompkins Square Park in lower Manhattan; barred "unauthorized persons" from public structures after homeless people were implicated in fires at the Staten Island ferry terminal and at an abandoned building in Brooklyn, where a firefighter was killed; and tentatively embraced a transit-authority policy of removing disorderly homeless people from the subway system.

Other News. Subway safety was catapulted into the public consciousness on August 28 when a motorman, who police said was drunk, apparently sped around a curve and crashed his train into station abutments, killing five passengers in the city's worst subway accident in 63 years.

The temperature also set records: The summer with the most 90°F (32°C) days ever recorded began in June after New York hosted a traditional ticker-tape parade to welcome returning veterans from the Persian Gulf.

SAM ROBERTS, *"The New York Times"*

NEW ZEALAND

Although victorious in the October 1990 elections, New Zealand's National Party government headed by Prime Minister Jim B. Bolger enjoyed an unprecedentedly brief political honeymoon. Unemployment rose, negative economic growth was recorded, and the government's showing in the polls gave it no cause for comfort.

The Economy. In March the Porter Report—a study on the quest for upgrading New Zealand's competitive advantage prepared under the direction of Harvard Business School Professor Michael Porter—exposed the futility of trying to maintain First World standards on a Third World income. New Zealand's standard of living had been borrowed, not earned. The report's prescription for recovery included opening up competition, repayment of the huge overseas debt—now NZ$70 billion (about $41 billion) or 70% of gross domestic product (GDP), lower wages, cuts in social spending, and incentives for saving.

Finance Minister Ruth Richardson believed that economic salvation lay in reducing the inflation rate. Mortgage-interest rates dropped from 15.4% in October 1990 to 12.6% by June 1991, and then slipped below 10%. By July the annual inflation rate stood at 2.8%. However, the downside of the assault on inflation was devastating. A 1% negative growth was seen in 1990. As 1991 began the unemployed numbered 9.5% of the work force (14.1% if all jobless were included). By September the tally had climbed to 200,000, or 16.7% of the work force, counting those on special training.

The Budget. In probably the most savage peacetime budget since the Great Depression, the government introduced a means test for use of public hospitals and for old-age benefits. Gasoline was to be levied two cents per liter and workers were to be taxed to help meet costs of accident compensation. The age of eligibility for a national retirement pension was to be lifted gradually to 65 and a severe income test applied. The end-of-July budget offered no incentives for saving, avoided directly addressing the unemployment crisis, and promised a continuation of rigid monetarist solutions.

Domestic Politics. Deeply divided over how to restore prosperity, the National government in August saw two members of Parliament resign from the party to form the New Zealand Liberal Party. A few weeks later Bolger reshuffled the cabinet and dismissed Minister of Maori Affairs Winston Peters, who had attacked monetarist strategies.

The government also encountered disaster at the public-opinion polls. In April it was 10% adrift of the opposition Labour Party. By Sep-

NEW ZEALAND • Information Highlights

Official Name: New Zealand.
Location: Southwest Pacific Ocean.
Area: 103,737 sq mi (268 680 km²).
Population (mid-1991 est.): 3,500,000.
Chief Cities (March 31, 1990 est.): Wellington, the capital, 325,700; Auckland, 864,700; Christchurch, 303,400; Napier-Hastings, 108,100.
Government: *Head of state,* Elizabeth II, queen, represented by Dame Catherine Tizard, governor-general (took office November 1990). *Head of government,* James Bolger, prime minister (took office November 1990). *Legislature* (unicameral) —House of Representatives.
Monetary Unit: New Zealand dollar (1.7762 N.Z. dollars equal U.S.$1, Oct. 23, 1991).
Gross Domestic Product (1989 est. U.S. $): $39,100,-000,000.
Economic Index (1990): *Consumer Prices* (1980 = 100), all items, 275.6; food, 259.1.
Foreign Trade (1990 U.S.$): *Imports,* $9,489,000,000; *exports,* $9,435,000,000.

tember it had slumped to 22% approval, the lowest level ever recorded for a party in power, while the minor parties—three of which formed an alliance—soared to a collective peak of 36%. Forty percent of those polled were unwilling to endorse any party.

Foreign Policy. The government supported the U.S.-led war to evict Iraq from Kuwait and dispatched a token contingent of air-transport and medical crews. Relations with the United States were less frigid than in recent years. In August, Minister of Foreign Affairs Don McKinnon hosted Assistant Secretary of State Richard H. Solomon, the highest-ranking U.S. official to visit since the 1985 banning of nuclear warships. After a September address to the UN General Assembly, Bolger met with President George Bush and signaled a further thaw in relations.

GRAHAM BUSH, *University of Auckland*

NIGERIA

The military government of Gen. Ibrahim B. Babangida concentrated much of its effort in 1991 toward establishing the complicated mechanisms necessary for returning Nigeria to civilian control as promised for 1992.

Domestic Development. The first step in the graduated process to end military rule was the local government election in December 1990. That vote, by open ballot, was to be followed by other elections. Voters stood behind a photograph of the candidate of choice to register their vote. On June 5 ward elections were held to choose delegates in the 5,575 wards who would monitor later elections. There was little violence at either election. Meanwhile, the National Election Commission (NEC) was establishing the 250,000 registration centers and screening candidates for the August 24 primary gubernatorial elections in 30 states. (Nine new states were created in August.) Only two political parties were recognized by the ruling Armed Forces Ruling Council (AFRC)—the Social Democratic Party and the National Republican Convention. Differences between the parties were minimal; the AFRC feared reigniting religious and tribal animosities. Additional elections for governors and state assembly members were held in December.

© Kenneth B. Noble/NYT Pictures

Gen. Ibrahim Babangida promised to turn Nigeria, which has been governed primarily by the military since 1960 independence, over to civilian rule after fall 1992 elections.

There was endemic violence unconnected with voting in all areas. In May a riot at Yaba College resulted in the deaths of two students. The NEC headquarters in Brass was bombed and there were religious riots in some cities. In May the government placed many churches and mosques under surveillance. Gen. Oladipo Diya, chief of the defense staff, noted increased discipline problems within the army and warned of the possible consequences. The 1990 report from the Committee for Defense of Human Rights castigated the AFRC for secret trials, executions, and establishing tribunals outside the judicial framework. It was particularly harsh in describing the foul conditions in prisons where a reported 2,000 persons die each year.

Economics. Babangida's Structural Adjustment Program produced mixed results. New credits from the International Monetary Fund (IMF) were obtained and $17 billion in debts to the Paris Club of lenders and $5.8 billion to the London Club were rescheduled. Inflation stood at 18% in 1990, compared with 51% the previous year. The projected budget of N38.6 billion (about $4 billion) was within revenue limits and would provide a surplus for the first time in a decade. The AFRC's attempts to increase

NIGERIA • Information Highlights

Official Name: Federal Republic of Nigeria.
Location: West Africa.
Area: 356,668 sq mi (923 770 km²).
Population (mid-1991 est.): 122,500,000.
Chief City: Abuja, the capital.
Government: *Head of state and government,* Maj. Gen. Ibrahim Babangida, president, federal military government (took office Aug. 27, 1985). *Legislature*—Armed Forces Ruling Council; National Council of Ministers and National Council of States.
Monetary Unit: Naira (9.699 naira equal U.S.$1, May 1991).
Economic Index (1989): *Consumer Prices* (1980 = 100), all items, 534.1; food, 578.0.
Foreign Trade (1989 U.S.$): *Imports,* $3,419,000,000; *exports,* $8,138,000,000.

nonpetroleum products made slight gains. Nigeria does not produce enough raw materials for a major growth in manufacturing. Petroleum exports continued to provide 95% of revenue. The government introduced incentives to encourage exploration of new fields with the goal of boosting production to 22 million barrels per day. It also continued to fund such major projects such as a new capital at Abuja and the multibillion-dollar Niara mining and steel complex at Ajaokuta.

Foreign Affairs. In April troops were sent to Sierra Leone to help repulse attacks from irregular troops fleeing Liberia. In May, Babangida announced willingness to resume relations with South Africa if all vestiges of apartheid were removed. Nigeria welcomed heads of state to the Organization of African Unity meeting at Abuja from June 3–5. It also supported the Economic Community of West African States' attempts to end civil war in Liberia with funds and soldiers.

HARRY A. GAILEY
San Jose State University

NORTH CAROLINA

The recession and opposition to waste-disposal facilities topped the news in North Carolina in 1991.

The Financial Crisis. Although unemployment barely exceeded 6%, the recession brought serious consequences to North Carolina. Legislative overestimation of tax revenues forced the Republican administration of Gov. James G. Martin to make sharp cutbacks in state spending. Even so, the General Assembly faced a $1.2 billion shortfall, and the $7.7 billion budget for the new fiscal year eliminated more than 3,000 state-funded jobs and required $657 million in new taxes. The sales tax was raised to 6%, the corporate-income tax to 7.75%, and the cigarette tax to 5 cents per pack. A half cent was added to the gasoline tax, and tuition was raised at state colleges. While $576 million in spending was cut, $160 million was added for programs relating to infant mortality, child abuse, mental health, medicaid, and financially pressed schools.

The Legislature. In other legislative news, Daniel T. Blue, Jr., became the first black to be elected speaker of the House of Representatives, and Marie W. Colton was the first woman to serve as speaker pro tem of the Senate. A gerrymandered congressional redistricting plan, featuring one district with a black majority, raised questions of whether it could survive a court challenge. Legislation was passed authorizing police to arrest, without a warrant, abusive spouses; requiring persons acquitted of violent crimes because of insanity to be committed to psychiatric hospitals; permitting the state to take over school districts that perform badly; and raising the minimum wage.

Waste Management. Legal maneuvering, unruly protests, and intimidated politicians forced North Carolina to renege on its commitment to provide adequately for waste disposal, depriving the state of satisfactory disposal facilities both within and outside its borders.

Business and Labor. Despite campaigns against its use, tobacco was pumping $7.3 billion annually into the state's economy, including 281,000 jobs and more than $700 million in state and local taxes. Movie, television, and commercial productions added nearly $500 million to the economy. The Amalgamated Clothing and Textile Workers Union again lost a vote for recognition by workers of Fieldcrest Cannon Inc., in Cabarrus and Union counties.

Tragedies. Twenty-five persons died in a fire at a Hamlet, NC, chicken-processing plant. Locked doors in violation of fire codes were blamed, and the state was faulted for never having inspected the plant. As the year ended, the state labor department fined the plant $808,150 for safety violations. Tragedy of another kind struck Edenton, NC, where owners of a day-care center were charged with sexually abusing their students.

Other News. A survey during the year found that nearly half of all North Carolinians identified themselves as Baptists when asked about religious preferences; Methodists followed with 12.7% and Roman Catholics with 5.9%. Only 4.8% professed no religion. . . . North Carolina continued to receive the lowest per capita return from taxes paid into the federal treasury and had a higher percentage of working mothers than any other state. . . . Michael Van McDougall became the first convicted killer to be executed by the state in five years. . . . Duke University won the NCAA basketball championship.

H. G. JONES
University of North Carolina at Chapel Hill

NORTH CAROLINA • Information Highlights

Area: 52,669 sq mi (136 413 km²).
Population (1990 census): 6,628,637.
Chief Cities (1990 census): Raleigh, the capital, 207,951; Charlotte, 395,934; Greensboro, 183,521; Winston-Salem, 143,485; Durham, 136,611.
Government (1991): *Chief Officers*—governor, James G. Martin (R); lt. gov., Jim Gardner (R). *General Assembly*—Senate, 50 members; House of Representatives, 120 members.
State Finances (fiscal year 1990): *Revenue,* $14,485,000,000; *expenditure,* $13,493,000,000.
Personal Income (1990): $108,396,000,000; per capita, $16,293.
Labor Force (June 1991): *Civilian labor force,* 3,481,900; *unemployed,* 216,300 (6.2% of total force).
Education: *Enrollment* (fall 1989)—public elementary schools, 769,825; public secondary, 310,919; colleges and universities, 345,401. *Public school expenditures* (1989), $3,892,971,000.

NORTH DAKOTA

The last U.S. blue laws fell in 1991 when North Dakota retailers finally opened for business on Sundays. The abortion battle heated up in legislative meeting rooms and on city streets, and the state's farmers followed up a near-record harvest in 1990 with a so-so year.

Legislature. Lawmakers met for their biennial session in 1991 and increased spending—most notably for education—by 13.3% without raising taxes. The session produced several landmark changes, including a major consolidation of the state's court system and creation of a holiday honoring Martin Luther King, Jr. Lawmakers gave North Dakota schoolteachers the right to binding arbitration in contract negotiations. That law was suspended in June, however, after opponents filed referral petitions to force a public vote. Meeting in a special reapportionment session in November, lawmakers trimmed the number of legislative districts from 53 to 49.

Commerce. Most major retailers legally did business for the first Sunday ever in February just days after Democratic Gov. George Sinner signed legislation striking down the state's century-old blue laws. Sunday opening had been rejected twice at the polls and a Minot businessman filed petitions to refer the change to voters again in 1992. But an October survey by the University of North Dakota Bureau of Governmental Affairs indicated that more than 75% of the residents wanted the stores to stay open.

Abortion. Lawmakers also passed two bills that drastically would have changed abortion law. Governor Sinner, a father of ten who once studied for the Catholic priesthood, vetoed what would have been the nation's toughest anti-abortion law, cautioning that government "must not play God." Sinner signed another bill calling for a 24-hour waiting period before an abortion. The measure was suspended, however, in a challenge of the law's constitutionality. Meanwhile, protesters repeatedly stormed the Fargo Women's Health Organization Inc., the state's only abortion clinic, chaining themselves inside the facility and throwing themselves in front of cars entering clinic property. By late in the year more than 145 protesters had been arrested in a series of demonstrations, and in October a state judge ordered most demonstrators to stay at least 100 ft (30 m) from clinic property.

Agriculture. A hot, dry summer withered a promising crop. An estimated 212 million bushels of spring wheat were reaped, along with 88.6 million bushels of durum wheat, 137.2 million bushels of barley, 2.1 billion lbs (953 560 000 kg) of sunflowers, 3.2 million tons of sugar beets, and 17.7 million bushels of soybeans.

Politics and Other News. Governor Sinner underwent bypass surgery in July after developing chest pains. In announcing in October that he would not seek an unprecedented third consecutive four-year term in 1992, he said his health was not a factor. . . . North Dakotans were red-faced in 1991 when a $500,000 grant to build a museum in tiny Strasburg, ND, was ridiculed as an example of wasteful federal spending. Critics charged that the grant was to rebuild the boyhood home of entertainer Lawrence Welk.

The Federal Bureau of Investigation (FBI) reported in 1991 that North Dakota had the lowest violent crime rate in the nation

JIM NEUMANN, *Grand Forks, ND*

NORTH DAKOTA • Information Highlights

Area: 70,702 sq mi (183 119 km^2).
Population (1990 census): 638,800.
Chief Cities (1990 census): Bismarck, the capital, 49,256; Fargo, 74,111; Grand Forks, 49,425; Minot, 34,544.
Government (1991): *Chief Officers*—governor, George A. Sinner (D); lt. gov., Lloyd B. Omdahl (D). *Legislative Assembly*—Senate, 53 members; House of Representatives, 106 members.
State Finances (fiscal year 1990): *Revenue,* $1,810,000,000; *expenditure,* $1,755,000,000.
Personal Income (1990): $9,686,000,000; per capita, $15,215.
Labor Force (June 1991): *Civilian labor force,* 328,800; *unemployed,* 13,700 (4.2% of total force).
Education: *Enrollment* (fall 1989)—public elementary schools, 84,920; public secondary, 32,896; colleges and universities, 40,350. *Public school expenditures* (1989), $431,814,000.

NORTHWEST TERRITORIES

Agreement between the Inuit of the Northwest Territories and the government of Canada on the largest native land claim in Canadian history was the major event of 1991 in the Northwest Territories (NWT).

Nunavut. The settlement, which came on December 16, covers close to 770,000 sq mi (2 000 000 km^2)—about one fifth of the Canadian landmass—in the eastern Arctic, from the tree line at the 60th parallel to the North Pole. In that vast area, a new territory would be established and called Nunavut. The Inuit people make up about 80% of the population of Nunavut, an important factor for the Inuit negotiators who considered that the Inuit would have effective political control in the new territory.

The agreement remained to be approved by the Canadian Parliament and ratified by the Inuit people through a referendum, expected early in 1992. A plebiscite also would be held in the entire Northwest Territories in March 1992 to approve or reject the boundary line between the western portion of the NWT and the new Nunavut Territory. Some opposition to the agreement, particularly from the Indian leadership who had been pressing for recognition of "inherent rights to self-government" in any settlements, was expressed.

NORTHWEST TERRITORIES • Information Highlights

Area: 1,304,903 sq mi (3 379 700 km²).
Population (September 1991): 54,800.
Chief Cities (1986 census): Yellowknife, the capital, 11,753; Inuvik, 3,389; Hay River, 2,964.
Government (1991): *Chief Officers*—commissioner, Daniel L. Norris; government leader, Nellie Cournoyea. *Legislature*—Legislative Assembly, 24 elected members.
Public Finances (1989–90 fiscal year): *Revenues*, $965,280,000; *expenditures*, $971,999,000.
Education (1991–92): *Enrollment*—elementary and secondary schools, 14,750 pupils. *Public school expenditures* (1989–90), $170,587,000.
(All monetary figures are in Canadian dollars.)

New Government. In October residents of the NWT went to the polls in a general election for the 24 independent members of the Northwest Territories Legislative Assembly. On November 12, Nellie Cournoyea, the member for Nunakput, was elected by her Assembly colleagues as the new government leader. Cournoyea, an Inuvialuit (Western Arctic Inuit) became the first woman to head the government of the NWT. She indicated that she would take the title of premier, similar to what is used in the Yukon Territory and the provinces. Cournoyea, 51, a supporter of economic and social development in the Mackenzie Delta and Beaufort Sea regions, held four cabinet portfolios in the previous government and planned to maintain responsibility for energy, mines, and petroleum resources.

ROSS M. HARVEY
Television Northern Canada

NORWAY

Norway's King Olav V, who as crown prince became a national symbol of resistance against the German invaders during World War II, died on Jan. 17, 1991, from a heart attack. At 87 years of age, he was the oldest monarch in Europe and was revered by all Norwegians. He was succeeded by his son, King Harald V (*see* BIOGRAPHY).

Foreign Relations. Norway was in full agreement not only with the UN Security Council resolutions in the fall of 1990 which called upon Iraq to leave Kuwait, but also with the military actions taken by the allied coalition to evict the Iraqis from the conquered territory. Although not a full belligerent, the Norwegian government deployed a Coast Guard vessel to the Persian Gulf, offered humanitarian assistance to refugees and evacuees, and, together with Great Britain, provided a full field hospital in Saudi Arabia.

Like the other Scandinavian countries, Norway lost little time in recognizing the full independence of the three Baltic republics of Estonia, Latvia, and Lithuania. Full diplomatic relations were established at a meeting in Oslo on August 26 between Foreign Minister Thorvald Stoltenberg and the foreign ministers of the three countries. Norway actually had recognized the independence and sovereignty of the three republics in 1921 and never had withdrawn that action.

Norway's politicians as well as the general public supported arguments both pro and con regarding the possibility of Norway joining the European Community (EC). The planning for a new free-trade area to be known as the European Economic Area (EEA) seemed to complicate the situation. However, in Luxembourg on October 22 the 12 nations of the EC and the seven nations, including Norway, of the European Free Trade Association (EFTA) agreed in principle to establish the EEA.

Political Affairs. The Labor cabinet, headed by Gro Harlem Brundtland, which had taken office in November 1990, never was challenged seriously during the year. It, however, did face looming difficulties—including bankruptcies and mergers as well as wide retrenchment leading to increased unemployment in many fields. A grand exception was the oil industry, which grew at an unprecedented pace.

Local elections were held throughout Norway on September 9, with the Center Party and the Socialist Left making some progress. The ruling Labor Party lost 3.8% of its local representatives and the Progressive Party lost all 6% of its local strength. The Conservatives lost a mere 0.5%, and diminutive changes were recorded for the Christian Democrats, the Liberal Party, and the Red Electoral Alliance.

Vinland Revisited. In May replicas of Viking ships began a voyage across the Atlantic Ocean as part of a decade-long commemoration of the 1,000th anniversary of Leif Ericson's reported landing in North America. Norway and Iceland sponsored the expedition, which also was intended to call attention to the importance of the environment.

ERIK J. FRIIS
"The Scandinavian-American Bulletin"

NORWAY • Information Highlights

Official Name: Kingdom of Norway.
Location: Northern Europe.
Area: 125,182 sq mi (324 220 km²).
Population (mid-1991 est.): 4,300,000.
Chief Cities (Jan. 1, 1990): Oslo, the capital, 458,364; Bergen, 211,826; Trondheim, 137,346.
Government: *Head of state,* Harald V, king (acceded January 1991). *Head of government,* Gro Harlem Brundtland, prime minister (took office November 1990). *Legislature*—Storting: Lagting and Odelsting.
Monetary Unit: Krone (6.2750 kroner equal U.S.$1, Nov. 26, 1991).
Gross Domestic Product (1989 est. U.S.$): $75,800,000,000.
Economic Indexes (1990): *Consumer Prices* (1980 = 100), all items, 208.5; food, 217.6. *Industrial Production* (1980 = 100), 171.
Foreign Trade (1990 U.S.$): *Imports,* $26,905,000,000; *exports,* $34,702,000,000.

NOVA SCOTIA

The year 1991 brought Nova Scotians a new premier, tough legislation, racial tension, and an economic recession.

Legislation and Government. In 1991 the Conservative government, with Donald Cameron as its newly elected leader, sought to distance itself from John Buchanan's image of a scandalous premier by launching a tough legislative program. Several controversial bills, including financial disclosure and conflict of interest rules for politicians, human-rights protection for homosexuals and AIDs carriers, regulations to force compliance with child-support orders, and the deregulation of gas prices, were enacted. The government found time to strike a deal with Amherst Aerospace and bankers for keeping its plant in operation, named members to the Electoral Boundaries Commission, and created the Constitution Committee under the chairmanship of Eric Kierns.

The government also streamlined its operations and trimmed public expenditures on health, social welfare, and public administration. The size of the provincial cabinet shrunk from the previous 21 ministers to 16, while the pharmacare program was modified to raise the contribution of senior citizens toward drug costs. The availability of free dental care was restricted and financial assistance for seniors was reduced. In May a two-year wage freeze imposed on 40,000 public servants provoked teachers and government employees to demonstrate. In July, downtown Halifax became the scene of violent riots attributed to racial discrimination practiced by bar owners.

The government, despite its firmness in resolving disputes with public employees and controlling racism, failed to recover public support. The defeat of the conservative candidate by Robert Chisholm of the New Democratic Party (NDP) in an August Halifax-Atlantic by-election not only robbed the Tories of a one-seat majority in the legislature but showed voters' lack of confidence in the government.

© Michael Creagen

Donald Cameron (center), a 44-year-old former dairy farmer, was elected leader of Nova Scotia's ruling Conservatives on Feb. 9, 1991. He took office as premier on February 26.

Economy. The provincial economy continued its stay in recessionary doldrums. In August the total number of employed (seasonally adjusted) fell by 10,000 when compared with August 1990. A 2.9% gain in workers' earnings over the first five months of 1991 was eroded by a 6% upsurge in inflation. Production of lumber, fish landings, and power over the same period fell by 21%, 4.7%, and 2.7%, respectively. Similarly, the provincial housing industry was expected to slump in 1991 to its lowest level in seven years. The sluggishness of the resource sector, spurred by the weak international market, was reflected by the excess supply of coal experienced by the Cape Breton Development Corporation and deeper losses recorded by the Rio-Algoma tin and base-metal mines of Yarmouth.

Energy. LASMO and N.S. Resources Ltd. continued to develop the small Cohasset Panuke oil field near Sable Island. Discovery of another reserve (9,000 barrels per day) improved the viability of the project, even during a period of lower oil prices. The construction of the controversial Point Aconi power plant in Cape Breton also moved ahead. In April, Nova Scotians were hit by a third consecutive power-rate increase.

R.P. SETH
Mount Saint Vincent University, Halifax

NOVA SCOTIA • Information Highlights

Area: 21,425 sq mi (55 491 km²).
Population (September 1991): 900,800.
Chief cities (1986 census): Halifax, the capital, 113,577; Dartmouth, 65,243; Sydney, 27,754.
Government (1991): *Chief Officers*—lt. gov., Lloyd R. Crouse; premier, Donald Cameron (Progressive Conservative). *Legislature*—Legislative Assembly, 52 members.
Provincial Finances (1990–91 fiscal year budget): *Revenues*, $4,508,014,000; *expenditures*, $4,700,000,000.
Personal Income (average weekly earnings, August 1991): $484.73.
Labor Force (October 1991, seasonally adjusted): *Employed* workers, 15 years of age and over, 371,000; *Unemployed*, 12.5%.
Education (1991–92): *Enrollment*—elementary and secondary schools, 167,930 pupils; postsecondary—universities, 27,700; community colleges, 2,600.
(All monetary figures are in Canadian dollars.)

OBITUARIES

GRAHAM, Martha

U.S. dancer and choreographer: b. Allegheny, PA, May 11, 1894; d. New York City, April 1, 1991.

As the foremost American dancer and choreographer who helped establish modern dance as a new art form, Martha Graham became one of the 20th century's revolutionary artists.

Graham's legacy, going beyond her own legend as a performer and her pioneering masterworks, is represented by the codified movement vocabulary she invented. In their training and choreography, companies worldwide now use the Graham technique—dance's first enduring alternative to the idiom of classical ballet. The technique's principle of "contraction and release" created a jagged powerful dynamic—the intensified expression of emotion that defined the more than 180 works Graham choreographed over 65 years.

Like dominant modernists in painting and literature, Graham broke the traditional mold and rejected realistic imagery. "Dance is not representational," she said and focused on the distillation of feeling. An example was her 1930 solo, *Lamentation*, in which she sought to embody the essence of grief.

Initially recognized as a great dancer, Graham wished "to give visible substance to things felt" in her own performing (she retired from the stage in 1969) and then applied the same ideas to the group she formed in 1926. It now is the internationally acclaimed Martha Graham Dance Company, attached to Graham's school. The repertory, which the troupe plans to continue performing, ranges widely. Graham's early dances were spare and stark, exemplifying her desire to strip dance to its basic rudiments. In the 1930s and 1940s she composed works on American themes. The 1944 *Appalachian Spring*, with a commissioned score by Aaron Copland, expressed both Graham's open-frontier optimism and her typical warning against a narrow Puritanism.

A larger theme in Graham's work, beginning with the 1929 *Heretic*, spoke of the need for tolerance toward nonconformists. The choreographer took a more theatrical turn in the 1940s. After 1946 her psychological depiction of Medea, Jocasta, Clytemnestra, and other figures from Greek mythology stirred up controversy with frank acknowledgment of human sexuality. After she stopped dancing, Graham created new works more focused on an ensemble than a protagonist.

Background. Graham was the eldest of three daughters born to George Graham, a physician, and Jane Beers, a descendant of Miles Standish. (A brother died in infancy.) After the family moved to Santa Barbara, CA, Graham

was graduated from the Cumnock School of Expression and in 1916 entered the Los Angeles school run by two precursors of American modern dance, Ruth St. Denis and Ted Shawn. She danced with the Denishawn company, and in 1923 and 1924 performed in New York City with the Greenwich Village Follies.

After teaching dance at the Eastman School in Rochester, NY, Graham embarked upon her experiments and an independent career. She enlisted three of her students in her first concert at the 48th Street Theater in New York City on April 18, 1926. By 1929, Graham had formed an all-female troupe and shed the lyrical exotic influences of Denishawn. Her interest in the Indian rituals of the Southwest was seen in acknowledged Graham classics like *Primitive Mysteries* (1931) and *El Penitente* (1940). The music for both pieces was by Louis Horst, a composer who was Graham's mentor since Denishawn and with whom she had a long personal relationship. She married Erick Hawkins, the first male dancer in her company, in 1948. (They divorced in 1954.)

Among Graham's other celebrated works were *Frontier*, *Letter to the World*, *Deaths and Entrances*, *Cave of the Heart*, *Errand into the Maze*, *Night Journey*, *Diversion of Angels*, and *Clytemnestra*. She collaborated on dramatic productions with Katherine Cornell, among others; she taught budding actors like Gregory Peck at the Neighborhood Playhouse; she invited the sculptor Isamu Noguchi to create her sets. Her numerous awards included the Presidential Medal of Freedom (1976).

ANNA KISSELGOFF

Editor's Note: Special obituaries are arranged chronologically by date of death. Unsigned obituaries were written by the staff.

© Viking Photo by Karsh, Ottawa

GREENE, Graham

British author: b. Berkhamsted, Hertfordshire, England, Oct. 2, 1904; d. Vevey, Switzerland, April 3, 1991.

Graham Greene, a major 20th-century man of letters, declared early a distaste for an emphasis on artistic technique at the expense of content—an aesthetic tenet he held throughout his literary career. He considered himself "journalistically minded," and resented the assumptions of some critics that conditions described in the exotic settings of some of his novels did not exist. These critics referred instead to the general locale of Greene's fiction simply as Greeneland, a mix of a morally decadent and seedy landscape, whether it be West Africa or Malaysia, Mexico or Vietnam, or even England.

Despite such criticism and the fact that he never received the Nobel Prize in Literature (for which he long was mentioned as a possibility), he was a skilled writer of more than 20 novels and numerous collections of short stories, essays, plays, autobiographical works, and travel and children's books.

Of considerable interest, too, was his conversion to Catholicism following the persuasion of his fiancée, since he came to be known as a Catholic novelist.

Background. Graham Greene, one of four sons of Charles Henry Greene and Marion Raymond Greene, was schooled privately at Berkhamsted, where his father was headmaster, and then at Balliol College, Oxford. Early in his career he worked as a journalist and cinema critic.

Greene's so-called Catholic novels, notably *Brighton Rock* (1938), *The Power and the Glory* (1940), *The Heart of the Matter* (1948), and *The End of the Affair* (1951), won a wide readership, and for some, these remain the works on which his reputation was built. But his renown does not rest on these alone. Some of his mature works—*The Quiet American* (1955), *A Burnt-Out Case* (1961), *The Comedians* (1966), *Travels With My Aunt* (1969), and *The Honorary Consul* (1973)—added new readers to those already familiar with Greene's works that had been adapted for cinema.

Greene's oeuvre suggests a progression toward the comedic, as well as a lifelong preoccupation with crossing borders—those of allegiance of heart and mind as well as geography. Dictating his delineation of character and signaling his whole body of work, finally, was a clear focus on the underdog, whether the sinner in the eyes of God or those trodden under by the prevailing political power. His works treat prominently such themes as the nature of power and problems of belief.

Greene was married and later separated from Vivien Dayrell-Browning. He had one daughter and one son from that marriage.

DONALD JENNERMANN

SINGER, Isaac Bashevis

U.S. author: b. Radzymin, Poland, July 14, 1904; d. Miami, FL, July 24, 1991.

Isaac Bashevis Singer, the Polish émigré and 1978 Nobel laureate in literature, presented in his various works both a picture of Eastern European Jewish life and experiences of the immigrant in the United States. His more than 30 novels and short-story collections, all written in Yiddish but widely translated, deal with his upbringing as a rabbi's son and draw upon Jewish folklore and mysticism.

Background. Singer received a traditional Jewish schooling and, following his parents' wishes that he become a rabbi, enrolled for a time in a Warsaw rabbinical seminary. In 1935, alarmed by the growing menace of Nazism, he joined his brother, a Yiddish-language writer, in the United States, beginning his New York career as a journalist for *The Jewish Daily Forward,* where much of his fiction first appeared. Among his works are the trilogy *The Family Moskat* (1950), *The Manor* (1967), and *The Estate* (1969)—a family epic tracing the history of the Jews in Poland from the anti-tsarist uprisings of 1863 to World War II. Other works include the short-story collection *A Crown of Feathers* (1973) and the novel *Enemies: A Love Story* (1972; film 1989), the first of his novels set in the United States.

© Carol Halebian/Gamma-Liaison

GEISEL, Theodor Seuss

U.S. author of children's books: b. Springfield, MA, March 2, 1904; d. La Jolla, CA, Sept. 25, 1991.

Theodor Geisel, better known as Dr. Seuss to his many fans, was one of the most beloved children's authors. The 87-year-old Geisel, the author of such classics as *The Cat in the Hat* (1957), *How the Grinch Stole Christmas!* (1957), and *Green Eggs and Ham* (1960), wrote and illustrated 48 books that sold more than 200 million copies in 20 languages.

Seuss said that he wrote for everyone, not just for children. Though he was the stepfather to his second wife's children, he had no children of his own and often remarked, "You make 'em, I amuse 'em." He did that, and much more also—taught them to read, gave them

© Photofest

PAPP, Joseph

U.S. theatrical producer: b. Brooklyn, NY, June 22, 1921; d. New York, NY, Oct. 31, 1991.

"Theater is a social force," said Joseph Papp, "not just an entertainment." One of the most dominant figures in U.S. theater over the previous three decades, Papp proved his dedication to this maxim through his actions.

With his productions of *A Chorus Line* and *Hair,* Papp showed that Broadway hits could be nurtured in the less-commercial confines of alternative theaters. He also demonstrated how a blockbuster like *A Chorus Line,* the longest-running show in Broadway history—grossing almost $150 million—could pay for less-commercial projects, including free Shakespeare in New York's Central Park, which he produced for more than 30 years.

AP/Wide World

MAXWELL, Ian Robert

British publisher: b. Selo Slatina, Czechoslovakia, June 10, 1923; d. near the Canary Islands, Nov. 5, 1991.

At the time of his death, Robert Maxwell commanded a multibillion-dollar communications empire that included, among other major holdings, the New York *Daily News,* the *Daily Mirror* of London, and the Macmillan Company, along with a U.S. horse-racing newspaper and *The European,* an English-language weekly. Maxwell, known as the "citizen Kane of his time," was a political socialist who ran his companies with a well-known ruthlessness, often eliminating jobs after he acquired a business. Maxwell's business practices partly revolutionized the British newspaper industry, helping eliminate union control on Fleet Street.

messages about values, and made them sensitive to their surroundings.

Background. Theodor Seuss Geisel was born in Springfield, MA, on March 2, 1904, gaining an early interest in unusual creatures from his frequent visits to the zoo (his father was superintendent of parks). He graduated from Dartmouth College in 1925 and began his career writing two-line gags for humor magazines. In 1937 he got his start as a children's book writer with *And to Think That I Saw It on Mulberry Street*. Dr. Seuss (although he added the "Dr." to his middle name to sound more scientific, he later was given an honorary doctorate by Dartmouth) not only wrote his own books but illustrated them as well. His style was full of wordplay, ingenious rhyme, and amusing, if improbable, characters.

In 1957 he authored *The Cat in the Hat* for beginning readers, with a vocabulary of 220 words. In the sterile Dick-and-Jane era it became an immediate hit. Seuss founded and was a longtime executive of Beginner Books, now owned by Random House.

Later, Seuss wrote stories with messages like *The Lorax* (1971), about environmentalism and greed, and *The Butter Battle Book* (1984), on war and peace. His own favorite characters were the starbelly sneetches from *The Sneetches & Other Stories* (1961), who offered lessons about discrimination, and Yertle from *Yertle the Turtle* (1958). A recent book, *Oh, the Places You'll Go!* (1990) was aimed at adults.

Seuss also worked in the visual media, winning Academy Awards for his documentary films—*Hitler Lives* (1946) and *Design for Death* (1947). In 1951 a Seuss cartoon, *Gerald McBoing-Boing*, won an Oscar for animation. Seuss won a special Pulitzer citation in 1984.

ILENE COOPER

Papp proposed that art and culture should be regarded as a staple of human life. That was the idea of bringing Shakespeare to people who otherwise might not be exposed to theater. He likewise encouraged the often-controversial work of minority writers and players, knowing what it was like to be considered an outsider.

Background. Born Yosl Papirofsky, the Brooklyn native grew up in poverty and took to the theater after serving in the Navy during World War II. Working as a television stage manager for CBS in the 1950s, Papp began producing free performances of Shakespeare in 1954. Two years later he put on two plays in East River Park, including *The Taming of the Shrew*, starring a young Colleen Dewhurst. In 1957 the plays were moved to Central Park.

In 1966, Papp founded the Shakespeare Festival Public Theater—a six-theater complex where the works of many young playwrights were presented. Over the years, Papp nurtured the careers of numerous actors and playwrights. His productions won three Pulitzer Prizes and 28 Tony Awards.

Never afraid of controversy, in 1958, Papp took the 5th Amendment when called to testify before the House Committee on Un-American Activities, and thus lost his job at CBS. He sued and won back his position, becoming the first to break the blacklist in network television. More recently, Papp had criticized the National Endowment for the Arts for politicizing the awarding of grants, and refused funding when it required signing an anti-obscenity pledge.

The night after Papp died, Broadway theaters dimmed their lights in tribute. Then, as Papp would have wanted, it was on with the show.

JOHN MILWARD

His mysterious death off the Canary Islands during a yachting excursion came as mounting debt threatened his publishing empire. After his death, many of his business interests were placed under the control of two of his sons.

Background. Robert Maxwell was born Jan Ludvik Hoch in Czechoslovakia. In 1940 he settled in England, having left his native country to escape Hitler; most of his family perished in the Nazi death camps. Maxwell served in the British Army during World War II and was awarded a Military Cross for valor. During the war he met his French-born future wife, Elisabeth Meynard. He changed his name during this period to Ian Robert Maxwell.

After the war, Maxwell acquired a publishing company producing scientific journals and textbooks that he named the Pergamon Press. By 1964 the company was thriving, and Maxwell followed his political ambitions by winning election to the House of Commons as a Labour Party candidate. He served until 1970. In 1969, Maxwell lost Pergamon in a scandal after trying unsuccessfully to sell it to a U.S. financier. He repurchased Pergamon in 1974, but sold it in 1991.

In 1984, Maxwell acquired the Mirror Group Newspapers, including the *Daily Mirror*, Britain's second-largest daily. In 1988 he acquired Macmillan, and in 1991 he obtained the *Daily News*. During the final months of his life, Maxwell attempted to reduce debt accumulated as a result of his acquisitions. In addition to selling Pergamon, he offered 49% of the Mirror Group to the public. Shortly before his death, allegations by journalist Seymour Hersh linking Maxwell to the Israeli secret service angered the publisher, who filed a libel action against Hersh in the British courts.

DAVID PERRY

The following is a selected list of prominent persons who died during 1991. Articles on major figures appear in the preceding pages.

Abbott, Berenice (93), photographer; best known for her black and white photos of New York City in the 1930s. She began her career in Paris in 1923 as a darkroom assistant to the Surrealist Man Ray and in 1925 took up portrait photography. Four years later she began a major project—photographing New York City—the documentation of which continued for a number of years. Later she turned to scientific photography, which gained her new acclaim. Her books include *Greenwich Village Today and Yesterday* (1949) and *Photographs* (1970). She also was considered the person primarily responsible for the fame of French photographer Eugène Atget: d. Monson, ME, Dec. 10.

Akhromeyev, Sergei F. (68), marshal in the Soviet army and chief military adviser to Soviet President Mikhail Gorbachev; he committed suicide following the failed Soviet coup in August 1991: d. Moscow, Aug. 24.

Allen, Irwin (75), film producer of big-budget disaster films, including *The Towering Inferno* (1974) and *The Poseidon Adventure* (1972). He also was noted for the television series *Voyage to the Bottom of the Sea*, *Lost in Space*, *Time Tunnel*, and *Land of the Giants*: d. Santa Monica, CA, Nov. 2.

Anderson, Carl (85), physicist; shared the Nobel Prize in physics in 1936 for his discovery of the particle positron that grew out of his studies of cosmic rays; was with the California Institute of Technology (1930–76): d. San Marino, CA, Jan. 11.

Appling, Luke (83), baseball shortstop; played with the Chicago White Sox (1930–50). He won the American League batting title twice. He was elected to the Baseball Hall of Fame in 1964: d. Cumming, GA, Jan. 3.

Arrau, Claudio (88), Chilean-born pianist; his specialties included the works of Liszt and the sonatas and concertos of Beethoven. He studied in Germany in the early part of the century and in 1922 made his first London appearance. He made his New York debut in 1923. Between 1924 and 1940 he taught at the Stern Conservatory in Berlin. He returned to Chile in 1940 but as a political protest stopped performing there in 1967. He also toured extensively: d. Mürzzuschlag, Austria, June 9.

Arrupe y Gondra, Pedro (83), Spanish-born head of the Roman Catholic Jesuit Order (1965–83): d. Rome, Feb. 5.

Arthur, Jean (born Gladys Georgianna Greene) (90), film actress who made numerous light dramas in the 1930s and 1940s. Among her films are three that were directed by Frank Capra—*Mr. Deeds Goes to Town* (1936), *You Can't Take It with You* (1938), and *Mr. Smith Goes to Washington* (1939)—as well as *Shane* (1953): d. Carmel, CA, June 19.

Ashcroft, Dame Edith Margaret Emily (Peggy) (83), British actress; noted for her classical stage roles beginning in the 1930s; appeared with major British theater companies, including the Old Vic, the Royal Shakespeare Company, and the National Theatre. She was made a dame of the British Empire in 1956. More recently she won international acclaim for her roles in the film *A Passage to India* (1984), for which she won an Academy Award, and in the 1984 television series *The Jewel in the Crown*: d. London, June 14.

Ashman, Howard (40), lyricist, librettist, playwright, and director; wrote and staged the 1982 off-Broadway hit *Little Shop of Horrors*. In 1990 he won an Oscar for his song *Under the Sea*: d. New York City, March 14.

Atwater, Lee (40), manager of President George Bush's 1988 campaign and chairman of the Republican National Committee (1988–90): d. Washington, DC, March 29.

Axthelm, Pete (47), columnist, television sports commentator, and author; probably best known for his 20-year career as writer and editor with *Newsweek* magazine (1968–88). Between 1980 and 1985 he worked for NBC Sports as a commentator; in 1987 he joined the cable sports channel ESPN: d. Pittsburgh, PA, Feb. 2.

Baldwin, Hanson Weighman (88), Pulitzer Prize-winning military writer for more than 50 years. He joined *The New York Times* in 1929 and was the author of more than a dozen books on military and naval history and policy: d. Roxbury, CT, Nov. 13.

Ball, William (60), founder of the American Conservatory Theatre in San Francisco: d. Los Angeles, CA, July 30.

Barbie, Klaus (77), German Nazi war criminal; during World War II he commanded the Gestapo in Lyons, France, and sent many to gas chambers in Auschwitz. For many years after the war he prospered in Latin America. He was convicted of war crimes in 1987: d. Lyons, France, Sept. 25.

Bardeen, John (82), physicist and professor emeritus at the University of Illinois; the first person to receive two Nobel Prizes in the same field. He shared the 1956 Nobel Prize in physics for the invention of the transistor and in 1972 shared a second Nobel for his work on superconductivity, developing a theory of low-temperature superconductivity. He was at the University of Illinois from 1951 until his retirement in 1975: d. Boston, MA, Jan. 30.

Barrera, Lazaro (66), Cuban-born horse trainer; won the Kentucky Derby and Belmont Stakes with Bold Forbes in 1976 and the 1978 Triple Crown with Affirmed: d. Downey, CA, April 25.

Bell, James (Cool Papa) (87), baseball star of the Negro Leagues for 24 years beginning in 1922; was regarded widely as the fastest man ever to play baseball; inducted into the Hall of Fame in 1974: d. St. Louis, MO, March 7.

Bellamy, Ralph (87), film and stage actor; attained his greatest recognition on Broadway playing the stricken Franklin D. Roosevelt in *Sunrise at Campobello* (1958; film 1960). Earlier stage appearances were in *Tomorrow the World* (1943), *State of the Union* (1945), and *Detective Story* (1949). He was also a film actor, appearing in many low-budget movies as well as in such comedies as *The Awful Truth* (1937) and *His Girl Friday* (1940); and he had a career in television, appearing in many leading dramatic programs and in four television series: d. Los Angeles, CA, Nov. 29.

Bergalis, Kimberly (23), AIDS victim who gained national attention as the first known case of a patient contracting the virus from a health-care worker (her dentist). As such, she led a national debate over AIDS testing: d. Fort Pierce, FL, Dec. 8.

Bigart, Homer (83), journalist; wrote for both the *New York Herald Tribune* (1929–55) and *The New York Times* (1955–72). During his career he won many awards, including two Pulitzer Prizes: d. Portsmouth, NH, April 16.

Blatnik, John A. (80), U.S. representative (D-MN, 1947–75); served as chairman of the House Public Works Committee (1971–75): d. Forest Heights, MD, Dec. 18.

Bolling, Richard (74), U.S. representative (D-MO, 1949–83): d. Washington, DC, April 21.

Brinig, Myron (94), novelist; noted for his books on the settlement and development of Montana. Among his 20 novels is *Singermann* (1929): d. New York City, May 13.

Brooks, A. Raymond (95), the last surviving ace among U.S. fighter pilots in World War I: d. Summit, NJ, July 17.

Brown, Paul (82), founder of the Cleveland Browns and Cincinnati Bengals football teams and a successful football coach of championship high-school and college teams as well as military and professional teams. In 1941 he coached at Ohio State. After World War II, he became the founder, part owner, general manager, and coach of the Cleveland Browns. In 1968 he began his association with the Bengals. He was inducted into the Pro Football Hall of Fame in 1967: d. Cincinnati, OH, Aug. 5.

Peggy Ashcroft

© Evening Standard/Sipa

Lee Atwater

AP/Wide World

John Bardeen

AP/Wide World

Ralph Bellamy

AP/Wide World

Brunet, Pierre (89), French-born figure ice skater and Olympic champion of the 1920s and 1930s. He also was a renowned teacher: d. Boyne City, MI, July 27.

Burch, Dean (63), chairman of the Republican National Committee (1964–65) and of the Federal Communications Commission (1969–74); earlier had helped run Sen. Barry Goldwater's 1964 campaign for president. Since 1987 he was director general of Intelsat: d. Potomac, MD, Aug. 4.

Burleson, Omar (85), U.S. representative (D-TX, 1947–79): d. Abilene, TX, May 14.

Busch, Niven (88), screenwriter and novelist; among his 14 novels he is best known for *Duel in the Sun* (1944), which was made into a film in 1947. His screenwriting credits included *The Postman Always Rings Twice* (1946): d. San Francisco, CA, Aug. 25.

Bush, Dorothy V. (75), secretary of the Democratic National Committee; called the roll call at the party national conventions for more than 40 years from 1944 to 1988: d. Naples, FL, Dec. 21.

Capra, Frank (94), Italian-born film director; was the first director to win three directorial Oscars—for *It Happened One Night* (1934), *Mr. Deeds Goes to Town* (1936), and *You Can't Take It with You* (1938). Beginning in silent films, he rose to fame at Columbia Pictures. His typical hero was an honest and perhaps naive crusader threatened by evil forces. Among his other films are *Lost Horizons* (1937), *Mr. Smith Goes to Washington* (1939), *Arsenic and Old Lace* (1944), and *State of the Union* (1948). Capra's 1946 film *It's a Wonderful Life* is a favorite among television viewers each year around Christmas. His last film was *Pocketful of Miracles* (1961), a remake of his *Lady for a Day* (1933): d. La Quinta, CA, Sept. 3.

Carter, Harlon B. (78), chief executive officer and executive vice-president of the National Rifle Association (1977–85): d. Green Valley, AZ, Nov. 19.

Caulfield, Joan (69), film actress of the 1940s; appeared in *Blue Skies* (1946) and *Dear Ruth* (1947). During the 1950s she appeared in two television series—*My Favorite Husband* (1953–57) and *Sally* (1957–58): d. Los Angeles, CA, June 18.

Chandler, A. B. (Happy) (92), Democratic governor of Kentucky (1935–39; 1955–59); he also was a U.S. senator (1939–45) and commissioner of baseball (1945–51), who broke the color line in that sport in 1947 by supporting Jackie Robinson's entry into the major leagues. In 1982 he was elected to the Baseball Hall of Fame: d. Versailles, KY, June 15.

Chang, M. C. (82), scientist in the field of reproductive biology and a codeveloper of the birth-control pill: d. Worcester, MA, June 5.

Chaplin, Lady Oona O'Neill (65), wife of British comedian Charlie Chaplin and the daughter of U.S. playwright Eugene O'Neill. She and Chaplin had eight children. She became known as Lady Chaplin after Charlie Chaplin was knighted in 1975: d. Corsier-sur-Vevey, Switzerland, Sept. 27.

Clark, Steve (30), guitarist for the heavy-metal rock music group Def Leppard: d. London, Jan. 8.

Clayton, Buck (80), jazz trumpeter; a star of Count Basie's orchestra in the late 1930s and early 1940s, he later toured with his own groups. In recent years he did composing and arranging: d. New York City, Dec. 8.

Coleman, J[ames] P[lemon] (77), Democratic governor of Mississippi (1956–60); later was for 16 years a U.S. court of appeals judge. He retired from the bench in 1981: d. Ackerman, MS, Sept. 28.

Collins, LeRoy (82), Democratic governor of Florida (1955–61); he early on sought to promote racial justice in the region: d. Tallahassee, FL, March 12.

Combs, Bertram Thomas (80), Democratic governor of Kentucky from 1959 to 1963. A progressive, he worked for racial equality as governor and later was a federal-court judge. In 1989 he was the lead attorney (who worked without pay) in the successful civil suit brought by 66 state school districts challenging the way Kentucky's public schools were funded: d. East-central Kentucky, Dec. 4.

Conte, Silvio O. (69), U.S. representative (R-MA, 1959–91); considered a liberal Republican: d. Bethesda, MD, Feb. 8.

Convy, Bert (57), actor and host of television game shows; won an Emmy in 1977 as the host of *Tattletales*. His films include *Semi-Tough* (1977): d. Brentwood, CA, July 15.

Cooper, John Sherman (89), U.S. senator (R-KY, 1946-49; 1952–55; 1956–73). He was elected three times to fill unexpired terms of the Kentucky senators A. B. Chandler, Virgil Chapman, and Alben Barkley prior to winning election in his own right in 1960: d. Washington, DC, Feb. 21.

Coppola, Carmine (80), Italian-born conductor and Academy Award-winning composer for the film *The Godfather Part II* (1974), directed by his son Francis Ford Coppola: d. Northridge, CA, April 26.

Lord Cromer (George Rowland Stanley Baring) (72), member of a leading British banking family; the Third Earl of Cromer headed the Bank of England (1961–66): d. London, March 16.

Crosby, John (79), novelist and former syndicated radio and television columnist; wrote action and adventure novels, including *Men in Arms* (1983). He was a columnist for the New York *Herald Tribune* (1946–65) and for the British weekly, *The Observer* (1965–75): d. Esmont, VA, Sept. 7.

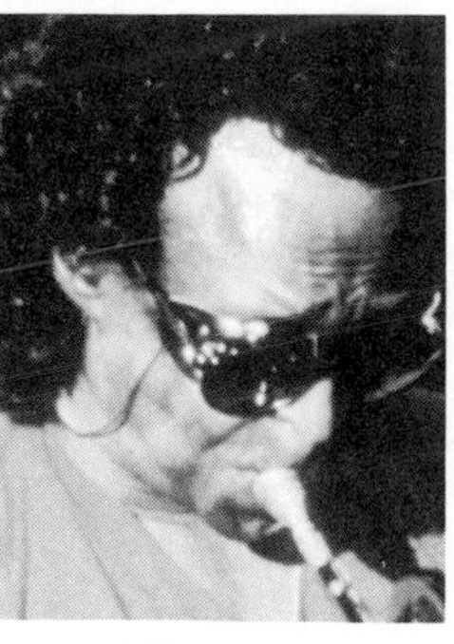
© Jeff Sedlick/Outline Press

Miles Davis

AP/Wide World

Colleen Dewhurst

Curtis, Ken (born Curtis Gates) (74), actor; best known as Festus on the television series *Gunsmoke*. He was on the show from 1964 to 1975: d. Fresno, CA, April 28.

Daly, John Charles, Jr. (77), radio news reporter who became known to millions as the host of the television game show *What's My Line* (1950–67): d. Chevy Chase, MD, Feb. 25.

Davis, Brad (41), stage, film, and television actor; appeared in the films *Midnight Express* (1978) and *Chariots of Fire* (1981): d. Studio City, CA, Sept. 8.

Davis, Miles Dewey, 3d (65), jazz trumpeter and composer; he came of age during the bebop era of the 1940s, but during the course of his career sparked many successive styles, including cool jazz, hard-bop, modal jazz, jazz-rock, and jazz-funk. He drew on many types of music, from blues to classical, in creating his sounds. Among his best known recordings are *The Miles Davis Chronicles, Vol. 2, Birth of the Cool, Miles Davis, Kind of Blue, Sorcerer, Bitches Brew, Dark Magnus, Star People*, and *Tutu*: d. Santa Monica, CA, Sept. 28.

de Castries, Christian (88), French general who in 1953 defended for 55 days but ultimately lost the fortress of Dien Bien Phu in Vietnam. The French, who had exercised colonial rule there, then negotiated a settlement that split Vietnam into north and south: d. (death reported July 30).

Decroux, Etienne (92), French actor and teacher; had been called the father of modern French mime: d. Boulogne-Billancourt, France, March 12.

Delacombe, Major General Sir Rohan (85), military officer who commanded British occupation forces in Berlin from 1959 to 1962 during the height of the Cold War. Later was the last British governor of the Australian state of Victoria (1963–74): d. Nov. 10.

Delacorte, George T. (97), founder of Dell Publishing and a philanthropist; he gave millions of dollars to New York City for the building of fountains, statues, theaters, and schools: d. New York City, May 4.

de Lubac, Cardinal Henri (95), French Roman Catholic Jesuit theologian who participated in the ecumenical council Vatican II in the 1960s. He wrote some 40 books and taught at the Catholic University in Lyons and the Jesuit faculty of Fourvière. After a falling-out with his superiors in Rome he was censured. He was forbidden to teach for eight years, but was rehabilitated in 1958 and elevated to the rank of cardinal in 1983: d. Paris, Sept. 4.

Dewhurst, Colleen (67), Canadian-born actress; she was especially identified with the works of Eugene O'Neill. She won a Tony Award in 1974 for her work in his *Moon for the Misbegotten*. Her films include *Annie Hall* (1977) and *Dying Young* (1991), in which she appeared with her son. She received television Emmys for *Between Two Women* and *And Those She Left Behind*, and in 1989 won a third Emmy for her performances on the CBS television series *Murphy Brown*: d. South Salem, NY, Aug. 22.

Dey, Joseph C., Jr. (83), executive director of the U. S. Golf Association (1934–69) and the first commissioner of the independent professional circuit now known as the PGA Tour: d. Locust Valley, NY, March 4.

Dickey, John Sloan (83), lawyer; president of Dartmouth College (1945–70): d. Hanover, NH, Feb. 9.

Dodd, Edward Benton (88), creator of the "Mark Trail" comic strip, currently syndicated in more than 200 newspapers. He stopped writing the strip in 1978: d. Gainesville, GA, May 27.

Donegan, Horace (91), Episcopal Church bishop; served as Episcopal bishop of New York from 1950 to 1972 and was an early church advocate for the rights of blacks, women, and the poor: d. Sanibel, FL, Nov. 11.

Dunnock, Mildred (90), film and stage actress who appeared in both the stage (1949) and film (1951) versions of *Death of a*

Leo Durocher

Dame Margot Fonteyn

Salesman, for which she was nominated for an Academy Award: d. Oak Bluffs, MA, July 5.

Durocher, Leo (86), major-league baseball player and manager; known for his win-at-all-cost philosophy, he gained notoriety by proclaiming that "nice guys finish last." He began playing major-league baseball in the 1920s with the New York Yankees and later played with the Cincinnati Reds and the St. Louis Cardinals prior to beginning a career as manager with the Brooklyn Dodgers in 1939. He became the New York Giants' manager in 1948 and enjoyed his greatest managerial acclaim in the early 1950s. In all, his teams won three pennants (the Dodgers in 1941 and the Giants in 1951 and 1954) and one World Series (1954): d. Palm Springs, CA, Oct. 7.

Eliot, Thomas H. (84), U.S. representative (D-MA, 1941–43); was political-science professor and chancellor of Washington University in Saint Louis (1962–71): d. Cambridge, MA, Oct. 14.

Elliott, Sumner Locke (73), Australian-born novelist, actor, and playwright; wrote for television during the so-called golden age of the 1950s. His first novel was *Careful, He Might Hear You* (1963), later made into a prizewinning Australian film: d. New York City, June 24.

Engle, Paul (82), poet and educator; a founder in 1967 of the International Writing Program at the University of Iowa where he worked from 1937 until his retirement in 1987: d. Chicago, IL, March 22.

Ennals, Martin (64), British-born secretary-general of the human-rights group Amnesty International (1968–80); he was credited with building the group into a major international human-rights organization: d. Saskatoon, Sask., Oct. 5.

Evers, Walter A. (Hoot) (69), baseball outfielder with the Detroit Tigers in the 1940s and the 1950s: d. Houston, TX, Jan. 25.

Fairbank, John K. (84), history professor at Harvard University (1936–77); widely credited with creating the field of modern Chinese studies. He wrote and edited more than 24 books, including *The United States and China* (1948): d. Cambridge, MA, Sept. 14.

Fender, Clarence Leo (82), designer of electric guitars who helped revolutionize popular music. His Fender Stratocaster was introduced in 1954: d. Fullerton, CA, March 21.

Ferber, Herbert (85), abstract expressionist sculptor; was among a small group of U.S. sculptors who broke with the idea of sculpture as a solid mass and created more open forms: d. North Egremont, MA, Aug. 20.

Finkelstein, Louis (96), chancellor emeritus of the Jewish Theological Seminary of America and the dominant leader of 20th-century Conservative Judaism. He headed the seminary from 1940 to 1972 and was the author or editor of more than 100 books: d. New York City, Nov. 29.

Fish, Hamilton (102), U.S. representative (R-NY, 1921–45); opposed U.S. World War II involvement until the attack on Pearl Harbor; also opposed President Franklin Roosevelt's New Deal policies: d. Cold Spring, NY, Jan. 18.

Fletcher, James C. (72), head of the National Aeronautics and Space Administration (1971–77; 1986–89); presided over the development of the space-shuttle program during his tenure: d. Washington, DC, Dec. 22.

Fletcher, Joseph F., 3d (86), Episcopal priest and professor of ethics; he was a founder of the field of biomedical ethics. He wrote many articles and 11 books, including *Situation Ethics* (1966): d. Charlottesville, VA, Oct. 28.

Fodor, Eugene (85), Hungarian-born creator of travel guidebooks: d. Torrington, CT, Feb. 18.

Fonteyn, Dame Margot (born Margaret Hookham) (71), British-born ballerina; noted as the prima ballerina of Britain's Royal Ballet. She long was associated with the ballets of Sir Frederick Ashton, many of which were created for her. Later in her career, she teamed with Russian defector Rudolf Nureyev, creating a partnership that brought new acclaim. She performed in Ashton's *Apparitions* (1936), *Nocturne* (1936), *A Wedding Bouquet* (1937), *Symphonic Variations* (1946), *Daphnis and Chloe* (1951), *Ondine* (1958), and *Marguerite and Armand* (1963). She also appeared in such classics as *The Sleeping Beauty, Swan Lake,* and *Romeo and Juliet*: d. Panama City, Panama, Feb. 21.

Ford, Tennessee Ernie (born Ernest Jennings Ford) (72), country-and-western singer, comedian, gospel singer, and television host; his 1955 song *16 Tons* became one of the biggest-selling records of all time. He hosted television's *The Ford Show*, a musical variety show that ran from 1956 to 1961: d. Reston, VA, Oct. 17.

Foxx, Redd (born John Sanford) (68), comedian; best known for his portrayal of the junk dealer Fred Sanford in television's *Sanford and Son* (1972–77). He collapsed on the set of his new television series *The Royal Family* and died soon thereafter. Prior to his television success, he had a long career in the black theater and on the nightclub circuit. He made numerous risqué "party records" and some films: d. Los Angeles, CA, Oct. 11.

Francescatti, Rene (Zino) (89), French violinist; renowned for his lyricism, he debuted at the Paris Opera in 1925 and often toured internationally. Along with pianist Robert Casadesus, he made sonata recordings: d. La Ciotat, France, Sept. 17.

Franciscus, James (57), film and television actor; first appeared on television in 1958 in *The Naked City,* but left after one season. Later he became popular in the series *Mr. Novak,* which began in 1963. In addition to these and other television series, he appeared in feature films: d. Los Angeles, CA, July 8.

Freeman, Lawrence (Bud) (84), tenor saxophonist; along with Eddie Condon and others, created what became known as Chicago jazz: d. Chicago, IL, March 15.

Friedman, Maurice Harold (87), physician and medical researcher who in the 1930s developed the "rabbit test," the first reliable and widely used test to determine human pregnancy: d. Sarasota, FL, March 8.

Frisch, Max (79), Swiss novelist, dramatist, and essayist; considered for some time a leading candidate for a Nobel Prize, he won the 1986 Neustadt International Prize for literature. His books, written in German, include *I'm Not Stiller* (1958), *Homo Faber* (1959), and *Man in the Holocene* (1980). His plays include *The Firebugs* (1958) and *Andorra* (1961): d. near Zurich, Switzerland, April 4.

Frye, (Herman) Northrop (78), Canadian literary theorist, critic, and educator; noted for his studies of myth and symbolism as unifying models of Western literature. A minister of the United Church of Canada, he became a professor at the University of Toronto in 1967. His books include *Fearful Symmetry* (1947), *Anatomy of Criticism* (1957), *The Great Code: The Bible and Literature* (1982), and *Words with Power: Being the Second Study of "The Bible and Literature"*: d. Toronto, Ont., Jan. 23.

Gaillard, Bulee (Slim) (74), jazz pianist and composer; part of the Slim and Slam duo (with bassist Slam Stewart): d. London, England, Feb. 26.

Gandhi, Rajiv *See* page 51 .

Gann, Ernest K. (81), author of adventure novels; his books include *Island in the Sky* (1944), *The High and the Mighty* (1952), and *Soldier of Fortune* (1955), all of which were made into films: d. San Juan Island, WA, Dec. 19.

García Robles, Alfonso (80), Mexican diplomat and Mexico's foreign minister in 1975; shared the Nobel Peace Prize in 1982 for his efforts to ban nuclear weapons from Latin America: d. Mexico City, Mexico, Sept. 2.

Garin, Mary S. Painter (71), economist; innovator in economic and statistical work. During World War II she served on the Board of Economic Warfare and then at the Office of Strategic Services. Later she served at the Federal Reserve Board in Washington and in 1948 was among the economists who set up the European headquarters of the Marshall Plan: d. Toulon, France, Oct. 21.

Garrison, Lloyd Kirkham (92), New York City lawyer and champion of civil rights; was dean of the University of Wisconsin Law School (1932–45) and president of the National Urban League (1947–52). He defended poet Langston Hughes and playwright Arthur Miller against charges by Sen. Joseph McCarthy and the House Un-American Activities Committee in the early 1950s and sought unsuccessfully in 1954 to have J. Robert Oppenheimer's security clearance restored by the Atomic Energy Commission: d. New York City, Oct. 2.

Getz, Stan (64), jazz tenor saxophonist; noted as one of the best improvisationists, as a superb melodist, and for his influence on the "cool school" of jazz in the 1950s and on the bossa nova in the 1960s: d. Malibu, CA, June 6.

Gilbert, Felix (85), German-born historian, educator, and author; wrote on Renaissance Italy, 18th-century North America, and 20th-century Europe and was a professor at Princeton University (1962-75): d. Princeton, NJ, Feb. 14.

Ginzburg, Natalia (75), Italian novelist, essayist, and translator; wrote six works of fiction, the play *I Married You for the Fun of It*, a biography of the novelist Alessandro Manzoni, and translations of Flaubert and Proust. Her first novel was *The*

Road to the City. She gained international recognition with the novel *Voices in the Evening* (1961) and an autobiography, *Family Savings* (1963): d. Rome, Oct. 7.

Gobel, George (71), nightclub and television comedian; became a sensation during the 1950s when his two hit television series, both titled *The George Gobel Show*, were broadcast (1954–57; 1957-59). During the 1970s and 1980s he appeared on *Hollywood Squares*: d. Encino, CA, Feb. 24.

Goody, Sam (born Samuel Gutowitz) (87), founder of the record-store chain: d. New York City, Aug. 8.

Goren, Charles (90), contract bridge expert; well known to many for his development of point-count bidding and for his many books, columns, and articles. His nearly 40 books include *Contract Bridge Complete* (1942) and *Point Count Bidding* (1949). Between 1959 and 1964 he was the star of the television show *Championship Bridge with Charles Goren*: d. Encino, CA, April 3.

Gouraud, Marie-Michel (86), former lieutenant general in the French army who was implicated in the 1961 mutiny aimed at keeping the de Gaulle government from entering negotiations on Algerian independence: d. Paris, March 20.

Gowing, Sir Lawrence (72), British painter, writer, curator, and teacher; was known beginning in the 1940s for his portrait paintings and landscapes. He was knighted in 1982: d. London, Feb. 5.

Graham, Bill (born Wolfgang Grajonca) (60), promoter of rock musicians; helped develop the mass rock-concert format and was for 25 years a central figure in organizing, producing, and marketing rock music in the United States and internationally: d. near San Francisco, CA, Oct. 25.

Graham, John (82), architect who in the late 1940s designed a shopping center that became a prototype for others; also designed the Space Needle for the 1962 Seattle World's Fair and created the first revolving restaurant (in Honolulu, HI): d. Seattle, WA, Jan. 29.

Grange, Harold (Red) (87), football running back in the 1920s for the University of Illinois and for the professional Chicago Bears (1925–26; 1929–34); known as the "Galloping Ghost." He also played two seasons with the New York Yankees football team. After his retirement as a player, he had a brief career as an assistant coach prior to becoming a radio and television analyst and announcer. He was a charter member of the Professional Football Hall of Fame (1963): d. Lake Wales, FL, Jan. 28.

Guard, Dave (56), a founding member of the Kingston Trio whose hit songs helped create the folk-music boom of the 1950s and 1960s: d. Rollinsford, NH, March 22.

Guthrie, A.B., Jr. (90), author; noted for his writings on the American West. He won a Pulitzer Prize in 1950 for *The Way West* (1949) and also wrote the screenplay for the 1953 film *Shane*. Earlier he was a journalist with the *Lexington* [KY] *Leader*: d. Choteau, MT, April 26.

Hannah, John (88), president of Michigan State University (1941–69); also first chairman of the U.S. Commission on Civil Rights (1957–69): d. Kalamazoo, MI, Feb. 23.

Harvey, Ralph M. (90), U.S. representative (R-IN, 1948–59; 1961–66): d. Fort Lauderdale, FL, Nov. 7.

Hatfield, Richard (60), Canadian Progressive Conservative senator since 1990; he was premier of New Brunswick (1970–87): d. Ottawa, Ont., April 26.

Heidelberger, Michael (103), pathologist; known as the father of modern immunology; credited with discovering that antibodies are proteins: d. New York City, June 25.

Heinz, John, III (52), U.S. senator (R-PA, 1977-91); he earlier had served as a U.S. representative and was an heir of the Heinz food-company fortune: d. Lower Merion Township, PA, April 4.

Hieu, Nguyen Van (68), founding member of the National Front for Liberation of South Vietnam (Vietcong), established in 1960. After the Vietnam war he served in the National Assembly: d. Ho Chi Minh City, March 6.

Hildesheimer, Wolfgang (74), German novelist, playwright, and painter; his 1977 biography of Mozart became an international best-seller: d. Poschiavo, Switzerland, Aug. 21.

Honda, Soichiro (84), Japanese automobile industrialist, who in order to build automobiles defied Japanese government bureaucrats who wanted him to stick to making motorcycles, which he had begun producing in the early post-World War II years. His greatest success came in the United States, where in the 1970s he won over a generation of young drivers drawn to fuel efficiency and low emissions. After his retirement in 1973, Honda Motor became the first Japanese company to build factories in the United States: d. Tokyo, Aug. 5.

Hunter, Ian McLellan (75), screen and television writer; won an Academy Award for the 1953 film *Roman Holiday*: d. New York City, March 5.

Hurwitz, Leo (81), documentary filmmaker; blacklisted in the 1950s for his left-wing political beliefs. His films include *Native Land* (1942): d. New York City, Jan. 18.

Husák, Gustav (1978), premier and general secretary of the Communist Party in Czechoslovakia (1969–87) and president of Czechoslovakia (1975–89). He rose to power after the reform movement was stamped out in 1968. Earlier he had spent years in jail during the Stalinist era: d. Bratislava, Czechoslovakia, Nov. 18.

Hyde-White, Wilfrid (87), British actor; known for his urbane characterizations in such films as *The Third Man* (1949), *My Fair Lady* (1964), and *Ten Little Indians* (1965). He also was a stage actor: d. Woodland Hills, CA, May 6.

Idris, Yusuf (64), a leading Egyptian playwright and short-story writer: d. London, Aug. 1.

Ikard, Frank Neville (78), U.S. representative (D-TX, 1951–61) and president of the American Petroleum Institute (1963–79): d. Washington, DC, May 1.

Princess Ileana (82), princess of Romania and aunt of the former King Michael of Romania; she became an Orthodox Church nun and founded a U.S. convent in 1968: d. Youngstown, OH, Jan. 21.

Irwin, James B. (61), U.S. astronaut; walked on the moon in July 1971 as a member of the crew of the Apollo 15 mission. He resigned from the space program in 1972 and established an evangelical religious organization, High Flight Foundation, based in Colorado Springs: d. Glenwood Springs, CO, Aug. 8.

Jackson, Sir Robert (79), Australian under secretary-general of the United Nations (1972–87); he was knighted in 1956: d. London, Jan. 12.

Jacoby, Jim (58), bridge player; considered among the world's best; won 16 national titles and four world titles: d. Dallas, TX, Feb. 8.

Jagger, Dean (87), film and television actor; during his 50-year career he made more than 120 films, winning an Academy Award for his performance in *Twelve O'Clock High* (1949). On television he appeared in the series *Mr. Novak* (1963–65) and in 1980 won an Emmy Award for his role in "Independence and '76," from the religious program *This Is the Life*: d. Santa Monica, CA, Feb. 5.

Jiang Qing (born Li Jin) (77), the widow of Chinese Communist Party Chairman Mao Zedong; she apparently committed suicide while serving a life prison sentence for her role as a leader of the Gang of Four who promoted the policies of the Cultural Revolution from 1966 to 1976. Despite her sentence she was allowed to leave prison for medical reasons in 1984: d. suburban Beijing, China, May 14.

Johansen, Gunnar (85), Danish-born pianist and composer; was the first musician to be appointed artist-in-residence at a U.S. university. He held that position at the University of Wisconsin (1939-76), where he both taught and performed: d. Blue Mounds, WI, May 25.

Johnson, Bob (born Bob Olars) (60), U.S. collegiate and professional ice-hockey coach who led the Pittsburgh Penguins to a Stanley Cup championship in 1991. He was the coach of the 1976 U.S. Olympic team and was inducted into the Hockey Hall of Fame in October: d. Colorado Springs, CO, Nov. 26.

Joxe, Louis (89), French public servant who as a member in the government of Charles de Gaulle negotiated Algeria's sovereignty in the early 1960s. He later was a justice minister but left the post in the late 1960s: d. Paris, April 6.

Kaganovich, Lazar M. (born Lazar M. Kogan) (97), Soviet aide to Stalin and the last surviving Bolshevik leader who joined the Communist Party before the revolution. Because of his association with Stalin, he sometimes was regarded as the number two man in the USSR: d. Moscow, July 25.

Kaye, Sylvia Fine (78), songwriter, lyricist, and composer; the widow of actor Danny Kaye, she wrote music and lyrics for many of his films: d. New York City, Oct. 28.

Kelso, Louis O. (77), lawyer, investment banker, and economist; advocated worker-capitalism through employee stock-ownership plans. He wrote, with Mortimer J. Adler, *The Capitalist Manifesto* (1958) and *The New Capitalists* (1961): d. San Francisco, CA, Feb. 17.

Charles Goren

AP/Wide World

Soichiro Honda

© P. Frilet/Sipa

Michael Landon

Archbishop Marcel Lefebvre

Keltner, Ken (75), baseball third baseman; began with the Cleveland Indians in 1937 and played 13 major-league seasons. He played one season with the Boston Red Sox. A highlight of his career was his backhanded stops of two grounders that helped end New York Yankee Joe DiMaggio's 56-game hitting streak in 1941: d. Milwaukee, WI, Dec. 12.

Kinski, Klaus (born Nikolaus Gunther Nakszynski) (65), Polish-born actor; especially noted for his performances in the films of Werner Herzog that include *Aguirre: The Wrath of God* (1972), *Nosferatu, The Vampyre* (1978), *Woyzeck* (1978), and *Fitzcarraldo* (1982): d. Lagunitas, CA, Nov. 23.

Klasen, Karl Ferdinand (81), president of the Bundesbank, West Germany's central bank (1970–77): d. Hamburg, Germany, April 22.

Knight, Etheridge (57), poet who began writing while in prison; his books include *Poems from Prison* (1968), *Black Voices from Prison* (1970), and *Born of a Woman* (1980): d. Indianapolis, IN, March 10.

Knight, James L. (81), chairman emeritus of Knight-Ridder Inc., one of the major U.S. newspaper chains. His career began in the 1930s when he and his older brother inherited the debt-ridden *Akron* [OH] *Beacon Journal*. In 1937 his brother acquired *The Miami Herald*, which along with the Akron paper started the brothers on their way to acquiring their newspaper chain. In 1974 the Knights merged their group with Ridder Publications: d. Santa Monica, CA, Feb. 5.

Kosinski, Jerzy (57), Polish-born writer; achieved great success with his first novel, *The Painted Bird* (1965), and with his second novel, *Steps* (1968), won a National Book Award. He was president of the U.S. chapter of PEN, the international writer's group, from 1973 to 1975. His novel *Being There* (1971) was made into a 1979 film. Earlier he published two collections of political essays under the pseudonym Joseph Novak. He was found dead, an apparent suicide: d. New York City, May 3.

Krenek, Ernst (91), Austrian-born composer; his most famous work remains the opera *Jonny Spielt Auf* (1925–26), a story of a black violinist: d. Palm Springs, CA, Dec. 23.

Kulp, Nancy (69), actress; best known as the secretary in the television series *The Beverly Hillbillies* (1962–71) who was in love with Jethro: d. Palm Desert, CA, Feb. 3.

Land, Edwin H. (81), inventor of the instant camera; founded the Polaroid Corporation in 1937 and helped provide a long line of photographic products: d. Cambridge, MA, March 1. (*See also* page 428.)

Landon, Michael (born Eugene Maurice Orowitz) (54), television actor; first gained fame in the role of Little Joe on the television series *Bonanza* (1959-73). He later played a frontier father in the series *Little House on the Prairie* (1974–83) and an angel in *Highway to Heaven* (1984–89): d. Malibu, CA, July 1.

Lawrence, John H. (87), founder of the Donner Laboratory, the world's first research laboratory devoted to nuclear medicine, and a pioneer in the use of nuclear radiation in diagnosing and treating cancer. He was also one of the first scientists to warn of the dangers of radiation. His center was affiliated with the Lawrence Berkeley Laboratory that was directed by Ernest O. Lawrence, a brother, whom the deceased followed to Berkeley in 1935 after serving as an instructor in medicine at Yale University: d. Berkeley, CA, Sept. 7.

Lean, Sir David (83), British director noted for both small, intimate films and grand epics. He directed such films as *In Which We Serve* (1942), *This Happy Breed* (1944), *Brief Encounter* (1945), and *Great Expectations* (1946) and won directorial Academy Awards for *The Bridge on the River Kwai* (1957) and *Lawrence of Arabia* (1962). Other of his important films are *Dr. Zhivago* (1965), *Ryan's Daughter* (1970), and *A Passage to India* (1984). He was knighted in 1984: d. London, April 16.

Lefebvre, Marcel (85), French archbishop of the Roman Catholic Church. A strong traditionalist who battled for the return of the Latin Mass and other practices rejected following the ecumenical council Vatican II, he caused a schism within the church by establishing his own order of priests and consecrating his own bishops. He was excommunicated in June 1988, but his followers set up schools and seminaries in several countries: d. Martigny, Switzerland, March 25.

Le Gallienne, Eva (92), British-born actress, producer, director, as well as a translator, writer, and teacher; she first attracted attention in 1919 in New York in *Not So Long Ago* and went on to become a leading U.S. stage actress. In 1926 she founded the Civic Repertory Theater, which operated until 1933. Of the 34 plays performed she directed 32 and starred in many as well. She later helped organize the American Repertory Theater, but it lasted only one season. In 1958 her television production of *The Bridge of San Luis Rey* was acclaimed critically. A memorable stage role was as Queen Elizabeth in *Mary Stuart*, which she periodically performed from 1957 to 1962: d. Weston, CT, June 3.

Léger, Cardinal Paul Emile (87), Canadian Roman Catholic churchman; was archbishop of Montreal from 1950 until 1968, when he resigned to work with lepers and handicapped children in Africa, spending 12 years in Cameroon. He was made a cardinal in 1953 at age 48, one of the youngest to be elevated to that position: d. Montreal, Que., Nov. 13.

Lewis, Herbert A. (85), ice-hockey player; was with the Detroit Red Wings (1928–39); later was inducted into the Hockey Hall of Fame: d. Indianapolis, IN, Jan. 20.

Lewis, Robert Q. (71), radio and television personality; known for his trademark horn-rimmed glasses. He made guest appearances on the television shows of such stars as Arthur Godfrey, Jack Paar, and Garry Moore and was a regular panelist on such shows as *What's My Line*, *To Tell the Truth*, and *Play Your Hunch*: d. Los Angeles, CA, Dec. 11.

Lewis, Sir William Arthur (76), Caribbean-born educator; shared the Nobel Prize in economic science in 1979. Among his major works was *The Theory of Economic Growth* (1954). He was a member of the faculty of Princeton University from 1963 until his retirement in 1983; thereafter he was professor emeritus: d. Barbados, June 15.

Lilly, Doris (60), gossip columnist for the *New York Post* newspaper (1958–68); wrote the books *How to Marry a Millionaire* (1951; film 1953) and *Glamour Girl* (1977). She was said to be the inspiration for the character "Holly Golightly" in Truman Capote's book *Breakfast at Tiffany's*: d. New York City, Oct. 9.

Luke, Keye (86), Chinese-born actor; was the Number One Son in Charlie Chan detective films of the 1930s and 1940s; most recently he appeared in Woody Allen's film *Alice* (1990): d. Whittier, CA, Jan. 12.

Luria, Salvador E. (78), Italian-born biologist and physician; shared a 1969 Nobel Prize in medicine and physiology with two others, cited for their "discoveries concerning the replication mechanism and the genetic structure of viruses." He taught at Indiana University (1943–59), then joined the faculty of the Massachusetts Institute of Technology, retiring in 1978. He was active in the peace movement. In 1969 his name appeared on a federal blacklist of 48 scientists: d. Lexington, MA, Feb. 6.

The Rev. Lord MacLeod (born George F. MacLeod) (96), founder of the ecumenical religious community on the Scottish island of Iona, where he and his followers restored the ruins of a 13th-century Benedictine abbey. Members of the community practice prayer and Bible study, share money and use of time, meet with fellow members, and maintain peace and justice commitments. In 1989 he received the Templeton Prize in religion: d. Edinburgh, Scotland, June 27.

MacMahon, Aline (92), stage, screen, radio, and television actress; was nominated for an Academy Award for the film *Dragon Seed* (1944). Among the memorable stage plays in which she performed were *Once in a Lifetime* and *All the Way Home*. Her films include *Ah, Wilderness!* (1935), *The Search* (1948), and *The Flame and the Arrow* (1950): d. New York City, Oct. 12.

MacMurray, Frederick Martin (Fred) (83), film and television actor; noted for the long-running television series *My Three Sons* (1960–72). While he often appeared in film comedies, he also made some important dramatic films, including *Double Indemnity* (1944), *The Caine Mutiny* (1954), and *The Apartment* (1960). He also starred in several Walt Disney films: d. Santa Monica, CA, Nov. 5.

Mann, Daniel (79), theater, motion-picture, and television director; his films include *Come Back Little Sheba* (1952), *The Rose Tattoo* (1955), and *Butterfield 8* (1960): d. Los Angeles, CA, Nov. 21.

Manzù, Giacomo (82), Italian sculptor; gained fame for his set of bronze doors for St. Peter's Basilica in Vatican City, commissioned in the early 1950s and completed in 1964: d. Ardea, Italy, Jan. 17.

McCone, John A. (89), chairman of the U.S. Atomic Energy Commission (1958–60) and director of Central Intelligence (1961–65); credited with being the first government official to foresee that the Soviet Union would place offensive weapons in Cuba: d. Pebble Beach, CA, Feb. 14.

McIntire, John (83), actor in films, radio, and television; was well known as the wagonmaster (1961-65) in the television series *Wagon Train.* (He had succeeded actor Ward Bond in the role.): d. Pasadena, CA, Jan. 30.

McKissick, Floyd Bixler (69), lawyer and civil-rights activist; was director of the Congress of Racial Equality (1966--67): d. Soul City, NC, April 28.

McMillan, Edwin (83), nuclear physicist; won the Nobel Prize in chemistry in 1951 as a codiscoverer of plutonium and neptunium. He was head of the Lawrence Berkeley Laboratory in Berkeley, CA (1958-73): d. El Cerrito, CA, Sept. 7.

McPartland, Jimmy (83), cornetist; one of the creators of a 1920s variation of Dixieland jazz that became known as Chicago-style jazz: d. Port Washington, NY, March 13.

Mercury, Freddie (45), lead singer of the hard-rock group Queen: d. Kensington, England, Nov. 24.

Michener, Daniel R. (91), governor-general of Canada (1967–74): d. Toronto, Ont., Aug. 6.

Miles, Lord Bernard (83), British actor and founder (in 1959) of the Mermaid Theatre in London. He was knighted in 1969 and made a life peer in 1979: d. Yorkshire, England, June 14.

Mollenhoff, Clark R. (69), reporter, author, and syndicated columnist; an investigative correspondent for Cowles Publications (1950–78). He won a Pulitzer Prize for national reporting in 1958 for his inquiries into corrupt labor practices. Since 1976 he had been a professor at Washington and Lee University: d. Lexington, VA, March 2.

Montalban, Carlos (87), Spanish-born actor and dancer; the brother of actor Ricardo Montalban, he was perhaps best known for his television commercials for Savarin coffee: d. New York City, March 28.

Montand, Yves (born Ivo Livi) (70), Italian-born French actor and singer; internationally known for his political views, which were at first leftist but later conservative, and for his affairs with famous women, including Marilyn Monroe and Edith Piaf. He was married to actress Simone Signoret until her death. He began his career as a singer but later was a noted film star. His films include *The Wages of Fear* (1953), *The Crucible* (1956), *Let's Make Love* (1960), *Is Paris Burning?* (1966), *Z* (1969), *The Confession* (1970), *Jean de Florette* (1986), and *Manon of the Spring* (1986): d. Senlis, France, Nov. 9.

Moorman, Charlotte (57), cellist of avant-garde works and pioneer performance artist; noted for her performances of New Music by such composers as Nam June Paik, Joseph Beuys, and Yoko Ono. Her best-known pieces include *Cello Sonata No. 1 for Adults Only* (1965). She gained attention in 1967 by performing a cello piece while nude from the waist up: d. New York City, Nov. 8.

Motherwell, Robert (76), painter; one of the last major artists of the abstract expressionist movement and a leading spokesman of what he called the New York school in art. Among his abstract works are series known as *Elegies to the Spanish Republic* and *Opens.* His work showed a major involvement with the culture of Mediterranean Europe, and he was also a master of the collage. In his later years he received many honors, and in 1982 a permanent Motherwell Gallery was installed at the Bavarian State Museum of Modern Art in Munich, Germany. In addition to his work as an artist he was both a teacher and editor: d. Provincetown, MA, July 16.

Muhammad Abu-Shakra, Sheikh (81), Lebanese spiritual leader of the Druze religion; was named supreme spiritual leader of the group in 1970: d. Badaran, Lebanon, Oct. 24.

Murray, Arthur (born Arthur Murray Teichman) (95), ballroom dance teacher; built a mail-order operation and then a network of franchised dance studios that were grossing $25 million annually when he stepped down as president of Arthur Murray Inc. in 1964: d. Honolulu, HI, March 3.

Nemerov, Howard (71), poet and educator; served as U.S. poet laureate from 1988 to 1990. He won a Pulitzer Prize and a National Book Award for *The Collected Poems of Howard Nemerov* (1977). He taught at several colleges and universities, most recently at Washington University: d. University City, MO, July 5.

Nikezic, Marko (69), a diplomat and foreign minister of Yugoslavia (1965–68); he was a leading liberal politician of Serbia in the post-World War II era. He headed the Serbian Communist Party but in 1972 was ordered by Josip Tito to resign: d. Belgrade, Yugoslavia, Jan. 6.

North, Alex (80), composer of film musical scores for *Death of a Salesman, A Streetcar Named Desire, Who's Afraid of Virginia Woolf,* and many other films over the course of his 40-year Hollywood career: d. Los Angeles, CA, Sept. 8.

Oduber Quiros, Daniel (70), president of Costa Rica (1974–78) and founder of the leftist National Liberation Party: d. San José, Costa Rica, Oct. 13.

O'Faolain, Sean (born John Francis Whelan) (91), Irish writer; noted for his short stories. Among his more than 20 books are his novels *A Nest of Simple Folk* (1933) and *Bird Alone* (1936), and the short-story collection *The Collected Stories of Sean O'Faolain* (1983). He also wrote several books on Ireland, including *The Irish: A Character Study* (1947): d. Dublin, Ireland, April 20.

Olav V, King of Norway (87), served as king from 1957 to 1991; as crown prince he became a national symbol of resistance to Nazi Germany's occupation of Norway during World War II: d. Norway, Jan. 17.

Page, Irvine H. (90), physician who pioneered in hypertension research; he was one of the first to recognize that high blood pressure was a disease that could be treated: d. Hyannisport, MA, June 10.

Page, Ruth (92), dancer and choreographer; she was one of the first ballet choreographers to use American subject matter. Her ballets include *Hear Ye, Hear Ye* (1934), *An American Pattern* (1937), and *Billy Sunday* (1948). With Bentley Stone she choreographed *Frankie and Johnny* (1938), a ballet that has been revived successfully by many companies: d. Chicago, IL, April 7.

Panufnik, Sir Andrzej (77), Polish-born composer and conductor; helped develop a contemporary Polish style but left Poland in 1954 in protest against the lack of freedom of expression. His works include ten symphonies, including *Sinfonia Votiva*, as well as concertos, chamber works, and choral and vocal music. He served as musical director of the City of Birmingham Symphony Orchestra (1957–59): d. London, Oct. 27.

Pasternak, Joe (89), Hungarian-born film producer of 105 films; noted for his family-oriented fare and musicals. His films include *Destry Rides Again, The Great Caruso,* and *Where the Boys Are*: d. Beverly Hills, CA, Sept. 13.

Payne, Ethel L. (79), black journalist; reported for the *Chicago Defender* newspaper; in the 1970s became the first black female commentator on network television, appearing on the *Spectrum* series: d. Washington, DC, May 28.

Penney, Lord (born William George Penney) (81), father of the British atomic bomb who in 1952 directed the test explosion of Britain's first atomic bomb in the Monte Bello Islands off the coast of Australia. Earlier he was an adviser on U.S. atomic projects, including the development program at Los Alamos, NM. He studied mathematics at London University, the University of Wisconsin, and Cambridge University. He was knighted in 1952 and made a life peer in 1967: d. East Hendred, England, March 3.

Perlman, Isador (76), nuclear chemist; was with the Lawrence Radiation Laboratory (1958–75) and the University of California at Berkeley (1945–74); later was with Hebrew University in Jerusalem: d. Los Alamitos, CA, Aug. 3.

Perry, Harold R. (74), Roman Catholic bishop; the first black American so consecrated in the 20th century. He had been auxiliary bishop of New Orleans since 1965: d. New Orleans, LA, July 17.

Pierce, Webb (65), country music singer; among his hits was *In the Jailhouse Now*: d. Nashville, TN, Feb. 24.

Pirie, (Douglas Alistair) Gordon (60), British runner; set five world records between 1953 and 1956 and won a silver medal at the 1956 Olympic Games: d. Dec. 7.

Pomus, Jerome (Doc) (born Jerome Solon Felder) (65), rock-and-roll songwriter who along with his partner Mort Shuman was very successful in the early 1960s. Among their hit songs were *Save the Last Dance for Me, A Teen-Ager in Love,* and *This Magic Moment*: d. New York City, March 14.

Popa, Vasko (68), modernist Yugoslav poet; his symbolist poetry with its mix of folk poetry and surrealism was considered by some as the finest in the Serbian language: d. Belgrade, Yugoslavia, Jan. 4.

Porter, Sylvia F. (77), author and newspaper columnist who reported business and financial news understandable to the general reader. Her newspaper column was syndicated by the *Los Angeles Times* and carried in 450 newspapers. She also wrote more than 20 books on financial and economic matters: d. Pound Ridge, NY, June 5.

Fred MacMurray

Sylvia Porter

Photos, AP/Wide World

Qin Benli (73), dissident Chinese newspaper editor of the *World Economic Herald*. He was fired by the government in 1989 for his support of the prodemocratic movement. His dismissal gave impetus to the Tiananmen democratic movement: d. Shanghai, China, April 15.

Quist, Adrian K. (78), Australian tennis player; won Wimbledon doubles championships in 1935 and 1950: d. Sydney, Australia, Nov. 17.

Racker, Efraim (78), biochemist at Cornell University (1966–91); was a leading researcher on energy storage in living cells and its implications for cancer: d. Syracuse, NY, Sept. 9.

Ragni, Gerome (48), cowrote the book and lyrics of the Broadway musical *Hair* (1968), which for many epitomized the youth culture of the 1960s: d. New York City, July 10.

Rains, Albert McKinley (89), U.S. representative (D-AL, 1945–65): d. Gadsden, AL, March 22.

Ray, Aldo (born Aldo DaRe) (64), film actor; noted for his husky, gravelly voice; played in numerous war films and in comedies. His films include *Pat and Mike* (1952), *Miss Sadie Thompson* (1953), *We're No Angels* (1955), *Battle Cry* (1955), and *The Naked and the Dead* (1958): d. Martinez, CA, March 27.

Reasoner, Harry (68), television newscaster who spent most of his career with CBS News, serving as reporter and correspondent there from 1956 to 1970 and from 1978 until 1991. From 1970 to 1978 he worked for ABC News, anchoring the evening news for a time with Barbara Walters. He appeared for many years on the series *60 Minutes*: d. Norwalk, CT, Aug. 6.

Remick, Lee (55), stage, film, and television actress; first appeared on Broadway in 1953 in the comedy *Be Your Age* and then moved on to various dramatic roles in television in the 1950s. She made a number of films in the 1950s, 1960s, and 1970s and also was a frequent star in television miniseries of the 1970s and 1980s. Her films include *A Face in the Crowd* (1957); *Anatomy of a Murder* (1959); and *The Days of Wine and Roses* (1963), in which her portrayal of the alcoholic housewife brought her an Academy-Award nomination. Her most successful stage role was in *Wait Until Dark* (1966): d. Los Angeles, CA, July 2.

Revelle, Roger (82), scientist who was an early predictor of global warming; he headed the Scripps Institution of Oceanography (1951–64), and in 1964 founded and became director of the Center for Population Studies at Harvard University: d. San Diego, CA, July 15.

Richardson, Tony (63), British film director; he won an Academy Award in 1963 for the film *Tom Jones*. He began his career with the British Broadcasting Company in 1953 and in 1955 joined the newly formed English Stage Company. The first play that he directed there was *Look Back in Anger*, which gained much attention and was made into a film in 1959. Among his other films are *The Entertainer* (1960), *A Taste of Honey* (1961), *The Loneliness of the Long Distance Runner* (1962), *Joseph Andrews* (1977), *The Border* (1982), and *The Hotel New Hampshire* (1984): d. Los Angeles, CA, Nov. 15.

Riding Jackson, Laura (born Laura Reichenthal) (90), an avant-garde poet of the 1920s; she contributed to a school of critical thought that became known as the New Criticism: d. Sebastian, FL, Sept. 2.

Rizzo, Frank (70), Democratic mayor of Philadelphia (1972–80) and a dominant Philadelphia political force for 25 years; he earlier had been the city's police commissioner. At the time of his death he was staging a political comeback. (He had switched to the Republican Party in 1986.): d. Philadelphia, PA, July 16.

Robinson, Earl (81), singer and composer; created songs honoring the U.S. labor movement, including *Joe Hill, The House I Live In*, and *Black and White*. He was blacklisted during the McCarthy era of the 1950s: d. Seattle, WA, July 20.

Roddenberry, Gene (70), writer and producer; created the 1960s science-fiction television series *Star Trek* (1966–69). The series inspired six feature films as well as a sequel television series, *Star Trek: The Next Generation*, which began in 1987: d. Santa Monica, CA, Oct, 25.

Roosevelt, James (83), U.S. representative (D-CA, 1955–65); he was the eldest son of U.S. President Franklin D. Roosevelt: d. Newport Beach, CA, Aug. 13.

Rose, Frank Anthony (70), president of the University of Alabama (1958–69), during which time the university was desegregated peacefully: d. Washington, DC, Feb. 1.

Ruffin, Davis Eli (David) (50), original member of the Temptations, a rock-music group that had the 1965 hit *My Girl*. He left the group in 1968: d. Philadelphia, PA, June 1.

Runnels, James Edward (Pete) (63), baseball infielder with the Washington Senators and the Boston Red Sox in the 1950s and 1960s. He twice won American League batting titles—in 1960 and 1962: d. Pasadena, TX, May 20.

Ryan, Jack (65), inventor and designer whose association with the toy company Mattel Inc., led to his designing the Barbie doll, the Chatty Cathy doll, and Hot Wheels motor vehicles: d. Los Angeles, CA, Aug. 13.

Sabry, Aly (71), Egyptian prime minister (1964–65) and vice-president (1965–67). He later was accused of plotting a coup against President Anwar el-Sadat and was imprisoned for ten years: d. Cairo, Aug. 3.

Scelba, Mario (90), founder of Italy's Christian Democratic Party; he served as Italy's prime minister in 1954 and 1955. He was president of the European Parliament from 1969 to 1971: d. Rome, Oct. 29.

Schaefer, Jack (83), author of Western novels; his best-known work was *Shane* (1949), which was made into a 1953 film: d. Santa Fe, NM, Jan. 24.

Schafer, Natalie (90), actress, best known as the stranded millionaire's wife in the television series *Gilligan's Island* (1964–67): d. Beverly Hills, CA, April 10.

Schuyler, James (67), poet; won the Pulitzer Prize in 1981 for *The Morning of the Poem* (1980): d. New York City, April 12.

Seibert, Florence B. (93), inventor of the first reliable tuberculosis test: d. St. Petersburg, FL, Aug. 23.

Serkin, Rudolf (88), Austrian-born concert pianist; noted for his ability in both the classical and romantic styles of piano playing. He first played in the United States in 1933 and made his formal debut as a soloist with the New York Philharmonic under Toscanini in 1936. He joined the faculty at the Curtis Institute in Philadelphia in 1939, where he taught for 36 years until 1975. In 1949 he helped found the Marlboro Festival, a summer music series, in Vermont: d. Guilford, VT, May 8.

Shea, William A. (84), New York City lawyer and power broker; was instrumental in establishing the New York Mets baseball team in the city in 1962. The stadium in Flushing Meadows that the Mets moved into in 1964 was named for Shea: d. New York City, Oct. 2.

Shoemaker, Vaughn (89), Pulitzer Prize-winning editorial cartoonist (1938; 1947); created the character John Q Public for the *Chicago Daily News*: d. Carol Stream, IL, Aug. 18.

Siegel, Don (78), director of such action-adventure movies as *Baby Face Nelson* (1957), *Coogan's Bluff* (1968), *Dirty Harry* (1971), and *Escape from Alcatraz* (1979). He also directed two short films that won Academy Awards—*Star in the Night* and *Hitler Lives*—and the 1956 science-fiction classic *Invasion of the Body Snatchers*: d. Nipomo, CA, April 20.

Siegmeister, Elie (82), music composer of eight operas and eight symphonies as well as songs, choral settings, concertos, orchestral works, and chamber pieces. He used folk music, jazz, and street songs to devise contemporary American classical music. Among his works is the 1933 composition *American Holiday*: d. Manhasset, NY, March 10.

Siskind, Aaron (85), photographer; best known for his nearly abstract, spare black-and-white photographs that often focused on close-up details. Among his books are *Places* (1976) and *Aaron Siskind: Pleasures and Terrors* (1983): d. Providence, RI, Feb. 8.

Harry Reasoner

AP/Wide World

Lee Remick

© S. Schapiro/Sygma

Tony Richardson

© NYT Pictures

Rudolf Serkin

AP/Wide World

Joseph R. Smallwood

Danny Thomas

John Tower

Marietta Tree

Smallwood, Joseph R. (90), Canadian politician; credited with leading Newfoundland and Labrador into federation with Canada in 1949. He was premier of Newfoundland (1949–72): d. near St. John's, Newfoundland, Dec. 17.

Snelling, Richard A. (64), Republican governor of Vermont (1977–85; 1991); known for blending fiscal conservatism with environmental concerns: d. Shelburne, VT, Aug. 14.

Spessivtzeva, Olga (96), Russian ballerina; her dancing was praised for its Romantic purity and spirituality, and she was acclaimed as one of the foremost interpreters of *Giselle*. She began her dancing career with the Maryinsky (now the Kirov) Ballet and during the 1920s danced with Sergei Diaghilev's Ballets Russes. She also appeared with the Paris Opera Ballet, the Colón ballet in Buenos Aires, and with the Camargo Society, one of the forerunners of the London Royal Ballet: d. Valley Cottage, NY, Sept. 16.

Staggers, Harley Orrin (84), U.S. representative (D-WV, 1949–81): d. Cumberland, MD, Aug. 20.

Stigler, George J. (80), economist; won the Nobel Prize in 1982. He was professor emeritus at the University of Chicago and wrote the classic study, *The Theory of Price*: d. Chicago, IL, Dec. 1.

Strugatsky, Arkady Natanovich (66), Soviet science-fiction writer, in collaboration with his brother Boris; their work blended adventure with criticism of the Soviet state and includes the novel *Prisoners of Power* (1977): d. Oct. 14.

Tamayo, Rufino (91), Mexican artist, one of the leaders of the Mexican Renaissance; best known for his painting, which drew from his Indian origins and Mexican folk art, he was also a printmaker and a sculptor. In the 20 years prior to his death he became a national celebrity, and two Mexican museums are named for him: d. Mexico City, Mexico, June 24.

Thomas, Danny (born Muzyad Yakhoob) (79), comedian and film and television actor; probably best known for his role as a nightclub entertainer in the television series *Make Room for Daddy* (later known as *The Danny Thomas Show*) (1953–64). As a nightclub entertainer he found his comedic voice through his storytelling ability rather than the delivery of one-liners. Earlier he was a radio performer, and he also appeared in several films, including *The Jazz Singer* (1953). He was a successful television producer and a founder and benefactor of the St. Jude Children's Research Hospital in Memphis, TN. He considered his hospital work his most important accomplishment: d. Los Angeles, CA, Feb. 6.

Tierney, Gene (70), movie actress of the 1940s; noted particularly for her performance in the title role of *Laura* (1944). Other films included *Leave Her to Heaven* (1945), for which she was nominated for an Academy Award; *Dragonwyck* (1946); *The Ghost and Mrs. Muir* (1947); and *The Left Hand of God* (1955): d. Houston, TX, Nov. 6.

Tinguely, Jean (66), Swiss sculptor, noted for his kinetic works made up of discarded wheels, bathroom fixtures, electronic parts, and other scraps. Some of his works are designed to self-destruct: d. Bern, Switzerland, Aug. 30.

Toomey, Regis (93), movie character actor; appeared in more than 200 films, including *The Big Sleep* (1946), *Guys and Dolls* (1955), and *You're in the Army Now* (1941): d. Los Angeles, CA, Oct. 12.

Towe, Harry L. (92), U.S. representative (R-NJ, 1943–51): d. Lakewood, NJ, Feb. 8.

Tower, John G. (65), U.S. senator (R-TX, 1961–85); served as chairman of the Armed Services Committee and was a leading advocate of modernizing and expanding the military. He was nominated by George Bush to be secretary of defense in 1989 but was rejected by the Senate: d. near Brunswick, GA, April 5.

Towns, Forrest G. (Spec) (77), champion hurdler of the 1930s; won a gold medal in the 1936 Olympic Games. Later he spent 34 years coaching championship track teams at the University of Georgia: d. Athens, GA, April 9.

Tree, Marietta Peabody (74), socialite active in Democratic Party politics; served at the U.S. Mission to the United Nations (1961–67): d. New York City, Aug. 15.

Tryon, Thomas (65), film actor who later became a writer. He appeared in the movie *The Cardinal* (1963). Among his novels is *The Other* (1971; film 1972): d. Los Angeles, CA, Sept. 4.

Tsedenbal, Yumjaagiyn (74), head of Mongolia's government and a Stalinist leader; prime minister of Mongolia in 1952, he combined that post with the post of Communist Party leader in 1958. In 1973 he also became head of state. He was overthrown in 1984: d. Moscow, April 20.

Ungo, Guillermo (59), political leader of the democratic left in El Salvador; in 1979 and 1980 he served on a junta that governed El Salvador. He was an unsuccessful political candidate in 1989: d. Mexico City, Mexico, Feb. 28.

Vercors (born Jean Bruller) (89), French author and publisher; wrote *The Silence of the Sea* (1942), which by 1948 had sold 1 million copies in 17 languages. After World War II he sold his publishing house but continued to write essays and fiction: d. Paris, June 10.

Voelker, John D. (87), former Michigan Supreme Court justice who under the pseudonym Robert Traver wrote the best-selling *Anatomy of a Murder* (1958; film, 1959) and other books: d. near Marquette, MI, March 10.

Wade, Leigh (93), U.S. Air Force major general and pioneer aviator who in 1924 participated in the first round-the-world flight. He saw duty during World War II and retired in 1955: d. Fort Belvoir, VA, Aug. 31.

Wagner, Robert F. (80), mayor of New York City (1954–65); a Democrat, he was first a protégé of Tammany Hall, New York's Democratic party machine, but eventually he broke with the organization and defeated it. Later he served as ambassador to Spain and envoy to the Vatican: d. New York City, Feb. 12.

Walters, Bucky (82), baseball pitcher for the Cincinnati Reds. In the years 1939, 1940, and 1944 he won 20 or more games each year, and in 1939 he was the National League's most valuable player: d. Abington, PA, April 20.

Watson, Phil (78), player for the National Hockey League New York Rangers between 1935 and 1948, except for a year with the Montreal Canadiens (1943-44). He later coached the Rangers (1955–59): d. Vancouver, Canada, Feb. 1.

Weist, Dwight (81), radio actor and announcer; known as "the man of 1,000 voices" for impersonations on the *March of Time* in the 1930s and 1940s: d. Block Island, RI, July 16.

Welensky, Sir Roy (81), prime minister of the Central African Federation that consisted of the British colonies of Southern Rhodesia, Northern Rhodesia, and Nyasaland (1956–63): d. near Blandford Forum, England, Dec. 5.

West, Dottie (58), country-music singer; probably best known for the song *Country Sunshine* and for her duets with Kenny Rogers: d. Nashville, TN, Sept. 4.

Wilson, Allan C. (56), New Zealand-born biochemist; involved in research relating to a genetic approach to the study of evolution that led to the theory that all humans descended from a single woman who lived in Africa some 200,000 years ago. He was a faculty member at the University of California at Berkeley (1964–91): d. Seattle, WA, July 21.

Wilson, Sir Angus (77), South African-born British writer; satirized the British middle class. He wrote some 50 books including *Hemlock and After, No Laughing Matter,* and *The Naughty Nineties* as well as biographies of Charles Dickens and Rudyard Kipling: d. Bury St. Edmunds, England, May 31.

Wolfson, Sir Isaac (93), British philanthropist; built a fortune as chairman of the retail firm Great Universal Stores (1946–86): d. Rehovot, Israel, June 20.

Zwicker, Ralph W. (88), U.S. Army major general; a highly decorated veteran of World War II, he was a central figure in the Senate censure of Sen. Joseph McCarthy in 1954. He retired in 1960: d. Fort Belvoir, VA, Aug. 9.

OCEANOGRAPHY

Awareness of change in delicately balanced climate systems has stimulated increased examination of the role of the ocean in control of world climate. The normal descent of cold surface water in the Greenland Sea, which helps pump the deep ocean circulation worldwide, reportedly slowed by about 80% during the 1980s. Since deep-water formation helps in the heat-exchange process between the deep ocean and the atmosphere, the observed changes indicate that even relatively small changes in ocean-surface conditions can cause great adjustments to the overall circulation. While the cause of the slowing descent of Greenland Sea water is unknown, reduced surface salinities may have been involved.

WOCE and JGOFS. U.S. and German scientists conducted a Deep Basin Experiment in the South Atlantic as part of the World Ocean Circulation Experiment (WOCE). In addition to the deployment of moored instruments for current measurement, hydrographic and bathymetric data were obtained. Recovery of the moored array was planned for late 1992 or early 1993. The measurements obtained will help determine the transports in the Brazil current and the deep western boundary currents, including the inflow of bottom water. Additional WOCE surveys planned for 1991 and 1992 involved the United States, Great Britain, Canada, France, and the USSR. The area of the North Atlantic between the Azores and Madeira would be studied for air/sea interactions and the sinking of near-surface layers to intermediate depths. A satellite launched by the European Space Agency would provide precise measurements to determine the absolute elevation of the ocean surface.

Scientists from the United States, Britain, the Netherlands, Germany, and Canada, using one aircraft and six ships, measured the development, spread, and decline of the phytoplankton bloom in the North Atlantic in 1989 for the Joint Global Ocean Flux Study (JGOFS). Changes in carbon-dioxide levels were correlated with chlorophyll content and seawater temperatures over the duration of the bloom period. The biological uptake of carbon dioxide at the sea surface is potentially important to climate regulation, but questions remain about winter conditions and the annual variability.

A 1992 JGOFS field study undertaken by the United States would aim to correlate the biological production with physical circulation such as the upwelling along the equator in the eastern Pacific Ocean. Preliminary computer analysis of this dynamic system has produced working models in three dimensions that include recycling of materials from inorganic nutrients through organic components of the food chain and demonstrate the physical forcing of observed variables in the upwelling area. Use of the computer model should help the researcher at sea interpret observations and clarify the relationship of physical, chemical, and biological cycles.

JGOFS and WOCE plan to collaborate on a survey of the bio-optical properties of the ocean through measurements of underwater irradiance and plant pigments during the WOCE hydrographic program. A remote ocean color satellite sensor, scheduled for 1993 launch, will expand the coverage from which oceanic primary productivity can be evaluated as a factor in the organic flux of carbon and the exchanges with the atmosphere and the ocean depths.

Global Warming. The theory that sound propagation in the ocean could reveal data on ocean-temperature change and hence indicate possible global warming was tested by a detonation of a low-frequency acoustical signal of about 200 decibels from a ship off Heard Island in the southern Indian Ocean. A sound signal was received on both the east and west coasts of the United States, as well as at several other stations up to 11,000 mi (18 000 km) away from the source. Temperature is the largest factor affecting sound spread over long ocean distances and hence the signal should travel measurably faster each year if global warming predictions are correct.

Much concern was expressed, however, that the sound waves could be damaging to marine mammals, possibly affecting their fertility, feeding behavior, and growth rates. Although much remains uncertain about the impact of this Heard Island Feasibility Test (HIFT) on marine life, lower sound levels would be used in future tests. It was shown that sound can be transmitted less frequently and at greater depth (with less effect on whales and seals) and still give good results.

Marine Species. A new species of whale was discovered and described in the Pacific Ocean off Peru. The new species of beaked whale has an elongated jaw, few teeth, and apparently feeds on squid; an adult male is about 12 ft (3.6 m) long. In the summer of 1991 numerous dolphins were washed ashore on the beaches of southern Italy, apparently victims of a virus that affected seals in the North Sea in 1989, then spread to dolphins off the coast of Spain and into the Mediterranean. Concern was expressed for the monk seal in the Ionian Sea near Greece, whose population already was down to an estimated 200.

Barrier Reef. Review of sediment samples from the Great Barrier Reef near Australia suggests an age for the reef's formation of less than 1 million years, rather than some 20 million years as previously thought. This reef has seen 24 global sea-level changes during its history, however, as recorded by the fossil evidence within the coral structure.

DAVID A. MCGILL
U.S. Coast Guard Academy

OHIO

Efforts to finance education and other state services without resorting to major statewide tax increases made news in Ohio in 1991, as did the mixed response of the legislature to Gov. George V. Voinovich's new legislative program.

Legislation. For the first time in ten years the General Assembly failed to pass a spending plan by the end of the fiscal year on June 30. Finally approved on July 12, the biennial budget called for $27.1 billion in outlays, an increase of 12%—about $250 million more than the governor had requested. Additional revenue from the extension of the sales tax to certain business services and contracts was earmarked for increased funding for higher education and environmental protection. However, certain welfare benefits were reduced.

The General Assembly, divided between a Democratic House and Republican Senate, rejected Republican Voinovich's request for more direct gubernatorial control over the state board of education and for greater regulation of private nursing homes, and only partially approved his plan for privatization of state liquor stores. The legislature also failed to act on measures involving recycling, campaign finance reform, and controls on rising medical costs. The lawmakers did act to maintain the Ohio Turnpike as a toll road, reversing a previous commitment to end tolls in 1991 upon final retirement of the original revenue bonds.

Governor Voinovich, an opponent of abortion, signed into law a bill requiring "informed consent" and a 24-hour waiting period before an abortion can be performed in Ohio. A new law authorizing living wills also went into effect. It enables people to declare against receiving life-sustaining treatment in cases of terminal illness or a permanently comatose state.

Education. More than 250 local school districts asked voters to approve property-tax increases for education, the largest number in 21 years. Approximately 50% of these issues passed. The state released almost $60 million in emergency loans to financially strapped school districts, with the largest single amount going to Cincinnati. Several courts heard cases challenging the present method of school financing that leads to inequities between rich and poor districts, but the issue remained unresolved. High-school students began taking a series of standardized statewide tests that will have to be passed in order to graduate in future years. Ohio's public-school students have scored slightly above the national average in recent achievement tests, but the state's high-school graduates were attending college at a rate 13% below the national average.

Economy. Dayton-based NCR Corp., a major international computer manufacturer, was acquired by AT&T on September 25 for $7.4 billion. Ohio's unemployment remained near the national average throughout the year as the recession slowed the manufacturing and service sectors. An unusually hot, dry summer in most of the state hurt farmers, and 80 of the state's 88 counties were declared agricultural disaster areas, making farmers eligible for federal assistance. Ohio's per-capita personal income ranked 23d among the states, down from 17th place 20 years earlier.

Other. Financier and former U.S. ambassador to Switzerland Marvin Warner began serving a three-and-one-half-year prison term on convictions growing out of the 1985 collapse of the former Home State Savings Bank. Warner also was ordered to pay $22 million in restitution to the state.

Three people were killed June 9 in two separate accidents at Kings Island amusement park near Cincinnati. One involved a fall from a high-level ride and the other an electrocution from a faulty aerator pump in a fountain.

JOHN B. WEAVER
Sinclair Community College

OHIO • Information Highlights

Area: 41,330 sq mi (107 044 km²).
Population (1990 census): 10,847,115.
Chief Cities (1990 census): Columbus, the capital, 632,910; Cleveland, 505,616; Cincinnati, 364,040; Toledo, 332,943; Akron, 223,019; Dayton, 182,044.
Government (1991): *Chief Officers*—governor, George V. Voinovich (R); lt. gov., Paul R. Leonard (D). *General Assembly*—Senate, 33 members; House of Representatives, 99 members.
State Finances (fiscal year 1990): *Revenue,* $28,516,000,000; *expenditure,* $25,237,000,000.
Personal Income (1990): $190,720,000,000; per capita, $17,564.
Labor Force (June 1991): *Civilian labor force,* 5,508,000; *unemployed,* 355,700 (6.5% of total force).
Education: *Enrollment* (fall 1989)—public elementary schools, 1,242,327; public secondary, 524,832; colleges and universities, 550,729. *Public school expenditures* (1989), $7,425,194,000.

OKLAHOMA

The educational-reform measure that was enacted in 1990 and controversies surrounding Democratic Gov. David Walters during his first year in office dominated Oklahoma news in 1991. The state's economy continued to be sluggish, as the national recession further dimmed prospects for a strong upturn.

Education and the Legislature. In 1990 the legislature passed amid much controversy a measure widely known as House Bill 1017 that mandated education reforms and increased taxes by about $220 million. To meet goals mandated by 1017, the 1991 legislature increased common education spending. The minimum teacher salary rose $3,000, and early-education programs were enhanced as were

Office of the Attorney General of Oklahoma

Oklahoma Gov. David Walters appointed Susan B. Loving, above, to take over as the state's attorney general in 1991. Women held several key government posts in the state.

measures to reduce class size gradually and strengthen the curriculum. Spending for higher education increased by $52.3 million or 10.3%. The legislature approved tuition increases that ran from 5% at the two-year colleges to 9% at the comprehensive universities. The School of Science and Mathematics for the state's top high-school seniors won an increase of $1.5 million. Spending for vocational-technology training increased by more than 9%.

Despite the legislative action, sentiment against 1017 continued during 1991 and opponents, upset about the tax increases, worked for its repeal. On October 15 voters rejected such a repeal by a narrow but adequate margin of 54%. Supporters of 1017 in Oklahoma and beyond hailed the vote as a major test of the willingness of the public to endorse education spending even in a weak economy.

In other actions the legislature increased funding for the elderly, for mental health, and for a public-defender system. Reapportionment passed and effectively protected incumbents at the state and federal levels. The redistricting plan also favored rural interests.

Other Government News. At the annual meeting of the National Conference of State Legislatures held in Florida in August, a survey revealed that Oklahoma ranked second nationally in the fiscal health of its state government as measured by the general-fund surplus in 1991 over that of 1990. The 10.3% increase in higher-education funding far exceeded the national average of 2.2%.

Susan Loving became Oklahoma's attorney general when Governor Walters appointed her to replace the incumbent, who resigned to become a law-school dean. Among top elective executive positions, women also held the positions of treasurer and state school superintendent.

Governor Walters became embroiled in controversies that gained attention far beyond the state and even led to talk of his resignation. Among the reports were those indicating that Walters had angered legislators by continued attacks on politicians long after the political campaign had ended. There also were allegations that he had promised state jobs in return for campaign contributions. A disgruntled former supporter, whom Walters had hired and then fired as state tourism director, aired charges of job selling.

The Federal Bureau of Investigation (FBI) was said to be checking possible violations of the law, and rumors appeared suggesting Walters would resign as part of a deal with the federal government. An August *USA Today* poll of 18 new governors by five political analysts showed that Walters ranked low. Another poll of voters in 12 Southern states ranked Walters at the bottom. Walters remained in office but the unfavorable publicity dimmed the luster of the state's efforts at education reform.

HARRY HOLLOWAY
University of Oklahoma (emeritus)

OKLAHOMA • Information Highlights

Area: 69,956 sq mi (181 186 km^2).
Population (1990 census): 3,145,585.
Chief Cities (1990 census): Oklahoma City, the capital, 444,719; Tulsa, 376,302; Lawton, 80,561.
Government (1991): *Chief Officers*—governor, David Walters (D); lt. gov., Jack Mildren (D). *Legislature*—Senate, 48 members; House of Representatives, 101 members.
State Finances (fiscal year 1990): *Revenue*, $7,201,000,000; *expenditure*, $6,515,000,000.
Personal Income (1990): $48,620,000,000; per capita, $15,457.
Labor Force (June 1991): *Civilian labor force*, 1,538,500; *unemployed*, 101,300 (6.6% of total force).
Education: *Enrollment* (fall 1989)—public elementary schools, 420,940; public secondary, 157,640; colleges and universities, 175,855. *Public school expenditures* (1989), $1,833,743,000.

ONTARIO

Ontario, Canada's most populous province, was battered by recession during 1991. This severely curtailed the opportunity for Premier Bob Rae's New Democratic Party (NDP) government to implement any of its political platform during its first full year in office.

Budget. Despite hopes for a balanced budget, Provincial Treasurer Floyd Laughren

© "Toronto Sun"/Canapress

With Canada introducing a goods and services tax and with the Canada dollar enjoying a good exchange rate against the U.S. dollar during 1991, many Ontarians were crossing the border into the United States to do their shopping.

chose to run a deficit of C$9.7 billion in his April budget to stimulate the faltering economy. Expenditures of C$52.8 billion were proposed, with revenues of C$43.03 billion. Of the expenditures, 32% was for health, 18% for education, 17% for social services, and 10% for debt service. Gasoline taxes were raised immediately by 1.7 cents per liter with a further 1.7 cents to be added in 1992. Taxes on diesel and aviation fuel also were raised, along with beer, liquor, and cigarette taxes. The capital tax on insurance companies, banks, and trust companies was increased from .8% to 1.0%.

In October spending cuts of C$600 million were announced to prevent the deficit from increasing as a result of greater expenditures for welfare and pensions. Salaries for legislature members and senior civil-service workers were frozen and civil-service wages were to be held down. Many programs were postponed until 1992 and C$219 million was cut from current grants—including C$75 million from hospital construction and C$13 million from base grants to colleges and universities. One factor putting pressure on the provincial treasury was the civil-service-wage bill, which grew by 14.5%. The increase was due to employment-equity provisions introduced into the public service in 1991 and to the hiring of new public servants by the attorney general's department to handle large backlogs in the courts and in the ministry of community and social services to deal with expanding welfare caseloads.

Business circles, already suspicious of a New Democratic government, were highly critical of the deficit budget and of the subsequent

ONTARIO • Information Highlights

Area: 412,580 sq mi (1 068 580 km²).
Population (September 1991): 9,919,400.
Chief Cities (1986 census): Toronto, the provincial capital, 612,289; Ottawa, the federal capital, 300,763; Scarborough, 484,676; Mississauga, 374,005; Hamilton, 306,728; London, 269,140.
Government (1991): *Chief Officers*—lt. gov., Hal Jackman; premier, Robert Keith Rae (New Democrat). *Legislature*—Legislative Assembly, 130 members.
Provincial Finances (1991–92 fiscal year budget): *Revenues,* $43,030,000,000; *expenditures,* $52,800,000,000.
Personal Income (average weekly earnings, July 1991): $569.51.
Labor Force (September 1991, seasonally adjusted): *Employed* workers, 15 years of age and over, 4,783,000; *Unemployed,* 9.2%.
Education (1991–92): *Enrollment*—elementary and secondary schools, 2,059,200 pupils; postsecondary—universities, 223,500; community colleges, 102,200.
(All monetary figures are in Canadian dollars.)

downgrading of the province's credit rating to AA status by Moody's Investors' Services.

Government and Legislation. While coping with the recession, the inexperienced NDP government suffered a series of embarrassing ministerial changes during the year. The problems began in March with the dismissal of Consumer Affairs Minister Peter Kormos, who appeared as a clothed "Sunshine Boy" pin-up in the Toronto *Sun* the day after he drafted new guidelines to eliminate sexism in beer advertising. Women's-rights advocates were especially upset. Further resignations followed during the summer. Premier Rae shuffled his cabinet in the fall in an effort to improve its image. Murray Elston became interim Liberal Party leader upon the resignation of former Treasurer Robert Nixon.

In legislative matters, little was done to curtail Sunday shopping, despite promises to introduce "a common pause day" in view of evidence that local options were favored and that more shoppers would be driven across the border on Sundays to shop in the United States. Because of the estimated cost, the government abandoned a major plank in its election platform for provincially run automobile insurance.

Business. Plans to keep de Havilland Aircraft, a major manufacturer of turboprop commuter aircraft, active in Ontario were set back in October when a proposal to buy it from Boeing Aircraft by a consortium consisting of Aerospatiale S.A. of France, Alenia S.p.A. of Italy, and the Ontario government was vetoed by the European Commission. De Havilland, with a work force of 4,300 (down from 6,200 in 1988) and the largest industrial employer in Toronto, later announced further cuts in its work force.

Ontario Hydro's nuclear-generation program brought it under increasing fire from both environmentalists opposed to nuclear power and consumers faced with price increases in excess of the cost of living due to the construction and maintenance costs of the generating stations. Some were urging that it be privatized.

PETER J. KING, *Carleton University*

OREGON

Oregon appeared to have escaped the effects of the recession that gripped much of the nation during 1991. Paul Werner, the state's economist, predicted economic acceleration for late 1991 and early 1992 despite job losses and lower revenues for many businesses. Although the timber industry faltered, population growth, almost double the national average, continued to buoy the economy. Unemployment reached 6% in August, but remained below the national average.

Business and the Environment. The spotted-owl issue continued to occupy both environmental interests and the timber and lumber industries, following the northern spotted owl's endangered-species designation in 1990. Congress had authorized the sale of 3.2 billion board feet of timber during fiscal 1991, but a federal-court injunction blocked the sale of about two thirds of the authorized cut. Judge William Dwyer removed 66,000 acres (26 709 ha) of northwest national forestlands from harvest, stating that there was a risk the owl population could not recover should that acreage be cut. The Forest Service was ordered to present a plan for the protection of the owl by March 1992.

Governmental Affairs. Laws passed by the legislature in 1991 made it illegal for minors to smoke cigarettes and extended jobless benefits for timber workers. A fee charged to petroleum distributors was to be used to finance loans to help service stations repair or replace leaky underground tanks as now required by federal law. The state lawmakers failed to pass reapportionment bills drawing new state house and senate districts as well as new congressional districts. Secretary of State Phil Keisling drew new state district boundaries, and the task of redrawing congressional districts fell to the federal courts.

Proposition 5, the property-tax limitation initiative passed in November 1990, prompted Gov. Barbara Roberts to ask all state agencies to prepare to cut budgets by as much as 25%. State workers were concerned that deep cuts would necessitate layoffs as the state agencies would have to share general-fund monies—derived from income taxes—with school districts, formerly financed by property taxes. Higher-education institutions raised tuition by 6.7% in addition to imposing an annual $500 surcharge per student. In spite of Proposition 5, many Oregon homeowners found their property taxes higher for 1991 because of increased

OREGON • Information Highlights

Area: 97,073 sq mi (251 419 km^2).
Population (1990 census): 2,842,321.
Chief Cities (1990 census): Salem, the capital, 107,786; Portland, 437,319; Eugene, 112,669.
Government (1991): *Chief Officers*—governor, Barbara Roberts (D); secretary of state, Phil Keisling (D); *Legislative Assembly*—Senate, 30 members; House of Representatives, 60 members.
State Finances (fiscal year 1990): *Revenue*, $7,001,000,000; *expenditure*, $6,352,000,000.
Personal Income (1990): $49,198,000,000; per capita, $17,196.
Labor Force (June 1991): *Civilian labor force*, 1,559,400; *unemployed*, 93,200 (6.0% of total force).
Education: *Enrollment* (fall 1989)—public elementary schools, 340,264; public secondary, 132,130; colleges and universities, 161,822. *Public school expenditures* (1989), $2,123,241,000.

property values. Governor Roberts planned to call the legislature into special session in early 1992 to enact a replacement-tax measure, which then would be referred to the voters in the summer of 1992.

Republican U.S. Sen. Bob Packwood announced that he would run for reelection, and Harry Lonsdale, narrowly defeated in 1990 by U.S. Sen. Mark Hatfield, planned to run against 1st District Congressman Les AuCoin in the Democratic primary for the Packwood seat. State Treasurer Tony Meeker, an unsuccessful challenger to AuCoin in the past, announced his intention to run for AuCoin's House seat.

Other News. In the state's most celebrated and most expensive murder trial, Frank Gable, habitual petty criminal, was convicted in the 1989 killing of Corrections Chief Michael Francke. . . . A part of the new $42 million Snake River Corrections Facility in Ontario was opened in July.

L. CARL and JOANN C. BRANDHORST
Western Oregon State College

OTTAWA

Ottawa, Canada's capital, seemed preoccupied during 1991 with its potential and existing sports teams. Mayoral and council elections also attracted interest.

Sports. In December 1990 a group of businessmen led by Mayor Jim Durrell had been successful in winning a National Hockey League (NHL) franchise for the city. The franchise was conditional on the new team, the Senators, having a major-league arena ready by 1994–95. In August 1991 the Ontario municipal board approved a proposed C$125 million arena-hotel-office in the suburb of Kanata, but reduced its projected size. It was hoped that the Senators would take to the ice in 1992–93, initially at the Ottawa Civic Centre.

Durrell accepted a senior executive post with the new NHL team, resigning the mayoralty when controversy cropped up over a possible conflict of interest. Ottawa's city council elected alderman Marc Laviolette to serve the nine months remaining in Durrell's term.

Three years of effort to bring Triple A baseball to the city paid off in September with the award of a franchise. Ottawa's role in financing a suitable stadium for the team had been highly contentious. After much debate, the city council agreed to contribute C$8 million toward the construction. Lobbying induced the provincial government to put up C$2 million.

The city's professional football team, the Ottawa Rough Riders of the Canadian Football League, attracted greater public interest in 1991. In midseason the team was taken over by the league after disagreements among the owners caused them to break up.

Elections. The post of regional-council chairman, being filled by direct election for the first time, attracted a wide field of candidates after incumbent Andrew Hayden declined to run. A 60% increase in development charges on new housing and property projects by the council provoked considerable opposition among builders and was opposed by many candidates running for the post.

In close races in November, Jacquelin Holzman was elected mayor of Ottawa and Peter Clark won as regional-council chairman. The new city council, with ten new members, seemed to favor restraint in city spending.

Other Events. Attempting to stay in the vanguard of the antismoking movement, the Ottawa city council passed a bylaw to ban smoking in shopping malls (except in food courts). It already was banned in stores and workplaces.

In September and early October the city was disrupted by a strike of federal civil servants. Picketing and demonstrations were widespread and occasionally violent, and many nonstriking government employees were prevented from going to work.

PETER J. KING
Carleton University

PAKISTAN

Nawaz Sharif, during his first year as Pakistan's prime minister, encountered some of the same political challenges that had befallen his predecessors, but he also managed to initiate some major economic and political reforms.

Political Developments. Nawaz Sharif's ruling alliance, the Islami Jamhoori Ittehad (IJI or, in English, the Islamic Democratic Alliance, IDA), in early 1991 extended the dominant position it had established in national and provincial elections the previous October. In by-elections on January 10, the IJI won 19 of 25 national and provincial assembly seats. On March 14, the IJI won 23 of 42 seats in elections to the Senate. Nawaz' political position also was strengthened by the departure of carryover cabinet members more loyal to President Ghulam Ishaq Khan, including veteran Foreign Minister Sahabzada Yaqub Khan.

In other respects, however, the prime minister continued to maneuver within an area circumscribed by the president, the military, competing forces within the IJI alliance, and the political opposition. Rumors arose of possible presidential or military intervention—such as President Ghulam Ishaq Khan's abrupt dismissal of Benazir Bhutto in August 1990—but no such disruption of representative government materialized.

Nawaz Sharif's support of the U.S.-led forces in the Persian Gulf war caused widespread public protests, but the rapid allied victory vindicated his position. Of more lasting damage was the persistent lawlessness in Sind province and the apparent spread of violence to other parts of the country. Urban violence in Sind generally had subsided since the 1990 elections, but attacks on journalists in Karachi shocked the country. In addition, at least seven foreigners were kidnapped in 1991, and there were outbreaks of violence in the North-West Frontier province and the Punjab region, all of which helped undermine confidence in the government's ability to maintain order.

Despite these and other political difficulties, Nawaz was able to demonstrate some major policy accomplishments in his first year. The most impressive was an agreement on the sharing of Indus River water among Pakistan's four provinces. Bringing an end to a dispute which had lasted at least 70 years, the agreement was expected to open at least 50 million acres (20 million ha) of land to agricultural production. The Nawaz Sharif government also succeeded in passing a watered-down version of the so-called Shariah Bill, legislation originally intended to make Islamic law the basic law.

© Nickelsberg/Gamma-Liaison

Pakistan Prime Minister Nawaz Sharif instituted a series of political and economic reforms, including legislation making Islam the nation's basic law, in his first year in office.

Economic Issues. Drawing upon his experience as a successful industrialist, Nawaz Sharif took several steps to liberalize, denationalize, and decentralize Pakistan's economy. In January he appointed a privatization commission, which subsequently targeted 160 state-run companies for public sale. In February he announced a set of wide-ranging economic reforms, including cuts in import duties and taxes, elimination of import licenses on many items, removal of restrictions on foreign investment, and loosening of foreign-exchange regulations. The declared objective of the reforms was to stimulate development of Pakistan's economy to the ranks of South Korea and other Asian "miracles." Although implementation of privatization encountered some snags, the government claimed by the end of the year that the reforms were having positive impact, including increases in exports and foreign investment.

PAKISTAN • Information Highlights

Official Name: Islamic Republic of Pakistan.
Location: South Asia.
Area: 310,402 sq mi (803 940 km²).
Population (mid-1991 est.): 117,500,000.
Chief Cities (1981 census): Islamabad, the capital, 204,364; Karachi, 5,180,562.
Government: *Head of state,* Ghulam Ishaq Khan, president (elected Dec. 12, 1988). *Head of government,* Nawaz Sharif, prime minister (took office Nov. 6, 1990). *Legislature*—Parliament: Senate and National Assembly.
Monetary Unit: Rupee (24.55 rupees equal U.S.$1, Nov. 19, 1991).
Gross National Product (1989 fiscal year U.S.$): $43,200,000,000.
Economic Index (1990): *Consumer Prices* (1982 = 100), all items, 165.3; food, 169.6.
Foreign Trade (1990 U.S.$): *Imports,* $7,356,000,000; *exports,* $5,522,000,000.

In April the National Finance Commission announced a new formula for the distribution of tax revenues, giving the provinces a greater share vis-à-vis the central government. One anticipated consequence would be an expansion of oil and gas exploration, particularly in Baluchistan, where large reserves were thought to exist. Pakistan planned to double its oil-refining capacity by 1996.

The annual budget, presented May 30, further incorporated the government's liberalization strategies, including tax reductions and other incentives, for private-sector investment. The tax incentives, combined with the new revenue-sharing formula, were expected to result in a wider national-budget deficit.

Pakistan's economic performance clearly would need to improve if it was to meet its severe economic challenges. Its economy grew at about 5% annually during 1989–91, down from 6.5% during the 1980s, but the population growth rate remained exceptionally high at more than 3%. Meanwhile, double-digit inflation (about 13%) and growing unemployment were concerns.

Foreign Affairs. Despite public protests, the Nawaz Sharif government supported the United States and Saudi Arabia in the Persian Gulf war with the dispatch of some 8,000 troops. Nawaz made a prewar tour of several Middle Eastern capitals urging a plan for negotiated settlement, but with little success. One result of the war was better relations with Iran, including prospective improvement of road, rail, and oil-pipeline links.

Pakistan and the United States remained deadlocked over the nuclear-proliferation issue. Aid was cut off in October 1990 in accordance with U.S. nonproliferation policies, although funds already committed to Pakistan might continue for as long as three years.

Tension with India over Kashmir continued throughout the year, though the two countries did sign agreements on other issues, including finalization of earlier pledges not to attack one another's nuclear facilities.

WILLIAM L. RICHTER
Kansas State University

PARAGUAY

The democratization process in Paraguay continued in 1991 as the first-ever municipal elections were held on May 26. The economy performed below levels of the previous year. And the country entered a regional common market.

Government and Politics. Independent Carlos Filizzola, 31, beat the ruling Colorado Party candidate in the mayoral race for Asunción, but the government won in most of the 206 municipalities. Accepting his party's loss of the most important municipal post, President Andrés Rodríguez was consoled by the Colorados winning 70% of districts nationwide in a fair, multiparty contest. Elections were held in December for a constituent assembly.

Economy. At midyear the cost of living had risen 6.1% and unemployment had surpassed 13%. Economic growth was forecast at 2.5% to 3%. In order to reach agreement on an International Monetary Fund (IMF) adjustment program, preliminary to rescheduling foreign loans worth about $800 million, the government endeavored to reduce inflation to 15%. The government also planned to sell state enterprises to private interests.

The 18th and final turbine at Itaipú, the world's largest hydroelectric dam, was completed in March. The $20 billion binational installation was inaugurated on May 6 by President Fernando de Collor de Mello of Brazil and President Rodríguez. While Paraguay was required to sell its unused electricity to Brazil, Brazilian consumers were not paying for it and, by August, owed $110 million to Asunción.

A 143,000-acre (58 000-ha) parcel of subtropical forest in eastern Paraguay was purchased in May by the U.S. land-preservation organization Nature Conservancy in order to avoid its destruction. It was to be turned into a nature preserve operated by a Paraguayan group.

Foreign Relations. Jon Glassman, a former assistant to U.S. Vice-President Dan Quayle, became U.S. ambassador to Paraguay in August. As of March 1, Paraguay again became a beneficiary of the U.S. Generalized System of Preferences (GSP). (It had been suspended in 1986 because of Paraguay's human-rights record.) Paraguayans expected that restoration of GSP trade benefits would encourage substantial U.S. investment. Direct U.S. investment in Paraguay amounted to only $9 million in 1991.

PARAGUAY • Information Highlights

Official Name: Republic of Paraguay.
Location: Central South America.
Area: 157,046 sq mi (406 750 km²).
Population (mid-1991 est.): 4,400,000.
Chief City (1985 est.): Asunción, the capital, 477,100.
Government: *Head of state and government,* Gen. Andrés Rodríguez, president (took office 1989). *Legislature*—Congress: Senate and Chamber of Deputies.
Monetary Unit: Guaraní (1,316.0 guaraníes equal U.S.$1, selling rate, July 1991).
Gross Domestic Product (1989 est. U.S.$): $8,900,-000,000.
Foreign Trade (1989 U.S.$): *Imports,* $695,000,000; *exports,* $1,163,000,000.

Restoration of diplomatic relations with Nicaragua took place in February, ten years after their suspension because of the assassination in Asunción of Nicaragua's former President Anastasio Somoza. Diplomatic ties were established with the Soviet Union for the first time in July.

President Rodríguez participated in a summit of Latin American chief executives in Mexico in July. He stressed that greater participation in the world market required a commercial order that was more just and that regional integration would raise living standards in member countries.

The Asunción Treaty was signed on March 26, creating MERCOSUR, a common market composed of Argentina, Brazil, Paraguay, and Uruguay. Paraguay would have until 1995 to eliminate all tariffs on imports from its neighbors.

In June, Labor Minister Hugo Estigarribia admitted to the International Labor Organization in Geneva, Switzerland, that Paraguay's labor legislation remained inadequate, even with recent improvements.

LARRY L. PIPPIN
University of the Pacific

PENNSYLVANIA

National attention focused on Pennsylvania on Nov. 5, 1991, when a little-known Democrat, Harris Wofford, defeated Richard L. Thornburgh, a former U.S. attorney general and state governor, in a special election to fill the final three years of the term of Republican Sen. John Heinz, who was killed in an April plane crash. On May 8, Democratic Gov. Robert P. Casey had appointed Wofford, the state's secretary of labor and industry, to fill the seat until the special election. Although the 65-year-old Wofford, a special assistant on civil rights for President John F. Kennedy, had little name recognition, the Democratic State Committee in June nominated him to run in the fall election. In August the Republican State Committee chose Thornburgh, who then resigned from the cabinet. During the campaign one survey showed Thornburgh leading Wofford by 44 percentage points, but in the November election Wofford received 55% of the vote and became the first elected Democratic senator from Pennsylvania since the 1960s. While campaigning, Wofford said he would work to establish a national health-care system.

William H. Gray 3d, the third-ranking Democrat in the U.S. House, resigned September 11 to become president of the United Negro College Fund. In Pennsylvania's only district with a predominantly minority population, Lucien F. Blackwell defeated three opponents in the special November election to hold the Democratic seat.

Legislation. The major legislative challenge was addressing the $454 million state budget deficit. On August 4, 34 days into the new fiscal year and facing 100,000 state workers unpaid for a month, the legislature agreed upon a $13.9 billion budget with $2.85 billion in new taxes. The state's income tax rose from 2.1% to 3.1%, but was to drop to 2.8% after July 1, 1992. Redistricting, usually a difficult task, was completed for state legislative seats with minimal controversy in the summer. Redistricting for Pennsylvania's seats in the federal House was complicated by the loss of two seats (from 23 to 21) and was not completed until late in 1991.

Economy. Unemployment in Pennsylvania reached 6.8% by the late fall, about the national average. The relative prosperity of southeastern counties outside Philadelphia was balanced by the decline in many western industrial counties.

Philadelphia. On January 18 the state's largest city narrowly avoided bankruptcy by procuring a $150 million short-term loan from sources including local banks and pension funds for teachers and city employees. The $5 million fee for the loan raised the effective interest rate to 24%. On June 5 the state legislature agreed to provide funding to help Philadelphia overcome its financial crisis but also put a financial-oversight board in place. The law required Philadelphia to plan balanced budgets for five years and empowered the financial-oversight board to stop state funding if the plans were not approved and implemented.

These financial problems were debated at length during the mayoral campaign. The flamboyant former Democratic Mayor Frank L. Rizzo, who became a Republican, won the GOP nomination over district attorney Ron Castille in a close race. After Rizzo suffered a fatal heart attack on July 16, the Republican City Committee chose Joseph M. Egan, Jr., former deputy city commerce director. Although the city has a black majority, the Democrats chose former district attorney Edward F. Rendell, a white candidate, over black city councilmen Lucien Blackwell and George Burrell. In the November election, Rendell won with more than 68% of the vote.

In February three firefighters died in a high-rise office fire that gutted floors 22-29 of a 38-story building. There were no sprinklers on the bottom 28 floors as they were not required when the building was constructed.

ROBERT E. O'CONNOR
Pennsylvania State University

AP/Wide World

In a big win for the Democrats, Harris Wofford, above, *defeated Richard Thornburgh (R) to fill the unexpired term of Pennsylvania's late U.S. Sen. John Heinz (R).*

PENNSYLVANIA • Information Highlights

Area: 45,308 sq mi (117 348 km²).
Population (1990 census): 11,881,643.
Chief Cities (1990 census): Harrisburg, the capital, 52,376; Philadelphia, 1,585,577; Pittsburgh, 369,379; Erie, 108,718; Allentown, 105,090.
Government (1991): *Chief Officers*—governor, Robert P. Casey (D); lt. gov., Mark A. Singel (D). *Legislature*—Senate, 50 members; House of Representatives, 203 members.
State Finances (fiscal year 1990): *Revenue,* $27,223,000,000; *expenditure,* $24,531,000,000.
Personal Income (1990): $222,228,000,000; per capita, $18,686.
Labor Force (June 1991): *Civilian labor force,* 6,024,200; *unemployed,* 406,400 (6.7% of total force).
Education: *Enrollment* (fall 1989)—public elementary schools, 1,150,653; public secondary, 504,626; colleges and universities, 610,357. *Public school expenditures* (1989), $8,597,355,000.

PERU

In 1991 a cholera epidemic was added to Peru's trio of chronic problems—economic decline, the Shining Path insurgency, and the drug trade. As of the end of August, 246,246 cases of cholera had been reported, resulting in 2,416 deaths (*see* SIDEBAR/LATIN AMERICA). President Alberto Fujimori's draconian economic-adjustment program dramatically reduced the inflation rate, though at an extremely high social cost. New efforts to combat the insurgency, which became increasingly intertwined with the drug trade, met only with escalating violence.

Economic-Adjustment Program. The economic-adjustment measures of 1990 were continued and expanded after February, when Carlos Boloña Bohl replaced Juan Carlos Hurtado Miller as the minister of economy. By May, Boloña had eliminated nontariff trade barriers for consumer goods, abolished monopoly status for state enterprises, allowed interest rates to float, slashed import tariffs, liberalized banking and foreign investment rules, and ended subsidies on foodstuffs, fuels, and medicines. By October the nuevo sol had replaced the inti as the national currency.

While the stabilization program prolonged the recession, it appeared to have been successful in controlling inflation. The annual rate of inflation was not expected to exceed 100%, a vast improvement on the 1990 rate of 7,650%. Another success was achieved in September, when the International Monetary Fund (IMF) announced an $845 million plan to help return Peru to the world's financial circuits.

These two developments, however, were the only positive notes in a declining and desperate economy. Since President Fujimori took office in July 1990, real wages decreased by one half to three quarters, open unemployment was 8% with underemployment estimated at more than 80%, and that part of the population falling below the poverty line increased to more than 50%. At a time when social conditions were worsening, social expenditures decreased. The gross domestic product (GDP) shrank by 4.5% in 1990, the third contraction in three years, and growth in 1991 was expected to be zero, if not negative. Growth was held back by declining wages, the scarcity of funds for investment, a prolonged drought, and the cholera epidemic. Fear of contamination caused domestic demand for fish, shellfish, and vegetables to fall; weakened tourism; and led to an international boycott of Peruvian produce. Exports also were frustrated by an overvalued currency.

Politics. Fujimori found diminishing support in Congress and lost further support when Hurtado, who had been associated with the conservative Acción Popular, and two left-wing ministers quit his cabinet. But the president was not stymied completely since he tended to bypass the Congress, issuing almost 90% of all new laws by decree. The military also became more important as a base of support. But the government found itself powerless to stop long strikes by teachers, health workers, some doctors, and university workers.

PERU • Information Highlights

Official Name: Republic of Peru.
Location: West coast of South America.
Area: 496,224 sq mi (1 285 220 km²).
Population (mid-1991 est.): 22,000,000.
Chief Cities (mid-1988 est.): Lima, the capital, 6,053,900; Arequipa, 591,700; Callao (mid-1985 est.), 515,200.
Government: *Head of state,* Alberto Fujimori, president (took office July 28, 1990). *Head of government,* Alfonso de los Heros, prime minister (took office November, 1991). *Legislature*—Congress: Senate and Chamber of Deputies.
Monetary Unit: new sol (.93 new sols equal U.S.$1, official rate, Oct. 24, 1991).
Gross Domestic Product (1989 est. U.S.$): $18,900,000,000.
Economic Index (Lima, 1990): *Consumer Prices* (1989 = 100), all items, 7,581.7.
Foreign Trade (1990 U.S.$): *Imports,* $2,455,000,000; *exports,* $3,274,000,000.

Guerrillas and Drugs. The war against the Shining Path appeared to be winding down in the first half of the year, but with a surge of 540 political deaths in June alone, the average for the year rose to 300 political deaths monthly, nearly twice the level of violence as under the previous government. Political violence left 37% of Peru under state-of-emergency rules, and forced the government to cancel local elections in 101 out of 371 districts. The official response was to arm the *rondas campesinas,* peasant self-defense groups that have been fighting guerrillas successfully.

New violence broke out in early November as the Shining Path increased its attacks on the militias. Dozens of Peruvians were killed in the unrest. In its midst, Carlos Torres y Torres resigned as premier. He was succeeded by Labor Minister Alfonso de los Heros, who reshuffled the cabinet.

The Shining Path's involvement in the drug trade complicated the antiguerrilla campaign. After having rejected U.S. military assistance in 1990, Fujimori bowed to pressure from the Bush administration and accepted $34.9 million in military aid and $60 million in economic aid, even though only $6.4 million of the aid package was slated for encouraging coca growers to cultivate alternative crops. The aid package was held up for five months by the U.S. Congress because of the Peruvian security forces' poor human-rights record.

Corruption was also an issue in 1991 with charges that officials in the previous government had diverted $270 million of reserves to the Bank of Credit and Commerce International.

MICHAEL COPPEDGE
Johns Hopkins University

PHILIPPINES

Negotiations regarding extending the Military Bases Agreement between the United States and the Philippines, first signed in 1947, and the eruption of the Mount Pinatubo volcano intertwined to dominate 1991 events in the Philippines. As the year ended, the nation was looking ahead to a 1992 presidential election.

The 1947 Military Bases Agreement, which established the U.S. Subic Bay Naval Base and the Clark Air Force Base in the Philippines, was expiring in mid-September 1991, and negotiations were under way early in the year regarding its renewal. Both bases had proven useful to the United States during the Korean and Vietnam wars and, more recently, during the 1991 Persian Gulf conflict. The Filipinos, however, were led by budgetary deficits to demand larger compensation from the United States for renewed leases for the bases. Passionate nationalism and concern for sovereignty also entered into the Philippines' position.

Mount Pinatubo. Although the Philippine American Cooperation Talks (PACT) regarding extending the lease on the two U.S. bases had ended without agreement in February and May, negotiations were continuing. Abruptly, however, national disaster intervened, having a major effect on the discussions. On June 12 the Mount Pinatubo volcano, about 55 mi (90 km) northwest of Manila, erupted spewing ash and rock throughout the region. Even after the eruption, mushroom clouds of gas and ash some 15 mi (24 km) high continued to form, and tropical storms during the regular typhoon season—July through October—caused giant mudflows to wash out bridges and bury small villages. By September more than 500 persons had been killed as a result of the volcano's eruption. Floodings and mud slides were caused by a clear-cutting of many mountain slopes.

Some 150,000 refugees from the volcano fled to Manila, where unemployment already had been approaching 30%. The city was clogged with squatters whose dreadful conditions became even more wretched from floods in July as sewers were blocked by volcanic ash that had fallen on and accumulated in the city. Many Manilans took to wearing surgical masks or head scarves in order to breathe.

The cataclysm caused by Mount Pinatubo had been unexpected. Although one of 22 officially active volcanoes in the Philippines, it had been quiet for 600 years. Equally unpredictable was its future behavior, according to the Philippines' Bureau of Volcanology, which considers that portion of Pampanga province indefinitely unstable. An even greater long-term concern about Mount Pinatubo's effects concerned the rehabilitation of overrun subsistence farms and agribusinesses. Although volcanic residue commonly is thought to be exceptionally fertile and constitutes most of the tillable soil in the entire Philippines, Mount

© Alberto Garcia/Saba

Several thousand supporters welcomed Imelda Marcos back to the Philippines on Nov. 4, 1991, following more than five years of exile in the United States. The former first lady of the Philippines faced criminal charges in her homeland.

Pinatubo's emissions included lahar, a gravelly substance resistant to growth. One congressman from the central island of Negros suggested using power tillers designed for deep plowing after the harvest of sugarcane. Such tillers have 3-ft (.9-m)-long spikes and blades which might be able to bury the sand and deep ash of Pampanga and the neighboring province of Zambales, thus restoring the topsoil. But relief efforts were directed mainly toward helping refugees survive, with no practical plan of action emerging for either recovery of the land or for employing those now landless. Some 500,000 persons lived within 25 mi (40 km) of Mount Pinatubo. Airborne volcanic material was expected to influence even global temperatures. (*See* SIDEBAR/GEOLOGY.)

U.S. Bases. Before the volcano's eruption, anticipation among Filipino negotiators regarding PACT had run high. Either the bases would be returned to the Philippine government or the Philippines would receive greater U.S. compensation for their continued use. If the bases were returned to the Philippines, they would be converted into an international airport with adjacent high-rise corporate centers or, in the case of Subic Bay, be leased to Japanese or Korean shipbuilders. Mount Pinatubo's effect on the negotiations was immediate. On June 10, as a result of preliminary warnings regarding the volcano, some 16,000 Air Force and nonmilitary personnel and their families were evacuated from Clark, only 10 mi (16 km) from the volcano, and transferred temporarily to Subic, 30 mi (48 km) to the southwest. When the volcano erupted on June 12, the 1,500 troops who had remained behind to guard the base joined them. Within a week, after ash began raining down on Subic, too, 20,000 U.S. military and civilian personnel and dependents boarded warships for Cebu island, from where they later were flown to the United States. Lease negotiations were stalled as Clark was written off as a total loss. It would have required some $800 million to dig out and repair the air base's 9,000 acres (3 600 ha), and even though it had served as a logistical center for U.S. forces in the Pacific, the cost and the base's vulnerability to Pinatubo was not worth it.

On July 17 the U.S. and Philippine negotiators agreed that U.S. use of Subic Bay could be extended ten years. Withdrawal from Clark airfield would take place in one year and the field would be turned over to the Philippines on Sept. 16, 1992. Under the agreement, the United States would pay the Philippines $323 million in 1992, together with other aid worth some $227 million. In addition, the Philippines would receive $203 million annually for the use of Subic. All excess base equipment, both medical and military, estimated to be worth $150 million, would be turned over to the Philippines. In addition, U.S. base commanders would be allowed to purchase Philippine goods and services in excess of $200 million each year. Finally, a joint program review group would meet annually to consider new economic developments and modernization of the Philippine armed forces.

Although the Philippines originally had demanded an annual compensation package of $825 million, the volcano's eruption had lessened its bargaining position. In turn, the United States, which had admitted that it was investigating the possibility of relocating its military bases, realized that labor costs at such installations elsewhere would be much higher.

After the treaty was signed on August 27, it had to be ratified by the Senates of both nations. Although the Philippine negotiators were content with the terms of the agreement, the Philippine Senate was not. Ratification required a two-thirds favorable vote by the Philippines' 23 senators. Anticipating opposition, President Corazon C. Aquino organized a pro-treaty rally in Manila for September 10. The president had hoped 1 million people would participate in the rally, but only one tenth that number appeared. In the end, Philippine nationalistic tendencies prevailed and the treaty was rejected by a vote of 12–11. Some senators had not forgotten that an overflight of U.S. fighters suppressed a 1989 coup attempt against Aquino. Some said they also were concerned that the possibility of nuclear weapons aboard U.S. ships docked at Subic defied the 1987 Philippine Constitution.

The senators' feelings found expression in the words of one of them, Teofisto Guingona: "We want friendship with America. We want trade. But we do not want servitude." President Aquino, believing that most Filipinos favored a continued U.S. presence, urged a referendum on the issue. However, 3 million signatures would be required just to petition a referendum; such a vote would take months to accomplish; and then it would face legal challenges. It also was not certain immediately that

PHILIPPINES • Information Highlights

Official Name: Republic of the Philippines.
Location: Southeast Asia.
Area: 115,830 sq mi (300 000 km^2).
Population: (mid-1991 est.): 62,300,000.
Chief Cities (1990 census): Manila, the capital, 1,598,918; Quezon, 1,666,766; Davao, 849,947; Caloocan, 761,011.
Government: *Head of state and government,* Corazon C. Aquino, president (took office Feb. 25, 1986). *Legislature* (bicameral)—Senate and House of Representatives.
Monetary Unit: Peso (26.15 pesos equal U.S. $1, floating rate, Dec. 31, 1991).
Gross National Product (1989 U.S.$): $40,500,-000,000.
Economic Index (1990): *Consumer Prices* (1980 = 100), all items, 359.8; food, 356.8.
Foreign Trade (1990 U.S.$): *Imports,* $12,206,000,000; *exports,* $8,186,000,000.

a "people's initiative," allowed under the constitution, could overturn a vote on a treaty, as opposed to a vote on regular legislation. On October 2 a compromise was reached allowing the United States three years to withdraw from Subic Bay. Part of the agreement required that the U.S. Navy leave behind its dry docks and much of its heavy equipment.

In view of its own budgetary concerns and the closing of U.S. bases at home, the United States seemed to have two remaining options. It could wait until after the Philippine presidential and senatorial elections of May 1992 to see if a change of policy emerged under a new administration. Election, rather than an unwieldy referendum, would decide the popularity or unpopularity of retaining the bases. (Fidel Ramos, who had resigned as secretary of defense in order to become a presidential candidate representing the LDP (Laban ng Demokratikong Pilipino) Party, already had expressed his concern that departure of the U.S. forces might leave the Philippines vulnerable to external attack.) The second U.S. option involved the gradual removal of Clark airfield functions elsewhere and the dispersal of the Subic Bay facilities to Hawaii, Guam, Japan, Singapore, or some other Southeast Asian countries.

The issue came to a head as the year ended, however, when the Philippines told the United States that it would have to withdraw from Subic Bay by the end of 1992. An impasse over further negotiations regarding the bases reportedly was behind the decision. A U.S. State Department official noted that "in the end, it proved impossible to achieve arrangements which would meets the need of our [the U.S.] military and be satisfactory to the Philippine government."

The greater burden of the closing of the two facilities, however, in the long run could fall on the Filipinos. Subic Bay had been the principal maintenance, support, and storage base for the U.S. Pacific fleet's 180 ships. It contributed some $344 million each year to the Philippine economy and employed some 20,000 Filipino workers. Cities adjacent to the bases, such as Angeles and Olongapo, would be affected. It was estimated that the bases provide less than 2% of the Philippines' gross national product (GNP); but in a developing nation no cut in the GNP can go unnoticed.

Political News. In the state of the nation address on July 22, President Aquino took credit for recovery of representative forms of self-government. At the same time she had to admit that she would be leaving her country an uncertain economy. President Aquino had indicated consistently that she did not plan to seek reelection in 1992.

Meanwhile, military coup attempts against Aquino had lost purpose with the onset of election campaigning and with the capture of most of the antigovernment rebel leaders. The Communist New People's Army, anxious to appear responsible for finally having driven the U.S. forces out, was in disarray. The collapse of communism in Eastern Europe left the rebels more isolated than before, so that a unilateral offer of a truce was taken as evidence of a need to regroup and reconsider their resources.

Late in 1990, Switzerland's Supreme Court had opened the way for the Philippine government to recover reported assets of its former President Ferdinand Marcos which had been held secretly in Swiss bank accounts. Such assets reportedly totaled as much as $500 million. The Swiss tribunal ruled that the funds could be returned to the Philippines only after a Philippine court had issued a "legally binding verdict" on whether the funds should go to the government or their claimants. On November 4, Imelda Marcos, the wife of the late president, returned to the Philippines, ending more than five years of exile in the United States. The following day she was arrested on charges of fraud and released on bail. Having pleaded not guilty to new corruption charges early in 1992, Mrs. Marcos announced that "after months of direct consultations" with the nation's "poor and oppressed citizens," she had "decided to run for office to seek the presidency." The effect of the Marcos candidacy on the political plans of former Marcos colleagues could not be determined. But Aquino's refusal to seek a constitutional amendment allowing a second presidential term seemed final.

Economics, Land Reform, and Emigration. Some positive economic events took place in the Philippines during 1991. They included offshore oil drilling in Palawan province that discovered a potential 100 million barrels of oil; the International Monetary Fund approving $900 million in loans to the Philippines; and eight new manufacturing corporations being installed in Export Processing Zones, chiefly in Cebu, bypassing the clogged capital, Manila. Nevertheless, the most crucial bill passed during the Aquino administration—land reform (CARP)—seemed to have been circumvented more often than implemented. More than 300,000 Filipinos continued to apply for U.S. visas every year, many in hope of permanent residence; and as a result of the U.S. Immigration Act of 1990, some 60,000 Filipino veterans of World War II became eligible for naturalization.

The Philippines was hit by another major natural disaster in November as Tropical Storm Thelma took as many as 3,500 lives and left more than 50,000 persons homeless. The islands of Leyte, Samar, and Negros particularly were affected due to excessive logging. Many of the dead lived in the city of Ormoc on the island of Ormoc.

LEONARD CASPER, *Boston College*
GRETCHEN CASPER, *Texas A&M University*

PHOTOGRAPHY

In 1991 it was apparent that photography had undergone a radical change. A decline in camera and film sales reflected not only a depressed economy but also the growing popularity of camcorders—one-piece video cameras and recorders—foretelling the dawn of a revolutionary electronic-imaging era.

Rushing to capture a piece of this new market, old-line camera and film manufacturers Kodak and Polaroid—whose strengths are in chemistry—were in a desperate race against electronics hardware masters Sony and Matsushita. Huge research budgets were aimed at creating products that would give consumers the power to edit photographs while making video-photo albums or appeal to the imaging needs of various professionals.

In the news media, electronic equipment's ability to alter images resulted in editors and art directors mapping out new rules so as not to cross the line between reporting the news and creating it.

In fine-art photography, an era that began in 1962 ended as John Szarkowski, photography department director at the Museum of Modern Art in New York City, stepped down; he practically had set the agenda for what is considered art photography. And at Sotheby's spring auction in New York, a record $165,000 was paid for Tina Modotti's "Roses."

Hardware and Software. While there were no big product breakthroughs and few new models introduced at the annual Photo Marketing Association show and throughout the year, beyond the seeming lull the industry prepared for better days ahead with downsizing, added features, and lots of product tweaking.

Among new 35mm single-lens-reflex (SLR) cameras, the very rapid advances in autofocus systems and controls have spawned an entirely new generation of autofocus SLRs. Minolta's 7xi, the third-generation Maxxum, brought "fuzzy logic"—a major step in artificial intelligence that enables cameras to analyze a scene and make exposure and focusing decisions—to SLRs for the first time. And Pentax's PZ-10 opened a new era in its autofocus SLR series.

In the point-and-shoot (P/S) 35mm sector, there were plenty of refinements, with flatter, more pocketable zoom models; and every new upgraded model had red-eye reduction, usually by preflash, to reduce the size of the pupil. Downsizing resulted in mini-mini models: Olympus' Infinity Stylus, which fits in a shirt pocket and has a 15-pop preflash; and the even smaller Big Mini from Konica.

There was a flurry of activity in the stretch-format (13x36mm), panoramic-effect arena, from Minolta's upscale Freedom Vista point-and-shoot to Fuji's QuickSnap Panoramic disposable (12 exposures, $13.95) and Konica's 17mm Panoramate. The latter two were just a few of the special-use, special-effects single-use cameras available in 1991.

The instant-photography market for the amateur declined more than ever. But depending on the results of an appeal, Polaroid could receive an $873 million settlement from Kodak, ending a 15-year battle over patent rights to instant cameras and films.

In the home-video revolution, one study showed one in five households owning a video camera. Compactness was a strong selling point, as video-making equipment continued to shrink in size while growing in capabilities.

The 8mm camera was coming into the fore in 1991, as Sony introduced an Hi8 camcorder —the CCD-TR81—with a much-improved autofocusing system, into its unprecedentedly popular TR series of small 8mm camcorders. Two products from Canon, the A1 Digital and L1, were 8mm dream machines for those limited by earlier technical constraints; the L1 had one feature unique to camcorders—the ability to accept a variety of lenses.

In the software arena, the story was revised films and packaging. Kodak introduced Ektachrome 64X, while altering its Ektachrome 100 Pro and Kodachrome 200 Pro slide films and resetting Ektar's 125 ISO rating to the internationally favored 100. In an ecological effort to reduce packing waste, Kodak eliminated the film box for all three Ektar pro films; the newly sealed film canister had a thumb tab and a peel-back resealable data label. At Fuji a new biodegradable film canister replaced clear-plastic print-film containers.

Exhibitions and Publications. At New York's Museum of Modern Art, a group show called "The Pleasures and Terrors of Domestic Comfort" included 150 images by 60 photographers, while a single photographer was spotlighted in "Lee Friedlander: Nudes," black-and-white everyday views of women done with a hand-held camera and flash. At the Baltimore Museum of Art, Mike and Doug Starn's cut, torn, bent, and taped constructions challenged conventional notions of the photograph.

Scheduled for extensive U.S. and international travel, two retrospective shows opened: "Annie Leibovitz: 1970–1990," comprising 100 portraits of the famous, opening at the National Portrait Gallery in Washington, D.C.; and Danny Lyon's documentary work, "Photo-Film, 1959–1990," at Arizona's Center for Creative Photography.

Individual photographers were headliners in book form: *Nature's Chaos*, with photos by Eliot Porter, was published a few weeks after Porter's death in 1990; Gordon Parks' latest autobiography, *Voices in the Mirror*, was released; and Alfred Stieglitz was featured in *O'Keeffe & Stieglitz: An American Romance* by Benita Eisler.

BARBARA LOBRON
Writer, Editor, Photographer

The Legacy of Edwin H. Land

Edwin H. Land, who invented instant photography and a long line of innovative products, died on March 1, 1991, at age 81. It was in response to his 3-year-old daughter's wanting to see a photograph her father just had taken of her that this self-taught physicist came up with the answer; within one hour he had envisioned the instant photography (camera, film, and chemistry) that today is associated with the company he founded in 1937 and led for 45 years—Polaroid.

In the 1960s a Polaroid marketing executive estimated that half the households in the United States had acquired Polaroid cameras. This pioneering by Dr. Land—an honorary title as he was a two-time Harvard dropout—led to 533 patents by the time he retired in 1982. He outinvented everyone but Thomas Edison, and was the recipient of both the Presidential Medal of Freedom and the National Medal of Science.

Polaroid Corporation

Edwin H. Land (May 7, 1909–March 1, 1991)

For Land, scientific achievement of the highest order meant more than abstract brilliance. "As I review the nature of the creative drive in . . . inventive scientists," he wrote, "I find the first event is an urge to make a significant intellectual contribution that can be tangibly embodied in a product or process."

And embody he did. Land's work led to myriad products and processes. His first important innovation, the light-polarizing plastic named Polaroid, spun off such products as polarized sunglasses, equipment for 3-D movies and for forestalling headlight glare, and the ever-popular polarizing filters for photography.

He pioneered both black-and-white (1947) and color (1959) instant photography, which he finally freed of the peel-away process in 1972 with the introduction of the ingenious SX-70 camera. He also is credited with other specialized products such as infrared night goggles, bombsights, and optical systems used in high-altitude surveillance.

Land retired at 73 following the commercial failure of one of his longtime pet projects: Polavision instant motion pictures for amateurs. In 1980 he founded and financed the Rowland Institute for Science, in Cambridge, MA, which in recent years developed microscopic laser "tweezer" beams capable of manipulating single-cell organisms as small as bacteria.

An ardent advocate of research, Land lavished energy and creativity on the art of running a technologically innovative company. As a result, although instant photography in the early 1990s is in serious decline and the patents for Land's SX-70 are about to run out, those at Polaroid today are hard at work in research and development to invent products that successfully will meet the needs of the computer age.

BARBARA LOBRON

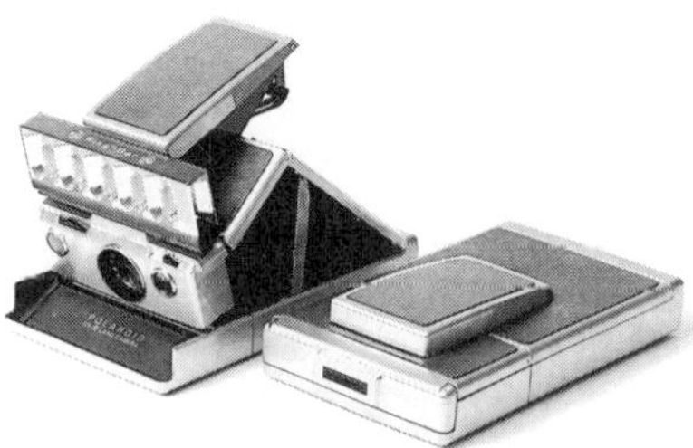

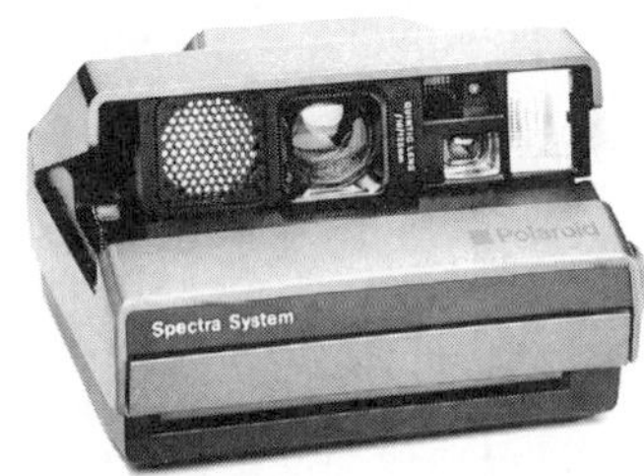

Photos, Polaroid Corporate Archives

The Polaroid Land Camera—including (l-r) *the 95 (introduced in 1948), the SX-70 (1974 issue), and the Spectra System (first presented in 1986)—made photo history.*

PHYSICS

Developments in physics during 1991 included controversial new evidence for a massive neutrino and hints of a solution to the solar-neutrino puzzle.

Solar Neutrinos. Detecting neutral, nearly massless particles which interact very weakly with matter is exceptionally difficult. Several experiments are attempting to resolve the discrepancy between the number of neutrinos expected to be emitted by the Sun and the number of neutrinos actually observed.

For many years the only data came from the neutrino detector at the Homestake Gold Mine in South Dakota. Giant liquid detectors are used, with chemical separation of the very few rare nuclei which are the end products of the neutrino interaction. This and all similar systems were located underground to minimize background. A second detector, the Japanese Kamiokande II, began operating in 1987. Two new systems—the Soviet-American Gallium Experiment (SAGE) in the Soviet Caucasus and the Gallex experiment in Italy—were coming on line in 1991. The results of the Homestake experiments were less than predicted and seemed to oscillate with time, leading to the solar-neutrino puzzle. The Kamiokande results also were less than expected but did not change with time. No solar neutrinos were observed in the first SAGE experiments. Since the three detectors measure different parts of the neutrino energy spectrum, the results are not directly comparable.

A possible solution to the puzzle is that the predicted number of neutrinos are created in the Sun but are transformed to another type of neutrino during passage to Earth—the Mikheyev-Smirnov-Wolfenstein (MSW) effect. John Bahcall of the Institute of Advanced Study in Princeton and Hans Bethe of Cornell found a solution consistent with present experimental data which supports the MSW theory.

Massive Neutrino. There was new but controversial evidence for the existence of a massive neutrino. In beta decay the electron and the electron neutrino share the energy released, resulting in a smooth energy spectrum from zero to a maximum energy. In 1985, John Simpson of the University of Guelph in Ontario presented evidence for a "kink" in the energy spectrum about 17 keV below the maximum energy. This was interpreted as evidence for a neutrino with 17 keV mass, in disagreement with standard views. Most physicists criticized the experimental techniques and analysis.

Simpson's new results indicated that the massive neutrino is emitted in 1% of the nuclear decays. Groups at Oxford, England, Berkeley, CA, and Zagreb, Croatia, have observed similar evidence for the massive neutrino. In all cases where observation of the new neutrino is claimed, solid-state detectors were used. In measurements which utilize magnetic spectrometers, no such effect was observed. A massive neutrino is so surprising that in spite of the new evidence most physicists remain skeptical and the new data was being examined for possible artifacts.

Anyons. In quantum mechanics identical particles have special properties: The wave function is symmetric under the interchange of the particles called bosons and antisymmetric under the interchange of the particles called fermions. This led to the Pauli exclusion principle that no two fermions can occupy the same quantum state. In contrast, many bosons can occupy the same state. Since two interchanges must return things to their original state, there are only two possibilities—that the amplitude is multiplied by either plus or minus one or equivalently that the phase changes by 0 or 180 degrees—and, therefore, there are only fermions and bosons. However, this logic does not apply for two-dimensional systems. In two dimensions the phase change can have any value. Then fermions and bosons are just the two limiting cases. The others are called anyons, which might have applications when electrons are confined to two dimensions.

Efforts to observe anyons have increased. Anyons violate time-reversal invariance and parity. The spirit of the experiments is to use these symmetry-breaking effects as a signature of anyons. Materials which violate time or parity invariance will show optical effects and absorb left-handed polarized light differently from right-handed polarized light. Thus far experiments have proved inconclusive, leaving the existence of anyons in doubt.

Superconducting Super Collider. The world's largest scientific instrument will be the Superconducting Super Collider (SSC), with a tunnel some 50 mi (80 km) long with two 20-TeV (1 TeV = 10^{12} electron volts) colliding proton beams. The SSC, to be constructed at Waxahatchie, TX, will provide unique tests of present theories of elementary particles. Its cost originally was figured at $4.5 billion but later estimates were between $8 billion and $10 billion. Efforts to obtain international scientific and financial support for the SSC were set back by 1991 decisions on the giant detectors to be used at the SSC. One major general-purpose detector, designed by a 60-institution consortium led by George H. Trilling of Lawrence Berkeley Laboratory, was approved in January. It would cost more than $500 million. Another major proposal for an L* (L-Star) detector, designed by a consortium of 90 institutions from 13 nations and led by Samuel C.C. Ting of MIT, was rejected in May because of "persistent management problems." Following the rejection, prospects appeared poor for major international contributions for the SSC.

GARY MITCHELL
North Carolina State University

AP/Wide World

Becoming the first Polish president to visit Israel, Lech Walesa (right) *conferred with Prime Minister Yitzhak Shamir in Jerusalem in May 1991. The visit was intended to ease strain between the two nations over the issue of anti-Semitism.*

POLAND

Poland confronted monumental economic and political challenges in 1991. As the economic crisis intensified, political fragmentation and conflict threatened to engulf the fledgling Polish democracy and impede progress toward economic recovery.

Politics and Government. On Jan. 4, 1991, Jan Krzysztof Bielecki, the nominee of President Lech Walesa, was confirmed as prime minister by the Sejm (lower house of parliament) by a vote of 276 to 58 with 52 abstentions. Bielecki, a 39-year-old businessman, was the youngest prime minister in post-World War II Polish history. He promised to steer Poland toward a free-market economy with all deliberate speed. To help him carry out this pledge, Bielecki retained Finance Minister Leszek Balcerowicz, the pioneer of free-market reform in the cabinet of former Premier Tadeusz Mazowiecki.

In late February, President Walesa was replaced as leader of the Solidarity trade union movement by Marian Krzaklewski. Walesa's personal choice, Bogdan Borusewicz, was rejected by the delegates at the Solidarity congress in Gdansk. Krzaklewski's election came as the trade union movement was turning toward a more militant policy of wage increases, now opposed by Walesa and his new prime minister, Bielecki. High unemployment, rising prices, and the bankruptcies of inefficient firms caused a tide of discontent to sweep over the country. In January, Polish miners protested and jeered President Walesa in Warsaw. Similar strikes and demonstrations became more frequent.

The Sejm, 65% of whose members were former Communists, grew increasingly restive. It opposed emergency legislation requests by the government, and in late August caused Premier Bielecki to offer his resignation. The Sejm rejected Bielecki's offer to resign by a vote of 211 to 114 with 28 abstentions, but continued to oppose and criticize his austerity policies and his program for a return to capitalism. The Sejm also quarreled with President Walesa on the nature of the electoral law under which Poland was to hold its first free parliamentary elections since the 1920s. Fearing that the Sejm versions of the electoral system would contribute to a debilitating excess of parties in Poland, Walesa twice—on June 10 and June 26—exercised a veto to block the Sejm's electoral proposals. Eventually the Sejm overrode Walesa's veto and approved a law with considerable emphasis on proportional representation.

Since some 300 political parties had organized themselves by the October 27 elections, including Stanislaw Tyminski's Party X and a Beer Lover's Party, the prospects for democratically achieved Polish stability were not reassuring. In June, President Walesa had told reporters, somewhat ominously, that "I shall be decisive if we begin to get into anarchy . . . I shall use all the powers at my disposal."

The October 27 election was even more disappointing than was anticipated. The results indicated dramatic divisions within the Polish body politic. The election also seemed to reflect widespread alienation and apathy, as only about 40% of Poland's eligible voters cast their ballots. The new 460-member Sejm was divided among representatives of 29 political parties, with no group receiving as much as 13% of the vote. A front-runner was the Democratic Union, a center-left splinter of the Solidarity movement, led by former Premier Mazowiecki. Closely behind were the former Communists, now named the Democratic Left Alliance. No other group reached 10% of the vote. Premier Bielecki's Liberal Democratic Congress, which had pledged to support his tough program of free-market reforms, received only 7% of the vote.

Responding to the crisis, Walesa offered to serve as prime minister, while retaining the presidency of the republic. This initiative was viewed by some as prelude to a possible strongman rule on the model of Marshal Jozef Pilsudski—the authoritarian leader of Poland from 1926 to 1935 and known to be a hero to Walesa.

After a two-month-long government crisis, the Sejm on December 27 finally confirmed a cabinet led by Jan Olszewski, who headed a six-party center-left coalition. The Sejm's vote was 235-60 in favor with 39 abstentions. This was only 17 votes above the minimum 218 needed for the investiture of the government. The general orientation of the Olszewski cabinet—to the dismay of President Walesa—was to slow down the pace of Poland's free-market reforms in the interest of greater social stability.

Economy. While the Bielecki government attempted to convert the Polish economy to a free-market system through privatization, the year was marked by continuing increases in prices, declining employment and production, and faltering exports. These trends generally continued the patterns established in 1990. Unemployment rose from about 1.12 million at the end of 1990 to about 2.0 million at the end of 1991, or roughly from 8% of the labor force to more than 10%.

The government privatized hundreds of state-owned enterprises by offering shares to employees and citizens-at-large, and minority shares for the state. Although many stores in Poland were stocked with ample supplies of goods, prices continued to rise and the number of those able to afford the more plentiful Polish and Western products seemed to shrink. In mid-May the government announced the country's trade deficit had reached $525.6 million after the first four months of the year. On May 17 it also devalued the zloty by 14.4% against the dollar to a new rate of 11,000 zlotys to one dollar.

According to Polish Press Agency reports in August, food prices had risen by 18.9% since December; the cost of electricity had risen by 147.4%; and the price of gas had jumped by 369.6%. Unsurprisingly, there were three times as many strikes protesting economic conditions in Poland in the first six months of 1991 as there were in 1990 (271 to 91). In the face of these conditions, Premier Bielecki continued to insist on wage restraints throughout the Polish economy. He also sought additional powers from the Sejm to deal with the economic emergencies.

Among unfavorable developments were many serious corruption cases reported in both the public and private sectors of the Polish economy. Banking seemed especially hard hit by the new wave of corruption. The manufacture and export of illicit drugs also appeared to be on the rise, with some sources claiming that Poland had become one of the world's leading producers of illegal amphetamines.

Church and State. The Catholic Church in Poland undertook several major initiatives in 1991. A January 20 pastoral letter, issued by the Polish episcopate under the auspices of the Cardinal Jozef Glemp, called for dialogue and cooperation between Christians and Jews. The letter, which was read in all Catholic churches in Poland, emphasized the common elements of faith and tradition uniting Christians and Jews in "the ethical principles of the decalogue." The letter generally was seen as an attempt by the Church to fight anti-Semitism in Poland and to overcome the legacy of old and recent charges of anti-Semitism by and among Church officials. The Polish church was particularly sensitive about its conduct during World War II, when 3.5 million Polish Jews perished in the Holocaust.

In late April the Polish bishops called for an end to the separation of church and state in Poland, in effect making Roman Catholicism the state religion of Poland. But in a May 12 interview, Cardinal Glemp backed away from this position, indicating that the continued separation of the two entities was acceptable if it allowed for fruitful cooperation. The Church also pressed parliament for the abolition of the

POLAND • Information Highlights

Official Name: Republic of Poland.
Location: Eastern Europe.
Area: 120,726 sq mi (312 680 km²).
Population (mid-1991 est.): 38,200,000.
Chief Cities (Dec. 31, 1989 est.): Warsaw, the capital, 1,655,100; Lodz, 851,700; Krakow, 748,400.
Government: *Head of state,* Lech Walesa, president (inaugurated Dec. 22, 1990). *Head of government,* Jan Olszewski, premier (confirmed December 1991). *Legislature* (bicameral)—Sejm and Senate.
Monetary Unit: Zloty (11,000 zlotys equal U.S.$1, May 1991).
Gross National Product (1989 est. U.S.$): $172,400,-000,000.
Economic Indexes (1990): *Consumer Prices* (1980 = 100), all items, 22,326; food, 24,984.8. *Industrial Production* (1980 = 100), 82.
Foreign Trade (1990 U.S.$): *Imports,* $8,160,000,000; *exports,* $13,627,000,000.

After being authorized by the Sejm (lower house of parliament) in March 1991, a Polish stock exchange opened in the former headquarters of the Communist Party's Central Committee in Warsaw. Stocks in five Polish companies that had been privatized by the government in January were traded on opening day, April 16.

© Szulecki/East News/Sipa

abortion law. One victory of their campaign was the government's decision to discontinue state subsidies for birth-control pills. Nevertheless, in late May, in what was seen widely as a political defeat for the Church, Parliament voted to postpone indefinitely discussion of the bill prohibiting abortion. Public-opinion polls indicated that only about 20% of the people favored a total ban on abortions.

In June, Pope John Paul II visited his native Poland and reinforced the "anti-anti-Semitism" campaign at a Mass in Kielce, site of a 1946 pogrom against Jews. The pope also appealed for a reversal of Communist-adopted policies allowing abortions on demand in Poland. On June 8, President Walesa received the pope in Warsaw. Walesa credited the pontiff with major contributions toward Poland's new freedom and for having been a spokesman for Solidarity during the 1980s.

Foreign Relations. Much of Polish diplomacy in 1991 was concerned with debt reduction, foreign investment, and various forms of financial assistance to the struggling Polish economy. In early February, Premier Bielecki traveled to Switzerland, where he called upon Western nations to reduce Poland's indebtedness—estimated at about $31 billion—by 80%. On February 5, Bielecki and President Walesa attended a meeting in Visegrad, Hungary, to develop trilateral economic cooperation among Poland, Czechoslovakia, and Hungary.

The International Monetary Fund (IMF) announced on April 18 a $2.4 billion aid package to Poland. However, it was based on certain contingencies—including reduction in the rate of inflation from 250% in 1990 to 36% in 1991; the privatization of at least half of Polish business firms; the privatization of agriculture; and the removal of all barriers to foreign investment. In late April the Club of Paris creditor nations agreed to "write off" 50% of Poland's $33 billion debt. This prompted Japan to block its projected $500 million in aid to Poland in protest of the Club of Paris decision.

In mid-February, Foreign Minister Krzysztof Skubiszewski threatened a unilateral Polish denunciation of the treaty that had allowed the USSR to station some 50,000 Soviet troops in Poland, unless the Soviets agreed to a pullout by the end of 1991. Some Soviet forces began withdrawals in April and, according to Polish officials, all Soviet troops would be out of Poland by the end of 1993. Polish authorities also indicated that claims, asking for compensation, would be pressed against the Soviets for unspecified environmental damage.

In late February, Poland's foreign minister traveled to Budapest for the signing of documents dissolving the military structure of the Warsaw Pact, a Soviet-dominated organization to which Poland had belonged since 1955.

President Walesa traveled to Washington on March 19 to ask U.S. President George Bush for financial aid and concessions for the struggling Polish economy. On March 20, President Bush responded with a cancellation of 70% of Poland's $3.8 billion debt to the United States. Walesa spent eight days in the United States, visiting New York, Chicago, and Los Angeles. Before returning home, Walesa announced the lifting of visa requirements for U.S. citizens visiting Poland as of April 15.

In early April, President Walesa addressed EC officials in Brussels, warning against a new division of Europe—"a silver curtain"—based on a rich West and a poor East. In mid- and late April, Walesa visited France and Britain, enlisting support for future Polish association in the EC. France agreed to a $500 million write-off from its $5.2 billion Polish debt.

In May, President Walesa embarked on a four-day trip to Israel. In an emotional appearance before the Israeli parliament, Walesa called for renewed cooperation between Poland and Israel. Speaking about the legacy of anti-Semitism in Poland, he said: "Here in Israel, the land of your culture and survival, I ask for your forgiveness." According to Polish foreign-ministry sources, the new relationship was reflected in the permission granted to some 29,000 Soviet Jews to travel to Israel through Poland during the previous 18 months.

On May 9 the Polish government announced that it would resume some interest payments on debts to foreign commercial banks. These payments had been suspended since 1989.

On June 17, a Polish-German treaty on "good neighborliness and friendly cooperation" was signed in Berlin. The treaty guaranteed the protection of the rights of Poland's German minority, and it pledged that the Federal Republic would help Poland become a member of the EC. The issue of German reparations to Poland for damages inflicted by the Nazis was left to future negotiation. On June 28, Foreign Minister Skubiszewski journeyed to Budapest for the formal dissolution by the original signatories of the old Soviet-trading and economic-cooperation bloc—COMECON—Council of Mutual Economic Cooperation.

On July 1 in Prague, Czechoslovakia, President Walesa attended the dissolution of the remaining political-diplomatic structure of the Warsaw Pact. On July 3, Walesa visited North Atlantic Treaty Organization (NATO) headquarters in Belgium in an effort to secure the protection of the Atlantic alliance for Poland.

On December 16, Poland joined Czechoslovakia and Hungary in signing an agreement with the European Community providing for associate membership for the three Eastern European states. Following a year of negotiations, the agreement was to facilitate freer entry of Polish goods into Western Europe in 1992.

ALEXANDER J. GROTH
University of California, Davis

POLAR RESEARCH

Antarctic. On Oct. 4, 1991, the 26 voting members of the Antarctic Treaty adopted a new environmental-protection protocol designating Antarctica as a natural reserve devoted to peace and science. It protects flora and fauna; limits tourism, waste disposal, and marine pollution; and bans mineral-resource activities. It would enter into force 30 days after all voting members signed the agreement.

The year's research highlights included two major fossil discoveries. Working in the Transantarctic Mountains, about 400 mi (643.7 km) from the South Pole, geologists discovered fossils of two types of dinosaurs—the southernmost discovery of its kind. The fossils were found in rocks about 200 million years old. At another site about 250 mi (402.3 km) from the South Pole, 3-million-year-old fossil leaves were discovered. They suggested the Antarctic ice sheet has not remained stable for the last 15 million years, as scientists believed, but has had a dynamic history. The leaves record a warmer climate—when temperatures probably were 50°F-59°F (10°C-15°C) warmer.

At a conference in March 1991, two U.S. geologists startled the scientific community with their assertion that North American and Antarctica once were joined. Using rock samples from Antarctica and the United States and computer simulations, they showed that 500-million-year-old sedimentary rocks found in the Transantarctic Mountains and southern Australia match sediments from the U.S. Rocky Mountains. These data, as well as similarities among older metamorphic rocks from both continents, suggest that the continents were joined at least from about 1 billion years ago to a little more than 500 million years ago.

Researchers observing the "ozone hole" above Antarctica recorded a third consecutive year of stratospheric ozone losses equal to 1987's record lows. Other early reports suggested the depletion began during the austral winter—earlier than ever before. Biologists also reported that a 40% decrease in ozone appears to slow growth in the Antarctic marine community by 6% to 12%.

In August the first of 490 U.S. investigators began 1991–92 fieldwork in Antarctica. Among the 112 projects to be conducted during the austral summer were the launch of two 28-million-cu-ft (792 872-m^3) high-altitude balloons, 16 geology and geophysics projects, nine projects on climate change, and a U.S.-Soviet study of the western Weddell Sea.

Arctic. Concern for recorded decreases in ozone above the Arctic prompted the National Science Foundation (NSF) to install an ultraviolet (UV)-radiation monitor in Barrow, AK. The monitor, part of a network including three monitors in Antarctica and one in Tierra del Fuego, would measure changes in incoming UV radiation. NSF established the network to record increases in UV-radiation exposure resulting from decreased ozone protection.

Ice-core drilling by U.S. scientists in central Greenland was completed on August 29 at a depth of 4,954 ft (1 510 m)—about halfway to the bottom of the Arctic ice sheet. The 5.2-inch (13.2-cm)-diameter core samples provided an 8,500-year record back to the end of the last ice age. When drilling reaches the bedrock, investigators hope to have a 200,000-year record providing information on climate, atmospheric chemistry, and volcanic activity.

European investigators drilling at another Greenland site announced that their measurements showed that antipollution measures were working. In the 1950s and 1960s researchers found dramatic increases in the lead levels in Greenland snow; the new data showed that since 1967 the amount of lead in the snow has decreased by 85%.

WINIFRED REUNING
National Science Foundation

PORTUGAL

Prime Minister Aníbal Cavaco Silva's decisive victory in the fall 1991 general election augured well for four more years of political stability, foreign investment, and sustained economic growth in Portugal.

Politics. On October 6, Portuguese voters expressed their appreciation of Cavaco Silva's prudent political and economic stewardship by awarding his center-right Social Democratic Party (PSD) 50.4% of the vote in parliamentary contests. This figure, which was slightly higher than the PSD's 1987 showing (50.2%), translated into 132 seats in the 230-member parliament. The Social Democrats scored a nationwide victory. The governing party won in every district in the country except Beja, a traditional Communist stronghold.

Cavaco Silva's major challenger was Jorge Sampaio, mayor of Lisbon and the soft-spoken, highly principled leader of the Socialist Party (PS). Samaio criticized the growing chasm between Portugal's "haves" and "have nots," while warning that tough times lay ahead. Even though boosting their share of the vote from 22% (1987) to 29% and winning 70 seats, the Socialists finished a distant second. The conservative Christian Democrats retained their 4.4% of the electorate to win five seats, while the Democratic Renewal Party—a personal vehicle of former President Antonio Eanes—failed to win a seat and faced extinction. Another notable loser was the pro-Stalinist Communist Party (PCP). It joined the Greens and other small parties in the United Democratic Coalition. This alliance obtained just 8.8% of the vote (17 seats) compared with 12.4% four years earlier.

One surprise in the outcome was the single seat captured by the newly created National Solidarity Party, most of whose members are pensioners. More vexing to the government was the 32% abstentionism rate, the highest since the 1974 revolution that paved the way for democracy in the Iberian nation. Even as he commands respect for his leadership, the stern, aloof Cavaco Silva has failed to develop a personal rapport with the electorate.

Boasting personal popularity was Alberto Mário Soares, who in January won reelection as the nation's president with 70.4% of the vote.

Economics. Central to Cavaco Silva's obtaining a second consecutive absolute parliamentary majority was five years of sustained growth that the PSD called an "economic miracle." Indeed, since Portugal joined the European Community (EC) in 1986, national income had expanded at an average rate of 4.6% annually. Powering this expansion were huge EC payments combined with influx of foreign investment—especially in tourism, real estate, financial operations, and manufacturing.

The country's greatest economic coup of the year occurred in April when Ford and Volkswagen signed a $2.8 billion deal to build a new multipurpose vehicle for the European market. The plant, to be located in the unemployment-ridden city of Setúbal, south of Lisbon, would employ 4,700 workers and create indirectly 10,000 additional jobs.

Growth slipped to approximately 3% in 1991 amid 12% inflation and a budget deficit that approached 6% of gross domestic product (GDP). Yet in the aftermath of his electoral triumph, Cavaco Silva rejected a new austerity program and pledged that Portugal would continue to enjoy one of Europe's most robust growth rates. The 52-year-old prime minister would continue, however, to privatize an economy whose efficiency still was constrained by government controls and regulations.

During 1991, Portugal's privatization scheme was the most ambitious one in Western Europe. On the auction block were banks, insurance companies, manufacturing firms, utilities, the tobacco monopoly, the national airline, and the last state-owned newspaper. Critics attacked the program as piecemeal (particularly in the financial sector), overly generous to foreign capital, and lacking a strategy to restructure the economy.

Foreign Relations. As a sign of its growing confidence, Portugal was to take over the EC presidency from the Dutch in January 1992. In 1991, Cavaco Silva emphatically rejected the idea of a "two-speed" Europe—that is, opening the EC to new affiliates from the former Communist Eastern bloc before deepening integration among the 12 EC members. Portugal, he argued, had made enormous adjustments to meet the challenges of membership. "We did not avoid the difficulties, and we want to strengthen the community, not divide and build walls within it." As part of the process, Cavaco Silva backed efforts toward common foreign and defense policies.

George W. Grayson
College of William & Mary

PORTUGAL • Information Highlights

Official Name: Portuguese Republic.
Location: Southwestern Europe.
Area: 35,552 sq mi (92 080 km²).
Population (mid-1991 est.): 10,400,000.
Chief Cities (1981 census): Lisbon, the capital, 807,167; Oporto, 327,368; Amadora, 95,518.
Government: *Head of state,* Alberto Mário Soares, president (took office March 1986). *Head of government,* Aníbal Cavaco Silva, prime minister (took office November 1985). *Legislature* (unicameral)—Assembly of the Republic.
Monetary Unit: Escudo (146.02 escudos equal U.S.$1, Oct. 24, 1991).
Gross Domestic Product (1989 est. U.S.$): $72,100,000,000.
Economic Indexes (1990): *Consumer Prices* (1980 = 100), all items, 485.6; food, 478.1. *Industrial Production* (1980 = 100), 161.
Foreign Trade (1990 U.S.$): *Imports,* $25,072,000,000; *exports,* $16,348,000,000.

POSTAL SERVICE

The United States Postal Service (USPS) celebrated two decades of operation on July 1, 1991, the 20th anniversary of the effective date of the Postal Reorganization Act of 1970. The service had reasons to celebrate.

While postal volume had doubled since 1971, extensive automation had doubled productivity. Postal employment remained at 748,000 in 1991, compared with 741,000 in 1970, the last year of the old Post Office Department. While the new government corporation did not run in the black until fiscal year (FY) 1979, its subsidies had been reduced by then from 25% of operating revenues to 4%. Between fiscal 1979 and 1990 the USPS was in the black half the time. At 29 cents the U.S. first-class postal rate was the world's lowest. And in the spring of 1991 the Opinion Research Corporation of Princeton, NJ, reported that a survey showed 87% of citizens found service to be good to excellent.

However, during FY 1991, ending September 30, the USPS posted a deficit of $1.5 billion on top of a deficit in FY 1990 of $874 million. This was caused by a congressionally mandated payment of $1.9 billion toward the federal deficit. Otherwise, the normal USPS operations were in the black for FY 1991, Postmaster General Anthony Frank reported in December. But this was by a much smaller margin than anticipated for the Postal Rate Commission (PRC) had reduced a late-1990 USPS first-class rate-increase request from 30 to 29 cents. To make up the loss in revenue (about $850 million over three years), the PRC proportionately increased the third-class bulk-mail (often termed junk mail) rates, which normally brought in 40% of USPS revenues.

During the remainder of FY 1991 the first-class volume remained high, but third class declined by more than 1 billion pieces as direct mailers reconsidered their options. Instead of an expected increase, the USPS saw a total mail-volume decline from a FY 1990 high of 166.3 billion pieces to 165.9 billion pieces, the first volume decline since 1975. Thus the USPS lost revenue as a result of both the lower first-class rate and a reduced third-class volume. Efforts to change the PRC position failed.

During much of FY 1991 the postal service also was engaged in unusually complicated union contract negotiations. Citing its fiscal problems and high USPS salaries compared to those of its private counterparts, the service

Direct ("Junk") Mail

"Junk" mail has become a popular epithet used to describe the great mass of advertising and solicitation copy flooding our mailboxes in recent years. To the U.S. Postal Service (USPS), it is "third-class bulk business mail" whose 1990 volume of more than 63.5 billion pieces provided USPS with more than one third of its volume. To "junk-mail" producers, the material is known as direct mail or mail order.

Origins and Success. The system of direct contact with prospective buyers began with a one-page mail-out by Montgomery Ward in 1872. He was followed in direct-mail marketing by Richard Sears in 1886. The success of these early attempts revolutionized selling. Today mass mailings not only provide a highly profitable way to do business, but are the mainstay of fund-raising for schools, the Red Cross and other nonprofit organizations, as well as for large membership organizations and political candidates.

This highly efficient sales method seems here to stay. Even the general public is ambivalent about direct mail. Many complain, but there is evidence that at least half of those solicited make a purchase.

Privacy Concerns and Regulation. There have been growing concerns about direct marketing, however. The key to successful direct mailing is the list. The development and sale of mailing lists constitute a multibillion-dollar industry. Modern research techniques using the computer to bring together vast amounts of data from credit agencies, the U.S. census, and the like to develop files on the consumer behavior of individuals have sparked some reforms in the name of privacy.

From the producers' side there is limited self-regulation. Persons wishing to have their names struck from most publicly traded lists can do so by writing the Direct Marketing Association in New York City.

Since the 1960s federal privacy laws have been strengthened. The Deceptive Mailings Preventions Act of 1990 bans mail pretending to be government related. But no regulations in the United States have matched those of the European Community, which has proposed that by 1992 companies must obtain consumer consent to give to others personal information in their files.

Finally, the USPS may be helping inadvertently to decrease junk mail. A 25% increase in third-class mail rates in 1991 (compared with 15% for first-class) caused postal volume to fall off for the first time in 15 years. A survey indicated that many direct mailers were reconsidering their options.

PAUL P. VAN RIPER

offered its unions little more in August 1991 than a continuation of existing salaries and working rules.

During the fall of 1990 two smaller unions had signed three-year contracts essentially accepting the USPS proposal plus some bonuses, productivity awards, and additional job security. The two largest unions did not agree and went to arbitration in late 1990. After prolonged hearings the arbitration committee awarded these unions small salary increases but no bonuses or productivity awards. The two unions signed four-year contracts on June 12, 1991.

Meanwhile, the postal service and the U.S. Department of Defense delivered 450,000 lbs (193 850 kg) of mail daily to troops during the Persian Gulf war.

Canada. With a FY 1991 surplus of $14.8 million, the Canada Post Corporation continued in the black for the third year in a row. The first-class rate went to 42 cents (Canadian) in early 1991. A postal strike was in mediation during the fall of 1991.

PAUL P. VAN RIPER, *Texas A & M University*

PRINCE EDWARD ISLAND

Prince Edward Island's potato industry was hard hit by a virus in 1991, but farmers were compensated. The Northumberland Strait crossing project received a boost, and a large drug-running operation was broken up by police.

Virus Affliction. A virus known as PVY-n continued to ravage the seed-potato industry, a mainstay of the province's economy, in 1991. In August the federal government announced a compensation package for farmers whose crops had been ordered destroyed. Payments ranged from C$2,500 to C$2,900 per hectare. To that point in 1991, more than 80 potato lots had tested positive for the virus, which does not affect table potatoes or endanger human beings, but can infect other crops.

Bridge Plan Still Alive. The idea of building a bridge between Prince Edward Island and the Canadian mainland showed its durability. In an April statement, a committee of experts concluded that a span across the 8-mi (12.9-km)-wide Northumberland Strait could be constructed without causing a massive ice jam. Less than a year earlier, a federal environmental panel had expressed concern that the piers of such a bridge might hinder the spring ice breakup. The committee of experts then was set up by the government in Ottawa to review the matter. Using what its chairman called a "new model," it found that a bridge that met all the ice-delay criteria could be built after all. Federal authorities later announced a pricing call to potential contractors for the estimated C$700 million project.

Goods and Services Tax Flip-Flop. Finance Minister Gilbert Clements executed an about-face on the controversial issue of harmonizing Prince Edward Island's sales tax with the federal government's highly unpopular goods and services tax (GST). On July 23, Clements said his government would go ahead with harmonization, arguing that a blended system would yield C$107 million in revenue annually. Two weeks later he backed off, saying that the government had "no plans" for harmonization. The switch reflected strong popular opposition to the integration plan.

Deficit Budget. The recession and declining transfer payments from Ottawa were contributing factors in a C$8.9 million deficit budget for 1991–92, unveiled in the legislature April 9.

Drug Case. In the biggest drug bust in the province's history, police swooped down on a north-shore beach August 26 and seized a huge load of marijuana destined for central Canada and the U.S. eastern seaboard. Ten suspects were arrested on various charges.

The 10,000 lbs (4 536 kg) of marijuana seized, valued at C$20 million, just had been smuggled ashore in six inflated boats and loaded onto a truck when police moved in. The event recalled a time more than half a century earlier when Prince Edward Island coves were frequent transit points for liquor cargoes destined for the Prohibition-bound United States.

Summerside. The town of Summerside, hard hit by the defense department's 1989 closing of an air base there, received further help to make up the loss. The federal government announced January 16 that an aerospace center would be built in Summerside with help from the federally funded Atlantic Canada Opportunities Agency. The first enterprises on the site would include a C$12 million engine-repair plant and a C$8 million airplane-accessory repair depot. A C$38 million federal data-processing center was announced earlier.

JOHN BEST, *"Canada World News"*

PRINCE EDWARD ISLAND • Information Highlights

Area: 2,185 sq mi (5 660 km²).
Population (September 1991): 130,100.
Chief Cities (1986 census): Charlottetown, the capital, 15,776; Summerside, 8,020.
Government (1991): *Chief Officers*—lt. gov., Marion Reid; premier, Joe Ghiz (Liberal). *Legislature*—Legislative Assembly, 32 members.
Provincial Finances (1991–92 fiscal year budget): *Revenues,* $766,100,000; *expenditures,* $775,000,000.
Personal Income (average weekly earnings, July 1991): $424.75.
Labor Force (September 1991, seasonally adjusted): *Employed* workers, 15 years of age and over, 53,000; *Unemployed,* 17.3%.
Education (1991–92): *Enrollment*—elementary and secondary schools, 24,570 pupils; postsecondary—universities, 2,740; community colleges, 1,070.
(All monetary figures are in Canadian dollars.)

PRISONS

The United States, with more than 1 million citizens behind bars in 1991, ranked first in the world in the proportion and number of its population in prison. Several violent prison riots erupted during the year. And U.S. Supreme Court rulings curbed the legal rights of prisoners, especially those on death row.

Population Trends. In recent years the United States stood third—behind South Africa and the Soviet Union—in the rate of imprisonment, but an increase in crime and strict sentencing polices now have put it in first place. In January 1991, The Sentencing Project, a nonprofit advocacy organization, reported that the United States' incarceration rate had reached 426 per 100,000 people, surpassing South Africa (333 per 100,000 people) and the Soviet Union (268 per 100,000 people). Of the 22 countries surveyed, the majority had rates below 100. In 1990 the United States had 1,176,563 citizens in prison; in 1989—the latest figures available—South Africa had 119,682 prisoners, and the Soviet Union, 769,000. Attention also was called to the heavy concentration of black males in prisons. Almost one in four American black men aged 20 to 29 was under some form of penal supervision—in prison or jail, on probation or parole.

A "get tough on crime" attitude by the U.S. public and its leaders has resulted in the massive construction of new prisons over the past decades and an increase in the sentencing rate and time served. One result of this policy is an increase in the number of older inmates; one estimate is of more than 20,000 prisoners nationwide over the age of 55. Largely because of legally required medical expenses, incarcerating older inmates costs two to three times the amount (more than $50,000 per year) of incarcerating younger people.

Violence. One of the bloodiest prison riots in recent years took place on September 22 at Montana's overcrowded maximum-security prison, located in Deer Lodge. Prisoners took five guards hostage and controlled an entire cell block for four hours. When a tactical force retook the unit, it freed the guards but found five dead inmates and eight seriously injured ones. Extensive fire and water damage was reported. The facility, designed to house 750 prisoners, contained 1,078, although officials listed "emergency" capacity at 1,135.

In January, New York state began the conversion of its 798-cell Southport Correctional Facility to a super-secure—so-called "maxi-maxi"—prison designed to contain inmates who had committed violent acts or serious crimes while confined in one of the state's 66 other prisons. Southport inmates are confined to their cells 23 hours a day, with one recreational hour in outdoor cages. In May, 53 prisoners managed to break through the yard fences, take five guards hostage, and seize control of a cell block for 26 hours. The inmates surrendered after being allowed to air their grievances on local television, but not before four guards were injured, one seriously.

In the investigations that followed, state prison officials blamed lax behavior on the part of some of the guards. Growing tensions between guards and prisoners at Southport had been reported for a number of months. But despite the violent outbreak, state officials announced they would continue to isolate prisoners identified as troublemakers to reduce tension in other parts of the system. The concept of maxi-maxi prisons was being explored by a number of other states as a way to contain the growing number of violent prisoners confined in their systems.

In October, U.S. District Court Judge David G. Larimer ruled that black and Hispanic inmates in New York state's Elmira Correctional Facility were subjected to discrimination in the areas of housing, job assignment, and disciplinary procedures, which often meant denial of early parole. New York and other states are faced with a continuing problem of containing largely minority, metropolitan inmates in prisons located in rural settings and staffed largely by white, local residents.

U.S. Supreme Court. The growing conservative trend of the U.S. Supreme Court was apparent especially in decisions which restrained and limited the rights of prisoners, particularly those on death row. In February, Justice Antonin Scalia announced that he no longer would extend the 90-day appeal deadline for death-row inmates in the U.S. Fifth Circuit Court of Appeals who could not find attorneys. In June the Supreme Court, in *Coleman v. Thompson,* severely limited a prisoner's right to appeal. Justice Sandra Day O'Connor, arguing for the majority, held that "attorney ignorance or inadvertence" could not form the basis of an appeal. The decision underlined a growing conviction of the court majority that state decisions in criminal matters should be viewed as carrying greater finality, and their review by federal courts should be curtailed sharply. Those who looked to the Supreme Court as a safety net for failures in the lower courts found such hopes severely frustrated.

Lawsuits protesting inhumane conditions of prison confinement as "cruel and unusual punishment," according to another court decision announced in June, now must prove that the conditions contested were caused directly by prison officials' "deliberate indifference" to substandard conditions. Insufficient funding from state legislatures would not be legally sufficient to turn aside court suits brought to improve deteriorating prison conditions.

DONALD GOODMAN
John Jay College of Criminal Justice

PRIZES AND AWARDS

NOBEL PRIZES[1]

Chemistry: Richard R. Ernst, Eidgenössische Technische Hochscule, Zurich, Switzerland, for refinements in nuclear magnetic resonance spectroscopy

Economics: Ronald H. Coase, University of Chicago Law School, for his work on the role of institutions in the economy

Literature: Nadine Gordimer, South Africa, for her "continual involvement on behalf of literature and free speech in a police state" *(See* LITERATURE—*Overview.)*

Peace Prize: Aung San Suu Kyi, Myanmar, for "her nonviolent struggle for democracy and human rights . . . one of the most extraordinary examples of civil courage in Asia in recent decades" *(See* BIOGRAPHY.)

Physics: Pierre-Gilles de Gennes, Collège de France, Paris, for research on liquid crystals, treating systems "so complicated that few physicists earlier thought it possible to incorporate them all in a general physical description"

Physiology or Medicine: Erwin Neher and Bert Sakmann, Max Planck Institute, Germany, for discoveries in basic cell function that have "revolutionized modern biology and facilitated research"

[1] About $1,000,000 in each category.

ART

American Academy and Institute of Arts and Letters Awards
- Academy-Institute Awards ($5,000 ea.): art—Robert Arneson, Chuck Close, Arthur Osver, Shirley Smith, William T. Wiley; architecture—Rodolfo Machado, Jorge Silvetti; music—Frederic Goossen, Donald Harris, Tania J. Leon, Nicholas Thorne
- Award for Distinguished Service to the Arts: Alexander Schneider
- Arnold W. Brunner Memorial Prize in Architecture: Tadao Ando
- Jimmy Ernst Award: Peter Agostini
- Gold Medal for Music: David Diamond
- Walter Hinrichson Award: Marjorie Merryman
- Charles Ives Fellowship ($10,000): Nathan Currier
- Charles Ives Scholarships ($5,000 ea.): Kendall Durelle Briggs, Edmund J. Campion, John Vascon celos Costa, Justin Davidson, Eric Sessler, Julia Wolfe
- Goddard Lieberson Fellowships ($10,000): Michael Daugherty, Paul Moravec
- Louise Nevelson Award in Art: Gabor Peterdi
- Richard and Hinda Rosenthal Foundation Award ($5,000): Nicholas Maravell

Capezio Dance Awards ($5,000 each): John Curry, Katherine Dunham, Darci Kistler, Igor Youskevitch

Grawemeyer Award for musical composition ($150,000): John Corigliano, *Symphony No. 1*

John F. Kennedy Center Honors for career achievement in the performing arts: Roy Acuff, Betty Comden, Adolph Green, Fayard and Harold Nicholas, Gregory Peck, Robert Shaw

Edward MacDowell Medal: David Diamond

National Academy of Recordings Arts and Sciences Grammy Awards for excellence in phonograph records
- Album of the year: *Back on the Block,* Quincy Jones
- Classical album: *Symphony No. 2, The Gong on the Hook and Ladder (Fireman's Parade on Main Street), Central Park in the Dark, The Unanswered Question,* Ives; Leonard Bernstein conducting
- Country music song: "Where've You Been," Kathy Mattea (songwriter's award)
- Jazz vocal performance: (female) "All That Jazz," Ella Fitzgerald; (male) "We Are in Love," Harry Connick
- New artist: Mariah Carey
- Pop vocal performance: (female) "Vision of Love," Mariah Carey; (male) "Oh Pretty Woman," Roy Orbison (posthumous)
- Record of the year: "Another Day in Paradise," Phil Collins
- Song of the year: "From a Distance," Julie Gold (songwriter)

National Medal of Arts: Maurice Abravanel, Roy Acuff, Pietro Belluschi, J. Carter Brown, Charles "Honi" Coles, John O. Crosby, Richard Diebenkorn, R. Philip Hanes, Jr., Kitty Carlisle Hart, Pearl Primus, Isaac Stern, Texaco Inc.

Praemium Imperiale for lifetime achievement in the arts ($100,000 ea.): Gyorgy Ligeti (music); Ingmar Bergman (theater and film); Eduardo Chillida (sculpture); Gae Aulenti (architecture); Klossowski de la Balthus (painting)

Pritzker Architecture Prize ($100,000): Robert Venturi

Pulitzer Prize for Music: Shulamit Ran, *Symphony*

Samuel H. Scripps/American Dance Festival Award ($25,000): Anna Sokolow

JOURNALISM

Maria Moors Cabot Prizes ($1,000 ea.): Octavio Frias Filho, editor in chief, *Folha de São Paulo,* São Paulo, Brazil; Eduardo Gallardo, bureau chief, Chile and Bolivia, The Associated Press; Lucia Newman, South American bureau chief, Cable News Network; Alejandro Junco de la Vega, publisher, *El Norte,* Monterrey, Mexico

National Magazine Awards
- Design: *Condé Nast Traveler*
- Essays and criticism: *The Sciences*
- Feature writing: *U.S. News & World Report*
- Fiction: *Esquire*
- General excellence: *Glamour, Condé Nast Traveler, Interview, The New Republic*
- Personal service: *New York*
- Photography: *National Geographic*
- Public-interest: *Family Circle*
- Reporting: *The New Yorker*
- Single-topic issue: *The American Lawyer*
- Special-interest: *New York*

Overseas Press Club Awards
- Book on foreign affairs: Tad Szulc, *Then and Now: How the World Has Changed Since World War II*
- Business or economic news reporting from abroad: (magazines)—Fiammetta Rocco, *Institutional Investor;* (newspapers and wire services)—James Risen, *The Los Angeles Times*
- Cartoon on foreign affairs: Mike Peters, *Dayton Daily News*
- Daily newspaper or wire-service interpretation on foreign affairs: Michael Dobbs, *The Washington Post*
- Daily newspaper or wire-service reporting from abroad: Geraldine Brooks and Tony Horwitz, *The Wall Street Journal*
- General magazine article from abroad: Louise Lief, *U.S. News & World Report*
- Magazine reporting from abroad: Peter McGrath and team, *Newsweek*
- Photographic reporting from abroad: (magazines and books)—Christopher Morris, Black Star, for *Time;* (newspapers and wire services)—Greg Marinovich, The Associated Press
- Radio interpretation or documentary on foreign affairs: Alex Chadwick, National Public Radio
- Radio spot-news reporting from abroad: Rich Lamb, WCBS Radio News, New York
- Special award for lifetime achievements in foreign reporting: Peter Arnett, CNN
- Television interpretation or documentary on foreign affairs: Ted Koppel and Phyllis McGrady, The Koppel Report/ABC News
- Television spot-news reporting from abroad (shared): Bob Simon, CBS; Brian Ross and Ira Silverman, NBC
- Eric and Amy Burger Award (for best entry dealing with human rights): Jon Sawyer, *The St. Louis Post-Dispatch*
- Robert Capa Gold Medal (photographic reporting from abroad requiring exceptional courage and enterprise): Bruce Haley, Black Star, for *U.S. News & World Report*
- Madeline Dane Ross Award (for foreign correspondent showing concern for the human condition): Tom Jariel and Janice Tomlin, ABC's *20/20*

George Polk Memorial Awards
- Business reporting: Dianna Marder, *The Philadelphia Inquirer*
- Career award: Fred Friendly
- Documentary television reporting: Hedrick Smith and Martin Smith, "Inside Gorbachev's USSR"
- Environmental reporting: Adam Seessel, *The Independent Weekly,* Durham, NC
- Foreign reporting: Caryle Murphy, *The Washington Post*
- Local reporting: Heidi Evans, *The* (New York) *Daily News*
- Local television reporting: Kevin Kerrigan, Guam Cable Television
- Metropolitan reporting: Laurie Bennett and Robert Ourlian, reporters, and Alan Fisk, editor, *The Detroit News*

National reporting: Susan F. Rasky and David E. Rosenbaum, *The New York Times*
Network television reporting: Peter Jennings, Tom Yellin, and Leslie Cockburn, ABC News
Regional reporting: Gayle Reaves, David Hanners, and David McLemore, *The Dallas Morning News*
Special broadcasting award: Globalvision, "South Africa Now"
Special publications award: Joseph Belth, *The Insurance Forum*

Pulitzer Prizes
Beat reporting: Natalie Angier, *The New York Times*
Commentary: Jim Hoagland, *The Washington Post*
Criticism: David Shaw, *The Los Angeles Times*
Editorial cartooning: Jim Borgman, *The Cincinnati Enquirer*
Editorial writing: Ron Casey, Harold Jackson, and Joey Kennedy, *The Birmingham* (AL) *News*
Explanatory journalism: Susan C. Faludi, *The Wall Street Journal*
Feature photography: William Snyder, *The Dallas Morning News*
Feature writing: Sheryl James, *St. Petersburg* (FL) *Times*
International reporting: Caryle Murphy, *The Washington Post*, and Serge Schmemann, *The New York Times*
Investigative reporting: Joseph T. Hallinan and Susan M. Headden, *The Indianapolis Star*
National reporting: Marjie Lundstrom and Rochelle Sharpe, Gannett News Service
Public service: *The Des Moines Register* for reporting by Jane Schorer
Spot news photography: Greg Marinovich, The Associated Press
Spot news reporting: staff of the *Miami Herald*

LITERATURE

American Academy and Institute of Arts and Letters Awards
Academy-Institute Awards ($5,000 ea.): Edgar Bowers, Christopher Davis, Jaimy Gordon, Rachel Ingalls, Harry Mathews, J.D. McClatchy, Albert F. Moritz, James Schevill
Award of Merit Medal for Novel: Walter Abish
Witter Bynner Prize for Poetry ($1,500): Thylias Moss
E.M. Forster Award: Alan Hollinghurst
Gold Medal for Poetry: Richard Wilbur
Sue Kaufman Prize for First Fiction ($2,500): Charles Palliser
Richard and Hinda Rosenthal Foundation Award ($5,000): Joanna Scott
Jean Stein Award ($5,000): Cormac McCarthy
Harold D. Vursell Memorial Award ($5,000): Ursula K. Le Guin
Morton Dauwen Zabel Award ($2,500): Gordon Rogoff

Bancroft Prizes ($4,000 ea.): Lizabeth Cohen, *Making a New Deal: Industrial Workers in Chicago, 1919-1939;* Laurel Thatcher Ulrich, *A Midwife's Tale: The Life of Martha Ballard Based on Her Diary, 1785–1812*

Bollingen Prize for Poetry ($10,000 shared): Laura Riding Jackson, Donald Justice

Canada's Governor-General Literary Awards ($10,000 ea.):
English-language awards
Drama—Anne-Marie MacDonald, *Goodnight Desdemona (Good Morning Juliet)*
Fiction—Nino Ricci, *Lives of the Saints*
Nonfiction—Stephen Clarkson and Christina McCall, *Trudeau and Our Times*
Poetry—Margaret Avison, *No Time*
French-language awards
Drama—Jovette Marchessault, *Le Voyage magnifique d'Emily Carr*
Fiction—Gerald Tougas, *La Mauvaise foi*
Nonfiction—Jean-François Lisée, *Dans l'oeil de l'aigle*
Poetry—Jean-Paul Daoust, *Les Cendres bleues*

Ruth Lilly Poetry Prize ($25,000): David Wagoner

Mystery Writers of America/Edgar Allan Poe Awards
First novel: Patricia Daniels Cornwell, *Post Mortem*
Novel: Julie Smith, *New Orleans Mourning*
Grandmaster award : Tony Hillerman

National Book Awards ($10,000 ea.):
Fiction: Norman Rush, *Mating*
Nonfiction: Orlando Patterson, *Freedom: Freedom in the Making of Western Culture*
Poetry: Philip Levine, *What Work Is*

National Book Critics Circle Awards
Biography/autobiography: Robert A. Caro, *Means of Ascent*
Criticism: Arthur C. Danto, *Encounters and Reflections: Art in the Historical Present*
Fiction: John Updike, *Rabbit at Rest*
Nonfiction: Shelby Steele, *The Content of Our Character: A New Vision of Race in America*
Poetry: Amy Gerstler, *Bitter Angel*

PEN/Faulkner Award ($7,500): John Edgar Wideman, *Philadelphia Fire*

Pulitzer Prizes
Biography: Steven Naifeh and Gregory White Smith, *Jackson Pollock: An American Saga*
Fiction: John Updike, *Rabbit at Rest*
General nonfiction: Bert Holldobler and Edward O. Wilson, *The Ants*
History: Laurel Thatcher Ulrich, *A Midwife's Tale: The Life of Martha Ballard, Based on Her Diary, 1785–1812*
Poetry: Mona Van Duyn, *Near Changes*

Rea Award for the Short Story ($25,000): Paul Bowles

MOTION PICTURES

Academy of Motion Picture Arts and Sciences ("Oscar") Awards
Actor—leading: Jeremy Irons, *Reversal of Fortune*
Actor—supporting: Joe Pesci, *GoodFellas*
Actress—leading: Kathy Bates, *Misery*
Actress—supporting: Whoopi Goldberg, *Ghost*
Cinematography: Dean Semler, *Dances with Wolves*
Director: Kevin Costner, *Dances with Wolves*
Film: *Dances with Wolves*
Foreign film: *Journey of Hope* (Switzerland)
Music—original score: John Barry, *Dances with Wolves*
Music—original song: Stephen Sondheim, "Sooner or Later (I Always Get My Man)," (from *Dick Tracy*)
Screenplay—original: Bruce Joel Rubin, *Ghost*
Screenplay—adaptation: Michael Blake, *Dances with Wolves*

American Film Institute's Life Achievement Award: Kirk Douglas

Cannes Film Festival Awards
Golden Palm Award (best film): Joel and Ethan Coen, *Barton Fink*
Grand Prix: Jacques Rivette, *La Belle Noiseuse (The Beautiful Troublemaker)* (France)
Jury Prize (shared): Lars von Trier, *Europa* (Denmark); Maroun Bagdadi, *Hors de Vie (Out of Life)* (Lebanon)
Best actor: John Turturro, *Barton Fink*
Best actress: Irène Jacob, *The Double Life of Veronique* (France/Poland)
Best director: Joel and Ethan Coen, *Barton Fink*

National Society of Film Critics Awards
Film: *GoodFellas*
Actor: Jeremy Irons, *Reversal of Fortune*
Actress: Anjelica Huston, *The Grifters* and *The Witches*
Director: Martin Scorsese, *GoodFellas*

PUBLIC SERVICE

Africa Prize for Leadership ($100,000): Maryam Babangida, Nigeria; Wangari Maathai, Kenya

Charles A. Dana Foundation Awards for pioneering achievements in health and higher education ($50,000 ea.): J. W. Carmichael, Jr., Xavier University, New Orleans, LA; James P. Comer, Yale University; Mary Catherine Swanson, Advancement Via Individual Determination (AVID) Project, San Diego county, CA; David L. Olds, University of Rochester; (shared) Phyllis T. Piotrow and Patrick L. Coleman, Johns Hopkins

American Institute for Public Service Jefferson Awards
National Awards ($5,000 ea.): Dick Cheney, Marian Wright Edelman, Wendy Kopp, Robert Macauley

Templeton Prize for Progress in Religion ($800,000 shared): Immanuel Jakobovits, chief rabbi, Great Britain

U.S. Presidential Citizens Medal (awarded by President George Bush on July 3, 1991): Don Atwood, Lawrence Eagleburger, Robert Gates, Richard Haass, David Jeremiah, Richard Kerr, Robert Kimmitt, Paul Wolfowitz

U.S. Presidential Medal of Freedom (awarded by President Bush on March 7, 1991): Margaret Thatcher; (awarded July 3, 1991): James Baker, Dick Cheney, Gen. Colin Powell, Gen. H. Norman Schwarzkopf, Brent Scowcroft; (awarded Nov. 18, 1991): William F. Buckley, Jr.,

Luis A. Ferré, Betty Ford, Hanna Holborn Gray, Thomas P. O'Neill, Leon Howard Sullivan, Russell E. Train, Friedrich August Von Hayek, Vernon A. Walters, Ted Williams; (awarded Dec. 12, 1991): Javier Pérez de Cuéllar

SCIENCE

ACM Turing Award for technical achievements in computer science and information technology ($25,000): Robin Milner, University of Edinburgh, Scotland

Bristol-Myers Squibb Award for distinguished achievement in cancer research ($50,000): Edward E. Harlow, Jr., Massachusetts General Hospital Cancer Center

Charles Stark Draper Prize ($375,000 shared): Hans J. P. von Ohain, Sir Frank Whittle

General Motors Cancer Research Foundation Awards ($130,000 ea.): Leland H. Hartwell, University of Washington, Seattle; Victor Ling, University of Toronto and Ontario Cancer Institute/Princess Margaret Hospital; Peter K. Vogt, University of Southern California School of Medicine

Louisa Gross Horwitz Prize for research in biology or biochemistry ($20,000 shared): Richard Ernst and Kurt Wüthrich, Eidgenössische Technische Hochschule, Zurich, Switzerland

Albert Lasker Medical Research Awards ($15,000 ea.): Edward B. Lewis, California Institute of Technology; Christiane Nüsslein-Volhard, Max-Planck Institute, Germany; Yuet Wai Kan, University of California

National Medal of Science (presented by President George Bush on Sept. 16, 1991): Mary Ellen Avery, Ronald Breslow, Alberto P. Calderon, Gertrude B. Elion, George H. Heilmeier, Dudley R. Herschbach, G. Evelyn Hutchinson, Elvin A. Kabat, Robert W. Kates, Luna B. Leopold, Salvador E. Luria, Paul A. Marks, George A. Miller, Arthur L. Schawlow, Glenn T. Seaborg, Folke K. Skoog, H. Guyford Stever, Edward C. Stone, Jr., Steven Weinberg, Paul C. Zamecnik

National Medal of Technology (presented by President George Bush on Sept. 16, 1991): Stephen D. Bechtel, Jr., C. Gordon Bell, Geoffrey Boothroyd, John Cocke, Peter Dewhurst, Carl Djerassi, James J. Duderstadt, Robert W. Galvin, Grace Murray Hopper, F. Kenneth Iverson, Frederick M. Jones, Joseph A. Numero, The Pegasus Team, Charles E. Reed, John Paul Stapp

Wolf Prizes ($100,000 shared): Maurice Goldhaber, Brookhaven National Laboratory; Valentine L. Telebdi, Zurich, Switzerland

TELEVISION AND RADIO

Academy of Television Arts and Sciences ("Emmy") Awards

Actor—comedy series: Burt Reynolds, *Evening Shade* (CBS)
Actor—drama series: James Earl Jones, *Gabriel's Fire* (ABC)
Actor—miniseries or a special: John Gielgud, "Summer's Lease," *Masterpiece Theatre* (PBS)
Actress—comedy series: Kirstie Alley, *Cheers* (NBC)
Actress—drama series: Patricia Wettig, *thirtysomething* (ABC)
Actress—miniseries or a special: Lynn Whitfield, *The Josephine Baker Story* (HBO)
Animated program: *The Simpsons* (Fox)
Cinematography—miniseries or a special: *Jackie Collins' Lucky-Chances, Part I* (NBC)
Cinematography—series: *Quantum Leap* (NBC)
Comedy series: *Cheers* (NBC)
Directing—comedy series: James Burrows, "Woody Interruptus," *Cheers* (NBC)
Directing—drama series: Thomas Carter, "In Confidence," *Equal Justice* (ABC)
Directing—miniseries or a special: Brian Gibson, *The Josephine Baker Story* (HBO)
Directing—variety or music program: "Show 1425," *Late Night with David Letterman* (NBC)
Drama series: *L.A. Law* (NBC)
Drama/comedy special or miniseries: *Separate But Equal* (ABC)
Supporting actor—comedy series: Jonathan Winters, *Davis Rules* (ABC)
Supporting actor—drama series: Timothy Busfield, *thirtysomething* (ABC)
Supporting actor—miniseries or a special: James Earl Jones, *Heatwave* (TNT)
Supporting actress—comedy series: Bebe Neuwirth, *Cheers* (NBC)
Supporting actress—drama series: Madge Sinclair, *Gabriel's Fire* (ABC)
Supporting actress—miniseries or a special: Ruby Dee, "Decoration Day," *Hallmark Hall of Fame* (NBC)
Variety, music, or comedy program: *The 63d Annual Academy Awards* (ABC)

George Foster Peabody Awards

Radio: Murray Street Enterprise, New York, in association with KQED-FM, San Francisco, *HEAT with John Hockenberry;* Connecticut Public Radio, New Haven, CT, *The Schubert Theater: 75 Years of Memories;* WXPN-FM, Philadelphia, PA, *Kid's Corner;* National Public Radio, Washington, *Manicu's Story: The War in Mozambique;* Vermont Folklife Center, Middlebury, VT, *Journeys' End: The Memories and Traditions of Daisy Turner and Family;* Southern Center for International Studies, Atlanta, for providing "an invaluable forum for the important decision-making of our time and [which] through its broadcasts and recordings has created an irreplaceable record for generations to follow"; Young Visions Inc. of Los Angeles and the Rotary Club of Los Altos, CA, *Rotary and AIDS: The Los Altos Story*

Television: KPTV News, Portland, OR, *Mount St. Helens: A Decade Later;* Blackside Inc., Boston, *Eyes on the Prize II: America at the Racial Crossroads (1965–1985);* Florentine Films and WETA-TV, Washington, *The Civil War;* CBS Music Video Enterprises and American Masters in association with Perry Films, *John Hammond: From Bessie Smith to Bruce Springsteen;* ABC News and Koppel Communications, New York, *The Koppel Report: Death of a Dictator;* Mouchette Films/P.O.V., copresented by the National Asian American Telecommunications Association, New York, *P.O.V.: Days of Waiting;* ABC News/Time, New York, *Peter Jennings Reporting: Guns;* KCTS-TV, Seattle, and *MacNeil/Lehrer News Hour*, New York, *Backhauling;* WKYC-TV, Cleveland, *Dick Feagler Commentaries;* CNN, Atlanta, for "unique 24-hour global coverage from the scene of the Persian Gulf crisis"; ABC Television and Lynch/Frost Productions in association with Propaganda Films in association with Worldvisions Enterprises Inc., *Twin Peaks*, premier episode; NBC Television, New York, *Saturday Night Live; American Playhouse* series, New York, for "an outstanding record of achievement over nine seasons"; Foundation for Advancement in Science and Education Productions, Los Angeles, *Futures;* Think Entertainment and the Disney Channel, *Mother Goose Rock 'n' Rhyme;* John D. and Catherine T. MacArthur Foundation, Chicago, for its "support of quality" TV

THEATER

New York Drama Critics Circle Awards

Best new play ($1,000): *Six Degrees of Separation*, by John Guare
Best foreign play: *Our Country's Good*, by Timberlake Wertenbaker
Best musical: *The Will Rogers Follies*, by Peter Stone, Betty Comden, Adolph Green, Cy Coleman
Special citation: Eileen Atkins, for her portrayal of Virginia Woolf in *A Room of One's Own*

Antoinette Perry ("Tony") Awards

Actor—play: Nigel Hawthorne, *Shadowlands*
Actor—musical: Jonathan Pryce, *Miss Saigon*
Actress—play: Mercedes Ruehl, *Lost in Yonkers*
Actress—musical: Lea Salonga, *Miss Saigon*
Choreography: Tommy Tune, *The Will Rogers Follies*
Director—play: Jerry Zaks, *Six Degrees of Separation*
Director—musical: Tommy Tune, *The Will Rogers Follies*
Featured actor—play: Kevin Spacey, *Lost in Yonkers*
Featured actor—musical: Hinton Battle, *Miss Saigon*
Featured actress—play: Irene Worth, *Lost in Yonkers*
Featured actress—musical: Daisy Eagan, *The Secret Garden*
Musical: *The Will Rogers Follies*
Musical—book: Marsha Norman, *The Secret Garden*
Musical—score: Cy Coleman, Betty Comden, Adolph Green, *The Will Rogers Follies*
Play: *Lost in Yonkers*
Reproduction of a play or musical: *Fiddler on the Roof*

Pulitzer Prize for Drama: Neil Simon, *Lost in Yonkers*

PUBLISHING

As the U.S. publishing industry awaited the 200th birthday of the 1st Amendment in late 1991, it faced a lingering economic downturn. Book sales fell early in the year, while magazines and newspapers experienced significant drops in advertising revenues, although circulations often remained stable. In response, many media companies raised prices, announced layoffs, and otherwise cut costs. And there was only guarded optimism for a 1992 rebound.

Books. For 1991 the U.S. Commerce Department predicted that book shipments would total $17.3 billion, a 3% rise from 1990, after adjustment for price increases. Increased school enrollments, international demand, and growing disposable income were expected to boost book sales.

Final figures from the Association of American Publishers indicated that 1990 book sales totaled about $15.43 billion, reflecting a moderate 5.3% increase from 1989. In 1990 publishers issued only about 44,000 titles, far less than the more than 50,000 titles published in most recent years. For 1991 the number of titles issued was expected to rebound to perhaps 48,000. Two notable areas of growth included U.S. book exports and audio books. Exports, which amounted to $1.43 billion in 1990, grew by 2.3% during the first half of 1991. By mid-1991 sales of audio books were approaching $1 billion per year, and stores devoted exclusively to them had appeared in a number of major cities. Also, many booksellers anticipated improved business following the fall release of new books by best-selling authors Tom Clancy and Stephen King and a sequel to *Gone with the Wind*.

Controversies about certain books were especially evident, with the resulting publicity often boosting sales. In late 1990 widespread protest helped persuade Simon & Schuster to cancel its planned publication of Bret Easton Ellis' *American Psycho,* a book containing descriptions of extreme violence, especially against women. Vintage Books then published it as an original trade paperback, and the novel briefly became a best-seller. Media publicity also evidently moved Derek Humphry's *Final Exit,* containing explicit details on how to commit suicide, onto the lists. Publishers also profitably issued a number of unauthorized and often less-than-flattering biographies, such as Kitty Kelley's book about Nancy Reagan. And the liberal People for the American Way reported that attempts to censor schoolbooks had increased dramatically.

Trouble followed Simon & Schuster's successful bid of $920,000 for Derek V. Goodwin's novel *Just Killing Time*. In April the company said it would not publish the manuscript, which it learned had been submitted with fictionalized endorsements from writers John le Carré and Joseph Wambaugh.

In September, author Salman Rushdie, whose best-seller *The Satanic Verses* offended many Muslims, spoke in public for the first time since Ayatollah Khomeini threatened his life in 1989. Rushdie, who has been in hiding, appeared at a Writers Guild award ceremony in London.

At least one notable international acquisition occurred. In late 1990, Japanese electronic giant Matsushita agreed to acquire MCA, the parent of the Putnam Berkley Group, marking the first Japanese acquisition of a major U.S. book publisher.

A number of book publishers won a legal battle in March when a U.S. District Court judge ruled that businesses that commercially copy college professors' collections of articles and excerpts without permission violate copyright law. As textbook prices have risen in recent years, some faculty have substituted photocopied class packets, which are cheaper for students. Kinko's Graphics Corp., the defendant, was ordered to pay $510,000 in damages, plus attorney and court fees.

Magazines. The U.S. magazine industry celebrated its 250th anniversary during 1991 amid very grim economic problems. Falling advertising revenues, declining single-copy sales, and increased postal rates all hit the industry. Nonetheless, lower paper prices helped cushion these setbacks, as did increases in paid circulation of many titles.

For the first six months of the year, advertising pages in consumer magazines tracked by the LNA/Magazine Week Consumer Advertising Monitor dropped a devastating 12.8%, compared with the same period in 1990. Ad revenues during this period dropped by about 5%, according to the Publishers Information Bureau. Second-class postal rates, used for mail subscriptions, rose by 22% early in 1991. On the other hand, some 63% of reporting titles registered increases in paid circulation during the first half of the year, according to the Audit Bureau of Circulations.

At midyear, signs of long-term hope appeared. Veronis Suhler & Associates, an investment-banking firm that specializes in media industries, predicted a 6.3% annual rate of growth in advertiser and reader spending on magazines through 1995. This would increase spending from $20 billion in 1990 to $27.1 billion in 1995. The firm also predicted that circulation revenues, which accounted for 52.1% of all spending on consumer magazines in 1990, would continue to grow faster than advertising.

The economic troubles created some notable casualties. In January, *Savvy Woman* closed shop, preceding the August collapse of its publisher, Family Media. Observers termed this failure one of the largest in publishing history. Family Media also had published *Golf Il-*

lustrated and *Health*. Many surviving publications cut staffs and trimmed editorial contents. Time Warner Inc. announced layoffs of 105 editorial employees at six titles. A number of important acquisitions also occurred. In late April, K-III Holdings agreed to purchase eight magazines and one newspaper from Rupert Murdoch's News Corp. for more than $600 million. The sale included such well-known titles as *New York, Seventeen,* and *New Woman*. Also in April, British media magnate Robert Maxwell (*see* OBITUARIES) announced the sale of Pergamon Press, a major part of his publishing empire, to Elsevier of the Netherlands for $764.9 million. Pergamon publishes about 400 academic and scientific journals. In June, Sussex Publishers, headed by British investor John Colman, purchased *Psychology Today* and *Mother Earth News,* both of which had suspended publication. In September, Disney Publishing agreed to buy Family Media's profitable *Discover* for about $15 million.

The appearance and contents of some notable titles also drew attention. Two business magazines, *Forbes* and *Changing Times,* were redesigned, and the latter changed its name to *Kiplinger's Personal Finance Magazine*. *Time* magazine planned to unveil a redesigned product in 1992. *Vanity Fair*'s cover photograph of nude and visibly pregnant actress Demi Moore dramatically increased sales of its August issue. And the Church of Scientology reacted to a negative May cover story in *Time* by launching a multimillion-dollar advertising campaign against the magazine.

The possibility that several states would impose taxes on magazines and newspapers also created concern. California lifted a sales-tax exemption, and large publishers were expected to respond by hiking single-copy and subscription prices.

Newspapers. Profits plummeted and advertising spending declined in newspaper publishing in 1991. Nonetheless, the economically sensitive industry signaled confidence in its long-term viability by spending an estimated $1.6 billion on new equipment and plant expansion in 1991, matching an all-time record. It also raised single-copy and circulation prices at a rate not seen since the early 1980s.

At midyear, Veronis Suhler & Associates predicted that total spending on newspapers would average increases of 5.5% annually through 1995, exceeding growth during the 1985–90 period. If so, total ad and circulation spending would increase from more than $44 billion in 1990 to more than $58 billion in 1995. Spending growth on weeklies was expected to be more rapid than on dailies. As of late 1990, about 1,611 dailies and some 865 Sunday papers were being published in the United States. Total Sunday circulation, about 62.4 million, exceeded total daily circulation, about 62.3 million, for the first time in modern history. *The Wall Street Journal,* with a circulation of about 1.9 million, continued as the largest daily. *USA Today* and *The Los Angeles Times* were in second and third place, respectively. As of early 1991, there were about 7,476 weeklies, with circulation of 54.7 million. Ad spending, which grew 1.1% in 1990, was expected to fall 1.3% in 1991. As the year progressed, circulation held its own at most large dailies, in part because of interest in the war with Iraq.

However, the lingering recession did contribute to the mergers and deaths of some noteworthy newspapers. In September, Media General Inc. announced plans to fold its evening Richmond (VA) *News-Leader* into the morning *Times-Dispatch*. In addition, the merger of the *San Diego Union* and the *Tribune* was planned. In June, *The National,* the first U.S. nationwide sports daily, died after 16 months of existence; the paper had been financed by Mexican media tycoon Emilio Azcárraga Milmo. The *Dallas Times Herald* (founded 1879) was bought in December by a rival Dallas newspaper and ceased publication. A number of newspapers, such as the *Star Tribune* of Minneapolis-St. Paul and the *Chicago Tribune,* canceled facsimile editions, often due to lower-than-expected demand.

A five-month strike that threatened to kill *The New York Daily News*—until then the nation's third-largest metropolitan daily, with a circulation of almost 1.1 million—ended in March when Robert Maxwell acquired it from the Tribune Co. Nine striking unions settled with Maxwell and agreed to the elimination of about 800 unionized jobs. After Maxwell's death in November, his son Kevin briefly served as chairman and publisher. His resignation, effective on Jan. 1, 1992, signaled the end of the Maxwell family's involvement with the newspaper. Editor James Willse was named as publisher. In general, sales of newspaper properties slowed in late 1990 and 1991, partly because owners demanded premium prices.

Legal issues continued to cause concern. In October a Florida judge dismissed all charges against a tabloid that was accused of violating a Florida law that prohibits the publication of the names of victims of sex crimes. The tabloid and several other newspapers and magazines had come under fire for publishing the name of the woman who alleged she was raped by William Kennedy Smith. The tabloid was the only one to be prosecuted, however, because it published in Florida. In two decisions against news defendants, the U.S. Supreme Court ruled that the 1st Amendment does not protect a journalist who breaks a promise of confidentiality to a source or who makes up defamatory quotes. The retirement of liberal Justice Thurgood Marshall also added to concern that an increasingly conservative Supreme Court might dilute constitutional protection for journalists.

DAVID K. PERRY, *The University of Alabama*

The Military and the Media in Wartime

The relationship between the military and the media—especially in time of war—never has been a particularly comfortable one, with the different culture and aims of the two institutions bringing repeated conflict.

The Issue and Its History. For the military and the media alike the central axis around which the military-media dispute revolves is the question of the media's access to information. If the press serve as a proxy for the public in gathering and disseminating information, what sort of information should they be allowed to gather and disseminate? Put another way, in a democracy, what is the public's right to know?

In the United States the media have come to be regarded as the fourth branch of government, with a central role in the democratic process. As former U.S. Supreme Court Justice William Brennan noted, the press perform "the communicative function necessary for democracy" in providing for an open discourse and public debate on public policy. And it is only through such a discourse, democratic theory holds, that a democracy will be able to function.

The rights of a free press guaranteed by the 1st Amendment and the right of the press to function without prior restraint then would seem to argue in favor of a press functioning unfettered and unrestricted in wartime as in peacetime. The press would be free to ferret out whatever information the public needs to know to be able to make an informed decision. Wartime by common consent seems to represent a special case in the function of the body politic: A "clear and present danger" is said to exist (for if not, why go to war?). That condition would seem to justify the curtailing of the regular functionings of a democracy, including that of the press.

Although Gen. Colin Powell (below) *held frequent news conferences during the Persian Gulf conflict, the press was restricted by the Pentagon in its coverage of the war.*

© D. Hudson/Sygma

The U.S. government has a long tradition of imposing wartime restrictions on the press. Andrew Jackson suppressed dispatches from journalists at the front during the War of 1812. More than 100 years later, *The New York Times*' William L. Laurence was recruited by the Manhattan Project to cover the development of the atomic bomb but was forbidden to report on it until after Hiroshima and Nagasaki had been destroyed. This is not to say that the military and the press never have cooperated. In World War II, united by a sense of common purpose, the two institutions cooperated, often without explicit rules of censorship. Gen. George Marshall regularly briefed senior reporters on the war's progress, and Gen. Dwight Eisenhower briefed reporters before the landings in Sicily and Normandy. Indeed, members of the press corps went in with the first waves landing on D-Day, June 6, 1944. The press did not disclose any of the key facts that it learned in these briefings until after the various battles were over.

This relationship unraveled in Vietnam, however, when press-military relations began to fray over the course of that conflict. As the war dragged on, the press began to claim a broader "right to know" (on behalf of the people) and engaged in more aggressive, investigative journalism about the war's conduct, purpose, and how the military was trying to "sell" the war. This sort of journalism quickly gained the enmity of the military, however, which accused the press of presenting a distorted picture of the war and, in some cases, of losing the war itself by doing so.

The myth that the press "lost" Vietnam is just that: By the Defense Department's own studies of the 2,000-plus accredited journalists who covered the Vietnam war, only six had their press credentials revoked because of security problems. Even so, there are no records that press reports compromised even one military operation.

When the United States invaded Grenada in 1983 and Panama in 1989, the military put in place restrictions on press operations that it hoped would prevent a replay of what it perceived as the "Vietnam syndrome"—the press bringing the war back home, with all its graphic brutality, and in so doing turning the public against the military and the war. The argument presented by the military—that neither troops or operational security could be risked by possible press leaks of operations—was one that was accepted by most of the American people, if not the journalists themselves.

The Gulf War. During the 1991 Persian Gulf war the Pentagon enacted even more stringent restrictions on the operations of the media. Reporters were restricted to "pools"—assigned to groups which were activated by the military, brought to designated locations for reporting, and accompanied by public-affairs officials as escorts. The pool system cut down on the ability of a reporter to investigate independently and, with public-affairs escorts looking over their shoulders, to conduct interviews freely. Outside of the pools individual journalists were not allowed access to the war. In addition the Pentagon's *Guidelines for News Media* called for journalists (both print and broadcast) to submit stories for "review to determine if they contain sensitive information."

These limits—virtually unprecedented rules in the history of U.S. government-press relations—were justified by the Pentagon, as before, as necessary to protect operational security and the lives of the troops. This was even more important, the military argued, in the age of satellites, television, and instant communication. The risk of a reporter broadcasting live from a battlefield, and in so doing providing intelligence to the enemy, was a risk that was simply too great to take. Members of the media, in turn, argued that the restrictions put on their movements and ability to investigate severely hampered their ability to report either the full or the accurate story back to the American people.

So long as the war went well this did not seem to matter so much to the U.S. public, the majority of whom supported the Pentagon's press restrictions. This raises the interesting paradox, however, of how the public would be able to know that a war was going anything but well if they supported restrictions on the media's ability to report on anything but the good news.

The military also exercised more subtle forms of control over the media during the course of the Gulf war through the exercise of what in political circles has become known as "spin." In determining what pictures were going to be cleared for viewing on the nightly television news—the dramatic "smart bomb" shoots, for example—the military was able to create the image of an effective, antiseptic war.

© Robert Trippett/Sipa

During the Gulf war reporters were forced to work in pools, in which small groups were taken to the battlefield under the supervision of military public-affairs officers.

Additionally, new questions about military-media relations were raised during the Gulf war due to the new news technology now in use. The dramatic reporting by Peter Arnett (*see* BIOGRAPHY) of CNN out of Baghdad during the initial stages of the war, for example, would not have been possible in earlier conflicts. But it also raised some interesting questions about the role of a reporter in reporting the "enemy beat" during wartime.

Although few, especially in the press corps, would argue in favor of reporting information that knowingly and intentionally puts the lives of U.S. soldiers in danger, there is a gray area that exists between censorship for military purposes and that which achieves political ends. As a military officer commented in the *Los Angeles Times* just prior to the onset of the ground war, the press restrictions were put in place "so the natural tendency in any democracy . . . which is to debate . . . can't work against us [the military]."

As both the military and the press work to assimilate the many lessons of the Gulf war, the question of the limits placed on the media's ability to report on the war surely will be one of the questions that merits further debate.

ROBERT KARL MANOFF and R. MICHAEL SCHIFFER

Editor's Note: Robert Karl Manoff is director of the Center for War, Peace, and the News Media at New York University; R. Michael Schiffer is director of international security programs at the center.

PUERTO RICO

As 1991 drew to a close, Puerto Rican voters gave a resounding "no" to a proposal that would have set guidelines for a future political-status vote determining whether Puerto Rico would remain a U.S. commonwealth, become independent, or become a U.S. state.

Referendum. With 59% of Puerto Rico's 2.1 million registered voters participating, a December 8 referendum that recommended amending the island's constitution on status-related issues was defeated by a 53% to 45% margin. Some saw the outcome as an indication of growing support for statehood. Others perceived discontent among the voters, who were viewed as being more concerned about crime, the economy, and other everyday problems. The island of 3.6 million has been a U.S. commonwealth since 1952 and has no voting representation in the U.S. Congress. Island residents do not pay federal taxes.

Favoring statehood for Puerto Rico, the New Progressive Party campaigned against the referendum, which included guarantees for Spanish language and culture should Puerto Rico ever become a state. The party argued the measure aimed to drive a wedge in the relationship between Puerto Rico and the United States.

Campaigning for the referendum was the Popular Democratic Party and Gov. Rafael Hernández Colón, who favors Puerto Rico remaining a U.S. commonwealth with greater autonomy. The small Puerto Rican Independence Party also supported the referendum.

The ballot called for barring a simple yes-or-no vote on the statehood question and would have required that any future vote on status include statehood, commonwealth, and independence choices on the ballot.

Another status related issue also received attention. The Puerto Rican legislature, dominated by the pro-commonwealth party, passed a law making Spanish the official language of the island government. That action repealed a 1902 law that had designated both Spanish and English as official languages. The new law, signed by the governor in April, won for Puerto Rico the Prince of Asturias award from Spain for the island's defense of the Spanish language. But it also drew fire from statehood supporters who saw it as a move to distance Puerto Rico from the United States.

PUERTO RICO • Information Highlights

Area: 3,515 sq mi (9 104 km²).
Population (1990 census): 3,599,000.
Chief Cities (1990 census): San Juan, the capital, 437,745; Bayamon, 220,262; Ponce, 187,749.
Government (1991): *Chief Officer*—governor, Rafael Hernández Colón (Popular Democratic Party). *Legislature*—Senate, 27 members; House of Representatives, 51 members.

Other News. New political faces emerged in 1991. Victoria Muñoz announced plans to run for governor in 1992, possibly challenging Governor Hernández Colón in a primary. The governor did not say whether he would seek reelection. In the pro statehood party, Pedro Rossello, a doctor, became his party's new leader and gubernatorial candidate for 1992.

The government of Puerto Rico suffered a setback when its plans to sell the state-owned telephone company collapsed in May. The money from the sale would have gone into public education and infrastructure improvements. The government ended negotiations after offers fell below the $3 billion asking price.

In November much of Puerto Rico was plunged into darkness after the sabotage of three high-power transmission towers cut electricity. The November 13 blackout lasted several hours and left 500,000 households without power, paralyzing traffic and closing businesses. The outage came in the midst of labor-contract talks between the government-owned power company and its 7,000-member union. The union denied involvement in the sabotage, and an investigation into the crime still was under way at the end of the year.

DEBORAH RAMIREZ, *"The San Juan Star"*

QUEBEC

Glimmerings of a possible constitutional settlement between Quebec and the rest of Canada began to appear in 1991. Provincial budgetary and fiscal policies were dominated by the impact of the recession. A troubled defense contractor received a C$363 million government bailout.

Constitutional Debate. The struggle for the soul of Quebec quickened in 1991, with federalist forces perhaps gaining a little.

In Montreal on March 10, Premier Robert Bourassa stressed that federalism was still the first choice of his Liberal Party. He told delegates to a party convention that French-speaking Quebec did not want to "cut the bridges" connecting it to the rest of Canada, as advocated by the Parti Québécois (PQ) opposition. However, major changes were required to make the federal system more "functional."

One day before the premier spoke, the convention adopted a party committee report calling for a massive transfer of federal powers to Quebec. The report also called for a referendum on Quebec sovereignty in the fall of 1992 unless a constitutional deal could be worked out.

Bourassa again struck a pro-federal note at a Quebec City news conference March 27, following the tabling of still another report urging a large-scale transfer of legislative powers to Quebec. This report—by a committee composed of prominent Quebecers—endorsed the idea of a referendum and proposed a deadline for getting what Quebec wanted: October 1992. However, an unruffled Bourassa told reporters he was confident the rest of Canada would come up with an acceptable deal.

A bill authorizing the holding of an independence referendum in late 1992 was passed by the National Assembly June 20.

A 28-point federal constitutional package unveiled September 24 in Ottawa received qualified endorsement from the premier. The federal blueprint provided for acceptance of Quebec's demand for recognition as a "distinct society" within Canada, and a realignment of legislative authority between the two levels of government, though not the sweeping devolution of federal powers that Quebec had demanded.

Though Bourassa appeared to accept the federal package as a basis for negotiation, PQ leader Jacques Parizeau rejected it outright and vowed to continue to fight for Quebec independence.

Economy and Budget. Early in the year, Premier Bourassa announced a series of pump-priming measures, including government-subsidized mortgages and additional funds for construction. Quebec residents who bought new homes before Sept. 30, 1991, had a choice of a guaranteed mortgage rate of 8.5% for three years or a subsidy equivalent to 4.5% of the cost of the house, to a maximum of C$5,000.

Trying hard to cushion the effects of the recession, the Bourassa government on March 19 froze the salaries of 410,000 provincial employees for the first six months of 1992. The freeze was expected to save the treasury more than C$1 billion in immediate and longer-term spinoff economies. Wages were to increase by 3% when the freeze was to be lifted, on June 30, 1992.

Another recession-era move came May 2 when Finance Minister Gérard Levesque tabled a budget that called for a near-record deficit of C$3.5 billion, with revenues of C$34.9 billion and expenditures of C$38.4 billion. The budget imposed stiffly higher taxes on cigarettes, liquor, and gasoline, but personal-income-tax levels remained unchanged.

© Jacques Boissinot/Canapress

On Sept. 25, 1991, Quebec's Premier Robert Bourassa called Canada's new constitutional-reform plan "a discussion document, useful, but certainly incomplete."

QUEBEC • Information Highlights

Area: 594,857 sq mi (1 540 680 km²).
Population (September 1991): 6,850,900.
Chief Cities (1986 census): Quebec, the capital, 164,580; Montreal, 1,015,420; Laval, 284,164.
Government (1991): *Chief Officers*—lt. gov., Gilles Lamontagne; premier, Robert Bourassa (Liberal). *Legislature*—National Assembly, 125 members.
Provincial Finances (1991–92 fiscal year budget): *Revenues,* $34,900,000,000; *expenditures,* $38,400,000,000.
Personal Income (average weekly earnings, July 1991): $529.85.
Labor Force (September 1991, seasonally adjusted): *Employed* workers, 15 years of age and over, 2,988,000; *Unemployed,* 12.1%.
Education (1991–92): *Enrollment*—elementary and secondary schools, 1,143,800 pupils; postsecondary—universities, 127,700; community colleges, 154,800.
(All monetary figures are in Canadian dollars.)

Shipyard Rescue. A C$363 million bailout package for the troubled MIL-Davie shipyard at Lauzon, Quebec, jointly funded by the federal and Quebec governments, was announced in Quebec City July 12. Of the total amount, C$263 million would be put up by Ottawa.

The package was to cover cost overruns on two major defense contracts: the construction of three new frigates and the updating of four 1970s-vintage destroyers for the Canadian navy.

Dam Assessment. The Quebec and federal governments announced October 24 an agreement on joint procedures for carrying out the environmental assessment of the proposed C$12.7 billion Great Whale hydroelectric development in northern Quebec. They also declared their intention to "explore all options" for carrying out the assessment in harmony with the Cree Indians and Inuit of the area. Aboriginal groups had voiced opposition to Hydro-Quebec's plan to harness rivers flowing into Hudson Bay.

Stemming the Tide. Against the background of a growing exodus of English-speaking Quebecers, the government on May 16 outlined steps to boost Anglophone representation in the Quebec civil service. The goal was to lift the proportion of Anglophones from less than 1% to 10%.

JOHN BEST, *"Canada World News"*

RECORDINGS

In 1991 the recording industry shipped a record $7.5 million worth of product in a forever-changing ratio of formats. Compact disc (CD) sales were flat, but were generating more revenue than cassettes. Cassette sales were beginning to fall, and the format was presumed to be on the path to extinction. The vinyl long-playing album (LP) was already dead; the major labels issued only two to five LPs a month, out of a total of about 40 releases.

Competing Technologies. The digital audio tape (DAT) format had been presumed to be the natural tape accompaniment to the compact disc. It had been stalled for years when the record industry resisted releasing prerecorded digital tapes for fear of ruining its CD bonanza. With its average $800 price tag, however, the DAT machine remained a recording tool of limited appeal to the average consumer.

Two lower-priced alternatives, to be introduced in 1992, would try to find the market that eluded the DAT. Philips would introduce the Digital Compact Cassette (DCC), a digital tape the size of a standard cassette. This 90 minute tape can be played on a DCC machine, which can be used to record digital tapes. Likely to help the DCC machine was the fact that it also can play analog cassettes, although DCC tapes would not play on analog machines. Sony planned to debut the Mini Disc, a pocket-sized machine that can play or record music on 2½-inch (6.35-cm) discs resembling computer floppy discs. This disc offers the same convenience as the compact disc. Yet while the Mini Disc could be used to copy a compact disc, the two discs would not be interchangeable.

The marketing showdown of competing technologies in 1991 recalled the deadly competition between the VHS and Beta videorecorder formats in the 1980s. Because the success of both DCC and the Mini Disc would depend on the availability of prerecorded music in the available format, it hardly was surprising that both Sony and Philips owned major U.S. record companies. Reflecting the consolidation of the record industry, 1990 sales figures showed that the three top companies controlled more than two thirds of the market: WEA (owned by Time Warner) with 37%, Sony with 16.9%, and CEMA with 16.4%.

CD Packaging. The industry reacted in 1991 to the complaints of environmentalists and some pop stars about the wasteful cardboard packaging of CDs. The cardboard longbox soon would be history, though what would take its place still was unclear. Some companies wanted to sell CDs in the plastic jewel box, the packaging standard in virtually every other country. But U.S. retailers were resistant, concerned that the jewel box would force them to refit their shelves and would increase the threat of shoplifting because of its small size.

WEA announced that, beginning in early 1992, it would release CDs in a cardboard and plastic package called the Eco-Pak Jewel Box. In the store the package would stand up like a longbox, but later would collapse to the size of the plastic jewel box. Other companies also were working on packaging alternatives.

JOHN MILWARD, *Free-lance Writer and Critic*

REFUGEES AND IMMIGRATION

During 1991 masses of refugees again were generated by the political upheavals that have come to characterize the post-Cold War world. The largest and most dramatic exodus was that of the 2 million Iraqi Kurds and Shiites who streamed toward the borders of Turkey and Iran following Iraqi President Saddam Hussein's genocidal attacks on them. (*See* FEATURE ARTICLE/THE KURDS, page 48.) But refugee movements always have been as diverse as humanity itself. Famine in Africa again forced millions of people into exile. Nearly 200,000 Soviet Jews moved to Israel in 1991, a record number that would continue to grow and that already has triggered alarm in neighboring Arab countries. More than 1 million ethnic Germans and Hungarians, Albanians, Romanians, and Yugoslavs sought asylum and economic opportunity in the West during the year. People continued to flee Vietnam.

End of the Cold War. With the end of the Cold War, conflicts in such far-flung places as Afghanistan, Angola, Cambodia, El Salvador, Ethiopia, Mozambique, and the Western Sahara seemed to be moving toward peaceful resolution. Yet, contrary to expectations, the ending of East-West confrontation in the Third World had not diminished the problems of displacement. The numbers of refugees and displaced persons, as well as migrants, were on the rise throughout the world.

Ethnic and Communal Conflict. In the 1990s most refugee movements are likely to be the result of ethnic and communal conflicts. The most common form of warfare in the developing world in the 1990s is internal, especially ethnic and religious conflict, with age-old hatreds fueled by sharp socioeconomic inequalities and the availability of modern weaponry. Internal wars in the Third World have been fought not only by military means but by preventing international aid from reaching people living in conflict areas. The most alarming examples in 1991 occurred in Sudan, Somalia, and Liberia. Currently, more than half of the world's refugees flee communally based violence. And there are fears that many more could become displaced in future years as nationalistic, ethnic, and religious tensions, previously suppressed by East-West conflict and totalitarian regimes, are unleashed. In order to deal more adequately with these new developments, Western governments in 1991 lobbied for the development of a stronger and more rapid UN response system for refugee emergencies.

Internally Displaced People. While there were almost 18 million recognized refugees worldwide in 1991, there were at least 20 million more people who had been displaced within their own countries. In 1991 huge internal displacements took place in Afghanistan, Burma, India, Liberia, the Philippines, Somalia, Sri Lanka, the Soviet Union, and Yugoslavia, to give but a few examples. A critical weakness of the international humanitarian system is that there is now no special international organization to protect and assist the internally displaced. There is a body of international law dealing with internal refugees, but it is regarded by many as too weak and inadequate to regulate their treatment by their own governments. Thus, internally displaced people have neither recourse to international refugee law nor, ordinarily, to international-relief agencies. They are unprotected mostly because while within the boundaries of their own countries they are by current definition not refugees.

Long-standing Refugee Populations. Even as new refugee crises emerge, there remain numerous long-standing refugee populations in the Third World, some in existence for 20 years or more. Unlike earlier forced migrations, which ultimately were resolved by repatriation or overseas resettlement, Third World refugees today find only temporary asylum in neighboring states. Some national groups have become more or less permanent refugees, such as the Palestinians who make up at least half of Jordan's population of 3 million or the hundreds of thousands of Cambodians who have spent more than a decade along the Thai-Cambodian border.

In October nearly 19 million foreigners took part in a U.S. immigration lottery, an innovation of the 1990 immigration law, vying for 40,000 permanent-residency slots.

© Kevin Mellema/Gamma-Liaison

Most of today's permanent refugees are the result of intense and long-standing conflicts in Afghanistan, the Horn of Africa, southern Africa, Indochina, and Central America. Because the international community has failed to resolve most current refugee situations, international aid for refugees has become increasingly bogged down with expensive and continuing care and maintenance programs.

The majority of these populations languish in camps or survive illegally without any hope of a permanent place of settlement or eventual return home. Desperate poverty, idleness, and stress often characterize camp environments. In some cases, as with the Vietnamese boat people in Hong Kong, forced repatriation has begun.

Costly care and maintenance programs for long-staying refugee populations also have drained the resources of the Office of the United Nations High Commissioner for Refugees (UNHCR). In recent years, donor countries' contributions have not kept pace with the ever-growing numbers of refugees. Without sufficient funds the UNHCR has been unable to fulfill its mandate, and for the first time in many years critical services have had to be cut back in refugee camps throughout the world.

Asylum Crisis in the West. While the contemporary situation is characterized by long-term care and maintenance in enclosed camps for the majority of refugees in the Third World and by the failure to provide any kind of alternatives to prolonged camp existence, Western countries—particularly Western European governments—increasingly are unwilling to let refugees enter their countries to apply for political asylum. While the United States took steps to implement a series of wide-ranging reforms in its asylum procedures initiated in 1990, Western Europe moved closer to a harmonized policy on asylum and entry as part of its overall plan to abolish internal customs and passport controls within the European Community by the end of 1992. The effect of this on asylum seekers in Europe in 1991 was diminished opportunity to register asylum claims. Western Europe's restrictionism was motivated in large part by increasing numbers of asylum seekers from the Middle East, Africa, South Asia, and southeastern Europe, in addition to concern about the prospect of mass migration from a deteriorating Soviet Union.

Late in 1991 in what some saw as a refugee-policy contradiction, the United States turned back hundreds of Haitian refugees attempting to reach the United States in the wake of a military takeover of Haiti's democratically elected government. U.S. government officials, however, categorized nearly all of the Haitians as economic migrants and thus, in accordance with long-standing immigration policies, not eligible for resident status.

GIL LOESCHER, *University of Notre Dame*

© Robert Trippett/Sipa

The Rev. Sharon Johnson gives Communion at the 203d General Assembly of the Presbyterian Church (USA) in June 1991. The delegates rejected a report urging the church to relax some strictures on sexual relations.

RELIGION

Overview

A survey conducted for the Graduate School of the City University of New York revealed that 90% of the U.S. population identify themselves with a religious denomination. Of that total, 60.2% said they belong to various Protestant denominations, 26.2% are Roman Catholics, and 3.7% are members of non-Christian faiths, including 1.8% Jewish and .5% Muslim. Of the latter group the survey noted that there are 1 million Buddhists and 500,000 Hindus in the nation. Some 7.5% responded that they are of no religion and 2.3% refused to participate.

Like other divisions of society, many U.S. religious denominations were facing economic difficulties in 1991. Although donations by churchgoers were at an all-time high, financial deficits were common. Increased expenses, inflation, and the fact that denominations had been assuming new responsibilities (for example, day-care centers and shelters for the homeless) contributed to the shortfall. Staff layoffs and a cutback in services within the individual denominations resulted.

Immanuel Jakobovits, Britain's chief rabbi and a member of the House of Lords, was awarded the 1991 Templeton Prize for Progress in Religion. He was the first Jew to receive the award, currently valued at some $800,000.

Far Eastern

On March 24, 1991, hundreds of thousands of Hindus visited a temple in Ayodhya, India, that is believed to be the birthplace of the god Rama. The peaceful nature of the annual birthday pilgrimage was notable because the shrine, housed in a 16th-century mosque, was the focal point of a bitter controversy between Hindus and Muslims in 1990 in which several hundred people were killed.

Fundamentalist Hindus have demanded that the mosque be torn down and replaced with a larger temple, while Muslims say there is no basis for the belief that a temple existed at the site before the mosque. Ayodhya has more than 6,000 temples, but the birthplace of Rama is the one that attracts the most pilgrims.

The dispute illustrates the persistence of historic tensions between the more than 600 million Hindus and 100 million Muslims in India. Despite the fact that Hindus are far and away the religious majority, some fundamentalist groups and the Hindu nationalist Bharatiya Janata Party (BJP) have complained about provisions in the law that grant non-Hindus special privileges. For example, the state cannot take over Muslim religious real estate but can appropriate Hindu land. The World Hindu Organization (Vishwa Hindu Parishad, VHP) has been campaigning to "liberate" about 3,000 temples, including the one in Ayodhya, which it says were destroyed and replaced by Muslim structures.

Henna, a motion picture by Indian director Randhir Kapoor that was released in India in 1991, is an Asian Romeo and Juliet story that features an Indian Hindu as the male lead and a Pakistani Muslim as the female lead. The film, which takes place in the disputed border territory of Kashmir, was promoted in both countries with the slogan, "God made land, Man made borders."

Mongolia. The Khama Lama, Mongolia's ranking Buddhist cleric, told Western visitors in 1991 that about 100 monasteries have been reoccupied by monks since the country's Communist dictatorship was ousted and replaced with a more reform-minded government in 1990. The repressive regime that had ruled the country for 70 years had destroyed more than 700 monasteries in the 1930s and executed thousands of lamas. The Khama Lama, who is in his eighties, said that restoration of the monasteries would be slow because of a lack of money and a shortage of monks.

DARRELL J. TURNER
Religious News Service

Islam

Islamic symbolism and rhetoric figured prominently in the 1991 Persian Gulf war as both predominantly Muslim Iraq and the Islamic states in the coalition arrayed against it sought to win the support of fellow Muslims by proclaiming that their approaches to the conflict were in accord with Islam. Parties with programs emphasizing Islamic values played pivotal roles in Jordan and Algeria in 1991. Pakistani leaders considered the imposition of Islamic law. The decline of communism gave Muslims expanded religious opportunities in the USSR and elsewhere.

Gulf War. Just before the U.S.-led offensive to liberate Kuwait began in mid-January, Iraqi President Saddam Hussein told world Muslim leaders meeting in Baghdad that his refusal to yield to United Nations demands represented a determination to safeguard Islam against non-Muslim incursions. Several days later, the president ordered the phrase "Allah Akbar" ("God is Great") added to the Iraqi flag. To counter Saddam's moves, religious authorities in Saudi Arabia and other coalition countries sanctioned the Gulf war as a *jihad*—a struggle to protect and defend Islamic interests.

Nevertheless, Iraq's assertions won widespread popular approval in many Muslim societies. Conservative Islamic organizations in Turkey protested against their government's willingness to facilitate the coalition's military plans in the Gulf, while Islamic groups in Egypt launched demonstrations to swing public opinion away from the government's policy of sending troops to the Gulf. Some Muslims in Jordan, India, Pakistan, Indonesia, Malaysia, and Nigeria expressed anger over non-Muslim military action against a Muslim state, frequently by vehement public demonstrations.

During the war itself, Muslim members of the coalition expressed the hope that the fighting would end quickly. In addition to concern about the human and material cost of the war, they pointed out that it would be inappropriate for the large number of non-Muslim troops deployed in and around Arabia to remain there during either the Islamic holy month of Ramadan (mid-March to mid-April 1991) or the annual Muslim pilgrimage to Mecca (June). The rapid coalition victory permitted both events to proceed more or less as normal.

Jordan and Algeria. In Jordan members of the Muslim Brotherhood, a political party that had won more than one quarter of the seats in the November 1989 parliamentary elections on a platform emphasizing Islamic values, received ministerial posts early in January. In Algeria in May the Islamic Salvation Front engineered a series of protests against government practices it feared would limit the Front's effectiveness on the national political scene. As the protests fueled widespread violence, a state of emergency was declared on June 5 and several key members of the Front, including its leader, Abbasi Madani, were arrested later in the month. Although the government subsequently agreed to open a dialogue with the opposition, the Front's refusal to participate in these talks and its insistence on its leaders' freedom and early presidential elections left Algeria's political future in doubt.

Pakistan and India. In April politicians in Pakistan considered a proposal to make the *Sharia* the supreme law of the land and to subject all aspects of life to Islamic tenets. Despite the country's 97% Muslim population, the plan met with a mixed reception and no immediate action was taken. The volatility of the mixture of politics and religion on the Asian subcontinent was demonstrated vividly as Muslims and Hindus argued, and occasionally came to blows, over the status of a shrine in the northeastern city of Ayodhya, India, that both religions claimed as their own.

Communism Collapses. In Albania, 1991 saw Muslims experience the right to worship publicly for the first time since 1967. The collapse of communism in the Soviet Union and the political turmoil in many of the republics also paved the way for Muslims, especially those in Central Asia, to practice their faith to a degree unprecedented in the days of Communist control. In the euphoria of this new freedom, some Central Asian Muslims began exploring the possibility of establishing relations with the Muslim states of Iran and Afghanistan, while others campaigned for strong ties with Turkey on the basis of their common Turkic ethnicity.

KENNETH J. PERKINS
University of South Carolina

Judaism

The dramatic events that convulsed much of the world during 1991—the Persian Gulf war and the abortive coup in the Soviet Union—had repercussions for Jews and Judaism.

The Gulf War. On January 17, Iraqi Scud missiles began falling on the state of Israel, even though the Jewish state was not a participant in the war. The possibility that the Scuds might carry chemical weapons evoked memories of the Nazi destruction of European Jewry, especially since Israel, heeding a U.S. request not to retaliate, had to maintain a passive stance. Jews around the world prayed and fasted for the success of the anti-Iraq coalition and the safety of Jews in Israel.

The outbreak of the Gulf war also prompted Jewish theologians to articulate a religious approach to questions of war and peace, and their position differed markedly from that of their Christian counterparts, who overwhelmingly opposed the war. Reflecting the absence of a strong pacifist tradition in Judaism, the Jewish thinkers justified the Gulf war as a legitimate step to check aggression.

In certain Orthodox Jewish circles, the whirlwind success of the United States and its allies—coming just when the tide of human freedom was pushing back the forces of Communism—was interpreted in messianic terms. This tendency was pronounced especially in the Lubavitch Hasidic sect, a group that originated 200 years ago in Russia and that now is headquartered in Brooklyn, NY. Citing medieval Jewish mystical writings, members of the group claimed that the defeat of Iraq could usher in the redemption of the world. A prediction allegedly made by Menachem Schneerson, the rabbi of Lubavitch, that the war would end on or near the Jewish holiday of Purim—which it did—confirmed the belief of some of his followers that he might be the Messiah.

Anti-Semitism. Fears of resurgent anti-Semitism in Eastern Europe continued in 1991. Ironically the new freedom of speech that came with the fall of Communism provided opportunities for extreme nationalist groups to malign Jews. Public-opinion polls conducted in the spring indicated especially high levels of hostility toward Jews in Poland, while in Romania an attempt to rehabilitate the reputation of Ion Antonescu, the pro-Hitler dictator of the country during World War II, carried clear anti-Jewish implications.

Similar Jewish concerns about the activities of anti-Semitic groups in the Soviet Union intensified on August 19 when a coup briefly removed Mikhail Gorbachev from power. Since the plotters came from hard-line circles within the Communist Party, a curb on Soviet Jewish emigration and a wave of government-sponsored anti-Semitism were clear possibilities. The collapse of the coup two days later eased those anxieties, though the movement toward increased autonomy of the individual Soviet republics that followed raised the specter of intensified ethnic chauvinism that might spill over into anti-Semitism.

© Little, Brown and Company

In "Chutzpah," Alan Dershowitz charges that Jewish leaders are not assertive enough in confronting anti-Semitism.

U.S. Developments. A new demographic survey of U.S. Jews also attracted attention. Commissioned by the Council of Jewish Federations and Welfare Funds, the study provided much cause for concern, showing that more than half of all the Jews who married since 1985 had married non-Jews—and in only a small percentage of these cases did the non-Jewish partner convert to Judaism. In the absence of such a conversion, the children generally were being raised as Christians or with no religion—a trend likely to reduce the number of Jews over the next generation. Equally striking was how few Jews expressed opposition to mixed marriage: Fully 87.5% of Jews said they would not object if their child married a non-Jew. Release of the report prompted discussion among rabbis about how to reach out to mixed-religion families in a way that nevertheless would maintain the traditional Jewish attitude of disapproval toward such marriages.

In late August the killing of a Jew in the Crown Heights neighborhood of Brooklyn, NY, by blacks enraged over the death of a black child accidentally run over by a Jewish motorist again raised, in a most agonizing way, the question of how Jews should respond to attacks on them.

LAWRENCE GROSSMAN
The American Jewish Committee

Orthodox Eastern

Metropolitan Bartholomeos of Chalcedon was elected ecumenical patriarch of Constantinople following the death of Patriarch Dimitrios I in October 1991. Unlike his predecessor, Bartholomeos was well known internationally and had served on the World Council of Churches' Central Committee and Faith Order Commission.

The USSR and Eastern Europe. New ecclesiastical structures for Orthodox churches in the independent Baltic states and in the Byelorussian and Ukraine republics were expected in the aftermath of the failed August coup in the USSR. Most Orthodox churches in these regions remained within the patriarchate of Moscow, although a small independent Ukrainian Orthodox Church was formed. Meanwhile thousands of new churches, parochial schools, and philanthropic agencies opened throughout the republics.

Eastern-rite Catholic bishops convened in the Vatican to plan strategies for gaining membership from among the Orthodox in Eastern Europe and the USSR, particularly in the Western Ukraine, Czechoslovakia, and Romania, where Eastern-rite Catholicism now is legal. A number of new bishops were consecrated for the task.

Patriarch Paul, formerly metropolitan of Rasko-Prizren, became the new primate of the Serbian Orthodox Church, centered in Belgrade, following the retirement and subsequent death of Patriarch German. Recognized as an ascetic man of prayer, Paul, with the church's synod of bishops, consecrated five new hierarchs for the Serbian Church. The new bishops are the spiritual children of Father Justin Popovich (d. 1979), a monastic priest, theologian, and author, who was detained under the old regime and now is venerated widely as a saint.

Conflict between Orthodox Serbs and Roman Catholic Croatians in Yugoslavia caused the bombing of the church in Jasenovac, recently constructed in memory of the thousands of Serbs who perished there in World War II death camps. The home of the Orthodox bishop of Pakrac, which housed an invaluable library, also was destroyed.

North America. The Serbian Orthodox Church raised its North American diocese to a metropolitanate on the occasion of the 70th anniversary of Serbian Orthodoxy as a distinct ecclesiastical entity in the New World. U.S.-born Archbishop Christopher Kovachevich of the Midwestern diocese was named metropolitan in October, a step that raised hopes for the unification of the expatriate Serbian "Free Church" with the patriarchate from which it has been in schism since the 1960s.

Archbishop Iakovos of the Greek Orthodox archdiocese in North America suspended relations during the summer with the National Council of Churches of Christ (NCCC) in the United States because of its pro-choice stand on abortion and the ordination of gay men and lesbians in some NCCC member churches. The move brought attempts to find a common ecumenical policy, particularly in regard to the NCCC, which now is presided over by Father Leonid Kishkovsky of the Orthodox Church in America (OCA).

THOMAS HOPKO, *St. Vladimir's Seminary*

© W. Laski/Sipa

In a new atmosphere of greater religious freedom, Patriarch Alexei of the Russian Orthodox Church took part in Boris Yeltsin's inaugural as president of the Russian Republic.

Protestantism

Proposals to change traditional Christian standards for sexual behavior, including homosexual practice and heterosexual activity outside of marriage, stirred turmoil in several Protestant bodies in 1991. However, no major denomination took an official stand endorsing such practices, although some decided to continue studying the subject.

Human Sexuality. The most controversy was generated by a report prepared by a task force of the 2.9-million-member Presbyterian Church (U.S.A.) that suggested replacing traditional Christian norms on sexuality with an ethic of "justice-love" focusing on the quality of relationships between sex partners. The denomination's annual General Assembly in June rejected the document and a minority report opposing it, while leaving the door open to continued study of both and calling for development of a program on issues of human sexuality.

The triennial General Convention of the 2.4-million-member Episcopal Church, meeting in July, affirmed the church's traditional teachings limiting sexual relations to married heterosexual couples, while acknowledging a "discontinuity" between these teachings and the experience of many Episcopalians. It asked each of the church's 121 dioceses to initiate studies of sexuality at the parish level to be used in development of a "pastoral teaching" on the subject by the House of Bishops.

Establishment of a task force on sexuality was endorsed by the biennial meeting of the 1.5-million-member American Baptist Churches in June, which also adopted a statement opposing homosexual clergy. The Southern Baptist Convention, which has ten times as many members, adopted a resolution at its annual convention earlier in the month reaffirming its commitment to traditional biblical principles of sexual morality and deploring what it called a nonbiblical "culture of moral relativism" in the United States.

The Rev. Michael Kinnamon failed to get the two-thirds vote needed to be elected president of the 1.1-million-member Christian Church (Disciples of Christ) at its convention in Tulsa, OK, in October, largely because of his refusal to condemn homosexual behavior. The Rev. C. William Nichols was named to head the church on a temporary two-year basis after Kinnamon, the official nominee, was defeated.

The 5.2-million-member Evangelical Lutheran Church in America adopted a statement on abortion at its biennial church assembly in Orlando, FL, in September. The document drew wide attention for its attempt to take a middle course, neither condemning all abortions outright nor giving unqualified support to a woman's right to abortion. The assembly also called for development of a process for study of a proposed concordat with the Episcopal Church that calls for "full communion" between the two bodies. Earlier the Episcopal Convention had approved the beginning of such a study in its churches.

The Southern Baptists. President George Bush was criticized by leaders of several denominations—including the Episcopal Church, of which he is a member—for his decision to go to war against Iraq in January. But he received a warm welcome at the annual meeting of the Southern Baptist Convention in June, where he praised that denomination for having "held to faith where others have lost it, gained in numbers where others haven't, made a difference where others couldn't."

The Southern Baptist Convention voted to cut its ties to the Baptist Joint Committee on Public Affairs, reflecting the deep division between the moderates who staff the ten-denomination agency and the fundamentalists who control the convention. Some 6,000 moderates met in Atlanta in May and elected the Rev. John Hewett of Asheville, NC, as moderator of their movement within the strife-torn denomination.

Continuing battles with trustees led to a rash of departures from the faculty of Southeastern Baptist Theological Seminary in Wake Forest, NC, while trustees at Southern Baptist Theological Seminary in Louisville, KY, adopted new faculty-hiring guidelines that were worked out in a compromise with faculty. The Rev. Lloyd Elder, who had been criticized by conservatives, agreed to retire early as head of the Southern Baptist Sunday School Board. He was succeeded by the Rev. Jimmy Draper, a past president of the denomination.

Organizations. South Korean feminist theologian Chung Hyun Kyung generated controversy with her address to the Seventh Assembly of the World Council of Churches, meeting in Canberra, Australia, in February. In the speech she invoked the spirits of martyrs and linked them to the Holy Spirit. Most of the audience gave her a standing ovation, but many Orthodox delegates, joined by some Anglicans and Lutherans, responded with shouts of "apostate" and "pagan."

In the United States the National Council of Churches (NCC) called for a "serious reflection of our national purpose and identity" in the wake of the Persian Gulf war. It launched a 16-month dialogue on the concept of a "new world order" that would include a series of conferences on such topics as the urban crisis; world economic realignment; racism; and security, arms, and peace. Under the leadership of its new general secretary, the Rev. Joan Brown Campbell, the organization worked to improve its relationships with evangelical Protestants. In late August, Campbell met with evangelist Billy Graham at NCC headquarters in New York City.

DARRELL J. TURNER

Roman Catholicism

For Roman Catholicism the year 1991 was one of coming to grips with the changes and challenges after the fall of Communist regimes in the Soviet Union and Eastern Europe. But while Roman Catholic leadership reveled along with others at the demise of communism, it was quick to point out capitalism's shortcomings. In an encyclical marking the 100th anniversary of modern Catholic social teaching, *Centesimus Annus,* Pope John Paul II said that Marxism failed to remedy—and even worsened—the problems of the working class, but unbridled capitalism has not supplied the solution either.

The World Scene. As religious freedom flowered in the post-Communist Soviet Union, the pope named the first resident bishop of Mos-

© Livio Anticoli/Gamma-Liaison

At a Vatican ceremony, June 28, Pope John Paul II elevated 23 members, including U.S. Archbishops Roger Mahony and Anthony Bevilacqua, to the College of Cardinals.

cow in 55 years, named bishops in Siberia and Kazakhstan, and created two new dioceses in Byelorussia. The Vatican formalized diplomatic relations with Lithuania, Latvia, Estonia, and Albania and named its first-ever ambassador to Bulgaria. But as ethnic tension rose in Eastern Europe, especially in Yugoslavia, which broke into a civil war, the Jesuit magazine *La Civilita Cattolica* said the Soviet breakup likely would give rise to "dangerous nationalism." Warning that a weakened Soviet Union would be less able to balance the "American superpower" in the world arena, the magazine said the Soviet Union should remain a "great power."

Doubting that war between the U.S.-led allied coalition and Iraq was morally justified, the Vatican supported plans to avoid armed conflict in the Persian Gulf. Many U.S. Catholic bishops publicly opposed the war or raised grave doubts about the morality of aggression. Opponents of the war did not believe the situation fulfilled the Catholic theory of a just war, which claims that war can be waged only as a last resort and that civilians cannot be targeted. The Gulf war prompted Catholic groups, such as Pax Christi USA, to question whether the just-war theory had become obsolete.

At a special meeting at the Vatican, the pope sought the views of the world's cardinals on the growing threats to human life. The Vatican group condemned RU-486, an abortion pill, as "a new serious threat to human life." In the United States, North Dakota and Michigan passed abortion restrictions; Maryland approved the most permissive abortion legislation in the nation.

In other Vatican news, Pope John Paul II traveled to Brazil, Portugal, Poland, and Hungary. He also named 23 new cardinals from six continents, including Archbishops Roger Mahony of Los Angeles and Anthony Bevilacqua of Philadelphia. Attacking the attitude that "one religion is as good as another," the pope issued an encyclical, *Redemptoris Missio,* criticizing widespread indifference to missionary activity in the church today.

At the urging of the U.S. bishops, the church discussed problems facing women in the Roman Catholic Church and in society at a two-day international consultation. However, U.S. church leaders, including Bishop Joseph L. Imesch, chairman of the committee writing a pastoral letter on women, said the Vatican's response was "frustrating and dismaying."

Worldwide, the number of priests declined 1.3% to 401,479. Asking for a broad discussion of issues related to vocations, the National Federation of Priests' Councils warned that the rule of celibacy is threatening opportunities for Catholics to receive the Eucharist regularly. However, a study indicated that most U.S. priests are generally happier in their work than were their counterparts 20 years earlier. Richard Turner, a 57-year-old North Carolina man, was the 50th married former Episcopal priest to join the Catholic priesthood in the United States.

Newsmakers. Richard John Neuhaus, a leading neoconservative voice and former Lutheran minister, was ordained a Roman Catholic priest by New York Cardinal John J. O'Connor. Seattle Archbishop Raymond Hunthausen, recognized internationally as a peace activist and the object of a controversial Vatican-ordered investigation, retired on his 70th birthday, five years before mandatory retirement. The Vatican gave permission for the archdiocese of Baltimore to begin the cause for sainthood for Mother Mary Elizabeth Lange, founder of the Oblate Sisters of Providence, the first order of black nuns. The cause of sainthood for Queen Isabella of Spain was suspended.

DANIEL MEDINGER
Editor, "The Catholic Review"

RETAILING

U.S. retailing wallowed in 1991 as sales and profits reacted sluggishly to the recession.

Early in 1991, Wal-Mart Stores, the Southern discounter, edged Sears Roebuck off its traditional perch as the largest U.S. retailer in sales. A revitalized K Mart Corporation, in turn, elbowed Sears into the number-three post. With 1990 sales of about $33 billion, both Wal-Mart and K Mart predicted they soon would rack up $50 billion in sales, with $100 billion by the turn of the century.

Although financially pressed Americans appeared to be favoring the discounters, two such companies, Ames and Hills, were unable to avoid bankruptcy. Two traditional companies, P. A. Bergner Company of Milwaukee, WI, which had purchased Carson Pirie Scott Inc., of Chicago, and Morse Shoe Company of Canton, MA, also filed for voluntary bankruptcy, as did Carter Hawley Hale Stores, Inc. However, Federated Department Stores and Allied Stores, the largest firms in voluntary bankruptcy, made progress in obtaining creditor approval for an emergence from insolvency in 1992. Carter Hawley, too, appeared to move in that direction as Zell/Chillmark Fund, an investment partnership, took over a substantial interest in the concern.

But the recession dogged some of the best-known companies. In August, Sears informed suppliers that it was extending payments from 30 to 60 days. After it was reported that Saks Fifth Avenue had sustained a $100 million loss in the first seven months of 1991 (a report which Saks denied), Heller Financial Inc., a leading factor—a financial go-between for retailers and suppliers—told its supplier clients that it no longer would guarantee payment for goods shipped to Saks. And when Nordstrom announced it would have an unfavorable third-quarter report, investors cut the price of its stock 25% in one day.

Not all was dour, however. Wal-Mart, K Mart, the Gap, the Limited, and Charming Shoppes outpaced others in sales and profits. In addition, they and many others so had altered their strategies to cope with the recession that analysts believed their restructuring would stand them well when the recession ended.

Nonetheless, Wall Street observers remained cautious. "Gains in market share by the growth companies, in merchandise units and dollar sales, would suffocate ineffectual and heavily leveraged retailers if economic growth were to be slow over an extended period," said Bernard Sosnick of Oppenheimer & Company, Inc.

Regionally, there were some surprising shifts in the retailing growth rate. In the first quarter, the Midwest supplanted the West as the area with highest growth, rising 3.6% while the West edged down 0.2% from 1990, according to the International Council of Shopping Centers (ICSC). And while the South jumped 3.3% in sales, the Northeast continued to languish, dropping 4.2%, the ICSC said. The fastest-growing locality was Bakersfield, CA, up a blistering 22.2%.

Like the nonfood retailing industry, food chains reflected the performance flux favoring nonleveraged companies against those extended in debt. Even those with strong sales/profit records were victims of a falling junk-bond market. Despite the recession, supermarket chains added specialty departments, boosted productivity in shelf space, and raised profits.

In the clothing war between name brands and private labels, the Gap stores resolved one battle. The 1,100-store chain said it would drop Levi Strauss clothes to push its own brand.

ISADORE BARMASH, *Free-lance Writer*

With the U.S. economy in a downturn, more and more consumers were turning to members-only discount warehouses for their shopping. Sales at such stores, including the Wal-Mart-owned Sam's, below, jumped 26% during 1990.

Courtesy, Wal-Mart Stores, Inc.

RHODE ISLAND

In mid-March, as the General Assembly neared its halfway point, House Speaker Joseph DeAngelis, a Democrat, told a reporter, "We have just come out of ten of the worst weeks in Rhode Island history." Most observers later would call 1991 the worst year in state history.

Bank Woes. On January 1, hours after his swearing in, Democratic Gov. Bruce Sundlun signed an executive order closing 45 banks and credit unions, freezing $1.7 billion in deposits held by some 300,000 depositors. The failure of a private insurer forced the action and the administration began a crash program to find means of heading off economic disaster. Federal insurance and takeovers by healthy banks saved some institutions, but many were near insolvency. A state takeover plan, including liquidation, was proposed by the governor and passed by the General Assembly with many misgivings and changes. Some depositors did get money back, but impatience triggered angry rallies and bitter denunciation of the governor.

Budget. Governor Sundlun also inherited a budget deficit of more than $220 million. Heavy revenue shortfalls demanded immediate action to meet the requirement of a balanced budget on June 30. The administration thus turned its attention from the credit unions to a revised 1991 budget with major cuts and tax increases. This, too, the assembly passed, after impassioned debate and largely fruitless efforts to soften the blows.

Next came the governor's 1992 budget. Revenue still was falling and the economic recession was deepening. Another 18.5% education cut, other reductions, and many fee increases were proposed, but Sundlun was adamantly against further tax increases. Again the legislature struggled to find alternatives and managed to restore some school money in an effort to fend off further political damage.

The legislature also enacted the state's first compulsory auto-insurance law, a major reform of the zoning code, and various departmental reorganizations.

Recession. The drama of the assembly session was played out against a background of serious economic recession. Unemployment at the start of the year was 7.3%, rose to 8% by February, dropped some in the spring, and resumed its climb, topping 9% in the fall. By then, growing numbers of residents had exhausted their unemployment benefits.

The real-estate boom sagged during the first six months of 1991, with home prices dropping to 1988 levels. Business bankruptcies soared; the Electric Boat division of General Dynamics, the submarine builder located in Groton, CT, and employing many Rhode Islanders, under threat of a drop in government contracts, announced layoffs totaling nearly 2,000. Defense cutbacks meant additional recessionary pressure. Only tourism increased.

Scandals. The state also was battered by scandals. The mayor of Pawtucket was indicted on a number of bribe solicitation counts; a recently retired Superior Court judge was arrested for taking kickbacks; and the press recounted a pattern of lush state pensions secured for favored individuals.

Disasters. Nature also dealt a blow in the form of hurricane *Bob,* which struck the state on August 19. The resulting damage was serious along the shore, but far less than some past storms. There was no loss of life.

By late in the year, polls reflected widespread public pessimism and unprecedented anger at politicians and government generally.

ELMER E. CORNWELL, JR., *Brown University*

RHODE ISLAND • Information Highlights

Area: 1,212 sq mi (3 140 km²).
Population (1990 census): 1,003,464.
Chief Cities (1990 census): Providence, the capital, 160,728; Warwick, 85,427.
Government (1991): *Chief Officers*—governor, Bruce G. Sundlun (D); lt. gov., Roger N. Begin (D). *General Assembly*—Senate, 50 members; House of Representatives, 100 members.
State Finances (fiscal year 1990): *Revenue,* $3,034,000,000; *expenditure,* $3,014,000,000.
Personal Income (1990): $18,894,000,000; per capita, $18,802.
Labor Force (June 1991): *Civilian labor force,* 510,600; *unemployed,* 38,800 (7.6% of total force).
Education: *Enrollment* (fall 1989)—public elementary schools, 98,412; public secondary, 37,317; colleges and universities, 76,503. *Public school expenditures* (1989), $736,942,000.

ROMANIA

In 1991, Romania continued to cope with a political system and an economy newly emerged from decades of dictatorship.

Protests, Riots, and Unrest. Early in 1991 the Civic Alliance group organized demonstrations across Romania, demanding the resignation of President Ion Iliescu and the National Salvation Front government. Waves of strikes swept the country, as Prime Minister Petre Roman warned against the danger of "union dictatorship." In June five trade-union groups set up an umbrella National Confederative Union, demanding installation of an emergency government to promote reforms and increase social benefits.

The worst violence since June 1990 gripped Romania in late September, when Bucharest residents joined thousands of miners in fierce rioting in the capital, demanding higher wages, lower prices, and the resignation of government leaders. The only victim of the antigovernment crusade was Roman, who was replaced as prime minister by former Finance Minister Theodor Stolojan on October 1.

The dissatisfaction of Romania's Hungarian minority continued unabated. The Hungarian Democratic Union of Romania, the country's second-largest opposition party, held its second national conference in the troubled district of Tîrgu-Mures in May, reconfirming its alliance with the Romanian democratic opposition. It issued resolutions accusing the government of orchestrating the Tîrgu-Mures violence of 1990 and demanded restoration of separate Hungarian schools. In October ethnic Hungarian newspapers in Transylvania called for a referendum on autonomy for that area.

The other major ethnic issue concerned the Soviet territory of Moldavia, formerly Romanian Bessarabia. A July poll found a majority of Romanians and nearly two thirds of Moldavians preferred to remain separate, but with close economic and cultural ties to Romania. However, after Moldavia declared its independence from the USSR following the failed August coup, Romania was the first country to recognize the republic's independence; while President Iliescu maintained the inviolability of current borders, he remained vague on the prospects for future union.

The Iliescu Regime. Public support for the Iliescu government remained low in the face of continued shortages, soaring inflation, and ongoing labor unrest. The Front redefined itself as a "center-leftist party of socialist orientation" at its convention in March, but no policy changes were evident. Repeated attempts to woo opposition groups went unheeded.

Helsinki Watch reports continued to criticize Romania's human-rights situation, noting that the development of civil society lagged behind other Eastern European countries.

On June 3 a military court sentenced Nicu Ceauşescu, the late dictator Nicolae Ceauşescu's son and heir apparent, to 16 years in prison on the charge of "instigation to murder" during the 1989 revolution.

Political Parties. In April the opposition umbrella organization Anti-Totalitarian Democratic Forum, comprised of seven major groups, rejected the Front's call for a coalition government and announced plans to leave the parliament and create a united opposition. Meanwhile, the opposition Civic Alliance movement formed a political branch called the All-Civic Party under the chairmanship of Nicolae Manolescu, a prominent activist. The rejuvenated Romanian Communist Party, with a revised platform supporting political pluralism and a mixed economy, publicized its intentions to participate in the fall elections, as did another offshoot of the party, the Socialist Labor Party, headed by Ilie Verdet, a former Ceauşescu regime prime minister.

After the December 1990 return to Romania and subsequent expulsion of the 70-year-old former King Michael, a public-opinion poll revealed that 80% of the Romanians questioned favored a presidential regime and only 13% favored monarchy.

ROMANIA • Information Highlights

Official Name: Romania.
Location: Southeastern Europe.
Area: 91,699 sq mi (237 500 km^2).
Population (mid-1991 est.): 23,400,000.
Chief Cities (July 1, 1986 est.): Bucharest, the capital, 1,989,823; Braşov, 351,493; Constanta, 327,676.
Government: *Head of state,* Ion Iliescu, president (took office December 1989). *Head of government,* Theodor Stolojan, prime minister (took office October 1, 1991). *Legislature* (unicameral)—Grand National Assembly.
Monetary Unit: Leu (60.770 lei equal U.S.$1, July 1991).
Gross National Product (1989 est. U.S.$): $79,800,-000,000.
Foreign Trade (1990 U.S.$): *Imports,* $9,249,000,000; *exports,* $6,095,000,000.

Economy. Romania's economy continued its downward slide in 1991. The leu's devaluation and 1990 price liberalizations raised the cost of living by 50%, while the Persian Gulf war worsened an already-severe energy shortage. In August the government estimated that 155,000 people were unemployed, triple the April level, and that industrial production had dropped by 18%.

Despite ongoing crises some advances were made. Faced with widespread social unrest, the Front government launched a second stage of price liberalizations in April and announced plans for a single exchange rate, a privatization law, and formation of a stock exchange. The first commercial bank opened in Bucharest in April; by September some 28,000 commercial companies existed in Romania, 3,200 created with foreign capital.

Outside aid, jeopardized in 1990 due to doubts about the Front's commitment to democracy, resumed in April with an International Monetary Fund $748 million package for economic reform. In June the World Bank granted a $180 million loan for energy and agricultural development, its first to Romania in nine years.

Foreign Affairs. Romania continued to be active diplomatically in 1991, especially toward the rest of Europe. It applied for association with the European Community (EC) in February, though following the September riots that removed Prime Minister Roman from power the Commission of the EC postponed planned talks on the association. Meanwhile, Romania received guest status in the Council of Europe.

In accordance with its support for allied actions in the Persian Gulf, the government sent two nonfighting units to Saudi Arabia. President Iliescu's visit to China, the first by any European leader since the Tiananmen Square riots in 1989, was seen by the opposition as a continuation of dictator Ceauşescu's friendly relations with that country.

In the wake of the Warsaw Pact's demise, Romania established bilateral military contacts with France, Spain, Italy, and Turkey, and concluded a 15-year treaty of cooperation and friendship with the USSR. Following the aborted hard-line coup in Moscow in late August, the Iliescu regime and opposition groups alike insisted on the need to maintain the Soviet Union's fledgling democratic tradition and the reform process begun by Soviet President Mikhail Gorbachev.

VLADIMIR TISMANEANU
University of Maryland

SASKATCHEWAN

A devastating election loss for Premier Grant Devine and an economy in severe decline dominated Saskatchewan headlines in 1991.

Election. Premier Grant Devine's 11-year-old Progressive Conservative (PC) government went down to stunning defeat before Roy Romanow's socialist New Democrat Party (NDP) in October. The NDP captured 55 seats, the PCs ten, and Liberal leader Lynda Haverstock won the only seat for her party. Devine, whose party had come to power in 1982, had stalled in calling an election, hoping that public-opinion polls would turn in his favor. Constitutionally forced to have an election by Nov. 12, 1991, Premier Devine finally selected October 21 as the date.

Budget. PC Finance Minister Lorne Hepworth unveiled a budget that increased expenditures by just under 4% to C$4.82 billion on expected revenues of C$4.55 billion, but the budget never won approval in the provincial legislature. The New Democrats, then in opposition, prevented its passage by technicalities. The government then closed down the legislature pending the election and financed its operations by having the lieutenant governor sign special spending warrants. The budget measures, however, which included cuts to public service and reductions in grants to arts, sports, and recreational and multicultural groups, did go ahead.

© Dave Buston/Canapress Photo Service

Following the New Democratic Party's victory in Saskatchewan's election on Oct. 21, 1991, Roy Romanow, a former provincial attorney general, took over as premier.

SASKATCHEWAN • Information Highlights

Area: 251,865 sq mi (652 330 km²).
Population (June 1991): 996,200.
Chief Cities (1986 census): Regina, the capital, 175,064; Saskatoon, 177,641; Moose Jaw, 35,073.
Government (1991): *Chief Officers*—lt. gov., F. W. Johnson; premier, Roy Romanow (New Democrat). *Legislature*—Legislative Assembly, 64 members.
Provincial Finances (1991–92 fiscal year budget): *Revenues,* $4,554,000,000; *expenditures,* $4,819,000,000.
Personal Income (average weekly earnings, June 1991): $476.46.
Labor Force (August 1991): *Employed* workers, 15 years of age and over, 446,000; *Unemployed,* 7.5%.
Education (1991–92): *Enrollment*—elementary and secondary schools, 211,300 pupils; postsecondary—universities, 22,300; community colleges, 3,600.
(All monetary figures are in Canadian dollars.)

Tax Change. On April 1 the government harmonized its provincial sales tax with the federal government's new goods and services tax (GST), which had been imposed nationally on January 1. The move extended the 7% provincial tax to an entire range of goods that previously had been untaxed. Hepworth said the tax would be extended to various other services in 1992. However, when New Democrat leader Roy Romanow was elected he immediately urged residents not to pay the expanded tax and told businesses not to charge it. He said he would make the changes official when the legislature was recalled.

Agriculture. The provincial economy was hit heavily by falling resource prices for uranium, potash, and oil, and by the lowest grain prices in 16 years. Some analysts said that real grain prices were now as low as during the Great Depression. The initial price for wheat in 1991 was 30% lower than in 1990. Economists said rural Saskatchewan particularly would be devastated by the low prices, but urban centers would suffer too. In October, 8,000 farmers rallied in Regina to urge politicians to come up with aid and solutions to the crisis.

Business and Labor. In a major coup a group of Regina businessmen, backed by a provincial-government loan guarantee, bought a 42% stake in Toronto-based Crown Life Insurance Co., Ltd., and announced it would transfer the company's head office and 1,200 jobs to Saskatchewan. The C$250 million deal enraged Toronto Mayor Art Eggleton, who said that Toronto could not afford to see its jobs stolen. The Saskatchewan government said the move was part of its plan to rejuvenate the province's fading economy.

The longest nurses' strike in Saskatchewan history ended after 11½ days when the nurses agreed to accept a 9.2% increase in pay over two years. They had been seeking a 19% increase. The strike hit 118 hospitals and 50 long-term-care facilities and involved some 5,500 of the province's 6,500 nurses.

Justice. During 1991 there was a growing chorus for the reexamination of a 1969 murder case in which 19-year-old David Milgaard was jailed for life for the rape and murder of Saskatoon nursing assistant Gail Miller. Milgaard constantly has pleaded his innocence. Although federal Justice Minister Kim Campbell initially rejected a new trial, as the controversy around the case grew—including the revelation that pertinent files were missing and charges that another suspect was not investigated properly—even Prime Minister Brian Mulroney promised he would look into the matter.

PAUL JACKSON
"Saskatoon Star-Phoenix"

SAUDI ARABIA

The early 1991 Persian Gulf war against Iraq for the liberation of Kuwait profoundly affected domestic and external aspects of Saudi Arabia's activities (*see* FEATURE SECTION, page 36).

The Gulf War. Saudi Arabia invited hundreds of thousands of foreign troops onto its soil in response to the Aug. 2, 1990, invasion of Kuwait by Iraq. On November 26, King Fahd warned Saudis to prepare for war; he also called on Iraq to withdraw unconditionally from Kuwait. Since despite repeated international condemnations Iraq refused to withdraw peacefully, a coalition of nations led by the United States and Saudi Arabia launched an air war on Iraq and Iraqi-occupied Kuwait on Jan. 17, 1991. A *jihad* or Muslim holy war was proclaimed officially by the chief religious official of Saudi Arabia on January 18. Iraq fired many Scud missiles at Saudi Arabia, especially aiming at Riyadh, but most of them were intercepted by U.S. Patriot missiles. The short ground war from February 24–28 resulted in an overwhelming military victory for the coalition. Saudi Arabia secured its goal of liberating Kuwait, but since Iraqi leader Saddam Hussein remained in office, Saudi hopes for a more peaceful regional balance of power were thwarted. Most U.S. troops had left Saudi Arabia by mid-1991, and a complete U.S. withdrawal was expected.

During the 43 days of war with Iraq a total of nearly 800,000 coalition military personnel were in or near Saudi Arabia. About 193,000 troops from 24 countries came under the control of Saudi Gen. Prince Khalid bin Sultan, who worked closely with U.S. Gen. Norman Schwarzkopf. The Saudi air force flew about 12,000 sorties and lost two airplanes. At the battle of Khafji, Saudi ground forces with U.S. air and naval assistance successfully evicted the Iraqis after heavy resistance. The Saudi National Guard, a lightly armed organization, was particularly effective in the attack on the coastal road leading to Kuwait during the ground war.

Economic Consequences. Saudi Arabia pledged the United States $16.8 billion to help pay for the war, and by September 1991 the Saudis actually had provided about $14 billion. Expenses resulting from the war were immense —increased expenditures on the Saudi armed forces; weapons purchases; petroleum, water, food, and other support given foreign troops; financial subsidies to coalition countries, such as Syria; loans to the Soviet Union; and reconstruction of areas damaged by Iraqi missile attacks and the Saudi border zones harmed during the fighting. On Dec. 1, 1990, Saudi Arabia had canceled Egypt's debt of $4 billion. From August to December 1990 the incipient war cost Saudi Arabia as much as $30 billion, and in 1991 costs resulting from the war were estimated to be at least $34 billion. Financial uncertainty was so great that a budget was not published, but a deficit of $35 billion was anticipated for 1991. In May, Saudi Arabia borrowed about $4.5 billion from international banks and raised more than $2.5 billion from internal loans.

Oil Policies. Saudi production of oil grew sharply from about 5.5 million barrels per day in July 1990 to about 8.5 million barrels per day in December. Sustainable production capacity

SAUDI ARABIA • Information Highlights

Official Name: Kingdom of Saudi Arabia.
Location: Arabian peninsula in southwest Asia.
Area: 829,996 sq mi (2 149 690 km^2).
Population (mid-1991 est.): 15,500,000.
Capital (1981 est.): Riyadh, 1,000,000.
Government: *Head of state and government,* Fahd bin 'Abd al-'Aziz Al Sa'ud, king and prime minister (acceded June 1982).
Monetary Unit: Riyal (3.7592 riyals equal U.S.$1, Dec. 12, 1991).
Gross Domestic Product (1988 U.S.$): $73,000,-000,000.
Economic Index (1989): *Consumer Prices* (1980 = 100), all items, 96.2; food, 102.2.
Foreign Trade (1989 U.S.$): *Imports,* $21,153,-000,000; *exports,* $28,369,000,000.

also was increased at a cost of about $4 billion; 146 oil wells and 17 gas-separation plants were brought into use. Since the world price of oil rose because of the Kuwait crisis, Saudi Arabia in 1990–91 received extra "windfall" profits of about $12 billion more than such production would have earned previously. Saudi Arabia remained the world's largest exporter of oil, with an average production of about 8 million barrels per day in 1991, and it also supplied more than 200,000 barrels per day of oil products to U.S. armed forces stationed in Saudi Arabia.

When Iraq asked the Organization of Petroleum Exporting Countries (OPEC) to support a lifting of UN oil sanctions, Saudi Arabia successfully opposed the idea. Saudi Oil Minister Hisham Nazer, at the September 24 OPEC meeting in Geneva, brought about an increase in OPEC total oil production so as to restrain a too-rapid price increase, while abolishing individual quotas for member nations.

Political Changes. In January 1991, King Fahd said that the crisis and the presence of non-Muslim armed forces in Saudi Arabia would not lead to great political change, but he did undertake some alterations in government. To reinforce his appeal to religious conservatives, the government provided extra money to the Committees for the Encouragement of Virtue and Discouragement of Vice. Three new ministers were appointed to the cabinet in August. In a March television address, King Fahd repeated his earlier announcement of research into the establishment of a consultative council. On May 24 a petition signed by dozens of prominent religious and academic figures asked the king for the council. The king on November 17 called for the consultative council to be formed no later than January 1992.

The Saudi government slowly resumed its civilian operations as most foreign troops pulled out. The June pilgrimage saw nearly 2 million pilgrims go to Mecca for the religious ceremonies that make Saudi Arabia the center of the Muslim world. On July 3, 1991, the Saudis completed the first stage of cleaning the Persian Gulf waters of the estimated 3.5 million barrels of oil Iraq had dumped there.

Diplomacy. Saudi Arabia remained deeply worried about its regional role even after the February victory over Iraq. Since past foreign policy had failed to deter war, the government sought new alternatives. Foreign aid became more selective as subsidies to the Palestine Liberation Organization (PLO) were eliminated. Saudi Arabia vigorously sought to punish countries—such as Jordan, Yemen, and the Sudan—that had been cool to the coalition's military activities. Hundreds of thousands of Yemeni workers were expelled in 1990–91 by the Saudi government. Neutral Iran and Saudi Arabia resumed diplomatic relations on March 26 and Iranians participated in the pilgrimage.

King Fahd opposed the permanent stationing of U.S. troops on Saudi soil, but he aided President Bush in a number of diplomatic endeavors. On May 11, Saudi Arabia and the other countries of the Gulf Cooperation Council agreed to a limited role in the Middle East peace conference that eventually met in Madrid, Spain, on October 30; the Saudis supported the U.S. peace initiative, while calling for a just and comprehensive solution for the Palestinian question.

The new status Saudi Arabia gained by such actions was reflected in the September 17 election of Saudi Ambassador Samir Shihabi as president of the United Nations General Assembly.

Military. In October 1990, Saudi Arabia signed contracts to buy weapons worth $7.3 billion from the United States. On Jan. 4, 1991, a further request for $13 billion of arms purchases was canceled by the United States after supporters of Israel in the U.S. Congress objected. On November 5, Saudi Arabia indicated it wished to purchase 72 F-15 fighters at a cost of $4 billion.

Future Saudi military security seemed dependent on outside guarantees. Saudi Arabia sought to have external military assistance available on a contingency basis, but without any permanent foreign military presence inside the country.

WILLIAM OCHSENWALD
Virginia Polytechnic Institute and State University

SINGAPORE

In 1991, Singapore, the island city-state, continued to prove itself worthy as the business and financial capital for the fast-developing ASEAN (Association of Southeast Asian Nations) region of Southeast Asia. Singapore could boast of having the world's best airport and the first telephone system to be fully computer-compatible, and of being one of the least-

SINGAPORE • Information Highlights

Official Name: Republic of Singapore.
Location: Southeast Asia.
Area: 244 sq mi (632.6 km²).
Population (mid-1991 est.): 2,800,000.
Capital: Singapore City.
Government: *Head of state,* Wee Kim Wee, president (took office September 1985). *Head of government,* Goh Chok Tong, prime minister (took office November 1990). *Legislature* (unicameral)—Parliament.
Monetary Unit: Singapore dollar (1.6465 S. dollars equal U.S. $1, Dec. 10, 1991).
Gross Domestic Product (1989 est. U.S.$): $27,500,000,000.
Economic Index (1990): *Consumer Prices* (1980 = 100), all items, 124.9; food, 118.1.
Foreign Trade (1990 U.S.$): *Imports,* $60,787,000,000; *exports,* $52,729,000,000.

© Miladinovic/Sipa

After the ruling People's Action Party of Goh Chok Tong (center) *lost strength in August 1991 elections, the prime minister said that he would "make sure" the government does not "go too far ahead of conservative sectors in the society" in its reform program.*

expensive cities for corporate-office operations in the world.

Politics. Singapore began 1991 under a new prime minister, Goh Chok Tong. Former Prime Minister Lee Kuan Yew was still a political factor, having been named senior minister in the prime minister's office. The presidential-election bill, which passed in January, took effect on November 30. President Wee Kim Wee would hold the office until the first election for the post in September 1993. The president has veto power over spending of national reserves and important public appointments. Many believed this post is slated for former Prime Minister Lee.

The Singapore Democratic Party won three parliamentary seats and the Workers' Party one in the national elections held on August 31. The prime minister, perhaps prematurely, announced that a two-party partisan system had arisen in Singapore. The election was a political setback for Prime Minister Goh Chok Tong. The percentage of votes received by the ruling People's Action Party (PAP) slipped to 61%, the lowest total ever for the party, which has dominated Singapore politics since the country gained independence in 1965.

Democracy. The government took tentative steps to increase press freedom and to lift some restrictions on motion pictures in 1991 in response to its own survey, which indicated that the country's highly educated citizens were becoming disillusioned with official policies. The world's longest-serving political detainee known, Chia Thye Poh, marked the 25th anniversary of his arrest under Singapore's Internal Security Act with a lengthy interview. Chia now was free to work in Singapore but had to return to Sentosa tourist island each night. As the year drew to a close, concerns from the opposition emerged over the fact that Prime Minister Goh Chok Tong had not convened Parliament following the August elections.

Foreign Affairs. Singapore worked to strengthen ties with Malaysia and Indonesia by supporting the former's proposal for an East Asian Economic Caucus and by working with both countries to make the "economic-growth triangle"—involving the southern Malaysian state of Johore, Singapore, and the Indonesian island of Batam—a success.

Singapore was involved in an international controversy toward the end of the year when the government threatened to turn ten Vietnamese boat people away and indicated that it no longer would accept guarantees for new refugees until certain third-party countries honored past pledges to remove approximately 150 refugees from the country.

On December 17, Singapore sent its first trade delegation to Vietnam since relations with that country were restricted after the latter invaded Cambodia. In November the Monetary Authority of Singapore (MAS) ended the ban on investment in Vietnam.

Economy. Singapore enjoyed another year of sustained economic growth projected to reach 6.5% for 1991. Inflation was anticipated to be the lowest in the ASEAN region. The country continued to face a labor shortage for skilled jobs and had virtually no foreign debt.

Education. July 1 marked the beginning for Singapore's second university, the Nanyang Technological University. The government also announced a new program, "Edusave," which would establish a savings account for every schoolchild between 6 and 16 which could be used to pay for future education costs.

PATRICK M. MAYERCHAK
Virginia Military Institute

SOCIAL WELFARE

The U.S. struggle to climb out of the economic recession in 1991 had wide-ranging repercussions on the general state of Americans' social welfare. Unemployment, which reached 7% in June, remained a nagging problem; welfare and food-stamp rolls rose to unprecedented levels even as many state governments, hit hard by lower tax revenues, instituted widespread funding cuts; and the disparity between income levels of the nation's richest and poorest citizens continued to grow. Troubling rates of joblessness, poverty, hunger, and malnutrition were reported among children and the elderly in general, and among Hispanics and African-Americans (blacks) in particular.

The annual Census Bureau report on family income reported a sharp rise in the poverty rate in 1990 and a corresponding drop in family income. The report, released September 26, found that in 1990 some 33.6 million Americans —about 13.5% of the population—lived below the poverty line, which was defined as a total cash income of $13,359 for a family of four. The poverty rate rose by some seven tenths of one percent compared with 1989. The number of those living in poverty increased by some 2.1 million. The report also estimated that median household income dropped 1.7% in 1990 from 1989's figure of $30,468, to $29,943. The poverty rate among blacks was 31.9%; for Hispanics, 28.1%; for whites, 10.7%; for the elderly, 12.2%; and for children, 20.6%.

There was disagreement about the significance of the Census Bureau report. In general, liberals and Democrats saw the statistics as a damning indictment of the Reagan and Bush administrations' economic and social policies of the 1980s and early 1990s. Conservatives and Republicans tended to take issue with the accuracy of the poverty statistics. They also pointed to the general decline of the poverty rate and rise of median family income in the 1980s, as well as to the relatively low overall rates of inflation and unemployment during that period.

The Census Bureau poverty figures "greatly exaggerate poverty because they count only cash income, not non-cash benefits such as food stamps, thereby ignoring $129 billion in welfare spending, and assets such as a house," said Kate Walsh O'Beirne, vice-president of the conservative Heritage Foundation. Sen. Paul Sarbanes (D-MD), chairman of the Joint Economic Committee, on the other hand, called the poverty figures "really distressing."

Reports and Studies. The annual Census Bureau report was far from the only survey issued in 1991 indicating that poverty was a severe and growing problem among certain sectors of U.S. society. A study released in April by the federal National Cancer Institute, for example, found evidence strongly linking the incidence of cancer with poverty. The survey, which focused on cancer's socioeconomic factors, reported that in some urban areas rates of lung and prostate cancer were 60% to 70% higher among blacks than whites—a disparity researchers partially attributed to the fact that many urban blacks lived in poverty and had limited access to health care and education.

A federal advisory panel, the Physician Payment Review Commission, reported to Congress in April that relatively low fees paid by the federal and state governments to doctors under the Medicaid program caused many physicians to refuse to care for many of the 27 million low-income Americans who qualify for the program. The committee reported that the problem was acute in areas of the country such as the Northeast where costs of living are high. The committee found that many poor people had limited access to private physicians in places such as New York City because Medicaid payments often were less than what it cost physicians to provide the service.

A series of reports issued throughout the year provided evidence that the income gap between affluent and poor Americans continued to widen. Those same reports also indicated that, in general, blacks and Hispanics suffered disproportionately. Census Bureau statistics released in January, for example, estimated that in 1988 the net assets of the median white household were $43,280, compared with just $4,170 for African-American households and $5,520 for Hispanic families. "It means that you have grinding poverty, the absence of amenities, books, newspapers, magazines, encyclopedias, health care, college funds—the kinds of things that build the environment that move people toward upward mobility," Benjamin Hooks, executive director of the National Association for the Advancement of Colored People (NAACP), said of the report.

The nonprofit Center on Budget and Policy Priorities, a liberal think tank, released a study in July indicating that the average income of those in the top 1% of U.S. households increased 122% percent from 1977 to 1988, while the average income for those in the bottom fifth of society fell 10%. "During the period examined . . . the incomes of the wealthiest households shot up dramatically but middle-income households received only a slight gain," said Isaac Shapiro, who coauthored the study based on data from the Congressional Budget Office. "Meanwhile, low-income households became poorer."

Perhaps the most publicized social-welfare report issued in 1991 came from the bipartisan National Commission on Children, a 34-member panel chaired by Sen. John D. Rockefeller IV (D-WV) set up by Congress and the White House in 1987. The commission's 557-page report, issued June 24, stressed the relationship between poverty and the widespread incidence

© Cynthia Carris

An undetermined number of homeless people remained a major social problem in the United States. A group of New York City homeless, above, erected a tent city after being evicted from a municipal park.

of divorce and out-of-wedlock births. "Nearly 75% of all American children growing up in single-parent families experience poverty for some period during their first ten years, compared with 20% of children in two-parent families," the report said. The panel proposed a $1,000 income-tax credit for each child to help ease families' financial burdens.

Another report focusing on children, released in March by the Food Research and Action Center, a nonprofit antihunger group, estimated that 5.5 million U.S. children under 12 suffered from hunger, and that many of those children had health problems such as unwanted weight loss, fatigue, headaches, and irritability. The group's executive director, Robert J. Fersh, said the data also suggested that one in eight U.S. children experienced hunger each year.

The Homeless. The overall problem of homelessness, which first became acutely apparent in the nation's largest cities in the early 1980s, continued in 1991. Many cities struggled to cope with large numbers of homeless persons, most of them single adults and single mothers with children. New York City provided shelter to some 25,000 single homeless persons and 11,000 homeless families in about 35 shelters and hotels in 1990–91. In Philadelphia city officials estimated the homeless population at some 25,000 persons, about 17% of whom were believed to be mentally ill.

In April the Census Bureau reported on its first attempt to count the nation's homeless. Based on information gathered by some 15,000 Census Bureau employees who spent two days in March 1990 at homeless shelters in selected cities, the agency reported that some 180,000 people were living in emergency shelters and 50,000 were living on the streets. The agency stressed that the figures were not an exact count of the number of homeless persons because of the extremely transient nature of the homeless population. Nevertheless, the report was greeted by intense criticism from homeless advocacy groups. Those groups estimated the number of homeless Americans to be significantly higher—as few as 600,000 and as many as 3 million, according to different estimates.

"The [Census Bureau's] shelter count is not as bad as the street count, but even the shelter count is extremely inaccurate," said Maria Foscarinis, director of the National Law Center on Homelessness and Poverty. "My fear is that this is an effort by the federal government to diminish the plight of the homeless by minimizing the numbers." Census officials denied the charge. "We admitted all along that you can't count everybody," said Paula Schneider, director of the bureau's population division. "Those who hide from the census can't be counted. There is no way you can count them. And some of the homeless are among them."

The concern about the census among homeless advocates came during the second consecutive year in which there was widespread evidence of a growing national backlash against the homeless among both government officials and the public at large. In addition to budget cuts in state and local government homeless-aid programs, 1991 saw a continuation of police crackdowns on homeless persons living in public places and a growing antipathy among the public at street begging, antisocial acts committed by mentally ill homeless persons, and the homeless situation in general.

In July, Atlanta passed a law giving police the right to arrest homeless persons for loitering in abandoned buildings and engaging in "aggressive panhandling." The previous year Atlanta had begun arresting homeless persons for loitering, public drunkenness, and blocking traffic in the city's downtown area. Police in New York City continued a tough crackdown on panhandling in the city's subways and mounted raids in June and October to dislodge hundreds of homeless persons living in makeshift encampments in a park and on city-owned property in Manhattan's East Village. Washington, DC, officials closed two of the city's emergency shelters in August and announced plans for further cutbacks. In 1990 the nation's capital had weakened an ordinance that guaranteed shelter to any homeless person requesting it.

The Disabled. The big news in 1990 for the nation's estimated 43 million disabled persons came when President Bush signed into law the Americans With Disabilities Act, which had been approved overwhelmingly in the Senate and House of Representatives. The new law for the first time prohibited private employers from denying jobs on the basis of disability. It also set up a timetable for the federal government to draw up guidelines for all businesses that deal with the public to make their facilities accessible to the disabled. The law additionally gave protection to the disabled from discrimination in public accommodations, transportation, and telecommunications.

In 1991 the government began the long regulatory process designed to implement the 1990 law. On January 21 the federal Architectural and Transportation Barriers Compliance Board proposed a sweeping group of new detailed regulations that would require nearly all newly built or remodeled retail stores, restaurants, banks, offices, hotels, private schools, and theaters to take specific steps to accommodate disabled persons. The regulations mandated that, among other things, hotels set aside at least 5% of their rooms for the disabled; grocery and other stores provide disabled people full access to all checkout stations; and libraries and restaurants reserve at least 5% of their tables for those with disabilities.

On February 21 the compliance board proposed a further set of rules requiring millions of existing commercial businesses to make changes to accommodate disabled persons. Businesses able to prove that such alterations would be a financial hardship were exempt from the regulations. A week later the federal Equal Employment Opportunities Commission issued a set of proposed rules dealing with hiring and accommodating disabled workers.

The International Situation

In 1991, U.S. social problems once again were dwarfed by those of hundreds of millions in Third World nations faced with overwhelming poverty; alarmingly high rates of infant and child mortality; short life expectancy; and severe problems with disease, malnutrition, and starvation. Some 440 million people lived in the 42 countries with national per capita income rates of less that $200 per year, according to a report issued in March by the United Nations Conference on Trade and Development (UNCTAD).

That report also found that Iraq's occupation of Kuwait and the subsequent Persian Gulf war exacerbated problems in virtually every economic sector—including unemployment, national debt, and export earnings—in the world's poorest nations. The war also resulted in the dislocation and social upheaval of an estimated 5 million people from more than two dozen countries in the Middle East, Africa, and Asia.

Other human tragedies took place in 1991 in many large cities and rural areas in Central and South America, South Asia, and throughout Africa. In Peru, for example, health officials estimated that about half the population—some 13 million persons—lived in extreme poverty and that some 60,000 children would die before their first birthdays as a result of malnutrition and disease. In Bangladesh, where a late April cyclone took an estimated 125,000 lives, some 870,000 children under age 5 were expected to die in 1991—most as a result of easily preventable diseases.

There were repeated warnings in 1991 of the threat of imminent widespread famine in Angola, Ethiopia, Liberia, Mozambique, Somalia and Sudan—six African nations beset by civil warfare in recent years. "Unless there is a massive acceleration of the flow of food aid to the affected populations [of some 30 million], we are going to see widespread deaths from starvation," said UN Food and Agriculture Organization (FAO) Director-General Edouard Saouma.

MARC LEEPSON, *Free-lance Writer*

SOMALIA

The 21-year reign of President Muhammad Siad Barre came to an end in 1991 during an extremely violent struggle for power led by three clan-based rebel groups. After the overthrow the victors continued to contest power in a country whose per capita income makes it one of the poorest in the world.

Political Developments. On January 26, President Muhammad Siad Barre, in power since 1969, was overthrown. The final stage of a civil war culminated in a ferocious battle for the capital, Mogadishu. The city virtually was destroyed, some 4,000 civilians were killed, while the Catholic cathedral and Central Bank were leveled by retreating troops. The former president, a member of the Marehan clan, fled. The United Somali Congress (USC), representing the Hawiye clan, led the battle for the capital.

In the north the Isaak-clan-based Somali National Movement (SNM) captured the major towns of the area, including Hargeisa, but not before they too virtually were obliterated. Normal life came to a halt as housing, water, communications, and electrical facilities were destroyed. Hundreds of thousands of refugees fled to Ethiopia and Djibouti, while in March 150 drowned while trying to flee to Kenya.

In the south the Marehan-clan-based Somali Patriotic Movement (SPM) occupied the region, taking the town of Kismayu in April. Throughout the country the violence, chaos, and savagery of the struggle for power during the last months of the revolution were extraordinary.

New Leadership. Ali Mahdi Mohamed, the head of the USC, became interim president and selected Omar Arteh Ghalib as interim prime minister. A cabinet that included some ten ministerial positions was appointed. Although the new government under the auspices of the USC took power, its authority was contested by the SNM and SPM.

The SNM viewed itself as having been the vanguard of the civil war, and in February refused to meet at a "unity conference" called by the USC. It continued to maintain power and authority in the north and demonstrated a desire to establish its own central position. The SPM, which maintained its position in the south, was accused by the USC of working together with the remaining authorities of Siad Barre's army to gain political leverage; it was a charge the SPM refuted.

Thus, at the end of 1991 the country remained divided, with the USC in control of the central government but holding effective authority over little else. Anarchy was widespread and country-wide looting and random killings continued.

International Affairs. During the final act of the civil war all embassies, except those of Egypt and Italy, were evacuated. With the Soviet Union no longer a threat and with the overthrow of Ethiopia's Marxist government in May, Western countries no longer saw Somalia as a necessary Cold War client with the result that no large aid programs were instituted.

PETER SCHWAB
State University of New York at Purchase

SOMALIA • Information Highlights

Official Name: Somali Democratic Republic.
Location: Eastern Africa.
Area: 471,776 sq mi (1 221 900 km²).
Population (mid-1991 est.): 7,700,000.
Chief City (1981 est.): Mogadishu, the capital, 500,000.
Government: *Head of government,* Ali Mahdi Mohamed, interim president (took office 1991). *Head of state,* Omar Arteh Ghalib, interim prime minister (appointed 1991).
Monetary Unit: Shilling (929.5 shillings equal U.S. $1, 1989).
Gross Domestic Product (1988 U.S. $): $1,700,000,000.

SOUTH AFRICA

The beginnings of the official dismantling of legislated segregation of the races, apartheid, dominated all levels of South African life in 1991.

Repeal of Apartheid Legislation. In a speech to the South African Parliament early in February, President F. W. de Klerk announced that he would introduce legislation to repeal remaining racially discriminatory laws and by so doing abolish apartheid as a legal system. The leader of the right-wing official opposition, Dr. Andries Treurnicht, and other members of the Conservative Party walked out of the Parliament in protest. In May, de Klerk announced plans to end preventive detention and remove other repressive provisions of the Internal Security Act of 1982, including restrictions on organizations and publications and the banning of individuals. Subsequently, in June, the infamous Group Areas Act of 1950—which dictated where people could live according to race, the Land Acts of 1913 and 1936—which had reserved 87% of the country's land for whites, and the Population Registration Act of 1950—which classified every South African by race, were repealed by the white Parliament and the repeals endorsed by the Coloured House of Representatives and the Asian House of Delegates. While the legal foundations of apartheid crumbled in such areas as residence, education, health care, and public amenities, in practice segregation continued to be active and widespread.

Toward Transitional Rule. Following earlier hints of a gradual approach to constitutional change, President de Klerk and Minister of Constitutional Development and Planning Gerrit Viljoen at the end of October announced the

In Johannesburg on Sept. 14, 1991, South Africa's President F. W. de Klerk, African National Congress (ANC) President Nelson Mandela (center), *and Inkatha President Mangosuthu Gatsha Buthelezi* (extreme right) *signed an accord to end violence in the black townships.*

AP/Wide World

government's willingness to negotiate fundamental constitutional amendments, and perhaps even to alter the status of Parliament to create a transitional authority. President de Klerk maintained, however, that such major changes would require a referendum—the first ever to include blacks—which could be held as early as 1992. De Klerk also suggested that in the meantime his government would continue to make decisions and that he would bind himself morally to consider recommendations made by an agreed-upon forum. This suggestion was unacceptable to the African National Congress (ANC), which was not prepared to leave crucial questions to such informal procedure.

In mid-September representatives of the National Party (NP), the ANC, and the Inkatha Freedom Party (IFP), who had been brought together by a mediating committee of church leaders and business representatives, signed a draft peace accord known as the National Peace Initiative. The draft proposed a political code of conduct which emphasized democratic tolerance, a commission to investigate the causes of violence, special courts to deal with cases of political violence, and the appointment of a special police unit and an ombudsman to investigate allegations of misconduct by the police. While ongoing violence following the signing of the accord undermined confidence in the prospects for peace, the long-awaited all-party conference, which was to lay the groundwork for the more formal negotiations over the political future of South Africa, began during the third week in December.

In the meantime, the NP's proposals for a democratic constitution were released in September and included a minority veto in the upper chamber, proportional representation in the cabinet, and a system of voting at the local level which would give extra votes to property owners, a system which obviously favored whites. Predictably, the ANC and other government opponents were highly critical of the NP plan, which they claimed would continue to entrench white-minority privilege. To counter what they characterized as the ruling party's "apartheid in disguise," opponents wanted the agenda at the all-party conference to include the creation of an interim government and the election of a popular assembly to draft a new constitution. President de Klerk, however, continued to insist on more limited transitional arrangements.

Lifting of International Sanctions. As a result of the government's moves against apartheid,

SOUTH AFRICA • Information highlights

Official Name: Republic of South Africa.
Location: Southern tip of Africa.
Area: 471,444 sq mi (1 221 040 km²).
Population (mid-1991 est.): 40,600,000.
Chief Cities (1985 census, city proper): Pretoria, the administrative capital, 443,059; Cape Town, the legislative capital, 776,617; Durban, 634,301; Johannesburg, 632,369.
Government: *Head of state and government,* Frederik W. de Klerk, state president (took office Sept. 1989). *Legislature*—Parliament (tricameral): House of Assembly, House of Representatives (Coloured), and House of Delegates (Indians).
Monetary Unit: Rand (2.79 rands equal U.S. $1, Dec. 3, 1991).
Gross Domestic Product (1988 U.S.$): $83,500,000,000.
Economic Index (1990): *Consumer Prices* (1980 = 100), all items, 392.2; food, 414.8.
Foreign Trade (1990 U.S.$): *Imports,* $17,075,000,000; *exports,* excluding exports of gold, $18,969,000,000.

on July 10, U.S. President George Bush lifted sanctions that had been imposed on South Africa by the U.S. Congress with the passage of the 1986 Comprehensive Anti-Apartheid Act. The provisions of the legislation had covered a wide variety of economic and political activities. It had prohibited new U.S. investments in South Africa as well as computer exports, loans and credits, the export of crude oil, and nuclear cooperation. It also had prohibited the importation of South African uranium ore, gold Krugerrand coins, coal, textiles, iron, steel, and sugar. South African Airways had been denied landing privileges throughout the United States and cooperation with the South African armed forces had been suspended. Members of the Black Caucus of the U.S. Congress and anti-apartheid groups in the United States had lobbied against the lifting of the sanctions, arguing that they should remain in place until all black South Africans had the right to vote.

Sanctions that had been imposed by many individual U.S. states, cities, and pension funds remained in effect as did the prohibition on arms sales, export-import loans, exports to the South African military and police, and a ban on intelligence cooperation, as well as the United Nations embargo and loans from the International Monetary Fund (IMF).

The European Community already had removed its ban on new investments in South Africa and on April 8 removed prohibitions on the importation of South African iron and steel and gold coins. On July 9 the International Olympic Committee lifted a 21-year exclusion on South African participation in the Olympic Games.

African National Congress Convention. Nelson Mandela, running unopposed, was elected president of the ANC in early July in Durban, at the first national conference held in three decades. Oliver Tambo, the former president, moved into the new position of national chairman, and Walter Sisulu replaced Mandela as deputy president. On the fourth day of the conference, in secret balloting, the more than 2,000 delegates elected Cyril Ramaphosa, a leading trade unionist and a prominent member of the Mass Democratic Movement, as secretary-general, defeating the incumbent Alfred Nzo. The election of Ramaphosa was significant because he represented leadership that had opposed apartheid from within South Africa. Until then ANC leadership had been dominated by returned exiles and former prisoners. At the end of the conference, Mandela maintained that a clear mandate had been given for continuing negotiations with the government.

Continuing Ethnic Violence. At the end of January a long-awaited meeting took place between Nelson Mandela and Chief Mangosuthu Buthelezi of the IFP. This was the first meeting between the two men in 30 years and ended with an agreement to set aside differences and to fight apartheid together. There were high expectations that this meeting might help to ease the violence among black ethnic groups that had dominated South Africa for so many months but, unfortunately, as the year progressed the violence intensified and spread from Natal to areas around Johannesburg. A second meeting between the two leaders on March 30 was similarly unsuccessful. In April the ANC warned President de Klerk that it would pull out of talks with the government unless there were moves to stop the violence in the townships. Late in May, de Klerk opened a two-day conference to examine the violence. The ANC boycotted the conference, claiming that government security forces were causing the clashes, but Inkatha attended. ANC allegations of government partiality toward Inkatha were substantiated in July when Minister of Law and Order Adriaan Vlok admitted that the government and its police had given as much as 1.5 million rand (about $525,000) to Inkatha for its trade-union and political activities.

In part as a result of the scandal over the government's Inkatha slush fund, Minister Vlok and Defense Minister Magnus Malan,

© Mark Peters/Sipa Press

A desegregated group of fans enjoys a South African sporting event. With South Africa working to abolish its apartheid rules, its athletes were being welcomed back into the world of international sports in 1991.

© Juhan Kuus/Sipa Press

Winnie Mandela, the wife of ANC President Nelson Mandela, was convicted of charges arising from the abduction and beating of four black youths at her Soweto home. After she was sentenced to six years in prison, her lawyer filed an appeal.

who had been implicated in the scandal, were demoted to minor cabinet portfolios.

Return of Political Refugees. In August an agreement was reached in Geneva, Switzerland, between the South African government and the United Nations High Commissioner for Refugees (UNHCR) for the voluntary return of as many as 40,000 political refugees. The agreement assured freedom of movement within South Africa for the returning refugees and UNHCR access to them. The United States reportedly would contribute $4 million of the $40 million needed for the repatriation.

The Trial of Winnie Mandela. The highly publicized trial of Winnie Mandela, the wife of the ANC's Nelson Mandela, and three codefendants on charges of assault and kidnapping in connection with the alleged abduction of four youths in December 1988 took place early in 1991. An earlier trial in May 1990 found Jerry Richardson, one of Mrs. Mandela's bodyguards, guilty of the murder of one of the youths, "Stompie" Moeketsi Seipei. During the trial three witnesses testified that before the murder Mrs. Mandela had taken part in the beatings and that they, along with Moeketsi, had been kidnapped. Mrs. Mandela's defense rested on the alibi that she was at a meeting in Brandfort in the Orange Free State, nearly 200 mi (320 km) away, when the assaults took place.

On May 13, Winnie Mandela was found guilty of kidnapping and for being an accessory after the fact to the assaults and was sentenced to six years in prison. Two of her codefendants also were found guilty, while the charges against the third were dropped because of insufficient evidence. Mrs. Mandela was released on bail and her lawyer immediately filed an appeal. Nelson Mandela, who was not present when the sentence was passed, insisted on his wife's innocence and maintained that the verdict would have no bearing on the ANC talks with the government.

The Economy. In March, Finance Minister Barend du Plessis presented a 1991–92 budget to Parliament that contained a 19% cut in defense spending, tax incentives to businesses, but only limited increases in spending for social programs. Because of South Africa's continuing recession, du Plessis maintained that the expenditure needed to narrow the economic gap between the races was not available. Du Plessis stated that over the previous two years there had been an increase in unemployment and that while a real economic growth rate of 2% had been achieved in 1989, in 1990 there had been a decrease of 1% and a 3% decline in gross domestic spending. South Africa also had been hit by increased oil prices as a result of the Persian Gulf war, which, he said, would contribute to an inflation rate of more than 15%.

The budget also introduced a value added tax (VAT), which took effect on September 30. The VAT of 10% on all foodstuffs (mealie meal and brown bread were exempted) replaced the existing general sales tax of 13%. Du Plessis hoped that after a period of adjustment the new tax would lead to lower prices and a decline in the inflation rate. Critics claimed that it would hurt the poor, who are disproportionately black, because it included food, medical care, and utilities. While the government set aside 200 million rand (approximately $73 million) for relief for the very poor, it was estimated that with more than 40% of the population living below the poverty level this amount would be far from adequate. Businesses were to benefit from the new tax because a VAT on capital and intermediate goods would be rebated. In addition, the corporate tax was cut from 50% to 48% and import surcharges were reduced.

In November black workers responded to the introduction of the VAT by calling a two-day nationwide strike in which an estimated 3.5 million workers stayed home in what was described as the largest such strike in the country's history. Health and hospital workers were exempted as were black high-school seniors taking final examinations, but trains and buses ran virtually empty and the South African Chamber of Business estimated that workers forfeited more than $70 million in wages. Members of the business community and the government said the strike cost the country hundreds of millions of dollars and a significant loss of jobs. The Congress of South African Trade Unions (COSATU) insisted that the mass-action campaign would end only when the government agreed to exempt all basic foods, medical services, and utilities from the new tax.

South Africa would continue to face the very difficult choice between using scarce resources for redistribution or to stimulate economic growth. The present government seemed to have made a choice in favor of incentives for business, and while the ANC toned down its views of nationalization of mines and industries, it remained deeply committed to redistribution as a means to redress the economic effects of generations of apartheid. At the same time leaders such as Nelson Mandela, Thabo Mbeki, and Cyril Ramaphosa realized that it would be unwise to alienate investors and frighten away skilled labor. Late in 1991, South African and overseas investors anxiously were awaiting the ANC's promised economic-policy statement.

PATRICK O'MEARA and
N. BRIAN WINCHESTER
Indiana University

SOUTH CAROLINA

The recession caused major reductions in state revenues and hampered the economy. South Carolina ended the 1990–91 fiscal year with a slight surplus only by reducing departmental expenditures, freezing employment, exhausting both reserve funds, and advancing reporting dates for sales taxes.

Scandal. A lengthy federal investigation of corruption in the state ended. Seventeen legislators, four other employees, six lobbyists, and one businessman were indicted in the case for violations of the Hobbs Act which prohibits vote buying and extortion. Twenty pleaded guilty, seven were convicted in trials, and one was acquitted by the jury. Growing out of the scandal, a special legislative session enacted a tough ethics law to control lobbyists and campaign contributions.

In an unrelated case, former University of South Carolina president James Holderman was found guilty of tax evasion and use of public office for private gain.

Government. Recessionary pressures forced a $4 million budget reduction for 1991–92. Furloughs for employees were authorized, raises were withheld for state employees and teachers, and cuts in education and health services were imposed. Fewer than 125 employees were laid off but local property-tax levies were increased.

Frustrated by the recession, legislative scandals, lack of leadership, and political differences with Republican Gov. Carroll A. Campbell, Jr., the General Assembly enacted only a few important laws. It authorized presidential primaries, broadened living wills to permit the withholding of food and water from certain patients, and established goals for reducing the amount of garbage sent to landfills. Proposals providing for state-conducted primaries and redistricting of the state failed. Strong political differences and disagreements over black majority districts meant that redistricting likely would have to be resolved by the federal courts. Meanwhile, Governor Campbell was urging a reorganization of the state's government to a cabinet form under gubernatorial control.

The Economy and Agriculture. The recession was felt most strongly in the first half of the year, with the economy beginning to rebound during the second half. Unemployment for July was 5.9%, nearly 1% less than the national average. About 30,000 more people were employed than in 1990. Textile and manufacturing jobs continued to decline and temporary help was the fastest-growing job segment. Two

SOUTH CAROLINA • Information Highlights

Area: 31,113 sq mi (80 582 km²).
Population (1990 census): 3,486,703.
Chief Cities (1990 census): Columbia, the capital, 98,052; Charleston, 80,414; North Charleston, 70,218.
Government (1991): *Chief Officers*—governor, Carroll A. Campbell, Jr. (R); lt. gov., Nick A. Theodore (D). *General Assembly*—Senate, 46 members; House of Representatives, 124 members.
State Finances (fiscal year 1990): *Revenue,* $8,750,000,000; *expenditure,* $7,910,000,000.
Personal Income (1990): $53,006,000,000; per capita, $15,151.
Labor Force (June 1991): *Civilian labor force,* 1,784,400; *unemployed,* 120,800 (6.8% of total force).
Education: *Enrollment* (fall 1989)—public elementary schools, 443,712; public secondary, 172,465; colleges and universities, 145,730. *Public school expenditures* (1989), $2,118,732,000.

major foreign companies planned to locate in the state.

Above-average rainfall benefited most crops but hurt peach and apple marketing, wheat, and small grains. Cotton, corn, and soybean yields were good. Tobacco still led as the chief cash crop. The number of farms in the state dropped by 1,000.

Education. Under the leadership of Superintendent of Education Barbara Nielsen, many of the public-school curriculum and testing programs were reevaluated and the department was reorganized to emphasize service. Levels of communication and command were reduced and funding increased slightly. Schoolteacher salaries slightly exceeded the average for the nation's Southeastern states and the number of schools permitting more local decision-making rose to 140.

The state's average scores on Scholastic Aptitude Tests (SATs), however, changed little, leaving the state at the bottom of the national rankings. Efforts were under way to recruit black students into teaching.

ROBERT H. STOUDEMIRE
University of South Carolina

SOUTH DAKOTA

The budget, economic growth, abortion issues, and continued tensions between Indians and whites dominated South Dakota's news in 1991.

Legislation. A 1991–92 budget of $1.3 billion was approved by the General Assembly with much of the expenditures earmarked for social services, transportation, and education. The largest burden on state taxpayers came in all levels of educational and cultural programs. The greatest reliance on federal funds—which provided 40% of budget revenues—was in allocations for social services and transportation.

Other important 1991 legislation involved farm-debt mediation, computer-service improvement, and health-care delivery. The legislature also established the Lonetree solid-waste disposal facility, which would receive garbage from out-of-state, and passed a bill facilitating Indian tribal and state government agreements on the collections of taxes and license fees. Especially controversial were the matters of tribal-state shares of road taxes and fishing and hunting-license fees.

Indian Affairs. Efforts at better relations between whites and Indians, which were begun during the "Year of Reconciliation" in 1990, continued in 1991. Most state-sponsored work in the field came in informational services and public programs, including more requirements for Indian studies in all public educational institutions. Missing, however, were efforts to reconcile historical confrontations over two matters of central importance to majorities in all the tribes. They were state governmental acceptance of tribal jurisdictional authority within reservation boundaries and a settlement of the Black Hills legal case to include not only financial remuneration for the 1876 surrender (by 1991 authorized congressional payment exceeded $250 million), but also the return of some Indian jurisdictional authority within parts of the Black Hills region.

In addition, there were threats of militant demonstrations for the Indian acquisition of Bear Butte, which under public management has been a center for tribal religious activities. Factions within the tribes were split on whether a transfer to intertribal management would be desirable.

Economy. South Dakota's economy fared better than those of most states, with an unemployment rate of only 3.5% recorded in the spring. Unemployment rates, generally, continued to decline from the early 1980s, due to a shift from primary reliance on agriculture to manufacturing, service, and public employment. Although average personal income among farmers fluctuated due to uncertainty regarding federal parity payments, incomes for nonagrarian citizens (89% of the population) increased by 1.6% over 1990. Income for construction was especially strong, increasing by 17%. Service industries also reported gains, averaging 2.4%.

Trends. Late in the 1980s, according to U.S. Census Bureau findings, South Dakota surpassed North Dakota in economic growth, personal income, business development, and general potential. Gains also were made on other neighboring states. Sioux Falls was ranked 12th in the nation by *Money* magazine in terms of overall desirability and potential for growth. The state's population continued to age, reaching a median of 32.5 years. Stability in family life was reflected in a decline of divorce rates over the previous decade—from 4.1% to 3.5%.

HERBERT T. HOOVER
University of South Dakota

SOUTH DAKOTA • Information Highlights

Area: 77,116 sq mi (199 730 km²).
Population (1990 census): 696,004.
Chief Cities (1990 census): Pierre, the capital, 12,906; Sioux Falls, 100,814; Rapid City, 54,523.
Government (1991): *Chief Officers*—governor, George S. Mickelson (R); lt. gov., Walter D. Miller (R). *Legislature*—Senate, 35 members; House of Representatives, 70 members.
State Finances (fiscal year 1990): *Revenue*, $1,494,000,000; *expenditure*, $1,344,000,000.
Personal Income (1990): $10,997,000,000; per capita, $15,797.
Labor Force (June 1991): *Civilian labor force*, 366,100; *unemployed*, 11,400 (3.1% of total force).
Education: *Enrollment* (fall 1989)—public elementary schools, 93,596; public secondary, 33,733; colleges and universities, 32,666. *Public school expenditures* (1989), $427,522,000.

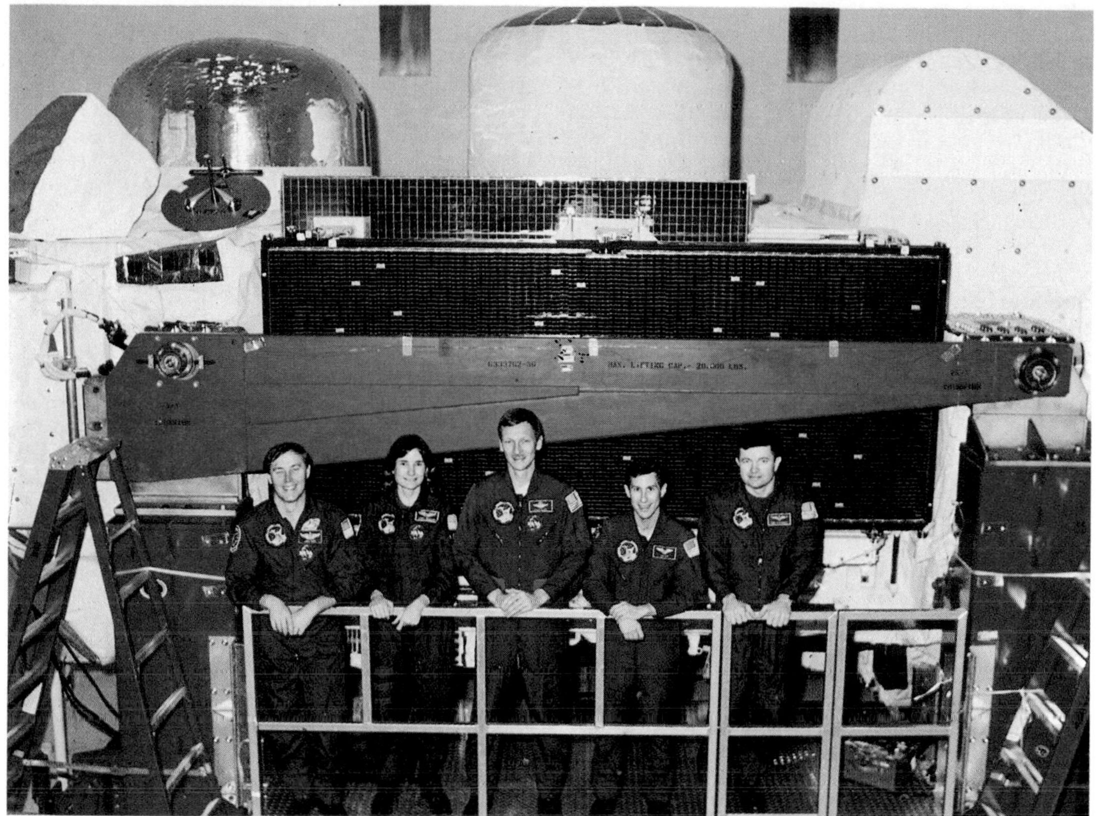

NASA

The U.S. STS-37 crew (l-r)—Jerry Ross, Linda Godwin, Steven Nagel, Jay Apt, and Ken Cameron—prepare for their April 5–11, 1991, flight aboard the space shuttle Atlantis, *during which the Gamma Ray Observatory* (rear) *was launched.*

SPACE EXPLORATION

Space exploration in 1991 was marked by a turning of scientific instruments toward the Earth as well as the scanning of the surrounding universe with powerful space-borne sensors. To study Earth's complex environment and chart climatic changes due to human activities around the globe, several environment-watching satellites were launched. The Magellan planetary spacecraft (launched in 1989) continued the detailed mapping of the fractured and rifted terrain of Venus. Still traveling a long and winding road to Jupiter for a December 1995 rendezvous, the Galileo spacecraft suffered from a stuck radio antenna that may reduce its scientific output when it reaches the giant planet. Throughout the year crews of U.S. astronauts and Soviet cosmonauts studied the reactions of the body to microgravity in experiments that eventually would help pave the way for a human return to the Moon and sending an expedition to Mars.

Shuttle Program. There were six shuttle flights during 1991, all by the United States. While some shuttle lift-offs were delayed by structural, mechanical, or computer problems, for the most part missions achieved all of their major objectives. In April a new space shuttle, the *Endeavour,* was added to the shuttle fleet. *Endeavour* replaced the *Challenger,* which was destroyed in the 1986 accident that cost the lives of seven astronauts.

The shuttle program's year began with the STS-37 (April 5–11) and saw the five-person crew of space shuttle *Atlantis* deploy the 17-ton Gamma Ray Observatory (GRO). An unscheduled space walk by two astronauts was needed to adjust manually a balky antenna on the GRO, which failed to deploy. *Atlantis* astronauts also used manual and electric carts to haul equipment on a monorail track. Operated in the craft's cargo bay, these carts were evaluated for use in the assembly of space station *Freedom* toward the end of the decade.

The *Discovery* STS-39 mission (April 28-May 6) was dedicated to select experiments and testing of hardware for the Strategic Defense Initiative, the "Star Wars" program. The seven-person crew deployed several small satellites that spewed chemicals into space to help design advanced missile-tracking sensors. A Shuttle Pallet Satellite housing an infrared sensor also was released from *Discovery,* then returned to the cargo bay by a robotic arm. The mission marked the 40th space-shuttle flight since the program's start in 1981.

The nine-day flight of *Columbia* on its STS-40/Spacelab Life Sciences (SLS-1) mission (June 5–14) focused on human and animal adaptation to space. Fit into the shuttle's cargo bay, a Spacelab module replete with racks of equipment allowed astronauts to explore how human bones, muscles, the heart, blood vessels, lungs, kidneys, and hormone-secreting glands respond to microgravity. Joining the four-man, three-woman crew were some 2,000 jellyfish, carried aloft to investigate their responses to a gravity-diminished environment.

The STS-43 mission of *Atlantis* (August 2-11) deployed the fifth Tracking and Data Relay Satellite (TDRS), joining three similar satellites that serve as communications relay points between low-orbit spacecraft and Earth. The five *Atlantis* astronauts carried out studies of hardware considered for use in building space station *Freedom*. The crew also studied flame propagation in microgravity to improve fire-safety technology for spacecraft.

Designed to help scientists learn more about the fragile mixture of gases protecting Earth from the harsh space environment, the Upper Atmosphere Research Satellite (UARS) was dispatched during the STS-48 mission (September 12–18) by the five-person *Discovery* crew. The 14,500-lb (6 500-kg) UARS began its planned 20-month mission that includes studying winters in the Northern Hemisphere and surveying the Antarctic ozone hole. UARS is the first major satellite of NASA's Mission to Planet Earth, a 15-year program using ground, airborne, and space-based sensors to study Earth as a complete environmental system. One crew member, on his fourth space voyage, commented that Earth's atmosphere appeared in worse condition, compared to his prior flights. During the mission the *Discovery* crew had to maneuver to avoid a large hunk of space debris—a spent Soviet booster.

The last shuttle mission of 1991 was STS-44 (November 24–December 1), a Department of Defense (DoD) flight that released a Defense Support Program (DSP) satellite that detects nuclear detonations and missile launches on Earth. On board *Atlantis,* the six-person crew used countermeasures to combat adverse effects of space, thereby gaining confidence in increasing the duration of shuttle missions.

Space Station. Despite political turmoil in their country below, cosmonauts circling Earth aboard the Soviet *Mir* space station continued throughout 1991 to utilize the orbiting research lab for materials processing, Earth remote sensing, and astronomical studies. Automatic spacecraft regularly docked to *Mir* in 1991. These Progress spacecraft supplied the complex with water, oxygen, food, and replacement parts, including a new computer. Maintenance to the station was performed regularly inside and outside the facility. On May 18 a Soyuz TM-12 docked with *Mir,* bringing to the complex Anatoly Artsebarsky, Sergei Krikalyov, and the first British astronaut to fly, Helen Sharman. Sharman, a former chemist with the Mars candy firm, earned her eight-day *Mir* trip through a British-Soviet commercial contract. On May 26, Sharman, along with Viktor Afanasyev and Musa Manarov, who had lived on board the station for 175 days, touched down on Earth in a Soyuz TM-11 vehicle. On October 2 a Soyuz TM-13 rocketed to *Mir* carrying Aleksandr Volkov, Toktar Aubakirov, and Austrian Franz Viehboeck. Eight days later they returned to Earth in a Soyuz TM-12 with long-duration cosmonaut Anatoly Artsebarsky, who had occupied *Mir* for 114 days. Soviet political and economic problems slowed *Mir* growth plans. The addition of two more *Mir* modules carrying Earth remote-sensing instruments, as well as a flight to the station by an automatically controlled Soviet shuttle, were delayed. Soviet space officials now were working to open the *Mir* station for expanded scientific and commercial use by other nations. A visit by a U.S. astronaut to the *Mir* station, and a reciprocal flight by a cosmonaut on a U.S. shuttle, were in the planning stages. A total reshaping of the Soviet space endeavor was expected to take place in 1992.

In the United States work on space station *Freedom* continued to be plagued by politics, cost overruns, and technical snags. The station's cost, projected to be $30 billion, became the subject of a heated debate in Congress, forcing NASA to downgrade the orbiting outpost. Originally designed to house a crew of eight, *Freedom* now initially will house four astronauts and will not be ready for permanent boarding until 1999. Astronauts, however, will make brief visits to the station in 1997.

Space Science. The high-resolution radar mapping of Venus by the U.S. Magellan spacecraft continued in 1991, providing staggering images of the planet's violent crustal deformations, giant volcanoes, and extremely long channel-like features. By mid-May, Magellan had succeeded in surveying more than 80% of the Venusian surface. That mission cycle covered 243 days, one Venus rotation. While similar in size to Earth, Venus is veiled by a visually impenetrable fog of carbon dioxide. This thick layer causes a greenhouse effect prompting surface temperatures to reach nearly 900°F (482°C). Using powerful radar pulses to cut through the planet's dense atmosphere, Magellan produced image mosaics of the Venus topography. Large circular features, called coronae, were imaged by Magellan. The pancake-like structures, ranging in size from about 100 mi (161 km) to more than 600 mi (965 km) in diameter, are surrounded by a ring of ridges or troughs. These coronae are associated with volcanism, with interior heat of the planet venting through the immense hot spots. Using an on-board altimeter, Magellan also is measuring the heights of features on Venus such as the continent-sized upland, Aphrodite Terra, or Maat Mons, a 5-mi (8-km)-high volcano that juts into the Venusian sky. As Magellan swings around Venus on several mapping cycles it will reimage volcanic regions. Scientists, therefore, are hopeful that changes in lava flows will be detected, indicating that volcanoes are erupting and that the planet is geologically active like Earth. (*See also* ASTRONOMY.)

It was announced in May that NASA's Astro-1 telescopes mounted in the cargo bay of space shuttle *Columbia* during its 1990 STS-35 mission (Dec. 2–11, 1990) imaged intense, hot stars in the Large Magellanic Cloud. Hundreds of the newly formed young, hot, energetic stars were imaged by Astro-1's Ultraviolet Imaging Telescope. The discovery points to the possibility that many of the new stars were formed at about the same time as the star which exploded as Supernova 1987A. The implication is that several of these stars one day could become supernovas as well.

Japan's Solar-A spacecraft was lofted from the Kagoshima Space Center, August 30, by a M3SII booster. High-energy phenomena in solar flares during the Sun's maximum solar activity were being eyed by Solar-A's soft X-ray telescope. A first image from the spacecraft, named *Yohko* (meaning sun ray or sunbeam), showed the structures of the X-ray corona, which extends far above the Sun's surface.

NASA's Hubble Space Telescope (HST) experienced more problems in 1991. One of the observatory's two ultraviolet detectors in a high-resolution spectrograph suffered intermittent power failure. In addition, two of Hubble's six gyroscopes, which keep the telescope finely targeted on celestial objects, malfunctioned. Lastly, a set of solar arrays mounted on HST were wobbling as they moved in and out of sunlight. The heating and cooling of the thin solar panels could cause their eventual mechanical failure, leaving HST without rechargeable power. A shuttle servicing of the orbiting telescope was slated for early 1994. This mission promises to relieve some of these problems. Included in the repairs would be the attachment of corrective lenses that would sharpen the focus of Hubble's primary mirror. Despite these technical snags HST continued to transmit impressive views of such astronomical bodies as Jupiter, Mars, and "blue stragglers," a class of star that appears to evolve from old age back to a hotter and brighter star.

Engineers also struggled with the U.S. Galileo spacecraft, trying to unfurl its main antenna properly. The large antenna is needed to relay quality data across interplanetary mileage. The spacecraft, however, did whisk by asteroid Gaspra on October 29, imaging that 10-mi (16-km) by 7.5-mi (12-km) irregularly shaped rocky world. Galileo is Jupiter-bound for a long scouting mission of that planet and its moons beginning December 1995.

The twin Voyager spacecraft, long since fulfilling their missions of exploring outer planets, continued to cruise gracefully on new interstellar missions. With much of their equipment still working, the Voyagers were searching for the elusive heliopause, the outermost boundary of the solar wind. Exactly where the heliopause is remains a mystery.

Applications Satellites. Satellites to monitor the complex nature of Earth's environment were launched by several nations in 1991, underscoring the global urgency of gaining better stewardship of the planet. The first Soviet Almaz (meaning "diamond") was rocketed into orbit atop a Proton booster on March 31 and carried a synthetic-aperture radar. Almaz can produce sharp radar images under all lighting and weather conditions, imaging objects down to 49 ft (15 m) in size. The Almaz, coupled with other remote-sensing satellites, was being used in oceanography, geological mapping, and forestry management. Joining Almaz, resource-monitoring Resurs-F satellites were launched by the Soviets in May, June, July, and August. On March 2 an Ariane rocket lifted off from the Kourou Space Center in French Guiana, placing into space the European Space Agency's Meteosat-5 (MOP-2) weather satellite. NASA launched the NOAA-12 meteorological satellite on May 14 on board an Atlas-E launch vehicle from Vandenberg Air Force Base, CA. A Soviet Okean-3 oceanographic and polar ice-watching satellite was orbited June 4 by a Tsiklon booster. Carrying radar similar to the Soviet Almaz, the European Remote Sensing-1 (ERS-1) spacecraft was orbited July 17 by an Ariane rocket. ERS-1 was set to chart Earth on a global and repetitive basis for upward of three years. In a joint U.S.-Soviet project, the Soviet Meteor-3 rocketed spaceward on August 15, carrying a NASA Total Ozone Mapping Spectrometer. An Indian Remote Sensing satellite (IRS-1B) was launched August 29 on behalf of India by the USSR. The 7-ton Upper Atmosphere Research Satellite (UARS) was dispatched by a U.S. shuttle September 12 to relay back a long-term, three-dimensional view of ozone in the Earth's upper atmosphere. Early data relayed from UARS supported aircraft and ground-based research about human-made chemical interactions with the atmosphere that lead to ozone destruction.

Communications Satellites. Providing communications services by satellite remains the largest application of space to global needs. The business end of boosting such satellites spaceward also has become profitable, sparking competition among nations, particularly between France's Ariane rocket and launchers built by U.S. firms.

Among the communications satellites orbited in 1991 was the NATO 4A satellite that links military commanders around the globe, launched January 8. The 41st Ariane launch boosted both the Italsat 1 and a Eutelsat II F2 telecommunications satellites into space January 15 for the Italian Space Agency and Eutelsat, a European consortium of satellite users.

An Ariane rocket also boosted on March 2 the Astra 1-B, a direct television satellite, launched for Luxembourg. The Canadian Anik E2 was orbited by an Ariane on April 5, although it was months before the spacecraft became fully operational, due to stuck antennas. The U.S. commercial satellite-launch business was set back on April 18 when an Atlas booster carrying a Japanese direct-broadcast satellite had to be destroyed. Cause of the mishap later was traced to possible debris in an upper-stage engine. A commercial Atlas did loft on December 7 an $85 million Eutelsat—a European-built satellite that would relay the 1992 Olympics.

A June 28 lift-off placed into space the U.S. Air Force Radiation Experiment (REX), a test of communications in a high-radiation environment. Also in June ground controllers were able to regain control of the nearly lost Olympus, a large European Space Agency telecommunications satellite. Soviet Gorizont communications satellites were orbited in July and October, as were Molinya satellites in February, March, June, August, and September. The second mission of the Pegasus air-launched space booster on July 17 deployed seven small U.S. DoD satellites around the Earth. The mammoth Intelsat 6 F-5 was launched on August 14 to provide global radio, television, and data services for Intelsat's 121-member nations. On August 25, Japan orbited the BS-3B, a powerful broadcast satellite. A September 26 Ariane mission dispatched the Anik E1 satellite for Canada. Yet another Ariane boost of an Intelsat 6 F-1 on October 29 placed the world's largest civil telecommunications satellite into orbit. The eighth and final Ariane flight for 1991 launched a French Telecom satellite and an Inmarsat maritime communications satellite on December 16.

LEONARD DAVID
Space Data Resources & Information

SPAIN

SPAIN • Information Highlights

Official Name: Kingdom of Spain.
Location: Iberian Peninsula in southwestern Europe.
Area: 194,884 sq mi (504 750 km²).
Population (mid-1991 est.): 39,000,000.
Chief Cities (Jan. 1990 est.): Madrid, the capital, 3,120,732; Barcelona, 1,707,286; Valencia, 758,738.
Government: *Head of state,* Juan Carlos I, king (took office Nov. 1975). *Head of government,* Felipe González Márquez, prime minister (took office Dec. 1982). *Legislature*—Cortés Generales: Senate and Congress of Deputies.
Monetary Unit: Peseta (103.0 pesetas equal U.S.$1, Dec. 3, 1991).
Gross National Product (1989 est. U.S.$): $398,700,-000,000.
Economic Indexes (1990): *Consumer Prices* (1980 = 100), all items, 243.5; food, 246.4. *Industrial Production* (1980 = 100), 120.
Foreign Trade (1990 U.S.$): *Imports,* $87,694,-000,000; *exports,* $55,640,000,000.

In 1991 the government of Prime Minister Felipe González stressed its support for free-market policies in order to stimulate Spain's economy and prepare it for the European Community's single market.

Politics. Since taking power in 1982, González had expended immense political energy building and repairing bridges between the two major factions in his Socialist Worker's Party (PSOE). On the party's left were advocates of paternalistic socialism identified with González' longtime confidant Alfonso Guerra and labor leaders; on the right were free-market-oriented liberals associated with Finance Minister Carlos Solchaga.

Feuding sharpened in 1991 in the face of widespread rumors that González, who was completing his third term, would not serve beyond 1993. This prospect found potential successors jockeying for position.

An opportunity for González to show his preference for the liberals occurred in January when he accepted Guerra's resignation as deputy prime minister. Guerra had amassed enormous power in domestic affairs as González increasingly concentrated on international relations, and his brother, Juan Guerra, was alleged to have enriched himself at public expense. González' break with Guerra ended a 25-year alliance during which the two Seville natives lifted the PSOE to power.

The rift contributed to a PSOE setback in the May 26 local and regional elections. Notable were the party's losses in Madrid, Barcelona, Seville, Valencia, and other cities. Thus, the PSOE became ever more dependent on a large but poorly educated rural electorate.

These reverses aside, the Socialists were far stronger than the conservative Popular Party (PP) and the Communist-led United Left (IU). Still, the continual erosion of PSOE strength could force the party into a coalition after the 1993 parliamentary contests.

The center-right Democratic and Social Center Party polled so few votes in May that Adolfo Suárez, party founder and former prime minister, resigned as party head.

The respected newspaper *El País* reported that ultraconservative army officers plotted to murder King Juan Carlos, Queen Sofia, and González at the armed forces parade in mid-1985. These articles appeared as Spain marked the tenth anniversary of a coup attempt by civil guards that the king helped thwart in February 1981. Several hundred neo-Nazi skinheads, centered in Barcelona, declared war on immigrants, homosexuals, and drug addicts.

Economy. The foreign press often has presented González as a proponent of privatization; this image obscured the fact that the state still generated at least half of Spain's gross domestic income. Compared to Portugal, privati-

© Ralf-Finn Hestoft/Saba

© Frederico Mendes/Sipa Press

Major construction projects were under way in Spain in 1991 as the nation prepared to mark the quincentenary of Christopher Columbus' discovery of America in 1992. In Barcelona—the principal site of the 1992 Summer Olympics dedicated to Columbus—the Olympic Stadium (above) *neared completion. In Seville, the host of a 1992 Columbian world's fair, exhibits from more than 100 nations, including the Italian Pavilion* (left), *were being planned.*

zation of the government's large industrial holdings was proceeding slowly and timidly—with foreign investment still barred from key economic sectors. González' approach was to modernize public firms, not necessarily place them on the auction block.

Guerra's departure from the cabinet emboldened Finance Minister Solchaga to push for deregulating and streamlining the Spanish economy. In September, following the collapse of negotiations with organized labor over a social pact, the finance minister proposed in parliament a "surprise package" of reforms. Specifically, he announced a change in the National Employment Institute whereby rejecting a job or refusing employment training would disqualify applicants for unemployment benefits. He also championed higher indirect taxes, a leveling off of direct taxes, and the deregulation of capital markets.

Solchaga implied that an economic opening was necessary to boost national income, which grew 2.7% during 1991, compared with 3.6% and 5.2% in 1990 and 1989, respectively. Another goal was to curb inflation, which declined from 6.7% in 1990 to just above 5% in 1991. One obstacle to decisive action lay in the fear that deregulation might increase unemployment, which hovered around 15% in 1991.

Foreign Affairs. Spain played a pivotal role in the defeat of Iraq following its invasion of Kuwait. U.S. war supplies were routed through Spain to the Persian Gulf region, and the Spanish Air Force reportedly ferried bombs to U.S. bases to supply allied air strikes. González kept these operations secret both to avoid domestic protests and to obviate friction with Arab states in North Africa.

In October, King Juan Carlos urged support for Third World countries in a speech before the UN General Assembly, and Madrid hosted a Middle East peace conference.

GEORGE W. GRAYSON
College of William and Mary

© N. Tavernier/Sipa

SPORTS

Overview

Veteran athletes added a whiff of old spice to the world of sports in 1991.

Forty-four-year-old Texas Ranger pitcher Nolan Ryan finished his 23d season in the major leagues at the top of his form, give or take some aches, continuing to confound opposing batters and breaking records—some his own—in the process. Boxer George Foreman, at age 42 and weighing 257 lbs (117 kg), went the 12-round distance against 28-year-old heavyweight champion Evander Holyfield, losing on points but earning $12.5 million in the process. Tennis great Jimmy Connors set fire to the U.S. Open, reaching the quarterfinals on his 39th birthday before being defeated by Jim Courier, 21, in the semis.

Other seniors who threw themselves up against the brick wall of age were 45-year-old Hall-of-Fame pitcher Jim Palmer, who called off a comeback with the Baltimore Orioles after tearing a hamstring during spring training. Former Olympic swimming marvel Mark Spitz, 41, stumbled in an attempt at the 1992 Olympics after being beaten badly in a two-man race. Tennis player Björn Borg, 34, and boxer Sugar Ray Leonard, 34, also experienced failed resurrections in 1991.

© Bob Martin/Allsport

In sports action at opposite ends of the globe, Fu Mingxia, a 12-year-old diver from China, won the ladies' World Platform Diving Championship in Perth, Australia, to become the youngest world champion ever of an aquatic event; while four-time winner Susan Butcher came in third in the 1,163-mi (1 872-km) Iditarod Trail Sled Dog Race from Anchorage to Nome, behind Rick Swenson, who won the race for a record fifth time. Judy Sweet won another kind of race and was elected the first woman president of the National Collegiate Athletic Association (NCAA).

© Bob Martin/Allsport © David Cannon/Allsport © Tony Triolo

Sports Milestones: *In Tokyo on Aug. 30, 1991, Mike Powell,* top page 476, *a 27-year-old American, leaped 29'4.5" (8.95 m) to surpass Bob Beamon's long-standing long-jump record. Canada's Kurt Browning and Kristi Yamaguchi, above, a 19-year-old Californian, reigned supreme at the World Ice Skating Championships in Munich in March. Ian Woosnam of Wales pared the final hole for a dramatic win at the 55th Masters golf tournament in Augusta, GA, on April 14. Preakness winner Hansel surpassed Kentucky Derby victor Strike the Gold (11) to capture the 123d Belmont Stakes in June.*

Meanwhile, the 22-member Knight Foundation Commission of Intercollegiate Athletics—headed by the Rev. Theodore Hesburgh, former Notre Dame president, and William C. Friday, former president of the University of North Carolina—issued its report. Considered the most extensive investigation of intercollegiate athletics in more than 60 years, the report recommended that university heads should be active in NCAA affairs, booster clubs and trustees should relinquish control of collegiate athletics and its finances to school presidents, and athletes unlikely to graduate from college should not be admitted in the first place.

In September, Robert Helmick resigned as president of the U.S. Olympic Committee (USOC) after it was revealed he had accepted consulting fees from companies looking to do business with the USOC.

ARTHUR KAPLAN

Auto Racing

Ayrton Senna of Brazil defended his Formula One world driving championship by winning the first four races of the 16-event season. He outpointed Nigel Mansell of Great Britain, 96–72. Italy's Riccardo Patrese was third with 53 points. Senna captured seven races in earning his third world championship. He clinched the crown with a second-place finish behind McLaren-Honda teammate Gerhard Berger in the Japanese Grand Prix, the next-to-last race on the schedule, and then won a rain-shortened finale in Australia.

Senna became the first driver to open the Formula One season with four victories, capping off his streak with a win in the Monaco Grand Prix. Senna ended 1991 with 33 career wins, second only to France's Alain Prost's 44.

Rick Mears of Bakersfield, CA, joined A. J. Foyt and Al Unser, Sr., in becoming the third driver to win four Indianapolis 500s. The 39-year-old Mears beat Michael Andretti of Nazareth, PA, by 3.1 seconds at a winning speed of 176.46 mph (284 km/h). A record four members of the Andretti family started in the Indianapolis 500. Michael's younger brother, Jeff, joined their father Mario and cousin John in the 33-car field. Michael, John, and Mario finished first, second, and third, respectively, at the Miller 200 in Milwaukee June 2.

Michael Andretti dominated the Indy-car season and won the Championship Auto Racing Teams (CART) title with 234 points to 200 for runner-up Bobby Rahal of Dublin, OH. Andretti won eight of the 17 events and clinched the crown by winning the final race at Monterey, CA. He also won the pole for eight races, set seven qualifying and six race records, and led during a record 45.7% of the laps.

AUTO RACING

Major Race Winners, 1991

Indianapolis 500: Rick Mears, United States
Marlboro 500: Mears
Daytona 500: Ernie Irvan, United States

1991 Champions

World Championship: Ayrton Senna, Brazil
CART: Michael Andretti
NASCAR: Dale Earnhardt

Grand Prix for Formula One Cars, 1991

United States: Ayrton Senna, Brazil
Brazilian: Senna
San Marino: Senna
Monaco: Senna
Canadian: Nelson Piquet, Brazil
Mexican: Riccardo Patrese, Italy
French: Nigel Mansell, Great Britain
British: Mansell
German: Mansell
Hungarian: Senna
Belgian: Senna
Italian: Mansell
Portuguese: Patrese
Spanish: Mansell
Japanese: Gerhard Berger, Austria
Australian: Senna

Stock Cars. Dale Earnhardt of Kannapolis, NC, won his fifth Winston Cup stock-car championship by outpointing runner-up Ricky Rudd of Chesapeake, VA, 4,287–4,092. Davey Allison of Hueytown, AL, was third with 4,088 points. Earnhardt had four first-place finishes.

STAN SUTTON
"Louisville Courier-Journal"

Baseball

Before the Minnesota Twins and Atlanta Braves both did it in 1991, no major-league team of the 20th century had gone from last place one year to first place the next. The Twins, winning the American League West title for the first time since 1987, went from 74-88 and 29 games behind in 1990 to 95–67 and eight games ahead in 1991. The Braves, who had not won a National League West crown since 1982, jumped from 65–97 (baseball's worst record in 1990) and 26 games behind to 94–68, one game ahead of the Los Angeles Dodgers in a grueling title chase.

Play-offs and World Series. In the National League Championship Series (NLCS), the Braves were decided underdogs against the heavy-hitting Pittsburgh Pirates, whose 98–64 regular-season record had been baseball's best. Pittsburgh took a 5–1 win behind Doug Drabek in the opener on October 9 but lost the next day, 1–0, to 21-year-old southpaw Steve Avery. After Atlanta hit three home runs in a 10–3 win in game three on October 12, the Pirates bounced back to win two in a row, 3–2 in ten innings and 1–0—taking the best-of-seven series back to Pittsburgh with a lead of three games to two. But the Braves got consecutive 1–0 and 4–0 shutouts from Avery (with ninth-inning help from Alejandro Pena) and John Smoltz to win their first pennant since 1958. Avery was named most valuable player (MVP) of the play-offs for pitching a record 16⅓ consecutive scoreless innings. The three 1–0 games were also a postseason-series record.

The NLCS ended on a sour note for Pittsburgh, which failed to score in its final 22 innings overall and in the last 27 innings in its home ballpark. During the regular season, the Pirates had led the league with a .263 batting average and 768 runs scored, an average of 4.7 per game.

By the end of the American League Championship Series (ALCS), the Toronto Blue Jays also had become a symbol of futility. After winning the Eastern Division title by seven games, they lost their third ALCS without a win by bowing to Minnesota in five games.

The Twins took the October 8 opener, 5–4, but lost a 5–2 verdict a day later. After regrouping during an off-day, Minnesota swept all three games in Toronto's SkyDome, 3–2 on Mike Pagliarulo's pinch-homer in the tenth,

© Focus on Sports

Minnesota Twins pitcher Jack Morris won two games in the American League Championship Series and two games in the World Series. He was most valuable player of the latter.

then 9–3 and 8–5. Kirby Puckett, who led the Twins with a .429 average, two homers, and six runs batted in, was named play-off MVP.

Minnesota maintained its momentum in the first two games of the World Series. Jack Morris, who had won two games in the ALCS, took the October 19 opener, 5–2, and Kevin Tapani won the second game, 3–2, after rookie Scott Leius snapped a tie with a solo homer in the eighth. Once the series switched to Atlanta, however, the tables were turned. The Braves took 12 innings to win game three, 5-4, on October 22, then won again in their last at bat with a 3–2 victory the next day. Atlanta rode three home runs to a 14–5 win—and a three-games-to-two lead—in game five.

The Twins proved invincible in the Metrodome, however. Puckett's 11th-inning homer won game six, 4–3, and Morris worked ten tense but scoreless innings to win a 1–0 finale—only the second game seven to be decided by that score. With two wins and a 1.17 earned run average, Morris was named the MVP of the World Series that many experts felt was the most dramatic in history. The match of two Cinderella teams produced many records, including the most games decided in a club's last at bat (five), the most decided on the last pitch (four), and the most extra-inning affairs (three).

Regular Season. Of the four divisional winners, the Pirates took the easiest path to post-season play. They held first place from April 27 to the end of the season, romping to their second straight NL East title 14 games ahead of the St. Louis Cardinals.

In the Western Division, the Cincinnati Reds sought to defend their 1990 world championship from a strong challenge by the Los Angeles Dodgers. The Dodgers led the Reds by five games at the break for the All-Star Game, with Atlanta third, nine and one-half games back. Then Atlanta's young pitching staff caught fire, enabling the team to lead both leagues with a 55–28 second-half record and finish first by a single game. The Braves

BASEBALL

Professional—Major Leagues

Final Standings, 1991

AMERICAN LEAGUE

Eastern Division	W	L	Pct.	Western Division	W	L	Pct.
Toronto	91	71	.562	Minnesota	95	67	.586
Boston	84	78	.519	Chicago	87	75	.537
Detroit	84	78	.519	Texas	85	77	.525
Milwaukee	83	79	.512	Oakland	84	78	.519
New York	71	91	.438	Seattle	83	79	.512
Baltimore	67	95	.414	Kansas City	82	80	.506
Cleveland	57	105	.352	California	81	81	.500

NATIONAL LEAGUE

Eastern Division	W	L	Pct.	Western Division	W	L	Pct.
Pittsburgh	98	64	.605	Atlanta	94	68	.580
St. Louis	84	78	.519	Los Angeles	93	69	.574
Philadelphia	78	84	.481	San Diego	84	78	.519
Chicago	77	83	.481	San Francisco	75	87	.463
New York	77	84	.478	Cincinnati	74	88	.457
Montreal	71	90	.441	Houston	65	97	.401

Play-offs—American League: Minnesota defeated Toronto, 4 games to 1; National League: Atlanta defeated Pittsburgh, 4 games to 3.

World Series—Minnesota defeated Atlanta, 4 games to 3. First Game (Hubert H. Humphrey Metrodome, Minneapolis, Oct. 19, attendance 55,108): Minnesota 5, Atlanta 2; Second Game (Metrodome, Oct. 20, attendance 55,145): Minnesota 3, Atlanta 2; Third Game (Atlanta-Fulton County Stadium, Oct. 22, attendance 50,878): Atlanta 5, Minnesota 4; Fourth Game (Fulton County Stadium, Oct. 23, attendance 50,878): Atlanta 3, Minnesota 2; Fifth Game (Atlanta-Fulton County Stadium, Oct. 24, attendance 50,878): Atlanta 14, Minnesota 5; Sixth Game (Metrodome, Oct. 26, attendance 55,155): Minnesota 4, Atlanta 3; Seventh Game (Metrodome, Oct. 27, attendance 55,118): Minnesota 1, Atlanta 0.

All-Star Game (SkyDome, Toronto, July 9, attendance 52,383): American League 4, National League 2.

Most Valuable Players—American League: Cal Ripken, Jr., Baltimore; National League: Terry Pendleton, Atlanta

Cy Young Memorial Awards (outstanding pitchers)—American League: Roger Clemens, Boston; National League: Tom Glavine, Atlanta

Managers of the Year—American League: Tom Kelly, Minnesota; National League: Bobby Cox, Atlanta

Rookies of the Year—American League: Chuck Knoblauch, Minnesota; National League: Jeff Bagwell, Houston

Leading Hitters—(Percentage) American League: Julio Franco, Texas, .341; National League: Terry Pendleton, Atlanta, .319. (Runs Batted In) American League: Cecil Fielder, Detroit, 133; National League: Howard Johnson, New York, 117. (Home Runs) American League: Fielder and Jose Canseco, Oakland, 44; National League: Johnson, 38. (Hits) American League: Paul Molitor, Milwaukee, 216; National League: Pendleton, 187. (Runs) American League: Molitor, 133; National League: Brett Butler, Los Angeles, 112. (Slugging Percentage) American League: Danny Tartabull, Kansas City, .593; National League: Will Clark, San Francisco, .536.

Leading Pitchers—(Earned Run Average) American League: Roger Clemens, Boston, 2.62; National League: Dennis Martinez, Montreal, 2.39. (Victories) American League: Scott Erickson, Minnesota, and Bill Gullickson, Detroit, 20; National League: John Smiley, Pittsburgh, and Tom Glavine, Atlanta, 20. (Strikeouts) American League: Clemens, 241; National League: David Cone, New York, 241. (Shutouts) American League: Clemens, 4; National League: Dennis Martinez, Montreal, 5. (Saves) American League: Bryan Harvey, California, 46; National League: Lee Smith, St. Louis, 47.

Professional—Minor Leagues, Class AAA

American Association: Denver
International League: Columbus
Pacific Coast League: Tucson

Amateur

NCAA: Louisiana State University
Little League World Series: Tai Chung, Taiwan

1941—The Year of Ted and Joe

© UPI/Bettmann

Baseball, a game that never forgets its larger-than-life heroes, paused in 1991 to salute the 50th anniversary of two of its most celebrated batting feats: Joe DiMaggio's 56-game hitting streak and Ted Williams' .406 batting average. In addition to tributes at various ballparks and much press coverage, DiMaggio *(right in photo)* and Williams *(left in photo)* were honored at the White House on July 9, then flown to Toronto for the All-Star Game aboard Air Force One. Pregame ceremonies honored the living legends.

DiMaggio, right-handed-hitting center fielder of the New York Yankees, was 26 and the winner of consecutive batting crowns when the 1941 season started. Williams, 22-year-old left-handed-hitting left fielder of the Boston Red Sox, was starting his third season after hitting .327 and .344 in his first two years.

On May 15 both men began hitting streaks. Williams hit .487, while connecting in 23 straight games; DiMaggio's streak continued until July 17, when two backhanded grabs by Cleveland's third baseman Ken Keltner left the Yankee Clipper hitless. DiMaggio batted .408 during his record-setting period.

It took a six-for-eight performance in a season-ending doubleheader for Williams to become baseball's first .400 hitter since Bill Terry of the New York Giants in 1930. No one has hit higher than .390 since. During the 1941 season, Williams had 145 walks and struck out only 27 times. He led the American League with 37 home runs, while DiMaggio, a .357 hitter for the season, was first in runs batted in (RBIs)—125. DiMaggio won the second of three most-valuable-player (MVP) awards that fall as the Yankees won the World Series.

During 19 seasons, Williams took the triple crown twice and won six batting crowns. Finishing with a .344 lifetime average and 521 home runs, he hit below .300 only once. DiMaggio, who played 13 seasons, had a .325 career average, with 361 home runs and an average of 118 RBIs per season.

DAN SCHLOSSBERG

clinched on October 5, the next-to-last day of the season, with their eighth straight victory—six of them on the road. The Dodgers dropped three of their last four. Atlanta and Los Angeles had been tied entering the final weekend.

In the American League East, the defending champion Boston Red Sox overcame Toronto's 11-game August 7 lead to close to within one game by mid-September. A Red Sox slump, coupled with a Blue Jay revival, enabled Toronto to clinch the title on October 2.

Six teams were separated by six and one-half games in the AL West race at the All-Star break before Minnesota pulled away from the pack, ending a string of three straight pennants by the Oakland Athletics. Each of the seven teams in the division finished at .500 or better—a baseball first.

The heroes of Atlanta's surprise season monopolized the postseason awards. Terry Pendleton was named National League MVP and comeback player of the year after leading the league with a .319 average, 187 hits, and 303 total bases (tied with San Francisco's Will Clark). Tom Glavine, who shared the league leadership in most wins with Pittsburgh's John Smiley (20) and complete games with Montreal's Dennis Martinez (nine), won the NL's Cy Young Award for pitching excellence.

Jeff Bagwell of the Houston Astros was NL rookie of the year after hitting .294 with 15 homers and mastering a new position (first base). Chuck Knoblauch took AL rookie honors for filling Minnesota's second-base hole, while hitting .281. His 15 postseason hits were a record for a rookie. Cal Ripken, Jr., was named American League MVP for the second time. The Baltimore shortstop reached career highs with a .323 average, 34 home runs, and 114 runs batted in (RBIs); led the league with 85 extra-base hits and a .986 fielding percentage; and extended his streak of consecutive games played to 1,546. Texas pitcher Jose Guzman was comeback player of the year.

Detroit's Cecil Fielder led the league in home runs (44) and RBIs (133) for the second straight year, though he shared the home-run crown with Oakland's Jose Canseco. Julio Franco of the Texas Rangers hit .341 to win his first batting crown, while Rickey Henderson of

Oakland stole 58 bases to lead the league in that department for the 11th time, four in a row.

Roger Clemens (*see* BIOGRAPHY) of the Boston Red Sox won his third AL Cy Young Award after posting an 18–10 record and leading the league with a 2.62 earned run average, 241 strikeouts, four shutouts, and 271.1 innings pitched. Minnesota's Scott Erickson and Detroit's Bill Gullickson led the league with 20 victories each, while Bryan Harvey of the California Angels had the most saves (46).

Howard Johnson of the New York Mets led the National League with 38 home runs and 117 RBIs and posted his third 30/30 (home runs and stolen bases) season. Atlanta's Ronnie Gant, the other 30/30 player of 1991, joined Willie Mays and Bobby Bonds as the only men to perform the rare feat in consecutive campaigns. Brett Butler of Los Angeles led the NL with 112 runs scored and had a 23-game hitting streak, the best in baseball.

Marquis Grissom of the Montreal Expos topped the majors with 76 stolen bases, while teammate Dennis Martinez led both leagues with a 2.39 ERA. New York's David Cone struck out 19 men on the season's last day to tie Clemens for the major-league strikeout crown (241).

Lee Smith of the St. Louis Cardinals saved 47 games, an NL record, and moved into elite company with his 300th career save. Jeff Reardon of the Boston Red Sox also passed the 300-save plateau while posting his third 40-save season, matching a record achieved two days earlier by Oakland's Dennis Eckersley.

On May 1, the same day Henderson stole his 939th base to break Lou Brock's career record, 44-year-old Nolan Ryan of the Texas Rangers became the oldest man in baseball history to pitch a no-hitter. The season's first no-hitter, a 3–0 win over Toronto, was Ryan's seventh, extending his own record. Although there were six other 1991 no-hitters, the best was the 2–0 perfect game pitched by Dennis Martinez at Los Angeles on July 28. It was the 13th perfect game in major-league history. No-hitters also were pitched by Tommy Greene (Phillies), Bret Saberhagen (Royals), Wilson Alvarez (White Sox), and tandems of four Orioles and three Braves. Alvarez had made only one previous big-league start.

The American League got its fifth win in the last six All-Star Games with a 4–2 win in the July 9 game at Toronto. Ripken was All-Star MVP for his three-run homer.

Two weeks later, on July 21, the Hall of Fame inducted five new members: former pitchers Gaylord Perry and Ferguson Jenkins; seven-time batting champion Rod Carew; the late Tony Lazzeri, slugging second baseman of the Babe Ruth era; and Bill Veeck, innovative owner of several big-league clubs.

Also in 1991, the official baseball family grew with the announcement that two new teams, the Colorado Rockies and Florida Marlins, would join the National League in 1993, equalizing the size of both leagues at 14 clubs. The 26 current clubs agreed to supply players for a draft to stock the new teams.

DAN SCHLOSSBERG, *Baseball Writer*

With a seasonal batting average of .319, 22 home runs, and 86 runs batted in, Terry Pendleton helped lead the Braves to the World Series. He was the National League's MVP.

© Lonnie Major/Allsport

Basketball

After 25 frustrating years, the Chicago Bulls finally won their first National Basketball Association (NBA) title by defeating the Los Angeles Lakers, four games to one, to capture the 1991 championship. The Bulls were led by the marvelous performance of Michael Jordan, who was selected most valuable player (MVP) of the final series.

Another frustrated squad, the Blue Devils of Duke University, finally won their first National Collegiate Athletic Association (NCAA) basketball crown by downing the Kansas Jayhawks, 72–65, in the championship game. Duke, which had lost the title contest in two of the previous five years, beat undefeated and favored Nevada-Las Vegas in a semifinal game. Tennessee upset second-ranked Virginia to win the women's NCAA title.

The Professional Season

The Detroit Pistons, who had won two straight NBA championships, were hoping to become only the third franchise in league history to win three titles in a row. But injuries and improved competition proved too much for the Pistons, who finished with only the ninth-best regular-season record (50–32) in the league, then lost in the Eastern Conference play-off finals to Chicago.

Regular Season. The league's best record was captured by the Portland Trail Blazers (63–19), who had lost in the 1990 championship series to Detroit. But the Blazers did not have an easy time. They were pressed by the Los Angeles Lakers, whose late-season rush left them trailing by just five games in the Pacific Division standings. The San Antonio Spurs, behind their outstanding center, David Robinson, won their second straight Midwest Division title, outlasting the Utah Jazz by one game and the Houston Rockets by three. Boston, despite Larry Bird's season-long back problems, ran away with the Atlantic Division race, finishing 12 games ahead of Philadelphia. Chicago, which slowly had been building a contender since Michael Jordan joined the Bulls as a rookie in 1984, beat out both Detroit and Milwaukee in the Central Division, compiling the league's second-best record and the franchise's best ever while winning its first division title since 1974–75.

Golden State, despite playing without a legitimate center, finished with a winning record (44–38). But two other franchises, Cleveland (33–49) and Dallas (28–54), played poorly after being rated as play-off contenders. The New York Knicks were so disappointed in their season that they went through two coaches, Stu Jackson and John MacLeod. The Minnesota Timberwolves fired their coach, Bill Musselman, and the coach of the Miami Heat, Ron Rothstein, resigned.

Jordan had a magnificent season. He won his fifth straight scoring championship; only Wilt Chamberlain had won more in a row (seven). He averaged 31.5 points and 5.5 assists, was third in the league in steals, and shot 53.9% from the field, a career high. He was named both to the all-NBA team and to the league's all-defensive team. More significantly, he was voted the NBA's most valuable player, the second time he had won the award. Magic Johnson of Los Angeles, who had won the pre-

The Los Angeles Lakers stood defenseless in the play-off finals as MVP Michael Jordan (23) led the Chicago Bulls to their first NBA championship. Jordan also won the regular-season scoring and MVP awards.

© Focus on Sports

Magic Johnson

Basketball fans everywhere suffered a great loss in the early days of the 1991–92 season when Earvin ("Magic") Johnson announced that he had contracted the HIV virus that causes AIDS (*see* MEDICINE AND HEALTH) and that he, therefore, would retire immediately as a player for the Los Angeles Lakers. Johnson was not only one of the game's most popular but also one of its best players. During his 12 seasons with the Lakers, Magic had been voted the season's most valuable player (MVP) three times, MVP of the play-offs three times, MVP of the 1990 All-Star game, a member of the All-NBA first team (1983–91), and a member of five NBA championship teams. The 6'9" (2.05-m), 32-year-old point guard also had led the league in assists four times and had set the NBA career record for assists (9,921). Prior to joining the Lakers he helped lead Michigan State to a national title in 1979.

vious two MVP awards, finished second in the voting, while Robinson was third. Philadelphia's Charles Barkley was fourth, Utah's Karl Malone fifth, and Portland's Clyde Drexler sixth.

Utah's John Stockton broke his own NBA single-season assist record with 1,164. His old mark was 1,134. Johnson finished second, but more important, he broke Oscar Robertson's career assist record. Jordan ran away with the scoring title; second was Utah's Malone, who had a 29.0 average, with Washington's Bernard King third (28.4). Robinson was the rebounding leader (13.0). Second was Detroit forward Dennis Rodman (12.5). Hakeem Olajuwon was the Number 1 shot blocker (3.95), barely finishing ahead of Robinson (3.9). Boston's Bird became the fifth player in league history to collect more than 20,000 points, 5,000 rebounds, and 5,000 assists in a career.

Joining Jordan on the all-NBA team were Robinson, Johnson, Malone, and Barkley. Robinson, Rodman, Jordan, Portland's Buck Williams, and Milwaukee's Alvin Robertson made the all-defensive squad. Rodman was the defensive player of the year for the second straight season. Derrick Coleman of New Jersey was chosen rookie of the year.

The Play-offs. On the strength of their regular-season showing, the Portland Trail Blazers were slight favorites to win the NBA title, with Chicago and Detroit considered the main contenders from the Eastern Conference. But Portland never made it to the finals. The Trail Blazers struggled in the opening round of the play-offs against Seattle, the weakest play-off team in the Western Conference. Portland had to win the fifth, and last, game of the series to prevail, three games to two. After defeating Utah in the semifinals, the Trail Blazers met Los Angeles in the conference finals.

The Lakers had breezed to the finals after downing both Houston and Golden State,

PROFESSIONAL BASKETBALL

National Basketball Association
(Final Standings, 1990–91)

Eastern Conference

Atlantic Division	W	L	Pct.	Games Behind
*Boston	56	26	.683	—
*Philadelphia	44	38	.537	12
*New York	39	43	.476	17
Washington	30	52	.366	26
New Jersey	26	56	.317	30
Miami	24	58	.293	32
Central Division				
*Chicago	61	21	.744	—
*Detroit	50	32	.610	11
*Milwaukee	48	34	.585	13
*Atlanta	43	39	.524	18
*Indiana	41	41	.500	20
Cleveland	33	49	.402	28
Charlotte	26	56	.317	35

Western Conference

Midwest Division	W	L	Pct.	Games Behind
*San Antonio	55	27	.671	—
*Utah	54	28	.659	1
*Houston	52	30	.634	3
Orlando	31	51	.378	24
Minnesota	29	53	.354	26
Dallas	28	54	.341	27
Denver	20	62	.244	35
Pacific Division				
*Portland	63	19	.768	—
*Los Angeles Lakers	58	24	.707	5
*Phoenix	55	27	.671	8
*Golden State	44	38	.537	19
*Seattle	41	41	.500	22
Los Angeles Clippers	31	51	.378	32
Sacramento	25	57	.305	38

*In play-offs

Play-Offs

Eastern Conference

First Round	Boston	3 games	Indiana	2
	Chicago	3 games	New York	0
	Detroit	3 games	Atlanta	2
	Philadelphia	3 games	Milwaukee	0
Second Round	Chicago	4 games	Philadelphia	1
	Detroit	4 games	Boston	2
Finals	Chicago	4 games	Detroit	0

Western Conference

First Round	Golden State	3 games	San Antonio	1
	Los Angeles	3 games	Houston	0
	Portland	3 games	Seattle	2
	Utah	3 games	Phoenix	1
Second Round	Los Angeles	4 games	Golden State	1
	Portland	4 games	Utah	1
Finals	Los Angeles	4 games	Portland	2
Championship	Chicago	4 games	Los Angeles	1
All-Star Game	East 116, West 114			

Individual Honors

Most Valuable Player: Michael Jordan, Chicago
Most Valuable Player (championship): Michael Jordan
Most Valuable Player (All-Star Game): Charles Barkley, Philadelphia
Rookie of the Year: Derrick Coleman, New Jersey
Coach of the Year: Don Chaney, Houston
Defensive Player of the Year: Dennis Rodman, Detroit
Leader in Scoring: Michael Jordan, 31.5 points per game
Leader in Assists: John Stockton, Utah, 14.2 per game
Leader in Rebounds: David Robinson, San Antonio, 13.0 per game
Leader in Field-Goal Percentage: Buck Williams, Portland, .602

which had advanced to the conference semifinals by registering the biggest upset of the play-offs. The Warriors were too quick for San Antonio and won in four games. In its matchup against Los Angeles, Portland never recovered from losing the opening game on its home court. With Magic Johnson and forward James Worthy playing splendidly, the Lakers ultimately took the series, four games to two, and advanced to the NBA championship round.

Chicago was waiting to play the Lakers after sweeping through the Eastern Conference play-offs. The Bulls were not pressed by either the New York Knicks or the Philadelphia 76ers, losing only once. That set up a conference final meeting with Detroit, which had beaten the Bulls in the finals the previous two years. This time, however, the Pistons were no match for Chicago. The Bulls overwhelmed the limping Pistons in four straight games to advance to the league championship round.

On the strength of their home-court advantage, Chicago figured to beat the Lakers, who had more play-off experience. But Los Angeles began by upsetting the Bulls, 93–91, in the opening game on the Bulls' home court. Sam Perkins won it for Los Angeles by making a three-point field goal with 14 seconds left. Chicago came back in game two to win, 107–86, with Jordan scoring 33 points and the Bulls setting several records, including best shooting percentage in play-off competition (.617). The series moved to Los Angeles, where the Bulls quickly reclaimed home-court advantage by outlasting L.A. in overtime, 104–96. Jordan made a jump shot with three seconds left to send the game into the extra period. In game four, another balanced team effort by Chicago overwhelmed the Lakers, 97–82. Los Angeles was trying to avoid a sweep at home but Chicago wrapped up the championship by winning game five, 108–101. Scottie Pippen had 32 points and Jordan, who won the series' MVP, had 30.

In a big upset, Duke, led by Christian Laettner, stopped undefeated UNLV in the NCAA-tournament semifinals. The Blue Devils then defeated Kansas, 72–65, for the title.

The College Season

The 1990–91 season was dominated by the University of Nevada-Las Vegas (UNLV), which was the top-ranked team throughout the year, while at the same time being the subject of a major investigation by the NCAA regarding the conduct of its basketball program. In addition, UNLV's coach, Jerry Tarkanian, was involved in an ongoing controversy with the NCAA, which had been resolved when the Rebels were allowed to play in the 1991 NCAA tournament and then put on a year's probation in 1992 which banned them from the tournament and television appearances.

UNLV had four starters returning from its 1989–90 national champions and a deep bench. The Rebels were favored heavily to win a second straight national title, something that had not been done since UCLA accomplished the feat in the early 1970s. Their major challengers were expected to be Arkansas, Arizona, Michigan State, and North Carolina, although no other college team was considered to be nearly as good as UNLV. The Rebels did not disappoint. They breezed through their regular-season schedule with hardly a stumble, including a crushing victory over then Number 2-ranked Arkansas in February, breaking the Razorbacks' streak of 20 straight wins.

Michigan State did not play up to its potential, and fell behind both Ohio State, which was better than expected, and Indiana in the Big Ten. North Carolina emerged as the best team in the Atlantic Coast Conference and in the East, playing just a shade better than Duke. The Big East Conference was not as dominant as usual, with regular-season champion Syracuse considered only a long-shot contender for the national title. Kansas, which figured to have a rebuilding year, finished strongly in the

Big Eight, where Nebraska also excelled. Arizona dominated West Coast teams. The best conferences were the Big Ten and the Atlantic Coast.

Forward Larry Johnson, who had passed up a lucrative professional contract to play his senior season at UNLV, was the consensus player of the year. He was joined on most All-America teams by teammate Stacey Augmon, LSU center Shaquille O'Neal, Kenny Anderson from Georgia Tech, and Billy Owens from Syracuse. Other standout players included guards Rodney Monroe of North Carolina State, Steve Smith of Michigan State, Jim Jackson of Ohio State, and Keith Jennings of East Tennessee State; centers Christian Laettner of Duke and Dikembe Mutombo of Georgetown, and forwards Doug Smith of Missouri, Calbert Cheaney of Indiana, and Rick Fox of North Carolina. Johnson wound up being the first player selected in the NBA draft in June.

In late spring, Tarkanian announced that he would coach one more season and then quit. He was pressured into the resignation after a Las Vegas newspaper printed a photo showing three of his players in a hot tub with a reputed gambler. Another prominent coach, Richard (Digger) Phelps, resigned after a 20-year career at Notre Dame. John MacLeod left the New York Knicks to take over for Phelps at South Bend.

The Tournament. The four top-seeded teams in the NCAA tournament were UNLV, North Carolina, Arkansas, and Ohio State. UNLV and North Carolina reached the Final Four but Arkansas and Ohio State were upset in regional play. UNLV won the West Region, having trouble only against Georgetown. The Rebels defeated Seton Hall for the regional title. North Carolina held off Temple for the East Region crown. Arkansas got to the Southeast Region final against Kansas, where the underdog Jayhawks ran away with the victory. Duke breezed to the Midwest Region championship by downing St. John's, which earlier had an easy time upending Ohio State.

In the Final Four at the Indianapolis' Hoosier Dome, Kansas and North Carolina met in one semifinal, while Duke and UNLV met in the other in a rematch of the 1990 championship game. The 1990 contest was won by UNLV by 30 points. But this time the Blue Devils sprung one of the greatest upsets in NCAA-tournament history. Playing just as aggressively as the highly favored Rebels, Duke took an early lead and refused to fold against UNLV's relentless attempts to take control of the game. Guard Bobby Hurley and center Christian Laettner were particularly outstanding. UNLV took a five-point lead late in the game, but Laettner put Duke ahead, 79–77, with two foul shots 11 seconds before the end of the game. The loss broke UNLV's 45-game winning streak and set up a final between Duke and Kansas, which had defeated North Carolina in the other semifinal.

Duke was too strong for the Jayhawks. Laettner, who scored 28 points against UNLV, added 18 points and ten rebounds against Kansas and was selected most valuable player of the Final Four. Hurley played another splendid floor game and Duke neutralized the inside strength of Kansas. The Blue Devils held off a last-gasp rally by Kansas and won, 72–65.

Women's. In the women's NCAA tournament, Virginia came into the Final Four as the favorite after being ranked Number 1 for most of the season. But the Cavaliers were upset in the finals, 70–67, in overtime by Tennessee, giving the Lady Vols their third national title in five years. Center Daedra Charles of Tennessee scored 19 points and had 12 rebounds and guard Dena Head had 28 points. But guard Dawn Staley of Virginia was chosen MVP. She also was player of the year in women's college basketball. In the semifinals, Tennessee had beaten Stanford and Virginia had defeated Connecticut.

PAUL ATTNER
Senior Writer, "The Sporting News"

COLLEGE BASKETBALL

Conference Champions

American South: New Orleans[r], Louisiana Tech[t]
Atlantic Coast: Duke[r], North Carolina[t]
Atlantic 10: Rutgers[r], Penn State[t]
Big East: Syracuse[r], Seton Hall[t]
Big Eight: Oklahoma State, Kansas (tied)[r]; Missouri[t] (ineligible for NCAA tournament)
Big Sky: Montana[r,t]
Big South: Coastal Carolina[r,t] (defeated Jackson State, Southwestern Athletic tournament champion, in a play-in game for an NCAA tournament berth)
Big Ten: Ohio State, Indiana (tied)
Big West: UNLV[r,t]
Colonial Athletic: James Madison[r], Richmond[t]
East Coast: Towson State[r,t]
Ivy League: Princeton
Metro: Southern Mississippi[r], Florida State[t]
Metro Atlantic Athletic: Siena, LaSalle (tied)[r]; St. Peter's[t]
Mid-American: Eastern Michigan[r,t]
Mid-Continent: Northern Illinois[r], Wisconsin-Green Bay[t]
Mid-Eastern Athletic: Coppin State[r], Florida A&M[t]
Midwestern: Xavier[r,t]
Missouri Valley: Creighton[r,t]
North Atlantic: Northeastern[r,t]
Northeast: St. Francis, PA[r,t] (defeated Fordham, Patriot League tournament champion, in a play-in game for an NCAA tournament berth)
Ohio Valley: Murray State[r,t]
Pacific-10: Arizona
Patriot League: Fordham[r,t]
Southeastern: Mississippi State, LSU (tied)[r]; Alabama[t]
Southern: Furman[r]; East Tennessee State[t]
Southland: Northeast Louisiana[r,t] (defeated Florida A&M, Mid-Eastern Athletic tournament champion, in a play-in game for an NCAA tournament berth)
Southwest: Arkansas[r,t]
Southwestern Athletic: Jackson State[r,t]
Sun Belt: South Alabama[r,t]
Trans America Athletic: University of Texas, San Antonio[r], Georgia State[t]
West Coast: Pepperdine[r,t]
Western Athletic: Utah[r], Brigham Young[t]
[r]regular-season winner; [t]conference-tournament winner

Tournaments

NCAA: Duke
NCAA Division II: North Alabama
NCAA Division III: Wisconsin-Platteville
NIT: Stanford
NAIA: Oklahoma City
NCAA Division I (women): Tennessee

Boxing

Heavyweights drew most of the attention on boxing's calendar in 1991.

The Heavyweights. On April 19 the highly publicized bout between the 28-year-old heavyweight champion, Evander Holyfield, and the ageless challenger, 42-year-old George Foreman, took place in Atlantic City, NJ. Foreman, a former champion, went into the bout weighing 257 lbs (116.57 kg) while Holyfield entered at a lean 208 lbs (94.35 kg). Few ringside observers gave Foreman a chance to last beyond the first few rounds, but from the outset he took Holyfield's best punches and let fly with rolling uppercuts, long rights, and short left hooks that found their mark and kept Holyfield from delivering a knockout blow.

Foreman forced Holyfield to go the 12-round distance before the champion received a unanimous decision from the three judges. They scored the fight 116-111, 115-112, 117-110 for Holyfield, but Foreman had won a moral victory. Foreman was guaranteed $12.5 million and Holyfield $20 million.

In December in Reno, NV, Foreman was back in the ring, earning $5 million for administering a legal beating to Jimmy Ellis, a former football player, who was knocked out at 1:36 of the third round. Foreman immediately began drumbeating for another title match with Holyfield.

Meanwhile, the fighter most fans wanted to see in the ring with Holyfield—Mike Tyson, the former champion—had many problems, legal and otherwise, to overcome. He managed to defeat Donovan (Razor) Ruddock by decision in a 12-round summer rematch of their March bout (where Tyson had stopped Ruddock in the seventh) at Las Vegas, but some thought Tyson was beginning to lose his edge.

Promoters and TV entrepreneurs working for a Tyson-Holyfield match became snarled in legal wrangling before they could settle on a date for a bout. First it was listed for November 8, but finally it was moved to November 23 in Las Vegas. The projected gate was $100 million, with Holyfield to take home $30 million and Tyson $15 million. During the wrangling, Tyson was accused of raping a beauty-pageant contestant in Indianapolis in the summer and was indicted after a grand-jury investigation. The trial was scheduled for early 1992.

On October 18, Tyson pulled out of the fight, claiming he had an injured rib cage. In his place, Holyfield lined up Italian Francesco Damiani, who also withdrew abruptly, with an ankle injury, a week before the bout. The gap was filled by Bert Cooper, a 22–1 underdog who stunned Holyfield early in the fight. Referee Mills Lane stopped the bout in the seventh round after the champion had dealt severe punishment. No one had given Cooper a chance, but he gave Holyfield, fighting in his hometown of Atlanta, the toughest fight of his pro career. Cooper earned $750,000; Holyfield $6 million.

WORLD BOXING CHAMPIONS*

Heavyweight: World Boxing Council (WBC)—Evander Holyfield, United States, 1990; World Boxing Association (WBA)—Holyfield, 1990; International Boxing Federation (IBF)—Holyfield, 1990.

Cruiserweight: WBC—Anaclet Wamba, France, 1991; WBA—Bobby Czyz, United States, 1991; IBF—James Warring, United States, 1991.

Light Heavyweight: WBC—Jeff Harding, Australia, 1991; WBA—Thomas Hearns, United States, 1991; IBF—Charles Williams, United States, 1990.

Super Middleweight: WBC—Mauro Galvano, Italy, 1990; WBA—Victor Cordova, Panama, 1991; IBF—Darren Van Horn, United States, 1991.

Middleweight: WBC—Julian Jackson, Virgin Islands, 1990; WBA—vacant; IBF—James Toney, United States, 1991.

Junior Middleweight: WBC—Terry Norris, United States, 1990; WBA—Vinny Pazienza, United States, 1991; IBF—Gianfranco Rosi, Italy, 1989.

Welterweight: WBC—James McGirt, United States, 1991; WBA—Meldrick Taylor, United States, 1991; IBF—Maurice Blocker, United States, 1991.

Junior Welterweight: WBC—Julio César Chávez, Mexico, 1989; WBA—Edwin Rosario, United States, 1991; IBF—Rafael Pineda, Colombia, 1991.

Lightweight: WBC—Pernell Whitaker, United States, 1989; WBA—Whitaker, 1990; IBF—Whitaker, 1989.

Junior Lightweight: WBC—Azumah Nelson, Ghana, 1988; WBA—Ganaro Hernandez, United States, 1991; IBF—Brian Mitchell, South Africa, 1991.

Featherweight: WBC—Paul Hodkinson, Great Britain, 1991; WBA—Yung-kyun Park, South Korea, 1991; IBF—Manuel Medina, Mexico, 1991.

Junior Featherweight: WBC—Daniel Zaragoza, Mexico, 1991; WBA—Raul Perez, Mexico, 1991; IBF—Welcome Ncita, South Africa, 1990.

Bantamweight: WBC—Joichiro Tatsuyoshi, Japan, 1991; WBA—Israel Contreras, Venezuela, 1991; IBF—Orlando Canizales, United States, 1988.

Junior Bantamweight: WBC—Sunkil Moon, South Korea, 1990; WBA—Kaosai Galaxy, Thailand, 1984; IBF—Robert Quiroga, United States, 1990.

Flyweight: WBC—Muangchai Kittikasem, Thailand, 1991; WBA—Yongkang Kim, South Korea, 1991; IBF—Dave McAuley, Great Britain, 1989.

Junior Flyweight: WBC—Humberto Gonzalez, Mexico, 1989; WBA—Myung Woo Yuh, South Korea, 1985; IBF—Michael Carbajal, United States, 1990.

Strawweight: WBC—Ricardo Lopez, Mexico, 1990; WBA—Hiyong Choy, South Korea, 1991; IBF—Fah-Lan Lookmingkwan, Thailand, 1990.

*As of Dec. 31, 1991; date indicates year title was won.

Other Divisions. A fighter who had held five different weight-division titles added still another in June when 32-year-old Thomas Hearns used his legendary jab to win the World Boxing Association (WBA) light-heavyweight crown from Virgil Hill in Las Vegas in a unanimous 12-round decision. Hearns, a 2–1 underdog in the fight, won his sixth championship and his second as a light heavyweight.

In January at Atlantic City, Meldrick Taylor, whose loss to Julio César Chávez in March 1990 seemed to have demoralized him, won a unanimous decision to take the WBA welterweight title from Aaron Davis.

The 34-year-old Sugar Ray Leonard, who had undergone surgery for a detached retina in 1982 and had made several comebacks after that, attempted one more in the ring at Madison Square Garden. But it was to be his last, as he struggled in losing a 12-round unanimous decision to Terry Norris, the World Boxing Council (WBC) junior-middleweight champion. After the fight, Leonard told the crowd of 7,495, "This is my last fight."

GEORGE DE GREGORIO
"The New York Times"

Football

There was a sense of predictability to the 1991–92 National Football League (NFL) season. For a change, the preseason favorites to reach the Super Bowl—the Buffalo Bills and Washington Redskins—fulfilled expectations. The two teams compiled the best records in their respective conferences and then marched through the play-offs to set up a long-expected showdown in the NFL title game. But it was not a good year for league coaches, one third of whom were fired by season's end.

Despite the Bills' successful season, it was not a good championship appearance for them either, as the Redskins completely dominated Super Bowl XXVI before 63,130 at the Metrodome in Minneapolis. Washington jumped off to a 17–0 halftime lead, never was challenged, and won, 37–24. Redskins' quarterback Mark Rypien, who completed 18 of 33 passes for 292 yards and two touchdowns, was the game's most valuable player. The Redskins' defense also was particularly effective, limiting Thurman Thomas, who led the league in rushing, to 13 yards; intercepting Bills' quarterback Jim Kelly four times; and sacking him five times. It was Washington's third Super Bowl win in ten years (*see* FEATURE ARTICLE, page 70).

In college competition, the mythical national title was shared by Washington and Miami after both schools won their New Year's Day bowl games to finish undefeated. Michigan receiver/kick returner Desmond Howard, the most exciting player in the game, won the Heisman Trophy as the nation's top player.

In the Canadian Football League, the Toronto Argonauts defeated the Calgary Stampeders, 36–21, for the Grey Cup championship. The victory was clinched by Raghib (Rocket) Ismail with an 87-yard kickoff return for a fourth-quarter touchdown. Ismail was voted the game's most valuable player.

The Professional Season

It was not a very good season for National Football League (NFL) coaches. By the end of the regular schedule, there was so much unhappiness with the performance of many teams that numerous coaches lost their jobs, including John Robinson of the Los Angeles Rams, Chuck Knox of the Seattle Seahawks, Richard Williamson of the Tampa Bay Buccaneers, Lindy Infante of the Green Bay Packers, Dan Henning of the San Diego Chargers, Sam Wyche of the Cincinnati Bengals, and Jerry Burns of the Minnesota Vikings. It was the

AP/Wide World

Carlton Bailey (54), a right inside linebacker, scored Buffalo's only touchdown following an interception to lead the Bills to a 10–7 win over Denver in the American Football Conference championship game. The Bills then were defeated by the Redskins, 37–24—their second consecutive Super Bowl loss.

PROFESSIONAL FOOTBALL

National Football League

Final Standings, 1991

AMERICAN CONFERENCE

Eastern Division	W	L	T	Pct.	Points For	Points Against
Buffalo	13	3	0	.813	458	318
N.Y. Jets	8	8	0	.500	314	293
Miami	8	8	0	.500	343	349
New England	6	10	0	.375	211	305
Indianapolis	1	15	0	.063	143	381
Central Division						
Houston	11	5	0	.688	386	251
Pittsburgh	7	9	0	.438	292	344
Cleveland	6	10	0	.375	293	298
Cincinnati	3	13	0	.188	263	435
Western Division						
Denver	12	4	0	.750	304	235
Kansas City	10	6	0	.625	322	252
L.A. Raiders	9	7	0	.563	298	297
Seattle	7	9	0	.438	276	261
San Diego	4	12	0	.250	274	342

PLAY-OFFS
Kansas City 10, L.A. Raiders 6
Houston 17, N.Y. Jets 10
Denver 26, Houston 24
Buffalo 37, Kansas City 14
Buffalo 10, Denver 7

NATIONAL CONFERENCE

Eastern Division	W	L	T	Pct.	Points For	Points Against
Washington	14	2	0	.875	485	224
Dallas	11	5	0	.688	342	310
Philadelphia	10	6	0	.625	285	244
N.Y. Giants	8	8	0	.500	281	297
Phoenix	4	12	0	.250	196	344
Central Division						
Detroit	12	4	0	.750	339	295
Chicago	11	5	0	.688	299	269
Minnesota	8	8	0	.500	301	306
Green Bay	4	12	0	.250	273	313
Tampa Bay	3	13	0	.188	199	365
Western Division						
New Orleans	11	5	0	.688	341	211
Atlanta	10	6	0	.625	361	338
San Francisco	10	6	0	.625	393	239
L.A. Rams	3	13	0	.188	234	390

PLAY-OFFS
Atlanta 27, New Orleans 20
Dallas 17, Chicago 13
Washington 24, Atlanta 7
Detroit 38, Dallas 6
Washington 41, Detroit 10

SUPER BOWL XXVI: Washington 37, Buffalo 24

heaviest coaching turnover in the league in two decades. The NFL announced plans to expand by two more teams for the 1994 season. The biggest question mark entering the season was whether Ray Handley, who replaced the retired Bill Parcells as coach of the Super Bowl XXV champions, the New York Giants, could return the Giants to the title game.

Regular Season. Injuries to star quarterbacks marred the regular season. San Francisco's Joe Montana, the best in the league, never played after undergoing elbow surgery. Philadelphia's Randall Cunningham hurt a knee in the opening game and missed the rest of the season. Both of their teams failed to qualify for the play-offs. Detroit guard Mike Utley fell on his neck during a game and was paralyzed from the neck down.

The Giants stumbled in their quest for a postseason spot behind quarterback Jeff Hostetler, the hero of Super Bowl XXV, who beat out veteran Phil Simms for the starting spot. With their toughest National Football Conference (NFC) Eastern Division foes struggling, the Washington Redskins easily won the division, at one point putting together an 11-game winning streak, thanks in large part to the play of quarterback Rypien. Dallas of the NFC East carried a six-game winning streak into the play-offs, two years after finishing 1–15.

The Detroit Lions, for years one of the league's worst teams, were a major surprise, winning the NFC Central Division title despite losing quarterback Rodney Peete to an Achilles injury. The Lions beat out traditional rival Chicago, which also qualified for the play-offs. In the NFC Western Division, New Orleans won the first title in its history while the Atlanta Falcons, another longtime also-ran, made it into the play-offs after a slow start.

Buffalo running back Thurman Thomas emerged as the league's most valuable player and also helped the Bills romp to the American Football Conference (AFC) Eastern Division title. Teammate Jim Kelly was the league's best quarterback. Houston, behind the play of quarterback Warren Moon, won the AFC Central Division crown and Denver, rebounding from a 5–11 season, captured the AFC Western Division title, just beating out play-off qualifiers Kansas City and the Los Angeles Raiders. The New York Jets, despite an 8–8 record, got into the play-offs by beating the Miami Dolphins on the final week of the season.

The most disappointing teams included the Cincinnati Bengals, who finished with a 3–13 record after being considered play-off contenders, and the San Francisco 49ers, who missed out on the play-offs two years after being league champions.

Individual Performances. Emmitt Smith of Dallas won the league rushing title on the final week of the season. He gained 1,563 yards, beating out Barry Sanders of Detroit (1,548) and Thurman Thomas (1,407). Houston's Haywood Jeffires caught 100 passes and Dallas' Michael Irvin gained 1,523 passing yards, both league bests. The top quarterback, statistically, was Warren Moon, who threw for 4,690 yards. Buffalo's Kelly had 33 touchdown passes, followed by Washington's Mark Rypien (28). Washington's Chip Lohmiller was the leading scorer (149 points) and Rick Robey of Miami the leading punter (45.7-yard average). The best defensive players were Philadelphia end Reggie White, Philadelphia tackle Jerome Brown, New Orleans linebacker Pat Swilling, and Denver safety Steve Atwater.

Play-offs. In the opening round of the play-offs, Dallas upset the Bears in Chicago, 17–13, and Atlanta upended the Saints in New Orleans, 27–20. In the AFC, Houston held off the Jets, 17–10, and Kansas City outlasted the Los Angeles Raiders, 10–6. In the second round, Detroit quarterback Erik Kramer threw for 372 yards and the Lions beat Dallas, 38-6. In heavy rain, the Redskins used a superior ground game to down Atlanta, 24–7. In the AFC, John Elway led Denver on an 87-yard drive at the end of the game that set up a field goal for a 26–24 triumph over Houston. Buffalo had a much easier time defeating outmanned Kansas City, 37–14.

In the AFC title game, Buffalo used an interception return for a touchdown by linebacker Carlton Bailey and a 44-yard field goal by Scott Norwood to beat Denver, 10–7. It was only the second time all season that the high-powered Buffalo offense did not score a touchdown. Denver's David Treadwell missed three first-half field-goal attempts. Bronco quarterback John Elway was forced to leave the game with an injury.

In the NFC title game, Rypien threw for two touchdowns and Washington converted three Detroit turnovers into 17 points as the Redskins trounced the Lions, 41–10. Washington limited Sanders, the Lions' star runner, to 44 rushing yards while its own running backs combined for 117 yards. The Redskins led 17–10 at halftime before putting away the game with 24 points in the last 30 minutes.

Honors and Expansion. In July five new members were admitted to the Pro Football Hall of Fame. They were former running back Earl Campbell, who played for the Houston Oilers and New Orleans Saints; Jan Stenerud, a former placekicker for the Kansas City Chiefs, Green Bay Packers, and Minnesota Vikings; former New England Patriots' offensive guard John Hannah; Stan Jones, a former lineman for the Chicago Bears and Washington Redskins; and Tex Schramm, the former general manager and president of the Dallas Cowboys.

In May the NFL owners voted to add two new teams for the 1994 season. It would be the league's first expansion since 1976.

The new World League of American Football—including six U.S., one Canadian, and three European teams owned by 26 NFL owners and consisting mainly of players who could not make the NFL and former European soccer players—completed its first season in the spring of 1991. The league was much more successful in Europe than in the United States, with the crowds at the European games much larger than at those in the United States. In addition, the league's U.S. television ratings were below expectations. However, the league's first World Bowl drew 61,108 fans to London's Wembley Stadium on June 9 as the London Monarchs defeated the Barcelona Dragons, 21–0.

The College Season

Florida State was the preseason favorite to capture the 1991 national football championship. The Seminoles—who never had been national titleholders—held on to the Number 1 position until late November but then lost to in-state rival Miami, 17-16, in Tallahassee, and the race for first in the country became wide open. It never did get settled satisfactorily. In the final polls following the annual bowl games, Miami and Washington wound up sharing the top spot. In the Associated Press (AP) ratings, where voting is done by broadcasters and writers, Miami was picked for first place. In the *USA Today*/CNN poll, where voting is done by a panel of coaches, Washington finished first. Both teams had compiled 12-0 records. This was the second year in a row that two teams shared the national title. The previous season, Georgia Tech and Colorado were cochampions.

Miami entered the Orange Bowl against Nebraska ranked Number 1 in the AP poll and tied with Washington in the coaches' poll. The Hurricanes overwhelmed Nebraska, 22-0, handing the Cornhuskers their first shutout since 1973

Michigan's junior wide receiver and kick returner Desmond Howard (21), who scored 23 touchdowns during the season, was an overwhelming choice for the 1991 Heisman Trophy.

© Jim Commentucci/Allsport

—a time period covering 220 games. Nebraska led the nation in rushing, averaging 353 yards, but gained only 82 yards on the ground against Miami. The Hurricane defense limited Nebraska to 171 total yards. Miami had opportunities to score another two or three touchdowns, but 143 penalty yards hurt their chances considerably. The most valuable player award for the game was won by Miami freshman running back Larry Jones, who gained 144 yards.

Washington, which was second in the AP poll entering the Rose Bowl against Michigan, never had finished a season undefeated. The Huskies were dominant against then fourth-ranked Michigan, winning easily, 34-14. Quarterback Billy Joe Hobert completed 18 of 34 passes for 192 yards and two touchdowns, and shared the game's most valuable player honors with teammate Steve Emtman, a defensive tackle. Michigan's Desmond Howard, the Heisman Trophy winner, was held to just one catch, for 35 yards and no touchdowns. The Wolverines, whose strength was their running game, gained only 72 yards on the ground against Washington, which had one of the best defenses in the nation. The victory wound up securing Washington's first-ever national championship. They had finished the season ranked Number 2 in 1984.

Florida, which had been ranked Number 3, hoped that upsets in the Rose and Orange bowls would give it a chance to finish atop the polls. Instead, the Gators would up losing in the Sugar Bowl to Notre Dame, 39-28, and dropped to Number 7 in the AP rankings. Notre Dame had been a national championship contender until a late-season slump, but used an effective ground game (279 yards) to overcome 370 passing yards by Florida quarterback Shane Matthews.

Florida State (FSU) had lost back-to-back games to Miami and Florida entering the Cotton Bowl. But the Seminoles stopped their losing streak by outlasting Texas A&M, 10-2, despite a combined 13 turnovers by both teams. The only touchdown of the game was scored by quarterback Casey Weldon on a four-yard run in the first half. FSU finished fourth in the polls.

Howard, Michigan's talented receiver, easily won the Heisman Trophy voting as the best player in college football, leading by one of the widest margins in Heisman history. Howard led the nation with 23 touchdowns and was considered the country's most dangerous kick returner. Weldon finished second and Brigham Young quarterback Ty Detmer was third. Detmer was the 1990 Heisman winner, but lost any chance of repeating when Brigham Young lost its opening three games. He finished his career as the NCAA's all-time passing leader and set more than 50 individual and career major-college records.

COLLEGE FOOTBALL

Conference Champions	Atlantic Coast—Clemson Big Eight—(tie) Colorado, Nebraska Big Ten—Michigan Big West—(tie) San Jose State, Fresno State Ivy League—Dartmouth Mid-American—Bowling Green Pacific Ten—Washington Southeastern—Florida Southwest—Texas A&M Western Athletic—Brigham Young
NCAA Champions	Division I-AA—Youngstown State Division II—Pittsburgh State (KS) Division III—Ithaca
NAIA Champions	Division I—Central Arkansas Division II—Georgetown University (KY)
Individual Honors	Heisman Trophy—Desmond Howard, Michigan Lombardi Award—Steve Emtman, Washington Outland Trophy—Emtman

Major Bowl Games

Aloha Bowl (Honolulu, HI, Dec. 25)—Georgia Tech 18, Stanford 17
Blockbuster Bowl (Miami, FL, Dec. 28)—Alabama 30, Colorado 25
California Bowl (Fresno, CA, Dec. 14)—Bowling Green 28, Fresno State 21
Citrus Bowl (Orlando, FL, Jan. 1)—California 37, Clemson 13
Copper Bowl (Tucson, AZ, Dec. 31)—Indiana 24, Baylor 0
Cotton Bowl (Dallas, Jan. 1)—Florida State 10, Texas A&M 2
Fiesta Bowl (Tempe, AZ, Jan. 1)—Penn State 42, Tennessee 17
Freedom Bowl (Anaheim, CA, Dec. 30)—Tulsa 28, San Diego State 17
Gator Bowl (Jacksonville, FL, Dec. 29)—Oklahoma 48, Virginia 14
Hall of Fame Bowl (Tampa, FL, Jan. 1)—Syracuse 24, Ohio State 17
John Hancock Bowl (El Paso, TX, Dec. 31)—UCLA 6, Illinois 3
Holiday Bowl (San Diego, CA, Dec. 30)—Iowa 13, Brigham Young 13
Independence Bowl (Shreveport, LA, Dec. 29)—Georgia 24, Arkansas 15
Liberty Bowl (Memphis, TN, Dec. 29)—Air Force 38, Mississippi State 15
Orange Bowl (Miami, FL, Jan. 1)—Miami 22, Nebraska 0
Peach Bowl (Atlanta, GA, Jan. 1)—East Carolina 37, North Carolina State 34
Rose Bowl (Pasadena, CA, Jan. 1)—Washington 34, Michigan 14
Sugar Bowl (New Orleans, LA, Jan. 1)—Notre Dame 39, Florida 28

Howard also was named winner of the Maxwell Award, another major player-of-the-year selection, and Detmer won the Davey O'Brien Award as the nation's best quarterback for the second straight season. Weldon received the Johnny Unitas Golden Arm Award as the nation's top senior quarterback. Washington's Emtman won the Outland Trophy as the nation's best interior lineman, edging Baylor's Santana Dotson and Michigan's Greg Skrepenak, as well as the Lombardi Award for top lineman or linebacker. Rice's Trevor Cobb, the nation's third-leading rusher, was named Doak Walker Award winner as the country's top running back. Florida State's Terrell Buckley won the Jim Thorpe Award as the nation's best defensive back.

Other standout players included running backs Vaughn Dunbar of Indiana and Marshall Faulk of San Diego State; receiver Mario Bailey of Washington; kicker Carlos Huerta of Miami; linebacker Marvin Jones of Florida State; and Houston quarterback David Klingler, who had been the preseason choice to win the Heisman but whose chances were hurt when his team played poorly most of the season.

PAUL ATTNER
"The Sporting News"

Golf

The big event in golf in 1991 was the biennial Ryder Cup match, as the United States defeated Europe, 14½-13½. The Cup has become golf's most intense competition. The winners were led by Fred Couples and Lanny Wadkins, each of whom had 3–1–1 records in four-ball, foursomes, and singles play. Chip Beck defeated Ian Woosnam and Paul Azinger beat José-María Olazábal in critical singles matches on the last day. But it came down to a 6-ft (1.83-m) putt by Europe's Bernhard Langer on the final hole of the final match against American Hale Irwin. He missed, the two players finished in a tie, and the Cup belonged to the United States for the first time since 1983.

In major men's competition, Wales' Ian Woosnam won the Masters and the individual World Cup title and was named world player of the year by *Golf Digest*. Payne Stewart won the U.S. Open in a play-off over Scott Simpson and Ian Baker-Finch won the British Open. John Daly was a surprise winner of the PGA

GOLF

1991 PGA Tour

Infiniti Tournament of Champions: Tom Kite (272)
Northern Telecom Tucson Open: Phil Mickelson (272)
United Airlines Hawaiian Open: Lanny Wadkins (270)
Phoenix Open: Nolan Henke (268)
AT&T Pebble Beach National Pro-Am: Paul Azinger (274)
Bob Hope Chrysler Classic: Corey Pavin (331)
Shearson Lehman Brothers Open: Jay Don Blake (268)
Nissan Los Angeles Open: Ted Schulz (272)
Doral Ryder Open: Rocco Mediate (276)
Honda Classic: Steve Pate (279)
Nestle Invitational: Andrew Magee (203)
USF&G Classic: Ian Woosnam (275)
The Players Championship: Steve Elkington (276)
Masters: Ian Woosnam (277)
Deposit Guaranty Golf Classic: Larry Silveira (266)
MCI Heritage Classic: Davis Love III (271)
K Mart Greater Greensboro Open: Mark Brooks (275)
GTE Byron Nelson Classic: Nick Price (270)
BellSouth Atlanta Classic: Corey Pavin (272)
Memorial Tournament: Kenny Perry (273)
Southwestern Bell Colonial: Tom Purtzer (267)
Kemper Open: Billy Andrade (263)
Buick Classic: Billy Andrade (273)
U.S. Open: Payne Stewart (282)
Anheuser-Busch Classic: Mike Hulbert (266)
Federal Express St. Jude Classic: Fred Couples (269)
Centel Western Open: Russ Cochran (275)
New England Classic: Bruce Fleisher (268)
Chattanooga Classic: Dillard Pruitt (260)
Canon Greater Hartford Open: Billy Ray Brown (271)
Buick Open: Brad Faxon (271)
PGA Championship: John Daly (276)
The International: José-María Olazábal (+10)
NEC World Series of Golf: Tom Purtzer (279)
Greater Milwaukee Open: Mark Brooks (270)
Canadian Open: Nick Price (273)
Hardee's Golf Classic: D. A. Weibring (267)
B.C. Open: Fred Couples (269)
Ryder Cup: United States 14 1/2, Europe 13 1/2
Buick Southern Open: David Peoples (276)
H.E.B. Texas Open: Blaine McCallister (269)
Las Vegas Invitational: Andrew Magee (329)
Walt Disney World/Oldsmobile Classic: Mark O'Meara (267)
Independent Insurance Agent Open: Fulton Allem (273)
Tour Championship: Craig Stadler (279)
Asahi Glass Four Tours WCOG: PGA European Tour
Kapalua International: Mike Hulbert (276)
Shark Shootout: Tom Purtzer-Lanny Wadkins (189):
Skins Game: Payne Stewart ($260,000)
J.C. Penney Mixed Team Classic: Billy Andrade-Kris Tschetter (266)

LPGA Tour

The Jamaica Classic: Jane Geddes (207)
Oldsmobile LPGA Classic: Meg Mallon (276)
The Phar-Mor at Inverrary: Beth Daniel (209)
Orix Hawaiian Ladies Open: Patty Sheehan (207)
Women's Kemper Open: Deb Richard (275)
Inamori Classic: Laura Davies (277)
Desert Inn LPGA International: Penny Hammel (211)
Standard Register Ping: Danielle Ammaccapane (283)
Nabisco Dinah Shore: Amy Alcott (273)
Ping/Welch's Championship: Chris Johnson (273)
Sara Lee Classic: Nancy Lopez (206)
Crestar-Farm Fresh Classic: Hollis Stacy (282)
Centel Classic: Pat Bradley (278)
LPGA Corning Classic: Betsy King (273)
Rochester International: Rosie Jones (276)
Atlantic City Classic: Jane Geddes (208)
Lady Keystone Open: Colleen Walker (207)
McDonald's Championship: Beth Daniel (273)
Mazda LPGA Championship: Meg Mallon (274)
Jamie Farr Toledo Classic: Alice Miller (205)
U.S. Women's Open: Meg Mallon (283)
JAL Big Apple Classic: Betsy King (279)
LPGA Bay State Classic: Juli Inkster (275)
The Phar-Mor in Youngstown: Deb Richard (207)
Stratton Mountain LPGA Classic: Melissa McNamara (278)
Northgate Computer Classic: Cindy Rarick (211)
Chicago Sun-Times Shoot-Out: Martha Nause (275)
Rail Charity Golf Classic: Pat Bradley (197)
Ping-Cellular One LPGA Golf Championship: Michelle Estill (208)
Du Maurier Ltd. Classic: Nancy Scranton (279)
Safeco Classic: Pat Bradley (280)
MBS LPGA Classic: Pat Bradley (277)
Daikyo World Championship: Meg Mallon (216)
Nichirei International: United States 21.5, Japan 10.5
Mazda Japan Classic: Liselotte Neumann (211)
JBP Cup LPGA Match Play Championship: Deb Richard

Senior PGA Tour

Infiniti Tournament of Champions: Bruce Crampton (279)
Senior Skins Game: Jack Nicklaus ($310,000)
Royal Caribbean Classic: Gary Player (200)
GTE Suncoast Classic: Bob Charles (210)
Aetna Challenge: Lee Trevino (205)
Chrysler Cup: United States 58.5, International 41.5
GTE West Classic: Chi Chi Rodriguez (132)
Vantage at the Dominion: Lee Trevino (137)
The Vintage Arco Invitational: Chi Chi Rodriguez (206)
Fuji Electric Grand Slam: Miller Barber (202)
The Tradition at Desert Mountain: Jack Nicklaus (277)
PGA Seniors Championship: Jack Nicklaus (271)
Doug Sanders Kingwood Celebrity Classic: Mike Hill (203)
Las Vegas Senior Classic: Chi Chi Rodriguez (204)
Murata Reunion Pro-Am: Chi Chi Rodriguez (208)
Liberty Mutual Legends of Golf: Lee Trevino-Mike Hill (252)
Bell Atlantic Classic: Jim Ferree (208)
NYNEX Commemorative: Charles Coody (193)
Mazda Senior Players Championship: Jim Albus (279)
MONY Syracuse Senior Classic: Rocky Thompson (199)
PaineWebber Invitational: Orville Moody (207)
Southwestern Bell Classic: Jim Colbert (201)
Kroger Senior Classic: Al Geiberger (203)
Newport Cup: Larry Ziegler (199)
Ameritech Senior Open: Mike Hill (200)
U.S. Senior Open: Jack Nicklaus (282)
Northville Long Island Classic: George Archer (204)
Showdown Classic: Dale Douglass (209)
GTE Northwest Classic: Mike Hill (198)
Sunwest Bank/Charley Pride Senior Classic: Lee Trevino (200)
GTE North Classic: George Archer (199)
First of America Classic: Harold Henning (202)
Digital Seniors Classic: Rocky Thompson (205)
Nationwide Championship: Mike Hill (212)
Bank One Classic: DeWitt Weaver (207)
Vantage Championship: Jim Colbert (205)
Raley's Senior Golf Rush: George Archer (206)
Transamerica Senior Golf Championship: Charles Coody (204)
Security Pacific Senior Classic: John Brodie (200)
Du Pont Cup: United States 24, Japan 8
First Development Kaanapali Classic: Jim Colbert (265)
New York Life Champions: Mike Hill (202)

Other Tournaments

British Open: Ian Baker-Finch (272)
World Match Play: Severiano Ballesteros
World Cup: Individual: Ian Woosnam, Wales (273); Team: Sweden (563)
Walker Cup: United States 14, Great Britain/Ireland 10
U.S. Men's Amateur: Mitch Voges
U.S. Women's Amateur: Amy Fruhwirth
U.S. Men's Public Links: David Berganio
U.S. Women's Public Links: Tracy Hanson
U.S. Mid-Amateur: Jim Stuart
U.S. Women's Mid-Amateur: Sarah Ingram
U.S. Senior Men's Amateur: Bill Bosshard
U.S. Senior Women's Amateur: Phyllis Preuss
U.S. Junior Boys: Eldrick Woods
U.S. Junior Girls: Emilee Klein
NCAA Men: Individual: Warren Schutte; Team: Oklahoma State
NCAA Women: Individual: Annika Sorenstam; Team: UCLA

Championship and was named rookie of the year by *Golf Digest*.

Corey Pavin, one of eight players to win two tournaments on the tour, won the Arnold Palmer Award as leading money winner with $979,430 and was named the PGA player of the year. Couples, also a two-time winner, won the Vardon Trophy with a 69.59 scoring average and was named player of the year by the Golf Writers Association of America.

Senior Tour. On the Senior PGA tour, Jack Nicklaus played in only five events but won three, including two majors—the PGA Seniors Championship and the U.S. Senior Open. Jim Albus, a club professional from Long Island, NY, won the other senior major, the Mazda Senior Players Championship. Mike Hill, winner of five tournaments, took the money title with $1,065,657 and was the consensus player of the year. Lee Trevino, who won three tournaments, earned his second straight Byron Nelson Trophy for scoring average at 69.50.

LPGA Tour. Pat Bradley won her way into the LPGA Hall of Fame with four victories, the last of which got her to the 30-win mark and made her eligible. She led the LPGA with $763,118, won the Vare Trophy with a scoring average of 70.66, and was named the LPGA player of the year. With four wins, Meg Mallon was chosen player of the year by the golf writers. Rookie of the year honors went to Brandie Burton, who won the LPGA award, and Michelle Estill, who was *Golf Digest*'s pick.

LARRY DENNIS, *Creative Communications*

Horse Racing

In 1991 the Breeders' Cup returned to Churchill Downs in Louisville, KY, where Black Tie Affair led wire-to-wire in the $3 million Classic while holding off Twilight Agenda.

The Irish-bred 5-year-old winner, ridden by Jerry Bailey in the Classic on November 2, covered the 1.25 mi (2 km) in 2:02⅖ for owner Jeffrey Sullivan and trainer Ernie Poulos. Bailey had substituted for Black Tie Affair's regular jockey, Pat Day, when Day opted to ride 1990 Preakness Stakes champion Summer Squall in the Classic. Summer Squall finished ninth in the field of 11. Defending champion Unbridled was third.

Long shot Miss Alleged paid backers $86.20 to win in the $2 million Breeders' Cup Turf at 1.5 mi (2.4 km). Miss Alleged was not admitted to the field until two other entrants were withdrawn, but she beat Itsallgreektome by half a length with the slow time of 2:30⅘.

Arazi showed great speed in capturing the $1 million Breeders' Cup Juvenile. Allen Paulson's colt appeared pinned along the rail in 13th place among the 14 2-year-olds in the field as he headed into the far turn, but then showed such speed that he was first entering the stretch and won by 4¾ lengths. The time for the 1.06-mi (1.7-km) race was 1:44⅗.

Strike the Gold captured the 117th Kentucky Derby on May 4 by 1¾ lengths over Best Pal under jockey Chris Antley. Strike the Gold was the ninth Derby winner bred at Calumet Farm in Lexington, KY, but was the first of the group not to have Calumet ownership. B. Giles Brophy, William Condren, and Joseph Cornacchia posted their first Kentucky Derby victory as owners.

Hansel won the second leg of the Triple Crown for 3-year-olds with the fifth-fastest time in Preakness history—1:54 for 1.19 mi (1.9 km). Hansel, who was tenth as the Kentucky Derby favorite, won by seven lengths over Corporate Report. Hansel then completed the Triple Crown by beating Strike the Gold by a head in the Belmont Stakes.

STAN SUTTON

HORSE RACING

Major U.S. Thoroughbred Races

Arlington Million: Tight Spot, $1 million (total purse)
Belmont Stakes: Hansel, $695,800
Blue Grass Stakes: Strike the Gold, $400,800
Breeders' Cup Classic: Black Tie Affair, $3 million
Breeders' Cup Turf: Miss Alleged, $2 million
Breeders' Cup Juvenile: Arazi, $1 million
Breeders' Cup Juvenile Fillies: Pleasant Stage, $1 million
Breeders' Cup Mile: Opening Verse, $1 million
Breeders' Cup Distaff: Dance Smartly, $1 million
Breeders' Cup Sprint: Sheikh Albadou, $1 million
Coaching Club American Oaks: Lite Light, $250,000
Florida Derby: Fly So Free, $500,000
Haskell Invitational: Lost Mountain, $500,000
Hollywood Gold Cup: Marquetry, $1 million
Iselin Handicap: Black Tie Affair, $500,000
Jim Beam Stakes: Hansel, $500,000
Jockey Club Gold Cup: Festin, $850,000
Kentucky Derby: Strike the Gold, $905,800
Kentucky Oaks: Lite Light, $318,900
Metropolitan Handicap: In Excess, $500,000
Mother Goose Stakes: Meadow Star, $224,000
Oak Leaf Stakes: Pleasant Stage, $260,900
Pacific Classic: Best Pal, $1 million
Pimlico Special: Farma Way, $750,000
Preakness Stakes: Hansel, $665,800
Santa Anita Derby: Dinard, $500,000
Santa Anita Handicap: Farma Way, $1 million
Strub Stakes: Defensive Play, $500,000
Suburban Handicap: In Excess, $500,000
Travers Stakes: Corporate Report, $1 million
Whitney Handicap: In Excess, $250,000
Wood Memorial: Cahill Road, $500,000
Woodward Stakes: In Excess, $500,000

Major North American Harness Races

Breeders Crown Horse and Gelding Trot: Billyjojimbob, $394,000
Breeders Crown Mare Pace: Delinquent Account, $300,000
Breeders Crown Mare Trot: Me Maggie, $300,000
Breeders Crown Horse and Gelding Pace: Camluck, $347,250
Cane Pace: Silky Stallone, $523,190
Hambletonian: Giant Victory, $1 million
Kentucky Futurity: Whiteland Janice, $178,140
Kentucky Pacing Derby: Caprock, $282,628
Little Brown Jug: Precious Bunny, $575,150
Meadowlands Pace: Precious Bunny, $1 million
Woodrow Wilson Pace: Sportsmaster, $889,000
World Trotting Derby: Somatic, $700,000
Yonkers Trot: Crowns Invitation, $370,393

Ice Hockey

The Pittsburgh Penguins won the first Stanley Cup in their 24-year history, ending the Cinderella ride of the Minnesota North Stars in May 1991. The Penguins, who finished seventh in the regular season with 88 points, beat the North Stars, who were 16th, four games to two in the finals. The surprising North Stars, who had the second-fewest points (68) of the 16 teams to make the play-offs, had shocked the Number 1 Chicago Black Hawks (106 points), the Number 2 St. Louis Blues (105), and the defending National Hockey League (NHL) champion Edmonton Oilers in the play-offs to reach the finals. Pittsburgh rallied to win the opening-round series four games to three over New Jersey but never faltered after that, beating Washington, Boston, then the North Stars behind captain Mario Lemieux, who was hampered by a sore back but led everybody with 44 play-off points.

Regular Season. The Black Hawks beat the Detroit Red Wings, 5–1, on the final night of the season to edge the Blues for the overall points championship. The Los Angeles Kings were third with 102 and the Calgary Flames and Boston Bruins tied for fourth with 100. The Oilers were 11th with just 80 points, their worst finish since the 1980–81 season. Pittsburgh overcame the New York Rangers in the final week to take the Patrick Division. Boston won the Adams Division for the second consecutive year. Chicago's rookie goaltender Ed Belfour carried the Hawks to the best defensive record (211 goals) and the Number 1 position in the Norris Division. Los Angeles edged Calgary to win the Smythe. Calgary led the league in offense, though, with 344 goals.

Los Angeles center Wayne Gretzky won his ninth Ross (scoring) Trophy with 163 points, 32 more than St. Louis winger Brett Hull. Hull, who led the league with 72 goals in the 1989–90 season, scored 86 this time. Only Gretzky (92 and 87) ever has scored more in a single season. Hull also joined Gretzky and Lemieux as the only players in NHL history to score 50 goals in fewer than 50 games; he accomplished the feat in 49. He also joined his dad Bobby (1965–66) as the first father and son to capture the Hart (MVP) Trophy. St. Louis center Adam Oates was third with 115 points, two more than Pittsburgh winger Mark Recchi. Lemieux, who missed all but one of the final 22 games of the 1989–90 season with a disc problem in his back, did not return until late January. He had 45 points in 26 games.

In all, ten players had at least 100 points. Hull, who scored at least one goal against the other 20 teams, became the third player to surpass 80 goals in a season. Only Gretzky and Lemieux (85) ever have done it. Only four players—Hull, Boston's Cam Neely, Detroit's Steve Yzerman, and Calgary's Theoren Fleury—had 50 or more goals. Gretzky moved past Phil Esposito into third place on the all-time goals list with 718.

The Play-offs. Edmonton's reign as NHL champion ended in the fifth game of the Campbell Conference finals when Minnesota's Bobby Smith scored with 16 minutes left for a 3–2 victory. The Oilers had overcome Calgary in overtime in the seventh game of the first

ICE HOCKEY

National Hockey League
(Final Standings, 1990–91)

Wales Conference

Patrick Division	W	L	T	Pts.	Goals For	Goals Against
*Pittsburgh	41	33	6	88	342	305
*N.Y. Rangers	36	31	13	85	297	265
*Washington	37	36	7	81	258	258
*New Jersey	32	33	15	79	272	264
Philadelphia	33	37	10	76	252	267
N.Y. Islanders	25	45	10	60	223	290
Adams Division						
*Boston	44	24	12	100	299	264
*Montreal	39	30	11	89	273	249
*Buffalo	31	30	19	81	292	278
*Hartford	31	38	11	73	238	276
Quebec	16	50	14	46	236	354

Campbell Conference

Norris Division	W	L	T	Pts.	Goals For	Goals Against
*Chicago	49	23	8	106	284	211
*St. Louis	47	22	11	105	310	250
*Detroit	34	38	8	76	273	298
*Minnesota	27	39	14	68	256	266
Toronto	23	46	11	57	241	318
Smythe Division						
*Los Angeles	46	24	10	102	340	254
*Calgary	46	26	8	100	344	263
*Edmonton	37	37	6	80	272	272
*Vancouver	28	43	9	65	243	315
Winnipeg	26	43	11	63	260	288

*In play-offs

Stanley Cup Play-Offs
Wales Conference

Round	Winner		Loser	
First Round	Boston	4 games	Hartford	2
	Montreal	4 games	Buffalo	2
	Pittsburgh	4 games	New Jersey	3
	Washington	4 games	N.Y. Rangers	2
Second Round	Boston	4 games	Montreal	3
	Pittsburgh	4 games	Washington	1
Finals	Pittsburgh	4 games	Boston	2

Campbell Conference

Round	Winner		Loser	
First Round	Edmonton	4 games	Calgary	3
	Los Angeles	4 games	Vancouver	2
	Minnesota	4 games	Chicago	2
	St. Louis	4 games	Detroit	3
Second Round	Edmonton	4 games	Los Angeles	2
	Minnesota	4 games	St. Louis	2
Finals	Minnesota	4 games	Edmonton	1

Stanley Cup Finals

Winner		Loser	
Pittsburgh	4 games	Minnesota	2

Individual Honors

Hart Trophy (most valuable player): Brett Hull, St. Louis
Ross Trophy (leading scorer): Wayne Gretzky, Los Angeles
Vezina Trophy (top goaltender): Ed Belfour, Chicago
Norris Trophy (best defenseman): Ray Bourque, Boston
Selke Trophy (best defensive forward): Dirk Graham, Chicago
Calder Trophy (rookie of the year): Ed Belfour
Lady Byng Trophy (sportsmanship): Wayne Gretzky
Conn Smythe Trophy (most valuable in play-offs): Mario Lemieux, Pittsburgh
Adams Trophy (coach of the year): Brian Sutter, St. Louis
King Clancy Trophy (humanitarian service): Dave Taylor, Los Angeles

NCAA: Northern Michigan

AP/Wide World

Mario Lemieux led the Pittsburgh Penguins to their first Stanley Cup. He was named the play-offs' MVP.

round on a goal by Esa Tikkanen, then sent Los Angeles to the sidelines on Craig MacTavish's goal in overtime in the sixth game of the Smythe Division final. Minnesota ended Edmonton's hopes for a sixth Stanley Cup in eight years with a four-games-to-one win in the third round, however. The North Stars, who finished 38 points behind Chicago, beat the Hawks in six games and did the same against St. Louis to take the Norris.

In the Adams Division, Boston, who lost the 1988 and 1990 Stanley Cup finals to Edmonton, got past Hartford and Montreal in six and seven games, respectively. Pittsburgh got a huge scare from New Jersey, then subdued Washington in five games to take the Patrick. In the Wales Conference final, Pittsburgh spotted Boston a 2–1 series lead, then won three straight over the injury-plagued Bruins. It set up the first all-U.S. final since 1981 when the New York Islanders defeated the North Stars. There had been a Canadian winner since 1984.

Stanley Cup Finals. Neal Broten, who played on the 1980 U.S. Olympic gold-medal team, scored two goals in the first game of the finals to give Minnesota a 5–4 win in Pittsburgh. It was the fourth straight time the North Stars had won the opening game of a play-off series, all in the other team's rink. The Penguins won game two, 4–1, as Lemieux broke open a 2–1 game late in the second period with a brilliant breakaway goal.

In Minnesota the North Stars took advantage of Lemieux removing himself from the lineup with back spasms and won, 3–1. Dave Gagner and Bobby Smith scored 33 seconds apart in the second period as Minnesota won its eight consecutive play-off home game. The Penguins tied it, 2–2, when they scored three times in the first three minutes for a 5–3 victory in game four. Lemieux was back to score one of the quick goals and add an assist on an empty-net goal with 15 seconds to play.

In game five, Pittsburgh jumped to a 4–0 lead before the game was 14 minutes gone and held on for a 6–4 victory. Lemieux led the way with a goal and two assists. In the final, Lemieux scored once and added three assists in an 8–0 rout—the most lopsided finals game since 1917 when the Seattle Metropolitans beat the Montreal Canadiens, 9–1, in the deciding game. Lemieux's four points gave him 44.

JIM MATHESON, *"Edmonton Journal"*

Ice Skating

For the first time ever, three women from the same country captured the gold, silver, and bronze medals in the women's singles competition at the world figure-skating championships. Three Americans—Kristi Yamaguchi, 19, of Freemont, CA, Tonya Harding, 20, of Portland, OR, and Nancy Kerrigan, 21, of Stoneham, MA—finished first, second, and third, respectively, in Munich, Germany, in March 1991. Canada's Kurt Browning won the men's world title for a third consecutive time. A free-skating program filled with triple jumps contributed to his victory.

Completing a successful triple axel, the first by a U.S. woman in competition, Tonya Harding had taken the women's title at the U.S. championships in Minneapolis in February. Todd Eldredge, 19, of Chatham, MA, edged out Christopher Bowman of Los Angeles to retain the U.S. men's singles crown.

Speed Skating. Norway's Johann Olav Koss and Gunda Kleeman won the overall men's and women's crowns at the world speed-skating championships in Heerenveen, the Netherlands, in February. Koss set world records in the 5,000- and 10,000-meter events.

ICE SKATING

World Figure-Skating Championships

Men: Kurt Browning, Canada
Women: Kristi Yamaguchi, United States
Pairs: Natalia ("Natasha") Mishkuteniok and Artur Dmitriev, USSR
Dance: Isabelle and Paul Duchesnay, France

U.S. Figure-Skating Championships

Men: Todd Eldredge
Women: Tonya Harding
Pairs: Natasha Kuchiki and Todd Sand
Dance: Elizabeth Punsalan and Jerod Swallow

World All-Around Speed-Skating Championships

Men's Overall: Johann Olav Koss, Norway
Men's 500 meters: Peter Adeberg, Germany
Men's 1,500 meters: Johann Olav Koss
Men's 5,000 meters: Johann Olav Koss
Men's 10,000 meters: Johann Olav Koss
Women's Overall: Gunda Kleeman, Germany
Women's 500 meters: Ye Qiaobo, China
Women's 1,500 meters: Gunda Kleeman
Women's 3,000 meters: Gunda Kleeman
Women's 5,000 meters: Gunda Kleeman

The XI Pan American Games

The XI Pan American games had as many political as athletic overtones when Havana, Cuba, served as host for the Aug. 2–18, 1991, contests between nations of the Western Hemisphere. Cuban fans reveled in the successes of their athletes, even to the point of beating drums and ringing cowbells as U.S. athletes performed. But out of the arena they warmed to the some 2,000 U.S. athletes and tourists who were given a rare opportunity to travel in Cuba, largely a closed nation since the 1959 revolution. The games attracted about 14,000 visitors.

The Cubans had accepted the host's role in 1986 before the dissolution of communism in Eastern Europe left them without some of their most reliable trading partners and led to strict rationing of such staples as bread and shoes within their nation. Nevertheless, Cuba built 21 new facilities and renovated 46 others for the games and did not get a proposed $6.5 million in rights fees from ABC Sports, which was prohibited by the U.S. government from paying.

Some of the new facilities, including the track-and-field stadium, barely were completed in time, and some of the works represented progress for a deprived nation. The Pan American Village, which housed 4,000 competitors from 39 nations, later was converted to provide housing for some of the thousands of Cubans who voluntarily assisted in its construction.

The Competition. With Cuba's President Fidel Castro frequently in attendance, the Cubans astounded the United States by winning 140 gold medals to 130 for the U.S. athletes. The United States had not finished second in the gold-medal count since the inaugural games in 1951. Canada's 22 and Brazil's 21 were next best as 13 nations and Puerto Rico collected golds. Still, the U.S. depth gave them a 352-265 edge over the Cubans in total medals as the United States added 125 silvers and 97 bronzes to Cuba's 62 and 63, respectively. Canada was third with 127 top-three finishes.

AP/Wide World

President Castro, right, *was an ardent fan as Cuba hosted the 1991 Pan Am Games. Before a crowd of 60,000, Cuba defeated the United States in baseball,* below, *and went on to beat Puerto Rico for the gold medal in the sport.*

© Rick Stewart/Allsport

XI JUEGOS DEPORTIVOS PANAMERICANOS

Some 60,000 Cuban fans especially savored their 3–2 victory over the United States in baseball, a national pastime in both nations, and cheered their dominant boxers to 11 gold medals. It was Cuba's sixth straight Pan Am baseball championship. Another loss to Puerto Rico led to the United States winning only a bronze medal in baseball.

Cuba's record-setting 11 gold medals in boxing included three victories over Americans as the U.S. team endured its worst showing ever in the Pan Am Games. Only Steve Johnston, who won a decision over Mexico's Edgar Ruiz Burges for the 139-lb (63-kg) championship, interrupted the Cuban dominance. The Cuban boxers, who had won ten gold medals in the 1987 games, posted four first-round knockouts.

A major disappointment for the United States was its failure to win another international men's basketball championship. Puerto Rico won the gold medal by beating Mexico, 77-65, after first defeating the United States, 73-68. The United States, which was upset by Brazil at the 1987 games and then lost to the Soviets in the 1988 Olympics, beat Cuba, 93-74, for the bronze. The U.S. women's basketball team lost to Cuba, 86-81, in the semifinals, reversing a 20-point U.S. victory two days earlier.

U.S. swimmers won 24 of the 32 races and 49 of a possible 58 medals, although many of the best Americans skipped the games to concentrate on the Pan-Pacific Games later in August. The United States defeated Mexico, 2-1, for its first gold medal in soccer.

STAN SUTTON

Skiing

In March 1991, Luxembourg's Marc Girardelli, 27, accumulated 242 points to defeat Italy's Alberto Tomba for the World Cup overall trophy. Girardelli, who missed much of the 1989–90 season due to injury, thereby joined Gustavo Thoeni of Italy and Pirmin Zurbriggen of Switzerland as the only four-time World Cup overall champions. Austria's Petra Kronberger, 22, captured her second consecutive overall title in the women's World Cup.

A. J. Kitt of Rochester, NY, and Eva Twardokens of Santa Cruz, CA, each captured double crowns at the U.S. Alpine Championships in Crested Butte, CO. Kitt won the men's downhill and super-giant slalom events, while Twardokens took the women's slalom and giant slalom.

SKIING

World Cup

Men's Downhill: Franz Heinzer, Switzerland
Men's Slalom: Marc Girardelli, Luxembourg
Men's Giant Slalom: Alberto Tomba, Italy
Men's Super-Giant Slalom: Franz Heinzer
Men's Overall: Marc Girardelli
Women's Downhill: Chantal Bournissen, Switzerland
Women's Slalom: Petra Kronberger, Austria
Women's Giant Slalom: Vreni Schneider, Switzerland
Women's Super-Giant Slalom: Carol Merle, France
Women's Overall: Petra Kronberger

World Alpine Championships

Men's Downhill: Franz Heinzer
Men's Slalom: Marc Girardelli
Men's Giant Slalom: Rudolf Nierlich, Austria
Men's Super-Giant Slalom: Stefan Eberharter, Austria
Men's Combined: Stefan Eberharter
Women's Downhill: Petra Kronberger
Women's Slalom: Vreni Schneider
Women's Giant Slalom: Pernilla Wiberg, Sweden
Women's Super-Giant Slalom: Ulrike Maier, Austria
Women's Combined: Chantal Bournissen

U.S. Alpine Championships

Men's Downhill: A. J. Kitt
Men's Slalom: Joe Levins
Men's Giant Slalom: Alain Feutrier
Men's Super-Giant Slalom: A. J. Kitt
Women's Downhill: Megan Gerety
Women's Slalom: Eva Twardokens
Women's Giant Slalom: Eva Twardokens
Women's Super-Giant Slalom: Julie Parisien

NCAA: Colorado

© Bob Martin/Allsport

The performance of Switzerland's Franz Heinzer was a highlight of the 1991 World Cup season. He captured both the downhill, right, *and the super-giant slalom titles.*

Soccer

With the World Cup soccer tournament, scheduled for the United States in 1994, only three years away, the U.S. national team made remarkable progress in 1991 under the guidance of new coach Bora Milutinovic, a Yugoslavian who formerly had coached World Cup teams from Costa Rica (1990) and Mexico (1986).

World. The world's most famous soccer player, Diego Maradona, was banned in April 1991 from international competition for 15 months after he tested positive for cocaine. Maradona, from Argentina, was playing in the Italian professional league when he was banned.

The European Cup Winners Cup went to Manchester United of England, which defeated Barcelona, 2-1, in Rotterdam, the Netherlands, in May. This was a significant event for Great Britain, since its teams had been banned from European club soccer after a series of rowdy incidents involving fans. The English had not participated in the tournament since the 1985–86 season.

Red Star Belgrade defeated Olympique Marseille of France, 5-3, on penalty kicks in May to capture its first European Championship Cup. To win the game, which was played in Bari, Italy, Red Star had to rely on those penalty kicks after regulation play, plus overtime, resulted in a scoreless game. The Union of European Football Associations Cup went to Internazionale of Milan in May. The Italian team overcame AS Roma with an aggregate score of 2-1. Milan won the first game, 2-0, and AS Roma the second, 1-0. It was Milan's first European cup in 26 years.

In English soccer, Arsenal won the English Football League First Division title for the second straight year, with Liverpool taking second. Tottenham Hotspur took the English Football Association Cup, 2-1, in overtime over Nottingham Forest.

United States. Bora Milutinovic won his first significant event as coach of the U.S. national team when the Americans took the Gold Cup title in July. The tournament, staged in the United States, ended with the Americans and the team from Honduras still scoreless after both regulation and overtime. The teams then held a long shootout, eventually won by the United States, 4-3. Fernando Clavijo made what proved to the be the winning kick.

In the Major Indoor Soccer League, the San Diego Sockers won their second straight title by beating the Cleveland Crunch in the championship series, four games to two. Paul Dougherty scored two goals and had two assists in the final game, which San Diego won, 8-6.

Virginia defeated Santa Clara for the NCAA Division I title.

PAUL ATTNER

Swimming

With six new records set at the world championships at Perth, Australia, and several other marks registered during the season, swimming's record keepers were busy in 1991.

World Championships. At the world meet in January, Tamás Darnyi of Hungary, who registered new records in the 200-m and 400-m individual medleys, was named the meet's outstanding performer. In the 400, Darnyi bettered his own record by 2.39 seconds with a time of 4:12.36. He had set the previous mark in the 1988 Summer Olympics. His effort of 1:59.36 in the 200 clipped .75 seconds from the record set in 1989 by U.S. swimmer David Wharton.

Two Americans set world records at Perth. Mike Barrowman, who set the 200-m breaststroke standard in 1990, bettered his mark by .30 seconds with a time of 2:11.23. Barrowman later lowered the mark to 2:10.60 and *U.S. Swimming* named him 1991 Swimmer of the Year. Melvin Stewart swam the 200-m butterfly .55 seconds faster than the mark of 1:56.24 set by Michael Gross of West Germany in 1986.

Janet Evans, winner of three gold medals at the 1988 Olympics, was the only U.S. participant to win more than one gold at the world meet. She took the 400-m and 800-m freestyles. Matt Biondi, winner of seven medals in the 1988 Olympics, won the 100-m freestyle but lost to his archrival, Tom Hager, in the 50.

Joerg Hoffman of Germany was a standout, clipping more than four seconds off the 1983 mark set by Vladimir Salnikov of the USSR in the 1,500-m freestyle with a time of 14:50.36.

Norbert Rozsa of Hungary swam 1:01.45 in the 100-m breaststroke, beating the record holder, Great Britain's Adrian Moorhouse. In the Athens meet, Rozsa bettered the mark with 1:01.29.

Other Meets. Hungarian swimmers were especially effective in 1991. Krisztina Egerszegi, a backstroke specialist, cracked two world records at the European championships in Athens, Greece. She and Darnyi accounted for four of the new records achieved during the year. Egerszegi churned the 200-m backstroke in 2:06.62 to better the 2:08.60 achieved by Betsy Mitchell of the United States in 1986. Earlier in the same meet, Egerszegi broke the 100-m backstroke mark with 1:00.31, breaking the 1984 mark of 1:00.59 by Ina Kleber of East Germany.

A 1985 record in the 200-m backstroke by Igor Polyansky fell to Martin Zubero at the U.S. outdoor nationals at Fort Lauderdale, FL, with a time of 1:57.30.

Comeback Attempt. In April, Jager and Biondi frustrated the comeback attempt of Mark Spitz, 41, the star of the 1972 Olympics. Spitz hoped to qualify for the 1992 Olympics.

GEORGE DE GREGORIO

© Bob Martin/Allsport

© Focus on Sports

Tennis highlights of 1991 included Michael Stich (left) *defeating fellow German Boris Becker at the Wimbledon singles final and the play of Yugoslav Monica Seles, who won three of the major crowns, including the U.S. Open* (right).

Tennis

Ungainly but powerful and deadly effective, 17-year-old Yugoslav Monica Seles (*see* BIOGRAPHY) took the female tennis lead—in accomplishment and attention—during 1991. But once again the male side of the tennis game was fragmented: The four major championships were split four ways for the second successive year.

Unorthodox in strokemaking (two hands on both sides) and in mysteriously skipping Wimbledon, Seles nevertheless won the other three major Open crowns—beating Czechoslovakia's Jana Novotna at the Australian, 5-7, 6-3, 6-1; Spain's Arantxa Sánchez Vicario at the French, 6-3, 6-4; and American Martina Navratilova at the United States, 7-6, 6-1.

Although Sweden's Stefan Edberg held the men's Number 1 ranking at season's end and performed devastatingly to win the U.S. Open on his ninth try (6-2, 6-4, 6-0 over American Jim Courier), the startlers were relative newcomers—Courier and the German, Michael Stich. A determined scrapper, Courier won the French over countryman Andre Agassi, 3-6, 6-4, 2-6, 6-1, 6-4. Putting on a show of freewheeling power, Stich won Wimbledon on only a second try, dethroning Edberg in the semis, then depriving compatriot Boris Becker of a fourth title, 6-4, 7-6, 6-4.

Becker had begun the year impressively by winning his first Australian (and fifth major), 1-6, 6-4, 6-4, 6-4, over Czechoslovakia's Ivan Lendl. That gave him the Number 1 ranking for awhile, but he was unable to follow up, winning only one more tournament, Stockholm. Edberg and France's Guy Forget were high with six victories, while Pete Sampras of the United States won four, including the season-ending ATP Championship, 3-6, 7-6, 6-3, 6-4 over Courier. Lendl's three tourney wins gave him a career total of 91-18 short of the United States' Jimmy Connors' record. Unexpected acclaim was earned by 39-year-old Connors, five-time U.S. champ, who zigzagged his way through a series of unlikely victories at the U.S. Open to attain the semis for a 14th time in 21 years.

Steffi Graf, the German who lost the uppermost perch to Seles after a reign of 186 weeks, rehabilitated herself at Wimbledon to win for a third time—a 6-4, 3-6, 8-6 thriller over the Argentine, Gabriela Sabatini. Sabatini, who beat Seles for the Italian title, 6-3, 6-2, seemed headed for her best year. However, two points from triumph at Wimbledon, she could not hold serve and her quest for a U.S. crown was knocked off in the quarterfinals by the 15-year-old U.S. phenom, Jennifer Capriati. Capriati, who then narrowly lost to Seles in the semis (a 7-3 third-set tiebreaker), had led the United States to the final of the Federation Cup at Nottingham, England. However, Sánchez Vicario and Conchita Martinez gave Spain its first Cup, 2-1 over the United States.

Seles became only the second woman in pro-tennis history to attain the final of every tournament she entered. (Graf had done so in 1987 and 1989). She won ten of 16 tournaments, including the season-concluding Virginia Slims Championship in New York, 6-4, 3-6, 7-5, 6-0 over Navratilova. But Navratilova, still formidable at 35, beat Seles twice and won five tournaments to equal Chris Evert's all-time record of 157 victories. Although Navratilova lost the Slims singles crown, she teamed with Pam Shriver for an exciting win in the Virginia Slims doubles championship. Overall, Graf won seven tournaments, Sabatini five.

France took its first Davis Cup since 1932. France's Guy Forget and Henri Laconte both beat Pete Sampras in singles matches and teamed for a doubles win over the U.S. collaborators Ken Flach and Robert Seguso. Favored Germany's chances evaporated with a back injury to Becker, keeping him out of the semifinals, a 3-2 U.S. win.

BUD COLLINS, *"The Boston Globe"*

TENNIS

Davis Cup: France
Federation Cup: Spain

Leading Tournaments

Australian Open—men's singles: Boris Becker (Germany); men's doubles: Scott Davis and David Pate; women's singles: Monica Seles (Yugoslavia); women's doubles: Patty Fendick and Mary Joe Fernandez; mixed doubles: Jeremy Bates (Great Britain) and Jo Durie (Great Britain).
International Players Championships—men's singles: Jim Courier; men's doubles: Wayne Ferreira (South Africa) and Piet Norval (South Africa); women's singles: Monica Seles (Yugoslavia); women's doubles: Mary Joe Fernandez and Zina Garrison.
Italian Open—men's singles: Emilio Sanchez (Spain); men's doubles: Omar Camporese (Italy) and Goran Ivanisevic (Yugoslavia); women's singles: Gabriela Sabatini (Argentina); women's doubles: Monica Seles (Yugoslavia) and Jennifer Capriati.
French Open—men's singles: Jim Courier; men's doubles: John Fitzgerald (Australia) and Anders Jarryd (Sweden); women's singles: Monica Seles (Yugoslavia); women's doubles: Gigi Fernandez and Jana Novotna (Czechoslovakia); mixed doubles: Helena Sukova (Czechoslovakia) and Cyril Suk (Czechoslovakia).
Wimbledon—men's singles: Michael Stich (Germany); men's doubles: John Fitzgerald (Australia) and Anders Jarryd (Sweden); women's singles: Steffi Graf (Germany); women's doubles: Larisa Savchenko (USSR) and Natalia Zvereva (USSR); mixed doubles: John Fitzgerald (Australia) and Elizabeth Smylie (Australia).
Canadian Open—men's singles: Andrei Chesnokov, USSR; women's singles: Jennifer Capriati; men's doubles: Patrick Galbraith and Todd Witsken; women's doubles: Larisa Savchenko (USSR) and Natalia Zvereva (USSR).
U.S. Open—men's singles: Stefan Edberg (Sweden); men's doubles: John Fitzgerald (Australia) and Anders Jarryd (Sweden); women's singles: Monica Seles (Yugoslavia); women's doubles: Pam Shriver and Natalia Zvereva (USSR); mixed doubles: Manon Bollegraf (Netherlands) and Tom Nijssen (Netherlands); senior men's singles: Hank Pfister; senior men's doubles: Peter Fleming and Hank Pfister; senior women's doubles: Rosie Casals and Billie Jean King; senior mixed doubles: Wendy Turnbull (Australia) and Bob Hewitt (South Africa); boys' singles: Leander Paes (India); boys' doubles: Karim Alami (Morocco) and John DeJager (South Africa); girls' singles: Karina Habsudova (Czechoslovakia); girls' doubles: Kristin Godrige (Australia) and Nicole Pratt (Australia).
A.T.P. Finals—singles: Pete Sampras; doubles: Anders Jarryd (Sweden) and John Fitzgerald (Australia).
Virginia Slims Championship—singles: Monica Seles (Yugoslavia); doubles: Martina Navratilova and Pam Shriver.
Grand Slam Cup: David Wheaton
NCAA (Division I)—men's singles: Jared Palmer, Stanford; men's team: Southern California; women's singles: Sandra Birch, Stanford; women's team: Stanford.

N.B. All players are from the United States unless otherwise noted.

Track and Field

Some of the most spectacular world records in track and field were toppled in 1991.

Field Events. Mike Powell and Carl Lewis, both of the United States, put on one of the most astounding performances ever in the world championships at Tokyo in August. Powell, 27, startled the athletic world when he shattered Bob Beamon's 23-year-old world long-jump record. Many observers had believed Lewis was the only athlete capable of breaking Beamon's mark of 29′2½″ (8.90 m), set in the high altitude of Mexico City at the 1968 Olympics.

Lewis, 30, turned in six leaps all over 28′ (8.53 m) and at one point surpassed Beamon's distance at 29′2¾″ (8.91 m), but the judges ruled the distance was wind-aided.

Powell botched his first four attempts. But on his fifth try, he cracked Beamon's record by 2 inches (5.08 cm) with a jump of 29′4½″ (8.95 m). Lewis' best effort was a remarkable 29′1¼″ (8.87 m).

Sergei Bubka of the USSR became the first man to pole-vault over 20′ (6.10 m) both indoors and outdoors. He broke the barrier on March 15 at an indoor meet in San Sebastian, Spain, clearing 20′¼″ (6.102 m). During the season he soared over 20′ four times, three times indoors and once for the world outdoor mark of 20′¼″ at Malmo, Sweden, on August 5. Four days after his vault in Spain he did 20′½″ (6.11 m) at his hometown of Donetsk, and four days later at Grenoble, France, he went 20′1″ (6.12 m).

In the javelin throw, Finland's Seppo Räty improved on his world mark by more than 16″ (40.6 cm) with a throw of 318′1″ (96.96 m) in Finland in June. Inessa Kravets of the USSR set a world triple-jump record of 49′¾″ (14.95 m) among the women competitors.

Running Events. At the world championships, Lewis raced to a new world record in the 100-m dash with a time of 9.86 seconds, again claiming the title of "world's fastest human." Lewis' run led an amazing field in which U.S. athletes scored a one, two, three sweep and six of the eight runners in the event finished under ten seconds. Ten weeks earlier the 24-year-old American Leroy Burrell, who finished second at Tokyo, had lowered the world mark to 9.90 at the national championships in New York. Burrell's time behind Lewis was 9.88, good enough to have broken his previous mark.

Lewis and Burrell also led the U.S. team to a world record of 37.50 seconds in the 400-m relay. Dennis Mitchell and Andre Cason ran the other legs, improving on the 37.67 that Burrell, Mitchell, Lewis, and Mike Marsh had clocked in Zurich three weeks earlier.

Diane Dixon became the first U.S. woman to win a gold medal at the world indoor championships when she ran the 400 m in 50.64

Sergei Bubka of the USSR became the first to pole-vault over 20' (6.10 m) and set new indoor and outdoor records.

© Pressens Bild AB/Allsport

seconds for a U.S. record in Seville, Spain, in March.

Ben Johnson of Canada, who was stripped of the gold medal in the 100-m event in the 1988 Olympics for testing positive for drug use, returned to competition and scored his first victory since then, running 55 m in 6.2 seconds at the Ottawa Winternational in January. In July, Johnson and Lewis went head-to-head in France, but it proved anticlimactic as Lewis finished second and Johnson seventh in a 100-m race won by Dennis Mitchell in 10.09.

Marathons. The winners of the Boston Marathon were Ibrahim Hussein of Kenya and Wanda Panfil, a Polish runner who lives in Mexico. In the New York City Marathon the victors were Salvador Garcia of Mexico and Liz McColgan of Scotland, who was competing in a marathon for the first time.

GEORGE DE GREGORIO

Yachting

An Italian yacht won the first world championships for America's Cup class boats early in May 1991 off San Diego in a competition designed as a warm-up for the America's Cup racing scheduled for 1992. The boat, *Il Moro di Venezia,* skippered by Paul Cayard of San Francisco, beat out the *New Zealand* in the final match to secure the victory.

The world event proved a disappointment for the United States, however, as Team Dennis Conner withdrew from the nine-boat event. Conner had placed third in the five-day fleet-racing phase and had qualified for the semifinal in the match-racing segment. His reasons for withdrawing were that his boat, *Stars & Stripes,* had insufficient sails, and that it might be damaged by the stress of match-racing.

Later in the year, Britain, a competitor in all events in the America's Cup's 141-year history, announced it would not compete in 1992 because of the high cost of high—ech sailing.

In single-handed racing around the world, a Frenchman, Christophe Auguin, captured the BOC Challenge race. He arrived at Newport, RI, on April 23, sailing *Group Sceta,* a 60-ft (20-m) sloop. He won the 27,000-mi (43 452-km) event with an elapsed time in the four-stage race of 120 days, 22 hours, 36 minutes, and 35 seconds.

French sailors also won the prestigious Admiral's Cup for the first time in August. The French chartered the 50-ft (15.24-m) *Corum Saphir* from Italy and *Corum Diamant,* a 40-ft (12.19-m) one-ton class yacht, from the Netherlands to form a three-vessel challenge with their own yacht, *Corum Rubis,* a two-tonner. *Corum Saphir,* sailing in the Fastnet competition, was the first of the Admiral's Cup boats to reach Plymouth, England. *Corum Diamant,* however, won its class and also beat all the other two-tonners to win the Fastnet Cup.

Three of New Zealand's America's Cup team skippers dominated the Omega Gold Cup match-race tournament in Bermuda in October. Eddie Warden Owen of Britain, alternate skipper for New Zealand, beat Rod Davis, a colleague on the New Zealand team, for the Omega trophy and $30,000. Russell Coutts was third.

Chris Dickson, the 29-year-old New Zealander who is skipper for Japan's America's Cup team, retained his world match-racing title late in October by winning the $135,000 Mazda championship of Bermuda.

GEORGE DE GREGORIO

SPORTS SUMMARIES[1]

ARCHERY—World Champions: men: Simon Fairweather, Australia; women: Soo-nyung Kim, South Korea. **U.S. Champions:** men: Ed Eliason, Stansbury Park, UT; women: Denise Parker, South Jordan, UT.

BADMINTON—World Champions: men: Jianhua Zhao, China; women: Jiuhong Tang, China. **U.S. Champions:** men: Chris Jogis, Palo Alto, CA; women: Liz Aronsohn, Tempe, AZ.

BIATHLON—U.S. Champions: men: 10k: Curtis Schreiner, Day, NY; 20k: Curtis Schreiner; women: 7.5k: Patrice Anderson, Eden, UT; 15k: Anna Sonnerup, Hanover, NH.

BILLIARDS—World Champions: men's 9-ball: Earl Strickland, Greensboro, NC; women's 9-ball: Robin Bell, Costa Mesa, CA.

BOBSLEDDING—World Champions: world 2-man: Germany; world 4-man: Germany; World Cup 4-man: Switzerland.

BOWLING—Professional Bowlers Association Tour: Firestone Tournament of Champions: David Ozio, Vidor, TX; National Championship: Mike Miller, Albuquerque, NM; Bud Light Touring Players Championship: Dave Ferraro, Kingston, NY; Ebonite Senior Championship: Gene Stus, Allen Park, MI. **American Bowling Congress:** singles: Ed Deines, LaPorte, CO; doubles: Jimmy Johnson, Columbus, OH, and Dan Nadeau, Las Vegas, NV; all events: Tom Howery, Madison, WI; team all events: Nadeau's Pro Shop, Las Vegas, NV; regular team: Tri-State Lane No. 1, Chattanooga, TN; Masters Tournament: Doug Kent, Canandaigua, NY.

CANOEING—U.S. Champions: canoe: 1,000 m: Wyatt Jones, Honolulu, HI; men's kayak: 1,000 m: Patrick Richardson, Newport Beach, CA; women's kayak: 500 m: Sheila Conover, Newport Beach.

COURT TENNIS—World: Wayne Davies, New York. **U.S. Open:** Lockland Deuchar, Australia; doubles: Wayne Davies and Lockland Deuchar. **U.S. Amateur:** Morris Clothier, New York.

CROSS-COUNTRY—World Champions: men: Khalid Skah, Morocco; women: Lynn Jennings, Newmarket, NH. **U.S. Champions:** men: Todd Williams, Knoxville, TN; women: Lynn Jennings.

CURLING—World Champions: men: David Smith, Scotland; women: Dordi Nordby, Norway. **U.S. Champions:** men: Steve Brown, Madison, WI; women: Maymar Gemmell, Houston, TX.

CYCLING—Tour de France: men: Miguel Indurain, Spain.

DOG SHOWS—Westminster: best-in-show: Ch. Whisperwind on a Carousel, standard poodle, owned by Joan and Frederick Hartsock, Potomac, MD.

FENCING—U.S. Fencing Association: men's foil: Nick Bravin, Los Angeles; men's épée: John Normile, New York City; men's saber: Michael Lotton, New York City; women's foil: Mary Jane O'Neill, Concord, MA; women's épée: Margo Miller, Santa Monica, CA.

FIELD HOCKEY—NCAA Division I: women: Old Dominion.

GYMNASTICS—U.S. Champions: men's all-around: Chris Waller, Los Angeles, CA; women's all-around: Kim Zmeskal, Houston, TX.

HANDBALL—U.S. Handball Association: men's one-wall: Joe Durso, Brooklyn, NY; men's four-wall: John Bike, Fairfield, CT; women's one-wall: Rosemary Bellini, Brooklyn, NY; women's four-wall: Anna Engele, St. Paul, MN.

HORSESHOE PITCHING—World Champions: men: Walter Ray Williams, Jr., Stockton, CA; women: Tari Powell, Rantoul, IL.

HORSE SHOWS—U.S. Equestrian Team: dressage: Carol Lavell, Fairfax, VT, riding Gifted; three-day event: Karen Lende, Upperville, VA, riding Mr. Maxwell; show jumping: Lisa Jacquin, Collegeville, PA, riding For the Moment. **U.S. League Volvo World Cup:** Carol Lavell, riding Gifted.

JUDO—U.S. Champions: men: heavyweight: John Serbin, San Jose, CA; open: Johnny Walker, Colorado Springs, CO; women: heavyweight: Cheryl Stephens, Los Angeles, CA; open: Grace Jividen, Colorado Springs, CO.

KARATE—U.S. Champions: men: Advanced WUKO Mandatory Kata: Ferdie Allas, San Diego, CA; Advanced Open Kata: Shane Mata, Neptune, NJ; 35 and over Advanced Open Kata: Michael Cain, Bellingham, WA; 45 and over Advanced Open Kata: William Damon, Tucson, AZ; Advanced Weapons Kata: Brian Hobson, Hampton, VA; 35 and over Advanced Weapons Kata: Jimmy Blann, Southhaven, MA; 45 and over Advanced Weapons Kata: James Keahan, Hamilton Square, NJ; women: Advanced WUKO Mandatory Kata: Melanie Genung, Seattle, WA; Advanced Open Kata: Gwen Hoffman, Freehold, NJ; 35 and over Advanced Open Kata: Elaine Rhodes, Warren, PA; 45 and over Advanced Open Kata: Pat Wright, Newark, OH; Advanced Weapons Kata: Carolyn Giardina, Westwood, NJ; 35 and over Advanced Weapons Kata: Norma Kaiser, Tucson, AZ, 45 and over Advanced Weapons Kata: Pat Wright.

LACROSSE—NCAA Division I: men: North Carolina; women: Virginia. **Major Indoor League:** Detroit Turbos.

LUGE—U.S. Champions: men: Duncan Kennedy, Lake Placid, NY; women: Cammy Myler, Lake Placid. **World Champions:** men: Arnold Huber, Italy; women: Susi Erdmann, Germany. **World Cup:** men: Markus Prock, Austria; women: Susi Erdmann.

MODERN PENTATHLON—U.S. Champions: men: Rob Stull, Austin, TX; women: Kim Arata, Vandenberg Air Force Base, CA. **World Champions:** men: Arkad Skrzypaszek, Poland; women: Eva Fjellerup, Denmark.

PADDLE TENNIS—U.S. Champions: men's singles: Scott Freedman, Culver City, CA; women's singles: Kelly Chase, Los Angeles, CA.

PLATFORM TENNIS—U.S. Champions: men's singles: Scott Staniar, Greenwich, CT; women's singles: none; men's doubles: Steve Baird, Harrison, NY, and Rich Maier, Scarsdale, NY; women's doubles: Robin Fulton, Stamford, CT, and Diane Tucker, Bedford, NY; mixed doubles: Patty Hogan, Summit, NJ, and David Ohlmuller, Montclair, NJ.

POLO—Rolex Gold Cup: Cellular One, Greenwich, CT. **International Gold Cup:** JM Lexus, Boca Raton, FL. **International Open:** Michelob Dry, St. Louis, MO. **World Cup:** Michelob, St. Louis.

RACQUETBALL—U.S. Champions: men: Andy Rogers, Memphis, TN; women: Michelle Gilman, Ontario, OR.

RACQUETS—U.S. Open: Neil Smith, England. **U.S. Professional:** Wayne Davies, New York. **U.S. Amateur:** William Boone, England. **World:** James Male, England.

ROWING—U.S. Collegiate Champions: men: Pennsylvania; women: Boston University. Intercollegiate Rowing Association: Northeastern. Eastern Sprint: Pennsylvania. Dad Vail Regatta: Temple. **World Champions:** men's eights: Germany; women's eights: Canada; men's lightweight eights: Italy.

SHOOTING—U.S. International Champions: men's free rifle, three position: Thomas Tamas, Fort Benning, GA; men's air rifle: Matt Suggs, Roanoke, VA; women's standard rifle, three position: Launi Meili, Cheney, WA; women's air rifle: Ann-Marie Pfiffner, Dubuque, IA.

SOFTBALL—U.S. Champions: men's fast pitch: Guanella Brothers, Rohnert Park, CA; women's fast pitch: Raybestos Brakettes, Stratford, CT; men's major-slow pitch: Riverside, Louisville, KY; women's major slow pitch: Cannan's Illusion, San Antonio, TX; men's super-slow pitch: Sunbelt/Worth, Centerville, GA; U.S. college women: Arizona.

SQUASH TENNIS—U.S. Champion: men: Gary Squires, Darien, CT.

TEAM HANDBALL—U.S. Champions: men: Garden City, NY; women: Colorado Springs Stars. **Collegiate Champions:** men: Army; women: Army.

TRIATHLON—World Champions: Ironman men: Mark Allen, Cardiff, CA; Ironman women: Paula Newby-Fraser, Encinitas, CA.

VOLLEYBALL—NCAA Division I: men: Long Beach State; women: UCLA. **World Cup:** men: Soviet Union; women: Cuba.

WATER POLO—U.S. Champions: men's outdoor: Newport A (CA); women's outdoor: California at Berkeley. **NCAA:** California at Berkeley.

WATER SKIING—U.S. Overall: men's open: Sammy Duvall, Windermere, FL; women's open: Karen Neville, Australia. **World Overall:** men's: Patrice Martin, France; women's: Karen Neville.

WRESTLING—World Champions: freestyle: 48 kg: Vugar Orudzhev, Soviet Union; 52 kg: Zeke Jones, Bloomsburg, PA; 57 kg: Sergei Smai, Soviet Union; 62 kg: John Smith, Stillwater, OK; 68 kg: Arsen Fadzaev, Soviet Union; 74 kg: Amir Khaden, Iran; 82 kg: Kevin Jackson, Ames, IA; 90 kg: Maharbek Khadartsev, Soviet Union; 100 kg: Leri Khabelov, Soviet Union; 130 kg: Andreas Schroder, Germany; team: Soviet Union; Greco-Roman: 48 kg: Duk-Yong Gooun, Korea; 52 kg: Raul Martinez, Cuba; 57 kg: Rifat Yildiz, Germany; 62 kg: Sergei Martynov, Soviet Union; 68 kg: Islam Duguchiev, Soviet Union; 74 kg: Mnatsakan Iskandarian, Soviet Union; 82 kg: Peter Farkus, Hungary; 90 kg: Maik Bullman, Germany; 100 kg: Hector Millian, Cuba; 130 kg: Alexander Karelin, Soviet Union; team: Soviet Union.

[1]Sports for which articles do not appear in pages 476–500.

SRI LANKA

In addition to the continuing eight-year-old civil war between government forces and militant Tamil groups, Sri Lanka in 1991 experienced an unexpected constitutional crisis, which threatened to topple the United National Party (UNP) government and President Ranasinghe Premadasa. While Sri Lanka's north and northeast areas remained troubled, the security situation improved elsewhere. A stagnant economy was weakened further, but there were some signs of recovery.

Continuing Violence. On Jan. 1, 1991, the major Tamil militant group, the Liberation Tigers of Tamil Eelam (LTTE), declared a unilateral truce and said that it was prepared to enter into unconditional peace talks. Ten days later the government charged that the LTTE had violated the proclaimed truce and began preparations for a major offensive in the north.

On March 2, Deputy Minister of Defense and former Foreign Minister Ranjan Wijeratne was killed along with 24 others when a car bomb exploded in the capital city of Colombo. The bomb was believed to have been planted by LTTE guerrillas. More than 400 people were killed in the first week in April in battles between security forces and Tamil guerrillas. In May a bloody offensive lifted the siege of an army camp guarding the key Elephant Pass, gateway to the Jaffna Peninsula. Army sources estimated the number of government losses at 170 men, with 1,400 guerrillas killed; independent estimates were lower. This battle was heralded in progovernment circles as a turning point in the prolonged civil war. The LTTE was more than ever on the defensive and seemed to be losing support, even among the Tamils; but the group still retained control of the Jaffna Peninsula and continued its activities more sporadically in the northeast.

The Constitutional Crisis. An August petition charged President Premadasa with treason for allegedly supplying arms to the LTTE and many lesser crimes and abuses. A call for his impeachment, led by two former UNP cabinet ministers—Lalith Athulathmudali and Gamini Dessanayake—was signed by a majority of the members of Parliament. In an attempt to prevent a vote of impeachment and win back dissidents from his own party who had signed the petition, Premadasa suspended Parliament on August 30. When it reassembled on September 24, it soon became apparent that the impeachment forces did not have the required two-thirds vote to remove the president. The episode, however, was a sign of the growing dissatisfaction with Premadasa's rule and of the weakness of the political system.

The Economy. The civil strife remained a great obstacle to any substantial improvement in Sri Lanka's economy. Expenditures for defense had accelerated by nearly 50% since June 1990. The civil strife also was a major cause of the rising inflation rate of between 15% and 25%. It increased the national debt and discouraged foreign trade, foreign investment, tourism, and foreign contacts generally. The impact of the Gulf war was an added burden. About 100,000 Sri Lankan expatriate laborers in Iraq and Kuwait were suddenly out of work. Most of them had to be assisted in returning to their homes and in finding means of survival after they returned. Remittances from these expatriates had been a major contribution to the country's revenues. The loss of markets for major exports was another severe blow.

Following the Gulf war, exports of tea, textiles, petroleum products, and other key products increased substantially. Foreign companies—especially Japanese—took a renewed interest in investment and joint ventures in Sri Lanka, and tourists began to return. Overall, the growth rate reached 6.5%. To speed economic development further, the government relaxed the rather stringent foreign-exchange controls and removed many onerous barriers to foreign trade and investment. In September the International Monetary Fund granted Sri Lanka $455 million for "extended structural adjustment."

Foreign Relations. In spite of the tensions created by the presence of more than 200,000 Sri Lankan Tamils in the adjoining Indian state of Tamil Nadu, relations between Sri Lanka and India seemed to improve early in the year. However, they again became strained because of the alleged involvement of the LTTE in the assassination of India's former Prime Minister Rajiv Gandhi on May 20. Relations became worse when the sixth summit of the South Asian Association for Regional Cooperation (SAARC), scheduled to be held in Colombo in early November, suddenly was postponed. Sri Lanka alleged that India had "sabotaged" the meeting.

NORMAN D. PALMER, *Professor Emeritus*
University of Pennsylvania

SRI LANKA • Information Highlights

Official Name: Democratic Socialist Republic of Sri Lanka.
Location: South Asia.
Area: 25,332 sq mi (65 610 km²).
Population (mid-1991 est.): 17,400,000.
Chief Cities (mid-1988 est.): Colombo, the capital, 609,000; Dehiwala-Mount Lavinia, 190,000.
Government: *Head of state,* R. Premadasa, president (took office Jan. 1989). *Head of government,* D. B. Wijetunga, prime minister (appointed March 3, 1989). *Legislature* (unicameral)—Parliament.
Monetary Unit: Rupee (41.5 rupees equal U.S.$1, July 1991).
Gross Domestic Product (1988 U.S.$): $6,100,-000,000.
Economic Index (Colombo, 1990): *Consumer Prices* (1980 = 100), all items, 317.0; food, 321.1.
Foreign Trade (1990 U.S.$): *Imports,* $2,634,000,000; *exports,* $1,912,000,000.

STAMPS AND STAMP COLLECTING

U.S. Postal Service

The U.S. stamp program for 1991 mirrored events of the year. Included were new issues honoring "those who served in the Desert Shield/Desert Storm" campaign and hailing "Old Glory" and Mount Rushmore for the 50th anniversary of the mountain sculpture. The environment and nature were noted with colorful wildlife stamps issued in sheets of 50. Also offered were ten stamps featuring eight of the nine planets and the Moon.

Rates and New Issues. In 1990 the U.S. Postal Service had proposed an increase in the postal rate. Nondenominated "flower" stamps were released until the rates were established definitely (29¢ for most letters and 19¢ for postcards) and printing presses could be prepared.

New sports-related commemoratives spotlighted Olympic events with a multistamp issue to promote the 1992 Summer Games. A stamp issued for the centennial of basketball was released in the fall. Laughter was instilled with a booklet of five stamps honoring U.S. comedians; the five designs were done by caricaturist Al Hirschfeld.

A joint issue by the United States and Switzerland marked the 700th birthday of the founding of Switzerland. New stamps recognized a competitive hobby—coin collecting—and the 200th anniversary of the District of Columbia. A ten-stamp commemorative issue initiated a series recalling U.S. involvement in World War II. To be issued annually from 1991 to 1995, the stamps will focus on the war from the battlefield to the factory.

The annual Black Heritage Series paid tribute to inventor Jan E. Matzeliger. The Performing Arts Series spotlighted musical-comedy composer and lyricist Cole Porter. Pulitzer Prize-winning novelist William Saroyan received accolades in the Literary Arts Series. The Historic Preservation Series was furthered by the issuance of postal cards dedicated to the centennial of Carnegie Hall, Notre Dame University's 150th anniversary, and the centennial of the University of Texas Medical School. Special issues included one- and two-ounce-rate "Love" stamps, the traditional and contemporary Christmas stamps, and the third American Series stamps (both airmail and domestic) with the theme "Pre-Columbian Voyages of Discovery."

In the "Great Americans" series, a 35¢ stamp honored Dennis Chavez, who represented New Mexico in Congress for many years, and a 52¢ stamp paid tribute to Hubert H. Humphrey, 38th U.S. vice-president.

SYD KRONISH, *The Associated Press*

Selected U.S. Stamps for 1991

Subject	Denomination	Date	Subject	Denomination	Date	Subject	Denomination	Date
Extraordinary Flag	29¢	Jan. 22	Eagle Aerogramme	45¢	May 17	Eagle Priority Mail	$2.90	July 7
Steam Carriage (coil)	4¢	Jan. 25	William Saroyan	29¢	May 22	Summer Olympics	29¢	July 12
Switzerland	50¢	Feb. 22	Tractor	10¢	May 25	Fishing Boat	19¢	Aug. 8
Vermont Statehood	29¢	March 8	Canoe	5¢	May 25	Numismatics	29¢	Aug. 13
Fawn	19¢	March 11	Fishing Flies	29¢	May 31	Niagara Falls Card	30¢	Aug. 21
Carnegie Hall	19¢	April 1	Hubert H. Humphrey	52¢	June 3	Basketball	29¢	Aug. 28
Dennis Chavez	35¢	April 3	Cole Porter	29¢	June 8	Comedians	29¢	Aug. 29
Flower	29¢	April 5	Olympic Track & Field	29¢	June 12	Int. Express Mail	$14.00	Aug. 31
Flag with Olympic Rings	29¢	April 21	Jan Matzeliger	29¢	June 14	World War II minisheet	29¢	Sept. 3
Harriett Quimby	50¢	April 27	Antarctic Treaty	50¢	June 21	USPS Logo w/Olympic Rings	$9.95	Sept. 29
Savings Bonds	29¢	April 30	Birds	30¢, 3¢, 1¢	June 22	Space Exploration	29¢	Oct. 1
Love (one-ounce)	29¢	May 9	Yankee Clipper	40¢	June 28	America Series	50¢	Oct. 12
Love (two-ounce)	52¢	May 9	Desert Shield/Desert Storm	29¢	July 2	Traditional Christmas	29¢	Oct. 17
Balloon	19¢	May 17	Flag Over Mount Rushmore	29¢	July 4	Contemporary Christmas	29¢	Oct. 17
William Piper (airmail)	40¢	May 17						

STOCKS AND BONDS

Against a background of war in the Persian Gulf, recession in the domestic economy, and financial scandals around the world, the stock and bond markets in the United States demonstrated their stubborn contrariness by posting strong gains in 1991. Most analysts agreed that the main forces behind the rally were a sharp decline in U.S. interest rates and hopes for stable growth in the economy once the debts and speculative excesses of the 1980s could be worked off.

Overall Trends. The Dow Jones average of 30 industrials, a representative sample of big-name stocks traded on the New York Stock Exchange, closed on December 31 at 3,168.83, up 535.17 points or 20.32% from the end of 1990. Many smaller stocks fared even better, after lagging behind the blue chips for most of the previous seven years. The NASDAQ composite index for the over-the-counter market, home to thousands of smaller stocks, sported a gain of 56.8%.

The action was equally dramatic in the markets for bonds and other interest-bearing securities, where prices rose as interest rates fell. Short-term rates, in particular, tumbled as the Federal Reserve Board pursued a yearlong policy of easing credit conditions. Yields on Treasury bills of three-month to one-year duration dropped below 4.5% late in the year, down from about 7% in late 1990. Yields on long-term Treasury bonds, with lives of as much as 30 years, came down more grudgingly, to about 7.75% from about 8.3% a year earlier.

The Fed made its intentions clear with a series of reductions in the discount rate, the charge set by the central bank on loans to private financial institutions, bringing it down from 7% starting in late December 1990 to 3.5% on Dec. 20, 1991. The prime lending rate, a benchmark set by commercial banks to determine rates charged on many types of adjustable-rate loans, dropped over the same span from 10% to 7.5%.

The Fed was impelled on this course by an economy that encountered heavy resistance as it struggled to recover from the recession that began in the latter stages of 1990. Declines in total economic output, after adjustment for inflation, in the fourth quarter of 1990 and the first quarter of 1991 met the official definition of recession—at least two consecutive quarters of contraction in business activity. By the second quarter of 1991, signs of recovery were stirring. But six months later, there was little evidence that the upswing had gathered any significant momentum, and many economists and politicians were talking anxiously about a "double dip" recession of uncertain duration.

The stock market recorded gains in the first few months of the year, inspired in part by swift and decisive victory for the U.S.-led coalition against Iraq in the Gulf war. Among other things, that success touched off hopes of improved confidence among consumers and business planers and relieved fears of a major disruption in energy supplies to the United States. As the year passed, world events stirred even more expansive visions of economic possibilities for the future with the crumbling of the Soviet Union. But by then, investors had other, more immediate worries about domestic growth and corporate profits on their minds. Nevertheless, after the discount rate was dropped a full percentage point on December 20, the market closed the year with a major rally, with the Dow Jones exceeding 3,100 for the first time.

In early summer, the Dow had closed above 3,000 for the first time. It went on over the next few months to post marginally higher records, but the long market rally by then was showing signs of flagging as economic statistics registered disappointment after disappointment. On Friday, November 15, the Dow tumbled more than 120 points for its biggest point loss in more than two years, under the weight of accumulated worries about where the economy was headed and what desperate measures the Bush administration and Congress might take to try to revive it. Most unsettling to Wall Street was a proposal, soon thereafter abandoned, to set administered limits on credit-card interest rates. Indeed, the November 15 market drop played a central role in chilling enthusiasm for that idea, providing what many analysts regarded as a striking case study of securities markets' functioning as a potent force in the nation's political and legislative process.

The stock and bond markets drew a direct, if hard to measure, benefit from the economy's weakness and the Fed's stimulative policies. As interest rates fell, they reduced the appeal of many conservative investments, such as bank certificates of deposit (CDs), that compete with the securities markets for the investor's dollar. At mid-December, the rate offered on a typical six-month CD, as tracked by the Fed, had fallen to 4.13% from 7.49% a year earlier. Savers never before had been faced with such unappetizing returns in the era of deregulated banking dating back to the 1970s and early 1980s.

The Funds Industry. The resulting search for better-yielding alternatives represented a boon to mutual-funds investing in both stocks and bonds and kept alive a decade-old period of spectacular growth for the fund industry. At the end of October, total assets of mutual funds, as reported by the Investment Company Institute trade group, surpassed $1.3 trillion, up from a little more than $1 trillion a year earlier. Over that interval, bond-fund assets swelled from $312.41 billion to $417.84 billion and stock-fund assets from $225.85 billion to $337.49 billion.

Designed by George Stewart

To the surprise of many observers, growth also persisted in money-market and short-term municipal funds, even with yields at the lowest levels in well more than a decade. The two categories together held $546.26 billion at the end of October, up from $495.73 billion 12 months before. This came as persuasive evidence that money funds had established themselves as a prime savings vehicle for Americans, just 20 years after the first of their breed was organized. It remained to be seen, however, how they might fare in an extended period of low short-term interest rates.

The fund industry, among several types of financial organizations, also benefited from burgeoning growth in a type of retirement savings program known as the 401(k) plan (named after the section of the tax code that authorized it). In a typical 401(k) plan, sponsored by an employer, employees make tax-deductible contributions to an account offering several investment choices. By some estimates, more than 40 million Americans were eligible to take part in 401(k) programs in 1991, up from about 7 million eight years earlier. Total assets in the plans were estimated at $300 billion and were rising fast. About half that money reposed in an insurance-industry product called a guaranteed investment contract (GIC). These interest-bearing contracts, long assumed to be supersafe, came under much closer scrutiny in 1991 as many insurance companies, like banks, confronted problems such as shaky real-estate investments.

Scandals. Three financial scandals unfolded during 1991. In June the world's strongest stock market of the past several years, in Tokyo, was rocked by disclosures that some major Japanese brokerage firms had financed a major underworld figure and reimbursed clients covertly for some $464 million in investment losses. The news led to resignations from some of the top jobs in the Japanese securities business.

Just a few weeks later came the abrupt collapse of the Bank of Commerce and Credit International (BCCI), an organization with depositors in close to 70 countries that was accused of a broad range of fraudulent practices, including bogus accounting and failure to disclose deposits from shady sources as well as loans gone bad. BCCI never had been permitted to operate as a commercial bank in the United States, but it had major investors and depositors internationally. (*See* SPECIAL REPORT/INTERNATIONAL TRADE AND FINANCE.)

Much closer to home for U.S. investors, the Wall Street firm of Salomon Brothers Inc. acknowledged that it had acted improperly as it participated in auctions of Treasury securities that are a routine part of the functioning of the huge market through which the U.S. government manages its debts. Financier Warren Buffett, a legendary figure who earlier had made a large investment in Salomon, was summoned to take the reins of the troubled firm, and several of its former top officials resigned.

International Markets. Worldwide, nine of the 12 major foreign stock markets tracked by Datastream International and reported in *The Wall Street Journal* showed gains for the year through the end of November. Number 1, ranked by results in local currencies, was the Hong Kong market, up 37.20%; it was followed by two other Pacific Basin markets—Singapore, up 25.87%, and Australia, up 25.46%. Next came France, up 14.61%; the Netherlands, up 14.02%; Britain, up 12.91%; Germany, up 12.04%; Spain, up 10.38%; and Canada, up 5.89%. The three in the minus column were Italy, down 0.30%; Switzerland, down 1.42%; and Japan, down 4.87% after a year of wide fluctuations.

CHET CURRIER, *The Associated Press*

SUDAN

For Sudan the year 1991 was one of civil war, major economic problems, and political disunity.

Domestic Affairs. In 1991 the government of Omar Hassan Ahmed al-Bashir undertook a number of policy initiatives, with limited results. It continued the process of developing a political system it had initiated upon assuming power in 1989. The government was committed to a federal system and by late summer 1991 the outlines of a central structure for organizing popular congresses at all levels were established. Opposition parties were not legalized, but in April the government announced the release of all political detainees. There was, however, no indication that the Revolutionary Command Council for National Salvation, headed by Bashir, was reducing its control over government policies.

The Bashir government continued to be identified with the National Islamic Front. Measures implementing Islamic law proceeded throughout 1991. Application of Islamic punishments continued to arouse criticism from the regime's opponents.

Little progress was made during 1991 toward bringing an end to the civil war or the localized conflicts among ethnic groups in the western regions. The Sudan People's Liberation Movement (SPLM) continued to control substantial parts of the southern region. While leaders of both the government and the SPLM spoke of their willingness to open negotiations, neither suggested new approaches. The SPLM remained committed to its goal of a secular state in the context of a countrywide social revolution, while the government maintained its commitment to Islamization.

SPLM's situation changed dramatically early in 1991 when the Mengistu government in Ethiopia was overthrown. Ethiopia had provided both material support and base areas for the SPLM. In addition, significant divisions within the SPLM surfaced in August when three of its army commanders declared the ouster of SPLM leader John Garang. Garang survived the threat but charges of dictatorial leadership and corruption opened the way for discussion of the need for reform of the movement.

Economic Affairs. Sudan continued to face many critical economic problems. At the end of 1990 the Food and Agriculture Organization (FAO) listed Sudan as an area of ''most concern'' for famine, and throughout 1991 issues of supplying relief aid to the country were debated. Both the government and the SPLM had disputes with aid agencies and restricted access to areas under their control. The government disputed claims that a major famine existed, but noted that there were some problems of food shortage. Others estimated continuing high levels of hunger and hardship in many areas of the country.

SUDAN • Information Highlights

Official Name: Republic of the Sudan.
Location: Northeast Africa.
Area: 967,494 sq mi (2 505 810 km^2).
Population (mid-1991 est.): 25,900,000.
Chief Cities (1983 census): Khartoum, the capital, 476,218; Omdurman, 526,287; Khartoum North, 341,146.
Government: *Head of government,* Omar Hassan Ahmed al-Bashir, prime minister (took over June 30, 1989). A 15-member Revolutionary Command Council for National Salvation serves as the supreme executive, legislative, and judicial body.
Monetary Unit: Pound (4.5 pounds equal U.S.$1, June 1991).
Foreign Trade (1988 U.S.$): *Imports,* $1,060,000,000; exports, $509,000,000.

Sudan also faced significant financial problems. The large international debt inherited from preceding regimes continued to dominate the economy. In May the government completed a major currency change in an effort to combat tax evasion and speculation and to bring cash flows under governmental control.

International Affairs. During the Persian Gulf crisis, Sudan gave diplomatic support to Iraq and was an active opponent of the growing role of the United States in the Middle East. This represented a significant change from the policies of earlier regimes, which had been closer to the United States. In 1991, Sudan became identified more clearly with Libya and strengthened its ties with Iran.

Sudanese leadership was prominent in the emergence of a new international organization, the Islamic Arab Popular Conference, which held a meeting in Khartoum in August. The Islamic emphasis in foreign policy also was seen in the role of Hassan al-Turabi, leader of the National Islamic Front. He was a key figure in an international group of Islamist leaders who met regularly to find an Islamic and Arab solution to the Persian Gulf conflict.

JOHN O. VOLL
University of New Hampshire

SWEDEN

Sweden changed its political course in 1991 with the triennial elections for the Riksdag (parliament). The September 15 election, which had a turnout of 85% of the 6.4 million voters, resulted in an astonishing defeat for the Social Democrats, who had governed almost continuously for 60 years.

The Social Democrats lost 18 seats, while the Left Party (formerly the Communists) lost five seats. The 138 seats retained by the Social Democrats and the 16 retained by the Left Party added up to only 154 seats for the ruling coalition. This compared with 170 seats for the

© Tony Sica/Gamma-Liaison

Sweden's new Prime Minister Carl Bildt, the leader of the Moderate Party, headed up a new coalition government following September elections that saw the defeat of the Social Democrats, who had governed for most of the previous 60 years.

nonsocialist alliance, made up of the Moderates with 80 seats, the Liberals with 33 seats, the Center Party with 31 seats, and the Christian Democrats with 26 seats, while a newcomer to the political scene, the New Democracy, won 25 seats.

The day after the election, Premier Ingvar Carlsson and his entire cabinet resigned. The speaker of the Parliament proposed that Carl Bildt, the leader of the Moderates, be made prime minister and head a coalition cabinet of Moderates, Liberals, Christian Democrats, and Center Party members. The right-wing New Democracy was unaligned and did not participate in forming a new government. On October 3, Bildt accepted his election as the first conservative prime minister in 63 years. He also presented a new cabinet with eight women members, including Foreign Minister Margaretha af Ugglass.

SWEDEN • Information Highlights

Official Name: Kingdom of Sweden.
Location: Northern Europe.
Area: 173,730 sq mi (449 960 km^2).
Population (mid-1991 est.): 8,600,000.
Chief Cities (Dec. 31, 1990 est.): Stockholm, the capital, 674,452; Göteborg, 433,042; Malmö, 233,887; Uppsala, 167,508.
Government: *Head of state,* Carl XVI Gustaf, king (acceded Sept. 1973). *Head of government,* Carl Bildt, prime minister (took office Oct. 4, 1991). *Legislature* (unicameral)—Riksdag.
Monetary Unit: Krona (5.971 kronor equal U.S.$1, Nov. 12, 1991).
Gross Domestic Product (1989 est. U.S.$): $132,700,000,000.
Economic Indexes (1990): *Consumer Prices* (1980 = 100), all items, 207.6; food, 229.2. *Industrial Production* (1980 = 100), 114.
Foreign Trade (1990 U.S.$): *Imports,* $54,580,000,000; *exports,* $57,423,000,000.

Economic Affairs. A top priority of the new coalition government was to vitalize the Swedish economy through deregulation, lower taxes, and a so-called "revolutionary policy of freedom of choice" within the welfare policy. Bildt also promised to rescind a recently passed increase in the value-added tax (VAT) on food.

Sweden and Denmark on March 23 signed an official agreement to build a road and rail bridge linking the two countries. The project was expected to cost a minimum of $2.5 billion. Plans called for the bridge to open in 1999.

On May 17 the Swedish krona was pegged to the so-called ECU, the European currency unit. The value of the krona remained the same; the action was a first step in the adjustment of the Swedish exchange-rate system to the principles of the European Monetary System (EMS).

Foreign Relations. The Swedish government was in full sympathy with the UN Security Council resolutions condemning the Iraqi invasion of Kuwait and the subsequent allied military action against Iraq. But the government stated that Sweden was not to be considered a cobelligerent. Sweden instead provided humanitarian assistance, including a 200-bed hospital in Saudi Arabia staffed with 500 volunteers, $16.5 million in aid to help Kurdish refugees from Iraq, and about $70 million to help those hit hardest by the Gulf crisis, particularly children.

On July 1, Sweden applied for membership in the European Community (EC), a move that had been a topic of discussion for a number of years. The government, however, stressed that Sweden would retain its neutrality on the off chance the EC would develop into a military alliance. A final decision on whether to enter the EC was to be based on a national referendum.

On August 27, Sweden recognized the sovereignty of Estonia, Latvia, and Lithuania, and authorized the establishment of embassies in the three nations. Bilateral cooperation commissions were charged with drawing up mutual trade agreements and other mechanisms for solidifying trans-Baltic relations.

King Carl Gustaf and Queen Silva made a state visit to Italy, April 8-10. The royal couple also was greeted by Pope John Paul II at the Vatican.

Environmental Conference. World Environmental Day was celebrated in Stockholm on June 5, with King Carl Gustaf and Brazilian President Fernando Collor de Mello in attendance. It commemorated the first UN conference on the Human Environment held in Stockholm in 1972. At the close of the conference, a symbolic torch was passed to Rio de Janeiro, which would host World Environmental Day in 1992.

ERIK J. FRIIS
"The Scandinavian-American Bulletin"

SWITZERLAND

In 1991, Switzerland observed the 700th anniversary of the founding of the Swiss Confederation. Yet even as they celebrated, the Swiss faced new challenges to their traditional political and economic independence.

The European Community. Plans for the 1992 creation of a true economic union within the European Community raised Swiss governmental and business concerns about the potentially harmful economic impact if Switzerland failed to participate in these developments. Popular opinion, however, remained suspicious of formal international commitments. Nonetheless, in October, Switzerland agreed to become part of a European free-trade area—the European Economic Area (EEA)—effective in 1993. Earlier, on June 2, Swiss voters had defeated two government proposals that would have brought Switzerland's revenue system more in accord with those of other Western European states. A value-added tax (VAT) along with tax reductions on various securities transactions were rejected.

International Cooperation. In many areas, however, Swiss governmental and economic leadership cooperated in joint activities with other nations. On May 30 the Swiss government joined with 18 nations in an agreement to restrict the exportation of 50 common chemicals that could be used to produce chemical weapons. On July 5, Swiss bank regulators, along with regulators in six other countries, shut down the financially troubled and allegedly corrupt multinational Bank of Commerce and Credit International (BCCI)—*see also* SPECIAL REPORT/INTERNATIONAL TRADE AND FINANCE. Perhaps most important, however, was a May 3 announcement that so-called Form B anonymous bank accounts (in which a lawyer or administrative group could establish and have access to an account without disclosure of its actual ownership) would be eliminated by Sept. 30, 1992, although divulging information regarding account ownership still would be governed by Swiss federal law.

On the diplomatic front, Switzerland, which since 1977 had served as the sponsor of a U.S. "interest section" at the Swiss embassy in Havana, Cuba, announced on February 11 that it would assume from Czechoslovakia the sponsorship of a similar Cuban "interest section" at the Swiss embassy in Washington.

Domestic Issues. In October general elections, the four-party coalition that had governed since 1959 was returned to power, although rightist anti-immigrant sentiment was reflected in the vote. Earlier, in a March national referendum, voters had approved a reduction in the voting age from 20 to 18 in federal elections.

Resolving an issue that had caused tensions in recent years, Swiss voters in June ended the practice of imposing prison sentences on conscientious objectors who refused to perform military-service obligations, mandating instead human-services work.

Fresh from finally attaining in 1990 the right to vote in all cantons, 500,000 Swiss women went "on strike" on June 14, the tenth anniversary of the passage of the nation's equal-rights law, demonstrating for pay and job opportunities equal to those accorded men.

PAUL C. HELMREICH
Wheaton College, MA

SWITZERLAND • Information Highlights

Official Name: Swiss Confederation.
Location: Central Europe.
Area: 15,942 sq mi (41 290 km²).
Population (mid-1991 est.): 6,800,000.
Chief Cities (Dec. 31, 1989 est.): Bern, the capital, 134,393; Zurich, 342,861; Basel, 169,587.
Government: *Head of state,* Arnold Koller, president (took office Jan. 1990). *Legislature*—Council of States and National Council.
Monetary Unit: Franc (1.3890 francs equal U.S.$1, Dec. 10, 1991).
Gross Domestic Product (1989 est. U.S.$): $119,500,000,000.
Economic Indexes (1990): *Consumer Prices* (1980 = 100), all items, 139.6; food, 145.1. *Industrial Production* (1980 = 100), 122.
Foreign Trade (1990 U.S.$): *Imports,* $69,869,000,000; *exports,* $63,884,000,000.

SYRIA

In 1991, Syria's President Hafiz al-Assad continued to pursue his new policy of cooperation with the West, particularly with the United States. In 1990, Syria had joined the majority of Arab states in condemning Iraq's annexation of Kuwait; in 1991 it participated in the U.S.-led coalition that defeated Iraq in the Persian Gulf war. Its image as a radical state and supporter of terrorism thus was transmuted in a matter of months into one of international respectability. This policy shift was no doubt the result of calculation on the part of Assad, one of the shrewdest wielders of power in the Middle East; and it paid handsome dividends—Syria became the object of a virtual courtship by many Western countries and was rewarded with substantial financial assistance. Assad's new attitude was equally evident in his support for the Arab-Israeli peace conference, which met in Madrid on October 30. Syria's participation in the conference, however reluctant and conditional, actually did occur—an event noteworthy in itself.

Domestic Affairs. The change in foreign policy was not accompanied by any increase in political liberty at home. The Syrian government in 1991 was still, as it has been for two decades, an autocratic regime dominated by the Baath Party under Hafiz al-Assad.

While in all probability the majority of Syrians sympathized with Iraq rather than Kuwait, there was little overt sign of public dissent during the Gulf war. Although the official Iraqi news agency carried a report on May 16 that Syrian intelligence had arrested 20 high-ranking officers for disloyalty, the public mood seemed to be one of fatalistic resignation.

The average Syrian's standard of living did not improve, especially for those on small official salaries. Life was made more tolerable by a policy of subsidizing, and thus keeping low, the prices of basic foodstuffs—such as wheat, rice, sugar, tea, and coffee. But there was little incentive for farmers to increase production, since produce must be sold at low prices fixed by the government. Near hardship for the majority contrasted sharply with the fact that during 1991 the stores were filled with a great variety of consumer goods available to the middle and upper classes who could afford them.

Increased oil production was one of the bright spots in the economy. Since 1987, Syria had signed 13 oil-exploration and production agreements with foreign oil companies; and Syrian output, averaging about 400,000 barrels per day in 1991, showed a 250% increase in four years.

A new investment law signed by President Assad on May 4 aimed at encouraging investment in Syria's mixed economy. It created a Higher Council for Investment headed by the prime minister, facilitated dealings in hard currencies, and granted a complete seven-year tax exemption for new projects with at least 25% state ownership.

Foreign Aid. Soon after the conclusion of the Gulf war, Saudi Arabia furnished Syria with $2 billion in aid; most of this was spent on the purchase of 300 T-72 tanks from Czechoslovakia and on missiles from China. Some 60% of the Syrian budget went to military expenditures.

On February 4 the European Community agreed to end a freeze on aid to Syria in force since 1987 because of suspected Syrian complicity in terrorist actions. This step unblocked some $200 million in various forms of financial assistance, and the community contemplated further grants later in the year. Germany's Foreign Minister Hans-Dietrich Genscher, visiting Damascus on February 13, offered Syria $85 million in grants and loans. Also noteworthy was Japan's decision to extend a loan package to Syria totaling $500 million.

Reconciliation with the West. The change of course in Syrian foreign policy presumably was based on a clear-sighted acceptance of the fact that Soviet support and financial aid, on which Syria depended for many years, could not be expected in the future. Thus, Syria restored good relations with the U.S. ally Egypt, broken off in 1977, and backed U.S. efforts in the Gulf. An immediate reward was U.S. acquiescence in Syria's ending the civil war in Lebanon and establishing predominance there in October 1990.

Gulf War and Gulf Security. Syria contributed one of the largest contingents—more than 20,000 troops—to the anti-Iraqi coalition, but the force played little part in actual fighting and seemed to have suffered no casualties. Also, the controlled Syrian press made no reference to the troops' participation, and when they returned there were no official welcomes.

The foreign ministers of the Arab states that had participated in the Desert Storm allied co-

SYRIA • Information Highlights

Official Name: Syrian Arab Republic.
Location: Southwest Asia.
Area: 71,498 sq mi (185 180 km²).
Population (mid-1991 est.): 12,800,000.
Chief Cities (1987 est.): Damascus, the capital (1988 est.), 1,326,000; Aleppo, 1,216,000; Homs, 431,000.
Government: *Head of state,* Gen. Hafiz al-Assad, president (took office officially March 1971). *Head of government,* Mahmoud Zubi, prime minister (took office Nov. 1987). *Legislature* (unicameral)—People's Council.
Monetary Unit: Pound (11.225 pounds equal U.S.$1, July 1991).
Gross Domestic Product (1989 est. U.S.$): $18,500,000,000.
Economic Index (Damascus, 1990): *Consumer Prices* (1980 = 100), all items, 715.4; food, 795.5.
Foreign Trade (1990 U.S.$): *Imports,* $2,526,000,000; *exports,* $4,062,000,000.

© Ismail Handan/Gamma-Liaison

In Damascus in May, Syria's President Hafiz al-Assad (right) *and Lebanon's President Elias Hrawi signed a treaty of "brotherhood, cooperation, and coordination." Syrian predominance in Lebanon continued during 1991.*

alition—the six states of the Gulf Cooperation Council plus Egypt and Syria—met in Damascus on March 5 and 6. They issued a statement called the "Damascus Declaration," which among other things addressed the question of future security arrangements in the Gulf. It envisaged that Syrian and Egyptian forces would be stationed permanently in the Gulf states to form the nucleus of a new joint Arab defense. However, this idea steadily dwindled as a probability later in the year. (*See also* FEATURE SECTION/MIDDLE EAST, page 36.)

Syria-Lebanon Treaty. Syria's new position in Lebanon was recognized formally when the two presidents of the two countries signed a six-point treaty of "brotherhood, cooperation, and coordination" in Damascus on May 22. The treaty provided for cooperative arrangements which were in form entirely symmetrical, but served to mask the reality that Syria had established a unique position of predominance over its small neighbor.

The Middle East Peace Process. Syria's new centrality in the affairs of the Middle East was reflected by a number of visits to Damascus by U.S. Secretary of State James Baker in the spring, summer, and fall of 1991. The Syrians were at first very reluctant to take part in the proposed Arab-Israeli peace conference, but Secretary Baker's diplomacy achieved a breakthrough on July 14, when Hafiz al-Assad agreed to a compromise plan. Syria remained the most recalcitrant of the Arab states that met with Israel at the opening conference in Madrid on October 30. In the Madrid negotiations, Syrian representatives confined themselves to insisting that Israel return the Golan Heights, which it took from Syria in 1967. No progress was made, but the Syrians attended the second round of talks in Washington on December 4.

ARTHUR CAMPBELL TURNER
University of California, Riverside

TAIWAN

The government on Taiwan made several major decisions in 1991 that would reshape the island's economy as well as its political system. In light of these decisions, Taiwan was reconsidering its relationships with the outside world. Some of its neighbors, in turn, were considering how to restore to the government on Taiwan a role in international affairs commensurate with its position in the world economy.

Politics and Government. The Kuomintang (KMT) or Nationalist Party had based the legitimacy of its claim to monopoly control of the government on Taiwan on an election held on the mainland of China in 1947. Representatives elected at that time had continued to occupy seats in the national legislature and to dominate the political scene.

In April the party approved a plan for restructuring the government to conform to current political realities. Those elected in 1947 were required to retire at year's end. The National Assembly was reduced in size from 613 members to 327 members, of whom 227 henceforth would be elected on Taiwan. Eighty seats would be "national representatives" appointed by the political parties based on the proportion of the vote each took in a December 21 election. The remaining 20 seats were reserved for representatives of overseas Chinese communities. Amendments to the constitution would require a 75% majority vote.

More than 450 candidates stood for the National Assembly election and an additional 166 put their names forward for the appointed seats. The results proved disappointing to the opposition Democratic Progressive Party (DPP). Although it captured 24% of the popular vote, only 66 of its 94 candidates were elected. In the end, the KMT took 254 seats, which, combined with the 86 already held from an earlier election, gave the majority party control of 79% of the National Assembly.

Relations With the Mainland. In May the government announced a three-phase plan for the gradual reunification of Taiwan with the mainland provinces and the creation of a single Chinese state.

During the first phase, which Taiwan's President Lee Teng-hui estimated might last as long as 20 years, the government of the People's Republic of China (PRC) must encourage reform leading to the creation of an economy driven by market forces, renounce the use of force in bringing about reunification with Taiwan, and accede to the return of Taiwan as a full participant in the international community.

During phase two, direct and official communications would be established, including trade relations and air and sea travel. In the third phase, the two sides would work together toward what is referred to as "long-term consultation and unification."

Responding to this scenario leading toward reunification, the DPP met in October and took the dramatic step of calling for the establishment of an independent Republic of Taiwan with no claim to authority over China's mainland provinces. The call for independence was rejected by the Taiwan and PRC governments.

Meanwhile, de facto reunification continued apace. Taiwan investments on the mainland exceeded $1 billion, and two-way trade reached a projected $7 billion in 1991. Moreover, by year's end nearly 2 million Taiwan citizens had visited the mainland since the loosening of travel restrictions in 1988. A new airline was inaugurated with a view toward capturing the potential Taiwan to Fujian travel market, and property values soared in the city of Taichung, slated to be the port for direct sea communications with the mainland.

Economy. The Taiwan economy grew at a healthy 7.3% in 1991 with inflation estimated at just above 4%. Two-way foreign trade grew at a rate of 43% during the year, reaching a total of nearly $150 billion and making Taiwan the world's 13th-largest trading nation. The trade surplus exceeded $12 billion, and foreign-exchange reserves were more than $75 billion at year's end.

Nonetheless, economists doubted Taiwan's ability to continue to grow without substantial investment in economic infrastructure. A third major government decision, announced in February, addressed this problem by calling for a total of more than 750 infrastructure construction projects to be undertaken over the next six years. The cost of this development plan was estimated to exceed $300 billion.

Already under way was construction of a subway network for the capital city of Taipei. Delays in this project called into question the government's ability to carry out its ambitious developmental program. Questions also were asked about its ability to raise the needed capital without jeopardizing the stability of the economy and about the prudence of importing workers to fill the projected shortfall of 120,000 laborers required to complete the work.

International Status. Given Taiwan's important and growing role in the world economy, many had begun to argue that the island state should be accorded greater international legitimacy. U.S. President George Bush, responding to critics in Congress of his support for continued economic ties with Beijing, committed his administration to supporting Taiwan's application for membership in the General Agreement on Tariffs and Trade (GATT)—a step actively opposed by the PRC government. In the same spirit, some 10,000 demonstrators took to the streets of Taipei in October calling for a seat in the United Nations.

JOHN BRYAN STARR, *Yale-China Association*

TAIWAN • Information Highlights

Official Name: Taiwan.
Location: Island off the southeastern coast of mainland China.
Area: 13,892 sq mi (35 980 km²).
Population (mid-1991 est.): 20,500,000.
Chief Cities (Dec. 31, 1989 est.): Taipei, the capital, 2,702,678; Kaohsiung, 1,374,231; Taichung, 746,780; Tainan, 675,685.
Government: *Head of state,* Lee Teng-hui, president (installed Jan. 1988). *Head of government,* Hau Pei-tsun, prime minister (appointed March 1990). *Legislature* (unicameral)—Legislative Yuan.
Monetary Unit: New Taiwan dollar (25.56 NT dollars equal U.S.$1, Dec. 31, 1991).
Gross National Product (1989 U.S.$): $121,400,000,000.

TANZANIA

Political and economic reforms continued to dominate Tanzanian affairs in 1991. Tanzania's attempts to emerge as a regional transportation center faced increased competition from alternative southern African routes.

Political Reform. The National Executive Committee (NEC) of Tanzania's only party, Chama Cha Mapinduzi (CCM), met in late February to discuss President Ali Hassan Mwinyi's proposal for creating a commission to discuss the future of party politics, the party's commitment to the Arusha Declaration—which commits the party to "socialism and self-reliance," and the leadership code—which prohibits CCM leaders from having outside sources of income. Reformers sought to scrap the code in an effort to attract business leaders to the CCM. While the NEC failed to act decisively, President Mwinyi unilaterally implemented the changes.

Opposition to the CCM was led by the Steering Committee for the Seminar on the Course of the Transition to Multiparty Democracy in Tanzania that was organized on February 23 and chaired by Chief Abdullah Fundikira, Tanzania's first minister of justice. In order to frustrate the committee, President Mwinyi appointed one of its leading members, Mabere Marando, to the commission on the constitution. Marando declined the appointment, however. The committee also was set back when its vice-president, James Mupalala, resigned.

Within the government, Mwinyi undertook an anticorruption campaign led by Minister of Home Affairs Augustine Mrema. Mwinyi himself dedicated the last Wednesday of each month to meeting directly with citizens to address problems of public corruption and incompetence. In addition, the government began a process of laying off redundant and unqualified civil servants.

Economic Recovery. Rising oil prices due to the Persian Gulf war, along with low rainfall, threatened Tanzania's economic-recovery program. In order to facilitate getting products to market, Tanzania had undertaken a massive $700 million project to rehabilitate its roads. It also continued to rehabilitate and expand both the port at Dar es Salaam and the Tazara railway. Unfortunately, these projects would face increased competition from alternative outlets to the sea that inevitably would become available with the independence of Namibia, the peace settlement in Angola, and the pending settlement in Mozambique.

WILLIAM CYRUS REED
The American University in Cairo

TANZANIA • Information Highlights

Official Name: United Republic of Tanzania.
Location: East coast of Africa.
Area: 364,900 sq mi (945 090 km^2).
Population (mid-1991 est.): 26,900,000.
Chief City (1985 est.): Dar es Salaam, the capital, 1,096,000.
Government: *Head of state,* Ali Hassan Mwinyi, president (took office Nov. 1985). *Head of government,* Joseph S. Warioba, prime minister (took office Nov. 1985). *Legislature* (unicameral)—National Assembly, 233 members.
Monetary Unit: Tanzanian shilling (230 shillings equal U.S.$1, July 1991).
Gross Domestic Product (1989 est. U.S.$): $5,920,000,000.
Foreign Trade (1988 U.S.$): *Imports,* $1,495,000,000; *exports,* $337,000,000.

TAXATION

With the United States in the midst of a recession, the federal budget deficit growing, and many states facing severe fiscal crises (*see* SPECIAL REPORT/UNITED STATES), the issue of taxation was a major headline item throughout the nation in 1991.

The 1991 fiscal year (FY)—Oct. 1, 1990-Sept. 30, 1991—had started with a negotiated agreement between President George Bush and the Congress to raise taxes in order to reduce the federal deficit. The Omnibus Budget Reconciliation Act of 1990 raised income and excise taxes by more than $140 billion over the following five years. It was designed to reduce the federal budget deficit by $40 billion in FY 1991 and by about $500 billion in total over the five fiscal years. The deepening U.S. recession, however, forced President Bush and Congress to reconsider this agreement.

As a consequence, the 1991 debate over taxes centered on the proper way to encourage economic growth rather than to reduce the budget deficit. Specifically, many in Congress promoted a cut in taxes for the middle class in order to spur the slumping economy, while others in Congress and the Bush administration proposed cuts in business and investment taxes as the way to end the recession. In fact, pressure for action on the tax question became so great late in the year that the finance committees of the Senate and House scheduled tax hearings in December, following the adjournment of Congress in late November. Final congressional action was not anticipated before 1992, however.

On the international scene, several countries changed their tax systems in response to the ever-changing world political and economic structures. Germany increased taxes to help finance the unification of East and West Germany. Spain undertook major tax revisions in preparation for the European Community alliance in 1992. The new government in Great Britain proposed reversing the Thatcher government's imposition of a "poll tax" to fund local government expenditures and reduced taxes on corporate profits.

United States

Federal. Federal tax collections during FY 1991 were estimated to be $1,148,400,000,000. The bulk of this was composed of individual income taxes, social-insurance taxes and contributions (Social Security and unemployment insurance), and corporation income taxes. An estimated $503 billion in individual income taxes made up 43.8% of total tax revenue; $461.5 billion in social-insurance taxes (payroll taxes) represented 40.2% of collections; and $113.4 billion in corporation income taxes made up about 10% of federal tax revenue. The remaining 6% of tax collections were composed of excise taxes, estate and gift taxes, and customs duties and fees. Corporate-tax revenues continued to decline as a percentage of federal tax revenues, while social-insurance taxes continued to represent an increasingly important portion of tax revenue.

The federal tax code is governed by two recent revisions—the Tax Reform Act of 1986 (TRA-86) and the Omnibus Budget Reconciliation Act of 1990 (OBRA-90). TRA-86 was the last major federal tax-reform legislation. It lowered the highest income-tax bracket from 50% to 33% and reduced the total number of personal-income-tax bracket rates (the tax rate applied to the portion of personal income falling into each bracket) from 14 to four (15%, 28%, 33%, and 28%). The increase from 28% to 33% occurred as the advantages of the lower 15% tax bracket on the first $32,400 of income and personal exemptions from taxable income were removed for higher-income taxpayers. As a result, taxable income between $78,400 and $185,760 was taxed at 33%. Any income exceeding $78,400 was taxed once again at 28%. This increase in marginal tax rates to 33% and then the decrease back to 28% created a "bubble" in the income-tax brackets.

© Najlah Feanny/Saba

Taxation was a key issue as many U.S. states faced severe financial crises in 1991. "Ax the tax" became a rallying cry for those opposed to Connecticut's new income tax.

The purpose of OBRA-90 was to reduce the federal budget deficit. To achieve this goal, OBRA-90 modified the TRA-86 by establishing three marginal tax rates (15%, 28%, and 31%), thereby removing the tax-rate bubble. These changes effectively increased the tax rate on the highest income level. Taxable family income between $0 and $34,000 faced a 15% marginal tax rate, taxable family income between $34,00 and $82,150 was taxed at 28%, and family income greater than $82,150 now was taxed at the 31% marginal tax rate.

The federal income tax historically has been considered a fair or progressive tax in public-opinion polls. (A progressive-tax system means that individuals with higher income pay a greater tax as a proportion of their total income. In a regressive tax system, they pay a smaller proportion of their income in taxes.) Since higher marginal tax brackets still were being applied to larger incomes, and with the increases in the personal exemption and standard deduction and a general decrease in number of "tax loopholes" after the TRA-86 and OBRA-90, the individual income tax still was considered to be the most progressive federal tax. It also generally was considered fairer than the social-insurance tax (payroll taxes).

Payroll taxes are considered to be regressive, since a flat statutory tax rate of 6.2% of labor income (e.g., interest and capital gains are not covered by this tax) is placed on both the employee and the employer. However, no tax is paid on income beyond $53,400. Moreover, it is probably the case that employers can shift part or all of their share to the employee by paying a lower wage. An additional flat tax on the employer and employee of 1.45% of labor income is designated for the medical-insurance program (Medicare) for the elderly. OBRA-90 increased the cap on employee wages subject to the Medicaid portion of the payroll tax to $125,000 from $53,400. The regressivity of this tax is reduced when the payments from these taxes (Social Security, Medicare, and unemployment insurance) are taken into consideration.

Tax Fairness. One of the major issues in the budget negotiations between the Bush administration and Congress continued to be the proper distribution of any deficit-reduction taxes or expansionary tax policies across high-, middle-, and low-income taxpayers. Some members of Congress believed that the bulk of tax benefits in the 1980s was skewed toward individuals in the upper income brackets, so that many of the proposed expansionary tax proposals are aimed at individuals in the middle-income group. On the other hand, the Bush administration and other members of Congress favored tax measures designed to encourage economic investment, such as reductions in the capital-gains tax. The major arguments for this preferential treatment is that gains in the value of assets reflect general price-level increases and not real wealth increases and that this preferential tax treatment will encourage saving and investment and promote economic growth.

Congress refused to reinstate the significant differential treatment of capital gains that was part of the pre-TRA-86 tax code. The feeling was that since capital gains are realized disproportionately by upper-income individuals, the preferential tax treatment of these gains was unfair. However, as part of the agreement to raise taxes on the highest income levels, OBRA-90 reestablished the differential treatment of ordinary income and income from capital gains by setting a maximum capital-gains-tax rate at 28%.

State and Local. States and municipalities also levy taxes. In FY 1991 states obtained about 75% of their revenue from income taxes on individuals and corporations, sales taxes, and federal grants. State revenues from their own sources (nonfederal grant revenues) amounted to about $285 billion. Local governments receive the bulk of their revenue from property taxes, state grants, and, in a few localities, income taxes.

There are many differences in tax structures and burdens across the states and localities. For example, several states impose no individual income tax, while the numbers of tax brackets and the levels of the tax rates in these brackets in the states that do have one vary widely. In addition, a few states do not levy a general sales tax. Finally, local taxes on property vary across jurisdictions with regards to tax rates, tax base, and definition of property. As a result, it is difficult to summarize the tax burden of these state and local levies.

Since the major sources of tax revenue for the states (income and sales taxes) are based on economic activity, the 1991 national recession imposed severe revenue constraints on the states. At the same time, the states had increased expenditure responsibilities, since welfare and other social-services expenditures rise during a recession. The states are often reluctant to increase major taxes, because policymakers are concerned about the migration of individuals and corporations out of the state in response to relatively high tax burdens. Nevertheless, state income, sales, and corporate taxes increased more than $10 billion in FY 1991. In addition, many states increased their excise taxes on cigarettes, motor fuels, and, to a lesser extent, alcohol. In one of the more drastic measures to obtain additional tax revenue, Connecticut introduced a personal income tax for FY 1992.

International

Several countries changed their tax systems in response to changing events.

Spain. Since there are significant legislated freedoms in capital movement within the European Community alliance beginning in 1992, European countries with relatively high tax rates were concerned about capital flight to escape high tax burdens. Spanish personal-income taxes were one of the highest in the European Community, and to protect itself from capital flight, Spain adopted major revisions to its tax code. Specifically, it lowered the tax burden on the highest personal incomes and exempted long-term capital gains on sales of property and securities from tax. The value added tax, however, increased from 12% to 14%.

Germany. Germany increased taxes on income, natural gas, gasoline, heating oil, tobacco, and insurance to pay for the 1990 unification of West and East Germany. Taxes were increased to avoid enlarging the budget deficit.

Great Britain. Prime Minister John Major's government proposed eliminating the controversial and widely unpopular "community tax" that was designed by the Thatcher government to replace a complex local tax-rate system. The community tax first was implemented in Scotland in 1989 and then in England and Wales in early 1990. Unlike taxes that are related to economic activity (e.g., sales, excise, and wage taxes) or economic measures (e.g., income, wealth, or property), the community tax was uniform across all adult-age individuals and, as a result, it was considered by many individuals to be unfair. A new property-based council tax would replace the community tax. In an additional tax-policy change, the Major government reduced the corporate-tax rate to 34%, which is the lowest rate in the European Community.

Canada. A 7% goods and services tax went into effect on Jan. 1, 1991. Its introduction raised a furor among consumers and, in part, was blamed for dampening consumer spending and prolonging the recession.

THOMAS A. HUSTED
The American University

TELEVISION AND RADIO

The October 1991 televised congressional confirmation hearings of U.S. Supreme Court nominee Clarence Thomas—culminating in charges of sexual harassment in testimony by his former employee, Anita Hill—galvanized U.S. attention as only a television event can.

The revelations of alleged sexual shenanigans were even more titillating than those of the soap operas they preempted. The hearings even topped the Columbia Broadcasting System's (CBS') third game of the World Series in the ratings, 12.5 to 10.1. The hearings—covered in depth by the three major networks, the Public Broadcasting Service (PBS), and Cable News Network (CNN)—spun off numerous debates in the nation's homes and workplaces and in the news media on the subjects of sexual harassment and race.

In a rare case of a network entertainment program addressing a topical issue within its brief life in the national attention span, the CBS sitcom *Designing Women* in early November aired an episode in which the cast debated the Thomas hearings.

Another highly charged television event, the William Kennedy Smith rape trial in December, led some commentators to speculate that jurors experienced unusual, judgment-bending pressures in the national video glare. Another issue in the area of television ethics and the law was whether to reveal the name or face of Smith's accuser. All the networks blocked out her face during her testimony, but CNN took heavy criticism for letting her face appear at one point due to technical error.

Network Programming. With the cancellation of the American Broadcasting Companies' (ABC's) Philadelphia-set *thirtysomething,* the new programming of ABC, CBS, and the National Broadcasting Company (NBC) fled the cities and their seemingly intractable problems in 1991. The networks sought, for the most part, down-home settings and characters with funny, small-town idiosyncrasies.

Perhaps the most bracing, successful foray into the hinterlands, with both audiences and critics, was CBS' 1990–91 entry, *Northern Exposure,* a hip, intelligently quirky ensemble comedy about the adventures in a remote Alaskan hamlet of a young New York doctor (Rob Morrow) suffering culture shock. The series also broke ground with its textured portrayals of Native Americans.

But the down-home television migration mainly was southerly—and escapist. The modest success of the 1990–91 CBS sitcom *Evening Shade,* with its warm, humorous writing and classy acting ensemble (Burt Reynolds, Marilu Henner, Ossie Davis, Hal Holbrook), suggested a ripe market for more Dixie fare. These programs were prevalent especially on NBC, including the continuing crime drama *In the Heat of the Night* and the new 1991–92 entries *The Torkelsons* (set in rural Oklahoma) and the critically well-received *I'll Fly Away,* starring Sam Waterston as a district attorney in a southern town affected by the fledgling black civil-rights movement.

Significantly, at the head of the city-streets-to-country-sticks movement was the trend-setting production team of Joshua Brand and John Falsey, creators of *St. Elsewhere* in the 1980s, and *Northern Exposure* and *I'll Fly Away* in the 1990s.

Meanwhile on the urban-contemporary scene, another innovative producer of the 1980s, Steven Bochco (*Hill Street Blues*), weighed in with *Civil Wars* on ABC. Starring Peter Onorati and Mariel Hemingway as divorce lawyers, it was praised for its typically "Bochco-esque" irreverence, quick-cutting

Janine Turner and Rob Morrow are stars of the CBS hit "Northern Exposure," an ensemble comedy series centering on the adventures of a New York Jewish doctor who suffers culture shock as he practices medicine in a remote Alaskan village to pay off his medical-school bills.

pace, and realistic detail. Two 1990–91 midseason replacement shows were brought back for full-season runs by virtue of their good reviews: NBC's *Seinfeld* (with witty young comic Jerry Seinfeld blending traditional sitcom with club stand-up routines) and the gritty ABC crime series *Equal Justice*.

A symbolic milestone—closing the era of the nighttime serials oriented toward sex, power, and money, so popular in the 1980s—was the cancellation of CBS' *Dallas* after a run of 13 years.

Still, sex, power, and money remained important ingredients in program appeal, as evidenced by the Fox Network's one new hit of 1991, *Beverly Hills 90210*. Although *The Simpsons, In Living Color,* and *Married . . . With Children* remained popular, Fox had a difficult year as it expanded its schedule.

PBS also had its troubles in 1991. The independent film series, *P.O.V.* (for "Point of View") was the target of attack and fierce controversy, first for "Tongues Untied," about growing up black and gay, and later for "Stop the Church," a film by the AIDS advocacy group ACT-UP about its confrontations with Catholic hierarchy. The network canceled the latter film at the last minute because, in a spokesman's words, "it crosses the line of being responsible programming into being ridicule."

Cable and Syndicated TV. *Variety* newspaper observed that made-for-cable films were

Among the acclaimed shows of the year was "I'll Fly Away." Set in the late 1950s, it stars Sam Waterston as a liberal Southern lawyer and Regina Taylor as his housekeeper.

© Ruth Leitman/1991 NBC, Inc.

© Bob D'Amico/ABC

"Civil Wars" in its premiere season on ABC had two winning stars in Mariel Hemingway and Peter Onarati. The pair portray Manhattan lawyers specializing in divorce law.

the "first alternative" in the video world for major movie talent. For Home Box Office (HBO), Melanie Griffith starred in the film adaptation of an Ernest Hemingway story, *Hills Like White Elephants,* and Richard Dreyfuss played the 19th-century political martyr Alfred Dreyfus in *Prisoners of Honor*. Even producer-director George Lucas (known for the *Star Wars* film series) got into the original-cable-programming act, creating *Maniac Mansion,* a comedy horror series for The Family Channel. A broadcast network, ABC, even paid a cable network, the Lifetime Channel, the rare compliment of rerunning one of its original movies, the suspense drama *Stop at Nothing,* which starred Veronica Hamel.

The tenth anniversary of MTV, the music-video network, was an additional symbol of the coming-of-age of original cable programming. Perhaps, however, the most dramatic symbolic sign of the rising stock of syndicated television and the falling fortunes of the three major networks was the defection of television's biggest star of the 1980s, Bill Cosby. The actor-producer announced that he would star in the Groucho Marx moderator role in a new version of the 1950s game show, *You Bet Your Life,* to be sold directly into syndication in the fall of 1992 without an initial network run. This plan would cut out the networks' customary role as profit-sharing middlemen.

With above-the-waist shots of romantic clinches fairly common on television in 1991—especially on the afternoon and evening "soaps"—it took a fairly brazen program to generate a new controversy about bad taste. *Studs* did just that. The syndicated game show, in which single women "rated" their single male dates in thinly veiled sexual innuendoes, enjoyed generally strong ratings in its 40 markets. However, it was canceled in Cleveland due to viewer protest.

News. Another blow to the major networks' collective ego was the *TV Guide* cover story, "Look What They've Done to the News." The grim account of falling ratings and profits for the news shows was illustrated with a mock-up of Mount Rushmore consisting of the heads of network anchors Peter Jennings, Dan Rather, and Tom Brokaw, with large cracks running down their stone faces.

NBC News, particularly, seemed vulnerable as two of its newsmagazines, *Expose* with Brokaw and *Real Life with Jane Pauley,* were canceled due to low ratings after only one full season each.

Not all the changes in network news were perceived as bad, however. A *New York Times* analysis indicated that, in fact, network national newscasts now may be paying "more sustained attention to such subjects as the jobless and the homeless, health care and education."

Another symbolic benchmark in the balance of power, reflecting the newly matured status of cable television relative to the networks, was the widespread admiration for CNN's coverage of the Persian Gulf war. Even U.S. Secretary of Defense Richard Cheney, during a news conference, gave the Atlanta-based cable network the highest marks. CNN jumped into the lead with a major journalistic coup, its spectacular footage of Baghdad under night bombardment by the only U.S. news team still inside the city. But the network's coups were tainted by critics' charges that correspondent Peter Arnett (*see* BIOGRAPHY) received his exclusive access inside Iraq because of the pro-Iraqi tone of his reports.

People. "Here we go again!" said a *Time* magazine headline for an item about perky, down-to-earth Katie Couric replacing the short-lived Deborah Norville as co-anchor on *Today*. However, the move appeared finally to stabilize the NBC show, plagued by almost continuous gossip and criticism in recent years.

Carol Burnett, one of the queens of CBS' glory years in the 1960s and 1970s, attempted a comeback in 1991, headlining a new variety show—a vanished genre since the early 1980s. The CBS venture was canceled after a few episodes, however.

Johnny Carson announced that he would leave as the host of *Tonight* after 30 years, in May 1992. Jay Leno was to replace him.

Danny Thomas, one of the beloved father figures of the golden age of television in the 1950s and 1960s, both as an actor (*Make Room for Daddy*) and as a producer (*The Dick Van Dyke Show, The Andy Griffith Show*), died at age 77. Another beloved dad of television, Fred MacMurray of *My Three Sons,* also died during the year. When comedian Redd Foxx collapsed on the set of his new CBS sitcom, *The Royal Family,* some cast members assumed it was an-

Courtesy, Lifetime Television

In the made-for-cable movie "Stop at Nothing," Veronica Hamel (right), who earlier appeared on the television series "Hill Street Blues," assists Annabella Price (left) in her efforts to attain custody of her daughter, played by Deborah Anne Gorman. The movie was rerun during 1991 on network television, showing the new clout of cable television.

TELEVISION | 1991

Some Sample Programs

Antony and Cleopatra—A *Great Performances* telecast of the Samuel Barber opera. Performed by the Lyric Opera of Chicago. PBS, Dec. 16.

Best of Disney: 50 Years of Magic—A retrospective of the Disney Studio's 50 years in show business. ABC, May 20.

Born at the Right Time—A live telecast of Paul Simon's concert in New York City's Central Park. HBO, Aug. 15.

Columbus and the Age of Discovery—A seven-hour series chronicling the explorer and his times. PBS, Oct. 6.

Conagher—A made-for-cable movie based on a Louis L'Amour novel about a young widow who finds love with a cowhand. With Katharine Ross, Sam Elliott. TNT, July 1.

Crazy from the Heart—A made-for-cable movie about a Texas principal who falls romantically for a Mexican-American rancher who moonlights as a janitor. With Christine Lahti, Ruben Blades. TNT, Aug. 19.

The Crucifer of Blood—A made-for-cable Sherlock Holmes mystery movie. With Charlton Heston. TNT, Nov. 4.

Die Kinder—A six-part thriller from the *Mystery* series set in contemporary Germany; about a former husband who abducts his children and the subsequent investigation of his 1960s revolutionary activities. With Frederic Forrest, Miranda Richardson. PBS, March 28.

Finding the Way Home—A TV movie about a Texas merchant in financial and emotional trouble who rediscovers himself after a bout with amnesia. With George C. Scott, Hector Elizondo. ABC, Aug. 26.

Fire in the Dark—A TV movie about a woman who is growing old, but does not want to surrender her independence. With Olympia Dukakis. CBS, Oct. 6.

Frank Sinatra: The Voice of Our Time—Documentary of the famous singer's career; includes movie and television clips. Hosted by Mel Torme. PBS, March 3.

Going Home to Gospel with Patti LaBelle—A concert of gospel music from historic Quinn Chapel in Chicago. PBS, March 6.

The Grapes of Wrath—An *American Playhouse* telecast of the stage adaptation of the John Steinbeck novel. With Gary Sinise, Lois Smith. PBS, March 22.

The House of Bernarda Alba—A *Great Performances* adaptation of Federico García Lorca's play. With Glenda Jackson, Joan Plowright. PBS, Dec. 18.

House of Cards—A *Masterpiece Theatre* four-part drama of political intrigue in Britain. With Ian Richardson. PBS, March 31.

In a Child's Name—A TV movie of a murder and subsequent custody battle between a woman and her murdered sister's in-laws, whose son has been convicted of the crime. With Valerie Bertinelli. CBS, Nov. 17.

An Inconvenient Woman—A two-part TV movie based on the Dominick Dunne novel about wealthy Californians. With Jason Robards, Jill Eikenberry, Rebecca De Mornay, Peter Gallagher. ABC, May 12.

Into the Woods—An *American Playhouse* telecast of the fairy-tale musical. PBS, March 20.

Johnny Carson's 29th Anniversary—Johnny Carson celebrates his 29th year on *Tonight.* NBC, Oct. 3.

LBJ—An *American Experience* two-part telecast of a Lyndon Johnson political biography. PBS, Sept. 30.

Live from Lincoln Center—The Mostly Mozart Festival opens its 25th-anniversary season. With James Galway, Andre Watts. PBS, July 10.—The New York Philharmonic opens its 150th season, introducing its new music director, Kurt Masur. PBS, Sept. 11.

Longtime Companion—An *American Playhouse* dramatization of a 1990 study of the effects of AIDS on a circle of gay New Yorkers. PBS, Sept. 29.

Lucy & Desi: Before the Laughter—A TV movie about Lucille Ball and Desi Arnaz in the years before the *I Love Lucy* show. With Frances Fisher, Maurice Benard. CBS, Feb. 10.

The Mahabharata—A three-part *Great Performances* telecast of a dramatization of India's epic Sanskrit poem. PBS, March 25.

Michael Landon—A tribute to the late television star who died in July 1991. NBC, Sept. 17.

Mrs. Lambert Remembers Love—A TV movie about a grandmother in the early stages of Alzheimer's disease. With Ellen Burstyn. CBS, May 12.

MTV 10—A celebration of the tenth anniversary of the music-video cable channel. With appearances by Madonna, Michael Jackson, and others. ABC, Nov. 27.

Murder in New Hampshire: The Pamela Smart Story—A fact-based TV movie dramatizing the case of a schoolteacher who seduces her high-school student and gets him to murder her husband. With Helen Hunt, Chad Allen, Ken Howard, Michael Learned. CBS, Sept. 24.

A Murder of Quality—A *Masterpiece Theatre* dramatization of the John le Carré 1962 novel. With Denholm Elliott, Glenda Jackson. PBS, Oct. 13.

Night of the Hunter—A TV remake of the 1955 feature film about a con man who tries to get a hidden cache from a widow's young son. With Richard Chamberlain, ABC, May 5.

One Against the Wind—A fact-based TV movie about an English woman estranged from her French aristocratic husband who helps entrapped Allies during World War II. With Judy Davis, Sam Neill. CBS, Dec. 1.

Our Sons—A TV movie about two mothers coping with crises relating to their gay sons. With Julie Andrews, Ann-Margret. ABC, May 19.

Pearl Harbor: Two Hours that Changed the World—An *ABC News Special* on the 50th-anniversary commemoration of the attack. Host, David Brinkley. ABC, Dec. 5.

The Perfect Tribute—A TV movie based on a 1905 fictional account of an encounter between Abraham Lincoln and a young Southern boy. With Jason Robards, Lukas Haas. ABC, April 21.

Perry Mason: The Case of the Glass Coffin—A TV movie about a magician indicted for murder. With Raymond Burr, Peter Scolari, Barbara Hale. NBC, May 14.

Prisoner of Honor—A made-for-cable movie on the court-martial of French Army Captain Alfred Dreyfus and its aftermath. With Richard Dreyfuss. HBO, Nov. 2.

Ray Charles: 50 Years of Music—A celebration of Ray Charles and his music. With Quincy Jones, MC Hammer, Stevie Wonder, Willie Nelson. Fox, Oct. 6.

Sarah, Plain and Tall—A *Hallmark Hall of Fame* drama set in 1910 Kansas about a widowed father who advertises for a woman to care for his family. With Glenn Close, Christopher Walken. CBS, Feb. 3.

Semiramide—A *Metropolitan Opera Presents* telecast of the Rossini 1823 opera. With June Anderson, Marilyn Horne, Samuel Ramey. PBS, Oct. 16.

Separate But Equal—A two-part, fact-based TV movie that tells the story of Thurgood Marshall, later a Supreme Court justice, as the chief counsel in a civil-rights case involving bus transportation for a South Carolina school district. With Sidney Poitier, Burt Lancaster. ABC, April 7.

She Stood Alone—A TV movie about a schoolteacher in Connecticut who opens a school for young black women. With Mare Winningham. NBC, April 15.

Son of the Morning Star—A two-part TV movie centering on the figure of Gen. George Custer. With Gary Cole, Rosanna Arquette, Rodney A. Grant. ABC, Feb. 3.

The Story Lady—A TV movie about a widow who begins a career reading fairy tales on television. With Jessica Tandy. NBC, Dec. 9.

The Sunset Gang: Yiddish—An *American Playhouse* drama set in a Florida retirement community. With Harold Gould, Tresa Hughes, Doris Roberts. PBS, April 5.

Uncle Vanya—A *Great Performances* telecast of the Anton Chekhov stage classic, adapted by playwright David Mamet. With David Warner, Ian Bannen, Mary Elizabeth Mastrantonio. PBS, Feb. 22.

Whatever Happened to Baby Jane?—A TV movie recreating the original 1962 horror feature film. With Vanessa Redgrave and Lynn Redgrave. ABC, Feb. 17.

When It Was a Game—A tribute to the game of baseball. Narrated by Peter Kessler. HBO, July 8.

Who Will Teach for America?—An examination of the "Teach for America" program set up in inner-city and rural areas and modeled after the Peace Corps. PBS, Sept. 3.

Wild Texas Wind—A TV movie about a country singer whose husband/manager batters her. With Dolly Parton, Gary Busey. NBC, Sept. 23.

A Woman Named Jackie—A three-part miniseries adapted from C. David Heymann's biography of Jacqueline Kennedy Onassis. With Roma Downey. NBC, Oct. 13.

Young Catherine—A made-for-cable, two-part movie focusing on the early years of Catherine the Great of Russia. With Vanessa Redgrave. TNT, Feb. 17.

Competition for the Big Three Networks

By the 1990–91 season, the three fat slices of television viewership pie that for decades had belonged to the American Broadcast Companies (ABC), the Columbia Broadcasting System (CBS), and the National Broadcasting Company (NBC) had been sliced, slivered, and subdivided into see-through wafers of audience by cable TV, syndicated shows, and the still-young Fox Network.

Many observers blamed the general TV malaise on the ubiquitousness of remote-control channel changers in the hands of itchy-fingered, option-glutted viewers. And an even bigger culprit was the recession-spurred plunge of the advertising market, which cut deeply into the growth rates of both cable and Fox.

"It's mass chaos," ABC Entertainment Chief Robert A. Iger told *Fortune* magazine. He was describing a competition-leveled landscape in which the overall percentage of viewers tuning in the Big Three networks had dropped from 90% to 65% from 1980 to 1990; in which 70% of all new shows never made it to a second season; and in which even a popular show might switch time slots to latch onto an extra percentage point or two of ratings advantage.

Part of the trend resulted from an originality drought among the Big Three networks. *Time* magazine reported in late November 1990 that not one of the 22 new network shows introduced that season was a hit, and only ABC's *America's Funniest People* (a spin-off of the popular *America's Funniest Home Videos*) even finished in the top 30 of the Nielsen rankings. Neither were there any new programs to rival the previous season's *Twin Peaks* (ABC) and *The Simpsons* and *In Living Color* (both on Fox) in breaking new creative ground. *Time* quoted an industry executive as saying, "The networks are crying out for new stuff. But they're not sure what 'new' is or what to do with it when they find it." This crisis was crystallized in a summer 1991 issue of *Spy* magazine, which stated, "All you need to know is, the single hit of the year was PBS' *The Civil War*."

Meanwhile, however, some of the shift in TV-industry power did reflect well on higher production quality beyond the Big Three networks. *The Arsenio Hall Show* was a classic model of the new-wave syndicated show of network-level quality. The stylish late-night talk show with crossover appeal for both blacks and whites was picked up by so many independent stations—and even some CBS affiliates, lacking their own late-night alternative to NBC's *Tonight* and ABC's *Nightline*—that it was easy to mistake the show for a CBS-generated product.

The Arts and Entertainment Network (A&E) exemplified the network-caliber quality so long sought-after in cable but relatively late in arriving. For instance, in the 1991 fall season, A&E's *General Motors Playwrights Theater* was in some ways a throwback to the dramatic anthology programs in the golden age of live TV, offering recent one-act plays by dramatists such as Arthur Miller and Robert Anderson whose newest works had become hard-sells even on their home turf of the theater.

Even the basic lexicon of the TV industry had changed to reflect the profundity of the decade-long shift from network dominance: "Broadcast" was becoming obsolete, while "narrowcast" was the coming word. The continuing proliferation of new cable channels aimed at increasingly specific audiences—The Cowboy Channel, part-owned by singer Willie Nelson; and the Science Fiction Channel—showed just how narrow the casting, so to speak, had become.

DAN HULBERT

other of his trademark mock heart attacks from his old series *Sanford and Son*. But the flamboyant performer, who in the words of *People* magazine "brought the harsh black comedy of the Chitlin Circuit into mainstream American culture and cleared the road for such disciples as Richard Pryor and Eddie Murphy," was dead at 68. Michael Landon, who had starred in *Bonanza, Little House on the Prairie,* and *Highway to Heaven*, also died during the year.

Radio. In contrast to its long-beleaguered video cousin, PBS, National Public Radio (NPR) saw an upswing in its fortunes in 1991. Long admired for some of the best seasoned correspondents in the country (Nina Totenberg, Cokie Roberts, Noah Adams), and on the verge of bankruptcy as recently as 1983, the network enjoyed a larger listenership and budget in 1991, the *Washington Journalism Review* reported. During the year, veteran reporter Nina Totenberg scored a major scoop for NPR by her revelations of Anita Hill's charges of sexual harassment against the then-nominee for the U.S. Supreme Court, Clarence Thomas.

A radio industry report revealed that 4% of all U.S. stations on the AM dial—suffering from years of erratic business—shut down in 1990.

DAN HULBERT
"The Atlanta Journal and Constitution"

TENNESSEE

Members of Tennessee's legislature were frustrated in 1991 by increasing government costs accompanied by a decline in tax revenue caused by the lingering recession. Although it was not a good year for state agriculture, the state's economy as a whole showed growth.

Politics and Government. To meet increased government costs and also fund educational reforms proposed by Gov. Ned McWherter, the state legislature pondered tax reform; more particularly, they seriously examined McWherter's proposed tax on income—a revenue-producing stratagem carefully and methodically avoided by state leaders for many years. McWherter's plan would levy a 4% tax and remove the sales tax from utility and grocery items entirely while reducing it by nearly one third on everything else. This proposal would fund adequately all state business and also provide for sweeping improvements in public schools.

A vigorous minority supported the governor's plan, but others reported that ingrained opposition to any form of income tax was so pronounced among their constituents that they must oppose it. In the meantime, lawmakers discussed other proposals such as an intangible property tax, an increase in the sales tax, and a tax on incomes of $50,000 or more.

In early June when legislators recessed for two weeks, Governor McWherter stumped the state in vain to arouse interest in his tax plan. Ultimately, in late June lawmakers adjourned after accepting nearly $300 million in cuts which would leave many school systems gasping for survival. State educators termed the situation "the worst budget crisis in two generations."

Meanwhile, a lawsuit filed by a coalition of 77 rural counties and schools seeking a more equitable distribution of educational funds among Tennessee's 95 counties resulted in a court decision voiding the state's public-school-funding system and ordering that the funding formula be corrected by mid-1992 so that funds are distributed equally among all public schools. At year's end, Governor McWherter and legislators continued to debate various plans for increased taxes designed to raise funds adequate to ensure quality education in all public schools.

Economy. The overall state economy displayed growth, owing in large measure to a continued expansion of foreign investments. Smyrna's Nissan Motors announced plans to employ 2,200 additional people and pump a $200 million annual payroll into the economy. Several Canadian companies also increased their presence in the state with expansions; they were led by Heil Quaker, which was employing more than 2,000 Tennesseans in making central heat and cooling systems.

Agriculture. While in the past farmers have complained of drought, in 1991 it was the heavy spring rains—especially in the western counties—which hindered planting and curtailed production. Cotton farmers in the Memphis and Jackson areas received April and May rainfall of 10 inches (25 cm) or more in excess of needs. Hay harvesting also was hindered in May in all sections of the state.

People in the News. Former Gov. Lamar Alexander (*see* BIOGRAPHY), vacating the presidency of the University of Tennessee, became U.S. secretary of education. He was replaced as university president by Joe Johnson, previously vice-president for administration. James Walker, named president of Middle Tennessee State University at Murfreesboro, became the first black to head a predominantly white state university. James Hefner became president of predominantly black Tennessee State University in Nashville, V. L. Rawlins was named president of Memphis State University, and Bert Bach became acting president of East Tennessee State University at Johnson City.

Willie Herenton was elected mayor of Memphis, becoming the first black mayor of a major Tennessee city. Nashville businessman Phil Bredesen, elected to his first political office, became mayor of Nashville, and Victor Ashe was reelected Knoxville mayor. Roy G. Lillard, widely recognized state and local historian, died at his home in Cleveland.

ROBERT E. CORLEW
Middle Tennessee State University

TENNESSEE • Information Highlights

Area: 42,144 sq mi (109 152 km^2).
Population (1990 census): 4,877,185.
Chief Cities (1990 census): Nashville-Davidson, the capital, 510,784; Memphis, 610,337; Knoxville, 165,121; Chattanooga, 152,466; Clarksville, 75,494.
Government (1991): *Chief Officer*—governor, Ned McWherter (D); *General Assembly*—Senate, 33 members; House of Representatives, 99 members.
State Finances (fiscal year 1990): *Revenue,* $9,110,000,000; *expenditure,* $8,403,000,000.
Personal Income (1990): $77,540,000,000; per capita, $15,866.
Labor Force (June 1991): *Civilian labor force,* 2,440,800; *unemployed,* 167,600 (6.9% of total force).
Education: *Enrollment* (fall 1989)—public elementary schools, 590,121; public secondary, 229,539; colleges and universities, 218,866. *Public school expenditures* (1989), $2,668,341,000.

TERRORISM

The year 1991 was one of the most paradoxical in the history of terrorism, beginning on a pessimistic note with the highest worldwide security alert ever for international terrorism but ending on an optimistic one with the apparent conclusion to the hostage dramas in Lebanon.

In between, there were enough incidents to indicate that terrorism would remain an international problem.

Persian Gulf War. The fear of an Iraqi-sponsored terrorist campaign during the early 1991 Gulf war led to increased security measures at airports and border points around the globe. It also raised public fears to unprecedented heights as Americans rushed to buy gas masks in anticipation of terrorists unleashing chemical and biological agents on U.S. soil. While this did not happen, there were several conventional terrorist attacks in other regions related to the war. These included the assassinations of a retired U.S. serviceman on February 7 and a retired chief master sergeant on March 22 in Turkey. The leftist extremist group Dev Sol claimed credit for the attacks. On February 3 a sniper attack on a shuttle bus in the Red Sea port of Jidda, Saudi Arabia, injured two U.S. soldiers. There also were bombings at the Bank of Egypt to protest Cairo's role in the multinational force. Abu Iyad, the second in command of the Palestine Liberation Organization (PLO), and Hayel Abdel-Hamid, the PLO security chief, were assassinated in Tunis on January 14. The assassin was the bodyguard for one of the victims and was reported to be a former member of the Abu Nidal organization.

Assassinations. The leftist German Red Army Faction was suspected of killing a leading German industrialist, Detlev Karsten Rohwedder, on April 1, while the leftist Greek terrorist group November 17 was suspected of the assassination of a Turkish diplomat in Athens on October 7. Meanwhile, Palestinian terrorists were suspected of setting off a parcel bomb in the port city of Patras, Greece, on April 19 that killed seven people, including the Palestinian student who carried the explosives. A U.S. Air Force sergeant was killed by a remote-control bomb on March 12 outside his suburban Athens home. November 17 was suspected.

The long reach of state-sponsored terrorism was illustrated when former Iranian Premier Shahpur Bakhtiar was assassinated in Paris. French authorities on September 18 charged an Iranian businessman and former correspondent for Iran's state broadcasting service as an accomplice. Bakhtiar had been a critic of the Islamic government in Iran.

A Cuban exile was arrested in Miami on April 23 and later was convicted in connection with the 1976 killing of Orlando Letelier, the former Chilean ambassador to the United States. Letelier had been the ambassador during the regime of Salvador Allende, which was toppled by a military coup led by Gen. Augusto Pinochet. In a related development, the Chilean Supreme Court upheld indictments of two chiefs of the former military government's secret police who were charged with the assassination of Letelier. Meanwhile, a rightist senator and former aide to Pinochet, Jamie Guzman, was assassinated on April 1.

IRA. The Irish Republican Army (IRA) launched one of its most daring attacks on February 7 when three mortar rounds were fired at 10 Downing Street, barely missing a room where Prime Minister John Major was holding a cabinet meeting. The attack was launched from a van across the street. The IRA followed these attacks with two more bombings on February 18 in railway stations in London, killing one person and injuring 38 other people during the early-morning rush hour.

India and Pakistan. The year 1991 also demonstrated that suicide terrorist attacks were not just the domain of religious fanatics in the Middle East. In India the Liberation Tigers of Tamil Eelam (TTE) were suspected of assassinating former Indian Prime Minister Rajiv Gandhi as he campaigned on May 21. A woman detonated a bomb that was tied around her waist as she bowed down to greet Gandhi. In Pakistan, Justice Nabi Sher Jujeno, a senior judge who heard cases of terrorism, was killed in Karachi on June 18.

India also was plagued with terrorist violence in the Punjab, where Sikh separatists were waging a violent campaign. Among the incidents was the June 15 massacre by Sikh militants of 76 Hindus on two passenger trains. An Indian security operation in Punjab in mid-July resulted in more than 60 deaths.

Hijackings. Hijackings continued to occur in 1991. A Soviet Aeroflot plane was hijacked by Chechen-Ingush separatists and flown to Ankara, Turkey, on November 9, while an Italian jet en route to Tunis from Rome was hijacked by a young Arab man on September 19. Both incidents were resolved peacefully.

The legacy of violence surrounding Salman Rushdie's novel *The Satanic Verses* continued in 1991. In Japan a translator of the book was stabbed to death on July 12, while another translator in Italy was attacked with a knife on July 3. Many Muslims continued to find the book blasphemous.

Middle East. Only two Germans remained in captivity—and an Italian was presumed dead—following the dramatic release of the remaining British and U.S. hostages in Lebanon late in the year. Meanwhile the United States and Scotland indicted two Libyans for the 1988 bombing of Pan Am flight 103 over Lockerbie, Scotland, which killed 270 people. Despite the indictment—and the unlikely prospects the Libyans ever would be handed over to the United States by Libyan leader Muammar el-Qaddafi—many analysts still believed that Syria and Iran also were involved in the bombing. In a separate case, a French judge issued arrest warrants for four Libyans in connection with the 1989 bombing of a French UTA airliner en route from the Congo capital, Brazzaville, to Paris, which killed 170 people. The same type of triggering device was used in both cases, and both bombs were plastic explosive Semtex.

Terrorists struck prior to the beginning of the Mideast peace talks in Madrid in the fall, with Islamic extremists claiming responsibility for two car bombings in Ankara that killed a U.S. serviceman and injured an Egyptian diplomat in October. An ambush on a bus in the occupied West Bank killed two Israeli settlers and wounded five people.

JEFFREY D. SIMON, *Free-lance Writer*

TEXAS

Economic conditions in Texas took a turn for the better in 1991, despite announced layoffs at the Frito-Lay and Shell Oil companies. In the aftermath of the war in the Persian Gulf, oil prices remained stable, encouraging increased drilling activity. Unemployment remained below the national average, and Houston boasted of creating 4,000 new jobs, more than any other comparable U.S. city. Other welcome news for Houston was its selection in January as the site of the 1992 Republican National Convention. The prospect of a mutually beneficial trade agreement between the United States and Mexico added to the economic luster of Laredo and El Paso, and San Antonio, Dallas, and Austin continued to attract new high-tech industries.

Politics. Gov. Ann Richards, who took office in January, had stressed fiscal responsibility during the 1990 campaign, while also emphasizing increased state funding for education and social services. In the early months of her tenure the governor made many minority appointments, seized control of insurance regulation, and forced a moratorium on new hazardous-waste sites.

A blue-ribbon committee, chaired by former Gov. John Connally, recommended a state income tax to handle a budget shortfall of $4.6 billion, but the proposal failed in the state legislature. The legislature granted approval to a French consortium to build a "bullet train" to run from Houston to Dallas, but no state bonds were issued to facilitate construction. Reflecting the 1990 census returns, the legislature crafted three new electoral districts assuring additional Democratic seats in the U.S. House of Representatives.

AP/Wide World

Bob Lanier, 66-year-old real-estate developer, defeated state Rep. Sylvester Turner, a black, in Houston's nonpartisan mayoralty runoff election on Dec. 3, 1991.

In 1991 mayoral races, Bob Lanier was elected mayor of Houston; former U.S. Rep. Steve Bartlett was chosen mayor of Dallas; Kay Granger was the first woman to be elected mayor of Fort Worth; and City Councilman Nelson Wolff was selected as San Antonio's mayor. In November, Texans voted to establish a state lottery, which would begin some operations in 1992.

Education. Lower revenues than anticipated in Dallas forced teacher and staff firings. Parents protested and demanded reinstatement of the teachers, which eventually was done. In order to meet the Texas Supreme Court's guidelines for essentially equal funding for every school district, local property taxes were raised throughout the state. Declining Scholastic Aptitude Test (SAT) scores and a soaring minority-dropout rate were major disappointments. Higher-education tuition was raised again with particular emphasis on out-of-state students. A lawsuit was filed by Hispanic groups, charging state officials with intentionally underfunding colleges and universities in south and west Texas. The suit alleged that Hispanics in a 41-county region from El Paso to Corpus Christi to the Mexican border were denied equal educational opportunities, violating the Texas constitution.

TEXAS • Information Highlights

Area: 266,807 sq mi (691 030 km²).
Population (1990 census): 16,986,510.
Chief Cities (1990 census): Austin, the capital, 465,622; Houston, 1,630,553; Dallas, 1,006,877; San Antonio, 935,933; El Paso, 515,342; Fort Worth, 447,619; Corpus Christi, 257,453.
Government (1991): *Chief Officers*—governor, Ann Richards (D); lt. gov., Bob Bullock (D). *Legislature*—Senate, 31 members; House of Representatives, 150 members.
State Finances (fiscal year 1990): *Revenue,* $30,975,000,000; *expenditure,* $26,027,000,000.
Personal Income (1990): $285,085,000,000; per capita, $16,716.
Labor Force (June 1991): *Civilian labor force,* 8,644,800; *unemployed,* 523,400 (6.1% of total force).
Education: *Enrollment* (fall 1989)—public elementary schools, 2,443,245; public secondary, 885,269; colleges and universities, 877,859. *Public school expenditures* (1989), $11,761,447,000.

Other News. Urban crime was on the rise in Houston, Dallas, and other major Texas cities. Many homicides were drug-related, but demands for increased police protection conflicted with declining local revenues. Public-opinion polls in Houston, where the murder rate was the highest in the South, indicated that voters preferred more resources dedicated to fighting crime than to a proposed monorail transportation system.

Tragedy struck Killeen, TX, in October when gunman George Hennard went on a shooting spree in a restaurant, leaving 24 persons, including himself, dead.

December flooding devastated parts of southeastern Texas, taking at least 15 lives and causing millions of dollars in property damage.

STANLEY E. SIEGEL, *University of Houston*

THAILAND

On Feb. 23, 1991, a military junta led by Gen. Suchina Kraprayoon overthrew Thailand's elected government of Premier Chatichai Choonhavan. Many Thais were upset by the setback to democracy, but Chatichai's government was considered deeply corrupt and had little popular support. An event that helped precipitate the coup was Premier Chatichai's February 20 appointment of Deputy Prime Minister Arthit Kamlang-ek, who was unpopular among army commanders, as deputy defense minister.

Politics. The new regime was headed by Anan Panyarachun, a highly respected former diplomat and business leader. Many of the people Anan chose for his cabinet, including Deputy Prime Minister Sano Unakun and Finance Minister Suthi Singsane, had served under Chatichai's predecessor, Prem Tinsulanonda.

Anan showed his independence from the junta by warning its members publicly to keep their promise to hold elections and not cling to power. But in November the junta produced a new constitution that gave the appointed Senate the right to participate in choosing the prime minister and to vote with the elected lower house in budget and no-confidence debates. Anan denounced these provisions, and the major parties and civil-rights groups held rallies in Bangkok.

Economics. The Thai economy grew at a spectacular rate of 10% per year from 1986-90. Although the 1991 Persian Gulf war briefly undermined Thailand's major industry—tourism—the economy continued to grow rapidly in 1991. This allowed Anan's cabinet much leeway to carry out reforms desired by the business community, which included privatizing state industries and curbing the powers of public-sector labor unions. Anan also favored moving ahead with vast multibillion-dollar infrastructure projects begun by Chatichai's government.

The military junta courted public support by reducing taxes and gasoline prices, but it lacked the moral and political strength to prevail when its policies clashed with those of Anan's cabinet. Thus, the generals wanted to develop northeast Thailand and other border regions where the military controlled the economy. But Anan won out with infrastructure projects.

In one important test of wills, the military deputy communications minister threatened to resign when his civilian minister proposed rewriting a $3.9 billion contract to upgrade the telephone system. The minister's aim was to make the system less monopolistic. Anan stepped in and mediated the dispute in favor of the civilian minister.

By casting aside the traditional Thai parties and politicians, the junta cleared the way for rapid growth of the New Aspiration Party (NAP). Its leader, Gen. Chaovalit Yongchaiyut, once had been the mentor of coup leader Suchina, and Chaovalit seemed at first to favor the coup. But as the months passed, he became increasingly critical of the coup leaders, who were all members of the influential fifth graduating class of Chulachomklao Military Academy.

Foreign Relations. The junta was anxious to protect the security of Thai borders as well as a range of cross border economic operations run by the military. Thus, it pursued close ties with the military regime in Myanmar (Burma) and allowed Anan and Foreign Minister Asa Sarasin to improve relations with the Communist regimes in Vietnam, Laos, and Cambodia in order to expand trade. This was similar to the foreign policy pursued by the previous government. But Anan was more careful than Chatichai to avoid getting out of step with Thailand's partners in the Association of Southeast Asian Nations.

PETER A. POOLE
Author, "The Vietnamese in Thailand"

THAILAND • Information Highlights

Official Name: Kingdom of Thailand (conventional); Prathet Thai (Thai).
Location: Southeast Asia.
Area: 198,456 sq mi (514 000 km²).
Population (mid-1991 est.): 58,800,000.
Chief City (June 30, 1989 est.): Bangkok, the capital, 5,845,152.
Government: *Head of state,* Bhumibol Adulyadej, king (acceded June 1946). *Head of government,* Anan Panyarachun, prime minister (took power Feb. 1991).
Monetary Unit: Baht (25.73 baht equal U.S.$1, July 1991).
Gross National Product (1989 est. U.S.$): $64,500,000,000.
Economic Index (Bangkok, 1990): *Consumer Prices* (1980 = 100), all items, 157.8; food, 150.5.
Foreign Trade (1990 U.S.$): *Imports,* $32,746,000,000; *exports,* $22,972,000,000.

THEATER

The U.S. theater enjoyed some memorable achievements in 1991: Robert Shenkkan's sprawling *The Kentucky Cycle* epic of Appalachian history at the Intiman Theatre of Seattle, the opening of a state-of-the-art theater (with a guest performance by Albert Finney) for the renowned Steppenwolf Theatre Company in Chicago, and a stupendously successful tour of *The Phantom of the Opera* that brought back hundreds of thousands of patrons who had not seen a live theatrical performance in years. But like soldiers reveling for all they are worth on the eve of terrible battle, the artists could not quite shake the doomsday mood. From Broadway to the furthest corners of the resident-theater map, the U.S. theater was in grave trouble.

In addition to the perennial bugaboo of money—stagnant funding levels from a recession-hit private sector and a Republican administration unfriendly to helping the arts, resulting in the closing of the multiculturally progressive Los Angeles Theater Center—there was a disturbing drought of creativity. There simply were not enough good new plays. New musicals, because they are even more expensive, were even scarcer. Writers as well as actors and directors were breaking ranks and heading for the alluring lucre of Hollywood (playwright David Mamet, for example, scored solidly as writer-director of the film *Homicide*).

Nor were there enough new big-stature artistic directors to reinforce the aging ranks of the founders of the nonprofit theater movement, decimated by death (Joseph Papp of the New York Shakespeare Festival Public The-

Keith Carradine found himself up in the air as the folksy humorist Will Rogers in The Will Rogers Follies, *a nostalgic revue directed by dancer-choreographer Tommy Tune. The production garnered several Tony Awards, including those for best musical and for best musical direction.*

atre and William Ball of the American Conservatory Theatre in San Francisco)—*see* OBITUARIES—and by retirement or semiretirement (Zelda Fichandler of Washington's Arena Stage and Lloyd Richards of the Yale Repertory Theatre). Deprived of the built-in charisma and freedom of vision that goes with being a founder, the new caretaker generation of artistic directors struggled with the questions of where, artistically, they wanted to go and how they possibly could get there on their dwindling budgets.

There were no clear answers on the horizon.

Broadway. The unhealthy "blockbuster syndrome" (a few splashy productions masking the shriveled reality of the Broadway scene) became even more exaggerated in 1991. The deceptive "busters" of the spring were *Miss Saigon* and *The Will Rogers Follies*. Among the spring 1991 entries, they dominated the theater talk and box office, but they hardly could have been more different.

Miss Saigon was a high-tech pop-opera epic from the British master of the form, Cameron Mackintosh (*Cats*), reunited with the French composer-lyricist team, Claude-Michel Schonberg and Alain Boublil of *Les Misérables* fame. Boublil's book and lyrics rather simplistically synthesize the U.S. experience in Vietnam. Updating the West-betrays-East theme of *Madame Butterfly*, it is the effectively tear-jerking tale of a Vietnamese "bar girl" who is abandoned by her G.I. lover during the fall of Saigon, bears his child, and then is revisited by him and his American wife after the war.

Coolly manipulative compared to the authentically moving *Les Misérables, Miss Saigon* was memorable mainly for its spectacular designs, the cinematic sweep of Nicholas Hytner's direction, and the lead performances (each rewarded with a Tony Award) of Lea Salonga as the courageous girl and Jonathan Pryce as her sublimely slimy procurer. The showstopper (with Boublil's best lyrics and Schönberg's best tune), was "The American Dream," which could have been another tiresome capitalism-is-bad lesson if not for the delightfully demonic performance of Pryce, simulating sex with a white Cadillac gliding across the stage.

It was a double triumph for Pryce, who had much to prove. Spurred by complaints by Asian-Americans (including *M. Butterfly* author David Henry Hwang) that the role of the French-Vietnamese pimp should go to an Asian, not the white Englishman Pryce, Actor's Equity threatened not to issue him a permit to work in the United States. Producer Mackintosh countered by threatening to keep the show in London (where Pryce's performance was deemed unbeatable) and never open it in New York. Equity, criticized by several newspaper commentators for its misplaced sense of minority advocacy, caved in and reversed its decision.

© Michael LePoer Trench

In the British musical import Miss Saigon, *Lea Salonga won a Tony Award for best actress as a Vietnamese girl abandoned by her G.I. lover during the fall of Saigon.*

However, the British Mackintosh probably paid a price for his power play among the clannish U.S. theater professionals who make up the Tony Awards voters. *The Will Rogers Follies*—a lavish revue wallowing in nostalgia that starred Keith Carradine as the folksy humorist of the title who emcees an imaginary edition of the Ziegfeld Follies—was redeemed from sheer blandness mainly by the clever production numbers of director-choreographer Tommy Tune (*see* BIOGRAPHY). And yet it won the Tony for best musical, probably a beneficiary of *Saigon*'s backstage controversy.

Likewise *The Secret Garden,* a slow and moody musicalization of the Edwardian mystery-fantasy novel, as popular with women and girls as it was unstimulating to most men, was an upset Tony Award winner for Marsha Norman's book.

The upset among plays was the dominance of the Tony Awards by Neil Simon's *Lost in Yonkers,* named best play over John Guare's *Six Degrees of Separation.* Simon's moving family comedy-drama, set in the 1930s, cast the great Irene Worth as a tyrannical mother and Mercedes Ruehl as her heartbreakingly repressed daughter—both sterling performances for which the women won Tonys. The play also won the 1991 Pulitzer Prize for drama.

Six Degrees, based on the true case of a young black man who bilked wealthy whites by impersonating the son of Sidney Poitier, was a provocative inquiry into the mysteries of identity and race, liberally sprinkled with suspense and witty comedy-of-the-times. It provided excellent vehicles for Courtney B. Vance as the gracefully cunning con artist and Stockard Channing as the stylish Manhattanite that he dupes.

The only Broadway period that conceivably could have been worse than the spring of the 1990–91 season was the fall of the 1991–92 season. *Nick and Nora,* as the only new musical, became the hapless emblem of the funereal fall. After lurching through frantic rewrites over a nine-week preview period, surrounded by bad word of mouth, the comedy-mystery musical based on the *Thin Man* films only lasted a week. This demise occurred despite a distinguished—if aging—creative team: author-director Arthur Laurents (*Gypsy*), composer Charles Strouse (*Annie*), and lyricist Richard Maltby, Jr. The only redeeming feature in the flat, muddled show was the wry Joanna Gleason, perhaps Broadway's most dependable actress since the mid-1980s, in the Myrna Loy role of Nora.

A godsend to the otherwise barren dramatic scene was *Dancing at Lughnasa* (pronounced LOO-na-sa), from Dublin's Abbey Theatre by way of London's West End. A lyrical, funny, haunting memory play from Brian Friel, it evoked Chekhov in the way that it captured the thwarted lives of the narrator's mother and her four grown sisters (all unmarried) in a small Irish village, set against the ghostly pagan resonance of a Celtic harvest festival. The production, with most of its original Abbey cast intact, was stunning.

Tony Randall (left), *founder in 1991 of New York's National Actors Theatre, understudied an ailing actor in* The Crucible, *the company's first production.*

© Jim Estrin/NYT Pictures

Another hopeful beacon was the enlistment of an astonishing 28,000 season subscribers to the first, sight-unseen season of Tony Randall's National Actors Theatre. Although reviews were mixed on the first of the limited-run productions in the Belasco theater—Arthur Miller's *The Crucible,* starring Martin Sheen as the courageous Salem-witch-hunt martyr John Proctor—it was inspiring to see a new classical-repertory troupe so enthusiastically supported in the United States of 1991.

Nonprofit Theater. In the nonprofit resident theaters (the preferred name for what used to be known as regional theaters), 1991 was a kind of unnaturally quiet intermission, as theaters paused to wonder where the next wave of leaders would come from.

In the New York institutions, there was an extensive directorial shuffle. After leading a five-year rebirth of Lincoln Center Theater, Gregory Mosher was edged out in favor of Playwrights Horizons founding director Andre Bishop, leaving a void of new Lincoln Center entries in the fall. As actor-director Don Scardino took Bishop's old post, one of Bishop's final Horizons offerings—*Marvin's Room* by Scott McPherson, an inky black comedy about love and compassion in the midst of overwhelming medical calamities—was greeted by major New York critics as one of the most important new plays of the year.

But the most forbiddingly difficult of the director transitions was at the New York Shakespeare Festival Public Theatre. Although the visionary and colorful Joseph Papp left the institution in relatively strong shape, his death from cancer was a devastating symbolic blow not only to the Public Theatre but to the whole nonprofit-theater movement. His hand-picked successor, JoAnne Akalaitis, was an avant-garde iconoclast with just a fraction of his base of popular support. From her severe presentation of Brecht's *In the Jungle of Cities*—one of the few stagings in the Public Theatre's autumn of disarray—it appeared she was not about to change her style.

The leadership gap was also conspicuous outside New York, with interim directors stretching out unusually long tenures as permanent artistic directors were sought by the Trinity Square Repertory in Providence, RI, and the Dallas [TX] Theater Center.

It was a relatively smooth and productive season for two off-Broadway resident theaters: The New York Theatre Workshop presented the U.S. premiere of Caryl Churchill's *The Mad Forest,* impressions of exhilaration and terror at the fall of the Nicolae Ceaușescu regime in Romania; and Lynn Meadows' Manhattan Theatre Club had a productive stable for playwrights that included Terrence McNally (the popular comedy about relationships, *Lips*

BROADWAY OPENINGS | 1991

MUSICALS

Gypsy!, music by Jule Styne; lyrics by Stephen Sondheim; book by Arthur Laurents; directed by Laurents; with Tyne Daly, Jonathan Hadary, Crista Moore; April 28-July 14.

Miss Saigon, music by Claude-Michel Schönberg; lyrics by Alain Boublil and Richard Maltby, Jr.; directed by Nicholas Hytner; with Jonathan Pryce (April 11–Dec. 15), Francis Ruivivar (Dec. 16–), Lea Salonga, Willy Falk (April 11–Dec. 15), Sean McDermott (Dec. 16–), Hinton Battle; April 11–.

Nick & Nora, music by Charles Strouse; lyrics by Richard Maltby, Jr.; book by Arthur Laurents; directed by Laurents; with Christine Baranski, Barry Bostwick, Joanna Gleason, Chris Sarandon; Dec. 8–15.

Peter Pan, lyrics by Carolyn Leigh, with additional lyrics by Betty Comden and Adolph Green; music by Moose Charlap, with additional music by Jule Styne; directed by Fran Soeder; with Cathy Rigby; Nov. 26–.

The Secret Garden, book and lyrics by Marsha Norman, based on the novel by Frances H. Burnett; music by Lucy Simon; directed by Susan H. Schulman; with Mandy Patinkin, Daisy Eagan, Rebecca Luker; April 25–.

The Will Rogers Follies, book by Peter Stone; lyrics by Betty Comden and Adolph Green; music by Cy Coleman; directed by Tommy Tune; with Keith Carradine, Dee Hoty; May 1–.

PLAYS

La Bête, by David Hirson; directed by Richard Jones; with Tom McGowan, Michael Cumpsty, James Greene, Dylan Baker; Feb. 10–March 2.

The Big Love, by Brooke Allen and Jay Presson Allen; directed by Jay Presson Allen; with Tracey Ullman; March 3–April 7.

Catskills on Broadway, conceived by Freddie Roman; with Roman, Marilyn Michaels, Mal Z. Lawrence, Dick Capri; Dec. 5–.

The Crucible, by Arthur Miller; directed by Yossi Yzraely; with Maryann Plunkett, Martin Sheen, Fritz Weaver, Michael York; Dec. 10–.

Dancing at Lughnasa, by Brian Friel; directed by Patrick Mason; with Bríd Brennan, Catherine Byrne, Donal Donnelly, Robert Gwilym, Rosaleen Linehan, Gerard McSorley, Dearbhla Molloy, Bríd Ní Neachtain; Oct. 24–.

Getting Married, by George Bernard Shaw; directed by Stephen Porter; with Victoria Tennant, Simon Jones, Lee Richardson, Elizabeth Franz; June 26–Aug. 25.

I Hate Hamlet, by Paul Rudnick; directed by Michael Engler, with Nicol Williamson, Evan Handler, Celeste Holm; April 8-June 22.

The Homecoming, by Harold Pinter; directed by Gordon Edelstein; with Lindsay Crouse, Roy Dotrice, Daniel Gerroll, Jonathan Hogan; Oct. 27–Dec 8.

Lost in Yonkers, by Neil Simon; directed by Gene Saks; with Mark Blum, Mercedes Ruehl (Feb. 21–Aug. 25), Jane Kaczmarek (Aug. 26–), Irene Worth (Feb. 21–Aug. 25), Mercedes McCambridge (Aug. 26–), Kevin Spacey (Feb. 21–Aug. 11), Bruno Kirby (Aug. 12–), Lauren Klein; Feb. 21–.

Lucifer's Child, by William Luce, based on the writings of Isak Dinesen; directed by Tony Abatemarco; with Julie Harris; April 4–27.

Mule Bone, by Langston Hughes and Zora Neale Hurston; directed by Michael Schultz; with Arthur French, Eric Ware, Kenny Neal, Leonard Jackson, Akosua Busia; Feb. 14–April 14.

On Borrowed Time, by Paul Osborn (based on the novel by L.E. Watkin); directed by George C. Scott; with Scott, Conrad Bain, Nathan Lane, Teresa Wright; Oct. 9–.

Our Country's Good, by Timberlake Wertenbaker, based on a novel by Thomas Keneally; directed by Mark Lamos; with Tracey Ellis, Richard Poe, Peter Frechette; April 29–June 8.

Park Your Car in Harvard Yard, by Israel Horovitz; directed by Zoe Caldwell; with Jason Robards, Judith Ivey; Nov. 7–.

The Speed of Darkness, by Steve Tesich; directed by Robert Falls; with Len Cariou, Stephen Lang, Lisa Eichhorn; Feb. 28–March 30.

Taking Steps, by Alan Ayckbourn; directed by Alan Strachan; with Jane Summerhays, Christopher Benjamin, Jonathan Hogan, Pippa Pearthree, Bill Buell, Spike McClure; Feb. 20–April 28.

OTHER ENTERTAINMENT

André Heller's Wonderhouse, by André Heller; directed by Heller; with Billy Barty, Patty Maloney, Gunilla Wingquist; Oct. 20–27.

A Christmas Carol, with Patrick Stewart; Dec. 19–29.

Moscow Circus, Nov. 6–.

Penn & Teller, comedy; with Penn Jillette and Teller; April 3–.

Together, Teeth Apart) and John Patrick Shanley (the dark family memory play, *Beggars in the House of Plenty*).

It was a quiet, unexceptional year for other well-known playwrights. Among the few who were heard from were August Wilson (*Two Trains Running* at Washington's Kennedy Center) and Sam Shepard (*States of Shock* at off-Broadway's American Place Theatre), both of who were not up to their usual form.

The Royal Shakespeare Company's distinguished Ron Daniels guest-directed *Hamlet* at Boston's American Repertory Theatre and the Pittsburgh Public Theatre (an increasingly common instance of a cost-saving joint production by two or more theaters). Meanwhile, artistic directors Mark Lamos and Michael Kahn continued their high standards of classics productions at the Hartford [CT] Stage and the Shakespeare Theatre at the Folger in Washington, DC, respectively.

At the Humana Festival of New American Plays at Actors Theatre of Louisville, the greatest emotional impact was scored by Shirley Lauro's *A Piece of My Heart,* based on the experiences of U.S. women in the Vietnam war (although the play fared less well in its remounting at the Manhattan Theatre Club).

As for good new musicals, their requirements for larger collaborative teams and budget demands threatened to make them obsolete; Hal Prince's New Musicals Workshop, based in the New York suburbs, went under, as if to press home the specter. Even the superb composer-lyricist Stephen Sondheim faltered with *Assassins,* a typically bold off-Broadway attempt to musicalize those who kill or attempt to kill presidents.

Happily there were a few glimmers of musical success. William Finn's *Falsettoland* at New York's Playwrights Horizons, John Bishop's *Elmer Gantry* at the La Jolla [CA] Playhouse, and *The Harvey Milk Show,* by the unknown Dan Pruitt and Patrick Hutchinson at Atlanta's Actors Express, were among those offerings that tried to present real issues and provocative ideas within the naturally emotional, manipulative form of the musical.

DAN HULBERT
"The Atlanta Journal and Constitution"

TRANSPORTATION

Transportation did not enjoy a prosperous 1991. Continuing weakness in general business conditions depressed traffic and decreased earnings of freight and passenger carriers, and triggered significant corporate failures and changes in the structure of the industry.

Airlines. Top events in air transport in 1991 included the cessation of operations by Pan American World Airways (Pan Am), Eastern Airlines, and Midway Airlines, and the emergence of United Airlines, American Airlines, and Delta Air Lines as major international carriers. First to close was Eastern, which stopped flying in January after its earnings proved insufficient to meet creditors' claims and support emergence from protection of the bankruptcy laws. Eastern's demise was preceded by years of labor-management strife and by allegations of managerial incompetence traceable to its founder, World War I flying ace Eddie Rickenbacker.

Midway Airlines, founded in 1979 and one of the few surviving carriers spawned by deregulation, ceased flying on November 14. In March it had filed for bankruptcy protection but continued to fly in an effort to restructure and regain solvency. However, higher fuel prices and declines in traffic induced by the Persian Gulf war and the recession cut too deeply into the company's resources. Midway then entered into an agreement to be acquired by Northwest Airlines. The agreement included a $40 million line of credit to cover Midway's operating expenses. Northwest withdrew from the agreement on November 13, leaving Midway with insufficient cash to continue operations.

Pan Am began 1991 by filing for bankruptcy protection on January 8, while continuing to operate. On July 28 it agreed to sell its European and Asian routes, Frankfurt-hub assets, East Coast shuttle, and various aircraft to Delta Air Lines for $460 million. As part of the purchase agreement Delta was to fund Pan Am's operating losses while Pan Am worked to regain profitability by transforming itself into a smaller airline focusing primarily on routes to the Caribbean and Latin America. In return Delta was to receive a 45% share in Pan Am when it emerged from bankruptcy. However, after having paid $115 million in operating assistance, Delta indicated on December 3 that it would provide no more funds. Unable to arrange alternative financing, Pan Am terminated all operations on December 4. This marked the end of what had been considered the world's premier airline during the 1940s and 1950s.

Several carriers quickly bid for Pan Am's remaining assets. Its commuter affiliate, Pan Am Express, was split between Trans World Airlines' (TWA's) commuter subsidiary, TW Express, and Business Express, Delta's commuter affiliate. On December 9, United Airlines purchased Pan Am's Latin American operations for $135 million. This made United the only airline with major operations on Pacific, North Atlantic, and Latin American routes, and also the top airline in the world ranked by total number of revenue passenger miles per year. By the same measure, American Airlines and Delta stood as the world's second- and third-largest air carriers.

Dec. 4, 1991: Passengers planning to travel to San Domingo aboard a Pan American World Airways flight are stranded in New York as the 64-year-old airline terminates all operations.

Other carriers' actions also reflected the trend toward continuing shrinkage in airline population and concentration of traffic on relatively few very large carriers and their affiliates. British Airways and KLM proposed a merger, with Northwest Airlines as a possible third party to the combination. USAir, which lost $225 million in the first half of the year, and Air Canada, which lost $114 million during the same period, formed a strategic alliance covering marketing, operational, and technical activities. TWA and Continental Airlines, both burdened by heavy debts, began talks on a possible consolidation.

Sluggishness in traffic contributed to this trend. The number of international passengers carried by major U.S.-based airlines during January-July declined 6.25% from the same period in 1990, while the number of domestic passengers carried increased 1.36%. International-revenue passenger-kilometers declined 3.75%, and domestic-revenue passenger-kilometers increased 1.71%. Cargo traffic also was slow for the major carriers, with international-revenue ton-kilometers increasing 0.70% and domestic-revenue ton-kilometers decreasing 2.09% within the same time period.

Airlines specializing in cargo traffic also experienced difficulties. Emery Worldwide's deficit for the third quarter was $29.6 million, compared with a loss of about $9 million for the same period in 1990. This increased Emery's total losses to $300 million since its purchase in 1989 by Consolidated Freightways, a major trucking company. Revenue ton-kilometers on Federal Express in January-July declined 9.04% from the same period in 1990. Federal, along with competitors United Parcel Service, TNT Express Worldwide, and DHL Worldwide, continued efforts to achieve profitability in the operation of pan-European air-highway express-package service. All lost money on the service in 1991.

Bus. In October, Greyhound Lines, Inc. (GLI) successfully completed a financial reorganization and emerged from one and one half years of operation under protection of the bankruptcy laws. This accomplishment raised confidence in the long-term viability of the company, which operates the only nationwide intercity bus system in the United States. The number of revenue passengers carried by GLI during January-June increased 12.6% over the same period in 1990, and its net deficit decreased from $118.8 million to $15.5 million. Revenue ridership on the nine largest regional intercity bus lines during the first six months of the year decreased 4.4% from the same period in 1990, while the lines' aggregate deficit increased from almost $1.4 million to $2.7 million.

Rail. Total carload shipments on major U.S. freight railroads between January 1 and December 7 declined 4.8% from the same period in 1990, while estimated ton-miles increased 15.1%. Aggregate gross operating revenue for these carriers for the 12 months ended June 30 totaled $27.7 billion, a decline of 1.2% from the previous 12 months; net income from railway operation declined 24.6%, to $1.7 billion.

Many months of negotiations between the carriers and 11 unions over wages, benefits, work rules, and crew sizes resulted in the issuance on January 15 of a nonbinding Presidential Emergency Board (PEB) report recommending terms of settlement, such as an increase in the basic day from 108 to 130 mi (174 to 209 km) for train crews by 1995. Inability to reach full agreement precipitated a one-day national rail strike on April 17. Congress immediately passed legislation ending the strike, imposing PEB's recommendations, and creating an arbitration board to mandate settlement of remaining issues by June 21.

By year's end six carriers had negotiated agreements providing for crew-size reductions on part or all of their systems. The agreements, some still awaiting ratification by union members at year's end, typically provided for the operation of through freight trains by two-person crews (conductor and engineer). The position of brakeman was to be eliminated, except on wayfreight (local) trains and in yard switching operations, with ultimate elimination of an estimated 20,000 jobs. Such changes in labor agreements should enable carriers to cut costs and compete more effectively against other forms of transport.

Union Pacific, Santa Fe, and other large carriers continued efforts to transfer light- and medium-density line segments to short-line and regional railways. In December, Consolidated Rail Corporation (Conrail) announced that it would take an after-tax charge against income of between $420 million and $450 million, part of it to result from the future sale or abandonment of more than 2,000 mi (3 200 km) of underused facilities and lines in its 13,000-mi (21 000-km) system. Conrail also began a supplier program for regional and short-line carriers, offering locomotive repair, leasing and sales services, and locomotive-parts sales.

Wisconsin Central, the largest of the new regionals with more than 2,000 mi (3 200 km) of line, successfully completed a public stock offering and entered the Duluth-Chicago market by acquiring line segments in northern Wisconsin. This opened access to Canadian traffic through interchange with carriers at Duluth.

In the passenger sector, National Railroad Passenger Corporation (Amtrak) celebrated its 20th anniversary on May 1. The number of passengers carried from October 1990 through September 1991 declined slightly, to 22,031,972 from 22,186,300 in 1989–90. Passenger miles per train mile increased from 183.3 to 184.5 between the same periods. Amtrak's revenue-to-expense ratio (percentage of costs covered by company-generated revenues as distinguished from government subsidies) rose to 79% from 72% in 1990.

On April 7, Amtrak consolidated its New York City services into one station by moving all Empire Service trains from Grand Central Terminal to Pennsylvania Station. Two weeks later it signed a contract to purchase 140 new double-deck, long-distance Superliner cars. Wyoming regained Amtrak service in June after an eight-year absence. In California service (three daily round-trips) to Sacramento from San Jose—with intermediate stops at Oakland, Berkeley, and other important points —was initiated on December 11.

The German Federal Railway (Deutsche Bundesbahn—DB) opened its new 203-mi (327-km) Hannover-Würzburg line in June, equipped with new Inter-City Express (ICE) passenger trains operating at up to 175 mph (282 km/h). DB also inaugurated express freight trains over the line, with a maximum speed of 100 mph (160 km/h). On October 3, Japan's only working (experimental) magnetic-levitation (Maglev) train was destroyed by fire during test runs at speeds up to 320 mph (515 km/h).

Shipping. Ocean carriers grappled with the challenge of traffic volumes insufficient to utilize available capacity. Cargo volume between Europe and North America dropped by about 18% in 1991. Eastbound volume increased some 7%, but unused capacity remained. Eurocorde, a group of 11 North Atlantic carriers, met in November in Amsterdam to discuss ways of ending the rate-cutting that generated operating losses. No solutions resulted.

In the Pacific trade, Sea-Land Services and Maersk announced a vessel-sharing agreement in April. Under the agreement three containerships were withdrawn from the trade by each carrier and capacity on the remaining vessels was used for movement of container traffic of both carriers. American President Lines initiated a similar slot-chartering agreement with Orient Overseas Container Line in December. Other vessel-sharing and capacity-reduction agreements in the Atlantic and Gulf trades also were announced during the year. Participants included Atlantic Container Line and Hapag-

SPECIAL REPORT/TRANSPORTATION

U.S. Highways—New Policy Directions

On Nov. 27, 1991, the U.S. Congress passed the Intermodal Surface Transportation Efficiency Act of 1991, a six-year, $151 billion measure covering highway and other surface-transportation programs. For a highway system universally acknowledged to be in trouble, the legislation came none too soon. The U.S. Department of Transportation's (DOT's) 1991 biennial report on the status of the nation's highways and bridges found 265,000 mi (426 000 km) of arterial and collector highways in poor condition in 1989, and some 642,000 mi (1.03 million km)—approximately half of nonlocal roads—at or near the point at which their deteriorating conditions would impair vehicle operations. The DOT report also found about 70% of daily peak-hour travel on the urban segments of the Interstate System subjected to congestion, causing more than 8 billion hours of delays and costing an estimated $120 billion in lost time. Structural deficiencies were reported to exist in 23% of the nation's 134,000 highway bridges.

The new act, signed by President Bush on December 18, not only changes the way highways and public transportation are financed, it provides research funds for, among other things, finding ways to tax motorists by the amount of congestion they cause rather than by the amount of gasoline they use; development of Intelligent Vehicle Highway Systems (IVHS)—the use of satellites, video, and subsurface sensors to monitor traffic; electronic toll-collecting systems that would eliminate toll-booth tie-ups; and "smart car" devices that provide dashboard navigation and traffic information.

Passage of the act involved ten months of arduous political effort extending nearly two months beyond the expiration of predecessor legislation. Contentious points included the amount of motor-fuel taxes, transferability of funding between highway and mass-transit programs, and federal-state ratios for funding. In final form, the new act's major provisions include the following highlights:

- *Highway System.* A new, 155,000-mi (250 000-km) National Highway System, consisting of the existing 44,000-mi (71 000-km) Interstate System and other roads to be selected by the states, is designated. It includes 31 corridors seen by Congress as deserving top priority in project funding.
- *Funding.* Highway and bridge construction and repair funding of $119.5 billion and $31.5 billion for mass-transit capital and operating assistance are earmarked over six years. Flexibility provisions permit much of this money to be shifted from one program to another. States can transfer up to 50% of the

Lloyd, and Compagnie Générale Maritime and Sea-Land.

Barge-lines' earnings suffered from recession-induced declines in petroleum and chemical traffic and other industrial freight, and weak grain movements. Infrastructure difficulties also impacted carriers at different times. They included low-water conditions extending to the lower Mississippi River, flooding on the Ohio, and ice jams on the upper Mississippi.

Trucking. Intercity truck tonnage moved by 143 motor carriers of general freight declined 1.2% in the second quarter, but rose 5.6%—from 49.5 million tons to 52.2 million tons—in the third quarter, according to the American Trucking Associations. However, the carriers' aggregate-net-profit margin shrank from 2.94% to 2.48%, and net income fell 12.4%, from $156 million to $136.7 million. Unused capacity and strong bargaining power among shippers prevented carriers from implementing significant rate increases. Efforts to increase carriers' productivity through expansion of the highway mileage on which long combination vehicles (triple 28-ft (8.5-m) trailers, and double 45-, 48-, or 53-ft (13.7-, 14.6-, or 16.1-m) trailers pulled by a single tractor) can be operated lawfully were thwarted in Congress. (*See* SPECIAL REPORT, page 530.)

Leading carriers such as Yellow Freight System, Roadway Express, CRST, and United Parcel Service expanded their links with Mexico in response to existing and expected growth in U.S.-Mexican trade. J.B. Hunt Transport expanded its partnership with the Santa Fe Railway by adding Los Angeles-Fort Worth truck-rail service to its existing West Coast-Midwest intermodal lines. Hunt also began moving trailerload freight between the Midwest and Pacific Northwest via Burlington Northern Railroad's priority intermodal trains on August 1.

Compliance with the Clean Air Act of 1990 compelled truckers and truck manufacturers to search for cleaner-burning power units. Toward this end, Roadway Express began a one-year experiment with liquefied-natural-gas-powered trucks operating out of its Copley, OH, break-bulk facility.

JOHN C. SPYCHALSKI
The Pennsylvania State University

money planned for highways to mass transit. In states that do not comply with the Clean Air Act, up to 100% of highway-program money can be applied to mass transit if the states obtain permission from the DOT. Of the $31.5 billion for mass transit, $18.2 billion is to come from the Mass Transit Account within the Highway Trust Fund, and $13.3 billion from the General Fund. The federal-state match for completion and repair of the Interstate System remains at 90–10. A ratio of 80–20 applies to all other programs. The sum of $16 billion is authorized for rebuilding and replacement of highway bridges, and $7.2 billion is authorized for Interstate System completion.

• *Fuel Taxes.* One half of the 5-cent-per-gallon fuel-tax increase imposed in 1990 is extended through 1999. The entire 1990 increase otherwise would have expired in 1995. In 1996 the federal diesel tax will drop from 20.1 cents per gallon to 17.6 cents, and the gasoline tax will drop to 11.6 cents.

• *Toll Facilities.* Rehabilitation of existing toll roads, bridges, and tunnels—with an 80% federal match—and construction of new toll facilities not on the Interstate System—with a maximum federal match of 50%—is authorized.

• *Research.* Funding of $35 million is provided for university transportation-research centers, $660 million is provided for IVHS development, and $725 million is provided for construction of an operating magnetic-levitation (Maglev) train prototype within seven years. An amount of $6.5 billion is earmarked for special projects specified by individual members of Congress.

• *LCVs.* Operation of longer combination vehicles (LCVs), such as triple 28-ft (9-m) trailers, twin 48-ft (15-m) trailers, and Rocky Mountain Doubles, is restricted to the 20 states that allowed them prior to this legislation.

• *Motor-Carrier Registration.* By 1996 states must join registration-fee and fuel-tax collection systems that enable motor carriers to pay state fees and taxes only to their home states. Home states will act as collectors for other states in which the carriers operate.

Issues. The scope of intermodal flexibility provisions within the act represents an unprecedented and radical departure from previous federal surface-transport funding legislation. Highway-transport interests feared that these provisions could result in insufficient funding of road construction and maintenance. But supporters of the new flexibility provisions contended that congestion could not be relieved by new highway construction alone. Instead, they argued, it must be countered by other means such as more efficient use of existing road capacity—which is a major objective of the act's IVHS program—and more use of mass transit.

Some advocates of high-speed, intercity, surface passenger transport viewed the Maglev project funded by the act as ignoring the potential of steel-wheel-on-steel-rail technology which, unlike Maglev, already has been proven in Japan, France, and Germany.

JOHN C. SPYCHALSKI

TRAVEL

War and recession sent U.S. travelers into a retreat in 1991. Early in the year the Persian Gulf war made travelers worldwide fearful of leaving home due to possible terrorism. And as the year progressed, economic concerns were an even stronger deterrent to travel.

Overseas trips by Americans fell by 10% from 1990, a dramatic reversal of the gains of recent years. Americans still traveled, but they did not venture as far and they looked for ways to save money. Business travel fell several more percentage points from the 8.3% drop of 1990. As the travel industry tightened its belt, there were layoffs at travel agencies, airlines, hotels, and other providers of travel services.

Bargains abounded for those who could be flexible about when and where they traveled. Hotel chains offered special rates to boost business, and there was deep discounting by cruise lines. Even Disneyland cut its admission price. Air fares bounced up and down, but at times travelers could fly cross-country for $198 round trip or to Europe and back for $360.

Of the 14.4 million Americans who did travel overseas during the year, according to U.S. Travel & Tourism Administration projections, only 6.35 million were bound for Europe—a 16% drop-off. Even Canada, despite its proximity, attracted 1.5% fewer Americans (12.5 million) than in 1990. Only Mexico, seen as a less-expensive destination, showed a gain—15.4 million U.S. visitors, up 3.4%.

Domestic Travel. On the domestic front, Americans took shorter vacations closer to home, visited friends and relatives, and used their cars more—anything to cut costs and still be able to travel. While the American Automobile Association estimated a 2% increase in summer travel by motor vehicle, vacationers did not seem to be spending as much. Many chose national parks (*see* FEATURE ARTICLE, page 62) or beaches over pricier destinations, and budget hotels were in demand.

One success story was Amtrak's first-ever rail-air plan, offered in cooperation with United Airlines. The packages, starting at $419 for transcontinental travel, proved to be Amtrak's most popular travel product. Overall, Amtrak noted a 3% rise in revenue passenger miles for the fiscal year ending in September 1991, although actual rider numbers dipped slightly.

While overall travel costs were up 6% to 7% for Americans over 1990, according to the U.S. Travel Data Center, dollar exchange rates still created bargains for foreign visitors. Final figures were expected to show 41.6 million inbound travelers, a 6.4% increase over 1990. Of those, an estimated 19 million came from Canada (up 9.8%), 15.7 million from overseas (up 4%), and 6.9 million from Mexico (up 1.5%).

U.S. President George Bush joined in the effort to drum up more travel business, videotaping an invitation to the world to visit the United States. The message was planned as part of an overseas promotional campaign by an industry-wide "Go USA" travel coalition.

Cruising. Despite the recession, cruising posted a 14% gain in passengers for the year, attracting some 4 million North American vacationers.

The Gulf war did have some effect: Ships were repositioned from the Mediterranean to "new" waters along the East Coast of the United States and Canada and in the Pacific Northwest, as well as to such old favorites as Alaska and the Caribbean.

Several brand-new ships entered service during the year. Among them were the 2,354-passenger *Monarch of the Seas,* operated by Royal Caribbean Cruise Line; the 2,040-passenger *Ecstasy,* Carnival Cruise Lines' newest megaship; Princess Cruises' 1,590-passenger *Regal Princess;* Star Clippers' 180-passenger sailing ship *Star Flyer;* and a trio of 100-passenger Renaissance Cruises vessels, the *Renaissance V, VI,* and *VII.* And cruise lines were readying more than a dozen new ships for 1992.

PHYLLIS ELVING, *Free-lance Writer*

Although the Persian Gulf war and poor economic conditions contributed to a downturn in the tourism industry, adventure travel, sometimes called "eco-tourism," was in the midst of a boom in 1991. Several agencies specialize in adventure travel and offer tours to a wide variety of destinations. At right, a group of brave fun seekers explores the Zambezi River in Zambia.

TUNISIA

Like the rest of North Africa, Tunisia was the site in early 1991 of some of the strongest pro-Iraq sentiment seen anywhere during the Persian Gulf conflict. Large demonstrations in Tunis, the capital, were encouraged by what initially was a frankly pro-Iraq stance from the government of President Zine El Abidine Ben Ali, a stance Tunisian leaders later in the year insisted had been misinterpreted by the West.

The country's emotional reaction to the war was explained not so much by any affinity for President Saddam Hussein as by a feeling that the Persian Gulf war was a Western conspiracy to crush a country that through economic and technological advancement—as well as a refusal of Islamic fundamentalism—had come to represent a kind of model for the Arab world.

Islamic Fundamentalism. Tunisia's preoccupation with the Gulf was relegated abruptly to secondary importance on the morning of February 17, however, when young Islamic fundamentalists attacked a Tunis branch office of the ruling political party, the Constitutional Democratic Rally (RCD). The particularly violent event—one guard died after he and two others were bound, doused with gasoline, and set afire—shocked the country and provided the government with a pretext for intensifying its continuing repression of the outlawed Islamic fundamentalist party, Hisb An-Nahda.

By October 9, when three fundamentalists convicted in the burning death were hanged, Tunisian prisons held hundreds of other Islamists who, President Ben Ali insisted, were involved in plots designed to foment an Islamic revolution and overthrow the government.

Tunisian leaders called on the neighboring governments of Algeria and France to become more vigilant about exiled fundamentalist leaders operating from their territories. What earlier had been minimal cooperation at best from Algeria improved after it was rocked in May and June by fundamentalist rioting. The Algerian situation reinforced the Tunisian government's conviction that, despite a desire to foster democracy, it was justified in banning Islamic political parties.

To offset the action against fundamentalists, Ben Ali in April approved measures designed to encourage the country's legal opposition parties, including financing and better access to government-controlled media.

On November 7, Ben Ali celebrated his four years in power by holding an international symposium on the new democracies of the Third World and the "new world order."

U.S. Secretary of State James Baker visited Tunis on August 4 as part of his effort to line up Arab support behind the Middle East peace process. Secretary Baker said he anticipated that cuts in U.S. aid to Tunisia would be reinstated in 1992.

The Economy. Tunisia's economy, in which tourism plays a major part, was thrown into a tailspin by the Persian Gulf war. A downfall in tourism due to the war put off hopes for strong economic growth, at least until 1992. Nevertheless, the country persevered in economic reforms already under way, with plans to privatize more of the some 300 companies still in the public sector. In October, Tunisian economic leaders announced they anticipated receiving more than $400 million in loans—primarily from the World Bank, the European Community, and Japan—to continue the reform process over the next two years.

HOWARD LAFRANCHI
"The Christian Science Monitor"

TUNISIA • Information Highlights

Official Name: Republic of Tunisia.
Location: North Africa.
Area: 63,170 sq mi (163 610 km²).
Population (mid-1991 est.): 8,400,000.
Chief City (1987 est.): Tunis, the capital, 1,600,000, district population.
Government: *Head of state,* Zine El Abidine Ben Ali, president (took office Nov. 7, 1987). *Head of government,* Hamed Karoui, prime minister (took office Sept. 27, 1989). *Legislature* (unicameral)—National Assembly.
Monetary Unit: Dinar (0.992 dinar equals U.S.$1, June 1991).
Gross Domestic Product (1989 est. U.S.$): $8,700,000,000.
Economic Index (1990): *Consumer Prices* (1980 = 100), all items, 218.4; food, 225.4.
Foreign Trade (1990 U.S.$): *Imports,* $5,550,000,000; *exports,* $3,595,000,000.

TURKEY

Three major topics dominated Turkish public affairs in 1991: a general election and a new government, the Persian Gulf war and its aftermath, and the Kurdish problem.

Domestic Affairs. A new government led by Prime Minister Suleyman Demirel (who had held that office six previous times) and his True Path Party (DYP), in coalition with the Social Democratic Populist Party (SHP), took power in Turkey in November. Growing disenchantment with the government of the Motherland Party (ANAP) that had ruled Turkey since the armed forces returned power to political parties in 1983 culminated in its election defeat on October 20, when it received only 24% of the popular vote and 115 seats in the 450-member Assembly. DYP, its chief rival on the moderate right, came in first with about 27% of the vote and 179 seats. Two socialist parties together polled just a third of the votes. The SHP, led by Erdal Inönü (son of Turkey's second president), finished with 20.8% and 88 seats, and the Democratic Left Party (DSP) of Bülent Ecevit, another former prime minister, received 10.7% and seven seats under Turkey's somewhat

© Diana Walker/"Time" Magazine

George Bush discussed the Cyprus issue with Turkey's President Turgut Özal (second from right) *in Ankara, July 20, 1991. The U.S. president also expressed gratitude for Turkey's support during the Persian Gulf war.*

skewed proportional-representation electoral system. Some concern was raised at the showing of the far-right Welfare Party (RP) (16.8% and 62 seats), led jointly by two more leaders from the not-too-distant past: Necmettin Erbakan, who had headed several religious fundamentalist parties, and veteran ultranationalist Alparslan Turkes.

The first sign that the ANAP thought itself in possible trouble had developed in the spring when the party replaced its leader, Prime Minister Yildirim Akbulut, with former Foreign Minister Mesut Yilmaz. In June, President Turgut Özal (*see* BIOGRAPHY) named Yilmaz as the prime minister.

The most important single reason for the government's defeat was the economy. Although it continued to grow (the final growth figure for 1990 was about 9%, with the per capita gross national product reaching $2,595), the country also continued to be plagued with inflation estimated at 70% at midyear. A contributing cause was the unpopularity of Özal, stemming from his autocratic manner as prime minister from 1983 until 1989 and from charges that he gave political favors to members of his family.

The number of pre-1980 leaders who reemerged into the political forefront dismayed some observers who saw possibilities of a return to the atmosphere of bitterness among many of them that often had characterized Turkish politics before 1980.

Positive longer-range economic developments, on the other hand, were the doubling of the U.S. import quota for Turkish textiles, something which Turkey long had sought; progress on privatization of government enterprises; many increases in production and exports; continued high revenues from tourism; and further progress on the huge Southeast Anatolia Project, centered around the development of the vast water resources of one of Turkey's least-developed regions. In the latter connection there began to be international consideration of harnessing Turkey's resources toward a possible wider scheme for providing water to Syria, Jordan, and Israel. Disappointing, however, was the little progress made in Turkey's campaign to be admitted to the European Community.

On other matters, the final results of the 1990 census were announced and showed that the population had reached 57 million, with an annual growth rate of 2.3%. Other notable events were the holding of the annual conference of the Organization of Islamic States in Turkey for the second time, the first appointment of a woman to be a provincial governor, and the death of world-famous composer Adnan Saygun.

TURKEY • Information Highlights

Official Name: Republic of Turkey.
Location: Southeastern Europe and southwestern Asia.
Area: 301,382 sq mi (780 580 km²).
Population (mid-1991 est.): 58,500,000.
Chief Cities (1985 census): Ankara, the capital, 2,235,035; Istanbul, 5,475,982; Izmir, 1,489,772.
Government: *Head of state,* Turgut Özal, president (took office November 1989). *Head of government,* Suleyman Demirel, prime minister (took office November 1991). *Legislature*—Grand National Assembly.
Monetary Unit: Lira (5,035.02 liras equal U.S. $1, Dec. 18, 1991).
Gross Domestic Product (1989 est. U.S.$): $75,000,-000,000.
Economic Index (1990): *Consumer Prices* (1982 = 100), all items, 2,570.6; food, 2,430.8.
Foreign Trade (1990 U.S.$): *Imports,* $21,810,-000,000; *exports,* $12,922,000,000.

Foreign Affairs. In foreign affairs the most important matters were the Persian Gulf war and its aftermath. In 1990, Turkey had become a staunch member of the anti-Iraq coalition through its closing of the Iraqi oil pipelines through Turkey and the basing of U.S. air power on Turkish soil. Despite some public misgivings about involvement in regional quarrels, Turkey remained firmly in the coalition, rejecting an Iraqi request to reopen the pipelines and agreeing to the continued stationing of some allied forces in Turkey. Cooperation was hailed in a March visit by President Özal to Washington and a July visit to Turkey by U.S. President George Bush.

More difficult were dilemmas related to the effects of the war on Turkey's Kurdish problem, particularly the flood of Iraqi Kurdish refugees who crossed into Turkey. Recalling a similar experience in 1988 when the country felt unfairly burdened by the lack of financial help from other countries when Kurdish refugees flooded in at the end of the Iran-Iraq war, Turkey insisted that it could not bear the burden alone again. The help from the Gulf war coalition was short of Turkey's request, however. Most of the refugees eventually were returned to an allied-protected enclave near the Turkish border, but the activity of Iraqi Kurds for autonomy stimulated new strivings among Turkish Kurdish separatists and provided the latter with bases. As a result, Turkish forces made several assaults on them in northern Iraq, increasing tensions between separatists and Turkish army units, both of whom suffered considerable casualties. An unfortunate related event occurred when a gesture designed to decrease Kurdish discontent—the government's proposed lifting of restrictions on the use of Kurdish language—was rejected by the Turkish parliament. (*See also* SPECIAL SECTION/MIDDLE EAST, page 36.)

In other matters, the United States made an unsuccessful attempt to convene negotiations between Greece, Turkey, and the Greek and Turkish sections of Cyprus. Tensions with Greece also increased over allegations that the Turkish minority in western Thrace was being persecuted, and a Turkish diplomat stationed in Athens was assassinated in October. In March, President Özal visited the Soviet Union, and at year's end the prospects for increased trade were judged to be good.

WALTER F. WEIKER
Rutgers University

UGANDA

Uganda's economic growth continued at an impressive rate of 6% in 1991, yet the country faced a mounting domestic economic crisis. Regionally, its ties with Kenya deteriorated, while rebels based in Uganda invaded Rwanda.

UGANDA • Information Highlights

Official Name: Republic of Uganda.
Location: Interior of East Africa.
Area: 91,135 sq mi (236 040 km^2).
Population: (mid-1991 est.): 18,700,000.
Chief Cities (1982 est.): Kampala, the capital, 460,000; Jinja, 55,000.
Government: *Head of state,* Yoweri Museveni, president (Jan. 29, 1986). *Head of government,* George Adyebo, prime minister (took office Jan. 22, 1991). *Legislature* (unicameral)—National Assembly.
Monetary Unit: Uganda shilling (700 shillings equal U.S. $1, June 1991).
Foreign Trade (1988 U.S.$): *Imports,* $544,000,000; *exports,* $274,000,000.

Economic Affairs. The Ugandan economy continued to be plagued by the rising costs of imports, particularly oil, and low prices for its exports, especially coffee. As a result, President Yoweri Museveni's government cut public spending by nearly 30%, thereby eliminating any new development projects. Uganda also was unable to meet its international financial obligations, including those to the International Finance Corporation (IFC) of the World Bank. In response the IFC froze new investments. Uganda's shortage of foreign exchange also forced it to sign a barter deal with Iran in which it swapped coffee and tea for oil and manufactured goods.

There also was declining agricultural productivity. While the number of acres planted had grown dramatically over the previous few years, total output barely inched upward and did not keep pace with Uganda's 3.8% population-growth rate.

Political Affairs. In January, President Museveni appointed George Adyebo, an economist, as prime minister, replacing the ailing Samson Kisekka, who became vice-president. Adyebo is from the north, an area that has been plagued by armed banditry. In March, Uganda's National Resistance Army (NRA) swept through the area and detained large numbers of civilians for "screening"; more than 50 people were thought to have been killed.

Regionally the NRA also came under fire from Rwanda, which claimed that it was the principal backer of the Ugandan-based Rwandan Patriotic Front (RPF). Many members of the NRA as well as Uganda's security service are ethnic Tutsi refugees from the Hutu-dominated government in Rwanda. The RPF's October 1990 invasion of Rwanda and its continued activities there cast serious doubts upon Museveni's ability to control the NRA and his willingness to pursue peaceful relations with his neighbors. The tension also undermined the international stature Museveni had achieved as a result of his success in ending his country's civil war and unifying its population. Such a situation also was embarrassing for Museveni in his position as the chairman of the

Organization of African Unity, which he held until mid-1991.

Uganda's relations with Kenya also were tense. Each side accused the other of supporting rebel movements and of attempting to topple the other's government. Kenya's close ties to Rwanda, coupled with its decision to host anti-Qaddafi guerrillas from Chad, irritated Uganda, given its ties to Libya. Economic tensions between Kenya and Uganda also emerged as a result of the reconstruction of Uganda's manufacturing base and subsequent decline in imports from Kenya. In a November meeting, however, Kenya's President Daniel arap Moi and President Museveni pledged themselves to peaceful cooperation.

WILLIAM CYRUS REED
The American University in Cairo

USSR

History will record 1991 as the last year of the Soviet system born of the Bolshevik Revolution in 1917. By year's end, just short of its 75th year of existence, the Communist system and the Soviet state had collapsed, freeing Russia, the other union republics, and the many peoples of the former USSR to begin shaping their own destinies. (*See* FEATURE SECTION, page 24.) The abortive coup in late August served as the catalyst, precipitating the final collapse of a country which had fallen into disarray in previous years. *Perestroika,* President Mikhail Gorbachev's grand program for reforming the Soviet system, had spun out of control and instead brought about the demise of Communist Party rule over the vast internal empire of the Union of Soviet Socialist Republics.

Well before the summer coup, signs were abundant that Gorbachev's leadership, the national economy, and the union state were in serious trouble. Conservative political leaders had become concerned gravely for the fate of the country, radical reformers and would-be democrats had found a new champion in Boris Yeltsin, and the West was becoming increasingly skeptical of Gorbachev's ability to control the powerful centrifugal forces his reforms had released. The USSR was engulfed in multiple crises which strained the government's capacity to cope.

After the brief, failed coup, things came apart very quickly. The governmental system, compromised by involvement in the coup, was replaced by a patchwork "transitional" arrangement incapable of asserting central authority as nearly all of the "sovereign" republics raced for the exits. Their declarations of independence left Gorbachev the president of a hollow shell, still, for want of a better term, called the Soviet Union. Nonetheless, even with his party and country collapsing around him, Gorbachev continued plying his magic on the international circuit in London, Madrid, Moscow, and Tokyo, trying to convert the USSR's fatal weaknesses into phantom strengths.

Domestic Affairs

Efforts by Soviet troops and paramilitary police to win back control of the breakaway Baltic republics early in 1991 did not succeed, but the attempt signaled a sharp swing to the right by the Gorbachev leadership, frustrated by ethnic nationalism and deepening economic problems.

Political Developments. In the first months of 1991, President Gorbachev sent the army to patrol city streets, empowered the KGB or secret police to carry out warrantless searches of economic enterprises, and deployed 50,000 troops in Moscow in an attempt to block a huge demonstration in support of his political rival, Boris Yeltsin, president of the Russian Republic parliament. By early spring, however, with important international meetings looming ahead, Gorbachev—ever the skillful navigator—reversed his course and tacked back in the direction of the reformers led by Yeltsin. Gorbachev's effort to fend off secessionist pressures by gathering support for a restructured union had prevailed by a good margin in the first nationwide referendum held in March. Beginning in April, Gorbachev opened negotiations with the leaders of all but the most intransigent republics on working out the details for a new union treaty, to replace the one still in place from 1922.

Relations remained strained between Gorbachev and Yeltsin, his major competitor for public affection, but the two worked together in the difficult process of redefining the relationship between the central government and the republics.

The first direct election of a Russian president was held on June 12, and Yeltsin won with almost 60% of the vote. Yeltsin's new mandate for radical reform as well as the deteriorating condition of the USSR, however, evoked a reaction from conservative leaders. A week after the election, the USSR Supreme Soviet went into special closed session to hear alarming reports on the burgeoning crime problem, the crumbling of the union state, and putative foreign conspiracies against the Soviet Union. Prime Minister Valentin Pavlov, without prior approval from Gorbachev, took the floor and asked the legislature to give him extraordinary powers to deal with the country's crises. Only a last-minute intervention by Gorbachev blocked this attempt by Pavlov to seize power.

By midsummer, with negotiations on the union treaty nearing success, Gorbachev was confronted by another conservative thrust—this time an effort by the hard-line Communist

© Novosti/Gamma-Liaison

During his final weeks as Soviet president, Mikhail Gorbachev reappointed his colleague Eduard Shevardnadze (right) *as foreign minister. Shevardnadze had given up the post in December 1991 and warned of an "approaching dictatorship."*

Party leadership to unseat him as party leader. Beating back the challenge, Gorbachev proposed to the chastened Central Committee Plenum a new radical program for the party containing ideas fundamentally anathema to its Marxist-Leninist ideology. Temporarily having neutralized the party conservatives, Gorbachev deferred to the fall a full-scale congress which he envisioned as the funeral congress of the party as the world had known it. It was to be changed beyond recognition.

In August the union treaty transferring considerable powers away from the center was ready, but its scheduled signing was blocked by the coup against Gorbachev. Thanks to Yeltsin's bold opposition, however, the coup quickly fizzled out, and the negative developments, which the conservative conspirators had set out to stop, were accelerated as the USSR went into free-fall. In an effort at damage control, Gorbachev, Yeltsin, other republic leaders, and union parliamentarians struggled in the ensuing weeks to reestablish some semblance of public authority and national unity, but to no avail. The interim institutions fashioned to guide the country through a "transitional period" failed to take hold, and Gorbachev's efforts to negotiate a common economic space as well as a confederative political union attracted nominal support at most.

Economy. Throughout 1991 the economy of the USSR was in steep decline, with nearly every economic indicator—industrial production, real income, gross national product—falling steadily toward depression levels. The standard of living and quality of life fell in tandem, intensifying already-serious social tensions, especially in the larger cities and towns where the daily search for affordable food turned citizens into foragers. As in previous years, Gorbachev continued to pursue the mirage of marketization just over the horizon, but, as before, he temporized, resisting the policies that decisively would move Soviet society in the desired direction. In the course of *perestroika,* Gorbachev had set in motion successfully the dismantling of the centrally planned economy, but he had been unable to replace it with an alternate economic mechanism. By 1991 economic life was getting worse by the month as internal commerce broke down and trade was reduced to bartering of goods between factories and farms, and between great cities and agricultural regions.

Incapable of coping with the faltering economy, Gorbachev and his conservative advisers started blaming the democrats and ethnic nationalists who, it was claimed, had carried Gorbachev's earlier policies of *glasnost* or openness and democratization to the excess, rending the social fabric and stimulating runaway nationalism.

The new conservative Prime Minister Pavlov's proposed solution in the spring was an "anti-crisis" program, which would have imposed a one-year moratorium on strikes and demonstrations while reinstituting central controls. Never gaining a strong consensus, the program soon was overtaken by events. Pavlov's attempt a few months later to obtain emergency powers from the legislature also failed. Meanwhile, a series of ad hoc policies over the months—such as confiscation of large-denomination currency in January, steep price increases in April, wage indexation, and several devaluations of the ruble—did little to arrest the downward spiral and, in fact, made life more difficult for many citizens.

The short-lived August coup, with its negative impact on the already weakened and fragile Soviet federal system, increased the velocity of economic decline. The now com-

© Rob Rogers; reprinted by permission of UFS, Inc.

pletely free press fed the public a daily diet of depressing economic news. Inflation was soaring, organized crime preyed on private business, black-market prices were skyrocketing, gold reserves had dwindled, and the foreign debt had climbed $80 billion. Added to this was a mediocre harvest, with collective and state farms withholding products from the market for still higher prices, food stocks in the great urban centers getting low, and winter fast approaching.

Gorbachev, reduced in power since the coup, could do little more than call for an economic union among the newly independent republics, while repeating more urgently his persistent appeals for Western foreign aid, especially food aid for winter, for the Soviet Union. In contrast, Yeltsin, his prestige greatly enhanced by his resistance to the coup, steadily accumulated more administrative power as the Russian government progressively took over the institutions of the declining USSR. Moving into the vacuum at the center, Yeltsin extended economic control over Soviet oil, gas, diamonds, gold on Russian territory, the central banks, and the diminished and restructured yet usable Soviet governmental institutions whose payrolls Russia now assumed. (The latter included a shrunken ministry of external relations.) Of greater importance, Yeltsin announced his radical program for marketization, including privatizing property, decontrolling the fixed value of the ruble, introducing a steep value-added tax to raise revenue, and freeing nearly all prices by the turn of the year. Populist politician that he is, Yeltsin promised his constituents that after only six months of social pain, positive results would appear. By the end of 1991, Gorbachev's calls and appeals for economic solutions had produced little or nothing and the battered Russian public awaited tremulously the impact of Yeltsin's economic "shock therapy."

Foreign Affairs

As Gorbachev's fortunes faded at home, his practice of turning to foreign affairs as a fillip to his sagging popularity and a panacea for the country's domestic problems continued. By 1991, however, he no longer could dominate the Soviet dialogue with the West, having to share the international stage with Yeltsin as well as other republic leaders, who were receiving warm receptions abroad as foreign statesmen became increasingly concerned about the stability of Gorbachev's stewardship and the question of who might inherit the future. The leitmotif of Gorbachev's foreign policy was the need for Western aid, expressly to support the much-discussed transition to the market and to revitalize his reputation as an economic reformer.

Thus, the foreign-aid appeal was his pitch in the spring in Japan, at the meeting of the leaders of the seven major industrial democracies (G-7) in London in mid-July, and in his Moscow summit with President Bush a few weeks later. Gorbachev smoothly played what foreign-policy cards he had, but they were not enough to persuade the West, which was beginning to have doubts about his ability to control events at home and about the soundness of sinking large sums of money into the still largely unreformed Soviet economy. During his visit to Japan—the first by a Soviet leader—he was willing to discuss the long-standing Japanese demand for the return of the tiny Kurile Islands seized by Stalin after World War II, but this was not sufficient for tough-minded Japanese industrialists who had concluded that the Soviet economy was not a promising investment opportunity at this time.

During the summer in England, Gorbachev, the first Soviet leader to be invited to a G-7 meeting, hoped that his democratic friends would reward financially his support of the allied side in the brief Persian Gulf war against Iraq several months earlier. But G-7 leaders, beset by recessions at home, offered him only a few symbolic tokens and some small change for his trip to London. Finally, at the July superpower summit where he signed the historic START treaty with President Bush to reduce long-range missiles by 30%, Gorbachev tried to lobby Bush for aid, but to little avail. President Bush, with budget problems of his own and a Democratic-controlled Congress at his back, would not go much beyond his earlier commitment of $1.5 billion in food aid over a nine-month period.

By the time of the coup in August, Gorbachev, the polished, urbane, international trouper, had largely come up empty-handed for his overseas efforts, while Yeltsin's reputation abroad was rising. After his June election victory, Yeltsin had made a highly successful visit to Washington, where his bluff charm and Siberian demeanor had played well. Later in a post-coup visit to Germany, Yeltsin was less successful, finding the German bankers skeptical of both his ability and political resolve to stay the course to the market with all the attendant hardship that would entail. As for the USSR, the July East-West summit confirmed the country's condition as a dying superpower. In the wake of the coup, after the republics had bolted the union, the Soviet Union's diminished stature was fully apparent at the fall Mideast peace conference in Madrid, where Gorbachev was at best only a peripheral player and the Soviet Union at most merely a symbolic partner of the United States in the global arena.

The End of the Union State

When Gorbachev came to power in 1985, the USSR was composed of 15 union republics and many more autonomous republics, regions and districts within those larger entities. By fall 1991, Gorbachev and the transitional union government had recognized the independence of Lithuania, Latvia, and Estonia. The Georgian and Moldavian republics had declared their independence earlier and, after the collapse of the coup, eight of the ten union state's remaining republics had followed suit. Only Russia and Kazakhstan had remained nominally in the decimated USSR as their presidents, Yeltsin and Nursultan Nazarbayev, worked unsuccessfully with Gorbachev to design some kind of loose confederative political union as successor to the imperial state. However, it was too late as the republics, seized by nationalistic fervor, sought their own destinies.

Gorbachev based his arguments for staying together in some fashion on the idea of a unified military, a coordinated foreign policy, a single currency, a common economic space, and—perhaps his most persuasive argument—the need for a center and some degree of unity as a condition for Western aid. However, as it became apparent to the former republics that the Western states had become hesitant and even reluctant donors, Gorbachev's pleas fell on deaf ears. Conversely, the ongoing breakup of the USSR presented the United States and the West with a worrisome problem. Who now would control the tens of thousands of all kinds of nuclear weapons on Soviet soil? Presidents Reagan and Bush signed major nuclear-disarmament treaties with Gorbachev, who was no longer in a position to ensure they were carried out. While the strategic weapons were concentrated in Russia, Ukraine, Belarus (Byelorussia), and Kazakhstan, the even-more-numerous short-range, field-level nuclear weapons were dispersed far more widely throughout the territory of the former Soviet Union.

The rush to republican independence, however, was not without problems for the newly arisen nations. Russia, the largest, richest and most powerful of the republics, inherited the USSR's two greatest problems—economic collapse and ethnic rebellion. It now would be Yeltsin's turn to fend off the bogeys which, far more than the clumsy coup attempt, brought Gorbachev down. Yeltsin already boldly had linked his political fortunes to the elusive market on the economic front, but his best efforts on the ethnic front *within* the giant Russian Federation were stymied in 1991. Just as the titular nations of the union republics initially sought sovereignty and then, in most cases, independence, several of the large and small nations living in enclaves within the Russian Federation also were seeking their independence, but in this case from Russia. It was one of the small nations, the Chechens, who dealt Yeltsin his major political setback of 1991. Declaring their independence in the northern Caucasus region, the Chechens prevailed (for the time being at least) in a tense face-off with federation police and troops. Subsequently the Russian Supreme Soviet denied Yeltsin its support and he had to back down.

Elsewhere the problems were similar and different. Moldavia contained two restive and potentially rebellious minorities, Russians and Gagauzi, while in Georgia and Azerbaijan heavy fighting continued against the South Ossetian and Armenian minorities, respectively. In several former republics, in particular Ukraine, Belarus, Azerbaijan, and Tajikistan the independence drive encapsulated an internal power struggle between anticommunist democrats or nationalists and the former party elite operating with newly adopted political identities. In most places in 1991 the former Communists with their greater organizational experience rode the wave of nationalism to victory one way or another. In Ukraine, Leonid Kravchuk, a former senior official of the now banned Ukrainian branch of the Communist Party, scored a victory at the ballot box, easily winning the presidency against several contenders.

In early December, Yeltsin joined with Ukraine and Belarus to declare the Soviet Union dead and proclaim as its successor the Commonwealth of Independent States. As all of the remaining republics but Georgia, by then engulfed in civil war, joined the loose commonwealth, Gorbachev reluctantly acknowledged the demise of his dream of a renewed Soviet Union and resigned his presidency. Whatever the durability of this initiative, it was clear that the future of that vast land no longer belongs to communism; it belongs, for better or worse, to the republics of the former Union of Soviet Socialist Republics.

ROBERT SHARLET
Union College

UNITED NATIONS

The United Nations, which had entered 1991 under the shadow of the Persian Gulf conflict, ended the year on standby involvement in Yugoslavia's devastating civil war.

Operation Desert Storm was launched just 16 days into the new year by the U.S.-crafted alliance to drive Iraq out of Kuwait. While not a UN operation, the coalition struck under a UN Security Council resolution authorizing any member state "to use all necessary means" to force Iraq out of Kuwait unless it withdrew by January 15.

Following Baghdad's defeat and subsequent pullout from Kuwait, the Security Council authorized a series of humanitarian, monitoring, and arms-destruction operations in Iraq, all of which would continue into 1992. In northern Iraq some 500 UN guards (as distinct from peacekeeping troops) were posted to discourage any acts of vengeance by Baghdad's military against the restive Kurdish population. In the south the UN Iraq-Kuwait Observation Mission (UNIKOM) monitored a demilitarized zone along the Iraq-Kuwait border.

UN inspectors dispatched to verify Iraq's mandated destruction of suspected nuclear-, biological-, and chemical-weapons capabilities were frustrated repeatedly by Baghdad's refusal to cooperate. Despite Iraq's denials, inspectors uncovered clandestine weapons-manufacturing facilities. On December 11 one team reported discovering chemical-bomb-making equipment in a Mosul sugar factory.

On October 24 chairman Rolf Ekeus of the UN's Commission on Iraqi Disarmament announced that together with the International Atomic Energy Agency (IAEA), the commission had fielded 20 inspection teams involving 300 experts from 34 countries.

IAEA Director-General Hans Blix reported that Iraq had violated pledges not to develop or acquire nuclear weapons. IAEA's General Conference condemned Iraq's noncompliance —the first such action that ever was taken against an agency member. Blix said inspectors had found vast undisclosed programs in the billion-dollar range for the enrichment of uranium plus conclusive evidence that Iraq was "well advanced in the production of nuclear weapons" as well as of lithium-6, used to produce hydrogen bombs.

For those and other reasons the Security Council concluded that conditions did not exist to justify easing Council-imposed sanctions against Iraq.

General Assembly. The twin highlights of the 46th General Assembly were the September 17 opening-day election to its presidency of Samir S. Shihabi and the simultaneous admission to UN membership of seven nations. Shihabi, Saudi Arabia's UN ambassador, succeeded Guido de Marco of Malta. UN membership rose to a record 166 with the admission of Lithuania, Latvia, Estonia, Micronesia, the Marshall Islands, and North and South Korea.

A total of 162 delegation leaders, including 24 heads of state, ten premiers, and 94 foreign ministers, addressed the Assembly. Speaking for the host country, U.S. President George Bush highlighted a domestic political demand: the revocation of the Assembly's 1975 resolution equating Zionism with racism. The Assembly acceded to Bush's appeal on December 16 by a 111–25 vote.

Before it adjourned for the year on December 20, the Assembly had dealt with more than 145 agenda items, ranging from voting for a global moratorium on drift-net fishing to a call for the protection of the human rights of AIDS victims.

Security Council. Dominated though its proceedings were by the Gulf war, the Security Council nevertheless was kept on an almost constant state of alert by other peace-and-security issues. On October 3 the Security Council issued a compromise statement that disapproved rather than condemned the coup that ousted President Jean-Bertrand Aristide of Haiti. Though Aristide had been voted into office in an election monitored and judged fair by a UN observer team, some Council members, like China, did not want to set a precedent for UN interference in what they saw as internal affairs.

The breakup of the Soviet Union caused uncertainty about the USSR's successor as a veto-wielding permanent Council member, along with Britain, China, France, and the United States. The matter was solved in a letter dated December 24 from Russian President Boris Yeltsin to the secretary-general. It announced that the Soviet membership on the Security Council and all other UN bodies would be taken over by Russia under that name and "with the support" of the new Commonwealth of Independent States of the former USSR.

Following the Paris agreement among Cambodia's four rival factions in October, the UN was poised at year's end to field in that battle-scarred nation what was expected to be the largest and costliest Council-authorized operation ever launched. A survey mission was dispatched to pave the way for the UN Transitional Authority in Cambodia (UNTAC). Comprising some 10,000 military and civilian personnel and budgeted at between $1 billion and $2 billion, UNTAC would administer the country and conduct elections scheduled for 1993.

In war-torn Yugoslavia a Council-authorized UN team surveyed the prospects of deploying a force to help restore peace. In addition the secretary-general dispatched Cyrus Vance, a former U.S. secretary of state, on a series of missions to Yugoslavia to determine whether a Security Council-mandated

ORGANIZATION OF THE UNITED NATIONS

THE SECRETARIAT

Secretary-General: Boutros Boutros-Ghali (until Dec. 31, 1996)

THE GENERAL ASSEMBLY (1991)

President: Samir S. Shihabi, Saudi Arabia
The 166 member nations were as follows:

Afghanistan
Albania
Algeria
Angola
Antigua and Barbuda
Argentina
Australia
Austria
Bahamas
Bahrain
Bangladesh
Barbados
Belarus
Belgium
Belize
Benin
Bhutan
Bolivia
Botswana
Brazil
Brunei Darussalam
Bulgaria
Burkina Faso
Burundi
Cambodia
Cameroon
Canada
Cape Verde
Central African Republic
Chad
Chile
China, People's Republic of
Colombia
Comoros
Congo
Costa Rica
Cuba
Cyprus
Czechoslovakia
Denmark
Djibouti
Dominica
Dominican Republic
Ecuador
Egypt
El Salvador
Equatorial Guinea
Estonia
Ethiopia
Fiji
Finland
France
Gabon
Gambia
Germany
Ghana
Greece
Grenada
Guatemala
Guinea
Guinea-Bissau
Guyana
Haiti
Honduras
Hungary
Iceland
India
Indonesia
Iran
Iraq
Ireland
Israel
Italy
Ivory Coast
Jamaica
Japan
Jordan
Kenya
Korea, Democratic People's Republic of
Korea, Republic of
Kuwait
Laos
Latvia
Lebanon
Lesotho
Liberia
Libya
Liechtenstein
Lithuania
Luxembourg
Madagascar
Malawi
Malaysia
Maldives
Mali
Malta
Marshall Islands
Mauritania
Mauritius
Mexico
Micronesia
Mongolia
Morocco
Mozambique
Myanmar
Namibia
Nepal
Netherlands
New Zealand
Nicaragua
Niger
Nigeria
Norway
Oman
Pakistan
Panama
Papua New Guinea
Paraguay
Peru
Philippines
Poland
Portugal
Qatar
Romania
Russia
Rwanda
Saint Kitts and Nevis
Saint Lucia
Saint Vincent and The Grenadines
Samoa
São Tomé and Príncipe
Saudi Arabia
Senegal
Seychelles
Sierra Leone
Singapore
Solomon Islands
Somalia
South Africa
Spain
Sri Lanka
Sudan
Suriname
Swaziland
Sweden
Syria
Tanzania
Thailand
Togo
Trinidad and Tobago
Tunisia
Turkey
Uganda
Ukraine
United Arab Emirates
United Kingdom
United States
Uruguay
Vanuatu
Venezuela
Vietnam
Yemen
Yugoslavia
Zaire
Zambia
Zimbabwe

COMMITTEES

General. Composed of 29 members as follows: The General Assembly president; the 21 General Assembly vice-presidents (heads of delegations or their deputies of Australia, Belize, Botswana, China, Ecuador, France, Guinea, Honduras, Italy, Malaysia, Myanmar, Oman, Qatar, Russia, Togo, Tunisia, Ukraine, United Kingdom of Great Britain and Northern Ireland, Tanzania, United States, Zaire); and the chairmen of the main committees at right, which are composed of all 166 member countries.

First (Political and Security). Robert Mroziewicz (Poland)
Special Political: Nitya Pibulsonggram (Thailand)
Second (Economic and Financial): John Burke (Ireland)
Third (Social, Humanitarian and Cultural): Mohammad Hussain Al-Shaali (United Arab Emirates)
Fourth (Decolonization): Charles Fleming (Saint Lucia)
Fifth (Administrative and Budgetary): Ali Sunni Muntasser (Libya)
Sixth (Legal): Pedro Comissario Afonso (Mozambique)

THE SECURITY COUNCIL

Membership ends on December 31 of the year noted; asterisks indicate permanent membership.

Austria (1992)
Belgium (1992)
Cape Verde (1993)
China*
Ecuador (1992)
France*
Hungary (1993)
India (1992)
Japan (1993)
Morocco (1993)
Russia*
United Kingdom*
United States*
Venezuela (1993)
Zimbabwe (1992)

THE ECONOMIC AND SOCIAL COUNCIL

President: Hocine Djoudi (Algeria)
Membership ends on December 31 of the year noted.

Algeria (1992)
Angola (1994)
Argentina (1993)
Australia (1994)
Austria (1993)
Bahrain (1992)
Bangladesh (1994)
Belarus (1994)
Belgium (1994)
Benin (1994)
Botswana (1993)
Brazil (1994)
Bulgaria (1992)
Burkina Faso (1992)
Canada (1992)
Chile (1993)
China (1992)
Colombia (1994)
Ecuador (1992)
Ethiopia (1994)
Finland (1992)
France (1993)
Germany (1993)
Guinea (1993)
India (1994)
Iran (1992)
Italy (1994)
Jamaica (1992)
Japan (1993)
Kuwait (1994)
Madagascar (1994)
Malaysia (1993)
Mexico (1992)
Morocco (1993)
Pakistan (1992)
Peru (1993)
Philippines (1994)
Poland (1994)
Romania (1992)
Russia (1992)
Rwanda (1994)
Somalia (1993)
Spain (1993)
Suriname (1994)
Swaziland (1994)
Sweden (1992)
Syria (1993)
Togo (1993)
Trinidad and Tobago (1993)
Turkey (1993)
United Kingdom (1992)
United States (1994)
Yugoslavia (1993)
Zaire (1992)

THE TRUSTEESHIP COUNCIL

President: (to be elected in 1992)

China[2] France[2] Russia[2] United Kingdom[2] United States[1]

[1] Administers Trust Territory. [2] Permanent member of Security Council not administering Trust Territory.

THE INTERNATIONAL COURT OF JUSTICE

Membership ends on February 5 of the year noted.

President: Sir Robert Y. Jennings (United Kingdom, 2000)
Vice-President: Shigeru Oda (Japan, 1994)

Roberto Ago (Italy, 1997)
Andres Aguilar Mawdsley (Venezuela, 2000)
Bola Ajibola (Nigeria, 1994)
Mohammed Bedjaoui (Algeria, 1997)
Jens Evensen (Norway, 1994)
Gilbert Guillaume (France, 2000)
Manfred Lachs (Poland, 1994)
Ni Zhengyu (China, 1994)
Raymond Ranjeva (Madagascar, 2000)
Stephen Schwebel (United States, 1997)
Mohamed Shahabuddeen (Guyana, 1997)
Nikolai Konstantinovich Tarassov (Russia, 1997)
Christopher G. Weeramantry (Sri Lanka, 2000)

INTERGOVERNMENTAL AGENCIES

Food and Agricultural Organization (FAO); General Agreement on Tariffs and Trade (GATT); International Atomic Energy Agency (IAEA); International Bank for Reconstruction and Development (World Bank); International Civil Aviation Organization (ICAO); International Fund for Agricultural Development (IFAD); International Labor Organization (ILO); International Maritime Organization (IMO); International Monetary Fund (IMF); International Telecommunication Union (ITU); United Nations Educational, Scientific and Cultural Organization (UNESCO); United Nations Industrial Development Organization (UNIDO); Universal Postal Union (UPU); World Health Organization (WHO); World Intellectual Property Organization (WIPO); World Meteorological Organization (WMO).

arms embargo was being observed and the political and military state of the conflict. Vance reported that the embargo was being violated widely, that repeated cease-fires were being broken, and that the fighting was continuing. Secretary-General Pérez de Cuéllar, therefore, concluded that a peacekeeping operation could not be fielded until the rival factions implemented an effective truce.

In May the Security Council extended for six months the mandate of the UN Observer Group in Central America, or ONUCA. It was established in 1989 to monitor compliance with an agreement by El Salvador, Guatemala, Honduras, Costa Rica, and Nicaragua. The key commitment was to stop aiding insurgents and to deny them sanctuary for operating against other states in the region. Meanwhile, in 1991 a UN representative sat in on continuing peace talks between the Guatemalan government and the insurgents, trying to negotiate a cease-fire, human rights guarantees, democratization, and constitutional reforms.

Arab-Israeli talks opened October 30 in Madrid with Security Council Resolution 242 of Nov. 22, 1967, as the basic formula for achieving regional peace. While not convened under the UN's aegis, the Madrid conference was attended by an observer representing the secretary-general.

In Western Sahara the UN-brokered agreement between Morocco and the rebel Polisario Front bogged down throughout 1991, in part because of the efforts of Moroccan King Hassan II to influence the disputed area's future by moving thousands of Moroccans into the region before a scheduled UN-supervised referendum on a choice between independence or integration with Morocco. With a 350-member UN advance team already in the territory, the deployment of the 3,000-member UN Mission for the Referendum of Western Sahara, or MINURSO, was put on hold despite the Security Council's December 31 endorsement of a plan put forth by Pérez de Cuéllar that would permit tens of thousands of Moroccans to vote in the referendum; the Council also asked for continuing efforts to settle further disagreements between the two sides.

In East Timor, a thorn on the UN agenda even before Indonesia forcibly annexed the former Portuguese territory in 1976, progress toward an accommodation was checked when Indonesian troops massacred Timorese mourners at a funeral in Dili, the territory's capital.

On October 16 the 15-nation Security Council elected Cape Verde, Morocco, Japan, Hungary, and Venezuela as nonpermanent members to replace Ivory Coast, Cuba, Romania, Yemen, and Zaire, whose two-year terms expired on the last day of the year.

Agencies. Sadako Ogata, the UN high commissioner for refugees, appealed for greater international assistance to cope with the global surge of refugees. The number cited, some 17 million, did not include another 15 million to 25 million displaced within their own countries. Toward the end of the year, Pérez de Cuéllar asked Ogata's office to assist the estimated 300,000 internally displaced victims of the Yugoslav war.

On October 8 the UN Children's Fund (UNICEF) and the World Health Organization (WHO) certified that 80% of young children had been immunized against lethal childhood diseases, the target under a global program launched in 1985.

On October 14 the WHO projected a cumulative total of 35 million to 40 million HIV infections in men, women, and children throughout the world, 90% of them in Third World countries.

The UN Environment Program's executive director, Dr. Mostafa K. Tolba, warned on October 22 that atmospheric ozone depletion was worsening. Reporting on the findings of scientists from 25 countries, he called the situation "very disturbing." At the same time he announced a multifaceted "Caring for the Earth" program in advance of the UN Conference on Environment and Development, to convene in June 1992 in Rio de Janeiro.

Finance. The year found the UN in what the secretary-general called the "worst financial crisis" since it was founded 46 years earlier. As of December, the membership was in arrears some $781 million against an Assembly-adopted zero-growth budget of $2.4 billion for the 1992–93 biennium. Despite its last-minute payments totaling more than $78 million, the United States headed the list of delinquents with a debt of more $266 million.

Secretary-General. After two five-year terms as secretary-general, Peruvian diplomat Pérez de Cuéllar turned over the office to Deputy Prime Minister Boutros Boutros Ghali of Egypt, appointed by the General Assembly on December 3 as the UN's sixth chief executive, effective Jan. 1, 1992.

Pérez de Cuéllar's term ended in a swirl of diplomatic successes. His personal initiative was largely responsible for the release of all but two Western hostages in Lebanon. Reciprocally, scores of Arab detainees held by Israel were released. And just minutes before he was to leave office—at the stroke of midnight December 31—he was in his 38th-floor UN headquarters suite presiding over the signing of a historic accord between El Salvador's President Alfredo Cristiani and leaders of the rebel Farabundo Martí Liberation Front (FMLN). Emerging from the session, Cristiani said the signing of the peace agreement would put a final end to the conflict that had torn El Salvador for more than 11 years.

TED MORELLO
United Nations Correspondent
"Far Eastern Economic Review"

© Rick Falco/Sipa

The United States was in a euphoric mood following its victory over Iraq in the early 1991 Persian Gulf war. Victory parades were held in many locales, including New York City (above), to welcome the troops home from Operation Desert Storm.

UNITED STATES

For the United States, 1991 was a year of triumph abroad marred by tribulations at home. The military success in the Persian Gulf war, achieved at relatively low cost in U.S. lives, combined with the end of the Cold War gave the nation reason for confidence and hope early on. But by the time the year ended, this bright outlook had been dimmed by the impact of an unexpectedly severe and sustained economic recession.

Domestic Affairs

The Presidency. In his State of the Union address delivered January 29, President George Bush cited "the conviction and courage we see in the Persian Gulf today" as reflecting "the same spirit that gives us the power and the potential to meet our toughest challenges at home." Issuing "an appeal for renewal," the president promised to submit detailed proposals "to achieve excellence in education," to establish a national energy strategy, and to finance a new national highway system. But as events unfolded, the Democratic opposition complained that the president's actions failed to match the promise of his rhetoric.

The centerpiece of Bush's domestic agenda, representing an attempt to keep his campaign promise to become "the education president," was his "America 2000" education program unveiled April 18 to a group of educators, business leaders, governors, and members of Congress at the White House. Its features included: broad national standards for students in five core subjects—English, math, science, history, and geography; a new voluntary nationwide examination system—the American Achievement Tests—to measure whether those standards were being met; and incentives for local school systems to allow parents greater opportunity to choose to which school they could send their children, while extending that choice to private as well as public schools.

While educators generally praised the president for focusing public attention on the need to remedy weaknesses in the nation's school system, some questioned whether the plans he outlined were adequate for meeting some of his own key goals, such as achieving better preschool preparation, lowering the dropout rate, and eliminating the scourge of drugs from schools. Perhaps the most controversial element of the program was the plan to promote school choice. This drew the fire of the leaders of the nation's two largest teachers' unions, the National Education Association and the American Federation of Teachers, who voiced fears that by encouraging parents to choose private schools, the program would undermine the public-school system. The president, however, stuck to his position that federal aid should be available to parents whose children chose private schools.

Spurred by the nation's dependence on oil imports, which had been underlined by the Gulf war, the president on February 20 unveiled his "national energy strategy." His proposals, he contended, would result in "an energy future that is secure, efficient, and environmentally sound." Bush said his intention was to establish enough diverse sources of energy "so that never again will this nation's energy well-being be swayed by events in any single foreign country." But Bush conceded that "under any realistic scenario," the United States still would have to depend on Middle East oil supplies for the foreseeable future.

The strategy depended heavily on expanding domestic supplies of oil and increasing the use of nuclear power. The president proposed opening 1.5 million acres (600 000 ha) of Alaskan wildlife areas for oil exploration and also expanding drilling in the Gulf of Mexico and off the California coast. License renewal for existing nuclear-power plants would be expedited as would the approval process for new facilities. Meanwhile the ability of states to block nuclear-waste repositories within their borders would be curbed. Democrats immediately charged that Bush's strategy gave too little attention to conservation and development of renewable fuels. California Rep. George Miller, at the time acting chairman of the House Interior Committee, dismissed Bush's plan as "the tired wish list of the energy companies."

Keeping another State of the Union promise, President Bush on February 13 set forth a five-year, $105 billion transportation program that emphasized improving roads rather than developing mass transportation. He called for $87.7 billion in federal spending on highways in addition to mandating increased spending on the states. By contrast, mass transportation outlays would total only $16.3 billion over the five-year period. Critics charged that the plan put too little emphasis on cutting back energy consumption and Jack Gilstrap, executive vice-president of the American Public Transit Association, labeled it "a recipe for more traffic jams, air pollution, and wasted energy."

In dealing with these and other domestic problems, the president's tasks were complicated by the continuing huge budget deficit. On February 4 in his fiscal 1992 budget message to Congress, Bush estimated that the deficit for fiscal 1991 would be a record $318.1 billion—five times higher than the estimate made a year earlier in the fiscal 1991 budget proposal. The 1992 deficit initially was forecast at $280.9 billion. But on July 15, Budget Director Richard G. Darman pushed that figure upward drastically, to $348.3 billion. Economists said that the cost of the Persian Gulf war and of the savings and loan bailout had contributed significantly to the boost. The Treasury Department had estimated the cost of the savings and loan bailout at $130 billion, excluding interest. But testifying before Congress June 10, Comptroller General Charles A. Bowsher, head of the General Accounting Office, said this figure was too low and that it was impossible to give an accurate figure because of the accounting system used by the Resolution Trust Corporation charged with supervising the bailout.

Many members of Congress were dismayed at the news of the higher deficit figure. It dashed hopes for deficit reduction that had been raised by the compromise budget agreement reached with the White House in the fall of 1990 that included a controversial tax increase. Moreover, efforts to reduce the deficit in the near future were crippled by the recession that by the end of the year clearly had become the nation's number one problem. The Bush administration initially had predicted that the slump, which began in the fall of 1990, would be short and would have only a shallow impact. But these rosy forecasts were belied by a flood of negative statistics signaling soaring rates of unemployment, welfare cases, bankruptcies, and foreclosures, as well as declining industrial production, personal income, and real-estate values.

Also on the descent as a result were the president's poll ratings. A *Washington Post* poll released December 17 showed that the president's approval rating, which had been in the 80% range right after the U.S. victory in the Gulf war in the spring, had dropped to 47%, the lowest level of his tenure. Nearly nine out of ten persons interviewed said the economy was "not so good" or "poor." And only one in four said they approved of the president's handling of the economy, compared to roughly half of those interviewed in June. In the face of the continued bad news, the White House abandoned its effort to persuade the public to look at the bright side of the economic news.

UNITED STATES • Information Highlights

Official Name: United States of America.
Location: Central North America.
Area: 3,618,768 sq mi (9 372 610 km^2).
Population (1990 census): 248,709,873.
Chief Cities (1990 census): Washington, DC, the capital, 606,900; New York, 7,322,564; Los Angeles, 3,485,398; Chicago, 2,783,726; Houston, 1,630,553; Philadelphia, 1,585,577; San Diego, 1,110,549.
Government: *Head of state and government,* George Bush, president (took office Jan. 20, 1989). *Legislature*—Congress: Senate and House of Representatives.
Monetary Unit: Dollar.
Gross National Product (1989): $5,233,300,000,000.
Merchandise Trade (1990): *Imports,* $516,575,000,000; *exports,* $393,893,000,000.

Before he could take on this formidable challenge, the president was forced to put his own White House in order by replacing his chief of staff, John Sununu. Long resented by many in Washington because of his abrasive, egocentric style, Sununu became the center of unwelcome public attention in April because of his use of military aircraft for dozens of trips that were personal or political in nature. He subsequently was ordered to clear all use of military aircraft with White House Counsel C. Boyden Gray. But in November he stirred another and more serious controversy when he blamed President Bush for publicly suggesting that banks lower interest rates on credit cards, a remark which many believed helped bring on a disastrous drop in the stock market. By then, Sununu had become what *The New York Times* called a "symbol of disarray" at the White House. His resignation was announced on December 3 and he was replaced by Transportation Secretary Samuel K. Skinner.

In the midst of his other difficulties the president had to contend with health problems. After being hospitalized May 4 with an erratic heartbeat while jogging at Camp David, he was diagnosed as having Graves' disease, an ailment of the thyroid gland. After treatment he was able to resume normal physical activity.

Congress. When the 102d Congress concluded its first session on November 27, House Majority Leader Tom Foley (D-WA) declared: "We have a solid record of achievement." And in the other body, Senate Minority Leader Robert Dole (R-KS) turned to his Democratic colleagues on the floor and said: "I think we had a pretty good year." Evidence could be found to support such positive assessments. Congress had begun the year in January with three days of solemn debate on the Persian Gulf crisis, culminating with a vote to authorize the war against Iraq, a decision that most Americans clearly approved. And during the next ten months it wrote into law a number of significant measures in such areas as transportation, banking, and civil rights. Final action on the president's education and energy plans was not taken, however.

For all of that, many felt that the Congress had slipped badly in public esteem during the session. Democratic Rep. Charles E. Schumer of Brooklyn, NY, citing the failure of both the legislative and executive branches to deal more effectively with such pressing problems as crime and the recession, said: "Paralysis of government is making the American people sick of the president, sick of the Congress, and sick of the system." In addition to its sins of omission, Congress' image also was tarnished during the year by a series of misadventures involving the conduct and standards of its own members. Also hurtful was the tawdry tone of the nationally televised Senate hearings that culminated in the confirmation of Clarence

Reuters/Bettmann

In mid-December, U.S. Transportation Secretary Samuel K. Skinner (left) succeeded John Sununu (right) as White House chief of staff. Sununu had been under fire.

Thomas (*see* BIOGRAPHY) as a Supreme Court justice.

These well-publicized episodes sometimes seemed to overshadow substantive achievements on a range of issues. These included:

• *Civil Rights.* A compromise between President Bush and congressional leaders ended two years of bitter controversy and made possible enactment of an anti-job-discrimination measure. The president initially had attacked such legislation being pushed in Congress as designed to force employers to adopt racial quotas as a basis for hiring and promotion. But he shifted ground after drafters of the legislation agreed to make a technical change in its language. Many believed that the president wanted to ease racial tensions stirred by the gubernatorial candidacy of former Ku Klux Klansman David Duke in Louisiana.

The legislation overturned a series of Supreme Court decisions that made it harder for workers to get judicial relief from discrimination. The new law placed the burden on employers to justify practices that resulted in indirect discrimination and it extended to victims of discrimination based on sex, religion, national origin, or disability the same right to sue for monetary damages previously granted to victims of race discrimination.

• *Recession Relief.* Legislation to extend benefits to the jobless was enacted, as in the case of the civil-rights bill, only after a long and bitter political controversy. The battle started in August when Congress passed legislation that would have provided up to $5.8 billion to pay for additional benefits to the long-term unemployed. The president signed the bill but refused to make the declaration of fiscal emergency that would have been necessary

AP/Wide World

In a November 21 White House ceremony attended by Vice-President Quayle and acting Attorney General William Barr (top right), *President Bush signed the 1991 civil-rights act.*

under the 1990 budget agreement to release the funds.

In October, Congress passed a $6.4 billion measure to extend benefits for 20 weeks which was written so that simply by signing it the president in effect would be declaring an emergency. But Bush vetoed the bill and Congress failed to override. Finally in November, Congress passed a new version of the bill, which included mechanisms for funding additional benefits amounting to $5.3 billion mainly by requiring larger advance income-tax payments from high-income earners. The compromise provided benefits for up to 3 million workers for periods of six, 13, or 20 weeks, depending on state unemployment rates.

• *Banking*. To help the Federal Deposit Insurance Corporation (FDIC) continue to play its role in the badly shaken banking industry, Congress agreed to let the FDIC borrow up to $70 billion to cover losses in failed banks and also toughened some bank regulations.

Similarly, Congress appropriated $30 billion in March to pay off insured depositors in failed savings and loans. Congress later cut back an administration request for $80 billion more for the same purpose to $25 billion. It also approved structural changes in the Resolution Trust Corporation to make it more efficient and accountable.

• *Transportation*. Congress enacted its own version of the president's transportation proposal, authorizing $151 billion to be spent over six years. Of that sum, $31.5 billion was earmarked for mass transit, nearly twice what the president had sought for that purpose. One major impact of the new legislation would be to shift to states and cities many of the decisions about transportation policy that long had been left to Washington. The administration had objected to earlier versions of the bill, contending that the states should pay a greater share of the costs of transportation projects. But the president signed the final compromise in the hope that the jobs it would create would curb unemployment caused by the recession.

But during the course of the year, Congress itself created a number of distractions from its record of accomplishment. One was the vote by the Senate in July to give itself a $23,000 pay raise, bringing its members' annual salary up to the House level of $125,100. At the same time the Senate voted to ban its members from accepting honoraria for speeches. The action stirred widespread public criticism in part because the Senate gave no advance notice of its action and also because of the hard times afflicting the country.

In the fall another furor was stirred when it was disclosed that some members of the House of Representatives routinely wrote checks on the private bank maintained for them without funds to cover them. Reacting to the wave of public indignation, the House shut down the bank and launched an inquiry into the bouncing of more than 8,300 checks by at least 134 lawmakers.

On November 20 the Senate Ethics Committee "strongly and severely" reprimanded Democratic Sen. Alan Cranston of California for "improper and repugnant" conduct in seeking to help thrift operator Charles H. Keating, Jr., a major fund-raiser, in his dealings with federal regulators. Cranston apologized but showed little remorse, contending that many other senators had been similarly helpful to contributors. Earlier in the session four other senators—Republican John McCain of Arizona and Democrats John Glenn of Ohio, Donald W. Riegle, Jr., of Michigan and Dennis DeConcini of Arizona—were given lighter rebukes for their efforts on behalf of Keating, who also contributed to their campaigns.

But perhaps the most spectacular blow to the image of Congress was the Senate Judiciary Committee inquiry into charges of sexual harassment brought by law-school professor Anita Hill against her former boss, Clarence Thomas. Committee members were criticized widely for not taking Hill's charges seriously enough and then for allowing the hearings to degenerate into a tasteless free-for-all in which the reputations of both the accuser and accused were damaged. One senator who at times seemed particularly uncomfortable with the proceedings was Democrat Edward Kennedy of Massachusetts. His own conduct had come under question because of his behavior earlier in the year when his nephew, William Kennedy Smith, was accused of rape. The charges were brought against Smith by a woman he met Good Friday night in a Palm Beach bar to which his uncle had taken him. Smith ultimately was acquitted after a trial at which Kennedy appeared to make a positive impression testifying on his nephew's behalf.

Politics. The presidential campaign got off to an abnormally slow start in 1991. In the wake of the Gulf war triumph, Bush and the GOP were riding high early in the year. Democrats seemed discouraged by the president's high poll ratings and the fact that most members of their party in Congress had opposed the war. But as the year wore on and economic conditions worsened, the political climate began to shift against Bush and in favor of the Democrats.

The most dramatic evidence of changing voter sentiment came in Pennsylvania on November 5 with the upset victory of Democratic Sen. Harris Wofford over Republican Richard Thornburgh. Wofford, appointed to fill the vacancy created by the plane-crash death of Republican Sen. John Heinz, was a relative unknown. Thornburgh by contrast had been a two term governor and Bush's attorney general. But Wofford set out to make the campaign a referendum on the Bush administration. He won by a 55% to 45% margin.

Meanwhile in Kentucky, in another sign of voter discontent, Democratic Lt. Gov. Brereton C. Jones defeated Republican Congressman Larry J. Hopkins for the governorship. Hopkins, for whom Bush campaigned, was among the lawmakers who had written bad checks on their accounts in the House of Representatives bank. Republicans took some satisfaction in the victory in the Mississippi governor's race of their candidate Kirk Fordice over Democratic incumbent Ray Mabus.

But the GOP and Bush had plenty of trouble in Louisiana, where former Ku Klux Klan leader David Duke eliminated Republican incumbent Gov. Buddy Roemer in the October 18 gubernatorial primary. Democrats sought to link Duke's strong showing to what they charged was Bush's exploitation of racial tensions in his 1988 presidential campaign. To avoid further embarrassment, the president and other Republican leaders reluctantly backed Democrat Edwin Edwards in the November 16 runoff election, which Edwards won by a 61% to 39% margin. Duke was not finished, however. On December 4 he announced his candidacy for the Republican presidential nomination, proclaiming himself the champion of middle-class America. He also threatened to run against the president in the November elections on a third-party slate.

The very next week another challenger to Bush entered the race. Patrick J. Buchanan, conservative columnist and former Nixon and Reagan White House aide, called for a "new nationalism" and an "America first" philosophy to safeguard U.S. interests in the post-Cold War world. Buchanan, who never had run for office, described Bush as "a man of graciousness, honor, and integrity," but added: "The differences between us are now too deep. He would put America's wealth and power at the service of some vague New World Order; we will put America first."

Meanwhile six Democrats had taken the field against Bush. They were former California Gov. Edmund G. (Jerry) Brown, Jr., Arkansas Gov. Bill Clinton, Iowa Sen. Tom Harkin, Nebraska Sen. Bob Kerrey, former Massachusetts Sen. Paul E. Tsongas, and Virginia Gov. L. Douglas Wilder. In a nationally televised debate December 15 they attacked Bush sharply for allegedly neglecting the nation's domestic problems, notably the economy. They also sought to introduce themselves to the viewing public.

Harkin took the part of the spokesman for economic populism and traditional Democratic liberalism. He described Bush as "a president completely out of touch with the American people" who "doesn't understand ordinary working people." Clinton, in contrast, depicted himself as loyal to his party's fundamental liberal creed but mindful of the need to adjust to changing times. Kerrey presented himself as the advocate of fundamental change: "I want to go into a different kind of a future, to build a great economic base in the United States." He took every opportunity to refer to his combat experience in Vietnam, which cost him his right leg and won him the Medal of Honor. Wilder, the only black among the candidates, cited his achievement as the grandson of slaves who in 1989 became the nation's first elected black governor. He also emphasized his record of fiscal discipline in Virginia. "I balanced my budget without raising taxes," he said. "And if I can do this in Virginia . . . then we can do that for the nation." Tsongas sought to live up to his self-billing as a probusiness liberal critical of traditional Democratic economic nostrums. Brown used the debate to define his candidacy further as a crusade against the political Establishment, which he contended is corrupted totally by the practices of campaign financing.

Meanwhile, New York Gov. Mario Cuomo (D) said he could not become a candidate in light of his state's budget problems. (Citing Virginia's financial difficulties, Governor Wilder withdrew from the race in early 1992.)

ROBERT SHOGAN, *"Los Angeles Times"*

Redistricting

The results of the 1990 census led to a renewed interest in the issue of redistricting throughout the nation in 1991.

Background. The vast majority of U.S. elected officials are selected from districts. For example, members of the U.S. House of Representatives are elected from congressional districts. Through districting, the boundaries of the geographical areas from which government officials are elected are drawn. Thus, if a city has a five-member city council, the city would be divided into five districts. Larger cities might have two or three council members from each district, but the process is the same. Lines must be drawn that divide the city into distinct geographical areas.

A series of decisions by the U.S. Supreme Court dating back to the 1960s require that political districts be "substantially equal" in population. Every ten years, immediately following the U.S. census, district lines must be redrawn to adjust the size of the districts to the latest population figures. This process is known as redistricting.

The most hotly debated part of congressional redistricting is gerrymandering—attempting to draw district lines so as to favor your political party over the opposition party. There are two ways to gerrymander. One is called cracking—taking a concentration of opposition-party voters and splitting them into two or three different districts. If these opposition-party voters had been kept together, they probably could have elected a House member from that party. Split apart, however, these voters easily are outvoted. The second way to gerrymander is by packing—creating congressional districts with huge concentrations of opposition-party voters. Although the opposition party wins the "packed" House seat, so many of its voters are concentrated in that district that the other party wins most or all of the rest of the state's seats.

The 1990s. At the time of redistricting, states with rapidly growing populations add representatives, while states that are not growing lose representatives. Following the 1990 census, southern states—such as California, Texas, and Florida—gained representatives in the House. Many northern and eastern states—including Illinois, Ohio, Pennsylvania, and New York—lost representatives. Congressional redistricting is particularly painful in states that lost representation. For example, the 1990 census decreed that Michigan should have 16 House members, two less than it had prior to the census. Since none of the 18 incumbent House members indicated a willingness to retire or run for a different office in 1992, the line-drawers had no choice but to put some of the incumbents in the same district, thereby forcing incumbents to run against each other and guaranteeing that at least two members of the delegation would not be returning as House members in January 1993.

Some observers argued that the Democrats benefited the most from the 1990–91 redistricting, because in most states the state legislature draws the new district lines and most of the state legislatures have Democratic majorities and draw district lines so as to elect more Democrats. Others point out that most of the 1980s' population growth occurred in the well-to-do suburbs of major cities, and these areas tend to vote Republican. Even Democratic state legislatures, the argument goes, had to create congressional districts in the Republican-oriented suburbs.

Further complicating the redistricting picture is the Voting Rights Act of 1965, which requires that district lines be drawn in such a way that minority groups—primarily blacks and Hispanics—will be able to elect their own people to political office. At first glance this requirement helps the Democrats, because minority voters, who tend to be concentrated in major cities, vote Democratic. A closer look reveals, however, that creating "minority districts" in center cities forces the boundary makers to create "all-suburban districts" outside the city line. This leads to one of the newest criticisms of redistricting—the district makers tend to create safe Democratic seats in the cities and safe Republican seats in the suburbs. The end result is that incumbent officeholders from either party face little or no competition when they come up for reelection.

ROBERT D. LOEVY

The New U.S. House of Representatives—States That Gained or Lost Seats

STATE	HOUSE SEATS	CHANGE FROM 1980	STATE	HOUSE SEATS	CHANGE FROM 1980	STATE	HOUSE SEATS	CHANGE FROM 1980
Arizona	6	+1	Kentucky	6	−1	North Carolina	12	+1
California	52	+7	Louisiana	7	−1	Ohio	19	−2
Florida	23	+4	Massachusetts	10	−1	Pennsylvania	21	−2
Georgia	11	+1	Michigan	16	−2	Texas	30	+3
Illinois	20	−2	Montana	1	−1	Virginia	11	+1
Iowa	5	−1	New Jersey	13	−1	Washington	9	+1
Kansas	4	−1	New York	31	−3	West Virginia	3	−1

Campaign Finance

The cost of getting elected to political office in the United States is high and, if present trends continue, going higher. In the 1988 general elections, candidates for the U.S. Senate spent $1.41 for each vote cast. In 1990 they spent $1.87 per voter, an increase of 33%.

There are a number of reasons why running for political office, particularly major offices such as state governor or U.S. senator, has become so expensive. Candidates have come to rely heavily on television advertising to carry their message to the voters, and the cost of making good television ads and paying for the time to put them on the air is very high. In addition, more candidates are using computers to poll the electorate and send "personalized" letters to prospective voters, another expensive item.

One side effect of the increasingly high cost of political campaigns is that political candidates, both incumbents and challengers, have to spend a great deal of time raising money. In the case of the U.S. Congress, some senators and representatives who face tough reelection campaigns spend more time trying to raise money than they do serving their constituents or studying and voting on legislation. The "money chase" thus has become a major part of modern political life.

For years Congress has considered a variety of reforms designed to reduce the importance—and the influence—of money in congressional-election campaigns. In the early 1970s, Congress legalized political action committees (PACs), organizations that could raise money and make contributions to candidates for public office. The major benefit of PACs was that they raised and spent their money publicly, thereby enabling the press and public to see the extent to which economic interests—both business and labor—were contributing to various politicians' election campaigns.

By the early 1990s, PACs appeared to be more of the problem than the solution to escalating campaign costs. House and Senate incumbents, respectively, received approximately 40% and 20% of their campaign contributions from PACs, and many observers suspected that the business and labor groups that contributed to PACs wanted favors from elected officials in return for their big campaign contributions.

Most proposals for campaign-spending reform fall into two categories—ceilings and subsidies. Ceilings would put a cap on the amount of money a congressional candidate could receive from PACs ($100,000 often has been mentioned) or would limit all campaign expenditures to a set figure ($250,000 per candidate per election has been recommended frequently). Subsidies would provide for public financing of congressional campaigns, with those candidates who accepted public money voluntarily agreeing to spending limits. In 1976, Congress applied such public financing and voluntary-spending limits to presidential-election campaigns, and almost all observers are pleased with the results, but Congress has declined steadfastly to impose a similar reform on itself.

1991 Reform Proposals. A bill passed in the U.S. Senate in May 1991 was typical of the current efforts of Congress to regulate campaign finance. The bill banned campaign contributions by PACs outright. In addition it offered candidates who accepted voluntary spending ceilings a partial public subsidy and reduced television rates for campaign advertising. The campaign limits, subsidies, and cut-rate TV would be provided equally to incumbents and challengers.

In turn, the House of Representatives passed its version of a campaign-financing bill on November 25 by a 273-156 vote. The House bill, which Speaker Thomas Foley called "one of the [House's] great achievements" of the year, would set a $600,000 optional spending limit for House primary and general elections. Candidates who accept the limit would receive such benefits as reduced postage and up to $200,000 in public funds to match the first $200 of each individual contribution. The bill also would establish a $200,000 aggregate cap on the amount a candidate could receive for PACs and a $200,000 cap on individual contributions of more than $200.

The House of Representatives and Senate were expected to try to iron out the differences between their two bills early in 1992. Such a Senate-House conference was considered to be difficult in light of the vast differences between the two measures. In addition, President Bush had indicated that he would veto any legislation that calls for public financing or spending limits or that sets up separate campaign-financing systems for House and Senate candidates. Both the Senate and House measures passed in 1991 included provisions limiting public financing but neither prescribed ways to pay the cost.

ROBERT D. LOEVY

The States' Fiscal Crisis

In Annapolis, on Oct. 1, 1991, dozens of Maryland state troopers formed ranks on the steps of the State House, bearing a huge banner with the words: "Save Your Troopers." They were protesting Gov. William Donald Schaefer's cost-cutting proposal to shut down two state police barracks and fire nearly 100 troopers. "Everyone has something they want to save," complained the hard-pressed governor.

In Hartford four days later, more than 40,000 angry taxpayers massed in front of Connecticut's Capitol in the largest protest demonstration in the state's history, to vent their anger at the state's new income tax. The chief sponsor of the tax, Gov. Lowell Weicker, was spat upon as he fought his way through the crowd but stuck to his guns. "I don't intend to back down to that kind of stuff ever," he declared.

In varying degrees and forms "that kind of stuff" confronted politicians of both parties in every corner of the United States in 1991, forcing a Hobson's choice between making drastic cuts in services, as in Maryland, or imposing new taxes, as in Connecticut, or doing both. It was the bitter harvest of an unprecedented fiscal crisis gripping state and city governments in 1991, the seeds of which had been sown in the freewheeling era of the 1980s.

Causes. The most immediate cause for the flood tide of red ink that engulfed state houses and city halls was not hard to identify. It was the economic recession that had struck in late 1990 and persisted well into 1991. State governments usually suffer more from recession than does the federal government because they are more dependent on consumption taxes, such as the sales tax, for revenue. The proceeds from such taxes drop dramatically in hard times when worried consumers cut back on spending, a behavioral pattern which was particularly evident in the current slump. As for local governments, the widespread collapse of the real-estate market, which antedated and brought on the recession, cut into the property taxes which are their main source of funding. And to make matters worse, as income dropped, pressure for spending increased as the recession fostered demand for health, welfare, and other social services.

Aggravating the impact of the recession was the failure of many national economic analysts, on whom state and local governments rely, to predict the recession far enough in advance for the states and cities to make preparations for meeting it. Not until spring did Commerce Department figures belatedly show that a recession officially had arrived as a result of declines in the gross national product for the last quarter of 1990 and the first quarter of 1991. Among the states taken unaware was the largest, California, where a January prediction of a shortfall of $7 billion over two years had to be doubled to more than $14 billion in May, while unemployment and welfare rolls also rose alarmingly.

That same month the Center for the Study of the States at New York's Nelson A. Rockefeller Institute of Government reported that tax revenues in the first quarter of 1991 were merely .9% over the same period in 1990.

In Boston demonstrators protest against Gov. William Weld's plan to force thousands of state employees to take unpaid furlough days. The measure was in response to the state's fiscal crisis.

Moreover, the center's figures, collected from every state except Alaska, showed that if the 5% inflation rate was taken into account tax revenue measured in "real dollars" actually had declined by 6%. Center officials said the growth of tax revenue was even weaker than in the 1982 recession, when relatively high inflation boosted these proceeds, particularly from sales taxes, at a faster rate than costs.

But the recession was only one of several causes for the fiscal conundrum. A more fundamental factor was a change in federal policy in the previous decades which led to imposition of greater burdens on the states and at the same time a lessening of federal support through the shrinking or outright elimination of such programs as revenue sharing. In part this trend was driven by ideology, that is, the conviction held by the Reagan administration that government power better was wielded by state and local officials who were supposedly more responsive to the citizenry than was the federal bureaucracy. Another, more pragmatic reason for the burden shifting was the increasing pressure on Washington to cut back spending because of the burgeoning federal deficit.

As year after year the national government continued to do business more or less as usual despite the huge national debt, taxpayers and politicians seem to have been lulled into a false sense of security about the financial condition of state and local government. Forgotten for the time being was the fact that unlike the federal government, 49 states and most local governments are prohibited legally from operating at a deficit. This difference was dramatized in July, when as states and citizens desperately pinched pennies to make ends meet, the Bush administration announced that the federal budget deficit in fiscal 1992 would reach an estimated $348 billion.

But all this had seemed far away during the booming 1980s when with their revenues on the rise and demands from the electorate for services increasing, states responded by stepping up their spending at a much faster rate than they should have, according to some critics. With their economies flourishing during the 1980s, spending rose 134% in Massachusetts, 119% in California, and 169% in Florida.

In its own analysis of the predicament, the Cato Institute, a Washington-based conservative think tank, contended that the "primary culprit" for the crisis was "a decade of runaway state-government expenditures." The analysis cited Census Bureau data showing that state spending between 1982 and 1988 increased at a rate of 8.5% or about twice the inflation rate. And it charged that double-digit annual percentage expenditure growth became the norm for state-funded programs such as education, health care, welfare, and corrections.

Reckoning. Whatever the causes, it soon became clear that the day of reckoning was at hand. In April the *Fiscal Survey of the States* compiled by the National Governors' Association and the National Association of State Budget Officers reported that 29 states had cut more than $8 billion out of their enacted budgets for fiscal year 1991, while 26 states were in the process of raising taxes by more than $10 billion—the largest tax increase since the survey began in 1978. More than $6 billion was expected in additional tax increases for 1992.

The biggest state, California, led the way. Republican Gov. Pete Wilson and the Democratic legislature agreed on a record $7.7 billion tax package, built around a $4.1 billion sales-tax rise which would lift the state sales tax to 8.25%, and including an income-tax hike on its wealthiest citizens. In New York, which was facing a $6 billion shortfall, agreement was reached on a $52 billion budget package built mainly around drastic spending cuts but also including an income tax on residents with incomes earning more than $100,000 and designed to raise $100 million a year. The plan was reached after a bitter battle between Governor Cuomo and the legislature.

In some ways the problem was even worse for cities, which experienced a significant decline in federal aid during the 1980s. To help out, states had boosted their aid to cities during that period. But as the states struggled to deal with their own fiscal burdens, they often chose to cut back the help they had given to their municipalities. This economic squeeze was driven home dramatically in June when the city of Bridgeport, CT, facing a $12 million imbalance in its budget, filed bankruptcy papers rather than boost taxes or further curtail services.

In July the National League of Cities, reporting on a survey of 525 cities of all sizes, said that one out of four was facing a budget gap of more than 5%, with seven out of ten complaining that they were less able to meet their financial needs than they had been a year earlier. In New York City, after months of wrangling, Mayor David Dinkins and the City Council agreed to a budget plan that would boost income and property taxes by $735 million and impose $1.5 billion in service cuts and layoffs of 10,000 workers. But hardly had this plan been approved when city officials said the tax boost was not big enough to meet the problem over the long run and anticipated a $4.3 billion shortfall through 1995.

Smaller cities were struggling, too. The League of Cities found that nearly 30% of communities with populations below 100,000 re-

With three out of five states facing serious financial trouble during 1991, cuts in services, such as much-needed highway repairs, as well as tax increases were enacted.

© Chris Gierlich/Saba

ported revenues running 5% behind outlays, and for some the gap was more than 25%. To make things even tougher for cities, many were forced to operate under restrictions on their ability to raise taxes. Thus in Montana, where a 1986 vote initiative froze property-tax rates, city officials in Billings watched their revenues from the property levy drop by $1 million per year, forcing them to eliminate 25 full-time and 50 part-time jobs, close the city's six ice-skating rinks, reduce recreation programs by one third, and eliminate two street-repair crews.

In the absence of such legal inhibitions, imposing new taxes or raising old ones was a common answer to the problem. California expanded its sales tax to take in bottled water and newspapers, New York to dating services. In Wisconsin fees for hunting licenses went up, while Oregon hiked the charge for birth-certificate copies to $13 from $10. But some politicians balked at paying the political price a tax hike would extract. In Illinois, where the budget debate dragged on past the July starting date for the new fiscal year, Republican Gov. Jim Edgar kept his campaign promise to balance the state's $25.6 billion budget without a new general tax increase. But the agreement with Democratic legislators to cover a $1.8 billion revenue shortfall did include an extension of an income-tax surcharge—along with about $1 billion in spending cuts. Similarly, in Texas, newly elected Democratic Gov. Ann Richards rejected proposals to enact an income tax or a big sales-tax increase to help the state fund its badly strapped school and prison systems. Instead she decided to push ahead on a massive cost-cutting plan to save $4 billion in expenditures through such measures as eliminating jobs, consolidating funds, and doubling tuition at state colleges and universities.

According to the National Conference of State Legislatures about 30 states resorted to deep cutbacks in services. Some targeted the poor, such as Michigan where the legislature eliminated the general-assistance welfare program that covered more than 80,000 adults. Others aimed at public employees, as in Iowa where Republican Gov. Terry E. Branstad vetoed $34 million in pay raises for state workers. But a good many of the cuts reached across the socioeconomic spectrum, affecting middle-class citizens. Though members of this group had not thought of themselves as clients of government they now were hurt as the budget axe bit deeply into spending for schools, libraries, roads, parks, and law enforcement.

Seeking an alternative to such cuts, more and more cities began to contract out services to private companies at savings ranging from 10% to 40%, according to various studies. Spurring this trend to privatization was the chance to avoid fast-growing costs for pensions. Proponents argued that private contractors often could offer cost-efficient equipment cities could not afford, and also could pay lower wages. But even advocates conceded that privatization needs intensive monitoring.

Hard times for states also seemed to be spurring interest in state lotteries, which already were proliferating rapidly. Between 1970 and 1990 the number of state lotteries jumped from three to 32 (plus the District of Columbia), while annual proceeds soared from $49 million to more than $20 billion. Other forms of gambling also were becoming increasingly popular as revenue sources.

More fundamentally, the nation's governors called on the federal government to increase support by fostering economic development through such measures as educational reform, infrastructure improvement, and energy conservation. Pointing out that the states had sought to pick up the slack in public services created by federal budget cuts, the governors warned in a policy statement adopted at their winter meeting that they could "no longer afford—and our federal partners could no longer ask us—to make up the difference." In the face of the fiscal squeeze, the governors declared: "It is time to work together . . . to maintain critical services and to make the long-term investments necessary for our country's continued growth."

ROBERT SHOGAN

The Economy

The U.S. economy in 1991 was one of repeated disappointments—to the White House, the Federal Reserve, businesses, and households. Hopes were dashed; forecasts were revised; plans were abandoned; purchases and investments were postponed. Except for a brief midsummer period, the pattern persisted throughout the year. While economists and government officials looked for improvement, they generally were greeted instead with news of further deterioration.

Recession and Weakness. By late in the year, however, almost everyone agreed that the recession was deeper and more persistent than at first believed, and that in some ways it might be worse than indicated by the traditional indices. The news for just two pre-Christmas days, December 17 and 18, gave some indication of the shock waves that reverberated almost daily through the economy near the end of the year, fraying nerves of the political leadership and depressing consumer confidence to lows not seen since 1980.

• The White House abandoned its insistence that the economy was rebounding. "For all practical purposes the recession continues," said White House spokesman Marlin Fitzwater. "People are unemployed; people are hurting; the economy is very slow," he said.

• The Commerce Department announced a 2.1% decline in housing starts during November. Building permits, precursor of future activity, fell 2.9%. The figures erased signs of improvement and undermined hopes of a quick recovery spurred by lowered interest rates.

• R.H. Macy & Co., one of the nation's largest retailers, said losses for the most recent quarter more than doubled to $155.4 million from $56.5 million a year earlier. It blamed a weak economy and predicted that the Christmas selling season, ordinarily the source for more than half of all retail profits, would be a poor one.

• General Motors announced plans to close 21 more factories, cut 74,000 jobs by the end of 1995, and slash capital spending in an attempt to end huge losses in North America. The downsizing would reduce the company's continental operations to 1985 size. Just three weeks earlier, International Business Machines had announced plans for cutting 20,000 more jobs in 1992, atop a similar cut in 1991.

• Digital Equipment Corp. said it would lose money in the quarter to end December 28, the first loss in the company's 34-year history which was not a result of restructuring or other special charges. It blamed weak sales throughout the industry.

• Alan Greenspan, Federal Reserve chairman, said the recovery that had appeared to take hold during the summer "clearly has faltered." He blamed much of the problem on resistance to more debt by already debt-burdened households and businesses.

After five fractional cuts in a year, the Federal Reserve lowered the discount rate, or loan rate to commercial banks, a full point to 3.5% on December 20. It was that rate's lowest level since 1964, and it was followed immediately by a cut to 6.5% in the prime lending rate, or the hypothetical base rate at which banks lend to their best corporate customers. The move, a drastic one for the usually cautious Fed, was made possible by evidence that no longer was inflation from overborrowing a threat. The urban consumer price index was running at less than 3.5%, growth of installment debt had ceased, and banks were only reluctant lenders. Some observers contended, however, that the Federal Reserve had no choice but to cut sharply because the economy was weak and otherwise would remain so. Moreover, Congress and the White House were stymied from adding stimulus because of budget deficits.

The evidence of weakness was everywhere, but perhaps the most serious aspect of the weakness was its location—in the very industrial and financial heart of the nation, in the esteemed manufacturing companies, and in banks and insurance companies. By year's end, 124 banks had failed and some insurers too. The institutional pillars of the economy were tilting badly. The banks, for example, were being dragged down by their nonperforming loans. The insurers, many of whom had invested heavily in junk bonds and almost all of whom owned real estate more vacant than utilized, found their assets shrinking in value. Part of the Federal Reserve's job, therefore, was to pump up the value of those assets via lower interest rates that, presumably, would create greater marketplace demand and, in so doing, would assure the collateral on loans. Many observers believed that the Fed's repeated lowering of interest rates propped up the stock market, and the Dow Jones industrial average seemed to reflect that belief, shrugging off occasional dips and closing at 3,168.83, 20.3% higher for the year.

These worries and fears contrasted with the earlier pronouncements of confidence. Economists and officials at every level, including those in the White House, seemed at first to believe the downturn would be short and shallow, especially if the Persian Gulf war were brief and successful. The recession that began at midyear 1990 at first was denied by some economists, then was conceded reluctantly, forecast to be over quickly and even, as events were to show, was declared over prematurely. A remarkable dichotomy developed: Households and many businesses, especially small ones, emitted signals of great financial distress, but many economists and officials dismissed their complaints as "anecdotal." They continued to insist that the consumer—though burdened by debts, overloaded with "stuff" from the buying binge of the 1980s, financially stressed by only slow gains in real income, and fearful of losing employment—would lead the nation into an economic recovery. Though the hope was held by supposedly the best economic minds, it was an unrealistic one that would be dashed by events.

Debt. Americans who had bought and borrowed with abandon in the 1980s clearly were frightened. While it might have contributed to the downturn, the reluctance of Americans to take on more debt was seen by many analysts as healthy over the longer term. Debts—government, business, and household—already totaled about $11 trillion and posed a formidable obstacle to future sales and services, to say nothing about the American quality of life. From 1966 to 1977, the ratio of household debt to disposable income was about 68% and the long-term average was only 75%. But total household debt in 1991, including mortgage and consumer borrowing of all types, jumped to an unsustainable 94% of disposable income. The Mortgage Bankers Association announced that payments 90 days or more past due rose in the third quarter at the fastest rate in five years and that a further deterioration was likely.

At first, the Fed lowered interest rates as much to help debtors pay down their loans as to spur economic activity through new lending. Those who owned homes benefited immediately and even enormously. With fixed-rate mortgages already down to about 8.5% in mid-December from 10% at the beginning of the year, some people who refinanced enjoyed savings of more than $200 per month, and the prospect was of even more savings to come. Economists at the National Association of Realtors forecast a drop to 8% by January 1992, which would mean a one-year decline of $288 per month on a $200,000 fixed-rate, 30-year mortgage. Variable-rate mortgages were headed toward a nationwide average of just more than 6% at the end of the year, and some banks offered loans with first-year rates less than 5%. Carmakers offered rates even lower, but neither housing nor industry could shake their depression. For the year, housing starts fell to just more than 1 million, the lowest level since 1945, and 12.3 million new cars and light trucks were sold in the United States, the lowest since 1983.

Interest Rates. Welcome as they were to most people, lower interest rates were not sought by all. While estimates varied, as much as 16% of the population relied to some extent on interest income. For them, the declines made the recession the more distressing, and since many were elderly they could do little to offset the loss. Based on telephone calls to about 1,000 heads of household each week, employees of Sindlinger & Co., a market-research firm, said they could measure a perceptible decline in consumer confidence, already at depressed levels, each time rates were lowered. Early in December, Citicorp's Chicago thrift subsidiary, Citibank FSB, cut the rate paid on savings accounts to 3.15% from 4.34%. Potentially, said Albert Sindlinger, in solving one problem the Fed might create another.

One beneficiary would be the federal government, since the national debt stood at $3,113,300,000,000 in 1990 and rising budget deficits—$268.7 billion in fiscal 1991—would add to that. Businesses and households had begun cutting their debts, but government at all levels still wrestled with expenses out of control. At the local level, real-estate-tax increases were common. Among states, income taxes proliferated in an attempt to reduce budget gaps.

Businesses benefited greatly from lower rates, especially since they had loaded up on debt financing during the 1980s. Now, however, many were reluctant to carry that debt in spite of lower interest rates. They opted for equity financing instead, and commentators said that if the 1980s was the decade of debt, the 1990s would be marked by a return to equity financing.

The Job Scene. Whereas various techniques for spurring growth marked every decade since World War II, the 1990s began with companies seeking to pare down their girths for the more competitive global economy. White-collar workers, once secure in their jobs, were dismissed by the tens of thousands, and many found their skills could not be transferred to jobs paying half what they had earned previously.

While downsizing, as it was called, might have prepared businesses for the future, it had devastating consequences in the short term. While the unemployment rate held fairly steady, varying only between 6.5% at the start of the year to under 7% at year's end, the job situation deteriorated badly. Officially, about 8.5 million Americans were unemployed late in the year, but many of those said to have jobs were employed only marginally. More than 6 million people worked part-time, many of them because they could not obtain full-time work. About 1.1 million were listed as discouraged, and since they had given up the active pursuit of work they were not counted in the labor force. In addition, the long-term growth in labor-force participation slowed, especially among women. Most importantly, the popularly cited statistics failed to reveal that many of the unemployed had lost their jobs forever, since their positions had been eliminated.

Business failures grew. Dun & Bradstreet found that in just the first seven months of the year, 50,641 companies went under, more than in all of 1989. The highest rates were in the New England, mid-Atlantic, and Pacific regions, and the weakest industries were transportation and finance. Also reflecting the distressed business climate, government figures showed that corporate profits, compared with periods a year earlier, fell throughout the year and for nine straight quarters in all. The decline in this and other aspects of the economy was reflected in a gross domestic product (GDP) that fell 2.5% in the first quarter, rose 1.4% and 1.8% in the second and third quarters, respectively, and fell as the year ended.

JOHN CUNNIFF, *The Associated Press*

Foreign Affairs

President George Bush's domestic political critics began speaking of a "feel good" foreign policy in 1991, one serving in part to divert attention from severe U.S. domestic problems. This followed earlier euphoria from the success of the Persian Gulf war and the momentum toward Middle East peace talks. After the Iraqi surrender, President Bush announced that the "Vietnam syndrome" of defeatism in U.S. foreign policy had been buried. In many respects the administration continued trying to build international consensus for a post-Cold War order under U.S. leadership, but it was not clear how that consensus would hold up in future crises.

The year's other main foreign events included a failed Soviet coup attempt and subsequent breakup of the Soviet Union, full-scale Yugoslav civil war, and an economic summit of the major industrial democracies (G-7). Other concerns involved an antidemocratic coup in Haiti, a North Atlantic Treaty Organization (NATO) summit, general progress toward democracy in Latin America and Africa, gradual momentum in peace talks for Cambodia and Central America, and continued trade negotiations.

The Middle East. The Gulf war ended with remarkably few U.S. casualties. Iraqi forces fought less well than had been predicted, and allied forces enjoyed a major advantage in modern weaponry. With the sweeping U.S. military victory, however, came a much less certain political outcome. In the interest of a stable Iraqi state, Saddam Hussein was allowed to remain in power and even to repress Kurdish and Shiite Muslim resistance that the United States had encouraged during the war.

This caused Washington to revive its "new international order" diplomacy, accepting a British suggestion to lead a United Nations (UN) multinational force to protect the Kurds, even as the bulk of U.S. forces returned home to a heroes' welcome. A UN inspection team also was dispatched to determine the extent of Iraqi nuclear- and chemical-weapons development. Washington threatened further air at-

U.S. diplomacy in 1991 included keeping pace with the historic changes in the USSR. Meetings between Secretary of State James Baker and Russia's President Boris Yeltsin—third from left, below, were a part of the process.

AP/Wide World

tacks against Iraq when the inspectors were impeded, and by the end of the year the Bush administration appeared to be pushing for Saddam Hussein's overthrow.

The war also profoundly affected the administration's Middle East security policy. Riding the crest of victory, and with the Soviet Union in trouble, the United States emerged as the only superpower to which Arab states and groups could turn. New security pacts were forged with several Gulf states, including Kuwait and Saudi Arabia, for a long-term U.S. military presence. As relations with Syria improved, the administration, in conjunction with Moscow, applied pressure and inducements for an Arab-Israeli peace conference.

Significant assistance and arms supplies went to Israel, in part as payment for Tel Aviv's restraint in the Gulf war. But signs of friction with the Jewish state caused some to question President Bush's long-term need for Israeli security partnership. Through September the two governments quarreled over a delayed U.S. loan-guarantee program for Israeli settlement of new Soviet immigrants as jockeying over terms of Arab-Israeli peace talks continued. The long-sought peace conference finally opened in late October at the summit level in Madrid, a monumental diplomatic achievement for persistent Secretary of State James Baker. However, haggling over the site of the next round of negotiations, plus Israel's reluctance to follow a "land for peace" formula, produced a stalemate. The Israelis and Arabs met again in December, in Washington, again with little achievement, while the UN General Assembly voted to rescind its previous resolution equating Zionism with racism.

By year's end all U.S. hostages held in Lebanon had been released, a further sign that profound changes had taken place in the Middle East. (*See also* FEATURE SECTION, page 36.)

The USSR. As Soviet leaders struggled to rescue their economy, constitution, and then the union itself, U.S. leaders expressed cautious support. President Mikhail Gorbachev joined his Western counterparts at the end of the London G-7 economic summit in July, hoping for assistance on the level of the post-World War II Marshall Plan; instead he got agreement for cooperation through the International Monetary Fund (IMF) and some bilateral promises of further humanitarian and economic assistance. The United States followed European leaders in recognizing the early independence of the Baltic republics.

The press of events pushed Congress and the administration to work out a Soviet aid package, with some funds to dismantle nuclear weapons and some for food shipments. By August the Soviet economy was in shambles as a result of attempted transition to market reform. Even so, the abortive army-KGB-Communist Party coup apparently caught Washington as well as the rest of the world by surprise. President Bush quickly signaled opposition to the coup and expressed solidarity with Russian Republic President Boris Yeltsin.

As events unfolded and the Soviet Union disintegrated, Washington grew increasingly uncertain about control over the nuclear weapons scattered among the various independence-minded Soviet republics. Thus in September, President Bush made a historic unilateral nuclear-disarmament offer. Going beyond the limits in the newly agreed-to but still nonratified Strategic Arms Reduction Treaty (START), Washington's cutbacks—also partly dictated by budgetary concerns—covered all short-range nuclear weapons on land and sea (aircraft excepted), the end to U.S. strategic-bomber alerts, cancellation of rail-mobile long-range missile development, and a further curb on land-based multiple-warhead missiles. Moscow seemed willing to reciprocate, but pushed as well for a comprehensive nuclear-test ban

With the Middle East a center of U.S. foreign policy in 1991, President Bush met with the emir of Bahrain, a U.S. ally in the Persian Gulf war, at the White House in mid-October.

© Cynthia Johnson/"Time" Magazine

and submarine-based-missile reductions to cut into U.S. advantages.

In remarks on Christmas night, the president praised Mikhail Gorbachev, who just had resigned as Soviet leader, and said the United States would recognize the independence of the 11 republics that had joined the newly formed Commonwealth of Independent States as well as Georgia, which had not. (*See also* FEATURE SECTION, page 24.)

Yugoslavia. The bitter interethnic violence tearing Yugoslavia apart in the autumn drew a much less urgent U.S. response than had the occupation of Kuwait or the Soviet breakup. Basically, formal mediation and conciliation attempts were left to the European Community (EC). At the NATO summit in November, President Bush formally endorsed an EC-proposed oil embargo of Yugoslavia to break the federal army's attacks on Croatia; subsequently, with former Secretary of State Cyrus Vance acting as UN mediator, the warring parties agreed in principle to a UN peacekeeping force.

NATO. NATO struggled to define its meaning, given the vanished Soviet threat and new European ethnic tensions. During his November visit, President Bush joined his allies in proposing vague political cooperation to address common security concerns, including Eastern Europe. Yet the alliance got no new powers or members and was left to find a role in relation to the quickly forming new international system. The result of the visit was that U.S. forces would remain in Europe for the time being, but without a clear mission.

The Third World. In U.S.-Third World relations, democratic reform was a commonly, though not uniformly, stressed theme. New accords between the government and guerrilla forces in El Salvador and an agreement for Panama to join Costa Rica in eliminating its armed forces seemed to open the way for peace in the Americas. The Bush administration was sensitive to counterdemocratic trends, however, and when the Haitian military overthrew President Jean-Bertrand Aristide in late September, Washington—rejecting military options—backed strict Organization of American States (OAS) economic sanctions against Haiti.

While supporting sanctions in Latin America and Yugoslavia, however, the Bush administration called for their elimination against South Africa, given that country's domestic peace agreements and despite its continued violence. Elsewhere in Africa, Washington hoped to bring Zaire into the growing circle of multiparty governments through cautious pressure on President Mobutu Sese Seko amid popular unrest. Despite its opposition to forced annexation of territory by Iraq, Washington continued to accept, with only mild protest, Indonesia's control of East Timor and the repression of the opposition there.

China. Commercial and strategic relations with China also seemed to override human-rights concerns; the U.S. trade deficit with Beijing was second only to that with Tokyo. Restrictions on high-technology trade were lifted despite Beijing's rights abuses and record of expanding arms trade. Nevertheless, considerable trade pressure was applied to China to protect U.S. copyrights and open restricted markets. During November, Secretary Baker obtained general agreement by Chinese leaders to join the nuclear-nonproliferation and missile-export-control agreements and to account for political prisoners.

Elsewhere in Asia, Baker expressed a growing U.S. concern about reports of fairly advanced North Korean nuclear research. Earlier, North Korea had indicated a desire for relaxed tensions with South Korea and had repeated its objections to U.S. nuclear weapons in the south. On December 18, South Korea declared that the United States had withdrawn all nuclear arms from its territory, and on December 31 the two Koreas signed a pact to ban nuclear weapons from the peninsula.

Economics. On the economic front, 1991 saw progress on a North American (U.S., Canada, and Mexico) free-trade zone. While a proposed U.S.-Mexico trade pact was politically controversial among organized labor and environmentalists, it was seen as a prelude to possible hemisphere-wide agreements in an attempt to counter European and East Asian moves toward restrictive regional common markets. (*See also* SPECIAL REPORT/MEXICO.)

Although some argued that the persistent U.S. trade deficit had more to do with deficient domestic productivity and marketing, "structural impediment talks" continued with Japan, addressing informal Japanese trade barriers such as dealer distribution networks. As the year ended, President Bush led a contingent of 21 U.S. industry executives to Japan to press these points. Also, successful renewal of the suspended Uruguay round of tariff-reduction talks would depend on reduced Japanese as well as European farm subsidies.

During the year less-developed countries—hard-pressed by higher oil prices, debts, and shrinking world markets—grew alarmed at the new focus of Western economic assistance on Eastern Europe. Some, like India, having lost Soviet support, tried to open commercial linkages and joint ventures with the United States. With the end of fighting in Cambodia, and with cooperation in identifying Americans missing in action (MIAs), Vietnam shared such hopes. Although the United States and Cuba remained estranged, Havana opened its tourist resorts and invited foreign investments, and the U.S. base at Guantánamo Bay was used to house fleeing Haitian refugees.

FREDERIC S. PEARSON, *Wayne State University*

URUGUAY

Although the ruling coalition of Luis Alberto Lacalle broke apart in 1991, postponing legislative approval of a modernization drive, the president received substantial assistance from abroad. Such aid reduced the foreign debt and expedited the president's plan to correct major problems in the nation's ailing economy. Uruguay also joined a new regional common market in 1991.

Politics and Government. Without a majority in the legislative branch or even solid backing from his own National Party, President Lacalle had to depend on support from the opposition for approval of his modernization program. By the end of May, when a bill privatizing state firms was to be debated, a strong faction of the Colorado Party withdrew its support from the cross-party coalition. The administration's program restructuring the public sector and encouraging competition had to be shelved. While labor also was opposed to privatization plans, a 24-hour general strike called on May 21 was motivated by a collapse of eight months of peaceful negotiations over the government's failure to fulfill its campaign pledge to raise the purchasing power of public-sector employees.

Debt. A debt- and debt-service-reduction package was signed in February with Uruguay's commercial-bank creditors. Banks holding 39% of the $1.6 billion indebtedness would sell their debt to the government for 56 cents cash on the dollar. Holders of one third of the debt were to exchange it for bonds, and those holding 28% of the debt would be repaid over a longer period than first stipulated. Funding for the proposal came from international lending agencies. One fourth of a $137 million standby loan from the International Monetary Fund (IMF), authorized in January, was set aside to finance debt relief. The World Bank approved a $65 million debt-reduction loan on May 14. And $58 million of an Inter-American Development Bank loan also would be used in the debt buyback. Thus, Uruguay's debt and debt-service obligations would be cut by $503 million. The relief enhanced prospects of Uruguay's achieving an average growth rate of 2.5% to 3% annually. (The rate in 1990 was about 0.3%.)

Foreign Affairs. President George Bush paid a visit to Uruguay on Dec. 4, 1990, during a tour that was to have promoted free trade, democracy, and growth in the Western Hemisphere. But the visit was dominated by the Uruguayan president's concern about the approaching war in the Persian Gulf and a consequent rise in the price of oil. Lacalle returned the visit in May. In Washington, DC, the Uruguayan chief executive predicted that his country would become the gateway to a market of 200 million people joined in a Southern Cone regional-trading bloc. Marking the first anniversary of President Bush's Enterprise for the Americas Initiative, Uruguayan Foreign Minister Héctor Gros Espiell went to the White House on June 19 to sign a framework for relaxing trade barriers between Uruguay and the United States.

Another problem treated bilaterally with the United States was that of the laundering of dollars from the narcotics trade through Uruguay's offshore banking system, with its secret accounts. While Uruguay had no intention of modifying the country's strict banking-secrecy laws or regulating the operations of numerous exchange houses in Montevideo and Punta del Este, it did sign a legal-assistance treaty in May that provided for some aid in criminal trials.

President Lacalle traveled to Asunción, Paraguay, in March to participate in the creation of MERCOSUR, a common market with Argentina, Brazil, and Paraguay. While it was to be in operation by Jan. 1, 1995, Uruguay would have an extra year to eliminate tariffs and coordinate relevant policies. Montevideo was to serve as headquarters for the trade pact and, Uruguayans hoped, the financial and services center for the whole MERCOSUR area.

LARRY L. PIPPIN
University of the Pacific

URUGUAY • Information Highlights

Official Name: Oriental Republic of Uruguay.
Location: Southeastern coast of South America.
Area: 68,039 sq mi (176 220 km²).
Population (mid-1991 est.): 3,100,000.
Capital (1985 census): Montevideo, 1,246,500.
Government: *Head of state,* Luis Alberto Lacalle, president (took office March 1, 1990). *Legislature*—National Congress: Senate and House of Deputies.
Monetary Unit: Peso (2,298.85 pesos equal U.S.$1, financial rate, Nov. 6, 1991).
Gross Domestic Product (1989 est. U.S.$): $8,800,-000,000.
Foreign Trade (1990 U.S.$): *Imports,* $1,343,000,000; *exports,* $1,693,000,000.

UTAH

A restrictive abortion law, an Olympic Games bid, construction of a new sports arena, and a new University of Utah president made news in Utah in 1991.

Utah's Abortion Law. The 1991 Utah legislature passed the most restrictive abortion law in the United States early in the year. The legislation prohibited abortion except in cases where the mother's life was jeopardized; where there was serious fetal deformity; and, during the first 20 weeks of pregnancy, for reported cases of incest or rape. Gov. Norman Bangerter signed the bill into law within hours of its passage by the House and Senate, after just three days of deliberation. Those on both sides

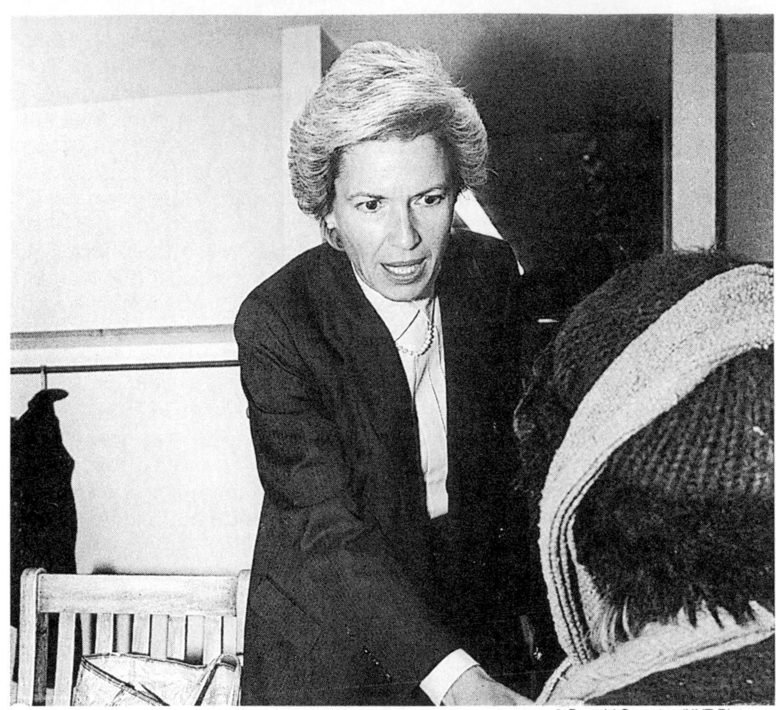

© Donald Grayston/NYT Pictures

On Nov. 5, 1991, Deedee Corradini became the first woman to be elected mayor of Salt Lake City, UT. The 47-year-old Democratic businesswoman had urged the city's electorate to vote for her because of her qualifications, not because of her gender. She won the post by a margin of 55% to 45%.

of the debate agreed that the law would prohibit 90% of all abortions and was a direct challenge to *Roe v. Wade* (1973).

The Utah legislature also appropriated $100,000 for the Utah attorney general's office to defend the law against any legal challenges. Governor Bangerter, a Republican, directed Attorney General Paul Van Dam, a Democrat, to retain a private law firm to defend the law. In October attorneys from the selected firm, after having been paid $95,000 in tax money, were removed from the case when the American Civil Liberties Union found that the firm also represented the Utah Women's Clinic, a plaintiff in the abortion suit.

Winter Olympic Bid. Utah made a strong bid to host the 1998 Winter Olympic Games with a commitment to the U.S. Olympic Committee to create Olympic facilities. In a 1988 referendum Utah voters had approved the spending of $56 million in sales-tax revenue to construct a speed-skating oval, bobsled/luge run, ski jumps, and other facilities. In the final round of voting in Birmingham, England, in June, the International Olympic Committee dismissed Salt Lake City's bid by a 46 to 42 vote, choosing instead Nagano, Japan.

The Delta Center. The construction of a $93 million sports arena was completed in Salt Lake City in October, after less than 16 months of construction. Made possible in part by the efforts of Larry Miller; a local automobile dealer and owner of the Utah Jazz National Basketball Association (NBA) basketball team and the Salt Lake City Golden Eagles hockey team, the 20,400-seat arena ranked third nationally in capacity for NBA teams. Although designed primarily for basketball, it is adaptable for hockey, concerts, and other events.

University of Utah. Amid controversy concerning his administration, University of Utah President Chase Peterson announced that he would leave at the end of the 1991 academic year. Peterson had been criticized strongly for his involvement in the decision to donate $500,000 of university funds to the National Cold Fusion Institute and was denounced for his effort to rename the University Health Sciences Center for Utah businessman James L. Sorenson, who had promised to donate $15 million to the center.

Arthur K. Smith, a native of New Hampshire, was named the new president by the Utah state board of regents in June. Smith is the first non-Mormon ever to head the institution. He is a graduate of the U.S. Naval Academy and holds a master's degree from the

UTAH • Information Highlights

Area: 84,899 sq mi (219 889 km²).
Population (1990 census): 1,722,850.
Chief Cities (1990 census): Salt Lake City, the capital, 159,936; West Valley City, 86,976; Provo, 86,835.
Government (1991): *Chief Officers*—governor, Norman H. Bangerter (R); lt. gov., W. Val Oveson (R). *Legislature*—Senate, 29 members; House of Representatives, 75 members.
State Finances (fiscal year 1990): *Revenue,* $4,302,000,000; *expenditure,* $3,857,000,000.
Personal Income (1990): $24,199,000,000; per capita, $13,993.
Labor Force (June 1991): *Civilian labor force,* 810,600; *unemployed,* 44,700 (5.5% of total force).
Education: *Enrollment* (fall 1989)—public elementary schools, 322,889; public secondary, 114,557; colleges and universities, 114,815. *Public school expenditures* (1989), $1,040,104,000.

University of New Hampshire and a Ph.D from Cornell University. Smith most recently served in various capacities at the State University of New York-Binghamton (1982-88) and the University of South Carolina (1988–91).

LORENZO K. KIMBALL, *University of Utah*

VENEZUELA

The year 1991 was one of paradox for Venezuela. Economic recovery, which began in 1990, a year after President Carlos Andrés Pérez launched his far-reaching economic program, continued and accelerated. After experiencing 5% growth in 1990, the highest in Latin America, the economy was expected to grow as much as 7% in 1991. Nevertheless, the better the economy performed, the more the government was criticized, both by the opposition and by the governing party, Acción Democrática (AD).

The Economy. The government was vulnerable to criticism that the economy had not recovered as much as promised. After the Persian Gulf crisis, oil prices fell below the level budgeted for 1991. Consequently, government revenues, largely derived from oil, lagged, creating an unexpected deficit. Disagreement about the size of a budget cut required to restore fiscal discipline prompted the International Monetary Fund (IMF) to delay disbursement of an $800 million loan installment. Deficit spending also may have been responsible for the stubbornness of the inflation rate, which seemed unlikely to fall much below 1990's 36.5%. Unemployment remained high at 10%, foreign investment did not increase as much as expected, and some exports actually declined.

Despite these disappointments, economic performance in 1991 represented an impressive turnaround in comparison with the previous decade. Gross domestic product (GDP) grew at an annual rate of 10% in the first half of 1991. During the year Venezuela negotiated agreements to pursue free trade with Mexico, Colombia, and the members of the Andean Pact. The state oil company, Petróleos de Venezuela S.A. (PDVSA), announced plans to expand and diversify by starting extractive activities elsewhere in Latin America and joint ventures with foreign oil companies at home. Economic prospects were so good that Venezuela and Mexico agreed to liberalize the San José Pact, which offers inexpensive oil to poor Central American and Caribbean nations.

Dissatisfaction and Conflict. While outside observers and investors were optimistic, domestic political groups manifested increasing dissatisfaction. When meat prices rose 30%, Pérez responded by threatening to reimpose state price controls. Merchants quickly lowered prices, but diverted their anger into criticism of the disappointing performance in privatizing state enterprises. In two and one half years the government had privatized three banks, sold 60% interest in VIASA Venezuelan International Airways, and accepted a bid for a 40% stake in the state telephone company, Compañía Anónima Nacional Teléfonos de Venezuela. In July, Pérez promised to obtain congressional approval for more of his economic policies, satisfying a demand business had been making for 30 years.

Conflicts also surfaced within the government. Oil Minister Celestino Armas and the IMF criticized the ambitious plans of PDVSA director Andrés Sosa Pietri to expand the company's operations as too expensive. The government also clashed with the Venezuelan Workers Confederation (CTV), which requested a 45% wage increase when Pérez was willing to offer no more than 20%. The Pérez administration also was criticized for not having dealt adequately with the social costs associated with its economic program, for relying excessively on devaluations, for failing to curb price speculation, and for not following through with promised administrative reforms.

Criticism from within the governing party well may have been motivated by the pressures of electoral competition. Internal party elections were scheduled for August—and then postponed—to prepare the party for local and state elections in 1992 and national elections in 1993. Various candidates for president already were competing for the nomination, and in the process challenging Pérez' authority.

Drugs. Fearing the country was becoming a base of operations for drug traffickers, President Pérez declared an "all out war" against the drug trade. Authorities seized about 94 tons (85 000 kg) of cocaine in 1991, ten times the total seized in 1990. Several high-ranking military and Interior Ministry officials, reportedly corrupted by traffickers, were forced to resign.

MICHAEL COPPEDGE
Johns Hopkins University

VENEZUELA • Information Highlights

Official Name: Republic of Venezuela.
Location: Northern coast of South America.
Area: 352,143 sq mi (912 050 km²).
Population (mid-1991 est.): 20,100,000.
Chief Cities (June 30, 1989 est., incl. suburbs): Caracas, the capital, 3,373,059; Maracaibo, 1,365,308; Valencia, 1,227,472.
Government: *Head of state and government,* Carlos Andrés Pérez, president (took office February 1989). *Legislature*—National Congress: Senate and Chamber of Deputies.
Monetary Unit: Bolívar (60.14 bolívares equal U.S.$1, floating rate, Oct. 28, 1991).
Gross Domestic Product (1989 est. U.S.$): $52,000,-000,000.
Economic Index (Caracas, 1989): *Consumer Prices* (1984 = 100), all items, 380.2; food, 652.1.
Foreign Trade (1990 U.S.$): *Imports,* $6,365,000,000; *exports,* $17,586,000,000.

VERMONT

Vermont citizens were shocked by the sudden death on Aug. 14, 1991, of Gov. Richard A. Snelling (R), who had been elected in November 1990 to his fifth term after a gap of six years. Lt. Gov. Howard B. Dean (D), a medical doctor and former legislator, took the oath of office to fill Snelling's unexpired term.

Vermont also was hard hit during the year by the national economic recession, which brought budget and program cuts at all governmental levels. The legislature (led by Democrats in both houses) made history by recessing for three weeks in May during which a Senate-House conference committee was deadlocked over state spending. Governor Snelling at that time threatened to veto the resulting $664 million compromise for fiscal year 1992 until the legislature agreed to cut another $1 million as well as to raise income and rooms and meals taxes. Meanwhile, the state ended fiscal 1991 in June with a $58.4 million deficit.

The vacancy in the lieutenant governorship resulting from Snelling's death required Senate President pro tem Douglas Racine (D) to preside over that body, leaving the Republicans with a 15–14 majority on the floor.

Local Government. On Town Meeting Day in March, tax-weary voters defeated school budgets in many communities. In Burlington, Vermont's largest city, Progressive Coalition Mayor Peter Clavelle was reelected without major-party opposition, but the Democrats displaced the Progressives as the largest bloc in the City Council. An October referendum to approve the Burlington electric company's purchase of power from Hydro-Quebec was defeated. An earlier vote approving the contract was nullified by court order because literature favoring the deal had been placed in some voting booths.

Higher Education. The year was also one of unprecedented tumult for higher education in Vermont. The University of Vermont in Burlington already was trying to cope with a cut in state appropriations when 22 black, Hispanic, and Asian students plus white sympathizers occupied the president's office for three weeks in April and May to demand fulfillment of goals set in 1988 to increase recruitment of minority faculty and students and to expand ethnic studies in the curriculum. The sit-in ended just prior to graduation with the arrest of protesters and the coincidental firebombing of several university buses. The student protesters erected a shantytown known as Diversity University on the university green and engaged in more sit-ins during the fall 1991 semester. In September the university celebrated its bicentennial without disruption, but in October, after little more than a year in office, President George Davis resigned after release of a recommendation to eliminate engineering and other programs. The trustees replaced him with former Gov. Thomas Salmon as interim president.

Presidents of Norwich University in Northfield, Johnson State College, and Middlebury College also resigned during the year.

Other News. Vermont had a mediocre skiing season and an excellent maple-syrup season. . . . Acid rain remained a problem for Vermont's mountain forests, and the number of Vermont farms continued to decline. . . . Abenaki Indians clashed with authorities over tribal rights, and in May, Chief Homer St. Francis was arrested for assaulting a police officer. He charged the state with conspiracy and disputed its authority to try him.

ROBERT V. DANIELS and SAMUEL B. HAND
University of Vermont

VERMONT • Information Highlights

Area: 9,614 sq mi (24 900 km²).
Population (1990 census): 562,758.
Chief Cities (1990 census): Montpelier, the capital, 8,247; Burlington, 39,127; Rutland, 18,230.
Government (1991): *Chief Officer*—governor, Howard B. Dean (D). *General Assembly*—Senate, 30 members; House of Representatives, 150 members.
State Finances (fiscal year 1990): *Revenue*, $1,592,000,000; *expenditure*, $1,565,000,000.
Personal Income (1990): $9,889,000,000; per capita, $17,511.
Labor Force (June 1991): *Civilian labor force*, 309,700; *unemployed*, 21,600 (7.0% of total force).
Education: *Enrollment* (fall 1989)—public elementary schools, 69,103; public secondary, 25,676; colleges and universities, 35,946. *Public school expenditures* (1989), $485,226,000.

VIETNAM

Despite a wholesale change of top leaders in 1991, Vietnam continued to follow the Chinese model: one-party rule with some tolerance for free-market practices. Hanoi's acceptance of a United Nations (UN) effort to pacify nearby Cambodia was linked to improved ties with China. Hanoi also sought to normalize relations with the United States and other Western powers, but the end of Soviet aid reduced Moscow's influence. In other news, at year's end two coastal provinces of Vietnam suffered high winds that killed at least 100 people and left about 500 missing.

Politics. At the congress of the Vietnamese Communist Party in June, the ailing head of the party, Nguyen Van Linh, asked to retire and was replaced by Premier Do Muoi. Both men favored moving Vietnam's economy toward more of a free market by promoting compromise between hard-line Communists and more liberal young reformers. The new premier, Vo Van Kiet, belonged to the liberal group.

Seven out of the 12 members of the party's ruling Politburo were replaced in June. Vo Chi Cong lost his Politburo seat, but he remained

© Reuters/Bettmann

Nguyen Van Linh, secretary-general of the Vietnamese Communist Party from 1986 to 1991, delivered the opening address at Vietnam's Seventh Party Congress in June shortly before his retirement due to ill health.

chairman of the State Council. Defense Minister Le Duc Anh was one of the few survivors. As second-ranking party member (after Do Muoi), he was expected to run defense and foreign policy. Anh favored closer ties with China, and he defeated his rival, Foreign Minister Nguyen Co Thach, who left the Politburo and government in June. Thach had sought to improve relations with the United States, but Washington was slow to respond. In another political development, Truong My Hoa became the first woman to be named to the party secretariat. When she was appointed head of the Vietnamese Women's Union, National Assembly members said the party should let women choose their own leaders. Party chief Do Muoi bowed to his critics and said Hoa was only the party's "recommended" candidate.

Economics. Vietnam's movement toward a market economy began after the 1987 party congress. By mid-1991, 273 foreign investment projects worth $2.1 billion had been approved. But despite efforts to streamline the bureaucracy, the party remained the leading force, both in law and in reality. This meant that even the simplest economic decisions were based on political factors. For example, the government allowed the first foreign bank to open in 1991. But it was a small, Indonesian joint venture, unable to meet even a fraction of Vietnam's banking needs. Its charter was a reward to Indonesia for diplomatic support of Vietnam.

Almost two thirds of all joint ventures were in southern Vietnam. Many of Vietnam's former capitalists, who are often ethnic Chinese, live in this region. Taiwan now was Vietnam's major foreign investor with many projects based on family ties which span the two countries. Australia, France, Britain, and the Netherlands were the largest Western investors. In 1991, Japan replaced the USSR as Vietnam's major trading partner. The loss of cheap Russian oil, machinery, and other goods was a major blow to Vietnam.

Foreign Affairs. A visit by party leader Do Muoi to China in November marked an improvement in relations between former enemies. Better ties with the West also were needed for Vietnam to obtain aid from the World Bank. In return for Vietnam's willingness to support UN peace efforts in Cambodia, the United States agreed to begin discussing the normalization of relations.

PETER A. POOLE
Author, "Eight Presidents and Indochina"

VIETNAM • Information Highlights

Official Name: Socialist Republic of Vietnam.
Location: Southeast Asia.
Area: 127,243 sq mi (329 560 km^2).
Population (mid-1991 est.): 67,600,000.
Chief Cities (April 1, 1989 prelim. census): Hanoi, the capital, 1,088,862; Ho Chi Minh City, 3,169,135.
Government: Communist Party secretary, Do Muoi.
Monetary Unit: Dong (7,600 dongs equal U.S.$1, July 1991).
Gross National Product (1989 est. U.S.$): $14,200,-000,000.

Virginia Gov. L. Douglas Wilder, "unable to stand on the sidelines" while the country he loves "stumbles further backwards," declares his candidacy for the Democratic presidential nomination on Sept. 13, 1991. He later withdrew.

VIRGINIA

Gov. L. Douglas Wilder dominated 1991 news in Virginia as he decided to run for president in September. The heavy cutting of the state budget that he engineered and his frequent absences from the state led to public disenchantment that ultimately was blamed for the unprecedented state-election losses for his Democratic Party. In early January 1992, however, the governor withdrew from the presidential race to devote himself to "guiding Virginia through these difficult times."

During the first half of the year, Wilder shared the spotlight with his fellow Democrat, U.S. Sen. Charles S. Robb. They were involved in a highly publicized feud surrounding taped telephone calls that surfaced in the midst of a scandal about Robb's alleged consorting with a former Miss Virginia USA.

Elections. Virginia Republicans were ecstatic after the statewide elections in November that put all the seats in the legislature up for grabs. The GOP increased its number in the 40-member state Senate from ten to 18 and in the 100-member House from 40 to 41. Many Republicans had campaigned against Wilder, whose approval rating had dropped to an all-time low for a Virginia governor.

The anti-incumbent mood apparently did not translate to Buchanan county, however, where two incumbent supervisors were reelected despite what was apparently the largest municipal-fraud case in state history. Two hundred ninety-three criminal indictments were issued against the entire board of supervisors, the county administrator, and other current or former county employees.

In a special U.S. congressional race in the 7th District in November, the easy election of George F. Allen, Jr., a state legislator from Charlotteville and the son of a famous National Football League coach, brought the Republican Party a rising star. The seat had become vaçant following the resignation of Rep. D. French Slaughter, Jr., for health reasons.

Senator Robb. In April the television program *Exposé* aired old charges that Robb, while governor, had attended parties where cocaine was used. What galvanized attention on the son-in-law of the late President Lyndon B. Johnson, however, was the on-air allegation by former beauty queen Tai Collins that she and Robb had had sexual relations in a New York City hotel room in 1984. Robb, long mentioned as presidential material, denied the charges but said Collins had given him a massage after they shared a bottle of wine at the hotel.

VIRGINIA • Information Highlights

Area: 40,767 sq mi (105 586 km²).
Population (1990 census): 6,187,358.
Chief Cities (1990 census): Richmond, the capital, 203,056; Virginia Beach, 393,069; Norfolk, 261,229; Newport News, 170,045; Chesapeake, 151,976.
Government (1991): *Chief Officers*—governor, L. Douglas Wilder (D); lt. gov., Donald S. Beyer, Jr. (D). *General Assembly*—Senate, 40 members; House of Delegates, 100 members.
State Finances (fiscal year 1990): *Revenue,* $13,607,000,000; *expenditure,* $12,632,000,000.
Personal Income (1990): $122,215,000,000; per capita, $19,671.
Labor Force (June 1991): *Civilian labor force,* 3,316,600; *unemployed,* 198,600 (6.0% of total force).
Education: *Enrollment* (fall 1989)—public elementary schools, 712,297; public secondary, 273,049; colleges and universities, 344,284. *Public school expenditures* (1989), $4,151,050,000.

The press scrutiny of Robb led to more damaging consequences, including the resumption of public antagonism with Wilder, the firing of three top Robb aides, and a subsequent grand-jury investigation after he acknowledged that his office had kept a transcript of a secret tape recording of Wilder talking on his car phone in 1988.

Legislature. In the midst of the economic recession, the Virginia General Assembly was preoccupied with trying to erase a $2.1 billion deficit. As a cornerstone of his platform, Wilder had pledged no new taxes and already had worked toward budget reductions, including eliminating pay raises for state workers. The legislature plugged most of the budget gap by cutting agency budgets, including taking more than $100 million from education aid.

In the fall the legislature created new districts for the U.S. House of Representatives. As a result of the 1990 census, Virginia had gained one House seat, bringing its total to 11.

VMI. The federal government moved to end the all-male admissions policy of Virginia Military Institute (VMI). But the school, one of only two state-supported military colleges in the United States, won a federal-court ruling that the policy was constitutional because the school's unique focus contributed to overall diversity in education in the state.

ED NEWLAND
"Richmond Times Dispatch"

WASHINGTON

The Persian Gulf war dominated Washington state news in early 1991. Antiwar demonstrations preceding the Persian Gulf war drew up to 30,000 participants in Seattle. Thousands of reservists and troops from bases around Puget Sound served in the war, with 14 servicemen from Washington reported killed or missing. Returning troops were welcomed at Seattle's annual Seafair parade drawing more than 250,000 spectators.

Elections and Politics. In November elections state voters passed an initiative strengthening abortion rights, but defeated measures that would have limited terms for public officials, allowed physicians to help end lives of the terminally ill, and rolled back tax rates on homes purchased before 1985. Gov. Booth Gardner announced he would not run for a third term in 1992.

Economy. State employment growth slowed dramatically in 1991 as wholesale, retail, and service sectors cooled. Total nonfarm employment averaged 2.18 million for the first three quarters of 1991, up 1.9% from 1990, but following three straight years in which jobs increased by about 5%.

Business. Frederick & Nelson, a 62-year-old Seattle-based chain of department stores, filed for Chapter 11 bankruptcy protection, putting several stores up for sale. The parent companies of the state's two largest banks, Seafirst and Security Pacific, announced plans to merge in a move expected to mean a significant reduction in the two banks' total state work force of 10,400.

Census. The 1990 census showed Washington's population increasing 18% during the 1980s to 4.87 million, giving the state a ninth seat in the U.S. Congress. The state's minority population was 11.5% at the time of the 1990 census.

Oil Spills. Three oil spills in 1991 fueled public concern about environmental damage. In January, 600,000 gallons (2 271 247 l) seeped from a pipeline at a Tacoma refinery; the following month, 210,000 gallons (794 937 l) spilled when a pump broke at a refinery at Anacortes. In both of these cases, most of the spilled oil remained on dry ground. But oil coated some Pacific beaches when about 100,000 gallons (378 541 l) spilled from a Japanese fish-processing boat that collided with a

WASHINGTON • Information Highlights

Area: 68,139 sq mi (176 479 km²).
Population (1990 census): 4,866,692.
Chief Cities (1990 census): Olympia, the capital, 33,840; Seattle, 516,259; Spokane, 177,196; Tacoma, 176,664.
Government (1991): *Chief Officers*—governor, Booth Gardner (D); lt. gov., Joel Pritchard (R). *Legislature*—Senate, 49 members; House of Representatives, 98 members.
State Finances (fiscal year 1990): *Revenue,* $14,999,000,000; *expenditure,* $13,567,000,000.
Personal Income (1990): $92,174,000,000; per capita, $18,775.
Labor Force (June 1991): *Civilian labor force,* 2,558,700; *unemployed,* 152,200 (5.9% of total force).
Education: *Enrollment* (fall 1989)—public elementary schools, 585,818; public secondary, 224,414; colleges and universities, 255,760. *Public school expenditures* (1989), $3,204,265,000.

Chinese freighter and sank outside the Strait of Juan de Fuca in July.

Weather. A dry summer and early fall increased fire danger and prompted warnings for water conservation. In Seattle a record 45-day dry spell ended October 16. Near Spokane, October fires scorched 46,000 acres (18 616 ha), destroyed 110 homes, and killed one person.

Crime. Two Washington residents died and a third became seriously ill after taking cyanide-laced capsules of Sudafed, a cold medicine, in February. Three other cyanide-laced capsules were found in Sudafed packs pulled from store shelves. The incident triggered a Federal Bureau of Investigation (FBI) investigation and a nationwide recall of the product.

U.S. District Judge William Dwyer overturned the death sentence of Kwan Fai "Willie" Mak, convicted in the 1983 massacre of 13 people at a gambling club in Seattle.

Sports. With a 83-79 record, the Seattle Mariners had the first winning season in the major-league baseball team's 14-year history. The University of Washington football team completed the season undefeated and beat Michigan in the 1992 Rose Bowl. Washington shared the national championship with Miami.

JACK BROOM, *"Seattle Times"*

WASHINGTON, DC

In 1991, District of Columbia residents and elected officials vented their collective frustrations as the city grappled with a homicide rate that for the third consecutive year generated headlines calling Washington, DC, the murder capital of the nation. The search continued for tangible solutions to the crisis.

Crime. By year's end the city recorded 490 killings, up from 483 in 1990. Both were records, and on a per capita basis, both were the worst murder rates in the country for their respective years. Several of the deaths were of innocent victims caught in the cross fire of drive-by shootings—the seemingly preferred method of retribution among many of the area's drug traffickers.

After a campaign led by a coalition of the city's clergy, voters in November overwhelmingly approved the reinstatement of the nation's first gun-liability law, which would hold manufacturers and sellers responsible for bodily injuries and deaths caused by their products. Fourteen semiautomatic weapons—among them the Tec 9, the Street Sweeper, and the Uzi—would be included under the law.

The referendum forced the City Council to reverse its February repeal of the gun law, which it had adopted in December 1990. The request for repeal was made by Mayor Sharon Pratt Kelly, who stated that repeal was necessary in order to win a special $100 million appropriation from Congress.

The mayor (who in December married New York City businessman James Kelly III and officially dropped the last name of her former husband, Arrington Dixon) responded to the increased incidence of crime and violence during a pre-Thanksgiving address to the city, which was broadcast live on local television news programs. Her proposed anticrime package called for increased police presence on the streets and more patrols around public-housing complexes, where officials claimed 80% of the drug-related violence was occurring. The plan also would double the number of homicide investigations with assistance from the Federal Bureau of Investigation (FBI), charge 14-year-olds as adults in murder cases, improve the delivery of services to families in crisis, and offer more programs designed to steer youths away from crime.

City Council members also were offering a flurry of legislative proposals to combat crime. Most of the measures were introduced after the Patricia Lexie murder. A newlywed, Lexie was shot in the head as she sat on the passenger side of a car being driven by her husband. The couple was traveling to their home in suburban Washington when a stray bullet struck her. The 19-year-old man charged with her murder allegedly had told friends hours before the act, "I feel like killing somebody." "Sometimes, unfortunately, it takes bad times to force your hand," said at large council member John Ray.

Finances. Mayor Kelly began her first year in office with a whirlwind of activity focused on reducing a $316 million deficit in the city's $3.6 billion budget and cutting the government's 48,000-member work force.

While she succeeded in reducing the deficit, she was far shy of her campaign pledge to rid the bureaucracy of 2,000 midlevel managers. By September 30 the mayor had been able to find only 334 excess management positions, with 162 of them being actual workers.

Marion Barry. In October 1991 former Mayor Marion Barry exhausted all legal appeals and began a six-month sentence at a federal prison in Petersburg, VA. Barry was convicted in 1990 on one misdemeanor count of cocaine possession. Though he was not to be released until April 1992, it already was speculated that he would seek to unseat veteran council member Wilhelmina Rolark, who represents the poorest section of the city.

Sports. Football's Washington Redskins roused the city with their impressive 14–2 record, clinching a division championship and winning home-field advantage in the National Football League (NFL) play-offs. They went on to defeat Atlanta and Detroit and were headed for Super Bowl XXVI. The team was expected to play in a new home by 1993, if Kelly and team owner Jack Kent Cooke could complete negotiations for a new stadium.

VINCENT MCCRAW, *"The Washington Times"*

WEST VIRGINIA

As in many of its sister states, West Virginia legislators, businesses, and citizens spent much of 1991 wrestling with financial issues relating to public health and safety and environmental concerns. In West Virginia, however, the issues often were made more pressing by the continued high rate of unemployment in most counties, the lack of a vibrant industrial base to replace yesteryear's coal and steel giants, and general economic anemia.

Rankings of the states—both official and unofficial—consistently placed West Virginia near the bottom in overall environmental health conditions. One poll near the end of the year actually rated it 50th.

There were some signs of economic progress, however. Ground was broken for a major fingerprint center for the Federal Bureau of Investigation (FBI) near Clarksburg, for a Central Intelligence Agency (CIA) unit near Martinsburg, and for a new $75 million radio telescope at Green Bank. The latter will replace the nation's largest and most sophisticated radio telescope, which collapsed there in 1988.

Health Care. The legislature convened in February to face a multitude of concerns in the field of health care—access to primary medical attention, a lack of minimal rural health facilities, and unsatisfactory performance by regulatory agencies. Early in the year, the state's largest Blue Cross/Blue Shield agency folded. Criticism of hospital-regulatory rules mounted, and even solid-waste-disposal matters were tied to public health.

The most acrimonious debate centered on the state's three medical schools—at West Virginia University, Marshall University, and the Osteopathic Medicine unit at Lewisburg. The legislative leadership, allied with Gov. Gaston Caperton, sought to merge the three into one unit. Opponents termed the plan a potential disaster, pointing out that it actually would decrease the number of doctors available for primary health care.

WEST VIRGINIA • Information Highlights

Area: 24,232 sq mi (62 760 km²).
Population (1990 census): 1,793,477.
Chief Cities (1990 census): Charleston, the capital, 57,287; Huntington, 54,844; Wheeling, 34,882.
Government (1991): *Chief Officers*—governor, Gaston Caperton (D); secy. of state, Ken Hechler (D). *Legislature*—Senate, 34 members; House of Delegates, 100 members.
State Finances (fiscal year 1990): *Revenue*, $4,435,000,000; *expenditure*, $4,212,000,000.
Personal Income (1990): $24,622,000,000; per capita, $13,755.
Labor Force (June 1991): *Civilian labor force*, 793,100; *unemployed*, 76,800 (9.7% of total force).
Education: *Enrollment* (fall 1989)—public elementary schools, 227,251; public secondary, 100,289; colleges and universities, 82,455. *Public school expenditures* (1989), $1,202,486,000.

A tougher health-care regulatory plan, including tighter controls over Blue Cross and related health-insurance groups, was adopted. Ohio's Blue Cross entity took over the West Virginia system. A vice-chancellor for medical education was named to coordinate that field, with the three medical-school units remaining intact. During a special session in October, money also was appropriated to match a Kellogg Foundation grant for rural health care, and various other fiscal measures were passed to beef up the state's Medicare and Medicaid matching program.

Other Legislative Issues. Alleged shortcomings in the performance of the agency charged with regulating mining laws—particularly those dealing with safety—led to a near-stalemate that threatened to surrender such supervision to federal authorities. And solid-waste matters—including proposed limits on landfill capacities, mandatory recycling, and the financing of new landfills—consumed extensive committee-hearing time.

The legislature finally passed a budget of $1.94 billion, with 78% of it earmarked for education and including a $1,000 raise for public-school teachers. A mandatory seat-belt law, however, failed for the sixth time.

Because West Virginia was one of the states found to have lost population during the 1980s, a redistricting plan to reduce the U.S. congressional delegation from four to three was mandated by federal law. The special session finally approved a plan, which was headed for the federal courts.

DONOVAN H. BOND
West Virginia University

WISCONSIN

A serial killer's rampage in Milwaukee left at least 17 young men dead and resulted in international attention for the city in 1991, but it also left the community with deepening divisions along racial lines.

Milwaukee Conflicts. Jeffrey L. Dahmer's confessions to years of killing young men horrified the city. The murders, however, soon were overshadowed by factional disputes and charges of police insensitivity. The disputed incident took place on May 27 when three Milwaukee police officers responded to a call that a 14-year-old boy was naked and bleeding in the street. The officers took the boy back to the apartment he was visiting, where Dahmer convinced them that the boy was older and that they were homosexual lovers. Within hours the boy was dead. Before his arrest on July 22, Dahmer reportedly killed three others.

Because Dahmer is white, the boy was Laotian, and most of the other victims were minorities, the police were accused of racial bias. Homosexual groups accused the police of in-

WISCONSIN • Information Highlights

Area: 56,153 sq mi (145 436 km²).
Population (1990 census): 4,891,769.
Chief Cities (1990 census): Madison, the capital, 191,262; Milwaukee, 628,088; Green Bay, 96,466.
Government (1991): *Chief Officers*—governor, Tommy G. Thompson (R); lt. gov., Scott McCallum (R). *Legislature*—Senate, 33 members; Assembly, 99 members.
State Finances (fiscal year 1990): *Revenue,* $13,388,000,000; *expenditure,* $11,416,000,000.
Personal Income (1990): $86,147,000,000; per capita, $17,560.
Labor Force (June 1991): *Civilian labor force,* 2,627,100; *unemployed,* 141,000 (5.4% of total force).
Education: *Enrollment* (fall 1989)—public elementary schools, 549,143; public secondary, 233,762; colleges and universities, 290,672. *Public school expenditures* (1989), $3,688,311,000.

sensitivity. After an internal investigation, Police Chief Philip Arreola fired the three officers, letting one stay on for a year. The police union accused the chief of bowing to minority demands and not providing leadership.

In the fall a mayoral commission recommended that the chief produce a plan to increase cooperation between police and minorities, to provide more training in cultural awareness, to discipline officers who are insensitive, to streamline the process of reporting police insensitivity, and to develop strategies to reduce crime and drug activity.

Legislative Action. Republican Gov. Tommy Thompson came up with yet another innovative proposal to reform welfare: The state would pay larger welfare grants to teenage mothers who married, and it would put a cap on benefits for unwed mothers regardless of whether they had more children. Democrats said the plan amounted to "state-sponsored shotgun weddings" and was a form of social engineering. A modified version of the "bridefare" program was passed and the state sought federal approval to implement it.

Thompson scored a victory in the biennial budget battle, exercising his veto power a record 457 times on the Democratic-controlled legislature's $28.3 billion budget. Thompson cut state spending by about $22 million and avoided more than $500 million in new taxes the first year. He vetoed every appropriation that exceeded by more than $100,000 the level of financing he had proposed in the second year. As a result, homeowners did not get a $30,000 exemption on the value of their property on tax bills from school districts. State credits on property-tax bills were preserved.

Thompson was able to carve his own budget out of the Democrats' version because the state constitution gives the governor powers to delete words and even individual digits from numbers. In October the U.S. Supreme Court rejected a Democratic appeal of a lower court ruling upholding the powers.

Economy. Per capita income reached $17,000, an increase of nearly 6% over the previous year. Cash receipts for farm commodities totaled $5.7 billion, also up 6%. Total nonfarm wage and salaried employment reached an all-time high of 2.28 million.

Treaty. Wisconsin officials and Chippewa Indians ended a 17-year battle over treaty rights. One ruling prevents the Chippewas from seeking $325 million in damages over loss of treaty rights and a second protects the Indians' rights to gather plants, hunt, and spear fish off reservations in northern Wisconsin.

PAUL SALSINI, *"The Milwaukee Journal"*

WOMEN

Women continued to make gains in politics and to establish themselves in the workplace, but issues of sex discrimination and sexual harassment took on new importance in 1991.

The World's Women. In its first attempt to document statistically women's standing in the world, the United Nations found that most women lagged far behind men in power, wealth, and opportunity. The numbers varied by country and region, but generally women worked in less-prestigious and lower-paid jobs than did men. Only 10%-20% of managerial and administrative jobs were held by women worldwide.

While health and education gains were seen among urban women in Latin America, the Caribbean, and parts of Asia, the worldwide illiteracy rate for women rose from 543 million in 1970 to 597 million in 1985. In almost all countries, women tended to outlive men, with a life expectancy of 75 years or more in developed regions, more than 70 years in developing countries, and 54 years in Africa. The number of households headed by women grew worldwide, with more single mothers and more elderly women living alone.

Sexual Harassment and Discrimination. The battle of the sexes took a different turn in October when University of Oklahoma law professor Anita Hill accused U.S. Supreme Court nominee Clarence Thomas of sexually harassing her when they worked together in the early 1980s. For Congress and the public alike, the televised Senate hearings brought a new awareness.

The hearings also raised questions as to when an act or remark was truly sexual harassment. Much like the issue of pornography, it appeared that people knew sexual harassment when they saw it but could provide only ambiguous definitions. The Equal Employment Opportunity Commission (EEOC) in 1980 defined it as any behavior that has "the purpose or effect of unreasonably interfering with an individual's work performance or creating an intimidating or hostile or offensive environ-

Patricia Ireland (extreme right), *a graduate of the University of Miami Law School and a former flight attendant for Pan American World Airways, succeeded Molly Yard* (right) *as president of the National Organization for Women in December 1991.*

© Alain McLaughlin/Impact Visuals

ment.'' The U.S. Supreme Court has upheld that definition and a federal appeals court in San Francisco has ruled that sexual harassment has to be judged from the viewpoint of a ''reasonable woman'' rather than a man.

Hill's accusations unleashed a flurry of comments from women, many of whom admitted that they, too, had experienced sexual harassment. Earlier, Dr. Frances Conley, a female surgeon at California's Stanford Medical School, cited 25 years of sexist attitudes and unwelcome advances when she resigned her post in June. She returned to the job following an outpouring of support and national attention focused on her case.

Politics. A National League of Cities survey found that in 1991 women accounted for 14.3% of the 2,610 mayors in the United States, up from 10.4% in 1986. The number of women on city councils also grew, climbing above the 20% mark at the time of the survey. And in March a woman was elected to the Louisiana Senate, marking the first time that women held seats in every state legislative body.

There was also some discouraging news for women at the polls in 1991. Kathryn Whitmire, the five-term mayor of Houston, was defeated in November as was Democrat Katherine Slaughter, seeking a U.S. House seat in Virginia's 7th District. On a brighter note were the victories of Kay Granger, elected mayor of Fort Worth earlier in 1991, and of Deedee Corradini, who was elected mayor of Salt Lake City. Women also made gains in the federal executive branch with 185 women named to full-time positions by U.S. President George Bush in his first two years in office. Former U.S. Rep. Lynn Martin (R-IL)—*see* BIOGRAPHY—succeeded Elizabeth Dole as secretary of labor.

Internationally, Rita Johnston served briefly in 1991 as premier of British Columbia, the first woman in Canada to gain that office. Socialist Edith Cresson was named premier of France, the first woman to hold that post. In Bangladesh, Khaleda Zia, widow of Gen. Ziaur Rahman, became prime minister. Aung San Suu Kyi (*see* BIOGRAPHY), the principal opposition leader in Myanmar (Burma), was awarded the Nobel Peace Prize.

New Leadership for NOW. Patricia Ireland became president of the National Organization for Women (NOW) in December, after the retirement of Molly Yard. Ireland, who had been executive vice-president of the 200,000-member organization, is an attorney and onetime flight attendant for Pan American World Airlines. She developed Project Stand Up for Women and organized attorneys to fight the U.S. Supreme Court nominations of Antonin Scalia, Robert Bork, Anthony Kennedy, and Clarence Thomas. She promised to follow much the same agenda as her predecessor.

Gender Issues. The role of women in combat received increased attention with the outbreak early in the year of war in the Persian Gulf. In separate bills the House and Senate approved assigning women to combat air crews. If enacted, such legislation could be a first step in expanding the military roles of women. (*See also* SPECIAL REPORT/FAMILY.)

Women's-rights issues were upheld when the U.S. Supreme Court ruled that potential health risks to a fetus were not sufficient reason to keep women from high-risk jobs. The ruling resulted from a case in which Johnson Controls, Inc., of Milwaukee excluded women capable of bearing children from jobs where they were exposed to high levels of lead.

KRISTI VAUGHAN

WYOMING

Finances and the environment dominated Wyoming's news for 1991.

Legislature. The state legislature authorized spending about $11 million more than Democratic Gov. Mike Sullivan recommended, pushing the 1991–92 state budget to more than $2 billion. Other key legislative issues included educational funding, reapportionment, and reorganization of the state government.

In passing the 1991 Reapportionment Act, the legislature essentially guaranteed each county at least one vote regardless of its population. However, in November a three-judge federal panel declared the law unconstitutional and gave the state until Feb. 21, 1992, to develop an acceptable plan. If it did not, the federal court would draft its own plan in time for the 1992 election. One of Governor Sullivan's top priorities—a $50 million education trust fund—passed. Also enacted were a school-funding bill raising the per classroom unit allocation 5.2% and a bill designed to create "drug-free zones" around public schools.

Economy. In his annual legislative address, Governor Sullivan said that the state has come through a period of great economic "uncertainty and turmoil," with slumps in the energy, mineral, and agricultural sectors affecting citizens throughout the state. In November he announced a "serious revenue shortfall" of more than $150 million and placed a ban on state hiring and most out-of-state travel by state employees.

The state's economy is based on three main industries: minerals, tourism, and agriculture. The coal industry led the nation in 1990—producing more than 184 million tons—and was expected to be the number one producer again in 1991. Increased demand for Wyoming's low-sulfur coal, most of which is mined in Campbell county, might create a bonanza. An agreement between Decker Coal of Sheridan and the United Mine Workers ended a four-year strike, bringing economic relief to the community. The state's natural gas, trona, and bentonite industries remained strong, as did the tourist industry. Final 1990 figures showed record numbers of visitors to Yellowstone, Grand Teton, and other sites. Amtrak resumed train service to the state.

On the downside, the state Geological Survey was predicting a continuing decline in oil production. Amoco's decision to close its Casper refinery after 78 years would affect 210 employees and have an impact on the community. Despite fluctuating prices in the beef market and declining prices in the sheep and wool industry, the agricultural component of Wyoming's economy remained a key force.

The Environment and Other Developments. A variety of environmental issues—including the reintroduction of wolves into the Yellowstone ecosystem, the use of poison to control predators, the proposed development of Medicine Wheel National Historic Landmark, the roundup of wild horses by the federal Bureau of Land Management, eagle poisonings, a proposed gold mine near Cooke City (MT), proposed new sites for a toxic-waste dump, recycling, and acquisition of Red Rim lands by the state Game and Fish Department for an antelope winter range—attracted attention.

Improving health care and recruiting new doctors to serve Wyoming remained key problems. . . . A federal Occupational Safety and Health Administration study showed Wyoming's job-related death and injury rate to be the second-worst in the nation. . . . The long dispute over water rights on the Wind River Indian Reservation continued.

ROBERT A. CAMPBELL
University of Wyoming

WYOMING • Information Highlights

Area: 97,809 sq mi (253 326 km²).
Population (1990 census): 453,588.
Chief Cities (1990 census): Cheyenne, the capital, 50,008; Casper, 46,742; Laramie, 26,687.
Government (1991): *Chief Officers*—governor, Michael J. Sullivan (D); secretary of state, Kathy Karpan (D). *Legislature*—Senate, 30 members; House of Representatives, 64 members.
State Finances (fiscal year 1990): *Revenue,* $1,900,000,000; *expenditure,* $1,641,000,000.
Personal Income (1990): $7,378,000,000; per capita, $16,314.
Labor Force (June 1991): *Civilian labor force,* 249,700; *unemployed,* 11,400 (4.6% of total force).
Education: *Enrollment* (fall 1989)—public elementary schools, 70,130; public secondary, 27,042; colleges and universities, 29,159. *Public school expenditures* (1989), $491,930,000.

YUGOSLAVIA

In 1991 act two of the transformation of Yugoslavia into a multiparty political system featured the leading politicians of 1990 with a new cast of largely inexperienced political actors jockeying for position on a radically restructured political stage. The political spectrum ranged from center-right coalitions in Slovenia and Croatia and national-ethnic dominated governments in Macedonia and Bosnia-Herzegovina, to the Socialist Party of Serbia and the Communist Party of Montenegro.

Anatomy of a Civil War. This mix became a struggle between supporters of the Slovene and Croatian confederal vision of Yugoslavia and Serbian insistence on federation. Those favoring confederation thought along the lines of the European Community (EC). Advocates of federation wanted to stop what they viewed as the "parcelization" of power that paralyzed decision making under the 1974 constitution.

Prime Minister Ante Marković represented a tenuous center. Marković had made good on his promise that Yugoslavia would continue to function "with or without the Communist Party." Despite subsequent wage hikes and the Persian Gulf war, his 1990 austerity program had reduced 2,500% inflation to zero by midsummer. Policymakers in Washington, Moscow, and Brussels much preferred to deal with Marković than with his political competition.

In Yugoslavia, however, there was less enthusiasm for the prime minister. His decision to compete in republic elections had created a credibility gap, while the weak showing of his Alliance of Reform Forces seriously undermined the government's ability to act.

Strongman Slobodan Milošević kept his job as president of the Serbian republic. His party dominated the republic's parliament. At the same time alleged rigging of the republic's election tarnished Milošević's once-iconic image, and his fiscal policies intensified doubts about his economic management. There were complaints that Serbia never had been so isolated at home or abroad.

The need of Croatian President Franjo Tudjman and his Croatian Democratic Union to respond to public pressure from Croatian constituents to make Croatia visibly the republic of the Croatians stirred fears among the 600,000 Serbian minority. The Croatian flag, under which Croatian fascists conducted what Serbs considered to be genocidal policies against them during World War II, was everywhere, even on packets of sugar in Zagreb cafes. Lack of reference to political rights of the Serbian minority in the new Croatian constitution brought Serbian backlash.

Serbian militants declared themselves unwilling to live in a Croatia that was not part of Yugoslavia. They asserted their autonomy not only via a referendum that changed the predominantly Serbian city of Knin and its environs into the self-proclaimed autonomous province of Krajina, but by closing the road from Zagreb to the Dalmatian coast and harassing tourists. Croatian nationalist fever rose. In response, Tudjman set up an ethnically pure Croatian paramilitary force that heightened fear for the physical safety of the Serbian minority.

Alija Izetbegović, leader of the Muslim Party for Democratic Action, who became the head of the collective republic presidency in Bosnia-Herzegovina, tilted toward confederation as the best chance for peace in his own multinational republic. He was joined by Macedonian President Kiro Gligorov in the belief that only a confederal Yugoslavia could protect Macedonia from Serbian, Greek, and Bulgarian territorial ambitions. Conversely—notwithstanding what amounted to an Albanian underground independence movement in Kosovo—Serbian spokesmen from autonomous provinces Kosovo and Vojvodina joined the chorus for federation, as did Montenegrin President Momir Bulatović.

In both the territorial and bureaucratic arenas, militant nationalists and dogmatic former Communists alike considered sovereignty synonymous with separation. While separation was preferred by nationalists and unacceptable to the dogmatists, both opposed moderates and centrists who saw sovereignty as compatible with confederation.

Finally, with the collapse of the once-dominant League of Communists, the primary channel of political access had disappeared for politicians in the Yugoslav Armed Forces (JNA) who had been accustomed to a constitutionally defined political role. Throughout 1990 the JNA had redefined its mission as protecting the unity of Yugoslavia. Now Defense Minister Veljko Kadijević repeatedly warned squabbling civilian politicians that the army would not allow the country to disintegrate or be pushed into civil war.

Meanwhile, the Yugoslav economy staggered under Serbian refusal to adhere to agreed-upon fiscal restraints and general unwillingness by all the republics to pay federal taxes. Thus, economic decline, constitutional gridlock, inability to agree on procedures for the promised federal election, and manipulation of ethnic passions by Serbian Milošević and Croatian Tudjman alike strengthened demands for separation.

After a massive March 9 demonstration of Serbian students and opposition parties against his economic mismanagement and undemocratic policies, Milošević's de facto abandonment of the goal of a Yugoslav federation was seen in Croatia and Slovenia as a Serbian land grab. When the eight-member collective federal presidency refused by one vote to give the army emergency powers, Serbia proved to be as unwilling to be outvoted as those whom Serbian leaders accused of attempting to destroy Yugoslavia. The brief window of opportunity that opened when Slovenia and Croatia unexpectedly came to the defense of the federation did not survive the Serbian and Montenegrin refusal to accept Croatian representative Stjepan Mesić as head of the collective presidency in May, as mandated by the rotation schedule. Politically, the June declarations of independence in Slovenia and Croatia served notice that federation was no longer an option. The choice now was between confederation and separation. Sectarian rhetoric drowned out calls for compromise from Bosnia-Herzegovina and Macedonia.

The Fighting. Slovenia's decision to renege on prior agreements to allow joint customs presence on Slovene borders while negotiations continued added to the recipe for disaster. When federal troops were sent in to escort federal customs officers back to their posts, the Slovene defense minister insisted that the federal government had "declared war." That was when the shooting started.

The political future of Yugoslavia came into question in 1991 as the neighboring northwestern republics of Croatia and Slovenia declared their independence in June. A devastating civil war followed.

Fearful of the accelerating violence, the EC brokered a cease fire (with EC observers) and a political cooling-off period. Serbia agreed to accept Mesić as head of the federal presidency. Slovenia and Croatia put their declarations of independence on hold for a three-month period of negotiation over the future Yugoslavia and/or the mechanism of separation.

More importantly, however, in terms of the subsequent unraveling of Yugoslavia, Croatia paid the price of the Slovene humiliation of the federal army. The body count of roughly 100 army recruits to four members of the Slovene defense forces supported the view that when the army stopped firing during the first cease-fire, Slovenes kept shooting.

Visually, the JNA "lost" to Slovenia. The pictures on Belgrade television of soldiers being stripped of their clothes as well as their weapons, sent back to Belgrade in pajamas, strengthened hard-liners in the military. Thus, as Yugoslavia moved in slow motion toward civil war, moderate military officers were purged or silenced. Not surprisingly, serious fighting erupted after Croatian forces took the army base at Bijelovar.

In these circumstances the EC peace conference made little headway. Cease-fire agreements became a revolving door to rising violence. Serbia, Montenegro, and the increasingly Serbian-dominated federal army fought to expand control over territory and resources. In October, Slovenia and Croatia declared that the three-month negotiating period was up; the only solution was separation. Macedonia and Bosnia-Herzegovina joined the march toward independence, insisting they would not stay in any "Greater Serbia," hiding behind a rump Yugoslavia.

As the war progressed, Marković became largely irrelevant. The prime minister was frequently absent from EC cease-fire negotiations with Defense Minister Veljko Kadijević (who Marković tried and failed to fire), Tudjman, and Milošević. Thereby, the EC de facto recognized what amounted to a civilian-military coup by the Serbian-Montenegrin faction of the federal presidency and the JNA, while it continued to attempt to impose acceptance of a confederal Yugoslav solution on all parties.

While Croatia's military position weakened, divisions appeared within the EC, the United Nations (UN) arms embargo backfired, and violence against civilian targets escalated. Desperate and in need of weapons, the Tudjman government gambled that by blockading or capturing federal-army garrisons in Croatia, JNA retaliation would force Germany to follow through on Chancellor Helmut Kohl's threat to recognize Slovenia and Croatia if the Yugoslav army did not exercise restraint.

Once the Croatian blockade deprived army garrisons of food, water, and electricity, the character of the civil war changed. For the JNA the battle was no longer over territory and future political position. It had become a war between Croatia and a professional military that viewed its primary mission as rescuing some 25,000 army hostages and their families.

Defense Minister Kadijević declared that for every army installation lost, something of importance to the Croatian republic would be destroyed. The army that in March still defined its job as separating warring paramilitary groups became the accelerator of the civil war. In short, the militarily senseless bombardment of the walled city of Dubrovnik must be seen as a consequence of German and Croatian miscalculation as well as of excessive army violence.

In Bosnia-Herzegovina a mass peace movement grew side by side with that violence. Opposition to the war spread throughout other republics as well. Even in Serbia many reservists went into hiding or left the country. Democratic Serbs feared that in Milošević's "Greater Serbia" they would be prisoners of an authoritarian war economy. Differences appeared within the Serbian leadership and between that leadership and the JNA.

Meanwhile, although Croatian censorship prevented criticism of the government's conduct of the war, the resignation of Vice-Premier Vladimir Veselica signaled tensions at the highest level. The Macedonian government openly supported war resisters. Students demonstrated in Titograd, and 40 families held a sit-in in Montenegrin President Bulatović's office.

International Reaction. International pressure intensified with EC economic sanctions against Serbia and Montenegro. Throughout December, the shuttle diplomacy of UN special envoy and former U.S. Secretary of State Cyrus R. Vance produced an agreement on UN peacekeeping forces by all sides. However, the precondition for such peacekeeping forces collapsed along with the fourth cease-fire.

The prospect of German recognition kept Croats fighting in hope of international protection and arms assistance. Serbian forces fought to improve their military positions. Politically, the policy of moving Serbian refugees into the homes of Croats running away from the fighting created a problem for future negotiations. War clouds darkened in Serbian-dominated districts of Bosnia-Herzegovina ready to declare for Serbia if the possibility of a confederal Yugoslavia disappeared.

Yugoslavia was suspended from the Council of Europe and deprived of its role in the Conference on Security and Cooperation in Europe (CSCE) Crisis Committee on the grounds that "Yugoslavia no longer exists." The United States imposed economic sanctions against all six republics and President George Bush joined UN Secretary-General Javier Pérez de Cuéllar's unsuccessful attempt to block Chancellor Kohl's promised recognition of Slovenia and Croatia "before Christmas." This succeeded only in pushing back Bonn's timetable. The EC compromise, adopted December 17, promised community recognition on Jan. 15, 1992, for all separatist republics conditional on protection of democratic and minority rights, and rejection of border changes by violence. Germany postponed formal "implementation" of recognition.

Thus as the year ended, the EC record of resolving conflicts between Serbs and Croats was not encouraging. EC involvement had escalated the violence, widened the war, jeopardized UN peace efforts, and split the EC itself. German insistence on recognition whether "any, all, or none of the European states join us" added fear of German expansion to that of a "Greater Serbia." It remained to be seen whether the New Year's Eve agreement negotiated during Vance's fifth peace mission could overcome the damage.

ROBIN ALISON REMINGTON
University of Missouri-Columbia

YUKON

The year 1991 in Yukon brought minor political changes, economic cutbacks, and continuing progress in Indian land-claims agreements.

Politics. Progressive Conservative Opposition Leader Willard Phelps stepped down as party leader in the spring of 1991 amid internal squabbling and discontent. A successor, 21-year-old Chris Young, took over the reins at a party leadership convention, only to step down three months later because some party supporters thought he was too young and inexperienced. Legislative Assembly member Dan Lang took over as interim leader. However, the Progressive Conservatives later disbanded in the territory and a Yukon Party with John Ostashek as leader was formed.

Meanwhile with the Tory Party in disarray, a moribund Liberal Party, and growing evidence of dissatisfaction with the ruling socialist New Democratic Party (NDP) government of Premier Tony Penikett, Yukon residents faced a likely general election in 1992.

Economy. Despite the opening of a high-grade lead/zinc mine north of Watson Lake in southeast Yukon, the territory's major private-sector employer, Curragh Resources Inc., was facing possible shutdown at its Fargo operation 250 mi (402.3 km) north of Whitehorse, and mineral exploration remained at a paltry C$14 million.

In addition, economic belt-tightening was expected to be the general rule as the territorial government scaled down its spending as Can-

YUKON • Information Highlights

Area: 186,660 sq mi (483 450 km²).
Population (September 1991): 27,000.
Chief city (Dec. 1990): Whitehorse, the capital, 21,112.
Government (1991): *Chief Officers*—commissioner, J. Kenneth McKinnon; premier, Tony Penikett (New Democratic Party); leader of official opposition, Dan Lang (Progressive Conservative Party). *Legislature*—16-member Legislative Assembly.
Public Finance (1990–91 fiscal year budget est.): *Revenues,* \$355,498,000; *expenditures,* \$346,-602,000.
Personal Income (average weekly earnings, July 1991): \$634.52.
Education (1991–92): *Enrollment*—elementary and secondary schools, 5,450 pupils.
(All monetary figures are in Canadian dollars.)

ada continued to weather the problems of a recession, low base-metal prices, the high Canadian dollar vis-à-vis the U.S. dollar, and reduced federal formula financing arrangements by Ottawa.

Indian Land Claims. Band-by-band negotiations for Indian land claims continued in 1991, and several Indian groups expected to complete their talks in 1992.

"Transboundary" aboriginal claims by Indians in the adjoining Northwest Territories who were demanding ownership of thousands of square miles of Yukon territory caused consternation throughout Yukon. The result might be further delays in reaching a final agreement with the Yukon Indians.

DON SAWATSKY, *Whitehorse*

ZAIRE

President Mobutu Sese Seko's failure to honor his promise to hand over power to a democratically elected government, combined with the decades-old economic distress, culminated in the mutiny of soldiers in Kinshasa, the capital. Quickly joined by civilians, the disturbances spread throughout Zaire in 1991.

Despite more than $4 billion in U.S. aid and constant shoring up by the World Bank and International Monetary Fund (IMF), the economy of Zaire was in shambles. The static nature of the economy combined with substantial reports of corruption at all levels and a variety of human-rights violations brought pressure on Mobutu from the creditor nations for reform. In April 1990 he announced that Zaire was to have a new constitution with multiple parties contesting the elections. However, little was done, and the military continued to crush demonstrations throughout the country.

Finally in February 1991, Mobutu allowed political exiles to return and in April announced that a conference to draw up a new constitution and plan for elections would be held on April 29. The date for this meeting was changed to July 10 and then to July 31 for "technical reasons." Meanwhile dozens of political parties were formed, the most important being the Union for Democracy and Social Progress led by Etienne Tshisekedi wa Mulumba and the Union of Federalist and Independent Republicans led by Nguza Karl-I-Bond; both leaders had served in Mobutu's governments. They and the leaders of the United Front, a coalition of 23 parties, stated that any conference convened while Mobutu was in power would be a farce. Mobutu countered by announcing that he would remain in control to prevent chaos and that the convention would not be sovereign. Peaceful demonstrations by thousands of persons protesting against Mobutu were broken up by his security forces.

ZAIRE • Information Highlights

Official Name: Republic of Zaire.
Location: Central equatorial Africa.
Area: 905,564 sq mi (2 345 410 km²).
Population (mid-1991 est.): 37,800,000.
Chief City (1987 est.): Kinshasa, the capital, 2,500,000.
Government: *Head of state,* Mobutu Sese Seko, president (took office 1965). *Head of government,* Nguza Karl-I-Bond, prime minister (appointed Nov. 25, 1991). *Legislature* (unicameral)—National Legislative Council.
Monetary Unit: Zaire (4,361.2 zaires equal U.S.$1, May 1991).
Foreign Trade (1989 U.S.$): *Imports,* $849,000,000; *exports,* $1,249,000,000.

The already explosive situation in Zaire detonated on September 23 when soldiers of the Kinshasa garrison, rebelling against poor treatment and lack of pay, rampaged through the capital looting, burning, and killing. The rebellion soon included civilians and spread to Zaire's other major cities.

Kinshasa was wrecked, the central business districts were destroyed, more than 100 persons were killed, and many others were wounded. France and Belgium immediately sent in paratroopers to protect foreigners and to speed the evacuation of approximately 8,000 persons. Mobutu announced a curfew and adopted an emergency food plan to help avert famine. He attempted to form a "government of national crisis," naming Tshisekedi as prime minister of a coalition government. Tshisekedi soon made it clear that he and not Mobutu would run the country. He, however, was dismissed by Mobutu on October 21, and soon thereafter Bernardin Mungul-Diaka, head of a small opposition party, was named as prime minister. As unrest, corruption, lawlessness among the armed forces, and economic chaos continued, Mungul-Diaka was succeeded on November 25 by Nguza Karl-I-Bond.

In early December, as his presidential term officially ended, Mobutu indicated that he would remain in power until new elections were held, a stance that Nguza appeared to support as a means of avoiding anarchy. Nguza requested, however, that international donors, including the IMF and World Bank, take over the management of Zaire's central bank.

HARRY A. GAILEY
San Jose State University

ZIMBABWE

In 1991 the government of Zimbabwe made significant changes in its economic and political policies. In an effort to boost the country's flagging economy, it abandoned its former socialist ideology and moved toward what some Zimbabweans have referred to as "indigenous capitalism."

Structural Adjustment. In contrast to other African nations which have introduced structural adjustment because of conditions for loans imposed by the International Monetary Fund (IMF), the government of Zimbabwe unveiled its own program in February 1991. The program includes the removal of price controls, cutting the budget deficit and the size of the bureaucracy, and ending government subsidies. In the same month, Michel Camdessus, managing director of the IMF, visited Zimbabwe and indicated that the fund would be willing to enter into negotiations for loans with the government.

Even with an economy far stronger and more diversified than most on the African continent, Zimbabwe faced significant economic problems. It has suffered from foreign-exchange shortages, heavy debt, budget deficits, and unemployment, and has had difficulty attracting foreign investment, largely as a result of its socialist orientation.

At the end of March representatives of Western governments and funding agencies attending a donors' conference in Paris pledged $700 million for Zimbabwe's structural-adjustment program. Immediately following the conference, Bernard Chidzero, Zimbabwe's finance minister, said that among the issues raised were the need to increase the role of the private sector and to make all publicly owned institutions or parastatals commercially viable. Zimbabwe was urged to reduce its budget and the size of its bureaucracy. It also was advised to take into account the effects of structural adjustment on the nation's vulnerable groups. Chidzero said that the government would set aside a fund to address temporary hardships.

The donors also were concerned about protection for foreign investment, particularly in connection with Zimbabwe's Land Acquisition Act, which authorized government purchase of 12 million acres (4.9 million ha)—mainly large, white-owned commercial farms—to acquire land for resettling peasant farmers and their families. Chidzero assured the donors that the law would not be carried out in ways that might discourage investment. In fact, land acquisition was proceeding cautiously, since the white commercial farmers most directly affected by it produced more than 40% of the country's foreign exchange. After discussions with the government, the Commercial Farmers Union (CFU), which initially had opposed the law, backed Zimbabwe's efforts to attract foreign aid and investment.

Budget. Changes to be brought about by structural adjustment, including restrictions on parastatal spending, were reflected in the 1991–92 budget submitted to the Zimbabwean parliament early in August. The budget also offered tax concessions to individuals and companies. In response to an inflation rate of more than 20%, some government ministries faced severe budget cuts, although the ministries of health, education, national housing, and labor received increases. The budget deficit would amount to 7.6% of the country's gross domestic product (GDP) for 1991–92 compared with 10.3% of GDP in 1990–91.

Ideological Changes. On June 22 the ruling Zimbabwe African National Union-Patriot Front (ZANU-PF) decided to delete all references to Marxism and socialism from the party constitution. President Robert Mugabe maintained that the changes were in response to events taking place all over the world and that "there was no reason why we should continue to stick to it." In July, in a joint appearance with President Mugabe in Washington, President George Bush announced that U.S. aid to Zimbabwe would be doubled because of the changes which had occurred—including "the removal of the state of emergency, the adoption of the multiparty policy, abandoning Marxism-Leninism as a guiding principle, and the institution of the structural-adjustment program."

University Unrest. In the spring, University of Zimbabwe students staged a three-week boycott of classes to protest the University Amendment Act (1991), which imposed direct political control over the university. In July the institution's vice-chancellor, Walter Kamba, resigned because of political interference.

Leader of ZUM Dismissed. In June, Edgar Tekere, the leader of the opposition Zimbabwe Unity Movement (ZUM), was dismissed by the organization's executive council. Tekere, an outspoken opponent of President Mugabe, had refused to accept a new ZUM constitution and leadership structure which had been agreed to by the party's council.

Commonwealth Summit. In October, Harare enjoyed the prestige of hosting the 1991 meeting of Commonwealth countries, officially opened by Queen Elizabeth II in the conference center adjacent to the Harare Sheraton Hotel. The hotel, damaged by a bomb of unknown origin in July, had been refurbished for the occasion.

PATRICK O'MEARA, *Indiana University*

ZIMBABWE • Information Highlights

Official Name: Republic of Zimbabwe.
Location: Southern Africa.
Area: 150,803 sq mi (390 580 km^2).
Population (mid-1991 est.): 10,000,000.
Chief Cities (1983 est.): Harare (formerly Salisbury), the capital, 681,000; Bulawayo, 429,000; Chitungwiza, 202,000.
Government: *Head of state and government,* Robert Mugabe, executive president (sworn in Dec. 31, 1987). *Legislature*—unicameral Parliament.
Monetary Unit: Zimbabwe dollar (3.444 Z dollars equal U.S.$1, July 1991).
Economic Index (1990): *Industrial Production* (1980 = 100), 134.
Foreign Trade (1987 U.S.$): *Imports,* $1,046,000,000; *exports,* $1,419,000,000.

ZOOS AND ZOOLOGY

Zoos around the world helped the San Diego Zoo celebrate its 75th birthday during 1991. Kicking off the festivities, the government of Australia presented San Diego with four koalas on January 5. Other exotic birthday gifts included mishmi takins (shaggy-haired Asian mammals) from Tierpark Berlin, Siberian weasels from the Leningrad Zoo, and babirusas (wild Indonesian pigs with tusks) from the Cincinnati Zoo. Continuing its celebration, San Diego unveiled two new exhibits on March 23—Gorilla Tropics and the completely renovated Scripps Aviary, which originally opened in 1923. The zoo's lowland gorillas now roam 2.5 acres (1 ha) of grassy hillsides with fallen trees for climbing and pools for bathing. Visitors to the Scripps Aviary walk on an elevated pathway to see tropical birds that live high in the treetops.

A brand-new zoo made its debut in Tennessee: The Nashville Zoo opened on May 17 with more than 500 animals on 135 acres (54.7 ha). In the African Savannah, visitors can stand atop a 14-ft (4.27-m) platform and stare giraffes right in the eye, as well as watch zebras, elands, gemsbok, and other plains animals graze. Tigers, lynx, mountain lions, and snow leopards inhabit the Valley of the Cats. And blackbuck and nilgai antelopes and fallow deer roam the Wilds of India exhibit.

Exhibits. On January 5, Lowry Park Zoo in Tampa, FL, opened its $3.3 million Florida Aquatics Exhibit, which features the endangered West Indian manatee. Manatees are extremely gentle marine mammals that look somewhat like walruses without tusks. About 1,200 of these animals inhabit Florida's coastal waters. They are threatened by habitat loss due to resort and housing development, collisions with boats (at least 27 were killed by powerboats in the first six months of 1990), and sudden cold weather. In addition to displaying these fascinating creatures, Lowry Park has built a research laboratory so zoo staff can educate people about manatees, study the species' ecology, and help save injured individuals.

The new Baboon Kingdom at the Phoenix Zoo, which opened in December 1990, features two colorful cousins: the hamadryas baboon of Somalia and Ethiopia; and the mandrill, native to the rain forests of west central Africa. Male hamadryas baboons can weigh up to 50 lbs (22.7 kg) and have capes of silvery gray fur and naked red skin on their faces and rumps. The larger mandrill males look even more spectacular, sporting a red stripe on the muzzle, flanked by blue ridges, and a yellow beard.

It may seem strange to see sharks in Minnesota, but Minnesota Zoo visitors now can stroll along a South Pacific beach in the new Coral Reef Sharks display. Butterfly fish, damselfish, and hundreds of other brightly colored tropical fishes dart in and out of staghorn, rose, and brain corals. Descending to an underwater viewing area and walking past a waterfall, spectators come to floor-to-ceiling windows, where they can stand nose-to-nose with white- and black-tipped, nurse, and bonnethead sharks. Both corals and sharks are threatened by human activities such as pollution, overcollecting, damage from boats and swimmers, and killing for food.

Moray eels lurk in caves and lemon sharks prowl in search of prey in Sea World of Florida's newest exhibit—Terrors of the Deep. Many deadly sea creatures surround visitors as they walk through the world's largest acrylic tunnel, which supports more than 500 tons of water. Venomous sea snakes slither among rock outcrops, surgeonfish with spines as sharp as scalpels inhabit a cave, and sleek barracudas slice through the water with amazing speed (they often are called torpedoes with teeth).

The world's largest indoor marine mammal habitat opened in Chicago on June 1. The new $45 million Oceanarium at the John G. Shedd Aquarium features Alaska sea otters, beluga whales, Pacific white-sided dolphins, and gentoo and rockhopper penguins.

At California's Monterey Bay Aquarium, visitors can see what life is really like in the bay and how underwater research is carried out via Live Link—the first permanent exhibit of its kind in the world. With a series of special video cameras mounted on a submersible vessel, scientists can transmit images from the bottom of the bay to a surface research ship. Those images then are sent by microwave to a

The clouded leopard is one of the more than 500 animal attractions at the Nashville Zoo, which opened in 1991.

© Tom Brakefield/Nashville Zoo

More and More Deer

Annually they cause untold motor-vehicle-related damage; destroy millions of garden plants, crops, and priceless native and exotic plant specimens; and host the ticks that carry the potentially crippling Lyme disease. What manner of malevolent creature is responsible for wreaking such havoc? It is the gentle 250-lb (113-kg) white-tailed deer, *Odocoileus virginianus*.

Background. In the past ten years or so, the number of white-tailed deer has doubled, even tripled, in many states, adding to the problems caused by deer. Experts estimate there are now 25 million such deer in the United States, about the same number as when the Pilgrims stepped ashore. Following the arrival of European settlers, hunting of white-tailed deer became so intense that legal protection was instituted in some areas. But unregulated hunting and clearing of forests decimated the deer population, and by 1900, only about 500,000 survived. Subsequent regulations and management policies began to reverse the downward trend, and by the 1950s most states had enough deer to establish hunting seasons.

Why have their numbers increased so dramatically? White-tailed deer live in small groups—basically the adult female, her yearling daughter, and her fawns (usually two) of the season. They are extremely adaptable and can live in a variety of habitats. While suburban sprawl has eaten up much of their former territory, it creates more forest edge, which deer seem to prefer to the deep woods. In addition, hunters kill only 2 to 3 million deer per year. The regulations in most states prohibit hunting in suburban areas, where most of the deer are, and traditionally encourage the killing of male deer with antlers. This leaves white-tail populations in which females may outnumber males by as many as nine to one, and a single buck is capable of breeding with many females each year.

© Charlie Palek/Animals Animals

Solutions. One of the most effective solutions to the deer problem would be to extend the deer-hunting season and to insist that hunters kill only antlerless deer. Pennsylvania is doing just that, in hopes of cutting its current deer herd of 1.3 million by more than one third. Vigilance on the roads is vital, particularly during the autumn rut when the behavior of males is unpredictable. Automobile drivers also must remember that when they see one deer, there is liable to be another deer following closely behind.

Although deer eat about 600 species of plants, deer-proof types—such as holly, barberry, English ivy, irises, daffodils, spruce, fir, and cactus—can be cultivated. Covering plants and putting up tall fences—deer easily can jump 7 ft (2.1 m)—also will limit damage.

DEBORAH A. BEHLER

relay station atop a local mountain and beamed to a satellite dish at the aquarium. Visitors can watch live pictures from the ocean floor and then look at a computer encyclopedia, which helps explain what they are seeing on the bottom of the bay and the technology oceanographers use to study underwater.

Zoological Research. A bonanza of belugas at the New York Aquarium may help zoologists understand these whales' social behavior. Two belugas were born in August 1991—both males. The aquarium was the first marine facility ever to exhibit belugas, in 1897. And the first beluga ever bred in captivity was born there in 1972. In the wild, these white whales travel in small groups of three or four, but in summer they migrate by the hundreds or even thousands to Arctic rivers where the females give birth. By studying the interactions of the two mother-and-calf sets, aquarium biologists hope to discover how the whales communicate.

Some fish are known to be good monitors of water pollution. The trout, for example, reacts to various chemical pollutants but is too sluggish in winter to be an accurate gauge. John Lewis, a biologist at London University, has discovered a better indicator—the elephant-nosed mormyrid, an African species that has evolved a navigational radar using electrical impulses that it sends out from an organ in its tail. Lewis found that the fish can detect variations in levels of mercury, copper, and arsenic in the Thames River in England. Pulses from the fish are linked via computer to an alarm system that can warn technicians when pollutants have been released into the river.

DEBORAH A. BEHLER
"Wildlife Conservation" Magazine

Statistical and Tabular Data

NATIONS OF THE WORLD[1]

A Profile and Synopsis of Major 1991 Developments

Nation, Region	Population in millions	Capital	Area Sq mi (km^2)	Head of State/Government
Angola, W. Africa	8.5	Luanda	481,351 (1 246 700)	José Eduardo dos Santos, president Fernando Jose Franca van Dunem, prime minister

The government of Angola and the rebel National Union for the Total Independence of Angola (UNITA) signed a peace agreement on May 31, 1991. The office of prime minister was reestablished in July. In September rebel leader Jonas Savimbi returned to Angola and began campaigning for presidential elections scheduled for 1992. Gross Domestic Product (GDP) (1988 est.): $5.0 billion. Foreign Trade (1989 est.): Imports, $2.5 billion; exports, $2.9 billion.

Antigua and Barbuda, Caribbean	0.1	St. John's	170 (440)	Sir Wilfred E. Jacobs, governor-general Vere C. Bird, prime minister

Prime Minister Vere C. Bird, Sr., shuffled his cabinet March 15, soon after reports that seven members of parliament had threatened to call for a parliamentary vote if he did not retire. Bird remained in power at year's end, however. GDP (1989 est.): $353.5 million. Foreign Trade (1988 est.): Imports, $302.1 million; exports, $30.4 million.

Bahamas, Caribbean	0.3	Nassau	5,382 (13 940)	Sir Henry Taylor, governor-general Lynden O. Pindling, prime minister

A report released in 1991 by the Pan American Health Organization stated that the Bahamas had one of the highest incidences of AIDS cases in the world. GDP (1988 est.): $2.4 billion. Foreign Trade (1989): Imports, $3.0 billion; exports, $2.8 billion.

Bahrain, W. Asia	0.5	Manama	[illegible]	Isa bin Salman Al Khalifa, emir Khalifa bin Salman Al Khalifa, prime minister

On July 2, 1991, Bahrain announced that it would allow foreign-owned companies to conduct their own business operations in the country. The government previously had required that all businesses on the Island have at least 51% Bahraini ownership. GDP (1987): $3.5 billion. Foreign Trade (1990): Imports, $3.7 billion; exports, $3.4 billion.

Barbados, Caribbean	0.3	Bridgetown	166 (430)	Dame Nita Barrow, governor-general L. Erskine Sandiford, prime minister

GDP (1988 est.): $1.3 billion. Foreign Trade (1990): Imports, $700 million; exports, $209 million.

Benin, W. Africa	4.8	Porto Novo	43,483 (112 620)	Nicephore Soglo, president

The first free presidential elections in almost 30 years were held in Benin in March 1991. Prime Minister Nicephore Soglo defeated President Gen. Mathieu Kérékou to become president. GDP (1988): $1.7 billion. Foreign Trade (1988): Imports, $413 million; exports, $226 million.

Bhutan, S. Asia	0.7	Thimphu	18,147 (47 000)	Jigme Singye Wangchuck, king

Bhutan's king continued to develop and modernize the nation's economy. New industries were sought to produce hard-currency exports. Priority also was given to skilled labor. The nation was troubled by a campaign of violence and terror by ethnic Nepalese guerrillas. GDP (1988 est.): $273 million. Foreign Trade (1989): Imports, $138.3 million; exports, $70.9 million.

Botswana, S. Africa	1.3	Gaborone	231,803 (600 370)	Quett Masire, president

GDP (1988): $1.87 billion. Foreign Trade (1988): Imports, $1.1 billion; exports, $1.3 billion.

Brunei Darussalam, S.E. Asia	0.3	Bandar Seri Begawan	2,288 (5 770)	Sir Muda Hassanal Bolkiah, sultan and prime minister

GDP (1989 est.): $3.3 billion. Foreign Trade (1987): Imports, $800 million; exports, $2.07 billion.

Burkina Faso, W. Africa	9.4	Ouagadougou	105,869 (274 200)	Blaise Compaoré, president

A new constitution was approved by voters in Burkina Faso on June 2, 1991, and was implemented by President Blaise Compaoré on June 11. GDP (1988): $1.40 billion. Foreign Trade (1988): Imports, $591 million; exports, $249 million.

Burundi, E. Africa	5.8	Bujumbura	10,745 (27 830)	Pierre Buyoya, president Adrien Sibomana, prime minister

GDP (1988): $1.3 billion. Foreign Trade (1990): Imports, $236 million; exports, $75 million.

Cameroon, Cen. Africa	11.4	Yaoundé	183,568 (475 440)	Paul Biya, president Sadou Hayatou, prime minister

In 1991, Cameroon's government braced against a campaign of civil disobedience orchestrated by opposition groups. In June the antigovernment coalition called for a general strike to weaken President Paul Biya's government. Biya promised revisions to the constitution and a new election code, pledged amnesty for political prisoners, and appointed a new prime minister. GDP (1988): $12.9 billion. Foreign Trade (1988): Imports, $2.3 billion; exports, $2.0 billion.

Cape Verde, W. Africa	0.4	Praia	1,556 (4 030)	Antonio Monteiro Mascarenhas, president Carlos Alberto Wahnon de Carvalho Veiga, prime minister

Cape Verde held its first multiparty elections since independence in January 1991. The African Party for the Independence of Cape Verde (formerly Marxist) lost its majority in parliament, with the Movement for Democracy (MPD) receiving at least 65% of the vote. Carlos Veiga, MPD leader, became prime minister. Antonio Monteiro Mascarenhas, backed by the MPD, was elected president in February. GDP (1987): $158 million. Foreign Trade (1989): Imports, $112 million; exports, $7.0 million.

[1] Independent nations not covered separately in alphabetical section.

Nation, Region	Population in millions	Capital	Area Sq mi (km²)	Head of State/Government
Central African Republic, Cen. Africa	3.0	Bangui	240,533 (622 980)	André-Dieudonné Kolingba, president Edouard Franck, prime minister

GDP (1988 est.): $1.27 billion. Foreign Trade (1989): Imports, $150 million; exports, $134 million.

Chad, Cen. Africa	5.1	Ndjamena	495,753 (1 284 000)	Gen. Idriss Déby, president Jean Bawoyeu Alingue, prime minister

A national charter was adopted in February 1991 establishing a cabinet and advisory council to replace the provisional Council of State created in December 1990. President Déby in March appointed a new government, to be headed by Jean Bawoyeu Alingue. The charter would remain in effect for 30 months; then a referendum would be held on a new constitution for Chad. GDP (1988): $902 million. Foreign Trade (1988): Imports, $214 million; exports, $432 million.

Comoros, E. Africa	0.5	Moroni	838 (2 170)	Said Mohammed Djohar, president

In early August 1991 an unsuccessful attempt to depose President Said Mohammed Djohar was mounted by a senior judge and members of an opposition party. GDP (1988 est.): $207 million. Foreign Trade (1987): Imports, $52 million; exports, $12 million.

Congo, Cen. Africa	2.3	Brazzaville	132,046 (342 000)	Denis Sassou-Nguesso, president Andre Milongo, prime minister

A national conference was convened in Brazzaville in 1991. (See also Africa.) GDP (1988 est.): $2.2 billion. *Foreign Trade (1988): Imports, $544 million; exports, $751 million.*

Djibouti, E. Africa	0.4	Djibouti	8,494 (22 000)	Hassan Gouled Aptidon, president Barkat Gourad Hamadou, premier

In November 1991 Amnesty International accused Djibouti's security police of torturing prisoners. The group claimed police brutality had led to ten deaths and charged the government with detaining political opponents without charges or trials. Gross National Product (GNP) (1986): $333 million. Foreign Trade (1986): Imports, $198 million; exports, $128 million.

Dominica, Caribbean	0.1	Roseau	290 (750)	Clarence A. Seignoret, president Eugenia Charles, prime minister

Dominica, Grenada, St. Lucia, and St. Vincent and the Grenadines began public assemblies in 1991 which it was hoped would lead to the creation of a single state. GDP (1988 est.): $137 million. Foreign Trade (1990): Imports, $118 million; exports, $55 million.

Dominican Republic, Caribbean	7.3	Santo Domingo	18,815 (48 730)	Joaquín Balaguer Ricardo, president

In April 1991, President Joaquín Balaguer, 84, announced he would retire when his term expired in 1994. Salvador Jorge Blanco, president from 1982 to 1986, and Manuel Cuervo Gomez, former armed forces chief, were convicted of corruption and sentenced to 20 years in prison in August. Also in August, the nation ousted thousands of Haitian sugar-plantation workers. GDP (1988): $5.1 billion. Foreign Trade (1989): Imports, $2.0 billion; exports, $924 million.

Equatorial Guinea, Cen. Africa	0.4	Malabo	10,830 (28 050)	Obiang Nguema Mbasogo, president Cristino Seriche Bioko Malabo, prime minister

GNP (1987): $103 million. Foreign Trade (1988 est.): Imports, $50 million; exports, $30 million.

Estonia, N.E. Europe	1.6	Tallinn	17,400 (45 066)	Arnold Ruutel, president

Estonia declared its independence of the Soviet Union in August 1991, and was recognized as independent by the USSR in September. See also Feature Article, *page 33.*

Fiji, Oceania	0.7	Suva	7,054 (18 270)	Sir Penaia Ganilau, president Kamisese Mara, prime minister

GDP (1989 est.): $1.32 billion. Foreign Trade (1990): Imports, $735 million; exports, $234 million.

Gabon, Cen. Africa	1.2	Libreville	103,348 (267 670)	El Hadj Omar Bongo, president Casimir Oye Mba, premier

GDP (1989): $3.2 billion. Foreign Trade (1989): Imports, $0.76 billion; exports, $1.14 billion.

Gambia, W. Africa	0.9	Banjul	4,363 (11 300)	Sir Dawda Kairaba Jawara, president

GDP (1989 est.): $195 million. Foreign Trade (1989): Imports, $105 million; exports, $133 million.

Ghana, W. Africa	15.5	Accra	92,100 (238 540)	Jerry Rawlings, chairman of the Provisional National Defense Council

Jerry Rawlings in December 1990 told the National Commission for Democracy (NCD) to present a report as to whether democracy was feasible in Ghana. The NCD concluded that it was, and Rawlings announced that a National Consultative Assembly would start work in July on drafting a constitution. Student demonstrators complained, however, that the new assembly would be subject to government influence and demanded the replacement of the NCD by a neutral body. GNP (1988): $5.2 billion. Foreign Trade (1988): Imports, $907 million; exports, $1.01 billion.

Grenada, Caribbean	0.1	St. George's	131 (340)	Sir Paul Scoon, governor-general Sir Nicholas Brathwaite, prime minister

On August 14, Prime Minister Brathwaite announced that he would commute the death sentences of 14 persons convicted in 1986 of the killings of former Prime Minister Maurice Bishop and ten others in an attempted 1983 coup foiled by U.S. intervention. Brathwaite made the announcement after appeals from Amnesty International and other human-rights groups. GDP (1988): $129.7 million. Foreign Trade (1988 est.): Imports, $92.6 million; exports, $31.8 million.

Guinea, W. Africa	7.5	Conakry	94,927 (245 860)	Lansana Conté, president

GDP (1988): $2.5 billion. Foreign Trade (1988 est.): Imports, $509 million; exports, $553 million.

Nation, Region	Population in millions	Capital	Area Sq mi (km²)	Head of State/Government
Guinea-Bissau, W. Africa	1.0	Bissau	13,946 (36 120)	João Bernardo Vieira, president
	Opposition political parties were legalized in Guinea-Bissau on May 4, 1991. The decision ended 17 years of one-party rule. GDP (1987): $152 million. Foreign Trade (1987): Imports, $49 million; exports, $15 million.			
Guyana, N.E. South America	0.8	Georgetown	83,000 (214 970)	Hugh Desmond Hoyte, president Hamilton Green, prime minister
	GDP (1988 est.): $323 million. Foreign Trade (1988 est.): Imports, $216 million; exports, $215 million.			
Ivory Coast, W. Africa	12.5	Yamoussoukro	124,502 (322 460)	Félix Houphouët-Boigny, president Alassane Ouattara, prime minister
	GDP (1988): $10.0 billion. Foreign Trade (1988): Imports, $1.3 billion; exports, $2.2 billion.			
Kiribati, Oceania	0.07	Tarawa	277 (717)	Teatao Teannaki, president
	General elections for the House of Assembly were held in May 1991. President Ieremia Tabai, prohibited by the constitution from seeking another term, won reelection to the legislature. Vice-President Teatao Teannaki was elected president. GDP (1989): $34 million. Foreign Trade (1988): Imports, $21.5 million; exports, $5.1 million.			
Latvia, N.E. Europe	2.7	Riga	24,600 (63 714)	Anatolijs Gorbunovs, president
	Latvia declared independence from the Soviet Union in August 1991, and was recognized by the USSR in September. See also FEATURE ARTICLE, *page 33.*			
Lesotho, S. Africa	1.8	Maseru	11,718 (30 350)	Letsie III, king Elias Phisoana Ramaema, chairman, military council
	Justin Lekhanya, military ruler of Lesotho since 1986, was deposed in April 1991. The reins of government were taken by Col. Elias P. Ramaema. In November 1990 exiled King Moshoeshoe II's son, Letsie III, had been elected king by a tribal assembly. GDP (1989 est.): $412 million. Foreign Trade (1989 est.): Imports, $526 million; exports, $55 million.			
Liberia, W. Africa	2.7	Monrovia	43,000 (111 370)	Amos Sawyer, president
	In 1991 the halt in the Liberian civil war was holding. See also AFRICA. *GDP (1988): $988 million. Foreign Trade (1989 est.): Imports, $394 million; exports, $505 million.*			
Liechtenstein, Cen. Europe	0.03	Vaduz	62 (160)	Hans Adam II, prince Hans Brunhart, prime minister
	Prince Hans Adam II announced in August 1991 that Liechtenstein would not seek membership in the European Community. However, Liechtenstein did join the European Free Trade Area (EFTA) during the year.			
Lithuania, N.E. Europe	3.9	Vilnius	25,200 (65 200)	Vytautas Landsbergis, president
	Lithuania, which had declared itself independent of the Soviet Union in 1990, was recognized as independent by the USSR in September 1991. See also FEATURE ARTICLE, *page 33.*			
Luxembourg, W. Europe	0.4	Luxembourg	998 (2 586)	Jean, grand duke Jacques Santer, prime minister
	GDP (1989 est.): $6.3 billion. (Luxembourg's foreign trade is recorded with Belgium's.)			
Madagascar, E. Africa	12.4	Antananarivo	226,656 (587 040)	Didier Ratsiraka, president Guy Razanamasy, prime minister
	In June 1991 a coalition of opposition parties began a campaign of strikes and demonstrations to force President Didier Ratsiraka to make democratic reforms or to resign. The coalition demanded a new constitution. Although Ratsiraka offered concessions, he refused to leave office. In August, Ratsiraka handed over power to his recently appointed prime minister, and in November he agreed to take part in a joint transitional government. GDP (1988): $1.7 billion. Foreign Trade (1989): Imports, $340 million; exports, $312 million.			
Malawi, E. Africa	9.4	Lilongwe	45,745 (118 480)	Hastings Kamuzu Banda, president
	GDP (1988): $1.4 billion. Foreign Trade (1990): Imports, $573 million; exports, $418 million.			
Maldives, S. Asia	0.2	Malé	116 (300)	Maumoon Abdul Gayoom, president
	GDP (1988): $136 million. Foreign Trade (1988 est.): Imports, $90.0 million; exports, $47.0 million.			
Mali, W. Africa	8.3	Bamako	478,764 (1 240 000)	Amadou Toumani Toure, chief of state Soumana Sako, prime minister
	Following strikes and protests in March, President Moussa Traoré's government was overthrown. The new ruling junta was headed by Lt. Col. Amadou Toumani Toure. Soumana Sako, a senior official of the UN Development Program, was named interim prime minister in a transitional government. In July a coup attempt was blocked. GDP (1988 est.): $1.94 billion. Foreign Trade (1989): Imports, $500 million; exports, $271 million.			
Malta, S. Europe	0.4	Valletta	124 (320)	Vincent Tabone, president Edward Fenech Adami, prime minister
	GDP (1988): $1.9 billion. Foreign Trade (1989): Imports, $1.51 billion; exports, $858 million.			
Mauritania, W. Africa	2.1	Nouakchott	397,954 (1 030 700)	Maaouiya Ould Sid Ahmed Taya, president
	In a July 12 referendum, Mauritanians approved a new constitution. The military government legalized political opposition and freed the press; Islamic opposition groups were not permitted. In late March the government declared amnesty for political prisoners (all of whom were black) and released its detainees in an attempt to improve Mauritania's international image, tarnished by its pro-Iraqi stance during the Persian Gulf war. The detainees, however, were in poor condition, having been tortured and abused. GDP (1988): $1.0 billion. Foreign Trade (1989): Imports, $222 million; exports, $437 million.			

Nation, Region	Population in millions	Capital	Area Sq mi (km^2)	Head of State/Government
Mauritius, E. Africa	1.1	Port Louis	718 (1 860)	Sir Veerasamy Ringadoo, governor-general Anerood Jugnauth, prime minister

GDP (1988): $1.9 billion. Foreign Trade (1990): Imports, $1.6 billion; exports, $1.2 billion.

Nation, Region	Population in millions	Capital	Area Sq mi (km^2)	Head of State/Government
Monaco, S. Europe	0.03	Monaco-Ville	0.7 (1.9)	Rainier III, prince M. Jean Ausseil, minister of state
Mongolia, E. Asia	2.2	Ulan Bator	604,247 (1 565 000)	Punsalmaagiyn Ochirbat, president

U.S. Secretary of State James Baker addressed the Mongolian parliament in July. Baker promised U.S. aid for Mongolia's economy, which was struggling to make the transition to free markets. In September, Mongolia was visited by the Dalai Lama, the Buddhist spiritual leader. GDP (1985 est.): $1.7 billion. Foreign Trade (1985): Imports, $1.0 billion; exports, $388 million.

Nation, Region	Population in millions	Capital	Area Sq mi (km^2)	Head of State/Government
Nauru, Oceania	0.009	Nauru	8 (21)	Bernard Dowiyogo, president

Foreign Trade (1984): Imports, $73 million; exports, $93 million.

Nation, Region	Population in millions	Capital	Area Sq mi (km^2)	Head of State/Government
Niger, W. Africa	8.0	Niamey	489,189 (1 267 000)	Ali Saibou, president

Niger would be the first nation to benefit from a World Bank plan enabling poor countries to reduce their international commercial-bank debts by buying them off at heavy discounts. By early 1991, 15 countries had applied for the facility. GDP (1988 est.): $2.4 billion. Foreign Trade (1988 est.): Imports, $441 million; exports, $371 million.

Nation, Region	Population in millions	Capital	Area Sq mi (km^2)	Head of State/Government
Oman, W. Asia	1.6	Muscat	82,031 (212 460)	Qaboos bin Said, sultan and prime minister

GDP (1987 est.): $7.8 billion. Foreign Trade (1990): Imports, $2.7 billion; exports, $5.2 billion.

Nation, Region	Population in millions	Capital	Area Sq mi (km^2)	Head of State/Government
Papua New Guinea, Oceania	3.9	Port Moresby	178,259 (461 690)	Wiwa Korowi, governor-general Rabbie Namaliu, prime minister

Governor-general Sir Vincent Serei Eri resigned Oct. 1, 1991, after Papua New Guinea's government asked Britain's Queen Elizabeth II to dismiss him; Eri had refused to oust Deputy Prime Minister Ted Diro, who had been found guilty of corruption. Diro also resigned October 1. The parliament on November 11 elected Wiwa Korowi as the governor-general. GDP (1988 est.): $3.26 billion. Foreign Trade (1990): Imports, $1.1 billion; exports, $1.1 billion.

Nation, Region	Population in millions	Capital	Area Sq mi (km^2)	Head of State/Government
Qatar, W. Asia	0.5	Doha	4,247 (11 000)	Khalifa bin Hamad Al Thani, emir and prime minister

GDP (1987): $5.4 billion. Foreign Trade (1988 est.): Imports, $1 billion; exports, $2.2 billion.

Nation, Region	Population in millions	Capital	Area Sq mi (km^2)	Head of State/Government
Rwanda, E. Africa	7.5	Kigali	10,170 (26 340)	Juvénal Habyarimana, president

In January 1991 up to 600 rebels invaded Rwanda from Uganda. The rebels were part of a force of Rwandan exiles that had staged an unsuccessful large-scale invasion in October 1990. In March the Rwandan government signed a cease-fire with the rebels. The agreement called for the release of all political detainees and prisoners of war before talks on a permanent settlement were held. In June a new constitution was signed by President Habyarimana. GDP (1988 est.): $2.3 billion. Foreign Trade (1988): Imports, $278 million; exports, $118 million.

Nation, Region	Population in millions	Capital	Area Sq mi (km^2)	Head of State/Government
Saint Kitts and Nevis, Caribbean	0.04	Basseterre	139 (360)	Clement A. Arrindell, governor-general Kennedy A. Simmonds, prime minister

GDP (1988 est.): $119 million. Foreign Trade (1988): Imports, $94.7 million; exports, $30.3 million.

Nation, Region	Population in millions	Capital	Area Sq mi (km^2)	Head of State/Government
Saint Lucia, Caribbean	0.2	Castries	239 (620)	Sir Stanislaus A. James, governor-general John Compton, prime minister

GDP (1988 est.): $172 million. Foreign Trade (1987): Imports, $178.1 million; exports, $76.8 million.

Nation, Region	Population in millions	Capital	Area Sq mi (km^2)	Head of State/Government
Saint Vincent and the Grenadines, Caribbean	0.1	Kingstown	131 (340)	David Jack, governor-general James F. Mitchell, prime minister

GDP (1988): $136 million. Foreign Trade (1986): Imports, $87.3 million; exports, $63.8 million.

Nation, Region	Population in millions	Capital	Area Sq mi (km^2)	Head of State/Government
San Marino, S. Europe	0.023	San Marino	23 (60)	Coregents appointed semiannually
São Tomé and Príncipe, W. Africa	0.1	São Tomé	371 (960)	Miguel Trovoada, president Daniel Lima dos Santos Daio, prime minister

São Tomé and Principe in 1991 held its first multiparty elections since independence in 1975. In January elections the ruling party lost its majority in the 65-seat parliament. In the March presidential election, former premier Miguel Trovoada was voted in as president. GDP (1986): $37.9 million. Foreign Trade (1988 est.): Imports, $17.3 million; exports, $9.1 million.

Nation, Region	Population in millions	Capital	Area Sq mi (km^2)	Head of State/Government
Senegal, W. Africa	7.5	Dakar	75,749 (196 190)	Abdou Diouf, president Habib Thiam, prime minister

The Casamance region of Senegal suffered from separatist violence in 1991, with the Movement for the Democratic Forces of Casamance seeking self-rule for the region. Both terrorist assaults by the movement and the harsh retaliatory crackdown by the government caused great tension. During a visit to the United States by President Diouf, U.S. President George Bush forgave Senegal's $42 million debt and pledged financial assistance to Senegal if it contributed troops to a peacekeeping force in Liberia. President Diouf was elected chairman of the Economic Community of West African States in July. GDP (1988 est.): $5 billion. Foreign Trade (1988): Imports, $1.1 billion; exports, $761 million.

Nation, Region	Population in millions	Capital	Area Sq mi (km^2)	Head of State/Government
Seychelles, E. Africa	0.1	Victoria	176 (455)	France Albert René, president

GDP (1988 est.): $255 million. Foreign Trade (1990): Imports, $187 million; exports, $39 million.

Nation, Region	Population in millions	Capital	Area Sq mi (km^2)	Head of State/Government
Sierra Leone, W. Africa	4.3	Freetown	27,699 (71 740)	Joseph Momoh, president

Nation, Region	Population in millions	Capital	Area Sq mi (km²)	Head of State/Government

Clashes between Sierra Leone troops and rebels invading from neighboring Liberia began in March 1991. Troops from Nigeria and Guinea were deployed in April to help repulse the incursion. By mid-April it was reported that 150 persons had been killed in the fighting. A rebel leader calling himself Corporal Zanco claimed responsibility for the invasion. In August the United States increased military assistance to Sierra Leone—reportedly the second time assistance was sent since March. GDP (1987): $965 million. Foreign Trade (1990): Imports, $152 million; exports, $143 million.

Solomon Islands, Oceania	0.3	Honiara	10,985 (28 450)	Sir George Lepping, governor-general Solomon Mamaloni, prime minister

GDP (1988): $156 million. Foreign Trade (1989): Imports, $114 million; exports, $75 million.

Suriname, S. America	0.4	Paramaribo	63,039 (163 270)	Ronald Venetiaan, president

In May elections, political groups favoring renewed ties between Suriname and the Netherlands won 38 of the National Assembly's 51 seats. These were the first elections since a provisional civilian government had been installed by the army, led by Lt. Col. Dési Bouterse, who had taken power in a December 1990 coup. In September a special assembly elected Ronald Venetiaan as president. GDP (1988 est.): $1.27 billion. Foreign Trade (1988 est.): Imports, $365 million; exports, $425 million.

Swaziland, S. Africa	0.8	Mbabane	6,703 (17 360)	Mswati III, king Obed Mfanyana Dlamini, prime minister

GNP (1989 est.): $539 million. Foreign Trade (1988): Imports, $386 million; exports, $394 million.

Togo, W. Africa	3.8	Lomé	21,927 (56 790)	Gnassingbé Eyadéma, president Joseph Kokou Koffigoh, prime minister

A national conference on democracy on August 27 elected Joseph Kokou Koffigoh premier of an interim government, stripping President Gnassingbé Eyadéma of all but ceremonial duties. Later in the year soldiers loyal to Eyadéma made several unsuccessful coup attempts against the interim government. Koffigoh was seized by the rebels on December 3. The prime minister remained under loose military guard late in the year, and Eyadéma issued a statement saying that he and Koffigoh would form a provisional government together. GDP (1988 est.): $1.35 billion. Foreign Trade (1988): Imports, $369 million; exports, $344 million.

Tonga, Oceania	0.1	Nuku'alofa	289 (748)	Taufa'ahau Tupou IV, king Baron Vaea, prime minister

GDP (1989 est.): $86 million. Foreign Trade (1990 est.): Imports, $65 million; exports, $13 million.

Trinidad and Tobago, Caribbean	1.3	Port of Spain	1,981 (5 130)	Noor Hassanali, president Patrick Manning, prime minister

Parliamentary elections were held in December 1991. Patrick Manning of the People's National Movement was voted in as prime minister, defeating Arthur Robinson and his National Alliance for Reconstruction by a landslide. The People's National Movement had ruled the nation for 30 years until being defeated by Robinson's party in 1986. GDP (1988 est.): $3.75 billion. Foreign Trade (1990): Imports, $1.2 billion; exports, $2.0 billion.

Tuvalu, Oceania	0.009	Funafuti	10 (26)	Sir Tupua Leupena, governor-general Bikenibeu Paeniu, prime minister

GNP (1989 est.): $4.6 million. Foreign Trade (1983 est.): Imports, $2.8 million; exports, $1 million.

United Arab Emirates, W. Asia	2.4	Abu Dhabi	32,278 (83 600)	Zayid bin Sultan Al Nuhayyan, president Rashid bin Said Al Maktum, prime minister

The United Arab Emirates began recruiting female soldiers during the year in a departure from the observance of Islamic religious laws. GNP (1988): $23.3 billion. Foreign Trade (1988 est.): Imports, $8.5 billion; exports, $10.6 billion.

Vanuatu, Oceania	0.2	Port-Vila	5,699 (14 760)	Frederick Timakata, president Donald Kalpokas, prime minister

Vanuatu's ruling party voted in August 1991 to remove Prime Minister and President Walter Lini. Donald Kalpokas was named prime minister. GDP (1987 est.): $120 million. Foreign Trade (1988 est.): Imports, $58 million; exports, $16 million.

Vatican City, S. Europe	0.001	Vatican City	0.17 (0.438)	John Paul II, pope

In September 1991 the Vatican and Albania established diplomatic relations. The Vatican thus had established relations with all the Eastern European nations and with Moscow.

Western Samoa, Oceania	0.2	Apia	1,104 (2 860)	Tanumafili II Malietoa, head of state Tofilau Eti Alesana, prime minister

GDP (1989 est.): $112 million. Foreign Trade (1988): Imports, $51.8 million; exports, $9.9 million.

Yemen, S. Asia	10.1	San'a	203,850 (527 970)	Ali Abdullah Saleh, president

On Feb. 24, 1991, thousands of Yemeni citizens marched on embassies of nations in the U.S.-led allied coalition against Iraq to protest the ground offensive of the Persian Gulf war. After the war unrest and economic problems mounted in the country, principally because Saudi and other Gulf nations had expelled almost 1 million Yemeni workers in retaliation for Yemen's support of Iraq. GDP (North—1987): $4.5 billion; (South—1986): $1.01 billion. Foreign Trade (North—1987): Imports, $1.4 billion; exports, $51.1 million; (South—1987 est.): Imports, $497 million; exports, $54 million.

Zambia, E. Africa	8.4	Lusaka	290,583 (752 610)	Frederick Chiluba, president Malimba Masheke, prime minister

In the first multiparty presidential elections since 1972, Zambia's President Kenneth Kaunda was defeated overwhelmingly by Frederick Chiluba. Kaunda, who had been president since independence in 1964, had legalized opposition parties in 1990. Chiluba was sworn in November 2. In September the World Bank suspended about $75 million in funds for Zambia after the country missed a payment deadline. GDP (1988): $4 billion. Foreign Trade (1990): Imports, $1.2 billion; exports, $899 million.

WORLD MINERAL AND METAL PRODUCTION

ALUMINUM, primary smelter (thousand metric tons)	1989	1990
United States	4,030	4,048
USSR[e]	2,400	2,200
Canada	1,555	1,567
Australia	1,244	1,234
Brazil	890	931
China[e]	750	850
Norway	863	845
West Germany	742	720
Venezuela	540	546
India	423	433
Spain	352	355
France	335	326
United Kingdom	297	290
Netherlands	279	258
Other countries[a]	3,218	3,212
Total	18,018	17,815

ANTIMONY, mine[b] (metric tons)	1989	1990
China[e]	30,000	30,000
USSR[e]	9,600	9,000
Bolivia	9,189	8,454
South Africa	6,167	6,000[e]
Mexico	1,906	2,627
Australia	1,419	1,300[e]
Guatemala	1,343	1,200[e]
Thailand	495	537
Canada	2,818	463
Yugoslavia	798	409
Turkey	1,031	400[e]
Other countries[a]	2,232	1,941
Total	66,998	62,731

ASBESTOS[c] (thousand metric tons)	1989	1990
USSR[e]	2,600	2,400
Canada	701	682
Brazil	206	210[e]
Zimbabwe	187	190[e]
China[e]	160	160
South Africa	155	148
Greece	73	73[e]
Other countries[a]	161	117
Total	4,243	3,980

BARITE[c] (thousand metric tons)	1989	1990
China[e]	1,750	1,750
USSR[e]	540	500
India	548	475[e]
United States	290	439
Turkey	435	430[e]
Morocco	370	370[e]
Mexico	325	332
West Germany	160	144
France	100	100[e]
Other countries[a]	1,059	1,037
Total	5,577	5,577

BAUXITE[d] (thousand metric tons)	1989	1990
Australia	38,583	40,697
Guinea	16,523	16,500[e]
Jamaica	9,601	10,921
Brazil	8,665	9,876
USSR[e]	5,737	5,294
India	4,768	4,340
China[e]	4,800	4,200
Suriname	3,530	3,267
Yugoslavia	3,252	2,952
Greece	2,576	2,504
Hungary	2,644	2,333
Sierra Leone	1,562	1,445
Guyana	1,321	1,424
Indonesia	862	1,206
Other countries[a]	3,208	3,125
Total	107,632	110,084

CEMENT[c] (thousand metric tons)	1989	1990
China	203,844	218,000[e]
USSR	140,436	137,328
Japan	80,316	84,444
United States	71,268	71,310
India	44,568	45,000[e]
Italy	39,708	41,800[e]
South Korea	30,474	33,600
West Germany	28,499	30,432
Spain	27,372	28,092
France	25,992	26,508
Brazil	25,883	25,848
Turkey	23,808	24,408[e]
Mexico	22,766	22,762
Other countries[a]	375,823	376,076
Total	1,140,757	1,165,608

CHROMITE[c] (thousand metric tons)	1989	1990
South Africa	4,951	4,497
USSR[e]	3,800	3,800
India	1,003	995
Turkey	1,000	850[e]
Albania[e]	610	600
Zimbabwe	627	600[e]
Finland	499	500[e]
Brazil	476	476[e]
Philippines	173	198
Other countries[a]	403	330
Total	13,542	12,846

COAL, anthracite and bituminous[c] (million metric tons)	1989	1990
China	1,021	1,051
United States	811	861
USSR	575	545[e]
Australia	190	200[e]
South Africa	176	180[e]
India	199	180[e]
Poland	178	148
United Kingdom	101	93
West Germany	71	76
North Korea[e]	65	55
Canada	60	52
Other countries[a]	192	195
Total	3,640	3,636

COAL, lignite[c,f] (million metric tons)	1989	1990
East Germany	301	290[e]
USSR	164	158[e]
West Germany	110	108
Czechoslovakia	94	86
United States	78	83
Poland	72	68
Yugoslavia	74	65
Greece	52	52
Australia	48	48
Turkey	52	47
Romania	53	34
Other countries[a]	128	105
Total	1,226	1,144

COPPER, mine[b] (thousand metric tons)	1989	1990
Chile	1,628	1,603
United States	1,497	1,587
Canada	705	780
USSR[e]	640	600
Zambia	470	496
China[e]	375	375
Zaire	467	372
Peru	373	334
Poland	384	329
Australia	296	316
Mexico	254	291
South Africa	192	188
Philippines	190	182
Papua New Guinea	204	170
Other countries[a]	1,082	1,185
Total	8,757	8,808

COPPER, refined, primary and secondary (thousand metric tons)	1989	1990
United States	1,957	2,012
Chile	1,071	1,192
Japan	990	1,008
USSR[e]	1,000	930
China[e]	540	560
Canada	515	516
West Germany	475	476
Zambia	464	443
Belgium	344	361
Poland	390	346
Australia	255	274
South Korea	180	186
Peru	220	182
Zaire	204	174
Spain	166	171
Other countries[a]	1,811	1,807
Total	10,582	10,638

DIAMOND, natural (thousand carats)	1989	1990
Australia	35,080	034,662
Zaire	17,755	18,000[e]
Botswana	15,252	17,352
USSR[e]	15,000	15,000
South Africa	9,116	8,694
Angola	1,245	1,280[e]
China[e]	1,000	1,000
Namibia	927	748
Other countries[a]	2,368	2,360
Total	97,743	99,096

FLUORSPAR[g] (thousand metric tons)	1989	1990
China[e]	1,700	1,500
Mongolia[e]	750	750
Mexico	779	634
USSR[e]	410	380
South Africa	368	311
France[e]	209	205
Spain[e]	135	135
Italy	126	127[e]
Other countries[a]	1,109	1,064
Total	5,586	5,106

GAS, natural[h] (billion cubic meters)	1989	1990
USSR	796	850
United States	489	497
Canada	98	100
Netherlands	75	75
Indonesia	40	65[e]
Algeria	48	50[e]
United Kingdom	41	42
Mexico	35	36[e]
Romania	32	30[e]
Norway	32	28
Other countries[a]	333	350
Total	2,019	2,123

GOLD, mine[b] (kilograms)	1989	1990
South Africa	607,460	602,789
United States	265,541	290,202
USSR[e]	285,000	250,000
Australia	203,563	242,299
Canada	159,494	164,991
China[e]	90,000	100,000
Brazil[e]	100,000	80,000
Philippines	35,300	35,000[e]
Papua New Guinea	27,538	31,035
Colombia	27,090	28,000[e]
Chile	22,559	27,591
Poland[e]	31,000	26,500
Other countries[a]	175,913	198,039
Total	2,030,458	2,076,446

GYPSUM[c] (thousand metric tons)	1989	1990
United States	15,988	14,883
Canada	8,196	8,202
China[e]	8,100	8,000
Iran[e]	8,000	8,000
Japan[e]	6,300	6,400
Mexico	5,390	6,001
Thailand	5,477	5,753
France	5,684	5,600[e]
Spain[e]	5,500	5,000
USSR[e]	4,900	4,700
United Kingdom[e]	4,000	4,000
West Germany[e]	1,850	1,800
Australia[e]	1,800	1,800
Romania[3]	1,600	1,500
Other countries[a]	16,199	15,999
Total	98,984	97,638

IRON ORE, marketable equivalent[c] (thousand metric tons)	1989	1990
USSR	241,348	236,160
Brazil	153,700	153,696
China[e]	100,000	118,000
Australia	105,810	110,884
United States	59,032	55,464
India	51,434	52,000[e]
Canada	39,445	36,443
South Africa	29,958	30,347
Venezuela	18,390	20,365
Sweden	21,578	19,812
Mauritania	11,138	11,200[e]
North Korea[e]	9,500	9,500
France	9,319	8,720
Other countries[a]	74,217	61,905
Total	924,869	924,496

IRON, crude steel (thousand metric tons)	1989	1990
USSR	160,092	154,416
Japan	107,908	110,339
United States	88,852	89,726
China	64,212	64,656
West Germany	41,073	38,435
Italy	25,213	25,439
South Korea	21,873	23,125
Brazil	25,018	20,572
France	19,286	19,017
United Kingdom	18,813	17,908
Czechoslovakia	15,465	14,813
Canada	15,456	14,500
Poland	15,094	13,553
India	12,782	13,000[e]
Spain	12,684	12,705
Belgium	10,948	11,426
Romania	14,415	10,700
Other countries[a]	117,287	113,421
Total	786,171	768,351

LEAD, mine[b] (thousand metric tons)	1989	1990
Australia	495	563
United States	420	495
USSR[e]	500	450
China[e]	341	315
Canada	275	236
Peru	192	189
Mexico	163	180
North Korea[e]	120	120
Sweden	89	84
Yugoslavia	86	73
Other countries[a]	687	656
Total	3,368	3,361

LEAD, refined, primary and secondary[i] (thousand metric tons)	1989	1990
United States	1,288	1,327
USSR[e]	745	700
West Germany	350	349
United Kingdom	350	329
Japan	333	329
China[e]	300	290
France	267	260
Canada	245	224
Australia	208	224
Mexico	197	214[e]
Italy	186	171
Belgium	109	92
Other countries[a]	1,409	1,370
Total	5,987	5,879

MAGNESIUM, primary (thousand metric tons)	1989	1990
United States	152	139
USSR[e]	91	88
Norway	50	48
Canada	7	25
France	15	15
Japan	8	13
Brazil	6	9
Other countries[a]	15	15
Total	344	352

MANGANESE ORE[c] (thousand metric tons)	1989	1990
USSR[e]	9,100	8,800
South Africa	3,623	3,672
China[e]	3,200	3,200
Gabon	2,593	2,630[e]
Brazil	2,280	2,000[e]
Australia	2,124	1,988
India	1,334	1,360[e]
Other countries[a]	1,060	1,046
Total	25,314	24,696

MERCURY, mine (metric tons)	1989	1990
USSR[e]	2,300	2,100
Spain	1,380	962
China[e]	700	750
Algeria	586	639
United States	414	460[e]
Mexico	345	345[e]
Other countries[a]	538	350
Total	6,263	5,606

MOLYBDENUM, mine[b] (metric tons)	1989	1990
United States	63,105	61,611
Chile	16,550	13,830
Canada	13,543	13,481
USSR[e]	11,500	11,000
Mexico	4,189	4,000[e]
Peru	3,177	3,000[e]
Other countries[a]	4,735	4,730
Total	116,799	111,652

NATURAL GAS LIQUIDS (million barrels)	1989	1990
United States	570	569
USSR[e]	330	274
Saudi Arabia	154	174
Mexico	137	155
Canada	150	145
United Kingdom	56	58[e]
Other countries[a]	365	370
Total	1,762	1,745

NICKEL, mine[b] (thousand metric tons)	1989	1990
USSR[e]	281	259
Canada	200	199
New Caledonia	80	85
Australia	67	67
Indonesia	60	54
Cuba[e]	44	43
South Africa	36	34
Dominican Republic	32	29
Other countries[a]	150	150
Total	950	920

NITROGEN, content of ammonia (thousand metric tons)	1989	1990
USSR[e]	19,500	18,500
China[e]	17,000	18,000
United States	12,201	12,646
India	6,661	7,022
Netherlands	3,001	3,163
Canada	3,340	2,964
Indonesia	2,526	2,600[e]
Mexico	2,100	2,164
Poland[e]	2,300	1,950
Romania[e]	2,600	1,900
France	1,476	1,500
Other countries[a]	26,311	25,530
Total	99,016	98,025

PETROLEUM, crude (million barrels)	1989	1990
USSR	4,180	3,899
United States	2,786	2,685
Saudi Arabia	1,853	2,364
Iran	1,048	1,127
China	1,010	1,011
Mexico	920	930
Venezuela	698	780
United Arab Emirates	717	774

PETROLEUM, crude (cont'd)	1989	1990
Iraq	1,033	732
Nigeria	620	668
United Kingdom	654	666
Canada	571	558
Indonesia	516	511
Libya	419	493
Algeria	403	429
Kuwait	660	427
Other countries[a]	3,731	3,895
Total	21,819	21,949

PHOSPHATE ROCK[c] (thousand metric tons)	1989	1990
United States	48,866	46,343
USSR[e]	34,400	33,500
Morocco	18,067	21,396
China[e]	17,000	17,300
Tunisia	6,610	6,259
Jordan	6,900	5,925
Israel	3,922	3,516
South Africa	2,963	3,165
Brazil	3,655	2,968
Togo	3,355	2,314
Senegal	2,273	2,147
Other countries[a]	10,955	9,273
Total	158,966	154,106

POTASH, K_2O equivalent basis (thousand metric tons)	1989	1990
USSR	10,200	9,500
Canada	7,074	7,372
East Germany	3,200	2,700[e]
West Germany	2,182	2,200[e]
United States	1,595	1,713
Israel	1,338	1,350[e]
France	1,195	1,300[e]
Other countries[a]	2,426	2,175
Total	29,210	28,010

SALT[c] (thousand metric tons)	1989	1990
United States	35,202	36,959
China[e]	28,000	20,000
USSR	15,000	14,500
West Germany	13,100	12,550[e]
Canada	11,057	11,097
India	9,693	9,500[e]
France	7,500	7,450[e]
Australia[e]	7,345	7,400
Mexico	6,942	7,135
Romania	6,771	6,500[e]
United Kingdom[e]	5,700	5,700
Poland[e]	4,670	4,800
Brazil	3,653	3,800[e]
Other countries[a]	35,844	35,920
Total	190,477	183,311

SILVER, mine[b] (metric tons)	1989	1990
Mexico	2,306	2,346
United States	2,007	2,170
Peru	1,840	1,725
USSR[e]	1,520	1,400
Canada	1,262	1,380
Australia	1,075	1,273
Poland	1,003	1,000[e]
Chile	545	633
Bolivia	267	280[e]
Spain	250	270
Morocco	195	235
Sweden	200	185
South Africa	182	161
Other countries[a]	1,677	1,626
Total	14,329	14,684

SULFUR, all forms[j] (thousand metric tons)	1989	1990
United States	11,601	11,500
USSR[e]	9,900	9,025
Canada	6,697	6,947
Poland	5,150	5,030[e]
China[e]	4,900	4,900
Japan	2,623	2,703
Mexico	2,369	2,340[e]
West Germany	1,885	1,835
Saudi Arabia[e]	1,400	1,500
Spain	1,058	1,085[e]
Iraq[e]	1,270	1,050
France	1,036	1,045[e]
Other countries[a]	8,837	8,048
Total	58,716	57,668

TIN, mine[b] (metric tons)	1989	1990
Brazil	50,232	39,149
China[e]	33,000	33,000
Indonesia	31,263	30,200
Malaysia	32,034	28,468
Bolivia	15,849	17,273
USSR[e]	16,000	15,000
Thailand	14,922	14,635
Australia	7,709	7,377
Other countries[a]	25,764	26,504
Total	226,773	211,606

TITANIUM MINERALS[c k] (thousand metric tons)	1989	1990
ILMENITE		
Australia	1,714	1,619
Norway	930	900[e]
Malaysia	521	502
USSR[e]	460	430
India[e]	160	160
China[e]	150	150
Brazil	147	150[e]
Other countries[a]	154	140
Total	4,236	4,051
RUTILE		
Australia	243	226
Sierra Leone	128	144
South Africa[e]	60	60
Other countries[a]	23	22
Total	454	452
TITANIFEROUS SLAG		
Canada	1,040	760
South Africa[e]	725	725
Total	1,765	1,485

TUNGSTEN, mine[b] (metric tons)	1989	1990
China[e]	21,000	21,000
USSR[e]	9,300	8,800
Portugal	1,382	1,405
South Korea	1,701	1,255
Austria	1,177	1,200[e]
Peru	961	1,200[e]
Bolivia	1,118	1,200[e]
Australia	1,371	900[e]
Other countries[a]	4,022	3,340
Total	42,099	40,300

URANIUM OXIDE (U_3O_8)[l] (metric tons)	1989	1990
Canada	12,965	11,153
United States	6,276	6,300[e]
Australia	4,311	4,909
Namibia	3,629	3,800
Niger	3,514	3,600[e]
France	3,781	3,302
South Africa	3,456	2,875
Other countries[a]	1,958	1,850
Total	39,669	37,789

ZINC, mine[b] (thousand metric tons)	1989	1990
Canada	1,273	1,177
Australia	803	937
USSR[e]	810	750
China[e]	620	619
Peru	597	577
United States	288	543
Mexico	284	322
Spain	282	258
Ireland	169	167
Sweden	174	160
Poland	170	153
Other countries[a]	1,708	1,638
Total	7,178	7,301

ZINC, smelter, primary and secondary (thousand metric tons)	1989	1990
USSR[e]	977	890
Japan	664	687
Canada	670	592
China[e]	451	470
United States	358	358
West Germany	343	338
Australia	296	308
Belgium	287	290
France	266	264
Spain	246	253
Italy	246	248
South Korea	240	248
Netherlands	203	208
Mexico	193	199
Other countries[a]	1,716	1,681
Total	7,156	7,034

[a] Estimated in part. [b] Content of concentrates. [c] Gross weight. [d] Includes calculated bauxite equivalent of estimated output of aluminum ores other than bauxite (nepheline concentrate and alunite ores) that are produced for the recovery of aluminum only in the USSR. [e] Estimate. [f] Includes coal classified as brown coal in some countries. [g] Gross weight of marketable product. [h] Marketable production (includes gas sold or used by producers as fuel, but excludes gas reinjected to reservoirs for pressure maintenance, as well as that flared or vented to the atmosphere, and hence not used either as a fuel or as an industrial raw material, and thus having no economic value). [i] Data for each country exclude bullion produced for refining elsewhere. [j] Includes: (1) Frasch process sulfur; (2) elemental sulfur mined by conventional means; (3) by-product recovered elemental sulfur; and (4) elemental sulfur equivalent of sulfur recovered in the form of sulfuric acid or other chemicals from pyrite and other materials. [k] Excludes output in the United States, which cannot be disclosed because it is company proprietary information. [l] Excludes output, if any, by Albania, Bulgaria, China, Cuba, Czechoslovakia, East Germany, Hungary, North Korea, Mongolia, Poland, Romania, USSR, and Vietnam.

UNITED STATES: Major Legislation Enacted During the First Session of the 102d Congress

SUBJECT	PURPOSE
Persian Gulf	Authorizes the use of U.S. armed forces in the Persian Gulf area pursuant to United Nations Security Council Resolution 678. Signed January 14. Public Law 102–1.
Taxation	Gives individuals participating in Operation Desert Shield more time to perform certain measures required under internal-revenue laws. Signed January 30. Public Law 102–2.
Veterans	Provides a 5.4% increase in veterans' compensation and dependency and indemnity compensation benefits. Signed February 6. Public Law 102–3.
Agent Orange	Compensates veterans of the Vietnam War who were exposed to Agent Orange. Signed February 6. Public Law 102–4.
Portugal	Commemorates the 200th anniversary of U.S.-Portuguese diplomatic relations. Signed March 8. Public Law 102–8.
Savings and Loans	Provides an additional $30 billion for the Resolution Trust Corporation to close failed thrift institutions. Signed March 23. Public Law 102–18.
Amtrak	Expresses appreciation for the service provided by Amtrak during its 20-year history. Signed May 3. Public Law 102–38.
Astronauts	Recognizes the Astronauts Memorial at the John F. Kennedy Space Center as the national memorial to astronauts who die in the line of duty. Signed May 8. Public Law 102-41.
Education	Establishes a National Commission on Time and Learning and a National Council on Education Standards and Testing. Signed June 27. Public Law 102–62.
Literacy	Establishes new programs to promote literacy and provides higher authorization levels for some current adult-literacy programs. Signed July 25. Public Law 102–73.
Libraries	Improves the effectiveness of the U.S. National Commission on Libraries and Information Science. Signed August 14. Public Law 102–95.
African-American History	Directs the secretary of the interior to prepare a national historic landmark theme study on African-American history. Signed August 17. Public Law 102–98.
Immigration	Provides for special immigration status for certain aliens who have served honorably (or are enlisted to serve) in the U.S. armed forces for at least 12 years. Signed October 1. Public Law 102–110.
Striped Bass	Authorizes appropriations for certain programs for the conservation of the striped bass. Signed October 17. Public Law 102–130.
Census	Provides for a study by the National Academy of Sciences to investigate how the government can improve the decennial census. Signed October 24. Public Law 102–135.
Unemployment	Extends unemployment benefits for six, 13, or 20 weeks for workers who have exhausted their regular unemployment benefits through July 4, 1992. Signed November 15. Public Law 102–164.
Civil Rights	Makes it easier for workers to sue their employers and win financial damages for job discrimination. Allows limited monetary damages for victims of harassment and other discrimination based on sex, religion, or disability. Signed November 21. Public Law 102–166.
Constitution	Extends the Commission on the Bicentennial of the Constitution for six months. Signed December 3. Public Law 102–181.
Trade	Establishes most-favored-nation trade status for Czechoslovakia and Hungary. An amendment also extends jobless benefits for either 13 or 20 weeks (*see* Public Law 102–164). Signed December 4. Public Law 102–182.
Intelligence	Authorizes more than $30 billion in fiscal 1992 for intelligence activities, including the Central Intelligence Agency. Encourages, but does not require, the administration to disclose total spending authorized for intelligence activities. Signed December 4. Public Law 102–183.
American Indians	Requests the president to proclaim 1992 as the "year of the American Indian." Signed December 4. Public Law 102–188.
Defense	Restricts production of B-2 bombers, permits initial deployment of the Strategic Defense Initiative, and removes a ban on female combat pilots. Signed December 5. Public Law 102–190.
American Indians	Authorizes the establishment of a memorial at Custer Battlefield National Monument to honor the Indians who fought in the Battle of Little Bighorn. Signed December 10. Public Law 102–201.
Wildlife Refuge	Establishes the Connecticut River National Fish and Wildlife Refuge. Signed December 11. Public Law 102–212.
Soviet Aid	Gives the president the authority to use up to $400 million in defense funding to help the former Soviet Union dismantle its nuclear arsenal and to use up to $100 million from the Defense Department's budget to transport humanitarian aid to the Soviet people. Also implements the Conventional Forces in Europe Treaty. Signed December 12. Public Law 102-228.
Transportation	Authorizes $151 billion for highways and mass transit through fiscal 1997. Signed December 18. Public Law 102–240. *See* page 530.
Banking	Overhauls the federal bank deposit insurance system. Signed December 19. Public Law 102–242. *See* page 138.
Telephone	Protects consumers from unsolicited telephone calls and "junk faxes." Signed December 20. Public Law 102–243.

THE UNITED STATES GOVERNMENT

President: George Bush

Vice-President: Dan Quayle

Executive Office of the President
The White House

Chief of Staff to the President: Samuel K. Skinner
Assistant to the President for Communications: David F. Demarest, Jr.
Assistant to the President and Press Secretary: Max Marlin Fitzwater
Counsel to the President: C. Boyden Gray
Assistant to the President and Secretary of the Cabinet: Edith E. Holiday
Assistant to the President for Legislative Affairs: Nicholas Calio
Assistant to the President for Management and Administration: Timothy J. McBride
Assistant to the President and Director, Office of National Service: C. Gregg Petersmeyer
Assistant to the President for Economic and Domestic Policy: Roger B. Porter
Assistant to the President for Public Events and Initiatives: Sigmund A. Rogich
Assistant to the President for National Security Affairs: Gen. Brent Scowcroft, USAF (Ret.)
Assistant to the President for Media Affairs: J. D. Smith
Assistant to the President for Presidential Personnel: Constance Horner
Office of Management and Budget, Director: Richard G. Darman
Council of Economic Advisers, Chairman: Michael J. Boskin
Office of Policy Development, Deputy Assistant to the President for Domestic Policy: Charles Kolb
Office of United States Trade Representative, United States Trade Representative: Carla A. Hills
Council on Environmental Quality, Chairman: Michael R. Deland
Office of Science and Technology Policy, Assistant to the President for Science and Technology and Director: D. Allan Bromley
Office of National Drug Control Policy, Director: Bob Martinez
Office of Administration, Deputy Assistant to the President for Management and Director: P. W. Bateman

The Cabinet

Secretary of Agriculture: Edward R. Madigan
Secretary of Commerce: Barbara H. Franklin[1]
Secretary of Defense: Richard Cheney
  Joint Chiefs of Staff, Chairman: Gen. Colin L. Powell
Secretary of Education: Lamar Alexander
Secretary of Energy: James D. Watkins
Secretary of Health and Human Services: Louis W. Sullivan, M.D.
  Surgeon General: Antonia Coello Novello
  Commissioner of Food and Drugs: David A. Kessler
  Social Security Administration, Commissioner: Gwendolyn S. King
Secretary of Housing and Urban Development: Jack Kemp
Secretary of Interior: Manuel Lujan, Jr.
Department of Justice, Attorney General: William P. Barr
  Federal Bureau of Investigation, Director: William S. Sessions
Secretary of Labor: Lynn Martin
Secretary of State: James A. Baker III
  United Nations Representative: T. R. Pickering
Secretary of Transportation: A. H. Card, Jr.[1]
Secretary of the Treasury: Nicholas F. Brady
  Internal Revenue Service, Commissioner: S. D. Peterson[1]
Secretary of Veterans Affairs: Edward J. Derwinski

Independent Agencies

ACTION, Director: Jane A. Kenny
Central Intelligence Agency, Director: Robert M. Gates
Commission on Civil Rights, Chairman: Arthur A. Fletcher
Consumer Product Safety Commission, Chairman: Jacqueline Jones-Smith
Environmental Protection Agency, Administrator: William K. Reilly
Equal Employment Opportunity Commission, Chairman: Evan J. Kemp, Jr.
Export-Import Bank of the United States, President and Chairman: John D. Macomber
Farm Credit Administration, Chairman: Harold B. Steele
Federal Communications Commission, Chairman: Alfred C. Sikes
Federal Deposit Insurance Corporation, Chairman: William Taylor
Federal Election Commission, Chairman: J. W. McGarry
Federal Labor Relations Authority, Chairman: Jean McKee
Federal Maritime Commission, Chairman: C. L. Koch
Federal Mediation and Conciliation Service, Director: Bernard E. DeLury
Federal Reserve System, Chairman: Alan Greenspan
Federal Trade Commission, Chairman: Janet D. Steiger
General Services Administrator: Richard G. Austin
Interstate Commerce Commission, Chairman: Edward J. Philbin
National Aeronautics and Space Administration, Administrator: Richard H. Truly
National Foundation on the Arts and Humanities
  National Endowment for the Arts, Chairman: John E. Frohnmayer
  National Endowment for the Humanities, Chairman: Lynne V. Cheney
National Labor Relations Board, Chairman: James M. Stephens
National Science Foundation, Chairman: Mary L. Good
National Transportation Safety Board, Chairman: James L. Kolstad
Nuclear Regulatory Commission, Chairman: Ivan Selin
Office of Government Ethics, Director: Stephen D. Potts
Peace Corps, Director: Elaine L. Chao
Postal Rate Commission, Chairman: George W. Haley
Securities and Exchange Commission, Chairman: Richard C. Breeden
Selective Service System, Director: R. W. Gambino
Small Business Administrator: Patricia F. Saiki
Tennessee Valley Authority, Chairman: Marvin Runyon
U.S. Arms Control and Disarmament Agency, Director: Ronald F. Lehman II
U.S. Information Agency, Director: Henry E. Catto
U.S. International Development Cooperation Agency, Director: Ronald W. Roskens
U.S. International Trade Commission, Chairman: Don E. Newquist
U.S. Postal Service, Postmaster General: Anthony M. Frank[2]

The Supreme Court

Chief Justice, William H. Rehnquist

Byron R. White
Harry A. Blackmum
John Paul Stevens
Sandra Day O'Connor
Antonin Scalia
Anthony M. Kennedy
David H. Souter
Clarence Thomas

[1] Nomination not confirmed. [2] Resigned effective Feb. 28, 1992. Selected listing as of January 1992.

UNITED STATES: 102d CONGRESS
Second Session

SENATE MEMBERSHIP

(As of January 1992: 57 Democrats, 43 Republicans). Letters after names refer to party affiliation—D for Democrat, R for Republican, I for Independent. Single asterisk (*) denotes term expiring in January 1993; double asterisk (**), term expiring in January 1995; triple asterisk (***), term expiring in January 1997. [1]Elected in 1991 to fill unexpired term. [2]Appointed to fill vacancy.

Alabama
*** H. Heflin, D
* R. C. Shelby, D

Alaska
*** T. Stevens, R
* F. H. Murkowski, R

Arizona
** D. DeConcini, D
* J. McCain, R

Arkansas
* D. Bumpers, D
*** D. H. Pryor, D

California
* A. Cranston, D
** J. F. Seymour, R[2]

Colorado
* T. E. Wirth, D
*** H. Brown, R

Connecticut
* C. J. Dodd, D
** J. I. Lieberman, D

Delaware
** W. V. Roth, Jr., R
*** J. R. Biden, Jr., D

Florida
* B. Graham, D
** C. Mack, R

Georgia
*** S. Nunn, D
* W. Fowler, Jr., D

Hawaii
* D. K. Inouye, D
** D. K. Akaka, D

Idaho
* S. Symms, R
*** L. E. Craig, R

Illinois
* A. J. Dixon, D
*** P. Simon, D

Indiana
** R. G. Lugar, R
* D. Coats, R

Iowa
* C. E. Grassley, R
*** T. Harkin, D

Kansas
* R. Dole, R
*** N. L. Kassebaum, R

Kentucky
* W. H. Ford, D
*** M. McConnell, R

Louisiana
*** J. B. Johnston, D
* J. B. Breaux, D

Maine
*** W. Cohen, R
** G. J. Mitchell, D

Maryland
** P. S. Sarbanes, D
* B. A. Mikulski, D

Massachusetts
** E. M. Kennedy, D
*** J. F. Kerry, D

Michigan
** D. W. Riegle, Jr., D
*** C. Levin, D

Minnesota
** D. F. Durenberger, R
*** P. Wellstone, D

Mississippi
*** T. Cochran, R
** T. Lott, R

Missouri
** J. C. Danforth, R
* C. S. Bond, R

Montana
*** M. Baucus, D
** C. Burns, R

Nebraska
*** J. J. Exon, Jr., D
** J. R. Kerrey, D

Nevada
* H. Reid, D
** R. H. Bryan, D

New Hampshire
* W. B. Rudman, R
*** R. C. Smith, R

New Jersey
*** B. Bradley, D
** F. R. Lautenberg, D

New Mexico
*** P. V. Domenici, R
** J. Bingaman, D

New York
** D. P. Moynihan, D
* A. M D'Amato, R

North Carolina
*** J. Helms, R
* T. Sanford, D

North Dakota
** Q. N. Burdick, D
* K. Conrad, D

Ohio
* J. H. Glenn, Jr., D
** H. M. Metzenbaum, D

Oklahoma
*** D. L. Boren, D
* D. L. Nickles, R

Oregon
*** M. O. Hatfield, R
* B. Packwood, R

Pennsylvania
* A. Specter, R
** H. Wofford, D[1]

Rhode Island
*** C. Pell, D
** J. H. Chafee, R

South Carolina
*** S. Thurmond, R
* E. F. Hollings, D

South Dakota
*** L. Pressler, R
* T. A. Daschle, D

Tennessee
** J. R. Sasser, D
*** A. Gore, Jr., D

Texas
** L. Bentsen, D
*** W. Gramm, R

Utah
* J. Garn, R
** O. G. Hatch, R

Vermont
* P. J. Leahy, D
** J. M. Jeffords, R

Virginia
*** J. W. Warner, R
** C. S. Robb, D

Washington
* B. Adams, D
** S. Gorton, R

West Virginia
** R. C. Byrd, D
*** J. D. Rockefeller IV, D

Wisconsin
* R. W. Kasten, Jr., R
** H. Kohl, D

Wyoming
** M. Wallop, R
*** A. K. Simpson, R

HOUSE MEMBERSHIP

(As of January 1992, 268 Democrats, 166 Republicans, 1 independent.) "At-L." in place of congressional district number means "representative at large." * Indicates elected in special election in 1991.

Alabama
1. S. Callahan, R
2. W. L. Dickinson, R
3. G. Browder, D
4. T. Bevill, D
5. B. Cramer, D
6. B. Erdreich, D
7. C. Harris, Jr., D

Alaska
At-L. D. Young, R

Arizona
1. J. J. Rhodes, III, R
2. E. Pastor, D*
3. B. Stump, R
4. J. L. Kyl, R
5. J. Kolbe, R

Arkansas
1. B. Alexander, D
2. R. Thornton, D
3. J. P. Hammerschmidt, R
4. B. F. Anthony, Jr., D

California
1. F. Riggs, R
2. W. W. Herger, R
3. R. T. Matsui, D
4. V. Fazio, D
5. N. Pelosi, D
6. B. Boxer, D
7. G. Miller, D
8. R. V. Dellums, D
9. F. P. Stark, D
10. D. Edwards, D
11. T. Lantos, D
12. T. Campbell, R
13. N. Y. Mineta, D
14. J. T. Doolittle, R
15. G. Condit, D
16. L. E. Panetta, D
17. C. M. Dooley, Jr., D
18. R. H. Lehman, D
19. R. J. Lagomarsino, R
20. W. M. Thomas, R
21. E. Gallegly, R
22. C. J. Moorhead, R
23. A. C. Beilenson, D
24. H. A. Waxman, D
25. E. R. Roybal, D
26. H. L. Berman, D
27. M. Levine, D
28. J. C. Dixon, D
29. M. Waters, D
30. M. G. Martinez, Jr., D
31. M. M. Dymally, D
32. G. M. Anderson, D
33. D. Dreier, R
34. E. E. Torres, D
35. J. Lewis, R
36. G. E. Brown, Jr., D
37. A. A. McCandless, R
38. R. K. Dornan, R
39. W. E. Dannemeyer, R
40. C. Cox, R
41. B. Lowery, R
42. D. Rohrabacher, R
43. R. Packard, R
44. R. Cunningham, R
45. D. Hunter, R

Colorado
1. P. Schroeder, D
2. D. Skaggs, D
3. B. N. Campbell, D
4. A. W. Allard, R
5. J. Hefley, R
6. D. Schaefer, R

Connecticut
1. B. B. Kennelly, D
2. S. Gejdenson, D
3. R. DeLauro, D
4. C. Shays, R
5. G. Franks, R
6. N. L. Johnson, R

Delaware
At-L. T. R. Carper, D

Florida
1. E. Hutto, D
2. P. Peterson, D
3. C. E. Bennett, D
4. C. T. James, R
5. B. McCollum, R
6. C. B. Stearns, R
7. S. Gibbons, D
8. C. W. B. Young, R
9. M. Bilirakis, R
10. A. Ireland, R
11. J. Bacchus, D
12. T. Lewis, R
13. P. J. Goss, R
14. H. A. Johnston, D
15. E. C. Shaw, Jr., R
16. L. J. Smith, D
17. W. Lehman, D
18. I. Ros-Lehtinen, R
19. D. B. Fascell, D

Georgia
1. R. L. Thomas, D
2. C. Hatcher, D
3. R. Ray, D
4. B. Jones, D
5. J. Lewis, D
6. N. Gingrich, R
7. G. Darden, D
8. J. R. Rowland, D
9. E. Jenkins, D
10. D. Barnard, Jr., D

Hawaii
1. N. Abercrombie, D
2. P. Mink, D

Idaho
1. L. LaRocco, D
2. R. H. Stallings, D

Illinois
1. C. A. Hayes, D
2. G. Savage, D
3. M. Russo, D
4. G. E. Sangmeister, D
5. W. O. Lipinski, D
6. H. J. Hyde, R
7. C. Collins, D
8. D. Rostenkowski, D
9. S. R. Yates, D
10. J. E. Porter, R
11. F. Annunzio, D
12. P. M. Crane, R
13. H. W. Fawell, R
14. J. D. Hastert, R
15. T. W. Ewing, R*
16. J. W. Cox, Jr., D
17. L. Evans, D

18. R. H. Michel, R
19. T. L. Bruce, D
20. R. Durbin, D
21. J. F. Costello, D
22. G. Poshard, D

Indiana
1. P. J. Visclosky, D
2. P. R. Sharp, D
3. T. Roemer, D
4. J. Long, D
5. J. P. Jontz, D
6. D. Burton, R
7. J. T. Myers, R
8. F. McCloskey, D
9. L. H. Hamilton, D
10. A. Jacobs, Jr., D

Iowa
1. J. Leach, R
2. J. Nussle, R
3. D. R. Nagle, D
4. N. Smith, D
5. J. Lightfoot, R
6. F. L. Grandy, R

Kansas
1. P. Roberts, R
2. J. Slattery, D
3. J. Meyers, R
4. D. Glickman, D
5. D. Nichols, R

Kentucky
1. C. Hubbard, Jr., D
2. W. H. Natcher, D
3. R. L. Mazzoli, D
4. J. Bunning, R
5. H. Rogers, R
6. L. J. Hopkins, R
7. C. C. Perkins, D

Louisiana
1. B. Livingston, R
2. W. J. Jefferson, D
3. W. J. Tauzin, D
4. J. McCrery, R
5. J. Huckaby, D
6. R. H. Baker, R
7. J. A. Hayes, D
8. C. C. Holloway, R

Maine
1. T. H. Andrews, D
2. O. J. Snowe, R

Maryland
1. W. T. Gilchrest, R
2. H. D. Bentley, R
3. B. L. Cardin, D
4. C. T. McMillen, D
5. S. H. Hoyer, D
6. B. B. Byron, D
7. K. Mfume, D
8. C. A. Morella, R

Massachusetts
1. J. Olver, D*
2. R. E. Neal, D
3. J. D. Early, D
4. B. Frank, D
5. C. G. Atkins, D
6. N. Mavroules, D
7. E. J. Markey, D
8. J. P. Kennedy II, D
9. J. J. Moakley, D
10. G. E. Studds, D
11. B. J. Donnelly, D

Michigan
1. J. Conyers, Jr., D
2. C. D. Pursell, R
3. H. E. Wolpe, D
4. F. S. Upton, R
5. P. B. Henry, R
6. B. Carr, D
7. D. E. Kildee, D
8. B. Traxler, D
9. G. Vander Jagt, R
10. D. Camp, R
11. R. W. Davis, R
12. D. E. Bonior, D
13. B. R. Collins, D
14. D. M. Hertel, D
15. W. D. Ford, D
16. J. D. Dingell, D
17. S. M. Levin, D
18. W. S. Broomfield, R

Minnesota
1. T. J. Penny, D
2. V. Weber, R
3. J. Ramstad, R
4. B. F. Vento, D
5. M. O. Sabo, D
6. G. Sikorski, D
7. C. C. Peterson, D
8. J. L. Oberstar, D

Mississippi
1. J. L. Whitten, D
2. M. Espy, D
3. G. V. Montgomery, D
4. M. Parker, D
5. G. Taylor, D

Missouri
1. W. Clay, D
2. J. K. Horn, D
3. R. A. Gephardt, D
4. I. Skelton, D
5. A. Wheat, D
6. E. T. Coleman, R
7. M. D. Hancock, R
8. B. Emerson, R
9. H. L. Volkmer, D

Montana
1. P. Williams, D
2. R. Marlenee, R

Nebraska
1. D. Bereuter, R
2. P. Hoagland, D
3. W. E. Barrett, R

Nevada
1. J. H. Bilbray, D
2. B. F. Vucanovich, R

New Hampshire
1. B. Zeliff, Jr., R
2. D. Swett, D

New Jersey
1. R. E. Andrews, D
2. W. J. Hughes, D
3. F. Pallone, Jr., D
4. C. H. Smith, R
5. M. Roukema, R
6. B. J. Dwyer, D
7. M. J. Rinaldo, R
8. R. A. Roe, D
9. R. G. Torricelli, D
10. D. M. Payne, D
11. D. A. Gallo, R
12. D. Zimmer, R
13. H. J. Saxton, R
14. F. J. Guarini, D

New Mexico
1. S. Schiff, R
2. J. Skeen, R
3. B. Richardson, D

New York
1. G. J. Hochbrueckner, D
2. T. J. Downey, D
3. R. J. Mrazek, D
4. N. F. Lent, R
5. R. J. McGrath, R
6. F. H. Flake, D
7. G. L. Ackerman, D
8. J. H. Scheuer, D
9. T. J. Manton, D
10. C. E. Schumer, D
11. E. Towns, D
12. M. R. Owens, D
13. S. J. Solarz, D
14. S. Molinari, R
15. B. Green, R
16. C. B. Rangel, D
17. T. Weiss, D
18. J. Serrano, D
19. E. L. Engel, D
20. N. Lowey, D
21. H. Fish, Jr., R
22. B. A. Gilman, R
23. M. R. McNulty, D
24. G. B. H. Solomon, R
25. S. L. Boehlert, R
26. D. O'B. Martin, R
27. J. T. Walsh, R
28. M. F. McHugh, D
29. F. Horton, R
30. L. McI. Slaughter, D
31. B. Paxon, R
32. J. J. LaFalce, D
33. H. J. Nowak, D
34. A. Houghton, R

North Carolina
1. W. B. Jones, D
2. T. Valentine, D
3. H. M. Lancaster, D
4. D. E. Price, D
5. S. L. Neal, D
6. H. Coble, R
7. C. Rose, D
8. W. G. Hefner, D
9. J. A. McMillan, R
10. C. Ballenger, R
11. C. H. Taylor, R

North Dakota
At-L. B. L. Dorgan, D

Ohio
1. C. Luken, D
2. W. D. Gradison, Jr., R
3. T. P. Hall, D
4. M. G. Oxley, R
5. P. E. Gillmor, R
6. B. McEwen, R
7. D. L. Hobson, R
8. J. A. Boehner, R
9. M. C. Kaptur, D
10. C. E. Miller, R
11. D. E. Eckart, D
12. J. R. Kasich, R
13. D. J. Pease, D
14. T. C. Sawyer, D
15. C. P. Wylie, R
16. R. Regula, R
17. J. A. Traficant, Jr., D
18. D. Applegate, D
19. E. F. Feighan, D
20. M. R. Oakar, D
21. L. Stokes, D

Oklahoma
1. J. M. Inhofe, R
2. M. Synar, D
3. B. K. Brewster, D
4. D. McCurdy, D
5. M. Edwards, R
6. G. English, D

Oregon
1. L. AuCoin, D
2. R. F. Smith, R
3. R. Wyden, D
4. P. A. DeFazio, D
5. M. Kopetski, D

Pennsylvania
1. T. M. Foglietta, D
2. L. E. Blackwell, D*
3. R. A. Borski, Jr., D
4. J. Kolter, D
5. R. T. Schulze, R
6. G. Yatron, D
7. C. Weldon, R
8. P. H. Kostmayer, D
9. B. Shuster, R
10. J. M. McDade, R
11. P. E. Kanjorski, D
12. J. P. Murtha, D
13. L. Coughlin, R
14. W. J. Coyne, D
15. D. Ritter, R
16. R. S. Walker, R
17. G. Gekas, R
18. R. Santorum, R
19. W. F. Goodling, R
20. J. M. Gaydos, D
21. T. J. Ridge, R
22. A. J. Murphy, D
23. W. F. Clinger, Jr., R

Rhode Island
1. R. K. Machtley, R
2. J. F. Reed, D

South Carolina
1. A. Ravenel, Jr., R
2. F. D. Spence, R
3. B. C. Derrick, Jr., D
4. E. J. Patterson, D
5. J. M. Spratt, Jr., D
6. R. Tallon, D

South Dakota
At-L. T. Johnson, D

Tennessee
1. J. H. Quillen, R
2. J. J. Duncan, Jr., R
3. M. Lloyd, D
4. J. Cooper, D
5. B. Clement, D
6. B. Gordon, D
7. D. K. Sundquist, R
8. J. S. Tanner, D
9. H. E. Ford, D

Texas
1. J. Chapman, D
2. C. Wilson, D
3. S. Johnson, R*
4. R. M. Hall, D
5. J. Bryant, D
6. J. L. Barton, R
7. B. Archer, R
8. J. M. Fields, Jr., R
9. J. Brooks, D
10. J. J. Pickle, D
11. C. Edwards, D
12. P. Geren, D
13. B. Sarpalius, D
14. G. Laughlin, D
15. E. de la Garza, D
16. R. D. Coleman, D
17. C. W. Stenholm, D
18. C. Washington, D
19. L. Combest, R
20. H. B. Gonzalez, D
21. L. S. Smith, R
22. T. DeLay, R
23. A. G. Bustamante, D
24. M. Frost, D
25. M. A. Andrews, D
26. R. K. Armey, R
27. S. P. Ortiz, D

Utah
1. J. V. Hansen, R
2. W. Owens, D
3. B. Orton, D

Vermont
At-L. B. Sanders, I

Virginia
1. H. H. Bateman, R
2. O. B. Pickett, D
3. T. J. Bliley, Jr., R
4. N. Sisisky, D
5. L. F. Payne, Jr., D
6. J. R. Olin, D
7. G. F. Allen, R*
8. J. P. Moran, Jr., D
9. R. Boucher, D
10. F. R. Wolf, R

Washington
1. J. Miller, R
2. A. Swift, D
3. J. Unsoeld, D
4. S. Morrison, R
5. T. S. Foley, D
6. N. D. Dicks, D
7. J. McDermott, D
8. R. Chandler, R

West Virginia
1. A. B. Mollohan, D
2. H. O. Staggers, Jr., D
3. R. E. Wise, Jr., D
4. N. J. Rahall II, D

Wisconsin
1. L. Aspin, D
2. S. Klug, R
3. S. Gunderson, R
4. G. D. Kleczka, D
5. J. Moody, D
6. T. E. Petri, R
7. D. R. Obey, D
8. T. Roth, R
9. F. J. Sensenbrenner, Jr., R

Wyoming
At-L. C. Thomas, R

AMERICAN SAMOA
Delegate E. F. H. Faleomavaega, D

DISTRICT OF COLUMBIA
Delegate Eleanor Holmes Norton, D

GUAM
Delegate, Ben Blaz, R

PUERTO RICO
Resident Commissioner
J. B. Fuster, D

VIRGIN ISLANDS
Delegate, Ron de Lugo, D

SOCIETIES AND ORGANIZATIONS

This listing includes some of the most noteworthy associations, societies, foundations, and trusts of the United States and Canada. The information was verified by the organization concerned.

Academy of Motion Picture Arts & Sciences. Membership: 5,411. Executive director, Bruce Davis. Headquarters: 8949 Wilshire Blvd., Beverly Hills, CA 90211.

Alcoholics Anonymous (The General Service Board of A.A., Inc.). Membership: 1.8 million in 136 countries. Chairman, Michael Alexander. Headquarters: 468 Park Ave. S., New York, NY. Mailing address: Box 459, Grand Central Station, New York, NY 10163.

American Academy and Institute of Arts and Letters. Membership: 250. Executive director, Virginia Dajani. Headquarters: 633 W. 155th St., New York, NY 10032.

American Academy of Political and Social Science. Membership: 5,500. President, Marvin E. Wolfgang. Headquarters: 3937 Chestnut St., Philadelphia, PA 19104.

American Anthropological Association. Membership: 10,529. Executive director, Eugene Sterud. Headquarters: 1703 New Hampshire Ave. NW, Washington, DC 20009.

American Association for the Advancement of Science. Membership: 132,000 and 285 affiliated scientific and engineering societies and academies of science. Meeting: Chicago, IL, Feb. 6–11, 1992. President, Leon M. Lederman; executive officer, Richard S. Nicholson. Headquarters: 1333 H St. NW, Washington, DC 20005.

American Association of Museums. Membership: 11,300. Meeting: Baltimore, MD, April 24–28, 1992. Executive director, Edward H. Able. Headquarters: 1225 Eye St. NW, Washington, DC 20005.

American Association of Retired Persons. Membership: 32,000,000. Biennial convention: San Antonio, TX, June 2–4, 1992. Executive director, Horace B. Deets. Headquarters: 1909 K St., NW, Washington, DC 20049.

American Association of University Professors. Membership: 41,000. General secretary, Ernst Benjamin. Headquarters: 1012 14th St. NW, Washington, DC 20005.

American Association of University Women. Membership: 140,000. President, Sharon Schuster. Headquarters: 1111 16th Street NW, Washington, DC 20036.

American Astronomical Society. Membership: 5,700. Meetings: Atlanta, GA, Jan. 5–9, 1992; Columbus, OH, June 7–11, 1992. Executive officer, Peter B. Boyce. Headquarters: 2000 Florida Ave. NW, Suite 300, Washington, DC 20009.

American Automobile Association. Membership: 30,000,000 in 154 affiliated clubs. President, James B. Creal. Headquarters: 1000 AAA Drive, Heathrow, FL 32746.

American Bankers Association (ABA). Membership: nearly 13,000. President, Richard A. Kirk. Headquarters: 1120 Connecticut Ave. NW, Washington, DC 20036.

American Bar Association. Membership: 370,000. Annual meeting: San Francisco, CA, Aug. 6–13, 1992. President, John J. Curtin, Jr.; president-elect, Talbot D'Alemberte; executive director, David Ja Hayes, Jr. Headquarters: 750 N. Lake Shore Dr., Chicago, IL 60611.

American Bible Society. Distribution: U.S. 91,434,834; overseas, 167,495,444. Annual meeting, New York City, May 14, 1992. Chairman, James Wood; vice chairman, Mrs. Norman Vincent Peale; president/CEO, Eugene B. Habecker; vice president, Maria I. Martinez; treasurer, Daniel K. Scarberry. Headquarters: 1865 Broadway, New York, NY 10023.

American Booksellers Association, Inc. Membership: 8,500. Convention: Anaheim, CA, May 23–26, 1992. President, Joyce Meskis; executive director, Bernard Rath. Headquarters: 137 W. 25th St., New York, NY 10001.

American Cancer Society, Inc. Membership: 124 voting members; 57 chartered divisions. Executive vice-president, William M. Tipping. Headquarters: 1599 Clifton Rd. NE, Atlanta, GA 30329.

American Chemical Society. Membership: 144,000. National meetings, 1992: San Francisco, CA, April 5–10; Washington, DC, Aug. 23–28. President, Ernest L. Eliel. Headquarters: 1155 16th St. NW, Washington, DC 20036.

American Civil Liberties Union. Membership: 290,000. President, Nadine Strossen; executive director, Ira Glasser. Headquarters: 132 W. 43rd St., New York, NY 10036.

American Correctional Association. Membership: 24,000. Executive director, James A. Gondles, Jr. Headquarters: 8025 Laurel Lakes Court, Laurel, MD 20707–5075.

American Council of Learned Societies. Membership: 51 professional societies concerned with the humanities and the humanistic aspects of the social sciences. President, Stanley N. Katz. Headquarters: 228 East 45th St., New York, NY 10017.

American Council on Education. Membership: 1,523 institutional members, 70 national associates, 95 regional associates, 14 affiliates, 59 international associates, and 33 corporate associates. Annual meeting: Washington, DC, January 1992. President, Robert H. Atwell. Headquarters: One Dupont Circle, Washington, DC 20036.

American Dental Association. Membership: 139,154. Annual session: Orlando, FL, Oct. 17–20, 1992. President, Eugene J. Truono, D.D.S.; executive director, Thomas J. Ginley, Ph.D. Headquarters: 211 E. Chicago Ave., Chicago, IL 60611.

American Economic Association. Membership: 21,000 and 6,500 subscribers. President, William Vickrey. Headquarters: 2014 Broadway, Suite 305, Nashville, TN 37203.

American Farm Bureau Federation. Membership: 3.8 million families. President, Dean R. Kleckner. Headquarters: 225 Touhy Ave., Park Ridge, IL 60068.

American Geographical Society. Fellows and subscribers: 8,500. President, John E. Gould; director, Mary Lynne Bird. Headquarters: 156 Fifth Ave., Suite 600, New York, NY 10010.

American Geophysical Union. Membership: about 28,000 individuals. Meetings: spring—Montreal, Que., May 11–15, 1992; fall—San Francisco, CA, Dec. 7–11, 1992. President, Brent Dalrymple. Headquarters: 2000 Florida Ave. NW, Washington, DC 20009.

American Heart Association. Membership: 3,200,000 medical and lay volunteers in 56 affiliates and more than 1,800 local divisions. 1991–92 president, W. Virgil Brown, M.D. Headquarters: 7320 Greenville Ave., Dallas, TX 75231.

American Historical Association. Membership: 14,000. Annual meeting: Washington, DC, Dec. 27–30, 1992. President: William E. Leuchtenburg; executive director, Samuel Gammon. Headquarters: 400 A St. SE, Washington, DC 20003.

American Horticultural Society. Membership: 22,000. Annual meeting: Washington, DC, 1992. President, George C. Ball, Jr. Headquarters: 7931 East Blvd. Dr., Alexandria, VA 22308.

American Hospital Association. Membership: 48,357 persons; 5,500 institutions. Annual meeting: Washington, DC, Jan. 26–29, 1992. Convention: Denver, CO, July 27–29, 1992. Chairman of the board, D. Kirk Oglesby, Jr.. Headquarters: 840 North Lake Shore Drive, Chicago, IL 60611.

American Hotel & Motel Association. Membership: 10,000 properties, 1.4 million rooms. Annual convention: Toronto, Ont., April 30-May 4, 1992. President/chief executive officer, Kenneth F. Hine. Headquarters: 1201 New York Avenue NW, Washington, DC 20005.

American Institute of Aeronautics and Astronautics. Membership: more than 40,000. Annual meeting: Crystal City, VA, April 27–29, 1992. Executive director, Cort Durocher. Headquarters: 370 L'Enfant Promenade SW, Washington, DC 20024–2518.

American Institute of Architects. Membership: 57,000. Convention: Boston, MA, June 19–22, 1992. President, W. Cecil Steward, FAIA. Headquarters: 1735 New York Avenue NW, Washington, DC 20006.

American Institute of Biological Sciences. Membership: 8,000 with 35 societies and 6 affiliate organizations. Annual meeting: Honolulu, HI, Aug. 9–13, 1992. President, Charles M. Chambers. Headquarters: 730 11th St. NW, Washington, DC 20001–4521.

American Institute of Certified Public Accountants. Membership: 300,000. Annual meeting: Washington, DC, Oct. 10, 1992. Chairman, Gerald A. Polansky; president, Philip B. Chenok. Headquarters: 1211 Avenue of the Americas, New York, NY 10036–8775.

American Institute of Chemical Engineers. Membership: 52,000. President, Gary L. Leach. Headquarters: 345 E. 47th Street, New York, NY 10017.

American Institute of Graphic Arts. Membership: 6,968. President, Anthony Russell; executive director, Caroline Hightower. Headquarters: 1059 Third Ave., New York, NY 10021.

American Institute of Mining, Metallurgical and Petroleum Engineers, Inc. 4 member societies: Society for Mining, Metallurgy, and Exploration; The Minerals, Metals & Materials Society; Iron and Steel Society; Society of Petroleum Engineers. Annual meeting: San Diego, CA, March 1–2, 1992. President, Roshan B. Bhappu. Headquarters: 345 E. 47th St., New York, NY 10017.

American Institute of Nutrition. Membership: 2,950. Annual meeting: Anaheim, CA, April 5–10, 1992. Executive officer, R. G. Allison, Ph.D. Headquarters: 9650 Rockville Pike, Bethesda, MD 20814.

American Legion, The. Membership: 3,050,000. National Executive Committee is chief administrative body between national conventions. National convention: Chicago, IL, Sept. 1–3, 1992. Headquarters: 700 N. Pennsylvania St., Indianapolis, IN 46204.

American Library Association. Membership: 52,000. Meetings, 1992: Midwinter—San Antonio, TX, Jan 24–30. Annual conference—San Francisco, CA, June 25–July 2. Executive director, Linda F. Crismond. Headquarters: 50 E. Huron, Chicago, IL 60611.

American Lung Association. Membership: 132 affiliated groups. Annual meeting: Miami Beach, FL, May 17–20, 1992. President, Lee B. Reichman, M.D., M.P.H. Headquarters: 1740 Broadway, New York, NY 10019–4374.

American Management Association. Membership: 75,000. Chairman of the board, Thomas R. Horton; president and CEO, David Fagiano. Headquarters: 135 W. 50th St., New York, NY 10020.

American Mathematical Society. Membership: 28,710. President, Michael Artin. Headquarters: P.O. Box 6248, Providence, RI 02940.

American Medical Association. Membership: 299,017. President, John Ring, M.D.; executive vice-president, James S. Todd, M.D. Headquarters: 515 N. State St., Chicago, IL 60610.

American Meteorological Society. Membership: 10,000 including 128 corporate members. Executive director, Dr. Richard E. Hallgren. Headquarters: 45 Beacon St., Boston, MA 02108.

American Newspaper Publishers Association. Membership: 1,425. Annual convention: New York, NY, May 4–6, 1992. Chairman, Robert F. Erburu, Times-Mirror Company, Los Angeles, CA; president, Jerry W. Friedheim. Executive offices: The Newspaper Center, 11600 Sunrise Valley Dr., Reston, VA 22091. Mailing Address: The Newspaper Center, Box 17407, Dulles International Airport, Washington, DC 20041.

American Nurses' Association. Membership: 201,000 in 53 state and territorial associations. National convention: Las Vegas, NV, June 22–27, 1992. President, Lucille Joel. Headquarters: 2420 Pershing Road, Kansas City, MO 64108.

American Physical Society. Membership: 38,000 American and foreign. President, Ernest M. Henley; executive secretary, N. Richard Werthamer. Headquarters: 335 E. 45th St., New York, NY 10017.

American Psychiatric Association. Membership: 36,900. Annual meeting: Washington, DC, May 2–7, 1992. President, Lawrence Hartmann, M.D. Headquarters: 1400 K Street NW, Washington, DC 20005.

American Psychological Association. Membership: 108,000. Annual meeting: Washington, DC, Aug. 14–18, 1992. President, Jack G. Wiggins, Ph.D. Headquarters: 1200 17th Street NW, Washington, DC 20036.

American Red Cross. Chapters: 2,880. National convention: Baltimore, MD, May 31-June 3, 1992. Chairman, George F. Moody; president, Elizabeth H. Dole. Headquarters: 17th and D Sts. NW, Washington, DC 20006.

American Society of Civil Engineers. Membership: 108,000. Executive director, Edward O. Pfrang. Headquarters: 345 E. 47th St., New York, NY 10017–2398.

American Society of Composers, Authors, and Publishers. Membership: 33,145 writer members; 1,605 associate members; 14,550 publisher members. President, Morton Gould; managing director, Gloria Messinger. Headquarters: One Lincoln Plaza, New York, NY 10023.

American Society of Mechanical Engineers. Membership: 118,000. President, Nathan H. Hurt, Jr.. Headquarters: 345 E. 47th St., New York, NY 10017.

American Sociological Association. Membership: 13,000. Meeting: Pittsburgh, PA, Aug. 20–24, 1992. President, James S. Coleman. Executive office: 1722 N St. NW, Washington, DC 20036.

American Statistical Association. Membership: 15,000. President, Katherine Wallman. Meeting: Boston, MA, Aug. 10–13, 1992. Headquarters: 1429 Duke Street, Alexandria, VA 22314–3402.

American Youth Hostels, Inc. Membership: 100,000; 40 councils in the United States. Executive director, Richard Martyr. Headquarters: P. O. Box 37613, Washington, DC 20013–7613.

Archaeological Institute of America. Membership: more than 10,000. President, Martha S. Joukowsky; executive director, Mark J. Meister. Annual meeting: New Orleans, LA, Dec. 27–30, 1992. Headquarters: 675 Commonwealth Ave., Boston, MA 02215.

Arthritis Foundation. Membership: 71 chapters. Annual scientific meeting: Miami, FL, Nov. 7–9, 1992. Chairman, James R. Klinenberg, M.D.; president, Don L. Riggin, C.A.E., C.F.R.E. Headquarters: 1314 Spring St. NW, Atlanta, GA 30309.

Association of American Publishers. Membership: approximately 230. Annual meeting: Washington, DC, March 1992. Chairman of the board, Jerome Rubin; president, Ambassador Veliotes; vice president, Thomas McKee. Addresses: 220 E. 23rd St., New York, NY 10010; and 1718 Connecticut Ave. NW, Washington, DC 20009.

Association of Junior Leagues International, Inc. Membership: 277 member leagues in U.S., Canada, Mexico, and the United Kingdom. Annual conference: New York, NY, May 1992. President, Suzanne Bond Plihcik. Headquarters: 660 First Ave., New York, NY 10016.

Association of Operating Room Nurses, Inc. Membership: 47,000 with 381 local chapters. Convention: Dallas, TX, March 15–20, 1992. President, Jean Reeder; executive director, Lola Fehr. Headquarters: 10170 East Mississippi Avenue, Denver, CO 80231.

Benevolent and Protective Order of Elks. Membership: 1,500,000 in 2,300 lodges. Convention: Dallas, TX, July 5–9, 1992. Grand exalted ruler, James W. Damon; grand secretary, James C. Varenhorst. Headquarters: 2750 Lake View Ave., Chicago, IL 60614.

Bide-A-Wee Home Association, Inc. Executive director, Gary Kesner. Headquarters: 410 E. 38th St., New York, NY 10016.

Big Brothers/Big Sisters of America. Membership: 490+ local affiliated agencies. National conference: Indianapolis, IN, June 17–19, 1992. President, Edward L. Gardner. Headquarters: 230 North 13th St., Philadelphia, PA 19107.

B'nai B'rith International. Membership: 500,000 in approximately 3,000 lodges, chapters, and units. President, Kent E. Schiner; executive vice-president, Dr. Sidney Clearfield. Headquarters: 1640 Rhode Island Ave. NW, Washington, DC 20036.

Boat Owners Association of the United States. Membership: 400,000. President, Richard Schwartz. Headquarters: 880 S. Pickett St., Alexandria, VA 22304.

Boys and Girls Clubs of America. Youth served: 1,600,000 in 1,200 affiliated Boys and Girls Clubs. Chairman, Jeremiah Milbank; national director, Thomas G. Garth. Headquarters: 771 First Ave., New York, NY 10017.

Boy Scouts of America. Membership: total youth members and leaders, 5,445,899 in 397 local councils. Annual meeting: Cincinnati, OH, May 13–15, 1992. President, Richard H. Leet; chief scout executive, Ben H. Love. National office: 1325 Walnut Hill Lane, P.O. Box 152079, Irving, TX 75015–2079.

Camp Fire, Inc. Membership: 600,000 boys and girls in more than 35,000 communities. President, Linda Sanders; national executive director, K. Russell Weathers. Headquarters: 4601 Madison Ave., Kansas City, MO 64112.

Canadian Library Association. Membership: 3,600 personal, 800 institutional, 4,400 total. 1992 annual conference: Winnipeg, Manitoba, June 11–14, 1992. Executive director, Karen Adams. Headquarters: 200 Elgin Street, #602, Ottawa, Ont. K2P 1L5.

Canadian Medical Association. Membership: 45,000. Annual meeting: St. John's, Newfoundland, Aug. 16–21, 1992. Secretary-general, Leo Paul Landry, M.D. Address: 1867 Alta Vista Drive, Ottawa, Ont. K1G 3Y6.

Chamber of Commerce, U.S. Membership: approximately 4,200 associations and state and local chambers; approximately 180,000 business members. Annual meeting: Washington, DC, February 24, 1992. President, Richard L. Lesher; chairman, C. J. Silas. Headquarters: 1615 H Street NW, Washington, DC 20062.

Common Cause. Membership: 270,000. Chairman, Archibald Cox. Headquarters: 2030 M St. NW, Washington, DC 20036.

Consumers Union of United States, Inc. Executive director, Rhoda H. Karpatkin. Headquarters: 101 Truman Ave., Yonkers, NY 10703.

Council of Better Business Bureaus. Membership: 600. Headquarters: 4200 Wilson Blvd., Suite 800, Arlington, VA 22203.

Council on Foreign Relations, Inc. Membership: 2,750. Annual meeting: New York City, fall 1992. President, Peter Tarnoff. Headquarters: 58 E. 68th St., New York, NY 10021.

Daughters of the American Revolution (National Society). Membership: 204,000 in 3,011 chapters. Continental congress: Washington, DC, April 20–24, 1992. President general, Mrs. Eldred Martin Yochim. Headquarters: 1776 D St. NW, Washington, DC 20006.

Esperanto League for North America, Inc. Membership: 1,000+. President, Angela Harlow. Headquarters: P.O. Box 1129, El Cerrito, CA 94530.

Foreign Policy Association. President, R. T. Curran. Headquarters: 729 Seventh Ave., New York, NY 10019.

Freemasonry, Ancient Accepted Scottish Rite of (Northern Masonic Jurisdiction): Supreme Council, 33°. Membership: 412,612 in 110 valleys. Sovereign grand commander, Francis G. Paul. Headquarters: 33 Marrett Rd., Lexington, MA 02173.

Freemasonry, Ancient and Accepted Scottish Rite of (Southern Jurisdiction): Supreme Council, 33°. Membership: 552,000 in 221 affiliated groups. Sovereign grand commander, C. Fred Kleinknecht. Headquarters: 1733 16th Street NW, Washington, DC 20009.

Gamblers Anonymous. Groups worldwide: 1,400. Headquarters: 3255 Wilshire Blvd., Suite 610, Los Angeles, CA 90010.

Garden Club of America, The. Membership: 16,000 in 189 clubs. Annual meeting: Baltimore, MD, May 10–14, 1992. President, Mrs. Sellers J. Thomas, Jr. Headquarters: 598 Madison Ave., New York, NY 10022.

General Federation of Women's Clubs. Membership: 350,000 in 8,500 U.S. clubs and 10,000,000 worldwide. International president, Mrs. Phyllis Dudenhoffer. Headquarters: 1734 N St. NW, Washington, DC 20036.

Geological Society of America. Membership: 17,000. President, E-an Zen; executive director, F. Michael Wahl. Headquarters: 3300 Penrose Place, P.O. Box 9140, Boulder, CO 80301.

Girl Scouts of the U.S.A. Membership: 3,268,630. National president, B. LaRae Orullian; national executive director, Mary Rose Main. Headquarters: 830 Third Ave., New York, NY 10022.

Humane Society of the United States. Constituency: more than 1,000,000. Annual convention: Boulder, CO, October 1992. President, John A. Hoyt. Headquarters: 2100 L St. NW, Washington, DC 20037.

Institute of Electrical and Electronics Engineers, Inc. Membership: 300,000. President, Merrill W. Buckley, Jr. Headquarters: 345 E. 47th St., New York, NY 10017.

Jewish War Veterans of the U.S.A. Membership: 100,000 in 450 units. Annual national convention: Atlanta, GA, Aug. 18–25, 1992. National commander, Albert L. Cohen; executive director, Col. Herb Rosenbleeth (ret.). Headquarters: 1811 R St. NW, Washington, DC 20009.

Kiwanis International. Membership: 325,000 in 8,700 clubs in U.S. and abroad. President, John D. Morton, Sr. Headquarters: 3636 Woodview Trace, Indianapolis, IN 46268.

Knights of Columbus. Membership: 1,503,362. Supreme knight, Virgil C. Dechant. Headquarters: Columbus Plaza, New Haven, CT 06507.

Knights of Pythias of the World, Supreme Lodge. Membership: 86,000 in 888 subordinate lodges. Supreme chancellor, James E. Hess, Sparks, NV; supreme secretary, Jack R. Klai. Executive office: 2785 East Desert Inn Rd., #150, Las Vegas, NV 89121.

League of Women Voters of the U.S. Membership: 100,000. President, Dr. Susan S. Lederman. Headquarters: 1730 M Street NW, Washington, DC 20036.

Lions Clubs International. Membership: 1,376,470 in 39,872 clubs in 171 countries and areas. Annual convention: Hong Kong, June 22–27, 1992. Executive administrator, Mark C. Lukas. Headquarters: 300 22nd St., Oak Brook, IL 60521–8842.

March of Dimes Birth Defects Foundation. Membership: 133 chapters. President, Jennifer L. Howse. Headquarters: 1275 Mamaroneck Ave., White Plains, NY 10605.

Modern Language Association of America. Membership: 30,000. Annual convention: New York, NY, Dec. 27–30, 1992. President, Houston A. Baker, Jr. Headquarters: 10 Astor Place, New York, NY 10003–6981.

National Academy of Sciences. Membership: 1,583. Annual meeting: Washington, DC, April 1992. President, Frank Press. Headquarters: 2101 Constitution Ave. NW, Washington, DC 20418.

National Association for the Advancement of Colored People. Membership: 500,000 in 1,800 branches and 600 youth and college chapters. National convention: Nashville, TN, July 11–16, 1992. President, Hazel Dukes; board chairman, William S. Gibson; executive director, Benjamin Hooks. Headquarters: 4805 Mt. Hope Dr., Baltimore, MD 21215–3297.

National Association of Manufacturers. Membership: 12,500. President, Jerry J. Jasinowski. Headquarters: 1331 Pennsylvania Ave. NW, Suite 1500 North Lobby, Washington, DC 20004–1703.

National Audubon Society. Membership: 550,000 in 500 local groups. President, Peter A. A. Berle. Headquarters: 950 Third Ave., New York, NY 10022.

National Committee for Prevention of Child Abuse. Executive director, Anne H. Cohn. Headquarters: 332 S. Michigan Ave., Suite 1600, Chicago, IL 60604.

National Conference of Christians and Jews, Inc. Membership: 75 regional offices. President, Gillian Martin Sorensen. Headquarters: 71 Fifth Ave., Suite 1100, New York, NY 10003.

National Council of the Churches of Christ in the U.S.A. Membership: 32 Protestant, Anglican, and Orthodox denominations. Headquarters: 475 Riverside Dr., New York, NY 10115.

National Council on the Aging, Inc. Membership: 7,000. President, Dr. Daniel Thursz. Annual conference: Washington, DC, April 29-May 2, 1992. Headquarters: 409 Third Street SW, Washington, DC 20024.

National Easter Seal Society. Annual conference: Tampa, FL, Nov. 18–21, 1992. Chairman of the board, Kenneth Wells Parkinson. Headquarters: 70 East Lake St., Chicago, IL 60601.

National Education Association of the U.S. Membership: more than 2,000,000. Annual convention: Washington, DC, July 3–8, 1992. President, Keith Geiger. Headquarters: 1201 16th St. NW, Washington, DC 20036.

National Federation of Business and Professional Women's Clubs, Inc. (BPW/USA). Membership: 93,000 in 2,800 clubs. President, Pat Taylor. Headquarters: 2012 Massachusetts Ave. NW, Washington , DC 20036.

National Federation of Independent Business, Inc. Membership: 560,000. President, John Sloan, Jr. Administrative office: 150 W. 20th Ave., San Mateo, CA 94403. Legislative and research office: 600 Maryland Ave. SW, Suite 700, Washington, DC 20024.

National Federation of Music Clubs. Membership: 500,000 in 4,500 clubs and 12 national affiliates. President, Virginia F. Allison. Headquarters: 1336 North Delaware St., Indianapolis, IN 46202.

National FFA Organization. Membership: 382,643 in 53 state associations. National convention: Kansas City, MO, Nov. 12–14, 1992. Executive secretary, Coleman Harris. Headquarters: 5632 Mt. Vernon Memorial Hwy., P.O. Box 15160, Alexandria, VA 22309.

National Fire Protection Association. Membership: 56,000. Annual meeting: New Orleans, LA, May 18–21, 1992; fall meeting: Dallas, TX, Nov. 17-19, 1992. President, Robert W. Grant. Headquarters: Batterymarch Park, Quincy, MA 02269.

National Grange. Membership: 300,000; local chapters: 4,000. Annual meeting: Denver, CO, Nov. 9–15, 1992. National master, Robert E. Barrow. Headquarters: 1616 H St. NW, Washington, DC 20006.

National Mental Health Association, Membership: 550 state and local chapters. Headquarters: 1021 Prince St., Alexandria, VA 22314–2971.

National Organization for Women. Membership: 200,000 in 750 local groups. President, Patricia Ireland. Headquarters: 1000 16th St. NW, Suite 700, Washington, DC 20036.

National PTA (National Congress of Parents and Teachers Association). Membership: 6,858,550 in 27,771 local units. National convention: San Diego, CA, June 20–23, 1992. President, Pat Henry. Headquarters: 700 N. Rush St., Chicago, IL 60611.

National Safety Council. Membership: 12,500. President, T. C. Gilchrest. Headquarters: 444 N. Michigan Ave., Chicago, IL 60611.

National Urban League, Inc. President and chief executive officer, John E. Jacob. Annual conference: San Diego, CA, July 26–29, 1992. Headquarters: 500 East 62nd St., New York, NY 10021.

National Woman's Christian Temperance Union. Membership: approximately 50,000 in 4,000 local unions. National convention: Tampa, FL, Aug. 17–23, 1992. President, Mrs. Rachel B. Kelly. Headquarters: 1730 Chicago Ave., Evanston, IL 60201.

Parents Without Partners, Inc. International membership: 115,000. International convention: Winston-Salem, NC, June 29-July 4, 1992. Executive administrator, Carolyn Nelson. International office: 8807 Colesville Rd., Silver Spring, MD 20910.

Phi Beta Kappa. Membership: 440,000. Headquarters: 1811 Q St., NW, Washington, DC 20009.

Photographic Society of America. Membership: 12,000. President, James H. Turnbull. Headquarters: 3000 United Founders Blvd., Suite 103, Oklahoma City, OK 73120.

Planned Parenthood Federation of America, Inc. (Planned Parenthood-World Population). Membership: 169 U.S. affiliates. President, Faye Wattleton; chairperson of the Federation, Kenneth C. Edelin, M.D. Headquarters: 810 Seventh Ave., New York, NY 10019.

Rotary International. Membership: 1,116,722 in 25,191 clubs internationally. International convention: Orlando, FL, June 14–17, 1992. General secretary, Spencer Robinson, Jr. Headquarters: 1560 Sherman Ave., Evanston, IL 60201–3698.

Salvation Army, The. Membership: 445,556. National commander, James Osborne. National headquarters: 615 Slaters Lane, Alexandria, VA 22314.

Special Libraries Association. Membership: 13,000. Annual conference: San Francisco, CA, June 1992. President, Catherine B. Scott. Headquarters: 1700 18th St. NW, Washington, DC 20009.

United Dairy Industry Association. Annual convention: Orlando, FL, Sept. 16–18, 1992. Chief executive officer: M. F. Brink. Headquarters: Dairy Center, 6300 N. River Rd., Rosemont, IL 60618.

United States Junior Chamber of Commerce. Membership: 230,000 in 5,000 affiliated chapters. Annual meeting: Portland, OR, June 22–25, 1992. President, Greg Thomes. Headquarters: P.O. Box 7, Tulsa, OK 74121. Shipping address: 4 W. 21st St., Tulsa, OK 74114.

U.S. Metric Association. Membership: 2,500. Executive director, Valerie Antoine. Headquarters: 10245 Andasol Ave., Northridge, CA 91325.

United Way of America. Service organization for more than 2,300 autonomous local United Ways. 1992 volunteer leaders conference: Indianapolis, IN, March 21–23, 1992. Chairman of the board of governors, John F. Akers, chairman of the board, IBM Corporation. Address: 701 N. Fairfax St., Alexandria, VA 22314–2045.

Veterans of Foreign Wars of the United States. Membership: VFW and Auxiliary 2,900,000. Adjutant general, Howard E. Vander Clute, Jr. Headquarters: Broadway at 34th St., Kansas City, MO 64111.

World Council of Churches (U.S. Conference). Membership: 31 churches or denominations in U.S. Moderator, Bishop Vinton Anderson. Headquarters: 150 route de Ferney, 1211 Geneva 20, Switzerland. New York office: 475 Riverside Dr., Room 915, New York, NY 10115.

YMCA of the USA. Membership: 12,800,000 in some 2,000 associations. Board chairman, Barbara Roper. Headquarters: 101 North Wacker Dr., Chicago, IL 60606.

YWCA of the USA. Members and participants: approximately 2,000,000. President, Ann Stallard. Headquarters: 726 Broadway, New York, NY 10003.

Zionist Organization of America. Membership: 130,000 in 600 districts. President, Sidney Silverman; executive vice-president, Paul Flacks. Headquarters: 4 East 34th St., New York, NY 10016.

Contributors

ADRIAN, CHARLES R., Professor of Political Science, University of California, Riverside; Author, *A History of City Government: The Emergence of the Metropolis 1920–1945;* Coauthor, *State and Local Politics, A History of American City Government: The Formation of Traditions, 1775–1870, Governing Urban America:* CALIFORNIA; LOS ANGELES

AMBRE, AGO, Economist, Office of Economic Affairs, U.S. Department of Commerce: INDUSTRIAL PRODUCTION

ARNOLD, ANTHONY, Visiting Scholar, Hoover Institution, Stanford, CA; Author, *Afghanistan: The Soviet Invasion in Perspective, Afghanistan's Two-Party Communism: Parcham and Khalq:* AFGHANISTAN

ATTNER, PAUL, Senior Writer, *The Sporting News:* THE SUPER BOWL AT 25; BIOGRAPHY—*Mike Krzyzewski;* SPORTS—*Basketball, Football, Soccer*

AUSTIN, TERESA, Free-lance Writer and Editor: ENGINEERING, CIVIL

BARMASH, ISADORE, Free-lance Writer; Author, *Always Live Better Than Your Clients, More Than They Bargained For, The Chief Executives:* RETAILING

BATRA, PREM P., Professor of Biochemistry, Wright State University: BIOCHEMISTRY

BEAUCHAMP, LANE, *The Kansas City Star:* MISSOURI

BECK, KAY, Department of Communications, Georgia State University: GEORGIA

BEHLER, DEBORAH A., Senior Editor, *Wildlife Conservation* magazine: ZOOS AND ZOOLOGY; ZOOS AND ZOOLOGY—*More and More Deer*

BEST, JOHN, Chief, *Canada World News,* Ottawa: NEW BRUNSWICK; PRINCE EDWARD ISLAND; QUEBEC

BOND, DONOVAN H., Professor Emeritus of Journalism, West Virginia University: WEST VIRGINIA

BOULAY, HARVEY, Director of Development, Rogerson House; Author, *The Twilight Cities:* MASSACHUSETTS

BOWER, BRUCE, Behavioral Sciences Editor, *Science News:* ANTHROPOLOGY; ARCHAEOLOGY

BRAMMER, DANA B., Director, Public Policy Research Center, University of Mississippi: MISSISSIPPI

BRANDHORST, L. CARL, and JoANN C., Department of Geography, Western Oregon State College: OREGON

BRITENRIKER, NAWANA MOS, American Numismatic Association: COINS AND COIN COLLECTING

BROOM, JACK, Reporter, *The Seattle Times:* WASHINGTON

BUGAJSKI, JANUSZ, Associate Director of East European Studies, Center for Strategic and International Studies; Author, *Fourth World Conflicts: Communism and Rural Societies, Sandinista Communism and Rural Nicaragua, East European Fault Lines: Dissent, Opposition, and Social Activism, Czechoslovakia: Charter 77's Decade of Dissent:* ALBANIA

BURKS, ARDATH W., Professor Emeritus Asian Studies, Rutgers University; Author, *Third Order of the Rising Sun, Japan: A Postindustrial Power:* BIOGRAPHY—*Kiichi Miyazawa;* JAPAN

BUSH, GRAHAM W. A., Associate Professor of Political Studies, University of Auckland; Author, *Governing Big Cities, Advance in Order: The Auckland City Council 1971–89:* NEW ZEALAND

CAMPBELL, ROBERT, University of Wyoming; Coauthor, *Discovering Wyoming:* WYOMING

CASEY, DAN, Staff Writer, *The* (Annapolis) *Capital:* MARYLAND

CASPER, GRETCHEN, Department of Political Science, Texas A&M: PHILIPPINES

CASPER, LEONARD, Professor of English, Boston College; Past Recipient of Fulbright grants to lecture in the Philippines: PHILIPPINES

CASSIDY, SUZANNE, Free-lance U.S. Journalist, London: GREAT BRITAIN; GREAT BRITAIN—*The Arts, The Royalty Issue*

CHRISTENSEN, WILLIAM E., Professor of History, Midland Lutheran College; Author, *Saga of the Tower: A History of Dana College and Trinity Seminary, New Song to the Lord: A History of First Lutheran Church, Fremont, Nebraska, In Such Harmony: A History of the Federated Church, Columbus, Nebraska:* NEBRASKA

COLE, JOHN N., Founder, *Maine Times;* Author, *Fishing Came First, In Maine, Striper, Salmon:* MAINE

COLLINS, BUD, Sports Columnist, *The Boston Globe;* Author, *My Life With The Pros:* SPORTS—*Tennis*

COLTON, KENT W., Executive Vice-President and Chief Executive Officer, National Association of Home Builders, Washington, DC: HOUSING

CONRADT, DAVID P., Professor of Political Science, University of Florida; Author, *The German Polity, West European Politics, Comparative Politics:* GERMANY

COOPER, ILENE, Children's Book Editor, *Booklist Magazine:* LITERATURE—*Children's;* OBITUARIES—*Theodor Seuss Geisel*

COOPER, MARY H., Staff Writer, *CQ* [Congressional Quarterly] *Researcher;* Author, *The Business of Drugs:* ENERGY; FOREIGN AID; INSURANCE, LIABILITY

COPPEDGE, MICHAEL, Deputy Director, Latin American Studies, Johns Hopkins University: ECUADOR; PERU; VENEZUELA

CORLEW, ROBERT E., Dean, Middle Tennessee State University: TENNESSEE

CORNWELL, ELMER E., JR., Professor of Political Science, Brown University: RHODE ISLAND

CUNNIFF, JOHN, Business News Analyst, The Associated Press; Author, *How to Stretch Your Dollar:* BUSINESS AND CORPORATE AFFAIRS; UNITED STATES—*The Economy*

CURRIER, CHET, Financial Writer, The Associated Press; Author, *The Investor's Encyclopedia, The 15-Minute Investor;* Coauthor, *No-Cost/Low-Cost Investing:* STOCKS AND BONDS

CURTIS, L. PERRY, JR., Professor of History, Brown University: IRELAND

DANIELS, ROBERT V., Professor of History, University of Vermont; former Vermont state senator; Author, *Russia: The Roots of Confrontation:* VERMONT

DARBY, JOSEPH W., III, Reporter, *The Times-Picayune,* New Orleans: LOUISIANA

DAVID, LEONARD, Director, Space Data Resources and Information: SPACE EXPLORATION

De GREGORIO, GEORGE, Sports Department, *The New York Times;* Author, *Joe DiMaggio, An Informal Biography:* SPORTS—*Boxing, Swimming, Track and Field, Yachting*

DELZELL, CHARLES F., Professor of History Emeritus and Adjunct Professor, Vanderbilt University; Author, *Italy in the Twentieth Century, Mediterranean Fascism, Mussolini's Enemies:* ITALY

DENNIS, LARRY, Golf Writer, Creative Communications: SPORTS—*Golf*

DUFF, ERNEST A., Professor of Politics, Randolph-Macon Woman's College; Author, *Agrarian Reform in Colombia, Violence and Repression in Latin America, Leader and Party in Latin America:* COLOMBIA

ELKINS, ANN M., Fashion Director, *Good Housekeeping Magazine:* FASHION

ELVING, PHYLLIS, Free-lance Travel Writer: TRAVEL

ENSTAD, ROBERT H., Writer, *Chicago Tribune:* CHICAGO; ILLINOIS

ENTER, JACK E., Specialist in Criminology; Free-lance Writer: CRIME

EWEGEN, ROBERT D., Editorial Writer, *The Denver Post:* COLORADO

FAGEN, MORTON D., Formerly, AT&T Bell Laboratories; Editor, *A History of Engineering and Science in the Bell System,* Vol. 1, *The Early Years, 1875–1925,* and Vol. II. *National Security in War and Peace, 1925–1975:* COMMUNICATION TECHNOLOGY

FISHER, JIM, Editorial Writer and Columnist, *Lewiston Morning Tribune:* IDAHO

FRANCIS, DAVID R., Economy Page Editor, *The Christian Science Monitor:* INTERNATIONAL TRADE AND FINANCE; INTERNATIONAL TRADE AND FINANCE—*The BCCI Scandal*

FRIIS, ERIK J., Editor and Publisher, *The Scandinavian-American Bulletin;* Coauthor and translator, *Nordic Democracy:* BIOGRAPHY—*Harald V;* DENMARK; FINLAND; NORWAY; SWEDEN

GAILEY, HARRY A., Professor of History, San Jose State University; Author, *History of the Gambia, History of Africa, Road to Aba:* MOZAMBIQUE; NIGERIA; ZAIRE

GEORGE, PAUL S., Department of History, University of Miami; Author, *Florida: Yesterday and Today, A Guide to the History of Florida:* FLORIDA

GIBSON, ROBERT C., Associate Editor, *The Billings Gazette;* Coauthor, *The Big Drive;* Editor, *Yellowstone on Fire, Wagons Across Wyoming:* MONTANA

GOODMAN, DONALD, Associate Professor of Sociology, John Jay College of Criminal Justice, City University of New York: PRISONS

GORDON, MAYNARD M., Detroit Editor, *Auto Age* magazine; Author, *The Iacocca Management Technique:* AUTOMOBILES; AUTOMOBILES—*The Electric Car*

GOUDINOFF, PETER, Professor, Department of Political Science, University of Arizona; Author, *People's Guide to National Defense:* ARIZONA

GRAYSON, GEORGE W., John Marshall Professor of Government and Citizenship, College of William and Mary; Author, *The Politics of Mexican Oil, The United States and Mexico: Patterns of Influence, Oil and Mexican Foreign Policy:* BRAZIL; PORTUGAL; SPAIN

GROSSMAN, LAWRENCE, Director of Publications, The American Jewish Committee: RELIGION—*Judaism*

GROTH, ALEXANDER J., Professor of Political Science, University of California, Davis; Author, *People's Poland, Contemporary Politics: Europe, Comparative Resource Allocation, Public Policy Across Nations:* POLAND

HALLER, TIMOTHY G., Department of Political Science, Western Nevada Community College: NEVADA

HALSEY, MARGARET BROWN, Professor of Art History, New York City Technical College of the City University of New York: ART

HAND, SAMUEL B., Professor of History, University of Vermont: VERMONT

HARMON, CHARLES, American Library Association: LIBRARIES

HARVEY, ROSS M., Executive Director, Television Northern Canada: NORTHWEST TERRITORIES

HELMREICH, ERNST C., Professor Emeritus of History, Bowdoin College; Author, *The German Churches under Hitler: Background, Struggle, and Epilogue:* AUSTRIA

HELMREICH, JONATHAN E., Professor of History, Allegheny College; Author, *Belgium and Europe: A Study in Small Power Diplomacy, Gathering Rare Ores: The Diplomacy of Uranium Acquisition, 1943–54:* BELGIUM

HELMREICH, PAUL C., Professor of History, Wheaton College; Author, *Wheaton College: The Seminary Years, 1834–1912; From Paris to Sèvres: The Partition of the Ottoman Empire at the Peace Conference of 1919–1920:* SWITZERLAND

HINTON, HAROLD C., Professor of Political Science and International Affairs, The George Washington University; Author, *Korea under New Leadership: The Fifth Republic, Communist China in World Politics, The China Sea: The American Stake in Its Future:* KOREA

HOLLOWAY, HARRY, Professor Emeritus, Department of Political Science, University of Oklahoma; Coauthor, *Public Opinion: Coalitions, Elites, and Masses, Party and Factional Division in Texas:* OKLAHOMA

HOOVER, HERBERT T., Professor of History, University of South Dakota; Author, *South Dakota Leaders, The Yankton Sioux, To Be an Indian, The Chitimacha People, Higher Education in South Dakota:* SOUTH DAKOTA

HOPKO, THE REV. THOMAS, Assistant Professor, St. Vladimir's Orthodox Theological Seminary: RELIGION—*Orthodox Eastern*

HOWARD, CARLA BREER, Furnishings and Antiques Editor, *Traditional Home:* INTERIOR DESIGN

HOYT, CHARLES K., Senior Editor, *Architectural Record;* Author, *More Places for People, Building for Commerce and Industry:* ARCHITECTURE; BIOGRAPHY—*Robert Venturi*

HUFFMAN, GEORGE J., Universities Space Research Association: METEOROLOGY

HULBERT, DAN, *Atlanta Journal & Constitution:* TELEVISION AND RADIO; TELEVISION AND RADIO—*Competition for the Big Three Networks;* THEATER

HUSTED, THOMAS A., Assistant Professor, Department of Economics, The American University: TAXATION

JACKSON, PAUL CONRAD, Editor, *The Calgary Sun;* Columnist, *Saskatoon Star-Phoenix;* Author, *Battleground: The Socialist Assault on Grant Devine's Canadian Dream:* ALBERTA; SASKATCHEWAN

JENNERMANN, DONALD, Director, University Honors Program, Indiana State University; Author, *Born of a Cretan Spring, Literature for Living:* LITERATURE—*English;* OBITUARIES—*Graham Greene*

JONES, H.G., Curator, North Carolina Collection, University of North Carolina at Chapel Hill; Author, *North Carolina Illustrated, 1524–1984:* NORTH CAROLINA

JUDD, DENNIS R., Professor and Chair, Department of Political Science, University of Missouri-St. Louis; Coauthor, *The Development of American Public Policy, Leadership and Urban Regeneration;* Coeditor, *Urban Affairs Quarterly:* CITIES AND URBAN AFFAIRS

KARNES, THOMAS L., Professor of History Emeritus, Arizona State University; Author, *Latin American Policy of the United States, Failure of Union: Central America 1824–1960:* CENTRAL AMERICA

KIMBALL, LORENZO K., Professor Emeritus, Department of Political Science, University of Utah: UTAH

KIMBELL, CHARLES L., Senior Foreign Mineral Specialist, U.S. Bureau of Mines: STATISTICAL AND TABULAR DATA—*Mineral and Metal Production*

KING, PETER J., Professor of History, Carleton University, Ottawa; Author, *Utilitarian Jurisprudence in America:* ONTARIO; OTTAWA

KINNEAR, MICHAEL, Professor of History, University of Manitoba; Author, *The Fall of Lloyd George, The British Voter:* MANITOBA

KISSELGOFF, ANNA, Chief Dance Critic, *The New York Times:* DANCE; OBITUARIES—*Martha Graham*

KOZINN, ALLAN, Music Critic, *The New York Times;* Author, *Mischa Elman and the Romantic Style, The Guitar: The History, The Music, The Players:* MUSIC—*Classical*

KRONISH, SYD, Stamp Editor, The Associated Press: STAMPS AND STAMP COLLECTING

KUNZ, KENEVA, University of Iceland: ICELAND

LABATON, STEPHEN, Washington Bureau, *The New York Times:* BANKING; BANKING—*Banking Reform*

LaFRANCHI, HOWARD, Staff Correspondent, *The Christian Science Monitor:* BIOGRAPHY—*Edith Cresson;* FRANCE; MOROCCO; TUNISIA

LAI, DAVID CHUENYAN, Professor of Geography, University of Victoria, British Columbia; Author, *Chinatowns: Towns Within Cities in Canada:* HONG KONG

LANCASTER, CAROL, Director, African Studies Program, Georgetown University; Coeditor, *African Debt and Financing:* AFRICA

LAWRENCE, ROBERT M., Professor of Political Science, Colorado State University; Author, *The Strategic Defense Initiative:* ARMS CONTROL AND DISARMAMENT; MILITARY AFFAIRS

LEE, STEWART M., Professor, Department of Economics and Business Administration, Geneva College; Coauthor, *Consumer Economics: The Consumer in Our Society:* CONSUMER AFFAIRS

LEEPSON, MARC, Free-lance Writer: DRUGS AND ALCOHOL; SOCIAL WELFARE

LESHNER, ALAN I., Acting Director, National Institute of Mental Health: MEDICINE AND HEALTH—*Mental Health*

LEVINE, LOUIS, Professor, Department of Biology, City College of New York; Author, *Biology of the Gene, Biology for a Modern Society:* BIOTECHNOLOGY; GENETICS; MICROBIOLOGY

LEWIS, ANNE C., Education Policy Writer: EDUCATION

LEWIS, JEROME R., Director for Public Administration, College of Urban Affairs and Public Policy, University of Delaware: DELAWARE

LINES, PATRICIA M., Professor of Education, Catholic University of America: EDUCATION—*Home Schooling*

LOBRON, BARBARA L., Editor, Photographer, Writer: PHOTOGRAPHY; PHOTOGRAPHY—*The Legacy of Edwin H. Land*

LOESCHER, GIL, Professor of International Relations, University of Notre Dame; Author, *Calculated Kindness: Refugees and America's Half-Open Door, Refugees and International Relations:* REFUGEES AND IMMIGRATION

LOEVY, ROBERT D., Professor of Political Science, Colorado College; Author, *To End All Segregation: The Politics of the Passage of the Civil Rights Act of 1964:* UNITED STATES—*Campaign Finance, Redistricting*

MABRY, DONALD J., Professor of History, Mississippi State University; Author, *Mexico's Acción Nacional, The Mexican University and the State;* Coauthor, *Neighbors—Mexico and the United States:* MEXICO; MEXICO—*The Free-Trade Issue*

MANOFF, ROBERT KARL, Director, Center for War, Peace and the News Media, New York University: PUBLISHING—*The Military and the Media in Wartime*

MARCOPOULOS, GEORGE J., Associate Professor of History, Tufts University: CYPRUS; GREECE

MATHESON, JIM, Sportswriter, *Edmonton Journal:* SPORTS—*Ice Hockey*

MAYERCHAK, PATRICK M., Professor of Political Science, Virginia Military Institute; Author, *Scholar's Guide to Southeast Asia;* Coauthor, *Linkage or Bondage: US-ASEAN Economic Relations:* MALAYSIA; SINGAPORE

McCORQUODALE, SUSAN, Professor of Political Science, Memorial University of Newfoundland: NEWFOUNDLAND

McCRAW, VINCENT D., *The Washington Times:* WASHINGTON, DC

McGILL, DAVID A., Professor of Marine Science, U.S. Coast Guard Academy: OCEANOGRAPHY

McLAURIN, RONALD D., President, Abbott Associates, Inc.; Author, *The Emergence of a New Lebanon: Fantasy or Reality?, Lebanon and the World in the 1980s:* LEBANON

MEDINGER, DANIEL, Editor, *Baltimore Catholic Review:* RELIGION—*Roman Catholicism*

MICHAELIS, PATRICIA A., Curator of Manuscripts, Kansas State Historical Society: KANSAS

MICHIE, ARUNA NAYYAR, Associate Professor of Political Science, Kansas State University: BANGLADESH

MILLER, PENNY M., Professor, Department of Political Science, University of Kentucky; Coauthor, *Political Parties and Primaries in Kentucky, The Kentucky Legislature: Two Decades of Change:* KENTUCKY

MILLER, RANDALL M., Department of History, St. Joseph's University; Author, *Immigration to New York, "Dear Master": Letters of a Slave Family; Shades of the Sunbelt: Essays on Race, Ethnicity and the Urban South:* ETHNIC GROUPS

MILWARD, JOHN, Free-lance Writer and Critic: MUSIC—*Popular and Jazz;* OBITUARIES—*Joseph Papp;* RECORDINGS

MITCHELL, GARY, Professor of Physics, North Carolina State University: PHYSICS

MONASTERSKY, RICHARD, Earth Sciences Editor, *Science News:* GEOLOGY; GEOLOGY—*The Eruption of Mount Pinatubo*

MORELLO, TED, United Nations Correspondent, *Far Eastern Economic Review;* Author, *Official Handbook of the Hall of Fame:* UNITED NATIONS

MORTIMER, ROBERT A., Professor, Department of Political Science, Haverford College; Author, *The Third World Coalition in International Politics;* Coauthor, *Politics and Society in Contemporary Africa:* ALGERIA

MORTON, DESMOND, Professor of History and Principal, Erindale College, University of Toronto; Author, *A Short History of Canada, Bloody Victory: Canadians and the D-Day Campaign, Working People: An Illustrated History of the Canadian Labour Movement, A Military History of Canada, Winning the Second Battle: Canadian Veterans and the Return to Civilian Life, 1915–1930;* Coauthor, *Marching to Armageddon: Canadians in the First World War, 1914–1919:* CANADA

MURPHY, ROBERT F., Editorial Writer, *The Hartford Courant:* CONNECTICUT

MURRAY, THOMAS H., Director, Center for Biomedical Ethics, Case Western Reserve University: MEDICINE AND HEALTH—*Medical Ethics*

NAFTALIN, ARTHUR, Professor Emeritus of Public Affairs, University of Minnesota: MINNESOTA

NEUMANN, JAMES, Free-lance Writer, Grand Forks, ND: NORTH DAKOTA

NEWLAND, ED, Assistant City Editor, *Richmond Times-Dispatch:* VIRGINIA

OCHSENWALD, WILLIAM, Professor of History, Virginia Polytechnic Institute; Author, *The Middle East: A History, The Hijaz Railroad, Religion, Society, and the State in Arabia:* KUWAIT; SAUDI ARABIA

O'CONNOR, ROBERT E., Associate Professor of Political Science, The Pennsylvania State University; Author, *Politics and Structure: Essentials of American National Government:* PENNSYLVANIA

O'MEARA, PATRICK, Director, African Studies Program, Indiana University; Coeditor, *Africa, International Politics in Southern Africa, Southern Africa, The Continuing Crisis:* BIOGRAPHY—*Mangosuthu Gatsha Buthelezi;* NAMIBIA; SOUTH AFRICA; ZIMBABWE

PALMER, NORMAN D., Professor Emeritus of Political Science and South Asian Studies, University of Pennsylvania; Author, *Westward Watch: The United States and the Changing Western Pacific, The United States and India: The Dimensions of Influence, Elections and Political Development: The South Asian Experience, The New Regionalism in Asia and the Pacific:* INDIA AFTER THE NEHRU-GANDHI DYNASTY: A NEW CHAPTER?; INDIA; SRI LANKA

PEARSON, FREDERIC S., Director, Center for Peace and Conflict Studies, Wayne State University, Detroit; Author, *International Relations: The Global Condition in the Late Twentieth Century, The Weak State in International Crisis:* UNITED STATES—*Foreign Affairs*

PERETZ, DON, Professor of Political Science, State University of New York at Binghamton; Author, *The West Bank—History, Politics, Society & Economy, Government and Politics of Israel, The Middle East Today:* EGYPT; ISRAEL

PERKINS, KENNETH J., Assistant Professor of History, University of South Carolina: LIBYA; RELIGION—*Islam*

PERRY, DAVID K., Associate Professor, Department of Journalism, The University of Alabama: OBITUARIES—*Robert Maxwell;* PUBLISHING

PIPPIN, LARRY L., Professor of Political Science, University of the Pacific; Author, *The Remón Era:* ARGENTINA; PARAGUAY; URUGUAY

PLATT, HERMANN K., Professor of History, Saint Peter's College: NEW JERSEY

POOLE, PETER A., Author, *The Vietnamese in Thailand, Eight Presidents and Indochina;* Coauthor, *American Diplomacy:* CAMBODIA; LAOS; THAILAND; VIETNAM

RALOFF, JANET, Senior Editor, *Science News:* ENVIRONMENT

RAMIREZ, DEBORAH, Reporter, *San Juan Star:* PUERTO RICO

REED, WILLIAM CYRUS, Director of African Studies, The American University in Cairo (Egypt): KENYA; TANZANIA; UGANDA

REMINGTON, ROBIN ALISON, Frederick A. Middlebush Professor of Political Science, University of Missouri-Columbia: YUGOSLAVIA

REUNING, WINIFRED, Writer, Polar Program, National Science Foundation: POLAR RESEARCH

RICHTER, LINDA K., Professor, Department of Political Science, Kansas State University; Author, *Land Reform and Tourism Development: Policy-Making in the Philippines, The Politics of Tourism in Asia:* BIOGRAPHY—*Aung San Suu Kyi;* MYANMAR

RICHTER, WILLIAM L., Professor and Head, Department of Political Science, Kansas State University: NEPAL; PAKISTAN

RIGGAN, WILLIAM, Associate Editor, *World Literature Today,* University of Oklahoma; Author, *Picaros, Madmen, Naïfs, and Clowns, Comparative Literature and Literary Theory:* LITERATURE—*World*

ROBERTS, SAM, Urban Affairs Columnist, *The New York Times;* Coauthor, *I Never Wanted To Be Vice-President of Anything:* NEW YORK CITY

ROBINSON, LEIF J., Editor, *Sky & Telescope,* Author, *Outdoor Optics:* ASTRONOMY

RODGERS, THOMAS E., University of Southern Indiana: INDIANA

ROSS, RUSSELL M., Professor of Political Science, University of Iowa; Author, *State and Local Government and Administration, Iowa Government and Administration:* IOWA

ROVNER, JULIE, *Congressional Quarterly:* MEDICINE AND HEALTH—*Health Care*

ROWEN, HERBERT H., Professor Emeritus, Rutgers University; Author, *The Princes of Orange, John de Witt: Statesman of the "True Freedom," The King's State, John de Witt: Grand Pensionary of Holland:* NETHERLANDS

RUBIN, JIM, Supreme Court Correspondent, The Associated Press: BIOGRAPHY—*Clarence Thomas;* LAW

RUFF, NORMAN J., Assistant Professor, Department of Political Science, University of Victoria, B.C.; Coauthor, *The Reins of Power: Governing British Columbia:* BRITISH COLUMBIA

SALSINI, PAUL, Staff Development Director, *The Milwaukee Journal:* WISCONSIN

SAVAGE, DAVID, Free-lance Writer: CANADA—*The Arts;* LITERATURE—*Canadian*

SAWATSKY, DON, Free-lance Writer/Broadcaster; Author, *Ghost Town Trails of the Yukon:* YUKON

SCHIFFER, R. MICHAEL, Director, International Security Programs, Center for War, Peace, and the News Media, New York University: PUBLISHING—*The Military and the Media in Wartime*

SCHLOSSBERG, DAN, Baseball Writer; Author, *The Baseball IQ Challenge, The Baseball Catalog, The Baseball Book of Why, Cooperstown: Baseball's Hall of Fame*

Players: BIOGRAPHY—*Roger Clemens;* SPORTS—*Baseball, 1941—The Year of Ted and Joe*

SCHROEDER, RICHARD, Consultant, Organization of American States: THE ADMIRAL OF THE OCEAN SEA; LATIN AMERICA THEN AND NOW; BOLIVIA; CARIBBEAN; CHILE; HAITI; LATIN AMERICA

SCHWAB, PETER, Professor of Political Science, State University of New York at Purchase; Author, *Ethiopia: Politics, Economics, and Society, Human Rights: Cultural and Ideological Perspectives:* ETHIOPIA, SOMALIA

SEGAL, MADY WECHSLER, Department of Sociology, University of Maryland at College Park; Recipient, Outstanding Civilian Service Medal, Department of the Army: FAMILY—*Today's Military Family*

SEIDERS, DAVID F., Chief Economist and Senior Staff Vice-President, National Association of Home Builders, Washington, DC: HOUSING

SENSER, ROBERT A., Free-lance Writer specializing in human-rights issues, Washington, DC: HUMAN RIGHTS

SETH, R.P., Professor of Economics, Mount Saint Vincent University, Halifax: CANADA—*The Economy;* NOVA SCOTIA

SEYBOLD, PAUL G., Professor, Department of Chemistry, Wright State University: CHEMISTRY

SHARLET, ROBERT, Professor of Political Science, Union College; Author, *Soviet Constitutional Crisis:* THE SECOND SOVIET REVOLUTION; USSR

SHEPRO, CARL E., Professor of Political Science, University of Alaska-Anchorage: ALASKA

SHOGAN, ROBERT, National Political Correspondent, Washington Bureau, *Los Angeles Times;* Author, *A Question of Judgment, Promises to Keep:* UNITED STATES—*Domestic Affairs, The States' Fiscal Crisis*

SIEGEL, STANLEY E., Professor of History, University of Houston; Author, *A Political History of the Texas Republic, 1836–1845:* TEXAS

SIMON, JEFFREY D., Free-lance Writer, Santa Monica, CA: TERRORISM

SIMON, SHELDON W., Professor of Political Science and Faculty Associate, Arizona State University-Tempe; Author, *The Future of Asian-Pacific Security Collaboration:* ASIA

SMITH, REX, Editor, *The* (Troy, NY) *Record:* NEW YORK

SNODSMITH, RALPH L., Horticulturist; Author, *Ralph Snodsmith's Tips from the Garden Hotline, Garden Calendar and Record Keeper 1985–1988:* GARDENING AND HORTICULTURE

SPYCHALSKI, JOHN C., Chairman, Department of Business Logistics, College of Business Administration, The Pennsylvania State University; Editor, *Transportation Journal:* TRANSPORTATION; TRANSPORTATION—*U.S. Highways—New Policy Directions*

STAFFORD-VAUGHAN, BETH, Women's Studies/Women in International Development Librarian and Associate Professor, University of Illinois, Urbana; Editor, *Directory of Women's Studies Programs and Library Resources:* CRIME—*Rape*

STARR, JOHN BRYAN, President, Yale-China Association; Author, *Continuing the Revolution: The Political Thought of Mao;* Editor, *The Future of U.S.-China Relations:* CHINA; TAIWAN

STERN, JEROME H., Professor of English, Florida State University; Author, *Making Shapely Fiction:* LITERATURE—*American*

STEWART, WILLIAM H., Professor of Political Science, The University of Alabama; Coauthor, *Alabama Government and Politics;* Author, *Leadership in the Public Service, The Alabama Constitution:* ALABAMA

STIEBER, JACK, Professor Emeritus, School of Labor and Industrial Relations and Department of Economics, Michigan State University; Author, *U.S. Industrial Relations: The Next Twenty Years, Governing the UAW, Public Employee Unionism:* LABOR

STOUDEMIRE, ROBERT H., Distinguished Professor Emeritus, University of South Carolina: SOUTH CAROLINA

SUTTON, STAN, Sportswriter, *The Courier-Journal,* Louisville, KY: SPORTS—*Auto Racing, Horse Racing, The XI Pan American Games*

TABORSKY, EDWARD, Professor of Government, University of Texas at Austin; Author, *Communism in Czechoslovakia, 1948–1960, Communist Penetration of the Third World:* CZECHOSLOVAKIA

TAYLOR, WILLIAM L., Professor of History, Plymouth State College: NEW HAMPSHIRE

TESAR, JENNY, Science and Medicine Writer; Author, *Introduction to Animals, Parents as Teachers:* THE NATIONAL PARK SERVICE AT 75; COMPUTERS; COMPUTERS—*Ever-Broadening Applications, Virtual Reality;* LATIN AMERICA—*The 1991 Cholera Epidemic;* MEDICINE AND HEALTH

THEISEN, CHARLES W., Assistant News Editor, *The Detroit News:* MICHIGAN

TISMANEANU, VLADIMIR, Assistant Professor of Government, University of Maryland (College Park); Author, *Reinventing Politics: Eastern Europe from Stalin to Havel:* BULGARIA; ROMANIA

TRUSCHKE, EDWARD, President, Alzheimer's Association: ALZHEIMER'S DISEASE

TURNER, ARTHUR CAMPBELL, Professor of Political Science, University of California, Riverside; Coauthor, *Ideology and Power in the Middle East:* THE MIDDLE EAST: THE INTERTWINING OF WAR AND DIPLOMACY; THE KURDS: A DISTINCT AND ANCIENT MOUNTAIN PEOPLE; IRAN; IRAQ; JORDAN; SYRIA

TURNER, CHARLES H., Free-lance Writer: HAWAII

TURNER, DARRELL J., Associate Editor, Religious News Service, New York, NY: BIOGRAPHY—*George Leonard Carey;* RELIGION—*Far Eastern, Protestantism*

VAN RIPER, PAUL P., Professor Emeritus and Head, Department of Political Science, Texas A&M University; Editor and Coauthor, *The Wilson Influence on Public Administration:* POSTAL SERVICE; POSTAL SERVICE—*Direct ("Junk") Mail*

VOLGYES, IVAN, Department of Political Science, University of Nebraska: HUNGARY

VOLL, JOHN O., Department of History, University of New Hampshire; Author, *Islam: Continuity and Change in the Modern World;* Coauthor, *Sudan: Unity and Diversity in a Multicultural Society;* Editor, *Sudan: State and Society in Crisis:* SUDAN

VOLSKY, GEORGE, Center for Advanced International Studies, University of Miami: CUBA

WALKER, SAMUEL, Department of Criminal Justice, University of Nebraska; Author, *The Police in America, In Defense of American Liberties: A History of the ACLU:* CRIME—*Police Misconduct*

WEATHERBEE, DONALD E., Department of Government, University of South Carolina: INDONESIA

WEAVER, JOHN B., Department of History, Sinclair Community College (Dayton, OH): OHIO

WEIKER, WALTER F., Professor of Political Science, Rutgers University: BIOGRAPHY—*Turgut Özal;* TURKEY

WELLER, MARC, Research Fellow and Lecturer, University of Cambridge; Coeditor, *The Kuwait Crisis, Volumes I and III:* LAW—*International*

WHELPLEY, KEITH, Writer, *Las Cruces Sun-News;* Contributing writer, *New Mexico* magazine: NEW MEXICO

WILLIAMS, C. FRED, Professor of History, University of Arkansas at Little Rock; Author, *Arkansas: An Illustrated History of the Land of Opportunity, Arkansas: A Documentary History:* ARKANSAS

WILLIS, F. ROY, Professor of History, University of California, Davis; Author, *France, Germany and the New Europe, 1945–1968, Italy Chooses Europe, The French Paradox:* EUROPE

WINCHESTER, N. BRIAN, Associate Director, African Studies Program, Indiana University: NAMIBIA; SOUTH AFRICA

WISNER, ROBERT N., Professor, Iowa State University; Coeditor, *Marketing for Farmers;* Author, *World Food Trade and U.S. Agriculture:* AGRICULTURE; FOOD

WOLF, WILLIAM, New York University; Author, *The Marx Brothers, Landmark Films, The Cinema and Our Century:* BIOGRAPHY—*Kevin Costner, Spike Lee;* MOTION PICTURES

WOLFE, JOHN, New York Bureau Chief, *Advertising Age:* ADVERTISING

YOUNGER, R.M., Journalist and Author; Author, *Australia and the Australians, Australia! Australia! A Bicentennial Record:* AUSTRALIA

Acknowledgments

We also wish to thank the following for their services: typesetting, Dix Type Inc.; color separations, Gamma One, Inc. and Colotone Graphics; text stock printed on Champion's 60# Courtland Matte; covers printed by Mid-City Lithographers; cover materials provided by Holliston Mills, Inc. and Decorative Specialties International, Inc.; and printing and binding by R. R. Donnelley & Sons, Co.

Index

Index

Main article headings appear in this index as bold-faced capitals; subjects within articles appear as lower-case entries. Both the general references and the subentries should be consulted for maximum usefulness of this index. Illustrations are indexed herein. Cross references are to the entries in this index.

A

B

C

F

G

J

K

L

M

N

O

P

Q

R

S

V

W

Y

Z